Sarah Wolkovitz

Sarah Wolkovitz

A Child's World

Eighth Edition

A Child's World

Infancy Through Adolescence

Diane E. Papalia

·

Sally Wendkos Olds

·

Ruth Duskin Feldman

Boston   Burr Ridge, IL   Dubuque, IA   Madison, WI   New York   San Francisco   St. Louis
Bangkok   Bogotá   Caracas   Lisbon   London   Madrid
Mexico City   Milan   New Delhi   Seoul   Singapore   Sydney   Taipei   Toronto

WCB/McGraw-Hill

A Division of The **McGraw·Hill** *Companies*

A CHILD'S WORLD: INFANCY THROUGH ADOLESCENCE, EIGHTH EDITION

This book is printed on acid-free paper.

2 3 4 5 6 7 8 9 0 VNH/VNH 9 3 2 1 0 9 8

ISBN 0–07–048785–5

Editorial director: *Jane E. Vaicunas*
Executive editor: *Mickey Cox*
Editorial assistant: *Sarah C. Thomas*
Developmental editor: *Jeaninne Ciliotta*
Marketing manager: *James Rozsa*
Project manager: *Sue Dillon/Cathy Ford Smith*
Senior production supervisor: *Sandra Hahn*
Designer manager: *Stuart D. Paterson*
Photo research coordinator: *Lori Hancock*
Supplement coordinator: *Stacy A. Patch*
Compositor: *Shepherd, Inc.*
Typeface: *10/12 Palatino*
Printer: *Von Hoffmann Press, Inc.*

Cover/interior design: *Elise Lansdon/Lansdon Design*
Cover image: *Charles Thatcher/Tony Stone*

The credits section for this book begins on page 669 and is considered an extension of the copyright page.

Library of Congress Cataloging-in-Publication Data

Papalia, Diane E.
    A child's world : infancy through adolescence / Diane E. Papalia,
Sally Wendkos Olds, Ruth Duskin Feldman. — 8th ed.
        p.   cm.
    Includes bibliographical references and index.
    ISBN 0–07–048785–5
    1. Child development.   2. Child psychology.   3. Adolescence.
I. Olds, Sally Wendkos.   II. Feldman, Ruth Duskin.   III. Title.
HQ767.9.P36   1999
305.231—dc21   98–5943
                                                                                      CIP

www.mhhe.com

About the Authors

As a professor, **Diane E. Papalia** taught thousands of undergraduates at the University of Wisconsin–Madison. She received her bachelor's degree, majoring in psychology, from Vassar College and both her master's degree in child development and family relations and her Ph.D. in life-span developmental psychology from West Virginia University. She has published numerous articles in such professional journals as *Human Development, International Journal of Aging and Human Development, Sex Roles, Journal of Experimental Child Psychology,* and *Journal of Gerontology.* Most of these papers have dealt with her major research focus, cognitive development from childhood through old age. She is especially interested in intellectual development and factors that contribute to the maintenance of intellectual functioning. She is a Fellow in the Gerontological Society of America. She is the coauthor, with Sally Wendkos Olds and Ruth Duskin Feldman, of *Human Development,* now in its Seventh Edition, and of *Adult Development and Aging,* with Cameron J. Camp and Ruth Duskin Feldman.

Sally Wendkos Olds is an award-winning professional writer who has written more than 200 articles in leading magazines and is the author or coauthor of six books addressed to general readers, in addition to the textbooks she has coauthored with Dr. Papalia. Her book The *Complete Book of Breastfeeding,* a classic since its publication in 1972, was issued in 1987 in a completely updated and expanded edition and is now in press for its third edition; more than 2 million copies are in print. She is also the author of *The Working Parents' Survival Guide* and *The Eternal Garden: Seasons of Our Sexuality* and the coauthor of *Raising a Hyperactive Child* (winner of the Family Service Association of America National Media Award) and *Helping Your Child Find Values to Live By.* She has spoken widely on the topics of her books and articles to both professional and lay audiences, in person and on television and radio. She received her bachelor's degree from the University of Pennsylvania, where she majored in English literature and minored in psychology. She was elected to Phi Beta Kappa and was graduated summa cum laude.

Ruth Duskin Feldman is an award-winning writer. She is the author or coauthor of four books addressed to general readers, including *Whatever Happened to the Quiz Kids?* and *Perils and Profits of Growing Up Gifted.* She is coauthor of the Fourth and Seventh Editions of Diane E. Papalia and Sally Wendkos Olds's widely used textbook *Human Development* and is coauthor, with Dr. Papalia and Cameron J. Camp, of *Adult Development and Aging.* A former teacher, she has developed educational materials for all levels from elementary school through college. She has written for numerous newspapers and national magazines on education and other topics and has lectured extensively throughout the United States. She prepared the test banks to accompany the Fifth Edition of *Human Development* and the Sixth Edition of *A Child's World,* as well as the *Study Guide with Readings* to accompany the Fifth, Sixth, Seventh, and Eighth Editions of *A Child's World.* She received her bachelor's degree from Northwestern University, where she was graduated with highest distinction and was elected to Phi Beta Kappa.

To our parents,
Madeline and Edward Papalia,
Leah and Samuel Wendkos,
and Boris and Rita Duskin,
for their unfailing love, nurturance, and
confidence in us, and for their abiding conviction
that childhood is a wondrous time of life.

And to our children,
Anna Victoria,
Nancy, Jennifer, and Dorri,
Steven, Laurie, and Heidi,
and our grandchildren,
Stefan, Maika, Anna, and Lisa,
Daniel, Emmett, Rita, and Carol,
who have helped us revisit childhood
and see its wonders and challenges
with new eyes.

Contents in Brief

Middle Childhood 390

Adolescence 502

Contents

Beginnings   50

Chapter 7

Psychosocial Development During the First Three Years 231

Early Childhood 276

Chapter 8

Physical Development and Health in Early Childhood 279

Chapter 9

Cognitive Development in Early Childhood 309

Adolescence 502

Chapter 14

Physical Development and Health in Adolescence 505

Chapter 15

Cognitive Development in Adolescence 541

Chapter 16

Psychosocial Development in Adolescence 571

List of Vignettes

List of Boxes

Preface

With the publication of the previous, seventh edition, *A Child's World* celebrated its twenty-first birthday. Now, with this eighth edition, *A Child's World* is "reborn." Virtually the entire book has been revamped—its design, content, and pedagogical features. At the same time, we have sought to retain some of the engaging qualities of tone, style, and substance that have contributed to its popularity over the years.

One notable change is the expansion of the author team. Ruth Duskin Feldman has been added as a coauthor, bringing a fresh perspective to the organization and writing of the text. Feldman coauthored the fourth and seventh editions of another widely used Papalia-Olds text, *Human Development*, and prepared the *Study Guide with Readings* to accompany the past three editions of *A Child's World*. ("About the Authors," details the professional backgrounds of all three authors.)

Our Aims for This Edition

Our primary aims for this edition remain the same as in previous editions: to emphasize the continuity of development from conception through adolescence and the interrelationships among the physical, cognitive, and psychosocial realms of development.

To initiate students into the dynamic discipline of child development, we have given special attention to the introductory sections of the book. A new *Prologue* lays the groundwork for the study of child development by summing up recent methodological advances and thematic shifts, as well as fundamental points on which a consensus has emerged. In *Chapter 1*, we expand our coverage of the history of the field with a time line of its major pioneers. This first chapter includes a new section on the influences of family type, socioeconomic status, ethnicity, and culture. Our intensified discussion of theoretical perspectives begins by highlighting three key issues: the relative importance of heredity and environment, whether development is active or passive, and whether development occurs in stages. We also present an expanded and revised description of research methods and designs and, as before, a discussion of the ethics of research.

As always, we seek to make the study of child development come alive by telling stories about actual incidents in the lives of children, which illustrate principles of child development. In this edition, each chapter opens with a fascinating *biographical vignette* from the childhood of a well-known person (such as Elvis Presley, Eva Perôn, Anne Frank, and Nelson Mandela) or a classic case (such as the wild boy of Aveyron and Louise Brown, the first "test-tube baby"). The subjects of these vignettes are people of diverse racial, national, and ethnic origins, whose experiences dramatize important themes in the chapter. Students will enjoy and identify with these stories, which lead directly and smoothly into the body of the chapter and are woven into its fabric. These vignettes, along with the shorter true anecdotes that appear throughout the book, underline the fact that there is no "average" or "typical" child, that each child is an individual with a unique personality and a unique set of life circumstances. They are reminders that whenever we talk about child development, we talk about real children in a real world.

The Eighth Edition: An Overview

Organization

There are two major approaches to the study of child development: the *chronological approach* (which describes all aspects of development at each period of infancy, childhood, or adolescence) and the *topical approach* (which focuses on one aspect of development, such as memory or sensory perception, at a time). We have chosen the chronological approach, which provides a sense of the multifaceted sweep of child development, as we get to know first the developing person-to-be in the womb, then the infant and toddler, then the preschool child, the schoolchild, and finally the adolescent on the brink of adulthood.

Following this chronological approach, we have divided the book into five parts. After the introductory chapter, which presents basic concepts, theories, and research methods, Part I describes the beginnings of life: conception, the influences of heredity and environment, pregnancy and prenatal development, birth, and the newborn baby. The next four parts cover physical, cognitive, and psychosocial development during each of the age-based periods from infancy through adolescence.

In this edition, we have looked with particular care at the internal organization of the text. To improve its clarity, logic, and readability, we have reorganized many sections and even whole chapters, have retitled some chapters, and have moved material from one chapter to another. For example, discussions of infertility and assisted reproduction are now in Chapter 2 (Forming a New Life: Conception, Heredity, and Environment); prenatal assessment is now in Chapter 3 (Pregnancy and Prenatal Development); Robert Sternberg's triarchic theory of intelligence is now in Chapter 12 (Cognitive Development in Middle Childhood); and a significantly updated discussion of sexual orientation is now in Chapter 14 (Physical Development and Health in Adolescence). Chapter 6 organizes the study of cognitive development under classic (behaviorist, psychometric, and Piagetian) and newer (information-processing, cognitive neuroscience, and social-contextual) approaches. Chapter 7 separates the psychosocial issues that arise during infancy from the very different issues characteristic of toddlerhood. In Chapter 16, the topic of teenage pregnancy immediately follows discussions of sexual activity and sexual risk taking.

Content

In this revision, we have made important improvements in scope and emphasis and have taken special pains to draw on the most recent information available. In line with the growing recognition of child development as a rigorous scientific enterprise, we have broadened the research base of each chapter more extensively than ever before. Dana Gross, Associate Professor of Psychology at St. Olaf College in Northfield, Minnesota, has served as a consultant for this edition, helping us keep up with the latest findings in a rapidly expanding field. We have added many new tables and figures and have updated statistics.

We are more keenly aware than ever that children grow up in diverse social contexts. This edition continues to extend our cross-cultural coverage, reflecting the diversity of children's lives in the United States and in other countries around the world. Both in *Around the World boxes* and in the main text, we show how cultural beliefs and practices affect children's development and how normal development varies in different settings. Our photo illustrations reflect an ever greater commitment to depicting this diversity. We continue to be sensitive to gender roles and the effects of divorce, single parenthood, and parents' employment.

Among the topics given new or significantly revised coverage (in addition to those already mentioned) are:

- *New discussions* of Esther Thelen's work on infant maturation in context; early intervention in cognitive development; elicited imitation; cognitive neuroscience and the brain's memory structures; Lev Vygotsky's concept of guided participation in cognitive learning; grandparents' roles and relationships; attachment patterns that may span generations; development of conscience; effects of exposure to smoking; self-esteem and "helplessness"; the schema confirmation-deployment model; body image; spatial thinking; selective attention; information processing and Piagetian tasks; Howard Gardner's theory of multiple intelligences; emotional growth; bullying; leptin and the onset of puberty; beginnings of sexual attraction, adrenarche, and gonadarche; health in context (protective factors); Robert Sternberg's work on matching teaching styles and student abilities; and Daniel Offer's study of self-image and the "universal adolescent."
- *Important revisions or expansions* of material on the information processing, neo-Piagetian, and social-contextual perspectives; genome imprinting; how heredity and environment work together; influences on intelligence; fetal abilities; the fetal environment; maternal factors affecting prenatal development; early feeding; growth of the brain and effects of environmental deprivation; smell and taste perception; infant mortality; sudden infant death syndrome; immunization; infant memory; influences on measured intelligence; invisible and deferred imitation; early language development; attachment; social referencing; emotional communication and maternal depression; socialization; effects of early day care; thumbsucking; diet and obesity; handedness; socioeconomic and ethnic factors in health and safety; cognitive training; predicting school success; friendships and family and peer relationships; growth hormones; discipline and corporal punishment; influences of family structure and family atmosphere; eating disorders; drug abuse; sexually transmitted diseases; abuse and neglect in adolescence; teenage suicide; development of formal reasoning; contextual influences on school achievement; sexual activity; teenage pregnancy; and juvenile delinquency.

Boxed Material in This Edition

This edition includes four kinds of boxed material:

- *The Research World.* These boxes (reinstated from earlier editions) appear in almost every chapter. They report on exciting new developments or current controversies in the field of child development. In this category are such contemporary topics as the adaptive value of immaturity; pregnancy in the twenty-first century; whether a supportive environment can overcome effects of birth complications; toddlers' ability to "read" others' wishes; early signs of conscience; whether musical training can improve spatial reasoning; Robbie Case's theory and research on central conceptual structures; and how psychosocial issues affect adolescents' moral judgments.
- *Around the World.* Almost all chapters contain one of these boxes, which present windows on child development in various cultures and subcultures. Among the new or greatly revised subjects are: sex selection through prenatal assessment; day care in Sweden; cultural attitudes toward

handedness; the implications of the one-child family in China; female genital mutilation; moral perspectives on care of the environment; cross-cultural findings on popularity; and continuity of personality from childhood to adolescence.

- *The Everyday World.* Nearly every developmental chapter presents one of these boxes, which highlight practical applications of research findings. Among the new or greatly revised subjects are: obesity in infancy; choosing a good day-care facility; building narrative skills as preparation for literacy; imaginary playmates; phonics versus whole-language reading instruction; and the pros and cons of part-time work for teenagers.
- *The Social World.* This box series, new to this edition, covers such social issues as: genetic testing; fetal welfare versus mothers' rights; homelessness; the reliability of young children's eyewitness testimony; dropping out of high school; and preventing teenage pregnancy and suicide.

Learning Aids

Some of the most conspicuous innovations in this edition are its new and improved teaching and learning aids:

- *Part openers* begin with *Bird's-eye-view tables,* visually keyed to each chapter of the text, which preview the main features of each period of development. *Part overviews* have been revised to stress the interaction of physical, cognitive, and psychosocial spheres.
- Frequent marginal *Checkpoints* enable students to test their understanding of what they have read.
- *Chapter summaries* at the end of each chapter briefly restate the most important points. The summaries are now organized by major topics and include all key terms (in **boldface**).
- *Questions for Thought and Discussion* at the end of each chapter challenge students to interpret, apply, and evaluate information presented in the text.
- A reinstated end-of-book *Glossary* assembles the definitions of key terms highlighted throughout the book.

We also continue to provide the following:

- *Chapter-opening outlines:* At the beginning of each chapter, an outline previews the major topics included in the chapter.
- *Preview questions and chapter overviews:* At the beginning of each chapter, a few key questions and a brief overview paragraph focus attention on important topics to be addressed in the chapter.
- *Key terms and "running glossary":* Whenever an important new term is introduced in the text, it is highlighted in **boldface italic** and defined in the margin.
- *End-of-chapter lists of key terms:* At the end of every chapter, key terms are listed in the order in which they first appear and are cross-referenced to pages where they are defined.
- *Bibliography:* A complete listing of references enables students to check the sources of statements of fact or theory.
- *Resource guide:* This front-of-book reference list helps interested readers seek information and assistance with regard to practical concerns related to topics discussed in the book.
- *Index:* Separate indexes, by subject and by author, appear at the end of the book.
- *Illustrations:* A full-color illustration program of photographs and art underscores and expands upon the textual discussions. The illustration program includes many new figures and new, larger photographs.

Supplementary Materials

An extensive package of supplementary materials adds to the value of this book as a teaching and learning tool. The supplements listed here may accompany *A Child's World,* eighth edition. Please contact your local McGraw-Hill representative for details concerning policies, prices, and availability as some restrictions may apply.

1. *Student Study Guide*
   Written by Ruth Duskin Feldman, coauthor of *A Child's World,* eighth edition, the 16-chapter *Study Guide with Readings* corresponds directly to Chapters 1–16 of the text. Each chapter begins with a brief overview of the text chapter and has the following six major parts: chapter review, chapter quiz, topics for thought and discussion, chapter reading, suggestions for further reading, and answer key.

2. *Instructor's Manual*
   Written by Peggy Skinner, this manual offers a variety of resources designed to help instructors plan their courses around the text, prepare for lecture and discussion sessions, and implement these lectures and discussions to prompt critical thinking. Featured in this manual are new web links to promote student use of multimedia resources.

3. *Test Bank*
   Written by Dana Gross, this test bank is designed to closely correspond with the eighth edition of *A Child's World.* There are approximately 110 multiple choice questions for each of the 16 chapters. Featured in this edition are application and comprehension style questions in addition to questions that test retention of factual knowledge.

4. *Computerized Test Bank MAC*
   Formatted test questions in MAC to accompany *A Child's World,* eighth edition. This computerized test bank makes the task of creating tests and exams easier and faster than ever.

5. *Computerized Test Bank WIN*
   Formatted test questions in WINDOWS to accompany *A Child's World,* eighth edition. This computerized test bank makes the task of creating tests and exams easier and faster than ever.

6. *Overhead Transparencies*
   McGraw-Hill has developed a comprehensive set of overhead transparencies for the child development course. It consists of 175 four color images. These images have been formatted for enhanced classroom presentation.

7. *Videocases in Human Development: Infancy*
   This video is one of a four-part series on human development. It consists of four interviews covering various topics pertaining to prenatal issues. The subjects addressed include: Alternative Ways to Parenthood; Teratogens: Fetal Alcohol Syndrome and Fetal Alcohol Effects; Preterm Babies; and the Birth Process.

8. *Videocases in Human Development: Childhood*
   This video is one of a four-part series on human development. It consists of four interviews covering childhood issues. The subjects addressed include: Biracial Adoption; Child Prostitution; Attention Deficit Disorder and Attention Deficit Hyperactivity Disorder; and Chronic Life-Threatening Illness.

9. *Newsletter*
   A supplementary newsletter will be posted biannually to accompany the eighth edition of *A Child's World.* The items discussed serve a number of purposes: to present new findings, to expand upon the presentation of

material in the text, to shed light on controversial issues, and, as in the text itself, to highlight development in diverse cultures. You can access the newsletter through McGraw-Hill's website at *www.mhhe.com* or order a copy through your sales representative.

10. *Presentation Manager*
    This CD-ROM is available to faculty to help organize and custom design their lectures. This product offers a variety of supplementary materials to choose from, including videos, instructor manual material, powerpoint slides, student study guide resources and images.

11. *Powerpoint Slide Presentation*
    This set of approximately 130 powerpoint slides follows the chapter organization of the text *A Child's World,* eighth edition.

12. *Web Site*
    The address of this book's web site is: *www.mhhe.com/developmental.* Text-specific and general resources are available, including an outline of the features of the book, all available supplements, and both student and instructor resource areas complete with practice tests and links.

13. *The Critical Thinker*
    Richard Mayer and Fiona Goodchild of the University of California, Santa Barbara, use excerpts from introductory psychology textbooks to show students how to think critically about psychology.

14. *The AIDS Booklet*
    The fourth edition by Frank D. Cox of Santa Barbara City College is a brief but comprehensive introduction to acquired immune deficiency syndrome, which is caused by HIV (human immunodeficiency virus).

15. *Guide to Life-Span Development for Future Educators*
    New course supplement that helps students apply the concepts of human development to education. The supplement contains information, exercises, and sample tests designed to help students prepare for certification and understand human development from a professional perspective.

16. *AE: Child Growth and Development 98/99*
    Thirty-six articles covering developmental issues from conception to birth; cognition, language, and learning; social and emotional development; parenting and family issues; and cultural and societal influences.

17. *TS: Clashing Views on Controversial Issues in Childhood and Society, second edition*
    A debate-style reader designed to introduce students to controversies in childhood and society. The readings represent the arguments of leading child behaviorists and social commentators, reflect a variety of viewpoints, and have been selected for their liveliness and substance and for their value in a debate framework.

Ancillaries available with the adoption of the text. Please consult your sales representative for specific details and qualifying conditions.

Acknowledgments

We would like to express our gratitude to the many friends and colleagues who, through their work and their interest, helped us clarify our thinking about child development. We are especially grateful for the valuable help given by those who reviewed the published seventh edition of *A Child's World* and the manuscript drafts of this eighth edition, whose evaluations and suggestions helped greatly in the preparation of this new edition:

Special Contributors

Dana Gross
St. Olaf College

Tiffany Fields
University of Miami School of Medicine

Cindy S. Bergeman
University of Notre Dame

Dr. James Johnson
Department of Pediatrics
New York University Medical Center

Reviewers

Vance Rhoades
Brewton-Parker College

Susan Giboney
Pepperdine University

Andrew R. Eisen
Fairleigh Dickinson University

Elaine Hauff
Minneapolis Community College

Trisha Folds-Bennett
College of Charleston

Joan T. Bihun
University of Wisconsin-Madison

Joseph M. Price
San Diego State University

Debra L. Schwiesow
Creighton University

We appreciate the strong support we have had from our publisher and would like to express our special thanks to Jane Vaicunas, editorial director; Mickey Cox, our sponsoring editor; Sarah Thomas, her capable assistant; Jeannine Ciliotta, our insightful developmental editor; Sue Dillon, our project manager; Molly Middlecamp, our conscientious research assistant; Kerime Toksu, who carefully compiled the bibliography; Rose Kramer, our thorough copy editor; and above all, Dana Gross, whose painstaking contributions went far beyond the call of duty. Inge King, photo editor of all seven previous editions of *A Child's World,* again used her good eye and sensitivity to developmental issues to find outstanding photographs. Elise Lansdon produced a strikingly new and attractive book design to "clothe" our reborn "baby."

As always, we welcome and appreciate comments from readers, which help us continue to improve *A Child's World.*

Diane E. Papalia
Sally Wendkos Olds
Ruth Duskin Feldman

Resource Guide

✓ Adoptive and Stepfamilies

Adoptive Families of America
333 Highway 100 North
Minneapolis, MN 55422
Tel. 612-645-9955; fax 612-645-0055
800-372-3300
Umbrella organization for adoptive parent support groups; offers information and support in adoption and adoptive family problems; 24-hour hotline.

National Adoptive Information Clearinghouse
P.O. Box 1182
Washington, DC 20013-1182
Tel. 703-352-3488; fax 703-385-3206
E-mail: naic@calib.com; Internet:
http://www.calib.com/naic
800-251-0075
Information on all aspects of adoption, including intercountry adoption, adoption of children with special needs, state and federal adoption laws.

Stepfamily Foundation
333 West End Avenue
New York, NY 10023
Tel. 212-877-3124; fax 212-362-7030
E-mail: stepfamily@aol.com; Internet:
www.stepfamily.org
Counseling; information packets; seminars for social workers and medical personnel; cable show "Family Matters" in Manhattan.

✓ Alcohol and Drug Abuse

Al-Anon Family Group Headquarters
1600 Corporate Landing Parkway
Virginia Beach, VA 23454-5617
Tel. 757-563-1600; fax 757-563-1655
800-356-9996
Internet: http://www.al-anon.alateen.org;
e-mail: www.aa.org
Offers information and help to family and friends of people with drinking and drug problems.

Alcoholics Anonymous World Services
475 Riverside Drive
New York, NY 10115
Tel. 212-870-3400; fax 212-870-3003
The largest and most successful organization in the world for recovery from alcoholism, through meetings and peer support. All services are free.

Center for Substance Abuse and Treatment
Tel. 1-800-662-HELP
A 24-hour hotline sponsored by the federal government and affiliated with the National Institute of Drug Abuse.

Hazelden Educational Materials
Pleasant Valley Road
Box 176
Center City, MN 55012-0176
Tel. 800-328-9000; fax 612-257-1331
Website: www.hazelden.org
Nonprofit organization that publishes and sells a wide range of books, pamphlets, and video and audio cassettes about chemical dependency, both for users and those close to them. Free catalog.

National Clearinghouse for Alcohol and Drug Information
P.O. Box 2345
Rockville, MD 20847
Tel. 301-468-2600; fax 301-468-6433
Website: www.health.org
Government-sponsored source of literature.

✓ Birth Defects and Diseases

National Down Syndrome Society
666 Broadway, Room 810
New York, NY 10012
Tel. 212-460-9330; fax 212-979-2873
Website: www.ndss.org
Gives information about parent support groups, publications, and special programs

National Multiple Sclerosis Society
733 Third Avenue New York, NY 10017
Tel. 212-986-3240; fax 212-986-7981
Website: www.nmss.org
Gives information about research and treatment.

National Muscular Dystrophy Association
3300 East Sunrise Drive
Tucson, AZ 85718
Tel. 520-529-2000; fax 520-529-5300
E-mail: arb@mdausa.org;
Website: www.mdausa.org
Supplies general information about the disease and services offered.

Spina Bifida Association of American
4590 MacArthur Boulevard NW, Suite 250
Washington, DC 20007-4226
Tel. 202-944-3285; fax 202-944-3295; 800-621-3141
E-mail: sbaa@sbaa.org; Website: www.sbaa.org
Provides general information and referrals.

✓ Cancer

American Cancer Society (National Office)
1599 Clifton Road NE
Atlanta, GA 30329
Tel. 800-ACS-2345; fax 404-325-1467
For free information on almost any concern about cancer, this number will aid you in finding local resources.

National Cancer Institute
Building 31, Room 10-A-24
9000 Rockville Pike
Bethesda, MD 20892
Tel. 800-4-CANCER
Website: http://cancernet.nci.nih.gov;
http://rex.nci.nih.gov
Persons at this number will answer cancer-related
questions in addition to providing free
information on cancer prevention.

✓ Child Abuse and Advocacy

American Coalition for Abuse Awareness
PO Box 27959
1858 Park Road NW, 2d floor
Washington, DC 20038-7959
Tel. 202-462-4688; fax 202-462-4689
E-mail: acaad@aol.com
Champions rights of victims and survivors of
childhood sexual abuse; provides information on
legal issues.

Childhelp USA
15757 North 78th Street
Scottsdale, AZ 85260
Tel. 800-423-4453; 800-4-A-CHILD
Website: http://www.charities.org/chidhelp/
index.html.
Dedicated to treatment and prevention of child
abuse; operates residential centers, recovery
programs, referral services; 24-hour hotline.

✓ Disabilities

Center on Human Policy
Syracuse University
805 S. Crouse Avenue
Room 101
Syracuse, NY 13244-2280
Tel. 315-443-3851; fax 315-443-4338; 800-894-0826
E-mail: thechp@sued.syr.edu; Internet:
www.soeweb.syr.edu/thechp/
Disseminates information on laws, regulations
and programs affecting those with disabilities,
especially developmental disabilities.

Disability Resources
4 Glatter Lane
Centereach, NY 11720-1032
Tel. 516-585-0290; fax (same #)
E-mail: jklaubere@suffolk.lib.ny.us;
Internet: www.diabilitiesresources.org
Provides information to help those with
disabilities to live independently.

International Dyslexia Association
8600 LaSalle Road
Chester Building, Suite 382
Baltimore, MD 21286-2044
Tel. 410-296-0232; fax 410-321-5069
E-mail: info@interdys.org
Provides information about reading and writing
disorders.

**National Information Center for Children
and Youth with Disabilities**
PO Box 1492
Washington, DC 20013
Tel. 202-884-8200; fax 202-884-8441; 800-695-0285
E-mail: nichcy@aed.org;
Website: www.nichcy.org
Provides information to parents, educators,
caregivers, and advocates to help children and
youth with disabilities participate at home, in
school, and in the community.

Pilot Parents
3610 Dodge Street, Suite 101
Omaha, NE 68131
Tel. 402-346-5220; fax 402-346-5253
Support for new parents of children with special
needs; parent matching program matches
experienced parents with parents of newly
diagnosed children to share expertise and
experiences.

✓ Divorce/Custody

Fathers' Rights and Equality Exchange
3140 Delacruz Blvd., Suite 200
Santa Clara, CA 95054
Tel. 415-853-6877; e-mail FREE@VIX.com
Website: http://www.free@vix.com
Offers educational programs, referrals, and
support for noncustodial divorced fathers.

Joint Custody Association
10606 Wilkins Avenue
Los Angeles, CA 90024
Tel. 310-475-5352; fax 310-474-4859
Disseminates information on joint custody for
children of divorce; assists children, parents,
attorneys, and jurists.

✓ Education and Child Care

ChildCare Action Campaign
330 Seventh Avenue, 17th floor
New York, NY 10001
Tel. 212-239-0138; fax 212-268-6515
National coalition of leaders from various
institutions and organizations serves as an
advocacy group offering information on many
aspects of child care through individual
information sheets, a bimonthly newsletter, and
audio training tapes for family day-care providers.

National Association of Bilingual Education
1220 L Street NW, Suite 605
Washington, DC 20005-4018
Tel. 202-898-1829; fax 202-789-2866
E-mail: NABE@nabe.org
A nationwide advocacy organization that
promotes equal opportunity for language-
minority students and academic excellence for all
students.

National Association for the Education of Young Children
1509 16th Street NW
Washington, DC 20036-1426
Tel. 800-424-4260; fax 202-328-1846
Website: www.naeyc.org/naeyc
Professional association that accredits child-care
centers and preschools around the country, holds
regional and national meetings, and distributes
publications for both professionals and parents.

National Black Child Development Institute
1023 15th Street NW, Suite 600
Washington, DC 20005
Tel. 202-387-1281; fax 202-234-1738
E-mail: moreinfo@nbcdi.org
Website: www.nbcdi.org
This national nonprofit organization focuses on
child care, health, education, and welfare. It holds
conferences, conducts tutorial programs, and
helps homeless children find adoptive families.

✓ Family Support

Alternative Family Project
PO Box 16631
San Francisco, CA 94116
Tel. 415-566-5683
Provides affordable therapy for nontraditional
families.

Family Resource Coalition
20 North Wacker Drive, Suite 1100
Chicago, IL 60606
Tel. 312-338-0900; fax 312-338-1522
Provides information on support groups
nationwide, offering a broad array of services.

Mothers Network
70 West 36 Street, Suite 900
New York, NY 10018
Tel. 800-7769-6667; fax 212-239-0510
Provides information on services and products
for parents with children under 5.

Parents Without Partners
401 North Michigan Avenue
Chicago, IL 60611-4267
Tel. 312-644-6610; fax 312-321-5194; 800-637-7974
E-mail: pwp@sba.com;
Website: www.parentswithoutpartners.org
Provides information on problems of single
parents.

✓ Grandparenting

AARP Grandparenting Information Center
Tel. 202-424-2296
Connects grandparents with local support groups
and resources; works with national and local
agencies involved in child care, aging issues, and
legal and family services.

Grandparents'-Children's Rights, Inc.
5728 Bayonne Avenue
Haslett, MI 48840
Tel. 517-339-8663
Information and counseling for grandparents
whose relationship with grandchildren is
changed or broken by divorce; problems with
custodial grandparenting, visitation rights,
stepgrandchildren, other issues.

Grandparents Raising Grandchildren
Barbara Kirkland
PO Box 104
Colleyville, TX 76034
Tel. 817-577-0435
Information on issues; support for starting local
self-help groups.

National Coalition of Grandparents
137 Larkin Street
Madison, WI 53705
Tel. 608-238-8751
A nationwide consortium of groups and
individuals concerned with grandparents and
children. A source of information, support, and
attorney referrals.

✓ Infant Mortality

Compassionate Friends, Inc.
P.O. Box 3696
Oak Brook, IL 60522-3696
Tel. 708-990-0010
Offers support to bereaved parents and siblings of infants and older children through 660 chapters in the United States.

National Sudden Infant Death Syndrome Resource Center
2070 Chain Bridge Road, Suite 450
Vienna, VA 22182
Tel. 703-821-8955; fax 703-821-2098
E-mail: sids@circsol.com
Website: www.circsol.com.sids
Provides resources and information.

✓ Infertility

Resolve
1310 Broadway
Somerville, MA 02144-1731
Tel. 617-623-0744
National, nonprofit organization that offers counseling services to infertile couples.

✓ Medical Help

American Trauma Society
8903 Presidential Parkway, Suite 512
Upper Marlboro, MD 20772-2656
Tel. 800-556-7890; fax 301-420-0617
E-mail: atstrauma@aol.com;
Website: www.amtrauma.org
Offers literature on accident prevention.

✓ Mental Health

National Institute of Mental Health
Public Inquiries Branch
5600 Fishers Lane, Room 7C02
Rockville, MD 20857
Tel. 301-443-4513; fax 301-443-4279
E-mail: nimhunfo@nih.gov
Website: www.nimh.nih.gov
Federally sponsored agency that answers questions about depression and other psychological disorders.

✓ Missing and Runaway Children

Child Find
P.O. Box 277
New Paltz, NY 12561
Tel. 914-255-1848; fax 914-255-5706; 800-I AM LOST
Hotline to report disappearances or sightings.

National Center for Missing and Exploited Children
2101 Wilson Boulevard, Suite 550
Arlington, VA 22201
Tel. 800-843-5678; fax 703-235-4069
E-mail: nemec@cis.compusene.com
Website: www.missingkids.com
Hotline to report disappearances or sightings.

National Runaway Switchboard
3080 North Lincoln Avenue
Chicago, IL 60657
Tel. 800-621-4000
Confidential crisis intervention and referral for runaway homeless youth and their families; and youth in crisis throughout the country.

✓ Pregnancy and Childbirth

American Society for Psychoproplylaxis in Obstetrics/Lamaze
1200 19th Street NW, Suite 300
Washington, DC 20036
Tel. 202-223-4579; 800-368-4404
E-mail: lamaze@dc.sba.com;
Website: www.lamaze-childbirth.com
Makes referrals to local Lamaze instructors, which help prospective parents prepare for childbirth and infant care.

Center for the Study of Multiple Birth
333 East Superior Street, Suite 464
Chicago, IL 60611
Tel. 312-266-9093
Disseminates information on the risks of multiple birth; resource center for media and the public.

International Childbirth Education Association
P.O. Box 20048
Minneapolis, MN 55420
Tel. 612-854-8660; fax 612-854-8872; 800-624-4934
E-mail: info@icea.org; Website: www.icea.org
Offers a free catalog of materials on pregnancy, childbirth, and child care.

✓ Sexually Transmitted Diseases and Aids

AIDS Hotline/American Social Health Association
Tel. 800-324-AIDS
Spanish: 800-344-7432 8 AM–2 AM EST 7 days a week
Hearing impaired: 800-243-7889 10 AM–10 PM EST M–F
Run by the Centers for Disease Control, this 24-hour hotline provides basic information on AIDS, HIV testing, prevention, and referral to treatment centers.

American Foundation for the Prevention of Venereal Disease
799 Broadway, Suite 638
New York, NY 10003
Tel. 212-759-2069
Publishes a booklet and other education materials on sexually transmitted diseases.

Children's Defense Fund
25 E Street NW
Washington, DC 20001
Tel. 202-628-8787; fax 202-662-3510
E-mail: cdfinfo@childrensdefense.org
Website: www.childrensdefense.org
Provides information and resources on a wide range of issues concerning children.

National AIDS Clearinghouse
P.O. Box 6003
Rockville, MD 20849-6003
Tel. 800-458-5231; fax 301-738-6616
Website: www.cdcnac.org
Provides information, publications, and public assistance concerning HIV and AIDS. Has reference and referral staff.

VD/STD National Hotline
Tel. 800-227-8922
Provides basic information on sexually transmitted diseases, as well as referrals to free or low-cost clinics in your area.

✓ Speech and Hearing

National Center for Stuttering
200 East 33rd Street
New York, NY 10016
Tel. 800-221-2483; 212-532-1460 (in New York); fax 212-683-1372
Website: www.stuttering.com
Provides information and literature on treatment programs.

Prologue
Reentering a Child's World

When you look through your family photo album and see pictures of yourself during your childhood, it may seem as if you are stepping back onto a terrain that is familiar yet strange. Is that really you in those images frozen in time? When you see that first portrait of yourself, soon after birth, do you wonder how it felt to come into this world? There you are on your bicycle. Do you remember how easy or hard it was to learn to ride? Did you take a lot of spills? How about that photo taken on your first day of school—were you nervous about meeting your teacher? Now flip ahead to your high school graduation picture. How did that helpless baby turn into the sturdy child on the two-wheeler and then into the cap-and-gowned young person about to step into the world of adulthood?

Snapshots tell us little about the processes of change that take place as a child grows up. Even a series of home videos, which can follow children from moment to moment as they get older, will not capture a progression of changes so subtle that we often cannot detect them until after they have occurred. The influences that produce those developmental changes are the subject of this book.

Child Development: An Exciting, Evolving Field

Children have been the focus of scientific study for more than one hundred years. This exploration is an ever-evolving, dynamic endeavor. The questions that developmentalists—people engaged in the professional study of human development—seek to answer, the methods they use, and the explanations they propose are not the same today as they were even 25 years ago. These shifts reflect progress in understanding, as new investigations build on or challenge those that went before. They also reflect the changing cultural and technological context, which influences the goals, attitudes, and tools that scientists bring to their work.

Advances in neuroscience and brain imaging are making it possible to probe the mysteries of temperament—tracing overanxiety, for example, to the chemical makeup of the brain. Advances in behavioral genetics enable scientists to assess more precisely the relative influences of inheritance and experience. Cameras, videocassette recorders, and computers allow investigators to scan infants' facial expressions for early signs of emotions and to analyze moment-by-moment how mothers and babies communicate with and respond to one another. Sensitive instruments that measure eye movements, heart rate, blood pressure, muscle tension, and the like are turning up intriguing connections between biological functions and psychological or social ones: between infant visual attentiveness and childhood intelligence, between electrical brain wave patterns and the emergence of logical thought, and between the chemical content of blood plasma and the likelihood of delinquency. New methods of assessing abilities have led to greater appreciation of the physical, cognitive (mental), emotional, and social competencies of young children.

Guideposts for Exploring a Child's World

As the study of children has matured, a broad consensus has emerged on several fundamental points. We list them here, in summary form, as guideposts to help you find your way more easily as you venture further into a child's world.

1. *All domains of development are interrelated.* Although developmentalists often look separately at various aspects of development, each affects the others. For example, increasing physical mobility affects a baby's knowledge of the world, sense of competence, and self-esteem; the growth of memory allows preschoolers to obey their parents' rules even when the parents are out of sight; and the hormonal and physical changes of puberty affect emotional and cognitive development.

2. *Normal development includes a wide range of individual differences.* Each child, from the start, is unlike anyone else in the world. One is outgoing, another shy. One is agile, another awkward. How those differences, and a multitude of others, come about is one of the fascinating questions we address in this book. Some of the influences on individual differences are inborn. Others come from experience. Family characteristics, the effects of gender, social class, race, and ethnicity, and the presence or absence of physical, mental, or emotional disability all make a difference.

3. *Children help shape their own development and influence others' responses to them.* Right from the start, through the responses they evoke in others, infants mold their environment and then respond to the environment they have helped create. Influence is *bidirectional:* parents treat a cheerful baby differently from an irritable one, and their treatment may in turn encourage the infant to become more cheerful or irritable. When babies babble and coo, adults are more likely to talk to them, which then makes the baby "talk" more.

4. *The historical and cultural contexts strongly influence development.* Each child develops within a specific environment, bounded by time and place. In studying children, we need to determine whether patterns of development are universal or specific to a given culture. And, since what happens around children affects them in many ways, it is important to look at development in context. Major historical events such as wars, depressions, and famines impinge profoundly on the development of entire generations. So do revolutionary new technologies, such as the computer. Medical advances, as well as improvements in nutrition and sanitation, have dramatically reduced infant and child mortality. Social changes, such as the increasing proportion of mothers in the workplace, have altered the landscape of the world of children.

5. *Early experience is important, but children can be remarkably resilient.* A traumatic incident or a severely deprived childhood may well have grave emotional consequences, but the life histories of countless people show that a single experience—even one as painful as the death of a parent in childhood—does not necessarily cause irreversible damage. On the other hand, in some ways, the ability to overcome early experience is limited; certain connections in the brain, if not stimulated at critical times in its growth, may shut down permanently, restricting development.

6. *Development in childhood is connected to development throughout the rest of the life span.* At one time, it was believed that growth and development end, as this book does, with adolescence. Today most developmentalists agree that development goes on throughout life. People continue to change as long as they live.

Studying Real Children in the Real World

The scientific study of children reflects the belief that knowledge is useful. The classic distinction between *basic research,* the kind undertaken purely in a spirit of intellectual inquiry, and *applied research,* which addresses an immediate practical problem, is becoming less meaningful; increasingly, research findings have direct application to child rearing, education, health, and social policy. For example, research into preschool children's understanding of death can enable adults to help a child deal with bereavement; research on children's memory can help determine the weight to be given children's courtroom testimony; and research on factors that increase the risks of low birthweight, antisocial behavior, and teenage suicide can suggest ways to prevent these ills.

Ultimately, it is *you* who will be able to apply what you learn from this book. Real children are not abstractions on the printed page. They are living, laughing, crying, shouting, tantrum-throwing, question-asking human beings. Observe the children about you. Listen to them. Look at them. Pause to pay attention as they confront and experience the wonder of life. Look too at the child you once were, and try to understand what made you the person you are. With the insights you gain as you read this book, you will be able to look at yourself and at every child you see with new eyes.

About a Child's World: History, Theory, and Research Methods

CHAPTER

1

There is one thing even more vital to science than intelligent methods; and that is, the sincere desire to find out the truth, whatever it may be.

Charles Sanders Peirce, *Collected Papers*, vol. 5

Focus
Victor, the Wild Boy of Aveyron

On January 8, 1800, a naked boy, his face and neck heavily scarred, appeared on the outskirts of the village of Saint-Sernin in the sparsely populated province of Aveyron in south central France. The boy, who was only four and a half feet tall but looked about 12 years old, had been spotted several times during the previous two and a half years, climbing trees, running on all fours, drinking from streams, and foraging for acorns and roots. He had been caught twice but had escaped. Then, in the unusually cold winter of 1799–1800, he had begun showing up at farmhouses seeking food.

When the dark-eyed boy came to Saint-Sernin, he neither spoke nor responded to speech, yet would turn around instantly at the sound of walnuts being cracked or a dog barking. He spurned prepared foods, preferring raw potatoes, which he threw into a fire, quickly retrieved with his bare hands, and devoured burning hot. Like an animal accustomed to living in the wild, the boy seemed insensitive to both extreme heat and extreme cold, and he tore off the clothing people tried to put on him. It seemed clear that he had either lost his parents or been abandoned by them, but how long ago this had occurred was impossible to tell.

The boy appeared during a time of intellectual and social ferment, when a new, scientific outlook was beginning to replace mystical speculation. Philosophers debated questions about the essential nature of human beings—questions that would, within the next two centuries, become central to the study of child development. Are the qualities, behavior, and ideas that define human beings innate or acquired? What is the effect of social contact during the formative years, and can its lack be overcome? A carefully documented study of a child who had grown up in isolation might provide evidence of the relative impact of "nature" (a child's inborn characteristics) and "nurture" (upbringing, schooling, and other societal influences).

After initial observation, the boy, who came to be called Victor, was sent to a school for deaf-mutes in Paris. There, he was turned over to Jean-Marc-Gaspard Itard, an ambitious 26-year-old practitioner of the emerging science of "mental medicine," or psychiatry. The boy was, Itard wrote, "a disgustingly dirty child . . . , who bit and scratched those who opposed him, who showed no affection for those who took care of him; and who was, in short, indifferent to everything and attentive to nothing" (Lane, 1976, p. 4). Some observers concluded that he was an "idiot," incapable of learning. But Itard believed that Victor's development had been limited by isolation and that he simply needed to be taught the skills that children in civilized society normally acquire through everyday living.

Itard took Victor into his home and, during the next five years, gradually "tamed" him. Itard first awakened his pupil's ability to discriminate sensory experience through hot baths and dry rubs, and then moved on to painstaking, step-by-step training of emotional responses and instruction in moral and social behavior, language, and thought. The methods Itard used—based on principles of imitation, conditioning, and behavioral modification, all of which we discuss later in this chapter—were far ahead of their time, and he invented many teaching devices used today. Indeed, Itard, refining the techniques he had used with Victor, went on to become a pioneer in special education.

But the education of Victor, which was dramatized in Francois Truffaut's film *The Wild Child,* was not an unqualified success. The boy did make remarkable progress: he learned the names of many objects and could read and write simple sentences; and he could express desires, obey commands, and exchange ideas. He showed affection, especially for Itard's housekeeper, Madame Guérin, as well as such emotions as pride, shame, remorse, and the desire to please. However, aside from uttering some vowel and consonant sounds, he never learned to speak. Furthermore, he remained totally focused on his own wants and needs, and, as Itard admitted in his final report, never seemed to lose his yearning "for the freedom of the open country and his indifference to most of the pleasures of social life" (Lane, 1976, p. 160). When the study ended, Victor—no longer able to fend for himself, as he had done in the wild—went to live with Madame Guérin (who received a stipend from the French government for his care) until his death in his early forties in 1828.

Sources of information about the wild boy of Aveyron were Frith, 1989, and Lane, 1976.

• • •

hy did Victor fail to fulfill Itard's initial hopes for him? It has been suggested that the boy was a victim of brain damage, autism (a disorder involving lack of social responsiveness), or severe early maltreatment. Itard's instructional methods, advanced as they were, may have been inadequate. Itard himself came to believe that the effects of long isolation could not be fully overcome, and that Victor may have been too old, especially for language learning.

Although Victor's story does not yield definitive answers to the questions Itard set out to explore, it is important because it was one of the first systematic attempts to study a child's development. Since Victor's time, we have learned much about the development of children, but developmentalists are still investigating such fundamental questions as the relative importance of nature and nurture. Victor's story dramatizes the challenges and complexities of the scientific study of a child's world—the study on which you are about to embark.

This first chapter is like an atlas for the world of children. It presents routes for studying child development; traces journeys that investigators have followed in the quest for information about what makes children grow up the way they do; points out the main directions theorists and researchers follow today; and poses questions about the best way to reach the destination: knowledge.

After reading this chapter, you should be able to answer and elaborate on such questions as these:

Preview Questions

- What does *development* mean, and why and how do scientists study it?

- What are the main aspects of children's development, and how do they overlap?

- How has the study of child development evolved, and who were some of its pioneers?

- What major theoretical perspectives try to explain child development, on what central issues do they differ, and what are their strengths and weaknesses?

- How do developmentalists study children, and what are the advantages and disadvantages of each research method?

A Child's World: Basic Concepts

child development Scientific study of change and continuity throughout childhood.

The field of *child development* is concerned with the scientific study of ways in which children change, as well as ways in which they stay the same, from conception through adolescence. Developmentalists focus on *developmental change*, which is both *systematic* and *adaptive* (effective in dealing with the conditions of existence). It may take more than one route and may or may not have a definite goal, but there is some connection between the often-imperceptible changes of which it is composed.

There are two kinds of developmental change: *quantitative* and *qualitative*. *Quantitative change* is a change in number or amount, such as growth in height, weight, vocabulary, or frequency of communication. *Qualitative change* is a change in kind, structure, or organization, such as the development from a nonverbal child to one who understands words and can communicate verbally. Qualitative change is marked by the appearance of new phenomena not readily predictable from earlier functioning, such as the use of language.

quantitative change Change in number or amount, such as in height, weight, or size of vocabulary.

qualitative change Change in kind, structure, or organization, such as the change from nonverbal to verbal communication.

Despite these changes, most children show an underlying continuity, or consistency, of personality and behavior. For example, about 10 to 15 percent of children are consistently shy, and another 10 to 15 percent are very sociable. Although various influences can modify these traits somewhat, they seem to persist to a moderate degree, especially in children at one extreme or the other (see Chapter 2). Which of a child's characteristics are most likely to endure? Which are likely to change, and why? These are among the questions that the study of child development seeks to answer.

Although the basic physical and psychological processes of development are the same for every normal child, their outcome is different—as different as you are from each of your classmates. Students of development are interested in factors that affect everyone, but they also want to know why one child turns out so different from another. Because development is complex and cannot always be precisely measured, scientists cannot answer that question fully. However, they have learned much about what children need to develop normally, how they react to the many influences upon and within them, and how they can best fulfill their potential.

Aspects and Periods of Development

One reason for the complexity of child development is that change and continuity occur in various aspects of the self. To simplify discussion, we talk separately about *physical development, cognitive development,* and *psychosocial development* at each period of childhood. Actually, though, these aspects of development are intertwined. Throughout life, each affects the others.

Growth of the body and brain, sensory capacities, motor skills, and health are part of *physical development* and may influence other aspects of development. For example, a child with frequent ear infections may develop language more slowly than a child without this problem. During puberty, dramatic physiological and hormonal changes affect the developing sense of self.

Changes in mental abilities, such as learning, memory, language, thinking, reasoning, and creativity constitute *cognitive development.* They are closely related to physical and emotional growth. The ability to speak depends on the physical development of the mouth and brain; and a child who has difficulty with expressive language may evoke negative reactions in others, influencing his or her popularity and self-esteem.

personality Person's unique and relatively consistent way of feeling, reacting, and behaving.

Personality is a person's unique and relatively consistent way of feeling, reacting, and behaving. *Social development* concerns relationships with others. Taken together, personality and social development constitute *psychosocial development.* This can affect both cognitive and physical functioning. For example, anxiety about taking a test can impair physical or intellectual performance. Social support can help children cope with the potentially negative effects of stress on physical and mental health. Conversely, physical and cognitive capacities contribute to self-esteem and can affect social acceptance.

In this book we explore child development chronologically by looking at the various aspects of development during the five periods of childhood (see Table 1-1): (1) prenatal (before birth), (2) infancy and toddlerhood, (3) early childhood, (4) middle childhood, and (5) adolescence. These divisions are, of course, approximate and somewhat arbitrary, and many individual differences exist in the way children deal with the characteristic events and issues of each period.

Influences on Development

Each child is like other children in some ways but unique in others. Children differ in height, weight, and body build; in constitutional factors such as health and energy level; in intelligence; and in personality characteristics and emotional reactions. The contexts of their lives differ too: the homes, communities, and societies they live in, the relationships they have, the kinds of schools they go to (or whether they go to school at all), and how they spend their leisure time.

A child's development is subject to countless influences. Some originate with *heredity*—the inborn genetic endowment that human beings receive from their biological parents. Others come from the external *environment*—the world outside the self, beginning in the womb. Individual differences increase as children grow older. Many typical changes of infancy and childhood seem to be tied to *maturation* of the body and brain—the unfolding of a natural, genetically influenced sequence of physical changes and behavior patterns, including readiness to master new abilities such as walking and talking. As children grow into adolescents and then into adults, differences in innate characteristics and life experience play a greater role.

Even in processes that all children go through, rates and timing of development vary. Throughout this book, we talk about average ages for the occurrence of certain behaviors: the first word, the first step, the first menstruation or "wet dream," the development of logical thought. But these ages are merely averages. Although children typically proceed through the same general sequence of development, there is a wide range of normal individual differences. Only when deviation from a norm is extreme is there cause to consider a child's development exceptionally advanced or delayed.

In trying to understand the similarities and differences in children's development, then, we need to look at the *inherited* characteristics that give each child a unique start in life. We also need to consider the many *environmental* factors, or contexts, that affect children—such factors as family, socioeconomic status, race or ethnicity, and culture. We need to look at influences that affect many or most children at a certain age or a certain time in history, and also at those that affect only certain individuals. Finally, we need to look at how timing can affect the impact of certain influences.

Family, Socioeconomic Status, Ethnicity, and Culture

Family may mean something different in different societies. Even its definition in American society has changed greatly. At one time, the **nuclear family,** a two-generational kinship, economic, and household unit consisting of two parents and their biological or adopted children, was the form in which the vast majority of children in the United States grew up. Today increasing numbers of children live in single-parent families, in stepfamilies, or with homosexual parents. In many societies, such as those of Asia and Latin America, and among some cultural minorities in the United States, the **extended family**—a multigenerational kinship

heredity Inborn influences on development, carried on the genes inherited from the parents.

environment Totality of nongenetic influences on development, external to the self.

maturation Unfolding of a genetically influenced, often age-related, sequence of physical changes and behavior patterns, including the readiness to master new abilities.

nuclear family Two-generational economic, kinship, and living unit made up of parents and their biological or adopted children.

extended family Multigenerational kinship network of parents, children, and more distant relatives, sometimes living together in an *extended-family household.*

Table 1-1   Major Developments in Five Periods of the Life Span

Age Period	Major Developments
Prenatal Stage *(conception to birth)*	Basic body structure and organs form. Physical growth is most rapid in the life span. Vulnerability to environmental influences is great.
Infancy and Toddlerhood *(birth to age 3)*	All senses operate at birth; vision improves during first few months. The brain grows in complexity and is highly sensitive to environmental influence. Physical growth and development of motor skills are rapid. Ability to learn and remember is present, even in early weeks. Use of symbols and ability to solve problems develop by end of second year. Comprehension and use of language develop rapidly. Attachments to parents and others form. Self-awareness develops. Shift from dependence to autonomy occurs. Interest in other children increases.
Early Childhood *(3 to 6 years)*	Growth is steady; appearance becomes more slender and proportions more adultlike. Appetite diminishes, and sleep problems are common. Handedness appears; fine and gross motor skills and strength improve. Thinking is somewhat egocentric, but understanding of other people's perspectives grows. Cognitive immaturity leads to some illogical ideas about the world. Memory and language improve. Intelligence becomes more predictable. Preschool experience is common. Self-concept and understanding of emotions become more complex; self-esteem is global. Gender identity develops. Play becomes more imaginative, more elaborate, and more social. Independence, initiative, self-control, and self-care increase. Altruism, aggression, and fearfulness are common. Family is still focus of social life, but other children become more important.
Middle Childhood *(6 to 11 years)*	Growth slows. Strength and athletic skills improve. Respiratory illnesses are common, but health is generally better than at any other time in life span. Egocentrism diminishes. Children begin to think logically but concretely. Memory and language skills increase. Cognitive gains permit children to benefit from formal schooling. Some children show special educational needs and strengths. Self-concept becomes more complex, affecting self-esteem. Coregulation reflects gradual shift in control from parents to child. Peers assume central importance.
Adolescence *(11 to about 20 years)*	Physical growth and other changes are rapid and profound. Reproductive maturity arrives. Major health risks arise (eating disorders, drug abuse, sexually transmitted diseases). Ability to think abstractly and use scientific reasoning develops. Immature thinking persists in some attitudes and behaviors. Education focuses on preparation for college or vocation. Search for identity, including sexual identity, becomes central. Relationships with parents are generally good. Peer groups help develop and test self-concept but also may exert an antisocial influence.

The typical family unit in many nonwestern societies, such as Turkey, is a multigenerational *extended family,* which may include grandparents, uncles, aunts, cousins, and even more distant relatives.

network of grandparents, aunts, uncles, cousins, and more distant relatives—is an intimate part of children's lives, and many or most people live in *extended-family households.*

Socioeconomic status (SES) involves a variety of related factors, including income, education, and occupation. Throughout this book, we describe many studies that relate SES to developmental outcomes, such as health, cognitive performance, and differences in mothers' verbal interaction with their children. However, it is generally not SES itself that affects these outcomes, but factors associated with SES, such as the kind of home and neighborhood a child lives in and the quality of medical care and schooling a child receives.

An **ethnic group** is a group of people united by ancestry, race, religion, language, and/or national origins, which contribute to a sense of shared identity. Most ethnic groups have, or originally had, a common *culture. Culture* refers to a society's or group's total way of life, including customs, traditions, beliefs, values, language, and physical products, from tools to art works—all of the learned behavior that is passed on from adults to children. Culture is not static; it is constantly changing, often through interaction with other cultures. In large, multi-ethnic societies such as the United States, cultural change is particularly noticeable among immigrant or minority ethnic groups, which adapt, or *acculturate,* to the majority culture while preserving or modifying some aspects of their own.

When we talk about influences of ethnicity and culture, especially on members of minority groups, it is important to distinguish between effects of shared biological traits, of SES (which may result from prejudice or lack of educational and employment opportunity), and of cultural attitudes that help

socioeconomic status (SES) Combination of economic and social factors, including income, education, and occupation.

ethnic group Group united by ancestry, race, religion, language, and/or national origins, which contribute to a sense of shared identity.

culture A society's or group's total way of life, including customs, traditions, beliefs, values, language, and physical products—all learned behavior passed on from adults to children.

Box 1-1 Purposes of Cross-Cultural Research

When David, an American child, was asked to identify the missing detail in a picture of a face with no mouth, he said, "The mouth." But Ari, an Asian immigrant child in Israel, said that the *body* was missing. Since art in his culture does not present a head as a complete picture, he thought the absence of a body was more important than the omission of "a mere detail like the mouth" (Anastasi, 1988, p. 360).

By looking at people from different cultural and ethnic groups, researchers can learn in what ways development is universal (and thus intrinsic to the human condition) and in what ways it is culturally determined. For example, children everywhere learn to speak in the same sequence, advancing from cooing and babbling to single words and then to simple combinations of words. The words vary from culture to culture, but around the world toddlers put them together to form sentences similar in structure. Such findings suggest that the capacity for learning language is universal and inborn.

On the other hand, culture can exert a surprisingly large influence on early motor development. African babies, whose parents often prop them in a sitting position and bounce them on their feet, tend to sit and walk earlier than American babies (Rogoff & Morelli, 1989).

One hundred years ago, most developmentalists assumed that the fundamental processes of development were universal. Cross-cultural research, when done, was seen as a way to highlight the workings of these universal processes under contrasting environmental conditions. Today it is becoming more and more evident that the cultural context can make a critical difference in the timing and expression of many aspects of development (Parke, Ornstein, Rieser, & Zahn-Waxler, 1994).

The society that children grow up in influences the skills they learn. In the United States, children learn to read, write, and operate computers; in rural Nepal, they learn how to drive water buffalo and find their way along mountain paths. The Russian psychologist Lev Vygotsky, whose sociocultural theory we discuss later in this chapter, analyzes how specific practices in a culture affect development. When, for example, a Hindu girl in a small village in Nepal touched the plow that her older brother was using, she was severely rebuked. In this way she learned that as a female she was restricted from acts her brothers were expected to perform (D. Skinner, 1989).

One important reason to conduct research among different cultural groups is to recognize biases in traditional western theories and research that often go unquestioned until they are shown to be a product of cultural influences. "Working with people from a quite different background can make one aware of aspects of human activity that are not noticeable until they are missing or differently arranged, as with the fish who reputedly is unaware of water until removed from it" (Rogoff & Morelli, 1989, p. 343). For example, in Chapter 7 we cite studies done in Sweden, Germany, Africa, and India that contradict the common assumption that fathers the world over play more roughly with infants than mothers do.

Since so much research in child development has focused on children in western industrialized societies, many people have defined the typical development of western children as the norm, or standard of behavior. Measuring against this "norm" leads to narrow—and often, wrong—ideas about development. Pushed to its extreme, this belief can cause the development of children in other ethnic and cultural groups to be seen as deviant (Rogoff & Morelli, 1989).

In Chapter 15, we discuss Lawrence Kohlberg's influential theory of moral development. As we will see, this and other theories that were developed from research on western participants do not always hold up when tested on people in other cultures. Throughout this book, we consistently look at children in cultures other than the dominant one in the United States to show how closely development is tied to society and culture and to add to our understanding of normal development in many settings.

shape children's development (such as the value placed on education by members of different groups).

Normative and Nonnormative Influences

Some experiences are purely individual; others may be universal (see Box 1-1). Still others are common to certain groups—to age groups, to generations, or to people who live in or were raised in particular societies and cultures at particular times.

Developmentalists distinguish between normative and nonnormative (or idiosyncratic) influences on development (Baltes, Reese, & Lipsitt, 1980). An event is *normative* when it occurs in a similar way for most people in a group. *Normative age-graded influences* are highly similar for people in a particular age group. They include biological events (such as puberty) and cultural events (such as entry into formal education).

Normative history-graded influences are common to a particular *cohort:* a group of people who share a similar experience, in this case growing up at the same time in the same place. Depending on when and where they live, children may feel the impact of wars, famines, economic depressions, or nuclear explosions. Historical changes in medical practice, technology, and social organization have changed the very nature of child development. Babies born in the United States today are less likely than in the past to be subjected to heavy maternal sedation during labor and delivery and more likely to have their fathers present at the birth. As they grow up, they are likely to be influenced by digital television, the Internet, and other technological developments yet undreamed of. Already most children are affected by the widespread participation of women in the work force.

Nonnormative life events are unusual events that have a major impact on individual lives and may cause stress because they are unexpected. They are either typical events that happen at an atypical time of life (such as the death of a parent when a child is young) or atypical events (such as having a birth defect or being in an automobile crash). They can also, of course, be happy events, such as winning a scholarship. Young people may help create their own nonnormative life events—say, by driving after drinking, or applying for a scholarship—and thus participate actively in their own development.

Timing of Influences: Critical or Sensitive Periods

A *critical period* is a specific time during development when a given event, or its lack, has the greatest impact. For example, if a woman receives X rays, takes certain drugs, or contracts certain diseases at specific times during pregnancy, the fetus may show specific ill effects. The amount and kind of damage will vary, depending on the nature of the "shock" and on its timing.

In Chapter 5, we point to several instances in which a child deprived of certain kinds of experiences during a critical period is likely to show permanent stunting of physical development. Undernourishment during the critical period of brain growth just after birth can result in brain damage. In addition, postnatal exposure to certain specific sensory experiences is necessary to complete the brain's "wiring." For example, mutual, face-to-face interactions with an adult caregiver during the first 6 months to 1 year of life may stimulate the brain to grow circuits that regulate emotional excitement (Pally, 1997). The first 3 years seem to be a critical period for development of binocular vision (ability to focus the eyes). If a physical problem interfering with visual coordination, such as crossed eyes, is not corrected during that period, binocular vision will not develop as well as it otherwise would. Conversely, enriched sensory or motor experience during a critical period in early infancy may speed up development; giving 1-week-old infants an opportunity to practice stepping movements may lead to early walking.

The concept of critical periods is more controversial when applied to cognitive and psychosocial development. For these aspects of development there seems to be greater *plasticity,* or modifiability of performance. Although the human organism may be particularly *sensitive* to certain psychological experiences at certain times of life, later events can often reverse the effects of early ones. As we report in Chapter 7, for example, early attachment patterns between infants and parents are generally stable, but those patterns can change: a baby's attachment to the mother may become more secure as she gains experience and skill. On the other hand, Lenneberg (1969) proposed a critical period for language development, before puberty. As we have seen, this concept was advanced as one explanation for the "wild child's" limited progress in learning to talk (Lane, 1976). More research is needed to determine which aspects of development are decisively formed during critical or sensitive periods and which aspects remain modifiable.

cohort Group of people who share a similar experience, such as growing up at the same time and in the same place.

critical period Specific time during development when a given event will have the greatest impact.

plasticity Modifiability of performance.

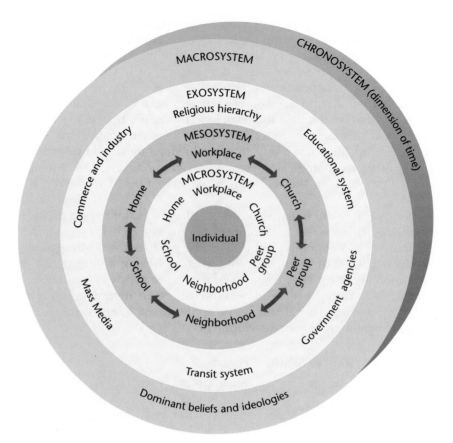

Figure 1-1
Bronfenbrenner's ecological model. Concentric circles show five levels of environmental influence, from the most intimate environment (innermost circle) to the broadest—all within the dimension of time.

Source: Adapted from M. Cole & Cole, 1989.

Contexts of Development: An Ecological Approach

A useful way of classifying environmental influences is by immediacy of impact. The American psychologist Urie Bronfenbrenner's (1979, 1986, 1994) *ecological approach* identifies five interlocking levels of external influence, or contexts of development, from the most intimate to the broadest (see Figure 1-1). To understand individual development, says Bronfenbrenner, we must study a child in the context of the multiple environments, or ecological systems, in which she or he develops. These begin with the intimate surroundings of the home, move outward to larger institutions such as the school system, and finally encompass cultural and sociohistorical patterns and conditions that affect home, school, and virtually everything in a child's life.

- The *microsystem* is the immediate everyday environment of home, school, or neighborhood. It includes personal, face-to-face relationships with parents, siblings, caregivers, classmates, and teachers, in which influences flow back and forth. Analyses of the microsystem have come up with some surprises: for example, the extent to which the environment differs for individual children within the same family.
- The *mesosystem* is the interaction of various microsystems that contain the developing child—in other words, a system of microsystems. These may include linkages between home and school, such as parent-teacher conferences, or between the family and the peer group.

ecological approach
Bronfenbrenner's system of understanding development, which identifies five interlocking levels of environmental influence: the microsystem, mesosystem, exosystem, macrosystem, and chronosystem.

- The *exosystem* refers to linkages between two or more settings, at least one of which does not contain the developing child but affects him or her indirectly. For example, a mother who is frustrated at work may mistreat her children.
- The *macrosystem* consists of cultural patterns: dominant beliefs, ideologies, and economic and political systems, such as capitalism and socialism.
- The *chronosystem* adds the dimension of time—the influence of normative or nonnormative change or constancy in the child and the environment. This can include changes in family structure, place of residence, or parents' employment, as well as larger cultural changes such as wars and economic cycles.

By looking at systems that affect individuals in and beyond the family, this ecological approach shows the variety of interrelated influences on child development. Attention to context can also alert us to differences in the way the same child may act in different settings. A child who can satisfactorily complete a school assignment at home may become tongue-tied when called upon to answer a question about the assignment in class. A child who is a terror on the playground may be docile as a lamb while having lunch at Grandma's house. For this reason, developmentalists need to pay attention to behavior in a variety of contexts and to the linkages between contexts.

A Child's World: How Its Study Evolved

Child development has, of course, been going on as long as children have existed, but its formal scientific study is relatively new. Looking back, we can see dramatic changes in the way adults have viewed and investigated the world of childhood.

Historic Views of Childhood

According to the French historian Philippe Ariès (1962), not until the seventeenth century were children in western societies seen as qualitatively different from adults; before that, children were considered simply smaller, weaker, and less intelligent. Ariès based his opinion on historical sources. Old paintings showed children dressed like their elders. Documents described children working long hours, leaving their parents at early ages for apprenticeships, and suffering brutality at the hands of adults.

Ariès's view has been widely accepted, but more recent analyses paint a different picture. The psychologist David Elkind (1986) found recognition of children's special nature in the Bible and in the works of the ancient Greeks and Romans. And, after examining more than 400 autobiographies, diaries, and other sources closer to the actual day-to-day experience of family life than those Ariès used, Linda A. Pollock (1983) makes a strong argument that, at least as far back as the sixteenth century, children have been seen and treated differently from adults.

Diaries of both parents and children portrayed parents who loved their children and saw them as playful beings in need of guidance, care, and protection. Parent-child relationships were *not* described as formal or distant, and there was little evidence of harsh discipline or abuse. Most parents wanted their children and enjoyed their company, were concerned about such issues as weaning and teething, and suffered when children fell ill or died. Parents regarded child rearing as one of the most important challenges in life.

The Study of Child Development: Early Approaches

Early forerunners of the scientific study of child development were *baby biographies,* journals kept to record the early development of a single child. One early journal, published in 1787 in Germany, contained Dietrich Tiedemann's

CHECKPOINT

Can you . . .
- Define two types and three aspects of developmental change?
- Briefly discuss the roles of family structure, socioeconomic status, ethnicity, and culture in child development?
- Give examples of normative age-graded, normative history-graded, and nonnormative influences and of critical or "sensitive" periods?
- Describe Bronfenbrenner's five interlocking levels of contextual influence and give an example of each?

(1787/1897) observations of his son's sensory, motor, language, and cognitive behavior during the first 2½ years. Typical of the speculative nature of such observations was Tiedemann's conclusion, after watching the infant suck more continuously on a cloth tied around something sweet than on a nurse's finger, that sucking appeared to be "not instinctive, but acquired" (Murchison & Langer, 1927, p. 206).

It was Charles Darwin, originator of the theory of evolution, who first emphasized the *developmental* nature of infant behavior. In 1877, in the belief that human beings could be better understood by studying their origins—both as a species and as individuals—Darwin published an abstract of his notes on his son's sensory, cognitive, and emotional development during the first 12 months (see Focus vignette at the beginning of Chapter 6). Darwin's journal gave "baby biographies" scientific respectability; about 30 more were published during the next three decades (Dennis, 1936).

Meanwhile, during the eighteenth and nineteenth centuries, several important trends were preparing the way for the scientific study of child development. Scientists had unlocked the mystery of conception and (as in the case of the wild boy of Aveyron) were arguing about the relative importance of "nature" and "nurture." The discovery of germs and immunization allowed parents to protect their children from the plagues and fevers that had made survival so uncertain. Because of an abundance of cheap labor, children were less needed as workers, and new laws protecting them from long workdays let them spend more time in school. The new science of psychology taught that people could understand themselves by learning what had influenced them as children.

By the end of the nineteenth century, scientists were devising ways to study children, but this new discipline still had far to go. Adolescence, for example, was not considered a separate period of development until the early twentieth century, when G. Stanley Hall, a pioneer in child study, published a popular though unscientific book called *Adolescence* (1904/1916). Figure 1-2 presents summaries, in historical order, of the ideas and contributions of Darwin, Hall, and some of the other early pioneers in the study of child development.

Studying the Life Span

Full life-span studies in the United States grew out of programs designed to follow children through adulthood. The Stanford Studies of Gifted Children (begun in 1921 under the direction of Lewis Terman) continue to trace the development of people (now in old age) who were identified as unusually intelligent in childhood. Other major studies that began around 1930—the Fels Research Institute Study, the Berkeley Growth and Guidance Studies, and the Oakland (Adolescent) Growth Study—have given us much information on long-term development.

Today the study of child development is part of the broader study of *human development*, which covers the entire life span from conception to death. Although growth and development are most obvious in childhood, they occur throughout life. Students of child development draw on a wide range of disciplines, including psychology, psychiatry, sociology, anthropology, biology, genetics (the study of inherited characteristics), family science (the interdisciplinary study of family relations), education, history, philosophy, and medicine. This book includes findings from research in all these fields.

Child Development: The Science and Its Goals

The purpose of any scientific study is to obtain knowledge that is verifiably accurate, through open-minded, objective investigation. As the field of child development became a scientific discipline, its goals evolved to include *description, explanation, prediction,* and *modification* of behavior. *Description* enables scientists to establish norms (averages) for behavior at various ages. *Explanation* is the un-

John Locke
1632–1704

English philosopher. Forerunner of behaviorism. Viewed infant as a "blank slate" on whom parents and teachers can "write" to create the kind of person they want.

Jean Jacques Rousseau
1712–1778

French philosopher. Believed that development occurs naturally in a series of predestined, internally regulated stages. Viewed children as "noble savages" who are born good and become warped only by repressive environments.

Charles Darwin
1809–1882

English naturalist. Originated theory of evolution, which held that all species developed through *natural selection*—reproduction by individuals best fitted to survive by adaptation to the environment.

G. Stanley Hall
1844–1924

American psychologist. Called "father of the child study movement." Invented questionnnaire method for studying children and wrote first book about adolescence.

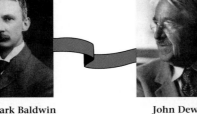

James Mark Baldwin
1861–1934

American psychologist. Helped organize psychology as a science. Established journals and university psychology departments; one of first presidents of American Psychological Association. Applied genetic concepts to psychology; stressed interaction of nature and nurture.

John Dewey
1859–1952

American philosopher and educator. Viewed developmental psychology as a tool for growth and fostering of socially desirable values. Initiated study of children in their social setting.

Alfred Binet
1857–1911

French psychologist. Developed the first individual intelligence test, in collaboration with Theodore Simon. The Binet-Simon Scale, published in 1905, was the basis for the Stanford-Binet IQ test, still widely used.

Maria Montessori
1870–1952

Italian physician and educator. Developed method of early childhood education based on self-chosen activities in a carefully prepared environment that encourages orderly progress from simple to complex tasks.

John B. Watson
1878–1958

American psychologist. Called "father of modern behaviorism." Saw no limits to trainability of human beings.

Arnold Gesell
1880–1961

American psychologist. Student of Hall; stressed importance of maturation. Conducted studies of normative change, showing that normal children go through the same stages in development.

Figure 1-2
A time line of pioneers in the study of a child's world.

covering of causes for behavior. *Prediction* is forecasting later development. *Modification* is intervention to promote optimal development.

By looking at language development, we can see how these four functions work together. For example, to *describe* when most normal children say their first word or how large their vocabulary typically is at a certain age, developmentalists observe large groups of children and establish norms, or averages,

CHECKPOINT

Can you . . .

• Trace how the study of child development evolved?

• Name four goals of the scientific study of child development, and explain the usefulness of each?

theory Coherent set of related concepts that seeks to organize and explain data.

data Information obtained through research.

hypotheses Possible explanations for phenomena, used to predict the outcome of research.

for behavior at various ages. They then attempt to *explain* what causes or influences the observed behavior—for example, how children acquire and learn to use language, and why a child like Victor of Aveyron, who may have lacked early exposure to language, did not learn to speak. This knowledge may make it possible to *predict* what language ability at a given age can tell about later behavior—for example, about the likelihood that a child like Victor could still be taught to speak. Finally, awareness of how language develops may be used to *modify* behavior by intervening to promote optimal development, as Itard attempted to do with Victor.

Even in less dramatic cases, the study of child development has practical implications. By learning about the normal course of development, we can look at various factors in a child's life and attempt to predict future behavior. If our predictions suggest possible future problems, we can try to modify development through training or treatment, or both.

A Child's World: Issues and Theoretical Perspectives

The way we explain development depends on the way we view the nature of human beings. Developmentalists have come up with many theories about why children behave as they do. A *theory* is a set of related concepts, which seeks to organize and explain *data,* the information gathered through research. Theories also predict what data might be obtained under certain conditions; thus they serve as a source of *hypotheses*—explanations or predictions that can be tested by research. Theories are dynamic; they change to incorporate new findings. Sometimes research supports a hypothesis and the theory on which it was based. At other times, scientists must modify their theories to account for unexpected data, as Itard may have had to do when he failed to teach Victor to speak. Whether research findings support a theory or not, they often suggest additional issues and hypotheses to be researched.

Theories, then, help scientists achieve the goals noted earlier—to *describe, explain, predict,* and *modify* behavior. As we will see, particular theories give greater emphasis to one or another of these goals. Early theories concentrated mainly on description and explanation. Theories and research that captured the popular imagination, as well as much scientific attention, during the 1960s—notably behaviorism—focused on attempts to predict and control behavior. Today the emphasis again is on precise, detailed description and explanation of the complex processes of development and their many overlapping contexts.

No one theory of human development is universally accepted, and no one theory explains all facets of development. Indeed, the trend today is away from "grand," all-encompassing theories (such as the classic theories of Sigmund Freud and Jean Piaget) and toward smaller, more limited "minitheories" aimed at explaining specific phenomena, such as how poverty influences family relations. Different investigators look from different perspectives at how children develop. These perspectives, which are generally affected by the culture in which they arose, influence the questions researchers ask, the methods they use, and the ways they interpret data. Therefore, to evaluate and interpret research, it is important to know the theoretical perspective on which it is based.

In this section, we'll examine key features of five perspectives (summarized in Table 1-2) that underlie influential theories and research on child development: (1) *psychoanalytic* (which focuses on unconscious emotions and drives); (2) *learning* (which emphasizes observable behavior); (3) *cognitive* (which stresses thought processes); (4) *ethological* (which considers evolutionary underpinnings of behavior); and (5) *contextual* (which emphasizes the impact of the social and cultural context). But first, let's look at three interconnected issues on which various theorists differ.

Table 1-2 Five Perspectives on Human Development

Perspective	Important Theories	Basic Beliefs	Technique Used	Stage-Oriented	Causal Emphasis	Active or Passive Individual
Psychoanalytic	Freud's psychosexual theory	Behavior is controlled by powerful unconscious urges.	Clinical observation	Yes	Innate factors modified by experience	Passive
	Erikson's psychosocial theory	Personality is influenced by society and develops through a series of crises.	Clinical observation	Yes	Interaction of innate and experiential factors	Active
	Miller's relational theory	Personality develops in the context of emotional relationships.	Clinical observation	No	Interaction of innate and experiential factors	Active
Learning	Behaviorism, or traditional learning theory (Pavlov, Skinner, Watson)	People are responders; the environment controls behavior.	Rigorous scientific (experimental) procedures	No	Experience	Passive
	Social-learning (social-cognitive) theory (Bandura)	Children learn in a social context by observing and imitating models; person is an active contributor to learning.	Rigorous scientific (experimental) procedures	No	Experience modified by innate factors	Active and passive
Cognitive	Piaget's cognitive-stage theory	Qualitative changes in thought occur between infancy and adolescence. Person is active initiator of development.	Flexible interviews; meticulous observation	Yes	Interaction of innate and experiential factors	Active
	Information-processing theory	Human beings are processors of symbols.	Laboratory research; technological monitoring of physiologic responses	No	Interaction of innate and experiential factors	Active and passive
Ethological	Bowlby's and Ainsworth's attachment theory	Human beings have the adaptive mechanisms to survive; critical or sensitive periods are stressed; biological and evolutionary bases for behavior and predisposition toward learning are important.	Naturalistic and laboratory observation	No	Interaction of innate and experiential factors	Active or passive (theorists vary)
Contextual	Vygotsky's sociocultural theory	Child's sociocultural context has an important impact on development.	Cross-cultural research; observation of child interacting with more competent person	No	Experience	Active

Three Developmental Issues

In trying to explain how children develop, some theories give more weight to innate factors (heredity), others to environment, or experience. Theories also differ as to whether they view children as active or passive in their own development and whether they view development as occurring in stages.

(1) Which Is More Important—Heredity or Environment?

Which has more impact on a child's development—heredity or environment? This issue has aroused intense debate for at least 200 years. Although any theory of child development must take account of both, theorists differ in the relative importance they give to *nature* (the traits and characteristics inherited from the biological parents) and *nurture* (environmental influences, both before and after birth, including influences of family, peers, schooling, society, and culture).

How much is inherited? How much is environmentally influenced? These questions matter. If parents believe that intelligence can be strongly influenced by experience, they may make special efforts to talk to and read to their children and offer them toys that help them learn. If parents believe that intelligence is inborn and unchangeable, they may be less likely to make such efforts.

Today, advances in behavioral genetics are enabling scientists to measure more precisely the roles of heredity and environment in accounting for individual differences in specific traits, such as intelligence, and how the strength of those influences can shift throughout life (Neisser et al., 1995). When we look at a specific child, however, research with regard to almost all characteristics points to an intermingling or interaction of inheritance and experience. Thus, even though intelligence has a strong hereditary component, parental stimulation, education, and other variables do make a difference. And while there is still considerable dispute about the relative impact of nature and nurture, many contemporary theorists and researchers (as we discuss in Chapter 2) are less interested in arguing about which of these forces is more important than in finding ways to explain how they work together to influence development.

(2) Is Development Active or Passive?

Closely related to the nature-nurture debate is the second issue: Are children active initiators of their own development or passive sponges, soaking up influences? This controversy goes back to the eighteenth century (refer back to Figure 1-2), when the English philosopher John Locke held that a young child is a *tabula rasa*—a "blank slate"—on which society "writes." In contrast, the French philosopher Jean Jacques Rousseau believed that children are born "noble savages" who would develop according to their own positive natural tendencies unless corrupted by a repressive society. We now know that both views are too simplistic. Children have their own internal drives and needs, as well as hereditary endowments, that influence development; but children are also social animals, who cannot achieve optimal development in isolation.

Locke's view was the forerunner of what came to be called the *mechanistic model* of development. In the mechanistic model, people are like machines (Pepper, 1942). They do not act of their own will; they simply react. Fill a car with gas, turn the ignition key, press the accelerator, and the vehicle will move. In the mechanistic view, human behavior is much the same. If we know enough about how the human "machine" is put together and about the internal and external forces impinging on it, we can predict what the person will do. Just as we can understand the operation of a machine by studying the operation of its parts, mechanistic research seeks to identify and isolate the factors that make people behave as they do, by breaking down complex stimuli and responses into simpler elements.

mechanistic model Model, based on the machine as a metaphor, that views development as a passive, predictable response to internal and external stimuli, focuses on quantitative development, and studies phenomena by analyzing the operation of their component parts.

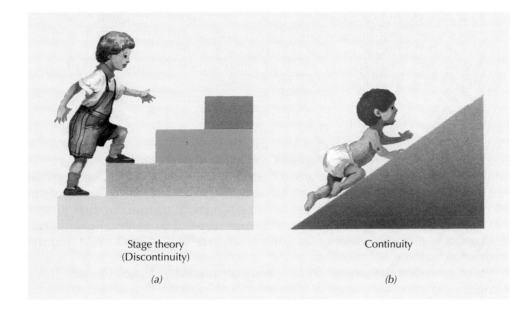

Figure 1-3
A major difference among developmental theories is (*a*) whether development occurs in distinct stages, as Piaget, Freud, and Erikson maintained or (*b*) whether it proceeds continuously, as learning theorists and information-processing theorists propose.

Rousseau was the precursor of the *organismic model* of development. This model sees people as active organisms who set their own development in motion (Pepper, 1942). They initiate events; they do not just react. The impetus for change is internal. Environmental influences do not cause development, though they can speed it up or slow it down. The whole of a human being's behavior is greater than the sum of the parts that make it up. Thus, say organicists, we cannot predict behavior simply by breaking it down into smaller elements, as the mechanistic model suggests.

organismic model Model that views development as internally initiated by an active person, or organism, and as occurring in a universal sequence of qualitatively different stages of maturation.

(3) Does Development Occur in Stages?

The two basic theoretical models also differ on the third issue: Does development occur in stages? Mechanistic theorists say no. They see development as continuous—always governed by the same processes, allowing prediction of earlier behaviors from later ones. These theorists focus on *quantitative* change: for example, changes in the frequency with which a response is made, rather than changes in the kind of response.

Organicists emphasize *qualitative* change. Development occurs in a series of distinct stages, like steps rising from one level to the next with rests on the "landings," rather than gradually and continuously, like walking up a ramp (see Figure 1-3). Each stage builds on the previous one and prepares the way for the next. At each stage, people cope with different kinds of problems and develop different kinds of abilities. Organicists see this orderly course of unfolding development as universal: every person in every culture goes through the same stages in the same order, though the precise timing may vary.

An Emerging Consensus

As the study of child development has evolved, the mechanistic and organismic models have shifted in influence and support (Parke et al., 1994). Most of the early pioneers in the field, such as Hall, Alfred Binet, James Mark Baldwin, and Arnold Gesell (refer back to Figure 1-2), favored organismic or stage approaches. So did Freud, Erikson, and Piaget. However, the mechanistic view gained support during the 1960s with the popularity of learning theories derived from the work of John B. Watson.

Today the pendulum has swung back—but not all the way. Quasi-organismic approaches, such as ethological theories centered on the biological bases of behavior, are on the rise; but instead of an emphasis on broad stages, there is an effort to discover what specific kinds of behavior show continuity or lack of continuity and what processes are involved in each.

Just as a consensus is emerging about how heredity and environment work together, many developmentalists are coming to a more balanced view of active versus passive development. There is wide agreement that influence is bidirectional: children change their world even as it changes them (Parke et al., 1994). A baby girl born with a cheerful disposition is likely to get positive responses from adults, which strengthen her trust that her smiles will be rewarded and motivate her to smile more. As children grow older, their natural tendencies lead them to choose or initiate activities, such as studying a musical instrument, that further develop those tendencies. The way children respond to external events can change them, too; it is not only the parents' divorce that affects a child, but the child's reaction to it.

Most developmentalists today take an open-minded, eclectic approach. They recognize that no single theory or theoretical perspective has all the answers; each has something to contribute to our understanding of child development.

Psychoanalytic Perspective

psychoanalytic perspective
View of development concerned
with unconscious forces
motivating behavior.

The *psychoanalytic perspective* is concerned with unconscious forces that motivate human behavior. This view originated at the beginning of the twentieth century, when a Viennese physician named Sigmund Freud (1856–1939) developed *psychoanalysis,* a therapeutic approach aimed at giving people insight into unconscious emotional conflicts. Freud believed that the source of emotional disturbances lay in repressed traumatic experiences of early childhood. The psychoanalytic perspective has been expanded and modified by other practitioners, including Erik H. Erikson and Jean Baker Miller. Their theories, like Freud's, are based largely on clinical observation.

Sigmund Freud: Psychosexual Theory

psychosexual development
In Freudian theory, an unvarying
sequence of stages of
personality development during
infancy, childhood, and
adolescence, in which
gratification shifts from the
mouth to the anus and then to
the genitals.

Freud (1953, 1964a, 1964b) believed that personality is formed in the first few years of life, as children deal with conflicts between their inborn biological, sexually related urges and the requirements of society. He proposed that these conflicts occur in an unvarying sequence of maturationally based stages of *psychosexual development,* in which pleasure shifts from one body zone to another—from the mouth to the anus and then to the genitals. At each stage, the behavior that is the chief source of gratification changes—from feeding to elimination and eventually to sexual activity.

Of the five stages of personality development that Freud described (see Table 1-3), he considered the first three—those of the first few years of life—crucial. He suggested that if children receive too little or too much gratification in any of these stages, they are at risk of *fixation*—an arrest in development—and may need help to move beyond that stage. He believed that evidence of childhood fixation shows up in adult personality. For example, babies whose needs are not met during the *oral stage* of infancy, when feeding is the main source of sensual pleasure, may grow up to become nail-biters or develop "bitingly" critical personalities.

According to Freud, a key event in psychosexual development occurs during the *phallic stage* of early childhood, when the site of pleasure shifts to the genitals. Boys develop sexual attachment to their mothers and girls to their fathers, and they regard the same-sex parent as a rival. The boy learns that a girl does not have a penis, assumes that it was cut off, and worries that his father

The Viennese physician Sigmund Freud developed an original, influential, and controversial theory of emotional development in childhood, based on his adult patients' recollections. His daughter, Anna, shown here with her father, followed in his professional footsteps and constructed her own theories of personality development.

will castrate him too. The girl experiences what Freud called *penis envy* and blames her mother for not having given her a penis. Children eventually resolve their anxiety by identifying with the same-sex parent and move into the relatively calm *latency stage* of middle childhood. They become socialized, develop skills, and learn about themselves and society. The *genital stage,* the final one, lasts throughout adulthood. The physical changes of puberty reawaken the *libido,* the energy that fuels the sex drive. The sexual urges of the phallic stage, repressed during latency, now resurface to flow in socially approved channels, which Freud defined as heterosexual relations with persons outside the family of origin.

Freud proposed three hypothetical parts of the personality: the *id,* the *ego,* and the *superego.* Newborns are governed by the *id,* a source of motives and desires that is present at birth. The id seeks immediate satisfaction under the *pleasure principle.* When gratification is delayed (as when they have to wait for food), infants begin to see themselves as separate from the outside world. The *ego,* which represents reason or common sense, develops sometime during the first year of life and operates under the *reality principle.* The ego's aim is to find realistic ways to gratify the id. At about age 5 or 6, as the child identifies with the parent of the same sex, the *superego* develops. It includes the conscience and incorporates socially approved "shoulds" and "should nots" into the child's own value system.

Freud's theory made historic contributions. Freud made us aware of unconscious thoughts and emotions, the ambivalence of early parent-child relationships, and the presence from birth of sexual urges. His psychoanalytic method greatly influenced modern-day psychotherapy. However, Freud's theory grew out of his place in history and in society. Much of it seems to demean women, no doubt because of its roots in the male-dominated social system of a Victorian-era European culture. Also, Freud based his theories about normal development

id In Freudian theory, the instinctual aspect of personality (present at birth) that operates on the pleasure principle, seeking immediate gratification.

ego In Freudian theory, an aspect of personality that develops during infancy and operates on the reality principle, seeking acceptable means of gratification in dealing with the real world.

superego In Freudian theory, the aspect of personality that represents socially-approved values; it develops around the age of 5 or 6 as a result of identification with the parent of the same sex.

Psychosexual Stages (Freud)	Psychosocial Stages (Erikson)	Cognitive Stages (Piaget)
Oral (birth to 12–18 months). Baby's chief source of pleasure involves mouth-oriented activities (sucking and eating).	*Basic trust versus mistrust (birth to 12–18 months).* Baby develops sense of whether world is a good and safe place. Virtue: hope.	*Sensorimotor (birth to 2 years).* Infant gradually becomes able to organize activities in relation to the environment through sensory and motor activity.
Anal (12–18 months to 3 years). Child derives sensual gratification from withholding and expelling feces. Zone of gratification is anal region.	*Autonomy versus shame and doubt (12–18 months to 3 years).* Child develops a balance of independence over shame and doubt. Virtue: will.	*Preoperational (2 to 7 years).* Child develops a representational system and uses symbols to represent people, places, and events. Language and imaginative play are important manifestations of this stage.
Phallic (3 to 6 years). Child becomes attached to parent of the other sex and later identifies with same-sex parent. Zone of gratification shifts to genital region.	*Initiative versus guilt (3 to 6 years).* Child develops initiative when trying out new things and is not overwhelmed by guilt. Virtue: purpose.	
Latency (6 years to puberty). Time of relative calm between more turbulent stages.	*Industry versus inferiority (6 years to puberty).* Child must learn skills of the culture or face feelings of incompetence. Virtue: skill.	*Concrete operations (7 to 12 years).* Child can solve problems logically if they are focused on the here and now, but cannot think abstractly.
Genital (puberty through adulthood). Time of mature adult sexuality. Reemergence of sexual impulses of phallic stage.	*Identity versus identity confusion (puberty to young adulthood).* Adolescent must determine own sense of self or experience confusion about roles. Virtue: fidelity.	*Formal operations (12 years through adulthood).* Person can think abstractly, deal with hypothetical situations, and think about possibilities.
	Intimacy versus isolation (young adulthood). Person seeks to make commitments to others; if unsuccessful, may suffer from isolation and self-absorption. Virtue: love.	
	Generativity versus stagnation (middle adulthood). Mature adult is concerned with establishing and guiding the next generation or else feels personal impoverishment. Virtue: care.	
	Integrity versus despair (late adulthood). Elderly person achieves acceptance of own life, allowing acceptance of death, or else despairs over inability to relive life. Virtue: wisdom.	

Note: All ages are approximate.

not on a population of average children, but on a clientele of upper-middle-class adults in therapy. His narrow concentration on biological and maturational factors and on early experience does not take into account other, and later, influences on personality. His theories, and those of other psychoanalytic theorists, are hard to test. Research has questioned or invalidated many of his concepts,

The psychoanalyst Erik H. Erikson departed from Freudian theory in emphasizing societal, rather than chiefly biological, influences on personality. Erikson described development as proceeding through eight crises, or turning points, throughout the life span.

for example, his idea that the superego and gender identity are outcomes of children's conflicts during the phallic stage (Emde, 1992).

Erik Erikson: Psychosocial Theory

Erik Erikson (1902–1994), a German-born psychoanalyst, was part of Freud's inner circle in Vienna until he fled from the threat of Nazism and came to the United States in 1933. His broad personal and professional experience led him to modify and extend Freudian theory by emphasizing the influence of society on the developing personality.

Whereas Freud maintained that early childhood experiences permanently shape personality, Erikson contended that ego development is lifelong. Erikson's (1950, 1982; Erikson, Erikson, & Kivnick, 1986) theory of *psychosocial development* covers eight stages across the lifespan (listed in Table 1-3 and discussed in later chapters). Each stage involves a "crisis" in personality—a major issue that is particularly important at that time and will remain an issue to some degree throughout life. The crises emerge according to a maturational timetable and must be satisfactorily resolved for healthy ego development. Successful resolution of each of the eight crises requires the balancing of a positive trait and a corresponding negative one. Although the positive quality should predominate, some degree of the negative is needed too. The crisis of infancy, for example, is *trust versus mistrust*. People need to trust the world and the people in it, but they also need to learn some mistrust to protect themselves from danger. The successful outcome of each crisis is the development of a particular "virtue" or strength—in this first crisis, the "virtue" of *hope*.

A major theme for Erikson, particularly in adolescence but also throughout adult life, was the quest for *identity*, which he defined as confidence in one's inner continuity amid change. He himself, growing up in Germany as the son of a Danish mother and a Jewish adoptive father, had felt confusion about his identity. He never knew his biological father; he floundered before settling on a vocation; and when he came to the United States, he needed to redefine his identity as an immigrant. All these issues found echoes in the "identity crises" he observed among disturbed adolescents, soldiers in combat, and members of minority groups (Erikson, 1968, 1973; R. I. Evans, 1967).

psychosocial development In Erikson's theory, the socially and culturally influenced process of development of the ego, or self; it consists of eight maturationally determined stages throughout the life span, each revolving around a particular crisis or turning point in which the person is faced with achieving a healthy balance between alternative positive and negative traits.

According to the psychiatrist Jean Baker Miller's relational theory, personality growth—beginning in infancy—occurs within emotional connections, or relationships.

relational theory Theory, proposed by Miller, that all personality growth occurs within emotional connections, not separate from them.

Jean Baker Miller: Relational Theory

The psychiatrist Jean Baker Miller (b. 1927) originally criticized the classic psychoanalytic theories as male-oriented, and thus as failing to explain women's development. She and her colleagues came to believe that such theories do not accurately describe what occurs in men, either.

A key issue for Miller and other current psychoanalytic theorists is whether healthy development rests more on *individuation* (development of the self) or on *connectedness* (relationships with other people). According to Miller's (1991) *relational theory*, personality growth occurs within relationships. The concept of self begins in dynamic interaction with another. The infant identifies with the first caregiver, not because of who that person *is,* but because of what the person *does.* The baby responds to other people's emotions, becomes comfortable when others are comfortable, and acts to build closer relationships. During toddlerhood and early childhood, rather than striving for autonomy and individuation, both boys and girls continue to place the highest importance on intimate connections. However, a split between male and female development occurs during the school years, when girls' interest in relationships, family, and emotional issues is encouraged, while boys are steered toward competition and personal achievement. This dichotomy widens during adolescence and adulthood, to the detriment of both men and women. Women's growth within relationships is devalued, and men's deficiencies in participating in growth-fostering relationships are not addressed early enough.

A newer proposal (Guisinger & Blatt, 1994) seeks to combine the concepts of individuation and connectedness. This theory suggests that healthy development for both men and women depends on the lifelong interaction of a continually maturing individuality with a continually maturing sense of connectedness.

Learning Perspective

learning perspective View of development concerned with changes in behavior that result from experience, or adaptation to the environment; the two major branches are behaviorism and social-learning theory.

learning Long-lasting change in behavior that occurs as a result of experience.

The *learning perspective* is concerned with behavior that can be observed and studied objectively and scientifically. Learning theorists maintain that development results from *learning,* a long-lasting change in behavior based on experience, or adaptation to the environment. Learning theorists see development as continuous (rather than occurring in stages) and emphasize quantitative change.

Learning theorists have helped to make the study of human development more scientific. Their terms are defined precisely, and their theories can be tested in the laboratory. By stressing environmental influences, they help explain cultural differences in behavior. However, they underplay the importance of heredity and biology. And, since they apply the same principles to behavior from infancy through adulthood, they do not deal with age-related development.

Two important learning theories are *behaviorism* and *social-learning theory.*

Behaviorism

Behaviorism is a mechanistic theory, which describes observed behavior as a predictable response to experience. Although biology sets limits on what people do, behaviorists view the environment as much more influential. They hold that human beings at all ages learn about the world the same way other animals do: by reacting to conditions, or aspects of their environment, that they find pleasing, painful, or threatening. Behaviorists look for events that determine whether or not a particular behavior will be repeated. Behavioral research deals with two kinds of learning: *classical conditioning* and *operant conditioning.*

Classical Conditioning Eager to capture Anna's memorable moments on film, her father took pictures of the infant smiling, crawling, and showing off her other achievements. Whenever the flash went off, Anna blinked. One evening when Anna was 11 months old, she saw her father hold the camera up to his eye—and she blinked *before* the flash. She had learned to associate the camera with the bright light, so that the sight of the camera activated her blinking reflex.

Anna's blinking is an example of *classical conditioning,* a kind of learning in which a person or animal learns a response to a stimulus that did not originally evoke it, after the stimulus is repeatedly associated with a stimulus that *does* elicit the response. Figure 1-4 shows the steps in classical conditioning.

behaviorism Learning theory that emphasizes the study of observable behaviors and events and the predictable role of environment in causing behavior.

classical conditioning Kind of learning in which a previously neutral stimulus (one that does not originally elicit a particular response) acquires the power to elicit the response after the stimulus is repeatedly associated with another stimulus that ordinarily does elicit the response.

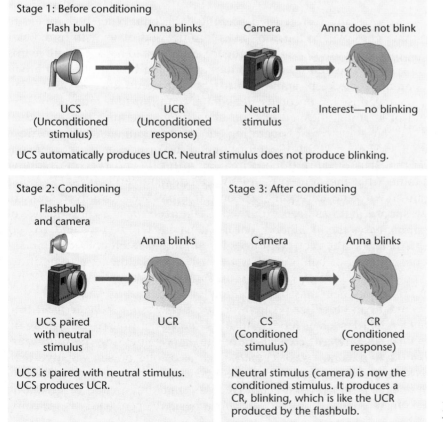

Figure 1-4
Three steps in classical conditioning.

The American psychologist B. F. Skinner formulated the principles of operant conditioning. He maintained that the same principles that governed the behavior of rats and pigeons also applied to human beings.

The principles of classical conditioning were developed by the Russian physiologist Ivan Pavlov (1849–1936), who devised experiments in which dogs learned to salivate at the sound of a bell that rang at feeding time. The American behaviorist John B. Watson (1878–1958) applied stimulus-response theories of learning to children. Watson (refer back to Figure 1-2) claimed that he could mold any infant in any way he chose. Using classical conditioning, he taught one baby, known as "Little Albert," to fear furry white objects (see Chapter 4).

Operant Conditioning Baby Terrell lies peacefully in his crib. When he happens to smile, his mother goes over to the crib, picks him up, and plays with him. Later his father does the same thing. As this sequence continues to occur, Terrell learns that something he does (smiling) can produce something he likes (loving attention from a parent); so he keeps smiling to attract his parents' attention. An originally accidental response has become a deliberate, conditioned response.

This kind of learning is called *operant conditioning* because the individual learns from the consequences of "operating" on the environment. The American psychologist B. F. Skinner (1904–1990) formulated the principles of operant conditioning on the basis of work done primarily with rats and pigeons. Skinner (1938) maintained that the same principles applied to human beings. He found that an organism will tend to repeat a response that has been reinforced and will suppress a response that has been punished. *Reinforcement* is a consequence of behavior that increases the likelihood that the behavior will be repeated; in Terrell's case, his parents' attention reinforces his smiling (see Figure 1-5). *Punishment* is a consequence of behavior that *decreases* the likelihood of repetition. Whether a consequence is reinforcing or punishing depends on the person. What is reinforcing for one person may be punishing for another.

Reinforcement can be either positive or negative. *Positive reinforcement* consists of *giving* a reward, such as food, gold stars, money, or praise—or picking up a baby. *Negative reinforcement* consists of *taking away* something the individual does not like (known as an *aversive event*), such as a loud noise. Negative reinforcement is sometimes confused with punishment. Punishment suppresses a behavior by *bringing on* an aversive event (such as spanking a child or giving an electric shock to an animal), or by *withdrawing* a positive event (such as watching

operant conditioning Kind of learning in which a person tends to repeat a behavior that has been reinforced or to cease a behavior that has been punished.

reinforcement In operant conditioning, a stimulus experienced following a behavior, which increases the probability that the behavior will be repeated.

punishment In operant conditioning, a stimulus experienced following a behavior, which decreases the probability that the behavior will be repeated.

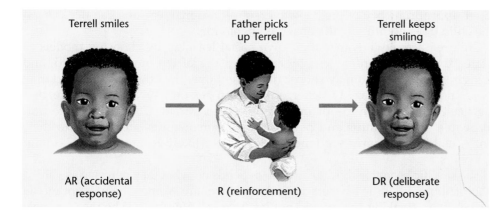

Terrell smiles   Father picks up Terrell   Terrell keeps smiling

AR (accidental response)   R (reinforcement)   DR (deliberate response)

Figure 1-5
Operant conditioning has three steps. An accidental response that is reinforced will be repeated.

television). Negative reinforcement encourages repetition of a behavior by *removing* an aversive event.

✸ Reinforcement is most effective when it immediately follows a behavior. If a response is no longer reinforced, it will eventually return to its original (baseline) level. This is called *extinction*. If, after a while, no one picks up Terrell when he smiles, he may not stop smiling but will smile far less than if his smiles still brought reinforcement.

Behavioral modification is a form of operant conditioning used to eliminate undesirable behavior or to instill positive behavior, such as using the toilet. This may be done by *shaping*: reinforcing responses that are more and more like the desired one. Behavioral modification can bring about rapid changes in behavior. It is particularly effective among children with special needs, such as youngsters with mental or emotional disabilities. However, because behaviorists are not interested in the causes of symptoms, they may eliminate one undesirable behavior (say, stealing) by punishing it, only to see the substitution of another negative behavior (say, bed-wetting), leaving the basic problem unresolved.

Social-Learning (Social-Cognitive) Theory

Social-learning theory maintains that children learn social behaviors by observing and imitating models (usually their parents). The American psychologist Albert Bandura (b. 1925) developed many of the principles of modern social-learning theory, also known as *social-cognitive theory*, which today is more influential than behaviorism.

Unlike behaviorism, social-learning theory (Bandura, 1977, 1989) regards the learner as active. Whereas behaviorists see the environment as molding the child, social-learning theorists believe that the child also acts upon the environment—in fact, *creates* the environment to some extent. Although social-learning theorists, like behaviorists, emphasize laboratory experimentation, they believe that theories based on animal research cannot explain human behavior. People learn in a social context, and human learning is more complex than simple conditioning. Social-learning theory also acknowledges the importance of cognition: children's cognitive responses to their perceptions, rather than reflexive responses to reinforcement or punishment, are seen as central to development.

Of particular importance in social-learning theory is observation and imitation of models. Children acquire new abilities through *observational learning*—by watching others. They demonstrate their learning by imitating the model, sometimes when the model is no longer present. According to social-learning theory, imitation of models is the most important element in how children learn a language, deal with aggression, develop a moral sense, and learn

social-learning theory
Theory, proposed by Bandura, that behaviors are learned by observing and imitating models. Also called *social-cognitive theory*.

observational learning
In social-learning theory, learning that occurs through watching the behavior of others.

gender-appropriate behaviors. However, observational learning can occur even if the child does not imitate the observed behavior.

Children actively advance their own social learning by choosing models to imitate. The choice is influenced by characteristics of the model, the child, and the environment. A child may choose one parent over the other. Or the child may choose another adult (say, a teacher, a television personality, a sports figure, or a drug dealer) in addition to—or instead of—either parent. Children tend to imitate people of high status and people whose personalities are similar to their own. A child with aggressive tendencies is more likely to imitate Rambo than Mr. Rogers.

The specific behavior children imitate depends on what they perceive as valued in their culture. If all the teachers in Carlos's school are women, he will not model their behavior, thinking that would not be "manly." However, if he meets a male teacher he likes, he may change his mind about the value of teachers as models.

Cognitive factors, such as the ability to pay attention and to mentally organize sensory information, affect the way people incorporate observed behavior into their own. Cognitive processes are at work as people observe models, learn "chunks" of behavior, and mentally put the chunks together into complex new behavior patterns. Rita, for example, imitates the toes-out walk of her dance teacher but models her dance steps after those of Carmen, a slightly advanced student. Even so, she develops her own style of dancing by putting her observations together into a new pattern. Children's developing ability to use mental symbols to stand for a model's behavior enables them to form standards for judging their own behavior.

Social-learning theory, in acknowledging cognitive influences on behavior and the active role people play in their own learning, serves as a bridge between behaviorism and the cognitive perspective.

Cognitive Perspective

cognitive perspective View of development concerned with thought processes and the behavior that reflects those processes.

The *cognitive perspective* is concerned with thought processes and the behavior that reflects these processes. This perspective encompasses both organismic and mechanistically influenced theories: the cognitive-stage theory of Piaget, the newer information-processing approach, and neo-Piagetian theories, which combine elements of both.

The Cognitive-Stage Theory of Jean Piaget

Much of what we know about how children think is due to the Swiss theoretician Jean Piaget (1896–1980). Piaget was the forerunner of today's "cognitive revolution" with its emphasis on internal mental processes, as opposed to classical learning theory's concern with external influences and overt behaviors. He inspired more research on children's cognitive development than any other theorist.

As a young man studying in Paris, Piaget set out to standardize the tests Alfred Binet had developed to assess the intelligence of French schoolchildren. Piaget became intrigued by the children's wrong answers, finding in them clues to their thought processes. From his observations of his own and other children, Piaget created a comprehensive theory of cognitive development.

Piaget's *clinical method* combined observation with flexible questioning. To find out how children think, Piaget followed up their answers with more questions. In this way, he discovered, for example, that a typical 4-year-old child believed that pennies or flowers were more numerous when arranged in a line than when heaped or piled up.

Piaget viewed children organismically, as active, growing beings with their own internal impulses and patterns of development. He believed that the core of intelligent behavior is an inborn ability to adapt to the environment. He saw every normal child, from infancy on, as a doer who constructs his or her world.

The Swiss psychologist Jean Piaget studied children's cognitive development by observing and talking with his own youngsters and others.

Piaget described cognitive development as occurring in a series of qualitatively different stages (listed in Table 1-3 and discussed in later chapters). At each stage a child develops a new way of operating—of thinking about and responding to the environment. Cognitive growth at all stages of development occurs through three interrelated principles: *organization, adaptation,* and *equilibration.*

Organization is a tendency to create increasingly complex systems of knowledge. From infancy on, building on their reflex, sensory, and motor capacities—by rooting for a nipple or exploring the boundaries of a room—children create increasingly accurate mental representations of reality that help them make sense of and act upon their world. Underlying these representations of reality lie cognitive structures called *schemes:* organized patterns of behavior that a person uses to think about and act in a situation. As children acquire more information, their schemes become more and more complex. An infant has a simple scheme for sucking, but soon develops varied schemes for how to suck at the breast, a bottle, or a thumb. At first schemes for looking and grasping operate independently. Later, infants integrate these separate schemes into a single scheme that allows them to look at an object while holding it.

Adaptation is Piaget's term for how a person deals with new information. Adaptation involves two steps: (1) *assimilation,* taking in information and incorporating it into existing cognitive structures, or ways of thinking, and (2) *accommodation,* changing one's ideas, or cognitive structures, to include the new knowledge. A breastfed baby who begins to suck on a rubber nipple is showing assimilation—using an old scheme to deal with a new object or situation. When the infant discovers that sucking on a bottle requires somewhat different tongue and mouth movements from those used to suck on a breast, she accommodates by modifying the old scheme. She has adapted her original sucking scheme to deal with a new experience: the bottle. Thus, assimilation and accommodation work together to produce cognitive growth. *Equilibration*—a constant striving for a stable balance, or equilibrium—leads a child to shift from assimilation to accommodation. When children cannot handle new experiences with their existing structures, they organize new mental patterns, restoring equilibrium.

organization In Piaget's terminology, integration of knowledge into a system to make sense of the environment.

schemes In Piaget's terminology, basic cognitive structures consisting of organized patterns of behavior used in different kinds of situations.

adaptation In Piaget's terminology, adjustment to new information about the environment through the complementary processes of assimilation and accommodation.

assimilation In Piaget's terminology, incorporation of new information into an existing cognitive structure.

accommodation In Piaget's terminology, changes in an existing cognitive structure to include new information.

equilibration In Piaget's terminology, the tendency to strive for equilibrium (balance) among cognitive elements within the organism and between it and the outside world.

Piaget's careful observations have yielded a wealth of information, including some surprising insights. Who, for example, would have thought that not until about age 7 do children realize that a ball of clay that has been rolled into a "worm" before their eyes still contains the same amount of clay? Or that an infant might think that a person who has moved out of sight may no longer exist? Piaget has shown us that children's minds are not miniatures of adults' minds. Understanding how children think makes it easier for parents and teachers to teach them.

Yet Piaget spoke primarily of the "average" child and took little notice of individual differences. He said little about emotional development or about how education and motivation affect performance. As we will see in Chapters 6 and 9, more recent research suggests that he seriously underestimated the abilities of infants and young children. Some contemporary psychologists question his clearly demarcated stages; they view cognitive development as more gradual and continuous (Flavell, 1992). More fundamentally, psychologists coming from a variety of perspectives have challenged Piaget's basic idea that children's thinking develops in a single, universal progression leading to formal thought. Instead, research beginning in the late 1960s suggests that children's cognitive processes are closely tied to specific content (what they are thinking *about*), as well as to the context of a problem and the kinds of information and thought a culture considers important (Case & Okamoto, 1996).

The Information-Processing Approach

The newer *information-processing approach* attempts to explain cognitive development by observing and analyzing the mental processes involved in perceiving and handling information, which underlie intelligent behavior. Scientists who take this approach study how people acquire, remember, and use information through manipulation of symbols, or mental images. The information-processing approach is quite eclectic. It is not a single theory but a framework, or set of assumptions, that underlies a wide range of theories and research.

Information-processing theorists compare the mind to a computer. Sensory impressions go in; behavior (including speaking, writing, and other responses) comes out. But what happens in between? How does the mind transform sensation and perception (say, of an unfamiliar face) into usable information (the ability to recognize that face again)? To behaviorists, the question does not matter. Piaget attempted to find out how children think by asking them, but neither children nor adults can be fully aware of complex mental processes.

Information-processing researchers *infer* what goes on in the mind. For example, they may ask a child to recall a list of words and then observe any difference in performance if the child repeats the list over and over before being asked to recall the words. Through such studies, information-processing theorists have developed models or flow charts of how an item is stored in memory and then retrieved when needed.

The information-processing approach is quasi-mechanistic in that it attempts to break the processes of thinking and remembering into their component parts. Despite the use of the "passive" computer model, information-processing theorists, like Piaget and unlike the behaviorists, see people as active thinkers about their world. Unlike Piaget, they generally do not propose age-related stages of development, but they do note increases in the speed, complexity, and efficiency of mental processing and in the amount and variety of material that can be stored in memory.

The information-processing approach is highly influential today. It provides a valuable way to assess intelligence and to gather information about the development of memory and other cognitive processes. However, it pays little or no attention to such important aspects of cognitive development as creativity, motivation, and social interaction, and it does not deal directly with the question of how development progresses.

information-processing approach Approach to the study of cognitive development by observing and analyzing the mental processes involved in perceiving and handling information.

Information-processing theory has at least two useful applications for child development. First, by understanding how information is gained, recalled, and used, parents and teachers can help children become more aware of their own mental processes and of strategies to enhance them. Second, information-processing models can be used to test, diagnose, and treat learning problems by pinpointing the weakness in the system: whether the difficulty is with vision or hearing, attentiveness, or getting information into memory (R. M. Thomas, 1996).

Neo-Piagetian Theories

In response to criticisms of Piaget's theory, neo-Piagetian developmental psychologists during the 1980s tried to integrate some elements of his theory with the information-processing approach. Instead of describing a single, general system of increasingly logical mental structures, or operations, which can be applied to any kind of problem, neo-Piagetians such as Robbie Case, Kurt Fischer, Graeme Halford, and Juan Pascual-Leone focused on specific concepts, strategies, and skills. They suggested that children develop cognitively by becoming more efficient at processing information. According to Case (1985, 1992), there is a limit to the number of schemes a child can keep in mind. A child who practices a skill, such as counting or reading, becomes able to do it faster and more proficiently, freeing some mental "space" for additional information and more complex problem solving. Maturation of the child's neurological processes also expands available memory capacity.

More recently, Case (Case & Okamoto, 1996) has been testing a model which goes back to Piaget's idea of central cognitive structures. However, these are *conceptual* structures within specific, major domains of thought, such as number, story understanding, and spatial relations, and they reflect the knowledge children acquire within their culture. In Case's model (discussed in Chapter 12), children go through four stages in which their structures become more complex and better coordinated, enabling them to deal with more and more dimensions of a problem.

The neo-Piagetian approach is a promising effort to explain the processes by which qualitative changes in cognition occur and the constraints on learning at any given stage. Because of its emphasis on efficiency of processing, it helps account for individual differences in cognitive ability and for uneven development in various domains.

Ethological Perspective

The *ethological perspective* focuses on biological and evolutionary bases of behavior. It looks beyond the immediate adaptive value of a behavior for an individual to its function in promoting the survival of the group or species.

ethological perspective View of development that focuses on the biological and evolutionary bases of behavior.

In the 1930s, two European zoologists, Konrad Lorenz and Niko Tinbergen, developed the scientific discipline of *ethology*, the study of the behavior of species of animals by observing them, usually in their natural surroundings. In the 1950s, the British psychologist John Bowlby extended ethological principles to human development.

Ethologists believe that, for each species, a variety of innate, species-specific behaviors have evolved to increase its odds of survival. They do comparative research to identify which behaviors are universal and which are specific to a particular species or are modified by culture. They also identify behaviors that are adaptive at different parts of the life span; for example, an infant needs to stay close to the mother, but for an older child more independent exploration is important. (Box 1-2 discusses the adaptiveness of immaturity from an evolutionary perspective.)

Bowlby (1951) was convinced of the importance of the mother-baby bond and warned against separating mother and baby without providing good substitute caregiving. His conviction arose partly from examining ethological studies

Box 1-2 The Adaptive Value of Immaturity

In comparison with other animals, and even with other primates, human children take a long time to grow up. For example, it takes chimpanzees about 8 years to reach reproductive maturity, rhesus monkeys about 4 years, and lemurs only about 2 years. Human beings, by contrast, do not mature physically until early in the teenage years and, at least in modern industrialized societies, typically reach cognitive and psychosocial maturity even later.

From the point of view of Darwinian evolutionary theory, this prolonged period of immaturity is essential to the survival and well-being of the species. Human beings, more than any other animal, live by their intelligence. Human communities and cultures are highly complex, and there is much to learn in order to "know the ropes." A long childhood serves as essential preparation for adulthood.

Apart from their long-term value, some aspects of immaturity (discussed in more detail later in this book) serve immediate adaptive purposes. For example, some primitive reflexes, such as rooting for the nipple, are protective for newborns and disappear when no longer needed. The development of the human brain is much less complete at birth than that of the brains of other primates; if the fetus's brain attained full human size before birth, its head would be too big to go through the birth canal. Instead, the human brain continues to grow throughout childhood, eventually far surpassing the brains of our simian cousins in the capacities for language and thought.

The human brain's slower development gives it greater flexibility, or *plasticity*, as not all connections are "hard wired" at an early age. "This behavioral and cognitive flexibility is perhaps the human species's greatest adaptive advantage" (Bjorklund, 1997, p. 157). It helps account for the resiliency of children who are victims of war, malnourishment, or abuse, yet manage to overcome the effects of early environmental deprivation.

The extended period of immaturity and dependency during infancy and childhood allows children to spend much of their time in play; and, as Piaget maintained, it is largely through play that cognitive development occurs. Play also enables children to develop motor skills and experiment with social roles. It is a vehicle for creative imagination and intellectual curiosity, the hallmarks of the human spirit.

Research on animals suggests that the immaturity of early sensory and motor functioning may protect infants from overstimulation. By limiting the amount of information they have to deal with, it may help them make sense of their world and focus on experiences essential to survival, such as feeding and attachment to the mother. Later, infants' limited memory capacity may simplify the processing of linguistic sounds and thus facilitate early language learning.

The differing rates of development of the various senses may minimize competition among them. In many species the sense of sight is the last to develop. Studies have found that premature visual stimulation can interfere with newborn rats' ability to smell (Kenny & Turkewitz, 1986); and quail chicks that have received prenatal visual stimulation cannot tell their mother's call from that of another quail (Lickliter & Hellewell, 1992). On the other hand, much research supports the value of early sensory stimulation for human infants. The animal studies reported above merely provide a warning that such stimulation should be within a normal range, and that extraordinary stimulation can have unintended negative effects.

Limitations on young children's thought may have adaptive value. For example, Piaget observed that young children are *egocentric;* they tend to see things from their own point of view. Some research suggests that a tendency toward egocentrism may actually help children learn. In one study (Ratner & Foley, 1997), 5-year-olds took turns with an adult in placing furniture in a doll house. In a control group, the adult had already placed half of the items, and the children were then asked to place the other half. When questioned afterward, the children who had taken turns with the adult were more likely than those in the control group to claim that they had placed pieces of furniture the adult had actually placed, but they also remembered more about the task and were better able to repeat it.

It may be that an "I did it!" bias helps young children's recall by avoiding the need to distinguish between their own actions and the actions of others. Young children also tend to be unrealistic in their assessment of their abilities, believing they can do more than they actually can. This immature self-judgment can be beneficial in that it encourages children to try new things and reduces their fear of failure.

continued

of bonding in animals and partly from seeing disturbed children in a psychoanalytic clinic in London. Mary Ainsworth, originally a junior colleague of Bowlby, studied African and American babies and devised the now-famous "Strange Situation" (see Chapter 7) to measure attachment to parents. Research on attachment is based on the belief that infant and parent are biologically predisposed to becoming attached to each other and that such attachment is important for the baby's survival.

So far, the ethological approach has been applied chiefly to only a few other specific developmental issues, such as dominance and aggression among peers

From an evolutionary perspective, the prolonged period of immaturity known as *childhood* permits human beings to develop adaptive skills. One important way this happens is through "pretend" play. This girl playing "doctor" with her teddy bear is developing her imagination and experimenting with social roles.

All in all, evolutionary theory and research suggest that immaturity is not necessarily equivalent to deficiency, and that some attributes of infancy and childhood have persisted because they are appropriate to the tasks of a particular time of life. That does not mean, of course, that *all* early behavior is adaptive, or that children should be "babied" indefinitely; "maturity is still the goal of development" (Bjorklund, 1997, p. 166). What it does mean is that each phase of development is entitled to respect and understanding in its own right, and not just as a pathway to a later phase.

Source: Bjorklund, 1997.

and everyday problem-solving skills, but has had little to say about other aspects of human development. Its methods, which involve long, tedious observation, may be more suited to studying animals than people. For example, it would be unethical to purposely deprive a human child of social contact to see what the results would be. (That is why the discovery of the wild boy of Aveyron was such a rare scientific opportunity.) However, the ethological perspective does point up the value of careful observation of children in their natural settings, and its methods can fruitfully be combined with those favored by other theoretical perspectives (P. H. Miller, 1993).

Contextual Perspective

contextual perspective View of development that sees the individual as inseparable from the social context.

According to the *contextual perspective,* human development can be understood only in its social context. The individual is not a separate entity interacting with the environment but an inseparable part of it. This emphasis on the context of development finds echoes in Bronfenbrenner's ecological approach.

Contextualists emphasize individual differences. Individuals set goals within a particular context as they perceive it and then select new goals within the new context that they seek out or that then presents itself. Success depends on how appropriate a behavior is to its context. For example, a girl growing up on a Sioux reservation, where females are trained to serve their future hunter husbands, will need different personality patterns and different skills from a girl growing up in an urban neighborhood.

The Russian psychologist Lev Semenovich Vygotsky (1896–1934) was a prominent proponent of the sociocultural perspective. His interest in cognitive development arose from his efforts to help blind, deaf, and mentally retarded children fulfill their potential. With the translation of his work into English and the increasing recognition of sociocultural contexts of development and the importance of cross-cultural research, his views have become more influential.

sociocultural theory Vygotsky's theory that analyzes how specific cultural practices, particularly social interaction with adults, affect children's development.

Vygotsky's (1978) *sociocultural theory* is concerned mainly with higher mental activities and has implications for education and cognitive testing. It emphasizes social interaction with adults, especially within the home, as a key factor in children's learning. According to Vygotsky, adults must direct and organize a child's learning before a child can master and internalize it.

zone of proximal development (ZPD) Vygotsky's term for the level at which children can *almost* perform a task on their own and, with appropriate teaching, *can* perform it.

Vygotsky's best-known concept is the *zone of proximal development (ZPD).* ("Proximal" means "near.") Children in the zone of proximal development for a particular task (such as multiplying fractions) can almost, but not quite, perform the task on their own. With the right kind of teaching, however, they can accomplish it successfully. Researchers have applied the metaphor of scaffolds—the temporary platforms on which construction workers stand—to this way of teaching. *Scaffolding* is the temporary support that parents, teachers, or other adults give a child to do a task until the child can do it alone. The more difficulty a child has, the more direction the adult needs to provide. When the child can do the task unaided, the adult takes away the scaffold, which is no longer needed.

scaffolding Temporary support given to a child who is mastering a task.

A major contribution of the contextual perspective has been its recognition of the social component in cognitive, as well as psychosocial, development. One result of the revival of interest in Vygotsky has been to shift research attention from the individual to larger, interactional units—parent and child, sibling and sibling, or even the entire family. The contextual perspective, and Vygotsky's theory in particular, also suggests that the development of children from one culture or one group within a culture (such as white, middle-class Americans) may not be an appropriate norm for children from other societies or cultural groups.

CHECKPOINT

Can you . . .

- Differentiate among five major theoretical perspectives on child development and state strengths and weaknesses of each?

Tests based on Vygotsky's theory, which focus on a child's potential, provide a welcome change from standard intelligence tests that assess only what the child has already learned; and many children may benefit from the sort of guidance Vygotsky prescribes. However, the concept of the ZPD may not lend itself to precise measurement. It also leaves unanswered questions: for example, how influential are a child's motivation and learning ability? Furthermore, the theory pays little attention to developmental issues, such as the role of maturation (P. H. Miller, 1993).

A Child's World: How We Discover It

Theories of child development grow out of, or are tested by, research. Although researchers coming from the various theoretical perspectives we have described use a variety of methods to study children in a variety of settings, the *scientific method* refers to an overall process that characterizes scientific inquiry in any field. Only by following the scientific method can researchers come to sound conclusions about children's development. The steps in this method are:

1. Identification of a problem to be studied, typically on the basis of a theory of development or of previous research.
2. Formulation of hypotheses to be tested by research; these often reflect the theoretical orientation of the researcher.
3. Collection of data.
4. Statistical analysis to determine whether or not the data support the hypothesis.
5. Public dissemination of findings so that other observers can check, learn from, analyze, repeat, and build on the work.

Two key issues at the outset of any investigation are how the participants will be chosen—the sampling method—and how the data will be collected. These decisions often depend on what questions the research is intended to answer. All of these issues play a part in a research design, or plan.

Sampling

How can we be sure that the results of research are true generally, and not just for the participants? First of all, we need to determine who gets into the study. Because studying an entire *population* (a group to which we want to apply the findings) is usually too costly and time-consuming, investigators select a *sample*, a smaller group within the population. The sample must adequately represent the population under study—that is, it must show relevant characteristics in the same proportions as in the entire population. Otherwise the results will be skewed and cannot properly be *generalized,* or applied to the population as a whole.

One way to ensure representativeness is by *random selection,* in which each person in a population has an equal and independent chance of being chosen. If we wanted to study the effects of day care on children in a given center, one way to select a random sample would be to put all the names of the children at the center into a hat, shake it, and then draw out a certain number of names. A random sample, especially a large one, is likely to represent the population well.

Forms of Data Collection

Common ways of gathering data (see Table 1-4) include self-reports (verbal reports by study participants), tests and other behavioral measures, and observation. Depending in part on time and financial constraints, researchers may use one or more of these data collection techniques in any research design. Currently there is a trend toward increased use of self-reports and observation in combination with more objective measures.

Self-Reports: Diaries, Interviews, and Questionnaires

The simplest form of self-report is a *diary* or log. Adolescents may be asked, for example, to record what they eat each day, or the times when they feel depressed. In studying young children, *parental self-reports*—diaries, journals, interviews, or questionnaires—are commonly used, often together with other methods, such as videotaping or recording. Parents may be videotaped playing with their babies and then may be shown the tapes and asked to explain why they reacted as they did.

In a face-to-face or telephone *interview,* researchers ask questions about attitudes, opinions, or behavior. To reach more people, researchers sometimes distribute a printed *questionnaire,* which participants fill out and return. Interviews

scientific method System of established principles and processes of scientific inquiry, including identification of a problem to be studied, formulation and testing of alternative hypotheses, collection and analysis of data, and public dissemination of findings so that other scientists can check, learn from, analyze, repeat, and build on the results.

sample Group of participants chosen to represent the entire population under study.

random selection Sampling method that ensures representativeness because each member of the population has an equal and independent chance to be selected.

Table 1-4   Characteristics of Major Methods of Data Collection

Type	Main Characteristics	Advantages	Disadvantages
Self-report: diary, interview, or questionnaire	Participants are asked about some aspect of their lives; questioning may be highly structured or more flexible.	Can provide firsthand information about a person's life, attitudes, or opinions.	Participant may not remember information accurately or may distort responses in a socially desirable way; how question is asked or by whom may affect answer.
Behavioral measures	Participants are tested on abilities, skills, knowledge, competencies, or physical responses.	Provides objectively measurable information; avoids subjective distortions.	Cannot measure attitudes or other nonbehavioral phenomena; results may be affected by extraneous factors.
Naturalistic observation	People are observed in their normal setting, with no attempt to manipulate behavior.	Provides good description of behavior; does not subject people to unnatural settings that may distort behavior.	Lack of control; observer bias.
Laboratory observation	Participants are observed in the laboratory, with no attempt to manipulate behavior.	Provides good descriptions; greater control than naturalistic observation.	Observer bias; controlled situation can be artificial.

or questionnaires may cover such topics as parent-child relationships, sexual activities, and occupational goals. In a *structured* interview, each participant is asked the same set of questions. An *open-ended* interview is more flexible; as in Piaget's clinical method, the interviewer can vary the topics and order of questions and can ask follow-up questions based on the responses.

By questioning a large number of people, investigators get a broad picture—at least of what the respondents *say* they believe or do or did. However, some people forget when and how events actually took place, and others consciously or unconsciously distort their replies to please the researchers. Furthermore, people willing to participate in interviews or fill out questionnaires tend to be a skewed sample. Also, how a question is asked, and by whom, can affect the answer. When researchers at the National Institute on Drug Abuse reworded a question about alcohol use to indicate that a "drink" meant "more than a few sips," the percentage of teenagers who reported drinking alcohol dropped significantly (see Table 14-5 in Chapter 14). For many kinds of research, then, investigators use more objective measures instead of, or in addition to, self-reports.

Behavioral Methods: Tests and Other Measures

A behavioral measure, such as an intelligence test, *shows* something about a child rather than asking the child or a parent to *tell* about it. Tests and other behavioral measures, including mechanical and electronic devices, may be used to assess abilities, skills, knowledge, competencies, or physiological responses, such as heart rate. Although tests are less subjective than self-reports, results can be affected by such factors as fatigue and self-confidence.

Observation

Observation can take two forms: *naturalistic observation* and *laboratory observation*. In **naturalistic observation,** researchers look at children in real-life settings. The researchers do not try to alter behavior or the environment; they simply record what they see. In **laboratory observation,** researchers observe and record behavior in a controlled situation, such as a laboratory. By observing all participants under the same conditions, investigators can more clearly identify any differences in behavior not attributable to the environment.

naturalistic observation
Research method in which behavior is studied in natural settings without the observer's intervention or manipulation.

laboratory observation
Research method in which the behavior of all participants is noted and recorded in the same situation, under controlled conditions.

Table 1-5   Basic Research Designs

Type	Main Characteristics	Advantages	Disadvantages
Case study	Study of single individual in depth.	Flexibility; provides detailed picture of one person's behavior and developments; can generate hypotheses.	May not generalize to others; conclusions not directly testable; cannot establish cause and effect.
Correlational study	Attempt to find positive or negative relationship between variables.	Allows prediction of one variable on basis of another; can suggest hypotheses about causal relationships.	Cannot establish cause and effect.
Experiment	Controlled procedure in which an experimenter manipulates the independent variable to determine its effect on the dependent variable; may be conducted in the laboratory or field.	Establishes cause-and-effect relationships; highly controlled procedure that can be repeated by another investigator. Degree of control is greatest in the laboratory experiment.	Findings, especially when derived from laboratory experiments, may not generalize to situations outside the laboratory.

Both naturalistic and laboratory observation can provide good descriptions of behavior, but they have limitations. For one, they do not explain *why* children behave as they do. Then, too, an observer's presence can alter behavior. Even when observers stay behind one-way mirrors, where they can see but cannot be seen, children may know that they are being watched and may act differently. Finally, there is a risk of *observer bias:* the researcher's tendency to interpret data to fit expectations, or to emphasize some aspects and minimize others. During the 1960s, laboratory observation was most commonly used so as to achieve more rigorous control. Currently, there is growing use of naturalistic observation supplemented by such technological devices as portable videotape recorders and computers, which enable researchers to analyze moment-by-moment changes in facial expressions or other behavior.

Basic Research Designs

A research design is a plan for conducting a scientific investigation: what questions are to be answered, how participants are to be selected, how data are to be collected and interpreted, and how valid conclusions can be drawn. Three of the basic designs used in developmental research are case studies, correlational studies, and experiments. Each design has advantages and drawbacks, and each is appropriate for certain kinds of research problems (see Table 1-5).

Case Studies

A *case study* is a study of a single case or individual, such as Victor, the wild boy of Aveyron. A number of theories, especially psychoanalytic ones, have grown out of clinical case studies—careful notes and interpretations of what patients have said. Case studies may also use biographical, autobiographical, and documentary materials.

Case studies offer useful, in-depth information. They can explore sources of behavior and can test treatments for problems; they can also suggest a need for other research. Another important advantage is flexibility: the researcher is free to explore avenues of inquiry that arise during the course of the study. But case studies have shortcomings. From studying Victor, for instance, we learn much about the development of a single child, but not how well the information applies to children in general. Furthermore, case studies cannot explain behavior with certainty, because there is no way to test their conclusions. Even though it

C H E C K P O I N T

Can you . . .

• Explain how random selection is achieved and why it is important?

• Discuss the relative advantages and disadvantages of various forms of data collection?

observer bias   Tendency of an observer to misinterpret or distort data to fit his or her expectations.

case study   Scientific study covering a single case or life, based on notes taken by observers or on published biographical materials.

Figure 1-6

Correlational studies may find positive or negative correlations or no correlation. In a positive, or direct, correlation (a), data plotted on a graph cluster around a line showing that one variable (X) increases as the other variable (Y) increases. In a negative, or inverse, correlation (b), one variable (X) increases as the other variable (Y) decreases. No correlation, or a zero correlation (c), exists when increases and decreases in two variables show no consistent relationship (that is, data plotted on a graph show no pattern).

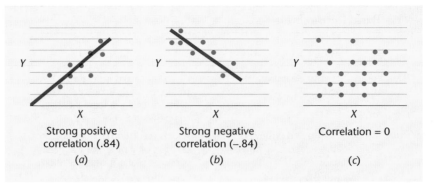

correlational study Research design intended to discover whether a statistical relationship between variables exists, either in direction or in magnitude.

seems reasonable that Victor's severely deprived environment caused or contributed to his language deficiency, it is impossible to know whether he would have developed normally if he had had a normal upbringing.

Correlational Studies

A *correlational study* is an attempt to find a *correlation,* or statistical relationship, between *variables,* phenomena that change or vary among people or can be varied for purposes of research. Correlations are expressed in terms of direction (positive or negative) and magnitude (degree). Two variables that are related *positively* increase or decrease together. A positive, or direct, correlation between televised violence and aggressiveness would exist if children who watched more violent television hit, bit, or kicked more than children who watched less violent television. Two variables have a *negative,* or inverse, correlation if, as one increases, the other decreases. Studies show a negative correlation between amount of schooling and the risk of developing dementia due to Alzheimer's disease in old age. In other words, the less schooling, the more dementia (Katzman, 1993).

Correlations are reported as numbers ranging from –1.0 (a perfect negative relationship) to +1.0 (a perfect positive relationship). Perfect correlations are rare. The closer a correlation comes to +1.0 or –1.0, the stronger the relationship, either positive or negative. A correlation of zero means that the variables have no relationship (see Figure 1-6).

Correlations allow us to predict one variable on the basis of another. If, for example, we found a positive correlation between watching televised violence and fighting, we would predict that children who watch violent shows are more likely to get into fights. The greater the magnitude of the correlation between two variables, the greater the ability to predict one from the other.

Although correlations *suggest* possible causes, they do not support conclusions about cause and effect. We cannot conclude from a positive correlation between televised violence and aggressiveness that watching televised violence *causes* aggressive play; we can conclude only that the two variables are related. It is possible that a third variable—perhaps an inborn predisposition toward aggressiveness—causes a child both to watch violent programs and to act aggressively. Similarly, we cannot be sure that schooling protects against dementia; it may be that another variable, such as socioeconomic status, might explain both lower levels of schooling and higher levels of dementia. To be certain that one variable causes another, we would need to design a controlled experiment—something that, in studying human beings, is not always possible for practical or ethical reasons.

Experiments

experiment Rigorously controlled, replicable (repeatable) procedure in which the researcher manipulates variables to assess the effect of one on the other.

An *experiment* is a rigorously controlled procedure in which the investigator, called the *experimenter,* manipulates variables to learn how one affects another. Scientific experiments must be conducted and reported in such a way that another

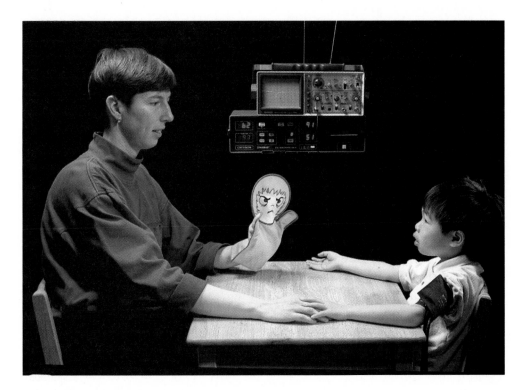

Experiments use strictly controlled procedures that manipulate variables to determine how one affects another. To study emotional resiliency, this research project at the University of California at San Francisco monitors the heart rate and blood pressure of young children as they explain their feelings in response to a hand puppet's happy or angry face.

investigator can *replicate* them, that is, repeat them in exactly the same way with different participants to verify the results and conclusions. Figure 1-7 shows how an experiment might be designed.

Groups and Variables To conduct an experiment, the experimenter needs to divide the participants into two kinds of groups. An **experimental group** is composed of people who are to be exposed to the experimental manipulation or *treatment*—the phenomenon the researcher wants to study. Afterward, the effect of the treatment will be measured one or more times. A **control group** is composed of people who are similar to the experimental group but do not receive the treatment. An experiment must include one or more of each type of group. Ideally, as we've already mentioned, the sample should be randomly selected.

Let's look at how one team of researchers (G. J. Whitehurst, Falco, et al., 1988) designed an experiment to find out what effect a special method of reading picture books to very young children might have on their language and vocabulary skills. The researchers compared two groups of middle-class children ages 21 to 35 months. In the *experimental group,* the parents adopted the new reading method (the treatment), which involved encouraging children's active participation and giving frequent, age-based feedback. In the *control group,* parents simply read aloud as they usually did. The parents of the children in the experimental group asked the children challenging open-ended questions rather than questions calling for simple yes/no answers. (Instead of asking, "Is the cat asleep?", they would ask, "What is the cat doing?") They expanded on the children's answers, corrected wrong answers, gave alternative possibilities, and bestowed praise. After 1 month of the program, the children in the experimental group were 8.5 months ahead of the control group in level of speech and 6 months ahead in vocabulary; 9 months later, the experimental group was still 6 months ahead of the controls. It is fair to conclude, then, that this reading method improved the children's language and vocabulary skills.

In the experiment just described, the type of reading approach was the *independent variable,* and the children's language skills were the *dependent variable.* An **independent variable** is something over which the experimenter has direct control. A **dependent variable** is something that may or may not change

experimental group In an experiment, the group receiving the treatment under study; any changes in these people are compared with changes in the control group.

control group In an experiment, a group of people who are similar to the people in the experimental group but who do not receive the treatment whose effects are to be measured; the results obtained with this group are compared with the results obtained with the experimental group.

independent variable In an experiment, the condition over which the experimenter has direct control.

dependent variable In an experiment, the condition that may or may not change as a result of changes in the independent variable.

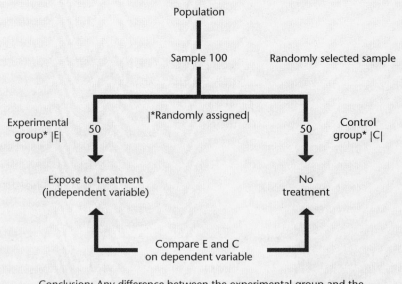

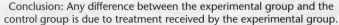

Population

Sample 100   Randomly selected sample

|*Randomly assigned|

Experimental group* |E| 50

Control group* |C| 50

Expose to treatment (independent variable)

No treatment

Compare E and C on dependent variable

Conclusion: Any difference between the experimental group and the control group is due to treatment received by the experimental group.

Figure 1-7
Design for an experiment. This experiment takes a random sample from the larger population being studied, randomly assigns participants to either the experimental (E) or control (C) group, and exposes the experimental group to a treatment that is not given to the control group. By comparing the two groups after the experimental group has received the treatment, the researcher can conclude that any difference between them is due to the experimental treatment.

random assignment
Technique used in assigning members of a study sample to experimental and control groups, in which each member of the sample has an equal chance to be assigned to each group and to receive or not receive the treatment.

as a result of changes in the independent variable; in other words, it *depends* on the independent variable. In an experiment, a researcher manipulates the independent variable to see how changes in it will affect the dependent variable.

If an experiment shows a significant difference in the performance of the experimental and control groups, how do we know that the cause was the independent variable? For example, in the read-aloud experiment, how can we be sure that the reading method and not some other factor (such as intelligence) caused the difference in language development of the two groups? The answer lies in controlling who gets the treatment. This can be done by *random assignment:* assigning the participants to experimental and control groups in such a way that each person has an equal chance of being placed in either group. If assignment is random and the sample is large enough, differences in such factors as age, sex, race, IQ, and socioeconomic status will be evenly distributed so that the groups are as alike as possible in every respect except for the variable to be tested.

Laboratory, Field, and Natural Experiments   Methods such as random assignment are most easily used in *laboratory experiments.* In a laboratory experiment the participants are brought to a special place where they experience conditions manipulated by the experimenter. The experimenter records the participants' reactions to these conditions, perhaps comparing them with their own or other participants' behavior under different conditions.

Not all experiments can be readily done in the laboratory. A *field experiment* is a controlled study conducted in a setting that is part of everyday life, such as a child's home or school. The experiment in which parents adopted a new way of reading aloud was a field experiment.

Laboratory and field experiments differ in two important respects. One is the *degree of control* exerted by the experimenter; the other is the degree to which findings can be *generalized* beyond the study situation. Laboratory experiments are more rigidly controlled and thus are easier to replicate. However, the results may be less generalizable to real life; because of the artificiality of the situation, participants may not act as they normally would. For example, if children who watch violent television shows in the laboratory become more aggressive in that

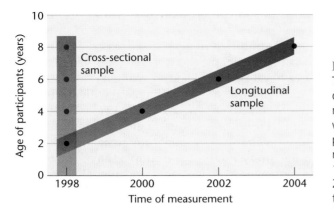

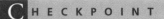

Figure 1-8
The two most common ways to obtain data about age-related development. In a *cross-sectional* study, people of different ages are measured at one time. Here, groups of 2-, 4-, 6-, and 8-year-olds were tested in 1998 to obtain data about age differences in performance. In a *longitudinal* study, the same people are measured more than once. Here, a sample of children were first measured in 1998, when they were 2 years old; follow-up testing is done in 2000, 2002, and 2004, when the children are 4, 6, and 8, respectively. This technique shows age changes in performance.

setting, we cannot be sure that children who watch a lot of violent shows at home hit their little brothers or sisters more often than children who watch fewer such shows.

When, for practical or ethical reasons, it is impossible to conduct a true experiment, a *natural experiment* may provide a way of studying certain events. A natural experiment compares people who have been accidentally "assigned" to separate groups by circumstances of life—one group of children who were exposed, say, to famine or AIDS or a birth defect or superior education, and another group who were not.

There is no one "right" way to study human beings. Many questions can be approached from several angles, each yielding different kinds of information. Experiments have important advantages over other research designs: the ability to establish cause-and-effect relationships and to permit replication. However, experiments can be too artificial and too narrowly focused. In recent decades, therefore, many researchers have concentrated less on laboratory experimentation or have supplemented it with a wider array of methods.

Developmental Research Designs

The two most common research strategies used to study children's development are *longitudinal* and *cross-sectional* studies (see Figure 1-8). Longitudinal studies reveal how children change or stay the same as they grow older; cross-sectional studies show similarities and differences among age groups. Because each of these designs has drawbacks, researchers have also devised *sequential* designs.

In a **longitudinal study**, researchers study the same person or persons more than once, sometimes years apart. They may measure a single characteristic, such as vocabulary size, IQ, height, or aggressiveness, or they may look at several aspects of development to find relationships among them. One example, the Oakland (Adolescent) Growth Study (part of the Berkeley Longitudinal Studies), which began in 1932, was initially designed to assess social and emotional development from the preteens through the senior high school years. Ultimately, many of the participants were followed into old age. All participants had medical examinations, and gave family histories. They took periodic intelligence and psychological tests, including personality inventories (instruments that yield quantitative ratings of certain traits or groups of traits). On the basis of recorded data and interviews, the researchers developed detailed life histories of 60 participants. Eventually the research began to focus on *planful competence,* a combination of self-confidence, intellectual commitment, and dependable effectiveness, which helps people mobilize resources and cope with difficulties. People who as teenagers showed planful competence made good choices in adolescence and early adulthood, which often led to promising opportunities (scholarships, good jobs, and competent spouses). Less competent

CHECKPOINT

Can you . . .

- Compare the uses and drawbacks of case studies, correlational studies, and experiments?

- Explain why and how a controlled experiment can establish causal relationships?

- Distinguish among laboratory, field, and natural experiments?

longitudinal study Study design in which data are collected about the same people over a period of time, to assess developmental changes that occur with age.

cross-sectional study Study design in which people of different ages are assessed on one occasion, providing comparative information about different age cohorts.

teenagers made poorer early decisions and then tended to lead crisis-ridden lives (Clausen, 1993).

In a *cross-sectional study*, people of different ages are assessed at one time. In one cross-sectional study, described in Chapter 9, researchers asked 3-, 4-, 6-, and 7-year-olds questions about what a pensive-looking woman was doing, or about the state of someone's mind. There was a striking increase with age in children's awareness of mental activity (Flavell, Green, & Flavell, 1995). These findings strongly suggest that as children become older, their understanding of mental processes improves, but we cannot draw such a conclusion with certainty. The younger children in the study might, for example, have come from homes in which their parents commented less frequently on mental states. The only way to see whether change occurs with age is to conduct a longitudinal study of a particular person or group.

Both longitudinal and cross-sectional designs have strengths and weaknesses. Longitudinal research, by repeatedly studying the same people, can track individual patterns of continuity and change. It avoids confounding developmental effects with effects of cohort membership (the differing experiences of children born, for example, before and after the advent of the Internet). However, a longitudinal study done on a particular cohort may not apply to a different cohort. (In other words, the results of a study of people born in the 1920s, such as the Oakland Growth Study, may not apply to people born in the 1990s.) Furthermore, longitudinal studies are more time-consuming and expensive than cross-sectional studies; it is hard to keep track of a large group of participants over the years, to keep records, and to keep the study going despite turnover in research personnel. Then there is the problem of attrition: participants may die or drop out. Another likely difficulty is bias in the sample: people who volunteer for such studies, and especially those who stay with them, tend to be above average in intelligence and socioeconomic status. Also, results can be affected by repeated testing: people may do better in later tests because of familiarity with test materials and procedures.

CHECKPOINT

Can you . . .

• List advantages and disadvantages of cross-sectional and longitudinal research?

Advantages of cross-sectional research include speed and economy; data can be gathered fairly quickly from large numbers of people. And, since participants are assessed only once, there is no problem of attrition. A drawback of cross-sectional studies is that they mask individual differences by looking only at group averages. Their major disadvantage, however, is that the results may be affected by cohort influences. Cross-sectional studies are sometimes interpreted as yielding information about developmental changes in groups or individuals, but such information is often misleading. Thus, although cross-sectional studies still dominate the field—no doubt because they are so much easier to do—the proportion of research devoted to longitudinal studies, especially short-term ones, is increasing (Parke et al., 1994).

cross-sequential study Study design that combines cross-sectional and longitudinal techniques by assessing people in a cross-sectional sample more than once.

The *cross-sequential study* is one of several strategies designed to overcome the drawbacks of longitudinal and cross-sectional studies. This method combines the other two: researchers assess a cross-sectional sample more than once to determine how members of each age cohort have changed. This procedure permits researchers to separate age-related changes from cohort effects. The major drawbacks of sequential studies involve time, effort, and complexity. Sequential designs require large numbers of participants and the collection and analysis of huge amounts of data over a period of years. Interpreting their findings and conclusions can demand a high degree of sophistication.

Ethics of Research

Should research that might harm its participants ever be undertaken? How can we balance the possible benefits against the risk of mental, emotional, or physical injury to children? What happens when the quest for useful knowledge conflicts with participants' rights? Such ethical dilemmas are particularly troubling when prospective participants are young and vulnerable—for example, if they are abused or socially disadvantaged.

In resolving such dilemmas, researchers try to be guided by three principles first stated by the National Commission for the Protection of Human Subjects of Biomedical and Behavioral Research (1978). These principles are (1) *beneficence:* the obligation to maximize possible benefits to participants and minimize possible harm; (2) *respect* for participants' autonomy and protection of those who are unable to exercise their own judgment; and (3) *justice:* inclusion of diverse groups while being sensitive to any special impact the research situation may have on them.

Since the 1970s, federally mandated committees have been set up at colleges, universities, and other institutions to review proposed research from an ethical standpoint. Guidelines of the American Psychological Association (1992) and the Society for Research in Child Development (1993) cover such points as protection of participants from harm and loss of dignity; guarantees of privacy and confidentiality, informed consent, avoidance of deception, and the right to decline or withdraw from an experiment at any time; and the responsibility of investigators to correct any undesirable effects. Still, despite the stringent rules and vastly improved ethical climate that prevail today, specific situations often call for hard judgments. Let's look more closely at some key issues.

Right to Informed Consent

Informed consent exists when participants voluntarily agree to be in a study, are competent to give consent, are fully aware of the risks as well as the potential benefits, and are not being exploited. Of course, children may not be able to give meaningful consent. But when parents, guardians, or school personnel consent to a child's participation in research, can we be sure that they are acting in the child's best interests? Obviously, passive consent forms, which guardians are asked to send back only if they do *not* want the child to participate, do not give enough assurance of informed consent (Fisher, 1993). The National Commission for the Protection of Human Subjects of Biomedical and Behavioral Research (1978) recommends that children age 7 or over be asked to give their own consent to take part in research and that children's objections should be overruled only if the research promises direct benefit to the child, as in the use of a new experimental drug.

If there is a language barrier, it is important to make sure that prospective participants are properly informed about any aspect of the study that might influence their decision. Sometimes families who are receiving health services from an institution sponsoring a study fear that if they withhold consent, they will lose the services. Sometimes, if financial incentives are offered, poor families may be willing to take on risks they otherwise would not assume. Parents may not realize that the objectives of a study (say, encouraging children to make their own decisions and question adult standards) are contrary to the parents' cultural values. Parents may think that participation in a study of a promising new treatment will benefit a child, even though the child may be assigned to a control group that does not receive the treatment. Some studies have been stopped early, when it became clear that a treatment was beneficial, so that it could be offered to the control group (Fisher, 1993).

Can informed consent exist if participants are deceived about the nature of a study? Suppose that children are told they are trying out a new game when they are actually being tested on their reactions to success or failure? Suppose that adults are told they are participating in a study on learning when they are really being tested on their willingness to inflict pain? Experiments like these, which cannot be carried out without deception, have been done—and they have added significantly to our knowledge, but at the cost of the participants' right to know what they were getting involved in.

Right to Self-Esteem

Should people be subjected to research that may damage their self-esteem? Studies on limits of memory, for example, have a built-in "failure factor": the researcher keeps asking question until the participant is unable to answer. Might this inevitable failure affect a participant's self-confidence? Similarly, when researchers publish findings that middle-class children are academically superior to poor children, unintentional harm may be done to the latter's self-esteem. Furthermore, such studies may become self-fulfilling prophecies, affecting teachers' expectations and students' performance.

Right to Privacy and Confidentiality

Is it ethical to use one-way mirrors and hidden cameras to observe people without their knowledge? How can we protect the confidentiality of personal information that participants may reveal in interviews or questionnaires (for example, about income or family relationships or even about illegal activities, such as smoking marijuana or shoplifting)?

On the other hand, what if, during the course of research, an investigator notices that a child seems to have a learning disability or some other treatable condition? What is a researcher's obligation to share such information with parents or guardians, or to recommend services that may help the child, especially if sharing the information would jeopardize the study? Such a decision should not be made lightly, since sharing information of uncertain validity may create damaging misconceptions about a child. Furthermore, researchers should not overstep the bounds of their own competence in making diagnoses and referrals. Researchers do need to know, and inform participants of, their legal responsibilities regarding reporting of child abuse or neglect or any other illegal activities of which they become aware.

Our final word in this introductory chapter is that this entire book is far from the final word. While we have tried to incorporate the most important and the most up-to-date information about how people develop, developmentalists are constantly learning more. As you read this book, you are certain to come up with your own questions. By thinking about them, and perhaps eventually conducting research to find answers, it is possible that you yourself, now just embarking on the study of child development, will someday add to our knowledge about the interesting species to which we all belong.

SUMMARY

A Child's World: Basic Concepts

- The scientific study of **child development** is concerned with both **quantitative change** and **qualitative change,** as well as with continuity of behavior.
- The various aspects of development (physical, cognitive, and psychosocial, which includes **personality** and social development) do not occur in isolation. Each affects the other.
- Influences on development come from both **heredity** and **environment.** Many typical changes during childhood are related to **maturation.** Individual differences increase as children grow older.
- One important influence is whether a child grows up in a **nuclear family** or an **extended family** household. Other important environmental influences stem from **socioeconomic status (SES), ethnic group,** and **culture.** Cross-cultural research can indicate whether certain aspects of development are universal or culturally influenced.
- Normative age-graded influences affect people of the same age. Normative history-graded influences affect a particular **cohort.** Nonnormative life events are unusual in themselves or in their timing.

- There is strong evidence of **critical periods** for certain kinds of early physical development; however, for cognitive and psychosocial development, there appears to be more **plasticity.**
- Bronfenbrenner's **ecological approach** identifies five interlocking levels of environmental influences, from the most intimate to the broadest.

A Child's World: How Its Study Evolved

- The question of how children were treated in earlier times is controversial, but recent analyses suggest that children have historically been regarded as qualitatively different from adults.
- The scientific study of child development began in the nineteenth century. Adolescence was not considered a separate phase of development until the twentieth century. The field of child development is now part of the study of the entire life span. It focuses on describing, explaining, predicting, and modifying development.

A Child's World: Issues and Theoretical Perspectives

- A **theory** is used to explain **data** and to generate **hypotheses,** which predict the results of research.
- Many influential theories of development stem from one of five theoretical perspectives: psychoanalytic, learning, cognitive, ethological, and contextual.
- The five perspectives vary in their positions on three central issues: the relative importance of heredity and environment, the active or passive character of development, and the existence of stages of development.
- Some perspectives are influenced by a **mechanistic model** of development; others by an **organismic model.**
- The **psychoanalytic perspective** sees development as motivated by unconscious emotional conflicts. Freud described five stages of **psychosexual development,** in which gratification shifts from one body zone to another. Freud also identified three hypothetical parts of the personality: the **id, ego,** and **superego.** Erikson proposed eight stages of **psychosocial development** between infancy and old age, each involving the resolution of a crisis. Miller's **relational theory** focuses on differences between male and female development.
- The **learning perspective** views development as a result of **learning,** a response to external events. Research based on **behaviorism** has shown that behavior can be predictably altered by **classical conditioning** or **operant conditioning,** which uses **reinforcement** and **punishment.** Bandura's **social-learning theory** stresses **observational learning** and imitation of models.
- The **cognitive perspective** describes children as active initiators of development. In Piaget's cognitive-stage theory, development results from the increasingly complex **organization** of mental and behavioral **schemes** through **adaptation (assimilation** and **accommodation)** and **equilibration.** The newer **information-processing approach** analyzes the mental processes underlying intelligent behavior. Neo-Piagetian theorists, such as Robbie Case, have combined elements of Piaget's theory with the information-processing approach.
- The **ethological perspective,** represented by Bowlby and Ainsworth, looks at specific behaviors that promote group survival and are adaptive at critical periods of the life span.
- The **contextual perspective** focuses on interaction between the individual and the social context. Vygotsky's **sociocultural theory** includes the concepts of the **zone of proximal development (ZPD)** and **scaffolding,** which have implications for cognitive testing and teaching.

A Child's World: How We Discover It

- Research, to produce sound conclusions, must be based on the **scientific method.**
- A research **sample** achieved through **random selection** can ensure generalizability.
- Forms of data collection include self-reports (diaries, interviews, and questionnaires); tests and other behavioral measures; **naturalistic observation;** and **laboratory observation.** The value of observation may be limited by **observer bias.**

- Three basic designs used in developmental research are the **case study, correlational study,** and **experiment.** Only experiments can establish causal relationships, but case studies and correlational studies can provide hypotheses or predictions to be tested by experimental research.

- In an experiment, the experimenter manipulates the **independent variable** to see its effect on the **dependent variable.** Experiments must be rigorously controlled so as to be valid and replicable. **Random assignment** of participants to the **experimental group** and **control group** is necessary to make sure that the effect of the independent variable, and not some other factor, is being tested.

- Laboratory experiments are easiest to control and replicate, but findings of field experiments may be more generalizable beyond the study situation. Natural experiments may be useful in situations in which true experiments would be impractical or unethical.

- The two most common designs used to study age-related development are the **longitudinal study** and the **cross-sectional study.** Cross-sectional studies compare age groups; longitudinal studies describe continuity or change in the same participants. The **cross-sequential study** is intended to overcome the weaknesses of the other two designs.

- Ethical issues in research on human development include informed consent, self-esteem, and privacy of participants.

KEY TERMS

child development (8)
quantitative change (8)
qualitative change (8)
personality (8)
heredity (9)
environment (9)
maturation (9)
nuclear family (9)
extended family (9)
socioeconomic status (SES) (11)
ethnic group (11)
culture (11)
cohort (13)
critical period (13)
plasticity (13)
ecological approach (14)
theory (18)
data (18)
hypotheses (18)
mechanistic model (20)
organismic model (21)
psychoanalytic perspective (22)
psychosexual development (22)
id (23)
ego (23)
superego (23)
psychosocial development (25)
relational theory (26)
learning perspective (26)
learning (26)
behaviorism (27)
classical conditioning (27)
operant conditioning (28)
reinforcement (28)

punishment (28)
social-learning theory (29)
observational learning (29)
cognitive perspective (30)
organization (31)
schemes (31)
adaptation (31)
assimilation (31)
accommodation (31)
equilibration (31)
information-processing approach (32)
ethological perspective (33)
contextual perspective (36)
sociocultural theory (36)
zone of proximal development (ZPD) (36)
scaffolding (36)
scientific method (37)
sample (37)
random selection (37)
naturalistic observation (38)
laboratory observation (38)
observer bias (39)
case study (39)
correlational study (40)
experiment (40)
experimental group (41)
control group (41)
independent variable (41)
dependent variable (41)
random assignment (42)
longitudinal study (43)
cross-sectional study (44)
cross-sequential study (44)

QUESTIONS FOR THOUGHT AND DISCUSSION

1. What practical or other reasons do you have for wanting to learn more about child development? Do some of the four goals mentioned in your text seem more important to you than others?

2. In which period of a child's life does change seem to be most dramatic?

3. Can you think of ways in which some aspect of your development as a child affected one or more other aspects?

4. Can you describe some of the childhood influences that helped make you the person you are today? How might you be different if you had grown up in a culture other than your own?

5. Because of ethical limitations on experimentation with humans, researchers often must rely on correlational studies to suggest links, for example, between televised violence and aggression. How would you evaluate the usefulness of information gained from such studies?

6. Some people have raised ethical objections to behaviorists' goal of controlling or shaping behavior. If developmentalists *could* mold children so as to eliminate antisocial behavior, *should* they?

7. What contributions can animal research make to the study of children? What might be some limitations of such research?

8. What kinds of research seem most suitable to a laboratory setting and what kinds to a natural field setting?

Beginnings: *A Bird's-Eye View*

Beginnings

By the time babies are born, they already have an impressive history. Part of this early history, which began long before conception, is the hereditary endowment passed on at that moment. Another part is environmental, for the new organism is affected by many events that occur during its nine months in the womb. As this organism grows from a single cell to a newborn baby, both inheritance and experience affect its development. At birth, children are already individuals, distinguishable not just by sex, but by size, temperament, appearance, and history.

The changes that occur between conception and the first months after birth are broader and faster-paced than any a person will ever experience again. Although these initial changes may seem to be mostly physical, they have repercussions on other aspects of development. For example, the physical growth of the brain before and immediately after birth makes possible a great burst of cognitive and emotional growth.

In Part I, we focus on this earliest period of development. Chapter 2 examines the two great forces—heredity and environment—that make each child a unique person. Chapter 3 considers effects of the prenatal environment. Chapter 4 describes the birth process and the tiny traveler who emerges into a child's world.

Forming a New Life: Conception, Heredity, and Environment

Of the cell, the wondrous seed
Becoming plant and animal and mind
Unerringly forever after its kind
In its omnipotence, in flower and weed
And beast and bird and fish, and many a breed
Of man and woman from all years behind
Building its future.

William Ellery Leonard, *Two Lives,* 1923

FOCUS
Louise Brown, the First "Test-tube Baby"

The writer Aldous Huxley foresaw it in 1932: human life created in the laboratory. As Huxley described it in his novel *Brave New World,* the feat would be accomplished by immersing female *ova* (egg cells), which had been incubated in test tubes, in a dish of free-swimming male sperm. Huxley envisioned his "brave new world" as 600 years into the future; yet it took only 46 years before a birth through *in vitro fertilization,* or fertilization outside the mother's body, became a reality.

Louise Brown, the world's first documented "test-tube baby," was born July 25, 1978, in a four-story red brick hospital in the old textile mill town of Oldham in northwest England. She had been conceived, not in a test tube, but by placing a ripe ovum from her 30-year-old mother, Lesley Brown, in a shallow glass dish with fluid containing sperm from her 38-year-old father, John Brown. After two days, during which the resulting single-celled organism multiplied to eight cells, it had been implanted in Lesley's womb.

Until this precedent-shattering event, Lesley and her husband, a truck driver for the British Railway Network, were—by their own description—an ordinary couple who lived in a low-rent, government-subsidized row house in Bristol. Although they were raising John's 17-year-old daughter from a previous marriage, they desperately wanted to have a baby together. After seven years of failure to conceive, they turned to the then-experimental *in vitro* method.

The fulfillment of the Browns' wish, two years later, was the culmination of more than a decade of painstaking preparatory research by Patrick Steptoe, a gynecologist in Manchester, and Robert Edwards, a physiologist at Cambridge University. The outcome was far more than a single baby. Steptoe's and Edwards's work gave birth to a new branch of medicine, known as *assisted reproductive technology.*

By now, in the United States alone, more than 26,000 babies have gotten their start *in vitro,* and 40,000 couples tried the method in 1996 alone. Many of the women, like Lesley

Brown, who have successfully conceived in this way have fallopian tubes that are blocked or scarred beyond surgical repair, which prevent ova from reaching the uterus on their own. However, as we'll see, this and other methods of assisted reproduction raise troubling ethical and practical issues, among them the great expense and effort coupled with a relatively low success rate.

Some questions were already in the air as Lesley and John Brown awaited the birth of what was to be called, in banner headlines, the "Miracle Baby" and "Baby of the Century." Despite strenuous efforts by the couple and their doctors to keep the birth secret, the news leaked out. Hordes of newspaper and television reporters from around the world hovered outside the hospital and, later, camped on the Browns' front lawn. Some of the couple's neighbors, and even some of their relatives, sold information to the press.

The story launched a debate about the moral implications of tampering with nature—and, down the road, the possibility of mass baby farms and reproductive engineering, which could alter or custom design the "products" of reproduction. More immediately, what about the risks to mother and baby? What if the baby was born grossly deformed? Could *any* baby conceived in a laboratory dish have a normal life?

Lesley was checked and monitored more frequently than most expectant mothers are, and, as a precaution, spent the last three months of her pregnancy in the hospital, while John took a leave from his job to be with her. The birth took place about two weeks before the due date, by cesarean delivery, because Lesley had developed toxemia (blood poisoning) and the fetus did not seem to be gaining weight. But all went smoothly; there were no further complications.

The blonde, blue-eyed, 5-pound-12-ounce baby was, from all accounts, a beautiful, normal infant, who emerged crying lustily. "There's no difference between her and any other little girl," her father maintained. "We just helped nature a bit, that's all" ("Louise Brown," 1984, p. 82).

By the time Louise celebrated her fourth birthday, she had a "test-tube" sister, Natalie, born June 14, 1982. Lesley and John used part of the nest egg obtained from interview, book, and film rights to buy a modest house; the rest remained in trust for the children. At last report, in 1996, 18-year-old Louise Brown was studying to be a school nurse and planned to have her own babies, "whatever it takes" (Faltermayer et al., 1996, p. 18).

Sources of information about Louise Brown were Barthel, 1982; Faltermayer et al., 1996; "The First Test-tube Baby," 1978; C. Lawson, 1993; "Louise Brown," 1984; "Louise Brown," 1994; "Test-tube Baby," 1978; Van Dyck, 1995.

● ● ●

What made Louise Brown the person she is today? Like any other child, she began with a hereditary endowment from her mother and father. For example, she has her father's stocky build, wide forehead, and chubby cheeks and her mother's tilted nose and curved mouth—as well as her mother's sudden temper. Louise has also been affected by a host of environmental influences, from that famous laboratory dish to the tremendous public interest in her story. As a preschooler, she was mentally precocious, mischievous, and (by her parents' admission) spoiled—the latter related, perhaps, to the constant, close attention she had received, not only from curious outsiders, but also from parents who wanted to be the perfect mother and father their "miracle baby" deserved. As a teenager, like many of her secondary school classmates, she liked to swim and ride horses, wore two gold studs in each ear, watched MTV, and had a crush on the actor Tom Cruise.

Most children do not become famous, especially at birth; but every child is the product of a unique combination of hereditary and environmental influences set in motion by the parents' decision to form a new life. We begin this chapter by exploring when and why people have children. We explain how normal conception works and what alternative technologies are available, some of them developed since Louise Brown's birth. We examine the mechanisms and patterns of heredity—the inherited factors that affect development—and how genetic counseling can help couples weigh the decision to become parents. We look at how heredity and environment work together.

After reading this chapter, you should be able to answer and elaborate on such questions as these:

Preview Questions

- Why and when do most people become parents?
- How does conception normally take place?
- What are some of the causes of, and remedies for, infertility?
- What mechanisms determine sex, physical appearance, and other characteristics?
- How are birth defects and disorders transmitted?
- How can the effects of heredity and environment be studied?

One reason why parents, like this couple in Nepal, have children is the complex, challenging, and gratifying intimacy that parenthood provides. Although large families were an economic asset in preindustrial societies, many people in developing countries beset by overpopulation and hunger now want smaller families.

Becoming Parents

The choice, timing, and circumstances of parenthood can have vast consequences for a child. Whether a birth was planned or accidental, whether the pregnancy was welcomed or unwanted, whether it came about through normal or extraordinary means, whether the parents were married or unmarried, and how old the parents were when a child was conceived or adopted are all factors in the microsystem identified in Bronfenbrenner's ecological approach (see Chapter 1). Whether the culture encourages large or small families, whether it values one sex over the other, and how much it supports families with children are macrosystem issues likely to influence that child's development.

Let's look at why and when people have children; then at how conception normally occurs and how multiple births occasionally come about; and finally, at options for couples unable to conceive in the normal way.

Why and When People Have Children

In preindustrial farming societies, large families were a necessity: Children helped with the family's work and would eventually care for aging parents. The death rate in childhood was high, and having many children made it more likely that some would reach maturity. Today, infant and child mortality rates have improved greatly (see Chapters 5 and 8), and, in industrial societies, large families are no longer an economic asset. In developing countries, too, where overpopulation and hunger are major problems, there is recognition of the need to limit family size and to space children farther apart.

In the United States today, many young adults are ambivalent about having children. Among 600 couples in the first 6 years of marriage, most saw children as necessary for "a real family life," as sources of love and affection, and as buffers against loneliness. However, they also saw disadvantages in parenthood: lifestyle changes, financial costs, and career problems for women. Almost half of these couples rated other values—a fulfilling career, time alone with a spouse, extra money, or a neat and orderly household—as equally or more important than having children (Neal, Grout, & Wicks, 1989).

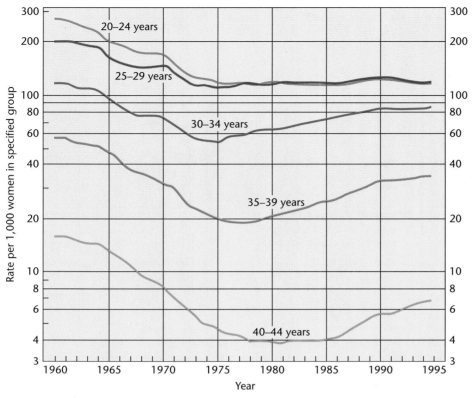

Figure 2-1

Birth rates by age of mother—United States, 1960–1995. Today women tend to have fewer children and to have them later in life than their mothers did. The birth rate for women in their twenties has declined, while the birth rate for women in their thirties and forties is increasing.

Source: Adapted from Ventura, Martin, Curtin, & Mathews, 1997, Figure 2.

NOTE: Rates are plotted on a log scale.

It is not surprising, then, that the birth rate has fallen. In 1955, the average American woman was likely to have 3.6 children; in 1994, she was likely to have only 2.1 (National Center for Health Statistics [NCHS], 1996; U.S. Bureau of the Census, 1995b). According to a projection by the U.S. Bureau of the Census, 16 percent of women in the "baby boom" generation born after World War II will *never* become mothers—about twice as many as in their mothers' generation (O'Connell, 1991). On the other hand, a growing number of single adults are choosing to have or adopt children (see Chapter 13).

Not only do people typically have fewer children today; they start having them later in life than was true 15 or 20 years ago, often because they spend their early adult years getting an education and establishing a career. Between 1970 and 1987, the percentage of women who had a first child after age 30 quadrupled, though most births were still to women in their twenties (NCHS, 1990). Between 1990 and 1995, live birth rates for women in their twenties fell by 6 to 7 percent, to their lowest point since 1987. Meanwhile, the rates for women age 30 and over continue to climb, though more slowly than before. More women are having babies after 40, too; the live birth rate for women ages 40 to 44 rose by 74 percent between 1981 and 1995 (Ventura, Martin, Curtin, & Mathews, 1997; see Figure 2-1).

Women with more education tend to have babies later. Although women without a high school education have the highest *overall* birth rate, among 30- to 39-year-old women the highest birth rate is for those with college degrees (Mathews & Ventura, 1997).

The risks of delayed childbearing (see Chapter 3) appear to be lower than was previously believed. After age 35 there is more chance of miscarriage and more likelihood of abnormalities, birth-related complications, or fetal death, but most risks to the infant's health are not much greater than for babies born to younger mothers (G. S. Berkowitz, Skovron, Lapinski, & Berkowitz, 1990; P. Brown, 1993). On the positive side, babies of older mothers may benefit from their mothers' greater ease with parenthood. When 105 new mothers ages 16 to 38 were interviewed

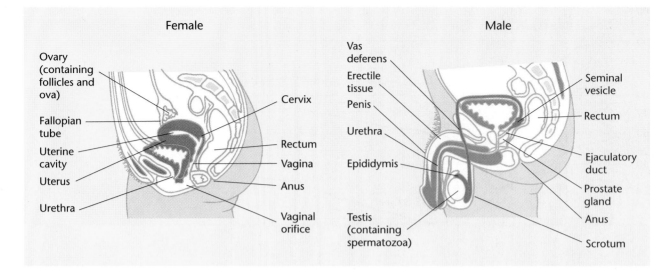

Female

Ovary (containing follicles and ova)
Fallopian tube
Uterine cavity
Uterus
Urethra

Cervix
Rectum
Vagina
Anus
Vaginal orifice

Male

Vas deferens
Erectile tissue
Penis
Urethra
Epididymis
Testis (containing spermatozoa)

Seminal vesicle
Rectum
Ejaculatory duct
Prostate gland
Anus
Scrotum

Figure 2-2
Human reproductive systems.

and observed with their infants, the older mothers reported more satisfaction with parenting and spent more time at it. They were more affectionate and sensitive to their babies and more effective in encouraging desired behavior (Ragozin, Basham, Crnic, Greenberg, & Robinson, 1982). And, among a large, nationally representative sample, a subsample of 47 men who became fathers after their 35th birthdays spent more leisure time with their children, had higher expectations for the children's behavior, and were more nurturing than a comparison group who became fathers before age 35 (Heath, 1994).

How Fertilization Takes Place

Regardless of why and when it occurs, the beginning of human life has always inspired wonder and curiosity. Every human being's biological beginning is a split-second event when a single spermatozoon, one of millions of sperm cells from the father, joins an ovum, one of the several hundred thousand ova produced by the mother's body. As we will see, which sperm meets which ovum has tremendous implications for the new person.

Fertilization, or conception, is the process by which sperm and ovum—the male and female *gametes,* or sex cells—combine to create a single cell called a *zygote,* which then duplicates itself again and again by cell division to become a baby. A girl is born with all the ova she will ever have—about 400,000. At birth, these immature ova are in her two ovaries (see Figure 2-2), each ovum in its own small sac, or *follicle.* The ovum—only about one-fourth the size of the period that ends this sentence—is the largest cell in the human body. In a mature woman, *ovulation*—rupture of a mature follicle in either ovary and expulsion of its ovum—occurs about once every 28 days until menopause. The ovum is swept along through the fallopian tube by tiny hair cells, called *cilia,* toward the uterus, or womb. Fertilization normally occurs during the brief time the ovum is passing through the fallopian tube.

The tadpolelike sperm—only 1/600 inch from head to tail—is one of the smallest cells in the body. Sperm are much more active than ova, and there are many more of them. Sperm are produced in the testicles (testes), or reproductive glands, of a mature male (refer back to Figure 2-2) at a rate of several hundred million a day and are ejaculated in the semen at sexual climax. They enter the vagina and try to swim through the cervix (the opening of the uterus) and into the fallopian tubes, but only a tiny fraction make it that far. Since sperm cells

fertilization Union of sperm and ovum to produce a zygote; also called *conception.*

zygote One-celled organism resulting from fertilization.

These 2-year-old monozygotic twins look so much alike that at first glance they could be mistaken for one child sitting by a mirror. Monozygotic twins have exactly the same genetic heritage and are of the same sex but may differ in temperament and other respects because of differences in prenatal and postnatal experience.

have odor receptors, like those in the nose, they may locate a fertile ovum by its scent (Parmentier et al., 1992).

Fertilization is most likely if intercourse occurs on the day of ovulation or during the five days before (Wilcox, Weinberg, & Baird, 1995). If fertilization does not occur, the ovum and any sperm cells in the woman's body die. The sperm are absorbed by the woman's white blood cells, and the ovum passes through the uterus and exits through the vagina. If sperm and ovum do meet, however, they conceive a new life and endow it with a rich genetic legacy.

What Causes Multiple Births?

Unlike most animals, the human baby usually comes into the world alone. Multiple births are thought to occur in two ways. Most commonly, the mother's body releases two ova within a short time (or sometimes, perhaps, a single ovum splits) and then both are fertilized. The resulting babies are *dizygotic (two-egg) twins,* commonly called *fraternal twins.* The second way is for a single fertilized ovum to split into two. The babies that result from this cell division are *monozygotic (one-egg) twins,* commonly called *identical twins.* Triplets, quadruplets, and other multiple births can result from either of these processes or a combination of both.

Monozygotic twins have the same genetic endowment and are the same sex, but—in part because of differences in prenatal as well as postnatal experience—they differ in some respects. They may not be identical in **temperament** (disposition, or style of approaching and reacting to situations). In some physical characteristics, such as hair whorls, dental patterns, and handedness, they may be mirror images of each other; one may be left-handed and the other right-handed. One may have a cleft palate (incomplete fusion of the roof of the mouth) while the other does not. Dizygotic twins, who are created from different sperm cells and usually from different ova, are no more alike in hereditary makeup than any other siblings and may be the same sex or different sexes.

Monozygotic twins—about one-third of all twins—seem to be the result of an "accident" of prenatal development; their incidence is about the same in all

dizygotic (two-egg) twins Twins conceived by the union of two different ova (or a single ovum that has split) with two different sperm cells within a brief period of time; also called *fraternal twins.*

monozygotic (one-egg) twins Twins resulting from the division of a single zygote after fertilization; also called *identical twins.*

temperament Person's characteristic disposition or style of approaching and reacting to situations.

CHECKPOINT

Can you . . .

- Summarize recent trends in birth rates, family size, and timing of first childbirth?

- Explain how and when fertilization normally occurs?

- Distinguish between monozygotic and dizygotic twins?

infertility Inability to conceive after 12 to 18 months of trying.

ethnic groups. Dizygotic twins are most common among African Americans, white northern Europeans, and east Indians and are least common among other Asians (Behrman, 1992). These differences may be due to hormonal tendencies that may make women of some ethnic groups more likely to release more than one ovum at the same time.

In 1995, the incidence of multiple births was 26.1 per thousand live births (Ventura et al., 1997), about a 33 percent increase since 1980. Although the vast majority of these births were twins, the proportion of all births that are triplets, quadruplets, or larger multiples tripled between 1980 and 1994, from about 1 in 2,500 to 1 in 860. The increase in multiple births may be due in part to delayed childbearing, since such births are more likely to happen to older women. A more important factor is increased use of fertility drugs, which spur ovulation, and of such techniques as in vitro fertilization. This is of concern, since multiple births are more likely to lead to disability or death in infancy (Guyer, Strobino, Ventura, MacDorman, & Martin, 1996).

When Conception Is an Issue: Alternative Ways to Parenthood

One risk in waiting to have children is failure to conceive. About 8 percent of American couples experience *infertility:* inability to conceive after 12 to 18 months of trying (Mosher & Pratt, 1991). Infertility can occur before or after having a first child (R. B. Glass, 1986).

The most common cause of infertility in men is production of too few sperm. Although only one sperm is needed to fertilize an ovum, a sperm count lower than 60 to 200 million per ejaculation makes conception unlikely. There is disputed evidence that sperm counts, as well as quality of sperm, in males worldwide have begun to decline, possibly due to drugs, tobacco, alcohol, gasoline fumes, industrial pollutants, stress, and other hazards of modern life (B. M. King, 1996; L. Wright, 1996; see Chapter 3). Sometimes an ejaculatory duct is blocked, making sperm unable to exit; or sperm may be unable to "swim" well enough to reach the cervix. Some cases of male infertility seem to have a genetic basis (B. M. King, 1996; Reijo, Alagappan, Patrizio, & Page, 1996).

If the problem is with the woman, she may not be producing ova; the ova may be abnormal; mucus in the cervix may prevent sperm from penetrating it; or a disease of the uterine lining may prevent implantation of the fertilized ovum. The most common female cause, however, is the problem Lesley Brown had: blockage of the fallopian tubes, preventing ova from reaching the uterus. In about half of these cases, the tubes are blocked as a result of scar tissue from sexually transmitted diseases (STDs), leading to pelvic inflammatory disease (PID) (B. M. King, 1996). The marked increase in adolescent sexual activity and in STDs, especially the human papilloma virus (HPV) (see Chapter 14), is likely to lead to sharp rises in infertility as today's teenagers enter adulthood (Shafer & Moscicki, 1991).

Infertility burdens a marriage emotionally. Women, especially, often have trouble accepting the fact that they cannot do what comes so naturally and easily to others. Partners may become frustrated and angry with themselves and each other and may feel empty, worthless, and depressed (Abbey, Andrews, & Halman, 1992; H. W. Jones & Toner, 1993). Their sexual relationship may suffer as sex becomes a matter of "making babies, not love" (Sabatelli, Meth, & Gavazzi, 1988). Such couples may benefit from professional counseling or support from other infertile couples; RESOLVE, a national nonprofit organization based in Boston, offers such services.

About 50 percent of infertile couples eventually conceive, with or without help. An increasing proportion get treatment (H. W. Jones & Toner, 1993). Hormone treatment may raise a man's sperm count or increase a woman's ovulation. Sometimes drug therapy or surgery can correct the problem. As we have seen,

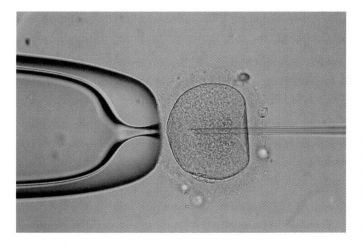

In *in vitro fertilization,* a microscopically tiny needle (right) injects the DNA from a man's sperm into a ripe ovum (center), which has been surgically removed from a woman's body. A flat-nosed pipette (left) is used to hold the ovum steady during the insertion. After cell division, the fertilized ovum is implanted in the womb. This technique is one of several forms of assisted reproduction that are helping some infertile couples to reproduce.

fertility drugs increase the likelihood of multiple, and often premature, births (B. M. King, 1996).

Since human beings seldom abandon their desires simply because they run into obstacles, it is no surprise that many infertile adults who want children, like Lesley and John Brown, eagerly embrace techniques that bypass ordinary biological processes. Others choose the more traditional route of adoption.

Assisted Reproduction

Many couples yearn to have children to carry on their hereditary legacy—to see in future generations the almond-shaped eyes of one ancestor or the artistic talent of another. Technology now enables many people to have children who are genetically at least half their own.

Artificial insemination—injection of sperm into a woman's cervix—can be done when a man has a low sperm count. Sperm from several ejaculations can be combined for one injection. If the man is infertile, a couple may choose *artificial insemination by a donor (AID).* The donor may be matched with the prospective father for physical characteristics, and the two men's sperm may be mixed so that no one knows which one is the biological father.

An increasing number of couples are attempting ***in vitro fertilization (IVF),*** fertilization outside the mother's body. First, fertility drugs are given to increase production of ova. Then a mature ovum is surgically removed, fertilized in a laboratory dish, and implanted in the mother's uterus. This method can also address male infertility, since a single sperm can be injected into the ovum. Usually several ova are fertilized and implanted, to increase the chances of success. Many couples conceive only after several tries, if at all; estimates of success rates range from 12 to 20 percent (de Lafuente, 1994; Gabriel, 1996). Sometimes the procedure results in multiple births (P. Brown, 1993).

Two newer techniques with higher success rates are *gamete intrafallopian transfer (GIFT)* and *zygote intrafallopian transfer (ZIFT),* in which the egg and sperm or the fertilized egg are inserted in the fallopian tube (Society for Assisted Reproductive Technology, 1993). Although children conceived through IVF tend to be small, their head circumference and mental development are normal (Brandes et al., 1992).

A major cause of declining fertility in women after age 30 is deterioration in the quality of their ova (van Noord-Zaadstra et al., 1991). A woman who is producing poor-quality ova or who has had her ovaries removed may try ***ovum transfer.*** In this procedure (the female counterpart of AID), an ovum, or *donor egg*—provided, usually anonymously, by a fertile young woman—is fertilized in

artificial insemination Injection of sperm into a woman's cervix in order to enable her to conceive.

in vitro fertilization (IVF) Fertilization of an ovum outside the mother's body.

ovum transfer Method of fertilization in which a woman who cannot produce normal ova receives an ovum donated by a fertile woman.

the laboratory and implanted in the prospective mother's uterus (Lutjen et al., 1984). Alternatively, the ovum can be fertilized in the donor's body by artificial insemination. The donor's uterus is flushed out a few days later, and the embryo is retrieved and inserted into the recipient's uterus. Ovum transfer has been used by women past menopause (Sauer, Paulson, & Lobo, 1990, 1993).

In *surrogate motherhood,* a fertile woman is impregnated by the prospective father, usually by artificial insemination. She carries the baby to term and gives the child to the father and his mate. Surrogate motherhood is in legal limbo; courts in most states view surrogacy contracts as unenforceable (A. Toback, personal communication, January 23, 1997), and some states have either banned the practice or placed strict conditions on it. The American Academy of Pediatrics (AAP) Committee on Bioethics (1992) recommends that surrogacy be considered a tentative, preconception adoption agreement in which the surrogate is the sole decision maker before the birth. The AAP also recommends a prebirth agreement on the period of time in which the surrogate may assert her parental rights.

Perhaps the most objectionable aspect of surrogacy, aside from the possibility of forcing the surrogate to relinquish the baby, is the payment of money (up to $30,000, including fees to a "matchmaker"). The creation of a "breeder class" of poor and disadvantaged women who carry the babies of the well-to-do strikes many people as wrong. Similar concerns have been raised about payment for donor eggs. Exploitation of the would-be parents is an issue, too. Some observers worry about the rapid growth of fertility clinics driven by the profit motive that may prey on desperate couples through misleading claims (Gabriel, 1996).

New and unorthodox means of conception raise other serious questions. Must people who use them be infertile, or should people be free to make such arrangements simply for convenience? Should single people and cohabiting and homosexual couples have access to these methods? What about older people, who may become frail or die before the child grows up? Should the children know about their parentage? Should genetic tests be performed on prospective donors and surrogates to identify potential abnormalities or susceptibility to certain diseases or disorders? What happens if a couple who have contracted with a surrogate divorce before the birth? When a couple chooses in vitro fertilization, what should be done with any unused embryos?

In one case, a couple who had arranged for IVF and the freezing of seven embryos later divorced. One of them then wanted to be able to use the embryos to conceive; the other wanted them destroyed. In another case, a couple conceived an embryo through IVF and hired another woman to carry it to term; she did not want to give up the infant until, in a Solomon-like judgment, the court threatened to send the baby to a foster home. Although the genetic parents agreed to this, the birth mother instead gave them temporary custody. These are just a few of the many complicated ethical quandaries that have arisen from new methods of reproduction (Angell, 1990).

Another concern is the psychological risk to children conceived with donated eggs or sperm. Will the lack of a genetic bond with one or both parents, together with strains created by the usual secrecy of such procedures and lingering disappointment about infertility, color the family atmosphere? One study suggests that the answer is no, and that a strong desire for parenthood is more important than genetic ties. The quality of parenting was *better* when a child was conceived by in vitro fertilization or donor insemination than in the usual way; and no overall differences appeared in the children's feelings, behavior, or relationships with their parents (Golombok, Cook, Bish, & Murray, 1995).

One thing seems certain: as long as there are people who want children but are unable to conceive or bear them, human ingenuity and technology will come up with new ways to satisfy their need.

Because of a decrease in the number of adoptable American babies, many children adopted today are of foreign birth. Adoptive parents face special challenges, such as the need to explain the adoption to the child. But most adoptive children view their adoption positively and see it as playing only a minor role in their identity.

Adoption

Anna Victoria Finlay, who was born in Santiago, Chile, is the adoptive daughter of Diane E. Papalia, one of the authors of this book. Anna is among the fewer than 2 percent of children in the United States who are adopted ("Effects of Open Adoption Vary," 1995). Married couples, single people, older people, and homosexual couples have become adoptive parents. Among African Americans, adoption is related less to infertility than to a wish to provide a family for a known child, often a relative (Bachrach, London, & Maza, 1991), and many of these adoptions are informal (L. Richardson, 1993). Advances in contraception and legalization of abortion have reduced the number of adoptable healthy white American babies; thus many of the children available for adoption are disabled, are beyond infancy, or are of foreign birth.

Although adoption is widely accepted in the United States, there are still prejudices and mistaken ideas about it. One seriously mistaken belief is that adopted children are bound to have problems because they have been deprived of their biological parents. Actually, a study of 715 families with teenagers who had been adopted in infancy found that nearly 3 out of 4 teens saw their adoption as playing only a minor role in their identity (Benson, Sharma, & Roehlkepartain, 1994). In another study of 85 adopted children, most viewed their adoption positively, though teenagers saw it less positively than younger children (D. W. Smith & Brodzinsky, 1994). In a study mentioned in the previous section, the quality of parenting was higher for adopted children, as well as for those born through assisted conception (Golombok et al., 1995).

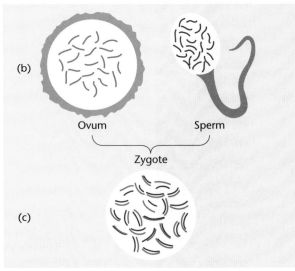

Figure 2-3

Hereditary composition of the zygote. (*a*) Body cells of women and men contain 23 pairs of chromosomes, which carry the genes, the basic units of inheritance. (*b*) Each gamete, or sex cell (ovum and sperm), has only 23 single chromosomes because of a special kind of cell division (meiosis) in which the total number of chromosomes is halved. (*c*) At fertilization, the 23 chromosomes from the sperm join the 23 from the ovum so that the zygote receives 46 chromosomes, or 23 pairs.

Ovum   Sperm

Zygote

CHECKPOINT

Can you . . .

- State at least three common causes of infertility in men and in women?

- Describe four leading methods of assisted conception?

- Assess the risks and challenges of adopting a child?

gene   Basic functional unit of heredity that contains all inherited material passed from biological parents to children.

deoxyribonucleic acid (DNA)
Chemical of which genes are composed that controls the functions of body cells.

chromosome   One of 46 rod-shaped structures that carry the genes.

Adopting a child does carry special risks and challenges. Besides the usual issues of parenthood, adoptive parents need to deal with acceptance of their infertility (if this is why they adopted), the need to explain the adoption to the child, and possible discomfort about the child's interest in the biological parents.

Mechanisms of Heredity

Before we can weigh the roles of heredity and environment in making children the people they are and will become, we need to see how heredity works.

Genes and Chromosomes

The basic unit of heredity is the *gene.* Genes contain all the hereditary material passed from biological parents to children, which affects inherited characteristics. Each cell in the human body contains an estimated 80,000 to 100,000 genes, which are made up of the chemical *deoxyribonucleic acid (DNA).* DNA carries the biochemical instructions that tell the cells how to make the proteins that enable them to carry out each specific body function. Each gene seems to be located by function in a definite position on a rod-shaped structure called a *chromosome.*

Every cell in the body except the sex cells has 23 pairs of chromosomes—46 in all. Through a complex process of cell division called *meiosis,* each sex cell, or gamete (sperm or ovum) ends up with only 23 chromosomes—one from each pair. Thus, when sperm and ovum fuse at conception, they produce a zygote with 46 chromosomes, half from the father and half from the mother (see Figure 2-3).

Three-fourths of the genes every child receives are identical to those received by every other child; they are called *monomorphic genes,* and they define characteristics that make a person recognizably human. The other one-fourth of the genes a child inherits are called *polymorphic genes,* and they define each person as

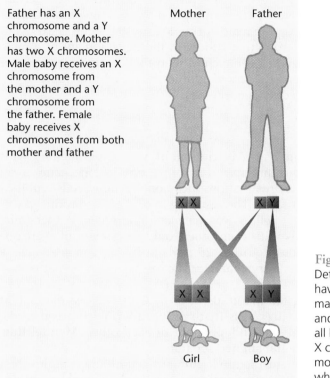

Father has an X chromosome and a Y chromosome. Mother has two X chromosomes. Male baby receives an X chromosome from the mother and a Y chromosome from the father. Female baby receives X chromosomes from both mother and father

Mother   Father

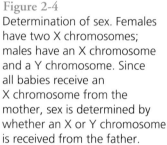

X X   X Y

X X   X Y

Girl   Boy

Figure 2-4

Determination of sex. Females have two X chromosomes; males have an X chromosome and a Y chromosome. Since all babies receive an X chromosome from the mother, sex is determined by whether an X or Y chromosome is received from the father.

an individual. Since there are about 20,000 or more polymorphic genes, many of which come in several variations, and since meiotic division is random, it is virtually impossible for any two children (other than monozygotic twins) to receive exactly the same combination of genes.

At conception, then, the single-celled zygote has all the biological information needed to guide its development into a unique human baby. This happens through *mitosis,* a process by which the cells divide in half over and over again. Each division creates a duplicate of the original cell, with the same hereditary information. When development is normal, each cell (except the gametes) continues to have 46 chromosomes identical to those in the original zygote.

What Determines Sex?

In many villages in Nepal, it is common for a man whose wife has borne no male babies to take a second wife. In some other societies, a woman's failure to produce sons is justification for divorce. The irony in these customs is that it is normally the father's sperm that determines a child's sex. Let's see how.

At the moment of conception, the 23 chromosomes from the sperm and the 23 from the mother's ovum form 23 pairs. Twenty-two pairs are *autosomes,* chromosomes that are not related to sexual expression. The twenty-third pair are *sex chromosomes*—one from the father and one from the mother—which govern the baby's sex.

Sex chromosomes are either *X chromosomes* or *Y chromosomes.* The sex chromosome of every ovum is an X chromosome, but the sperm may contain either an X or a Y chromosome. The Y chromosome contains the gene for maleness, the *SRY gene.* When an ovum (X) is fertilized by an X-carrying sperm, the zygote formed is XX, a female. When an ovum (X) is fertilized by a Y-carrying sperm, the resulting zygote is XY, a male (see Figure 2-4).

autosomes The 22 pairs of chromosomes not related to sexual expression.

sex chromosomes Pair of chromosomes that determines sex: XX in the normal female, XY in the normal male.

Still, if nothing further happens prenatally, the embryo will develop female sexual characteristics. For the embryo to develop male characteristics, certain events must occur about 6 to 8 weeks after conception. At this time human male embryos normally start producing the male hormone testosterone. It is exposure to steady, high levels of testosterone that results in the development of a male body plan with male sexual organs. Even a child with the masculine genetic endowment (XY) will retain the female body plan unless exposed prenatally to ongoing high levels of self-produced male hormones.

Patterns of Genetic Transmission

During the 1860s, Gregor Mendel, an Austrian monk who experimented with plants, laid the foundation for our understanding of patterns of inheritance in all living things. He crossbred pea plants that produced only yellow seeds with pea plants that produced only green seeds. The resulting hybrid plants produced yellow seeds, meaning, he said, that yellow was *dominant* over green. Yet when he bred the yellow-seeded hybrids with each other, only 75 percent of their offspring had yellow seeds, while the other 25 percent had green seeds. This proved, Mendel said, that a hereditary characteristic can be *recessive*, that is, carried by an organism that does not express, or show, it.

Mendel also tried breeding for two traits at once. Crossing pea plants that produced round yellow seeds with plants that produced wrinkled green seeds, he found that color and shape were independent of each other. Mendel thus showed that hereditary traits are transmitted separately.

Today we know that the genetic picture in humans is far more complex than Mendel imagined. Most human traits are not either-or; they fall along a continuous spectrum (for example, from light skin to dark). It is hard to find a single normal trait that people inherit through simple dominant transmission other than the ability to curl the tongue lengthwise! Let's look at various ways in which children inherit characteristics.

Dominant and Recessive Inheritance

If you are a "tongue curler," you inherited this ability through *dominant inheritance*. If you are a redhead but both your parents have dark hair, *recessive inheritance* operated. How do these two types of inheritance work?

Genes that can produce alternative expressions of a characteristic (such as ability or inability to curl the tongue) are called *alleles.* Every person receives a pair of alleles for a given characteristic, one from each biological parent. When both alleles are the same, the person is *homozygous* for the characteristic; when they are different, the person is *heterozygous.* In *dominant inheritance,* when a person is heterozygous for a particular trait, the dominant allele governs. In other words, when an offspring receives alleles for two contradictory traits, only one of them, the dominant one, will be expressed. *Recessive inheritance,* the expression of a recessive trait, occurs only when a person receives the recessive allele from both parents.

If you inherited one allele for tongue-curling ability from each parent, you are homozygous for tongue curling and you express the trait. If, say, your mother passed on an allele for the ability and your father passed on an allele lacking it, you are heterozygous. Since the ability is dominant and its lack is recessive, you can curl your tongue. But if you received the recessive allele from both parents, you would not be a tongue-curler (see Figure 2-5).

Most traits are transmitted by *polygenic inheritance,* the interaction of several genes. Skin color, for example, is the result of three or more sets of genes on three different chromosomes. These genes work together to produce different amounts of brown pigment, resulting in hundreds of shades of skin. Polygenic inheritance is one reason that simple dominance and recessiveness cannot

alleles Paired genes (alike or different) that affect a particular trait.

homozygous Possessing two identical alleles for a trait.

heterozygous Possessing differing alleles for a trait.

dominant inheritance Pattern of inheritance in which, when an individual receives contradictory alleles for a trait, only the dominant one is expressed.

recessive inheritance Pattern of inheritance in which an individual receives identical recessive alleles from both parents, resulting in expression of a recessive (nondominant) trait.

polygenic inheritance Interaction of several sets of genes to produce a complex trait.

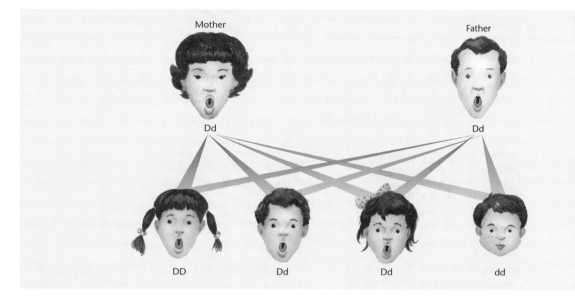

Figure 2-5

Phenotypes and genotypes. Because of dominant inheritance, the same observable phenotype (in this case, the ability to curl the tongue lengthwise) can result from two different genotypes (genetic patterns). This mother's and father's genotypes are heterozygous; each has one dominant gene (D) for the ability and one recessive gene (d) lacking the ability. Since the ability is dominant, both can curl their tongues. Each child receives one gene for this trait from each parent. Statistical averages predict that three out of four children in this family will express the trait in their phenotypes (that is, be able to curl their tongues). Two of these three children (*center*) will have heterozygous genotypes (Dd), like the parents; the third child (*left*) with the same phenotype will have a homozygous genotype (DD). The fourth child (*right*) will receive recessive genes from both parents and will be unable to curl the tongue. A phenotype expressing a recessive characteristic (such as inability to curl the tongue) must have a homozygous genotype (dd).

explain the inheritance of such complex human traits as intelligence. Indeed, whereas there are more than 1,000 rare genes for abnormal traits, there is no known single gene that significantly accounts for individual differences in any complex normal behavior. Instead, such behaviors are likely to be influenced by many genes, each with only a small effect. In addition, *multifactorial transmission,* a combination of genetic and environmental factors, plays a role in the expression of most traits. Let's see how.

Genotypes and Phenotypes: Multifactorial Transmission

If you can curl your tongue, that ability is part of your *phenotype,* the array of observable characteristics through which your *genotype,* or underlying genetic makeup, is expressed. Except for monozygotic twins, no two people have the same genotype. The phenotype is the product of the genotype and any relevant environmental influences.

As Figure 2-5 shows, the same phenotypical characteristic may arise from different genotypes: either a homozygous combination of two dominant alleles or a heterozygous combination of one dominant allele and one recessive allele. If you are heterozygous for tongue curling and you and a mate who is also heterozygous for the trait have four children, the statistical probability is that one child will be homozygous for the ability, one will be homozygous lacking it, and the other two will be heterozygous. Thus three of your children will have phenotypes that include tongue curling (they will be able to curl their tongues), but this ability will arise from two different genotypical patterns (homozygous and heterozygous).

Tongue curling has a strong genetic base; but for most traits, experience modifies the expression of the genotype. Let's say that Steven has inherited musical talent. If he takes music lessons and practices regularly, he may delight his

multifactorial transmission
Combination of genetic and environmental factors to produce certain complex traits.

phenotype   Observable characteristics of a person.

genotype   Genetic makeup of a person, containing both expressed and unexpressed characteristics.

Table 2-1   Birth Defects

Problem	Characteristics of This Condition	Who Is at Risk	What Can Be Done
Alpha$_1$ antitrypsin deficiency	Enzyme deficiency that can lead to cirrhosis of the liver in early infancy and pulmonary emphysema and degenerative lung disease in middle age.	1 in 1,000 white births	No treatment.
Alpha thalassemia	Severe anemia that reduces ability of the blood to carry oxygen; nearly all affected infants are stillborn or die soon after birth.	Primarily families of Malaysian, African, and southeast Asian descent	Frequent blood transfusions.
Beta thalassemia (Cooley's anemia)	Severe anemia resulting in weakness, fatigue, and frequent illness; usually fatal in adolescence or young adulthood.	Primarily families of Mediterranean descent	Frequent blood transfusions.
Cystic fibrosis	Body makes too much mucus, which collects in the lung and digestive tract; children do not grow normally and usually do not live beyond age 30; the most common inherited *lethal* defect among white people.	1 in 2,000 white births	Daily physical therapy to loosen mucus; antibiotics for lung infections; enzymes to improve digestion; gene therapy (in experimental stage).
Down syndrome	Minor-to-severe mental retardation caused by an extra twenty-first chromosome; the most common chromosomal defect.	1 in 350 babies born to women over age 35; 1 in 800 born to all women	No treatment, although programs of intellectual stimulation are effective.
Duchenne's muscular dystrophy	Fatal disease usually found in males, marked by muscle weakness; minor mental retardation is common; respiratory failure and death usually occur in young adulthood.	1 in 3,000 to 5,000 male births	No treatment.
Hemophilia	Excessive bleeding, usually affecting males rather than females; in its most severe form, can lead to crippling arthritis in adulthood.	1 in 10,000; families with a history of hemophilia	Frequent transfusions of blood with clotting factors.

CHECKPOINT

Can you . . .

- Explain why no two people, other than monozygotic twins, have the same genetic heritage?

- Explain why it is the sperm that normally determines a baby's sex?

- Tell how dominant inheritance and recessive inheritance work, and why most normal traits are not the products of simple dominant or recessive transmission?

family with his performances. If his family likes and encourages classical music, he may play Bach preludes; if the other children on his block influence him to prefer popular music, he may eventually form a rock group. However, if from early childhood he is not encouraged and not motivated, and if he has no access to a musical instrument or to music lessons, his genotype for musical ability may not be expressed (or may be expressed less fully) in his phenotype.

Some physical characteristics (including height and weight) and most psychological characteristics (such as intelligence and personality traits, as well as musical ability) are products of multifactorial transmission. Later in this chapter we discuss in more detail how environmental influences, together with the genetic endowment, influence many aspects of development.

Genetic and Chromosomal Abnormalities

About 6 percent of the nearly 4 million babies born in the United States each year are born with physical or mental disabilities. Although some inherited conditions are treatable, treatment is not always possible or successful. Birth disorders account for 22.4 percent of deaths in infancy—almost 1 in 4. Most of the serious malformations involve the circulatory or central nervous systems (Guyer et al., 1996; Wegman, 1994; see Table 2-1).

| Table 2-1 | Birth Defects (*continued*) |

Problem	Characteristics of This Condition	Who Is at Risk	What Can Be Done
Neural-tube defects. Two types of neural-tube defects together constitute the most common serious type of birth defect in the United States:			
Anencephaly	Absence of brain tissues; infants are stillborn or die soon after birth.	1 in 1,000	No treatment.
Spina bifida	Incompletely closed spinal canal, resulting in muscle weakness or paralysis and loss of bladder and bowel control; often accompanied by hydrocephalus, an accumulation of spinal fluid in the brain, which can lead to mental retardation.	1 in 1,000	Surgery to close spinal canal prevents further injury; shunt placed in brain drains excess fluid and prevents mental retardation.
Phenylketonuria (PKU)	Metabolic disorder resulting in mental retardation.	1 in 10,000 to 25,000 births	Special diet begun in first few weeks of life can offset mental retardation.
Polycystic kidney disease	*Infantile form;* enlarged kidneys, leading to respiratory problems and congestive heart failure. *Adult form:* kidney pain, kidney stones, and hypertension resulting in chronic kidney failure; symptoms usually begin around age 30.	1 in 1,000	Kidney transplants.
Sickle-cell anemia	Deformed, fragile red blood cells that can clog the blood vessels, depriving the body of oxygen; symptoms include severe pain, stunted growth, frequent infections, leg ulcers, gallstones, susceptibility to pneumonia, and stroke.	1 in 500 African Americans	Painkillers, transfusions for anemia and to prevent stroke, antibiotics for infections.
Tay-Sachs disease	Degenerative disease of the brain and nerve cells, resulting in death before age 5.	1 in 3,000 eastern European Jews, rarer in other groups	No treatment.

Source: Adapted from AAP Committee on Genetics, 1996; Tisdale, 1988, pp. 68–69.

It is in genetic defects and diseases that we see most clearly the operation of dominant and recessive transmission in humans, and also the operation of a variation, *sex-linked inheritance.* Some defects are due to abnormalities in genes or chromosomes. Some are due to *mutations:* permanent alterations in genes or chromosomes that often produce harmful characteristics. Mutations can occur spontaneously or can be induced by environmental hazards, such as radiation. Many disorders arise when an inherited predisposition interacts with an environmental factor, either before or after birth. Spina bifida (a defect in the closure of the vertebral canal) and cleft palate probably result from multifactorial transmission. Hyperactivity is one of a number of behavioral disorders thought to be transmitted multifactorially.

Not all genetic or chromosomal abnormalities show up at birth. Symptoms of Tay-Sachs disease (a degenerative disease of the central nervous system that occurs mainly among Jews of eastern European ancestry) and sickle-cell anemia (a blood disorder most common among African Americans) may not appear until at least 6 months of age; cystic fibrosis, not until age 4; and glaucoma and Huntington's disease (a progressive degeneration of the nervous system) usually not until middle age.

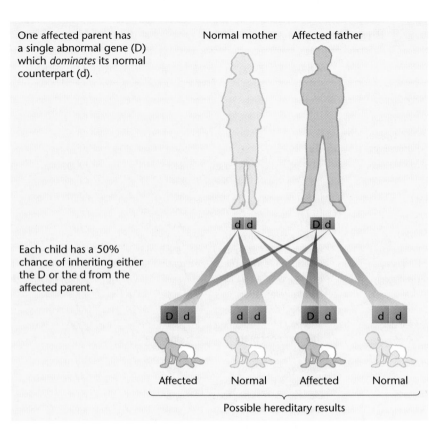

One affected parent has a single abnormal gene (D) which *dominates* its normal counterpart (d).

Normal mother   Affected father

Each child has a 50% chance of inheriting either the D or the d from the affected parent.

d d   D d

D d   d d   D d   d d

Affected   Normal   Affected   Normal

Possible hereditary results

Figure 2-6
Dominant inheritance of a birth defect.

Defects Transmitted by Dominant Inheritance

Most of the time, normal genes are dominant over those carrying abnormal traits, but sometimes an abnormal trait is carried by a dominant gene. When one parent has a dominant abnormal gene (D = dominant) and one recessive normal gene (d = recessive) and the other parent has two recessive normal genes, each of their children will have a 50-50 chance of inheriting the abnormal gene (see Figure 2-6). Because the abnormal gene is dominant, every child who receives it will have the defect. (Of course, if one parent has *two* dominant abnormal genes, that is, if one parent is homozygous for the condition, *all* the children will be affected.)

Among the 1,800 disorders known to be transmitted by dominant inheritance are achondroplasia (a type of dwarfism) and Huntington's disease. Defects transmitted by dominant inheritance are less likely to be lethal at an early age than those transmitted by recessive inheritance, since a dominantly transmitted defect that kills before the age of reproduction cannot be passed on to the next generation and therefore will soon disappear.

Defects Transmitted by Recessive Inheritance

Recessive defects are expressed only if a child receives the same recessive gene from each biological parent. Suppose that only one parent, say, the father, has a faulty recessive gene. If he is homozygous for the trait, that is, if he has two alleles for it, he has the disorder; if he is heterozygous, that is, has one normal and one defective allele, he is a *carrier* for the defect but does not suffer from it. In either case, none of his children will have it, but he can pass on the defective gene to them, and they have a 50-50 chance of being carriers and passing it on to future generations. If *both* parents carry the abnormal recessive gene (see Figure 2-7), although *they* are unaffected, each child has 1 chance in 4 of inheriting the abnormal gene from both of them and suffering the disorder, as well as

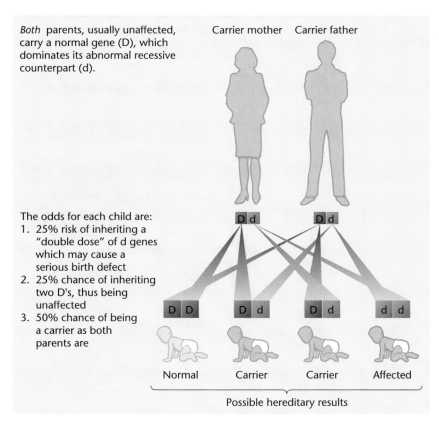

Both parents, usually unaffected, carry a normal gene (D), which dominates its abnormal recessive counterpart (d).

Carrier mother   Carrier father

The odds for each child are:
1. 25% risk of inheriting a "double dose" of d genes which may cause a serious birth defect
2. 25% chance of inheriting two D's, thus being unaffected
3. 50% chance of being a carrier as both parents are

D D   D d   D d   d d

Normal   Carrier   Carrier   Affected

Possible hereditary results

Figure 2-7
Recessive inheritance of a birth defect.

1 chance in 2 of being a carrier. Some defects transmitted recessively, such as Tay-Sachs disease and sickle-cell anemia, are more common among certain ethnic groups, which, through inbreeding (marriage within the group) have passed down recessive characteristics (see Table 2-2).

Defects Transmitted by Sex-Linked Inheritance

If you have trouble distinguishing red from green, you are probably male and you probably inherited your color blindness from your mother. In *sex-linked inheritance,* certain recessive disorders linked to genes on the sex chromosomes show up differently in male and female children. Red-green color blindness is one of these sex-linked conditions. Another is hemophilia, a disorder in which blood does not clot when it should.

Sex-linked recessive traits are carried on one of the X chromosomes of an unaffected mother. Sex-linked disorders almost always appear only in male children; in females, a normal dominant gene on the X chromosome from the father overrides the defective gene on the X chromosome from the mother. Boys are more vulnerable to these disorders because there is no opposite dominant gene on the shorter Y chromosome from the father to override a defect on the X chromosome from the mother.

Each son of a normal man and a woman who is a carrier has a 50 percent chance of inheriting the mother's harmful gene—and the disorder—and a 50 percent chance of receiving the mother's normal X chromosome and being unaffected (see Figure 2-8). Daughters have a 50 percent chance of being carriers. An affected father can never pass on such a gene to his sons, since he contributes a Y chromosome to them; but he can pass on the gene to his daughters, who then become carriers.

Occasionally, a female does inherit a sex-linked condition. For example, if her father is a hemophiliac and her mother happens to be a carrier for the

sex-linked inheritance
Pattern of inheritance in which certain characteristics carried on the X chromosome inherited from the mother are transmitted differently to her male and female offspring.

Table 2-2   Chances of Genetic Disorders for Various Ethnic Groups

If You Are	The Chance Is About	That
African American	1 in 12	You are a carrier of sickle-cell anemia.
	7 in 10	You will have milk intolerance as an adult.
African American and male	1 in 10	You have a hereditary predisposition to develop hemolytic anemia after taking sulfa or other drugs.
African American and female	1 in 50	
White	1 in 25	You are a carrier of cystic fibrosis.
	1 in 80	You are a carrier of phenylketonuria (PKU).
Jewish (Ashkenazic)	1 in 30	You are a carrier of Tay-Sachs disease.
	1 in 100	You are a carrier of familial dysautonomia.
Italian American or Greek American	1 in 10	You are a carrier of beta thalassemia.
Armenian or Jewish (Sephardic)	1 in 45	You are a carrier of familial Mediterranean fever.
Afrikaner (white South African)	1 in 330	You have porphyria.
Asian	almost 100%	You will have milk intolerance as an adult.

Source: Adapted from Milunksy, 1992, p. 122.

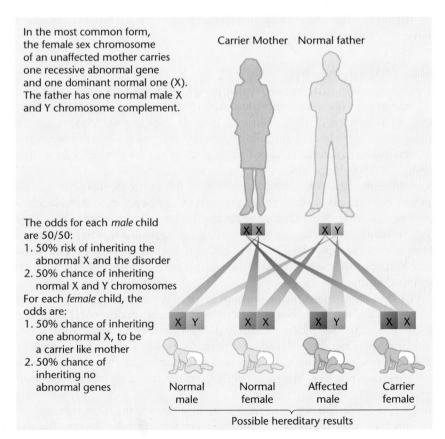

In the most common form, the female sex chromosome of an unaffected mother carries one recessive abnormal gene and one dominant normal one (X). The father has one normal male X and Y chromosome complement.

Carrier Mother   Normal father

The odds for each *male* child are 50/50:
1. 50% risk of inheriting the abnormal X and the disorder
2. 50% chance of inheriting normal X and Y chromosomes
For each *female* child, the odds are:
1. 50% chance of inheriting one abnormal X, to be a carrier like mother
2. 50% chance of inheriting no abnormal genes

Normal male   Normal female   Affected male   Carrier female

Possible hereditary results

Figure 2-8
Sex-linked inheritance of a birth defect.

Table 2-3	Sex Chromosome Abnormalities		
Pattern/Name	Characteristic*	Incidence	Treatment
XYY	Male; tall stature; tendency to low IQ, especially verbal.	1 in 1,000 male births	No special treatment
XXX (triple X)	Female, normal appearance, menstrual irregularities, learning disorders, mental retardation.	1 in 1,000 female births	Special education
XXY (Kleinfelter)	Male, sterility, underdeveloped secondary sex characteristics, small testes, learning disorders.	1 in 1,000 male births	Hormone therapy, special education
XO (Turner)	Female, short stature, webbed neck, impaired spatial abilities, no menstruation, infertility, underdeveloped sex organs, incomplete development of secondary sex characteristics.	1 in 1,500 to 2,500 female births	Hormone therapy, special education
Fragile X	Minor-to-severe mental retardation; symptoms, which are more severe in males, include delayed speech and motor development, speech impairments, and hyperactivity; the most common *inherited* form of mental retardation.	1 in 1,200 male births; 1 in 2,000 female births	Educational and behavioral therapies when needed

*Not every affected person has every characteristic.

disorder, the daughter has a 50 percent chance of receiving the abnormal X chromosome from each parent and having the disease.

Chromosomal Abnormalities

About 1 in every 156 children born in western countries is estimated to have a chromosomal abnormality (Milunsky, 1992). Some of these abnormalities are inherited; others result from accidents during prenatal development and are not likely to recur in the same family.

Some chromosomal disorders, such as Klinefelter syndrome, are caused by an extra sex chromosome (shown by the pattern XXY). Others, such as Turner syndrome, result from a missing sex chromosome (XO). Characteristics of the most common sex chromosome disorders are shown in Table 2-3.

Other chromosomal abnormalities occur in the autosomes. *Down syndrome,* the most common of these, is responsible for about one-third of all cases of moderate-to-severe mental retardation. The condition is also called *trisomy-21,* because it is usually caused by an extra twenty-first chromosome or the translocation of part of the twenty-first chromosome onto another chromosome. The most obvious physical characteristic associated with the disorder is a downward-sloping skin fold at the inner corners of the eyes. Other signs are a small head, a flat nose, a protruding tongue, motor retardation, and defective heart, gastrointestinal tract, eyes, and ears.

More than 90 percent of cases of Down syndrome are caused by a mistake in chromosomal distribution during development of the ovum, sperm, or zygote. (One of two identical twins may have the disorder, since such an accident can happen in the development of one twin and not the other.) When the mother is under age 35, the disorder is more likely to be hereditary; a clue to its genetic basis is the discovery of a gene on chromosome 21 responsible for a brain protein that seems to lead to Down syndrome (Allore et al., 1988).

About 1 in every 700 babies born alive has Down syndrome (Hayes & Batshaw, 1993). The risk is greatest with older parents: the chances rise from 1 such

Down syndrome
Chromosomal disorder characterized by moderate-to-severe mental retardation and by such physical signs as a downward-sloping skin fold at the inner corners of the eyes.

birth in 2,000 among 25-year-old mothers to 1 in 40 for women over 45. The risk also rises with the father's age, especially among men over 50 (Abroms & Bennett, 1981). DNA analysis has shown that the extra chromosome seems to come from the mother's ovum in 95 percent of cases (Antonarakis & Down Syndrome Collaborative Group, 1991); the other 5 percent of cases seem to be related to the father.

The prognosis for children with Down syndrome is brighter than was once thought. Many live at home until adulthood and then enter small group homes. Many can support themselves; they tend to do well in structured job situations. More than 70 percent of people with Down syndrome live into their sixties; they are at special risk of developing Alzheimer's disease (Hayes & Batshaw, 1993).

Genome Imprinting

genome imprinting
Process by which genes that have been temporarily chemically altered in the mother or father have differing effects when transmitted to offspring.

Through *genome imprinting,* some genes seem to be temporarily imprinted, or chemically altered, in either the mother or the father. These genes, when transmitted to offspring, have different effects than do comparable genes from the other parent. An imprinted gene will dominate one that has not been imprinted. Genome imprinting may explain why, for example, children who inherit Huntington's disease from their fathers are far more likely to be affected at an early age than children who inherit the Huntington's gene from their mothers (Sapienza, 1990).

A particularly dramatic example of genome imprinting appeared among 80 girls and young women with Turner syndrome (refer back to Table 2-3). Those who had received their lone X chromosome from their fathers were better adjusted socially and had stronger verbal and cognitive skills than those who had received the X chromosome from their mothers. This suggests that social competence is influenced by an imprinted gene or genes on the X chromosome, which is "turned off" when it comes from the mother. The findings may have even more far-reaching implications; they suggest a possible reason why men (whose X chromosome always comes from the mother) are more susceptible to such disorders as autism (discussed later in this chapter) and attention deficit hyperactivity disorder (see Chapter 12), which involve problems in social functioning (Skuse et al., 1997).

Genetic counseling can help prospective parents assess their risk of bearing children with genetic or chromosomal defects (see Box 2-1). Today, researchers are rapidly identifying genes that cause many serious diseases and disorders. Their work is likely to lead to widespread *genetic testing* to reveal genetic profiles—a prospect that involves dangers as well as benefits (see Box 2-2).

Nature and Nurture: Influences of Heredity and Environment

Which is more important, nature or nurture? The answer to this classic question varies. Some physical characteristics, such as eye color and blood type, are clearly inherited. As we have already mentioned, phenotypes for more complex traits having to do with health, intelligence, and personality are subject to both hereditary and environmental forces.

Research in *behavioral genetics*, the quantitative study of relative hereditary and environmental influences on psychological and behavioral traits, not only shows the importance of genetic influences on development, but also provides evidence of the importance of environment and of how heredity and environment work together. Let's see how scientists study and explain the influences of heredity and environment.

genetic counseling Clinical service that advises couples of their probable risk of having children with particular hereditary defects.

genetic testing Procedure for ascertaining a person's genetic makeup for purposes of identifying predispositions to specific hereditary diseases or disorders.

behavioral genetics Quantitative study of relative genetic and environmental influences on behavioral and psychological traits.

Box 2-1 Genetic Counseling for Prospective Parents

Genetic counseling helps people who believe that they may be at high risk of bearing a child with a birth defect to find out how great the risk is. People who have already had a child with a genetic defect, who have a family history of hereditary illness, who suffer from conditions known or suspected to be inherited, or who come from ethnic groups at higher-than-average risk of passing on genes for certain diseases can get information about their likelihood of producing affected children.

A genetic counselor may be a pediatrician, an obstetrician, a family doctor, or a genetic specialist. She or he takes a thorough family history and gives the prospective parents and any existing children physical examinations. Laboratory investigations of blood, skin, urine, or fingerprints may be performed. Chromosomes from body tissues may be analyzed and photographed, and the photographs enlarged and arranged according to size and structure on a chart called a *karyotype*. This chart can show chromosomal abnormalities and can indicate whether a person who appears normal might transmit genetic defects to a child (see accompanying figure in this box).

On the basis of these tests, the counselor calculates the mathematical odds of having an afflicted child. Prospective parents who feel the risk is too high may choose to have one partner sterilized, may consider adoption or another type of conception, or may choose to terminate a pregnancy. A genetic counselor does not give advice. Rather, the counselor tries to help clients understand the mathematical risk of a particular condition, explain its implications, and present information about alternative courses of action. A prediction that a child may be born with a hereditary disorder does not necessarily mean nothing can be done about it. For example, children born with the enzyme disorder phenylketonuria (PKU) will be mentally retarded if untreated; but if put on a special diet within the first 3 to 6 weeks of life, they develop normally.

Geneticists have made a great contribution to avoidance of birth defects. For example, since so many Jewish couples have been tested for Tay-Sachs genes, far fewer Jewish babies have been born with the disease; in fact, it is now far more likely to affect non-Jewish babies (Kaback et al., 1993). A national registry could help to identify people who may be at risk of specific birth defects, provide preventive services, and help agencies meet the needs of affected people and their families.

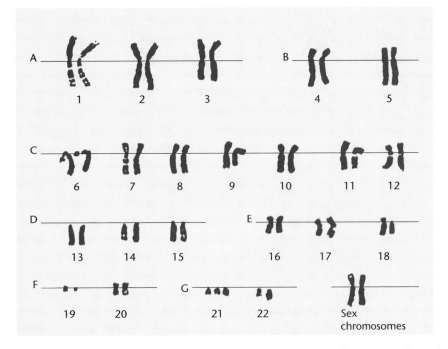

A karyotype is a chart that shows the chromosomes when they are separated and aligned for cell division. We know that this is a karyotype of a person with Down syndrome, because there are three chromosomes instead of the usual two on chromosome 21. Since pair 23 consists of two X's, we know that this is the karyotype of a female.

Source: Babu & Hirschhorn, 1992; March of Dimes Birth Defects Foundation, 1987.

Box 2-2 Genetic Testing: Benefits and Risks

What is your risk of developing colon cancer or Alzheimer's disease, or another genetically influenced condition? Genetic testing—formerly done mainly for reproductive counseling—is becoming more common as scientists find ways to identify people genetically likely to develop a variety of diseases and disorders.

The Human Genome Project, a 15-year, $3 billion research effort under the joint leadership of the National Institutes of Health and the U.S. Department of Energy, is designed to map the chromosomal locations of all the estimated 80,000 to 100,000 human genes and identify those that cause or trigger particular disorders. The first phase of this mapping was completed in 1996.

The genetic information gained from such research could save many lives and improve the quality of many others by increasing our ability to predict, control, treat, and cure disease. A person who learns of a genetic predisposition to lung cancer might be motivated to stop smoking. A woman who has a genetic tendency to breast cancer might be advised to undergo earlier and more frequent breast examinations. A person with a tendency to high cholesterol might be given a special diet or medication. *Gene therapy* (repairing or replacing abnormal genes) is considered experimental but is already a therapeutic option for some rare genetic disorders (J. Finlay, personal communication, October 7, 1997). In the meantime, genetic information may help people make important decisions—not only whether to have children and with whom, but what type of occupation to pursue and what climate to live in. It will also allow more time to plan what to do in the event of illness or death (Post, 1994).

Still, the prospect of widespread genetic testing is controversial. For one thing, genetic testing can be very costly. Given limited economic resources, the need for it must be weighed against other medical priorities.

Psychologically, it might be extremely anxiety-producing for a person to learn that she or he has the gene for an incurable disease. What is the point of knowing you have the gene for a potentially debilitating condition if you cannot do anything about it? For this reason, one panel of experts recommended against genetic testing for diseases for which there is no known cure (Institute of Medicine [IOM], 1993). On the other hand, some people who have family histories of a disease might be relieved once they know the worst that is likely to happen.

Specific issues need to be addressed when considering testing children. Whose decision should it be to have a child tested—the parent's or the child's? Should a child be tested to benefit a sibling or someone else? How will a child be affected by learning that he or she is likely to develop a disease twenty, thirty, or fifty years later? Will the child grow up thinking "There's something wrong with me"? Will parents who learn that a child has a gene for an incurable disease feel or act differently toward the child? Will they become overprotective? Or will they be afraid to become too attached to a child who may die young? If routine testing of new-

borns showed that a presumed biological father was not really the father of the child, might that information lead him to reject the child?

A major concern is *genetic determinism:* the misconception that a person with a gene for a disease is bound to get the disease. Actually, most diseases involve a complex combination of genes or depend in part on lifestyle or other environmental factors. Furthermore, our genetic knowledge is far from infallible. For example, research that seemed to identify a specific gene for alcoholism has not been confirmed by other investigators (Holden, 1994).

If a gene that controls alcoholism were to be identified, and a test developed for it, there would be pressure to screen airline pilots and other workers whose health and sobriety might affect public safety or welfare. But is it fair to use a genetic profile to deny employment to a currently healthy person? Discrimination on the basis of genetic information has already occurred—even though tests may be imprecise and unreliable, people deemed at risk of a disease may never develop it, and testing is largely unregulated.

What about privacy? Although medical data are supposed to be confidential, it is almost impossible to keep such information private. A study at the University of Minnesota found that at least 50 people had access to each patient's medical charts (Gruson, 1992). Then, do parents, children, or siblings have a legitimate claim to information about a patient that may affect them?

A broad-based panel of experts, including the official Working Group on Ethical, Legal, and Social Implications of the Human Genome Project, has recommended that employers be forbidden to request or require genetic information or to use such information to influence hiring, firing, or conditions of employment, unless the employer can prove that a worker's performance will be affected. The panel recommends that employers should be restricted from access to genetic information in an employee's medical records and should not be allowed to release such information without the employee's written consent (Rothenberg et al., 1997). In addition, the Institute of Medicine panel recommends that insurers be prevented from considering genetic risk in issuing or pricing insurance policies (IOM, 1993).

Some states, such as Wisconsin and New Jersey, have already passed laws prohibiting job or insurance discrimination on the basis of genetic information and/or protecting employees' privacy by denying employers access to such information. Federal laws offer limited protection against discrimination. The federal Equal Employment Opportunity Commission (EEOC) has stated that genetically based job discrimination violates the Americans with Disabilities Act. The Health Insurance Portability and Accountability Act of 1996 prohibits group health insurance plans from using genetic information to establish eligibility or from treating such information as a preexisting condition, in the absence of a diagnosis. However, existing federal laws do not protect privacy or restrict access to genetic information (Rothenberg et al., 1997).

The effects of heredity and environment are difficult to untangle. For one thing, human beings keep developing throughout life, and development generally reflects a combination of the two forces. Also, the mechanisms by which environment operates cannot be described as precisely as those of heredity. Nor can controlled comparisons readily be made, since no two children—not even twins growing up in the same household—have exactly the same environment. The best way to study genetic influences on animal behavior is to breed the animals for certain traits, such as aggressiveness. For ethical reasons, such studies cannot be done on human beings. Researchers in behavioral genetics therefore rely chiefly on three types of correlational research: family, adoption, and twin studies (Plomin, 1990; Plomin, Owen, & McGuffin, 1994).

Heritability is a statistical estimate of how great a contribution heredity makes toward individual differences in a specific trait at a certain time within a given population. Heritability does not refer to the relative influence of heredity and environment on a particular individual; as we will see, those influences may be virtually impossible to separate. Nor does heritability tell us how traits develop; it merely indicates the extent to which genes contribute to a trait.

Heritability is expressed as a percentage ranging from zero to 100 percent; the greater the percentage, the greater the heritability of a trait. Researchers usually measure heritability by calculating the incidence of a trait, or the degree of similarity for that trait, in members of the same family, in monozygotic twins as compared with dizygotic twins, or in adopted children as compared with their adoptive and biological parents or siblings.

Such studies are based on the assumption that immediate family members are more genetically similar than more distant relatives, monozygotic twins are more genetically similar than dizygotic twins, and children are genetically more like their biological families than their adoptive families. Thus, if heredity is an important influence on a particular trait, siblings should be more alike than cousins with regard to that trait, monozygotic twins should be more alike than dizygotic twins, and adopted children should be more like their biological parents than their adoptive parents. If heredity is *not* an important influence on a particular trait, such statistical differences should not appear. Also, if the shared environment exerts an important influence on a trait, persons who live together should be more similar than persons who do not live together (Plomin & Daniels, 1987).

In *family studies,* researchers measure the degree to which biological relatives share certain traits and whether the closeness of the genetic relationship is associated with the degree of similarity. If the correlation is strong, the researchers can infer a genetic influence. However, family studies cannot rule out environmental influences (Plomin, 1990). A family study alone cannot tell us whether obese children of obese parents inherited the tendency or whether they are fat because their diet is like that of their parents. For that reason, researchers do adoption studies, which can separate the effects of heredity from those of a shared environment (Plomin & Daniels, 1987).

Adoption studies look at similarities between adopted children and their adoptive families and also between adopted children and their biological families. When adopted children are more like their biological parents and siblings in a particular trait (say, obesity), we see the influence of heredity. When they resemble their adoptive families more, we see the influence of environment. The Colorado Adoption Project compares such data with data from control families in which parents are raising their biological children (Bergeman & Plomin, 1989; P. J. DeFries, Plomin, & Fulker, 1994).

Studies of twins compare pairs of monozygotic twins and same-sex dizygotic twins. (Same-sex twins are used so as to avoid any confounding effects of gender.) Monozygotic twins are twice as genetically similar, on average, as dizygotic

heritability Statistical estimate of contribution of heredity to individual differences in a specific trait within a given population.

concordant Term describing twins who share the same trait or disorder.

CHECKPOINT

Can you . . .

• State the basic assumption underlying studies of behavioral genetics and how it applies to family studies, twin studies, and adoption studies?

reaction range Potential variability, depending on environmental conditions, in the expression of a hereditary trait.

canalization Limitation on variance of expression of certain inherited characteristics.

twins, who are no more genetically similar than other same-sex siblings. When monozygotic twins are more *concordant* (that is, have a statistically greater tendency to show the same trait) than dizygotic twins, we see the likely effects of heredity. Concordance rates, which may range from zero to 100 percent, tell what percentage of pairs of twins in a sample are concordant, or similar.

When monozygotic twins show higher concordance for a trait than dizygotic twins, the likelihood of a genetic factor can be studied further through adoption studies. Studies of monozygotic twins separated in infancy and reared apart have found strong resemblances between the twins. Such findings support a hereditary basis for many physical and psychological characteristics.

Still, the heritability of traits rarely exceeds 50 percent, leaving a great deal of room for environmental influence (Plomin, 1990; Plomin & Daniels, 1987; Plomin et al., 1994). Furthermore, as we'll see in the next section, behavioral genetics has thrown a spotlight on the *kinds* of environmental factors that make the most difference.

How Heredity and Environment Work Together

Most developmentalists today see the relationship between genetic and environmental factors as fundamentally intertwined. Let's consider several ways in which heredity and environment work together.

Reaction Range and Canalization

Many characteristics vary within genetic limits. Developmentalists explain this variance through the concepts of *reaction range* and *canalization*.

Reaction range is a range of potential expressions of a hereditary trait under varying environmental conditions. Body size, for example, depends largely on biological processes, which are genetically regulated. Even so, a range of sizes is possible, depending upon environmental opportunities and constraints and a person's own behavior. In societies in which nutrition has drastically improved, an entire generation has grown up to tower over the generation before. The better-fed children share their parents' genes but have responded to a healthier world. Once a society's average diet becomes adequate for more than one generation, however, children tend to grow to heights similar to their parents'. Ultimately, height has genetic limits: we don't see people who are only a foot tall, or any who are 10 feet tall.

Heredity can influence whether a reaction range is wide or narrow. For example, a child born with a defect producing mild retardation is more able to respond to a favorable environment than a child born with severe limitations. A child of normal native intelligence is likely to have a higher IQ if raised in an enriched home and school environment than if raised in a more restrictive environment; but a child with more native ability will probably have a much wider reaction range (see Figure 2-9).

The metaphor of *canalization* may help explain why heredity restricts the range of development for some traits. After a heavy storm, the rainwater that has fallen on pavement has to go somewhere. If the street has potholes, the water will fill them. If deep canals have been dug along the edges of the street, the water will flow into the canals instead. Some human characteristics, such as eye color, are so strongly programmed by the genes that they are said to be highly canalized: there is little opportunity for variance in their expression. Certain behaviors also develop along genetically "dug" channels; it takes an extreme change in environment to alter their course.

Behaviors that depend largely on *maturation* (see Chapter 1) seem to appear when a child is ready. Normal babies follow a typical sequence of motor development: crawling, walking, and running, in that order, at certain approximate

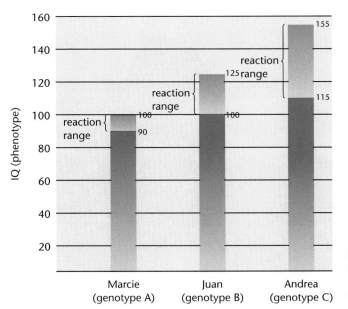

Figure 2-9

Intelligence and reaction range. Children with different genotypes for intelligence will show varying reaction ranges when exposed to a restricted (blue portion of bar) or enriched (entire bar) environment.

ages. Still, this development is not completely canalized; experience can affect its pace and timing.

Cognition and personality are more subject to variations in experience: the kinds of families children grow up in, the schools they attend, and the people they encounter. Consider language. Before children can talk, they must reach a certain level of neurological and muscular maturation. No 6-month-old could speak this sentence, no matter how enriched the infant's home life might be. Yet environment does play a large part in language development. If parents encourage babies' first sounds by talking back to them, children are likely to start to speak earlier than if their early vocalizing is ignored. Heredity, then, lays the foundation for development, but environment affects the pace at which construction proceeds and the form of the structure.

Genotype-Environment Interaction

Whereas reaction range and canalization affect the expression of the same hereditary trait under varying environmental conditions, *genotype-environment interaction* refers to the effects of similar environmental conditions on genetically different individuals. A child who inherits the gene for phenylketonuria (PKU) will become mentally retarded from eating foods containing phenylalanine, an amino acid, because an enzyme the child's body produces does not break down phenylalanine. A child without the PKU gene has no problem eating such foods. Thus an environmental factor (the child's diet) interacts with a genetic predisposition to produce retardation. However, a child with the PKU gene is not bound to become mentally retarded; this happens only when the PKU gene is combined with intake of phenylalanine. Controlling what the child eats can counteract the genetic influence (refer back to Table 2-1 and Box 2-1). The effect of genetic influences, then, is rarely inevitable: even in a trait strongly influenced by heredity, the environment can have substantial impact.

genotype-environment interaction The portion of phenotypic variation that results from the reactions of genetically different individuals to similar environmental conditions.

Genotype-Environment Correlation

The environment often reflects or reinforces genetic differences. In other words, certain genetic and environmental influences tend to act in the same direction. This is called *genotype-environment correlation,* or *genotype-environment covariance,* and it works in three ways to strengthen the

genotype-environment correlation Tendency of certain genetic and environmental influences to occur together; may be passive, reactive (evocative), or active. Also called *genotype-environment covariance.*

Musical ability is one of many characteristics passed on from parents to children through a combination of genetic and environmental influences. This father playing the guitar with his daughter may be more motivated to do so because she shows interest and ability in music. In turn, the enjoyable experience with her father is likely to strengthen the little girl's natural inclination toward music.

phenotypic expression of a genotypic tendency (Bergeman & Plomin, 1989; Scarr, 1992; Scarr & McCartney, 1983):

- *Passive correlations:* Often parents, who provide the genes that predispose a child toward a trait, also provide an environment that encourages the development of the trait. For example, a musical parent is likely to create a home environment in which music is heard regularly, to give a child music lessons, and to take the child to musical events. If the child inherited the parent's musical talent, the child's musicality will reflect a combination of genetic and environmental influences. This type of correlation is called *passive* because the child does not control it; it is most applicable to young children, whose parents, the source of their genetic legacy, have a great deal of control over their early experiences.
- *Reactive, or evocative, correlations:* Children with differing genetic makeups evoke different responses from adults. Parents may make a special effort to provide musical experiences to a child who shows interest and ability in music. This response, in turn, strengthens the child's genetic inclination toward music.
- *Active correlations:* As children get older and have more freedom to choose their own activities and environments, they actively select or create experiences consistent with their genetic tendencies. A child with a talent for music will probably seek out musical friends, take music classes, and go to concerts. A shy child is likely to spend more time in solitary pursuits than an outgoing youngster. This tendency to seek out environments compatible with one's genotype is called ***niche-picking;*** it helps explain why identical twins reared apart tend to be quite similar.

niche-picking Tendency of a person, especially after early childhood, to seek out environments compatible with his or her genotype.

What Makes Siblings So Different? The Nonshared Environment

Although two children in the same family may bear a striking physical resemblance to each other, siblings tend to be more different than alike in intellect and especially in personality (Plomin, 1989). One reason, of course, may be genetic differences, which lead children to respond differently to a similar environment

(Bergeman & Plomin, 1989). A child with a high IQ may be more stimulated by a roomful of books and puzzles than a child with a markedly lower IQ—an example of genotype-environment interaction. Surprisingly, though, the family environment itself seems to make siblings more different—as different, in fact, as any two unrelated children! Apparently, the experiences that strongly affect development are not those that are similar for all children in a family, but those that are different (Plomin & Daniels, 1987).

These *nonshared environmental effects* result from the unique environment in which each child in a family grows up. What factors contribute to this nonshared environment? One (which tends to be relatively unimportant) is family composition—the differences between boys' and girls' experiences, or between those of firstborns and laterborns. More important are effects of the way parents and siblings treat each child. Also, certain events, such as illnesses and accidents, and experiences outside the home (for example, with teachers and peers) affect one child and not another. While heredity accounts for most of the similarity between siblings, the nonshared environment accounts for most of the difference. Indeed, a great deal of research across the life span suggests that most of the variability in behavioral traits in the population as a whole is environmental, but of the nonshared type (McClearn et al., 1997; Plomin, 1996; Plomin & Daniels, 1987; Plomin et al., 1994).

Some investigators maintain that genotype-environment correlations play an important role in the nonshared environment. To some degree, children mold their own environments by the choices they make—what they do and with whom—and their genetic makeup influences these choices. In other words, "genes drive experience" (Scarr & McCartney, 1983, p. 425). A child who has inherited artistic talent may spend a great deal of time creating "masterpieces" in solitude, while a sibling who is athletically inclined spends more time playing ball with others. Thus, not only will the children's abilities (in, say, painting or soccer) develop differently, but their social lives will be different as well. These differences tend to be accentuated as children grow older and have more experiences outside the family. Furthermore, children's genetic differences lead parents and siblings to react to them differently and treat them differently. Genes also may influence how children perceive and respond to their treatment, and what the outcome of that treatment will be (Bergeman & Plomin, 1989; Bouchard, 1994; Plomin, 1990, 1996; Plomin et al., 1994; Scarr, 1992; Scarr & McCartney, 1983). The idea that genes may influence much of what children experience has led to sharp disagreements about the importance of the kind of environment parents create (see Box 2-3).

nonshared environmental effects The unique environment in which each child grows up, consisting of dissimilar influences or influences that affect each child differently.

CHECKPOINT

Can you . . .

- Explain and give at least one example of reaction range, canalization, genotype-environment interaction, and genotype-environment correlation?

- List three kinds of influences that contribute to nonshared environmental effects?

- Explain the meaning of the phrase, "genes drive experience"?

Some Characteristics Influenced by Heredity and Environment

Keeping in mind the complexity of unraveling the influences of heredity and environment, let's look more closely at their roles in producing certain characteristics.

Physical and Physiological Traits

Not only do monozygotic twins generally look alike; they are also more concordant than dizygotic twins in their risk for such medical disorders as hypertension (high blood pressure), heart disease, stroke, rheumatoid arthritis, peptic ulcers, and epilepsy (Brass, Isaacsohn, Merikangas, & Robinette, 1992; Plomin et al., 1994). *Obesity*—extreme overweight, sometimes defined in childhood as having a body mass index (comparison of weight to height) at or above the 85th percentile for age and sex—is strongly influenced by heredity. It is twice as likely that both monozygotic twins will be overweight as that both dizygotic twins will be (Stunkard, Harris, Pedersen, & McClearn, 1990). In fact, twin studies, adoption studies, and other research suggest that as much as 80 percent of the risk of obesity is genetic (Leibel, 1997). Researchers have now identified at least two

obesity Extreme overweight in relation to age, sex, height, and body type; sometimes defined as having a body mass index (weight-for-height) at or above the 85th percentile of growth curves for children of the same age and sex.

Box 2-3 Is "Good Enough" Parenting Good Enough?

How much difference do parents make in the way their child turns out? Not a great deal under most circumstances, says Sandra Scarr (1992). Scarr argues that being reared in one family rather than another—as long as the family is not violent, abusive, or neglectful—makes little difference in children's development. Diana Baumrind (1993) strongly disagrees; she maintains that parenting practices can and do influence children's lives. Jacquelyn Faye Jackson (1993) expresses concern that Scarr's view will harm children who need special help by giving policymakers less reason to support interventions. Let's summarize how each of these developmentalists supports her opinion.

Sandra Scarr

Scarr's Thesis: "Good Enough" Parenting Is Good Enough

Most families provide supportive environments for their children. It does not matter whether parents take children to a ball game or to a museum, since children's inherited characteristics will outweigh such environmental influences.

Twin studies and adoption studies have found a strong genetic influence on differences in intelligence and personality. "Parents do not have the power to make their children into whatever they want" (p. 15); children to a great extent create their own environment on the basis of their genetic tendencies. If the environment is varied enough so children can choose experiences that fit their inborn tendencies, the athletic child will end up playing ball and the artistic child will create, no matter what their parents do. This is not, of course, true of children in "very disadvantaged circumstances and adults with little or no choice about occupations and leisure activities" (Scarr, 1992, p. 9). Among environments that support normal development, however, variations in parenting are not very important in determining outcomes.

One reason developmentalists have overemphasized the role of the family environment is that parents also provide children's genes, and so genetic and environmental influences are correlated. Parents who read well bring books into the house, read to the child, and encourage reading. Parents with reading problems raise children in a less literate environment. When children's reading abilities are correlated with their parents' abilities, the effects of heredity can be confused with the effects of the environment.

Since ordinary parents are good enough, they can take comfort in raising their children in ways that are comfortable for them without feeling guilty when they do not conform to current wisdom about good parenting.

Baumrind's View: Excellent Parenting Is Better Than "Good Enough"

All nonabusive, nonpoor families are not alike in fostering healthy development. The person a child will become in one "normal" environment is different from what the same child would become in another.

continued

---

genes associated with obesity (R. S. Jackson et al., 1997; Montague et al., 1997). Of course, the environment also affects weight gain. The kind and amount of food eaten in a particular home or in a particular social or ethnic group, and the amount of exercise that is encouraged, can increase or decrease the likelihood that a person will become obese. The rapid rise in the prevalence of obesity in western countries seems to result from the interaction of a genetic predisposition with widespread environmental factors (Leibel, 1997; see Chapters 8, 11, and 14).

Our days on earth seem to be greatly affected by our genes. In one study, adopted children whose biological parents had died before age 50 were twice as likely to have died young themselves when compared to adopted children whose biological parents had lived past 49 (Sorensen, Nielsen, Andersen, & Teasdale, 1988). Still, sound health and fitness practices can increase longevity by tempering predispositions toward certain illnesses, such as cancer and heart disease.

Intelligence

Heredity seems to exert a strong influence on general intelligence and also on specific abilities (McClearn et al., 1997; Plomin et al., 1994). But experience counts

Diana Baumrind

Jacquelyn Faye Jackson

Scarr fails to specify what kinds of environment are "good enough" or what constitutes "normal development," making it hard to evaluate her thesis. She also fails to explore cross-cultural differences.

Many American children today—from both poor and well-off families—are growing up at risk of violence, drug abuse, poor reading and math skills, eating disorders, school failure, and sexually transmitted disease. "Thus, the average environment of most young people today is not really good enough" (Baumrind, 1993, p. 1302).

Biology is not destiny. Parents affect children's development by teaching knowledge and skills, monitoring children's activities, and modeling desirable behavior. All these practices take a high level of parental involvement and commitment, not just "good enough" parenting.

Scarr's thesis is dangerous because it may encourage parents to deny responsibility for children's healthy development. Parents who ascribe a child's dysfunctional behavior to the child's genes rather than to anything the parent did or did not do are less likely to try to improve the situation, and the child is less likely to turn out well.

Jackson's View: Interventions Can Be Effective

Research based on studies of twins and adopted children—who are atypical in important respects—cannot adequately support a theory about the development of "normal" children raised in "average" family environments. Scarr's theory can harm disadvantaged minority children by discouraging intervention to improve their environment. Interventions have been beneficial in boosting IQs of children of mothers with low IQs and in helping children with Down syndrome learn higher-order thinking skills.

Scarr's Response

"Both biological and environmental explanations are required to account for human development" (Scarr, 1993, p. 1334). What is normal for a given culture is not the same as what is normal for the human species; cultures define what behavior is desirable and provide a range of opportunities for development. But, because of their genetic makeup, different people—even siblings within the same household—react differently to the same environment. Biology and culture together shape behavior.

"Genetic does not mean intractable!" (Scarr, p. 1350). Minority and socially disadvantaged children do benefit from interventions that transmit values of the dominant culture. Still, this does not negate the strong effect of inherited characteristics.

It is important to recognize the power of heredity and not to bend scientific truth to a social agenda. "All children should have opportunities to become species-normal, culturally appropriate and uniquely themselves. . . . But humanitarian concerns should not drive developmental theory" (Scarr, p. 1350).

---

too; an enriched or impoverished environment can substantially affect the development and expression of innate ability (Neisser et al., 1995; see Chapter 12). Apparently, many genes, each with its own small effects, combine to establish a range of possible reactions to a range of possible experiences (Scarr, 1997; Weinberg, 1989; refer back to Figure 2-9).

Evidence for the role of heredity in intelligence has emerged from adoption and twin studies. Adopted children's IQs are consistently more similar to the IQs of their biological mothers than to those of their adoptive parents and siblings (J. Horn, 1983; Scarr & Weinberg, 1983). A widely accepted estimate of heritability of IQ, which holds true in studies of twins reared together, is about 50 percent, meaning that genetic differences explain about half of the observed variation among members of a population. In studies of twins reared apart (most of whom, when studied, were in middle age) heritability of IQ appears much higher (60 to 70 percent), suggesting that the genetic influence may increase with age (McClearn et al., 1997; McGue, 1997).

Additional evidence for an increasing genetic influence on IQ is that, in adoption studies, young siblings—whether related by blood or by adoption—score

Even very young babies show marked differences in temperament. These differences seem to be largely inborn but may be affected by parental handling and other environmental influences.

similarly, but adolescents' scores have zero correlation with those of adoptive siblings. Furthermore, adolescents' IQs correlate more closely with their biological mothers' levels of schooling than with their adoptive parents' IQs. This again suggests that the family environment has more influence on younger children; adolescents are more apt to find their own niche by actively selecting environments compatible with their hereditary abilities and related interests (McGue, Bouchard, Iacono, & Lykken, 1993; Scarr & Weinberg, 1983).

The main environmental influences on intelligence, then, seem to occur early in life (McGue, 1997). In fact, a recent analysis of 212 studies (Devlin, Daniels, & Roeder, 1997) points to the impact of the earliest shared environment: the womb. According to this analysis, the prenatal environment may account for 20 percent of the similarity in IQ between twins and 5 percent of the similarity in nontwin siblings (who occupy the same womb at different times), bringing heritability of IQ down to *below* 50 percent. These findings suggest that the influence of genes on intelligence may be weaker, and the influence of the prenatal environment stronger, than was previously thought, underlining the importance of a healthy prenatal environment (see Chapter 3). The possibility that prenatal intervention could raise the average IQ of the population as a whole is a fascinating one, though just what aspects of the prenatal environment are most influential is as yet unclear.

Personality

Specific aspects of personality appear to be inherited, at least in part. Analyses of five groupings of traits—extraversion, neuroticism, conscientiousness, agreeableness, and openness to experience—suggest a heritability of about 40 percent. Setting aside variances attributable to measurement error brings heritability closer to 66 percent for these trait groupings (Bouchard, 1994).

Temperament is an important aspect of personality. In 1956, two psychiatrists and a pediatrician (A. Thomas & Chess, 1984; A. Thomas, Chess, & Birch, 1968) launched the New York Longitudinal Study (NYLS), which followed 133 children from infancy into adulthood. These studies (more fully described in Chapter 7) found that temperament seems to be inborn. The researchers looked at how active children were; how regular they were in hunger, sleep, and bowel habits; how readily they accepted new people and situations; how they adapted to changes in routine; how sensitive they were to noise, bright lights, and other sensory stimuli; how intensely they responded; whether they tended to be cheerful or sad; and whether they persisted at tasks or were easily distracted.

The children varied enormously in all these characteristics, almost from birth, and the variances tended to continue. However, the environment, too, was important; many children changed their behavioral style, apparently reacting to special experiences or parental handling.

A more recent study, which focused on temperament in middle childhood, looked at 100 pairs of 7-year-old siblings (half of them adoptive siblings and half siblings by birth) in the Colorado Adoption Project. Ratings by teachers and by testers who observed the children in the laboratory found significant genetic influences on activity, sociability, and emotionality, but not on attention span (Schmitz, Saudino, Plomin, Fulker, & DeFries, 1996).

Other studies suggest ethnic differences in inborn temperament. If a Caucasian American newborn's nose is briefly pressed with a cloth, the baby will normally turn away or swipe at the cloth. Chinese American babies are more likely to open their mouths immediately to restore breathing, without a fight (Freedman & Freedman, 1969). Four-month-old American babies react more strongly than Irish babies to stimulating sights, loud sounds, and strong smells, by crying, fussing, kicking, arching their backs, and otherwise showing irritability; and Irish babies react more strongly than Chinese babies (Kagan et al., 1994). Such temperamental differences in infants tend to predict how fearful or outgoing they will be as toddlers (Kagan & Snidman, 1991a, 1991b). Shyness and sociability, then, may vary genetically among cultures.

A major body of research strongly suggests that shyness and its opposite, boldness, are largely inborn characteristics, which tend to stay with a person throughout life (Plomin, 1989). Jerome Kagan, a professor of psychology at Harvard University, and his colleagues have studied about 400 children longitudinally, starting in infancy (Arcus & Kagan, 1995; DiLalla, Kagan, & Reznick, 1994; Garcia-Coll, Kagan, & Reznick, 1984; Kagan, 1989, 1997; Kagan, Reznick, Clarke, Snidman, & Garcia-Coll, 1984; Kagan, Reznick, & Gibbons, 1989; Reznick et al., 1986; J. L. Robinson, Kagan, Reznick, & Corley, 1992). Shyness, or what these researchers call "inhibition to the unfamiliar," was present to a marked degree in about 15 percent of the children, first showing up in infancy and persisting in most cases until at least early adolescence. Boldness—comfort in strange situations—was especially strong in another 10 to 15 percent. Most of the children fell between the two extremes. Both the genetic influence and the stability of the traits were strongest for the children at either extreme.

These personality characteristics were associated with physiological signs, such as hormonal and brain activity, which may give clues to the heritability of the traits. The shyest children tended to have blue eyes and thin faces and to be subject to allergies, constipation, and unusual fears. When asked to solve problems or learn new information, they had higher and less variable heart rates than the other children, and the pupils of their eyes dilated more. The boldest children tended to be boys, to be energetic and spontaneous, and to have very low heart rates.

In another study, 2-year-olds who had been adopted soon after birth closely resembled their biological mothers in shyness. However, these babies also resembled their adoptive mothers, showing an environmental influence as well as a genetic one (Daniels & Plomin, 1985). The parents of shy babies tended to have less active social lives, exposing neither themselves nor their babies to many new social situations. Thus, although a tendency toward shyness may be inherited, the environment can either accentuate or modify the tendency.

Although the research we have discussed so far provides strong evidence of genetic effects on personality, this evidence is indirect. Now scientists have begun to identify genes directly linked with specific personality traits. One of these genes has been found to play a part in *neuroticism,* a group of traits involving anxiety, which may contribute to depression. An estimated 10 to 15 other genes may also be involved in anxiety (Lesch et al., 1996).

Personality Disorders

Certain personality disorders illustrate the interrelationship of heredity and environment. There is evidence for a strong hereditary influence on schizophrenia, alcoholism, and depression. (The latter two are discussed later in this book.) They all tend to run in families and to show greater concordance between monozygotic twins than between dizygotic twins. However, heredity alone does not produce such disorders; an inherited tendency can be triggered by environmental factors.

Many studies suggest that schizophrenia, a disorder marked by loss of contact with reality and by such symptoms as hallucinations and delusions, has a strong genetic component (Gottesman, 1993; McGuffin, Owen, & Farmer, 1995; Plomin et al., 1994; Plomin & Rende, 1991). European studies have found that the risk of schizophrenia is ten times as great among siblings and offspring of schizophrenics as among the general population; and twin and adoption studies suggest that this increased risk comes from shared genes, not shared environments. The estimated genetic contribution is between 63 and 85 percent. Researchers are investigating the possibilities of polygenic transmission, genome imprinting, or mutations (McGuffin et al., 1995). Since not all monozygotic twins are concordant for the illness, its cause cannot be purely genetic. So far, however, the contributing environmental causes are unknown ("Schizophrenia Update," 1995).

Autism is one of a group of severe *pervasive developmental disorders* of the brain; it is marked by a lack of normal sociability, impaired communication, and a restricted, narrow range of repetitive, often obsessive behaviors, such as spinning, rocking, hand-flapping, and head-banging. It develops within the first 2½ years, mostly in boys, and it continues to varying degrees throughout life (American Psychiatric Association [APA], 1994).

An autistic baby may fail to notice the emotional signals of others (M. D. Sigman, Kasari, Kwon, & Yirmiya, 1992) and may refuse to cuddle or make eye contact. These children may be affectionate, but only on their own terms; parents often describe them as independent. They do not know how to play and may show bursts of unprovoked aggression (Rapin, 1997). They may scream when their place at the table is changed, or insist on always carrying a particular object (such as a rubber band). About 3 out of 4 autistic children are mentally retarded (APA, 1994), but they often do well on tests of manipulative or visual-spatial skill and may perform unusual mental feats, such as memorizing entire train schedules.

Although "cold and unresponsive" parents once were blamed for autism, it is now recognized as a biological disorder of brain functioning (Rapin, 1997). It seems to have a strong genetic basis; concordance between monozygotic twins is more than 90 percent, as compared with 5 to 10 percent among same-sex dizygotic twins (Bailey, Le Couteur, Gottesman, & Bolton, 1995). A gene that regulates serotonin, a brain chemical, seems to be related to autism (Cook et al., 1997).

Autism has no known cure, but improvement—sometimes substantial improvement—does occur. Some autistic children can be taught to speak, read, and write; some never learn to speak but can sing a wide repertory of songs. During adolescence, autistic children may become more hyperactive and aggressive and may lose previous linguistic gains. Behavioral therapy (see Chapter 1) can help autistic children learn such basic social skills as paying attention, sustaining eye contact, and feeding and dressing themselves and can help control problem behaviors. Drugs may help manage specific symptoms but tend to be of limited use. Only about 5 to 10 percent of autistic children grow up to live independently; most need some degree of care throughout life ("Autism," 1997; Rapin, 1997).

In this chapter we have looked at some ways in which heredity and environment act to make children what they are. The first environment for every child is the world within the womb, which we discuss in Chapter 3.

---

autism One of a group of *pervasive developmental disorders (PDD)* of the brain that develops within the first 2½ years and is characterized by lack of sociability, impaired communication, and a narrow range of repetitive, often obsessive behaviors.

C H E C K P O I N T

Can you . . .

- Assess the evidence for genetic and environmental influences on obesity, intelligence, and temperament?

- Name and describe two personality disorders that show a large genetic influence?

SUMMARY

Becoming Parents

- People today tend to have fewer children than was true in the past and to start having them later.

- **Fertilization** results in formation of a one-celled **zygote,** which then duplicates itself by cell division.

- Although conception usually results in single births, multiple births can occur. **Dizygotic (two-egg) twins** (commonly called *fraternal twins*) have different genetic makeups and may be of different sexes; **monozygotic (one-egg) twins** (commonly called *identical twins*) have the same genetic makeup. Larger multiple births result from either one of these processes or a combination of the two. Because of differences in prenatal and postnatal experience, "identical" twins may differ in some respects, for example, in **temperament.**

- The most common cause of **infertility** in men is a low sperm count; the most common cause in women is blockage of the fallopian tubes. Infertile couples now have several options in addition to adoption: **artificial insemination, in vitro fertilization (IVF), ovum transfer,** and **surrogate motherhood.**

Mechanisms of Heredity

- The basic unit of heredity is the **gene,** which is made up of **deoxyribonucleic acid (DNA).** DNA carries the biochemical instructions that govern bodily functions and determine inherited characteristics. Each gene seems to be located by function in a definite position on a **chromosome.**

- At conception, each normal human being receives 23 chromosomes from the mother and 23 from the father. These form 23 pairs of chromosomes—22 pairs of **autosomes** and 1 pair of **sex chromosomes.** A child who receives an X chromosome from each parent will be a female. If the child receives a Y chromosome from the father, a male will be conceived.

- The simplest patterns of genetic transmission are **dominant inheritance** and **recessive inheritance.** When a pair of **alleles** are the same, a person is **homozygous** for the trait; when they are different, the person is **heterozygous.**

- Most normal human characteristics are transmitted by **polygenic inheritance** or **multifactorial transmission.** Except for monozygotic twins, each child inherits a unique **genotype,** or combination of genes. Dominant inheritance and multifactorial transmission explain why a person's **phenotype** does not always express the underlying genotype.

- Birth defects and diseases are generally transmitted through simple dominant, recessive, or **sex-linked inheritance** or by **genome imprinting.** Chromosomal abnormalities also can result in birth defects; **Down syndrome** is the most common.

- Through **genetic counseling,** prospective parents can receive information about the mathematical odds of having children with certain birth defects.

- **Genetic testing** to identify people likely to develop certain diseases is likely to become more widespread as scientists complete the identification and location of all human genes; however, such testing involves risks as well as benefits.

Nature and Nurture: Influences of Heredity and Environment

- It is hard to disentangle the relative contributions of heredity and environment to development. Today, developmentalists look at ways in which heredity and environment work together.

- Research in **behavioral genetics** is based on the assumption that if heredity is an important influence on a trait, genetically closer persons will be more similar in that trait. Family studies, adoption studies, and studies of twins have found the **heritability** of most traits to be no more than 50 percent. Monozygotic twins tend to be more **concordant** for genetically influenced traits than dizygotic twins.

- Developmentalists use the concepts of **reaction range, canalization, genotype-environment interaction, genotype-environment correlation** (or genotype-environment covariance), and **niche-picking** to describe the interrelationship of heredity and environment.

- Siblings tend to be more different than alike in intelligence and personality. Heredity accounts for most of the similarity; **nonshared environmental effects** account for most of the difference.

- **Obesity,** longevity, intelligence, temperament, and shyness are examples of characteristics influenced by both heredity and environment. The relative influences of heredity and environment may vary across the life span.

- Schizophrenia, alcoholism, and depression are examples of emotional and behavioral disorders influenced by both heredity and environment. **Autism** seems to be mostly inherited.

KEY TERMS

fertilization (58)

zygote (58)

dizygotic (two-egg) twins (59)

monozygotic (one-egg) twins (59)

temperament (59)

infertility (60)

artificial insemination (61)

in vitro fertilization (IVF) (61)

ovum transfer (61)

surrogate motherhood (62)

gene (64)

deoxyribonucleic acid (DNA) (64)

chromosome (64)

autosomes (65)

sex chromosomes (65)

alleles (66)

homozygous (66)

heterozygous (66)

dominant inheritance (66)

recessive inheritance (66)

polygenic inheritance (66)

multifactorial transmission (67)

phenotype (67)

genotype (67)

sex-linked inheritance (71)

Down syndrome (73)

genome imprinting (74)

genetic counseling (74)

genetic testing (74)

behavioral genetics (74)

heritability (77)

concordant (78)

reaction range (78)

canalization (78)

genotype-environment interaction (79)

genotype-environment correlation (79)

niche-picking (80)

nonshared environmental effects (81)

obesity (81)

autism (86)

QUESTIONS FOR THOUGHT AND DISCUSSION

1. In choosing to become parents, people today often face issues that were previously left to chance. What arguments do you see for and against the following choices? (a) Postponing parenthood until after age 30. (b) Having a child before age 30 even if financial security does not yet seem assured.

2. Should surrogate parenthood be made illegal? If not, under what conditions should it be allowed?

3. To prevent the transmission of hereditary disorders, should genetic counseling be made compulsory for all people wanting to get married? Or just for people in certain categories? Give reasons.

4. Would you want to know that you had a gene predisposing you to lung cancer? To Alzheimer's disease? If you had a family history of either of these diseases, would you want your child to be tested for the genes?

5. In what ways are you more like your mother and in what ways like your father? How are you similar and dissimilar to your siblings? After reading this chapter, which differences would you guess come chiefly from heredity and which from environment?

6. If and when scientists succeed in mapping all human genes, what effect will this accomplishment have on the study of child development?

7. In American culture, many people consider shyness undesirable. How should a parent handle a shy child? Is it best to accept the child's temperament or try to change it?

8. How strong a case do you think Sandra Scarr makes for the proposition that "good enough" parenting is good enough? Do you tend to agree more with Scarr or with her critics?

Pregnancy and Prenatal Development

If I could have watched you grow
as a magical mother might,
if I could have seen through my magical transparent belly,
there would have been such ripening within. . . .

Anne Sexton, 1966

Focus

Abel Dorris and Fetal Alcohol Syndrome

Today fetal alcohol syndrome (FAS), a cluster of abnormalities seen in children whose mothers drank during pregnancy, is recognized as a leading cause of mental retardation. But in 1971, when the part-Native American writer Michael Dorris adopted a 3-year-old Sioux boy whose mother had been a heavy drinker, the facts about FAS were not yet known. It was not until 11 years later—as Dorris relates in *The Broken Cord* (1989), the book that brought FAS to the forefront of public attention—that he discovered the source of his adopted son's developmental problems.

The boy, named Abel ("Adam" in the book), had been born almost seven weeks premature, with low birthweight, and had been abused and malnourished before being removed to a foster home. His mother (Dorris later found out) had died at age 35 of alcohol poisoning. His father had been beaten to death in an alley after a string of arrests for drunken and disorderly conduct, robbery, and assault. The boy was small for his age, was not toilet-trained, and could speak only about 20 words. He had been diagnosed as mildly retarded. Dorris, however, was certain that with a positive environment the boy would catch up.

Abel did not catch up. When he turned 4, he was still in diapers. He weighed only 27 pounds. He had trouble remembering names of playmates. His activity level was unusually high, and the circumference of his skull was unusually small. When alone, he would rhythmically rock back and forth.

At this time, he suffered the first of a series of severe seizures, which caused him to lose consciousness for days. The seizures seemed to emanate from a tiny lesion that produced unusual electrical activity in the left side of the brain. Doctors prescribed drug therapy three times a day, but the cause of the problem remained a mystery.

As the months went by, Abel had trouble learning to count, identify primary colors, and tie his shoes. His attention span was short; he had difficulty following simple instructions and made repeated mistakes. Before entering school, he was labeled "learning disabled." His IQ was, and remained, in the mid-60s. Thanks to the efforts of a devoted first-grade teacher, Abel did learn to read and write, but his comprehension was low. When the boy finished elementary school in 1983, he "still could not add, subtract, count money, or consistently identify the town, state, country, or planet of his residence" (Dorris, 1989, pp. 127–128).

By then, Michael Dorris had solved the puzzle of what was wrong with his son. As an associate professor of Native American studies at Darthmouth College, he was acquainted with the cultural pressures that make drinking prevalent among American Indians. In 1982, the year before Abel's graduation, Michael visited a treatment center for chemically dependent teenagers at a Sioux reservation in South Dakota. There he was astonished to see three boys who "could have been [Abel's] twin brothers" (Dorris, 1989, p. 137). They not only looked like Abel but acted like him.

Fetal alcohol syndrome had been identified during the 1970s, while Abel was growing up. A milder form reportedly afflicted Dorris's other adopted son, Sava, and his adopted daughter, Madeline—both of Native American descent—but did not become apparent until they reached adolescence (Streitfeld, 1997). Once alcohol enters a fetus's bloodstream, it remains there in high concentrations for long periods of time, causing brain damage and harming other body organs. There is no cure. As one medical expert wrote, "for the fetus the hangover may last a lifetime" (Enloe, 1980, p. 15).

For the family, too, the effects of FAS can be devastating. The years of constant attempts first to restore Abel to normalcy and then to come to terms with the irrevocable damage that had been done to all three adopted children in the womb may well have been a factor in the later problems in Dorris's marriage to the writer Louise Erdrich, which culminated in divorce proceedings and his suicide in 1997 at age 52. Five years earlier, Dorris noted that there had not been a period of more than three days during the previous four years when one of their alcohol-impaired adolescent or young adult children had not been in a serious crisis involving arrests, suicide attempts, violent behavior, expulsion from school, or "inappropriate sexual contact" (Streitfeld, 1997). Michael Dorris took his life after being alerted that Madeline and Sava were about to accuse him of physical, sexual, and emotional abuse—charges he could not fight without a vicious trial (Streitfeld, 1997).

As for Abel Dorris, at the age of 20 he had entered a vocational training program and moved into a supervised home, taking along his collections of stuffed animals, paper dolls, newspaper cartoons, family photographs, and old birthday cards. At 23, five years before his father's death, he was hit by a car and killed (Lyman, 1997).

• • •

or students of child development, the story of Abel Dorris is a devastating reminder of the responsibility prospective parents have for the crucial development that goes on before birth. The womb is the developing child's first environment, and its impact on the child is immense. In addition to what the mother does and what happens to her, there are other environmental influences, from those that affect the father's sperm to the technological, social, and cultural environment, which may affect the kind of prenatal care a woman gets.

In this chapter we begin by looking at the experience of pregnancy and at how prospective parents prepare for a birth. We trace how the fertilized ovum becomes an embryo and then a fetus, already with a personality of its own. Then we discuss environmental factors that can affect the developing person-to-be, describe techniques for determining whether development is proceeding normally, and explain the importance of prenatal care.

After reading this chapter, you should be able to answer and elaborate on such questions as these:

Preview Questions

- What happens during the three stages of prenatal development?
- What capabilities do fetuses have, and what kinds of individual differences do they show?
- How do both parents' lifestyles and other environmental factors affect prenatal development?
- What techniques are used to assess a fetus's health and well-being?

The Experience of Pregnancy

In Nepal, one term for pregnancy means "being with two bodies" (Escarce, 1989), a feeling shared by many pregnant women as their bellies inexorably expand. For the expectant mother the physiological changes during pregnancy are unlike those at any other time of her life. From the time a woman realizes she is pregnant, she makes many decisions, conscious or not, which have far-reaching effects on the creature growing in her womb. If she is wise, she will become more careful about her diet, give up smoking (if she ever started), and forego the occasional beer or wine she might ordinarily enjoy. Almost every choice she makes, and every experience she has, that affects her physical and emotional well-being may influence this child, whose presence will continue to alter her life in ways she cannot yet imagine.

Expecting a baby, especially a firstborn, changes more than the mother's body and lifestyle; it changes the life of everyone in the family. The months of preparing for a birth affect parents' personal identities, their emotional outlook, and their relationships with each other, with their own parents, and with the rest of the world.

As the new life develops, so do the parents-to-be. Even before they have a baby to hold, they begin to feel a strong emotional attachment to the developing being (Stainton, 1985). Still, they may be ambivalent. They may worry about the cost of having and raising a child, about being tied down, and about whether they are ready to be parents. Usually, positive feelings outweigh the negative ones, especially once the fetus makes its presence known by sudden kicks and thrusts. A man may experience "sympathetic" symptoms—nausea, backaches, and headaches—which help him feel like an active partner in the pregnancy.

By the eighth month, the prospective parents may be aware of a fetus's sleep-wake cycles and temperament (DiPietro, Hodgson, Costigan, & Johnson, 1996). They may wonder what it looks like and what its sex is, or they may already have found out the sex through prenatal assessment. The main purpose of such assessment, of course, is to confirm or put to rest the chief concern of most expectant parents: "Will my baby be born with a birth defect?" In the unlikely event that the answer is yes, there may be difficult decisions or preparations to make.

As expectant parents accept their relationship with the child they will have, they try to recognize that this child will be a distinct individual. As they acknowledge their willingness to raise and care for the child, their awareness of what parenthood entails may further their psychosocial development (Valentine, 1982). They may work out unresolved relationships with their own parents and gain new respect for them; or the pregnancy may trigger feelings of wanting to be *better* parents than their own parents and may raise anew issues and conflicts that had been buried for years. Parents may also have to deal with how the new baby will affect any children they already have.

Prenatal Development: Three Stages

If you had been born in China, you would probably celebrate your birthday on your estimated date of conception rather than your date of birth. This Chinese custom recognizes the importance of **gestation,** the approximately 9-month (or 266-day) period of development between conception and birth. Scientists, too, date *gestational age* from conception.

What turns a fertilized ovum, or *zygote,* into a creature with a specific shape and pattern? Research suggests that an identifiable group of genes is responsible for this transformation in vertebrates, presumably including human beings. These genes produce molecules called *morphogens,* which are switched on after fertilization and begin sculpting arms, hands, fingers, vertebrae, ribs, a brain, and other body parts (Echeland et al., 1993; Krauss, Concordet, & Ingham, 1993;

gestation The approximately 266-day period of development between fertilization and birth.

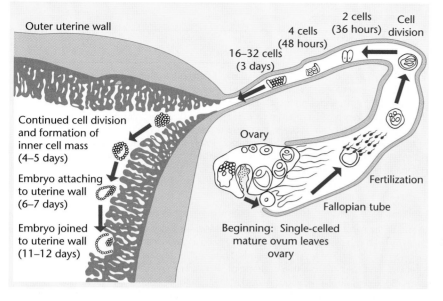

Figure 3-1

Early development of a human embryo. This simplified diagram shows the progress of the ovum as it leaves the ovary, is fertilized in the fallopian tube, and then divides while traveling to the lining of the uterus. It is implanted in the uterus, where it will grow larger and more complex until it is ready to be born.

Riddle, Johnson, Laufer, & Tabin, 1993). Scientists are also learning about the environment inside the womb and how it affects the developing person.

Prenatal development takes place in three stages: *germinal, embryonic,* and *fetal.* (Table 3-1 gives a month-by-month description.) During these three stages of gestation, the original single-celled zygote grows into an *embryo* and then a *fetus.* Both before and after birth, development proceeds according to two fundamental principles. Growth and motor development occur from top to bottom and from the center of the body outward.

The ***cephalocaudal principle*** (from Greek and Latin, meaning "head to tail") dictates that development proceeds from the head to the lower parts of the body. An embryo's head, brain, and eyes develop earliest and are disproportionately large until the other parts catch up. At 2 months of gestation, the embryo's head is half the length of the body. By the time of birth, the head is only one-fourth the length of the body but is still disproportionately large. According to the ***proximodistal principle*** (from Latin, "near to far"), development proceeds from parts near the center of the body to outer ones. The embryo's head and trunk develop before the limbs, and the arms and legs before the fingers and toes.

Germinal Stage (Fertilization to 2 Weeks)

During the ***germinal stage,*** from fertilization to about 2 weeks of gestational age, the fertilized ovum divides and becomes more complex, and the growing organism is implanted in the wall of the uterus (see Figure 3-1).

Within 36 hours after fertilization, the one-celled zygote enters a period of rapid cell division and duplication, or *mitosis* (see Chapter 2). Seventy-two hours after fertilization, it has divided into 16 to 32 cells; a day later it has 64 cells. This division continues until the original single cell has developed into the 800 billion or more specialized cells that make up the human body.

While the fertilized ovum is dividing, it is also making its way down the fallopian tube to the uterus, a journey of 3 or 4 days. Its form changes into a fluid-filled sphere, a *blastocyst,* which floats freely in the uterus for a day or two and then begins to implant (embed) itself in the uterine wall. As cell differentiation begins, some cells around the edge of the blastocyst cluster on one side to form the *embryonic disk,* a thickened cell mass from which the embryo begins to develop. This mass is already differentiating into two layers. The upper layer, the *ectoderm,* will become the outer layer of skin, the nails, hair, teeth, sensory organs,

cephalocaudal principle
Principle that development proceeds in a head-to-toe direction (i.e., that upper parts of the body develop before lower parts).

proximodistal principle
Principle that development proceeds from within to without (i.e., that parts of the body near the center develop before the extremities).

germinal stage First 2 weeks of prenatal development, characterized by rapid cell division, increasing complexity and differentiation, and implantation in the wall of the uterus.

Table 3-1   Prenatal Development

Month	Description

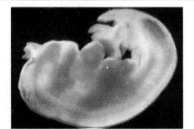

1 month

During the first month, growth is more rapid than at any other time during prenatal or postnatal life: the embryo reaches a size 10,000 times greater than the zygote. By the end of the first month, it measures about ½ inch in length. Blood flows through its veins and arteries, which are very small. It has a miniscule heart, beating 65 times a minute. It already has the beginnings of a brain, kidneys, liver, and digestive tract. The umbilical cord, its lifeline to the mother, is working. By looking very closely through a microscope, it is possible to see the swellings on the head that will eventually become eyes, ears, mouth, and nose. Its sex cannot yet be determined.

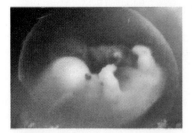

7 weeks

By the end of the second month, the organism is less than 1 inch long and weighs only ⅓ ounce. Its head is half its total body length. Facial parts are clearly developed, with tongue and teeth buds. The arms have hands, fingers, and thumbs, and the legs have knees, ankles, and toes. It has a thin covering of skin and can make handprints and footprints. Bone cells appear at about 8 weeks. Brain impulses coordinate the function of the organ system. Sex organs are developing; the heartbeat is steady. The stomach produces digestive juices; the liver, blood cells. The kidneys remove uric acid from the blood. The skin is now sensitive enough to react to tactile stimulation. If an aborted 8-week-old fetus is stroked, it reacts by flexing its trunk, extending its head, and moving back its arms.

3 months

By the end of the third month, the fetus weighs about 1 ounce and measures about 3 inches in length. It has fingernails, toenails, eyelids (still closed), vocal cords, lips, and a prominent nose. Its head is still large—about one-third its total length—and its forehead is high. Sex can easily be determined. The organ systems are functioning, and so the fetus may now breathe, swallow amniotic fluid into the lungs and expel it, and occasionally urinate. Its ribs and vertebrae have turned into cartilage. The fetus can now make a variety of specialized responses: it can move its legs, feet, thumbs, and head; its mouth can open and close and swallow. If its eyelids are touched, it squints; if its palm is touched, it makes a partial fist; if its lip is touched, it will suck; and if the sole of the foot is stroked, the toes will fan out. These reflexes will be present at birth but will disappear during the first months of life.

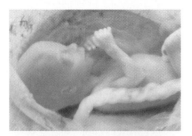

4 months

The body is catching up to the head, which is now only one-fourth the total body length, the same proportion it will be at birth. The fetus now measures 8 to 10 inches and weighs about 6 ounces. The umbilical cord is as long as the fetus and will continue to grow with it. The placenta is now fully developed. The mother may be able to feel the fetus kicking, a movement known as *quickening,* which some societies and religious groups consider the beginning of human life. The reflex activities that appeared in the third month are now brisker because of increased muscular development.

5 months

The fetus, now weighing about 12 ounces to 1 pound and measuring about 1 foot, begins to show signs of an individual personality. It has definite sleep-wake patterns, has a favorite position in the uterus (called its *lie*), and becomes more active—kicking, stretching, squirming, and even hiccuping. By putting an ear to the mother's abdomen, it is possible to hear the fetal heartbeat. The sweat and sebaceous glands are functioning. The respiratory system is not yet adequate to sustain life outside the womb; a baby born at this time does not usually survive. Coarse hair has begun to grow for eyebrows and eyelashes, fine hair is on the head, and a woolly hair called *lanugo* covers the body.

Table 3-1   Prenatal Development (*continued*)

Month	Description
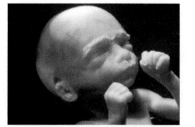 6 months	The rate of fetal growth has slowed down a little—by the end of the sixth month, the fetus is about 14 inches long and weighs 1¼ pounds. It has fat pads under the skin; the eyes are complete, opening, closing, and looking in all directions. It can hear, it cries, and it can make a fist with a strong grip. A fetus born during the sixth month still has only a slight chance of survival, because the breathing apparatus has not matured. However, some fetuses of this age do survive outside the womb.
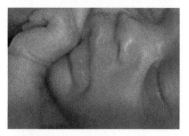 7 months	By the end of the seventh month, the fetus, about 16 inches long and weighing 3 to 5 pounds, now has fully developed reflex patterns. It cries, breathes, swallows, and may suck its thumb. The lanugo may disappear at about this time, or it may remain until shortly after birth. Head hair may continue to grow. The chances that a fetus weighing at least 3½ pounds will survive are fairly good, provided it receives intensive medical attention. It will probably need to be kept in an isolette until a weight of 5 pounds is attained.
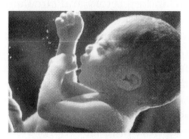 8 months	The 8-month-old fetus is 18 to 20 inches long and weighs between 5 and 7 pounds. Its living quarters are becoming cramped, and so its movements are curtailed. During this month and the next, a layer of fat is developing over the fetus's entire body, which will enable it to adjust to varying temperatures outside the womb.
 9 months–newborn	About a week before birth, the fetus stops growing, having reached an average weight of about 7½ pounds and a length of about 20 inches, with boys tending to be a little longer and heavier than girls. Fat pads continue to form, the organ systems are operating more efficiently, the heart rate increases, and more wastes are expelled through the umbilical cord. The reddish color of the skin is fading. At birth, the fetus will have been in the womb for about 266 days, although gestational age is usually estimated at 280 days, since most doctors date the pregnancy from the mother's last menstrual period.

Note: Even in these early stages, individuals differ. The figures and descriptions given here represent averages.

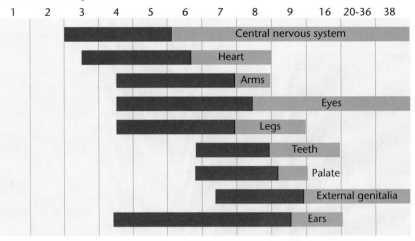

Weeks after conception:

| 1 | 2 | 3 | 4 | 5 | 6 | 7 | 8 | 9 | 16 | 20-36 | 38 |

Central nervous system

Heart

Arms

Eyes

Legs

Teeth

Palate

External genitalia

Ears

Figure 3-2
When birth defects occur. Body parts and systems are most vulnerable to damage when they are developing most rapidly (darkly shaded areas), generally within the first trimester of pregnancy.

Note: Intervals of time are not all equal.

Source: J. E. Brody, 1995; data from March of Dimes.

and the nervous system, including the brain and spinal cord. The lower layer, the *endoderm,* will become the digestive system, liver, pancreas, salivary glands, and respiratory system. Later a middle layer, the *mesoderm,* will develop and differentiate into the inner layer of skin, muscles, skeleton, and excretory and circulatory systems.

Other parts of the blastocyst begin to develop into organs that will nurture and protect the unborn child: the placenta, the umbilical cord, and the amniotic sac. The *placenta,* which has several important functions, will be connected to the embryo by the *umbilical cord.* Through this cord the placenta delivers oxygen and nourishment to the developing baby and removes its body wastes. The placenta also helps to combat internal infection and gives the unborn child immunity to various diseases. It produces the hormones that support pregnancy, prepare the mother's breasts for lactation, and eventually stimulate the uterine contractions that will expel the baby from the mother's body. The *amniotic sac* is a fluid-filled membrane that encases the developing baby, protecting it and giving it room to move. The *trophoblast,* the outer cell layer of the blastocyst (which becomes part of the placenta), produces tiny threadlike structures that penetrate the lining of the uterine wall and enable the developing organism to cling there until it is fully implanted in the uterine lining.

Embryonic Stage (2 to 8 Weeks)

embryonic stage Second stage of gestation (2 to 8 weeks), characterized by rapid growth and development of major body systems and organs.

During the **embryonic stage,** the second stage of gestation, from about 2 to 8 weeks, the organs and major body systems—respiratory, digestive, and nervous—develop rapidly. This is a critical period, when the embryo is most vulnerable to destructive influences in the prenatal environment (see Figure 3-2). An organ system or structure that is still developing at the time of exposure is most likely to be affected; a structure or organ that is already formed is in least danger. Defects that occur later in pregnancy are likely to be less serious.

The most severely defective embryos usually do not survive beyond the first *trimester,* or 3-month period, of pregnancy. A **spontaneous abortion,** commonly called a *miscarriage,* is the expulsion from the uterus of an embryo or fetus that is unable to survive outside the womb. Most miscarriages result from abnormal pregnancies; about 50 to 70 percent involve chromosomal abnormalities.

spontaneous abortion Natural expulsion from the uterus of an embryo or fetus that cannot survive outside the womb; also called *miscarriage.*

Women are at higher risk of miscarriage if they smoke, drink alcohol or coffee, have miscarried in the past, experience vaginal bleeding during pregnancy, are over 35, or have uterine abnormalities, endocrine problems, or certain infections (B. S. Apgar & Churgay, 1993; Mishell, 1993). The physical risks to a woman who has a miscarriage are small, but an infection, a hemorrhage, or an embolism (obstruction of a blood vessel) can sometimes occur. Women over 29 and those who miscarry in the second trimester are more likely to experience such complications, as are women who have limited access to health care, such as single women and members of minority groups (B. S. Apgar & Churgay, 1993; Berman, MacKay, Grimes, & Binkin, 1985).

Males are more susceptible than females to the effects of prenatal "shocks" and are more likely to be spontaneously aborted or *stillborn* (dead at birth). Thus, although about 120 to 170 males are conceived for every 100 females—a fact that has been attributed to the greater mobility of sperm carrying the smaller Y chromosome—only 106 boys are born for every 100 girls. Males' greater vulnerability continues after birth: more of them die early in life, and at every age they are more susceptible to many disorders. As a result, there are only 96 males for every 100 females in the United States (U.S. Department of Health and Human Services [USDHHS], 1996a).

Part of the explanation for male vulnerability may be that all zygotes start out with the female body plan. The fact that males undergo more alteration than females during early development may account at least in part for their poorer survival rates. Other possibilities are that the Y chromosome may contain harmful genes, or that the sexes may have different mechanisms for providing immunity to infections and diseases.

Fetal Stage (8 Weeks to Birth)

With the appearance of the first bone cells at about 8 weeks, the developing baby is in the *fetal stage*, the final stage of gestation. During this period, the fetus grows rapidly to about 20 times its previous length, and organs and body systems become more complex. Right up to birth, "finishing touches" such as fingernails, toenails, and eyelids develop.

fetal stage Final stage of gestation (from 8 weeks to birth), characterized by increased detail of body parts and greatly enlarged body size.

Fetal Activity and the Fetal Environment

Fetuses are not passive passengers in their mothers' wombs. They respirate, kick, turn, flex their bodies, do somersaults, squint, swallow, make fists, hiccup, and suck their thumbs. Nor does all this activity occur in a vacuum. Although the amniotic fluid provides a protective buffer, "the fetus . . . is surrounded by and interacts with a complex environment," bounded by the flexible uterine walls and the amniotic sac (Smotherman & Robinson, 1996, p. 426). These elastic membranes restrain the fetus but also stimulate some kinds of movement.

The fetus's isolation in the womb and dependence on the mother's body make it easier to study the effects of specific kinds of stimulation. Much of this research has been done with pregnant rats (Smotherman & Robinson, 1995, 1996). Human fetuses can be observed by *ultrasound,* a medical procedure using high-frequency sound waves to detect the outline of a fetus and observe its movements. New instrumentation allows the monitoring of a fetus's heart rate, changes in activity level, states of sleep and wakefulness, and cardiac reactivity. Through such technologies, scientists have learned much about fetal development.

ultrasound Prenatal medical procedure using high-frequency sound waves to detect the outline of a fetus and its movements, so as to determine whether a pregnancy is progressing normally.

In one study, 34 healthy fetuses were monitored at 4-week intervals from 20 weeks of gestation until term (DiPietro, Hodgson, Costigan, Hilton, & Johnson, 1996). As time went on, they had slower but more variable heart rates—possibly in response to the increasing stress of the mother's pregnancy—and greater cardiac response to stimulation. They also showed less, but more vigorous, activity—perhaps a result of the increasing difficulty of movement for a growing fetus in a constricted environment, as well as of maturation of the nervous system. A significant "jump" in all these aspects of fetal development seems to occur

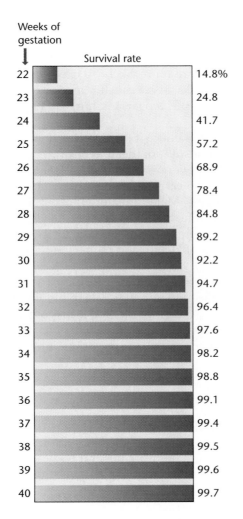

Weeks of
gestation

Survival rate

Weeks	Survival rate
22	14.8%
23	24.8
24	41.7
25	57.2
26	68.9
27	78.4
28	84.8
29	89.2
30	92.2
31	94.7
32	96.4
33	97.6
34	98.2
35	98.8
36	99.1
37	99.4
38	99.5
39	99.6
40	99.7

Figure 3-3

Fetal viability. Fetuses generally cannot survive outside the womb before about 22 weeks of gestation, and even then the survival rate is very low. Chances of survival improve greatly after about 28 to 32 weeks, perhaps due to maturation of the nervous system. Rates shown are the percentages of babies born in the United States after specified lengths of gestation who survive the first year of life.

Source: Stolberg, 1997; from Infant and Child Health Studies Branch, National Center for Health Statistics [NCHS]. Note: These survival rates are based on national birth and death data collected from 1989 to 1991.

between 28 and 32 weeks and may reflect an advance in brain development. It may also help explain why infants born prematurely at this age are more likely to survive and flourish than those born earlier (see Figure 3-3).

Even inside the womb, each individual is unique. The movements of fetuses differ, and their heart rates vary in regularity and speed. There are marked individual differences in activity level, and there are gender differences, too. One study using the fetal actocardiograph, which can detect even very slight movement changes, found that male fetuses are more active and tend to move more vigorously than female fetuses throughout gestation, even when they are the same size. This finding suggests that infant boys' tendency to be more active than girls (see Chapter 7) may be at least partly inborn (DiPietro, Hodgson, Costigan, Hilton, & Johnson, 1996).

Women who bear more than one child often notice differences in fetal activity from one pregnancy to another. One fetus kicks or punches, another squirms, and still another makes sharp, spasmodic movements. Such differences may predict how active, restless, or resistant to handling a baby will be during the first year (Sontag, 1966). Some of these patterns seem to persist into later childhood and adulthood, supporting the existence of inborn temperament. In one study, apparent differences in temperament appeared as early as 24 weeks of gestation and remained stable throughout the prenatal period and 3 to 6 months after birth. Infants who had moved around more in the womb tended to be more difficult, unpredictable, and active and less adaptable, according to their mothers, than infants whose fetal activity had been calmer (DiPietro, Hodgson, Costigan, & Johnson, 1996). It is possible, however, that the mothers' reports about their infants' temperament were influenced by perceptions formed during pregnancy. Attempts are now under way to confirm these findings with laboratory-based assessments.

Fetal Sensory Discrimination and Fetal Learning

Beginning at about the twelfth week of gestation, the fetus swallows and inhales some of the amniotic fluid in which it floats. This stimulation may affect the budding senses of taste and smell and may contribute to the development of the nose, tongue, palate, lungs, and other organs needed for breathing and digestion. Again, this process is not passive; the fetus's respiration, digestion, and elimination regulate the amount and composition of the surrounding amniotic fluid. This fluid also contains chemical substances that cross the placenta from the mother's bloodstream and enter the fetus's bloodstream. All of these sensations and experiences may help shape the development of body and brain (Mennella & Beauchamp, 1996a; Ronca & Alberts, 1995; Smotherman & Robinson, 1995, 1996).

Mature taste cells appear at about 14 weeks of gestation. The olfactory system, which controls the sense of smell, is also well developed before birth. The flavors and odors of foods the mother consumes may be transmitted to the fetus through the amniotic fluid. It is not yet clear whether the human fetus responds to odors, but rodent fetuses do. Whether odor preferences in the womb are related to preferences after birth also remains to be determined. Prenatal experience does not seem to significantly affect later taste preferences, which seem to be largely innate (Bartoshuk & Beauchamp, 1994; Mennella & Beauchamp, 1996a).

A fetus is continually exposed to other kinds of sensory stimuli, including the mother's voice and heartbeat and the vibrations of her body. Fetuses respond to these stimuli, showing that they can hear and feel.

Studies going back at least 60 years show that human fetuses, as early as 7 months of gestation, respond to bells and vibrations and can discriminate between different tones (Bernard & Sontag, 1947; Lecanuet, Granier-Deferre, & Busnel, 1995; Sontag & Richards, 1938; Sontag & Wallace, 1934, 1936). In one experiment, researchers turned on a hand-held vibrator and put its tip to the mother's abdomen, just over the place where the fetus's head was (as confirmed by ultrasound). Then they measured fetal heart rate and movements, again with ultrasound. After testing 60 fetuses, they found that the first responses to sound and vibration came at 26 weeks of gestation; response increased steadily over the next 6 weeks and reached a plateau at about 32 weeks (Kisilevsky, Muir, & Low, 1992). Fetal exposure to sounds, including speech sounds, may spur the ability to process such sounds after birth (Lecanuet et al., 1995). Familiarity with the mother's voice may have an even more basic function: to help newborns locate the source of food. Hungry infants, no matter on which side they are held, turn toward the breast in the direction from which they hear the mother's voice (Noirot & Algeria, 1983, cited in Rovee-Collier, 1996).

The fact that fetuses can discriminate what they have heard shows that they can learn and remember. Researchers tape-recorded pregnant women reading three different stories. One was an excerpt from *The Cat in the Hat* by Dr. Seuss; the second, *The Dog in the Fog*, was based on *The Cat in the Hat* with important nouns changed; the third was an unrelated story. During the last 6 weeks of pregnancy, the women recited just one of these stories an average of 67 times. On the third day after birth, their babies sucked more on a nipple that activated a recording of the story they had heard in the womb than on nipples that activated recordings of the other two stories. Apparently, then, the infants recognized the story they had heard in the womb. Babies in a control group, whose mothers had not recited a story before giving birth, responded equally to all three recordings (DeCasper & Spence, 1986).

Similar experiments have found that newborns 2 to 4 days old prefer musical and speech sequences heard before birth. They also prefer their mother's voice to

This pregnant woman reading nursery rhymes aloud may be familiar with research indicating that fetuses can hear and learn. Newborns prefer their own mother's voice to those of other women, and also seem to recognize stories they heard while in the womb.

CHECKPOINT

Can you . . .

- Identify two principles that govern physical development and give examples of their application during the prenatal period?

- Describe how a zygote becomes an embryo?

- Explain why defects and miscarriages are most likely to occur during the embryonic stage?

- Describe the fetal environment and its effects on fetal development?

those of other women, female voices to male voices, and their mother's native language to another language (DeCasper & Fifer, 1980; DeCasper & Spence, 1986; Fifer & Moon, 1995; Lecanuet et al., 1995; C. Moon, Cooper, & Fifer, 1993).

How do we know that these preferences develop before rather than after birth? To answer this question, newborns were given the choice of sucking to turn on a recording of the mother's voice or a "filtered" version of her voice as it might sound in the womb. The newborns sucked more often to turn on the filtered version, suggesting that fetuses develop a preference for the kinds of sounds they hear before birth (Fifer & Moon, 1995; C. Moon & Fifer, 1990).

Prenatal Development: Environmental Hazards

The pervasive influence of the prenatal environment underlines the importance of providing an unborn child with the best possible start in life. Only recently have scientists become aware of some of the myriad environmental influences that can negatively affect the developing organism. The role of the father used to be virtually ignored; today we know that various environmental factors can affect a man's sperm and the children he conceives. Although the mother's role has been recognized far longer, researchers are still discovering environmental hazards that can affect her fetus. Some of these findings have led to ethical debate over a woman's responsibility for avoiding activities that may harm her unborn child (see Box 3-1).

Box 3-1 Fetal Welfare Versus Mothers' Rights

A young German woman is rendered brain-dead in a car crash in her twelfth week of pregnancy. Although her parents want her to be disconnected from life support, the hospital's ethics committee plans to keep her alive until doctors can deliver a viable infant (Fisher, 1992).

The normal vaginal birth of a healthy baby boy in Chicago ends a long dispute with county officials who tried to force the mother to have a cesarean delivery that doctors said was needed to protect her fetus ("Woman Delivers Baby Boy," 1993).

A woman convicted of forging a check to support her crack habit is jailed for the remainder of her pregnancy to prevent harm to her fetus (Chavkin & Kandall, 1990).

A drunken woman in Racine, Wisconsin, who vowed to kill her fetus by drinking herself to death, gives birth to a baby with fetal alcohol syndrome. The mother is charged with attempted murder (Terry, 1996).

In all of these cases, the issue is the conflict between protection of a fetus and a woman's right to privacy or to make her own decisions about her body. It is tempting to require a pregnant woman to adopt practices that will ensure her baby's health. But what about her personal freedom? Can civil rights be abrogated for the protection of the unborn?

Should a woman be forced to submit to intrusive procedures that pose a risk to her, such as a surgical delivery or intrauterine transfusions? Legal coercion could jeopardize the doctor-patient relationship. Such coercion also could open the door to further intrusion into pregnant women's lives—demanding prenatal screening and fetal surgery or restricting their diet, work, and ath-

letic and sexual activity (Kolder, Gallagher, & Parsons, 1987). For these reasons, the overwhelming attitude of medical, legal, and social critics is that the state should intervene only in circumstances in which there is a high risk of serious disease or a high degree of accuracy in the test for a defect, strong evidence that the proposed treatment will be effective, danger that deferring treatment until after birth will cause serious damage, minimal risk to the mother and modest interference with her privacy, and persistent but unsuccessful efforts at educating her and obtaining her informed consent.

Does a woman have the right to knowingly ingest a substance, such as alcohol or another drug, which can permanently damage her unborn child? Since the late 1980s (when *The Broken Cord* was published), at least 200 women in more than 30 states have been prosecuted for behavior that could injure an unborn baby. Most of these cases involved illegal drugs, and the usual charges were child abuse or delivering a controlled substance to a minor. Most of the cases were dismissed, but in July, 1996, the South Carolina Supreme Court upheld a guilty verdict for a woman who had taken drugs during her pregnancy (Terry, 1996).

Some advocates for fetal rights think it should be against the law for pregnant women to smoke or use alcohol, even though these activities are legal for other adults. But some experts argue that expectant mothers who have a drinking or drug problem need education and treatment, not prosecution. If failure to follow medical advice can bring forced surgery, confinement, or criminal charges, some women may avoid doctors altogether and deprive their fetuses of prenatal care.

Maternal Factors

Since the prenatal environment is the mother's body, she is greatly responsible for the earliest environmental influences on her child-to-be. Virtually everything that impinges on her well-being, from her diet to her moods, may alter her unborn child's environment and affect its growth.

Much of what we know about prenatal hazards we have learned either from animal research or from reports by mothers, after childbirth, on what they ate while pregnant, what drugs they took, how much radiation they were exposed to, what illnesses they had, and so forth. Both methods have limitations. It is not always accurate to apply findings from animals to human beings, and women do not always remember what they did during pregnancy. Because of ethical considerations, it is impossible to set up controlled experiments that might provide more definitive answers. Nevertheless, we know a great deal about the risks of such prenatal influences.

Particular factors in the prenatal environment affect different fetuses differently. Some environmental factors that are *teratogenic* (birth-defect-producing) in some cases have little or no effect in other cases. The timing of an environmental event, its intensity, and its interaction with other factors may be relevant (refer back to Figure 3-2).

teratogenic Capable of causing birth defects.

Vulnerability may depend on a gene either in the fetus or in the mother. One study found that fetuses with a particular variant of a growth gene, called *transforming growth factor alpha,* have 6 times more risk than other fetuses of developing a cleft palate if the mother smokes while pregnant, and almost 9 times more risk if she smokes more than 10 cigarettes a day (S. J. Hwang et al., 1995). Women without the abnormal allele who smoke at least 20 cigarettes a day are at heightened risk of having babies with cleft palates, but their risk is even greater if the abnormal gene is present (G. M. Shaw, Wasserman et al., 1996). Other influences on prenatal development may turn out to be similarly multifactorial.

Nutrition

Even before she conceives, a woman's diet can affect her child's future health. A well-balanced diet during pregnancy may be even more vital. In rural Gambia, in western Africa, people born during the "hungry" season, when foods from the previous harvest are badly depleted, are 10 times more likely to die in early adulthood than people born during other parts of the year. This suggests that malnutrition during fetal growth may have permanent effects on the immune system (S. E. Moore et al., 1997).

Women need to eat more than usual when pregnant: typically, 300 to 500 more calories a day, including extra protein (Winick, 1981). Pregnant women who gain between 22 and 46 pounds are less likely to miscarry or to bear babies who are stillborn or whose weight at birth is dangerously low (Abrams & Parker, 1990). Gaining too little is riskier than gaining too much. In part because of societal pressures to look thin, many expectant mothers gain less than they should.

Malnourished women who take dietary supplements while pregnant tend to have bigger, healthier, more active, and more visually alert infants (J. L. Brown, 1987; Vuori et al., 1979); and women with low zinc levels in their blood who take daily zinc supplements are less likely to have babies with low birth weight and small head circumference (Goldenberg et al., 1995). However, certain vitamins (including A, B_6, C, D, and K) can be harmful in excessive amounts. Women who consume more than 15,000 units of vitamin A in foods or supplements, especially before the seventh week of pregnancy, have an increased risk of bearing babies with abnormalities of the head and face, central nervous system, thymus gland, and heart. This is not true of women who took betacarotene, which the body converts into vitamin A (Rothman et al., 1995).

Only recently have we learned of the critical importance of folic acid (a B vitamin) in a pregnant woman's diet. For some time, scientists have known that China has the highest incidence in the world of babies born with the neural-tube defects anencephaly and spina bifida (see Table 2-1 in Chapter 2), but it was not until the 1980s that researchers linked that fact with the timing of the babies' conception. Traditionally, Chinese couples marry in January or February and try to conceive as soon as possible. That means pregnancies often begin in the winter, when rural women have little access to fresh fruits and vegetables, important sources of folic acid.

After medical detective work established the lack of folic acid as a cause of neural-tube defects, China embarked on a massive program to give folic acid supplements to prospective mothers (Tyler, 1994). In the United States, women of childbearing age are now urged to include this vitamin in their diets, even before becoming pregnant (American Academy of Pediatrics [AAP] Committee on Genetics, 1993). Increasing women's folic acid consumption by just four-tenths of a milligram each day would reduce the incidence of neural-tube defects by about one-half (Daly, Kirke, Molloy, Weir, & Scott, 1995).

Some research points to a multifactorial effect. A randomized study in Dublin, Ireland, found that women who gave birth to babies with neural-tube defects were much more likely than women who gave birth to normal babies to have inherited a certain defective enzyme. This enzyme causes the fetus to be

Moderate exercise seems to be beneficial for pregnant women and their babies, as long as the women do not work out too strenuously.

exposed to a toxic substance unless the mother gets large amounts of folic acid (Mills, McPartlin, Kirke, Lee, & Conley, 1995).

Obese women also risk having children with neural-tube defects. Women who, before pregnancy, weigh more than 176 pounds or have an elevated body mass index (weight compared with height) are more likely to produce babies with such defects, regardless of folate intake. Obesity also increases the risk of other complications of pregnancy, including miscarriage, stillbirth, and *neonatal death* (death during the first month of life) (Goldenberg & Tamura, 1996; G. M. Shaw, Velie, & Schaffer, 1996; Werler, Louik, Shapiro, & Mitchell, 1996).

Physical Activity

Moderate exercise does not seem to endanger the fetuses of healthy women (Carpenter et al., 1988); an expectant mother can continue to jog, cycle, swim, or play tennis. Regular exercise prevents constipation and improves respiration, circulation, muscle tone, and skin elasticity, all of which contribute to a more comfortable pregnancy and an easier, safer delivery.

Employment during pregnancy generally requires no special accommodations. However, strenuous working conditions, occupational fatigue, and long working hours may be associated with a greater risk of premature birth (Luke et al., 1995).

The American College of Obstetrics and Gynecology's (1994) guidelines encourage women in low-risk pregnancies to be guided by their own stamina and abilities. The safest course seems to be for pregnant women to exercise moderately, not pushing themselves and not raising their heart rate above 150, and to taper off at the end of each session rather than stop abruptly.

Drug Intake

Almost everything an expectant mother takes in makes its way to the uterus. Drugs may cross the placenta, just as oxygen, carbon dioxide, and water do. Vulnerability is greatest in the first few months of gestation, when development is most rapid. Some problems resulting from prenatal exposure to drugs can be treated if the presence of a drug in a baby's body can be detected early.

What are the effects on children of the mother's use of specific drugs during pregnancy? Let's look first at medical drugs; then at alcohol, nicotine, and caffeine; and finally at widely used illegal drugs: marijuana, opiates, and cocaine.

Medical Drugs Medical drugs known to be harmful include the antibiotics streptomycin and tetracycline; the sulfanomides; certain barbiturates, opiates, and other central nervous system depressants; several hormones, including birth control pills, progestin, diethylstilbestrol (DES), androgen, and synthetic estrogen; Accutane, a drug often prescribed for severe acne; and even aspirin. The effects may be cognitive as well as physical and can be long-lasting. In one study, 34- to 36-year-old Danish men whose mothers had taken phenobarbitol, the most commonly prescribed barbiturate, during pregnancy (especially during the last trimester) had significantly lower verbal intelligence scores than a control group. Coming from a lower socioeconomic background or having been the product of an unwanted pregnancy tended to magnify the negative outcome, showing an interaction of environmental factors before and after birth (Reinisch, Sanders, Mortensen, Psych, & Rubin, 1995). The American Academy of Pediatrics (AAP) Committee on Drugs (1994) recommends that *no* medication be prescribed for a pregnant or breastfeeding woman unless it is essential for her health or her child's.

The effects of taking a drug during pregnancy do not always show up immediately. In the late 1940s and early 1950s, the synthetic hormone diethylstilbestrol (DES) was widely prescribed (ineffectually, as it turned out) to prevent miscarriage. Not until years later, when the daughters of women who had taken DES during pregnancy reached puberty, did about 1 in 1,000 develop a rare form of vaginal or cervical cancer (Melnick, Cole, Anderson, & Herbst, 1987). "DES daughters" also have had trouble bearing their own children, with higher than normal risks of miscarriage or premature delivery (A. Barnes et al., 1980).

fetal alcohol syndrome (FAS) Combination of mental, motor, and developmental abnormalities affecting the offspring of some women who drink heavily during pregnancy.

Alcohol Each year in the United States, more than 40,000 babies are born with alcohol-related birth defects. Like Abel Dorris, about 1 infant in 750 suffers from *fetal alcohol syndrome (FAS),* a combination of slowed prenatal and postnatal growth, facial and bodily malformations, and disorders of the central nervous system. Problems related to the central nervous system can include, in infancy, poor sucking response, brain-wave abnormalities, and sleep disturbances; and, throughout childhood, slow information processing, short attention span, restlessness, irritability, hyperactivity, learning disabilities, and motor impairments.

Some FAS problems recede after birth; but others, such as retardation, learning disabilities, and hyperactivity, tend to persist into adulthood. Unfortunately, enriching these children's education or general environment does not seem to enhance their cognitive development (Spohr, Willms, & Steinhausen, 1993; Streissguth et al., 1991; Strömland & Hellström, 1996).

The number of children known to have FAS has increased more than sixfold since 1979, to 6.7 per 10,000 births (Centers for Disease Control and Prevention [CDC], 1995). However, it is not clear whether this represents a real increase in the number of infants with FAS or merely an increase in awareness and reporting of the problem. For every child with fetal alcohol syndrome, as many as 10 others may be born with *fetal alcohol effects.* This less severe condition can include mental retardation, retardation of intrauterine growth, and minor congenital abnormalities.

Even moderate drinking may harm a fetus. One or two drinks a day can increase the risk of retarded growth (Mills, Graubard, Harley, Rhoads, & Berendes, 1984) and slow information processing (Jacobson, Jacobson, Sokol, Martier, & Ager, 1993). The more the mother drinks, the greater the effect. Alcohol consumption during pregnancy has also been linked with infant leukemia (Shu et al., 1996) and kidney abnormalities (C. A. Moore, Khoury, & Liu, 1997).

The impact of a mother's alcohol use on her baby's physical, cognitive, and psychosocial development shows the interrelationship among developmental realms and the bidirectional influences in a child's life. Moderate or heavy drinking during pregnancy seems to alter the character of a newborn's cry, an index of neurobehavioral status. (So does moderate smoking during pregnancy.)

Disturbed neurological and behavioral functioning may, in turn, affect early social interactions with the mother, which are vital to emotional development (Nugent, Lester, Greene, Wieczorek-Deering, & O'Mahony, 1996). Among 44 white, middle-class mothers, those who drank even moderately while pregnant had babies who were more irritable at 1 year of age than babies whose mothers did not drink during pregnancy. The babies' crying, whining, and tantrums annoyed their mothers, interfering with the relationship between them. These babies also tended to have low scores on tests of cognitive development (O'Connor, Sigman, & Kasari, 1993).

Since there is no known safe level of drinking during pregnancy, it is best to avoid alcohol from the time a woman begins *thinking* about becoming pregnant until she stops breastfeeding (AAP Committee on Substance Abuse, 1993).

Nicotine How harmful is nicotine to an unborn baby? An estimate based on data from almost 100 studies is that cigarette smoking by pregnant women causes the deaths of about 5,600 babies every year in the United States, as well as 115,000 miscarriages. Of the deaths, 1,900 are cases of *sudden infant death syndrome (SIDS)*, in which an apparently healthy infant is unexpectedly found dead (see Chapter 5); the other 3,700 infants die by the age of 1 month, many of them because they are too small to survive. Smoking during pregnancy is estimated to contribute to the births of 53,000 low-birthweight babies (weighing less than 5½ pounds at birth) annually and 22,000 babies who need intensive care (DiFranza & Lew, 1995). In addition, pregnant smokers are at higher risk than nonsmokers of complications ranging from bleeding during pregnancy to death of the fetus or newborn (Armstrong, McDonald, & Sloan, 1992; Chomitz, Cheung, & Lieberman, 1995; Landesman-Dwyer & Emanuel, 1979; A. D. McDonald, Armstrong, & Sloan, 1992; Sexton & Hebel, 1984). Women who cut down on smoking during pregnancy tend to have bigger babies than those who continue to smoke at the same rate (Li, Windsor, Perkins, Goldenberg, & Lowe, 1993).

Since women who smoke during pregnancy also tend to smoke after the birth, it is hard to separate the effects of prenatal and postnatal exposure. One study did this by examining 500 newborns about 48 hours after birth, while they were still in the hospital's nonsmoking maternity ward (Stick, Burton, Gurrin, Sly, & LeSouëf, 1996). Infants whose mothers had smoked during pregnancy were shorter and lighter and had poorer respiratory functioning than babies of nonsmoking mothers. Apparently exposure to smoke in utero may adversely affect lung development, which may lead to respiratory problems in childhood and adulthood.

Smoking during pregnancy seems to have some of the same effects on children when they reach school age as drinking during pregnancy: poor attention span, hyperactivity, anxiety, learning and behavior problems, perceptual-motor and linguistic problems, poor IQ scores, low grade placement, and minimal brain dysfunction (Landesman-Dwyer & Emanuel, 1979; Milberger, Biederman, Faraone, Chen, & Jones, 1996; Naeye & Peters, 1984; D. L. Olds, Henderson, & Tatelbaum, 1994a, 1994b; Streissguth et al., 1984; Wakschlag et al., 1997; Weitzman, Gortmaker, & Sobol, 1992; J. T. Wright et al., 1983). It is possible that smoking during pregnancy may alter the child's brain structure or function, with resulting long-term effects on behavior; that passive exposure to cigarette smoke after birth may affect a child's central nervous system; that smoking may alter the mother's behavior, thus affecting her child's; or that mothers who smoke may be less tolerant of their children's behavior.

Caffeine Can the caffeine a pregnant woman swallows in coffee, tea, cola, or chocolate cause trouble for her fetus? One study suggests that the amount of caffeine in 1½ to 3 cups of coffee a day may nearly double the risk of miscarriage,

A woman who drinks and smokes while pregnant is taking grave risks with her future child's health.

and drinking more than 3 cups nearly triples the risk (Infante-Rivard, Fernández, Gauthier, David, & Rivard, 1993). These findings appear to conflict with those of another study, which suggests that drinking up to 3 cups of coffee a day during pregnancy does not increase the risk of miscarriage or affect fetal development (Mills et al., 1993). Because serious questions remain, the U.S. Food and Drug Administration recommends that pregnant women avoid or use sparingly any food, beverages, or drugs that contain caffeine.

Marijuana   Findings about marijuana use by pregnant women are mixed. Some evidence suggests that heavy use can lead to birth defects. A Canadian study found temporary neurological disturbances, such as tremors and startles, as well as higher rates of low birthweight in the infants of marijuana smokers (Fried, Watkinson, & Willan, 1984). A study in the United States found that marijuana use just before and during pregnancy was linked with acute lymphoblastic leukemia, a childhood cancer, possibly because of pesticide contamination of the cannabis leaves (Robison et al., 1989).

In Jamaica (West Indies), where marijuana use is common, researchers who analyzed infants' cries concluded that a mother's heavy marijuana use affects her infant's nervous system (Lester & Dreher, 1989). On the other hand, in another study, 3-day-old infants of mothers who had used marijuana prenatally showed no difference from a control group of nonexposed newborns; and at 1 month, the exposed babies were more alert and sociable and less irritable (Dreher, Nugent, & Hudgins, 1994). The authors of this study suggest that rural Jamaican women who use marijuana are likely to be better educated, to have higher income, and to have more adults living in the household and that these factors may combine to create a more favorable child-rearing environment. Thus scientists cannot look at a single factor, such as marijuana use, in isolation, but must explore the cultural context in which it occurs. Still, the safest course for women of childbearing age is *not* to use marijuana.

Opiates Women addicted to morphine, heroin, and codeine are likely to bear premature, addicted babies who will be addicted to the same drugs and suffer the effects of addiction until at least age 6. Addicted newborns are restless and irritable and often suffer tremors, convulsions, fever, vomiting, breathing difficulties, and even death (Cobrinick, Hood, & Chused, 1959; Henly & Fitch, 1966; Ostrea & Chavez, 1979). As older babies, they cry often and are less alert and less responsive than other babies (Strauss, Lessen-Firestone, Starr, & Ostrea, 1975). In early childhood they weigh less, are shorter, are less well adjusted, and score lower on tests of perceptual and learning abilities (G. Wilson, McCreary, Kean, & Baxter, 1979). Later, these children tend not to do well in school, to be unusually anxious in social situations, and to have trouble making friends (Householder, Hatcher, Burns, & Chasnoff, 1982).

Cocaine Cocaine use seems to interfere with the flow of blood through the placenta, and it may act on fetal brain chemicals to cause neurological and behavioral problems. A pregnant woman's use of cocaine is associated with a higher risk of spontaneous abortion, prematurity, low birth weight, and small head circumference. "Cocaine babies" are generally not as alert as other babies and not as responsive, either emotionally or cognitively; or they may be more excitable and less able to regulate their sleep-wake patterns (Alessandri, Sullivan, Imaizumi, & Lewis, 1993; Kliegman, Madura, Kiwi, Eisenberg, & Yamashita, 1994; B. M. Lester et al., 1991; Napiorkowski et al., 1996; L. T. Singer et al., 1994; E. Z. Tronick, Frank, Cabral, Mirochnick, & Zuckerman, 1996; B. Zuckerman et al., 1989).

As newborns, they tend to smile less, to be more irritable and less consolable, and to suck more intensely, which may be related to early feeding problems (R. B. Phillips, Sharma, Premachandra, Vaughn, & Reyes-Lee, 1996). They may show either impaired motor activity (Fetters & Tronick, 1996) or excessive activity, as well as extreme muscular tension, jerky movements, startles, tremors, back arching, inability to follow an object with the eyes or turn toward the sound of a rattle, and other signs of neurological stress (Napiorkowski et al., 1996). Some of these behavior patterns may be due to the combined effects of maternal use of cocaine and other substances, such as alcohol and marijuana (Napiorkowski et al., 1996; E. Z. Tronick et al., 1996).

The far-reaching impact of cocaine exemplifies both the interconnectedness of development and its bidirectional influences. The mother's psychological reasons for using cocaine—which then affects her physically, cognitively, and emotionally—produce effects on her baby in all three domains. A baby's initial reaction to the drug may in turn frustrate the mother and interfere with her ability to form a close, caring relationship with her infant. The lethargic or irritable behavior of a cocaine-affected infant is not likely to inspire loving feelings. Since drug-abusing parents are often irritable themselves and are less able than most parents to cope with a difficult child, they may abuse or neglect the baby, making it less likely that the infant will recover from the initial effects of the drug (R. B. Phillips et al., 1996). Children of addicted mothers often face other environmental risks, such as poverty, unstable homes, inadequate prenatal care, and other lifestyle factors that may contribute to their problems (Fetters & Tronick, 1996; E. Z. Tronick et al., 1996).

The children's own behavior continues to affect their cognitive and emotional progress. For example, some research suggests that prenatal cocaine exposure affects the ability to regulate attention (Mayes, Granger, Frank, Schottenfeld, & Bornstein, 1993); and a very short attention span interferes with learning.

This 26-year-old mother contracted AIDS from her husband, who had gotten it from a former girlfriend, an intravenous drug user. The father died first, then the 21-month-old baby, and lastly the mother.

Later, organizational and language skills and emotional attachment may suffer (Azuma & Chasnoff, 1993; Hawley & Disney, 1992). In early childhood, many of these children have trouble loving their parents, making friends, and playing normally (B. M. Lester et al., 1991). Still, some studies have shown resilience in cocaine-exposed infants. Often—especially if they had good prenatal care—they catch up in weight, length, and head circumference by 1 year of age (Racine, Joyce, & Anderson, 1993; Weathers, Crane, Sauvain, & Blackhurst, 1993).

Human Immunodeficiency Virus (HIV) Infection and AIDS

acquired immune deficiency syndrome (AIDS) Viral disease that undermines effective functioning of the immune system.

Acquired immune deficiency syndrome (AIDS) is a disease caused by the human immunodeficiency virus (HIV), which undermines effective functioning of the immune system. A fetus may become infected with HIV if the mother has AIDS or has the virus in her blood. The contents of the mother's blood cross over to the fetus's bloodstream through the placenta. After birth, the virus can be transmitted through breast milk.

Advances in the prevention, detection, and treatment of HIV infection in infants include the successful use of the drug zidovudine, commonly called AZT, to curtail transmission, the recognition that women with HIV should not breastfeed, and the availability of new drugs to treat AIDS-related pneumonia. The chances that an infected woman will transmit the virus to her baby during pregnancy can be cut by nearly two-thirds, from about 14 percent to about 5 percent, by giving her AZT (Mayaux et al., 1997). The American Academy of Pediatrics (AAP) recommends that all pregnant women be given the opportunity for voluntary, confidential testing (AAP Provisional Committee on Pediatric AIDS, 1995).

Prospects for children born with HIV infection have improved. Current research indicates that the progress of the disease, at least in some of these children, is not as fast as was previously thought, even without treatment. While some develop full-blown AIDS by their first or second birthday, others live for years without apparently being affected much, if at all (European Collaborative Study, 1994; Nozyce et al., 1994). A recent study suggests that a gene mutation may slow the progress of AIDS (Misrahi et al., 1998). This also means, however, that infected children who appear healthy may not be diagnosed in the early stages.

One study looked at 197 children who were still alive at least 8 years after having been infected either at birth or through blood transfusions during the first month of life, and 9 out of 10 of whom had received treatment. Nearly half the children (48 percent) had developed AIDS-related conditions, such as inflammation of the lungs or recurrent bacterial infections; 20 percent showed no progression of the disease, or virtually none; and the rest were in various stages of progression (Nielsen et al., 1997). In a smaller study of 42 children and adolescents, ages 9 to 16, who had acquired HIV prenatally, 10 youngsters—nearly 1 out of 4—were living without symptoms and had relatively intact immune systems (Grubman et al., 1995). Most of the remaining youngsters, who had AIDS or chronic HIV-related symptoms that significantly affected their daily functioning, had not shown the signs until after 4 years of age. About three-fourths of the total group were attending regular schools, and the rest were enrolled in special education programs.

Other Maternal Illnesses

Some illnesses contracted during pregnancy can have serious effects on the developing fetus. However, medical advances have lowered the risks of many serious illnesses, at least among women with access to good medical care, and some can be prevented by immunization. Tests can determine whether a pregnant woman and her fetus may have been infected by a virus or parasite, and if so, the woman can be treated.

Rubella (German measles), if contracted by a mother before the eleventh week of pregnancy, is almost certain to cause deafness and heart defects in the baby. However, between 13 and 16 weeks of pregnancy, the chances of such effects are only about 1 in 3, and after 16 weeks, they are almost nil (E. Miller, Cradock-Watson, & Pollock, 1982). Such defects are rare these days, since most children are inoculated against rubella, making it unlikely that a pregnant woman will catch the disease. A woman who is not yet pregnant can find out through a blood test whether or not she is immune; and, if not, she can be immunized.

Diabetes, tuberculosis, and syphilis can cause problems in fetal development, and gonorrhea and genital herpes can have harmful effects on the baby at the time of delivery. The incidence of genital herpes simplex virus (HSV) has increased among newborns, who can acquire the disease from the mother or father either at or soon after birth (Sullivan-Bolyai, Hull, Wilson, & Corey, 1983). Newborns with HSV may suffer blindness, other abnormalities, or death.

A mild infection called *toxoplasmosis,* caused by a parasite harbored in the bodies of cattle, sheep, and pigs and in the intestinal tracts of cats, typically produces either no symptoms or symptoms like those of the common cold. In a pregnant woman, however, it can cause brain damage, blindness, or death of the baby. To avoid infection, expectant mothers should not handle cats or change their litter, should not eat raw or very rare meat or feed it to a cat, and should not dig in a garden where cat feces are buried.

Both prospective parents should try to prevent all infections—common colds, flu, urinary tract and vaginal infections, and sexually transmitted diseases—whenever possible. The father can transmit an infection to the mother, which could have dire effects. If the mother does contract an infection, she should have it treated promptly by a physician who knows she is pregnant.

Maternal Age

How does delayed childbearing affect the risks to mother and baby? Older pregnant women are more likely to suffer complications and possibly even death due to diabetes, high blood pressure, or severe bleeding. Also, there is greater likelihood of miscarriage, premature delivery, retarded fetal growth, stillbirth, or birth defects. However, due to widespread screening for fetal defects, deliveries of malformed fetuses have decreased (F. G. Cunningham & Leveno, 1995). At one Montreal hospital, while the overall fetal death rate has declined since 1961 for women of all ages, the risk of stillbirth remains greater for women over 35. Still, in absolute numbers the risk of fetal death among older mothers is low—about 6 per 1,000, as compared with 3 per 1,000 when the mother is 35 or under (Fretts, Schmittdiel, McLean, Usher, & Goldman, 1995). For prospective older mothers who are basically healthy, these findings are encouraging. (Risks of teenage pregnancy are discussed in Chapter 16.)

Incompatibility of Blood Types

Heredity can interact with the prenatal environment to cause incompatibility of blood type between mother and baby, most commonly due to the *Rh factor*, a protein substance found in the blood of most people. When a fetus's blood contains this protein (is Rh-positive) but the mother's blood does not (is Rh-negative), antibodies in the mother's blood may attack the fetus. The result can be miscarriage or stillbirth, jaundice, anemia, heart defects, mental retardation, or death soon after birth. Usually the first Rh-positive baby of an Rh-negative mother is not affected, but with each pregnancy the risk becomes greater. A vaccine administered to an Rh-negative mother within 3 days after childbirth or abortion will prevent her body from making antibodies that will attack future Rh-positive fetuses. Babies already affected by Rh incompatibility can receive blood transfusions, sometimes even before birth.

Environmental Hazards

Chemicals, radiation, extremes of heat and humidity, and other hazards of modern life can affect prenatal development. Infants exposed prenatally to high levels of lead score lower on tests of cognitive abilities than those exposed to low or moderate levels (Bellinger, Leviton, Watermaux, Needleman, & Rabinowitz, 1987; Needleman & Gatsonis, 1990). Children exposed prenatally to heavy metals have higher rates of childhood illness and lower levels of performance on a children's intelligence test (M. Lewis, Worobey, Ramsay, & McCormack, 1992). Women who work with chemicals used in manufacturing semiconductor chips have about twice the rate of miscarriage as other female workers (Markoff, 1992).

Chemicals called *PCBs* (polychlorinated biphenyls) have affected many children born before these pollutants were banned. Among 212 Michigan children born in 1980 and 1981, those whose mothers had eaten contaminated fish from Lake Michigan had lower IQs at age 11 than those whose mothers had not eaten contaminated fish (J. L. Jacobson & Jacobson, 1996). Memory and attention were particularly affected. The children with the greatest exposure to PCBs were 3 times as likely as unexposed children to have low IQs and twice as likely to be at least 2 years behind in reading comprehension. Apparently, then, the fetal stage is a critical period for brain development, when these chemicals can have a detrimental long-term effect.

Radiation can cause gene mutations. Nuclear radiation affected Japanese infants after the atomic bomb explosions in Hiroshima and Nagasaki (Yamazaki & Schull, 1990) and German infants after the spill-out at the nuclear power plant at Chernobyl in the Soviet Union (West Berlin Human Genetics Institute, 1987). In utero exposure to radiation has been linked to greater risk of mental retardation, small head size, chromosomal malformations, Down syndrome, seizures, and poor performance on IQ tests and in school. The critical period seems to be 8 through 15 weeks after fertilization (Yamazaki & Schull, 1990). Since the greatest damage seems to occur early in pregnancy, radiation exposure should be avoided especially during the first 3 months (Kleinman, Cooke, Machlin, & Kessel, 1983).

CHECKPOINT

Can you . . .

- Summarize recommendations concerning an expectant mother's diet and physical activity?

- Assess the short-term and long-term effects on the developing fetus of a mother's use of medical drugs, alcohol, tobacco, caffeine, marijuana, opiates, and cocaine during pregnancy?

- Summarize the risks of maternal illnesses, delayed childbearing, Rh incompatibility, and exposure to chemicals and radiation?

Paternal Factors

The father, too, can transmit defects, often environmentally caused. A man's exposure to lead, marijuana or tobacco smoke, large amounts of alcohol or radiation, DES, or certain pesticides may result in the production of abnormal sperm (R. Lester & Van Theil, 1977). Children of men who are electrical or electronic workers, auto mechanics, miners, printers, paper or pulp mill workers, or aircraft industry workers are more likely than other children to develop tumors in the nervous system (M. R. Spitz & Johnson, 1985). Fathers whose diet is low in vitamin C are more likely to have children with birth defects and certain types of cancer (Fraga et al., 1991).

One harmful environmental influence on both mother and baby is nicotine from a father's smoking. In one study, babies of fathers who smoked were lighter at birth by about 4 ounces per pack of cigarettes smoked per day by the father, or the cigar or pipe equivalent (D. H. Rubin, Krasilnikoff, Leventhal, Weile, & Berget, 1986). Another study found that children of men who smoked were twice as likely as other children to develop cancer in adulthood (Sandler, Everson, Wilcox, & Browder, 1985).

In such studies, it is hard to distinguish between prebirth and childhood exposure to smoke, and between a father's and a mother's smoking. To avoid the latter problem, researchers chose to do a study in Shanghai, China, where many men smoke but few women do. The study found a strong connection between paternal cigarette smoking and the risk of childhood cancer, particularly acute leukemia and lymphoma. The risk increased with the amount a man smoked and the length of time he had been smoking (Ji et al., 1997).

A man's use of cocaine can cause birth defects in his children. The cocaine seems to attach itself to his sperm, and this cocaine-bearing sperm then enters the ovum at conception. Other toxins, such as lead and mercury, may "hitchhike" onto sperm in the same way (Yazigi, Odem, & Polakoski, 1991). One route for the transmission of cocaine from sperm to baby may lie with the mother. When a cocaine-using woman has sexual intercourse, the man's sperm in her reproductive tract may pick up the drug and carry it to the ovum.

A later paternal age (averaging in the late thirties) is associated with increases in several rare conditions, including Marfan's syndrome (deformities of the head and limbs), dwarfism, and bone malformation (G. Evans, 1976). Advanced age of the father may also be a factor in about 5 percent of cases of Down syndrome (Antonarakis & Down Syndrome Collaborative Group, 1991). More male cells than female cells undergo mutations, and mutations may increase with paternal age. Older fathers may therefore be a significant source of birth defects in their children (Crow, 1993, 1995).

C H E C K P O I N T

Can you . . .

- Identify three ways in which a father can transmit environmentally caused defects?

- State some risks of advanced paternal age?

Monitoring Prenatal Development

Not long ago, almost the only decision parents had to make about their babies before birth was the decision to conceive; most of what happened in the intervening months was beyond their control. Now we have an array of tools to assess an unborn baby's progress and well-being. In line with these developments is a growing emphasis on the importance of early prenatal care. (See Box 3-2 for predictions about prenatal assessment and care in the twenty-first century.)

Prenatal Assessment Techniques

Normal prenatal development is overwhelmingly the rule. Most women feel good during pregnancy, both physically and emotionally, and their embryos and fetuses develop normally. Still, we need to be aware of the many ways development

Box 3-2 Pregnancy in the Twenty-First Century

At the end of the nineteenth century, in England and Wales, a woman who became pregnant had a risk of dying in childbirth almost 50 times as great as the risk facing a pregnant woman today (N. Saunders, 1997). A woman who conceived in 1950 in the United States was more than 3 times as likely as in 1993 to lose her baby either before or within 1 year after birth (USDHHS, 1996a).

The dramatic reductions in risks surrounding pregnancy and childbirth that have occurred, particularly during the past 50 years, are largely due to new technologies, such as the availability of antibiotics, blood transfusions, safe anesthesia, and drugs for inducing labor when necessary (see Chapter 4). In addition, improvements in prenatal assessment and care make it far more likely today that a baby will be born healthy.

What further progress will the next 50 to 100 years bring? Will today's practices seem archaic to people at the end of the twenty-first century? Looking ahead, one medical expert (N. Saunders, 1997) has made several predictions about the future of maternity care, most of them based on recent discoveries and advances that are already under way:

- *No more obstetrics.* Although there will continue to be a need for skilled persons to perform operative deliveries, medical attention will focus mainly on the beginning of pregnancy. A new medical specialty combining clinical genetics and fetal medicine will develop to do prepregnancy screening and counseling and diagnose abnormalities in the womb.
- *A massive increase in genetic screening.* The completion of the human genome map (see Chapter 2) will open virtually unlimited possibilities for advising couples of their risk of conceiving a child with an inherited defect or disorder.

- *For couples with potentially harmful genes, greater use of assisted conception and preimplantation genetic diagnosis* to make sure that affected offspring do not come into being.
- *Earlier detection of fetal malformations* by means of computer-assisted three-dimensional images and by examination of fetal cells obtained from the mother's blood.
- *Gene therapy and fetal surgery.* By manipulating genes or doing surgical corrections in the womb, doctors will be able to prevent certain predicted or diagnosed conditions from showing up in a child.
- *More emphasis on improving the fetal environment,* even before pregnancy begins. The recent discovery of the value of giving folic acid supplements to women of childbearing age to prevent them from bearing children with neural-tube defects is undoubtedly only one of a number of such measures that will prove to be beneficial. The impact of diet, exercise, work, and other lifestyle factors at critical periods of gestation will be more precisely known and closely monitored.
- *Better understanding of the causes of miscarriage,* which may make it preventable in some cases.
- *Prediction and prevention of premature delivery*—for example, through identification and treatment of genital tract infections.

Once a pregnancy is established, and it is clear that the fetus is well-formed and growing properly, not much will have to be done during the last half of pregnancy, other than to check for hypertension (high blood pressure), slowing of fetal growth, and the fetus's position in the womb. However, women probably will still be encouraged to see health-care professionals regularly—among other reasons, for the psychological reassurance such visits provide.

---

can go awry and how best to avoid problems. Techniques for monitoring fetal development, coupled with increased knowledge of ways to improve the child's prenatal world, make pregnancy much less a cause for concern than in earlier times. Access to prenatal diagnosis of birth defects, coupled with the legal availability of abortion and the possibility of fetal therapy, have encouraged many couples with troubling medical histories to take a chance on conception.

Ultrasound

Some parents see their baby for the first time in a *sonogram.* As we mentioned earlier in this chapter, this picture of the uterus, fetus, and placenta is created by *ultrasound,* high-frequency sound waves directed into the mother's abdomen. Ultrasound provides the clearest images yet of a fetus in the womb, with little or no discomfort to the mother. Ultrasound is used to measure fetal growth, to judge gestational age, to detect multiple pregnancies, to evaluate uterine abnormalities, to detect major structural abnormalities in the fetus, and to determine whether a fetus has died, as well as to guide other procedures, such as amniocentesis. Results from ultrasound can suggest what other procedures may be needed.

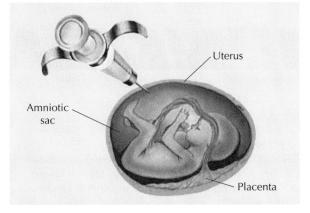

Figure 3-4
Amniocentesis. Through amniocentesis, a sample of amniotic fluid can be withdrawn and analyzed for the presence of a variety of birth defects. A needle is inserted through the mother's abdominal wall to remove the fluid. Analysis of the sampled fluid generally takes 2 to 4 weeks.
Source: F. Fuchs, 1980.

Uterus

Amniotic sac

Placenta

The use of ultrasound is increasingly common; 61 percent of mothers who had live births used it in 1995, as compared with only 48 percent in 1989 (Ventura, Martin, Curtin, & Mathews, 1997). However, ultrasound screening does not appear to reduce fetal and neonatal death (Ewigman et al., 1993). Thus there seems to be no reason to use it in low-risk pregnancies, especially since some research suggests that frequently repeated ultrasound may affect fetal growth (Newnham, Evans, Michael, Stanley, & Landau, 1993).

Amniocentesis

In *amniocentesis,* a sample of the amniotic fluid that surrounds the fetus is withdrawn and analyzed (see Figure 3-4). This fluid contains fetal cells, and its analysis enables physicians to detect the presence of a few hundred (out of 4,000) genetic defects, all recognizable chromosomal disorders, and other problems, including neural-tube defects. Amniocentesis, like ultrasound, can also reveal the sex of the fetus, which may help in diagnosing sex-linked disorders. In some cultures in which male births are prized, the procedure has been used for "sex-screening" of unborn babies (see Box 3-3).

Amniocentesis is much less common than ultrasound; only 3.2 percent of mothers with live births used it in 1995 (Ventura et al., 1997). It is recommended for pregnant women ages 35 and over. It is also recommended if the woman and her partner are both known carriers of diseases such as Tay-Sachs and sickle-cell anemia, or if they have a family history of such conditions as Down syndrome, spina bifida, Rh disease, and muscular dystrophy.

Although amniocentesis is generally considered safe, reliable, and accurate, one large-scale study found a slightly higher risk of miscarriage in women who had the procedure (Tabor et al., 1986). Amniocentesis is usually done between the fifteenth and eighteenth weeks of pregnancy. Women who have the test done earlier may greatly increase their risk of miscarriage, which is more common during the first trimester. A randomized Canadian study found a 7.6 percent rate of fetal loss when amniocentesis was done between the eleventh and twelfth weeks of gestation, as compared with 5.9 percent between the fifteenth and sixteenth weeks. There was also a greater incidence of foot deformities (Canadian Early and Mid-Trimester Amniocentesis Trial [CEMAT] Group, 1998). In another Canadian study, tested babies were no more likely than untested ones to have problems relating to intelligence, language, or behavior. They did, however, seem to be at slightly greater risk of ear infections and middle-ear abnormalities, though their hearing was not affected (Finegan et al., 1990).

Chorionic Villus Sampling

In *chorionic villus sampling (CVS),* tissue from the ends of villi—hairlike projections of the membrane around the fetus, which are made up of fetal cells—are

amniocentesis Prenatal diagnostic procedure in which a sample of amniotic fluid is withdrawn and analyzed to determine whether any of certain genetic defects are present.

chorionic villus sampling (CVS) Prenatal diagnostic procedure in which tissue from villi (hairlike projections of the membrane surrounding the fetus) is analyzed for birth defects.

Box 3-3   Ancient Cultures and New Technology

What happens when state-of-the-art technology is applied in the service of ancient cultural mores?

Amniocentesis and ultrasound were developed to detect birth defects; coincidentally, they can disclose the sex of the fetus. In the past 20 years, since these procedures became available in Asian countries where male babies have traditionally been preferred over female babies and efforts to fight poverty depend on holding down the birth rate, thousands of women have undergone amniocentesis or ultrasound solely to determine the sex of their unborn children. Many female fetuses have been aborted, with the result that in these populations males now predominate (J. F. Burns, 1994; Kristof, 1993; WuDunn, 1997).

In many male-dominated Asian countries, sons are wanted because they carry on the family name and family traditions, perform religious rituals, and often support aging parents. Since daughters usually go to live with their in-laws after marriage, their economic value to their parents is limited. Furthermore, their dowry can be costly; in India, although such payments are technically outlawed, in practice the expected sum can be more than 10 times a rural family's entire income for a year (J. F. Burns, 1994). One Indian woman pregnant with a fifth daughter burst into tears, crying that her husband would throw her out of the house if she did not produce a son (Weisman, 1988). In Korea, women who do not bear sons may fear their husbands will divorce them; in the past, men whose wives had not borne a male heir often took concubines, but that is no longer done (WuDunn, 1997). These customs and attitudes have resulted in mistreatment of girls, who often receive less food, less schooling, and poorer medical care than boys. Outright killing or abandonment of infant girls, as well as deaths from extreme neglect, have been common in some places.

In recent years, as a result of the new medical technology, far fewer girls have been born. In China, where the government since 1979 has decreed that families have no more than one child—a policy that still stands, even though it is unevenly enforced (see Box 10-3)—an estimated 12 percent of female fetuses were aborted in 1993. In one county alone, ultrasound was used in 2,316 cases, resulting in 1,006 abortions of female fetuses (Kristof, 1993). Laws to ban such testing except for medical reasons have been adopted, but their effectiveness is in question.

In India, ending a pregnancy just because the fetus is female has been against the law for several years, but the practice has continued; child welfare organizations estimate that tens of thousands of such abortions take place every year. As a result of protests by feminist groups and health officials, a new law was passed by the Indian Parliament in 1994 imposing fines and prison sentences on doctors or patients who give or take prenatal tests solely to determine the sex of the fetus. However, the penalties apply only to clinics, laboratories, and hospitals; thousands of mobile clinics equipped with compact ultrasound machines are beyond the reach of the law. Some women's advocates object to prosecuting women, whose husbands often are the ones who make the decision to abort (J. F. Burns, 1994).

In the face of the continuing pressure to bear sons, there is grave doubt about how effectively such a law can be enforced. And, unless social attitudes or economic realities change, the net effect in India, as in China, may be to drive families back to the ancient practice—outlawed under British colonial laws more than 100 years ago, but still common—of killing baby girls soon after birth or neglecting them so badly that they die of illness or starvation (J. F. Burns, 1994).

In South Korea, aborting female fetuses has been a crime since 1994, and disclosing the sex of a fetus is also against the law. Still, women who feel they have failed their husbands by conceiving girls often bribe doctors to perform secret tests and abortions. Indications are that 1 female fetus in 12 is aborted because of sex. In some regions, 125 boys are born for every 100 girls (WuDunn, 1997).

Women's low status in South Korea, as in some other Asian countries, is resistant to change because it is derived from traditional Confucian principles. But demographers anticipate a problem when today's lopsided cohort of babies reaches marriageable age (WuDunn, 1997). In China, with its one-child policy, the girl shortage is particularly dramatic: official data show that of the 25 million babies born each year, 750,000 more are males than females. Predictions are that eventually about 90 million men will be unable to find wives (Hutchings, 1997).

---

tested for the presence of birth defects and disorders. This procedure can be performed between 8 and 13 weeks of pregnancy (earlier than amniocentesis), and it yields results sooner (within about a week). However, one study found almost a 5 percent greater chance of miscarriage or neonatal death after CVS than after amniocentesis. Also, CVS diagnoses can be ambiguous, so women may need to undergo amniocentesis anyway (D'Alton & DeCherney, 1993).

Embryoscopy

Embryoscopy, insertion of a tiny viewing scope into a pregnant woman's abdomen, can provide a clear look at embryos as young as 6 weeks. The procedure

embryoscopy Prenatal medical procedure in which a scope is inserted in the abdomen of a pregnant woman to permit viewing of the embryo for diagnosis and treatment of abnormalities.

is promising for early diagnosis and treatment of embryonic and fetal abnormalities (Quintero, Abuhamad, Hobbins, & Mahoney, 1993).

Preimplantation Genetic Diagnosis

Preimplantation genetic diagnosis can identify genetic defects in embryos of four to eight cells, which were conceived by in vitro fertilization (see Chapter 2) and have not yet been implanted in the mother's uterus. In one study, researchers extracted and examined a single cell for cystic fibrosis (Handyside, Lesko, Tarín, Winston, & Hughes, 1992). Defective embryos were not implanted.

preimplantation genetic diagnosis Medical procedure in which cells from an embryo conceived by in vitro fertilization are analyzed for genetic defects prior to implantation of the embryo in the mother's uterus.

Umbilical Cord Blood Sampling

By inserting a needle into tiny blood vessels of the umbilical cord under the guidance of ultrasound, doctors can take samples of a fetus's blood. They can then get a blood count, examine liver function, and assess various other body functions. This procedure, called *umbilical cord sampling,* or *fetal blood sampling,* can test for infection, anemia, certain metabolic disorders and immunodeficiencies, and heart failure, and it seems to offer promise for identifying still other conditions. However, the technique is associated with miscarriage, bleeding from the umbilical cord, early labor, and infection (Chervenak, Isaacson, & Mahoney, 1986; Kolata, 1988). It should be used only when diagnostic information cannot be obtained by safer means (D'Alton & DeCherney, 1993).

umbilical cord sampling Prenatal medical procedure in which samples of a fetus's blood are taken from the umbilical cord to assess body functioning; also called *fetal blood sampling.*

Maternal Blood Tests

A blood sample taken from the mother between the sixteenth and eighteenth weeks of pregnancy can be tested for the amount of alpha fetoprotein (AFP) it contains. This *maternal blood test* is appropriate for women at risk of bearing children with defects in the formation of the brain or spinal cord, such as anencephaly or spina bifida, which may be detected by high AFP levels. To confirm or refute the presence of suspected conditions, ultrasound or amniocentesis, or both, may be performed.

maternal blood test Prenatal diagnostic procedure to detect the presence of fetal abnormalities, used particularly when the fetus is at risk of defects in the central nervous system.

Blood tests of samples taken between the fifteenth and twentieth weeks of gestation can predict about 60 percent of cases of Down syndrome. The diagnosis can then be confirmed by amniocentesis. This blood test is particularly important for women under 35, who bear 80 percent of all Down syndrome babies, because they are not usually targeted to receive amniocentesis (Haddow et al., 1992). Blood tests can identify carriers of such diseases as sickle-cell anemia, Tay-Sachs disease, and thalassemia. They also can reveal the sex of a fetus (Lo et al., 1989).

The discovery that fetal cells which "leak" into the mother's blood early in pregnancy can be isolated and analyzed (Simpson & Elias, 1993) will make it possible to detect genetic as well as chromosomal disorders from a maternal blood test without using more invasive, risky procedures, such as amniocentesis, chorionic villus sampling, or fetal blood sampling. Already researchers have succeeded in screening fetal blood cells for single genes for sickle cell anemia and thalassemia (Cheung, Goldberg, & Kan, 1996).

Fetal Therapy

In 1984, a Houston boy named David, who had spent almost his entire life inside a plastic tent designed to protect him from any contact with germs, died at the age of 12 after an unsuccessful bone marrow transplant. The transplant was an effort to cure him of a rare sex-linked genetic disorder, severe combined immunodeficiency, which prevented his own bone marrow from producing the white blood cells needed to fight off infection. The condition affects about 1 in 100,000 babies, mostly boys, and most of them die within the first year of life, even if a marrow transplant is performed shortly after birth ("Bone Marrow Transplant," 1996).

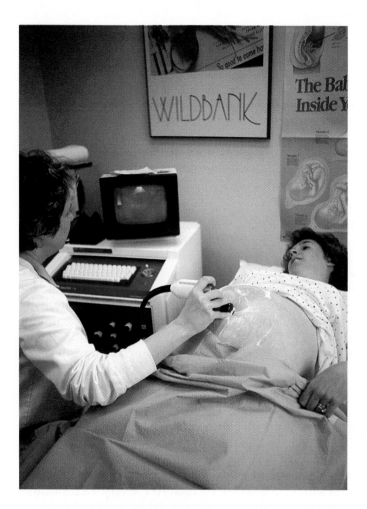

The most effective way to prevent birth complications is early prenatal care, which may include ultrasound checkups, such as this woman is having, to follow the fetus's development. Ultrasound is a diagnostic tool that presents an immediate image of the fetus in the womb.

CHECKPOINT

Can you . . .

- Describe some techniques for identifying defects or disorders in an embryo or fetus and discuss their advantages and disadvantages?

- Name three forms of fetal therapy?

In 1996, surgeons successfully performed a bone marrow transplant in the womb, preventing the development of the same immune disorder in an unborn male baby who had been identified by chorionic villus sampling as having the mutant gene for it (Flake et al., 1996). The baby was born healthy by cesarean delivery and showed no sign of the disorder throughout infancy. Similar transplantation procedures, used with caution, may be effective in treating other congenital diseases.

Surgery performed in the womb is not the only means of correcting conditions detected by prenatal assessment. Fetuses can swallow and absorb medicines, nutrients, vitamins, and hormones that are injected into the amniotic fluid. Blood can be transfused through the umbilical cord as early as the eighteenth week of pregnancy, and drugs that might not pass through the placenta can be injected through the cord.

Prenatal Care

Screening for treatable defects and diseases is only one reason for the importance of prenatal care. Early prenatal care, which also includes educational, social, and nutritional services, can help prevent maternal and infant death and other complications of birth. It can provide first-time mothers with information about pregnancy, childbirth, and infant care. Poor women who get prenatal care benefit by being put in touch with other needed services, and they are more likely to get medical care for their infants after birth (Shiono & Behrman, 1995).

Any pregnant woman in, for example, Belgium, Denmark, Germany, France, Ireland, Netherlands, Norway, Spain, Switzerland, Great Britain, or Israel can experience good maternity care. Every woman in these countries is entitled to

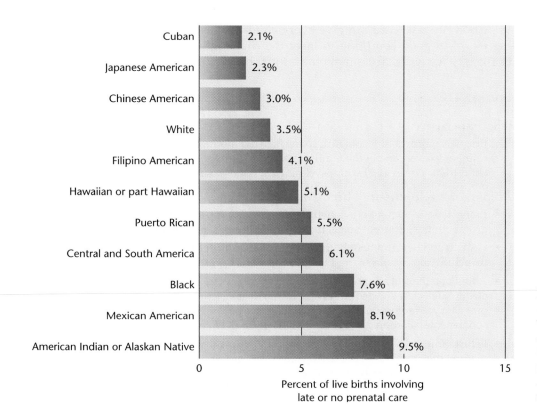

Cuban	2.1%		
Japanese American	2.3%		
Chinese American	3.0%		
White	3.5%		
Filipino American	4.1%		
Hawaiian or part Hawaiian	5.1%		
Puerto Rican	5.5%		
Central and South America	6.1%		
Black	7.6%		
Mexican American	8.1%		
American Indian or Alaskan Native	9.5%		

Percent of live births involving
late or no prenatal care

Figure 3-5
Proportion of American mothers with late or no prenatal care, according to race and ethnicity. Figures are for 1995. Late prenatal care begins in the last 3 months of pregnancy.
Source: NCHS, 1997.

health services and social support, including free or very low cost prenatal and postnatal care and paid maternity leave from work. The women tend to seek early prenatal care, which enables them to begin receiving such benefits as transportation privileges and preferential hospital booking for delivery. Typically, a general practitioner coordinates care with a midwife and an obstetrician; the midwife provides most of the prenatal care and attends the birth unless the pregnancy is considered high-risk.

Although prenatal care has become widespread in the United States, its form and quality vary greatly due to the absence of uniform national standards and guaranteed financial coverage. The percentage of pregnant women who start care during the first trimester of pregnancy has grown since 1970. Still, in 1995 about 19 percent of expectant mothers did not get care until after the first trimester, and 4.2 percent received no care until the last trimester or no care at all (National Center for Health Statistics [NCHS], 1997; Ventura et al., 1997). Women most at risk of bearing low-birthweight babies—teenage, unmarried, and some minority women, and women with little education—get the least prenatal care (S. S. Brown, 1985; Ingram, Makuc, & Kleinman, 1986; NCHS, 1994a; S. Singh, Forrest, & Torres, 1989; USDHHS, 1996a; see Figure 3-5).

Early prenatal care can reduce the incidence of low birth weight (discussed more fully in Chapter 4). Unfortunately, most prenatal care programs in the United States start too late to address this problem effectively, and they are not designed to attack its causes. Instead, the main focus is on screening for major complications (Shiono & Behrman, 1995).

A national panel has recommended that prenatal care be restructured to provide more visits early in the pregnancy and fewer in the last trimester, and that it be targeted to the specific needs of the woman and the fetus. In addition, care needs to be made more accessible to poor women and those from disadvantaged groups. In fact, care should begin before pregnancy. Prepregnancy counseling could make more women aware, for example, of the importance of getting enough folic acid in their diet and making sure that they are immune to rubella (Shiono & Behrman, 1995).

CHECKPOINT

Can you . . .

- Tell why early prenatal care is important?
- List at least three recommendations for improving prenatal care in the United States?

Good prenatal care can give every child the best possible chance of entering the world in good condition to meet the challenges of life outside the womb—challenges we will discuss in the next four chapters.

SUMMARY

The Experience of Pregnancy

- Pregnancy brings physiological changes to the mother's body and psychosocial changes to everyone in the family. Prospective parents develop an attachment to the child-to-be as they deal with psychological issues connected with the coming birth.

Prenatal Development: Three Stages

- Prenatal development is a genetically directed process that occurs in three stages of **gestation:** the **germinal stage,** the **embryonic stage,** and the **fetal stage.**

- Growth and development both before and after birth follow the **cephalocaudal principle** (top to bottom) and the **proximodistal principle** (center outward).

- About one-third of all conceptions end in **spontaneous abortion** (miscarriage). Nearly all birth defects and three out of four miscarriages occur in the first trimester of pregnancy. Chromosomal abnormalities are present in about 50 to 70 percent of spontaneous abortions. Males are more likely than females to be spontaneously aborted.

- Fetuses interact actively with their environment within the womb. As they grow and mature, they move less, but more vigorously, and show changes in heart rate, cardiac response, and coordination of sleep-wake states. Fetuses appear to be able to hear, exercise sensory discrimination, learn, and remember.

Prenatal Development: Environmental Hazards

- The developing organism can be greatly affected by its prenatal environment. Some environmental factors are **teratogenic;** the likelihood of birth defects may depend on the timing and intensity of an environmental event and its interaction with genetic factors.

- Important environmental influences involving the mother include nutrition, physical activity, smoking, drinking (which can produce **fetal alcohol syndrome,** or **FAS**), intake of other legal or illegal drugs, transmission of **acquired immune deficiency syndrome (AIDS),** other maternal illnesses or infections, maternal age, incompatibility of blood type, and external environmental hazards, such as chemicals and radiation. Such external influences may also affect the father's sperm.

Monitoring Prenatal Development

- **Ultrasound, amniocentesis, chorionic villus sampling (CVS), embryoscopy, preimplantation genetic diagnosis, umbilical cord sampling,** and **maternal blood tests** are used to determine whether an unborn baby is developing normally. Some abnormal conditions can be corrected through fetal therapy in the womb.

- One important ethical debate concerns the conflict between a fetus's right to be born healthy and a mother's right to privacy and bodily autonomy.

- Good prenatal care is essential for healthy development. It can lead to detection of defects and disorders and, especially if begun early in a pregnancy, can reduce maternal and infant death, low birthweight, and other birth complications.

KEY TERMS

gestation (94)
cephalocaudal principle (95)
proximodistal principle (95)
germinal stage (95)
embryonic stage (98)
spontaneous abortion (98)
fetal stage (99)
ultrasound (99)
teratogenic (103)

fetal alcohol syndrome (FAS) (106)
acquired immune deficiency syndrome (AIDS) (110)
amniocentesis (115)
chorionic villus sampling (CVS) (115)
embryoscopy (116)
preimplantation genetic diagnosis (117)
umbilical cord sampling (117)
maternal blood test (117)

QUESTIONS FOR THOUGHT AND DISCUSSION

1. During pregnancy, prospective parents usually have a number of emotional issues to resolve. If you have had a baby, which of the following issues were of most concern to you? If you have not yet had a child, which do you imagine would be most likely to affect you?
    *   Accepting the idea that your child will be an individual with his or her own interests, which may not be compatible with your own
    *   Anticipating the effect your new baby will have on your marriage
    *   Resolving your relationship with your own parents

2. Does society's interest in protecting an unborn child justify coercive measures against pregnant women who ingest alcohol or other drugs that could harm the fetus? If so, what form should such measures take? Should pregnant women who refuse to stop drinking or get treatment be incarcerated until they give birth? Should mothers of children with FAS be sterilized if they intend to keep drinking and reproducing? Should liquor companies be held liable if adequate warnings are not on their products? Would your answers be the same regarding smoking or use of cocaine or other potentially harmful substances? Since these substances can produce genetic abnormalities in a man's sperm, should men of childbearing age be forced to abstain from them? How could such a prohibition be enforced?

3. Hundreds of adults now alive suffered gross abnormalities of development because, during the 1950s, their mothers took the tranquilizer thalidomide during pregnancy. As a result, the use of thalidomide was banned in the United States and some other countries. Now thalidomide has been found to be effective in treating or controlling many illnesses, from cancer to leprosy. Should its use for these purposes be permitted even though there is a risk that pregnant women might take it?

4. In the United States, women who undergo ultrasound or amniocentesis are given the choice of whether or not they will be told their unborn babies' sex. Suppose it became known that substantial numbers of American women were aborting their fetuses for reasons of sex preference. In that case, would you favor a law forbidding use of a prenatal diagnostic procedure to reveal the sex of a fetus?

5. Should therapeutic abortions continue to be available to women who learn that they are carrying a fetus with a major defect?

6. Can you suggest ways to induce more pregnant women to seek early prenatal care?

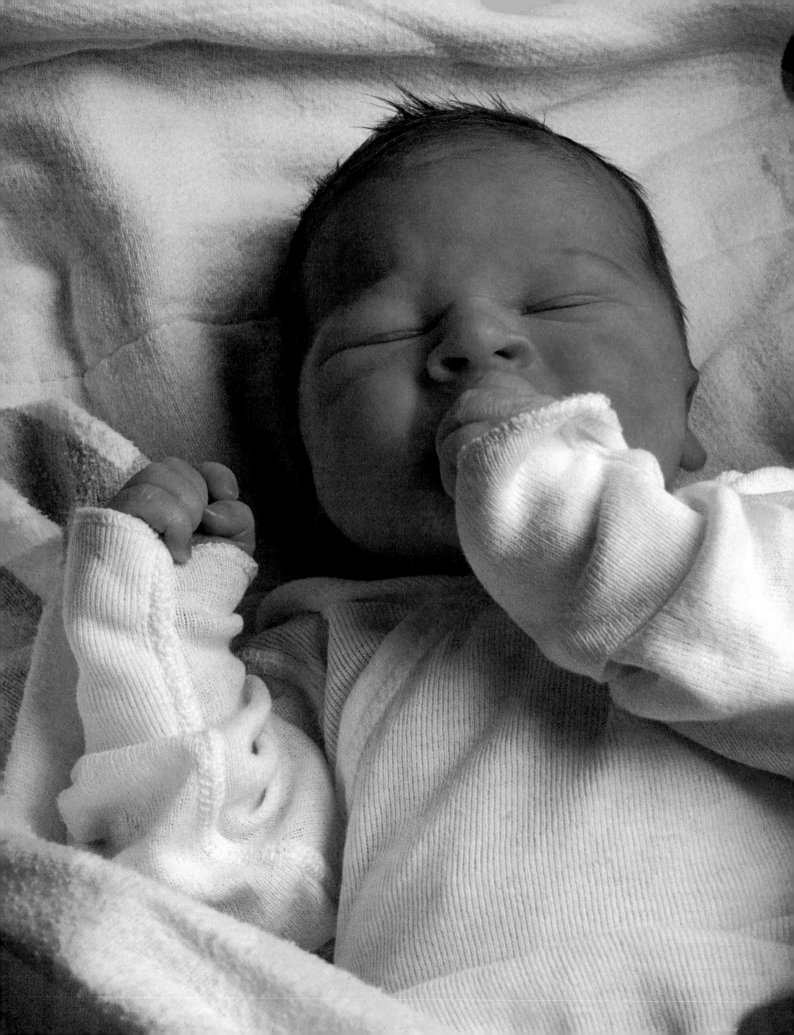

Birth and the Newborn Baby

*A newborn baby is an extraordinary event;
and I have never seen two babies who looked
exactly alike. Here is the breathing miracle
who could not live an instant without you,
with a skull more fragile than an egg, a miracle
of eyes, legs, toenails, and lungs.*

James Baldwin, *No Name in the Street,* 1972

Focus

The Birth of Elvis Presley

E lvis Presley was born on January 8, 1935, in a 30- by 15-foot cottage in East Tupelo,
Mississippi, in the lower Appalachian hill country. Today, the modest birthplace of
the now-legendary "king" of rock music is painted sparkling white, the walls are pa-
pered with primroses, and dainty curtains hang at the windows. A high chair, a sewing machine, a fan, a radio, a screen door, a porch swing, a brick walk, a lawn, and a boxwood
hedge are among the homey touches that have been added for the benefit of tourists. But,
like many of the popular myths about Elvis's early life, this "cute little doll house" (A. Goldman, 1981, p. 60) bears only slight resemblance to the reality: a bare board shack with no indoor plumbing or electricity, set on piles of rocks on a patch of hard-packed soil in a dirt-poor
hamlet that wasn't much more than "a wide spot in the road" (Clayton & Heard, 1994, p. 8).

During the Great Depression, Elvis's near-illiterate father, Vernon Elvis Presley, sometimes
picked up work as a carpenter or milk truck driver or did odd jobs for a farmer named Orville
Bean, who owned much of the town. Elvis's mother, born Gladys Smith, was vivacious and
high-spirited, as talkative as Vernon was taciturn. She, like Vernon, came from a family of
sharecroppers and migrant workers; she had grown up on a farm outside of town. Her father
had died when she was 20, and she had found a job in a garment factory in the nearby city
of Tupelo, earning about two dollars a day. It was then that she and her family had moved to
East Tupelo to be closer to her work.

East Tupelo was a town of maybe 20 houses, where everybody knew everybody else.
The Presley and Smith families lived a literal stone's throw from each other. Gladys first noticed handsome Vernon on the street and then, soon after, met him in church. They eloped
on June 17, 1933. Vernon, who was 17—not legally old enough to marry—put down his age
as 22. To minimize the difference in their ages, Gladys, who was 21, said she was 19. They
borrowed the three dollars for the license from friends.

At first the young couple lived with friends and family. When Gladys became pregnant the
following spring, Vernon borrowed $180 from his sometime employer, Bean, to buy lumber and

Focus—*Continued*

nails and, with the help of his father and older brother, built a two-room cabin next to his parents' house on Old Saltillo Road. According to Elvis's cousin Harold Loyd, Vernon's creation "wasn't much of a house," but Vernon and Gladys "were real proud of it" (Clayton & Heard, 1994). Bean, who owned the land, was to hold title to the house until the loan was paid off.

Vernon and Gladys moved into their new home in December, 1934, only about a month before she gave birth to twins. Her pregnancy was a difficult one; her legs swelled, and she finally quit her job at the garment factory, where she had to stand on her feet all day pushing a heavy steam iron.

The January night when Gladys delivered was bitterly cold. When Vernon got up for work in the wee hours of the morning, Gladys was hemorrhaging. The midwife told Vernon to get the doctor, Will Hunt. There is no indication that Dr. Hunt had seen Gladys before. Since the young parents could not afford his $15 fee, it was paid by welfare. At about 4 o'clock in the morning, Dr. Hunt delivered a stillborn baby boy, Jesse Garon. The second twin, Elvis Aron, was born about 35 minutes later. His father later claimed that he had gone out in the yard that night and had seen a ring of blue light in the sky.

Dr. Hunt, who doubled as a Sunday school teacher, announced the births in church, and neighbors came over to offer sympathy and help. Gladys was extremely weak from her ordeal and was losing blood. She and baby Elvis had to be taken to the hospital, where they stayed in the charity ward for more than 3 weeks. Gladys barely recovered and never had another child.

Baby Jesse was buried in an unmarked grave but remained an important part of the family's life. Gladys, who was highly superstitious, frequently talked to Elvis about his brother. "When one twin died, the one that lived got the strength of both," she would say (Guralnick, 1994, p. 13). Elvis, who was unusually attached to his mother, took her words to heart. Throughout his life, his twin's imagined voice and presence were constantly with him.

As for Elvis's birthplace, he lived there only until the age of 3. Vernon, who sold a pig to Bean for $4, was accused of altering the check to $40. He was sent to prison, and when the payment on the house loan came due, Bean evicted Gladys and her son, who had to move in with family members until Vernon was released. In later years, Elvis would drive back to East Tupelo (which since has been annexed to Tupelo and has become suburban Presley Heights). He would sit in his car in the dark, looking at the cottage on what is now called Elvis Presley Drive and "thinking about the course his life had taken" (Marling, 1996, p. 20).

Sources of information about Elvis Presley's birth were Clayton & Heard, 1994; Dundy, 1985; Goldman, 1981; Guralnick, 1994; and Marling, 1996.

• • •

Elvis Presley is just one of many well-known people—including almost all the presidents of the United States—who were born at home. At one time, medical care during pregnancy was rare, and births were usually attended by midwives. Birth complications and stillbirth were common, and many women died in childbirth. A rising standard of living—together with such medical advances as antibiotics, blood transfusions, and anesthesia—have eased childbirth and reduced its risks. Today, the overwhelming majority of births in the United States occur in hospitals. However, there is a small but growing movement back to home birth and delivery by midwives rather than physicians, as is still the custom in less-developed countries.

In this chapter we see how babies come into the world: the stages, methods, joys, and complications of birth. We describe how newborn infants look, how their body systems work, and how their brains grow. We discuss ways to assess their health, and how birth complications can affect development. We also consider how the birth of a baby affects the people most vital to the infant's well-being: the parents.

After reading this chapter, you should be able to answer and elaborate on such questions as these:

Preview Questions

- What happens during the four stages of childbirth?

- What are the advantages and disadvantages of various methods and settings of childbirth?

- What complications of childbirth can endanger newborn babies' adjustment or even their lives?

- How do newborn infants adjust to life outside the womb, and how can we tell whether they are healthy and developing normally?

- How do parents react to childbirth, and how does parenthood change their relationship?

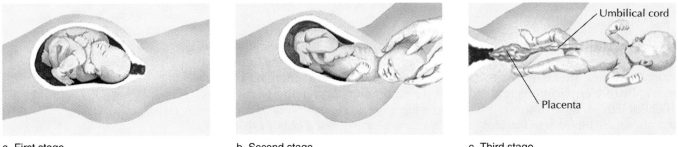

a. First stage   b. Second stage   c. Third stage

Figure 4-1

The first three stages of childbirth. (*a*) During the first stage of labor, a series of stronger and stronger contractions dilates the cervix, the opening to the mother's womb. (*b*) During the second stage, the baby's head moves down the birth canal and emerges from the vagina. (*c*) During the brief third stage, the placenta and umbilical cord are expelled from the womb. Then the cord is cut. During the fourth stage, recovery from delivery (not shown), the mother's uterus contracts.

Source: Adapted from Lagercrantz & Slotkin, 1986.

The Birth Process

Birth is both a beginning and an end: the climax of all that has happened from the moment of fertilization. *Labor* is an apt term. Birth is hard work for both mother and baby—but work that yields a rich reward. The work will continue for years as the parents learn to care for their child and the child learns how to make a life in the world.

The uterine contractions that expel the fetus begin as mild tightenings of the uterus. A woman may have felt similar contractions at times during the final months of pregnancy, but she may recognize birth contractions as the "real thing" because of their greater regularity and intensity.

As in many animal species, maturation of the human fetus determines when birth begins—typically, 266 days after conception. The process is controlled by the fetus's brain. When vital organs, such as the lungs, are ready for life outside the womb, endocrine changes in the fetus signal the mother's body to produce large quantities of estrogen, which stimulate the uterus to contract and the cervix to dilate, or widen (Nathanielsz, 1995). Thus, from the start, human beings act upon their environment to create conditions for development.

Stages of Childbirth

Childbirth, or labor, takes place in four overlapping stages (see Figure 4-1). The *first stage,* the longest, typically lasts 12 hours or more for a woman having her first child. However, there is a great deal of variability among women and even among different pregnancies of the same woman. In later births the first stage tends to be shorter. During this stage, uterine contractions cause the cervix to dilate. At first, contractions occur about every 8 to 10 minutes and last about 30 seconds; toward the end of labor, they may come every 2 minutes and last 60 to 90 seconds.

Much of the discomfort of labor is caused by the stretching of the lower part of the uterus, especially the cervix. Before the cervix can dilate enough to let the baby's head pass through, it needs to soften and thin out, through a process called *effacement.* Effacement and early dilation begin during the last weeks of pregnancy. If a woman's cervix dilates quickly during labor, she will feel little or no pain; but if her cervix is rigid and is forcibly dilated by the contractions of her uterus, the contractions will be painful.

The *second stage* typically lasts about 1½ hours or less. It begins when the baby's head starts to move through the cervix into the vaginal canal, and it ends when the baby emerges completely from the mother's body. It is also known as the "pushing" stage, since the mother feels the urge to push to help the baby in its efforts to leave her body by bearing down hard with her abdominal muscles at each contraction. If this stage lasts longer than 2 hours, signalling that the baby needs more help, a doctor may grasp the baby's head with forceps or use vacuum extraction to pull it out of the mother's body. At the end of this stage, the baby is born; but it is still attached to the placenta in the mother's body by the umbilical cord, which must be cut and clamped.

During the *third stage,* which lasts about 5 to 30 minutes, the placenta and the remainder of the umbilical cord are expelled from the mother. The couple of hours after delivery constitute the *fourth stage,* when the mother rests in bed while her uterus contracts and her recovery is monitored.

Methods of Delivery

The primary concerns in choosing a method for delivering a baby are the comfort of the mother and, especially, the safety of both mother and baby. Recently, as safety has become more assured in most normal births in developed countries, health workers have focused on making the experience more pleasant and on meeting emotional needs by bringing the father and other family members into the process.

Medicated Delivery

Most societies have evolved techniques to hasten delivery, make labor easier, and lessen discomfort. General anesthesia, which renders the woman completely unconscious, is rarely used today. More common is regional (local) anesthesia, which blocks the nerve pathways that would carry the sensation of pain to the brain; or the mother can receive a relaxing analgesic. All these drugs pass through the placenta to enter the fetal blood supply and tissues.

A number of studies indicate that obstetric medication may pose dangers to the baby. In women who have local spinal injections (epidurals), there is a heightened risk of fever, which may necessitate costly and uncomfortable testing and treatment of her newborn baby for possible infection—even though, in most cases, the fever turns out to be noninfectious. Women who are considering epidural anesthesia are advised to discuss this concern with their doctors (E. Lieberman et al., 1997).

In earlier studies, infants appeared to show immediate effects of obstetric medication in poorer motor and physiologic responses (A. D. (Murray, Dolby, Nation, & Thomas, 1981) and, through the first year, in slower motor development (Brackbill & Broman, 1979). In one study (A. D. Murray et al., 1981), the babies born in medicated deliveries had caught up by 1 month of age, but their mothers felt differently about them. Why? An alert infant, who nurses eagerly, generates positive feelings in the mother. If the first encounters between mother and baby do not draw a strong reaction from the baby, the mother's early impressions of her baby may dampen the interaction between them. On the other hand, it is possible that mothers who choose unmedicated deliveries may have more positive feelings about becoming parents, and these feelings may affect how they act with their babies.

Some research suggests, however, that medicated delivery may *not* do measurable harm. When babies born to medicated and nonmedicated mothers were compared on strength, tactile sensitivity, activity, irritability, and sleep patterns, no evidence of any drug effect appeared (Kraemer, Korner, Anders, Jacklin, & Dimiceli, 1985). The authors of this study suggest that poorly designed and misleading research may have kept appropriate drugs from some mothers, making them suffer unnecessary discomfort, while causing mothers who did receive drugs to feel guilty. Because the mother is the only person who can gauge her pain and is one of the two people most concerned about her child's well-being, she should be the one who decides about her obstetric medication.

In Lamaze classes for expectant parents, mothers learn breathing and muscular exercises to make labor easier, and fathers learn how to assist during labor and delivery.

natural childbirth Method of childbirth, developed by Dr. Grantly Dick-Read, that seeks to prevent pain by eliminating the mother's fear of childbirth through education about the physiology of reproduction and training in methods of breathing and relaxation during delivery.

prepared childbirth Method of childbirth, developed by Dr. Ferdinand Lamaze, that uses instruction, breathing exercises, and social support to induce controlled physical responses to uterine contractions and reduce fear and pain.

cesarean delivery Delivery of a baby by surgical removal from the uterus.

Natural and Prepared Childbirth

Two alternative methods of childbirth have been developed to minimize the use of drugs while maximizing the parents' active involvement. In 1914 a British physician, Dr. Grantly Dick-Read, claimed that pain in childbirth was not inevitable but was caused mostly by fear. To eliminate fear, he advocated *natural childbirth:* educating women about the physiology of reproduction and training them in physical fitness and in breathing and relaxation during delivery. By midcentury, Dr. Ferdinand Lamaze was using the *prepared childbirth* method of obstetrics. This technique substitutes controlled physical responses to the sensations of uterine contractions for the old responses of fear and pain.

The Lamaze method has become very popular in the United States. It entails (1) learning about the anatomy and physiology involved in childbirth to reduce fear, (2) training in such techniques as rapid breathing and panting "in sync" with the contractions to ease pain, and (3) concentrating on sensations other than the contractions. The mother learns to relax her muscles as a conditioned response to the voice of her "coach" (usually the father or a friend). The coach attends classes with her, takes part in the delivery, and helps with the exercises. This support enhances her sense of self-worth and reassures her that she will not be alone at the time of birth (Wideman & Singer, 1984).

Cesarean Delivery

Cesarean delivery is a surgical procedure to remove the baby from the uterus by cutting through the abdomen. Such deliveries have increased dramatically since 1970, when they accounted for only 5.5 percent of births in the United States (Centers for Disease Control and Prevention [CDC], 1993). By 1985, the cesarean birth rate in the United States was among the highest in the world (Notzon, 1990), but the rate has declined during the 1990s. Just over 1 in 5 babies—20.8 percent, or nearly 807,000—were delivered this way in 1995, an 8 percent decrease since 1991; and the rate of vaginal births for women who had previously had cesareans rose by 29 percent during the same period, from 21.3 to 27.5 percent (Curtin, 1997).

The operation is commonly performed when labor does not progress as quickly as it should, when the fetus seems to be in trouble, or when the mother is bleeding vaginally. Often a cesarean is needed when the fetus is in the breech position (feet first) or in the transverse position (lying crosswise in the uterus), or when its head is too big to pass through the mother's pelvis. Surgical deliveries are more likely when the birth involves a first baby, a large baby, or an older mother. Thus the increase in cesarean rates after 1970 was in part a reflection of a proportional increase in first births, a rise in average birthweight, and a trend toward later childbirth (Parrish, Holt, Easterling, Connell, & LeGerfo, 1994). The more recent decline in cesarean deliveries reflects a growing belief that this procedure is unnecessary or even harmful in many cases.

Disadvantages of cesarean deliveries for the mother include a longer hospital stay and recovery, greater expense, and the physical and psychological impacts of surgery (Sachs et al., 1983). About 4 percent of cesareans result in serious complications, such as bleeding and infections (K. B. Nelson, Dambrosia, Ting, & Grether, 1996). For the baby, there may be an important risk in bypassing the experience of labor, which may help in the adjustment to life outside the womb. The struggle to be born apparently stimulates the infant's body to produce huge amounts of two stress hormones, adrenaline and noradrenaline. The surge of these hormones at birth clears the lungs of excess fluid to permit breathing, mobilizes stored fuel to nourish cells, and sends blood to the heart and brain. Also, by making the baby more alert and ready to interact with another person, these hormones may promote the mother-infant bond (Lagercrantz & Slotkin, 1986).

Despite the advantages of vaginal birth, a vaginal delivery for a woman who has had an earlier cesarean delivery should be attempted with caution. Labor in such a subsequent birth is successful about 70 percent of the time, usually with good results (Hook, Kiwi, Amini, Fanaroff, & Hack, 1997). Among 6,138 women in Nova Scotia, the *overall* chances of complications (which are small in any case) were no greater than with a second cesarean. However, attempted vaginal delivery brought twice the risk of *major* complications to the mother, such as rupture of the uterus. The greatest risk of complications was to women whose labor was unsuccessful and who therefore had to undergo a cesarean after all (McMahon, Luther, Bowes, & Olshan, 1996). Among 1,007 births at three Cleveland hospitals to mothers who had had previous cesarean deliveries, babies born by elective cesarean surgery were more likely to have respiratory problems, while those born by cesarean after a failed attempt at normal labor were more apt to develop infections of the blood or tissues (Hook et al., 1997).

Settings and Attendants for Childbirth

In the Netherlands, pregnancy and labor are thought of as normal events that require medical intervention only when there is a specific reason. About 35 percent of Dutch babies are born at home, and about 43 percent of deliveries are attended by midwives. Most of these births are to women deemed to be at low risk, and their outcomes compare very favorably with hospital births attended by obstetricians (Treffers, Eskes, Kleiverda, & van Alten, 1990). In remote rural villages of less developed countries such as Nepal, virtually all births still occur in this traditional, natural way (see Box 4-1).

By contrast, 99 percent of U.S. births take place in hospitals, and nearly 94 percent are attended by physicians (Ventura, Martin, Curtin, & Mathews, 1997). In recent years, many hospitals have established birth centers, where fathers or other birth coaches may remain with the mother during labor and delivery. Many hospitals also have rooming-in policies, which allow babies to stay in the mother's room for much or all of the day and night. However, some women with good medical histories and normal, uncomplicated pregnancies opt for more intimate, personalized settings in their homes or in small, homelike birth centers. These freestanding centers generally offer prenatal care and are staffed principally by nurse-midwives.

Box 4-1 Having a Baby in the Himalayas

In 1993 and 1994, Sally Olds spent three weeks in Badel, a remote hill village in the small Asian country of Nepal. The following account from her journal describes a visit that she, the friend she traveled with, and their guide, Buddi, made to the village midwife.

Sabut Maya Mathani Rai has been helping childbearing mothers for almost 50 of her 75 years. Only three days ago she attended the birth of a baby girl.

When Sabut Maya attends a woman about to give birth, she says, "First I feel on the outside of the woman's belly. I look to see where is the head and the other organs. I help the mother push down when her time comes."

She does not use forceps. "I don't have any instruments," she says. "I just use my hands. If the baby is upside down, I turn it from the outside."

Nepali hill women usually give birth right after, or in the middle of, working in the house or in the fields. The delivery may occur inside or outside of the house, depending on when the woman goes into labor. Women usually give birth on their knees. This kneeling position allows the mother to use her strong thigh and abdominal muscles to push the baby out. If the mother has other children, they usually watch, no matter how small they are. But the husbands don't want to watch and the women don't want them there.

Most women are not attended by a midwife; they handle the delivery and dispose of the placenta and umbilical cord themselves. Buddi's mother once gave birth on the path as she was walking back from working in the fields, and then asked for her husband's knife to cut the cord.

"If the baby is not coming fast, I use special medicine," the midwife says. "I put grasses on the mother's body and I massage her with oil from a special plant. I don't give the mother any herbs or anything like that to eat or drink, only hot water or tea."

In a complicated birth—if, say, the baby is not emerging or the mother gets sick—the midwife calls the *shaman* (spiritual healer). Inevitably, some babies and some mothers die. In most cases, however, all goes well, and most deliveries are easy and quick.

How is the newborn cared for? "After the baby is born I wash the baby. I leave this much of the cord on the baby [indicating about half an inch] and I tie it up with very good cotton. Then I wrap a piece of cotton cloth around the baby's tummy. This stays on for a few days until the cord falls off." Sometimes a small piece of the umbilical cord is saved and inserted into a metal bead that will be given to the child to wear on a string around the neck, to ward off evil spirits. A family member flings the placenta high up on a tree near the house to dry out; it eventually is thrown away.

No one but the mother—not even the father—is allowed to hold the baby at first. This may help to protect both mother and baby from infection and disease when they are most vulnerable. Then, at three days of age for a girl or seven days for a boy (girls are thought to mature earlier), a purification rite and naming ceremony takes place.

My friend and I tell how in our culture women lie on their backs, a position unknown in most traditional societies, and how the doctor sometimes breaks the woman's water. We also describe how a doctor sometimes puts on surgical gloves and reaches inside the woman to turn a baby in a breech or other position. "We don't have gloves and we don't have instruments," Sabut Maya repeats. "We don't do any of those things. I'm just a helper." What Sabut Maya really is is a combination of midwife and doula (described in this chapter)—a kind of helper now seen with growing frequency in western delivery rooms. It seems ironic that it has taken the western world so long to rediscover some of the wisdom that "primitive" societies have known for centuries.

Source: © Sally Wendkos Olds, 1997.

In 1995, 6 percent of expectant mothers in the United States were attended by midwives (Ventura et al., 1997). Most midwives are registered nurses with special training in midwifery; some have been trained by apprenticeship. Midwives may or may not work under a doctor's direction. Women using nurse-midwives rather than doctors for low-risk hospital births tend to have equally good outcomes with less anesthesia. They are less likely to need episiotomies (incisions to enlarge the vaginal opening before birth), to have labor induced, or to end up having cesarean deliveries (Rosenblatt et al., 1997). Of course, these results may not be due to something the midwives did or did not do; rather, women who choose midwives may be more likely to take care of themselves during pregnancy, increasing their chances of normal delivery, and may be less willing to accept medical solutions to problems that arise during a birth.

Home birth is growing in popularity, especially in some western states. Unlike Gladys Presley, who had no choice but to give birth at home, women choosing home birth today are usually motivated by the desire to be in charge of their own birth process, to involve the entire family, and to make the experience as

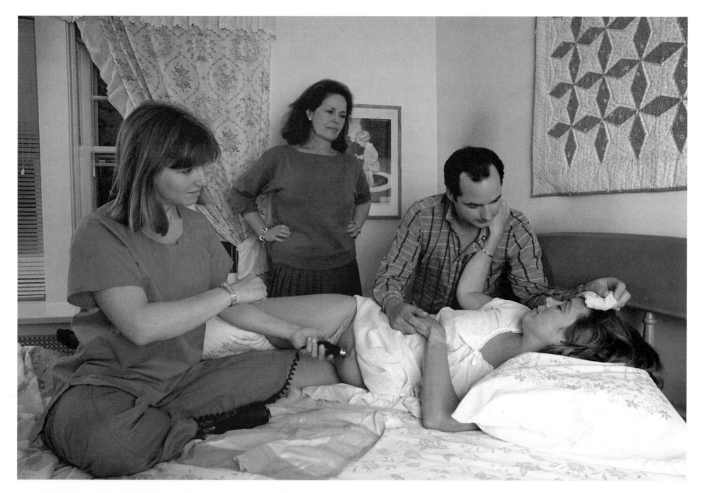

At a birth center in Princeton, New Jersey, a woman gives birth in a small house in a semiresidential area. Her husband and her mother give moral support as the midwife checks the fetal heartbeat. Informal, homelike settings for birth are growing in popularity for women with good medical histories and normal, uncomplicated pregnancies. However, it is essential to have arrangements with an ambulance service and a local hospital in case of emergency.

free and natural as possible. Studies of home births suggest that they can be at least as safe as hospital births in low-risk deliveries attended by skilled practitioners (Durand, 1992; Korte & Scaer, 1984). This may in part be due to the greater tendency in hospital deliveries to choose medical interventions that are not needed and may actually increase risks.

Since there may be a sudden emergency during any birth, it is vital to have backup plans. A good freestanding birth center will have a contract with an ambulance service, an agreement with a local hospital, and on-premises equipment for resuscitation and administration of oxygen. Plans for a home birth should include arrangements for emergency transportation to a nearby hospital.

In many cultures, childbearing women are attended by a *doula,* an experienced mother who can furnish emotional support. Among 412 women having their first babies in a U.S. hospital, 212 had a doula with them, and 200 did not (Kennell, Klaus, McGrath, Robertson, & Hinckley, 1991). The group attended by doulas had shorter labor, less anesthesia, and fewer forceps and cesarean deliveries. These findings argue for a female companion as part of the childbirth support team.

These "new-old" ways of giving birth have important implications. First, techniques that minimize drugs may give the baby a better start in life. Second, the active participation of both parents and other family members can reinforce family ties. Third, women's assumption of a major decision-making role in the

CHECKPOINT

Can you . . .

- Describe the 4 stages of childbirth?
- Compare medicated delivery, natural childbirth, and prepared childbirth?
- Discuss reasons for the decline in cesarean births?
- Assess the comparative advantages of various types of settings and attendants for childbirth?

neonate   Newborn baby, up to 4 weeks old.

neonatal period   First 4 weeks of life, a time of transition from intrauterine dependency to independent existence.

fontanels   Soft spots on head of young infant.

lanugo   Fuzzy prenatal body hair, which drops off within a few days after birth.

vernix caseosa   Oily substance on a neonate's skin that protects against infection.

birth of their children is consistent with the growing tendency for people to take responsibility for their own health. The crucial element is *choice*. Children born in a variety of ways and places can grow up physically and psychologically healthy.

The Newborn

A newborn baby, or *neonate,* is, in an extreme sense, an immigrant. After struggling through a difficult passage, the newcomer is faced with much more than learning a language and customs. A baby must start to breathe, eat, adapt to the climate, and respond to confusing surroundings—a mighty challenge for someone who weighs but a few pounds and whose organ systems are not fully mature. As we'll see, most infants arrive with systems ready to meet that challenge.

The first 4 weeks of life are the *neonatal period*—a time of transition from life in the uterus, when a fetus is supported entirely by its mother, to an independent existence. What are the physical characteristics of newborn babies? How do they function? How are they equipped for this crucial transition?

Size and Appearance

An average newborn in the United States is about 20 inches long and weighs about 7½ pounds. At birth, 95 percent of full-term babies weigh between 5½ and 10 pounds and are between 18 and 22 inches long. Boys tend to be slightly longer and heavier than girls, and a firstborn child is likely to weigh less at birth than later-borns. Size at birth is related to race, sex, parents' size, and the mother's nutrition and health, and tends to predict relative size later in childhood (Behrman, 1992).

In their first few days, neonates lose as much as 10 percent of their body weight, primarily because of a loss of fluids. They begin to gain weight again at about the fifth day and are generally back to birthweight by the tenth to the fourteenth day. Light full-term infants lose less weight than heavy ones, and firstborns lose less than later-borns (Behrman, 1992).

New babies have distinctive features, including a large head (one-fourth the body length) and a receding chin (which makes it easier to nurse). At first, a neonate's head may be long and misshapen because of the "molding" that eased its passage through the mother's pelvis. This temporary molding was possible because an infant's skull bones are not yet fused; they will not be completely joined for 18 months. The places on the head where the bones have not yet grown together—the soft spots, or *fontanels*—are covered by a tough membrane; they will close within the first month of life. Since the cartilage in the baby's nose also is malleable, the trip through the birth canal may leave the nose looking squashed for a few days.

Many newborns have a pinkish cast because their skin is so thin that it barely covers the capillaries through which blood flows. During the first few days, some neonates are very hairy because some of the *lanugo,* a fuzzy prenatal hair, has not yet fallen off. All new babies are covered with *vernix caseosa* ("cheesy varnish"), an oily protection against infection that dries within the first few days.

Body Systems

The newborn's need to survive puts a host of new demands on the body systems. Before birth, blood circulation, breathing, nourishment, elimination of waste, and temperature regulation were accomplished through the mother's body. After birth, babies must do all of this themselves (see Table 4-1). Most newborns do it so well that nobody even remarks on the feat.

Table 4-1	A Comparison of Prenatal and Postnatal Life	
Characteristic	**Prenatal Life**	**Postnatal Life**
Environment	Amniotic fluid	Air
Temperature	Relatively constant	Fluctuates with atmosphere
Stimulation	Minimal	All senses stimulated by various stimuli
Nutrition	Dependent on mother's blood	Dependent on external food and functioning of digestive system
Oxygen supply	Passed from maternal bloodstream via placenta	Passed from neonate's lungs to pulmonary blood vessels
Metabolic elimination	Passed into maternal bloodstream via placenta	Discharged by skin, kidneys, lungs, and gastrointestinal tract

Source: Timiras, 1972, p. 174.

Circulatory System

Before birth, the fetus and mother have separate circulatory systems and separate heartbeats; but the fetus's blood is cleansed through the umbilical cord, which carries "used" blood to the placenta and returns a fresh supply. After birth, the baby's circulatory system must operate on its own. A neonate's heartbeat is fast and irregular, and blood pressure does not stabilize until about the tenth day of life.

Respiratory System

The fetus gets oxygen through the umbilical cord, which also carries away carbon dioxide. A newborn needs much more oxygen than before and must now get it alone. Most babies start to breathe as soon as they are exposed to air. If breathing has not begun within about 5 minutes, the baby may suffer permanent brain injury caused by *anoxia,* lack of oxygen. Because infants' lungs have only one-tenth as many air sacs as adults' do, infants (especially those born prematurely) are susceptible to respiratory problems.

Gastrointestinal System

In the uterus, the fetus relies on the umbilical cord to bring food from the mother and to carry fetal body wastes away. At birth, babies have a strong sucking reflex to take in milk, and their own gastrointestinal secretions to digest it. During the first few days infants secrete *meconium,* a stringy, greenish-black waste matter formed in the fetal intestinal tract. When the bowels and bladder are full, the sphincter muscles open automatically; a baby will not be able to control these muscles for many months.

Three or four days after birth, about half of all babies (and a larger proportion of babies born prematurely) develop *neonatal jaundice:* Their skin and eyeballs look yellow. This kind of jaundice is caused by the immaturity of the liver; usually it is not serious and has no long-term effects. It is treated by medication and by putting the baby under fluorescent lights. Jaundice that is not monitored and treated promptly may result in brain damage.

Temperature Regulation

The layers of fat that develop during the last two months of fetal life enable healthy full-term infants to keep their body temperature constant after birth despite changes in air temperature. Newborn babies also maintain body temperature by increasing their activity when air temperature drops.

anoxia   Lack of oxygen, which may cause brain damage.

meconium   Fetal waste matter, excreted during the first few days after birth.

neonatal jaundice   Condition, in many newborn babies, caused by immaturity of liver and evidenced by yellowish appearance; can cause brain damage if not treated promptly.

CHECKPOINT

Can you . . .

- Describe the normal size and appearance of a newborn baby and mention at least three distinctive features that change within the first few days or first month of life?

- Compare the fetal and neonatal systems of circulation, respiration, digestion and excretion, and temperature regulation?

- Identify two dangerous conditions that can occur when a newborn's body systems are not functioning normally?

The Brain and Reflex Behavior

What makes newborns respond to a nipple? What tells them to start the sucking movements that allow them to control their intake of fluids? These are functions of the *central nervous system*—the brain and *spinal cord* (a bundle of nerves running through the backbone)—and of a growing peripheral network of nerves, which eventually reaches every part of the body. Through this network, sensory messages travel to the brain, and motor commands travel back.

central nervous system Brain and spinal cord.

Development of the Central Nervous System

The brain is unfinished at birth; its growth before and after birth is fundamental to future development (Behrman, 1992; Casaer, 1993; M.W. Cowan, 1979; Kolb, 1989). In the uterus an estimated 250,000 brain cells form every minute through cell division (mitosis); by birth most of the 180 billion nerve cells in a mature brain are already formed but are not yet fully developed. The brain at birth is only 25 percent of its adult weight. It reaches about 70 percent of its eventual weight during the first year and 80 percent by the end of the second year. It then continues to grow more slowly until, by age 12, it is almost adult size. Increases in brain weight and volume can be measured before birth by ultrasound and after birth by the circumference of the baby's head. These measurements provide a check on whether the brain is growing normally.

The number of cells in the central nervous system increases most rapidly between the 25th week of gestation and the first few months after birth. By the time of birth, the growth spurt of the *brain stem* (the part of the brain responsible for such basic bodily functions as breathing, heart rate, body temperature, and the sleep-wake cycle), the spinal cord, and much of the *cerebrum,* the upper and largest portion of the brain, has almost run its course (see Figure 4-2). However, the *cerebellum* (the part of the brain that maintains balance and motor coordination) grows fastest during the first year of life. When a particular part of the brain is growing most rapidly, it is most vulnerable to damage. Thus cerebral palsy is most likely to result from injuries occurring during the middle period of gestation—though a major trauma at any point, even after birth, can result in cerebral palsy, mental retardation, or both.

neurons Nerve cells.

There are two main kinds of brain cells: neurons and glial cells. *Neurons,* or nerve cells, send and receive information. *Glial cells* support and protect the neurons. Most of the neurons in the *cerebral cortex*—the outer part of the cerebrum, the front part of which modulates emotions and is responsible for thinking and problem solving—emerge by 20 weeks of gestation.

Neurons do not spring up fully formed. At first they are simply cell bodies with a nucleus, or center, composed of deoxyribonucleic acid (DNA), which contains the cell's genetic programming. As the brain grows, these rudimentary cells migrate to various parts of it and differentiate to perform various functions. The full timetable for differentiation is not known exactly. We do know that some changes in the primary visual cortex (the part of the cerebral cortex that controls vision) occur between 25 and 32 weeks of gestation, whereas in the cerebellum differentiation comes later and lasts until the end of the second year.

As the neurons differentiate, they sprout *axons* and *dendrites*—narrow, branching extensions. Axons send signals to other neurons, and dendrites receive incoming messages from them through *synapses,* the nervous system's communication links. The synapses are tiny gaps, which are bridged by means of chemicals called *neurotransmitters.* These early connections, prompted by sensory experience, refine and stabilize the brain's genetically designed "wiring." Thus environmental stimulation is crucial to the brain's postnatal development (see Chapter 5).

In a newborn infant, the structures below the cortex are the most fully developed; cells in the cerebral cortex are not yet well connected. *Positron*

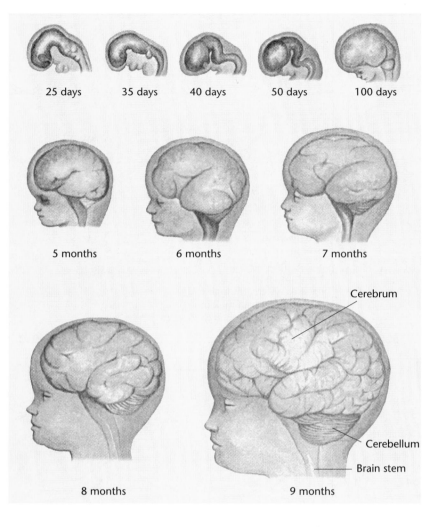

25 days   35 days   40 days   50 days   100 days

5 months   6 months   7 months

Cerebrum

8 months   9 months

Cerebellum

Brain stem

Figure 4-2
Fetal brain development from 25 days of gestation through birth. The *brain stem,* which controls basic biological functions such as breathing, develops first. As the brain grows, the front part expands greatly to form the *cerebrum* (the large, convoluted upper mass). Specific areas of the gray matter (the outer covering of the brain) have specific functions, such as sensory and motor activity; but large areas are "uncommitted" and thus are free for higher cognitive activity, such as thinking, remembering, and problem solving. The brain stem and other structures below the cortical layer handle reflex behavior and other lower-level functions. The *cerebellum,* which maintains balance and motor coordination, grows most rapidly during the first year of life.
Source: Casaer, 1993; Restak, 1984.

emission tomography (PET), a tool for measuring brain activity, suggests that this is because there are too many connections, not too few. The prenatal brain produces more cells and synapses than it needs. Those that are not used or do not function well die out after birth. This pruning of excess cells and connections, which begins during the neonatal period, helps to create an efficient nervous system (see Figure 4-3). Connections among cortical cells continue to improve throughout childhood and into adult life, allowing more flexible and more advanced motor and cognitive functioning.

A Newborn's Reflexes

When babies (or adults) blink at a bright light, they are acting involuntarily. Such automatic, innate responses to stimulation are called *reflex behaviors.*

Human beings have an array of reflexes, many of which are present by the time of birth or soon after (see Table 4-2). Some of these *primitive reflexes,* or newborn reflexes, such as rooting for food, are needed for early survival. Others may be part of humanity's evolutionary legacy. One example is the grasping reflex, by which infant monkeys hold on to the hair of their mothers' bodies.

Normally, the primitive reflexes disappear during the first year or so. For example, the Moro, or "startle," reflex drops out at 2 to 3 months, and rooting for the nipple drops out at about 9 months. Other reflexes, which continue to serve protective functions—such as blinking, yawning, coughing, gagging, sneezing, shivering, and the pupillary reflex (dilation of the pupils in the dark)—remain.

reflex behaviors Automatic, involuntary, innate responses to stimulation.

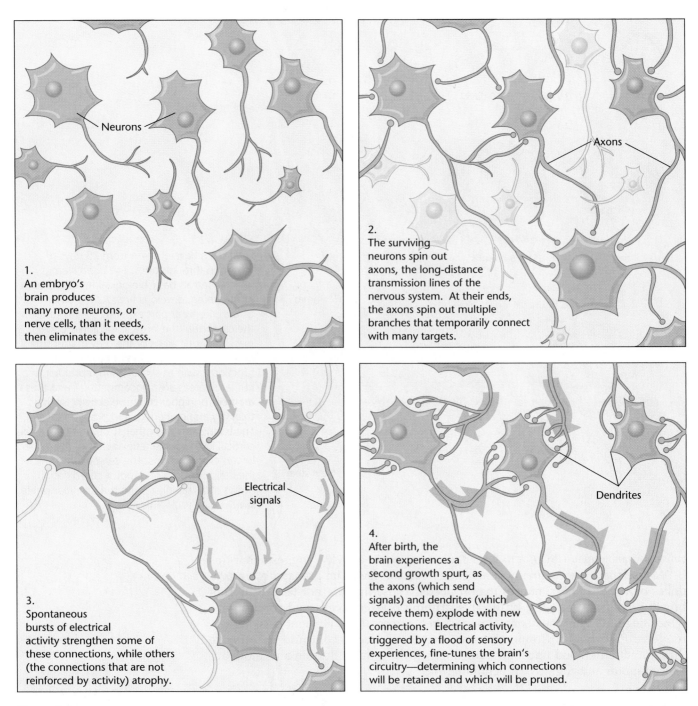

1.
An embryo's brain produces many more neurons, or nerve cells, than it needs, then eliminates the excess.

Neurons

2.
The surviving neurons spin out axons, the long-distance transmission lines of the nervous system. At their ends, the axons spin out multiple branches that temporarily connect with many targets.

Axons

3.
Spontaneous bursts of electrical activity strengthen some of these connections, while others (the connections that are not reinforced by activity) atrophy.

Electrical signals

4.
After birth, the brain experiences a second growth spurt, as the axons (which send signals) and dendrites (which receive them) explode with new connections. Electrical activity, triggered by a flood of sensory experiences, fine-tunes the brain's circuitry—determining which connections will be retained and which will be pruned.

Dendrites

Figure 4-3
Wiring the brain: development of neural connections before and after birth.
Source: Nash, 1997, p. 51.

Disappearance of the primitive reflexes on schedule is a sign that the cortex is maturing and developing normally, enabling a shift from reflex behavior to voluntary behavior. Thus we can evaluate a baby's neurological development by seeing whether certain reflexes are present or absent. As we'll see, one of the first tests after birth is for normal reflexes.

What is normal, however, varies somewhat from culture to culture; some reflex behaviors do not seem to be universal (Freedman, 1979). For example, differences show up in the Moro reflex. To elicit this reflex, the baby's body is lifted,

Table 4-2 Human Primitive Reflexes

Reflex	Stimulation	Baby's Behavior
Rooting	Baby's cheek or lower lip is stroked with finger or nipple.	Head turns; mouth opens; sucking movements begin.
Darwinian (grasping)	Palm of baby's hand is stroked.	Makes strong fist; can be raised to standing position if both fists are closed around a stick.
Swimming	Baby is put into water face down.	Makes well-coordinated swimming movements.
Tonic neck	Baby is laid down on back.	Turns head to one side, assumes "fencer" position, extends arms and legs on preferred side, flexes opposite limbs.
Moro (startle)	Baby is dropped or hears loud noise.	Extends legs, arms, and fingers; arches back; draws back head.
Babinski	Sole of baby's foot is stroked.	Toes fan out; foot twists in.
Walking	Baby is held under arms, with bare feet touching flat surface.	Makes steplike motions that look like well-coordinated walking.
Placing	Backs of baby's feet are drawn against edge of flat surface.	Withdraws foot.

Rooting reflex

Darwinian reflex

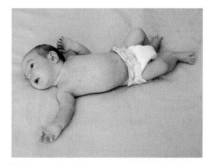

Tonic neck reflex

Moro reflex

Babinski reflex

Walking reflex

C HECKPOINT

Can you . . .

• Describe the most important features of brain development before and around the time of birth, and mention two ways of judging whether development is normal?

• Explain the functions of inborn reflex behaviors and why some of these reflexes drop out during the early months of life while others remain?

birth trauma Injury sustained at the time of birth due to oxygen deprivation, mechanical injury, infection, or disease.

low birthweight Weight of less than 5½ pounds at birth because of prematurity or being small for date.

preterm (premature) infants Infants born before completing the thirty-seventh week of gestation.

small-for-date (small-for-gestational age) infants Infants whose birthweight is less than that of 90 percent of babies of the same gestational age, as a result of slow fetal growth.

supporting the head. Then the head support is released, and the head is allowed to drop slightly. Caucasian newborns reflexively extend both arms and legs, cry persistently, and move about agitatedly. Navajo babies, however, do not extend their limbs in the same way, rarely cry, and almost immediately stop any agitated motion. It seems unlikely that such reflexive differences displayed soon after birth have much, if anything, to do with the cultural environment. Instead, it would seem that such instinctive behaviors show genetic variability among ethnic groups.

Is the Baby Healthy?

Although the vast majority of births result in normal, healthy babies, for a very small minority of infants the passage through the birth canal is a particularly harrowing journey. About 2 newborns in 1,000 are injured in the process (Wegman, 1994). *Birth trauma* (injury sustained at the time of birth) may be caused by anoxia (oxygen deprivation), diseases or infections, or physical harm. Sometimes the trauma leaves permanent brain damage, causing mental retardation, behavior problems, or even death. Early or late birth and low birthweight also can impair a baby's chances of survival and well-being. Modern methods of treating at-risk babies, of monitoring childbirth, and of screening newborns can increase their chances of survival and health. The resiliency of the human spirit, combined with medical progress and environmental support, enables many children to overcome a poor start in life.

Low Birthweight

In 1996, 7.4 percent of babies born in the United States (up from 6.8 percent in 1970) had *low birthweight*—they weighed less than 2,500 grams (5½ pounds) at birth. Much of this increased prevalence of low birthweight is attributed to the rise in multiple births, often due to use of fertility drugs, and to delayed childbearing (see Chapter 2). Very-low-birthweight babies weigh 1,500 grams (3⅓ pounds) or less; in 1995 they accounted for 1.35 percent of births. Low birthweight is the second leading cause of death in infancy, after birth defects (Guyer et al., 1997; National Center for Health Statistics [NCHS], 1997; Ventura et al., 1997).

Low-birthweight babies fall into two categories. Babies born before completing the thirty-seventh week of gestation are called *preterm (premature) infants;* they may or may not be the appropriate size for their gestational age. *Small-for-date (small-for-gestational age) infants,* who may or may not be preterm, weigh less than 90 percent of all babies of the same gestational age. Their delay in fetal growth is generally the result of inadequate prenatal nutrition. Preventing low birthweight and intervening when it occurs can increase the number of babies who survive the neonatal period and the first year of life.

Who Is Likely To Have a Low-Birthweight Baby?

Factors increasing the likelihood of having an underweight baby (see Table 4-3) include: (1) *demographic factors,* such as race, age, education, and marital status; (2) *medical factors predating the pregnancy,* such as previous abortions, stillbirths, or medical conditions; (3) *medical factors associated with the current pregnancy,* such as vaginal bleeding, infections, or too little weight gain; and (4) *prenatal behavioral and environmental factors,* such as poor nutrition, inadequate prenatal care, smoking, use of alcohol or other drugs, and exposure to stress or to toxic substances.

Many of these factors are interrelated, and socioeconomic status cuts across almost all of them. Teenagers' higher risk of having low-birthweight babies may stem more from malnutrition and inadequate prenatal care than from age, since teenagers who become pregnant are likely to be poor. At least one-fifth of all low birthweights are attributed to smoking. This proportion rises when the mother is

Table 4-3   Principal Maternal Risk Factors for Delivering Underweight Infants

Category	Risks	Category	Risks
Demographic and socio-economic factors	Age (under 17 or over 40)	Conditions of current pregnancy	Multiple pregnancy (twins or more)
	Race (African American)		Poor weight gain (less than 14 pounds)
	Poverty		Less than 6 months since previous pregnancy
	Unmarried		Low blood pressure
	Low level of education		Hypertension or toxemia
Medical risks predating current pregnancy	No children or more than four		Certain infections, such as rubella and urinary infections
	Low weight for height or short stature		Vaginal bleeding in the first or second trimester
	Genital or urinary abnormalities or past surgery		Placental problems
	Diseases such as diabetes or chronic hypertension		Anemia or abnormal blood count
	Lack of immunity to certain infections, such as rubella		Fetal abnormalities
			Incompetent cervix
			Spontaneous premature rupture of membranes
	Poor obstetric history, including previous low-birthweight infant and multiple miscarriages	Lifestyle factors	Smoking
			Poor nutritional status
	Genetic factors in the mother (such as low weight at her own birth)		Abuse of alcohol and other substances
			Exposure to DES and other toxins, including those in the workplace
			High altitude
			Stress
		Risks involving health care	Absent or inadequate prenatal care
			Premature delivery by cesarean section or induced labor

Sources: Adapted from S. S. Brown, 1985; additional data from Chomitz et al., 1995; Nathanielsz, 1995; Shiono & Behrman, 1995; Wegman, 1992.

underweight, does not gain enough during pregnancy, and also smokes—a combination that accounts for nearly two-thirds of cases of retarded fetal growth. Even before they become pregnant, women can cut down their chances of having a low-birthweight baby by eating well, not smoking or using drugs, drinking little or no alcohol, and getting good medical care (Chomitz, Cheung, & Lieberman, 1995; Shiono & Behrman, 1995).

Although the United States is more successful than any other country in the world in *saving* low-birthweight babies, the rate of such births to American women is higher than in 21 European, Asian, and Middle Eastern nations (UNICEF, 1996). Worse still, the rates of low birthweight for African American babies are higher than the rates in 73 other countries, including a number of African, Asian, and South American nations (UNICEF, 1992). African American babies are more than twice as likely as white babies to have low birthweight (see Table 5-2 in Chapter 5). Also at high risk—one and a half times the rate for white babies—are babies of Puerto Rican origin in the mainland United States. Rates for other minorities are about the same as for white births (Chomitz et al., 1995; NCHS, 1997).

The higher rates for African American women may in part reflect greater poverty, less education, less prenatal care, and a greater incidence of teenage and unwed pregnancy. However, such differences do not fully explain the disparities; Hispanic women, too, tend to have limited education and to lack early prenatal care. Also, even college-educated African American women are more likely than white women to bear low-birthweight babies (S. S. Brown, 1985; Chomitz et al., 1995; Schoendorf, Hogue, Kleinman, & Rowley, 1992). This may be due to poorer general health, or it may stem from specific health problems that span generations. The cause does not seem to be primarily genetic, since birthweights of babies of African-born black women are more similar to birthweights of infants of U.S.-born white women than of U.S.-born black women (David & Collins, 1997). In any case, the high proportion of low-birthweight babies in the African American population is the major factor in the high mortality rates of black infants (see Chapter 5).

Consequences of Low Birthweight

The most pressing fear for very small babies is that they will die in infancy; if not, they may have long-term health or developmental problems. Because their immune systems are not fully developed, they are especially vulnerable to infection. Their nervous systems may not be mature enough for them to perform functions basic to survival, such as sucking, and they may need to be fed intravenously (through the veins). Because they have insufficient fat to insulate them and to generate heat, it is hard for them to stay warm enough. Respiratory distress syndrome, also called *hyaline membrane disease,* is common. Many preterm babies with very low birthweight lack surfactant, an essential lung-coating substance that keeps air sacs from collapsing; they may breathe irregularly or stop breathing altogether and die.

Administering surfactant to high-risk preterm neonates has increased their survival rate (Corbet et al., 1995; Horbar et al., 1993), allowing significant numbers of infants who are born at 24 weeks of gestation and weigh as little as 500 to 750 grams (about 1 pound 2 ounces to 1 pound 10 ounces) to survive. However, these infants are as likely as before to be in poor health and to have neurological deficits—at age 20 months, a 20 percent rate of mental retardation and 10 percent likelihood of cerebral palsy (Hack, Friedman, & Fanaroff, 1996). Furthermore, these rescue efforts are extremely costly—as much as $1 million or more for one baby (Shiono & Behrman, 1995). Health care, special education, and child care for the 3.5 to 4 million children up to 15 years old whose weight was low at birth costs nearly $6 billion dollars more than if these children had been born with normal weight (Lewit, Baker, Corman, & Shiono, 1995). New research offers hope that giving magnesium sulfate to mothers before they give birth may drastically reduce the risk of cerebral palsy in very-low-birthweight babies—by as much as 90 percent—and possibly reduce the risk of mental retardation as well (Schendel, Berg, Yeargin-Allsopp, Boyle, & Decoufle, 1996).

Many low-birthweight babies who survive the dangerous early days do fairly well, owing in part to follow-up support. An analysis of 80 studies published since 1979 showed only about a 6-point difference in average IQ after age 2 between children of low and normal birthweight, and both groups were in the normal range for intelligence: 97.7 as compared with 103.78 (Aylward, Pfeiffer, Wright, & Verhulst, 1989). Very-low-birthweight babies have a less promising prognosis. In one study, about half of a sample of eighty-eight 7-year-olds who had weighed less than 3.3 pounds at birth needed special education, compared with 15 percent of a normal-weight, full-term control group (G. Ross, Lipper, & Auld, 1991). When low-birthweight children reach school age, those who weighed the least at birth have the most behavioral, social, attention, and language problems (Klebanov, Brooks-Gunn, & McCormick, 1994). Apparently it is not prematurity that makes the difference, but weight for gestational age. Small-for-gestational age infants are more likely to be neurologically and cognitively impaired during their first 6 years of life than equally premature infants whose weight was appropriate for their gestational age (McCarton, Wallace, Divon, & Vaughan, 1996). Male babies with very low birthweight are more likely than

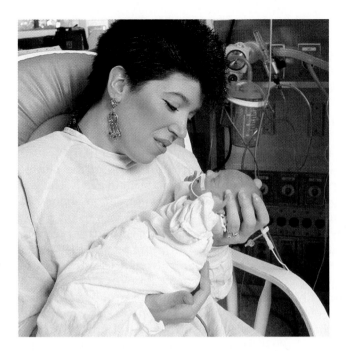

The tiniest babies thrive on human touch. This mother's holding and stroking of her low-birthweight baby girl will help establish a bond between mother and child, and will also help the baby grow and be more alert.

female babies to have problems during childhood that interfere with everyday activities, and to need special education or other special help (Verloove-Vanhorick et al., 1994).

Treatment of Low-Birthweight Babies

Much of the overall increase in survival of babies during the first 4 weeks of life (see Chapter 5) is due to improved care of low-birthweight babies. A low-birthweight baby is placed in an *isolette* (an antiseptic, temperature-controlled crib) and fed through tubes. To counteract the sensory impoverishment of life in an isolette, hospital workers and parents give these small babies special handling. Gentle massage seems to foster growth, behavioral organization, weight gain, motor activity, and alertness (T. M. Field, 1986; Schanberg & Field, 1987).

Some parents—anxious about a low-birthweight baby's health and fearful that the infant may die—are afraid of becoming too attached; they may feel uncomfortable with the baby and refrain from touching the infant (Stern & Hildebrandt, 1986). Frequent visits can give parents a more realistic idea of how the baby is doing and help them become more relaxed. Regularly visited babies seem to recover faster and leave the hospital sooner (Levy-Shiff, Hoffman, Mogilner, Levinger, & Mogilner, 1990; Zeskind & Iacino, 1984).

Long-Term Prospects for Low-Birthweight Babies

How do adolescents who were born dangerously small, many of whom have impaired health, judge their quality of life? Perhaps surprisingly, most call it quite satisfactory.

This finding emerged from a study (Saigal et al., 1996) of 150 young people ages 12 to 16 in Ontario, Canada, whose weight at birth had been extremely low (less than 1,000 grams, or 2 pounds 3 ounces). More than one-fourth of the group had neurological, sensory, or cognitive impairments, such as blindness, deafness, or cerebral palsy; and the group as a whole reported more, and more complex, limitations in sensory functioning, mobility, emotional state, cognitive performance, degree of pain, and ability to care for themselves than a comparison group of teenagers whose birthweight had been normal and few of whom had discernible impairments. Yet the two groups' ratings of their health-related quality of life were almost indistinguishable. Apparently most of the low-birthweight youngsters had learned to cope with any disabilities they had and to feel good about themselves and their lives.

A child's prospects for overcoming the early disadvantage of low birthweight seem to depend on several interacting factors. One is the family's socioeconomic circumstances (Aylward et al., 1989; McGauhey, Starfield, Alexander, & Ensminget, 1991; Ross et al., 1991). Another is the quality of the caregiving environment.

A large-scale study (Infant Health and Development Program [IHDP], 1990) followed 985 preterm, low-birthweight babies in eight parts of the United States—most of them from poor inner-city families—from birth to age 3. The parents of one-third of the babies received counseling and information about children's health and development and learned games and activities to play with their children; at 1 year, these babies entered an educational day-care program. At 30 months, children in this experimental group were more persistent, enthusiastic, and competent than a control group of low-birthweight children whose parents had not received counseling (Spiker, Ferguson, & Brooks-Gunn, 1993).

At age 3, when the program stopped, the experimental group were doing better on cognitive and social measures, were much less likely to show mental retardation, and had fewer behavioral problems than the control group (Brooks-Gunn, Klebanov, Liaw, & Spiker, 1993). However, two years later, at age 5, the children in the experimental group who had had the lowest birthweights no longer held a cognitive edge over children in the control group. Furthermore, having been in the program made no difference in health or behavior, regardless of how low the birthweight had been (Brooks-Gunn et al., 1994). By age 8, much of the cognitive advantage of the children in the experimental group had disappeared even for those whose birthweight had been heaviest. At this point, both the experimental and control groups had substantially below-average IQs and vocabulary scores. However, the children with heavier birthweights who had received the intervention had IQs about 4 points higher, on average, than children of equivalent birthweight who had not received help (McCarton et al., 1997). It seems, then, that for such an intervention to have lasting effects, it needs to continue beyond age 3.

Other studies of the full IHDP sample underline the importance of what goes on in the home. Children who got little parental attention and care were more likely to be undersized and to do poorly on cognitive tests than children from more favorable home environments (Kelleher et al., 1993). Those whose cognitive performance stayed high had mothers who scored high themselves on cognitive tests and who were responsive and stimulating to their children. Babies who had more than one risk factor (such as poor neonatal health combined with having a mother who did not receive counseling or was less well educated or less responsive) fared the worst (Liaw & Brooks-Gunn, 1993).

These studies make clear the need to look at child development in context. The studies show how biological and environmental influences interact, before and after birth; they show the complex consequences of such influences on all aspects of development; and they show that some resiliency is possible even among babies born with serious complications (see Box 4-2).

Other Birth Complications

Postmaturity

Close to 9 percent of pregnant women have not gone into labor 2 weeks after the due date, or 42 weeks after the last menstrual period (Ventura et al., 1997). At that point, a baby is considered *postmature.* Postmaturity can last as long as 5 weeks. Postmature babies tend to be long and thin, because they have kept growing in the womb but have had an insufficient blood supply toward the end

CHECKPOINT

Can you . . .

• Discuss the risk factors, outcomes, treatment, and long-term prospects for low-birthweight babies?

postmature Referring to a fetus not yet born as of 2 weeks after the due date or 42 weeks after the mother's last menstrual period.

Box 4-2   Can a Supportive Environment Overcome Effects of Birth Complications?

Can a favorable environment overcome the effects of birth injuries, low birthweight, or other complications of birth? According to a longitudinal study of all babies born on Kauai, Hawaii, in 1955, the answer is yes.

For more than three decades, Emmy E. Werner (1987, 1995) and a research team of pediatricians, psychologists, public health workers, and social workers have followed 698 children born in 1955 on the Hawaiian island of Kauai—from the prenatal period through birth, and then into young adulthood. The researchers interviewed the mothers; recorded their personal, family, and reproductive histories; monitored the course of their pregnancies; and interviewed them again when the children were 1, 2, and 10 years old. They also observed the children interacting with their parents at home and gave them aptitude, achievement, and personality tests in elementary and high school. The children's teachers reported on their progress and their behavior. The young people themselves were interviewed at ages 18 and 30. The researchers also reviewed records of community agencies and police and court files.

Of the original 1,000 live births, 865 children survived to age 2 with no apparent physical, cognitive, or social abnormalities. Stress at birth took its biggest toll during the first two years of life: All of the deaths during the first month and three-fourths of the deaths before the second birthday were attributed to birth complications. As time went on, however, the role of the environment became more pronounced.

Among the children who had suffered problems at or before birth, physical and psychological development were seriously impaired *only* when a child grew up in persistently poor environmental circumstances unless the early damage was so serious as to require institutionalization. From toddlerhood on, those children who had a stable and enriching environment did well (E. E. Werner, 1985,

1987). In fact, they had fewer language, perceptual, emotional, and school problems than children who had *not* experienced unusual stress at birth but who had suffered "environmental trauma" by receiving little intellectual stimulation or emotional support at home (E. Werner et al., 1968; E. E. Werner, 1989). The children who showed the worst health problems and whose development was most retarded were those who had been exposed to *both* reproductive problems and stressful experiences (E. E. Werner, 1987). Given a supportive environment, then, many children—even those who have suffered significant birth complications—can overcome a poor start in life.

Even more remarkable is the resilience of children who escape damage despite *multiple* sources of stress. Even when birth complications were combined with such environmental risks as chronic poverty, family discord, divorce, or parents who were mentally ill, many children came through relatively unscathed. Of the 276 children who at age 2 had been identified as having four or more risk factors, two-thirds developed serious learning or behavior problems by the age of 10 or, by age 18, had become pregnant, gotten in trouble with the law, or become emotionally troubled. Yet by age 30, one-third of these at-risk children had managed to become "competent, confident, and caring adults" (E. E. Werner, 1995, p. 82).

Protective factors fell into three categories: (1) individual attributes that may be largely genetic, such as energy, sociability, and intelligence; (2) affectionate ties with at least one supportive family member; and (3) rewards at school, work, or church that provide a sense of meaning and control over one's life (E. E. Werner, 1987). While the home environment seemed to have the most marked effect in childhood, the individuals' own qualities made more difference in their lives and in the environments they chose as adults (E. E. Werner, 1995).

---

of gestation. Possibly because the placenta has aged and become less efficient, it may provide less oxygen. The baby's greater size also complicates labor: the mother has to deliver a baby the size of a normal 1-month-old.

Since postmature fetuses are at risk of brain damage or even death, doctors sometimes induce labor with drugs or perform cesarean deliveries. However, if the due date has been miscalculated, a baby who is actually premature may be delivered. To help make the decision, doctors monitor the baby's status with ultrasound to see whether the heart rate speeds up when the fetus moves; if not, the baby may be short of oxygen. Another test involves examining the volume of amniotic fluid; a low level may mean the baby is not getting enough food.

Stillbirth

A stillbirth is a tragic union of opposites: birth and death. Sometimes fetal death is diagnosed prenatally; in other cases, as with Elvis Presley's twin brother, the baby's death is discovered during labor or delivery.

Table 4-4	Apgar Scale			
Sign*	0	1	2	
Appearance (color)	Blue, pale	Body pink, extremities blue	Entirely pink	
Pulse (heart rate)	Absent	Slow (below 100)	Rapid (over 100)	
Grimace (reflex irritability)	No response	Grimace	Coughing, sneezing, crying	
Activity (muscle tone)	Limp	Weak, inactive	Strong, active	
Respiration (breathing)	Absent	Irregular, slow	Good, crying	

*Each sign is rated in terms of absence or presence from 0 to 2; highest overall score is 10.
Source: Adapted from V. Apgar, 1953.

Parents of a stillborn baby need to grieve for the baby they have lost. To feel the reality of their loss, they may benefit from seeing and holding the dead infant, obtaining an autopsy report, and having a funeral. Some parents try to "find" the lost child by immediately beginning another pregnancy, but this seems only to complicate their grief rather than help resolve it. The period up to 6 months to a year after the stillbirth is usually a time of depression, apathy, and self-evaluation. Then, possibly after receiving counseling and emotional support, the parents begin to resume their roles in society. They do not forget their stillborn child, and they may commemorate the anniversary, but they can now focus on life and the living (Kirkley-Best & Kellner, 1982).

Medical Monitoring of Childbirth

electronic fetal monitoring Mechanical monitoring of fetal heartbeat during labor and delivery.

Some birth complications may be prevented through *electronic fetal monitoring,* the use of machinery to track the fetus's heartbeat during labor and delivery. This procedure is intended to detect a lack of oxygen, which may lead to brain damage. It can provide valuable information in high-risk deliveries, including those of low-birthweight babies and fetuses that seem to be in distress.

In 1995, electronic fetal monitoring was used in 81 percent of live births in the United States (Ventura et al., 1997). Yet monitoring has drawbacks when used routinely in low-risk pregnancies. It is costly; it restricts the mother's movements during labor; and, most important, it has an extremely high "false-positive" rate, suggesting that fetuses are in trouble when they are not. Such warnings may prompt doctors to deliver by the riskier cesarean method rather than vaginally (K. B. Nelson et al., 1996).

Medical and Behavioral Screening

The first few minutes, days, and weeks after birth are crucial for development. It is important to know as soon as possible whether a baby has any problem that needs special care.

Immediate Medical Assessment: The Apgar Scale

Apgar scale Standard measurement of a newborn's condition; it assesses appearance, pulse, grimace, activity, and respiration.

One minute after delivery, and then again 5 minutes after birth, most babies are assessed using the *Apgar scale* (see Table 4-4). Its name, after its developer, Dr. Virginia Apgar (1953), helps us remember its five subtests: *a*ppearance (color), *p*ulse (heart rate), *g*rimace (reflex irritability), *a*ctivity (muscle tone), and respiration (breathing). The newborn is rated 0, 1, or 2 on each measure, for a maximum score of 10. A 5-minute score of 7 to 10—achieved by 98.6 percent of babies born in the United States in 1995—indicates that the baby is in good to excellent condition (Ventura et al., 1997). A score below 7 means the baby needs help to establish breathing; a score below 4 means the baby needs immediate life-saving treatment. If resuscitation is successful, bringing the baby's score to 4 or more, no long-term damage is likely to result (American Academy of Pediatrics [AAP] Committee on Fetus and Newborn, 1986; AAP Committee on Fetus and Newborn and American College of Obstetricians and Gynecologists Committee on Obstetric Practice, 1996).

A low Apgar score does not always mean that a baby is suffocating. An infant's tone and responsiveness may be affected by the amount of sedation or pain-killing medication the mother received; or neurological or cardiorespiratory conditions may interfere with one or more vital signs. Premature infants may score low simply because of physiological immaturity. Scores of 0 to 3 at 10, 15, and 20 minutes after birth are increasingly associated with cerebral palsy or other future neurological problems, but such conditions may or may not be caused by oxygen deprivation (AAP Committee on Fetus and Newborn and American College of Obstetricians and Gynecologists Committee on Obstetric Practice, 1996).

Critics of the Apgar test point out that it is not as sensitive as newer measures, such as one new test that measures the oxygen in the newborn's blood. However, the Apgar test is quick, inexpensive, and easy to perform and, if administered carefully, has good predictive value.

Screening for Medical Conditions

Children who inherit the enzyme disorder phenylketonuria (PKU) will become mentally retarded unless they are fed a special diet beginning in the first 3 to 6 weeks of life. Screening tests that can be administered soon after birth can often discover such correctable defects.

Routine screening of all newborn babies for such rare conditions as PKU (1 case in 10,000 to 25,000 births), congenital hypothyroidism (1 in 3,600 to 5,000), and galactosemia (1 in 60,000 to 80,000)—or other, even rarer disorders—is expensive. Yet the cost of testing thousands of newborns to detect one case of a rare disease may be less than the cost of caring for a mentally retarded person for a lifetime. All states require routine screening for PKU and congenital hypothyroidism; states vary on requirements for other screening tests (AAP Committee on Genetics, 1996). However, there is some risk in doing these tests. They can generate false-positive results, suggesting that a problem exists when it does not, and triggering anxiety and costly, unnecessary treatment.

Assessing Neurological Status: The Brazelton Scale

The *Brazelton Neonatal Behavioral Assessment Scale* is a neurological and behavioral test used to measure neonates' responses to their environment; it is named for its designer, Dr. T. Berry Brazelton (1973). It assesses *interactive behaviors*, such as alertness and cuddliness; *motor behaviors*, such as reflexes, muscle tone, and hand-mouth activity; *physiological control*, such as a baby's ability to quiet down after being upset; and *response to stress* (the startle reaction). The test takes about 30 minutes, and scores are based on a baby's best performance. The Brazelton scale may be a better predictor of future development than the Apgar scale or standard neurological testing (Behrman & Vaughan, 1983).

Newborns and Their Parents

The birth process is a major transition not only for the baby but for the parents as well. The mother's body systems have undergone massive physical change. For

Brazelton Neonatal Behavioral Assessment Scale
Neurological and behavioral test to measure neonate's response to the environment; it assesses interactive behaviors, motor behaviors, physiological control, and response to stress.

CHECKPOINT

Can you . . .

• Discuss the uses and drawbacks of electronic fetal monitoring, the Apgar test, routine post-birth screening for rare disorders, and the Brazelton scale?

Newly hatched chicks will follow and become attached to the first moving object they see. The ethologist Konrad Lorenz, who got newborn ducklings to "love him like a mother," called this behavior *imprinting*.

both mother and father, especially with a first birth, the newcomer in their lives brings insistent demands that challenge their ability to cope and that force adjustments in their relationship. Meanwhile, parents (and, perhaps, siblings) are getting acquainted with this newcomer—developing emotional bonds and becoming familiar with the infant's patterns of sleeping, waking, feeding, and activity.

Childbirth and Bonding

How and when does the special intimacy between mothers and their babies develop? Some researchers have followed the ethological approach (introduced in Chapter 1), which considers behavior in human beings, as in animals, to be biologically determined and emphasizes critical, or sensitive, periods for development of certain behaviors.

In one well-known study, Konrad Lorenz (1957) waddled, honked, and flapped his arms—and got newborn ducklings to follow him as they would the mother duck. Lorenz showed that newly hatched ducklings will follow the first moving object they see, whether or not it is a member of their own species, and that they become increasingly attached to it. Usually, this first attachment is to the mother; but if the natural course of events is disturbed, other attachments (like the one to Lorenz) can form. This phenomenon is called *imprinting*, and Lorenz believed that it is automatic and irreversible.

imprinting Instinctive form of learning in which, during a critical period in early development, a young animal forms an attachment to the first moving object it sees, usually the mother.

Imprinting, said Lorenz, is the result of a *predisposition toward learning:* the readiness of an organism's nervous system to acquire certain information during a brief critical (or sensitive) period in early life. If ducklings had no object to follow during the critical period after birth, imprinting would not take place. Similarly, among goats and cows, certain ritual behaviors occur right after birth. If these rituals are prevented or interrupted, mother and offspring will not recognize each other. The results for the young animal are devastating: physical withering and death or abnormal development.

Does something similar to imprinting happen between human newborns and their mothers? Is there a critical period for bonding?

In 1976, two researchers concluded that if mother and baby are separated during the first hours after birth, the *mother-infant bond*—the mother's feeling of close, caring connection with her newborn—may not develop normally (Klaus & Kennell, 1976). However, follow-up research has not confirmed a critical time for bonding (Chess & Thomas, 1982; Lamb, 1983), and the original advocates of this idea later modified their position, saying that contact immediately after birth is *not* essential for strong mother-child bonding (Klaus & Kennell, 1982). Some mothers do seem to achieve closer bonding with their babies after early extended contact, as in hospitals that offer rooming-in, or when birth occurs at home; but no long-term effects have been shown. This finding has relieved the worry and guilt sometimes felt by adoptive parents and parents who had to be separated from their infants after birth.

Fathers, like mothers, form close bonds with their babies soon after birth. Proud new fathers admire their babies and pick them up. The babies contribute simply by doing the things normal babies do: opening their eyes, grasping their fathers' fingers, or moving in their fathers' arms.

In 1945, one small hospital in Texas began allowing fathers into the delivery room. By 1983, 99 percent of hospitals surveyed allowed fathers to attend a birth (May & Perrin, 1985; Wideman & Singer, 1984). Fathers who are present at the birth of a child often see the event as a "peak emotional experience" (May & Perrin, 1985). One psychiatrist argues that, since a father has not felt the baby inside his own body, his immediate physical contact with the infant after birth is vital in making the transition to fatherhood and forming an emotional bond with the child (Pruett, 1987). However, research shows that fathers become emotionally committed to their newborn babies, whether or not they attended the birth (Palkovitz, 1985).

Getting to Know the Baby: States of Arousal and Activity Levels

The bond between parents and infant helps them get to know their baby's needs. An important way in which newborns may express their individuality, as well as their unpredictability, is in their patterns of sleeping and waking and of activity when awake. An important way in which parents express their love for the baby is in their responsiveness to these patterns.

Babies have an internal "clock," which regulates their daily cycles of eating, sleeping, and elimination, and perhaps even their moods. These periodic cycles of wakefulness, sleep, and activity, which govern an infant's *state of arousal,* or degree of alertness, seem to be inborn. All neonates experience the same states of arousal (see Table 4-5), but each baby's cycle is different and varies from day to day. Newborn babies average about 16 hours of sleep a day, but one may sleep only 11 hours while another sleeps 21 hours (Parmelee, Wenner, & Schulz, 1964).

Although sleep dominates the neonatal period, the cliché "sleeping like a baby" is misleading. Most new babies wake up every 2 to 3 hours, day and night; short stretches of sleep alternate with shorter periods of consciousness, which are devoted mainly to feeding. Newborns have about six to eight sleep periods, which vary between quiet and active sleep. Active sleep is probably the equivalent of rapid eye movement (REM) sleep, which in adults is associated with dreaming. Active sleep appears rhythmically in cycles of about 1 hour and accounts for 50 to 80 percent of a newborn's total sleep time.

At about 3 months, babies grow more wakeful in the late afternoon and early evening and start to sleep through the night. By 6 months, more than half their sleep occurs at night. By this time, active sleep accounts for only 30 percent of sleep time, and the length of the cycle becomes more consistent (Coons & Guilleminault, 1982). The amount of REM sleep continues to decrease steadily throughout life.

Parents and caregivers spend a great deal of time and energy trying to change babies' states—for example, by soothing a fussy infant to sleep. Although

mother-infant bond
Mother's feeling of close, caring connection with her newborn.

state of arousal An infant's degree of alertness; his or her condition, at a given moment, in the periodic daily cycle of wakefulness, sleep, and activity.

Table 4-5	States of Arousal in Infancy			
State	**Eyes**	**Breathing**	**Movements**	**Responsiveness**
Regular sleep	Closed; no eye movement	Regular and slow	None, except for sudden, generalized startles	Cannot be aroused by mild stimuli
Irregular sleep	Closed; occasional rapid eye movements	Irregular	Muscles twitch, but no major movements	Sounds or light bring smiles or grimaces in sleep
Drowsiness	Open or closed	Irregular	Somewhat active	May smile, startle, suck, or have erections in response to stimuli
Alert inactivity	Open	Even	Quiet; may move head, limbs, and trunk while looking around	An interesting environment (with people or things to watch) may initiate or maintain this state
Waking activity and crying	Open	Irregular	Much activity	External stimuli (such as hunger, cold, pain, being restrained, or being put down) bring about more activity, perhaps starting with soft whimpering and gentle movements and turning into a rhythmic crescendo of crying or kicking, or perhaps beginning and enduring as uncoordinated thrashing and spasmodic screeching

Sources: Adapted from information in Prechtl & Beintema, 1964; P. H. Wolff, 1966.

crying is usually more distressing than serious, it is particularly important to quiet low-birthweight babies, because quiet babies maintain their weight better. Steady stimulation is the time-proven way to soothe crying babies: by rocking or walking them, wrapping them snugly, or letting them hear rhythmic sounds (see Box 4-3).

Beginning at birth, babies behave in different ways while awake. One baby sticks her tongue in and out, over and over; another makes rhythmic sucking movements. Some babies smile often; others, rarely. Some infant boys have frequent erections; others never do. Some new babies are more active than others. These activity levels reflect temperamental differences that continue throughout childhood, and often throughout life. In one study, children whose movements had been measured during the first days of life were assessed again at 4 and 8 years of age. The most vigorous newborns continued to be very active as 4- and 8-year-olds, while the least active infants were less active later (A. F. Korner et al., 1985). Even infants born prematurely show highly reliable individual differences in such ingredients of temperament as excitability, irritability, activity level, and sensitivity to stimulation (A. Korner, 1996).

How much a baby sleeps or fusses, but not how much the baby cries, may be an indicator of temperament. When 217 mothers who gave birth in London hospitals were asked to keep 24-hour diaries of their babies' behavior at 2, 6, 12, and 40 weeks, crying decreased with age, but individual patterns of sleeping and fussing were more stable. Birth order made a difference; later-born infants slept more and fussed less than firstborns (St. James-Roberts & Plewis, 1996).

As babies become more awake, alert, and active, their unique behavior patterns elicit varying responses from their caregivers. Adults react very differently to a placid baby than to an excitable one; to an infant they can quiet easily than to one who is often inconsolable; to a baby who is often awake and alert than to one who seems uninterested in the surroundings. Babies, in turn, respond to the way their caregivers treat them. This bidirectional influence can have far-reaching effects on what kind of person a baby turns out to be. Thus, from the start, children

Box 4-3 Comforting a Crying Baby

All babies cry. It is their only way to let us know they are hungry, uncomfortable, lonely, or unhappy. And since few sounds are as distressing as a baby's cry, parents or other caregivers usually rush to feed or pick up a crying infant. As babies quiet down and fall asleep or gaze about in alert contentment, they may show that their problem has been solved. At other times, the caregiver cannot figure out what the baby wants. The baby keeps crying. It is worth trying to find ways to help; babies whose cries bring relief seem to become more self-confident, seeing that they can affect their own lives.

Some parents worry that they will spoil a child by responding too much to crying, but there seems to be little danger of that. Some evidence suggests that, by the end of the first year, babies whose cries have brought tender, soothing care cry less, and communicate more in other ways, than babies of punitive or ignoring caregivers (Ainsworth & Bell, 1977; Bell & Ainsworth, 1972).

In Chapter 7, we discuss several kinds of crying and what the crying may mean. Unusual, persistent crying patterns may be early signs of trouble. For healthy babies who just seem unhappy, the following may help (Eiger & Olds, in press):

- Hold the baby, perhaps laying the baby on his or her stomach on your chest, to feel your heartbeat and breathing; or sit with the baby in a comfortable rocking chair.

- Put the baby in a carrier next to your chest and walk around.
- If you are upset, ask someone else to hold the baby; infants sometimes sense and respond to their caregivers' moods.
- Pat or rub the baby's back, in case a bubble of air is causing discomfort.
- Wrap the baby snugly in a small blanket; some infants feel more secure when firmly swaddled from neck to toes, with arms held close to the sides.
- Make the baby warmer or cooler; put on or take off clothing or change the room temperature.
- Give the baby a massage or a warm bath.
- Sing or talk to the baby, or provide a continuous or rhythmic sound, such as music from the radio, a simulated heartbeat, or background noise from a whirring fan, vacuum cleaner, or other appliance.
- Take the baby out for a ride in a stroller or car seat—at any hour of the day or night. In bad weather, some parents walk around in an enclosed mall; the distraction helps them as well as the baby.
- If someone other than a parent is taking care of the baby, it sometimes helps if the caregiver puts on a robe or a sweater that the mother or father has recently worn so the baby can sense the familiar smell.
- Pick up on the baby's signals.

Comforting a crying baby, as this mother is doing, will not spoil the child. Babies whose cries have been answered become more self-confident, and tend to cry less as they grow older, than babies whose cries have been ignored.

affect their own lives by molding the environment in which they grow. Babies are also affected by how mothers and fathers feel about being parents, and these feelings in turn may influence and be influenced by the marital relationship.

How Parenthood Affects a Marriage

Both women and men often feel ambivalent about becoming parents. Along with excitement, wonder, and awe, most new parents feel some anxiety about the responsibility of caring for a child, the commitment of time and energy it entails, and the feeling of permanence that parenthood imposes on a marriage. Pregnancy and the recovery from childbirth can affect a couple's sexual relationship, sometimes making it more intimate, sometimes creating barriers.

What happens in a marriage with the birth of a first child? One team followed 128 middle- and working-class couples in their late twenties from the first pregnancy until the child's third birthday. Although some marriages improved, many suffered overall, especially in the eyes of the wives (Belsky & Rovine, 1990). Many spouses reported that they loved each other less, became more ambivalent about their relationship, argued more, and communicated less. This was true no matter what the sex of the child and whether or not couples had a second child by the time the first was 3 years old.

What distinguished marriages that got stronger from those that deteriorated? In weaker marriages, the partners were likely to be younger and less well educated, to earn less money, and to have been married a shorter time. One or both partners tended to have low self-esteem, and husbands were likely to be less sensitive. The mothers who had the hardest time were those whose babies had "difficult" temperaments (see Chapter 7). Surprisingly, couples who were most romantic "pre-baby" had more problems "post-baby," perhaps because they had unrealistic expectations. Also, women who had planned their pregnancies were unhappier, possibly because they had expected life with a baby to be better than it turned out to be (Belsky & Rovine, 1990).

Are adoptive parents' experiences different from those of biological parents? Researchers in Israel looked at 104 couples before they became parents, and then again when their babies—half adopted, half biological offspring—were 4 months old (Levy-Shiff, Goldschmidt, & Har-Even, 1991). The adoptive parents reported more positive expectations and more satisfying parenting experiences than did the biological parents. The adoptive parents, who tended to be older and to have been married longer, may have been more mature and resourceful, or they may have appreciated parenthood more when it finally came.

One problem involves the division of household tasks. If a couple shared them fairly equally before becoming parents, but then, after the birth, the burden shifts to the wife, marital happiness tends to decline, especially for nontraditional wives (Belsky, Lang, & Huston, 1986). Since most mothers now work for pay, the fact that most husbands do not share equally in the burdens of homemaking and child care can be a source of stress (Apostal & Helland, 1993; Barnett, Brennan, Raudenbush, & Marshall, 1994; Clay, 1995; Greenstein, 1995; Olmsted & Weikart, 1994). Among young Israeli first-time parents, fathers who saw themselves as caring, nurturing, and protecting experienced less decline in marital satisfaction than other fathers and felt better about parenthood (Levy-Shiff, 1994).

Many elements go into the family relationships that exert a strong influence on a baby's development; and infants themselves exert a strong influence on the people who play the biggest role in their lives. We will see further examples of bidirectional influence in Part II, as we examine physical, cognitive, and psychosocial development in infancy and toddlerhood.

CHECKPOINT

Can you . . .

- Summarize the current status of research on bonding between parents and infants?

- Describe typical patterns of sleep and arousal during the first few months?

- Identify at least two ways in which a neonate may show the beginnings of temperament?

- Explain how a newborn's activity can have a bidirectional influence on the infant's development?

- Cite at least three factors that can influence a new baby's effect on the parents' marriage?

SUMMARY

The Birth Process

- Birth occurs in four stages: (1) dilation of the cervix; (2) descent and emergence of the baby; (3) expulsion of the umbilical cord and the placenta; (4) contraction of the uterus and recovery of the mother.

- Excessive anesthesia in medicated deliveries may have a harmful effect on the newborn. **Natural childbirth** or **prepared childbirth** can minimize the need for pain-killing drugs and maximize the parents' active involvement.

- About 21 percent of births in the United States are by **cesarean delivery.** Critics claim that many cesareans, which carry special risks to mother and baby, are unnecessary.

- Delivery at home or in birth centers attended by midwives are alternatives to physician-attended hospital delivery for women with normal, low-risk pregnancies. The presence of a doula can provide physical benefits as well as emotional support.

The Newborn

- The **neonatal period** is a time of transition from intrauterine to extrauterine life. During the first few days, the **neonate** loses weight and then regains it; the **lanugo** (prenatal hair) falls off and the protective coating of **vernix caseosa** dries up. The **fontanels** (soft spots) in the skull close within the first month.

- At birth, the circulatory, respiratory, gastrointestinal, and temperature regulation systems become independent of the mother's. Newborns have a strong sucking reflex and secrete **meconium** from the intestinal tract. They are commonly subject to **neonatal jaundice,** due to immaturity of the liver.

- The **central nervous system** controls a newborn's sensorimotor functioning. Most of the **neurons,** or nerve cells, in the brain are formed before birth. A neonate's brain grows most rapidly during the months before and immediately after birth as neurons migrate to their proper places, differentiate in function, and form connections.

- **Reflex behaviors** are indications of neurological maturation. Primitive reflexes drop out during the first year as voluntary, cortical control develops.

Is the Baby Healthy?

- A small minority of infants suffer lasting effects of **birth trauma,** sometimes due to **anoxia.** Other complications include **low birthweight, postmature** birth, and stillbirth. Low-birthweight babies may be either **preterm (premature) infants** or **small-for-date (small-for-gestational age) infants.** Low birthweight is a major factor in infant mortality and can cause long-term physical or cognitive problems.

- **Electronic fetal monitoring** is widely used (and may be overused) during labor and delivery to detect signs of fetal distress, especially in high-risk births.

- At 1 minute and 5 minutes after birth, the neonate is assessed by the **Apgar scale** to determine how well he or she is adjusting to extrauterine life. The **Brazelton Neonatal Behavioral Assessment Scale** may be given to assess responses to the environment and to predict future development.

Newborns and Their Parents

- Researchers following the ethological approach have suggested that—similar to **imprinting** in some animals—there is a critical period for the formation of the **mother-infant bond.** However, research has not confirmed this hypothesis. Fathers typically bond with their babies whether or not they are present at the birth.

- A newborn's **state of arousal** is governed by periodic cycles of wakefulness, sleep, and activity, which seem to be inborn. Sleep takes up the major (but a diminishing) amount of a neonate's time. Newborns' activity levels show stability and may be early indicators of temperament.

- Marital satisfaction often declines after the birth of a first baby. Expectations and sharing of tasks can contribute to a marriage's deterioration or improvement. Dual-earner couples have a particularly difficult challenge.

KEY TERMS

natural childbirth (128)
prepared childbirth (128)
cesarean delivery (128)
neonate (132)
neonatal period (132)
fontanels (132)
lanugo (132)
vernix caseosa (132)
anoxia (133)
meconium (133)
neonatal jaundice (133)
central nervous system (134)
neurons (134)
reflex behaviors (135)

birth trauma (138)
low birthweight (138)
preterm (premature) infants (138)
small-for-date (small-for-gestational age)
   infants (138)
postmature (142)
electronic fetal monitoring (144)
Apgar scale (144)
Brazelton Neonatal Behavioral
   Assessment Scale (145)
imprinting (146)
mother-infant bond (147)
state of arousal (147)

QUESTIONS FOR THOUGHT AND DISCUSSION

1. If you or your partner were expecting a baby, and the pregnancy seemed to be going smoothly, would you prefer (a) medicated or nonmedicated delivery, (b) hospital, birth center, or home birth, and (c) attendance by a physician or midwife? Give reasons. If you are a man, would you choose to be present at the birth? If you are a woman, would you want your partner present?

2. What aspects of traditional ways of delivering babies might enhance western childbearing practices without giving up medical techniques that save lives? Could advanced medical techniques be introduced into traditional societies without invalidating practices that seem to serve women in those societies well?

3. In view of the long-term outlook for very-low-birthweight babies and the expense involved in helping them survive, how much of society's resources should be put into rescuing these babies? If you had to choose between putting a very-low-birthweight baby in intensive care and providing therapy for a young adult with AIDS or breast cancer, which would you choose?

4. Do you think routine screening of newborns for such rare conditions as PKU is good public policy?

Infancy and Toddlerhood: *A Bird's-Eye View*

Infancy and Toddlerhood

Some of the most exciting developmental research during the past quarter-century has been on the period from birth to age 3, known as infancy and toddlerhood. By measuring how long infants look at objects or patterns, and how vigorously they suck on nipples that turn on recordings, researchers have discovered that even newborns can discriminate sights and sounds—and have definite preferences about what they see and hear. By noting babies' reactions to boxes teetering on the edge of tabletops, investigators have found that infants as young as 3 months understand basic principles that govern the physical world. By videotaping babies' facial expressions, researchers have documented when specific early emotions (such as joy, anger, and fear) first appear. Other researchers have described how the complex emotions of pride, shame, and guilt emerge with the cognitive growth that takes place during the second year. All in all, we now know that the world of infants and toddlers is far richer, and their abilities far more impressive, than was previously suspected.

Infancy begins at birth and ends when a child begins walking and stringing words together—two events that typically take place between 12 and 18 months of age. Toddlerhood lasts from about 18 months to 36 months, a period when children become more verbal, independent, and able to move about. As we study how neonates become infants and toddlers (and, later, grow into children and adolescents), we see how each of the three aspects of development is bound up with the others. Thus, while we focus on the *physical* development of infants and toddlers in Chapter 5, on their *cognitive* development in Chapter 6, and on their *psychosocial* development in Chapter 7, we will see many examples of how these aspects of development intertwine.

Cognitive abilities, for example, are based on physical connections in the brain, which are literally formed by early sensations—sights, sounds, smells, touches, and tastes. Furthermore, learning is not just a matter of the mind; infants learn by doing. They learn through their physical movements where their bodies end and everything else begins. By touching a pretzel, by picking up a shoe, by playing with their toes, they learn about the world and about themselves. They learn that they can drop a toy but that a thumb is always there for sucking. As they splash water and hurl sand, they learn how their bodies can change their world. This physical and cognitive exploration is a key to the psychosocial shift from the total dependence of the newborn to the growing self-awareness and independence of the 3-year-old.

Physical Development and Health During the First Three Years

There he lay upon his back
The yearling creature, warm and moist with life
To the bottom of his dimples,—to the ends
Of the lovely tumbled curls about his face.

Elizabeth Barrett Browning, *Aurora Leigh*, 1857

Focus

Helen Keller

"What we have once enjoyed we can never lose," the author Helen Keller once wrote. "A sunset, a mountain bathed in moonlight, the ocean in calm and in storm—we see these, love their beauty, hold the vision to our hearts. All that we love deeply becomes a part of us" (Keller, 1929, p. 2).

This quotation is especially remarkable—and especially poignant—in view of the fact that Helen Keller never saw a sunset, or a mountain, or moonlight, or an ocean, or anything else after the age of 19 months. It was then that she contracted a mysterious fever ("acute congestion of the stomach and brain," the doctor called it), which abated almost as quickly as it had come, leaving the child deaf and with inexorably ebbing sight.

As Keller later remembered, "I think I was lying in somebody's lap, and suddenly I was raised into a bright light. I felt a great pain which made me scream violently" (Lash, 1980, p. 43). The "someone" was her half-brother, who had found her lying on a sofa with her face buried in a pillow and had picked her up.

Helen Keller was born June 27, 1880 in Tuscumbia, Alabama. Her father was a farmer and small-town newspaper publisher; her mother was his second wife. Before her illness, Helen had been a normal, healthy baby—lively, friendly, and affectionate. Now she became expressionless and unresponsive. At 1 year, she had begun to walk; now she clung to her mother's skirts or sat in her lap. She had also begun to talk—one of her first words was "water"—and had given every indication of being a bright child. After her illness, she continued to say "wah-wah," but not much else.

Her distraught parents first took her to a mineral spa and then to medical specialists, but there was no hope for a cure. The light, Helen later wrote, "came to me dim and yet more dim each day. . . . Gradually I got used to the silence and darkness that surrounded me and forgot that it had ever been different" (1905, p. 8).

At a time when physical and cognitive development normally enter a major growth spurt, the sensory gateways to the exploration of Helen's world were slammed shut—but not entirely. Deprived of two senses, she leaned more heavily on the other three, especially smell and touch. She later explained that she could tell a doctor from a carpenter by the odors of ether or wood that emanated from them. She used her ever-active fingertips to trace the "delicate tremble of a butterfly's wings . . . , the soft petals of violets . . . , the clear, firm outline of face and limb, the smooth arch of a horse's neck and the velvety touch of his nose" (Keller, 1908/1920, pp. 6–7). Memories of the daylight world she had once inhabited helped her make sense of the unrelieved night in which she found herself. During her 19 months of sight, she "had caught glimpses of broad, green fields, a luminous sky, trees and flowers which the darkness that followed could not wholly blot out" (1905, p. 8).

Helen realized that she was not like other people, but at first she had no clear sense of who or what she was. "I lived in a world that was a no-world. . . . I did not know that I knew [anything], or that I lived or acted or desired. I had neither will nor intellect. I was carried along to objects and acts by a certain blind natural impetus" (1908/1920, p. 113). Sometimes, when family members were talking to each other, she would stand between them and touch their lips, and then frantically move her own—but nothing happened. Her frustration found its outlet in violent, inconsolable tantrums; she would kick and scream until she was exhausted.

Her parents, out of pity, indulged her whims. Finally, more in desperation than in hope, they engaged a teacher for her: a young woman named Anne Sullivan, who herself had limited vision and who had been trained in a school for the blind. Arriving at the Keller home, Miss Sullivan found 6-year-old Helen to be "wild, wilful, and destructive" (Lash, 1980, p. 348). She would grab food off other people's plates. Once, after figuring out how to use a key, she locked her mother in the pantry. Another time, frustrated by her teacher's attempts to spell the word *doll* into her palm, Helen hurled her new doll to the floor, smashing it to bits.

Yet, that same day, the little girl achieved her first linguistic breakthrough. As she and her teacher walked in the garden, they stopped to get a drink at the pump. Miss Sullivan placed Helen's hand under the spout, at the same time spelling "w-a-t-e-r" over and over into her other hand. "I stood still," Keller later wrote, "my whole attention fixed upon the motions of her fingers. Suddenly I felt a misty consciousness as of something forgotten—a thrill of returning thought; and somehow the mystery of language was revealed to me. I knew then that 'w-a-t-e-r' meant the wonderful cool something that was flowing over my hand. That living word awakened my soul, gave it light, hope, joy, set it free!" (Keller, 1905, p. 35)

Sources of information about Helen Keller include Keller, 1905, 1908/1920 and Lash, 1980.

• • •

The story of how Anne Sullivan tamed this unruly child and brought her into the light of language and thought is a familiar and inspiring one. For our present purposes, the lesson to be drawn from the story of Helen Keller's early development is the central importance of the senses—the windows to a baby's world—and their connection with all other aspects of development. Had Helen Keller not lost her vision and hearing, or had she been born without one or the other, or both, her physical, cognitive, and psychosocial development undoubtedly would have been quite different.

In this chapter, we show how sensory perception goes hand in hand with an infant's growing motor skills and shapes the astoundingly rapid development of the brain. We describe typical growth patterns of body and brain, and we see how a nourishing environment can stimulate both. We see how infants, who spend most of their time sleeping and eating, become busy, active toddlers and how parents and other caregivers can foster healthy growth and development. We discuss threats to infants' lives and health and what can be done to ward them off.

After reading this chapter, you should be able to answer and elaborate on such questions as these:

Preview Questions

- What influences physical growth?

- How and what should infants be fed?

- How does environmental stimulation or deprivation affect brain growth?

- How do the senses develop during infancy?

- What are the milestones in motor development during the first 3 years?

- How do motor development and perception influence each other?

- What role do environmental influences play in motor development?

- How can we enhance babies' chances of survival and health?

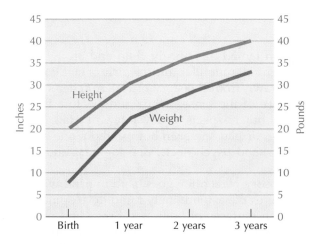

Figure 5-1
Growth in height and weight during infancy and toddlerhood. Babies grow most rapidly in both height and weight during the first few months of life, then taper off somewhat by age 3.

Growth of Body and Brain

Children grow faster during the first 3 years, especially during the first few months, than they ever will again (see Figure 5-1). At 5 months, the average baby's birthweight has doubled from 7½ pounds to about 15 pounds, and, by 1 year, has tripled to about 22 pounds. This rapid growth rate tapers off during the second year, when a child typically gains 5 or 6 pounds, quadrupling the birthweight by the second birthday. During the third year, the average gain is somewhat less, about 4 to 5 pounds. Height typically increases by about 10 to 12 inches during the first year (making the typical 1-year-old about 30 inches tall); by about 5 inches during the second year (so that the average 2-year-old is about 3 feet tall); and by 3 to 4 inches during the third year.

Teething usually begins around 3 or 4 months, when infants begin grabbing almost everything in sight to put into their mouths; but the first tooth may not actually arrive until sometime between 5 and 9 months of age, or even later. By the first birthday, babies generally have 6 to 8 teeth; by age 2½, they have a mouthful of 20.

As a baby grows, body shape and proportions change too; a 3-year-old typically is slender compared with a chubby, potbellied 1-year-old. Physical growth and development follow the maturational principles introduced in Chapter 3: the *cephalocaudal principle* and *proximodistal principle.* According to the *cephalocaudal principle,* growth occurs from top to bottom. Because the brain grows so rapidly before birth, a newborn baby's head is disproportionately large. By 1 year, the brain is 70 percent of its adult weight, but the rest of the body is only about 10 to 20 percent of adult weight. The head becomes proportionately smaller as the child grows in height and the lower parts of the body develop (see Figure 5-2). As we'll see later in this chapter, sensory and motor development proceed according to the same principle: infants learn to use the upper parts of the body before the lower parts. They see objects before they can control their trunk, and they learn to do many things with their hands long before they can crawl or walk. According to the *proximodistal principle* (inner to outer), growth and motor development proceed from the center of the body outward. In the womb (as we saw in Chapter 3), the head and trunk develop before the arms and legs, then the hands and feet, and then the fingers and toes. During infancy and early childhood, the limbs continue to grow faster than the hands and feet. Similarly, babies first develop the ability to use their upper arms and upper legs (which are closest to the center of the body), then the forearms and forelegs, then hands and feet, and finally, fingers and toes.

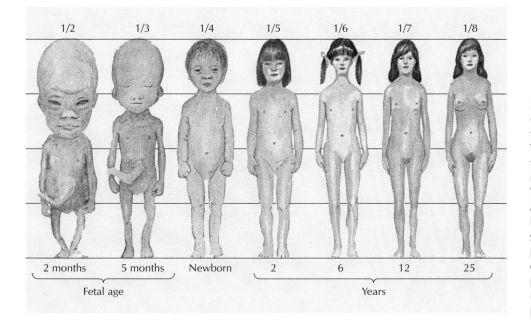

| 1/2 | 1/3 | 1/4 | 1/5 | 1/6 | 1/7 | 1/8 |

| 2 months | 5 months | Newborn | 2 | 6 | 12 | 25 |

Fetal age   Years

Figure 5-2
Changes in the proportions of the human body during growth. The most striking change is that the head becomes smaller relative to the rest of the body. The fractions indicate head size as a proportion of total body length at several ages. More subtle is the stability of the trunk proportions (from neck to crotch). The increasing leg proportion is almost exactly the reverse of the decreasing head proportion.

Influences on Growth: The Importance of Nutrition

The genes an infant inherits have a strong influence on body type; they help determine whether the child will be tall or short, thin or stocky, or somewhere in between (A. Stunkard, Harris, Pedersen, & McClearn, 1990; A. J. Stunkard, Foch, & Hrubec, 1986). This genetic influence interacts with such environmental influences as nutrition and living conditions, which also affect general health and well-being.

Well-fed, well-cared-for children grow taller and heavier than less well nourished and nurtured children. They also mature sexually and attain maximum height earlier, and their teeth erupt sooner. Today, children in many developed countries are growing taller and maturing sexually at an earlier age than a century ago (see Chapter 14), probably because of better nutrition, improved sanitation, and the decrease in child labor. Better medical care, especially immunization and antibiotics, also plays a part; heart disease, kidney disease, and some infectious illnesses can have grave effects on growth. Children who are ill for a long time may never achieve their genetically programmed stature because they may never make up for the loss of growth time while they were sick. Malnutrition, even apart from the effects of such related factors as low birthweight and illness, can interfere with normal cognitive growth (Rose, 1994).

Babies can grow normally and stay healthy under a variety of feeding regimens. Still, some feeding practices are more beneficial than others.

Early Feeding

From the beginnings of human history, babies were breastfed. A woman who was either unable or unwilling to nurse her baby had to find another woman to do it. Early in the twentieth century, with the advent of dependable refrigeration and pasteurization, manufacturers began to develop formulas to modify and enrich cow's milk for infant consumption.

During the next half-century, formula feeding became the norm in the United States and some other industrialized countries. By 1971, only 25 percent of American mothers even tried to nurse. Since then, recognition of the benefits of breast milk has brought about a reversal of this trend, so that today nearly 60 percent of new mothers in the United States breastfeed (A. S. Ryan, 1997). However, fewer

In accordance with the cephalocaudal principle, infants can use their hands adeptly before their legs are very useful, as this baby reaching for a toy demonstrates.

than 22 percent are still breastfeeding at 6 months, and many of these are supplementing breast milk with formula (American Academy of Pediatrics [AAP] Work Group on Breastfeeding, 1997).

Breast milk is almost always the best food for newborns and is recommended for at least the first 12 months. The only acceptable alternative is an iron-fortified formula based on either cow's milk or soy protein and containing supplemental vitamins and minerals. Breast milk is more digestible and more nutritious than formula, protects against infections and other diseases, and is less likely to produce allergic reactions (AAP, 1989a, 1996; AAP Work Group on Breastfeeding, 1997; Lindberg, 1996).

Human milk is a complete source of nutrients for at least the first 6 months, and possibly longer; during this time breastfed babies normally do not need any other food. Neither they nor formula-fed infants need additional water (AAP Committee on Nutrition, 1993; AAP Work Group on Breastfeeding, 1997). Neonates, particularly, if they drink too much water, are susceptible to water intoxication (which can lead to a drop in body temperature, swelling of the tissues, and seizures) because of difficulty eliminating excess water (Scariati, Grummer-Strawn, & Fein, 1997b).

The health advantages of breastfeeding are striking during the first 2 years and even later in life (A. S. Cunningham, Jelliffe, & Jelliffe, 1991; J. Newman, 1995; A. L. Wright, Holberg, Taussig, & Martinez, 1995). Among the illnesses prevented or minimized by breastfeeding are diarrhea, respiratory infections (such as pneumonia and bronchitis), otitis media (an infection of the middle ear), and staphylococcal, bacterial, and urinary tract infections (AAP Work Group on Breastfeeding, 1997; A. S. Cunningham et al., 1991; Dewey, Heinig, & Nommsen-Rivers, 1995; J. Newman, 1995; Scariati, Grummer-Strawn, & Fein, 1997a). Breast-feeding also seems to have benefits for visual acuity (Makrides, Neumann, Simmer, Pater, & Gibson, 1995), neurological development (Lanting, Fidler, Huisman, Touwen, & Boersma, 1994), and cognitive development (AAP Work Group on Breastfeeding, 1997; Horwood & Fergusson, 1998). The flavors and odors of the foods a nursing mother eats are transmitted through her milk, exposing her baby to a rich variety of sensory experiences (Bartoshuk & Beauchamp, 1994; Mennella & Beauchamp, 1996b).

Women least likely to breastfeed are African American and low-income mothers, those under age 25, those without a high school education, and those who work full time outside the home, though the rate of breastfeeding has risen

Breast milk can be called the "ultimate health food" because it offers so many benefits to babies—physical, cognitive, and emotional.

fastest among these groups in recent years (A. S. Ryan, 1997). It is ironic that many poor women do not breastfeed (MacGowan et al., 1991), since breast milk is far more economical than formula. One prenatal educational and counseling program boosted breastfeeding rates among urban African American low-income women by explaining the benefits to their babies' health (Kistin, Benton, Rao, & Sullivan, 1990). Facilities in the workplace for breastfeeding and for pumping and storage of mothers' milk, as well as on-site infant care, would encourage working mothers to continue nursing (Lindberg, 1996).

Almost every woman can breastfeed with proper information, encouragement, and support. However, breastfeeding is inadvisable if a mother is infected with the AIDS virus, which can be transmitted through her milk, or another infectious illness: if she has untreated active tuberculosis; or if she is taking any drug that would not be safe for the baby (AAP Committee on Drugs, 1994; AAP Committee on Infectious Diseases, 1994; AAP Work Group on Breastfeeding, 1997; WHO/UNICEF Constitution on HIV Transmission and Breastfeeding, 1992). Nursing mothers need to be as careful as pregnant women about what they take into their bodies (Eiger & Olds, in press).

Feeding a baby is an emotional as well as a physical act. Warm contact with the mother's body fosters emotional linkage between mother and baby. Such bonding can take place through either breast or bottle-feeding; and since bottle-feeding can be done by fathers, it can promote bonding with them as well. Babies who are fed with properly prepared formula and raised with love do grow up healthy. Despite the many advantages of breastfeeding, the quality of the relationship between parent and child and the affection and cuddling that accompany feeding sessions may be more important for a child's emotional development than the feeding method.

Cow's Milk, Solid Foods, and Juice

Because infants fed plain cow's milk in the early months of life suffer from iron deficiency (Sadowitz & Oski, 1983), the American Academy of Pediatrics (AAP, 1989b, 1996; AAP Committee on Nutrition, 1992b) recommends that babies receive breast milk or, alternatively, iron-fortified formula for the first year. At 1 year, babies can switch to cow's milk if they are getting a balanced diet of supplementary solid foods that provide one-third of their caloric intake (AAP, 1989b). The milk should be homogenized whole milk fortified with vitamin D, not skim milk or reduced-fat (1 or 2 percent) milk. Some parents believe that feeding with skim milk will prevent a baby from becoming too fat (see Box 5-1), but babies need the calories in whole milk for proper growth during the first 2 years. Also, the high protein and electrolyte content of skim or low-fat milk can be harmful (AAP, 1996).

The American Academy of Pediatrics recommends that iron-enriched solid foods—usually beginning with cereal or strained fruits—be gradually introduced during the second half of the first year (AAP Work Group on Breastfeeding, 1997). At this time, too, fruit juice may be introduced in moderation. A study of toddlers who had failed to grow normally found that large quantities of juice seemed to be interfering with the children's appetite for higher-calorie, more nutritious foods. Also, some got diarrhea (M. M. Smith & Lifshitz, 1994). In another study, 2-year-olds and 5-year-olds who drank 12 ounces or more of fruit juice daily were more likely to be short and obese than children who drank less juice; their diets did not differ significantly in other respects (Dennison, Rockwell, & Baker, 1997). To be on the safe side, children 2 or 3 years old should drink no more than 4 to 8 ounces of juice a day, and younger children should have less (M. M. Smith & Lifshitz, 1994).

"Nourishing" the Brain

Smiling, babbling, crawling, walking, and talking—all the major sensory, motor, and cognitive milestones of infancy—are made possible by the amazingly rapid development of the brain (see Figure 5-3), particularly the *cerebral cortex*. This outer layer of the front part of the brain, which is responsible for high-level functioning, continues to grow rapidly between birth and age 2.

The multiplication of *synapses,* or connections between nerve cells, during the early months of life accounts for much of the brain's growth in weight and permits the emergence of new perceptual, cognitive, and motor abilities (see Figure 5-4). Part of the credit goes to the *glial cells,* which coat the *axons*—nerve fibers that carry messages between neurons—with a fatty substance called *myelin.* This process of *myelination* permits faster travel times for, and responses to, sensory signals. For example, we know that certain visual pathways have been myelinated by 2 to 3 months after birth, when babies typically smile as soon as they see their caregivers.

Until the middle of the twentieth century, scientists believed that the brain grew in an unchangeable, genetically determined pattern. This does seem to be largely true before birth. But it is now widely agreed that the brain is "molded" by experience, especially during the early months of life, when the cortex is still growing rapidly and organizing itself. The technical term for this malleability, or modifiability, of the infant brain is ***plasticity.*** This molding goes on throughout life as nerve cells change in size and shape in response to environmental stimulation (M. C. Diamond, 1988; Pally, 1997).

Just as chronic malnutrition of a fetus can lead to brain damage, undernourishment after birth can have a similar effect. As we mentioned in Chapter 4, the brain also needs perceptual "nourishment," in the form of sensory stimulation. Not only early cognitive development but early emotional development may depend on experience. Infants whose mothers are severely depressed show less activity in the left frontal lobe, the part of the brain that is involved in positive

CHECKPOINT

Can you . . .

- Summarize typical patterns of growth during the first 3 years?
- Discuss how nutrition affects growth?
- Summarize pediatric recommendations regarding breastfeeding versus formula and the introduction of cow's milk, solid foods, and fruit juices?

plasticity Modifiability, or "molding," of the brain through early experience.

Box 5-1 Is Obesity a Problem in Infancy?

Seven babies on Long Island were fed a diet that sounds healthy: skim milk rather than whole milk, no animal fat or sugar, and restricted snacking. But their well-intentioned parents, trying to prevent obesity in their children, were starving them. The babies were not getting enough calories (Pugliese, Weyman-Daum, Moses, & Lifschitz, 1987).

In the United States, obesity—generally defined in children as having a body mass at or above the 85th percentile for age and sex— is the chief nutritional problem of all age groups. It occurs when people consume more calories than they expend as energy, and the excess calories are stored as fat. This imbalance reflects an interplay of physical, psychological, and cultural factors. Although a tendency toward overweight seems to be largely inherited, individual eating habits often follow patterns set in a particular household, which in turn are influenced by standards set by the larger

Contrary to popular belief, chubby babies rarely grow into obese adults—unless their parents are obese.

culture (Leibel, 1997; A. Stunkard et al., 1990; A. J. Stunkard et al., 1986; see Chapters 2, 8, 11, and 14).

Those Long Island parents may have underfed their babies because of a belief that overfeeding infants is likely to lead to obesity in later life. The scientific basis for this belief rests on research in rats; feeding rat pups too many calories makes them develop too many fat cells, which persist through life (J. Hirsch, 1972). But is that true of human infants?

Two factors seem to influence most strongly the chances that an obese child will grow up to be an obese adult: the age of the child and whether or not the child has an obese parent or parents. One study found almost no relationship between obesity before age 6 and at age 16. After age 6, however, obese children were increasingly likely to become obese adults (Roche, 1981). In a 40-year follow-up of Swedish children, whether obese infants became obese adults depended on obesity in the family, especially in the mother. If she was obese, her child was likely to remain obese, even if the child ate a recommended diet (Mossberg, 1989). In a more recent study in the state of Washington, obese children under age 3 who did not have an obese parent were unlikely to grow up to be obese, but among children above that age, obesity in childhood was an increasingly important predictor of adult obesity. Having an obese parent more than doubled the risk that a child under age 10 would be obese in adulthood, whether or not the child was currently obese (Whitaker, Wright, Pepe, Seidel, & Dietz, 1997).

There is no evidence that obesity hurts babies. For proper growth, children under 3 who do not have obese parents should not be on any kind of special diet without a clear indication that it is needed (AAP Committee on Nutrition, 1986). Since few of these children will be obese adults, adults should avoid calling attention to their obesity or suggesting that they are in danger of being fat when they get older. On the other hand, a 1- or 2-year-old who has an obese parent—or especially two obese parents—may be a candidate for prevention efforts, if it can be determined what factors, such as a too-rich diet or too little exercise, are contributing to the problem.

The ideal time to treat obesity in children is between 3 and 9 years of age, when it is more likely that the condition, if left untreated, will persist and when parents still have a strong influence on a child's diet and activities (Whitaker, et al., 1997). In the meantime, the best thing parents can do to avoid obesity in themselves and in their children is to adopt a more active lifestyle for the entire family.

emotions such as happiness and joy, and more activity in the right frontal lobe, which is associated with negative emotions (G. Dawson, Frey, Panagiotides, Osterling, & Hessl, 1997; G. Dawson, Klinger, Panagiotides, Hill, & Spieker, 1992).

Animal experiments suggest that impoverished sensory experience during early life can leave a permanent imprint on the brain. Kittens fitted with goggles that allowed them to see only vertical lines grew up unable to see horizontal lines and bumped into horizontal boards in front of them. Other kittens, whose goggles allowed them to see only horizontal lines, grew up blind to vertical columns (Hirsch & Spinelli, 1970).

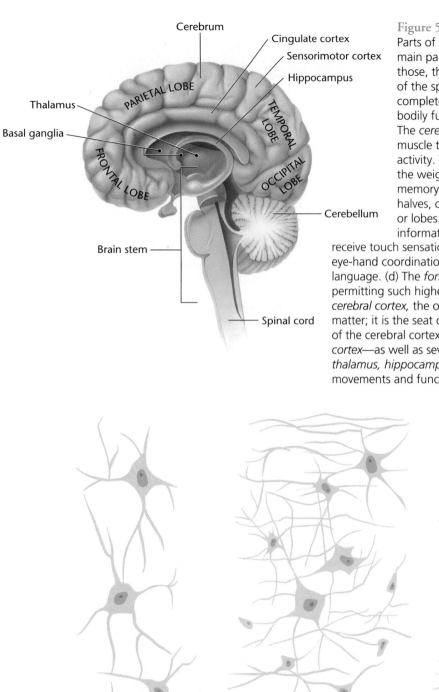

Cerebrum

Cingulate cortex

Sensorimotor cortex

Hippocampus

PARIETAL LOBE

TEMPORAL LOBE

Thalamus

Basal ganglia

FRONTAL LOBE

OCCIPITAL LOBE

Cerebellum

Brain stem

Spinal cord

Figure 5-3

Parts of the brain, side view. The brain consists of three main parts: the *brain stem,* the cerebellum, and, above those, the large cerebrum. The brain stem, an extension of the spinal cord, is one of the regions of the brain most completely developed at birth. It controls such basic bodily functions, as breathing, circulation, and reflexes. The *cerebellum,* at birth, begins to control balance and muscle tone; later it coordinates sensory and motor activity. The *cerebrum* constitutes almost 70 percent of the weight of the nervous system and handles thought, memory, language, and emotion. It is divided into two halves, or hemispheres, each of which has four sections, or lobes. (a) The *occipital lobe* processes visual information. (b) The *parietal lobe* allows an infant to receive touch sensations and spatial information, which facilitates eye-hand coordination. (c) The *temporal lobe* helps with hearing and language. (d) The *fontal lobe* develops gradually during the first year, permitting such higher-level functions as speech and reasoning. The *cerebral cortex,* the outer surface of the cerebrum, consists of gray matter; it is the seat of thought processes and mental activity. Parts of the cerebral cortex—the *sensorimotor cortex* and *cingulate cortex*—as well as several structures deep within the cerebrum, the *thalamus, hippocampus,* and *basal ganglia,* all of which control basic movements and functions, are largely developed at birth.

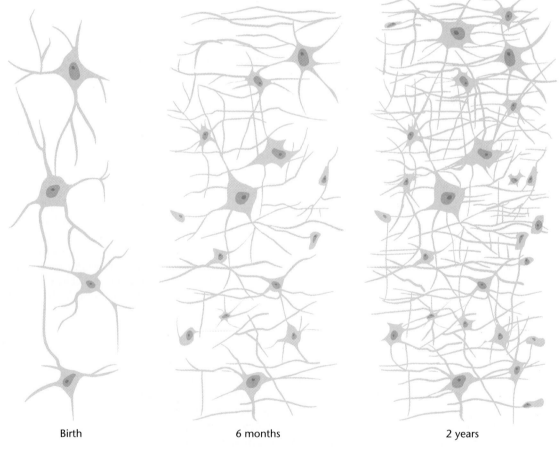

Birth

6 months

2 years

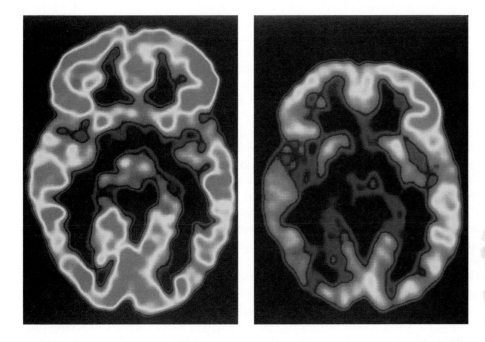

Extreme environmental deprivation in infancy can affect the structure of the brain, resulting in cognitive and emotional problems. A PET scan of a normal child's brain (left) shows regions of high (red) and low (blue and black) activity. A PET scan of the brain of a Romanian orphan institutionalized after birth (right) shows little activity.

This does not happen when the same procedure is carried out with adult cats. Apparently, early experience can modify the "wiring" of the visual cortex: neurons in that part of the brain become programmed to respond only to lines running in the direction the kittens are permitted to see. It appears that if certain cortical connections are not made early in life, these circuits "shut down" forever. Thus early experiences can have lasting effects on the capacity of the central nervous system to learn and store information (Greenough, Black, & Wallace, 1987; Pally, 1997; Wittrock, 1980; see Chapter 6). The implications of these findings for child development—and for social policy—are profound. Children deprived of stimulation early in life may be left with permanently stunted brains.

On the other hand, a stimulating environment can enhance brain growth and functioning. In one series of experiments, rats and other animals were raised in cages with wheels to run on, rocks to climb on, levers to manipulate, or other animals to interact with. These animals were then compared with littermates raised in standard cages or in isolation. The "enriched" animals had heavier brains with thicker cortical layers, more cells in the visual cortex, more complex cells, and higher levels of neurochemical activity, making it easier to form connections between axons and dendrites (Rosenzweig, 1984; Rosenzweig & Bennett, 1976). Even brain-damaged rats, when raised in an enriched setting, grow more dendritic connections (M. C. Diamond, 1988). Such findings have sparked successful efforts to stimulate the physical and mental development of children with Down syndrome and to help victims of brain damage recover function.

Of course, ethical constraints prevent controlled experiments on the comparative effects of environmental deprivation and enrichment on human infants. However, the discovery of thousands of infants and young children who had spent virtually their entire lives in overcrowded Romanian orphanages before the fall of the dictator Nicolae Ceausescu in December, 1989, offered an opportunity for a natural experiment (Ames, 1997). These abandoned children appeared to be starving, passive, and emotionless. They had spent much of their time lying quietly in their cribs or beds, with nothing to look at. They had had little contact with each other or with their caregivers and had heard little conversation or even noise. Most of the 2- and 3-year-olds did not walk or talk, and the older children played aimlessly. PET scans of their brains showed extreme inactivity in the temporal lobes, which regulate emotion and receive sensory input.

Many of these children were adopted by foreign families who wanted to help return them to normalcy. Researchers at Simon Fraser University in British Columbia studied 46 children, ages 8 months to 5½ years, who had been adopted by Canadian parents (Ames, 1997; S. J. Morison, Ames, & Chisholm, 1995). At the time of adoption, all showed delayed motor, language, or psychosocial development, and nearly 8 out of 10 were behind in all these areas.

How well did these children catch up? Three years later, when compared with children left behind in the Romanian institutions, they showed remarkable progress. Even when compared with Canadian children reared in their own homes from birth, about one-third had no serious problems and were doing well—in a few cases, better than the average home-raised child. Another one-third—generally those who had been in institutions the longest—still had serious developmental problems. The rest were moving toward average performance and behavior. Apparently, then, with proper environmental stimulation, the human brain's plasticity often makes it possible to overcome the effects of extreme early deprivation.

The current findings on brain development underline what many child development experts have long said: that parents are a child's first and most important teachers. As we will see in the next two chapters, parents who provide pleasantly stimulating (but not overstimulating) sensory experiences and who frequently talk to their babies give them an important cognitive boost. The findings also underline the need for high quality child care when parents work (see Chapter 7).

CHECKPOINT

Can you . . .

• Explain the role of early experience in brain growth and development and draw implications for social policy?

Early Sensory Capacities

"The baby, assailed by eyes, ears, nose, skin, and entrails at once, feels that all is one great blooming, buzzing confusion," wrote the psychologist William James in 1890. We now know that this is far from true. Thanks to their burgeoning brains, even newborn infants can make fairly good sense of what they touch, see, smell, taste, and hear; and sensory stimulation in turn can promote rapid brain development.

Touch and Pain

Touch seems to be the first sense to develop, and for the first several months it is the most mature sensory system. When a hungry newborn's cheek is stroked near the mouth, the baby responds by trying to find a nipple. Early signs of this rooting reflex show up in the womb, 2 months after conception. By 32 weeks of gestation, all body parts are sensitive to touch, and this sensitivity increases during the first 5 days of life (Haith, 1986). Parents and caregivers of premature infants take advantage of this early sensitivity when they give "preemies" a gentle back rub. Gentle massage seems to foster a variety of physical, sensory, and cognitive gains (Cigales, Field, Lundy, Cuandra, & Hart, 1997; T. M. Field, 1986; Schanberg & Field, 1987).

The sense of touch is what enables people to feel pain. Often physicians performing surgery on newborn babies have avoided giving anesthesia because of a mistaken belief that neonates cannot feel pain, or feel it only briefly. For example, pain-killing medication is rarely given during circumcision (removal of the foreskin from the penis of male newborns for religious or medical reasons). Actually, even on the first day of life, babies can and do feel pain; and they become more sensitive to it during the next few days. Furthermore, pain experienced during the neonatal period may sensitize an infant to later pain, perhaps by affecting the neural pathways that process painful stimuli. In one study, circumcised 4- and 6-month-olds had stronger reactions to the pain of vaccination than uncircumcised infants, but the reaction was muted among infants who had been treated with a painkilling cream before being circumcised (Taddio, Katz, Ilersich, & Koren, 1997).

Sight

By contrast with touch, vision is the least developed sense at birth. The eyes of newborns are smaller than those of adults, the retinal structures are incomplete, and the optic nerve is underdeveloped. Newborns blink at bright lights. Their peripheral vision is very narrow; it more than doubles between 2 and 10 weeks of age (E. Tronick, 1972). The ability to follow a moving target also develops rapidly in the first months, as does color perception. By about 2 months, babies can tell red from green; by about 3 months, they can distinguish blue (Haith, 1986). Four-month-old babies can discriminate among red, green, blue, and yellow; like most adults, they prefer red and blue (M. Bornstein, Kessen, & Weiskopf, 1976; Teller & Bornstein, 1987).

A neonate's eyes focus best from about 1 foot away, the typical distance from the face of a person holding the baby. Vision becomes much more acute during the first year, reaching the 20/20 level by about the sixth month (Aslin, 1987). (This measure of vision means that a person can read letters on a specified line on a standard eye chart from 20 feet away.) *Binocular vision*—the use of both eyes to focus, allowing perception of depth and distance—usually does not develop until 4 or 5 months (Bushnell & Boudreau, 1993).

From birth, babies can choose what to look at. The amount of time they spend looking at different sights is a measure of their ***visual preference,*** which is based on the ability to make visual distinctions. Babies less than 2 days old prefer curved lines to straight lines, complex patterns to simple patterns, three-dimensional objects to two-dimensional objects, pictures of faces to pictures of other things, and new sights to familiar ones (Fantz, 1963, 1964, 1965; Fantz, Fagen, & Miranda, 1975; Fantz & Nevis, 1967). By observing infants' visual preferences, researchers have found that neonatal *pattern vision,* the ability to distinguish between patterns, is related to future cognitive development. In one classic study, ratings on a neonatal visual pattern test predicted children's IQ scores at age 3 or 4 better than neonatal ratings on neurological tests (Miranda, Hack, Fantz, Fanaroff, & Klaus, 1977).

visual preference An infant's tendency to look longer at certain stimuli than at others, which depends on the ability to make visual distinctions.

Smell and Taste

The senses of smell and taste begin to develop in the womb (see Chapter 3). The flavors and odors of foods an expectant mother consumes may be transmitted to the fetus through the amniotic fluid. After birth, a similar transmission occurs through breast milk. In one study (Mennella & Beauchamp, 1996b), breast fed infants sucked longer and more strongly after their mothers drank diluted vanilla extract, as did bottle-fed infants when vanilla was added to their formula. Experience plays a bigger part in preferences for specific odors than in taste preferences, which seem to be largely innate (Bartoshuk & Beauchamp, 1994).

Newborns can tell where odors are coming from. When an ammonium compound is dabbed on one side of a newborn's nose, even a 1-day-old baby will turn the nose to the other side (Rieser, Yonas, & Wilkner, 1976). Newborns also can distinguish odors. They seem to show by their expression that they like the way vanilla and strawberries smell but do not like the smell of rotten eggs or fish (Steiner, 1979). The preference for pleasant odors seems to be learned in utero and during the first few days after birth, and the variety of odors transmitted through the mother's breast milk may contribute to this learning (Bartoshuk & Beauchamp, 1994).

Six-day-old breastfed infants prefer their mother's breast pad over that of another nursing mother, but 2-day-olds do not, suggesting that babies need a few days' experience to learn how their mothers smell (Macfarlane, 1975). Bottle-fed babies do not make such a distinction (Cernoch & Porter, 1985). From an evolutionary point of view, neonates' recognition of, and preference for, the odor of their own mother's breast may well have been a survival mechanism. Mothers and other family members also can identify their own infant's odor, suggesting that the sense of smell may aid in kinship recognition (Rovee-Collier, 1996).

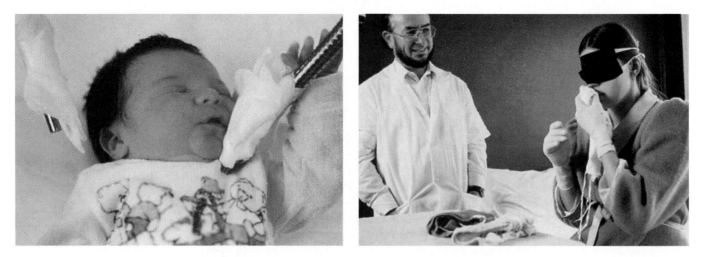

The nose knows. Three-day-old infants, like this one, are more peaceful when they smell pieces of gauze that their mothers have worn than when they smell cloth worn by other women. And blindfolded mothers can distinguish by smell the shirts their own babies have worn from shirts worn by other babies.

Newborns prefer sweet tastes to sour or bitter ones. The sweeter the fluid, the harder they suck and the more they drink (Haith, 1986). An inborn "sweet tooth" may help a baby adapt to life outside the womb; breast milk is quite sweet, and so are the ripe, nutritionally rich fruits and vegetables that soon become part of an infant's diet. Newborns' rejection of bitter tastes is probably a survival mechanism, since many bitter substances are toxic (Bartoshuk & Beauchamp, 1994).

Sweetened water calms crying newborns, whether full-term or two to three weeks premature—evidence that not only the taste buds themselves (which seem to be fairly well-developed by 20 weeks of gestation), but the mechanisms which produce this calming effect are functional before normal term (B. A. Smith & Blass, 1996). Sometime between 2 and 4 weeks of age, however, sweetened water seems to lose much of its power, unless it is combined with eye contact with the caregiver (Zeifman, Delaney, & Blass, 1996). This finding has fascinating implications regarding the coordination of the senses, as well as the interaction of physical, cognitive, and psychosocial aspects of the relationship between infants and their mothers or other caregivers. One-month-old babies can see the caregiver's features more clearly than before, and they actively seek eye contact. Furthermore, their cognitive recognition of the caregiver's face seems to have taken on emotional significance: it has a calming effect independent of its association with suckling or taste in the feeding situation.

Does a breastfeeding mother's diet have long-term effects on her baby's food preferences? Animal studies suggest that the answer may be yes. Young animals are more likely to accept a flavor if they were exposed to it in their mother's milk, and the amount of variety in the mother's diet seems to influence the young animal's later willingness to eat novel foods. Further research may determine whether early experience with flavors has similar effects on human babies (Mennella & Beauchamp, 1996b).

Hearing

Hearing is functional even before birth; fetuses respond to sounds and seem to learn to recognize them (see Chapter 3). Newborns' ability to distinguish sounds is well established. Three-day-old infants can tell new speech sounds from those they have heard before (L. R. Brody, Zelazo, & Chaika, 1984). At 1 month, babies can discriminate between sounds as close as "ba" and "pa" (Eimas, Siqueland, Jusczyk, & Vigorito, 1971). As we reported in Chapter 3, babies less than 3 days old respond differently to a story heard while in the womb than to other stories, by sucking more on a nipple that activates a recording of the story heard prenatally (DeCasper & Spence, 1986). They also can tell their mother's voice from a stranger's, and they prefer their native language to a foreign language (DeCasper & Fifer, 1980; C. Moon, Cooper, & Fifer, 1993). Early recognition of voices and language heard in the womb may be a mechanism for forming a relationship between parents and child.

Sensitivity to auditory distinctions may be an early indicator of cognitive abilities. One study found significant correlations between the ability to discriminate between sounds at 4 months of age and IQ scores at 5 years (O'Connor, Cohen, & Parmelee, 1984). In Chapter 6, we look further at the relationship between infants' processing of sensory information and childhood IQ.

Motor Development

Babies do not have to be taught such basic motor skills as grasping, crawling, and walking. They just need room to move and freedom to see what they can do. When the central nervous system, muscles, and bones are mature enough and the environment offers the right opportunities, babies keep surprising the adults around them with their new abilities. The more babies can do, the more they can explore; and the more they can explore, the more they can learn and do.

Maturation in Context

Newborn babies are busy. They turn their heads, kick their legs, flail their arms, and display an array of reflex behaviors. By about the fourth month, babies begin to make more deliberate movements. Increasing control over body parts is believed to reflect the growing role of the cerebral cortex, which allows infants to do specific motor tasks with growing accuracy. They master these tasks by repeated practice—a fact that can become tiresome for caregivers when the new skill involves dropping an object from the high chair and then crying for it until an adult picks it up so the baby can drop it again!

Babies develop motor skills in a certain sequence, which is generally believed to be genetically programmed. Infants must reach a certain level of physiological maturation before they are ready to exercise an ability; and each newly mastered ability prepares a baby to tackle the next. Skills follow the two principles of development outlined earlier: head to toe and inner to outer. Also, babies first learn simple skills and then combine them into increasingly complex *systems of action*, which permit a wider or more precise range of movement and more control of the environment. We can see these maturational principles at work in the development of two of the most distinctively human motor capacities that develop during infancy: the precision grip, in which thumb and index finger meet at the tips to form a circle, and the ability to walk on two legs. In developing the precision grip, an infant first learns to pick things up with the whole hand, fingers closing against the palm; later the baby begins to use neat little pincer motions with the thumb and forefinger to pick up tiny objects. In learning to walk, an infant first gains control of separate movements of the arms, legs, and feet before putting these movements together to take that momentous first step.

Today, some developmentalists are questioning the traditional view of motor development as a largely automatic, preordained series of stages directed by the maturing brain. Instead, according to Esther Thelen (1995) of Indiana University, it is a continuous, dynamic, multifactorial process of interaction between baby and environment. As evidence of the shortcomings of traditional maturational theory, Thelen points to what is usually called the walking reflex: stepping movements a neonate makes when held upright with the feet touching a surface. This behavior usually disappears in the second or third month; not until the latter part of the first year, when a baby is getting ready to walk, do such movements appear again. The usual explanation is a shift from subcortical to cortical control; an older baby's

CHECKPOINT

Can you . . .

- Give evidence for the early development of the senses of touch?
- List at least five ways in which newborns' vision is underdeveloped?
- Give evidence of newborns' sense of smell and taste and explain how breastfeeding plays a part in their development?
- Tell how auditory discrimination in newborns is related to fetal hearing and to intelligence in early childhood?

systems of action Increasingly complex combinations of simpler, previously acquired skills, which permit a wider or more precise range of movement and more control of the environment.

deliberate walking is seen as a new skill masterminded by the developing brain. But, Thelen observes, a newborn's stepping involves the same kinds of movements neonates make while lying down and kicking. Why would stepping stop, only to reappear months later, while kicking continues? The answer, she suggests, may be that babies' legs become thicker and heavier during the early months, but not yet strong enough to carry the increased weight (Thelen & Fisher, 1982, 1983). In fact, when young infants are held in warm water, which helps support the legs, stepping reappears. The ability to produce the movement has not changed—only the physical and environmental conditions that inhibit or promote it.

Maturation alone cannot adequately explain such observations, says Thelen; a baby must be studied in a physical and social context. Infant and environment form an interconnected system, and development has interacting causes. One is the infant's motivation to do something (say, pick up a toy or get to the other side of the room). The infant's physical characteristics and his or her position in a particular setting (for example, lying in a crib or being held upright in a pool) offer opportunities and constraints that affect whether and how the goal can be achieved. Ultimately, a solution emerges as a result of trying out behaviors and retaining those that most efficiently meet the goal. Babies' ongoing perceptions, including their recognition of what happens when they move in a certain way, may be the impetus for developmental change. Rather than being solely in charge of this process, says Thelen, the maturing brain is only one part of it.

According to Thelen, normal babies develop the same skills in the same order because they are built approximately the same way and have similar physical challenges and needs. Thus they eventually discover (for example) that walking is more efficient than crawling in most situations. The idea that this discovery arises from each particular baby's experience in a particular context may help explain why some babies learn to walk earlier than others.

Milestones of Motor Development

Motor development, however we explain it, is marked by a series of "milestones": achievements a child masters before going on to more difficult ones. The *Denver Developmental Screening Test* was designed to identify children who are not developing normally, but it can also be used to chart normal progress between the ages of 1 month and 6 years (Frankenburg, Dodds, Fandal, Kazuk, & Cohrs, 1975). The test covers such gross motor skills (those using large muscles) as rolling over and catching a ball, and such fine motor skills (using small muscles) as grasping a rattle and copying a circle. It also assesses language development (for example, knowing the definitions of words) and personality and social development (such as smiling spontaneously and dressing without help).

The newest edition, the Denver II Scale (Frankenburg et al., 1992), includes revised norms and many new items. The norms are the ages at which 25 percent, 50 percent, and 90 percent of children can perform each skill (see Table 5-1 for examples). A child who cannot yet do something that 90 percent of children the same age can already do is considered developmentally delayed. A child with two or more delays in two or more categories may need special attention.

In the following discussions, when we talk about what the "average" baby can do, we refer to the 50 percent Denver norms. There is, however, no "average" baby. Normality covers a wide range; about half of all babies master these skills before the ages given, and about half afterward. Also, it's important to remember that the Denver norms were standardized on a western population and are not necessarily valid in assessing children from other cultures. For example, southeast Asian children who were given the Denver did not play pat-a-cake, did not pick up raisins, and did not dress themselves at the expected ages (V. Miller, Onotera, & Deinard, 1984). Yet that did not indicate slow development: In their culture, children do not play pat-a-cake; raisins look like a

CHECKPOINT

Can you . . .

• Contrast Thelen's contextual explanation for motor development with the traditional maturational view, and tell how she supports her explanation?

Denver Developmental Screening Test Screening test given to children 1 month to 6 years old to determine whether they are developing normally; it assesses gross motor skills, fine motor skills, language development, and personality and social development.

Table 5.1	Milestones of Motor Development		
Skill	**25 Percent**	**50 Percent**	**90 Percent**
Rolling over	2.1 months	3.2 months	5.4 months
Grasping rattle	2.6 months	3.3 months	3.9 months
Sitting without support	5.4 months	5.9 months	6.8 months
Standing while holding on	6.5 months	7.2 months	8.5 months
Grasping with thumb and finger	7.2 months	8.2 months	10.2 months
Standing alone well	10.4 months	11.5 months	13.7 months
Walking well	11.1 months	12.3 months	14.9 months
Building tower of two cubes	13.5 months	14.8 months	20.6 months
Walking up steps	14.1 months	16.6 months	21.6 months
Jumping in place	21.4 months	23.8 months	2.4 years
Copying circle	3.1 years	3.4 years	4.0 years

Note: This table shows the approximate ages when 25 percent, 50 percent, and 90 percent of children can perform each skill, according to the Denver Training Manual II.
Source: Adapted from Frankenburg et al., 1992.

medicine they are taught to avoid; and their parents continue to help them dress much longer than western parents do.

Again, as we trace a typical infant's progress in head control, hand control, and locomotion during the first year, notice how these developments follow the cephalocaudal (head to toe) and proximodistal (inner to outer) principles.

Head Control

At birth, most infants can turn their heads from side to side while lying on their backs. While lying chest down, many can lift their heads enough to turn them. Within the first 2 to 3 months, they lift their heads higher and higher. By 4 months of age, almost all infants can keep their heads erect while being held or supported in a sitting position.

Hand Control

Babies are born with a grasping reflex. If the palm of an infant's hand is stroked, the hand closes tightly. At about 3½ months, most infants can grasp an object of moderate size, such as a rattle, but have trouble holding a small object. Next they begin to grasp objects with one hand and transfer them to the other, and then to hold (but not pick up) small objects. Sometime between 7 and 11 months, their hands become coordinated enough to pick up a tiny object, such as a pea, with pincer-like motion. After that, hand control becomes increasingly precise. By 15 months, the average baby can build a tower of two cubes. A few months after the third birthday, the average toddler can copy a circle fairly well.

Locomotion

After 3 months, the average infant begins to roll over purposefully, first from front to back and then from back to front. (Before this time, babies sometimes roll over accidentally, and so even the youngest ones should never be left alone on a surface from which they might roll off.)

Babies sit either by raising themselves from a prone (face down) position or by plopping down from a standing position. The average baby can sit without support by 6 months and can assume a sitting position without help about 2½ months later.

At about 6 months, most babies begin to get around under their own power. They may wriggle on their bellies and pull their bodies along with their arms, dragging their feet behind. They may hitch or scoot by moving along in a sitting position, pushing forward with their arms and legs. They may bear-walk, with hands and feet touching the ground. They may crawl on hands and knees with their trunks raised, parallel to the floor. By 9 or 10 months, most babies get around quite well by such means, and so parents have to keep a close eye on them. This new ability of self-locomotion has important cognitive and psychosocial implications (see Box 5-2).

By holding onto a helping hand or a piece of furniture, the average baby can stand at a little past 7 months of age, but will only occasionally stand erect. A little more than 4 months later, after dogged practice in pulling themselves to an upright posture, most babies let go and stand alone. The average baby can stand well about 2 weeks or so before the first birthday.

All these developments are milestones along the way to the major motor achievement of infancy: walking. Humans begin to walk later than other species, possibly because babies' heavy heads and short legs make balance difficult (Thelen, quoted in Bushnell & Boudreau, 1993). For some months before they can stand without support, babies practice "cruising" while holding onto furniture—sitting down abruptly when they reach table's end and crawling or lurching from chair to sofa. Soon after they can stand alone well, at about 11½ months, most infants take their first unaided steps, tumble, go back to crawling, and then try again. The average baby is walking regularly, if shakily, within a few days. Within a few weeks, soon after the first birthday, the child is walking well and thus achieves the status of toddler.

During the second year, children begin to climb stairs one at a time. (Since they can crawl upstairs before that—and tumble down long before—vigilance and baby gates are needed.) At first they put one foot and then the other on the same step before going on to the next higher one; later they will alternate feet. Walking down stairs comes later. In their second year, toddlers run and jump; their parents, trying to keep up with them, run out of energy. By age 3½, most children can balance briefly on one foot and begin to hop.

Motor Development and Perception

Perception allows an infant to learn about the environment and navigate in it; motor experience sharpens and modifies the infant's sensory perceptions. This bidirectional connection between perception and motion is an important topic of investigation.

A classic contribution to the study of infants' perceptions, and to the nature-nurture controversy, made use of a *visual cliff* (Walk & Gibson, 1961). Researchers tested the hypothesis that children are born with no knowledge of space and come to know about height, depth, and distance only through experience. The researchers put babies on a glass tabletop, over a checkerboard pattern. The glass formed a continuous surface; but, to an adult's eye, the pattern underneath made it appear that there was a vertical drop in the center of the table—a "visual cliff." Would infants see the same illusion of depth and feel themselves in danger?

Young infants did see a difference between the "ledge" and the "drop." Six-month-old babies crawled freely on the "ledge" but avoided the "drop," even when they saw their mothers on the far side of the table. When even younger infants, ages 2 and 3 months, were placed face down over the visual cliff, their hearts slowed down, probably in response to the illusion of depth (J. J. Campos, Langer, & Krowitz, 1970). However, a slowed heart rate, which indicates interest, does not mean that the younger infants were afraid of falling; fear would be indicated by a *faster* heart rate. Not until babies can get around by themselves do they generally learn from experience, or from a caregiver's warnings, that a steep dropoff can be dangerous (Bertenthal, Campos, & Kermoian, 1994).

The visual cliff experiments suggested that *depth perception,* the ability to perceive objects and surfaces three-dimensionally, is either innate or learned very early. More recent analysis indicates that it may depend, at least in part, on motor development.

visual cliff Apparatus designed to give an illusion of depth and used to assess depth perception in infants.

depth perception Ability to perceive objects and surfaces three-dimensionally.

Box 5-2   The Far-Reaching Effects of Crawling

Did you ever drive for the first time to a place where you had gone only as a passenger? As a driver, you probably saw landmarks and were aware of turns you had never noticed before. After getting to your destination on your own, you most likely felt more familiar with the route than you had earlier. Something similar seems to happen to babies when they begin to get around on their own, first by crawling and then by walking, after having always been carried or wheeled. The emergence of self-produced locomotion is a turning point in the second half of the first year of life, influencing all domains of development—physical, cognitive, emotional, and social.

Between 7 and 9 months, babies change greatly in many ways. They show an understanding of such concepts as "near" and "far." They imitate more complex behaviors, and they show new fears; but they also show a new sense of security around their parents or other caregivers. Since these changes, and others that occur around this time, involve so many different psychological functions and processes and occur during such a short time span, some observers tie them all in with a reorganization of brain function. This neurological development may be set in motion by a skill that emerges at this time: the ability to crawl, which makes it possible to get around independently. Crawling has been called a "setting event" because it sets the stage for other changes in the infant and his or her relationships with the environment and the people in it (Bertenthal & Campos, 1987; Bertenthal, Campos, & Barrett, 1984; Bertenthal, Campos, & Kermoian, 1994).

Crawling exerts a powerful influence on babies' lives by giving them a new view of the world. When carried, they need not pay much attention to their surroundings. When they begin to crawl, they become more sensitive to where objects are, how big they are, whether they can be moved, and how they look. Crawling babies can differentiate similar forms that are unlike in color, size, or location (J. Campos, Bertenthal, & Benson, 1980). Babies are more successful in finding a toy hidden in a box when they crawl around the box than when they are carried around it (Benson & Uzgiris, 1985); and when they see an object hidden in a new location, they look for it there (Bertenthal et al., 1994).

Crawling helps babies learn to judge distances and perceive depth. As they move about, they see that people and objects can look different depending on how close they are. Crawling babies also develop fear of heights. When babies start to move around by themselves, they are in danger of falling. To keep them from getting hurt, caregivers often hover over babies, remove them from dangerous locations, or cry out and jump up when a child is about to get into trouble. Babies are sensitive to these actions and emotions, and they learn to be afraid of places from which they might fall.

The ability to move from one place to another also has social implications. Crawling babies are no longer "prisoners" of place. If Milly wants to be close to her mother and far away from a strange dog, she can move toward the one and away from the other. This is an important step in developing a sense of mastery, enhancing self-confidence and self-esteem.

The ability to crawl gets babies into new situations. As they become more mobile, they begin to hear warnings like "Come back!" and "Don't touch!" They also receive loving help as adult hands pick them up and turn them in a safer direction. They learn to look to caregivers for clues as to whether a situation is secure or frightening—a skill known as *social referencing* (see Chapter 7). Crawling babies do more social referencing than babies who have not yet begun to crawl. They seem to pick up emotional signals from their caregivers' faces or gestures, which in turn influence their behavior (J. B. Garland, 1982). Thus the physical milestone of crawling has far-reaching effects in helping babies see and respond to their world in new ways.

When babies can get around under their own power, they can take the initiative in going after something they want, such as a furry cat's tail. Independent locomotion sets the stage for new cognitive and social skills.

No matter how enticing a mother's arms are, this baby is staying away from them. As young as she is, she can perceive depth and wants to avoid falling off what looks like a cliff.

haptic perception Ability to acquire information about properties of objects, such as size, weight, and texture, by handling them.

People perceive depth with the help of several kinds of cues affecting the image of an object on the retina of the eye. These cues involve not only eye coordination, but also motor control (Bushnell & Boudreau, 1993). *Kinetic cues* are changes in an image with movement either of the object or of the observer. To find out which is moving, a baby might hold his or her head still for a moment, an ability that is well established by about 3 months. As we have already mentioned, *binocular cues* (both eyes working together) for depth are present by about 5 months.

Sometime between 5 and 7 months, babies respond to such cues as relative size and differences in texture and shading. To judge depth from these cues, babies make judgments that depend on *haptic perception,* the ability to acquire information by handling objects rather than just looking at them. Haptic perception comes only after babies develop enough eye-hand coordination to reach for objects and grasp them. Up to 3 months of age, when infants clutch objects tightly in their fists, they can perceive temperature, size, and possibly hardness. Between about 4 and 10 months they make repetitive finger and hand movements that help them perceive texture and weight: scratching, rubbing, waving, banging, squeezing, and poking objects and passing them from one hand to the other. Toward the end of the first year, when infants are strong enough to sit without supporting themselves with one hand, they can use both hands to fondle an object and become better aware of its shape (Bushnell & Boudreau, 1993).

Environmental Influences on Motor Development

Although motor development does not seem to be affected by sex or by parents' education (Bayley, 1965), its pace does seem to respond to certain contextual factors. For example, one study found that babies born in the winter or spring begin to crawl about 3 weeks earlier than those born in summer or fall (Benson, 1993). It may be that with milder weather and more daylight, the winter and spring babies were more active at critical times in their development.

Cross-cultural studies show differences in how and when certain skills are typically acquired. Let's look at this evidence and then at how environmental influences affect the pace of development.

The major motor achievement of infancy, walking, occurs at varying ages. Environmental influences may affect how quickly a child learns to walk. Some babies find it easier to take their first steps when they have something to push, like this doll carriage.

Cross-Cultural Comparisons

Even for basic motor behaviors, what is normal in one culture may not be in another. African babies tend to be more advanced than Caucasian infants in standing and walking; Asian infants are apt to develop such gross motor skills more slowly. Some of these differences may be related to temperament. Asian babies, for example, are typically more docile; this may explain why they respond more calmly when a cloth is pressed to their noses, and why they tend to stay closer to their parents (H. Kaplan & Dove, 1987).

Some differences in the pace of motor development may reflect a culture's child-rearing practices. A study of 288 normal full-term babies from the Yucatan peninsula in Mexico found that at 3 months these babies were ahead of United States babies in motor skills. Yet by 11 months the Mexican babies lagged so far behind in their ability to move about that a U.S. baby at the typical level of these Mexican babies might be considered neurologically impaired (Solomons, 1978). However, the Mexican babies were *not* slow in developing according to standards and customs of their own culture. As infants, Mexican babies are swaddled, restricting their movement. Later they are restrained by being carried more than American babies, by sleeping in hammocks (which become net "cages" compared with the open space of a firm-mattressed crib), and by not being put on the ground to play (because of insects and local beliefs about the dangers of cold floors). On the other hand, Mexican babies may be more advanced in manipulative skills; without toys to play with, they discover and play with their fingers earlier than U.S. babies. Evidence *against* an environmental explanation for such differences, however, is that Navajo babies—also swaddled for most of the day—begin to walk at about the same age as other U.S. babies (Chisholm, 1983).

Other research found that children of the Ache in eastern Paraguay do not begin to walk until 18 to 20 months of age—about 9 months later than U.S. babies (H. Kaplan & Dove, 1987). Ache mothers pull their babies back to their laps when the infants begin to crawl away. The Ache mothers closely supervise their babies to protect them from the hazards of nomadic life, and also because the women's primary responsibility is child raising rather than subsistence labor. Children whose mothers spend less time with them may become independent sooner because their other caregivers may supervise them less closely. (This may now apply to U.S. babies, who, in an era of day care, seem to be developing some skills more quickly.)

Slower-developing children often catch up, given a supportive environment. Ache babies show the slowest motor development reported for any human group; but as 8- to 10-year-olds, they climb tall trees, chop branches, and play in ways that enhance their motor skills. Development, then, may be viewed as "a series of immediate adjustments to current conditions as well as a cumulative process in which succeeding stages build upon earlier ones" (H. Kaplan & Dove, 1987, p. 197).

Can Environment Slow or Speed Up Motor Development?

When children are well fed and well cared for and have physical freedom and the chance to practice motor skills, their motor development is likely to be normal for their culture. An environment grossly deficient in any of these areas, like that in the Romanian orphanages described earlier in this chapter, may retard motor development.

Can environmental influences speed up motor development? For many years, the answer was thought to be no. In a famous experiment, Arnold Gesell (1929) trained one monozygotic twin, but not the other, in stair-climbing, block-building, and hand coordination. As the children got older, the untrained twin became just as expert as the trained one, showing, said Gesell, "the powerful influence of maturation." According to Gesell, children perform certain activities when they are ready, and training gives no advantage.

However, later research indicates that early training can influence development. In one study, infants trained in stepping at 8 weeks walked at an average of 10 months, while those in an untrained control group did not begin walking until an average of 12⅓ months (P. R. Zelazo, Zelazo, & Kolb, 1972). Why did this happen? Perhaps there is a critical period during which the newborn's repetitive walking response can be translated into a specific later voluntary action. Then again, practice in one such behavior pattern might promote maturation of the brain's ability to control related activities. Another possibility, in line with Thelen's view, is that training strengthened the infants' legs, allowing them to resume stepping at an earlier-than-usual age.

A randomized follow-up experiment was designed to see whether effects of training are limited to the practiced ability. Six-week-old healthy baby boys who were trained for 7 weeks, either in stepping alone or in stepping and sitting, stepped more than those untrained in stepping movements; and infants trained either in sitting alone or in stepping and sitting sat more. Infants trained in sitting alone did not step more, and infants trained in stepping alone did not sit more (N. A. Zelazo, Zelazo, Cohen, & Zelazo, 1993; see Figure 5-5). Apparently early training can accelerate a specific behavior, but the training does not carry over to other abilities. These results do not indicate whether changes in the brain or in muscle strength, or both, are involved; but they do seem to rule out a view of maturation as purely biologically determined and suggest that learning plays a greater role in early motor development than has generally been believed.

In recent years, many parents have put their babies in mobile walkers, partly because the babies like them and also because the parents think the walkers help

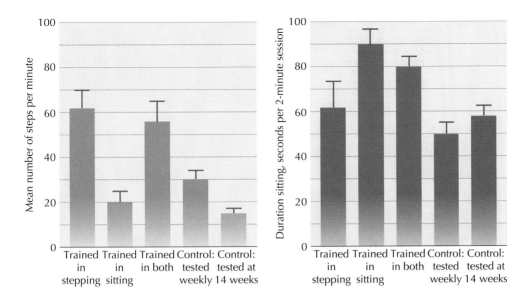

Figure 5-5
Infants trained in sitting and stepping for 7 weeks performed more of those activities than did untrained infants. (*left*) Mean number of steps per minute and standard error for five groups at 14 weeks of age; (*right*) mean duration of sitting per 2 minutes and standard error for five groups at 14 weeks of age.
Source: N. A. Zelazo, Zelazo, Cohen, & Zelazo, 1993, p. 689.

the babies learn to walk earlier. This belief is mistaken; use of baby walkers may discourage crawling and *delay* walking. Walkers were responsible for an estimated 25,000 injuries in the United States in 1993 and 11 deaths in the previous five years. Safety experts recommend not using them (C. Collins, 1994), and the American Academy of Pediatrics has called for a ban on their manufacture and sale (AAP Committee on Injury and Poison Prevention, 1995b).

Health

Infancy and toddlerhood are risky times of life, though far less so than they used to be. How many babies die during the first year, and why? What can be done to prevent dangerous or debilitating childhood diseases? How can we ensure that infants and toddlers will live, grow, and develop as they should?

Reducing Infant Mortality

One of the most tragic losses is the death of an infant. Great strides have been made in protecting the lives of new babies, but these improvements are not evenly distributed throughout the population. Too many babies still die—in 1995, nearly 30,000 in the United States alone (Anderson, Kochanek, & Murphy, 1997)—some without warning and for no apparent reason.

Trends in Infant Mortality

In the United States, the ***infant mortality rate***—the proportion of babies who die within the first year—is the lowest ever. In 1995, there were 7.6 deaths in the first year for every 1,000 live births, compared with 20 per 1,000 in 1970, a 62 percent drop. *Neonatal mortality,* deaths during the first four weeks, plunged even further, by about 68 percent. Still, more than two-thirds of infant deaths take place during the neonatal period. *Postneonatal mortality* (death after the first four weeks) has declined by about 45 percent (National Center for Health Statistics [NCHS], 1997), largely because of better nutrition and sanitation. However, because of the greater drop in neonatal mortality, proportionally more infant deaths occur after the first month, often in poor families with little or no access to medical care.

The continuing improvement in infant mortality rates during the 1990s, even at a time when more babies are born perilously small, has been due in part to effective treatment for respiratory distress and to prevention of sudden infant death

CHECKPOINT

Can you . . .

- Assess the significance of the Denver norms, and trace a typical infant's progress in head control, hand control, and locomotion?

- Explain the relationship between motor development and haptic perception?

- Give evidence for environmental influences on motor development?

infant mortality rate
Proportion of babies born alive who die within the first year.

Chapter 5 Physical Development and Health During the First Three Years **179**

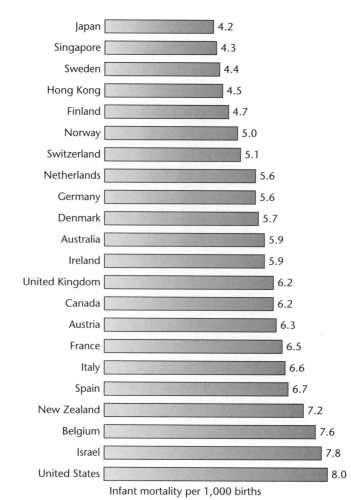

Figure 5-6

Infant mortality rates in industrialized countries. In 1994, the United States had a higher infant mortality rate than 21 other industrialized nations with populations of more than 1 million, largely because of its very high mortality rate for African American babies (see Table 5-2). In recent years, most nations, including the United States, have shown dramatic improvement.

Note: Rates for Hong Kong, Norway, Denmark, France, Spain, New Zealand, and Israel are for 1993. Rates for Denmark and Canada are based on provisional data.

Source: Wegman, 1996, Table 2, p. 1022, based on data from United Nations Statistical Division.

Country	Infant mortality per 1,000 births
Japan	4.2
Singapore	4.3
Sweden	4.4
Hong Kong	4.5
Finland	4.7
Norway	5.0
Switzerland	5.1
Netherlands	5.6
Germany	5.6
Denmark	5.7
Australia	5.9
Ireland	5.9
United Kingdom	6.2
Canada	6.2
Austria	6.3
France	6.5
Italy	6.6
Spain	6.7
New Zealand	7.2
Belgium	7.6
Israel	7.8
United States	8.0

syndrome (SIDS) (discussed in the next section), as well as to medical advances in keeping very small babies alive and treating sick newborns. Birth defects were the leading cause of infant deaths in 1995. Second was low birthweight, third was SIDS, and fourth was respiratory distress syndrome (NCHS, 1997).

Even though fewer infants are dying than in the past, death in infancy is still far too prevalent. The infant mortality rate in the United States in 1995 was higher than the mortality rate in any other age group below ages 55–64 (NCHS, 1997). U.S. babies have a poorer chance of reaching their first birthday than babies in many other large industrialized countries (NCHS, 1997; Wegman, 1996; see Figure 5-6).

Age of the mother is not a factor in neonatal mortality; pound for pound, babies born to teenagers and those born to adults have an equal chance of survival. What puts teenagers' babies at higher risk of dying in the first 4 weeks is the greater likelihood that they will be born very small (Rees, Lederman, & Kiely, 1996). This is especially likely to be true of African American babies.

Although infant mortality has declined for both black and white babies, the rates for white babies have fallen more (see Table 5-2). Black babies are still dying at nearly two and a half times the rate of white babies—15.1 as compared with 6.3 per 1,000 live births in 1995 (NCHS, 1997)—and this disparity is closely comparable to the disparity in the prevalence of low birthweight (see Chapter 4). Latino infants, as a group, die at only slightly higher rates than non-Hispanic white babies (NCHS, 1997; Wegman, 1993, 1994). White newborns are more likely to die of birth defects than of other causes, whereas black neonates are most likely to die of disorders related to low birthweight (Anderson et al., 1997).

These facts raise troubling questions. Why, in a wealthy country like the United States, is infant mortality not declining even faster? Why does the large

Table 5-2   Comparison of Black and White Infants

	Low Birthweight (less than 5½ pounds, or 2,500 grams), % of births (1995)	Very Low Birthweight (less than 3.3 pounds, or 1,500 grams), % of births (1994)	Decline in Infant Mortality Rate, per 1,000 (1995)	Neonatal Mortality Rate per 1,000 (1995)	Postneonatal Mortality Rate per 1,000 (1995)	Infant Mortality Rate, 1970–1995
Black infants	13.13	2.97	15.1	9.8	5.3	54%
White infants	6.22	1.06	6.3	4.1	2.2	65%

Note: Black infants are more likely than white infants to die in the first year from sudden infant death syndrome, respiratory distress syndrome, infections, injuries, disorders related to short gestation and low birthweight, pneumonia and influenza, and as a result of maternal complications of pregnancy.
Source: NCHS, 1997

disparity between black and white babies continue? Although physicians have the knowledge and technology to diagnose and treat high-risk pregnancies and help vulnerable infants, this know-how has not equally benefited all babies.

Sudden Infant Death Syndrome

Sudden infant death syndrome (SIDS), sometimes called "crib death," is the sudden death of an infant under 1 year of age in which the cause of death remains unexplained after a thorough investigation that includes an autopsy. In 1995, about 3,400 babies were victims of SIDS, approximately a 40 percent decrease since 1979 (Guyer, Strobino, Ventura, MacDorman, & Martin, 1996; NCHS, 1997). SIDS occurs most often between 2 and 4 months of age (Willinger, 1995).

A number of risk factors, such as being black, male, and of low birthweight, are associated with SIDS. Often SIDS mothers are young, unmarried, and poor; have received little or no prenatal care; have been ill during pregnancy; smoke or abuse drugs or both; and have had another baby less than a year before the one who died. The fathers, too, are likely to be young and to smoke (Babson & Clarke, 1983; C. E. Hunt & Brouillette, 1987; Kleinberg, 1984; Klonoff-Cohen et al., 1995; E. A. Mitchell et al., 1993; D. C. Shannon & Kelly, 1982a, 1982b; U.S. Department of Health and Human Services [USDHHS], 1990). The risk of SIDS is worsened by low socioeconomic circumstances, but SIDS also strikes infants in advantaged families.

What causes SIDS? The condition is not contagious, nor is it caused by choking or vomiting. One theory suggests a neurological anomaly, perhaps an abnormality in brain chemistry. Studies point to difficulties in the regulation of respiratory control (C. E. Hunt & Brouillette, 1987), in making the transition from sleep to wakefulness (Schechtman, Harper, Wilson, & Southall, 1992), or in arousal and ability to turn the head to avoid suffocation (K. A. Waters, Gonzalez, Jean, Morielli, & Brouillette, 1996). It seems likely that SIDS results from a combination of factors. An underlying biological defect may make some infants vulnerable, during a critical period in their development, to certain contributing or triggering factors, such as exposure to smoke or sleeping on the stomach (Cutz, Perrin, Hackman, & Czegledy-Nagy, 1996). However, some SIDS-labeled deaths may actually be the result of accidents (M. Bass, Kravath, & Glass, 1986) and a small porportion—perhaps 5 to 10 percent—of infanticide (Southall et al., 1997).

Research strongly supports the connection with parental smoking (Aligne & Stoddard, 1997; American Academy of Pediatrics Committee on Environmental Health, 1997; Haglund, 1993; E. A. Mitchell et al., 1993; Schoendorf & Kiely, 1992). In one nationally representative sample, the mother's smoking during pregnancy was the *only* risk factor independently associated with SIDS. Perhaps 30 percent of SIDS could be prevented if pregnant women did not smoke

sudden infant death syndrome (SIDS) Sudden and unexpected death of an apparently healthy infant.

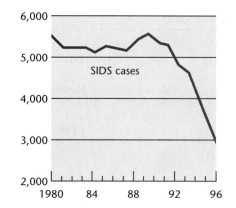

Figure 5-7

Number of deaths classified as sudden infant death syndrome (SIDS), 1980 to 1996. The sudden decline in SIDS cases after 1992 followed recommendations that babies be put to bed on their backs rather than their stomachs.

Source: Begley, 1997, p. 72; data from Centers for Disease Control and Prevention and National Center for Health Statistics.

(J. A. Taylor & Sanderson, 1995). Passive exposure to smoke is also a risk factor after birth; the more smoking around the baby, the greater the risk (Klonoff-Cohen et al., 1995). Exposure to smoke, both before and after birth, seems related to brain and lung development (Cutz et al., 1996; Milerad & Sundell, 1993). The 1993 International State of the Art Conference on SIDS recommended that parents and other caregivers stop smoking completely; at the very least, they should smoke less, and not around the baby (Köhler & Markestad, 1993).

A clue to what happens in SIDS has emerged from the discovery of a cell defect in a chemical receptor, or nerve ending, in the brain stem. This defect may prevent SIDS babies from awakening when they are breathing too much stale air containing carbon dioxide trapped under their blankets (Kinney et al., 1995). This may be especially likely to happen when the baby is sleeping face down; and it may be why SIDS deaths are more common in winter, when babies tend to be more heavily covered or tightly wrapped. Since many infants sleep face down at least part of the time, and relatively few succumb to SIDS, SIDS babies may be deficient in a protective mechanism that allows an infant to become aroused enough to turn the head when breathing is restricted (K. A. Waters et al., 1996).

Studies support the relationship between SIDS and sleeping on the stomach (J. A. Taylor et al., 1996). SIDS rates fell by as much as 70 percent in some countries following recommendations by the American Academy of Pediatrics and international medical authorities that healthy babies be put to sleep on their backs (Dwyer, Ponsonby, Blizzard, Newman, & Cochrane, 1995; C. E. Hunt, 1996; Skadberg, Morild, & Markestad, 1998; Willinger, Hoffman, & Hartford, 1994; see Figure 5-7). The only babies who should still be put to bed stomach-down are infants with swallowing or upper-airway difficulties or other special problems. Infants should not sleep on soft surfaces, such as pillows, quilts, or sheepskin (AAP Task Force on Infant Positioning and SIDS, 1992, 1996, 1997; Dwyer, Ponsonby, Newman, & Gibbons, 1991; Kemp, Livne, White, & Arfken, 1998).

Sharing a bed with the mother is a common practice in some cultures; its possible role in preventing or promoting SIDS has been controversial (see Box 5-3).

Immunization for Better Health

Since 1990, because of renewed public attention to the need to vaccinate children, both rates and number of cases of most vaccine-preventable illnesses in the United States have shown a downward trend (NCHS, 1997). More than 90 percent of the nation's children begin their immunizations on schedule, and more than 90 percent are fully inoculated by age 5, when it is required for school attendance, but there is often a lag in obtaining the recommended shots (Institute of Medicine [IOM], 1994). One report noted that fewer than half the 2-year-olds in major U.S. cities had gotten all their required shots, and those who *had* gotten them all had not received them at recommended intervals (Zell, Dietz, Stevenson, Cochi, &

Box 5-3 Sleep Customs

Until her first birthday, Maria shared the "family bed" with her parents. At first, Sean slept in a cradle next to his parents' bed but was soon moved into a crib in a separate room. There is considerable cultural variation in newborns' sleeping arrangements. In many cultures, infants sleep with their mothers for the first few years of life, often in the same bed. In the United States, it is common practice, reflecting the prevailing recommendations of childcare experts, to have a separate bed and a separate room for the infant. White and college-educated mothers are less likely to take their babies into bed with them than are African American mothers and mothers whose education ended with high school (Morelli, Rogoff, Oppenheim, & Goldsmith, 1992).

Some experts find benefits in the shared sleeping pattern. One research team that has been monitoring sleep patterns of mothers and their 3-month-old infants found that those who sleep together tend to wake each other up during the night and suggested that this may prevent the baby from sleeping too long and too deeply and having long breathing pauses that might be fatal (McKenna & Mosko, 1993). However, the American Academy of Pediatrics (AAP) Task Force on Infant Positioning and SIDS (1997) did not find this evidence persuasive. Instead, the Task Force found that, under some conditions, bed sharing can lead to SIDS (presumably, due to the danger that a sleeping mother may roll over onto her child).

Bed-sharing does promote breastfeeding, however. Infants who sleep with their mothers breastfeed about 3 times longer during the night than infants who sleep in separate beds (McKenna, Mosko, & Richard, 1997). By snuggling up together, mother and baby stay oriented toward each other's subtle bodily signals. Mothers can respond more quickly and easily to an infant's first whimpers of hunger, rather than having to wait until the baby's cries are loud enough to be heard from the next room.

In interviews, middle-class U.S. parents and Mayan mothers in rural Guatemala revealed their child-rearing values and goals in their explanations about sleeping arrangements (Morelli et al., 1992). The U.S. parents, many of whom kept their infants in the same room but not in the same bed for the first 3 to 6 months, said they moved the babies to separate rooms because they wanted to make them self-reliant and independent. The Mayan mothers kept infants and toddlers in their beds until the birth of a new baby, when the older child would sleep with another family member or in a bed in the mother's room. The Mayan mothers valued close parent-child relationships and expressed shock at the idea that anyone would put a baby to sleep in a room all alone.

Societal values influence parents' attitudes and behaviors. Throughout this book we will see many ways in which parents' attitudes and behaviors, often culturally determined, affect their children.

Bruce, 1994; Table 5-3 shows current recommendations). Immunization rates are lower among some minority groups and poor families (NCHS, 1997).

In 1994 Congress appropriated more than $800 million to improve community education, to make vaccines more available and less costly, and to provide free vaccine to the uninsured and those on Medicaid (Children's Defense Fund, 1995; Leary, 1994). By 1995, the proportion of 19- to 35-month-old children who were fully immunized had reached about 75 percent, but 1 in 4 children still lacked at least one of the required shots (Children's Defense Fund, 1996).

One reason some parents hesitate to immunize their children is fear that the vaccines may cause brain damage. This fear arose in response to cases of brain damage that some people attributed to injections of pertussis vaccine (to prevent whooping cough), which are usually given along with immunizations for diphtheria and tetanus in the DPT vaccine. However, the association between DPT and neurologic illness appears to be very small (Gale et al., 1994). The potential damage from the diseases that this vaccine prevents is far greater than the risks of the vaccine.

New and improved vaccines are being devised. For example, in 1995, the federal government approved a vaccine for chicken pox. It is recommended for all children over 1 year of age and for adolescents and adults who have not had the disease (Centers for Disease Control and Prevention [CDC], 1996a).

Immunization is cost-effective. Every dollar spent to immunize against measles, mumps, and rubella saves $13.40 as compared with the cost of treating these illnesses, and every dollar spent on pertussis immunization saves $11.10 (Harvey, 1990).

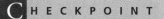

C H E C K P O I N T

Can you . . .

- Summarize trends in infant mortality and explain why black infants are more likely to die than white infants?

- Discuss risk factors, causes, and prevention of sudden infant death syndrome (SIDS)?

- Summarize trends in immunization and cite factors influencing these trends?

Table 5-3 Recommended Childhood Immunization Schedule*

Age ▶ Vaccine ▼	Birth	1 mo	2 mos	4 mos	6 mos	12 mos	15 mos	18 mos	4–6 yrs	11–12 yrs	14–16 yrs
Hepatitis B	Hep B–1									(Hep B)	
		Hep B–2			Hep B–3						
Diphtheria, Tetanus, Pertussis		DTaP† or DTP	DTaP or DTP	DTaP or DTP		DTaP or DTP			DTaP or DTP	Td††	
H influenzae type b		Hib	Hib	Hib		Hib					
Polio		Polio	Polio		Polio				Polio		
Measles, Mumps, Rubella (German measles)						MMR			MMR	(MMR)	
Varicella (Chicken pox)						Var				(Var)	

Approved by the Advisory Committee on Immunization Practices (ACIP), the American Academy of Pediatrics (AAP), and the American Academy of Family Physicians (AAFP).

*Vaccines are listed under the routinely recommended ages. Bars indicate range of acceptable ages for immunization. Catch-up immunization should be done during any visit when feasible. Ovals indicate vaccines to be assessed and given if necessary during the early adolescent visit.

†DTaP (diphtheria and tetanus toxoids and acellular pertussis vaccine) is the preferred vaccine for all doses in the vaccination series, including completion of the series in children who have received 1 or more doses of whole-cell DTP vaccine. Whole-cell DTP is an acceptable alternative to DTaP.

††Tetanus and diphtheria toxoids.

Source: Adapted from AAP Committee on Infectious Disease, 1998.

Fortunately, most babies survive and grow up healthy. The physical developments we have described in this chapter form the underpinning for cognitive and psychosocial developments that enable infants and toddlers to become more at home in their world, as we see in Chapters 6 and 7.

SUMMARY

Growth of Body and Brain

- A child's body grows most dramatically during the first year of life; growth proceeds at a rapid but diminishing rate during the next 2 years.
- Normal physical growth and motor development proceed according to the cephalocaudal and proximodistal principles.
- Breastfeeding offers many physiological and psychological benefits to the infant. However, the quality of the relationship between parents and baby is the most important element in promoting healthy psychological development.
- During the latter half of the first year, babies may begin to eat solid foods. Obesity in infancy does not necessarily predict obesity later in life.
- Much of the brain's growth after birth consists of the formation of synapses, or connections between nerve cells. Due to the brain's **plasticity,** especially during this critical period of growth, environmental experience can influence brain development positively or negatively.

Early Sensory Capacities

- Sensory capacities, present from birth and even in the womb, develop rapidly in the first months of life. Very young infants show pronounced abilities to discriminate between stimuli.
- Touch seems to be the first sense to develop and is the most mature sensory system for the first several months. Newborns are sensitive to pain.
- Smell, taste, and hearing begin to develop in the womb. A preference for sweet taste seems to be inborn and probably helps infants adapt to life outside the womb. Odor preferences develop with experience.

- Vision is the least well developed sense at birth. Peripheral vision, color perception, acuteness of focus, binocular vision, and the ability to follow a moving object with the eyes all develop within the first few months. **Visual preference** and auditory discrimination appear to be related to later cognitive functioning.

Motor Development

- During the first 3 months of life, infants begin to gain control over their body movements. Motor skills develop in a certain sequence, which may depend largely on maturation but also on experience and perception. Simple skills are combined into increasingly complex **systems of action.** Self-locomotion seems to be a "setting event," effecting changes in all domains of development.

- The **Denver Developmental Screening Test** is widely used to assess motor, linguistic, and personality and social development.

- Experiments with the **visual cliff** suggest that **depth perception** is present very early in life. It may depend in part on control of the head and on eye-hand coordination, which permits **haptic perception.**

- Environmental factors, including cultural patterns, may affect the pace of motor development. Extreme environmental deprivation can slow development, at least temporarily, and training or practice can accelerate certain specific skills.

Health

- Although the **infant mortality rate** in the United States has improved, it is still disturbingly high, especially for African American babies, among whom low birthweight is the biggest factor. White newborns are more likely to die of birth defects, the leading cause of infant deaths.

- **Sudden infant death syndrome (SIDS)** is the third leading cause of death in infants in the United States. Exposure to smoke and sleeping in the prone position are major risk factors.

- Rates of immunization have improved in the United States, but many preschoolers, especially among the poor and minority groups, are not protected.

KEY TERMS

plasticity (164)
visual preference (169)
systems of action (171)
Denver Developmental Screening
 Test (172)
visual cliff (174)

depth perception (174)
haptic perception (176)
infant mortality rate (179)
sudden infant death syndrome
 (SIDS) (181)

QUESTIONS FOR THOUGHT AND DISCUSSION

1. "Every mother who is physically able should breastfeed." Do you agree or disagree? Give reasons.

2. In view of what is now known about the plasticity of the infant brain, should society make sure that every baby has access to an appropriately stimulating environment? If so, how can and should this be done?

3. Is it advisable to try to teach babies skills such as walking before they develop them on their own?

4. In view of the facts presented in this and previous chapters, what more do you think can and should be done to reduce the incidence of low birthweight and bring down the infant mortality rate?

5. In view of preliminary medical evidence that bed sharing between mother and infant may contribute to SIDS, should mothers from cultures in which sharing a bed is customary be discouraged from doing so?

6. Who should be primarily responsible for ensuring that children are immunized: parents, community agencies, or government?

CHAPTER

6

Cognitive Development During the First Three Years

The experiences of the first three years of life are almost entirely lost to us, and when we attempt to enter into a small child's world, we come as foreigners who have forgotten the landscape and no longer speak the native tongue.

Selma Fraiberg, *The Magic Years*, 1959

Focus

William Erasmus (Doddy) Darwin

On December 27, 1839, when the naturalist Charles Darwin was 30 years old, his wife, Emma, gave birth to their first baby, William Erasmus Darwin, affectionately known as Doddy. That day—20 years before the publication of Charles Darwin's *Origin of Species,* which outlined his theory of evolution based on natural selection—the proud father began keeping a diary of observations of his newborn son. Doddy's birth inspired Darwin to look for parallels between the development of one small human being and the development of the human species.

What abilities are babies born with? How do they learn about their world? How do they communicate, first nonverbally and then through language? These were among the questions Darwin set out to answer—questions that are still central to the study of cognitive development today.

Darwin's keen eye illuminates how coordination of physical and mental activity helps an infant adapt to the world—as in this entry written when Doddy was 4 months old:

> Took my finger to his mouth & as usual could not get it in, on account of his own hand being in the way; then he slipped his own back & so got my finger in.—This was not chance & therefore a kind of reasoning. (Diary, p. 12, quoted in Keegan & Gruber, 1985, p. 135)

In Darwin's notes, we can see Doddy developing new cognitive skills through interaction not only with his father's finger, but with other objects as well. The diary depicts a series of recurring encounters with mirrors. In these episodes we see Doddy gaining knowledge, not in sudden bursts or jumps, but through gradual integration of new experience with existing patterns of mental and physical behavior. In Darwin's view—as, later, in Piaget's—this was not merely a matter of piling new knowledge upon old; it involved an actual transformation of the way the mind is organized.

The first time Doddy saw a mirror (as far as Darwin reported), he was 4½ months old. In it he saw his likeness and his father's (presumably holding him up to the glass). Darwin noted that the baby "seemed surprised at my voice coming from behind him, my image being in front" (Diary, p. 18, quoted in Keegan & Gruber, 1985, p. 135). Two months later, Doddy apparently had solved the mystery: now, when his father, standing behind him, made a funny face in the mirror, the infant "was aware that the image . . . was not real & therefore . . . turned round to look" (Diary, pp. 21–22, quoted in Keegan & Gruber, 1985, pp. 135–136).

However, this newfound understanding did not immediately generalize to other reflective materials. Two weeks later, Darwin observed that his son seemed puzzled to see his father's reflection in a window. By 9 months of age, however, the boy realized that "the shadow of a hand, made by a candle, was to be looked for behind, in [the] same manner as in [a] looking glass" (Diary, p. 23, quoted in Keegan & Gruber, 1985, p. 136). His recognition that reflections could emanate from objects behind him now extended to shadows, another kind of two-dimensional image.

Darwin was particularly interested in documenting his son's communicative progress. He believed that language acquisition was a natural process, akin to earlier physical expressions of feelings. Through smiling, crying, laughing, facial expressions, and sounds of pleasure or pain, Doddy managed to communicate quite well with his parents even before uttering his first word. One of his first meaningful verbal expressions was "Ah!"—uttered when he recognized an image in a glass.

The source for analysis of Darwin's diary is Keegan and Gruber, 1985.

● ● ●

Although Darwin made these observations more than 150 years ago, before the science of child development was well established, many of them have been borne out by later research. Darwin wrote his diary at a time when infants' cognitive abilities were widely underestimated. Today, our picture of these abilities has changed radically. During the past few decades, there has been more research on this topic than during all previous history. We now know that normal, healthy infants are born with the ability to learn and remember and with a capacity for acquiring and using speech. Newborns begin sizing up what their senses tell them. They use their cognitive abilities to distinguish between sensory experiences (such as the sounds of different voices), to build on their small inborn repertoire of behaviors (especially sucking), and to exert growing control over their behavior and their world. Evidence of infants' early cognitive competence has revived an old debate about whether infants have basic intuitive knowledge about the physical world, such as what happens when one object hits another (Spelke, 1994), or whether they are born with mental mechanisms that guide them in acquiring such knowledge (Baillargeon, 1994).

In this chapter we look at infants' and toddlers' cognitive abilities from three classic perspectives—behaviorist, psychometric, and Piagetian—and then from three newer perspectives: information-processing, cognitive neuroscientific, and social-contextual. Lastly, we trace the early development of language and discuss how it comes about. After reading this chapter, you should be able to answer and elaborate on such questions as these:

Preview Questions

- How do infants learn and how well can they remember?

- Is it possible to measure an infant's or a toddler's intelligence?

- When and how do babies begin to think?

- How do babies process information, and how do processing abilities relate to intelligence?

- When do babies develop concepts about characteristics of the physical world?

- How do interactions with parents and other adults advance cognitive competence?

- How do babies develop language, and what are some milestones of language development during the first 3 years?

Studying Cognitive Development: Classic Approaches

When Doddy Darwin, at 4 months, figured out how to get his father's finger into his mouth by moving his own hand out of the way, he showed ***intelligent behavior***, behavior involving complex, self-initiated learning. Intelligent behavior is generally agreed to have two key aspects. First, it is *goal-oriented*: conscious and deliberate rather than accidental. Second, it is *adaptive*: directed at adjusting to the circumstances and conditions of life. Intelligence—the array of mental abilities underlying intelligent behavior—is influenced by both inheritance and experience. Intelligence enables people to acquire, remember, and use knowledge, to understand concepts and relationships, and to solve everyday problems.

How and when do babies learn to solve problems? How and when does memory develop? What accounts for individual differences in cognitive abilities? Can we measure a baby's intelligence? Can we predict how smart that baby will be in the future? Many investigators of cognitive development have taken one of three classic approaches to the study of such questions:

- The ***behaviorist approach*** studies the basic mechanics of learning. It is concerned with how behavior changes in response to experience.
- The ***psychometric approach*** seeks to measure individual differences in quantity of intelligence. The higher a person scores on an intelligence test, the more intelligent he or she is presumed to be.
- The ***Piagetian approach*** looks at changes in the quality of cognitive functioning, or what people can do. It is concerned with the evolution of mental structures and how children adapt to their environment, and it maintains that cognition develops in stages.

All three approaches, as well as the three newer ones we discuss in the following section—the information-processing, cognitive neuroscience, and social-contextual approaches—help us understand intelligent behavior. Let us see what each can tell us about the cognitive development of infants and toddlers.

Behaviorist Approach: Basic Mechanics of Learning

Human beings are born with the ability to learn from experience. Babies learn from what they see, hear, smell, taste, and touch. Of course, maturation is essential to this process; certain neurological, sensory, and motor capacities must be developed before specific kinds of learning, such as learning to talk, can occur. But, while learning theorists recognize maturation as a limiting factor, they do not focus on it. Their main interest is in mechanisms of learning.

Let's look at two simple learning processes that behaviorists study: *classical conditioning* and *operant conditioning*. Later we will look at *habituation*, another simple form of learning, which information-processing researchers study. Social learning theory and research, discussed in Chapter 1, focus on learning that occurs through observation and imitation. More complex learning can involve combinations of these modes.

Classical and Operant Conditioning

In Chapter 1, we saw how Anna, after her father had taken many pictures of her, eventually blinked *before* the flashbulb on his camera went off (see Figure 1-4). This is an example of ***classical conditioning***, in which a person or an animal learns an automatic response (in this case, blinking) to a stimulus (the camera) that originally did not provoke the response. In classical conditioning, a person learns to anticipate an event before it happens by forming associations between stimuli (such as the camera and the flash) that regularly occur together.

Newborns can be classically conditioned most readily when the association between stimuli serves their survival needs. Babies only 2 hours old have been

---

intelligent behavior Behavior that is goal-oriented (conscious and deliberate) and adaptive to circumstances and conditions of life.

behaviorist approach Approach to the study of cognitive development based on learning theory, which is concerned with the basic mechanics of learning.

psychometric approach Approach to the study of cognitive development that seeks to measure the quantity of intelligence a person possesses.

Piagetian approach Approach to the study of cognitive development based on Piaget's theory, which describes qualitative stages, or typical changes, in children's and adolescents' cognitive functioning.

classical conditioning Kind of learning in which a previously neutral stimulus (one that does not originally elicit a particular response) acquires the power to elicit the response after the stimulus is repeatedly associated with another stimulus that ordinarily does elicit the response.

An Indian snake charmer's son eagerly plays with a snake the father has trained, showing that fear of snakes is a learned response. Children can be conditioned to fear animals that are associated with unpleasant or frightening experiences (as "Little Albert" was in a classic study by John B. Watson and Rosalie Rayner).

classically conditioned to turn their heads and suck when their foreheads are stroked, by stroking the forehead at the same time that they are given a bottle of sweetened water (Blass et al., 1984, in Rovee-Collier, 1987). Newborn babies have been conditioned to suck when they hear a buzzer or a tone; to show the Babkin reflex (turning their heads and opening their mouths) when their arms are moved (instead of the usual stimulus, pressure on the palm of the hand); to dilate and constrict the pupils of their eyes; and to blink (Rovee-Collier & Lipsitt, 1982).

One of the earliest demonstrations of classical conditioning in human beings showed that fear can be conditioned (Watson & Rayner, 1920). An 11-month-old baby known as "Little Albert," who loved furry animals, was brought into a laboratory. Just as he was about to grasp a furry white rat, a loud noise frightened him, and he began to cry. After repeated pairings of the rat with the loud noise, the child whimpered with fear whenever he saw the rat. The fear also generalized to rabbits, dogs, a Santa Claus mask, and other furry white objects. Under today's ethical standards, this research would never be permitted; it would be unethical to arouse fear in the name of science. However, the study did show that a baby could be conditioned to fear things he had not been afraid of before.

Terrell's smiling to get loving attention from his parents (described in Chapter 1; see Figure 1-5) is an example of *operant conditioning,* in which a baby learns to make a certain response (smiling) in order to produce a particular effect (parental attention). Operant conditioning, in which the learner operates on and influences the environment, enables infants to learn voluntary behaviors, such as smiling, as opposed to involuntary behaviors, such as blinking.

Many studies demonstrate that newborns can be operantly conditioned. In one study, 2-day-old infants sucked nipples connected to a music source. The babies kept sucking when their sucking turned on the music but stopped when their sucking turned off the music (Butterfield & Siperstein, 1972). Studies like this, which change what babies do (suck) by reinforcing certain behaviors (in this case, with music), show that neonates can learn by operant conditioning *if* the conditioning encourages them to perform some kind of behavior they can already do (such as sucking).

Classical and operant conditioning together can produce increasingly complex behavior. In studies with 1- to 20-week-old infants, the babies received milk if they turned their heads left at the sound of a bell. The babies who did not learn to turn their heads through this operant conditioning were then classically conditioned. When the bell sounded, the left corner of the baby's mouth was touched, and the baby turned his or her head and received the milk. (The touch was the

operant conditioning Form of learning in which a person tends to repeat a behavior that has been reinforced or to cease a behavior that has been punished.

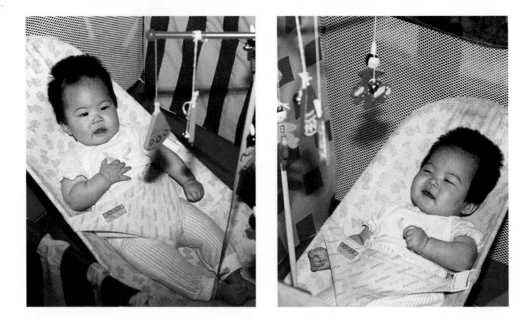

Babies 2 to 6 months old can remember, after a hiatus of 2 days to 2 weeks, that they were able to activate a mobile by kicking; they show this by kicking as soon as they see the mobile. The series of experiments in this research varied the contexts in which the babies learned, and contextual cues helped to establish memory.

unconditioned stimulus; turning the head was the unconditioned response. The bell was the conditioned stimulus; turning the head to the bell became the conditioned response.) By 4 to 6 weeks, all the babies had learned to turn their heads when hearing the bell. Then the babies learned to differentiate the bell from a buzzer (Papousek, 1959, 1960a, 1960b, 1961). When the bell rang, they were fed on the left; when the buzzer rasped, they were fed on the right. At about 3 months of age, the babies had learned to turn to whichever side brought food, as signaled by the bell or buzzer. By 4 months, they even learned to reverse their responses to bell and buzzer—an impressively complex feat.

Operant Conditioning and Infant Memory

If infants did not have a short-term ability to remember, at least unconsciously, they would not be able to learn. Studies using operant conditioning have found that babies 2 to 6 months old can repeat an action days or weeks later—*if* the testing situation is very similar to the one in which the initial training occurred.

In a series of experiments (Amabile & Rovee-Collier, 1991; Fagen, Morrongiello, Rovee-Collier, & Gekoski, 1984; Hayne & Rovee-Collier, 1995; Rovee-Collier, Schechter, Shyi, & Shields, 1992; Shields & Rovee-Collier, 1992), infants whose left legs were attached to a mobile above a crib or playpen quickly learned that kicking would activate the mobile. When they saw the mobiles again a few days later, the babies kicked even though their legs were no longer attached to the mobiles. Babies trained with different mobiles on different days learned to expect a different one each time. Furthermore, if, within a few days after training, 3-month-olds saw a *new* mobile (or another object) in motion, they would try to move it by kicking; but if the new object was stationary, they did not kick. Apparently, when the babies observed a new moving object, they associated it with their memory of the mobile they had been trained with (Rovee-Collier, 1996).

Contextual cues can help retention. Infants as young as 3 to 6 months of age recognize differences in their surroundings, and they seem to associate information about the setting with the behavior they are learning. Babies who were given the mobile training in playpens hung with patterns of stripes, squares, dots, or triangles remembered to kick if retested in a playpen with the same pattern; but if retested in a differently patterned playpen, or with the same pattern but in a different room, they did not kick. Furthermore, babies trained and tested in such distinctively patterned settings were more likely to respond differently to a new mobile than to the one they had originally seen. By contrast, 9- and 12-month-olds who can get around on their own *do* remember a task learned in a different room (pressing a lever to move a miniature train around a track). Apparently, self-locomotion allows them to construct a *cognitive map*, in which various places and the memories of events that occurred in those places become linked (Rovee-Collier, 1996).

The length of time an operantly conditioned memory is retained increases with age. In these studies, 2-month-olds remembered the kicking response for 2 days, 3-month-olds for 1 week, and 6-month-olds for 2 weeks; 9-month-olds remembered how to make the train go after 6 weeks, and 18-month-olds after 13 weeks. However, the memory span of 2-month-olds could be increased to equal that of 6-month-olds by dividing their training time into three sessions rather than two; and 3-month-olds could be reminded to kick as much as 6 weeks after training—just like 9-month-olds—by seeing a researcher move a mobile at two different times. This suggests that the capacity for longer-term retention is there at an early age if the circumstances for creating and activating a memory are right (Rovee-Collier, 1996).

Psychometric Approach: Developmental and Intelligence Tests

At the beginning of the twentieth century, school administrators in Paris asked the psychologist Alfred Binet to devise a way to identify children who could not handle academic work and who should be removed from regular classes and given special training. The test that Binet and his colleague Theodore Simon developed was the forerunner of psychometric tests, used for children of all levels of ability, which score intelligence by numbers. One is the Stanford-Binet Intelligence Scale, an American version of the traditional Binet-Simon tests (see Chapter 9).

The goals of psychometric testing are to measure quantitatively the factors that are thought to make up intelligence, such as comprehension and reasoning, and, from the results of that measurement, to predict future performance (such as school achievement). *IQ (intelligence quotient) tests* consist of questions or tasks that are supposed to show how much of the measured abilities a person has, by comparing her or his performance with that of other test-takers. A child's score is compared with *standardized norms:* standards obtained from the scores of a large, representative sample of children of the same age who were given the test while it was being developed.

Test developers devise techniques to try to ensure that tests have high *validity* (that is, the tests measure the abilities they claim to measure) and *reliability* (that is, the test results are reasonably consistent from one time to another). Tests can be meaningful and useful only if they are both valid and reliable. For school-age children, intelligence test scores can predict school performance fairly accurately and reliably. Testing infants' and toddlers' intelligence is another matter.

Testing Infants and Toddlers

Infants are intelligent from birth, but measuring their intelligence is not easy. Since babies cannot tell us what they know and how they think, the most obvious way to gauge their intelligence is by assessing what they can do. But if they do not grasp a rattle, it is hard to tell whether they do not know how, do not feel like doing it, do not realize what is expected of them, or have simply lost interest and turned their attention elsewhere.

Despite the difficulty of measuring infants' intelligence, sometimes it is advisable to do so. If parents are worried because a baby is not doing the same things as other babies the same age, developmental testing may reassure them that development is normal or may alert them to a problem. Developmental tests

C H E C K P O I N T

Can you . . .

- Summarize the distinguishing features of the behaviorist, psychometric, and Piagetian approaches to the study of cognitive development?

- Identify conditions under which newborns can be classically or operantly conditioned?

- Summarize what studies of operant conditioning have shown about infant memory?

IQ (intelligence quotient) tests Psychometric tests that seek to measure how much intelligence a person has by comparing her or his performance with standardized norms.

standardized norms Standards for evaluating performance of persons who take an intelligence test, obtained from scores of a large, representative sample who took the test while it was in preparation.

validity Capacity of a test to measure what it is intended to measure.

reliability Consistency of a test in measuring performance.

Table 6-1	Sample Tasks in the Bayley Scales of Infant Development

Age (in months)	Mental Scale*	Motor Scale*
1	Eyes follow moving person	Lifts head when held at shoulder
3	Reaches for suspended ring	Turns from back to side
6	Manipulates bell, showing interest in detail	Turns from back to stomach
9	Jabbers expressively	Raises self to standing position
12	Pats toy in imitation	Walks alone
14–16	Uses two different words appropriately	Walks up stairs with help
20–22	Names three objects	Jumps off floor with both feet
26–28	Matches four colors	Imitates hand movements
32–34	Uses past tense	Walks up stairs, alternating feet
38–42	Counts	Walks down stairs, alternating feet

*Task most children this age can do
Source: Bayley, 1993.

compare a baby's performance on a series of tasks with norms established on the basis of observation of what large numbers of infants and toddlers can do at particular ages.

The ***Bayley Scales of Infant Development*** (Bayley, 1969, 1993) are widely used for this purpose (see Table 6-1). The revised Bayley II is designed to assess the developmental status of children from 1 month to 3½ years. It is used primarily with children suspected of being at risk for abnormal development (B. Thompson et al., 1994). The Bayley II is organized into three categories: a *mental scale,* which measures such abilities as perception, memory, learning, and verbal communication; a *motor scale,* which measures gross (large-muscle) and fine (manipulative) motor skills; and a *behavior rating scale,* a 30-item rating of the child's test-taking behaviors. The separate scores calculated for each scale, which are called *developmental quotients,* are most useful for early detection of emotional disturbances and sensory, neurological, and environmental deficits (Anastasi, 1988).

Although these scores give a reasonably accurate picture of current developmental status, they tend to be unreliable and are generally considered to have little value in predicting future functioning. One reason for this unreliability is that the developmental tests traditionally used for babies measure mostly sensory and motor abilities, whereas intelligence tests for older children measure verbal abilities (Bornstein & Sigman, 1986; Colombo, 1993; McCall & Carriger, 1993). Not until at least the third year of life, when children may be tested with the Stanford-Binet, do a child's IQ scores, along with such factors as the parents' IQ and educational level, usually help to predict later test scores (Kopp & Kaler, 1989; Kopp & McCall, 1982; McCall & Carriger, 1993). But even for toddlers, predictions from psychometric tests are unreliable. As children are tested closer to their fifth birthday, the relationship between current IQ scores and those in later childhood becomes stronger (Bornstein & Sigman, 1986).

Psychologists are better able to predict the future IQ of infants with disabilities or prenatal problems, especially if they are raised in impoverished, unstimulating environments (McCall & Carriger, 1993). However, human beings have a strong *self-righting tendency;* given a favorable environment, infants will follow normal developmental patterns unless they have suffered severe damage. Children born with mental or motor problems can make impressive strides in tested intelligence as they grow older (Kopp & Kaler, 1989; Kopp & McCall, 1982).

Bayley Scales of Infant Development Standardized test of infants' mental and motor development.

Assessing the Impact of the Home Environment

What specific aspects of a baby's home environment affect future measures of intelligence? According to the *Home Observation for Measurement of the Environment (HOME)* (R. H. Bradley, 1989), one important factor is parental responsiveness. HOME gives credit to the parent of an infant or toddler for caressing or kissing the child during an examiner's visit; to the parent of a preschooler for spontaneously praising the child at least twice during the visit; and to the parent of an older child for answering the child's questions. Examiners evaluate how parent and child talk to each other, and they give high ratings for a parent's friendly, nonpunitive attitude. A longitudinal study found positive correlations between parents' responsiveness to their 6-month-old babies, as measured by HOME, and the children's IQ and achievement test scores at age 10, as well as teachers' ratings of classroom behavior (R. Bradley & Caldwell, 1982; R. Bradley, Caldwell, & Rock, 1988).

The HOME scale also assesses the number of books in the home, the presence of playthings that encourage the development of concepts, and parents' involvement in children's play. High scores on all these factors are fairly reliable in predicting children's IQ; when combined with the parents' level of education, they are even more accurate. In one study, researchers compared HOME scores for low-income 2-year-olds with the children's Stanford-Binet intelligence test scores two years later. The single most important factor in predicting high intelligence was the mother's ability to create and structure an environment that fostered learning (J. H. Stevens & Bakeman, 1985).

In another study of 931 African American, Mexican American, and white children up to age 3, socioeconomic status and other aspects of their inner-city environment were less closely related to cognitive development than were such day-to-day aspects of the home environment as parental responsiveness and access to stimulating play materials (R. H. Bradley et al., 1989). In all three ethnic groups, a responsive and stimulating home environment could offset problems in infancy; but when both early development *and* early home environment were poor, the chances for a good outcome were much smaller. In two other studies of low-income African American children, discussed in the next section, the home environment as measured by HOME had at least as strong an influence on cognitive development as the mother's IQ (Burchinal, Campbell, Bryant, Wasik, & Ramey, 1997).

Six *developmental priming mechanisms* have repeatedly been found to be associated with positive cognitive (as well as emotional and social) outcomes. These are called "priming" mechanisms because they help make children ready for schooling. The six mechanisms are: (1) encouragement to explore the environment, (2) mentoring in basic cognitive and social skills, such as labeling, sequencing, sorting, and comparing, (3) celebration and reinforcement of new accomplishments, (4) guidance in practicing and expanding new skills, (5) protection from inappropriate punishment, teasing, or disapproval for mistakes or unintended consequences of exploring and trying out new skills (such as breaking Mom's favorite vase), and (6) stimulation of language and other symbolic communication (discussed later in this chapter). The consistent presence of all six of these conditions seems to be essential to normal brain development; otherwise, important neuronal connections may not be made (C. T. Ramey & Ramey, 1998, in press; S. L. Ramey & Ramey, 1992; see Chapter 5). Box 6-1 has a fuller discussion of these and other suggestions for helping babies develop both cognitive and social competence.

Early Intervention

Early intervention, as defined under the Individuals with Disabilities Education Act (IDEA), is a systematic process of planning and providing therapeutic and educational services to families that need help in meeting infants', toddlers', and

Home Observation for Measurement of the Environment (HOME) Instrument to measure the influence of the home environment on children's cognitive growth.

developmental priming mechanisms Preparatory aspects of the home environment that seem to be necessary for normal cognitive and psychosocial development to occur.

early intervention Systematic process of planning and providing therapeutic and educational services to families that need help in meeting infants', toddlers', or preschool children's developmental needs.

Box 6-1 Fostering Competence

In 1965 Burton L. White and his colleagues began the Harvard Preschool Project to test and observe some 400 preschoolers and rate them on their cognitive and social competence, or ability to function effectively in their world (B. L. White, 1971; B. L. White, Kaban, & Attanucci, 1979). The researchers found significant individual differences related to factors in the children's environment. The major differences seemed to revolve around three aspects of child rearing: caregivers' ability to "design" a child's world, to serve as "consultants" for a child, and to provide a balance between freedom and restraint. Findings from the Harvard Preschool Project, from studies using the HOME (Home Observation for Measurement of the Environment) scales, and from recent neurological studies and other research suggest the following guidelines for fostering infants' and toddlers' cognitive development:

1. In the early months, *provide sensory stimulation.* During the first month, avoid overstimulation and distracting noises, which can produce stress. As sensory discrimination becomes more acute, let the baby watch a vividly patterned mobile swaying over the crib; babies especially like high-contrast, black-and-white patterns. Let babies handle household objects and toys, which enable them to learn about shapes, sizes, textures, and other characteristics of the physical world.

2. As babies grow older, *create an environment that fosters learning*—one that includes books, interesting objects (which do not have to be expensive toys), and a place to play.

3. *Respond to babies' signals.* This is probably the most important thing a caregiver can do. Meeting an infant's needs—whether for food, cuddling, comforting, or guidance in play—establishes a sense of trust that the world is a friendly place and gives babies a sense of control over their lives.

4. *Give babies the power to effect changes.* Provide toys that the baby can shake to make noise, or can mold or move. This, too, teaches babies that they have some control over their world and helps them learn about cause and effect. During the second six months, help a baby discover that turning a doorknob opens a door, flicking a light switch turns on a light, and opening a faucet produces running water for a bath.

5. *Give babies freedom to explore.* Do not confine them regularly in a playpen, crib, jump seat, or small room. It's better to baby-proof the environment by taking away things that can be broken or swallowed, by removing sharp objects that can injure, and by jamming books into a bookcase so tightly that a baby can't pull them out. Babies need opportunities to crawl and eventually to walk, not only to exercise their large muscles but also to learn about their environment and to develop a sense of independence. And they need to be protected from inappropriate disapproval, teasing, or punishment for exercising their normal curiosity.

6. *Talk to babies.* By hearing and responding to conversational speech (not just commands or warnings), babies improve

One way to help children become competent is to allow them freedom to explore in a safe environment full of interesting things to see and touch. Annie's mother is nearby, ready to answer the 2-year-old's questions about her exciting discovery, tell her what it is, and initiate a conversation about it.

their ability to express themselves. They will not pick up language from listening to the radio or television; they need interaction with adults.

7. In talking to or playing with babies, *enter into whatever they are interested in* at the moment instead of trying to redirect their attention to something else.

8. *Arrange opportunities to learn basic skills,* such as labeling, comparing, and sorting objects (say, by size or color), putting items in sequence, and observing the consequences of actions.

9. *Applaud new skills, and help babies practice and expand on them.* Give babies help when they need it rather than pressing it on them too soon, ignoring them, or seeing them as a burden to be dealt with quickly. Stay fairly close but do not hover so much that you discourage them from developing attention-seeking skills.

10. *Read to babies from an early age.* Reading aloud in a warm, caring atmosphere and asking challenging, open-ended questions about what's happening in the stories helps develop preliteracy skills.

11. *Use punishment sparingly, and do not punish or ridicule results of normal trial-and-error exploration.* Instead, find opportunities for positive feedback.

Sources: R. R. Bradley & Caldwell, 1982; R. R. Bradley, Caldwell, & Rock, 1988; R. H. Bradley et al., 1989; C. T. Ramey & Ramey, 1998, in press; S. L. Ramey & Ramey, 1992; Staso, quoted in Blakeslee, 1997; J. H. Stevens & Bakeman, 1985; B. L. White, 1971; B. L. White, Kaban, & Attanucci, 1979.

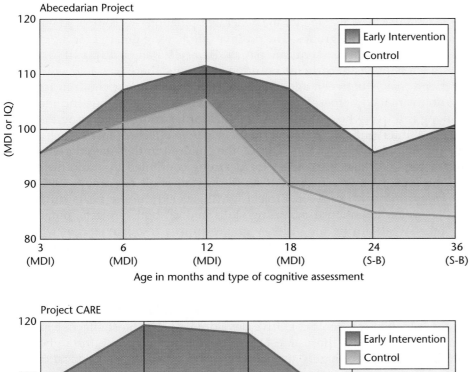

Abecedarian Project

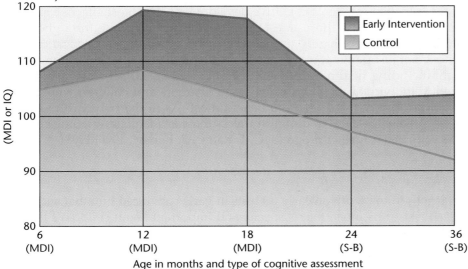

Project CARE

Figure 6-1
Effects of early childhood educational intervention on psychometric developmental and intelligence scores. In both the Abecedarian Project and Project CARE, infants randomly assigned to a university-based educational program throughout their preschool years did better on IQ tests than a control group, even after the dip in scores around age 2, which reflects the shift to IQ tests with more verbal content.

Note: *MDI* stands for Mental Development Index, one of the Bayley Scales, and *S-B* for Stanford-Binet Intelligence Scale.

Source: C. T. Ramey & Ramey, in press, Figure 3.

preschool children's developmental needs. According to the Centers for Disease Control and Prevention, early and continuing intervention could have prevented retardation in as many as 300,000 young people under age 21 (Boyle, Decoufle, & Yeargen-Allsopp, 1994, cited in C. T. Ramey & Ramey, 1998).

How effective is early intervention? Results from randomly assigned, controlled studies have found positive effects, especially among the most at-risk children—those whose parents are very poor, have little education, and in many cases are unmarried (C. T. Ramey & Ramey, in press-b). Project CARE (Wasik, Ramey, Bryant, & Sparling, 1990) and the Abecedarian project (C. T. Ramey & Campbell, 1991) involved a total of 174 North Carolina babies, almost all African American, from at-risk homes. In each project, from 6 weeks of age until kindergarten, an experimental group was enrolled in a full-day, year-round early childhood education program, Partners for Learning, at a university child development center. The program had a low child–teacher ratio and used learning games to foster specific cognitive, linguistic, perceptual-motor, and social skills.

Figure 6-1 shows the dramatic initial results: in both projects, the children who received the early educational intervention demonstrated a widening advantage in developmental test scores during the first 18 months. By age 3, the average IQ of the Abecedarian children was 101, and of CARE children, 105—equal to or better than average for the general population—as compared with only 84 and 93 for the control groups. The positive effects were greatest for the children whose mothers had the least education (C. T. Ramey & Ramey, in press).

As often happens in early intervention programs, there was a general downward trend in IQs between ages 3 and 8, especially among children from the most disadvantaged homes. However, scores tended to be higher and more stable among children who had been in Partners for Learning, suggesting that early educational intervention can moderate the negative effects of low socioeconomic status (Burchinal et al., 1997). At age 12, the children in the Abecedarian Project who had been enrolled in Partners for Learning continued to outdo the control group on both IQ and academic tests (F. A. Campbell & Ramey, 1994). Two home-based interventions—in Project CARE, weekly home visits during the preschool years to enhance parenting skills and, in both projects, home visits every other week during the primary grades from a resource teacher who provided supplementary educational activities—did not significantly affect the outcomes, perhaps because the visits were not frequent enough to make a difference or because it was difficult to get parents to change the way they interacted with their children.

These findings and those of a number of other studies show that early educational intervention can boost cognitive development. The most effective early interventions seem to be those that (1) start early and continue throughout the preschool years; (2) are highly time-intensive; (3) provide direct educational experiences, not just parental training; (4) take a comprehensive, multipronged approach, including health, family counseling, and social services; and (5) are tailored to individual differences and needs. Parents and children who participate actively and regularly tend to benefit most. As in the two North Carolina projects, initial gains tend to diminish unless there is adequate, ongoing environmental support for further progress (C. T. Ramey & Ramey, 1996, 1998).

Piagetian Approach: Cognitive Stages

Jean Piaget's initial work on early IQ tests in Paris convinced him that such standardized tests miss much that is special and important about children's thought processes. To examine these processes, Piaget observed his own and other children from infancy on. Children's thinking, he concluded, is qualitatively different (different in kind) from adult thought. Whereas psychometricians measured individual differences in how much intelligence children (or adults) have, Piaget proposed universal sequences of cognitive development throughout infancy, childhood, and adolescence. The first of Piaget's four stages of cognitive development (refer back to Table 1-3 in Chapter 1) is the *sensorimotor stage.*

Piaget's theory has inspired much research on cognition in infancy and early childhood. Some of this research, as we will see, has shown that—as important as Piaget's contributions were—he underestimated young children's abilities.

Piaget's Sensorimotor Stage: Birth to Age 2

During the *sensorimotor stage* (approximately the first 2 years of life), said Piaget, infants learn about themselves and their world through their own developing sensory and motor activity. Babies change from creatures who respond primarily through reflexes and random behavior into goal-oriented toddlers.

The sensorimotor stage consists of six substages (see Table 6-2), which flow from one to another as a baby's *schemes,* or organized patterns of behavior, become more elaborate. Much of this early cognitive growth comes about through what Piaget called *circular reactions,* in which an infant learns to reproduce pleasurable or interesting events originally discovered by chance. The process is based on operant conditioning. Initially, an activity produces a sensation so

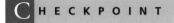

CHECKPOINT

Can you . . .

- Tell why developmental tests are sometimes given to infants and toddlers and describe one such widely used test?

- Explain why tests of infants and toddlers are unreliable in predicting later IQ?

- Identify factors in the home environment that affect cognitive development?

- Summarize findings about the value of early intervention in improving disadvantaged children's IQ scores?

sensorimotor stage In Piaget's theory, the first stage in cognitive development, during which infants (from birth to approximately 2 years) learn through their developing senses and motor activity.

schemes In Piaget's terminology, basic cognitive structures consisting of organized patterns of behavior used in different kinds of situations.

circular reactions In Piaget's terminology, processes by which an infant learns to reproduce desired occurrences originally discovered by chance.

Table 6-2   Six Substages of Piaget's Sensorimotor Stage of Cognitive Development

Substage	Description
Substage 1 (birth to 1 month) *Use of reflexes*	Infants exercise their inborn reflexes and gain some control over them. They do not coordinate information from their senses. They do not grasp an object they are looking at. They have not developed object permanence.
Substage 2 (1 to 4 months) *Primary circular reactions*	Infants repeat pleasurable behaviors that first occur by chance (such as sucking). Activities focus on infant's body rather than the effects of the behavior on the environment. Infants make first acquired adaptations; that is, they suck different objects differently. They begin to coordinate sensory information. They have still not developed object permanence.
Substage 3 (4 to 8 months) *Secondary circular reactions*	Infants become more interested in the environment and repeat actions that bring interesting results and prolong interesting experiences. Actions are intentional but not initially goal-directed. Infants show partial object permanence: they will search for a partially hidden object.
Substage 4 (8 to 12 months) *Coordination of secondary schemes*	Behavior is more deliberate and purposeful as infants coordinate previously learned schemes (such as looking at and grasping a rattle) and use previously learned behaviors to attain their goals (such as crawling across the room to get a desired toy). They can anticipate events. Object permanence is developing, although infants will search for an object in its first hiding place, even if they saw it being moved.
Substage 5 (12 to 18 months) *Tertiary circular reactions*	Toddlers show curiosity as they purposefully vary their actions to see results. They actively explore their world to determine how an object, event, or situation is novel. They try out new activities and use trial and error in solving problems. Concerning object permanence, they will follow a series of object displacements, but since they cannot imagine movement they do not see, they will not search for an object where they have not observed its being hidden.
Substage 6 (18 to 24 months) *Mental combinations*	Since toddlers can mentally represent events, they are no longer confined to trial and error to solve problems. Symbolic thought allows toddlers to begin to think about events and anticipate their consequences without always resorting to action. Toddlers begin to demonstrate insight. Object permanence is fully developed.

Note: Infants show enormous cognitive growth during Piaget's sensorimotor stage, as they learn about the world through their senses and their motor activities. Note their progress in problem solving, object permanence, and the coordination of sensory information. All ages are approximate.

welcome that the child wants to repeat it. The repetition then feeds on itself in a continuous cycle in which cause and effect keep reversing (see Figure 6-2).

During the first five substages of the sensorimotor stage, babies learn to organize their activities in relation to their environment and coordinate information they receive from their senses. During the sixth and last substage, they progress from trial-and-error learning to the use of symbols and insights to solve simple problems.

In the *first substage* (birth to about 1 month), as neonates exercise their inborn reflexes, they gain some control over them. They begin to engage in a behavior even when the stimulus that elicits it as an automatic reflex is not present. For example, newborns suck reflexively when their lips are touched. They soon learn to find the nipple even when they are not touched, and they suck at times when they are not hungry. Thus infants modify and extend the scheme for sucking as they begin to initiate activity.

In the *second substage* (about 1 to 4 months), babies learn to repeat a pleasant bodily sensation first achieved by chance (say, sucking their thumbs). Piaget called this a *primary circular reaction.* Babies also learn to adjust or accommodate their actions by sucking their thumbs differently from the way they suck on a nipple. They begin to turn toward sounds, showing the ability to coordinate different kinds of sensory information (vision and hearing).

The *third substage* (about 4 to 8 months) coincides with a new interest in manipulating objects. Babies engage in *secondary circular reactions:* intentional actions repeated not merely for their own sake, as in the second substage, but to get results beyond the infant's own body (for example, cooing when a friendly face appears, so as to make the face stay longer).

By the time they reach the *fourth substage, coordination of secondary schemes* (about 8 to 12 months), infants have built on the few schemes they were born with and have learned to generalize from past experience to solve new problems.

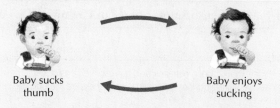

Baby sucks thumb → Baby enjoys sucking

(a) Primary circular reaction: Action and response both involve infant's own body (1 to 4 months).

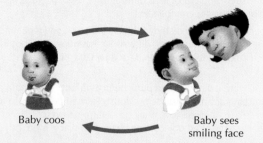

Baby coos ← Baby sees smiling face

(b) Secondary circular reaction: Action gets a response from another person or object, leading to baby's repeating original action (4 to 8 months).

Baby steps on rubber duck   Baby squeezes rubber duck   Duck squeaks

(c) Tertiary circular reaction: Action gets one pleasing result, leading baby to perform similar actions to gets similar results (12 to 18 months).

Figure 6-2
Primary, secondary, and tertiary circular reactions. According to Piaget, infants learn to reproduce pleasurable events they discover accidentally. (*a*) Primary circular reaction: A baby happens to suck a thumb, enjoys sucking, and puts the thumb back into the mouth or keeps it there. The stimulus (thumb) elicits the sucking reflex; pleasure then stimulates the baby to keep on sucking. (*b*) Secondary circular reaction: This involves something outside the baby's body. The baby coos; the mother smiles; and because the baby likes to see the mother smile, the baby coos again. (c) Tertiary circular reaction: The baby tries different ways to reproduce an accidentally discovered response. When the baby steps on a rubber duck, the duck squeaks. The baby then tries to produce the squeak in other ways, perhaps by squeezing it or sitting on it.

representational ability   In Piaget's terminology, capacity to mentally represent objects and experiences, largely through the use of symbols.

They will crawl to get something they want, grab it, or push away a barrier to it (such as someone else's hand). They try out, modify, and coordinate previous schemes, to find one that works.

In the *fifth substage* (about 12 to 18 months), babies begin to experiment with new behavior. Once they begin to walk, they can satisfy their curiosity by exploring their environment. They now engage in *tertiary circular reactions,* varying an action to see what will happen rather than merely repeating pleasing behavior they have accidentally discovered. For the first time, children show originality in problem solving. By trial and error, they try out new behaviors until they find the best way to attain a goal.

Representational ability—the ability to mentally represent objects and actions in memory, largely through symbols such as words, numbers, and mental pictures—blossoms in the *sixth substage, mental combinations,* between about 18 months and 2 years. Children in the sixth substage, a transition into the preoperational stage of early childhood, can use symbols to *think* about actions before taking them. Since they now have some understanding of cause and effect, they no longer have to go through laborious trial and error to solve new problems. Piaget's daughter Lucienne demonstrated this when, in figuring out how to pry open a partially closed matchbox to remove a watch chain, she opened her mouth wider to signify her idea of widening the slit in the box (Piaget, 1952).

This baby, in the stage of secondary circular reactions, is studying what happens when he pulls the string on his toy. Perhaps he discovered accidentally that the bells rang the first time he pulled the string and is now recreating that interesting experience.

This baby seems to be showing at least the beginning of the concept of object permanence by searching for an object that is partially hidden. She will probably have the complete concept by about 18 months of age, when she will look for objects or people even when she has not seen where they were hidden.

The ability to manipulate symbols frees children from immediate experience. They can now engage in *deferred imitation,* imitating actions they no longer see in front of them. They can pretend, as Anna did at 20 months when she was given a tea set and immediately "served tea" to her parents. This simple *pretend play* involving imaginary people or situations is the forerunner of the more elaborate dramatic play that occurs during the preoperational stage, as children become better able to remember and imagine.

During the sensorimotor stage, children gradually develop *object permanence:* the realization that an object or person continues to exist even when out of sight (refer back to Table 6-2). At first, infants have no such concept. By the third substage, according to Piaget, they will look for something they have dropped, but if they cannot see any part of it, they act as if it no longer exists. In the fourth substage, they will

deferred imitation In Piaget's terminology, reproduction of an observed behavior after the passage of time by calling up a stored symbol of it.

pretend play Play involving imaginary people or situations; also called *fantasy play, dramatic play,* or *imaginative play.*

object permanence In Piaget's terminology, the understanding that a person or object still exists when out of sight.

Box 6-2   Playing Peekaboo

In a mud hut in rural South Africa, a mother smiles at her 9-month-old son, covers her eyes with her hands, and asks, "Uphi?" (Where?) After 3 seconds, the mother says, "Here!" and uncovers her eyes to the baby's delight. In a Tokyo apartment a Japanese mother, using different language and covering her eyes with a cloth, plays the same game with her 12-month-old daughter, who shows the same joyous response.

Peekaboo is played across diverse cultures, using similar routines (Fernald & O'Neill, 1993). In all cultures in which the game is played,* the moment when the mother or other caregiver reappears is exhilarating. It is marked by exaggerated gestures and voice tones. Infants' pleasure from the immediate sensory stimulation of the game is heightened by their fascination with faces and voices, especially the high-pitched tones the adult usually uses.

The game is not only fun; it serves several important purposes. Psychoanalysts maintain that it helps babies master anxiety when their mother disappears. Cognitive psychologists see it as a way babies play with developing ideas about the existence, disappearance, and reappearance of objects—the concept of object permanence. It may also be a social routine that helps babies learn the kinds of rules that govern conversation, such as taking turns. It may provide practice in paying attention, a prerequisite for learning.

As babies develop the cognitive competency to predict future events, the game takes on new dimensions. Between 3 and 5 months, the baby's smiles and laughter as the adult's face moves in and out of view signal the infant's developing expectation of what will happen next. (The development of expectations at this age is the basis for research about babies' understanding of the physical world, discussed elsewhere in this section.) At 5 to 8 months, the baby shows anticipation by looking and smiling as the adult's voice alerts the infant to the adult's imminent reappearance. By 1 year, babies are no longer merely observers but usually initiate the game, actively engaging adults in play. Now it is the adult who generally responds to the baby's physical or vocal cues, which can become quite insistent if the adult doesn't feel like playing.

To help infants who are in the process of learning peekaboo or other games, parents often use *scaffolding* (discussed in Chapter 1 and elsewhere in this chapter). They encourage babies to move to a higher level of mastery by prompting them to perform at their highest current level of competence.

In a study at the University of Montreal, 25 mothers were videotaped playing peekaboo with their infants, using a doll as a prop, at 6, 9, 12, 15, 18, and 24 months (Rome-Flanders, Cronk, & Gourde, 1995). The amount of scaffolding on the mother's part, and the particular type of scaffolding behavior, varied with the infant's age and skill. For example, mothers frequently tried to attract a 6-month-old's attention to begin the game; this became less and less necessary as time went on. Modeling (performing the peekaboo sequence to encourage a baby to imitate it) was also most frequent at 6 months and decreased significantly by 12 months, when there was an increase in direct verbal instruction ("Cover the doll") as babies became more able to understand spoken language. However, indirect verbal instruction ("Where is the doll?"), used to focus attention on the next step in the game, remained constant throughout the entire age range. Reinforcement (showing satisfaction with the infant's performance, for example, by saying "Peekaboo!" when the infant uncovers the doll) was fairly constant from 9 months on. The overall amount of scaffolding dropped substantially at 24 months, by which time most babies have fully mastered the game.

Seeing her father's shirt on the floor, 2-year-old Cindy drapes it over her head and toddles over to him. "Where's Cindy?" he asks. Cindy laughs as she whips the shirt off her face and exclaims, "Peekaboo!"

*The cultures included in this report are found in Malaysia, Greece, India, Iran, Russia, Brazil, Indonesia, Korea, and South Africa.

look for an object in a place where they first saw it hidden, even if they have seen it being moved to another place. In the fifth substage, they will search for an object in the *last* place they saw it being hidden; but they will not search for it in a place where they did not see it being hidden. By the sixth substage, toddlers' imagination allows them to look for an object even if they did not see where it was hidden.

Object permanence is the basis for children's awareness that they exist apart from objects and other people. It also allows a child whose parent has left the room to feel secure in the knowledge that the parent continues to exist and will return. It is essential to understanding time, space, and a world full of objects and events. The development of this concept in many cultures can be seen in the game of peekaboo (see Box 6-2).

What Abilities May Develop Earlier than Piaget Thought?

Piaget has made monumental contributions to our understanding of cognitive development; but while research has supported some of his claims, it has challenged others. As we report later in this chapter, studies since the late 1970s, taking an information-processing approach, build an impressive case for babies' cognitive strengths. Studies using the *violation-of-expectations* method—based on infants' tendency to look longer at surprising rather than at familiar phenomena—suggest that infants as young as 3 or 4 months old may understand certain principles about the physical world, may have a sense of object permanence, and may have a rudimentary concept of number. Current research also challenges Piaget's view that babies up to 18 months cannot form mental representations or memories of objects not physically present. Some of this research, which is in dispute, deals with imitation in very young infants; other research deals with toddlers' long-term ability to remember and repeat actions they have previously learned.

Invisible and Deferred Imitation   How early do babies engage in *invisible imitation,* imitation using parts of the body that the baby cannot see, such as the mouth? Piaget maintained that invisible imitation develops at about 9 months, after *visible imitation*—the use of hands or feet, for example, which babies can see. Yet in a series of studies by Andrew Meltzoff and M. Keith Moore (1983, 1989), babies less than 72 hours old (including one who was tested only 42 minutes after birth) appeared to imitate adults by opening their mouths and sticking out their tongues, as well as duplicating adults' head movements.

A related question is the timing of the development of *deferred imitation.* According to Piaget, children under 18 months cannot imitate an action they saw some time before; yet babies have been found to display deferred invisible imitation as early as 6 *weeks* of age, suggesting that very young babies can retain a memory of an event and a mental representation of it, a "picture" in the mind. In one experiment, 6-week-old infants who were randomly assigned to four groups saw adults either open their mouths, stick out their tongues to the middle of the mouth, stick out their tongues to the side, or make no movement. Not only did the infants in the first three groups tend to immediately reproduce the type of movement they had seen, thus apparently demonstrating invisible imitation, but they also appeared to show deferred imitation by making similar movements 24 hours later in the presence of the same adult, who at that time was expressionless (Meltzoff & Moore, 1994). In successive trials, the infants became more and more accurate in matching the previous behavior of the adult. Since the infants in each group made a different type of movement—the one they had seen a particular adult make—their actions could not be reflexive, Meltzoff and Moore argue; instead, they had to be based on mental representations triggered by the sight of the person originally seen to make the movement. Meltzoff and his colleagues (Gopnik & Meltzoff, 1994, in press) suggest that such representations enable even very young infants to make a mental link between an expression on a face they see and the way they feel when their own unseen faces make similar expressions. If so, this may be a prelude to understanding of other people's mental states (Repacholi & Gopnik, 1997; see Box 6-3).

Provocative as all these findings are, they are controversial. A recent review of Meltzoff and Moore's work, and of attempts to replicate it, found clear, consistent evidence *only* with regard to sticking out the tongue (Anisfeld, 1996). Furthermore, the tongue thrust disappears by about 2 months of age (Bjorklund, 1997; S. S. Jones, 1996). Since it seems unlikely that an early and short-lived imitative capacity would be limited to one gesture, some researchers have suggested that the tongue thrust may serve different adaptive purposes for an infant than imitation does for an older child—the learning of new behavior patterns (Bjorklund, 1997).

One possibility is that a baby reproducing an adult's tongue thrust is making an automatic, reflexive response to facilitate nursing (Abravanel & Sigafoos, 1984; Kaitz, Meschulach-Sarfaty, Auerbach, & Eidelman, 1988). Because of newborns'

invisible imitation   Imitation with parts of one's body that one cannot see (e.g., the mouth).

visible imitation   Imitation with parts of one's body that one can see (e.g., the hands and the feet).

Box 6-3 Can Toddlers "Read" Others' Wishes?

At what age can babies begin to "read" what is on other people's minds? In Chapter 9, we will discuss the development of *empathy*, the ability to feel what another person is feeling, and its relationship to understanding of mental states. How far back do the beginnings of this understanding go?

Twelve-month-olds will give an object to a person who points to it and asks for it. But does the baby realize that the request reflects an inner desire, or is the child merely responding to observable behavior (pointing)? Eighteen-month-olds will offer a toy to a crying child. But do they realize that their comforting may change the other child's mental state, or are they merely trying to change an overt behavior (crying)? And, since they usually offer a toy they themselves would find comforting, are they capable of distinguishing another person's state of mind from their own?

It's hard to answer such questions, since most toddlers can't talk well enough to tell us what they are thinking. So one research team (Repacholi & Gopnik, 1997) designed a nonverbal experiment to test toddlers' ability to discern another person's food preferences.

The researchers recruited 159 children, about half of them 14 months old and the other half 18 months old. Each child was invited to participate in an individual free play session in a human development laboratory at the University of California–Berkeley. In the course of the session, the child and an experimenter were offered two bowls of snacks: one that young children typically like (goldfish crackers) and one that they typically do not like (raw broccoli flowerets). The child was first given a chance to taste the snacks, and then the experimenter did. As expected, more than 9 out of 10 children (93 percent) preferred the crackers.

Equal numbers of boys and girls of each age were randomly assigned to two testing conditions: one in which the experimenter's apparent food preference matched the child's expected preference and one in which it did not. In the "matched" condition, the experimenter showed pleasure after tasting the cracker ("Mmm!") and disgust after tasting the broccoli ("Eww"). In the "mismatched" condition, the experimenter acted as if she preferred the broccoli.

Next, the experimenter placed one hand, palm up, halfway between the two bowls, and asked the child to give her some food, without indicating whether she wanted the broccoli or the crackers. The child was also given another opportunity to taste the snacks. This was done to see whether the children's food preferences had been influenced by the experimenter's expressed preferences. Only 6 children (4 percent) changed their apparent preference.

What did the children do when the experimenter asked for some food? Nearly 7 out of 10 of the 14-month-olds did not respond, even when the request was repeated. About 1 in 3 "teased" the experimenter by offering the crackers and then pulling back. Most of the 14-month-olds who did respond (including the teasers) offered crackers, regardless of which food the experimenter seemed to prefer. By contrast, only 3 out of 10 of the 18-month-olds failed to respond to the request; and, of those who did, 3 out of 4 gave the experimenter the food she had shown a liking for, whether or not it was the one they themselves liked.

Thus 18-month-olds, but not 14-month-olds, seem able to use another person's emotional cues to figure out what that person likes and wants, even when that person's desire is different from their own, and then to apply the information in a different situation in which there are no visible cues to the other person's preference. This suggests a rather sophisticated understanding of mental states: an awareness that two people can have opposite feelings about the same thing.

An interesting finding is that 14-month-olds were much less likely to respond to the experimenter's request for food when she had seemed to like broccoli than when she had seemed to like crackers. Perhaps those who did not respond in the "mismatched" situation found it hard to believe that someone might like and want broccoli; but unlike the children who instead gave the experimenter crackers, they may have been in a transitional stage, in which they noticed that another person's desires were different from their own and did not know what to do with this surprising information.

Young children who can interpret another person's desire are on their way to developing a *theory of mind*, a topic we discuss in Chapter 9.

limited eyesight, a protruding tongue may look to them like a nipple, leading them to stick out their own tongues, as they often do when rooting for the breast. However, research testing this hypothesis has raised more questions than it answered (S. S. Jones, 1996). A second hypothesis, which has received some research support, is that the tongue thrust may be an early form of communication and social interaction with the mother, at a time when newborns cannot yet control their gaze and head movements (Bjorklund, 1997). Still another possibility, suggested by a study of 4-week-olds, is that what appears to be imitation may actually be exploratory behavior aroused by an intriguing sight—which may be an adult tongue, but also may be (for example) colored lights or dangling objects. Neonates' limited hand control makes movement of the tongue one of their few exploratory options, and they stop making this response when they become capable of using the hands to explore (S. S. Jones, 1996).

Until further research supports or refutes these hypotheses, the age when invisible deferred imitation begins will remain in doubt. However, *visible* deferred imitation of complex activities does seem to begin earlier than Piaget thought. In one study in New Zealand (Hayne & Campbell, 1997), 6-month-old babies who saw a researcher pull a mitten off a puppet, jingle a bell, and then put the mitten back on the puppet mimicked the same actions 24 hours later, if they were in the same place and with the same people. In previous Meltzoff (1988) research, infants had demonstrated similar abilities no earlier than 9 months of age.

In other studies, 14- to 18-month-olds who watched other toddlers play with objects (for example, putting beads in a cup or sounding a buzzer), either in a laboratory or in a day-care center, were more likely to do the same thing than a control group who had seen the objects but had not seen another child playing with them. The experimental groups then repeated the behavior when given the same objects at home 2 days later—evidence that toddlers are capable of deferred imitation even in a different context (Hanna & Meltzoff, 1993).

Elicited Imitation   Piaget (1952, 1969) believed that infants and toddlers cannot form lasting memories of specific events because they have not yet developed the cognitive structures to do so. Indeed, the idea that children under the age of 3 have no conscious memory has been widely accepted, in part because most people have few, if any, memories going back that far (see Chapter 9). However, it may well be that toddlers' memories have been underestimated because of their limited ability to talk about what they remember.

One line of research has attempted to get past the language barrier by inducing children to repeat actions they previously learned to do. In this procedure, called *elicited imitation,* a researcher shows a child how to use certain items in a certain way. The child does so. Then the child is again shown the same items, this time with no instruction. Babies as young as 11 months old were able to immediately reproduce a simple sequence, such as making a car roll down an incline, and toddlers from 13 to 20 months old could repeat an unfamiliar sequence (such as putting together a metal gong) a full eight months later—impressive evidence of long-term recall (Bauer, 1996).

Apparently, then, the ability to talk about an event is not necessary for a toddler to remember it. However, as we will discuss in Chapter 9, verbal skills may affect whether memories can be carried forward into later life.

elicited imitation   Research method in which a child copies a researcher's use of specific objects and later remembers how to repeat the procedure without instruction.

CHECKPOINT

Can you . . .

- Summarize major developments during Piaget's sensorimotor stage?
- Discuss the implications of research on imitation in infants and toddlers?

Studying Cognitive Development: Newer Approaches

During the past few decades, researchers have turned to three new approaches to add to our knowledge about infants' and toddlers' cognitive development:

- The *information-processing approach* focuses on how people use their minds—the processes involved in perception, learning, memory, and problem solving. It seeks to discover what children and adults do with information from the time they encounter it until they use it.
- The *cognitive neuroscience approach* examines the "hardware" of the central nervous system. It attempts to identify what brain structures are involved in specific aspects of cognition.
- The *social-contextual approach* examines environmental aspects of the learning process, particularly the role of parents and other caregivers.

Information-Processing Approach: Perceptions and Representations

At about 6 weeks, André makes sucking noises and waves his arms excitedly as his mother approaches. Anyone can see that he recognizes her and that the sight and sound of her fill him with joy. But how does recognition take place? What is

information-processing approach   Approach to the study of cognitive development by observing and analyzing the mental processes involved in perceiving and handling information.

cognitive neuroscience approach   Approach to the study of cognitive development by examining brain structures and measuring neurological activity.

social-contextual approach   Approach to the study of cognitive development by focusing on the influence of environmental aspects of the learning process, particularly parents and other caregivers.

Can this baby tell the difference between Raggedy Ann and Raggedy Andy? This researcher may find out by seeing whether the baby has habituated—gotten used to—one face and then stops sucking on the nipple when a new face appears, showing recognition of the difference.

going on in André's head? Information-processing research is coming up with answers to such questions. Like the psychometric approach, information-processing theory is concerned with individual differences in intelligent behavior, but it attempts to describe the mental processes involved in acquiring and remembering information or solving problems, rather than merely assuming differences in mental functioning from answers given or problems solved. Information-processing research provides new methods for testing ideas about children's cognitive development that sprang from the psychometric and Piagetian approaches.

Infants' Information Processing as a Predictor of Intelligence

Because of the weak correlation between infants' scores on developmental tests and their later IQ, many psychologists believed that the cognitive functioning of infants had little in common with that of older children and adults—in other words, that there was a discontinuity in cognitive development (Kopp & McCall, 1982). As we have seen, Piaget believed this too. However, when researchers assess how infants process information, some aspects of mental development seem to be fairly continuous from birth into childhood (Bornstein & Sigman, 1986; Colombo, 1993; Dougherty & Haith, 1997; McCall & Carriger, 1993; L. A. Thompson, Fagan, & Fulker, 1991). Much of this research with infants is based on the simple learning process called *habituation,* which can be used as an indicator of sensory discrimination.

Habituation is a type of learning in which repeated exposure to a stimulus (such as a sound or a sight) reduces attention to that stimulus. Habituation allows people to conserve mental energy by remaining alert to things and events in the environment only as long as they seem to merit attention. Cognitive development occurs as infants transform the novel into the familiar, the unknown into the known (Rheingold, 1985).

Researchers study habituation in newborns by repeatedly presenting a stimulus (usually a sound or visual pattern) and then monitoring such responses as heart rate, sucking, eye movements, and brain activity. A baby who has been sucking typically stops when the stimulus is first presented and does not start again until after it has ended. After the same sound or sight has been presented again and again, it loses its novelty and no longer causes the baby to stop sucking. Uninterrupted sucking shows that the infant has habituated to the stimulus.

habituation Simple type of learning in which familiarity with a stimulus reduces, slows, or stops a response. Compare *dishabituation.*

A new sight or sound, however, will capture the baby's attention and the baby will again stop sucking. This increased response to a new stimulus is called *dishabituation.*

Researchers gauge the efficiency of infants' information processing by measuring how quickly babies habituate to familiar stimuli, how fast their attention recovers when they are exposed to new stimuli, and how much time they spend looking at the new and the old (Bornstein, 1985a). Efficiency of habituation correlates with later signs of mental development, such as a preference for complexity, rapid exploration of the environment, sophisticated play, fast problem solving, and the ability to match pictures. In fact, speed of habituation and other information-processing abilities show promise as predictors of intelligence, especially of verbal abilities. Infants who are efficient at taking in and interpreting sensory information score well later on childhood intelligence tests. In many longitudinal studies, habituation and attention-recovery abilities as well as *visual recognition memory* (the ability to distinguish familiar sights from unfamiliar ones when shown both at the same time) during the first 6 months to 1 year of life were moderately useful in predicting scores on psychometric tests taken between ages 1 and 8 (Bornstein & Sigman, 1986; Colombo, 1993; McCall & Carriger, 1993).

If infants pay more attention to new stimuli than to familiar ones, they can tell the new from the old; therefore, say information-processing theorists, they must be able to remember the old. To compare new information with information they already have, they must be able to form mental images or representations of stimuli. The efficiency of information processing depends on the speed with which they form and refer to such images—in other words, on memory. Contrary to Piaget's view, habituation studies have found that this representational ability seems to be working at birth or very soon after, and it quickly becomes more efficient.

Newborns can tell sounds they have already heard from those they have not. In one study, infants who heard a certain speech sound one day after birth appeared to remember that sound 24 hours later, as shown by a reduced tendency to turn their heads toward the sound and even a tendency to turn away (Swain, Zelazo, & Clifton, 1993). Indeed, as we reported in Chapter 3, newborns seem to remember sounds they heard in the womb. Early sensitivity to sounds may predict aspects of later cognitive functioning: a high positive correlation was found between the ability of 4-month-old infants to discriminate sounds and their IQ scores at age 5 (O'Connor, Cohen, & Parmelee, 1984).

Visual novelty preference—an infant's preference for new rather than familiar sights—is measured by the decline in the amount of time spent looking at a sight to which the infant has habituated and the increase in time spent looking at a new sight. As a measure of memory for the familiar, visual novelty preference seems to predict general intelligence (Colombo, 1993; McCall & Carriger, 1993), as well as certain specific abilities. In one study, babies who, at 5 and 7 months, preferred looking at new pictures rather than ones they had seen before tended to score higher on the Bayley Scales at 2 years and the Stanford-Binet at 3 years. They also showed stronger language skills and memory ability at age 3 (L. A. Thompson et al., 1991). *Visual anticipation* (the tendency to look for the next in a series of computer-generated pictures) and *visual reaction time*, as measured by an infant's eye movements at 3½ months, correlate with IQ at age 4 (Dougherty & Haith, 1997).

Other research refutes Piaget's belief that the senses are unconnected at birth and are only gradually integrated through experience. We now know that newborns will look at a source of sound, showing a connection between hearing and sight. One-month-olds will look longer at either a bumpy or a smooth pacifier, depending on which kind they have sucked, suggesting an integration between vision and touch (Mandler, 1990; Meltzoff & Borton, 1979). *Cross-modal transfer,* the ability to identify by sight items an infant earlier felt with the hands but did

dishabituation Increase in responsiveness after presentation of a new stimulus. Compare *habituation*.

visual-recognition memory Ability to distinguish a familiar visual stimulus from an unfamiliar one.

visual novelty preference Infant's preference for new rather than familiar sights.

cross-modal transfer Ability to identify by sight an item earlier felt but not seen.

not see, develops later. This ability shows a fairly high level of abstraction; it implies central processing of tactile and visual information. In one longitudinal study, a combination of visual recognition memory at 7 months and cross-modal transfer at 1 year predicted IQ at age 11 and also showed a modest (but nonetheless remarkable after 10 years!) relationship to processing speed and memory at that age (S. A. Rose & Feldman, 1995, 1997). Thus processing speed and memory seem to be underlying factors in the continuity in cognitive development between infancy and childhood.

All in all, there is much evidence that the abilities infants use to process sensory information are related to the cognitive abilities intelligence tests measure in children and adults. Still, we need to be cautious in interpreting these findings. Most of these studies used small samples. Also, measurements of habituation and recognition memory tend to be unreliable. The predictability of childhood IQ from these measures is only modest; it is no higher than the predictability from parental education and socioeconomic status, and not as high as the predictability from some other infant behaviors, such as early vocalization. Finally, while information-processing abilities normally predict IQ better than standardized infant developmental tests, that is not true for infants who suffered birth complications or who have environmental risk factors pointing to later developmental disorders (Laucht, Esser, & Schmidt, 1994; McCall & Carriger, 1993).

Information Processing and Exploratory Competence

As babies begin to get around on their own, they show curiosity about their world. No longer limited to oral exploration, they now squeeze, jab, rub, shake, and bang objects. The degree to which a baby initiates such activities is related to competence in solving problems and provides clues to early cognitive development (Caruso, 1993).

One longitudinal study found that information-processing skills in early infancy help predict *exploratory competence* at 13 months—a cognitive capacity that seems to underlie the growing variance at that age in the sophistication of toddlers' play and their ability to sustain attention (Tamis-LeMonda & Bornstein, 1993). For example, 5-month-olds who looked longer at novel sights, such as a bull's-eye and a female face projected on a screen, had a longer attention span at 13 months and were more likely to engage in highly symbolic play (such as pretending a block is a spoon). The infants' activity also made a difference: the more the 5-month-olds cooed, looked at their mothers or at an object, or touched an object, the more exploratory competence they showed at 13 months.

Violation of Expectations and the Development of Thought

It appears that babies can think at a much earlier age than Piaget believed; either they are born with the capacity to reason about the physical world, or they acquire it very early in life. This conclusion has come from *violation-of-expectations* research. In this method, infants are first habituated to seeing an event happen as it normally would. Then the event is changed in a way that conflicts with the infant's expectations. An infant's tendency to look longer at the changed event (dishabituation) shows that the infant recognizes the changed event as surprising. Researchers have used this method to test the age at which some of the concepts Piaget described, such as object permanence, number, and causality, first arise.

Piaget may have underestimated infants' grasp of *object permanence* because of his testing methods. Babies may fail to search for hidden objects because they are not able to perform the sequence of actions necessary for solving a problem, such as moving a cushion to look for something hidden behind it. Infants as young as 3½ months, when tested by the more age-appropriate violation-of-expectations procedure, appeared to remember an object they could no longer

exploratory competence
Cognitive capacity underlying the variance in toddlers' ability to sustain attention and engage in sophisticated symbolic play.

violation-of-expectations
Research method in which an infant's tendency to dishabituate to a stimulus that conflicts with previous experience is taken as evidence that the infant recognizes the new stimulus as surprising.

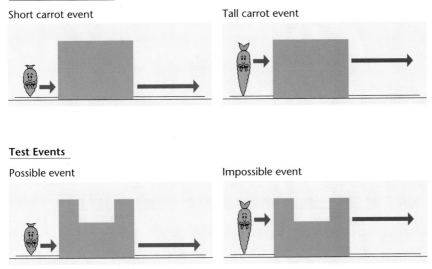

Habituation Events

Short carrot event

Tall carrot event

Test Events

Possible event

Impossible event

Figure 6-3

Object permanence in infants. In this experiment, 3½-month-old infants watched a short and then a tall carrot slide along a track, disappear behind a screen, and then reappear. After they became accustomed to seeing these events, the opaque screen was replaced by a screen with a large window at the top. The short carrot did not appear in the window when passing behind the screen; the tall carrot, which should have appeared in the window, also did not. The babies looked longer at the tall than at the short carrot event, suggesting that they were surprised that the tall carrot did not reappear.

Source: Baillargeon & DeVos, 1991.

see—a tall carrot that slid behind a screen and then failed to appear in a window (Baillargeon & DeVos, 1991; see Figure 6-3). Of course, since this task is so different from Piaget's, it may not be assessing precisely the same ability. Nevertheless, it does suggest that at least a rudimentary form of object permanence is present in the early months of life.

Likewise, an *understanding of number* may begin long before Piaget's sixth substage, when he claimed children first begin to use symbols. In a series of experiments, Karen Wynn (1992) used Mickey Mouse dolls to show that 5-month-old babies may be able to add and subtract small numbers of objects (see Figure 6-4). In all the experiments, the babies looked longer at surprising "wrong" answers than at expected "right" ones, suggesting (according to Wynn) that they had mentally "computed" the right answers.

This research suggests that an ability to grasp the rudiments of arithmetic may be inborn, and that when parents teach their babies numbers, they may only be teaching them the names ("one, two, three") for concepts the babies already know. Other researchers who replicated such experiments got similar results (Simon, Hespos, & Rochat, 1995). In follow-up experiments, Wynn (1996) showed that 6-month-old infants can tell the difference between a puppet jumping twice in a row and three times in a row, even when the puppet is in constant motion. This sophisticated achievement shows not only a sense of number but the ability to break up a continuous sequence of experiences into separate conceptual units.

Piaget believed that an understanding of **causality**, the awareness that one event causes another, develops slowly throughout the first year of life, as infants, at about 4 months, begin to recognize their own ability to act on their environment and then, close to 1 year, become aware that forces outside their own bodies can have causal effects. In habituation-dishabituation experiments, infants 4½ and 8 months old have seen a difference between events that flow into other events (such as a brick striking a second brick, which is then pushed out of position) and events that occur with no apparent cause (such as a brick moving away from another brick without having been struck by it). Thus, at an early age, infants may be aware of the continuity of relationships in time and space—a first step toward understanding causality (Leslie, 1982).

How does a baby come to understand that an unsupported object will fall? Renée Baillargeon (1994) and her colleagues showed infants a box, first resting on a platform and then pushed to the edge of it (see Figure 6-5). Three-month-old babies stared longer at the box when it had lost contact with the platform, apparently

causality Awareness that one event causes another.

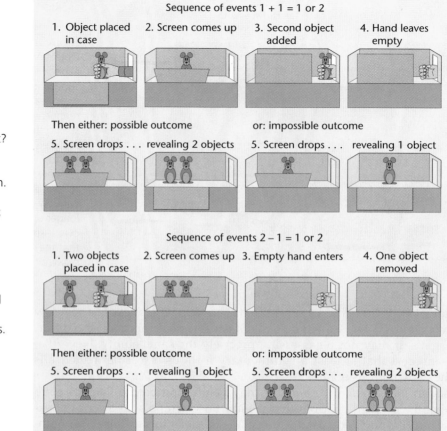

Figure 6-4

Can 5-month-old infants count? For the problem "1 plus 1," a researcher showed a baby 1 doll, then hid it behind a screen. The baby saw a hand place another doll behind the screen; then the screen was pulled away, revealing 2 dolls. Sometimes there was a false answer; the baby saw only 1 doll or 3 dolls. In the "2 minus 1" trials the researcher showed 2 dolls, then took 1 away, and the baby saw either 1 or 2 dolls. Babies consistently looked longer at the surprising "wrong" answers than at the expected right ones, which suggests that they had "computed" the right answers in their minds.

Source: Wynn, 1992.

Sequence of events 1 + 1 = 1 or 2

1. Object placed in case   2. Screen comes up   3. Second object added   4. Hand leaves empty

Then either: possible outcome   or: impossible outcome

5. Screen drops . . . revealing 2 objects   5. Screen drops . . . revealing 1 object

Sequence of events 2 – 1 = 1 or 2

1. Two objects placed in case   2. Screen comes up   3. Empty hand enters   4. One object removed

Then either: possible outcome   or: impossible outcome

5. Screen drops . . . revealing 1 object   5. Screen drops . . . revealing 2 objects

Figure 6-5

Test for infants' understanding of how objects are supported. A hand pushes a box toward the right edge of a supporting platform. In the possible event, the box stops when its bottom surface is still resting on the platform. In the impossible event, the box is pushed off the edge of the platform until only a small portion of its bottom surface rests on the platform. Six and a half-month-old infants, but not 3-month-olds, look longer at the impossible event than at the possible event, suggesting that they recognize that such a small area of contact cannot support the box.

Source: Baillargeon, 1994.

Possible Event

Impossible Event

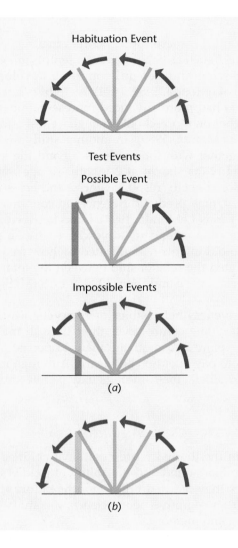

Habituation Event

Test Events

Possible Event

Impossible Events

(a)

(b)

Figure 6-6

Test for infants' understanding of how a barrier works. Infants first become accustomed to seeing a screen rotate 180 degrees on one edge. Then a box is placed beside the screen. In the possible event, the screen stops when it reaches the edge of the box. In the impossible events, the screen rotates through part or all of the space occupied by the box. On the basis of how long they stare at each event, 4½-month-old infants seem to know that the screen cannot pass through the entire box (b); but not until 6½ months do infants recognize that the screen cannot pass through 80 percent of the box (a).

Source: Adapted from Baillargeon, 1994.

realizing that the box should fall. By 6½ months, infants appeared to recognize the importance of two other factors: where the box touches the platform (on top or on the side) and how much of the box is touching the platform. In thinking about a physical phenomenon such as this one, infants may first form a general, "all-or-nothing" idea about it and later modify this initial concept by considering variables that enable them to make more accurate predictions.

The ability to reason about physical phenomena may be tied to motor development. Six-month-old babies who can sit up and handle objects learn from experience that an object placed on the edge of a table will fall unless enough of its bottom surface is on the table.

Babies first seem to reason qualitatively and then quantitatively, and their quantitative reasoning continuously improves. Baillargeon repeatedly showed infants a screen rotating through a 180-degree arc (see Figure 6-6). When the infants became accustomed to seeing the rotation, a barrier was introduced in the form of a box. At 4½ months of age, infants showed that they realized the screen could not move through the entire box but did not recognize the point at which the screen must stop. Six and a half-month-olds knew that the screen could not rotate through 80 percent of the box, but not until 8½ months did infants recognize that rotation through 50 percent of the box was impossible. Such findings, says Baillargeon, suggest that infants may have *innate learning mechanisms* that help them make sense of the information they encounter in the physical world.

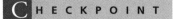

Can you . . .

- Briefly distinguish the information-processing, cognitive neuroscience, and social-contextual approaches to studying cognitive development?

- Summarize evidence that information-processing abilities in infants can predict later intelligence?

- Explain the relationship between information processing and exploratory competence?

- Describe the "violation-of-expectations" method and name three abilities which, according to research using this method, may develop earlier than Piaget believed?

- Discuss how maternal responsiveness may affect information-processing abilities?

explicit memory Memory, generally of facts, names, and events, which is intentional and conscious. Compare *implicit memory.*

implicit memory Memory, generally of habits and skills, which does not require conscious recall; sometimes called *procedural memory.* Compare *explicit memory.*

Caregivers' Influence

According to studies of American and Japanese mothers, maternal responsiveness to babies' "nondistress behavior," such as babbling and attempts at eye contact, influences information processing and general cognitive development (Bornstein, 1985b; Bornstein & Tamis-LeMonda, 1989, 1994). As toddlers, the children of the most responsive mothers had more advanced representational abilities. As 4-year-olds, they scored higher on a preschool intelligence test and other learning tasks (Bornstein & Tamis-LeMonda, 1989). In another study, maternal responsiveness to 5-month-olds, together with the mother's IQ and the infant's own early visual discrimination ability (as shown at 2 months of age), was related to the 5-month-olds' habituation, novelty responsiveness, and cross-modal transfer—skills that, as we have seen, may predict differences in cognitive abilities later in childhood (Bornstein & Tamis-LeMonda, 1994). Links between maternal responsiveness and intelligence even extend to adolescence. In one study, mothers' responsiveness to 1-month-old infants (as indicated by how frequently the mothers talked to them) moderated the relationship between the infants' attention span when looking at a checkerboard and their IQ at age 18 (M. Sigman, Cohen, & Beckwith, 1997).

How might an adult's responsiveness help babies develop cognitively? It may make them feel that they have some control over their lives. It may also make them feel secure enough to explore and motivate them to persist. And it may help them regulate themselves to pay attention and learn. Although most of these studies have been done with mothers, their findings may be relevant to fathers and other caregivers.

Cognitive Neuroscience Approach: The Brain's Memory Structures

What makes the difference between the limited representational abilities of infants who can turn away from a familiar sound and the ability of toddlers to reproduce complex action sequences they learned eight months before (Bauer, 1996)? Some answers are coming from cognitive neuroscience, the study of the brain structures that govern thinking and memory.

We are learning about infant neurological development both indirectly, from studies of monkeys, rabbits, and other animals, and directly, from instruments that measure human brain activity. Studies of infant brain functioning have made use of behaviorist principles (classical and operant conditioning) and Piagetian tasks (such as deferred imitation, elicited imitation, and object permanence). Other studies have looked at the physical side of information processing. Measurements taken on an infant's scalp have been used to record brain wave changes associated with visual recognition memory (C. A. Nelson & Collins, 1991, 1992), auditory recognition memory (D. G. Thomas & Lykins, 1995), and cross-modal transfer (C. A. Nelson, Henschel, & Collins, 1993), as well as physical responses involved in habituation, visual novelty preference, visual anticipation, and reaction time.

Studies of normal and brain-damaged adults suggest that people have two separate memory systems, which acquire and store different kinds of information. *Explicit memory* is conscious or intentional recollection, usually of facts, names, events, or other things that people can state, or declare. *Implicit memory* refers to remembering that occurs without effort or even conscious awareness; it generally pertains to habits and skills, such as knowing how to throw a ball or ride a bicycle. Until recently, direct physical evidence of the existence and location of these two distinct memory systems was lacking. Now, high-technology research, including magnetic resonance imaging (MRI) and positron emission tomography (PET), has provided such evidence (Squire, 1992; Vargha-Khadem et al., 1997). Scientists today are getting an increasingly clear picture of which brain structures control which aspects of memory (see Figure 6-7).

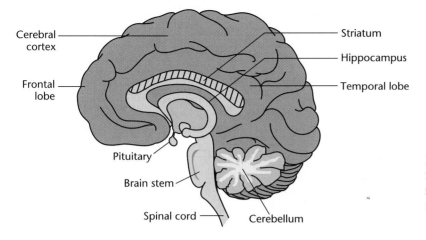

Cerebral cortex

Frontal lobe

Striatum

Hippocampus

Temporal lobe

Pituitary

Brain stem

Spinal cord

Cerebellum

Figure 6-7
Simplified side view of the human brain, showing structures involved in explicit, implicit, and working memory.

Implicit memory seems to develop earlier and mature more rapidly than explicit memory. Two kinds of implicit memory develop during the first few months of life: memory for procedures (such as anticipating the next light in a sequence), which seems to be centered in the *striatum;* and conditioning, which appears to depend on the *cerebellum* and cell nuclei deep in the *brain stem.* At the same time, an early, reflex-like form of explicit memory apparently develops; it is chiefly dependent on the *hippocampus,* a seahorse-shaped structure deep in the central portion of the brain, the *medial temporal lobe.* This preexplicit memory system permits infants to remember specific sights or sounds for no more than a few seconds—long enough to show simple preferences for novel sights or sounds (C. A. Nelson, 1995).

Sometime between 6 and 12 months, a more sophisticated form of explicit memory modifies or replaces the preexplicit form. It draws upon cortical structures, which are the primary site of general knowledge (*semantic memory*), as well as structures associated with the hippocampus, which govern memory of specific experiences (*episodic memory*) (C. A. Nelson, 1995; Vargha-Khadem et al., 1997). This advance is responsible for the emergence of such complex abilities as cross-modal transfer and elicited imitation.

During this same period, the *prefrontal cortex* (the portion of the frontal lobe directly behind the forehead) and associated circuitry develop the capacity for ***working memory.*** Working memory is short-term storage of information the brain is actively processing, or working on—either preparing for storage or recalling from storage. Its relatively late appearance seems to be largely responsible for the slow development of object permanence (C. A. Nelson, 1995).

Although explicit memory and working memory continue to develop during the ensuing months and years, the early emergence of memory structures underlines the importance of environmental stimulation during the critical first few months of life (see Chapter 5). Social-contextual theorists and researchers pay particular attention to the impact of these environmental influences.

working memory Short-term storage of information being actively processed.

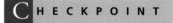

CHECKPOINT

Can you . . .

- Name the brain structures apparently involved in implicit, preexplicit, explicit, and working memory and mention at least one task that is made possible by each of these kinds of memory?

Social-Contextual Approach: Learning From Interactions With Caregivers

How do parents and caregivers contribute to infants' and toddlers' cognitive development? As we have seen, parental responsiveness is positively related to infants' information-processing abilities and future IQ. IQ is also related to parents' ability to create a stimulating home environment and involvement in children's play (refer back to Box 6-1.) Researchers coming from a social-contextual perspective look more closely at the *content* of early social interactions with adults.

Vygotsky's concept of ***guided participation*** broadens his idea of scaffolding (see Chapter 1) to encompass not only academic learning but also ordinary, everyday shared activities. Through guided participation, caregivers give greater

guided participation In Vygotsky's terminology, participation of an adult in a child's activity in a manner that helps to structure the activity and to bring the child's understanding of it closer to the understanding of the adult.

structure to children's activities and help bridge the gap between the child's understanding and the adult's. Guided participation can occur not only in play but in many other activities in which children learn informally from adults the skills, knowledge, and values important in their culture. The concept may be especially useful in describing early cognitive development in cultures in which learning is less tied to formal schooling than to observation of parents and other adults.

In one cross-cultural study (Rogoff, Mistry, Göncü, & Mosier, 1993), researchers visited the homes of fourteen 1- to 2-year-olds in each of four communities: San Pedro, a Mayan town in Guatemala; Dhol-Ki-Patti, a tribal village in India; and middle-class urban neighborhoods in Salt Lake City and Keçiören, Turkey. The investigators interviewed caregivers about their child-rearing practices and watched them help the toddlers learn to dress themselves and to operate objects the children had not seen before, such as a set of nesting dolls and a pencil box with a sliding lid and latch.

In everyday life, children in the various communities routinely interacted with their parents, but in different contexts. In the Guatemalan town, toddlers typically watched their mothers sewing and weaving at home to help support the family; in the Indian village, they accompanied their mothers at work in the fields. Unlike the children in these two developing countries, the Turkish toddlers had full-time homemaker mothers; in Salt Lake City, children either had homemaker mothers or were in day care. These urban middle-class children interacted with their parents more in the context of their own childhood milieu than in the parents' work or social worlds. Parents in these communities frequently played with their children, whereas toddlers in the Guatemalan and Indian communities were expected to play alone or with older siblings while the mother got her work done. She supervised the children's play but did not get involved in it.

These cultural differences were reflected in the types of guided participation the parents in the study used to help their children learn. After initial demonstration and instruction by a caregiver (the mother, the father, or another adult), the Guatemalan and Indian children took the lead in their own learning; the caregiver remained available to respond to requests for help. Communication was mostly nonverbal. The U.S. caregivers, by contrast, emphasized verbal instruction; they spoke with the children as peers and managed their learning, using praise, mock excitement, and other motivators. The Turkish families, who were in transition from a rural to an urban way of life, showed a pattern somewhere between these two.

The cultural context, then, influences the way caregivers contribute to cognitive development. These researchers suggest that direct adult involvement in children's play and learning may be less adaptive in a rural village or small town in a developing country, in which children more frequently observe and participate in adult activities, than in a middle-class urban community, in which homemaker mothers have more time, greater verbal skills, and possibly more interest in children's play and learning.

Interaction with caregivers plays an important part in language learning.

CHECKPOINT

Can you . . .

• Compare two cultural patterns of guided participation in toddlers' learning?

Language Development

At 4½ months, Stefan chuckles out loud. He also says "ngoo-ooo" and "ngaaah." At 7 months he makes more sounds, mostly sounding like "da" or "ga." At 11 months he says "dada," and at 14 months he points to everything, asking "What zis?" or saying "Da" for "I want that." At 17 months he points to the right places when asked "Where is your nose? Tongue? Belly button?" By 21 months, he says, or tries to say, at least 50 words, and he understands many more. He can now tell you, in his own language, exactly what he does or does not want. When asked "Do you want to go to bed?" he answers "Eh-eh-eh," accompanied by vigorous

Table 6-3 Language Milestones from Birth to 3 Years

Age in Months	Development
Birth	Can perceive speech, cry, make some response to sound.
1½ to 3	Coos and laughs.
3	Plays with speech sounds.
5 to 6	Makes consonant sounds, trying to match what she or he hears.
6 to 10	Babbles in strings of consonants and vowels.
9	Uses gestures to communicate and plays gesture games.
9 to 10	Begins to understand words (usually "no" and baby's own name); imitates sounds.
10 to 12	No longer can discriminate sounds not in own language.
9 to 12	Uses a few social gestures.
10 to 14	Says first word (usually a label for something).
10 to 18	Says single words.
13	Understands symbolic function of naming.
13	Uses more elaborate gestures.
14	Uses symbolic gesturing.
16 to 24	Learns many new words, expanding vocabulary rapidly, going from about 50 words to up to 400; uses verbs and adjectives.
18 to 24	Says first sentence (2 words).
20	Uses fewer gestures; names more things.
20 to 22	Has comprehension spurt.
24	Uses many two-word phrases; no longer babbles; wants to talk.
30	Learns new words almost every day; speaks in combinations of three or more words; understands very well; makes grammatical mistakes.
36	Says up to 1,000 words, 80 percent intelligible; makes some mistakes in syntax.

Sources: Bates, O'Connell, & Shore, 1987; Capute, Shapiro, & Palmer, 1987; Lalonde & Werker, 1995; Lenneberg, 1969.

arm waving—in other words, "No!" He has also said his first three-word sentence: "Choo-choo bye-bye da-da," meaning "The train went away, and now it's all gone."

Stefan's growing ability to use *language,* a communication system based on words and grammar, is a crucial element in his cognitive development. Once he knows words, he can use them to represent objects and actions. He can reflect on people, places, and things; and he can communicate his needs, feelings, and ideas in order to exert control over his life.

The growth of language illustrates the interaction of all aspects of development: physical, cognitive, emotional, and social. As the physical structures needed to produce sounds mature, and the neuronal connections necessary to associate sound and meaning become activated, social interaction with adults introduces babies to the communicative nature of speech. Let's look at the typical sequence of language development (see Table 6-3), at some characteristics of early speech, at how babies acquire language and make progress in using it, and at how parents and other caregivers help toddlers prepare for *literacy,* the ability to read and write.

Sequence of Early Language Development

The word *infant* is based on the Latin for "without speech." Before babies say their first words, they make sounds known as *prelinguistic speech,* sounds rich in emotional expression. Starting with crying and then contented cooing and babbling,

language Communication system based on words and grammar.

literacy Ability to read and write.

prelinguistic speech Forerunner of linguistic speech; utterance of sounds that are not words. Includes crying, cooing, babbling, and accidental and deliberate imitation of sounds without understanding their meaning.

the range of emotional tone increases steadily as babies progress to accidental imitation and then deliberate imitation. Before babies can express ideas in words, parents become attuned to their children's feelings through the sounds they make.

During this period, infants also grow in the ability to recognize and understand speech sounds and to use meaningful gestures. Around the end of the first year, babies typically say their first word, and about eight months to a year later, toddlers begin speaking in sentences.

Early Vocalization

Crying is the newborn's only means of communication. To a stranger, all cries may sound alike, but a baby's parents can often tell the cry for food from the cry of pain. Different pitches, patterns, and intensities signal hunger, sleepiness, or anger.

Between 6 weeks and 3 months, babies start to make sounds when they are happy. *Cooing* includes making squeals, gurgles, and vowel sounds like "ahhh." At about 3 to 6 months, babies begin to play with speech sounds, matching the sounds they hear from people around them (Bates, O'Connell, & Shore 1987).

Babbling—repeating consonant-vowel strings, such as "ma-ma-ma-ma"—occurs suddenly between 6 and 10 months of age and is often mistaken for a baby's first word. Babbling is not real language, since it does not hold meaning for the baby; but it becomes more wordlike.

Language development continues with accidental *imitation of language sounds* babies hear and then of themselves making these sounds. At about 9 to 10 months, they deliberately imitate sounds without understanding them. Once they have a repertoire of sounds, they string them together in patterns that sound like language but seem to have no meaning (Eisenson, Auer, & Irwin, 1963; Lenneberg, 1967).

Recognizing Language Sounds

Long before babies can utter anything but a cry, they can distinguish between speech sounds as similar as "ba" and "pa" (Eimas, Siqueland, Jusczyk, & Vigorito, 1971; see Chapter 5). This ability seems to exist in the womb. In one study, two groups of Parisian women in their ninth month of pregnancy each recited a different nursery rhyme, saying it 3 times a day for 4 weeks. A month later, researchers played recordings of both rhymes close to the women's abdomens. The fetuses' heart rates slowed when the rhyme the mother had spoken was played, but not for the other rhyme. Since the voice on the tape was not that of the mother, the fetuses apparently were responding to the linguistic sounds they had heard the mother use. This suggests that hearing the "mother tongue" before birth may "pre-tune" an infant's ears to pick up linguistic sounds (DeCasper, Lecanuet, Busnel, Granier-Deferre, & Maugeais, 1994). Indeed, as we reported in Chapters 3 and 5, even 2-day-old infants prefer to hear the language they heard in the womb rather than a foreign language (C. Moon, Cooper, & Fifer 1993).

Before 6 months of age, babies have learned the basic sounds of their native language. In one study, 6-month-old Swedish and U.S. babies routinely ignored variations in sounds common to their own language but noticed variations in an unfamiliar language (Kuhl, Williams, Lacerda, Stevens, & Lindblom, 1992). Recognition of metrical patterns (accented and unaccented syllables) seems to develop as babies become increasingly familiar with their own language. Nine-month-old U.S. babies, but not 6-month-olds, listened longer to words with the stress pattern most common in English: strong-weak, as in *butter* (but'-ter) rather than weak-strong as in *restore* (re-store'). This preference may be the beginning of the ability to segment continuous speech into words, an ability needed for acquiring a vocabulary (Jusczyk, Cutler, & Redanz, 1993).

By 10 to 12 months, babies lose their earlier sensitivity to sounds that are not part of the language they hear spoken. For example, Japanese infants no longer make a distinction between "ra" and "la," a distinction that does not exist in the

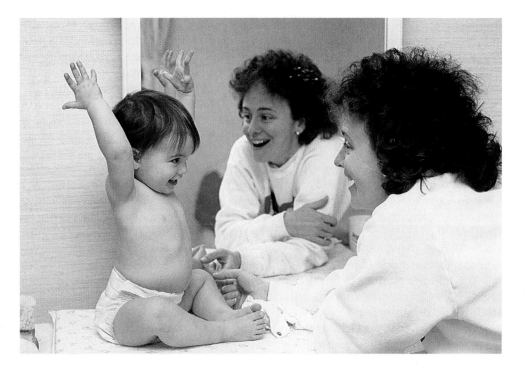

"So big!" Before babies say their first words, they have developed a repertoire of nonverbal gestures. When Mother asks, "How big is Alyssa?" the baby's hands are likely to shoot up. Later gestures will become more elaborate, expressing more complex meanings.

Japanese language. Although the ability to perceive nonnative sounds is not entirely lost—it can be revived, with effort, in adulthood—the brain no longer routinely discriminates them (Bates, O'Connell, & Shore, 1987; Lalonde & Werker, 1995; Werker, 1989).

Eight-month-olds pay attention to how words sound, and then store those sound patterns in memory. In one study, infants that age heard recordings of three children's stories 10 times during a 2-week period. Two weeks later, the infants listened longer to a list of words from the stories they had heard than to an unrelated list of words; a control group listened equally long to both lists. Apparently, in getting ready to understand speech, infants first become familiar with the sounds of words and later attach meanings to them (Jusczyk & Hohne, 1997).

Gestures

At 9 months Antonio *pointed* to an object, sometimes making a noise to show that he wanted it. Between 9 and 12 months, he learned a few *conventional social gestures:* waving bye-bye, nodding his head to mean *yes,* and shaking his head to signify *no.* By about 13 months, he used more elaborate *representational gestures;* for example, he would hold an empty cup to his mouth or hold up his arms to show that he wanted to be picked up.

Symbolic gestures, such as blowing to mean "hot," often emerge around the same time as babies say their first words; these gestures show that children understand that things and ideas have names and that symbols can refer to specific everyday objects, events, desires, and conditions. Among thirty-eight 17-month-olds, 87 percent used at least one such gesture, and the average child used four (Acredolo & Goodwyn, 1988). Gestures usually appear before children have a vocabulary of 25 words and drop out when children learn the word for the idea they were gesturing and can say it instead (A. Lock, Young, Service, & Chandler, 1990).

First Words

Doddy Darwin, at 11 months, said his first word—"ouchy"—which he attached to a number of objects. Doddy's development was typical in this respect. The average baby says a first word sometime between 10 and 14 months, initiating

linguistic speech Verbal
expression designed to convey
meaning.

holophrase Single word that
conveys a complete thought.

linguistic speech—verbal expression that conveys meaning. Before long, the baby will use many words and will show some understanding of grammar, pronunciation, intonation, and rhythm. For now, an infant's total verbal repertoire is likely to be "mama" or "dada." Or, as in Doddy's case, it may be a simple syllable that has more than one meaning depending on the context in which the child utters it. "Da" may mean "I want that," "I want to go out," or "Where's Daddy?" A word like this, which expresses a complete thought, is called a *holophrase.*

Babies understand many words before they can use them; that is, their *passive vocabulary* develops faster and is larger than their *active vocabulary.* The first words most babies understand, at about 9 or 10 months, are the ones they are likely to hear most often: their own names and the word "no." Babies also learn to recognize words with special meaning for them; Emma's parents may start spelling words in front of her if, for example, it is not time yet to give her a b-a-n-a-n-a. Babies listen especially closely to words they are getting ready to pronounce. In one study, French 11- to 12-month-olds who were just beginning to talk paid more attention to familiar words that French children typically begin to say at 14 to 18 months than to unfamiliar words of equal phonetic complexity (Hallé & de Boysson-Bardies, 1994).

By 13 months, most children understand that a word stands for a specific thing or event, and they can quickly learn the meaning of a new word (Woodward, Markman, & Fitzsimmons, 1994). Addition of new words to their *expressive* (spoken) vocabulary is slower at first. As children come to rely more on words to express themselves, the sounds and rhythms of speech grow more elaborate.

As babies work on attaching meaning to sounds, they temporarily pay less attention to fine auditory discrimination. In one study (Stager & Werker, 1997), when spoken nonsense words were paired with pictures of objects, 14-month-olds failed to notice the difference between "bih" and "dih," a distinction they easily detected when viewing a meaningless pattern. Eight-month-olds, who were not yet focused on learning word meanings, distinguished the sounds equally well in both kinds of tasks. Apparently inattention to phonetic detail is adaptive during the period when babies are concentrating their linguistic resources on understanding the sounds they hear and do not yet have to deal with many similar-sounding words.

Vocabulary continues to grow throughout the single-word stage, which generally lasts until about 18 months of age. The most common early spoken words in English are *names* of things (nouns), either general ("bow-wow" for dog) or specific ("Unga" for one particular dog). Others are *action* words ("bye-bye"), *modifiers* ("hot"), words that express *feelings or relationships* (the ever-popular "no"), and a few *grammatical* words ("for") (K. Nelson, 1973, 1981). Sometime between 16 and 24 months a "naming explosion" occurs. Within a few weeks, a toddler goes from saying about 50 words to saying about 400 (Bates, Bretherton, & Snyder, 1988).

Until recently, it was believed that the initial tendency to use more nouns than other kinds of words was universal—either because the underlying concept of a noun is simpler and more concrete or because toddlers, by the time they begin to learn language, already have mental concepts of objects to which they can readily affix names (Gentner, 1982; K. Nelson, 1974). Actually, as we have seen, babies as young as 4 months have concepts of movement and what brings it about (Leslie, 1982). It now appears that the kinds of words children initially use may depend in part on the characteristics of their native language and the social context in which they hear it. In one small study, 9 out of 10 Mandarin-speaking toddlers in Beijing, China, used more verbs than nouns—hardly surprising, since verbs are especially prominent in the Mandarin language (Tardif, 1996).

What about babies born into households where two languages are spoken? At first, such babies often use elements of both languages, sometimes in the same utterance—a phenomenon called *code-mixing.* Still, a study of five 2-year-olds in Montreal (Genesee, Nicoladis, & Paradis, 1995) suggests that children in dual-language households do differentiate between the two languages, using French, for example, with a predominantly French-speaking father and English with a predominantly English-speaking mother. This is called *code-switching* (see Chapter 12).

code-mixing Use of elements of two languages, sometimes in the same utterance, by young children in households where both languages are spoken.

Sentences, Grammar, and Syntax

The next important linguistic breakthrough comes when a toddler puts two words together to express one idea ("Dolly fall"). Generally, children do this between 18 and 24 months, about 8 to 12 months after they say their first word. However, this age range varies greatly. Although prelinguistic speech is fairly closely tied to chronological age, linguistic speech is not. Most children who begin talking fairly late catch up eventually—and many make up for lost time by talking nonstop to anyone who will listen!

A child's first sentence typically deals with everyday events, things, people, or activities (Braine, 1976; M. L. Rice, 1989; Slobin, 1973). Children at first use *telegraphic speech,* which, like most telegrams, includes only a few essential words. When Rita says, "Damma deep," she seems to mean "Grandma is sweeping the floor." Telegraphic speech was once thought to be universal, but we now know that children's use of it varies (Braine, 1976). Its form varies, too, depending on the language being learned (Slobin, 1983). Word order conforms to some degree to what a child hears; Rita does not say "Deep Damma" when she sees her grandmother pushing a broom.

telegraphic speech Early form of sentence consisting of only a few essential words.

Sometime between 20 and 30 months, children acquire the fundamentals of *syntax*—the rules for putting sentences together in their language. They begin to use articles (*a, the*), prepositions (*in, on*), conjunctions (*and, but*), plurals, verb endings, past tense, and forms of the verb *to be* (*am, are, is*). By age 3, speech is fluent, longer, and more complex; although children often omit parts of speech, they get their meaning across well (R. Brown, 1973a, 1973b). At 2 years, 10 months, Maika said clearly and grammatically (despite her frustration), "I can't get this glove on my hand." This simple sentence, which she had never heard before, showed the impressive achievement that command of language represents.

syntax Rules for forming sentences in a particular language.

Characteristics of Early Speech

Young children's speech is not just an immature version of adult speech; it has a character all its own. This is true no matter what language a child is speaking (Slobin, 1971).

As we already have seen, children *simplify.* They use telegraphic speech to say just enough to get their meaning across ("No drink milk!"). Early speech also has several other distinct characteristics.

Children *understand grammatical relationships they cannot yet express.* At first, Erica may understand that a dog is chasing a cat, but she cannot string together enough words to express the complete action. Her sentence comes out as "Puppy chase" rather than "Puppy chase kitty."

Children *underextend word meanings.* Miranda's uncle gave her a toy car, which Miranda, at 13 months, called her "koo-ka." Then her father came home with a gift, saying, "Look, Miranda, here's a little car for you." Miranda shook her head. "Koo-ka," she said, and ran and got the one from her uncle. To her, *that* car—and *only* that car—was a little car, and it took some time before she called any other toy cars by the same name. Miranda was underextending the word *car* by restricting it to a single object.

Children also *overextend word meanings.* At 14 months, Eddie jumped in excitement at the sight of a gray-haired man on the television screen and shouted, "Gampa!" Eddie was overgeneralizing, or *overextending,* a word; he thought that because his grandfather had gray hair, all gray-haired men could be called

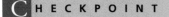
Can you . . .

• Trace the typical sequence of milestones in early language development, pointing out the influence of the language babies hear around them?

• State five ways in which young children's speech differs from adult speech?

"Grandpa." As children develop a larger vocabulary and get feedback from adults on the appropriateness of what they say, they overextend less. ("No, honey, that man looks a little like Grandpa, but he's somebody else's grandpa, not yours.")

Children *overregularize rules:* they apply them rigidly, not knowing that some rules have exceptions. When John says "mouses" instead of "mice" or Anna says "I thinked" rather than "I thought," this represents progress. Both children initially used the correct forms of these irregular words, but merely in imitation of what they heard. Once children learn grammatical rules for plurals and past tense (a crucial step in learning language), they apply them universally. The next step is to learn the exceptions to the rules, which they generally do by early school age.

How Do Babies Acquire Language? The Nature-Nurture Debate

How do babies figure out the secrets of verbal communication? Is this ability learned or inborn? In the 1950s, a debate raged between two schools of thought about language development: one led by B. F. Skinner, the foremost proponent of learning theory, the other by the linguist Noam Chomsky.

Skinner (1957) maintained that language learning, like other learning, is based on experience. According to learning theory, children learn language in the same way they learn other kinds of behavior, through operant conditioning and observational learning. At first, children utter sounds at random. Caregivers reinforce the sounds that happen to resemble adult speech by smiling, paying attention, and talking to a child. Children then repeat these reinforced sounds. Children also imitate the sounds they hear adults make and, again, are reinforced for doing so. As this process continues, children learn to produce meaningful speech by generalizing from their experience.

Almost all children, like this Japanese baby, learn their native language, mastering the basics in the same age-related sequence without formal teaching. Nativists say this shows that all human beings are born with the capacity to acquire language.

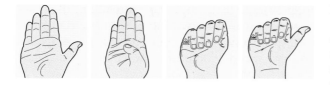

Figure 6-8
Example of hand-babbling by a nonhearing baby who had been exposed to sign language. The baby repeated this series of hand movements over and over again in sequence. Each motion is comparable to a syllable in a sequence of vocal babbling.
Source: Petitto & Marentette, 1991.

Reinforcement and imitation probably do contribute to language development, but, as Chomsky (1957) persuasively argued, they cannot fully explain it (Flavell, Miller, & Miller, 1993). For one thing, linguistic rules and nuances of meaning are so numerous and complex that they could not all be acquired by specific reinforcement and imitation. Furthermore, learning theory does not account for children's imaginative ways of saying things they have never heard. Anna, for example, described a sprained ankle as a "sprangle" and said she didn't want to go to sleep yet because she wasn't "yawny."

Chomsky's own view, more widely accepted today, is called *nativism.* Chomsky (1957) proposed that the human brain has an inborn capacity for acquiring language; babies learn to talk as naturally as they learn to walk. Nativists point out that almost all children master their native language in the same age-related sequence without formal teaching. Chomsky (1972) proposed that an inborn *language acquisition device (LAD)* programs children's brains to analyze the language they hear and to extract from it the rules of grammar and syntax.

Support for the nativist position comes from newborns' ability to differentiate similar sounds (Eimas et al., 1971). One researcher suggests that neonates can put sounds into categories because all human beings are "born with perceptual mechanisms that are tuned to the properties of speech" (Eimas, 1985, p. 49). Furthermore, human beings, the only animals with spoken language, are the only species whose brain is larger on one side than the other, suggesting that an inborn mechanism for language may be localized in the larger hemisphere (the left for most people). Still, the nativist approach does not explain why some children acquire language more rapidly and efficiently than others, why children differ in linguistic skill and fluency, how children come to understand the meanings of words, or why (as we'll see in a moment) speech development appears to depend on having someone to talk with, not merely on hearing spoken language.

Aspects of both learning theory and nativism have been used to explain how deaf babies learn sign language (which is structured much like spoken languages and is acquired in the same sequence). Deaf babies seem to copy the sign language they see their parents using, just as hearing babies copy vocal utterances. Using hand motions more systematic and deliberate than those of hearing babies, deaf babies first string together meaningless motions and repeat them over and over in what has been called *hand-babbling* (Petitto & Marentette, 1991; see Figure 6-8). As parents reinforce these gestures, the babies attach meaning to them.

However, the observation that deaf children make up their own sign language when they do not have models to follow strongly suggests that environmental influences alone cannot explain the capacity for linguistic expression. In one study, U.S. and Taiwanese deaf children developed complex systems of gestures that—despite the marked dissimilarity between the English and Chinese languages—resembled each other more than they did the gestures made by the children's hearing parents (Goldin-Meadow & Mylander, 1998). Furthermore, learning theory does not explain the uncanny correspondence between the ages at which linguistic advances in hearing and nonhearing babies occur. Deaf babies begin hand-babbling before 10 months of age, about the same period when hearing infants begin voice-babbling. Deaf babies also begin using sentences in sign language at about the same time hearing babies begin speaking in sentences. This suggests that an inborn language capacity may underlie the acquisition of both spoken and signed language and that advances in both kinds of language are tied to brain maturation rather than to maturation of the vocal cords.

nativism Theory that human beings have an inborn capacity for language acquisition.

language acquisition device (LAD) In Chomsky's terminology, an inborn mechanism that enables children to infer linguistic rules from the language they hear.

Most developmentalists today believe that language acquisition, like most other aspects of development, depends on an intertwining of nature and nurture. Children, whether hearing or deaf, probably have an inborn capacity to acquire language, which is activated and enhanced by maturation, cognitive development, and experience.

Influences on Linguistic Progress

What determines how quickly and how well children learn to understand and use language? Research during the past two or three decades has focused on specific influences, both within and outside the child.

Genes and Temperament

A genetic influence on language development is apparent in the moderate positive correlation between parents' intelligence and the rate at which their biological children develop communication skills during the first year of life. In adopted children, this correlation exists with their biological mothers but not with their adoptive parents (Hardy-Brown & Plomin, 1985; Hardy-Brown, Plomin, & DeFries, 1981).

Another influence likely to be inborn is temperament. This influence is probably bidirectional. According to one study (C. L. Slomkowski, Nelson, Dunn, & Plomin, 1992), children who at age 2 are happy, cooperative, and interested in other people are more advanced at ages 2, 3, and 7 in expressing themselves and responding to what other people say. This may be because extroverted children get more practice in speaking; they talk more, and they have the kind of personality that makes other people want to talk to them.

Indeed, a widespread view today is that *social interaction* is crucial to language acquisition. Many differences in language abilities, especially those that surface by the end of the second year, reflect differences in environment, including how and how much adults talk to a child.

Social Interaction: The Role of Parents and Caregivers

As the case of the wild boy of Aveyron (see Chapter 1) suggests, language is a social act, which requires practice from an early age. By talking to babies, adults show how to use new words, structure phrases, and carry on a conversation. They enable babies to pick up nuances and correct wrong assumptions. A review of the research literature concludes, "No child has been observed to speak a human language without having had a communicative partner from whom to learn" (Hoff-Ginsberg & Shatz, 1982, p. 22).

Parents and other caregivers play an important role at each stage of an infant's language development. At the babbling stage, adults help infants advance toward true speech by repeating the sounds a baby makes; the baby soon joins in the game and repeats the sounds back. Parents' imitation of babies' sounds affects the pace of language learning (Hardy-Brown & Plomin, 1985; Hardy-Brown, Plomin, & DeFries, 1981). It also helps babies experience the social aspect of speech, the sense that a conversation consists of taking turns, an idea most babies seem to grasp at about 7½ to 8 months of age.

Caregivers may help babies understand spoken words by, for example, pointing to a doll and saying, "Please give me Kermit." If the baby doesn't respond, the adult may pick up the doll and say, "Kermit." A baby's comprehension grows by discovering through language what another person is thinking. By 1 year, a baby has some sense of intentional communication, a primitive idea of reference, and a set of signals to communicate with familiar caregivers (Bates et al., 1987).

When babies begin to talk, parents or caregivers often help them by repeating their first words and pronouncing them correctly. A strong relationship has appeared between the frequency of various words in mothers' speech and the order in which children learn these words (Huttenlocher, Haight, Bryk, Seltzer, &

Lyons, 1991). Vocabularies get a boost when adults seize an appropriate opportunity to teach children new words. If Elijah's mother says, "This is a ball" when Elijah is looking at the ball, he is more likely to remember the word than if he were playing with something else and she tried to divert his attention to the ball (Dunham, Dunham, & Curwin, 1993). Adults help a toddler who has begun to put words together by expanding on what the child says. If Christina says "Mommy sock," her mother may reply, "Yes, that is Mommy's sock."

From early in their second year, children talk to their parents about what they see on television. They label objects, repeat slogans and jingles, and ask questions. Parents can build on the children's interest and lead them into exchanges that enhance language development (Lemish & Rice, 1986). These exchanges are crucial; hearing speech on television is not enough. Dutch children who watched German television every day did not learn German (C. E. Snow et al., 1976).

The value of frequent verbal interaction is supported by research on twins, who usually speak later than single-born children. An observational study of 15- and 21-month-olds suggests a reason: harried mothers who must divide their attention between two babies the same age cannot interact individually with each twin as much as mothers of single babies (Tomasello, Mannle, & Kruger, 1986). Mothers of twins speak less frequently to each child and have shorter conversations. Although twins have each other to talk to, and often develop a private language between themselves, their interaction is not as influential as the kind they would have with an adult.

What adults say to children may be almost as important as how much they speak. One factor in the delayed speech of twins is that when their mothers do speak to them, what they say consists mostly of telling the child what to do (Tomasello et al., 1986). Among 2-year-olds in day-care centers in Bermuda, children whose caregivers spoke to them often to give or ask for information rather than to control behavior had better language skills than children who did not have such conversations (McCartney, 1984; see Chapter 7).

Although the importance of conversation with caregivers is clear, there is disagreement over whether the primary initiative for linguistic progress comes from the caregiver or the child. According to the Vygotskyan *scaffolding model* (J. Bruner, 1983), caregivers structure conversation and guide learning as the child seems to be ready. Although the child is an active participant, the adult takes the lead. Adults start conversations, ask questions, and elaborate on what a child has said. According to the *intentionality model* (L. L. Bloom, 1993; Bloom, Margulis, Tinker, & Fujita, 1996), the child's desire to express, interpret, and share thoughts is the driving force behind adult-child conversations and language learning. Children start most conversations, using words relevant to the ideas they want to express; adults acknowledge or repeat what the child has said, and children use the adult's response to further their own conversational agenda.

In one study, researchers videotaped 40 mothers playing with their 9-month-old infants at home and observed the mothers' verbal sensitivity. Did a mother respond to her baby's interest in a toy by naming that toy? Did she continue to talk about the toy as long as the baby was paying attention to it and pick up on the baby's signal when the baby's attention shifted? If the baby was not paying attention to anything in particular, did she try to verbally focus the baby's attention? ("Look at the dolly.") The mother's verbal sensitivity turned out to be an important predictor of the baby's language comprehension (as reported by the mother) 4 months later. This was especially true of infants who initially showed lower comprehension (Baumwell, Tamis-LeMonda, & Bornstein, 1997).

Further research may continue to untangle the roles of caregiver and child, but it is clear that linguistic growth is a bidirectional process involving both.

Family Characteristics

Socioeconomic status seems to affect the amount and quality of verbal interaction between parents and children, and also the children's long-range language and cognitive development. In one longitudinal study, 40 midwestern families with 7-month-old babies were initially observed in their homes for an hour each month until the children were 3 years old. The children's language usage was taped and analyzed. The parents with lower incomes and educational and occupational levels tended to spend less time in positive verbal interaction with their children. The children were exposed to less varied language and were given less opportunity to talk, and their own spoken vocabulary was more limited (B. Hart & Risley, 1989). A follow-up study, which repeatedly assessed 32 of the children between ages 5 and 10, found that these differences in language experience and development in early childhood predicted linguistic and academic performance during the elementary school years (D. Walker, Greenwood, Hart, & Carta, 1994).

One factor in the favorable effect of high socioeconomic status on language development is that upper-middle-class American mothers tend to follow their children's conversational cues by answering questions or pursuing a topic the child has brought up, whereas working-class mothers are more likely to give orders or directions (Hoff-Ginsberg, 1991). As we have mentioned, too much direction—commands, requests, and instructions—does not help language development. Asking questions and elaborating on what children say is more effective (K. Nelson, 1973, 1981).

Parental speaking styles influence whether children are *referential*, using their first words (mainly nouns and verbs) to *refer* to objects and events by naming and describing them, or *expressive*, using first words (often pronouns) to *express* social routines and repeat formulas such as "stop it" (Lieven, 1978; K. Nelson, 1981; Olsen-Fulero, 1982). Referential children, who learn new words faster than expressive children (E. V. Clark, 1983), tend to be firstborns from better-educated families, whose parents encourage labeling by asking their children many questions. Parents of expressive children use more directive speech (K. Nelson, 1973).

The mother's age and marital status may make a difference. In one study of 32 infants, age 13 months, those born to unwed teenage mothers heard less speech than the babies of married mothers in their twenties, and the words the teenage mothers uttered did not tend to invite conversation. Their babies, in turn, engaged in significantly less vocalization than the infants of older mothers. In this case, socioeconomic status was not a likely factor, since the older mothers had no more than a high school education (Culp, Osofsky, & O'Brien, 1996).

Child-Directed Speech

You do not have to be a parent to speak "parentese." If, when you talk to an infant or toddler, you speak slowly in a high-pitched voice with exaggerated ups and downs, simplify your speech, exaggerate vowel sounds, and use short words and sentences and much repetition, you are using *child-directed speech (CDS)*. Most adults, and even children, do it naturally. Such "baby talk" may well be universal; it has been documented in many languages and cultures (Kuhl et al., 1997). Parents make similar adjustments when they sing to infants (Trehub et al., 1997).

Many researchers believe that CDS helps children to learn their native language, or at least to pick it up faster. In one study, mothers in the United States, Russia, and Sweden were audiotaped speaking to their 2- to 5-month-old infants. Whether the mothers were speaking English, Russian, or Swedish, they produced more exaggerated vowel sounds when talking to the infants than when talking to other adults. Apparently this kind of linguistic input helps infants hear the distinguishing features of speech sounds. At 20 weeks, the babies' babbling contained distinct vowels that reflected the phonetic differences to which their mothers' speech had alerted them (Kuhl et al., 1997).

CDS also seems to serve other cognitive, social, and emotional functions (Fernald, 1984; Fernald & Simon, 1984; C. E. Snow, 1972, 1977). It teaches babies how to carry on a conversation: how to introduce a topic, comment on and add to it, and take turns talking. It teaches them how to use new words, structure phrases, and

child-directed speech (CDS) Form of speech often used in talking to babies or toddlers; includes slow, simplified speech, a high-pitched tone, exaggerated vowel sounds, short words and sentences, and much repetition. Also called *parentese.*

"Parentese," or child-directed speech, is a simplified form of language used for speaking to babies and toddlers. It seems to come naturally, not only to parents, but also to other adults and slightly older children.

put ideas into language. Because CDS is confined to simple, down-to-earth topics, infants and toddlers can use their own knowledge of familiar things to help them work out the meanings of the words they hear. CDS also helps babies develop a relationship with adults and enables them to respond to emotional cues.

Adults' use of CDS teaches children the norms of their culture along with the rules of their language. In a study of 30 Japanese and 30 U.S. mothers with 6-, 12-, and 19-month-old babies (Fernald & Morikawa, 1993), both the Japanese and the U.S. mothers simplified their language, repeated often, and spoke differently to babies of different ages, but the mothers' ways of interacting with the babies reflected cultural values about child rearing. U.S. mothers labeled objects more, to expand the babies' vocabulary ("That's a car. See the car? You like it? It's got nice wheels"). Japanese mothers encouraged politeness by give-and-take routines ("Here! It's a vroom vroom. I give it to you. Now give this to me. Yes! Thank you"). Japanese mothers use CDS longer and more extensively than U.S. mothers, whose culture places a higher value on fostering independence in children.

Some investigators challenge the value of CDS. They contend that babies speak sooner and better if they hear and can respond to more complex adult speech. Children select from this speech the parts they are interested in and are able to deal with. In fact, some researchers say, children discover the rules of language faster when they hear complex sentences that use these rules more often and in more ways (Gleitman, Newport, & Gleitman, 1984).

Studies in nonwestern societies in which CDS is rarely used suggest that simplified speech is not necessary to language development. Normal adult conversations among older family members may be an important model, for example, for learning the correct usage of personal pronouns such as "you" and "me," which can refer to different people depending on the situation. Similarly, in a Canadian study, English-speaking secondborn 21-month olds, who experienced less speech directed *to* them than firstborn children and more complex *overheard* conversations between caregivers and older siblings, were more advanced in the use of personal pronouns at age 2 than were firstborns of the same age, though the general language development of the two groups was about equal (Oshima-Takane, Goodz, & Derevensky, 1996). Toddlers often break into these overheard conversations. Among six 2-year-old secondborns observed at home, a growing proportion—averaging more than one-fifth—of their talk over the course of a year consisted of such intrusions, and their contributions became increasingly relevant (Dunn & Shatz, 1989).

Whether or not simplified speech enhances language development, infants prefer it. This preference is clear before 1 month of age, and it does not seem to depend on any specific experience (R. P. Cooper & Aslin, 1990; Kuhl et al., 1997). Parents usually do not start speaking CDS until babies show by their expressions, actions, and sounds that they have some understanding of what is being said to them. This interactive behavior on the infant's part encourages the use of CDS; women tend to use it less when asked to speak on tape to unseen children (C. E. Snow, 1972).

Infants' preference for CDS crosses language barriers. In a Canadian study, 4½- and 9-month-old babies of immigrants from Hong Kong, whose native tongue was Cantonese, were more attentive, interested, happy, and excited when shown a videotape of a Cantonese-speaking woman using CDS than when the woman used normal adult speech—and so were babies of English-speaking parents (Werker, Pegg, & McLeod, 1994). The preference for CDS also does not seem to be limited to one language form. In a Japanese study, deaf mothers were videotaped reciting everyday sentences in sign language, first to their deaf 6-month-old infants and then to deaf adult friends. The mothers signed more slowly and with more repetition and exaggerated movements when directing the sentences to the infants, and other infants the same age paid more attention and appeared more responsive when shown these tapes (Masataka, 1996).

Preparing for Literacy: The Benefits of Reading Aloud

From an early age, most babies love to be read to, and the frequency with which parents or caregivers read to them, as well as the way they do it, can influence how well children speak and eventually how well they read. According to classic research, children who learn to read early are generally those whose parents read to them frequently when they were young (Durkin, 1966).

Reading to a child fosters parent-child conversation; when mothers and children play with toys together, the mothers are more likely to issue commands (Hoff-Ginsberg, 1991). Adults help a child's language development when they paraphrase what the child says, expand on it, talk about what interests the child, remain quiet long enough to give the child a chance to respond, and ask specific questions (M. L. Rice, 1989). Read-aloud sessions offer a perfect opportunity for this kind of interaction.

A child will get more out of such sessions if adults ask challenging, open-ended questions rather than those calling for a simple yes or no ("What is the cat doing?" instead of "Is the cat asleep?"). In one study, 21- to 35-month-olds whose parents did this—and who added to the child's answers, corrected wrong ones, gave alternative possibilities, encouraged the child to tell the story, and bestowed praise—scored 6 months higher in vocabulary and expressive language skills than did a control group whose parents did not use these practices in reading to the children. The experimental group also got a boost in *preliteracy skills,* the competencies helpful in learning to read, such as learning how letters look and sound (Arnold & Whitehurst, 1994; G. J. Whitehurst et al., 1988).

Children who are read to often, especially in this way, when they are 1 to 3 years old show better language skills at ages 2½, 4½, and 5 and better reading comprehension at age 7 (Crain-Thoreson & Dale, 1992; Wells, 1985). This may also be true of children with below-normal language abilities, who are at risk of developing reading problems. At a low-quality day-care center in Mexico, teachers were specially trained in these techniques, which are based on Vygotskyan principles. They then read to 2-year-olds from low-income homes, where the children were not read to frequently. After 6 or 7 weeks of one-on-one read-aloud sessions, these children did significantly better on standardized language tests and in spontaneous language usage than children whose teachers spent time with them individually doing arts and crafts (Valdez-Menchaca & Whitehurst, 1992).

CHECKPOINT

Can you . . .

- Summarize how learning theory and nativism explain language acquisition?

- Cite evidence for genetic and temperamental influences on linguistic development?

- Explain the importance of social interaction and give at least three examples of how parents or caregivers help babies learn to talk?

- Assess the arguments for and against child-directed speech (CDS)?

- Describe an effective way of reading aloud to infants and toddlers?

By reading aloud to his 2-year-old son and asking questions about the pictures in the book, this father is helping the boy build language skills and prepare to become a good reader.

Reading to an infant or toddler offers opportunities for emotional closeness and communication. Indeed, interaction in reading aloud, play, and other daily activities is a key to much of childhood development—cognitive, social, and emotional. Children call forth responses from the people around them and they, in turn, react to those responses. In Chapter 7, we will look more closely at these bidirectional influences as we explore early psychosocial development.

SUMMARY

Studying Cognitive Development: Classic Approaches

- Researchers take various approaches to the study of **intelligent behavior.**

- The **behaviorist approach** is concerned with the mechanics of learning. Two simple types of learning that occur early in infancy are **classical conditioning** and **operant conditioning.**

- The **psychometric approach** seeks to determine and measure quantitatively the factors that make up intelligence, usually through **IQ (intelligence quotient) tests** based on **standardized norms.** To be useful, psychometric tests must have **validity** and **reliability.**

- A widely used developmental test for infants and toddlers is the **Bayley Scales of Infant Development.** In normal infants, psychometric tests are generally poor predictors of intelligence in later childhood and adulthood.

- The home environment can affect measured intelligence. According to the **Home Observation for Measurement of the Environment (HOME),** parental responsiveness is one of the important factors associated with optimal cognitive development. If the **developmental priming mechanisms** necessary for normal development are not present, **early intervention** may be needed.

- The **Piagetian approach** is concerned with qualitative stages of cognitive development. During the **sensorimotor stage,** from about birth to 2 years, infants' cognitive and behavioral **schemes** become more elaborate. As they progress from primary to secondary to tertiary **circular reactions** and finally to the development of **representational ability,** babies change from primarily reflexive creatures to goal-oriented toddlers capable of symbolic thought, which makes possible **deferred imitation** and **pretend play. Object permanence** develops gradually throughout the sensorimotor stage.

- Research since Piaget's time suggests that a number of abilities develop earlier than he described. For example, **invisible imitation**—which, according to Piaget, develops at about 9 months, has been reported in newborns, though this finding is in dispute. More complex **visible imitation** has been reported as early as 6 months. Studies using **elicited imitation** suggest that toddlers as young as 13 months can form long-term memories.

Studying Cognitive Development: Newer Approaches

- The **information-processing approach** is concerned with how people manipulate symbols and what they do with the information they perceive. Information-processing research suggests that the ability to form and remember mental representations is present virtually from birth. Indicators of the efficiency of infants' information processing include speed of **habituation** and **dishabituation, visual recognition memory, visual novelty preference,** and **cross-modal transfer.** These abilities also tend to predict later intelligence. Early visual attentiveness is a predictor of a toddler's **exploratory competence.** Information processing ability is influenced by the responsiveness of significant adults.

- Studies based on the **violation-of-expectations** method suggest that infants as young as 3½ to 5 months may have a grasp of object permanence, a sense of number, and the beginning of an understanding of **causality.** The ability to reason about characteristics of the physical world appears to become more sophisticated during the second half of the first year, as babies gain experience in handling objects.

- The **cognitive neuroscience approach** is the study of brain structures that govern thought and memory. Such studies have found that some forms of **implicit memory** develop during the first few months of life. **Explicit memory** and **working memory** emerge between 6 and 12 months of age.

- The **social-contextual approach,** which is based on Vygotskyan principles, looks at the content of social interactions with adults and how they contribute to cognitive development. Through **guided participation** in play and other shared everyday activities, caregivers help children learn the skills, knowledge, and values important in their culture.

- Parents' child-rearing styles seem to affect children's cognitive and social competence. Parents of the most competent children are those who are skilled at "designing" a child's environment, are available as "consultants" to a child, and use appropriate controls.

Language Development

- The acquisition of **language** is a crucial aspect of cognitive development.
- **Prelinguistic speech** includes crying, cooing, babbling, and imitating language sounds. Neonates can distinguish speech sounds; by 6 months, babies have learned the basic sounds of their language. Before they say their first word, babies use gestures, including pointing, conventional social gestures, representational gestures, and symbolic gestures. By 9 or 10 months, babies begin to understand meaningful speech.
- The first word typically comes sometime between 10 and 14 months, initiating **linguistic speech;** often it is a **holophrase,** which expresses a complete thought. The kinds of words children initially use are influenced by the social context and the characteristics of their native language. Among English-speaking children, a "naming explosion" typically occurs sometime between 16 and 24 months of age. Children in households where two languages are spoken tend to do **code-mixing.**
- The first brief sentences, which are called **telegraphic speech,** generally come between 18 and 24 months. By age 3, grammar and **syntax** are fairly well developed. Early speech is characterized by simplification, underextending and overextending word meanings, and overregularizing rules.
- Historically, two opposing views about how children acquire language were learning theory, which emphasizes the roles of reinforcement and imitation, and **nativism,** which maintains that children have an inborn **language acquisition device (LAD).** Today, most developmentalists hold that this inborn capacity to learn language is activated and enhanced by maturation, cognitive development, and experience.

- Influences on language development include genetic factors, temperament, and social interaction. Communication between caregivers and children is essential to language development; however, children also learn from overheard speech between parents and older siblings.

- Family characteristics, such as socioeconomic status and mother's age and marital status, seem to affect verbal interaction and language learning.

- **Child-directed speech** seems to have cognitive, emotional, and social benefits, and infants show a preference for it. However, some researchers dispute its value.

- Reading aloud to a child from an early age helps pave the way for **literacy.**

KEY TERMS

intelligent behavior (190)
behaviorist approach (190)
psychometric approach (190)
Piagetian approach (190)
classical conditioning (190)
operant conditioning (191)
IQ (intelligence quotient) tests (193)
standardized norms (193)
validity (193)
reliability (193)
Bayley Scales of Infant Development (194)
Home Observation for Measurement of the Environment (HOME) (195)
developmental priming mechanisms (195)
early intervention (195)
sensorimotor stage (198)
schemes (198)
circular reactions (198)
representational ability (200)
deferred imitation (201)
pretend play (201)
object permanence (201)
invisible imitation (203)
visible imitation (203)
elicited imitation (205)
information-processing approach (205)

cognitive neuroscience approach (205)
social-contextual approach (205)
habituation (206)
dishabituation (207)
visual recognition memory (207)
visual novelty preference (207)
cross-modal transfer (207)
exploratory competence (208)
violation-of-expectations (208)
causality (209)
explicit memory (212)
implicit memory (212)
working memory (213)
guided participation (213)
language (215)
literacy (215)
prelinguistic speech (215)
linguistic speech (218)
holophrase (218)
code-mixing (219)
telegraphic speech (219)
syntax (219)
nativism (221)
language acquisition device (LAD) (221)
child-directed speech (CDS) (224)

QUESTIONS FOR THOUGHT AND DISCUSSION

1. Watson and Rayner's experiment which conditioned fear in "Little Albert" would violate today's ethical standards for research, yet it provided valuable information about human behavior. In an experiment such as this, where would you draw the line between society's need to learn and an infant's rights?

2. On the basis of observations by Piaget and others about early cognitive development, what factors would you consider in designing or purchasing a toy or book for an infant or toddler?

3. What practical and ethical questions should be considered in designing an intervention to enhance cognitive development of disadvantaged infants and toddlers?

4. The HOME scale assesses the relationship between the home environment and a child's later cognitive functioning. If you were designing such a measure, what aspects of the home situation, if any, would you add to those mentioned in the text?

5. Can you suggest any additional guidelines for fostering infants' and toddlers' competence, besides those in Box 6-1?

6. From your observations, which, if any, of the two patterns of guided participation in social interaction with toddlers do you consider more beneficial?

7. On the basis of your own experience and the information presented in this chapter, what is your opinion of the value of child-directed speech?

Psychosocial Development During the First Three Years

*I'm like a child
trying to do everything
say everything
and be everything
all at once*

John Hartford, "Life Prayer," 1971

Focus

Mary Catherine Bateson

Mary Catherine Bateson is an anthropologist, the daughter of two famous anthropologists: Margaret Mead and Gregory Bateson, who, before her birth, had collaborated on studies of childhood in Bali and New Guinea. Since her parents made a practice of blending their personal and professional lives, hers was probably one of the most documented infancies on record—her mother taking notes, her father behind the camera. Margaret Mead's memoir, *Blackberry Winter* (1972), and Mary Catherine Bateson's *With a Daughter's Eye* (1984) together provide a rare and fascinating dual perspective on the psychosocial dimensions of a child's first three years of life.

Cathy was born in 1939, when her mother was 38 years old. She was a very much wanted baby; Margaret had been told 13 years earlier that she could never bear a child, and she had had several miscarriages. Margaret's marriage to Gregory Bateson was her third; they divorced when Cathy was 11, after living apart during much of her childhood. Their work during World War II often pulled them in different directions and necessitated long absences from home. As their daughter grew up, she developed separate personal and, later, professional relationships with each of them. But during her infancy and toddlerhood, when her parents were together, she was the joint focus of their love and wholehearted attention.

Among Catherine's early, hazy memories are recollections of sitting with her parents on a blanket outdoors, her mother's lap providing a sheltering "nest" for cuddling up and reading aloud; riding atop her father's six-foot-five-inch frame, perched on his shoulders "far above the crowd, ducking down to pass under doorways or the branches of trees" (Bateson, 1984, p. 21); and watching the two of them at breakfast as they drank coffee and held up their spoons to reflect the morning light, making a pair of illusory "birds" flash across the walls and ceilings for her amusement.

Margaret arranged her professional commitments around breastfeeding. From the first, Cathy showed a quiet temperament and "did not fight for the nipple when it was taken away" (Mead, 1972, p. 259). To avoid subjecting her to frustration, her parents tried to respond so quickly to her needs that she would have little reason to cry. Rather than follow a

Focus—*Continued*

rigid, predetermined schedule, as was the practice at the time, Margaret nursed her baby "on demand," when the infant was hungry, as did the mothers in the South Pacific island cultures she had studied.

Like their friend Erik Erikson, Margaret and Gregory placed great importance on the development of trust in infancy. Cathy did not show anxiety in the presence of strangers. Her mother took care never to leave her in a strange place with a strange person; a new caregiver was always introduced to her in a familiar place. "Her warm responsiveness, her trustingness, and her outgoing interest in people and things all evoked lively responses from others and set the stage for her expectation that the world was a friendly place" (Mead, 1972, p. 266).

"How much was temperament? How much was felicitous accident? How much could be attributed to upbringing? We may never know," wrote Mead (1972, p. 268). "Certainly all a mother and father can claim credit for is that they have not marred a child in any recognizable way." As an adult, Catherine observed that, during difficult periods in her life, she often found "resources of faith and strength, a foundation that must have been built in those [first] two years" (Bateson, 1984, p. 35).

Margaret tried to avoid being an overprotective mother or projecting her own aspirations onto her child. Her overriding goal was to let Cathy be herself. Catherine remembers her father pushing her swing so high that he could run under it. Later he taught her to climb tall pine trees, testing every branch for firmness and making sure that she could find her way back down, while her mother, watching, tried not to betray the fear she felt.

When Cathy was 2, her parents merged their household with that of Lawrence Frank, a friend and colleague. The decision freed Margaret and Gregory for their increasing wartime travel. It also fit in with Margaret's belief, gleaned from her studies in Samoa, that children benefit from having multiple caregivers and from learning to adapt to different kinds of people and situations.

The ménage in Frank's five-story brownstone on Perry Street in Greenwich Village included his infant son, Colin, who was like a brother to Cathy, and five older children. "Thus," Catherine writes, "I did not grow up in a nuclear family or as an only child, but as a member of a flexible and welcoming extended family, full of children of all ages, in which five or six pairs of hands could be mobilized to shell peas or dry dishes." Her summertime memories are of a lakeside retreat in New Hampshire, where "each child was cared for by enough adults so that there need be no jealousy, where the garden bloomed and the evenings ended in song. . . . I was rich beyond other children . . . and yet there were all those partings. There were all those beloved people, yet often the people I wanted most were absent" (Bateson, 1984, pp. 38–39).

Sources of biographical information about Mary Catherine Bateson are Bateson, 1984, and Mead, 1972.

• • •

In Margaret Mead's and Mary Catherine Bateson's complementary memoirs, we can see how Mead, as a mother, put into practice the strong beliefs she had developed about child rearing, in part from her memories of her own childhood and in part from her observations of distant cultures. We can see her seeking innovative and comfortable solutions to a problem that has become increasingly perplexing in the United States: the problem of care for children of working parents. And we see again a bidirectionality of influence: not only how early experiences with parents help shape a child's development, but how the needs of a child can shape parents' lives.

This chapter is about the shift from the dependence of infancy to the independence of childhood and about the influences parents and children have on each other. We first examine foundations of psychosocial development: emotions, temperament, and early experiences with parents. We consider Erikson's views about the formation of trust and the growth of autonomy. We look at patterns of attachment and other developmental issues concerning relationships with caregivers, at the emerging sense of self, and at the foundations of conscience. We explore relationships with siblings and other children and with grandparents. Finally, we consider the increasingly widespread impact of early day care.

After reading this chapter, you should be able to answer and elaborate on such questions as these:

Preview Questions

- How do babies, their families, and others in their world contribute to their psychosocial development?

- When do emotions develop, and how do babies show them?

- What role does temperament play in personality development?

- What is the importance of early experiences with parents and grandparents?

- How do infants gain trust in their world and form attachments?

- How and when does the sense of self develop?

- How do toddlers develop autonomy and standards for socially acceptable behavior?

- How do infants and toddlers interact with siblings and peers?

- How does early day care affect children's cognitive, emotional, and social development?

Table 7-1	Highlights of Infants' and Toddlers' Psychosocial Development, Birth to 36 Months

Approximate Age, Months	Characteristics
0–3	Infants are open to stimulation. They begin to show interest and curiosity, and they smile readily at people.
3–6	Infants can anticipate what is about to happen and experience disappointment when it does not. They show this by becoming angry or acting warily. They smile, coo, and laugh often. This is a time of social awakening and early reciprocal exchanges between the baby and the caregiver.
6–9	Infants play "social games" and try to get responses from people. They "talk" to, touch, and cajole other babies to get them to respond. They express more differentiated emotions, showing joy, fear, anger, and surprise.
9–12	Infants are intensely preoccupied with their principal caregiver, may become afraid of strangers, and act subdued in new situations. By 1 year, they communicate emotions more clearly, showing moods, ambivalence, and gradations of feeling.
12–18	Toddlers explore their environment, using the people they are most attached to as a secure base. As they master the environment, they become more confident and more eager to assert themselves.
18–36	Toddlers sometimes become anxious because they now realize how much they are separating from their caregiver. They work out their awareness of their limitations in fantasy and in play and by identifying with adults.

Source: Adapted from Sroufe, 1979.

Foundations of Psychosocial Development

Although babies share common patterns of development, they also—from the start—show distinct personalities, which reflect both inborn and environmental influences. From infancy on, personality development is intertwined with social relationships (see Table 7-1).

Emotions

emotions Subjective feelings, such as sadness, joy, and fear, which arise in response to situations and experiences and are expressed through altered behavior.

Normal human beings have the same range of *emotions*. These pleasant or unpleasant subjective feelings, such as sadness, joy, and fear, motivate behavior. People differ in how often they feel a particular emotion, in the kinds of experiences that produce it, and in how they act as a result. Emotional reactions to events and people, which are tied to cognitive perceptions, are a basic element of personality.

Studying babies' emotions is a challenge. Does a baby's cry express anger, fear, loneliness, or discomfort? It will be a long time before the infant can tell us. Still, parents, caregivers, and researchers learn to recognize subtle cues. Carroll Izard and his colleagues, for example, have sought to identify infants' emotions from their facial expressions. In one study, the researchers videotaped 5-, 7-, and 9-month-olds playing games with their mothers; seeing a jack-in-the-box pop up; being given shots by a doctor; and being approached by a stranger. College students and health professionals who viewed the tapes interpreted the babies' facial expressions as showing joy, sadness, interest, and fear, and to a lesser degree anger, surprise, and disgust (Izard, Huebner, Resser, McGinness, & Dougherty, 1980). Of course, we do not know that these babies actually had the feelings they were credited with, but their facial expressions were remarkably similar to adults' expressions of these emotions; so it seems likely that they were experiencing similar feelings.

When Do Emotions Develop?

Very soon after birth, babies show signs of distress, interest, and disgust. Within the next few months these primary emotions differentiate into joy, anger, surprise, sadness, shyness, and fear. The emergence of these emotions seems to be

Table 7-2	Timetable of Emotional Development	

Emotion	Approximate Age of Emergence
Interest	
Distress (in response to pain)	Present at birth or soon after
Disgust (in response to unpleasant taste or smell)	
Anger, surprise, joy, fear, sadness, shyness	First 6 months
Empathy, jealousy, embarrassment	18–24 months
Shame, guilt, pride	30–36 months

Sources: Adapted from information in Izard & Malatesta, 1987; M. Lewis, 1987, 1992.

guided by the biological "clock" of the brain's maturation (see Table 7-2). From an ethological perspective, this timetable may have value for survival. Expressions of distress by helpless 2-month-olds may bring the help they need; expressions of anger may mobilize 9-month-olds to help themselves—for example, to push away an offender (Trotter, 1983). The emotional timetable can be altered by extreme environmental influences; abused infants show fear several months earlier than other babies (Gaensbauer & Hiatt, 1984).

Although the development of certain basic emotions seems to be universal, there may be cultural variations. In one study, 33 Japanese and U.S. babies were videotaped as experimenters gently but firmly restrained the babies' arms for up to 3 minutes. In both cultures, older babies seemed more distressed than younger ones. At 5 months, the Japanese babies showed a less intense reaction than the U.S. babies, but by 12 months babies in both cultures showed similar negative expressions (Camras, Oster, Campos, Miyake, & Bradshaw, 1992).

"Self-conscious" emotions, such as empathy, jealousy, embarrassment, shame, guilt, and pride, do not arise until the second and third year, after children have developed *self-awareness:* the understanding that they are separate from other people and things. Self-awareness, which has been found to be present by 18 months, is necessary before toddlers can reflect on their actions and measure them against social standards (Izard & Malatesta, 1987; Kopp, 1982; M. Lewis, 1987; D. J. Stipek, Gralinski, & Kopp, 1990).

How Do Infants Show Their Emotions?

Newborns plainly show when they are unhappy. They let out piercing cries, flail their arms and legs, and stiffen their bodies. It is harder to tell when they are happy. During the first month, they become quiet at the sound of a human voice or when they are picked up, and they smile when their hands are moved together to play pat-a-cake. Gradually infants respond more to people—smiling, cooing, reaching out, and eventually going to them.

These early signals or clues to babies' feelings are important steps in development. When babies want or need something, they cry; when they feel sociable, they smile or laugh. When their messages bring a response, their sense of connection with other people grows. Their sense of control over their world grows, too, as they see that their cries bring help and comfort and that their smiles and laughter elicit smiles and laughter in return.

As time goes by, the meaning of these emotional signals changes. At first, crying signifies physical discomfort; later, it more often expresses psychological distress. An early smile comes spontaneously as an expression of well-being; around 3 to 6 weeks, a smile may show pleasure in social contact (Izard & Malatesta, 1987).

This baby shows definite signs of interest in the toy train, and perhaps surprise as well. These early emotions emerge in a sequence apparently guided by the brain's maturation.

self-awareness Realization that one's existence is separate from other people and things.

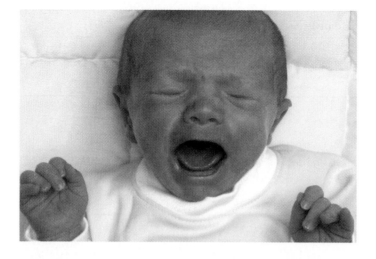

Crying is the most powerful way, and sometimes the only way, that babies can communicate their needs. Parents may soon learn to recognize whether their baby is crying because of hunger, anger, frustration, or pain.

Crying Crying is the most powerful way—and sometimes the only way—infants can communicate their needs. Babies have four patterns of crying (P. H. Wolff, 1969): the basic *hunger cry* (a rhythmic cry, which is not always associated with hunger); the *angry cry* (a variation of the rhythmic cry, in which excess air is forced through the vocal cords); the *pain cry* (a sudden onset of loud crying without preliminary moaning, sometimes followed by holding the breath); and the *frustration cry* (two or three drawn-out cries, with no prolonged breath-holding). Babies in distress cry louder, longer, and more irregularly than hungry babies and are more apt to gag and interrupt their crying (Oswald & Peltzman, 1974).

Babies' cries may reveal when they are sick or at risk of not developing normally. Sound-wave analyses show that many newborns cry at a very high pitch for the first day or two in response to the trauma of birth, but screeching that continues well into the first month may reflect problems in the central nervous system. The cries of newborn preterm and full-term babies have been associated with their scores on developmental tests at 18 months and at 5 years (B. M. Lester, 1987). Abnormal crying patterns have been linked with a number of medical conditions, including sudden infant death syndrome (B. M. Lester et al., 1989).

Parents tend to be sensitive to differences in babies' cries. When 28 mothers listened to a tape recording of the first 10 seconds of crying by 2-day-old infants who had been snapped on the soles of the feet with a rubber band, the mothers were especially distressed by the more high-pitched cries. When the cries included an up-and-down warbling, the mothers thought the babies sounded sick (Zeskind & Marshall, 1988).

Smiling and Laughing A baby's smile is irresistible. It sets in motion a cycle of trust and affection. Adults smile back, and the infant's smile widens. A happy, cheerful baby who rewards caregiving efforts with smiles and gurgles is likely to form better relationships than one who smiles less.

The earliest faint smile occurs spontaneously soon after birth, as a result of central nervous system activity. It frequently appears as the infant is falling asleep. In the second week, babies often smile drowsily after a feeding, possibly responding to the caregiver's sounds. After the second week, infants are more likely to smile when they are alert but inactive. At about 1 month, smiles become more frequent and more social. Babies this age smile when their hands are clapped together or when they hear a familiar voice. During the second month, as visual recognition develops, babies smile more at people they know. At about 3 months, their smiles become broader and longer lasting (Kreutzer & Charlesworth, 1973; Sroufe & Waters, 1976; P. H. Wolff, 1963).

At about the fourth month, infants start to laugh out loud—perhaps at being kissed on the stomach, hearing various sounds, or seeing a parent do something unusual. As babies grow older, they laugh more often and at more things. A 4- to 6-month-old may giggle in response to sounds and touch; a 7- to 9-month-old laughs during a game of peekaboo. This change reflects cognitive development: by laughing at the unexpected, older babies show that they know what to expect. Laughter also helps babies discharge tension, such as fear of a threatening object (Sroufe & Wunsch, 1972).

Temperament

Temperament, a person's characteristic way of approaching and reacting to people and situations, has been called the *how* of behavior: not *what* people do, but how they go about doing it (A. Thomas & Chess, 1984). Two toddlers, for example, may be equally able to dress themselves and equally motivated, but one may do it more quickly than the other, be more willing to put on a new outfit, and be less distracted if the cat jumps on the bed.

What are the aspects or components of temperament? How and when does it develop? How does it affect social adjustment? Is it subject to change?

Components and Patterns of Temperament

The New York Longitudinal Study (NYLS), begun in 1956 by Alexander T. Thomas, Stella C. Chess, and Herbert B. Birch, followed 133 infants into adulthood. Researchers interviewed, tested, and observed the participants and interviewed their parents and teachers.

This pioneering study found nine aspects or components of temperament, which can be seen soon after birth:

1. *activity level:* how and how much the baby moves;
2. *rhythmicity, or regularity:* predictability of biological cycles of hunger, sleep, and elimination;
3. *approach or withdrawal:* how the baby initially responds to a new stimulus, such as a new toy, food, or person;
4. *adaptability:* how easily an initial response is modified in a desired direction in a new or altered situation;
5. *threshold of responsiveness:* how much stimulation is needed to evoke a response;
6. *intensity of reaction:* how energetically a baby responds;
7. *quality of mood:* whether the baby's behavior is predominantly pleasant, joyful, and friendly or unpleasant, unhappy, and unfriendly;
8. *distractibility:* how easily an irrelevant stimulus can alter or interfere with the baby's behavior; and
9. *attention span and persistence:* how long the baby pursues an activity and continues in the face of obstacles (A. Thomas, Chess, & Birch, 1968).

To better appreciate how temperament affects behavior, let's look at three sisters. Amy, the eldest, was a cheerful, calm baby who ate, slept, and eliminated at regular times. She greeted each day and most people with a smile, and the only sign that she was awake during the night was the tinkle of the musical toy in her crib. When Brooke, the second sister, woke up, she would open her mouth to cry before she even opened her eyes. She slept and ate little and irregularly; she laughed and cried loudly, often bursting into tantrums; and she had to be convinced that new people and new experiences were not threatening before she would have anything to do with them. The youngest sister, Christina, was mild in her responses, both positive and negative. She did not like most new situations, but if allowed to proceed at her own slow pace, she would eventually become interested and involved.

Almost two-thirds of the children in the New York Longitudinal Study fell into one of three categories exemplified by these three sisters (see Table 7-3).

CHECKPOINT

Can you . . .

- Trace the typical sequence of emergence of emotions?
- Discuss the significance of patterns of crying, smiling, and laughing?

temperament Person's characteristic disposition, or style of approaching and reacting to people and situations.

Table 7-3	Three Temperamental Patterns	
Easy Child	**Difficult Child**	**Slow-to-Warm-Up Child**
Has moods of mild to moderate intensity, usually positive	Displays intense and frequently negative moods; cries often and loudly; also laughs loudly	Has mildly intense reactions, both positive and negative
Responds well to novelty and change	Responds poorly to novelty and change	Responds slowly to novelty and change
Quickly develops regular sleep and feeding schedules	Sleeps and eats irregularly	Sleeps and eats more regularly than difficult child, less regularly than easy child
Takes to new foods easily	Accepts new foods slowly	Shows mildly negative initial response to new stimuli (a first encounter with a new person, place, or situation)
Smiles at strangers	Is suspicious of strangers	
Adapts easily to new situations	Adapts slowly to new situations	
Accepts most frustrations with little fuss	Reacts to frustration with tantrums	
Adapts quickly to new routines and rules of new games	Adjusts slowly to new routines	Gradually develops liking for new stimuli after repeated, unpressured exposures

Source: Adapted from A. Thomas & Chess, 1984.

easy children Children with a generally happy temperament, regular biological rhythms, and a readiness to accept new experiences.

difficult children Children with irritable temperament, irregular biological rhythms, and intense emotional responses.

slow-to-warm-up children Children whose temperament is generally mild but who are hesitant about accepting new experiences.

Forty percent were *easy children* like Amy: generally happy, rhythmic in their biological functioning, and accepting of new experiences. Ten percent were what the researchers called *difficult children* like Brooke: more irritable and harder to please, irregular in their biological rhythms, and more intense in expressing emotion. Fifteen percent were *slow-to-warm-up children* like Christina: mild but slow to adapt to new people and situations (A. Thomas & Chess, 1977, 1984).

Many children (including 35 percent of the NYLS sample) do not fit neatly into any of these three groups. A baby may have regular eating and sleeping schedules but be afraid of strangers. A child may be easy most of the time, but not always. Another child may warm up slowly to new foods but adapt quickly to new baby-sitters. All these variations are normal (A. Thomas & Chess, 1984).

We need to recognize that ratings of infants' temperament are usually based on parents' reports, and those reports are subjective. Furthermore, many researchers have found the complex interviewing and scoring procedures used in the New York Longitudinal Study too cumbersome and have resorted to short-form questionnaires. Mothers' psychological characteristics, attitudes, or situation in life, which influence their interactions with their babies, may help account for their judgment about an infant's temperament. For example, mothers who, during pregnancy, had reacted more negatively than others to a recording of a baby crying were more likely to describe their 3-month-olds as fussy, difficult, or unpredictable (Pedersen, Huffman, del Carmen, & Bryan, 1996).

Effects of Temperament on Adjustment: "Goodness of Fit"

About one-third of the NYLS participants developed behavior problems at some time. Most were mild disturbances that appeared between ages 3 and 5 and had cleared up by adolescence, but some remained or had grown worse by adulthood. No temperamental type was immune to trouble. Even "easy" children had problems when they were expected to act contrary to their temperamental style.

According to the NYLS, the key to healthy adjustment is *goodness of fit*—the match between a child's temperament and the environmental demands and constraints the child must deal with. If a very active child is expected to sit still for long periods, if a slow-to-warm-up child is constantly pushed into new situations, if a persistent child is constantly taken away from absorbing projects,

goodness of fit Appropriateness of environmental demands and constraints to a child's temperament.

trouble may result. (Margaret Mead's awareness of the importance of goodness of fit led her to seek expert advice about her newborn daughter's temperament and how best to handle her.) When parents recognize that a child acts in a certain way, not out of willfulness, laziness, or stupidity, but largely because of inborn temperament, they are less likely to feel guilty, anxious, or hostile or to be rigid or impatient. Rather than seeing a child's temperament as an impediment, they can anticipate the child's reactions and help the child adapt. For example, a "difficult" child may need extra warning time before being expected to put toys away, or may require especially careful preparation before a family move.

Sometimes all that is required is a simple adjustment in parents' demands. A 6-year-old boy insisted on wearing the same outfit to school every day, claiming that his other clothes were tight and scratchy. His exasperated parents thought he was trying to annoy them; but when the NYLS researchers looked up the boy's records, they found that from at least the age of 3 months he had been extremely sensitive to sensory stimuli. Once his parents realized that his behavior was consistent with his basic temperament, they were willing to give him a veto over clothing purchases and to wash each item several times before he wore it (Chess, 1997).

How Stable Is Infant Temperament?

Even in the womb, fetuses show unique personalities. They have different activity levels and heart rates, which seem to forecast differences in disposition after birth (DiPietro, Hodgson, Costigan, & Johnson, 1996; see Chapter 3). This and other evidence (see Chapter 2) suggests that temperament is inborn and largely hereditary (Braungart, Plomin, DeFries, & Fulker, 1992; Emde et al., 1992; Schmitz, Saudino, Plomin, Fulker, & DeFries, 1996; A. Thomas & Chess, 1977, 1984). It also tends to be stable. Newborn babies show different patterns of sleeping, fussing, and activity, and these differences tend to persist (see Chapter 4). In a longitudinal study, infants whose parents rated them as difficult were perceived as negative and relatively unadaptable at every age from 2 through 12. They were seen as intense and irregular in their habits; and the boys, especially, as highly active (Guerin & Gottfried, 1994).

Some research (discussed in Chapter 2) has focused on an aspect of temperament called *inhibition to the unfamiliar*, which has to do with how sociable a child is with strange children and how boldly or cautiously the child approaches unfamiliar objects and situations. This characteristic seems to have a partial genetic basis and is associated with differences in physical features and brain functioning. Four-month-olds who are highly reactive—who show much motor activity and distress, or who fret or cry readily in response to new stimuli—are more likely to show the inhibited pattern at 14 and 21 months. Furthermore, babies who are highly inhibited or uninhibited to the unfamiliar seem to maintain these patterns to some degree, at least through the eighth year of life, and toddlers classified as inhibited are more likely to be extremely shy in early adolescence (Kagan, 1997; Kagan & Snidman, 1991a, 1991b).

In a study of 900 children, temperamental differences observed by an examiner at age 3 were linked to social adjustment 18 years later. Children who had been rated as well-adjusted, confident, or reserved showed normal social functioning at age 21, whereas those who had been rated as inhibited tended to be less sociable; they remained cautious and unassertive and were described by intimates as lacking vitality. However, they had fairly smooth romantic relationships, were seen as conscientious, and got along well with coworkers. On the other hand, as a group, children rated as undercontrolled (irritable, impulsive, overactive, inattentive, emotionally unstable, and lacking in persistence) grew up to have a broad array of social problems: conflicted relationships, inability to hold a job, and aggressive, risk-taking, or antisocial behavior (D. L. Newman, Caspi, Moffitt, & Silva, 1997).

Still, environmental factors, such as parental treatment, can bring about changes in temperament. Among 148 firstborn infants, some, who at 3 months cried a lot and were rated by their mothers as expressing highly negative emotion, by 9 months smiled, laughed, and vocalized frequently. This kind of change tended to occur when parents were psychologically healthy and in a good marriage, had high self-esteem, and had harmonious relationships with their babies. Parents of babies who went from generally positive emotional states at 3 months to negative ones 6 months later showed more negative characteristics themselves (Belsky, Fish, & Isabella, 1991).

The way a mother feels about her roles may affect her child's temperament. In one analysis of NYLS data, mothers who were dissatisfied either with their jobs or with being homemakers were more likely to show intolerance, disapproval, or rejection of their 3-year-olds' behavior, and the rejected children were apt to become "difficult" (J. V. Lerner & Galambos, 1985). However, disapproval may not always be a bad thing. In another study, firstborn male toddlers who were inclined to be fearful and shy were more likely to remain so at age 3 if their parents were highly accepting of the child's reactions. If parents were more critical and pushed their sons into new situations, the boys tended to become less inhibited. This research suggests that parents need not just passively accept a child's temperament; sometimes, by being less "sensitive" and more "intrusive," they may prompt the child to overcome tendencies that will make it harder to get along in the world (S. Park, Belsky, Putnam, & Crnic, 1997).

Earliest Social Experiences: The Infant in the Family

Right from the start, the family has an enormous influence on development. Was a birth planned and welcomed, like Mary Catherine Bateson's, or was it an "accident"? How well do the personalities of parent and child mesh? Does the child live in a nuclear family or (as Cathy Bateson did after the age of 2) in an extended or blended family, created by marriage or otherwise? Relationships formed in infancy affect the ability to form intimate relationships throughout life. Influence travels the other way, too. Children affect their parents' moods, priorities, plans, and even their marital relationship.

Family life near the turn of the twenty-first century is quite different from a century ago, and it probably will change even more in the future. A child growing up in the United States today is likely to have an employed mother, a father who is more involved in his children's lives than his own father was, and fewer siblings than in some earlier generations. The child is likely to receive a considerable amount of care from nonrelatives, perhaps outside the home. Today's children have a nearly 50 percent chance of living with only one parent at some point, usually the mother and generally because of divorce (Furukawa, 1994; P. C. Glick & Lin, 1986)—though 15 percent of children in single-parent families now live with their fathers (Eggebeen, Snyder, & Manning, 1996).

In the past, research on infant psychosocial development focused almost exclusively on mothers and babies, but now researchers are studying relationships between infants and their fathers, siblings, and other caregivers. Another trend is to examine the family as a whole. How old are the parents? Are they healthy? What is their financial status? How many people live at home? Do the parents act differently when either one is alone with a baby than when all three are together? How does the quality of the marital relationship affect the relationship each spouse has with the baby? How does living in a single-parent household, in a stepfamily, or with grandparents or other relatives affect a baby's development? By looking at the family as a functioning unit, we get a fuller picture of the network of relationships among all its members.

Since child-raising practices vary greatly around the world, we should be wary of conclusions drawn from experience in any one culture. For example, unlike infants in the United States, who first have a close relationship with the

CHECKPOINT

Can you . . .

- List and describe the nine components and three patterns of temperament identified by the New York Longitudinal Study?

- Discuss evidence for the stability of temperament, and explain the importance of "goodness of fit"?

In a series of classic experiments, Harry Harlow and Margaret Harlow showed that food is not the most important way to a baby's heart. When infant rhesus monkeys could choose whether to go to a wire surrogate "mother" or a warm, soft terry-cloth "mother," they spent more time clinging to the cloth mother, even if they were being fed by bottles connected to the wire mother.

mother and then pattern other ties on that one, infants among the Efe people of the African country of Zaire have intimate interactions with many adults from birth. Efe infants typically receive care from five or more people in a given hour and are routinely breastfed by other women as well as by their mothers. At age 3, they spend about 70 percent of their time with people other than their mothers (Tronick, Morelli, & Ivey, 1992). This social pattern may result in a distinctive set of social skills. Unlike U.S. babies, who spend more time alone or with just one or two family members and may learn to amuse themselves earlier than Efe babies, the Efe may learn to be more sociable at an earlier age. We need to remember, then, that patterns of psychological development we take for granted may be culture-based.

With that caution in mind, let's look first at the roles of the mother and father—how they care for and play with their babies, and how their influence begins to shape differences between boys and girls—and then at the changing roles of grandparents. Later in this chapter, we take an in-depth look at developmental issues involving relationships with parents and, still later, at interactions with siblings.

The Mother's Role

In a famous series of experiments done by Harry Harlow and his colleagues, rhesus monkeys were separated from their mothers 6 to 12 hours after birth and raised in a laboratory. The infant monkeys were put into cages with one of two kinds of surrogate "mothers": a plain cylindrical wire-mesh form or a form covered with terry cloth. Some monkeys were fed from bottles connected to the wire "mothers"; others were "nursed" by the warm, cuddly cloth ones. When the monkeys were allowed to spend time with either kind of "mother," they all spent more time clinging to the cloth surrogates, even if they were being fed only by the wire ones. In an unfamiliar room, the babies "raised" by cloth surrogates showed more natural interest in exploring than those "raised" by wire surrogates, even when the appropriate "mothers" were there.

Apparently, the monkeys also remembered the cloth surrogates better. After a year's separation, the "cloth-raised" monkeys eagerly ran to embrace the terry-cloth forms, whereas the "wire-raised" monkeys showed no interest in the wire forms (Harlow & Zimmerman, 1959). None of the monkeys in either group grew up normally, however (Harlow & Harlow, 1962), and none were able to nurture their own offspring (Suomi & Harlow, 1972).

It is hardly surprising that a dummy mother would not provide the same kind of stimulation and opportunities for development as a live mother. These experiments show that feeding is not the most important thing babies get from their mothers. Mothering includes the comfort of close bodily contact and, in monkeys, the satisfaction of an innate need to cling. Human infants also have needs that must be satisfied if they are to grow up normally, as the research on children raised in Romanian orphanages (discussed in Chapter 5) shows. A major task of developmental research is to find out what those needs are.

The Father's Role

Despite a common belief that women are biologically predisposed to care for babies, men can be just as sensitive and responsive to infants (Lamb, 1981). The amount of child care by men in industrialized countries is increasing (Lamb, 1987b). Still, although fathers generally believe they should be involved in their children's lives, most are not nearly as involved as mothers are (Backett, 1987; W. T. Bailey, 1994; M. G. Boulton, 1983; LaRossa, 1988; LaRossa & LaRossa, 1981). Fathers spend as much time playing with their babies as mothers do, but less time feeding or bathing them—a pattern that has been observed among white and African American middle-class families and in Jamaica as well (W. T. Bailey, 1994; Easterbrooks & Goldberg, 1984; Hossain & Roopnarine, 1994; Roopnarine, Brown, Snell-White, & Riegraft, 1995). Even mothers who work full time spend more time taking care of their babies than fathers do (W. T. Bailey, 1994; Pedersen, Cain, & Zaslow, 1982). However, fathers do more caregiving when the mother works than when she does not, and fathers spend more time caring for toddlers and preschoolers than for infants (W. T. Bailey, 1994).

Fathers who are closely involved with their babies exert a significant influence. One study of 48 working-class Irish fathers, which found a high level of child care, also found a strong relationship between father care and the babies' cognitive development at 1 year (Nugent, 1991). In another study, a group of toddlers, two-thirds of whose mothers worked outside the home, showed benefits of the father's involvement in caring for and playing with them, especially when his

Fathers can be as sensitive and responsive to infants as mothers and spend as much time playing with their babies as mothers do. This father, engrossed with his infant daughter, is likely to go on to exert a strong influence on her social, emotional, and cognitive development.

attitude was sensitive and positive. The father's behavior had a particularly strong influence on competence in problem solving (Easterbrooks & Goldberg, 1984).

In the United States, fathers tend to act differently with their babies than mothers do. Fathers "play rough": they toss infants up in the air and wrestle with toddlers, whereas mothers typically play gentler games and sing and read to babies (Lamb, 1977; Parke & Tinsley, 1981; Yogman, 1984; Yogman, Dixon, Tronick, Als, & Brazelton, 1977). Vigorous play with fathers offers an infant excitement and a challenge to conquer fears (Lamb, 1981). However, a highly physical style of play is not typical of fathers in all cultures. Swedish and German fathers usually do not play with their babies this way (Lamb, Frodi, Frodi, & Hwang, 1982; Parke, Grossman, & Tinsley, 1981). African Aka fathers (Hewlett, 1987) and fathers in New Delhi, India, also tend to play gently with their small children (J. L. Roopnarine, Hooper, Ahmeduzzaman, & Pollack, 1993; Roopnarine, Talokder, Jain, Josh, & Srivastav, 1992). Such cross-cultural variations cast doubt on the idea that rough play is a function of male biology; instead, it seems to be culturally influenced.

How Parents Shape Gender Differences

Measurable differences between baby boys and girls—physical, cognitive, and emotional—are few. As we discussed in Chapter 3, males are physically more vulnerable than females from conception on. On the other hand, baby boys are a bit longer and heavier than baby girls and may be slightly stronger. Newborn boys and girls react differently to stress, possibly suggesting genetic, hormonal, or temperamental differences (M. Davis & Emory, 1995). An analysis of a large number of studies found baby boys more active than baby girls, though this difference is not consistently documented (Eaton & Enns, 1986). In general, though, infant boys and girls are very similar. In a number of studies of infants' temperament—including irritability and interest in exploring their surroundings—findings of gender differences before age 2 have rarely been replicated (Birns, 1976). Other studies have found the two sexes equally sensitive to touch. Girls and boys tend to teethe, sit up, and walk at about the same ages (E. Maccoby, 1980).

Parental shaping of boys' and girls' personalities, however, begins very early. Consciously or not, parents behave differently toward baby boys than toward baby girls. Boys get more attention; girls are encouraged to smile more and be more social (Birns, 1976). Mothers' facial expressions show a wider range of emotion with baby daughters than with baby sons; perhaps this helps to explain why girls are better than boys at interpreting emotional expressions (Malatesta, in Trotter, 1983).

Fathers treat boys and girls more differently than mothers do, even during the first year (M. E. Snow, Jacklin, & Maccoby, 1983). During the second year, this difference intensifies: fathers talk more and spend more time with sons than with daughters (Lamb, 1981). Fathers, more than mothers, seem to promote *gender-typing,* the process by which children learn behavior that their culture considers appropriate for each sex (Bronstein, 1988).

Home observations of 12-month-old, 18-month-old, and 5-year-old children found the biggest gender differences at 18 months, when both mothers and fathers fostered gender-typed play. Parents encouraged girls to communicate but discouraged boys' efforts to do so. Boys received more positive reactions to aggressive behavior and to play with "boys' " toys and fewer positive responses from their fathers (but not their mothers) when they played with "girls' " toys. By the time children were 5 years old, parents treated both sexes about the same—possibly because the children had already become gender-typed and needed no more influence in that direction (Fagot & Hagan, 1991). We discuss gender-typing and gender differences in more depth in Chapter 10.

gender-typing Socialization process by which children, at an early age, learn behavior deemed appropriate by the culture for a boy or a girl.

The Grandparent's Changing Role

In traditional societies and in some minority communities in the United States characterized by large, multigenerational *extended-family households,* grandparents who live with the family play an integral role in child raising and family decisions. In the United States today, children typically grow up in *nuclear families* limited to parents and siblings, and many grandparents live far away or are busy with careers or other interests.

However, grandparents can play an important role in a child's life. When a new baby comes, grandparents may come over more often and help in many ways, large and small. They lavish affection on infants and toddlers, read books, sing songs, play games, and take children on outings. A grandparent can serve as caregiver, teacher, role model, confidant, and sometimes negotiator between child and parent. As children grow older, grandparents may have less frequent contact, but they still can be sources of guidance, links to the past, and symbols of the continuity of family life (Weissbourd, 1996).

A major study of a nationally representative three-generational sample found that "grandparents play a limited but important role in family dynamics," and many have strong emotional ties to their grandchildren (Cherlin & Furstenberg, 1986a, p. 26). Most grandparents (55 percent) fall into a *companionate* pattern; they do not intervene directly in the children's upbringing but are frequent, casual companions. Grandparents tend to be more *involved*—giving advice, helping out, providing care and nurturing, and discussing the child's problems with the parents—during the earliest years or in a time of family crisis. Younger grandparents, those who see their grandchildren almost every day, and those who have a close relationship with the child's mother are most likely to be involved (Cherlin & Furstenberg, 1986a, 1986b). Black grandparents tend to spend more time with their grandchildren than white grandparents, even when they live out of town, and are more likely to become involved in raising their grandchildren (Cherlin & Furstenberg, 1986a, 1986b; Strom, Collinsworth, Strom, & Griswold, 1992–1993).

Grandparents' involvement can make a positive difference in infants' cognitive and psychosocial development (Weissbourd, 1996). Babies whose grandparents are in frequent contact tend to score higher on the Bayley Scales (Tinsley & Parke, 1987). Infants become attached to grandmothers (and presumably to grandfathers, too), and that attachment can be an important part of their social development (Meyers, Jarvis, & Creasey, 1987). Many grandparents provide child care for working parents; in 1993, nearly 17 percent of preschool children of employed mothers were under a grandparent's daytime care (Casper, 1996).

Developmental Issues in Infancy

How does a dependent newborn, with a limited emotional repertoire and pressing physical needs, become a 3-year-old with complex feelings, a strong will, and the beginnings of a conscience? Much of this development revolves around issues regarding the self in relation to others. In this section, we look at the development of trust and attachment in infancy and at emotional communication between infants and caregivers—developments that pave the way for the very different issues of toddlerhood. We also look at three phenomena widely believed to be common during late infancy: stranger anxiety, separation anxiety, and social referencing.

Developing Trust

For a far longer period than the young of other mammals, human babies are dependent on other people for food, protection, and their very lives. How do they

C HECKPOINT

Can you . . .

- Explain the implications of research on infant monkeys "raised" by inanimate "mothers"?

- Discuss the role of fathers and describe cultural differences between the ways fathers and mothers play with their babies?

- Compare the influence of mothers and fathers on gender-typing?

- Discuss the changing role and influence of grandparents?

Diane's sensitivity to Anna's needs contributes to the development of Anna's sense of basic trust—her ability to rely on the people and things in her world. Trust is necessary, according to Erikson, for children to form intimate relationships.

come to trust that their needs will be met? According to Erikson (1950), early experiences are the key.

The first of the eight crises, or critical developmental stages, Erikson identified is *basic trust versus basic mistrust* (refer back to Table 1-3 in Chapter 1). This stage begins in infancy and continues until about 18 months. In these early months, babies develop a sense of the reliability of people and objects in their world. They need to develop a balance between trust (which lets them form intimate relationships) and mistrust (which enables them to protect themselves). If trust predominates, as it should, children develop the "virtue" of *hope:* the belief that they can fulfill their needs and obtain their desires (Erikson, 1982). If mistrust predominates, children will view the world as unfriendly and unpredictable and will have trouble forming relationships.

The critical element in developing trust is sensitive, responsive, consistent caregiving. Erikson saw the feeding situation as the setting for establishing the right mix of trust and mistrust. Can the baby count on being fed when hungry, and can the baby therefore trust the mother as a representative of the world? Trust enables an infant to let the mother out of sight "because she has become an inner certainty as well as an outer predictability" (Erikson, 1950, p. 247).

Mothers or other primary caregivers are not the only important influences on the development of trust or mistrust. A child's own contribution can be substantial.

Developing Attachments

When Ahmed's mother is near, he looks at her, smiles at her, "talks" to her, and crawls after her. When she leaves, he cries; when she comes back, he squeals with joy. When he is frightened or unhappy, he clings to her. Ahmed has formed his first attachment to another person.

Attachment is a reciprocal, enduring emotional tie between an infant and a caregiver, each of whom contributes to the quality of the relationship. Attachments have adaptive value for babies, ensuring that their psychosocial as well as physical needs will be met. As Mary Ainsworth (1979), a pioneering researcher on attachment, has said, it may be "an essential part of the ground plan of the human species for an infant to become attached to a mother figure" (p. 932).

basic trust versus basic mistrust In Erikson's theory, the first crisis in psychosocial development, occurring between birth and about 18 months, in which infants develop a sense of the reliability of people and objects in their world.

attachment Reciprocal, enduring relationship between infant and caregiver, each of whom contributes to the quality of the relationship.

Virtually any activity on a baby's part that leads to a response from an adult can be an attachment-seeking behavior: sucking, crying, smiling, clinging, and looking into the caregiver's eyes. As early as the eighth week of life, babies direct some of these behaviors more to their mothers than to anyone else. These overtures are successful when the mother responds warmly, expresses delight, and gives the baby frequent physical contact and freedom to explore (Ainsworth, 1969).

Ainsworth (1964) described four overlapping stages of attachment behavior during the first year:

1. Before about 2 months, infants respond indiscriminately to anyone.
2. At about 8 to 12 weeks, babies cry, smile, and babble more to the mother than to anyone else but continue to respond to others.
3. At 6 or 7 months, babies show a sharply defined attachment to the mother. Fear of strangers may appear between 6 and 8 months.
4. Meanwhile, babies develop an attachment to one or more other familiar figures, such as the father and siblings.

This sequence seems to be common in western societies but does not necessarily apply to babies in cultures in which there are numerous caregivers from birth on.

Studying Patterns of Attachment

Ainsworth first studied attachment in the early 1950s with John Bowlby (1951). Then, after studying attachment in African babies in Uganda through naturalistic observation in their homes (Ainsworth, 1967), Ainsworth changed her approach and devised the laboratory-based *Strange Situation,* a now-classic technique designed to assess attachment patterns between an infant and an adult. Typically, the adult is the mother (though other adults have taken part as well), and the infant is 10 to 24 months old.

The Strange Situation consists of a sequence of eight episodes (see Table 7-4), which take less than half an hour. During that time, the mother twice leaves the baby in an unfamiliar room, the first time with a stranger. The second time she leaves the baby alone, and the stranger comes back before the mother does. The mother then encourages the baby to explore and play again and gives comfort if the baby seems to need it (Ainsworth, Blehar, Waters, & Wall, 1978). Of particular concern is the baby's response each time the mother returns.

When Ainsworth and her colleagues observed 1-year-olds in the Strange Situation and also at home, they found three main patterns of attachment: *secure attachment* (the most common category, into which 66 percent of U.S. babies fell) and two forms of anxious, or insecure, attachment: *avoidant attachment* (20 percent of U.S. babies) and *ambivalent (resistant) attachment* (12 percent). Later, other researchers (Main & Solomon, 1986) identified a fourth pattern, *disorganized-disoriented attachment.*

Babies with *secure* attachment cry or protest when the mother leaves and greet her happily when she returns. They use her as a secure base, leaving her to go off and explore but returning occasionally for reassurance. They are usually cooperative and relatively free of anger. Babies with *avoidant* attachment rarely cry when the mother leaves, and they avoid her on her return. They tend to be angry and do not reach out in time of need. They dislike being held but dislike being put down even more.

Babies with *ambivalent (resistant)* attachment become anxious even before the mother leaves and are very upset when she goes out. When she returns, they show their ambivalence by seeking contact with her while at the same time resisting it by kicking or squirming. Resistant babies do little exploration and are hard to comfort. Babies with *disorganized-disoriented* attachment often show inconsistent, contradictory behaviors. They greet the mother brightly when she returns but then turn away or approach without looking at her. They seem confused and afraid. This may be the least secure pattern. It seems

Strange Situation Laboratory technique used to study attachment.

secure attachment Attachment pattern in which an infant separates readily from the primary caregiver and actively seeks out the caregiver upon the caregiver's return.

avoidant attachment Attachment pattern in which an infant rarely cries when separated from the primary caregiver and avoids contact upon his or her return.

ambivalent (resistant) attachment Attachment pattern in which an infant becomes anxious before the primary caregiver leaves, is extremely upset during his or her absence, and both seeks and resists contact on his or her return.

disorganized-disoriented attachment Attachment pattern in which an infant, after being separated from the primary caregiver, shows contradictory behaviors upon his or her return.

Table 7-4 Summary of Episodes in the Strange Situation

Episode	Persons Present	Duration	Brief Description of Action
1	Mother, baby, and observer	30 sec.	Observer introduces mother and baby to experimental room, then leaves.
2	Mother and baby	3 min.	Mother is nonparticipant while baby explores; if necessary, play is stimulated after 2 minutes.
3	Stranger, mother, and baby	3 min.	Stranger enters. First minute: Stranger silent. Second minute: Stranger converses with mother. Third minute: Stranger approaches baby. After 3 minutes mother leaves unobtrusively.
4	Stranger and baby	3 min. or less*	First separation episode. Stranger's behavior is geared to that of baby.
5	Mother and baby	3 min. or more†	First reunion episode. Mother greets and comforts baby, then tries to settle him or her again in play. Stranger leaves. Mother then leaves, saying "bye-bye."
6	Baby alone	3 min. or less*	Second separation episode.
7	Stranger and baby	3 min. or less*	Continuation of second separation. Stranger enters and gears behavior to that of baby.
8	Mother and baby	3 min.	Second reunion episode. Mother enters, greets baby, then picks him or her up. Meanwhile stranger leaves unobtrusively.

*Episode is curtailed if the baby is unduly distressed.
†Episode is prolonged if more time is required for the baby to become reinvolved in play.
Source: Adapted from Ainsworth et al., 1978, p. 37.

to occur in babies whose parents have suffered unresolved trauma, such as loss or abuse (Main & Hesse, 1990).

Almost all research on attachment has been based on the Strange Situation, but some investigators have questioned its validity. The Strange Situation *is* strange; it is also artificial. It sets up a series of eight brief, controlled episodes. It asks mothers not to initiate interaction, exposes babies to repeated comings and goings of adults, and expects the infants to pay attention to them. Since attachment influences a wider range of behaviors than are seen in the Strange Situation, some researchers have called for a more comprehensive, sensitive method to measure it, one that would show how mother and infant interact during natural, nonstressful situations (T. M. Field, 1987).

It has been suggested that the Strange Situation may be especially inappropriate for studying attachment in children of employed mothers, since these children are used to routine separations from their mothers and the presence of other caregivers (K. A. Clarke-Stewart, 1989; L. W. Hoffman, 1989). However, a comparison of 1,153 randomly sampled 15-month-olds born in 10 U.S. cities, who had received varying amounts, types, and quality of day care starting at various ages, found "no evidence . . . that the Strange Situation was less valid for children with extensive child-care experience than for those without" (NICHD Early Child Care Research Network, 1997a, p. 867). Babies who had received extensive child care showed no more or less distress during separations from the mother, and trained coders showed equal confidence in assigning them to attachment categories.

The Strange Situation may be less valid in some nonwestern cultures, which have different expectations for babies' interaction with their mothers and in which mothers may encourage different kinds of attachment-related behavior. Research on Japanese infants, who are less frequently separated from their mothers than U.S. babies, showed high rates of resistant attachment, which may reflect the extreme stressfulness of the Strange Situation for these babies (Miyake, Chen, & Campos, 1985). The Strange Situation also seems inappropriate for assessing the attachment of children with disabilities such as Down syndrome (Vaughn et al., 1994).

Some researchers have begun to supplement the Strange Situation with other methods that allow children to be studied in their natural settings. Using what is known as a Q-sort technique, observers may sort a set of descriptive words or phrases ("cries a lot"; "tends to cling") into categories ranging from most to least characteristic of the child. The Waters and Deane (1985) *Attachment Q-set (AQS)* has raters (either mothers or other observers) compare descriptions of children's everyday behavior with expert descriptions of the "hypothetical most secure child."

In a cross-cultural study using the AQS, mothers in China, Colombia, Germany, Israel, Japan, Norway, and the United States described their children as behaving more like than unlike the "most secure child." Furthermore, the mothers' descriptions of "secure-base" behavior were about as similar across cultures as within a culture. These findings suggest that the tendency to use the mother as a secure base is universal, though it may take somewhat varied forms. Mothers' preferences for "ideal" attachment behavior were also similar across cultures, though German and Israeli mothers, for example, tended to stress the comfort of physical contact between mother and child, while Chinese and Japanese mothers were more interested in having their babies interact with other adults (Posada et al., 1995).

A new instrument for measuring attachment after 20 months of age, the *Preschool Assessment of Attachment (PAA)* (Crittenden, 1993), takes into account older preschoolers' more complex relationships and language abilities. Evidence for its validity is rapidly accumulating (Teti, Gelfand, Messinger, & Isabella, 1995). We will undoubtedly learn more about attachment as researchers develop and use more diversified ways to measure it.

How Attachment Is Established

Both mothers and babies contribute to security of attachment by their personalities and behavior and the way they respond to each other. On the basis of a baby's interactions with the mother, said Ainsworth, the baby builds a "working model" of what can be expected from her. The various patterns of emotional attachment represent different cognitive representations that result in different expectations. As long as the mother continues to act the same way, the model holds up. If her behavior changes—not just once or twice but consistently—the baby may revise the model, and security of attachment may change.

A baby's working model of attachment is related to Erikson's concept of basic trust. Secure attachment evolves from trust; insecure attachment reflects mistrust. Securely attached babies have learned to trust not only their caregivers but their own ability to get what they need. Thus babies who fuss and cry a lot and whose mothers respond by soothing them tend to be securely attached (Del Carmen, Pedersen, Huffman, & Bryan, 1993).

Many studies show that mothers of securely attached infants and toddlers tend to be sensitive and responsive (Ainsworth, Blehar, Waters, & Wall, 1978; De Wolff & van IJzendoorn, 1997; Isabella, 1993; NICHD Early Child Care Research Network, 1997a). However, sensitivity is not the only important factor. Equally important are other aspects of mothering, such as mutual interaction, stimulation, a positive attitude, warmth and acceptance, and emotional support (De Wolff & van IJzendoorn, 1997).

Although the connection between a mother's behavior and her baby's attachment is strong in normal, middle-class homes, this connection is weaker among lower-class families and those troubled enough to seek clinical help. Thus contextual factors, in combination with what the mother does, may influence attachment (De Wolff & van IJzendoorn, 1997). One such factor is a mother's

---

Attachment Q-Set (AQS)
Instrument for measuring attachment, developed by Waters and Deane, in which observer sorts descriptive words and phrases into those most and least characteristic of a child and compares these descriptors with descriptions of the "hypothetical most secure child."

Preschool Assessment of Attachment (PAA)
Instrument for measuring attachment after 20 months of age, which takes into account the complexity of preschoolers' relationships and linguistic abilities.

This baby, like most infants, is developing a strong attachment to his mother. Both mother and baby contribute to the security of attachment by their personalities and behavior and their responsiveness to each other.

employment. In one study (Stifter, Coulehan, & Fish, 1993), babies of employed mothers who were highly anxious about being away from home tended to develop avoidant attachments, as measured at 18 months by the Strange Situation. The mothers' anxiety seemed to express itself in overintrusiveness. In a laboratory free-play session when the babies were 10 months old, these mothers had stimulated their babies too much, had taken away objects when the baby was still interested in them, and had not let the baby influence the focus and pace of play. The mother's employment itself does not seem to be at the root of such behaviors; rather, it is her *feelings* about working and the separation it causes. Some employed mothers may be overcontrolling because they feel a need to compensate for their frequent absences.

There has been less study of attachment to the father than of attachment to the mother, but both attachments follow similar patterns. Contrary to Ainsworth's original findings, babies seem to develop attachments to both parents at about the same time, and security of attachment to father and mother is quite similar (Fox, Kimmerly, & Schafer, 1991). As early as 3 months after birth, it may be possible to predict the security of attachment between father and baby. Fathers who show delight in their 3-month-olds, who see themselves as important in their babies' development, who are sensitive to their needs, and who place a high priority on spending time with them are likely to have infants who are securely attached at 1 year (M. J. Cox, Owen, Henderson, & Margand, 1992). Fathers of securely attached infants tend to be more extraverted and agreeable than fathers of insecure infants. They have more loving, communicative marriages and report more positive interaction between their work and family roles (Belsky, 1996).

The Role of Temperament

The similarity of attachment to both parents suggests that the baby's temperament may be an important factor, along with parents' shared behaviors and values (Fox, Kimmerly, & Schafer, 1991). However, researchers disagree about how much influence temperament exerts and in what way (Susman-Stillman, Kalkoske, Egeland, & Waldman, 1996; Vaughn et al., 1992). Some studies have identified frustration levels, amounts of crying, and irritability as temperamental predictors of attachment (Calkins & Fox, 1992; Izard, Haynes, Chisholm, & Baak, 1991). Neurological or physiological conditions may underlie temperamental differences in attachment. For example, variability in heart rate is associated with irritability, and heart rate seems to vary more in insecurely attached infants (Izard, Porges, Simons, Haynes, & Cohen, 1991).

A study of 6- to 12-month-old infants and their families (which used frequent home observations, maternal reports, and Q-sorts in addition to the Strange Situation) suggests that both a mother's sensitivity and her baby's temperament are important in establishing attachment patterns (Seifer, Schiller, Sameroff, Resnick, & Riordan, 1996). In another study, the mother's sensitivity predicted whether attachment would be secure or insecure, whereas the baby's temperament predicted the type of insecure attachment—avoidant or resistant (Susman-Stillman et al., 1996). Similarly, in a study of attachment to the father, the infant's temperament did not appear to influence whether attachment was secure or insecure, but *did* seem to affect whether insecure attachment was avoidant or resistant. Fathers tended to see avoidant babies as having more positive temperamental characteristics than resistant babies (Belsky, 1996).

A baby's temperament may have not only a direct impact on attachment but also an indirect impact through its effect on the parents. In one study of 114 white middle-class mothers and their 2½- to 13-month-old infants, insecurely attached babies (as measured by the Strange Situation) cried more, demanded more attention, and showed more sadness and anger than securely attached infants. The mothers of the insecurely attached babies also felt more insecure and helpless; they were angrier and sadder but were less open about showing these feelings than the mothers of the securely attached babies, who tended to be more sociable, nurturant, and empathic. The mothers' and babies' emotional states probably fed on each other. The insecure babies' behavior may have made their mothers feel sad, angry, and helpless; and the mothers' behavior, in turn, probably affected the babies (Izard, Haynes et al., 1991). As with other issues concerning temperament, "goodness of fit" between parent and child may well be a key to understanding security of attachment.

Intergenerational Transmission of Attachment Patterns

Can the way a mother remembers her attachment to her parents predict the way her children will be attached to *her*? The answer seems to be yes. Parents who can clearly, coherently, and consistently describe their own early experiences with attachment figures—whether those experiences were favorable or unfavorable, secure or insecure—tend to have babies who become securely attached to them (Main, 1995; Main, Kaplan, & Cassidy, 1985).

The *Adult Attachment Interview (AAI)* (C. George, Kaplan, & Main, 1985) is a semi-structured interview that asks adults to recall and interpret feelings and experiences related to their childhood attachment to parents or substitute caregivers. Participants are asked to describe their relationships with their parents and to say why they think their parents behaved as they did, how relationships with parents affected their own behavior, and how those relationships have changed. An analysis of 18 studies using the AAI found that the clarity, coherence, and consistency of responses to such questions reliably predicts the security with which the respondent's own child will be attached to him or her (van IJzendoorn, 1995).

Apparently, the way adults recall early experiences with parents or caregivers affects the way they treat their own children. Let's say that Katya, an insecurely attached baby with a rejecting mother, grows up with a mental working model of herself as unlovable. Unless this distorted self-image is later revised—perhaps through psychotherapy, through a secure attachment to her husband, or through mature, thoughtful reflection on her childhood experiences—Katya's memory of her relationship with her mother may lead her to misinterpret her baby's attachment behaviors and respond inappropriately. ("How can this child want to love me? How could anybody?") In turn, Katya's insensitivity to the baby's signals misleads the baby, making it difficult for the infant to form a

Adult Attachment Interview (AAI) Instrument for measuring the clarity, coherence, and consistency of an adult's memories of attachment to her or his parents.

Securely attached toddlers are more sociable with peers than anxiously attached toddlers, and their overtures are more likely to be accepted.

working model of a loving, accepting mother and a lovable self. On the other hand, a mother who was securely attached to *her* mother, or who understands why she was insecurely attached, can accurately recognize the baby's attachment behaviors, respond encouragingly, and help the baby form a secure attachment to her (Bretherton, 1990).

Furthermore, the working model a mother retains from her childhood relationships can affect her relationship with her child well beyond infancy. Forty-five mothers were videotaped helping their 16-month- to 5-year-old children solve a puzzle. Mothers with secure working models (as measured by the AAI) tended to have securely attached children (as measured by the Attachment Q-set) and to show more sensitivity in interacting with them than did insecure mothers. The quality of the mother's marriage made a difference; insecure mothers were more likely to have securely attached children if the marriage was strong (Eiden, Teti, & Corns, 1995).

This line of research shows promise for identifying prospective parents at risk of developing unhealthy attachment patterns with their children and developing interventions that might change the course of these at-risk relationships.

Long-Term Effects of Attachment

The more secure a child's attachment to a nurturing adult, the easier it seems to be for the child eventually to become independent of that adult and to develop good relationships with others. The relationship between attachment and characteristics observed years later underscores the continuity of development and the interrelationship of emotional, cognitive, and physical development.

Securely attached toddlers are more sociable with peers and unfamiliar adults than those who are anxiously attached (Elicker, Englund, & Sroufe, 1992; Main, 1983). At 18 to 24 months, they have more positive interactions with peers, and their friendly overtures are more likely to be accepted (Fagot, 1997). From ages 3 to 5, securely attached children are more curious, competent, empathic, resilient, and self-confident, get along better with other children, and are more likely to form close friendships (Arend, Gove, & Sroufe, 1979; Elicker et al., 1992; J. L. Jacobson & Wille, 1986; E. Waters, Wippman, & Sroufe, 1979; Youngblade & Belsky, 1992). They interact more positively with parents, preschool teachers, and peers and are better able to resolve conflicts (Elicker et al., 1992). They are also more independent, seeking help from teachers only when they need it (Sroufe, Fox, &

Pancake, 1983). As preschoolers and kindergartners, they tend to have a more positive self-image (Elicker et al., 1992; Verschueren, Marcoen, & Schoefs, 1996).

Their advantages continue into middle childhood and adolescence (Sroufe, Carlson, & Shulman, 1993). When 10- and 11-year-olds were observed in summer day camp, those with histories of secure attachment were better at making and keeping friends and functioning in a group than children who had been classified as avoidant or resistant. They were also more self-reliant, self-assured, and adaptable and better physically coordinated. In a reunion of 15-year-olds who had gone to camp together, the adolescents who had been securely attached in infancy were rated higher on emotional health, self-esteem, ego resiliency, and peer competence by their counselors and peers and by the researchers who observed them.

If children, on the basis of early experience, have positive expectations about their ability to get along with others and engage in social give and take, and if they think well of themselves, they may set up social situations that tend to reinforce these beliefs and the gratifying interactions that result from them (Elicker et al., 1992; Sroufe, Carlson et al., 1993). And if children, as infants, had a secure base and could count on parents' or caregivers' responsiveness, they are likely to feel confident enough to be actively engaged in their world. In one study, children with secure working models of attachment at age 7 were rated by teachers at ages 9, 12, and 15 as more attentive and participatory, as having better grades, and as seeming to feel more secure about themselves than children who had had insecure working models of attachment (Jacobsen & Hofmann, 1997). Conversely, insecurely attached children often have later problems: inhibitions at age 2, hostility toward other children at age 5, and dependency during the school years (Calkins & Fox, 1992; Lyons-Ruth, Alpern, & Repacholi, 1993; Sroufe, Carlson et al., 1993). However, it may be that the correlations between attachment in infancy and later development stem, not from attachment itself, but from personality characteristics that affect both attachment and parent-child interactions *after* infancy (Lamb, 1987a).

Emotional Communication with Caregivers

Max smiles at his mother. She interprets this signal as an invitation to play and kisses his stomach, sending him into gales of giggles. But the next day, when she begins to kiss his stomach again, he looks at her glassy-eyed and turns his head away. His mother interprets this as "I want to be quiet now." Following his cue, she tucks him into a baby carrier and lets him rest quietly against her body.

"Reading" Emotional Signals: Mutual Regulation

The interaction between infant and caregiver that influences the quality of attachment depends on the ability of both to respond appropriately to signals about each other's emotional states. This process is called *mutual regulation.* According to the *mutual-regulation model* (Tronick & Gianino, 1986), infants take an active part in this regulatory process. They do not just receive caregivers' actions; they affect how caregivers act toward them. These two-way signals become a precise language of emotional communication.

Babies differ in the amount of stimulation they need or want. Too little leaves them uninterested; too much overwhelms them. According to the mutual regulation model, healthy interaction occurs when a caregiver "reads" a baby's messages accurately and responds appropriately. When a baby's goals are met, the baby is joyful or at least interested (Tronick, 1989). If a caregiver ignores an invitation to play or insists on playing when the baby has signaled "I don't feel like it," the baby may feel angry or sad. When babies do not achieve the desired results, they usually keep on sending signals to repair the interaction. Normally, interaction moves back and forth between poorly regulated and well-regulated

CHECKPOINT

Can you . . .

• Explain the importance of Erikson's crisis of basic trust versus basic mistrust and identify what he saw as the critical element in its resolution?

• Identify four patterns of attachment?

• Explain how attachment is established, including the roles of mothers and fathers and of the baby's temperament?

• Describe long-term behavioral differences influenced by attachment patterns?

mutual regulation Process by which infant and caregiver communicate emotional states to each other and respond appropriately.

states, and babies learn from these shifts how to send signals and what to do when their initial signals do not result in a comfortable emotional balance.

Relationships with parents and other caregivers also help babies learn to "read" others' behavior and develop expectations about it. The ability to decipher other people's attitudes seems to be inborn; it helps human beings form attachments to others, live in society, and protect themselves. Even very young infants can perceive emotions expressed by others and can adjust their own behavior accordingly. At 10 weeks of age, they meet anger with anger (Lelwica & Haviland, 1983). Nine-month-olds show more joy, play more, and look at their mothers longer when the mothers seem happy; they look sad and turn away when their mothers seem sad (Termine & Izard, 1988).

The "still-face" paradigm is a research method used to measure mutual regulation in infants from 2 to 9 months old. In the "still-face" episode, which follows a normal face-to-face interaction, the mother suddenly becomes stony-faced, silent, and unresponsive. Then, a few minutes later, she resumes normal interaction (the "reunion" episode). During the still-face episode, infants tend to stop smiling and looking at the mother. They may make faces, sounds, or gestures or may touch themselves, their clothing, or a chair, apparently to comfort themselves or to relieve the emotional stress created by the mother's unexpected behavior (J. F. Cohn & Tronick, 1983; Tronick, 1980, 1989; M. K. Weinberg & Tronick, 1996).

How do infants react during the reunion episode? One study combined a microanalysis of 6-month-olds' facial expressions during this episode with measures of heart rate and nervous system reactivity. The infants' reactions were mixed. On the one hand, they showed even more positive behavior—joyous expressions and utterances, and gazes and gestures directed toward the mother— than before the still-face episode. On the other hand, the persistence of sad or angry facial expressions, "pick-me-up" gestures, distancing, and indications of stress, as well as an increased tendency to fuss and cry, suggested that while infants welcome the resumption of interaction with the mother, the negative feelings stirred by the still-face episode are not readily eased. These complex reactions indicate how difficult it must be for babies to cope with repairing a mismatched interaction (Weinberg & Tronick, 1996).

Mutual regulation continues during toddlerhood, though it takes somewhat different forms. In a study of 18- to 36-month-olds' reactions to a mother's simulated emotional withdrawal, the children first attempted to reengage the mothers' attention. When those attempts failed, they responded by moving away from her. Finally, they either showed unfocused behavior which resembled the mother's— staring vacantly, wandering around the room, or simply doing nothing—or they made negative bids for attention, such as hitting the mother or a toy, or throwing something at her (Seiner & Gelfand, 1995).

Reading emotional signals lets caregivers assess and meet babies' needs; and it lets babies influence or respond to the caregiver's behavior toward them. What happens, then, if that communication system seriously breaks down?

How a Mother's Depression Affects Mutual Regulation

Depression is more than ordinary sadness; it is an affective disorder (a disorder of mood) in which a person feels unhappy and often has trouble eating, sleeping, or concentrating (American Psychiatric Association [APA], 1994). While brief postpartum "blues" are common, true postnatal depression is much less so (American Psychological Association, 1997).

Temporary postpartum depression may have little or no impact on the way a mother interacts with her baby, but severe or chronic depression lasting 6 months or more can have serious effects (S. B. Campbell, Cohn, & Meyers, 1995; Teti et al., 1995). Babies of depressed mothers may give up on sending emotional signals and try to comfort themselves by sucking or rocking. If this

depression Affective disorder in which a person feels unhappy and often has trouble eating, sleeping, and concentrating.

defensive reaction becomes habitual, babies learn that they have no power to draw responses from other people, that their mothers are unreliable, and that the world is untrustworthy.

Some depressed mothers are overly intrusive: they ignore or override their babies' emotional signals. These mothers are hostile and punitive, consider their children bothersome and hard to care for, and feel as if their own lives are out of control (T. M. Field et al., 1985; Whiffen & Gotlib, 1989; B. S. Zuckerman & Beardslee, 1987). Their infants show elevated levels of stress hormones, possibly indicating anger (N. A. Jones et al., 1997). Other depressed mothers are withdrawn, unexpressive, anxious, and unresponsive (L. Murray, Fiori-Cowley, Hooper, & Cooper, 1996). Their babies are less active and look at them less than the babies of intrusive mothers, apparently mirroring the mothers' own behavior. At 1 year, these babies have lower scores on the Bayley Mental Scale, perhaps reflecting lack of stimulation (N. A. Jones et al., 1997).

Both as infants and as preschoolers, children with severely or chronically depressed mothers tend to be insecurely attached to them (D. M. Gelfand & Teti, 1995; Teti et al., 1995) and seem less upset than other infants when separated from their mothers (G. Dawson et al., 1992). Children of depressed mothers are also at risk of other emotional and cognitive disturbances (D. M. Gelfand & Teti, 1995). As infants, they are more likely than other babies to be drowsy or tense, to cry frequently, to look sad or angry more often, and to show interest less often (T. Field, Morrow, & Adelstein, 1993; Pickens & Field, 1993). They are less motivated to explore and more apt to prefer relatively unchallenging tasks (Redding, Harmon, & Morgan, 1990). As toddlers they are less likely to suppress frustration and tension (P. M. Cole, Barrett, & Zahn-Waxler, 1992) and to engage in symbolic play. Later they are likely to grow poorly and to perform poorly on cognitive measures, to have accidents, and to have behavior problems (T. M. Field et al., 1985; D. M. Gelfand & Teti, 1995; B. S. Zuckerman & Beardslee, 1987). They are also more likely to become depressed themselves (D. M. Gelfand & Teti, 1995).

Do infants become depressed through a failure of mutual regulation with a depressed, unresponsive mother? Or do they inherit a predisposition to depression, or acquire it prenatally through exposure to hormonal or other physiological influences? Evidence is inconclusive (T. Field, 1995). For example, newborns of mothers with depressive symptoms are less expressive, less active and robust, more excitable, and less oriented to sensory stimuli than other newborns. This would seem to indicate an inborn tendency; but it is possible that, even shortly after birth, negative interactions with a depressed mother have taken a toll (Lundy, Field, & Pickens, 1996). It may well be that a combination of genetic, prenatal, and environmental factors—including malnutrition, prenatal exposure to cocaine, preterm birth, and the absence of a father or grandmother who could assume some of a depressed mother's caregiving responsibilities—puts infants of depressed mothers at risk of becoming depressed (T. Field, 1995).

We do know that babies of depressed mothers tend to show unusual patterns of brain activity, similar to the mothers' own patterns. The left frontal region of the brain seems to be specialized for "approach" emotions such as joy and anger, whereas the right frontal region controls "withdrawal" emotions such as distress and disgust. In one study, 11- to 17-month-olds, while playing with their depressed mothers, showed less activity in the left frontal region than babies of nondepressed mothers (G. Dawson et al., 1992). Indeed, infants of depressed mothers have shown reduced activity in the left frontal region as early as 3 months and even 1 month of age (T. Field, Fox, Pickens, Nawrocki, & Soutollo, 1995; N. A. Jones, Field, Fox, Lundy, & Davalos, in press). Other research has found different neural patterns in babies of the two types of depressed mothers. As compared with infants of intrusive mothers, infants of withdrawn mothers have comparatively less activity in the left frontal region (N. A. Jones et al., 1997). Again, such findings can support genetic, prenatal, or environmental explanations.

Sitting on Santa's lap is not a very merry experience for this baby, who may be showing stranger anxiety. Wariness of unfamiliar people and places commonly occurs during the second half of the first year.

Professional or paraprofessional home visitors have helped depressed mothers by putting them in touch with community resources, such as parenting groups, and by modeling and reinforcing positive interactions. Techniques that may help improve a depressed mother's mood include listening to music, visual imagery, aerobics, yoga, relaxation, and massage therapy (T. Field, 1995). Massage can also help depressed babies. One- to 3-month-old infants of depressed teenage single mothers, when given 6 weeks of biweekly 15-minute massage treatments, were more alert, slept better, cried less, showed less stress, gained more weight, and were more soothable and more sociable than a control group who were rocked instead (T. Field et al., 1996). Interactions with a nondepressed adult—the father or a day-care teacher—can help compensate for the effects of depressed mothering (T. Field, 1995).

Stranger Anxiety and Separation Anxiety

Sophie used to be a friendly baby, smiling at strangers and going to them, continuing to coo happily as long as someone—anyone—was around. Now, at 8 months, she turns away when a new person approaches and howls when her parents try to leave her with a baby-sitter. Sophie is experiencing both *stranger anxiety,* wariness of a person she does not know, and *separation anxiety,* distress when a familiar caregiver leaves her.

Separation anxiety and stranger anxiety used to be considered emotional and cognitive milestones of the second half of infancy, reflecting attachment to the mother. However, research suggests (as does Margaret Mead's experience with Cathy Bateson) that although stranger anxiety and separation anxiety are fairly typical, they are not universal. Whether a baby cries when a parent leaves or when someone new approaches may say more about the baby's temperament or life circumstances than about security of attachment (R. J. Davidson & Fox, 1989).

stranger anxiety Wariness of strange people and places, shown by some infants during the second half of the first year.

separation anxiety Distress shown by an infant when a familiar caregiver leaves.

Babies rarely react negatively to strangers before 6 months of age, commonly do so by 8 or 9 months, and do so more and more throughout the rest of the first year (Sroufe, 1977). Even then, however, a baby may react positively to a new person, especially if the mother speaks positively about the stranger (Feinman & Lewis, 1983) or if the person waits a little while and then approaches the baby gradually, gently, and playfully.

Babies of different ages handle their anxiety differently. In one laboratory experiment, 6-month-olds tended to fuss and look away from a stranger, 12-month-olds to soothe themselves by sucking their thumbs, and 18-month-olds to turn their attention elsewhere or try to direct the interaction with the stranger. There were individual differences, too. Infants whose mothers described them as wary of strangers tended to avert their gaze from a strange woman longer than other infants and to cling more closely to their mothers (Mangelsdorf, Shapiro, & Marzolf, 1995).

Culture also makes a difference. Navajo infants show less fear of strangers during the first year of life than Anglo infants. Then, there are differences within a culture. Navajo babies who have many opportunities to interact with other people—who have frequent contact with relatives or live close to a trading post—are less wary of new people than are other Navajo infants (Chisholm, 1983).

Separation anxiety may be due less to the separation itself than to the quality of substitute care. Measurements of 9-month-olds' physiological and behavioral responses to brief separations from their mothers showed that when caregivers were warm and responsive and played with the infants *before* they cried, the babies cried much less than when they were with less responsive caregivers (Gunnar, Larson, Hertsgaard, Harris, & Brodersen, 1992). This was especially true of babies temperamentally disposed to be quick to anger in situations in which they seemed to feel a loss of control.

Stability of substitute care is also important. The pioneering work done by René Spitz (1945, 1946) on institutionalized children emphasized the need for care as close as possible to good mothering. Research has underlined the value of continuity and consistency in caregiving, so children can form early emotional bonds to their caregivers.

Today, neither early and intense fear of strangers nor intense protest when the mother leaves is considered to be a sign of secure attachment. Researchers now measure attachment more by what happens when the mother returns than by how many tears the baby sheds at her departure.

Social Referencing

social referencing
Understanding an ambiguous situation by seeking out another person's perception of it.

If, at a formal dinner party, you have ever cast a sidelong glance to see which fork the person next to you was using, you have read another person's nonverbal signals to get information on how to act. Through *social referencing,* one person forms an understanding of how to act in an ambiguous, confusing, or unfamiliar situation by seeking out and interpreting another person's perception of it. Babies seem to use social referencing when they look at their caregivers upon encountering a new person or toy. This pattern of behavior may begin sometime after 6 months of age, when infants begin to judge the possible consequences of events, imitate complex behaviors, and distinguish among and react to various emotional expressions.

In a study using the visual cliff (described in Chapter 5), when the drop looked very shallow or very deep, 1-year-olds did not look to their mothers; they were able to judge for themselves whether to cross over or not. When they were uncertain about the depth of the "cliff," however, they paused at the "edge," looked down, and then looked up at their mothers. Most of the babies whose mothers showed joy or interest crossed the "drop," but very few whose mothers looked angry or afraid crossed it (Sorce, Emde, Campos, & Klinnert, 1985).

However, the idea that infants engage in social referencing has been challenged (D. A. Baldwin & Moses, 1996). Are babies less than 1 year old aware of their own need for knowledge and someone else's ability to furnish it? Although infants as young as 8 or 9 months old do spontaneously look at caregivers in ambiguous situations, it is not clear that they are looking for information; they may be seeking comfort, attention, sharing of feelings, or simply reassurance of the caregiver's presence—typical attachment behaviors.

Social information gathering, as opposed to direct exploration or observation, is a complex process requiring several sophisticated cognitive abilities. Not only must an infant be able to decode another person's signals and know what situation they refer to, that is, be a *consumer* of social information, but the infant also must realize that such information is available, recognize the need to seek it out, and be able to elicit the information, that is, be an active *seeker* of social information. Infants by the end of the first year are becoming proficient as consumers of social information, but (it is argued) only gradually during the second year do they acquire the skills necessary to seek out such information before it is offered (D. A. Baldwin & Moses, 1996). That occurs as they become more aware of distinctions between themselves and others and better able to understand and use language. According to this analysis, true social referencing must await developments that seem to occur during toddlerhood and early childhood: the emergence of a sense of self and awareness of the difference between knowledge and ignorance, which necessitates a *theory of mind* (see Chapter 9).

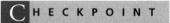

C HECKPOINT

Can you . . .

• Discuss factors affecting stranger anxiety and separation anxiety?

• Explain what social referencing is, and give arguments for and against infants' use of it?

Developmental Issues in Toddlerhood

About halfway between their first and second birthdays, babies become toddlers. This transformation can be seen not only in such physical and cognitive skills as walking and talking, but in how children express their personalities and interact with others. Let's look at three psychological issues that toddlers—and their caregivers—have to deal with: the emerging *sense of self;* the growth of *autonomy,* or self-determination; and the *internalization of behavioral standards.*

The Emerging Sense of Self

Before children can take responsibility for their own activities, they must have a cognitive sense of themselves as physically distinct persons—separate from the rest of the world—whose characteristics and behavior can be described and evaluated. Self-awareness is the first step toward developing standards of behavior; it lets children understand that a parent's response to something they have done is directed at *them* and not just at the act itself.

How does the ***self-concept,*** or sense of self, begin to develop? After interviewing the mothers of 123 children 14 to 40 months old, a team of researchers (Stipek et al., 1990) identified this sequence:

1. *Physical self-recognition and self-awareness:* Most toddlers recognize themselves in mirrors or pictures by 18 months, showing awareness of themselves as physically distinct beings. In an earlier study, researchers counted how often 6- to 24-month-old children touched their noses. Then the researchers dabbed rouge on the babies' noses and sat them in front of a mirror. The 18-month-olds touched their red noses much more often than younger babies did, suggesting that they knew they didn't normally have red noses and that they recognized the image in the mirror as their own (M. Lewis & Brooks, 1974).
2. *Self-description and self-evaluation:* Once they have a concept of themselves as distinct beings, children begin to apply descriptive terms ("big" or "little"; "straight hair" or "curly hair") and evaluative ones ("good," "pretty," or

self-concept Sense of self; descriptive and evaluative mental picture of one's abilities and traits.

According to Erikson, toddlers need to develop autonomy. During this stage, parents need to ignore messy faces, bibs, tables, and floors, and let children learn how to master such basic tasks as feeding themselves.

"mean") to themselves. This normally occurs sometime between 19 and 30 months, as representational ability and vocabulary expand.

3. *Emotional response to wrongdoing:* The third stage has arrived when children show that they are upset by a parent's disapproval and will stop doing something they are not supposed to do—at least while they are being watched. This stage, which lays the foundation for moral understanding and the development of conscience, comes about more gradually than the second stage, and there is some overlap.

According to the mothers in this study, children as young as 14 months showed an urge for autonomy, or self-determination—refusing help, acting contrary, and resisting attempts to dress or diaper them or pick them up (Stipek et al., 1990). Let's see what Erikson's theory has to say about this important development of toddlerhood.

Developing Autonomy

As children mature—physically, cognitively, and emotionally—they are driven to seek independence from the very adults to whom they are attached. "Me do!" is the byword as toddlers use their developing muscles and minds to try to do everything on their own: not only to walk, but to feed, dress, and protect themselves and to expand the boundaries of their world.

Erikson (1950) identified the period from about 18 months to 3 years as the second stage, or crisis, in personality development, *autonomy versus shame and doubt,* which is marked by a shift from external control to self-control. Having come through infancy with a sense of basic trust in the world and an awakening self-awareness, toddlers begin to substitute their own judgment for their caregivers'. The "virtue" that emerges during this stage is *will.* Toilet training is an important step toward autonomy and self-control. So is language; as children are better able to make their wishes understood, they become more powerful and independent.

Since unlimited freedom is neither safe nor healthy, said Erikson, shame and doubt have a necessary place. As in all of Erikson's stages, an appropriate balance is crucial. Self-doubt helps children recognize what they are not yet ready to do, and shame helps them learn to live by reasonable rules. Toddlers need adults to set appropriate limits, and shame and doubt help them recognize the need for those limits.

autonomy versus shame and doubt In Erikson's theory, the second crisis in psychosocial development, occurring between about 18 months and 3 years, in which children achieve a balance between self-determination and control by others.

Box 7-1 Dealing With the "Terrible Twos"

The following research-based guidelines can help parents and toddlers get through the "terrible twos" by discouraging negativism and encouraging socially acceptable behavior (Haswell, Hock, & Wenar, 1981; Kochanska & Aksan, 1995; Kopp, 1982; Kuczynski & Kochanska, 1995; Power & Chapieski, 1986):

- *Be flexible.* Learn the child's natural rhythms and special likes and dislikes. The most flexible parents tend to have the least resistant children.
- *Think of yourself as a safe harbor,* with safe limits, from which a child can set out and discover the world—and keep coming back for support.
- *Make your home "child-friendly."* Fill it with unbreakable objects that are safe to explore.
- *Avoid physical punishment.* It is often ineffective and may even lead a toddler to do more damage.
- *Offer a choice*—even a limited one—to give the child some control. For example, "Would you like to have your bath now, or after we read a book?"
- *Be consistent* in enforcing necessary requests. Many children refuse to obey to show their control—but do not really mean what they say and will eventually comply.
- *Don't interrupt an activity unless absolutely necessary.* Try to wait until the child's attention has shifted to something else.
- *If you must interrupt, give warning:* "We have to leave the playground soon." This gives the child time to

prepare and either finish an activity or think about resuming it another time.
- *Suggest alternative activities.* When Ashley is throwing sand in Keiko's face, say, "Oh, look! Nobody's on the swings now. Let's go over and I'll give you a good push!"
- *Suggest, don't command.* Accompany requests with smiles or hugs, not criticism, threats, or physical restraint.
- *Link requests with pleasurable activities:* "It's time to stop playing, so that you can go to the store with me."
- *Remind the child of what you expect:* "When we go to this playground, we *never* go outside the gate."
- *Wait a few moments before repeating a request* when a child doesn't comply immediately.
- *Use "time out"* to end conflicts. In a nonpunitive way, remove either yourself or the child from a situation. Very often this results in the resistance diminishing or even disappearing.
- *Expect less self-control during times of stress* (illness, divorce, the birth of a sibling, or a move to a new home).
- *Expect it to be harder for toddlers to comply with "do's" than with "don'ts."* "Clean up your room" takes more effort than "Don't write on the furniture."
- Above all, *keep the atmosphere as positive as possible.* Maintaining a warm, enjoyable relationship is the key to making children *want* to cooperate.

The "terrible twos" are a normal manifestation of the drive for autonomy. Toddlers have to test the new notion that they are individuals, that they have some control over their world, and that they have new, exciting powers. They are driven to try out their own ideas, exercise their own preferences, and make their own decisions. This drive typically shows itself in the form of *negativism,* the tendency to shout "No!" just for the sake of resisting authority. Almost all children show negativism to some degree; it usually begins before 2 years of age, tends to peak at about 3½ to 4, and declines by age 6. Parents and other caregivers who view children's expressions of self-will as a normal, healthy striving for independence, not as stubbornness, can help them learn self-control, contribute to their sense of competence, and avoid excessive conflict. (Box 7-1 gives specific, research-based suggestions for dealing with the "terrible twos.")

negativism Behavior characteristic of toddlers, in which they express their desire for independence by resisting authority.

Internalization: Developing a Conscience

Socialization is the process by which children develop habits, skills, values, and motives that make them responsible, productive members of society (Kochanska, 1993; E. E. Maccoby, 1992). Compliance with parental expectations is a first step toward compliance with societal standards (Kochanska & Aksan, 1995; Kopp, 1982; E. E. Maccoby & Martin, 1983). Socialization rests on *internalization* of these standards. Children who are successfully socialized no longer merely obey rules or commands to get rewards or avoid punishment; they have made society's standards their own (Grusec & Goodnow, 1994; Kochanska & Aksan, 1995). Let's see how internalization begins.

socialization Process of developing the habits, skills, values, and motives shared by responsible, productive members of a particular society.

internalization Process by which children accept societal standards of conduct as their own; fundamental to socialization.

Developing Self-Regulation

Katy is about to poke her finger into an electric outlet. In her "child-proofed" apartment, the sockets are covered, but not here in her grandmother's home. When Katy hears her father shout "No!" the toddler pulls her arm back. The next time she goes near an outlet, she starts to point her finger, hesitates, and then says "No." She has stopped herself from doing something she remembers she is not supposed to do. She is beginning to show *self-regulation:* control of her own behavior to conform to a caregiver's demands or expectations, even when the caregiver is not present.

Self-regulation is the foundation of socialization, and it links all domains of development—physical, cognitive, social, and emotional. Until Katy was physically able to get around on her own, electric outlets posed no hazard. To stop herself from poking her finger into an outlet requires that she consciously understand and remember what her father told her. Cognitive awareness, however, is not enough; restraining herself also requires emotional control.

Parents are the most important people in a toddler's life and the ones whose approval matters more than anything else in the world. By "reading" their parents' emotional responses to their behavior, children continually absorb information about what conduct their parents approve of. As children process, store, and act upon this information, their strong desire to please their parents leads them to do as they know their parents want them to, whether or not the parents are there to see. This growth of self-regulation parallels the development of the self-conscious emotions, such as empathy, shame, and guilt. It requires flexibility and the ability to wait for gratification. When young children want very badly to do something, however, they easily forget the rules; they may run into the street after a ball or take a forbidden cookie. In most children, then, the full development of self-regulation takes at least 3 years (Kopp, 1982).

Origins of Conscience: Committed Compliance

Internalization of societal standards is essential to the development of a *conscience,* which includes both emotional discomfort about doing something wrong and the ability to refrain from doing it (Kochanska, 1993; see Box 7-2). Conscience depends on willingness to do the right thing because a child believes it is right, not (as in self-regulation) just because someone else has said so. However, *inhibitory control*—conscious, or effortful, control of behavior, a mechanism of self-regulation which emerges during toddlerhood and may be linked to temperament—may contribute to the underpinnings of conscience by first enabling the child to comply with parental "dos" and "don'ts" (Kochanska, Murray, & Coy, 1997).

Grazyna Kochanska (1993, 1995, 1997a, 1997b) and her colleagues have sought the origins of conscience in a longitudinal study of a socioeconomically and ethnically mixed group of toddlers and mothers in urban and rural areas of Iowa. Researchers videotaped 103 children ages 26 to 41 months and their mothers playing together for two to three hours, both at home and in a homelike laboratory setting (Kochanska & Aksan, 1995). After a free-play period, the mother gave the child 15 minutes to put the toys away. The laboratory also had a special shelf with unusually attractive toys, such as a bubble gum machine, a walkie-talkie, a music box, a fishing set, and a beautiful doll. The child was told not to touch anything on the shelf during the entire session. After about an hour, the experimenter asked the mother to go into an adjoining room, leaving the child with the toys. A few minutes later, a strange woman entered, played with several of the toys on the forbidden shelf, and then left the child alone for 8 minutes.

The researchers assessed each child's compliance with the mother's demands by how willingly the child cleaned up and whether or not the child made any attempt to touch the forbidden toys while the mother was in the room. Children

Box 7-2 Early Signs of Conscience

Matthew, age 18 months, toddles across the living room floor and points to a chipped vase. "Broke?" he asks, with a worried look at his baby-sitter.

Does a toddler's concern with flawed objects—a concern that typically arises during the second year—have something to do with anxiety about his or her own wrongdoing, which also emerges around that time? Jerome Kagan (1984) thought so. By age 2, according to Piaget (1952), children understand that some actions are intentional and others are not. As part of their developing self-awareness, they also begin to understand and react emotionally to harm they have caused (Stipek et al., 1990). However, in ambiguous situations, young children's assessment of who caused what may be confused (Zahn-Waxler & Kochanska, 1990).

Grazyna Kochanska and her colleagues (Kochanska, Casey, & Fukumoto, 1995) videotaped 2- and 3-year-olds in laboratory interactions with whole and damaged objects. First, the experimenter showed a child four pairs of objects: teddy bears, beds, blankets, and cups. One object in each pair was defective—broken, torn, or stained, or missing a part—and the other was intact. The children were asked what they thought of each object, which of each pair they liked better, and why. Then the children were allowed to play with all the objects. The children were more interested in and concerned about the flawed items, even though by age 2½ they clearly preferred the undamaged versions.

The experimenters then set up two scenarios in which the child was led to believe that she or he had damaged the experimenter's doll or shirt. In the "doll mishap," the experimenter invited the child to play a game with two dolls. The experimenter would "walk" one doll, clap its hands, and make it do a somersault, and the child would do the same with the other doll. During the somersault, the head of the doll the child was playing with, which had been rigged, fell off. After the child had put the doll down, the experimenter asked a few questions about what had happened, then left the room briefly, came back with an identical but undamaged doll, and let the child play with it a little longer.

In the "shirt mishap," the experimenter asked the child to bring her a tee shirt from a nearby table. When the child picked up the shirt, a cup of ink, which had been hidden in its folds, spilled on the shirt. After questioning the child, the experimenter took responsibility for the mishap, took the shirt out of the room saying she would try to clean it, and came back with an identical, clean shirt.

Everything the child said during each mishap was transcribed. The statements fell into six categories: (1) *objective statements:* "Head fell off" or "There's a mess," (2) *apologies:* "Sorry" or "Didn't mean to," (3) *statements about repairing the damage:* "Put head back on" or "Wash this off," (4) *self-blaming statements:* "I did it," (5) *denials of blame:* "Nothing happened," "Doll did it," or "Not me," and (6) *statements of distress or withdrawal:* "I'm done with this doll," "Take this shirt away," or "Can we leave now?" The researchers also observed the children's emotional reactions.

Responses to the mishaps fit three patterns, which seem to correspond to the emotions of guilt, shame, or a combination of the two. "Amenders" accepted responsibility and sought to repair the damage (guilt). "Avoiders" showed distress and a desire to escape (shame). A third group made both apologetic and reparatory comments.

These children's reactions to flawed objects, both in an emotionally neutral situation and one in which they might conceivably be to blame, suggest a cognitive and emotional concern with violations of standards, which may be an early sign of emerging conscience. A fascination with flaws may develop cognitively as a result of repeated exposure to the way objects are supposed to look, and emotionally as a result of repeated exposure to caregivers' disapproval of damaging actions. As other research has shown, protection of personal property is one of the earliest and most effective demands parents make on young children (Gralinksi & Kopp, 1993). Research with younger children might show whether sensitivity to flawed objects is a forerunner of emotional responses to wrongdoing, or whether both develop at about the same time.

were judged to show **committed compliance**, which seems to be an early form of conscience, if they appeared to wholeheartedly accept the mother's orders, following them without reminders or lapses. Children showed **situational compliance** if they needed prompting to obey; their compliance depended on ongoing parental control.

Children whose mothers rated them as having internalized household rules showed the most committed compliance. These children refrained from touching the forbidden toys even when left alone with them, showing that they had internalized the prohibition. By contrast, children whose compliance was only situational tended to yield to temptation when their mothers were out of sight. The oldest children and those who had had positive interchanges with their mothers during play showed more committed compliance than younger children and those whose interactions with their mothers were characterized by irritation, boredom, anger, fear, or sadness.

committed compliance
In Kochanska's terminology, a toddler's wholehearted obedience of a parent's orders without reminders or lapses.

situational compliance
In Kochanska's terminology, a toddler's obedience of a parent's orders only in the presence of prompting or other signs of ongoing parental control.

A follow-up observation when the children were 3½ to 4½ years old provides further evidence that internalization grows out of committed, but not situational, compliance. Children who, as toddlers, had shown committed compliance were more likely to continue to show it as they got older, and they were also more likely to have internalized adult rules (Kochanska, Aksan, & Koenig, 1995).

Factors in the Success of Socialization

Some children internalize societal standards more readily than others. The way parents go about their job, together with a child's temperament and the quality of the parent-child relationship, may help predict how hard or easy it will be to socialize a child (Kochanska, 1993, 1995, 1997a, 1997b). Factors in the success of socialization may include security of attachment, observational learning of parents' behavior, and the mutual responsiveness of parent and child (E. E. Maccoby, 1992). All these, as well as socioeconomic and cultural factors (Harwood, Schoelmerich, Ventura-Cook, Schulze, & Wilson, 1996), may play a part in motivation to comply.

In a study that explored effects of parenting styles, 70 mothers and their 1½- to 3½-year-olds were videotaped through one-way mirrors in a naturalistic apartment setting. Two-thirds of the mothers and children participated in a follow-up study when the children were 5 years old (Kuczynski & Kochanska, 1995).

Mothers who had an *authoritarian* style of parenting—emphasizing strict supervision, power, control, and punishment—issued many prohibitions ("Don't hit," "Don't write on the wall," "Stop throwing the blocks around"). Mothers with an *authoritative* style—emphasizing rational guidance, encouragement of independence, and open communication of feelings—made demands that promoted social competence or gave instructions for future behavior ("Put the crayons away," "Share your cookies," "Be good while I'm gone"). Toddlers were more likely to comply with these demands, and those whose mothers made them had fewer behavior problems at age 5; those with authoritarian mothers had more problems. (Authoritarian and authoritative parenting, as well as a third style, *permissive* parenting, are more fully described in Chapter 10.)

A bidirectional influence appeared: children who actively resisted their mothers' demands received more regulatory and restrictive demands and fewer requests for cooperation and competence. A cycle may be created in which parents respond to resistant children by becoming overcontrolling and making even less effort to socialize the child in a positive way. Conversely, when parent and child get along well from the start, "a habit of competent and cooperative behavior" may develop (Kochanska & Aksan, 1995; Kuczynski & Kochanska, 1995, p. 625).

reciprocity In Maccoby's terminology, system of mutually binding, mutually responsive relationships into which a child is socialized.

A pleasant emotional atmosphere and cooperation with the other person's needs and goals are two aspects of *reciprocity:* a system of mutually binding, mutually responsive relationships. Eleanor Maccoby (1992; E. E. Maccoby & Martin, 1983) describes socialization as a process of initiating a child into this system of reciprocity, which begins with the parents and then extends to the community. Findings from Kochanska's (1997b) longitudinal study support this model. Mothers whose interactions with their toddlers were enjoyable and cooperative were less likely to have to depend on power to enforce their demands, and the children were more likely to have internalized the mothers' rules. In a second observation at preschool age, this correlation was less strong but still significant; by that time, other aspects of a reciprocal relationship, such as negotiation and agreement on rules, may become more important.

In any case, these findings suggest that a mutually responsive parent-child relationship during the toddler years can promote smoother, more successful socialization. In an earlier study of the same mothers and children, discussed above, a warm, mutually responsive relationship seemed to foster committed compliance. Mothers of committed compliers, as contrasted with mothers of situational compliers, tended to rely on gentle guidance rather than force, threats, or other forms of negative control (Kochanska & Aksan, 1995). Children may more readily comply with parental demands when the parent has repeatedly affirmed the child's autonomy (for example, by following the child's lead during play). Mothers who can readily see a child's point of view seem to be most successful in doing this (Kochanska, 1997b).

Gentle guidance seems particularly suited to temperamentally fearful or anxious children, who tend to become upset when they misbehave. Such a child will readily internalize parental messages with a minimum of prodding; displays of power would merely make the child more anxious. Something more is needed with bolder children, but they too are likely to respond better to appeals to cooperate than to threats, and they are more likely to comply if they are securely attached (Kochanska, 1995, 1997a).

Cultural and Class Influences on Socialization

The way children are socialized depends in large part on culture and socioeconomic class, which influence parents' beliefs about how children should behave (Harwood et al., 1996). In the United States, middle-class parents generally encourage self-direction and initiative, which have been found to promote competence, whereas lower-class parents are more likely to emphasize obedience to authority. But since many minority families in the United States are poor, it is difficult to separate the effects of culture and class. For example, Anglo-American parents (non-Hispanic white parents of European extraction), consistent with U.S. culture's emphasis on individualism, generally value independence and self-confidence, whereas Puerto Rican parents, consistent with their culture's emphasis on community well-being, value respectfulness and obedience. Is this difference primarily influenced by culture or socioeconomic status?

One research team sought to untangle these two factors by comparing beliefs about and perceptions of children's behavior among middle-class and lower-class Anglo mothers in Connecticut, middle-class and lower-class Puerto Rican mothers in Puerto Rico, and lower-class Puerto Rican mothers in Connecticut (Harwood et al., 1996). One hundred mothers (20 in each group) were asked about qualities they would and would not want their children to have as adults. They were also asked to describe toddlers they knew who showed tendencies in those directions. Anglo mothers, regardless of socioeconomic class, valued self-maximization (self-confidence, independence, happiness, development of skills and abilities) most highly, whereas Puerto Rican mothers, regardless of class or location, valued proper demeanor (respectfulness, politeness, gentleness, keeping quiet). It seems, then, that cultural values had a greater effect than socioeconomic status on these mothers' socialization goals.

CHECKPOINT

Can you . . .

- Trace three stages in the development of the sense of self during toddlerhood?
- Describe Erikson's crisis of autonomy versus shame and doubt?
- Explain why the "terrible twos" are a normal phenomenon?
- Tell when and how self-regulation develops and how it contributes to development of conscience?
- Discuss the roles of temperament, parenting styles, social class, and culture in socialization?

Contact with Other Children

Although parents exert a major influence on children's lives, relationships with other children—both in the home and out of it—are important too, from infancy on.

Siblings

If you have brothers or sisters, your relationships with them are likely to be the longest-lasting you'll ever have. You and your siblings may have fought continually as children, or you may have been each other's best friends. Either way, they share your roots; they "knew you when," they accepted or rejected the same parental values, and they probably deal with you more candidly than almost anyone else you know.

The Arrival of a New Baby

Children react in various ways to the arrival of a sibling. To bid for the mother's attention, some suck their thumbs, wet their pants, ask to suck from breast or bottle, or use baby talk. Others withdraw, refusing to talk or play. Some suggest taking the baby back to the hospital, giving it away, or flushing it down the toilet. Some take pride in being the "big ones," who can dress themselves, use the potty, eat with the grown-ups, and help care for the baby. Most behavioral problems related to the arrival of a new baby disappear by the time the baby is 8 months old (Dunn, 1985).

Much of the variation in children's adjustment to a new baby may have to do with such factors as the older child's age, the quality of his or her relationship with the mother, and the family atmosphere. Not surprisingly, attachment to the mother often becomes less secure, and the extent of this decline in security may indicate how a child is adjusting.

A study of 194 two-parent families suggests that firstborns who are more than 24 months old or whose mothers have emotional problems are more likely to have trouble (Teti, Sakin, Kucera, Corns, & Eiden, 1996). The researchers measured the security of the firstborn's attachment, using mothers' sortings with the Attachment Q-Set, during the third trimester of the mother's pregnancy and again one or two months after the birth. Security decreased more for 2- to 5-year-olds than for younger children, perhaps because children under 2 are not yet mature enough to see the newcomer as an intruder or a threat. Children whose mothers showed signs of depression, anxiety, or hostility also showed substantially diminished security.

This research may have practical implications in identifying firstborns who are at special risk of difficulty in adjusting to a new baby. However, we need to interpret the findings with caution. They do not necessarily suggest that it is best to space children closer than two years apart; it may be that firstborns younger than 24 months have a delayed reaction to a new baby as their social and cognitive awareness sharpens. Also, a child's temperament may make a difference. Furthermore, in most cases a lapse in secure attachment is likely to be only temporary unless the birth brings a serious disruption in the caregiving environment (Teti et al., 1996).

The birth of a younger sibling may change the way a mother acts toward an older child. The mother is likely to play less with the older child, to be less sensitive to her or his interests, to give more orders, to have more confrontations, and to initiate fewer conversations and games (Dunn, 1985; Dunn & Kendrick, 1982). Children who take the initiative to start a conversation or play with the mother show less sibling rivalry than those who withdraw. Also, older siblings generally adjust better if their fathers give them extra time and attention to make up for the mother's involvement with the infant (Lamb, 1978).

Parents are wise to prepare an older child for the birth of a new baby by making any changes in the child's life (such as moving to another bedroom or from a crib to a bed, or starting nursery school) well in advance, to minimize feelings of displacement (Spock & Rothenberg, 1992). Parents need to accept a child's anxiety and jealousy as normal, while protecting the new baby from any harmful expression of those feelings. They can encourage the older child to play and help with the baby and can emphasize how much they value *each* child.

How Siblings Interact

Young children usually become attached to their older brothers and sisters. Babies become upset when their siblings go away, greet them when they come back, prefer them as playmates, and go to them for security when a stranger enters the room. Although rivalry is often present, so is affection (Dunn, 1983; R. B. Stewart, 1983). The more securely attached siblings are to their parents, the better they get along with each other (Teti & Ablard, 1989).

Babies and toddlers become closely attached to their older brothers and sisters, especially when, as with these Chinese children, the older siblings assume a large measure of care for the younger ones.

Nevertheless, as babies begin to move around and become more assertive, they inevitably come into conflict with older siblings over toys and territory and begin to interfere with their freedom to play. Whereas an infant will give in to an older child who takes a toy away, a toddler is more likely to resist. Siblings who are close in age tend to fight more. An older child, especially a boy, is more likely to be the aggressor; the younger child may cry, pout, or get the mother to intervene. Conflict is particularly common between older brothers and younger sisters, who sometimes provoke it (Vandell & Bailey, 1992).

Sibling conflict increases dramatically during the second half of the younger child's second year (Vandell & Bailey, 1992). During this time, younger siblings begin to participate more fully in family interactions and become more involved in family disputes. As they do, they become more aware of others' intentions and feelings. Their actions and expressions suggest that they are beginning to recognize what kind of behavior will upset or annoy an older brother or sister and what behavior is considered "naughty" or "good." They can anticipate what will happen when rules are broken; they show a great deal of interest in older siblings' transgressions and may attempt to support or comfort a sister or brother in trouble. When quarreling with an older sibling, they increasingly focus their anger or frustration directly on him or her, rather than merely showing general distress, as a younger toddler would (Dunn & Munn, 1985).

This growing cognitive and social understanding accompanies changes in the quality of sibling conflict. By 24 months, children often tease older siblings, blame them for misdeeds, and deny their own. They may try to get their mothers to side with them and may appeal to family rules. Conflict tends to become more constructive and less coercive, with the younger sibling participating in attempts to reconcile. Constructive conflict is limited to the issue at hand, is not highly emotional, and usually leads to a negotiated settlement. Thus it can be an opportunity for growth. It helps children recognize each other's needs, wishes, and point of view, and it helps them learn how to fight, disagree, and compromise within the context of a safe, stable relationship (Vandell & Bailey, 1992).

Squabbling arises in part from what parents do—or fail to do. When parents show favoritism, are cold, hostile or punitive, depressed or unhappy, do not give their children enough attention, fight with each other, or deal inconsistently with sibling conflicts, such conflicts are more likely to occur. Conflicts are less frequent and more constructive when parents reason with children, recognize their feelings and needs, explain a younger child's behavior to the older one, refer to rules, and suggest solutions (Vandell & Bailey, 1992).

Parents walk a fine line in deciding when and how to intervene in children's quarrels. A parent's interference can make things worse by creating a winner and a loser, thus setting the stage for future trouble. In constructive conflicts, it is usually best for parents to stay out and let children work things out on their own. However, when anger is intense or someone is being victimized or abused, action is called for. Research suggests that parents should try not to lecture, take sides, or become emotionally involved but should defuse the conflict by calmly acknowledging each child's feelings and point of view, describing the problem, and then leaving the room so the children can resolve it. To reduce the frequency of sibling struggles, parents should avoid comparing their children, show pride in each child's achievements, treat each as an individual, and spend time alone with each (Vandell & Bailey, 1992).

The environment siblings create for each other affects not only their future relationship but the personality development of each child. Children also teach their younger siblings and thus influence their cognitive development (R. B. Stewart, 1983). Lack of siblings, too, affects children's lives; we consider the "only child" in Chapter 10.

Sociability with Nonsiblings

Although the family is the center of a baby's social world, infants and—even more so—toddlers show interest in people outside the home, particularly people their own size. Now that more infants and toddlers spend time in day-care settings in close contact with other children, researchers are better able to study how they react to each other.

In a hospital nursery, newborns who have been lying quietly in their cribs start to cry when they hear another baby's cries (G. B. Martin & Clark, 1982; Sagi & Hoffman, 1976; Simner, 1971). During the first few months, they show interest in other babies in about the same ways they respond to their mothers: by looking, smiling, and cooing (T. M. Field, 1978). During the last half of the first year, they increasingly smile at, touch, and babble to another baby, especially when they are not distracted by the presence of adults or toys (Hay, Pedersen, & Nash, 1982).

At about 1 year, when the biggest items on their agenda are learning to walk and to manipulate objects, babies pay more attention to toys and less to other people (T. M. Field & Roopnarine, 1982). This stage does not last long, though; from about 1½ years of age to almost 3, they show more interest in what other children do and increasing understanding of how to deal with them. This insight seems to accompany awareness of themselves as separate individuals. A 10-month-old who holds out a toy to another baby pays no attention to whether the other's back is turned, but an 18-month-old toddler knows when the offer has the best chance of being accepted and how to respond to another child's overtures (Eckerman, Davis, & Didow, 1989; Eckerman & Stein, 1982).

Toddlers learn by imitating one another. Fourteen- to 18-month-olds imitate each other's play as much as 2 days later and in a different context (Hanna & Meltzoff, 1993; see Chapter 6). Imitative games such as follow-the-leader help toddlers connect with other children and pave the way for more complex games during the preschool years (Eckerman et al., 1989).

Conflict, too, can have a purpose: helping children learn how to negotiate and resolve disputes. In one study, groups of three toddlers who had not known each other before were observed playing with toys. Overall, the children got along well—sharing, showing, and demonstrating toys to each other, even just before and after squabbling over them. Two-year-olds got into more conflicts than 1-year-olds but also resolved them more, often by sharing toys when there were not enough to go around (M. Caplan, Vespo, Pedersen, & Hay, 1991).

Some children, of course, are more sociable than others, reflecting such temperamental traits as their usual mood, readiness to accept new people, and ability to adapt to change. Sociability is also influenced by experience; babies who spend time with other babies become sociable earlier than those who spend all their time at home alone. As children grow older and enter more and more into the world beyond the home, social skills become increasingly important. For many children the first step into that wider world is entrance into day care.

The Impact of Early Day Care

What happens to the development of young children who are cared for by someone other than the parents? Does day care, especially infant day care, help or harm children? These questions are controversial, and the answers are important. In the United States, more than half of all mothers of children under 1 year of age are working for pay, full or part time, in or out of the home (Bachu, 1993)—a higher proportion than at any time in the nation's history.

The way we break down our questions is important, too. Where does care take place? What is high-quality care? How do we judge harm and benefit? How can we distinguish the effects of the day-care experience from the effects of parenting?

Many studies are open to criticism, and their findings are often contradictory. Furthermore, much of what we know about the effects of day care comes from studies of well-funded, university-based centers. We have relatively little information about the effects of the kinds of day care that children most commonly receive. Since organized group care or paid in-home care is costly, children in lower economic circumstances tend to be under the care of fathers, grandparents, or other relatives (L. M. Casper, 1996; NICHD Early Child Care Research Network, 1997b). Such socioeconomic distinctions are far less common in countries such as Sweden, where parental leave policies and child care subsidies make it possible for a very high percentage of parents to care for infants and toddlers at home during the first 18 months and then to put them into group care (see Box 7-3).

Recently, in the United States, there has been a shift from care by relatives to organized care in day-care centers or preschools. In 1993, relatives still cared for almost half (48 percent) of children under age 5 whose mothers were gainfully employed; but this figure was down from 53 percent in 1991, largely because, with the lifting of an economic recession, fewer fathers were serving as primary caregivers. Meanwhile, the proportion of these preschoolers who were in organized facilities jumped from 23 percent to 30 percent—an all-time high. Only 18 percent, an all-time low, were in family day care outside their own homes. The rest were in the care of nonrelatives in the children's homes (L. M. Casper, 1996; see Figure 7-1).

When we think about effects of day care, then, we need to consider variations in type, quality, and amount of care and also in the age at which children start day care. Economic factors, such as the family's total income and the mother's earning capacity, are major—but not the only—factors in such decisions. Mothers' personalities and attitudes and family characteristics make a difference. For example, mothers who believe that their working is beneficial to their children are more likely to place an infant in nonmaternal care during the early months of life and to do so for longer hours. Babies who spend a lot of time in day care tend to have few siblings; presumably, mothers with many children are less likely to work full

CHECKPOINT

Can you . . .

• Discuss factors affecting adjustment to a new baby?

• Trace changes in sibling interaction and sibling conflict during toddlerhood?

• Trace changes in sociability during the first 3 years?

Box 7-3   How Sweden Cares for Parents and Children

In most societies throughout history, other people have helped mothers care for children. Today the issue of nonparental child care in the United States has taken on a new urgency for several reasons: the great numbers of mothers now working outside the home, the rise of group day care as a business venture, and the belief that day care should enhance children's development rather than just offer baby-sitting. Sweden is often held up as a model.

Swedish family policy came about because of rapid industrialization and ensuing labor shortages. To enable women to work and also to bear and rear future workers, Sweden developed a system that included good pay, generous parental leaves, and high-quality early child care (C.-P. Hwang & Broberg, 1992; Lamb & Sternberg, 1992).

Every Swedish family receives an allowance from the state for each child, from birth through age 16. Both mothers and fathers can take parental leave for 10 months at 75 percent of regular salary, plus one month for each parent at 85 percent. Thus almost all Swedish babies have at least one parent home for most of the first year. In addition, to increase paternal involvement, Sweden in 1995 instituted a *mandatory* one-month paternity leave.

Since the national government sets guidelines for quality, municipal child care is of a very high caliber. Standards are set for the physical facility, staffing and staff training, size of groups, and so forth. However, family day care, which is common, is almost unregulated; efforts are being made to develop guidelines for "daymothers."

Research has shown positive effects of high-quality infant day care in Sweden (Andersson, 1992). Children ages 8 and 13 who had entered out-of-home care before age 1 (usually during the second half of the first year) were compared with children who had been cared for at home. The day-care youngsters generally did better in school, and their teachers gave them higher ratings for school adjustment and social competence. The *type* of day care did not affect children's social, emotional, or cognitive development; the most important factors seemed to be the quality of care children received in their own homes and the health of the emotional climate there.

However, a later longitudinal study in Göteborg, Sweden's second largest city, found that the type and quality of day care did make a difference. Researchers recruited 146 children between 12 and 24 months of age—before they entered day care—and followed them for the next 7 years. Within 3 months after the study began, 54 of the children were enrolled in day-care centers, 33 went into family day care, and 59 remained in exclusively parental care. At age 8, children who had spent more time in center-based care before age 3½ scored higher on tests of verbal and mathematical abilities than children in the other two groups; those who had been in family day care typically scored lowest. For children who had spent 3 or more years in care outside the home, the quality of care—as indicated by interactions with caregivers, child-staff ratio, group size, and age range—was also predictive of cognitive outcomes (Broberg, Wessels, Lamb, & Hwang, 1997). These findings are consistent with a growing body of research in several other countries, including the United States, which points to cognitive benefits from high-quality day care.

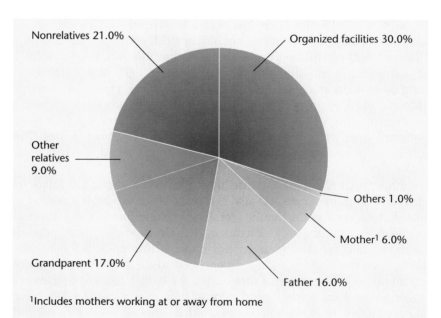

Figure 7-1
Primary child-care arrangements used by employed mothers for children under 5. In 1993, about 3 out of 10 of these children—more than ever before—were in group day-care centers.
Source: L. M. Casper, 1996.

Table 7-5	Checklist for Choosing a Good Day-Care Facility

- Is the facility licensed? Does it meet minimum state standards for health, fire, and safety? (Many centers and home care facilities are not licensed or regulated.)
- Is the facility clean and safe?
- Does the facility have small groups, a high adult-to-child ratio, and a stable, competent, highly involved staff?
- Are caregivers trained in child development?
- Are caregivers warm, affectionate, accepting, responsive, and sensitive? Are they authoritative but not too restrictive, and neither too controlling nor merely custodial?
- Does the program promote good health habits?
- Does it provide a balance between structured activities and free play?
- Do the children have access to educational toys and materials, which stimulate mastery of cognitive and communicative skills at a child's own pace?
- Does the program nurture self-confidence, curiosity, creativity, and self-discipline?
- Does it encourage children to ask questions, solve problems, and make decisions?
- Does it foster self-esteem, respect for others, and social skills?
- Does it help parents improve their child-rearing skills?
- Does it promote cooperation with public and private schools and the community?

Sources: American Academy of Pediatrics [AAP], 1986; Belsky, 1984; K. A. Clarke-Stewart, 1987; S. W. Olds, 1989.

time. Although income is generally related to quality of care, children in organized centers get better-quality care if they are from low-income families than if they are from moderate-income families, which do not usually benefit from federal subsidies (NICHD Early Child Care Research Network, 1997b).

The demand for day care is likely to rise dramatically as welfare reform requires poor mothers to go to work. As we look at what makes good day care (see Table 7-5) and at its impact on the interrelated areas of cognitive, emotional, and social development, our focus will be on organized centers, in part because their use is growing rapidly and in part because that is where most of the research on day care has been done.

The quality of care is particularly important for infants, since stimulating interactions with responsive adults are crucial to a baby's cognitive and linguistic as well as emotional and social development (Burchinal, Roberts, Nabors, & Bryant, 1996). By and large, children in good day-care programs do at least as well cognitively and socially as those raised at home. High-quality day care seems to enhance emotional development, too. Let's look more closely at each of these domains.

Day Care and Cognitive Development

The most clear-cut conclusions emerge in the cognitive realm for children ages 2 to 4 who attend day-care centers. For example, 3-year-olds with day-care experience engage in more sophisticated pretend play with peers than those without such experience (Aureli & Colecchia, 1996). On a number of other cognitive measures, children in adequate or superior group day care seem to do as well as, or better than, children who spend the day at home with parents or baby-sitters or in day-care homes (refer back to Box 7-3). Where differences appear, children in good group day care—regardless of how long they have been in day care or how old they were when they entered—tend to score higher on IQ tests, to show more advanced eye-hand coordination and language skills, to play more creatively, to know more about the physical world, and to count and measure better; they are also more likely to know their names and addresses. However, this cognitive edge may be temporary; in some studies, by the end of first grade, home-reared children have caught up (A. Clarke-Stewart, 1992).

These children in a high-quality group day-care program are likely to do at least as well cognitively and socially as children cared for full time at home. The most important element of infant day care is the caregiver or teacher, who exerts a strong influence on the children in her care.

The importance of quality of care emerges in a study of nine day-care centers in Bermuda, where 84 percent of 2-year-olds spend most of the workweek. When caregivers spoke often to children to give or ask for information and encouraged children to start conversations with them, the children (as we reported in Chapter 6) did better on tests of language development (McCartney, 1984). In a follow-up study (D. Phillips, McCartney, & Scarr, 1987), children who talked often with their caregivers were also more sociable and considerate, showing a link between cognitive influences and psychosocial development. The quality and amount of verbal stimulation seemed even more important for social development than the children's family background.

Children from low-income families or stressful homes benefit the most from good day care. Disadvantaged children in good programs tend not to show the declines in IQ often seen when such children reach school age, and they may be more motivated to learn (AAP, 1986; Belsky, 1984; Bronfenbrenner, Belsky, & Steinberg, 1977). In one study, children who had been in high-quality infant care were more likely to be assigned to gifted programs in elementary school and, as sixth graders, to get higher math grades (T. Field, 1991).

Even modest variations in care can make a difference, as seen in a study of 79 African American 12-month-olds who had been in poor to mediocre urban community-based day-care centers full time for 2 months or more. Their scores on the Bayley Scales, as well as on measures of language and communicative skills, were related to the quality of care they received, even after adjusting for such factors as gender, poverty, and characteristics of the home environment (Burchinal et al., 1996). The good news from this study is the possibility of nipping school failure in the bud by improving day care for at-risk infants; the bad news is that poor-quality programs, such as most of those observed in this study, may set the stage for future failure.

Day Care and Emotional Development

A complex issue is the effect of infant day care on attachment to the mother. Evidence suggests that regular, early care outside the home or by someone other than the mother does not in itself affect security of attachment; but unstable, poor-quality, or more-than-minimal amounts of child care—when added to the effects of insensitive, unresponsive mothering—make insecure attachment more likely (NICHD Early Child Care Research Network, 1997a).

An ongoing longitudinal study of 1,153 children and their families was designed to separate the effect of day care from effects of the mother's and child's personalities and of the care the child receives at home (NICHD Early Child Care Research Network, 1997a). The study began in 1991 in ten locations across the United States; samples reflect the economic, educational, and ethnic composition of each local area. Investigators observed mothers and babies in their homes when the babies were 1 month, 6 months, and 15 months old and observed the babies in their child care facilities at 6 and 15 months. The mothers filled out questionnaires and personality inventories, and observers rated how they cared for their babies. The observers also noted the infants' temperamental characteristics. At 15 months, the researchers assessed the children's attachment to their mothers by means of the Strange Situation.

The study found no direct, independent effect of child care on attachment, no matter how early infants entered nonmaternal care or how many hours they spent in it. Nor did the stability or quality of care make a difference. However, infants whose mothers were insensitive and unresponsive tended to be insecurely attached if they got poor-quality or unstable day care or received outside care for 10 or more hours a week. Apparently, children in unfavorable day-care arrangements are harmed more by a mother's negative behavior than are children in favorable care arrangements, who may be able to form secure attachments to other caregivers. One curious gender difference emerged: Boys who spent more than 30 hours a week in child care and girls who spent fewer than 10 hours a week were somewhat more likely to be insecurely attached, suggesting that boys react more negatively to a mother's prolonged absence. The reasons why girls do better with more extensive care may emerge with further analysis of the findings.

This research supports an earlier finding that boys who receive more than 35 hours a week of substitute care tend to be insecurely attached to both parents. This earlier research also found that factors other than day care affected attachment. The most vulnerable boys had been "difficult" babies and had mothers who were dissatisfied with their marriages, insensitive to other people, and strongly career-motivated (Belsky & Rovine, 1988).

Day Care and Social Development

Findings about effects of infant day care on social development are mixed. In general, children who have spent much of their first year in day care tend to be as, or more, sociable, self-confident, persistent, and achieving, and better at solving problems than children who were at home. Day-care-raised preschoolers also tend to be more comfortable in new situations, more outgoing, less timid and fearful, more helpful and cooperative, and more verbally expressive (A. Clarke-Stewart,

1992; K. A. Clarke-Stewart, 1989). One study of children who started day care, on average, at just under 7 months found that between 5 and 8 years of age they had more friends and were more physically affectionate with them, took part in more extracurricular activities, and were more assertive than children who had been at home as infants (T. Field, 1991). However, day-care children also have been found to be more disobedient and less polite to adults, bossier and more aggressive with other children, louder, more boisterous, and more demanding (A. Clarke-Stewart, 1992; K. A. Clarke-Stewart, 1989).

Among 36 children in a semirural area who entered day care before the age of 8 months, quality of care was a better predictor of social adjustment than age of entry or how many hours an infant spent in day care. Temperamentally vulnerable infants may be at risk of social difficulties if placed in poor-quality day care (Volling & Feagans, 1995).

The most important element in the quality of care is the caregiver or teacher. How children relate to caregivers can strongly influence their behavior with their peers. In one longitudinal study, 4-year-olds who had formed secure attachments to their earliest and current child-care teachers tended to be more sociable, sensitive, empathic, and better-liked than those who were insecurely attached (Howes, Matheson, & Hamilton, 1994). A relationship with a caregiver has several dimensions, each of which may affect social development in different ways and at different ages. Four-year-olds who as toddlers felt secure with their caregivers tend to be more gregarious and less aggressive. Those who got along well with the early teacher tend to be popular with other children. Children who are overly dependent on their current preschool teachers are more aggressive and socially withdrawn (Howes, Hamilton, & Matheson, 1994).

However infants and toddlers are cared for, the experiences of the first 3 years lay a foundation for future development. In Part III, we'll see how young children build on that foundation.

CHECKPOINT

Can you . . .

- Name at least five criteria for good day care?
- Cite evidence of the impact of day care on cognitive development, attachment, and social development?

SUMMARY

Foundations of Psychosocial Development

- Foundations of psychosocial development include **emotions, temperament,** and early experiences with parents.
- The development and expression of various emotions seem to be tied to brain maturation and cognitive development, including development of **self-awareness.**
- Infants show their emotions by crying, smiling, and laughing.
- Temperamentally, children seem to fall into three categories: **easy children, difficult children,** and **slow-to-warm-up children.** These temperamental patterns appear to be largely inborn and are generally stable. **Goodness of fit** between a child's temperament and environmental demands is important for adjustment.
- Infants have strong needs for closeness and warmth as well as physical care.
- Infants' and toddlers' experiences with mothers and fathers generally differ; mothers, even when employed outside the home, spend more time in infant care, and mothers and fathers in some cultures have different styles of play with babies.
- Significant physiological and behavioral differences between the sexes typically do not appear until after infancy. However, parents begin **gender-typing** boys and girls almost from birth.
- Most children today have two to four living grandparents. Geographic and emotional distance may diminish the connection with grandparents; but especially during infancy and toddlerhood, some grandparents are heavily involved in grandchildren's lives and strongly influence their development.

Developmental Issues in Infancy

- According to Erikson, infants in the first 18 months of life experience the first in a series of eight crises that influence personality development throughout life. Successful resolution of the first crisis, **basic trust versus basic mistrust,** results in the "virtue" of *hope.*

- On the basis of the **Strange Situation,** three main patterns of **attachment** to parents have been found: **secure attachment** and two types of insecure attachment, **avoidant attachment** and **ambivalent (resistant) attachment.** A fourth pattern, **disorganized-disoriented attachment,** may be the least secure.

- Newer instruments for measuring attachment in natural settings include the **Attachment Q-Set (AQS)** and the **Preschool Assessment of Attachment (PAA).** The **Adult Attachment Interview (AAI)** can predict the security of attachment on the basis of a parent's memories of her or his own childhood attachment.

- Attachment patterns may depend on a baby's temperament and other characteristics, as well as on the quality of parenting, and may have long-term implications for development.

- According to the **mutual regulation** model, babies play an active part in regulating their emotional states by sending and receiving emotional signals.

- A mother's **depression,** especially if severe or chronic, can have serious consequences for the infant's development.

- **Separation anxiety** and **stranger anxiety** may arise during the second half of the first year and appear to be related to temperament and life circumstances.

- The belief that babies, after about 6 months of age, display **social referencing** is in dispute.

Developmental Issues in Toddlerhood

- The **self-concept** begins to emerge in the following sequence: (1) physical self-recognition and self-awarenesss, (2) self-description and self-evaluation, and (3) emotional response to wrongdoing.

- Erikson's second crisis, which a toddler faces from about 18 months to 3 years, concerns **autonomy versus shame and doubt.** Successful resolution results in the "virtue" of *will.*

- **Negativism** is normal during this time.

- **Socialization,** which rests on **internalization** of societally approved standards, begins with the development of **self-regulation.** A precursor of **conscience** is **committed compliance** to a caregiver's demands; toddlers who show committed compliance tend to internalize adult rules more readily than those who show merely **situational compliance.**

- Parenting styles and demands, the **reciprocity** of the parent-child relationship, the child's temperament, and cultural and class standards may be factors in the ease and success of socialization.

Contact With Other Children

- Siblings influence each other both positively and negatively from an early age. Parents' actions and attitudes affect sibling relationships.

- Contact with other children, especially during toddlerhood, affects cognitive and psychosocial development.

- High-quality day care appears to have a generally positive impact on cognitive, emotional, and social development. Although the effect of early day care on attachment is complex, day care does not seem to be harmful unless it is poor-quality, unstable, or extensive and is combined with insensitive, unresponsive mothering.

KEY TERMS

emotions (234)
self-awareness (235)
temperament (237)
easy children (238)
difficult children (238)
slow-to-warm-up children (238)
goodness of fit (238)
gender-typing (243)
basic trust versus basic mistrust (245)
attachment (245)
Strange Situation (246)
secure attachment (246)
avoidant attachment (246)
ambivalent (resistant) attachment (246)
disorganized-disoriented attachment (246)
Attachment Q-Set (AQS) (248)
Preschool Assessment of Attachment
  (PAA) (248)
Adult Attachment Interview (AAI) (250)
mutual regulation (252)
depression (253)
stranger anxiety (255)
separation anxiety (255)
social referencing (256)
self-concept (257)
autonomy versus shame and doubt (258)
negativism (259)
socialization (259)
internalization (259)
self-regulation (260)
conscience (260)
committed compliance (261)
situational compliance (261)
reciprocity (262)

QUESTIONS FOR THOUGHT AND DISCUSSION

1. "Despite the increasingly active role today's fathers play in child care, a mother will always be more important to babies and young children than a father." Do you agree or disagree?

2. Should parents try to treat male and female infants and toddlers alike?

3. Do (or did) your grandparents fit the traditional role or the contemporary role described in this chapter? On the basis of your own early memories or of what family members have told you, can you assess your grandparents' impact on your development and on your family, especially during your first three years of life?

4. How would you expect each of the three stages in self-concept development described in this chapter to affect or change the parent-child relationship?

5. As reported in this chapter, Ainsworth's (1964) finding that attachment to the mother develops well before attachment to the father appears to be contradicted by more recent research. Can you suggest possible reasons for the difference in the later findings?

6. In line with stage theorists' belief that each developmental stage lays the groundwork for the next, what difference might security of attachment make in the way a child experiences the next developmental task, development of autonomy?

7. In view of Kochanska's research on the roots of conscience, what questions would you ask about the early socialization of antisocial adolescents and adults, whose conscience appears to be severely underdeveloped?

8. Given the cultural differences in socialization described in this chapter, would you expect to find the "terrible twos" to be a universal phase of development? Why or why not?

9. Would you like to see the United States adopt child-care policies similar to those in Sweden? Why or why not?

10. In light of the findings about cognitive, emotional, and social effects of day care, what advice would you give a new mother about the timing of her return to work and the selection of child care?

Early Childhood: *A Bird's-Eye View*

Early Childhood

During the years from 3 to 6, often called the *preschool years*, children make the transition from toddlerhood to childhood. Their bodies become slimmer, their motor and mental abilities sharper, and their personalities and relationships more complex.

Children who have celebrated their third birthday are no longer babies. They are capable of bigger and better things. The 3-year-old is a sturdy adventurer, very much at home in the world and eager to explore its possibilities, as well as the developing capabilities of his or her own body and mind. A child of this age has come through a relatively dangerous time of life—the years of infancy and toddlerhood—to enter a healthier, less threatening phase.

Change is less rapid in early childhood than in infancy and toddlerhood, but all aspects of development—physical, cognitive, emotional, and social—continue to intertwine. As muscles come under more conscious control, children can tend to more of their own personal needs, such as dressing and toileting, and thus gain a greater sense of competence and independence. Even the common cold can have cognitive and emotional implications, as we'll see in Chapter 8. Cognitive mastery of the rules of syntax and the secrets of conversation (Chapter 9) enables children to communicate more effectively with others, internalize societal standards, and develop friendships (Chapter 10). The neighborhood environment and wider societal influences can have a profound impact—for better or for worse—on physical health and cognitive growth. Yet, even as we describe general patterns that apply to many or most children, we need to look at each child as a unique person, setting more and more challenging goals and finding more and more diverse ways to meet them.

Physical Development and Health in Early Childhood

Children's playings are not sports and should be deemed as their most serious actions.

Montaigne, *Essays*

Focus
Wang Yani

Wang Yani is a gifted young Chinese artist. Now in her early twenties, she had her first exhibit in Shanghai at the age of 4 and produced 4,000 paintings by the time she turned 6. Since she was 10, her work has been shown throughout Asia and in Europe and the United States.

Yani (her given name)* began painting at 2½. Her father, Wang Shiqiang, was a professional artist and educator. One day she picked up a piece of charcoal and began drawing on the wall, imitating her father as she stood back, head tilted, arm on hip, to examine her creation. Another time, when her father was out, she mixed his oil paints and brushed them over a painting he had been working on. When he returned and started to punish her, she cried, "I was helping you paint. I want to paint like you!"

Her father, whose parents had responded to his own early artistic efforts by punishing him for making "messes," resolved to treat his daughter differently. He gave her big brushes and large sheets of paper to permit bold strokes. Rather than teach her, he let her learn by doing, in her own way, and always praised her work. In contrast with traditional Chinese art education, which emphasizes conformity and imitation, he allowed his daughter's spontaneity and imagination free rein. Later he even stopped painting himself, so she would not be influenced by his style.

Yani went through the usual stages in preschoolers' drawing, from scribbling to pictorial, far more quickly than usual. Her early paintings after the scribble stage were symbolic—made up of dots, circles, and apparently meaningless lines, which stood for people, birds, or fruit. By the age of 3, she painted recognizable but highly original forms. Yani painted nonstop every day. Once, at age 4, she refused to go to bed until almost midnight, making ten paintings in a row until she was satisfied that she had done her best.

Yani's father encouraged her to paint what she saw outdoors: the lotus flowers, pine trees, and animals near their home in the scenic riverside town of Gongcheng. Like traditional Chinese artists, she did not paint from life but constructed her brightly colored paintings from mental images of what she had seen. Her father helped develop her powers of observation, carrying her on his shoulders as he hiked in the mountains and fields or lying with her in the grass and telling stories about the passing clouds. In the pieces of pine bark Yani picked up, she saw shapes of dragons, chickens, or dogs. The pebbles along the riverbank reminded her of the monkeys that fascinated her at the zoo.

*In Chinese custom, the given name follows the family name.

Because of her short arms, Yani's brush strokes at first were short. Her father trained her to hold her brush tightly by trying to grab it from behind when she was not looking. She learned to paint with her whole arm, twisting her wrist to produce the effect she wanted. As her physical dexterity and experience grew, her strokes became more forceful, varied, and precise: broad, wet strokes to define an animal's shape; fuzzy, nearly dry ones to suggest feathers, fur, or tree bark. She listened to music as she painted, and her brush danced across the canvas.

With quick reflexes, a fertile imagination, strong motivation and persistence, beautiful natural surroundings, and her father's sensitive guidance, Yani's artistic progress has been swift. As a young adult, she is considered an artist of great promise. Yet she herself considers painting very simple: "You just paint what you think about. You don't have to follow any instruction. Everybody can paint" (Zhensun & Low, 1991, p. 9).

Sources of biographical information about Wang Yani are Bond, 1989; Costello, 1990; Ho, 1989; and Zhensun & Low, 1991.

• • •

Although Wang Yani's artistic growth has been unusual, it rested on a typical physical development of early childhood: improvement in the ability to make the hand do the eye's bidding. Youngsters between the ages of 3 and 6 grow less rapidly than before, but their muscular development and hand-eye coordination allow them to do much more. Like other children, Yani's gain in fine motor skills was accompanied by a growing cognitive understanding of the world around her, which helped her express her thoughts and feelings through art—an understanding guided by her social experiences with her father and others.

In this chapter, as we look at physical development during the years from 3 to 6, we will see other examples of its interconnection with cognitive and psychosocial development. Nutrition and handedness are influenced by cultural attitudes, and sleep patterns by emotional experiences. Environmental influences, including the parents' life circumstances, affect health and safety. The link between developmental realms is especially evident in the tragic results of child abuse and neglect, poverty, and homelessness; although the most obvious effects may be physical, these conditions affect other aspects of a child's development as well.

After reading this chapter, you should be able to answer and elaborate on such questions as these:

Preview Questions

- How do children grow and change physically between ages 3 and 6, and how do their diet and sleep patterns change?

- What are the major motor achievements of early childhood?

- How does children's artwork show their physical and cognitive maturation?

- How can young children be kept safe and healthy?

- What are the causes and consequences of child abuse and neglect?

Table 8-1	Physical Growth, Ages 3 to 6 (50th percentile)*			
	Height, Inches		**Weight, Pounds**	
Age	**Boys**	**Girls**	**Boys**	**Girls**
3	38	37¼	32¼	31¼
3½	39¼	39¼	34¼	34
4	40¼	40½	36½	36¼
4½	42	42	38½	38½
5	43¼	43	41½	41
5½	45	44½	45½	44
6	46	46	48	47

*Fifty percent of children in each category are above this height or weight level, and 50 percent are below it.
Source: Lowrey, 1978.

Physiological Growth and Change

At about age 3, children slim down and shoot up. They begin to lose their baby-ish roundness and take on the slender, athletic appearance of childhood. As abdominal muscles develop, the toddler potbelly tightens. The trunk, arms, and legs grow longer. The head is still relatively large, but the other parts of the body continue to catch up as body proportions steadily become more adultlike.

The pencil mark on the wall that shows Keisha's height at 3 years is a little more than 37 inches from the floor, and she now weighs more than 31 pounds. Boys at age 3 are slightly taller and heavier than girls and have more muscle per pound of body weight, while girls have more fatty tissue. Both boys and girls typically grow 2 to 3 inches a year during early childhood and gain 4 to 6 pounds annually (see Table 8-1). Boys' slight edge in height and weight continues until the growth spurt of puberty.

These changes in appearance reflect developments inside the body. Muscular and skeletal growth progresses, making children stronger. Cartilage turns to bone at a faster rate than before, and bones become harder and stronger, giving the child a firmer shape and protecting the internal organs. These changes, coordinated by the maturing brain and nervous system, promote the development of a wide range of motor skills. The increased capacities of the respiratory and circulatory systems build physical stamina and, along with the developing immune system, keep children healthier.

By age 3, all 20 primary, or deciduous, teeth are in place, and children can chew anything they want to. The widespread use of fluoride and high levels of dental care have dramatically reduced the incidence of tooth decay in children (Herrmann & Roberts, 1987).

Aside from giving a baby a pacifier to help satisfy sucking needs, parents usually can safely ignore the normal and common habit of thumb-sucking in children under 4 years of age. However, the permanent teeth, which begin to develop long before they appear at about age 6, may be affected if thumb-sucking does not stop after age 4. If children stop sucking thumbs or fingers by then, their teeth are not likely to be permanently affected (Herrmann & Roberts, 1987; Umberger & Van Reenen, 1995).

If thumb-sucking continues after age 4, treatment may be indicated, depending on the age of the child, the severity of the habit, and what emotional needs it may be meeting. If thumb-sucking has become an issue between parents and child, ignoring the habit for a month or so may cause it to stop. To help break the habit, the child may be fitted with a dental appliance that discourages sucking and corrects any existing malformation of the teeth. Success rates with these appliances have been high (Umberger & Van Reenen, 1995).

Box 8-1   Helping Children Eat and Sleep Well

One child refuses to eat anything but peanut butter and jelly sandwiches. Another seems to live on bananas. Mealtimes seem more like art class, as preschoolers make snowmen out of mashed potatoes or lakes out of applesauce, and food remains uneaten on the plate.

Although a diminished appetite in early childhood is normal, many parents make the mistake of insisting that children eat more than they want, setting in motion a contest of wills. Bedtime, too, often becomes an issue ("Daddy, leave the light on! . . . I want a drink of water. . . . What's that noise by the window? . . . I'm cold"). When a child delays or has trouble going to sleep or wakes often during the night, parents tend to become irritated, and the entire family feels the strain.

The following research-based suggestions can help make mealtimes and bedtimes pleasanter and children healthier (L. A. Adams & Rickert, 1989; American Academy of Pediatrics [AAP], 1992b; Graziano & Mooney, 1982; E. R. Williams & Caliendo, 1984):

Encouraging Healthy Eating Habits

- Keep a record of what a child eats. The child may in fact be eating enough.
- Serve simple, easily identifiable foods. Preschoolers often balk at mixed dishes such as casseroles.
- Serve finger foods as often as possible.
- Introduce only one new food at a time, along with a familiar one the child likes.
- Offer small servings, especially of new or disliked foods; give second helpings if wanted.
- After a reasonable time, remove the food and do not serve more until the next meal. A healthy child will not suffer from missing a meal, and children need to learn that certain times are appropriate for eating.
- Give the child a choice of foods containing similar nutrients: rye or whole wheat bread, a peach or an apple, yogurt or milk.
- Encourage a child to help prepare food by making sandwiches or mixing and spooning out cookie dough.
- Have nutritious snack foods handy and allow the child to select favorites.
- Turn childish delights to advantage. Serve food in appealing dishes; dress it up with garnishes or little toys; make a "party" out of a meal.

- Don't fight "rituals," in which a child eats foods one at a time, in a certain order.
- Make mealtimes pleasant with conversation on interesting topics, keeping talk about eating itself to a minimum.

Helping Children Go to Sleep

- Establish a regular, unrushed bedtime routine—about 20 minutes of quiet activities, such as reading a story, singing lullabies, or having quiet conversation.
- Allow no scary or loud television shows.
- Avoid highly stimulating, active play before bedtime.
- Keep a small night light on if it makes the child feel more comfortable.
- Stay calm but don't yield to requests for "just one more" story, one more drink of water, or one more bathroom trip.
- If you're trying to break a child's habit, offer rewards for good bedtime behavior, such as stickers on a chart, or simple praise.
- Try putting your child to sleep a little later. Sending a child to bed too early is a common reason for sleep problems.
- If a child's fears about the dark or going to sleep have persisted for a long time, look for a program to help the child learn how to relax, how to substitute pleasant thoughts for frightening ones, and how to cope with stressful situations.

Helping Children Go Back to Sleep

- If a child gets up during the night, take him or her back to bed. Speak calmly, pat the child gently on the back, but be pleasantly firm and consistent.
- After a nightmare, reassure a frightened child and occasionally check in on the child. If frightening dreams persist for more than 6 weeks, consult your doctor.
- After night terrors, do not wake the child. If the child wakes, don't ask any questions. Just let the child go back to sleep.
- Help your child get enough sleep on a regular schedule; overtired or stressed children are more prone to night terrors.
- Walk or carry a sleepwalking child back to bed. Child-proof your home with gates at the top of stairs and at windows and with bells on the child's bedroom door, so you'll know when she or he is out of bed.

As in infancy and toddlerhood, proper growth and health depend on good nutrition and adequate sleep (see Box 8-1). However, preschoolers' dietary and sleep needs are quite different from those of infants or toddlers. They are more likely to become overweight, especially if they are not very active, and many develop sleep-related problems.

Diet and Obesity

Preschoolers eat less in proportion to their size than infants do; as growth slows, they need fewer calories per pound of body weight. Parents often worry that their children are not eating enough, but preschool children seem to know how much food they need. In one study, 15 children ages 2 to 5 took in roughly the same number of calories every day for 6 days, even though they often ate very little at one meal and a great deal at another (Birch, Johnson, Andersen, Peters, & Schulte, 1991).

Preschoolers whose mothers let them eat when they are hungry and do not pressure them to eat everything given to them are more likely to regulate their own caloric intake than are children with more controlling mothers (S. L. Johnson & Birch, 1994). A child who is energetic, with good muscle tone, bright eyes, glossy hair, and the ability to spring back quickly from fatigue, is unlikely to be undernourished (E. R. Williams & Caliendo, 1984). (We discuss malnutrition in Chapter 11.)

What children eat is a different matter. According to a U.S. Department of Agriculture survey, only 1 percent of children and adolescents ages 2 to 19 meet all recommended dietary guidelines, and 16 percent meet none. Young people of all ages eat too much fat and sugar and too few servings of fruits, vegetables, grains, and dairy products. Diets of poor and minority children are especially deficient (Muñoz, Krebs-Smith, Ballard-Barbash, & Cleveland, 1997).

The nutritional demands of early childhood are easily satisfied. The daily protein requirement can be met with two glasses of milk and one serving of meat or an alternative such as fish, cheese, or eggs. Vitamin A can come from carrots, spinach, egg yolk, or whole milk (among other foods). Vitamin C is in citrus fruits, tomatoes, and leafy dark-green vegetables. Calcium, essential to build bone mass, can come from dairy products, broccoli, and canned salmon (especially the bones); lactose-intolerant children, who cannot digest milk, can get necessary nutrients from other foods. Children whose diets are high in "empty calories" from sugared cereal, cake, candy, and other low-nutrient foods will not have enough appetite for the foods they need; so parents should offer only nutritious foods, even for snacks.

Although preschoolers eat less in proportion to their size than infants do, they can fulfill their nutritional needs quite easily—and enjoyably. Since they eat so little, it's important that their snacks, as well as their regular meals, be nutritious.

Children over age 2 should get only about 30 percent of their total calories from fat, and less than 10 percent of the total from saturated fat. Meat and dairy foods should remain in the diet to provide protein, iron, and calcium; but meat should be lean, and milk and other dairy products can now be skim or low-fat (AAP Committee on Nutrition, 1992a). A study that followed a predominantly Hispanic group of 215 healthy 3- to 4-year-olds for 1 to 2 years found no negative effects on height, weight, or body mass from a moderately low-fat diet (Shea et al., 1993).

Today there are more obese preschoolers, especially girls (who tend to be less active than boys), than there were 25 years ago. Between the early 1970s and 1994, the proportion of 4- and 5-year-old girls who were above the 95th percentile of standard growth curves of weight for height increased from 5.8 percent to 10.8 percent; for boys, the increase was from 4.4 to 5 percent. Mexican American children of both sexes are most likely to be overweight. These patterns are similar to those seen for older children and adults (Ogden et al., 1997).

Although a fat baby is usually no cause for concern, a fat child may be. Overweight children, especially those who have overweight parents, tend to become overweight adults (Whitaker, Wright, Pepe, Seidel, & Dietz, 1997), and excess body mass can be a threat to health. A tendency to obesity is partly hereditary, but it also depends on fat intake and exercise (R. S. Jackson et al., 1997; Klesges, Klesges, Eck, & Shelton, 1995; Leibel, 1997; Ogden et al., 1997). Early to middle childhood is a good time to treat obesity, when a child's diet is still subject to parental influence or control (Whitaker et al., 1997). Obesity is discussed further in Chapters 11 and 14.

Sleep and Bedtime Patterns and Problems

Sleep patterns change throughout life, and early childhood has its own distinct rhythms (see Figure 8-1). Young children usually sleep more deeply at night than they will later in life, but they still need a daytime nap or quiet rest until about age 5.

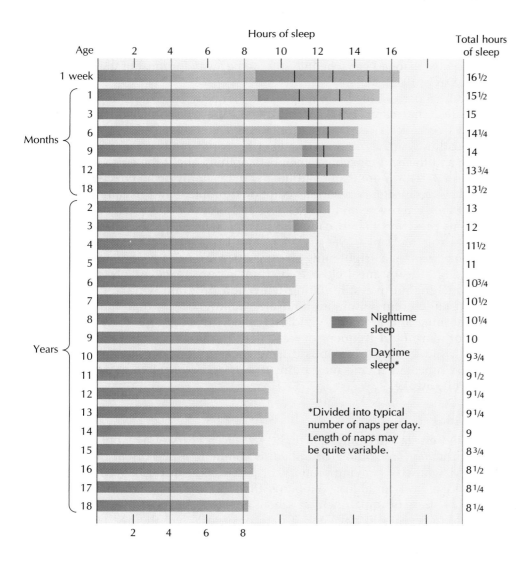

Age | Hours of sleep | Total hours of sleep

1 week — 16½

Months
1 — 15½
3 — 15
6 — 14¼
9 — 14
12 — 13¾
18 — 13½

Years
2 — 13
3 — 12
4 — 11½
5 — 11
6 — 10¾
7 — 10½
8 — 10¼
9 — 10
10 — 9¾
11 — 9½
12 — 9¼
13 — 9¼
14 — 9
15 — 8¾
16 — 8½
17 — 8¼
18 — 8¼

Nighttime sleep

Daytime sleep*

*Divided into typical number of naps per day. Length of naps may be quite variable.

Figure 8-1

Typical sleep requirements in childhood. Unlike infants, who sleep about as long day and night, preschoolers get all or almost all their sleep in one long nighttime period. The number of hours of sleep steadily decreases throughout childhood, but individual children may need more or fewer hours than shown here.

Source: Ferber, 1985.

Going to bed in the evening often becomes an issue. Young children may develop elaborate bedtime routines to put off retiring, and it may take them longer than before to fall asleep. They are likely to want a light left on and to sleep with a favorite toy or blanket (Beltramini & Hertzig, 1983). Such *transitional objects,* used repeatedly as bedtime companions, help a child shift from the dependence of infancy to the independence of later childhood. Parents sometimes worry if their child cannot fall asleep without a tattered blanket or stuffed animal, but such worry seems unfounded. In one longitudinal study, 11-year-olds who at age 4 had insisted on taking cuddly objects to bed were now outgoing, sociable with adults, and self-confident; they enjoyed playing by themselves and tended not to be worriers. At age 16, they were just as well adjusted as children who had not used transitional objects (Newson, Newson, & Mahalski, 1982).

Walking and talking during sleep are fairly common in early childhood and are usually harmless. However, persistent sleep disturbances may indicate an emotional problem that needs to be examined.

Sleep Disturbances

About 20 to 30 percent of children in their first 4 years engage in *bedtime struggles* lasting more than an hour and wake their parents frequently at night. Five experiences tend to distinguish children with these problems. One is sleeping in the same bed with parents; it is simply more tempting and easier to wake someone in the same bed than in the next room. The other four conditions signal family

transitional objects Objects used repeatedly by a child as bedtime companions.

stress. The family is likely to have experienced a stressful accident or illness; or the mother is likely to be depressed, to have mixed feelings about the child, or to have recently changed her schedule so as to be away for most of the day (Lozoff, Wolf, & Davis, 1985).

About 25 percent of children ages 3 to 8, mostly boys, have night terrors or nightmares (Hartmann, 1981). A child who experiences a *night terror* awakens abruptly from a deep sleep in a state of panic. The child may scream and sit up in bed, breathing rapidly and staring. Yet he is not really awake, quiets down quickly, and the next morning remembers nothing about the episode. Night terrors alarm parents more than children and may simply be an effect of very deep sleep; they rarely signify a serious emotional problem and usually go away by age 6. If they are severe and long-lasting and occur once a week or more, some physicians prescribe a short course of therapy with an antihistamine or antidepressant drug (McDaniel, 1986).

A *nightmare* is a frightening dream, often brought on by staying up too late, eating a heavy meal close to bedtime, or overexcitement—for example, from watching an overstimulating television program. Unlike night terrors, which usually occur within an hour after falling asleep, nightmares come toward morning and are often vividly recalled. An occasional bad dream is no cause for alarm, but frequent or persistent nightmares, especially those that make a child fearful or anxious during waking hours, may signal excessive stress. A repeated theme may point to a specific problem the child cannot solve while awake.

Bed-Wetting

enuresis Repeated urination in clothing or in bed.

Most children stay dry, day and night, by 3 to 5 years of age; but ***enuresis,*** repeated urination in clothing or in bed, is common, especially at night. A child may be diagnosed as having primary, or persistent, enuresis if wetting occurs at least twice a week for at least 3 months after age 5, or if the condition is causing significant stress or impairment at school or in other everyday activities. About 7 percent of 5-year-old boys and 3 percent of girls wet the bed regularly, but most outgrow the condition without special help (American Psychiatric Association [APA], 1994). Fewer than 1 percent of bed-wetters have a physical disorder. Nor is persistent enuresis primarily an emotional problem.

Enuresis runs in families. About 75 percent of bed-wetters have a close relative who also wets the bed, and identical twins are more concordant for the condition than fraternal twins (APA, 1994; Fergusson, Horwood, & Shannon, 1986). The discovery of the approximate site of a gene linked to enuresis (Eiberg, Berendt, & Mohr, 1995) points to heredity as a major factor, possibly in combination with such other factors as slow motor maturation, allergies, and poor behavioral control (Goleman, 1995). The gene does not appear to account for occasional bed-wetting.

CHECKPOINT

Can you . . .

- Describe typical physiological changes around the age of 3?
- Summarize preschoolers' dietary needs?
- Identify three common sleep problems and give recommendations for handling them?

Children and their parents need to be reassured that enuresis is common and not serious. The child is not to blame and should not be punished. Generally parents need not do anything unless children themselves see bed-wetting as a problem. The most effective treatments include rewarding children for staying dry; waking them when they begin to urinate by using devices that ring bells or buzzers; and teaching children to practice controlling the sphincter muscles and to stretch the bladder (Rappaport, 1993). As a last resort, hormones or antidepressant drugs may be given for a short time (Goleman, 1995; McDaniel, 1986).

Motor Development

Children ages 3 to 6 make great advances in motor skills—both *gross motor skills,* such as running and jumping, and *fine motor skills,* such as buttoning and

Table 8-2	Gross Motor Skills in Early Childhood		
	3-Year-Olds	**4-Year-Olds**	**5-Year-Olds**
	Cannot turn or stop suddenly or quickly	Have more effective control of stopping, starting, and turning	Can start, turn, and stop effectively in games
	Can jump a distance of 15 to 24 inches	Can jump a distance of 24 to 33 inches	Can make a running jump of 28 to 36 inches
	Can ascend a stairway unaided, alternating feet	Can descend a long stairway alternating feet, if supported	Can descend a long stairway unaided, alternating feet
	Can hop, using largely an irregular series of jumps with some variations added	Can hop four to six steps on one foot	Can easily hop a distance of 16 feet

Source: Corbin, 1973.

drawing. They also begin to show a preference for either the right or left hand. As with Wang Yani, artistic development reflects growing motor, cognitive, and emotional maturity.

Motor Skills

At 3, David could walk a straight line and jump a short distance. At 4, he could hop a few steps on one foot. On his fifth birthday, he could jump nearly 3 feet and hop for 16 feet and was learning to roller-skate—all *gross motor skills,* which involve the large muscles (see Table 8-2).

gross motor skills Physical skills that involve the large muscles.

During early childhood the sensory and motor areas of the cortex are more developed than before, permitting children to do more of what they want to do. Their bones and muscles are stronger, and their lung capacity is greater, making it possible to run, jump, and climb farther, faster, and better.

At about 2½, children begin to jump with both feet, a skill they have not been able to master before this time, probably because their leg muscles were not yet strong enough to propel their body weight upward. Hopping is hard to master until about 4 years of age. Going upstairs is easier than going down; by 3½, most children comfortably alternate feet going up, but not until about 5 do they easily descend that way. Children begin to gallop at about 4, do fairly well by 5, and are quite skillful by 6½. Skipping is harder; although some 4-year-olds can skip, most children cannot do it until age 6 (Corbin, 1973). Of course, children vary in adeptness, depending on their genetic endowment and their opportunities to learn and practice motor skills.

The gross motor skills developed during early childhood are the basis for sports, dancing, and other activities that begin during middle childhood and may continue for a lifetime. There seems to be virtually no limit to the number and kind of motor acts children can learn, at least to some degree, by the age of 6. However, those under 6 are rarely ready to take part in any organized sport. Only 20 percent of 4-year-olds can throw a ball well, and only 30 percent can catch well (AAP Committee on Sports Medicine and Fitness, 1992).

Young children develop best physically when they can be active at an appropriate maturational level in unstructured free play. Parents and teachers can help by offering young children the opportunity to climb and jump on safe, properly sized equipment, by providing balls and other toys small enough to be easily grasped and soft enough not to be harmful, and by offering gentle coaching when a child seems to need help.

Fine motor skills, such as tying shoelaces, cutting with scissors, drawing, and painting, involve eye-hand and small-muscle coordination. Gains in these skills allow young children to take more responsibility for their personal care.

fine motor skills Physical skills that involve the small muscles and eye-hand coordination.

Left-handed people, like this girl, are likely to be better at spatial tasks and may be more likely to be gifted. They also, however, are more likely to have accidents, allergies, and reading and behavior problems. For the most part, neither left- nor right-handedness is clearly superior.

systems of action
Combinations of motor skills that permit increasingly complex activities.

At 3, Winnie can pour milk into her cereal bowl, eat with silverware, and use the toilet alone. She can also draw a circle and a rudimentary person—without arms. At 4, Michael can dress himself with help. He can cut along a line, draw a fairly complete person, make designs and crude letters, and fold paper into a double triangle. At 5, Juan can dress himself without much help, copy a square or triangle, and draw a more elaborate person than before.

As they develop both types of motor skills, preschoolers continually merge abilities they already have with those they are acquiring, to produce more complex capabilities. Such combinations of skills are known as *systems of action.*

As we have mentioned, boys are slightly stronger than girls and have slightly more muscle (Garai & Scheinfeld, 1968). However, girls typically outshine boys in gross motor tasks involving limb coordination. For example, girls at age 5 are better than boys at playing jumping jacks, tapping feet, balancing on one foot, hopping, and catching a ball (Cratty, 1979). Girls also tend to excel at tasks requiring small-muscle coordination. Differences in boys' and girls' abilities may reflect societal attitudes that encourage gender-typed activities. By 6½, boys typically throw and catch a ball better than girls, probably because parents and coaches tend to spend more time teaching boys these skills, which depend not only on maturation but also on learning and practice (Corbin, 1973).

Handedness

In the 1992 United States presidential election all three candidates—Bill Clinton, George Bush, and Ross Perot—were left-handed, a statistical improbability since about 9 out of 10 people are right-handed.

handedness   Preference for using a particular hand.

Handedness, the preference for using one hand over the other, is usually evident by 3 years of age. Since the left hemisphere of the brain, which controls the right side of the body, is usually dominant, most people favor their right side. In people whose brains are more symmetrical, the right hemisphere tends to dominate, making them left-handed (Coren, 1992; Porac & Coren, 1981). Handedness is not always clearcut; not everybody prefers one hand for every task.

Is handedness genetic or learned? That question has been controversial. A new theory proposes the existence of a single gene for right-handedness (Klar, 1996). According to this theory, people who inherit this gene from either or both parents—about 82 percent of the population—are right-handed. Those who do not inherit the gene still have a 50-50 chance of being right-handed; otherwise

Box 8-2 Cultural Attitudes Toward Handedness

Around the world and across the ages, many cultures have viewed left-handedness as undesirable and have tried to discourage it. In Japan, for example, many parents try to force their children to use the right hand, even going so far as to bind the left hand with tape. In many Islamic societies, the left hand is used for private washing after toileting; using the same hand for writing, for eating, or for serving food (among other things) is considered offensive. In the United States, some elderly adults who showed an early preference for the left hand remember being forced to learn how to write with the right hand.

Traces of the idea that left-handedness is abnormal can be found in the English language. For example, the word *sinister,* which suggests something evil, comes from the Latin word meaning "on the left"; and *gauche,* meaning "awkward," is borrowed from the French word for "left." Favorable connotations of right-handedness are implied in such words as *dexterity* and *adroitness,* both meaning "skillfulness"—the first from the Latin and the second from the French word for "right." The

word *right* itself has favorable connotations: "correct," "moral," "fitting," and "proper."

No culture has encouraged left-handedness and, though none has completely abolished it, some societies have reduced its incidence. In the most permissive societies, 10.4 percent of the population is left-handed (about the proportion in the United States). In less permissive societies, the proportion drops to 5.9 percent. In harsh, restrictive societies, it is only 1.8 percent (Hardyck & Petrinovich, 1977).

Since scientific evidence does not provide any reason for favoring "righties," prejudice against the left-handed is on the wane in western industrial countries. However, in other parts of the world superstitions surrounding left-handedness continue, and left-handed children still are forced to use their right hand. If, as discussed in this chapter, handedness is primarily genetic, such beliefs and practices may eventually die out, and environments and tools may be designed to make life easier for the large left-handed minority (Klar, 1996).

they will be left-handed or ambidextrous. Random determination of handedness among those who do not receive the gene could explain why some monozygotic twins have differing hand preferences, as well as why 8 percent of the offspring of two right-handed parents are left-handed. The theory closely predicted the proportion of left-handed offspring in a three-generational sample of families recruited through advertisements.

Interestingly, it is only human beings who mostly tend to be "righties"; among mice, for example, paw preference is randomly distributed. In humans, there is some evidence of a partial correlation between handedness and the side of the brain that controls speech (Klar, 1996).

Although right-handedness is usually the culturally preferred characteristic (see Box 8-2), "lefties" seem to have certain advantages. Benjamin Franklin, Michelangelo, Leonardo da Vinci, and Pablo Picasso were all left-handed. All had unusual spatial imagination, a quality that may be more highly developed in left-handed people. This may explain the high proportion of left-handed architects. Left-handed people may be more likely to be academically gifted. Among more than 100,000 twelve- and thirteen-year-olds who took the Scholastic Aptitude Test (SAT), 20 percent of the top-scoring 300 children were left-handed, twice the rate in the general population (Bower, 1985).

On the other hand, left-handed children are more likely to have accidents (Graham, Dick, Rickert, & Glenn, 1993), as well as allergies, sleep problems, and migraine headaches. Left-handers are also more prone to stuttering. They have higher rates of dyslexia, a reading disability, and of attention deficit disorder, a behavior problem, both of which are discussed in Chapter 12 (Coren & Halpern, 1991; Geschwind & Galaburda, 1985). Some research suggests that "lefties" are likely to die younger than "righties" (Coren & Halpern, 1991; Halpern & Coren, 1993). However, a reexamination of the evidence questions this conclusion; the presence of fewer left-handers in the oldest age groups may be more readily explained by the pressures that existed when these people were young for natural left-handers to switch to the right hand (L. J. Harris, 1993a, 1993b).

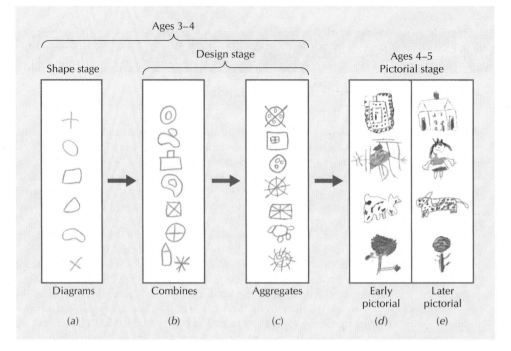

Figure 8-2
Artistic development in early childhood. There is a great difference between the very simple shapes shown in (a) and the detailed drawings in (e). The challenge for adults is to encourage children's creativity while acknowledging their growing facility in drawing.
Source: Kellogg, 1970.

On the whole, there is no compelling evidence that most left-handed people are significantly different from right-handed people in cognitive or physical abilities. Knowing which hand you hold your pencil in or pitch a ball with tells little about your skill as a writer or ballplayer.

Artistic Development

At 4, Demian draws one car or truck after another. When his mother encourages him to draw a person, he does—and then carefully draws wheels instead of feet. Demian's parents encourage his drawing, but they attach little importance to his artistic output. In this respect, they are similar to many early professional observers of child development. Now, however, we understand more about the significance of young children's art. With progress in fine motor coordination, children like Wang Yani are able to use their growing cognitive powers and express themselves emotionally in their art.

Stages of Children's Art Production

Rhoda Kellogg (1970) examined more than 1 million drawings by children, half of them under age 6. Since she found drawings by young children similar in different cultures, she concluded that stages in early drawing (see Figure 8-2) reflect maturation of the brain as well as of the muscles.

Two-year-olds *scribble.* Kellogg identified 20 basic scribbles, such as vertical and zigzag lines. In this first stage of drawing, the child is concerned chiefly with the placement of scribbles. Kellogg identified 17 patterns of placement of scribbles on paper that appear by age 2.

By age 3, the *shape* stage appears. Now a child draws diagrams in six basic shapes: circles, squares or rectangles, triangles, crosses, Xs, and odd forms. Next, children quickly move on to the *design* stage, in which they combine two basic shapes into a more complex abstract pattern.

Most children enter the *pictorial* stage between ages 4 and 5. Early drawings at this stage suggest real-life objects or people; later drawings are better defined. Although most adults see the later drawings as a sign of progress, Kellogg views the switch from abstraction to representation as a fundamental change in the purpose of children's drawing—a move away from a concern with form and design, primary elements in art—often under the "guidance" of adults who encourage children to portray reality (Kellogg, 1970).

Kellogg quotes artist Pablo Picasso: "Adults should not teach children to draw but should learn from them" (1970, p. 36). Like Wang Yani's father, adults can sustain children's early creativity by letting them draw what they like without imposing suggestions or standards.

Art Therapy

Therapists who help children deal with emotional trauma encourage them to draw pictures. A child who draws her feelings does not have to put them into words or understand them and does not have to worry about saying the wrong thing (Groth-Marnat, 1984).

The colors the child chooses and what the child depicts may express deep emotions (Garbarino, Dubrow, Kostelny, & Pardo, 1992). "The therapeutic use of play and art can help children reinstate their sense of inner control . . . and self-esteem, and develop . . . trust" (p. 204) and thus restore emotional health.

CHECKPOINT

Can you . . .

- List at least three gross motor skills and three fine motor skills, and tell when they typically develop?
- Discuss the incidence and possible cause of left-handedness?
- Describe four stages in young children's drawing?
- Explain how art therapy can help children deal with emotional trauma?

Health and Safety

What used to be a very vulnerable time of life is much safer now. Because of widespread immunization, many of the major diseases of childhood are now fairly rare, though minor illnesses are common. Children's death rates from all kinds of illness have come down in recent years. Deaths from influenza and pneumonia dropped by about 50 percent between 1950 and 1980 and remain at approximately the 1980 level (National Center for Health Statistics [NCHS], 1997). The 5-year disease-free survival rate for cancer (considered a cure in medical terms) has risen sharply for children under 15 (American Cancer Society, 1997). Deaths in childhood are relatively few compared with deaths in adulthood, and most are caused by injury rather than illness (NCHS, 1997). Still, environmental influences, such as parental smoking, stress, poverty, and homelessness, make this a less healthy time for some children than for others.

Minor Illnesses

Coughs, sniffles, stomach aches, and runny noses are a part of early childhood. These minor illnesses typically last a few days and are seldom serious enough to need a doctor's attention. Because the lungs are not fully developed, respiratory problems are common, though less so than in infancy. Three- to five-year-olds catch an average of seven to eight colds and other respiratory illnesses a year. It's a good thing they do, since these illnesses help build natural immunity (resistance to disease). During middle childhood, when the respiratory system is more fully developed, children average fewer than six such illnesses a year (Denny & Clyde, 1983). Minor illnesses may have emotional and cognitive as well as physical benefits. Repeated experience with illness helps children learn to cope with physical distress and understand its causes, and thus enhances their sense of competence (Parmelee, 1986).

Accidental Injuries

Because young children are naturally venturesome and often unaware of danger, it is hard for caregivers to protect them from harm without *over*protecting them. Although most cuts, bumps, and scrapes are "kissed away" and quickly forgotten, some accidental injuries result in lasting damage or death. Accidents are the leading cause of death in childhood in the United States, most often because of

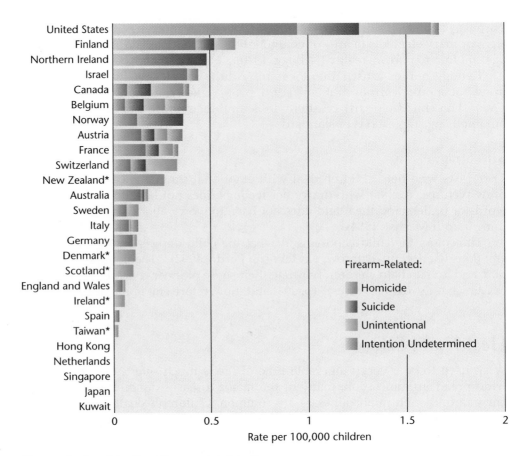

Firearm-Related:

- Homicide
- Suicide
- Unintentional
- Intention Undetermined

Rate per 100,000 children

Figure 8-3
Rates of firearm-related death among children less than 15 years old in 26 industrialized countries. Rates are for 1 year during the period 1990 to 1995.
Source: "Rates of Homicide," 1997.

*Reported only unintentional firearm-related deaths.

motor vehicle injuries, and next most often due to drowning (Rivara & Grossman, 1996; U. S. Department of Health and Human Services [USDHHS], 1996a; B. C. Williams & Miller, 1991, 1992). Young children are more likely to be hit *by* cars than to be injured *in* them (B. C. Williams & Miller, 1992).

Many injury-related deaths are preventable. Children's deaths from accidents in the United States declined 26 percent between 1978 and 1991 due largely to use of restraining devices in cars and fewer pedestrian injuries (Rivara & Grossman, 1996). All 50 states and the District of Columbia have laws requiring young children to be restrained in cars, either in specially designed seats or by standard seat belts. In 1991, 63 percent of children under age 5 who died in automobiles were unrestrained (Rivara & Grossman, 1996). Educating preschoolers about the importance of wearing restraints is more effective in securing compliance than is threatening parents with police checks and fines (Bowman, Sanson-Fisher, & Webb, 1987). Because airbags designed to inflate rapidly so as to protect adults riding in the front seat of a car in high-impact collisions can fatally injure young children, it is important that children always ride in the back seat.

Laws requiring "childproof" caps on medicine bottles, mandatory helmets for bicycle riders, and safe storage of firearms also have improved child safety. In 12 states that passed laws requiring that guns be inaccessible to children, unintentional shooting deaths of children younger than 15 fell by 23 percent (P. Cummings, Grossman, Rivara, & Koepsell, 1997). Still, the United States has by far the highest rates of childhood deaths due to homicide, suicide, and unintentional firearm-related injuries among 26 industrialized countries. Of all firearm-related deaths of children under age 15 in the most recently reported year in each of these countries, 86 percent occurred in the United States ("Rates of Homicide," 1997; see Figure 8-3).

Safety-approved helmets protect children of all ages from disabling or fatal head injuries.

Making playgrounds safer would be another valuable measure. An estimated 3 percent of children in day care are hurt badly enough each year to need medical attention. About half of accidents at day-care centers occur on playgrounds. Nearly 1 in 5 are from falls, often resulting in skull injury and brain damage (Briss, Sacks, Addiss, Kresnow, & O'Neil, 1994). Many of these could be averted by lowering the height of climbing equipment and covering the ground with impact-absorbing materials, such as wood chips, loose sand, or mats.

Children are less likely to be injured in day care, however, than in and around the home (Thacker, Addiss, Goodman, Holloway, & Spencer, 1992), where most fatal nonvehicular accidents occur. Children drown in bathtubs, pools, and buckets containing liquids (as well as in lakes, rivers, and oceans); are burned in fires and explosions; fall from heights; drink or eat poisonous substances; get caught in mechanical contrivances; and suffocate in traps, such as abandoned refrigerators. Another dangerous place is the supermarket shopping cart; the number of children injured in these carts doubled during the 1980s, and more than 12,000 serious head injuries to children under 5 were reported in 1989 (U.S. Consumer Product Safety Commission, 1991).

In a study of all children born in Tennessee between 1985 and 1994, a disproportionate number of accidental deaths during infancy and early childhood were related to the mother's youth or lack of education or the number of children she had to deal with. Children born to mothers under 20 years old, with less than a high school education and three or more other children, were 15 times as likely to die of injuries before the age of 5 as children whose mothers were college educated, more than 30 years old, and had fewer than three other children. If the mortality rate for all children could be reduced to that of this lowest-risk group, injury-related deaths might be reduced by more than 75 percent (Scholer, Mitchel, & Ray, 1997). Home visitation programs to teach parents to use car restraints and smoke detectors, lower water heater thermostats to avoid scalding, and undertake other safety measures can substantially reduce injuries (I. Roberts, Kramer, & Suissa, 1996). (Table 8-3 summarizes suggestions for reducing accident risks in various settings.)

Table 8-3	Reducing Accident Risks for Children

Activity	Precautions
Bicycling	Helmets reduce risk of head injury by 85 percent and brain injury by 88 percent.
Skateboarding and roller blading	Children should wear helmets and protective padding on knees, elbows, and wrists.
Using fireworks	Families should not purchase fireworks for home use.
Lawn mowing	Children under 12 should not operate walk-behind mowers; those under 14 should not operate ride-on mowers; small children should not be close to a moving mower.
Swimming	Swimming pools should not be installed in backyards of homes with children under 5; pools already in place need a high fence around all four sides, with gates having high, out-of-reach, self-closing latches. Adults need to watch children very closely near pools, lakes, and other bodies of water.
Playing on a playground	A safe surface under swings, slides, and other equipment can be 10-inch-deep sand, 12-inch-deep wood chips, or rubber outdoor mats; separate areas should be maintained for active play and quiet play, for older and younger children.
Using firearms	Guns should be kept unloaded and locked up, with bullets locked in separate place; children should not have access to keys; adults should talk with children about the risks of gun injury.
Eating	To prevent choking, young children should not eat hard candies, nuts, grapes, and hot dogs (unless sliced lengthwise, then across); food should be cut into small pieces; children should not eat while talking, running, jumping, or lying down.

Source: Adapted in part from American Academy of Pediatrics (AAP) Committee on Injury and Poison Prevention, 1995a; AAP and Center to Prevent Handgun Violence, 1994.

Health in Context: Environmental Influences

Why do some children have more illnesses or injuries than others? The genetic heritage contributes: some children seem predisposed toward some medical conditions. In addition, as Bronfenbrenner's ecological model (see Chapter 1) might predict, the home, the day-care center, the school, the neighborhood, and the larger society play major roles. Family situations involving stress or economic hardship increase vulnerability to illness and accidents.

Exposure to Smoking

Parental smoking is an important preventable cause of illness and death among children. In the United States, 43 percent of children 2 months to 11 years old live with smokers and are exposed daily to secondhand smoke (Pirkle et al., 1996). This passive exposure to tobacco smoke increases the risk of contracting a number of medical problems, including pneumonia, bronchitis, serious infectious illnesses, otitis media (middle ear infection), burns, and asthma. It also may lead to cancer in adulthood (Aligne & Stoddard, 1997; AAP Committee on Environmental Health, 1997; American Heart Association [AHA], 1994; U.S. Environmental Protection Agency, 1994). More young children die as a result of parental smoking than from accidental injuries (see Figure 8-4). Parental smoking is costly in economic terms as well; it results in $4.6 billion in medical expenditures and $8.2 billion in costs due to loss of life each year (Aligne & Stoddard, 1997). Because of the hazards of secondhand smoke, the American Academy of Pediatrics Committee on Environmental Health (1997) recommends that children be raised in a smoke-free environment.

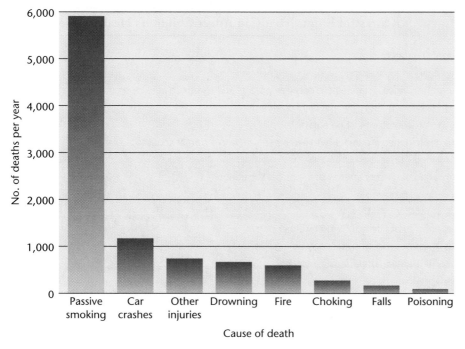

Figure 8-4

Passive smoking as compared with unintentional injuries as a cause of death in children younger than 5. The "other" column includes injuries from bicycling, boating, firearms, sports, farming, toy use, and other mishaps. Fire-related injuries were excluded from the passive smoking column, and the fire column was reduced by 14 percent to account for the proportion owing to parental smoking.

Source: Aligne & Stoddard, 1997, Figure 1, p. 652.

Exposure to Illness and Stress

Children in large families are sick more often than those in small families (Loda, 1980). Similarly, children in day-care centers, who come in contact daily with many other children, are 2 to 4 times more likely to pick up mild infectious diseases (such as colds, flu, and diarrhea) than are children who spend the day at home. They also have a higher risk of contracting more serious gastrointestinal diseases and hepatitis A (Thacker et al., 1992). However, children in high-quality day care, where nutrition is well-planned, hygiene is emphasized, and illnesses may be detected and treated early, tend to be healthier than those not in day-care programs (AAP, 1986).

Stressful events in the family, such as moves, job changes, divorce, and death, increase the frequency of minor illnesses and home accidents. In one study, children whose families had experienced 12 or more such stressful events were more than twice as likely to have to go into the hospital as children from families that had experienced fewer than 4 traumatic events (Beautrais, Fergusson, & Shannon, 1982; see Table 8-4). Entry into day care is stressful for many children. Children also can be affected by adults' stress. A distraught adult may forget to fasten a gate, put a cup of hot coffee, a kitchen knife, or a poisonous cleaning fluid out of a child's reach, or make sure that a child washes before eating (Craft, Montgomery, & Peters, 1992).

Poverty

Poverty is stressful, unhealthy, and dangerous. Low income is the *chief* factor associated with poor health of children and adolescents, over and above race and family structure (Montgomery, Kiely, & Pappas, 1996).

Young children are the largest age group living in poverty in the United States (Strawn, 1992). Children are nearly twice as likely as adults to be poor. In 1995, more than 1 in 5 children—and nearly 1 in 4 children under age 6—were poor, as defined by the official poverty level ($15,569 a year for a family of four). About 42 percent of black children and 40 percent of Hispanic children were poor (Children's Defense Fund, 1997a); and death rates for African American children and teenagers are considerably higher than for whites for every cause except suicide, car injuries, and accidental poisoning and falls (B. C. Williams &

Table 8-4	Stressful Events That Can Affect Children's Health

Moving to a different house

Parent's changing job, losing job, or starting new job

Serious or prolonged disagreement between parents and their own parents or in-laws

Death of close friend or relative of child or parents

Serious financial problems of parents

Serious or prolonged argument between parents or with a former spouse

Divorce or legal separation of parents

Reconciliation of parents after divorce or legal separation

Parents' sexual problems

Assault of mother by father

Serious illness or accident suffered by either parent

Serious illness or accident suffered by sibling

Serious illness among other family members

Mother's pregnancy

Court case involving either parent

Source: Adapted from Beautrais, Fergusson, & Shannon, 1982.

Miller, 1992). Child poverty rates in the United States are 1½ to 8 times as high as in other major industrialized countries (Children's Defense Fund, 1996, 1997a; see Figure 8-5).

The health problems of poor children often begin before birth. Many poor mothers do not eat well and do not receive adequate prenatal care; their babies are more likely than babies of nonpoor mothers to be of low birthweight, to be stillborn, or to die soon after birth. Poor children who do not eat properly do not grow properly, and thus are weak and susceptible to disease. Many poor families live in crowded, unsanitary housing, and the children may lack adequate supervision, especially when the parents are at work. They are more likely than other children to suffer lead poisoning, hearing and vision loss, and iron-deficiency anemia, as well as such stress-related conditions as asthma, headaches, insomnia, and irritable bowel. They also tend to have more behavior problems, psychological disturbances, and learning disabilities (J. L. Brown, 1987; Egbuono & Starfield, 1982; Santer & Stocking, 1991; Starfield, 1991). Poor children who do not have homes have the greatest problems of all (see Box 8-3).

Many poor children do not get the medical care they need. In 1993, more than 7.3 million children in the United States had health care needs (for medical care, dental care, prescription medicines, eyeglasses, or mental health care) that were either unmet or delayed because of cost. Nearly 4.2 million children—6 percent of the population under age 18—had no regular source of health care, in most cases because of low income and/or lack of insurance (G. Simpson, Bloom, Cohen, & Parsons, 1997).

During the 1990s, the number of uninsured families with children grew rapidly, largely due to a decline in employer-provided coverage. More than 1 million children, on average, lost private coverage each year between 1989 and 1994 (Children's Defense Fund, 1997a). By 1997, an estimated 10 million children—1 out of 7, most of them in low-income working families—were uninsured (Health Care Financing Administration, 1997).

Children who are uninsured see doctors less often, are in worse health, are less likely to have up-to-date immunizations, and—when they get sick—are more likely to require long hospital stays than children with health coverage. They are more likely to have no regular source of health care (Children's Defense Fund,

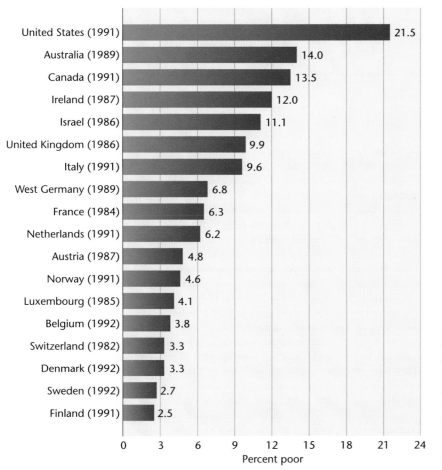

Figure 8-5
Child poverty rates in 18 industrialized countries. The poverty rate for children in the United States is higher than that in 17 other industrialized countries; yet upper- and middle-class children in the United States are much better off than in the other countries shown.

Source: Luxembourg Income Study; reprinted in Children's Defense Fund, 1996, p. 6.

1996, 1997a; Newacheck, Stoddard, Hughes, & Pearl, 1998; D. L. Wood, Hayward, Corey, Freeman, & Shapiro, 1990). Black and Hispanic children are more likely to lack regular care than white children (G. Simpson et al., 1997). Many minority families cannot afford private physicians, have no medical insurance, and, especially if they do not speak English, may have less access to doctors than white families do. As a result, minority children's conditions often are not reported or treated until they are severe enough to require hospitalization. When they do get outpatient care, it is more likely to be in a hospital emergency room than in a physician's office (McManus & Newacheck, 1993; Newacheck, Stoddard, & McManus, 1993). In 1993, black children were 8 times as likely as white children to get their regular care in a hospital emergency room (G. Simpson et al., 1997).

Important "safety nets" for poor children in the United States have been federally-funded Aid to Families with Dependent Children (AFDC) and Medicaid. AFDC has now been eliminated, responsibility for welfare for needy families has been shifted to the states, and Medicaid has not grown fast enough to offset losses in private insurance coverage. In 1997, the federal government authorized $24 billion in matching funds over a 5-year period to help states expand health care coverage to uninsured children (Health Care Financing Administration, 1997).

Exposure to Lead

Lead poisoning has been called the greatest hazard to the health of children under age 6. An estimated 3 million American children in that age group, especially in urban communities, have lead levels high enough to interfere with cognitive development (Tesman & Hills, 1994). However, there may be *no* safe level of exposure to lead. Furthermore, some of the effects of severe lead poisoning

Box 8-3 How Homelessness Affects Children

Children need homes if they are to thrive (AAP Committee on Community Health Services, 1996). An estimated 43 percent of the 2½ to 3 million homeless in the United States are families with children, the fastest-growing segment of this population. More than half (53 percent) of these families are headed by young single women, many of whom have abused alcohol or drugs or have been physically or sexually abused. In some cities, as many as 75 percent of the homeless are children, and a disproportionate number are black (AAP Committee on Community Health Services, 1996).

Why is the homeless population growing? Reasons include lack of affordable housing; cutbacks in rent subsidies and welfare programs; unemployment, especially among people with marginal skills; divorce and domestic violence; substance abuse; deinstitutionalization of the mentally ill; and poverty (AAP Committee on Community Health Services, 1996).

Many homeless children spend their crucial early years in an unstable, insecure, and often unsanitary environment. They sleep in emergency shelters, welfare hotels, abandoned buildings or cars, or on the street. Homeless children and their parents are cut off from a supportive community, family ties, and institutional resources and from ready access to medical care. The effects can be devastating, both physically and psychologically (AAP Committee on Community Health Services, 1996; J. L. Bass, Brennan, Mehta, & Kodzis, 1990; Bassuk, 1991; Bassuk & Rosenberg, 1990; Rafferty & Shinn, 1991).

From birth, these children suffer more health problems than do poor children who have homes (see figure). They are three times more likely than other children to lack immunizations, and two to three times more likely to have iron deficiency anemia. They experience high rates of diarrhea; hunger and malnourishment; obesity (from eating excessive carbohydrates and fats); tooth decay; asthma and other chronic diseases; respiratory, skin, and eye and ear infections; scabies and lice; trauma-related injuries; and elevated levels of lead. Homeless children tend to suffer severe depression and anxiety and to have neurological and visual deficits, developmental delays, behavior problems, and learning difficulties. Uprooted from their neighborhoods, as many as half do not go to school; if they do, they tend to have problems, partly because they miss a lot of it and have no place to do homework. They tend to do poorly on standardized reading and math tests, even when their cognitive functioning is normal, and they are more likely to repeat a grade or be placed in special classes than are children with homes (AAP Committee on Community Health Services, 1996; Bassuk, 1991; Rafferty & Shinn, 1991; D. H. Rubin et al., 1996).

To what extent are the problems of homeless children problems of poverty? In one study in Worcester, Massachusetts, preschoolers in 77 mother-only families living in homeless shelters were more likely to have experienced stressful events during the previous year than preschoolers in a comparison group of 90 low-income housed families. The homeless youngsters were more likely to have been investigated for neglect and to have been placed in foster care—itself a stressful event. However, while the homeless children showed more behavior problems than the comparison group, these problems were no more likely to merit professional attention. The mother's emotional status—which tended to suffer from the stress of raising children alone with few resources to rely on—strongly predicted the child's. Homeless mothers tended to live in worse circumstances than poor mothers with housing; they moved more often, were less educated, worked infrequently, and were more likely to be victims of violence or to have been hospitalized for emotional disturbances or substance abuse (Bassuk, Weinreb, Dawson, Perloff, & Buckner, 1997).

In 1994, a U.S. Court of Appeals in Washington, D.C., guaranteed homeless children in that city access to public education; and Congress directed school districts, wherever possible, to enroll homeless children in the schools their parents request (Children's Defense Fund, 1995). To combat homelessness, a number of communities and community development groups are building low-income housing units and reclaiming neighborhoods with the help of federal, state, local, foundation, and private financing (Children's Defense Fund, 1997a).

Homeless families need decent, permanent, and affordable housing. Failing that, they need safe, clean emergency shelters where they can get nutritious meals and have enough privacy so children can do their homework, get adequate sleep, and not be exposed to disease. These families also need health and child care, as well as other social services. Homelessness is a multifaceted problem requiring a multifaceted solution.

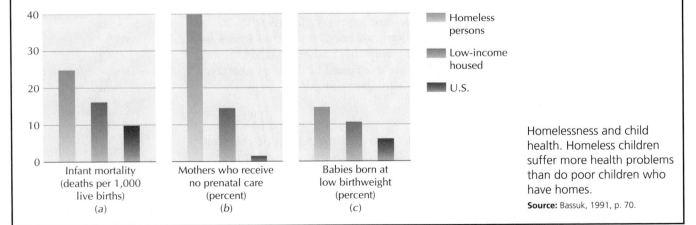

Homelessness and child health. Homeless children suffer more health problems than do poor children who have homes.
Source: Bassuk, 1991, p. 70.

Playing with peeling lead-based paint (often found in older buildings) can be hazardous to a child's health. Lead poisoning may cause irreversible cognitive damage.

may be irreversible (AAP Committee on Environmental Health, 1993). Yet lead poisoning is totally preventable by removing sources of lead from children's environment (Tesman & Hills, 1994).

Children can get lead in the bloodstream from lead-contaminated food or water, from putting contaminated fingers in their mouths, or from inhaling dust in homes or schools where there is lead-based paint (Baghurst et al., 1992; Bellinger, Stiles, & Needleman, 1992; Dietrich, Berger, & Succop, 1993). Although lead poisoning affects all economic levels, black children, many of whom live in homes with flaking lead paint and lead-contaminated dust, tend to have higher blood lead levels than white children (Lanphear, Weitzman, & Eberly, 1996). Problems associated with poverty, such as poor nutrition and poor medical care, may compound the effects of lead (Tesman & Hills, 1994).

Those effects may last for years. Lead exposure and high blood lead levels have been associated with sensorimotor deficits, lower IQ, and poorer academic achievement. (Which specific areas of cognition are affected is still unclear and may depend on the age of exposure and on socioeconomic status.) Lead is strongly linked to behavioral problems, such as hyperactivity (see Chapter 12), impulsiveness, irritability, distractibility, and a short attention span (Tesman & Hills, 1994). It is associated with antisocial and delinquent behavior (Needleman, Riess, Tobin, Biesecker, & Greenhouse, 1996) and can lead to seizures, mental retardation, or death (AAP Committee on Environmental Health, 1993). Because children with lead poisoning may be more difficult to raise than other children, they may be vulnerable to abuse (Bithoney, Vandeven, & Ryan, 1993).

Laws mandating removal of lead from gasoline, paints, and soldered food cans have helped prevention efforts, but dust and soil in many places are still contaminated, and an estimated 3 out of 4 housing units built before 1980 contain lead-based paint (Pirkle et al., 1994; Tesman & Hills, 1994). The Centers for Disease Control and Prevention (CDC, 1991) therefore recommends that virtually all children be routinely screened for lead exposure and lead poisoning. Screening is important because moderate lead poisoning can be successfully treated (Ruff, Bijur, Markowitz, Ma, & Rosen, 1993). Washing hands before meals and before bed, keeping fingernails clipped, and eating a well-balanced diet can help. Chipping or peeling paint should be removed carefully, and barriers can be put up to keep children away from areas known to contain lead (Kimbrough, LeVois, & Webb, 1994).

CHECKPOINT

Can you . . .

- Identify two benefits of minor illnesses?

- Tell where and how young children are most likely to be injured, and list at least five ways in which injuries can be avoided?

- Name and discuss several environmental influences that endanger children's health and development?

Maltreatment: Abuse and Neglect

physical abuse   Action taken to endanger a child involving potential injury to the body.

battered child syndrome Condition showing symptoms of physical abuse of a child.

physical neglect   Failure to meet a child's basic bodily needs, such as food, clothing, medical care, protection, and supervision.

sexual abuse   Sexual activity involving a child and an older person.

emotional (psychological) abuse   Nonphysical action that may damage children's behavioral, cognitive, emotional, or physical functioning.

emotional (psychological) neglect   Failure to give a child emotional support, love, and affection.

Although most parents are loving and nurturing, some cannot or will not take proper care of their children. *Maltreatment,* whether perpetrated by parents or others, is deliberate or avoidable endangerment of a child; it takes several specific forms. In general, *abuse* refers to action; *neglect* refers to inaction. Abuse is infliction of harm; *neglect* is failure to meet a child's basic needs. *Physical abuse* involves potential injury to the body, in a pattern often referred to as the *battered child syndrome* (Kempe, Silverman, Steele, Droegemueller, & Silver, 1962). *Physical neglect* is failure to provide such necessary physical care as food, clothing, medical care, protection, and supervision. *Sexual abuse* is any kind of sexual activity involving a child and an older person. *Emotional (psychological) abuse* is verbal or other nonphysical action which may damage a child's behavioral, cognitive, emotional, or physical functioning. It may include rejection, terrorization, isolation, exploitation, degradation, or ridicule. *Emotional (psychological) neglect* is failure to provide emotional support, love, and affection. Any one form of maltreatment is likely to be accompanied by one or more of the others (Belsky, 1993)

Although maltreatment is more widely recognized than in the past, its incidence is hard to determine. Methods for collecting data are flawed and interpretations difficult. The rise in reported cases and serious injuries since 1976, when the first national statistics were compiled, may reflect an increase in maltreatment, better recognition and reporting of abuse and neglect, or (more likely) both. Still, many cases are never reported to protective agencies, and many of those reported are not investigated. Figures may differ depending on whether we are considering children who are endangered by maltreatment or only those who have already been harmed (Sedlak & Broadhurst, 1996).

Children and families are often caught in a web of conflicting values: protecting children's safety versus preserving families and respecting privacy. Many allegations of maltreatment are never confirmed, and adults who are unjustly accused suffer grievously and unfairly. On the other hand, many children whose precarious situation is known to authorities or neighbors are left in the hands of abusive or neglectful parents, often with fatal results.

Overall, according to the most recent federal government estimate, the number of abused and neglected children nearly doubled between 1986 and 1993, from 1.4 million to 2.8 million (Sedlak & Broadhurst, 1996), though the number of cases investigated and confirmed by state child protective services in 1993, and again in 1995, was only a little over 1 million (National Clearinghouse on Child Abuse and Neglect Information, 1997; Sedlak & Broadhurst, 1996). Substantial increases occurred in all types of maltreatment except educational neglect. Of the 2.8 million children endangered by abuse and neglect according to the federal estimate, more than 1.5 million were actually harmed, and the rest were judged at risk of harm (Sedlak & Broadhurst, 1996). About half of all cases of maltreatment, whether reported or not, involve physical neglect, and one-fourth involve physical abuse (National Clearinghouse on Child Abuse and Neglect Information, 1997; Sedlak & Broadhurst, 1996).

Maltreatment has become a leading cause of death among young children; according to federal estimates, at least 2,000 die every year and 140,000 are seriously injured (U.S. Advisory Board on Child Abuse and Neglect, 1995). Parents were charged in 57 percent of murders of children under 12 years old in large urban areas in 1988, and in 8 out of 10 cases the parent had previously abused the child (J. M. Dawson & Langan, 1994). Often the killer is the mother's boyfriend, and the mother fails to intervene or tries to cover up. Sometimes the mother is a victim of abuse herself and is too intimidated to protect her child.

Contributing Factors: An Ecological View

Why do adults hurt or neglect children? Which children, in what kinds of families, are most likely to be mistreated? What are the characteristics of the perpetrators? What other influences are at work? We can look at factors contributing to maltreatment from Bronfenbrenner's ecological perspective (see Chapter 1), which considers the child in the family, the community, and the larger society.*

The Microsystem: The Child in the Family

Abused and neglected children are of all ages, but more than half of reported victims are 7 or younger, and about one-fourth are below age 4 (National Clearinghouse on Child Abuse and Neglect Information, 1997). However, maltreatment rates appear to be rising fastest for school-age children, ages 6 to 11; this may reflect the fact that children in this age group are more likely to be seen by community professionals. Vulnerability to sexual abuse is fairly consistent from age 3 on. Girls are three times as likely as boys to be sexually abused, whereas boys are more likely to be emotionally neglected or seriously injured. There are no significant racial differences in abuse or neglect (Sedlak & Broadhurst, 1996).

The people most likely to abuse or neglect a child are the child's natural parents. In more than 3 out of 4 cases in which children are harmed by maltreatment, including 9 out of 10 of those harmed by neglect, the birth parents are to blame. Mothers are more likely to abuse or neglect than fathers, but perpetrators other than the parents are more likely to be male. Nearly half of sexual abuse is done by someone other than a parent or caregiver, and nearly 9 out of 10 of these perpetrators are men or boys (Sedlak & Broadhurst, 1996). Sexual abusers have a wide range of personality disorders.

Maltreatment by parents is a symptom of extreme disturbance in child rearing; it usually appears in the context of other family problems, such as poverty, stress, alcoholism, or antisocial behavior. A disproportionate number of abused and neglected children are in large, poor, or single-parent families, which are likely to be under stress and to have trouble meeting children's needs (Sedlak & Broadhurst, 1996). Neglectful parents tend to be apathetic, incompetent, and irresponsible and emotionally withdrawn from spouse and children (D. A. Wolfe, 1985). Impulsive and infantile, many have trouble planning their own lives.

More than 9 out of 10 abusers are not psychotic and do not have criminal personalities, but many are lonely, unhappy, anxious, depressed, angry, or aggressive. They often have health or substance abuse problems that impair their ability to raise children, and they tend to have low self-esteem and poor impulse control. About one-third of abusing parents were abused themselves as children (NRC, 1993b; B. D. Schmitt & Kempe, 1983; D. A. Wolfe, 1985).

Unlike neglectful parents, who simply ignore their children, abusive parents are overly involved. They often hate themselves for what they do, yet feel powerless to stop. Often abuse begins when a parent who is already anxious, depressed, or hostile tries to control a child physically, but then loses control over his or her own behavior and ends up shaking, beating, or otherwise harming the child.

Abusive parents have trouble reading babies' emotional signals and may misinterpret their babies' needs (Kropp & Haynes, 1987). Often deprived of good parenting, they do not know how to be good parents; they tend to be ignorant of normal child development and are highly stressed by behavior that most parents take in stride. They are less effective in resolving problems and have more confrontations with their children (J. R. Reid, Patterson, & Loeber, 1982; D. A. Wolfe, 1985). They may expect their children to take care of *them* and may become

---

*Unless otherwise referenced, this discussion is indebted to Belsky (1993) and the National Research Council (NRC, 1993b).

enraged when this does not happen. Some abusive parents may use their power over their children in a misplaced effort to gain control over their own lives.

Abusive parents are more likely than others to have marital problems and to fight physically with each other. They tend to have more children and to have them closer together, and their households are more disorganized. They experience more stressful events than other families (J. R. Reid et al., 1982; Sedlak & Broadhurst, 1996). Abusive parents tend to cut themselves off from others, leaving them with no one to turn to in times of stress and no one to see what is happening. The arrival of a new man in the home (a stepfather or the mother's boyfriend) may lead to abuse.

When parents who think poorly of themselves, had troubled childhoods, and have problems handling negative emotions have children who are particularly needy or demanding, the likelihood of abuse increases. These children's greater needs may stem from poor health, "difficult" personalities, or physical disabilities. They are more likely than nonabused children to have been preterm or low-birthweight babies; to be hyperactive, mentally retarded, or physically handicapped; or to show behavioral abnormalities (J. R. Reid et al., 1982). Of course, most children with these characteristics are not abused; but if parents are prone to becoming abusive, such characteristics may provoke the abuse. Then too, abuse can make children more aggressive and defiant, perpetuating the cycle.

The Exosystem: Neighborhood and Social Support

The outside world can create a climate for family violence. Poverty, unemployment, job dissatisfaction, social isolation, and lack of assistance for the primary caregiver are closely correlated with child and spouse abuse. None of these, however, are determining factors.

What makes one low-income neighborhood a place where children are highly likely to be abused, while another, matched for ethnic population and income levels, is safer? In one inner-city Chicago neighborhood, the proportion of children who died from maltreatment (1 death for every 2,541 children) was about twice the proportion in another inner-city neighborhood. Researchers who interviewed community leaders found a depressed atmosphere in the high-abuse community. Criminal activity was rampant, and facilities for community programs were dark and dreary. This was an environment with "an ecological conspiracy against children" (Garbarino & Kostelny, 1993, p. 213). In the low-abuse neighborhood, people described their community as a poor but decent place to live. They painted a picture of a neighborhood with robust social support networks, well-known community services, and strong political leadership. In a community like this, maltreatment is less likely to occur.

The Macrosystem: Cultural Values and Patterns

Two cultural factors associated with child abuse are societal violence and physical punishment of children. In countries where violent crime is infrequent and children are rarely spanked, such as Japan, China, and Tahiti, child abuse is rare (Celis, 1990).

By comparison, the United States is a violent place. Homicide, wife battering, and rape are common. A 1977 Supreme Court ruling that school personnel may strike disobedient children is still in effect, with some qualifications. Many states still permit corporal punishment in schools; minority and handicapped children are paddled more often than their classmates. According to a 1995 Gallup poll, more than 5 percent of parents admit to punishing their children so brutally that it amounts to abuse.

Table 8-5	Developmentally Related Reactions to Sexual Abuse
Age	**Most Common Symptoms**
Preschoolers	Anxiety
	Nightmares
	Inappropriate sexual behavior
School-age children	Fear
	Mental illness
	Aggression
	Nightmares
	School problems
	Hyperactivity
	Regressive behavior
Adolescents	Depression
	Withdrawn, suicidal, or self-injurious behaviors
	Physical complaints
	Illegal acts
	Running away
	Substance abuse

Source: Adapted from Kendall-Tackett, Williams, & Finkelhor, 1993.

Long-Term Effects

Maltreatment can produce grave consequences—not only physical, but cognitive and psychosocial as well. Abused children often show delayed speech (Coster, Gersten, Beeghly, & Cicchetti, 1989). They are more likely to repeat a grade, to do poorly on cognitive tests, and to have discipline problems in school (Eckenrode, Laird, & Doris, 1993). They often have disorganized-disoriented attachments to their parents (see Chapter 7), have negative, distorted self-concepts, are deprived of positive social interactions, do not develop social skills, and thus have difficulty making friends (Price, 1996). They tend to be aggressive and uncooperative and, consequently, less well liked than other children (Haskett & Kistner, 1991; Salzinger, Feldman, Hammer, & Rosario, 1993). The friends they do make tend to be younger, and these friendships tend to be less intimate and more conflictual than the friendships of nonabused children (Parker & Herrera, 1996).

The severest emotional trauma generally occurs when a nonabusive parent does not believe a child's account of abuse and does not try to protect the child; when the child is removed from the home; or when the child has suffered more than one type of abuse (Browne & Finkelhor, 1986; Bryer, Nelson, Miller, & Krol, 1987; Burgess, Hartman, & McCormack, 1987; Kendall-Tackett, Williams, & Finkelhor, 1993). Although most abused children do not become delinquent or criminal as adults, abuse makes it likelier that they will (Dodge, Bates, & Pettit, 1990; Widom, 1989).

Teenagers who were abused when they were younger may react by running away, which may be self-protective, or may abuse drugs, which is not (NRC, 1993b). Teenagers who failed to thrive in infancy are likely to have physical, cognitive, and emotional problems, apparently due to emotional neglect (Oates, Peacock, & Forrest, 1985).

Consequences of sexual abuse vary with age (see Table 8-5). Sexually abused children are likely to be fearful, anxious, depressed, or unhappy, to have low self-esteem, to become preoccupied with sex, and to have problems with behavior and school achievement. As adolescents, they are more likely than other youngsters to engage in "binge" eating and to try to injure themselves or commit suicide (Einbender & Friedrich, 1989; Kendall-Tackett et al., 1993; Swanston, Tebbutt, O'Toole, & Oates, 1997). Fearfulness and low self-esteem often continue into adulthood. Adults who were sexually abused as children tend to be anxious, depressed, angry, or hostile; to distrust people; to feel isolated and stigmatized; and to be sexually maladjusted (Browne & Finkelhor, 1986). The effects of sexual abuse are more pronounced when the abuser is someone close to the child, when the sexual contact has been frequent and has persisted for a long period of time, when force has been used, when there has been oral, anal, or vaginal penetration, or when the child has a negative outlook or coping style (Kendall-Tackett et al., 1993).

Emotional maltreatment is more subtle than physical maltreatment, and its effects may be harder to pin down. It has been linked to lying, stealing, low self-esteem, emotional maladjustment, dependency, underachievement, depression, aggression, learning disorders, homicide, and suicide, as well as to psychological distress later in life (S. N. Hart & Brassard, 1987).

Still, many maltreated children show remarkable resilience, especially if they have been able to form an attachment to a supportive person (Egeland & Sroufe, 1981). Above-average intelligence, advanced cognitive abilities, and high self-esteem seem to help. Also important is the child's interpretation of the abuse or neglect. Children who see it as coming from a parent's weaknesses or frustrations seem to cope better than those who take it as parental rejection (Garmezy, Masten, & Tellegen, 1984; Zimrin, 1986).

Growing up to be an abuser is far from an inevitable result of being abused as a child. According to one analysis, two-thirds of abused children grow up to be nonabusing parents (J. Kaufman & Zigler, 1987). Abused girls who do *not* become abusers are likely to have had someone to whom they could turn for help, to have received therapy, and to have a good marital or love relationship. They usually are more openly angry about and able to describe their experience of abuse. They are likely to have been abused by only one parent and to have had a loving, supportive relationship with the other (Egeland, Jacobvitz, & Sroufe, 1988; J. Kaufman & Zigler, 1987).

Helping Families in Trouble or at Risk

Since abuse and neglect are much more common among young, poor, and uneducated parents, programs that seek to keep young people in school and prepare them for an occupation before they have children may forestall abuse. Specific abuse-prevention programs help parents overwhelmed by the demands of parenting by showing them how to care for babies, giving them pointers on how to encourage good behavior, and teaching them how to help children develop language and social skills (Wolfe, Edwards, Manion, & Koverola, 1988). Still other programs offer subsidized day care, volunteer homemakers, home visitors, and temporary "respite homes" or "relief parents" to occasionally take over for beleaguered parents. In one program in a semirural New York community, first-time expectant mothers were visited by nurses once a month during pregnancy and then during the child's first two years. Fifteen years later, these mothers were less likely than a comparison group to have been reported as abusers or neglectors (D. L. Olds et al., 1997).

When maltreatment is already occurring, several kinds of intervention are possible to stop the abuse or repair the damage. One way is to treat abusers as criminal offenders; people arrested for family violence are less likely to repeat the maltreatment (Bouza, 1990; L. W. Sherman & Berk, 1984). Sometimes a child

This adult volunteer uses dolls to help young children realize they have control over their bodies and need not let anyone—even friends or family members—touch them. Educational programs for preventing sexual abuse need to walk a fine line between alerting children to danger and frightening them.

must be separated from abusive parents; but if possible, it is usually better to keep the child in the family and stop the abuse. Services for abused children and adults include shelters, education in parenting skills, and therapy. Parents Anonymous and other organizations offer free, confidential support groups, which have been found to be effective in stopping physical and verbal abuse.

When authorities remove children from their homes, the usual alternative is foster care, which has increased markedly since the 1980s. Foster care removes a child from immediate danger, but it is often unstable, may also be an abusive situation, and further alienates the child from the family. It is intended as a temporary, emergency measure; but while the median stay in foster care is 1½ years, in some cities the average is 5 years, often with a series of placements in different homes (NRC, 1993b).

Medical treatment for abuse or neglect needs to be prompt and sensitive to the trauma a child has experienced. Physicians, nurses, social workers, day care workers, teachers, and lawyers need to be trained to identify abuse, collect evidence, document personal histories, and refer abusive families for help. Child protection agencies are supposed to investigate allegations of maltreatment and refer families for help, but because of underfunding and understaffing, many cannot do so. One national survey found that more than one-third of children involved in confirmed cases of maltreatment received no help (McCurdy & Daro, 1993).

The first step in helping victims of sexual abuse is to recognize the signs. These include any extreme change of behavior, such as loss of appetite; sleep disturbance or nightmares; regression to bed-wetting, thumb-sucking, or frequent crying; torn or stained underclothes; vaginal or rectal bleeding or discharge; vaginal or throat infection; painful, itching, or swollen genitals; unusual interest in or knowledge of sexual matters; and fear or dislike of being left in a certain place or with a certain person (USDHHS, 1984). Young children need to be told that their bodies belong to them and that they can say no to anyone who might try to touch them or kiss them against their will, even if it is someone they love and trust. They also need to know that they are never to blame for what an adult does and that they can talk to their parents about anything without fear of punishment. And they need to be reassured that most adults want to help and take care of children, not hurt them.

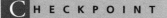

Can you . . .

- Define six types of child abuse and neglect?

- Summarize trends in the incidence of maltreatment and explain why it is hard to measure?

- Discuss contributing factors having to do with the child, the family, the neighborhood, and the wider society?

- Give examples of long-term effects of child abuse and neglect?

- Describe and assess approaches to preventing and stopping maltreatment and helping its victims?

Abused children may receive play or art therapy and day care in a therapeutic environment. In communities where abuse or neglect is widespread, school-based programs can be effective. In one preschool program for maltreated 3- to 5-year-olds who had become severely withdrawn, other preschoolers were trained to encourage the maltreated children to play with them. The trained "initiators" were better able to draw out the maltreated children than were trained adults (Fantuzzo et al., 1988).

The plight of abused and neglected children is one for which our society needs to find more effective remedies. Without help, maltreated children often grow up with serious problems, at great cost to themselves and to society, and may continue the cycle of maltreatment when they have children of their own.

Fortunately, most children are not maltreated. Preschool children who are in good health and whose basic physical needs are met are able to make major advances in cognitive development, as we'll see in Chapter 9.

SUMMARY

Physiological Growth and Change

- Physical growth increases during the years from 3 to 6, but more slowly than during infancy and toddlerhood. Boys are on average slightly taller, heavier, and more muscular than girls.

- The muscular, skeletal, nervous, respiratory, circulatory, and immune systems are maturing, and all primary teeth are present.

- Preschool children eat less than before and need a balanced diet. Obesity becomes a concern at this age; its prevalence has increased.

- Sleep patterns change during early childhood, as they do throughout life. Children generally sleep through the night, take one daytime nap, and sleep more deeply than later in life.

- It is normal for preschool children to develop bedtime rituals that delay going to sleep and to rely on **transitional objects.** Prolonged bedtime struggles or persistent night terrors or nightmares may indicate emotional disturbances that need attention.

- **Enuresis,** or bed-wetting, is common, especially at night, and is usually outgrown without special help.

Motor Development

- Motor development advances rapidly; children progress in **gross motor skills, fine motor skills,** and eye-hand coordination, developing more complex **systems of action.** Differences in boys' and girls' motor abilities may reflect skeletal differences or societal expectations, or both.

- **Handedness** is usually evident by age 3. Left-handed and right-handed people tend to differ in a number of other characteristics.

- Stages of art production, which appear to reflect brain development, are the scribbling stage, shape stage, design stage, and pictorial stage. Art therapy can help emotionally disturbed children.

Health And Safety

- Many major contagious illnesses are rare today due to widespread immunization, and death rates have declined.

- Minor illnesses, such as colds and other respiratory illnesses, are common during early childhood and help build immunity to disease.

- Accidents, most commonly motor vehicle injuries, are the leading cause of death in childhood in the United States but have declined since the late 1970s. Most fatal nonvehicular accidents occur at home.

- Environmental factors such as exposure to parental smoking, illness, stress, poverty, and homelessness increase the risks of illness or injury. Lead poisoning, a common environmental problem, can have serious physical, cognitive, and behavioral effects.

Maltreatment: Abuse and Neglect

- According to federal government estimates, 2.8 million American children are maltreated, resulting in at least 2,000 deaths annually.
- Characteristics of the abuser, the victim, the family, the community, and the culture all contribute to child abuse and neglect.
- Maltreatment, which may include **physical abuse** (the **battered child syndrome**), **physical neglect, sexual abuse, emotional (psychological) abuse,** and **emotional (psychological) neglect,** can have grave long-term effects.

KEY TERMS

transitional objects (285)
enuresis (286)
gross motor skills (287)
fine motor skills (287)
systems of action (288)
handedness (288)

physical abuse (300)
battered child syndrome (300)
physical neglect (300)
sexual abuse (300)
emotional (psychological) abuse (300)
emotional (psychological) neglect (300)

QUESTIONS FOR THOUGHT AND DISCUSSION

1. Much television advertising aimed at young children fosters poor nutrition by promoting fats and sugars rather than proteins and vitamins. How might parents counteract these pressures?

2. What do you think accounts for the rising prevalence of obesity in preschoolers? What suggestions can you make for preventing it?

3. In view of the differences in preschool boys' and girls' physical and motor development, should parents encourage different kinds of physical activity for boys and girls in that age group?

4. Drawings from children's early pictorial stage show energy and freedom; those from the later pictorial stage show care and accuracy. Why do you think these changes occur? How would you evaluate them?

5. Who should be responsible for children's well-being when parents cannot provide adequate food, clothing, shelter, and health care: government, religious and community institutions, or the private sector, or a combination of these?

6. Can you suggest strategies to deal with the problem of homelessness besides those mentioned in this chapter?

7. In a case of suspected child abuse by a parent, do you agree that the child should be kept in the family if possible? How can social policy balance the child's best interest with the rights of the alleged abuser and of any other parties, such as a spouse or other children in the home?

Cognitive Development in Early Childhood

Childhood is a world of miracle and wonder: as if creation rose, bathed in light, out of darkness, utterly new and fresh and astonishing. The end of childhood is when things cease to astonish us. When the world seems familiar, when one has got used to existence, one has become an adult.

Eugene Ionesco, *Fragments of a Journal,* 1976

Focus

Albert Einstein

In the public mind, Albert Einstein's name is synonymous with "genius." His general theory of relativity ("the greatest revolution in thought since Newton"), his discovery of the fundamental principle of quantum physics, and his other contributions to the reshaping of our knowledge of the universe caused him to be "universally recognized at 37 as the greatest theoretical physicist of his age" (M. Goldsmith, Mackay, & Woudhuysen, 1980, pp. 11, 4). Indeed, he is generally considered "one of the greatest physicists of all time" (Whitrow, 1967, p. 1).

Yet the young Einstein hardly seemed destined for intellectual stardom. Born in 1879 in the German town of Ulm, he was slow in learning to walk and did not begin talking until at least his third year of life; his parents consulted a doctor because they feared he might be mentally retarded. Einstein himself always insisted that he did not even try to speak until after the age of 3, thus skipping babbling and going directly into sentences. However, his sentences may have come a bit earlier. When his sister, Maja, was born four months before Albert's third birthday, Albert (who had been promised a new baby to play with and apparently thought it would be a toy) reportedly asked in disappointment, "Where are the wheels?"

Regardless of the exact timing, "Albert was certainly a late and reluctant talker" (Brian, 1996, p. 1). The reasons may have had more to do with personality than with cognitive development; he was a shy, taciturn child, whom adults thought backward and other children considered dull. He would not play marbles or soldiers or other games with his peers. His nurse called him *Pater Langweil* ("Father Bore"), and his schoolmates later called him *biedermeier* ("a square").

When he started school in Munich, where the family had moved a year after his birth, he did poorly in most subjects; the headmaster predicted he would never amount to anything. Albert hated the regimentation and rote learning that were stressed in German schools; he did not have a retentive memory and could not give clear answers to his teachers' questions. He would not even try to learn anything unless he was interested in it—and then his concentration was intense. Once his sister recalled seeing him painstakingly construct a house of cards fourteen stories high! As a young child, fascinated with nature, he would crouch for hours, observing an ant colony. He spent days trying to make friends with the chickens that roamed the garden of his family home, or exploring the nearby wooded hills.

Albert was a daydreamer, his questioning mind occupied with its own speculations. His wonder about the workings of the universe was awakened at the age of 4 or 5, when he was sick in bed and his father gave him a magnetic pocket compass to keep him amused. The boy was astonished: no matter which way he turned the compass, the needle pointed to "N" (for "north"). What controlled its motion? He pestered his Uncle Jacob—who had studied engineering and who lived with the family—with questions. His uncle told him about the earth's north and south poles and about magnetic fields, but Albert still was not satisfied. He believed there must be some mysterious force in what appeared to be the empty space around the needle. He carried the compass around for weeks, trying to figure out its secret. Years later, at the age of 67, he wrote: ". . . this experience made a deep and lasting impression upon me. Something deeply hidden had to be behind things" (Schilpp, 1970, p. 9).

That sense of wonder was reawakened several years later, when Uncle Jacob, noticing that Albert showed an interest in arithmetic, introduced him to algebra and geometry. Albert solved every problem in the books his uncle brought him and then went searching for more. It was that same insatiable curiosity and persistence—what Einstein himself called "a furious impulse to understand" (Michelmore, 1962, p. 24)—that underlay his lifetime quest for scientific knowledge.

Sources of biographical information about Albert Einstein are J. Bernstein, 1973; Brian, 1996; French, 1979; M. Goldsmith, Mackay, & Woudhuysen, 1980; Michelmore, 1962; Quasha, 1980; Schilpp, 1970; and Whitrow, 1967.

• • •

Albert Einstein's story touches on several themes of cognitive development in early childhood. One is the variation in normal language development. Although parents may be concerned about delayed development, the most serious implications may be social, influencing the way a child is perceived and treated by adults and peers. Einstein's reaction to the compass may have been unusually intense, but it was characteristic of young children's understanding of the physical world—their growing recognition that natural phenomena have causes, but also their tendency to confuse appearance and reality. Einstein's lifelong memory of that incident may shed light on why some kinds of early memories last while others do not. Finally, the underestimation of Einstein's cognitive abilities by his parents and teachers raises issues about how intelligence can best be assessed.

In this chapter, we examine all these aspects of cognitive development, as revealed by recent research as well as by such theorists as Piaget and Vygotsky. We see how preschool children's thinking has advanced since toddlerhood and in what ways it is still limited—particularly in their understanding of their own mental processes. We look at children's increasing fluency with language and what impact this has on other aspects of cognition, as well as on psychosocial development. We examine memory, drawing on the information-processing and social-contextual approaches; and we compare psychometric intelligence tests with assessments based on Vygotsky's theories. Finally, we look at the widening world of preschool and kindergarten.

After reading this chapter, you should be able to answer and elaborate on such questions as these:

Preview Questions

- What are some advances and limitations in preschool children's thinking?
- How does the ability to use language improve between ages 3 and 6?
- What influences affect young children's ability to remember?
- How is preschoolers' intelligence measured, and what factors influence it?
- What is the impact of early educational experiences?

Table 9-1	Cognitive Advances During Early Childhood*		
Advance	**Significance**		**Example**
Use of symbols	Children can think about something without needing to see it in front of them.		Jeffrey knows the name "Pumpkin" stands for his cat. He can talk or hear about her without having the cat in front of him. Words also stand for objects, people, and events.
Understanding of identities	The world is more orderly and predictable; children are aware that superficial alterations do not change the nature of things.		When Jeffrey cannot find his cat, he says, "Maybe Pumpkin put on a bear suit and went to someone else's house to be their pet bear." But when asked, Jeffrey shows that he knows that Pumpkin would—even if she put on a bear suit—still be his cat.
Understanding of cause and effect	It becomes more evident that the world is orderly; also, children realize that they can cause events to happen.		Marie knows that if she jumps into a puddle, she will get her sneakers dirty. She can choose to jump anyway; she can do it barefoot; or she can resist the temptation.
Ability to classify	It becomes possible to organize objects, people, and events into meaningful categories.		Marie lists which of her classmates are "nice" and which are "mean" and says, "The nice ones are my friends."
Understanding of number	Children can count and can deal with quantities.		Marie has two carrots on her plate. She leaves the table and comes back to find only one. "Who took my carrot?" she demands.
Empathy	Relationships with others become possible as children become able to imagine how others might feel.		Jeffrey tells a friend who brought him crayons, "I already have some." Then he quickly adds, "But I wanted more."
Theory of mind	It becomes possible to explain and predict other people's actions by imagining their beliefs, feelings, and thoughts.		Jeffrey wants to play ball with some bigger boys. His mother says no; so Jeffrey asks his father, but he does not tell his father that his mother has already said no. He knows that if his father knew, he would say no, too.

*Although the beginnings of these ways of thought are present in early childhood, their full achievement usually does not take place until middle childhood.

Piagetian Approach: The Preoperational Child

preoperational stage
In Piaget's theory, the second major stage of cognitive development (approximately from age 2 to age 7), in which children become more sophisticated in their use of symbolic thought but are not yet able to use logic.

Jean Piaget named early childhood the *preoperational stage.* In this second major stage of cognitive development, which lasts from approximately ages 2 to 7, children gradually become more sophisticated in their use of symbolic thought (see Chapter 6). However, according to Piaget, children cannot think logically until the stage of concrete operations in middle childhood (Chapter 12).

Among the cognitive advances of the preoperational stage identified by Piaget and other researchers are the *symbolic function, understanding of identities, understanding of cause and effect, ability to classify,* and *understanding of number.* Some of these abilities have roots in infancy and toddlerhood; others begin to develop in early childhood but are not fully achieved until middle childhood. Let's look at research on these advances and then at some limitations of preoperational thought (see Tables 9-1 and 9-2). We'll also consider more recent research that has challenged some of Piaget's conclusions. In Chapter 12, we'll examine more fundamental criticisms of Piaget's theory.

Cognitive Advances

"I want ice cream!" announces Cristina, age 4, trudging indoors from the hot, dusty backyard. She has not seen anything that triggered this desire—no open freezer door, no television commercial. She no longer needs this kind of sensory cue to think about something. She remembers ice cream, its coldness

Table 9-2 Limitations of Preoperational Thought (according to Piaget)

Limitation	Description	Example
Centration: inability to decenter	Child focuses on one aspect of a situation and neglects others.	Jeffrey cries when his father gives him a cookie broken in half. Because each half is smaller than the whole cookie, Jeffrey thinks he is getting less.
Irreversibility	Child fails to understand that an operation or action can go both ways.	Jeffrey does not realize that both halves of the cookie can be put next to each other to show the whole cookie.
Focus on states rather than transformations	Child fails to understand the significance of the transformation between states.	In the conservation task, Jeffrey does not understand that transforming the shape of a liquid (pouring it from one glass into another) does not change the amount.
Transductive reasoning	Child does not use deductive or inductive reasoning; instead, he jumps from one particular to another and sees cause where none exists.	"I had bad thoughts about my brother. My brother got sick. So I made my brother sick." Or "I was bad, so Mommy and Daddy got divorced."
Egocentrism	Child assumes everyone else thinks as she does.	Marie takes out a game and tells her mother, "This is *your* treat." She assumes her mother likes to play the game as much as she does.
Animism	Child attributes life to objects not alive.	Marie thinks clouds are alive because they move.
Inability to distinguish appearance from reality	Child confuses what is real with outward appearance.	Jeffrey thinks a sponge made to look like a rock really is a rock.

and taste, and she purposefully seeks it out. This absence of sensory or motor cues characterizes the **symbolic function**: the ability to use symbols, or mental representations—words, numbers, or images to which a person has attached meaning. Having symbols for things helps children to think about them and their qualities, to remember them and talk about them, without having them physically present. The development of symbolic thought makes possible other important advances.

symbolic function In Piaget's terminology, ability to use mental representations (words, numbers, or images) to which a child has attached meaning.

Children show the symbolic function through deferred imitation, symbolic play, and language. *Deferred imitation,* which appears to begin in infancy(see Chapter 6), is the repetition of an observed action after time has passed. In *symbolic play,* children make an object stand for (symbolize) something else; for example, a doll may represent a child. *Language,* which we discuss later in this chapter, involves the use of a common system of symbols (words) to communicate.

The world becomes more orderly and predictable as children develop a better understanding of *identities:* the concept that people and many things are basically the same even if they change in form, size, or appearance. This understanding underlies the emerging self-concept (see Chapters 7 and 10).

Young children's persistent "why" questions show that they can now link *cause and effect,* not only with regard to specific occurrences in the physical environment (as in infancy and toddlerhood), but in more complex social contexts. Very young children spontaneously use such words as *because* and *so.* "He's crying because he doesn't want to put his pajamas on," said Marie at 27 months, watching her brother cry loudly as he was being dressed for bed.

Researchers asked 3- and 4-year-olds to look at pictures like those on the top line of Figure 9-1 and then to choose the picture on the bottom line that would tell what happened (Gelman, Bullock, & Meck, 1980). The children showed an understanding of causality by telling such stories as: "First you have dry glasses, and then water gets on the glasses, and you end up with wet glasses."

Young children develop proficiency at *classifying,* or grouping objects, people, and events into categories based on similarities and differences. By the age of 4, many children can classify by two criteria, such as color and shape (Denney, 1972). As children use the ability to classify to order many aspects of their lives,

Story A

Choices for A

Figure 9-1
Example of sequence to test understanding of cause and effect. A child is asked to look at pictures like those in the top row, to pick the one in the bottom row that would show what happened, and to tell a story about what happened.
Source: Gelman, Bullock, & Meck, 1980.

they categorize people as "good," "bad," "friend," "nonfriend," and so forth. Thus classification is a cognitive ability with social and emotional implications.

Understanding of basic *number* concepts seems to begin in infancy. By early childhood, according to some research, children recognize five principles of counting (Gelman & Gallistel, 1978; Sophian, 1988):

1. The *1-to-1 principle:* You say only one number-name for each item being counted ("One . . . two . . . three . . .").
2. The *stable-order principle:* You say number-names in a set order ("One, two, three . . ." rather than "Three, one, two . . .").
3. The *order-irrelevance principle:* You can start counting with any item, and the total count will be the same.
4. The *cardinality principle:* The last number-name you use is the total number of items being counted. (If there are 5 items, the last number will be "5.")
5. The *abstraction principle:* You can count all sorts of things.

Children now have words for comparing quantities. They can say one tree is *bigger* than another, or one cup holds *more* juice than another. As early as age 3 or 4, they know that if they have one cookie and then get another cookie, they have more cookies than they had before, and that if they give one cookie to another child, they have less. Such quantitative knowledge appears to be universal, though it develops at different rates, depending on how important counting is in a particular family or culture and how much instruction parents, teachers, or educational television programs provide (L. B. Resnick, 1989; Saxe, Guberman, & Gearhart, 1987).

Limitations of Preoperational Thought

Although early childhood is a time of significant cognitive achievement, Piaget found important limitations in preoperational thinking compared with what children can do when they reach the stage of concrete operations in middle childhood. Awareness of these limitations is important for parents, teachers, health professionals, and other adults who need to explain things to children. Let's look at some of these limitations: *centration, irreversibility, focus on states, transductive reasoning,* and *egocentrism.* We'll also discuss more recent research that has challenged some of Piaget's observations.

Preoperational children show **centration** by focusing on one aspect of a situation and neglecting others. They come to illogical conclusions because they cannot *decenter*—think about several aspects of a situation at one time.

centration   In Piaget's theory, a limitation of preoperational thought that leads the child to focus on one aspect of a situation and neglect others, often leading to illogical conclusions.

decenter   In Piaget's terminology, to think simultaneously about several aspects of a situation; characteristic of operational thought.

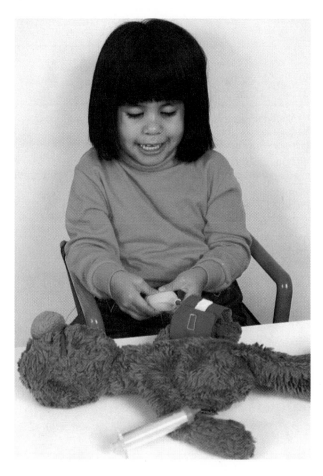

As Anna pretends to take Grover's blood pressure, she is showing a major cognitive achievement: a combination of symbolic play and deferred imitation, the ability to act out an action she observed some time before.

A classic example of centration is Piaget's famous experiment designed to test the development of *conservation*, the awareness that two things that are equal remain so if their appearance is altered, so long as nothing is added or taken away. Piaget found that children do not fully understand this principle until the stage of concrete operations and that they develop different kinds of conservation at different ages. Table 9-3 shows how various dimensions of conservation have been tested.

In one type of conservation task, conservation of liquid, 5-year-old Jeffrey is shown two identical clear glasses, each one short and wide and each holding the same amount of water. Jeffrey is asked whether the amount of water in the two glasses is equal. When he agrees, the water in one glass is poured into a third glass, a tall, thin one. Jeffrey is now asked whether both contain the same amount of water or whether one contains more, and why. In early childhood—even after watching the water poured out of one of the short, fat glasses into a tall, thin glass or even after pouring it himself—Jeffrey will say that either the taller glass or the wider one contains more water. When asked why, he says, "This one is bigger this way," stretching his arms to show the height or width. Preoperational children cannot consider height *and* width at the same time. Since they center on one aspect, they cannot think logically.

Preoperational logic is also limited by *irreversibility:* failure to understand that an operation or action can go two or more ways. Children show irreversibility by worrying that a cut will not heal or a broken leg cannot be mended. In the liquid conservation task, once Jeffrey can imagine restoring the original state of the water by pouring it back into the other glass, he will realize that the amount of water in both glasses is the same.

Preoperational children commonly think as if they were watching a filmstrip with a series of static frames: They *focus on successive states* and do not recognize

conservation In Piaget's terminology, awareness that two objects that are equal according to a certain measure (such as length, weight, or quantity) remain equal in the face of perceptual alteration (for example, a change in shape) so long as nothing has been added to or taken away from either object.

irreversibility In Piaget's terminology, a limitation on preoperational thinking consisting of failure to understand that an operation can go in two or more directions.

Table 9-3 Tests of Various Kinds of Conservation

Conservation Task	Show Child (and Have Child Acknowledge) That Both Items Are Equal	Perform Transformation	Ask Child	Preoperational Child Usually Answers
Number	Two equal, parallel rows of candies	Space the candies in one row farther apart.	"Are there the same number of candies in each row or does one row have more?"	"The longer one has more."
Length	Two parallel sticks of the same length	Move one stick to the right.	"Are both sticks the same size or is one longer?"	"The one on the right (or left) is longer."
Liquid	Two identical glasses holding equal amounts of liquid	Pour liquid from one glass into a taller, narrower glass.	"Do both glasses have the same amount of liquid or does one have more?"	"The taller one has more."
Matter (mass)	Two balls of clay of the same size	Roll one ball into a sausage shape.	"Do both pieces have the same amount of clay or does one have more?"	"The sausage has more."
Weight	Two balls of clay of the same weight	Roll one ball into a sausage shape.	"Do both weigh the same or does one weigh more?"	"The sausage weighs more."
Area	Two toy rabbits, two pieces of cardboard (representing grassy fields), with blocks or toys (representing barns on the fields); same number of "barns" on each board	Rearrange the blocks on one piece of board.	"Does each rabbit have the same amount of grass to eat or does one have more?"	"The one with the blocks close together has more to eat."
Volume	Two glasses of water with two equal-sized balls of clay in them	Roll one ball into a sausage shape.	"If we put the sausage back in the glass, will the water be the the same height in each glass, or will one be higher?"	"The water in the glass with the sausage will be higher."

transduction In Piaget's terminology, a preoperational child's tendency to mentally link particular experiences, whether or not there is logically a causal relationship.

egocentrism In Piaget's terminology, inability to consider another person's point of view; a characteristic of preoperational thought.

CHECKPOINT

Can you . . .

• List seven cognitive advances of the preoperational stage and discuss implications of these advances for children's daily lives?

• Identify seven limitations on preoperational thinking identified by Piaget, and give an example of each?

the transformation from one state to another. In the conservation experiment, they focus on the water as it stands in each glass rather than on the water being poured from one glass to another, and so they fail to realize that the amount of water is the same.

Preoperational children reason by *transduction*. They view one situation as the basis for another situation, often one occurring at about the same time, whether or not there is logically a causal relationship. For example, they may think that their "bad" thoughts or behavior caused their own or another child's illness, or feel guilty about their parents' divorce. ("I was bad today. Mom and Dad don't love each other anymore. I made them not love each other.")

Egocentrism is the inability to see things except from one's own point of view. It is not selfishness but self-centered understanding, and, according to Piaget, it is at the heart of much of the limited thinking of young children. Egocentrism is a form of centration: Piaget claimed that young children center so much on their own point of view that they cannot take in another's view. Three-year-olds are not, of course, as egocentric as newborn babies, who cannot distinguish between the universe and their own bodies; but, said Piaget, they still think the universe centers on them. Egocentrism may help explain why young children (as we will see) have trouble separating reality from what goes on inside their own heads and why they show confusion about what causes what. When Jeffrey believes that his "bad thoughts" have made his sister sick, or that he caused his parents' marital troubles, he is thinking egocentrically.

Challenges to Piaget's Conclusions

Piaget's theory and research form a valuable starting point for understanding young children's cognitive development. However, Piaget seems to have underestimated the capabilities of preoperational children, as he did with sensorimotor

Figure 9-2
Piaget's three-mountain task. A preoperational child is unable to describe the "mountains" from the doll's point of view—an indication of egocentrism, according to Piaget.

children. More recent research, using more age-appropriate language and tasks, has shown that certain abilities seem to develop earlier than he suggested and that many children show greater competence than Piaget thought possible.

Egocentrism, Animism, and Empathy

To study egocentrism, Piaget designed the *three-mountain task* (see Figure 9-2). A child sits facing a table that holds three large mounds. A doll is placed on a chair at the opposite side of the table. The investigator asks the child how the "mountains" would look to the doll. Piaget found that young children usually could not answer the question correctly; instead, they described the "mountains" from their own perspective. Piaget saw this as evidence that preoperational children cannot imagine a different point of view (Piaget & Inhelder, 1967).

However, another experimenter who posed a similar problem in a different way got different results (Hughes, 1975). In the *doll and police officer task,* the child sits in front of a square board with dividers that separate it into four sections. A toy police officer is put at the edge of the board; a doll is set in one section and then moved from one section to another. After each move the child is asked, "Can the police officer see the doll?" Then another toy police officer is brought into the action, and the child is told to hide the doll from both officers. In this study, 30 children between the ages of 3½ and 5 were correct 9 out of 10 times.

Why were these children able to take another person's point of view (the police officer's) when those doing the mountain task were not? It may be because the "police officer" task calls for thinking in more familiar, less abstract ways. Most children do not look at mountains and do not think about what other people might see when looking at one, but most 3-year-olds know about dolls and police officers and hiding. Thus, contrary to Piaget's claim, young children may show egocentrism primarily in situations beyond their experience.

Animism is the tendency to attribute life to objects that are not alive. When Piaget asked young children whether the wind and the clouds were alive, their answers led him to think they were confused about what is alive and what is not. Piaget attributed this to egocentrism; one child, for example, said the moon is alive "because we are."

However, when later researchers questioned 3- and 4-year-olds about differences between a rock, a person, and a doll, the children showed they understood that people are alive and rocks and dolls are not (Gelman, Spelke, & Meck, 1983). They did not attribute thoughts or emotions to rocks, and they cited the fact that dolls cannot move on their own as evidence that dolls are not alive. The "animism" Piaget saw in young children may have been due to the fact that the things he asked about (such as wind and clouds) show movement—and are very far away. Since children know so little about wind and clouds, they are less certain about them than about familiar things such as rocks and dolls.

Research also challenges Piaget's belief that egocentrism delays the development of *empathy*, the ability to understand what another person is feeling. Even 10- to 12-month-old babies cry when they see another child crying; by

animism Tendency to attribute life to objects that are not alive.

empathy Ability to put oneself in another person's place and feel what that person feels.

The young girl on the right is old enough to know that her cousin needs consoling. Empathy, the ability to understand another person's feelings, begins at an early age.

13 or 14 months, they pat or hug a crying child; by 18 months they may hold out a new toy to replace a broken one or give a bandage to someone with a cut finger (Yarrow, 1978). In early childhood, empathy, which is important for forming and maintaining relationships, shows itself more and more.

When Anna, at 4, was going home with her parents after a visit to her grandmother, she said, "Don't be sad, Grandma. We'll come see you again, and you can come see us in New York." Anna's grandmother had not cried or talked about feeling sad, but Anna imagined how she must have been feeling. This kind of understanding usually comes earlier to children in families that talk a lot about feelings and causality, underscoring the relationship between the cognitive and the emotional (Dunn, 1991; Dunn, Brown, Slomkowski, Tesla, & Youngblade, 1991).

Empathy is closely related to children's *theory of mind,* their emerging awareness of their own mental state and that of other people.

theory of mind Awareness and understanding of mental processes.

Do Young Children Have Theories of Mind?

"Why does Pedro look sad?" "What made Mommy mad at me?" The ability to make sense of how other people are acting is a major step in cognitive development. How and when do children come to understand what another person is thinking and feeling? For that matter, how and when do they come to be aware of their own state of mind?

Piaget (1929) was the first scholar to investigate children's conception of their mental life—their theory of mind. He asked children such questions as "Where do dreams come from?" and "What do you think with?" On the basis of the answers, he concluded that children younger than 6 cannot distinguish between thoughts or dreams and real physical entities and have no theory of mind. However, more recent research indicates that children do discover their minds sometime between the ages of 2 and 5, when their knowledge about mental states and attitudes grows dramatically (Astington, 1993; Bower, 1993; Flavell, Green, & Flavell, 1995).

Again, methodology appears to have made the difference. Piaget's questions were abstract, and he expected children to be able to put their understanding into words. Contemporary researchers use vocabulary and objects children are familiar with. Instead of talking in generalities, they observe children in everyday activities or give them concrete examples. In this way, we have learned, for example, that 3-year-olds can tell the difference between a boy who has a cookie and a boy who is thinking about a cookie; they know which boy can touch, share, and eat it (Astington, 1993). They know that people who get what they want are likely to feel happy, and people who don't get what they want are likely to feel sad (Flavell et al., 1995).

Young children's theory of mind continues to develop during early childhood. Let's look at some aspects of it: *knowledge about thinking, distinguishing fantasy from reality, awareness of false beliefs and deception,* and *distinguishing appearance from reality.*

Knowledge About Thinking   Young children know something about what thinking is, but they are less aware of when it occurs and what people are thinking about. Between ages 3 and 5, children come to understand that thinking goes on inside the mind; that it can deal with either real or imaginary things; that someone can be thinking of one thing while doing or looking at something else; that a person whose eyes and ears are covered can think about objects; that someone who looks pensive is probably thinking; and that thinking is different from seeing, talking, touching, and knowing (Flavell, Green, & Flavell, 1995).

However, preschoolers generally believe mental activity starts and stops; they assume that when the mind has nothing pressing to do, it does nothing. They do not seem to be aware that the mind is constantly engaged in thought. They tend not to realize that they have just been thinking, and they have trouble remembering what they were thinking about. Not until middle childhood do children realize that the mind is continuously active (Flavell, 1993; Flavell et al., 1995). Preschoolers also have little or no awareness that they or other people think in words, or "talk to themselves in their heads," or that they think while they are looking, listening, reading, or talking (Flavell, Green, Flavell, & Grossman, 1997).

Distinguishing Fantasy from Reality   Sometime between 18 months and 3 years, children learn to distinguish between real and imagined events. Three-year-olds know the difference between a real dog and a dog in a dream, and between something invisible (such as air) and something imaginary. They can pretend and can tell when someone else is pretending (Flavell et al., 1995). Still, the line between fantasy and reality may seem to blur at times. In one study (P. L. Harris, Brown, Marriott, Whittall, & Harmer, 1991), forty 4- to 6-year-olds were shown two cardboard boxes. They were asked to pretend that there was a monster in one box and a bunny in another. Each box had a small hole in it, and the children were asked whether they wanted to put a finger or a stick in the holes. The experimenter then left the room "to fetch something," and some of the children did touch the boxes. Even though most of the children claimed they were just pretending about both the bunny and the monster, most preferred to touch the box holding the imaginary bunny, and more put their finger in that box and put the stick in the monster box.

The researchers interpreted these results as suggesting that even though young children understand the distinction between fantasy and reality, they sometimes act as if the creatures of their imagination could exist. On the other hand, the children in that study may simply have been carrying on the unfinished pretend game in the experimenter's absence. That was the conclusion of later research (Golomb & Galasso, 1995), which failed to support the Harris team's findings. This time the experimenter (who was familiar to the children and thus may have made them feel more at ease) remained in the room and clearly ended the pretense. Under these conditions, and when other things were available to play with, only about 10 percent of the children touched or looked in the boxes. When questioned, almost all the children showed a clear understanding that the creatures were imaginary, though 4-year-olds were better than 3-year-olds at explaining the difference between "real" and "pretend."

Awareness of False Beliefs Five-year-old Mariella is shown a candy box and is asked what is in it. "Candy," she says. But when she opens the box, she finds crayons, not candy. "What will a child who hasn't opened the box think is in it?" the researcher asks. "Candy!" shouts Mariella, grinning at the joke. When the researcher repeats the same procedure with 3-year-old Bobby, he too answers the first question with "Candy." But after seeing the crayons in the box, when asked what another child would think was in the box, he says "Crayons." And then he says that he himself originally thought crayons would be in the box (Flavell, 1993; Flavell et al., 1995).

Not until children are 4 or 5 years old, according to this and some other research, do they understand that they or other people can hold false beliefs (Moses & Flavell, 1990). This understanding flows from the realization that people hold mental representations of reality, which can sometimes be wrong; and 3-year-olds, at least in some studies, appear to lack such an understanding (Flavell et al., 1995). However, other researchers claim that 3-year-olds have at least a rudimentary understanding of false beliefs but may not show it when presented with complicated situations (Hala & Chandler, 1996).

Three-year-olds' failure to recognize false beliefs may stem more from egocentric thinking than from lack of awareness of mental representations. Children that age do see a relationship between belief and surprise: they know, for example, that a child who believes she is getting hot oatmeal for breakfast will be surprised if she gets cold spaghetti instead (H. M. Wellman & Banerjee, 1991). But they have difficulty recognizing that another person's belief—or desire—may be different from a very strong belief or desire that they themselves hold (C. Moore et al., 1995).

Older preschoolers' more advanced understanding of mental representations seems to be related to a growing ability to recognize another person's point of view. Four-year-olds understand that people who see or hear different versions of the same event may hold different beliefs. Not until about age 6, however, do children realize that two people who see or hear the same thing may interpret it differently (Pillow & Henrichon, 1996).

Distinguishing Appearance from Reality Related to the understanding of false beliefs is the ability to distinguish between a misleading appearance and reality: both tasks require the child to refer to two conflicting mental representations at the same time. According to Piaget, not until about age 5 or 6 do children understand the distinction between what *seems* to be and what *is*. Much later research bears him out, though some studies have found this ability beginning to emerge between ages 3 and 4 (Friend & Davis, 1993; C. Rice, Koinis, Sullivan, Tager-Flusberg, & Winner, 1997). This flaw in thinking may explain why a younger child is frightened of something that looks scary, such as a witch on a movie screen.

In one series of experiments (Flavell, Green, & Flavell, 1986), 3-year-olds confused appearance and reality in a variety of tests. For example, the experimenters showed preschoolers a red car and then covered it with a filter that made it look black. When the children were asked what color the car really was, they said "Black." When the children put on special sunglasses that made milk look green, they said the milk *was* green, even though they had just seen white milk. When an experimenter put on a Halloween mask in front of the children, they thought the experimenter was someone else. In another study, which dealt not only with physical appearances (the colors of animal cutouts, which were altered by transparent plastic filters) but also with recognition of a story character's real versus feigned emotional state (looking happy while actually feeling sad), 5- and 6-year-olds did much better than 4-year-olds (Friend & Davis, 1993).

Can Training Help Children Acquire Cognitive Abilities?

Can the acquisition of cognitive abilities be speeded up? It depends on the ability, the timing, and the way a child is taught. Certain methods of teaching conservation seem to work when a child is already on the verge of acquiring the concept. In one study (D. Field, 1981), 3- and 4-year-olds were shown sets of checkers, candies, and sticks. A child was asked to pick the two rows that had the same number of items or to show which two objects were the same length. Then the objects were moved or changed, and the child was asked whether they were the same. The child was given one of three rules explaining *why* they were the same: (1) *identity* ("No matter where you put them, they're still the same candies"); (2) *reversibility* ("We just have to put the sticks back together to see that they are the same length"); or (3) *compensation* ("Yes, this stick does go farther in this direction, but at the other end the stick is going farther, and so they balance each other").

The type of training and the children's age affected how well they learned. Children who were told the identity rule made the most progress, and those who learned reversibility also advanced; but those who were taught compensation benefited little from the training. Four-year-olds (who presumably were closer to acquiring conservation on their own) were more apt than 3-year-olds to learn the concept and to retain it up to 5 months later. Three-year-olds were not able to conserve as many quantities and tended to lose whatever abilities they did gain.

Apparently, as Piaget held (and as Vygotsky's concept of the zone of proximal development suggests), only when children's cognitive structures are well enough developed to handle a principle such as conservation can training help. It gives children a strategy for integrating the principle into their thought processes. More recent attempts to train children who lag in such Piagetian skills as classification and number conservation also support Piaget in this (Pasnak, Hansbarger, Dodson, Hart, & Blaha, 1996).

Can training help children develop a theory of mind? Early attempts to train young children to distinguish appearance from reality were unsuccessful (Flavell, Zhang, Zou, Dong, & Qi, 1983). However, when 3-year-olds were shown a sponge that looked like a rock and were asked to help trick someone else into thinking it was a rock, the children were able to make the distinction between the way the sponge looked (like a rock) and what it actually was (a sponge). Apparently, putting the task in the context of a deception helped the children realize that an object can be perceived as other than what it actually is. Three-year-olds also did better when shown the rock-like sponge along with two objects that represented its real and apparent identities (a rock and a sponge). Now they did not have to hold the information about the two identities in their minds—a strain on their limited information-processing capacity (C. Rice, et al., 1997).

Development of Language

During early childhood Anna was full of questions: "How many sleeps until tomorrow?" "Who filled the river with water?" "Do babies have muscles?" "Do smells come from inside my nose?"

Young children are interested in the whole wide world. They ask questions about everything, and their linguistic skills improve rapidly. The child who, at 3, describes how Daddy "hatches" wood (chops with a hatchet), or asks Mommy to "piece" her food (cut it into little pieces), or says she is not ready to go to bed because she is not yet "yawny" may, by the age of 5, tell her mother, "Don't be ridiculous!" or proudly point to her toys and say, "See how I organized everything?"

Building Blocks of Speech

At the breakfast table, Terry, age 3½, overheard his grandparents discussing the number of square feet of tile needed for their kitchen. "But then," he piped up, "you'd need to have square shoes!"

CHECKPOINT

Can you . . .

• Give examples of research that challenges Piaget's views on young children's cognitive limitations?

• Describe changes in children's knowledge about the way their minds work between the ages of 3 and 6?

• Discuss the implications of efforts to train 3- and 4-year-olds' cognitive abilities?

Young children's growing facility with speech helps them form their own unique view of the world, in ways that often surprise and amuse adults. In vocabulary, grammar, and syntax, preschoolers make rapid advances, but they also show signs of linguistic immaturity.

Vocabulary

By the age of 6, the average child understands more than 14,000 words, having learned an average of 9 new words a day since about 1½ years of age (M. L. Rice, 1982). Apparently children do this by *fast mapping*, which allows them to absorb the meaning of a new word after hearing it only once or twice in conversation. On the basis of the context, children seem to form a quick hypothesis about the meaning of the word and store it in memory. Linguists are not sure how fast mapping occurs, but it seems likely that children draw on what they know about rules for forming words, similar words, grammatical contexts, and the subject under discussion.

Names of objects seem to be easier to fast map than names of actions (verbs). In trying to figure out the meaning of a new word, children generally attach it to an object or action whose name they have not yet learned (Golinkoff, Jacquet, Hirsh-Pasek, & Nandakumar, 1996). Yet many 3- and 4-year-olds also seem able to tell when two words refer to the same object or action—an impressive feat (Savage & Au, 1996).

Still, young children do not always use a word precisely as adults do (Pease & Gleason, 1985). For example, Anna at about age 4 used *tomorrow* to refer to any time in the future and *yesterday* for any time in the past. On the other hand, a child may be quite literal in interpreting a word and thus receive a different meaning from the intended one. When Diane told 5-year-old Anna that her shiny red boots were "sharp," Anna said, "No, they aren't—they don't have nails in them!"

The use of *metaphor*, a figure of speech in which a word or phrase that usually designates one thing is applied to another, becomes increasingly common during these years (Vosniadou, 1987). Once Anna, upset by her parents' quarreling, exclaimed, "Why are you two being such grumpy old bears?" Anna's use of metaphor reflected her growing ability to see similarities between (in this case) parents and bears, and thus was related to her ability to classify. The use of metaphors shows an ability to use knowledge about one type of thing to better understand another, an ability needed for acquiring many kinds of knowledge.

Grammar and Syntax

At 3, children typically use plurals and past tense and know the difference between *I, you,* and *we.* Between ages 4 and 5, sentences average four to five words. Children now use prepositions such as *over, under, in, on,* and *behind.* In some respects, though, their comprehension may be immature. For example, 4-year-old Noah can carry out a command that includes more than one step ("Pick up your toys and put them in the cupboard"). However, if his mother tells him "You may watch TV after you pick up your toys," he may process the words in the order in which he hears them and think he may first watch television and then pick up his toys. Around ages 5 and 6, children speak in longer and more complicated sentences. They use more conjunctions, prepositions, and articles. Between 6 and 7 years of age, children begin to speak in compound and complex sentences and use all parts of speech.

Although young children speak fluently, understandably, and fairly grammatically, they still have much to learn about language. For one thing, they rarely use the passive voice ("I was dressed by Grandpa"), conditional sentences ("If I were big, I could drive the bus"), or the auxiliary verb *have* ("I have seen that lady before") (C. S. Chomsky, 1969). They often make errors because they have

fast mapping Process by which a child absorbs the meaning of a new word after hearing it only once or twice in conversation.

Preschool children's mastery of vocabulary, grammar, and syntax helps them communicate more clearly. In social speech, they use words, phrases, and sentences to establish and maintain social contact, taking into account the other person's viewpoint. Sometimes a prop such as a toy phone can help conversation flow more easily.

not yet learned exceptions to rules. Saying "holded" instead of "held" or "eated" instead of "ate" is a normal sign of linguistic progress. When children discover a rule, such as adding -ed to a verb for past tense, they tend to *overregularize*—to use it even with words that do not conform to the rule. Eventually, they notice that -ed is not always used to form the past tense of a verb.

Communicative and Noncommunicative Speech

The form and function of speech are linked. As children master words, sentences, and grammar, they become more competent at communicating, and these verbal interactions help prepare them for literacy. Young children also spend a fair amount of time talking to themselves, a phenomenon that diminishes during middle childhood.

Pragmatics and Social Speech

Although Piaget characterized most of young children's speech as egocentric, research suggests that children use both gestures and verbal speech communicatively from an early age. Two-year-olds show objects to others (H. Wellman & Lempers, 1977), and 4-year-olds use "parentese" when speaking to 2-year-olds (Shatz & Gelman, 1973). Three- to 5-year-olds communicate very differently with a person who can see and with one who cannot; they will point to a toy for a sighted listener but describe it to a blindfolded one (Maratsos, 1973).

Pragmatics, the practical knowledge needed to use language for communicative purposes, includes learning how to ask for things, how to tell a story or joke, how to begin and continue a conversation, and how to adjust comments to the listener's perspective (M. L. Rice, 1982). These are all aspects of *social speech*—speech intended to be understood by a listener.

Social speech develops markedly during early childhood. At age 2½, children begin to engage in true conversation, in which they recognize the need to make their own speech clear and relevant to what someone else is saying. After the third birthday, children's pronunciation and grammar typically improve rapidly, making it easier for others to understand what they say. Children pay more attention to the effect of their speech on others. They want to be understood; if people cannot understand them, they try to explain themselves more clearly. By age 5, children understand and use such fundamentals of conversation as adjusting what they say to what the listener knows. They can now use words to resolve disputes.

pragmatics The practical knowledge needed to use language for communicative purposes.

social speech Speech intended to be understood by a listener.

Table 9-4	Types of Private Speech	
Type	**Child's Activity**	**Examples**
Wordplay, repetition	Repeating words and sounds, often in playful, rhythmic recitation	José wanders around the room, repeating in a singsong manner, "Put the mushroom on your head, put the mushroom in your pocket, put the mushroom on your nose."
Solitary fantasy play and speech addressed to nonhuman objects	Talking to objects, playing roles, producing sound effects for objects	Darryl says, "Ka-powee ka-powee," aiming his finger like a gun. Ashley says in a high-pitched voice while playing in the doll corner, "I'll be better after the doctor gives me a shot. Ow!" she remarks as she pokes herself with her finger (a pretend needle).
Emotional release and expression	Expressing emotions or feelings directed inward rather than to a listener	Keiko is given a new box of crayons and says to no one in particular, "Wow! neat!" Rachel is sitting at her desk with an anxious expression on her face, repeating to herself, "My mom's sick, my mom's sick."
Egocentric communication	Communicating with another person, but expressing the information so incompletely or peculiarly that it can't be understood	David and Mark are seated next to one another on the rug. David says to Mark, "It broke," without explaining what or when. Susan says to Ann at the art table, "Where are the paste-ons?" Ann says, "What paste-ons?" Susan shrugs and walks off.
Describing or guiding one's own activity	Narrating one's actions, thinking out loud	Omar sits down at the art table and says to himself, "I want to draw something. Let's see. I need a big piece of paper. I want to draw my cat." Working in her arithmetic workbook, Cathy says to no one in particular, "Six." Then, counting on her fingers, she continues, "Seven, eight, nine, ten. It's ten, it's ten. The answer's ten."
Reading aloud, sounding out words	Reading aloud or sounding out words while reading	While reading a book, Tom begins to sound out a difficult word. "Sher-lock Holm-lock," he says slowly and quietly. Then he tries again. "Sher-lock Holm-lock, Sherlock Holme," he says, leaving off the final *s* in his most successful attempt.
Inaudible muttering	Speaking so quietly that the words cannot be understood by an observer	Tony's lips move as he works a math problem.

Source: Adapted from Berk & Garvin, 1984.

Private Speech

Anna, age 4, was alone in her room painting. When she finished, she was overheard saying aloud, "Now I have to put the pictures somewhere to dry. I'll put them by the window. They need to get dry now. I'll paint some more dinosaurs."

private speech Talking aloud to oneself with no intent to communicate.

Private speech—talking aloud to oneself with no intent to communicate with others—is normal and common in childhood, accounting for 20 to 60 percent of what children say. The youngest children playfully repeat rhythmic sounds; older children "think out loud" or mutter in barely audible tones (see Table 9-4).

The purpose and value of private speech have been controversial. Piaget viewed it as egocentric. Also, he maintained, young children talk while they do things because the symbolic function is not fully developed: they do not yet distinguish between words and the actions the words stand for. Vygotsky, however, did not look upon private speech as immature. Instead, he saw it as a special form of communication: communication with oneself. Like Piaget, Vygotsky (1962) believed that private speech helps children integrate language with thought. Unlike Piaget, who saw private speech as characteristic of the preoperational stage, Vygotsky suggested that private speech increases during the early school years as children use it to guide and master their actions and then fades away as they become able to do this silently.

Research supports Vygotsky's interpretation. Among nearly 150 middle-class children ages 4 to 10, private speech rose and then fell with age. The most sociable children used it the most, apparently supporting Vygotsky's view that private speech is stimulated by social experience (Berk, 1986; Kohlberg, Yaeger, & Hjertholm, 1968). The brightest children used it earliest; for them, it peaked around age 4, compared with age 5 to 7 for children of average intelligence. By age 9 it had virtually disappeared in all the children.

Understanding the significance of private speech has practical implications, especially in school (Berk, 1986). Talking to oneself or muttering should not be considered misbehavior; a child may be struggling with a problem and may need to think out loud. Instead of insisting on perfect quiet, teachers can set aside areas where children can talk and learn without disturbing others. Children should also be encouraged to play with others to help them develop the internal thought processes that will eventually displace private speech.

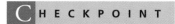

CHECKPOINT

Can you . . .

- Trace normal progress in 3- to 6-year-olds' vocabulary, grammar, syntax, and conversational abilities?

- Explain why children use private speech?

Delayed Language Development

The fact that Albert Einstein did not start to speak until he was close to 3 years old may encourage parents of children whose speech develops later than usual. Language development is delayed in about 3 percent of preschool-age children, though their intelligence is usually average or above (M. L. Rice, 1989). Some have a history of otitis media (an inflammation of the middle ear) between 12 and 18 months of age; these children improve in language ability when the infection, with its related hearing loss, clears up (Lonigan, Fischel, Whitehurst, Arnold, & Valdez-Menchaca, 1992).

It is unclear why children with no detectable problems speak late. They do not necessarily lack linguistic input at home. Some of their parents talk to them more in terms of what the children can say rather than what they can understand (Whitehurst, Fischel, Caulfield, DeBaryshe, & Valdez-Menchaca, 1989); but this may be more the result than the cause of their delay. These children may have a cognitive limitation that makes it hard for them to learn the rules of language (Scarborough, 1990).

Some current investigations focus on problems in fast mapping new words heard in conversation. Studies suggest that children with delayed language skills need to hear a word more often than other children do before they can incorporate it into their vocabulary (M. Rice, Oetting, Marquis, Bode, & Pae, 1994; M. L. Rice, 1989).

Delayed language development can have far-reaching cognitive, social, and emotional consequences. Children who show an unusual tendency to mispronounce words at age 2, who have poor vocabulary at age 3, or who have trouble naming objects at age 5 are apt to have reading disabilities later on (M. Rice et al., 1994; Scarborough, 1990). Children who do not speak or understand as well as their peers tend to be judged negatively by adults and other children.

In one study, kindergarten teachers, college students, laypersons, and specialists in speech problems listened to audiotaped samples of preschool children's speech. All four groups of adults rated children with delayed language skills as less bright, less likable, less socially mature, less likely to succeed in kindergarten, and less likely to be classroom leaders than other children (M. L. Rice, Hadley, & Alexander, 1993). Children whom adults view as unintelligent or immature may "live down" to these expectations. Also, peers are less likely to want to play with a child who does not understand what others are saying (Gertner, Rice, & Hadley, 1994), and children who are not accepted by peers have trouble making friends. In both respects, self-esteem suffers.

Speech and language therapy for children with delayed language development should begin with professional assessment of both child and family. It may include therapeutic strategies focusing on specific language forms, a specialized preschool program targeting language skills, and follow-up programs either in or out of school during the elementary school years (M. L. Rice, 1989).

One promising new technique involves reading picture books to the child using a method called *dialogic reading*. The method is based on one originally developed for younger children and described in Chapter 6. It includes asking "what" questions, following the child's answers with more questions, repeating and expanding on what the child says, asking open-ended questions, helping the child as needed, giving praise and encouragement, following the child's interests, and (above all) having fun.

Parents of thirty-three 3- to 6-year-olds with mild-to-moderate language delays were given two brief training sessions, 3 to 4 weeks apart, either in dialogic reading or in a conversational training method based on similar principles. About a month after completion of the training, the mothers were videotaped reading books and playing with toys with their children. The children whose mothers had had the dialogic reading training tended to give more verbal responses to questions than before and to use a more varied vocabulary and longer utterances, and their improvement was greater than that of the comparison group. However, the results were not dramatic, perhaps because the training and follow-up periods were so short. Children whose mothers' linguistic behavior was most affected by the training were most likely to improve (Dale, Crain-Thoreson, Notari-Syverson, & Cole, 1996).

Why is reading picture books more effective than just talking with a child? Shared reading affords a natural opportunity for giving information and increasing vocabulary. It provides a focus for both the adult's and child's attention and for asking and responding to questions. Shared reading is an important vehicle for language development, not only in children with language delays but also in those whose development is proceeding normally. Furthermore, it is usually enjoyable for both children and adults; it offers a way to foster emotional bonding while enhancing cognitive development.

Social Interaction and Preparation for Literacy

Social interaction, especially in the home, is a key factor in preparing young children for literacy. Children are more likely to become good readers and writers if, during the preschool years, parents provide conversational challenges the children are ready for—if they use a rich vocabulary and center dinner-table talk on the day's activities or on questions about why people do things and how things work. Such conversations help young children learn to choose words and put sentences together coherently (C. E. Snow, 1990, 1993). Interactive techniques for reading aloud, such as those described in Chapter 6 and in the preceding section, are also effective. Talking about books and, even more, about shared past events is an important contributor to literacy (E. Reese, 1995; see Box 9-1).

Preschool teachers have helped socioeconomically disadvantaged children expand their vocabularies by using relatively uncommon words. The children in these teachers' classes scored higher on vocabulary tests than children whose teachers did not use such words, and the children who heard the unfamiliar words used many of them in play (Dickinson, Cote, & Smith, 1993).

Educational television can help prepare children for literacy, especially if parents talk with children about what they see. In one study, the more time 3- to 5-year-olds spent watching *Sesame Street*, the more their vocabulary skills improved (M. L. Rice, Huston, Truglio, & Wright, 1990). The program teaches letters and numbers, as well as problem solving, reasoning, and understanding of the physical and social environments. The format is designed to attract children's attention and to get them to participate actively.

How children play is another factor in preliteracy development. Imaginative play, involving pretending or "make-believe," is most closely linked to literacy

Box 9-1 Building Narrative Skills as Preparation for Literacy

One day, on a walk with his mother, Emmett picked up a pine cone. "I'm going to take it to nursery school for 'show-and-tell,' " he said.

"Show-and-tell," a familiar part of the preschool day, is based on the importance of developing narrative skill. A child who can clearly tell classmates about finding a pine cone, or some other personal experience, is more likely to do well in school. The connection between being able to tell a story well and being able to read or write one hinges on the use of language to deal with things beyond the here and now. Thus talk about past events is good preparation for literacy (C. Peterson & McCabe, 1994; E. Reese, 1995).

How do young children learn to tell stories so others can understand them? According to Vygotskian theory and research, it happens through social interaction. When parents prompt 2- and 3-year-olds with frequent questions about the context of shared reminiscences ("When did you find the pine cone?" "Where did you find it?" "Who was with you?"), children soon learn to include this vital stage-setting information on their own (C. Peterson & McCabe, 1994).

A longitudinal study of 24 white, middle-class two-parent families (E. Reese, 1995) found that the Vygotskian assumption that parents need to do less prompting (scaffolding) as a child's skill increases may need to be qualified. Mother-child conversations about past events and during storybook reading were audiotaped when the children were 3 and almost 4 years old and again when they were nearly 5. Two months short of their sixth birthdays, before any of the children had entered first grade, they took a comprehensive test of literacy skills: knowledge of print concepts (such as the fact that books are read from left to right), receptive (understood) vocabulary, decoding (ability to figure out the sound and meaning of printed words), story comprehension, story recall, and ability to tell a story.

The quality of mother-child conversation—particularly about past events—was a strong predictor of literacy skills, especially print concepts, vocabulary, and comprehension. Most influential was mothers' increasing use of contextual questions and comments that helped children elaborate on events or link them with other incidents important to the child. Thus an expansion, not a withdrawal, of contextual cuing as children approach school age seems to promote these particular aspects of literacy. This cuing may help children recognize that words (whether spoken or written) have meaning.

On the other hand, as classic Vygotskian theory would predict, the child's own contribution to early conversations best predicted narrative skills. Children who took the lead in conversations at ages 3 and 4, rather than letting their mothers direct the content, were more likely to be competent storytellers as kindergartners. Narrative skill, then, may be an independent pathway to literacy—one in which the child, at least from age 3 on, takes an increasingly active part.

Still, another study of 15 of these same families (Haden, Haine, & Fivush, 1997) shows the importance of what mothers do. One role adults play in children's narrative development is to help bring out feelings about their experiences. When 3-year-olds' mothers, in the course of shared reminiscences, made frequent evaluative comments emphasizing subjective reactions ("You wanted to go on the slide," "It was a *huge* bowl," "Mommy was *wrong*"), the children were more likely to include their own evaluations 2½ years later in telling a story to a researcher who did not provide such cues.

Although mothers and fathers did not differ significantly in their handling of narrative conversations with their preschoolers and did not talk differently with their daughters than with their sons, girls showed more advanced narrative development than boys at age 3 and made more progress by age 5½. Also, both boys and girls gave longer, more contextually oriented, and more evaluative narratives with their fathers and with the unfamiliar researcher than with their mothers. It may be that young children see their fathers as representatives of the outside world and "expect to have to express themselves more fully with their fathers and with strangers than with their mothers" (Haden et al., 1997, p. 305).

Patterns of narration vary among cultures and are transmitted to children through parental conversation. Unlike the long, detailed exposition of a single experience, which is typical of North American preschoolers' narratives, Japanese children tend to tell shorter, more concise stories that combine several related experiences in a form resembling the lean, subtle structure of *haiku* (three-line poems). Mother-child conversations in the two cultures encourage these patterns. Japanese mothers are less likely than North American mothers to ask for descriptive information, they make fewer explicitly evaluative comments, and they frequently step in to cut short verbose statements. North American 5-year-olds make nearly twice as many utterances during each of their conversational turns as Japanese children. Japanese mothers also discourage overt expressions of emotion; in line with their culture's value of empathy, children are led to expect that listeners will put themselves in the speaker's position and fill in the blanks (Minami & McCabe, 1995).

There is, then, no single best way to promote literacy through shared narration; effective expression can develop within a range of narrative styles.

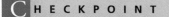

Can you . . .

- Discuss possible causes, consequences, and treatment of delayed language development?

- Identify factors in preparation for literacy?

recognition Ability to identify a previously encountered stimulus. Compare *recall.*

recall Ability to reproduce material from memory. Compare *recognition.*

(Christie, 1991). As children grow older, this kind of play becomes increasingly social, involving other people and a wide variety of objects. Story lines become more complex, evolving into well-coordinated scenarios, and roles and themes become more creative and unusual. All these changes offer children rich opportunities to learn, use, and practice language.

Information-Processing Approach: Development of Memory

When Anna was 3, she went on an apple-picking trip. Months later, she talked about riding on the bus, visiting a farm, picking apples, bringing them home, and eating them. She had a vivid memory of the event and enjoyed talking about it.

During early childhood, children show significant improvement in attention and in the speed and efficiency with which they process information. These advances allow cognitive strides, particularly in memory. Before the mid-1960s, there was little research on memory in children younger than 5; and until about the 1980s, most of that research was done in the laboratory. Now, with a surge of interest in information processing and the development of memory, we have a clearer picture of the "remembering child" in the everyday world.

Recognition and Recall

Recognition is the ability to identify something encountered before (for example, to pick out a missing mitten from a lost-and-found box). *Recall* is the ability to reproduce knowledge from memory (for example, to describe the mitten to someone). Preschool children, like all age groups, do better on recognition than on recall, but both abilities improve with age (Lange, MacKinnon, & Nida, 1989; N. Myers & Perlmutter, 1978).

The more familiar children are with an item, the better they can recall it. Also, young children can more easily recall items that have an understandable relationship to each other. When 3- and 4-year-olds were shown pairs of pictures, they did much better in recalling related pairs than unrelated ones (Staub, 1973). The type of relationship affects the degree of recall. Children are more likely to recall pictures when one member of a pair is a part of the other (say, a tire and a car) than when one item is the usual habitat of the other (say, a lake and a fish). They are least apt to recall pairs in which the two items belong to the same category (say, a hat and a sock).

Recall depends both on motivation to master skills and on how a child approaches a task. In one study (Lange et al., 1989), ninety-three 3- and 4-year-olds were tested on their knowledge of a variety of objects, were assessed on how reflective or impulsive they were, and were rated by preschool teachers and parents on such characteristics as initiative, use of problem-solving strategies, and pursuit of difficult tasks.

The children were videotaped as they handled two assortments of toys in succession and then tried to name them from memory. The best predictor of success was *mastery motivation:* the tendency to be independent, self-directed, and generally resourceful, as rated by the child's teacher. The only other relevant factor was what the child did while studying the toys. The more children named or grouped the toys, or spent time thinking about or repeating their names (in other words, used strategies to help them remember), the better their recall. These two factors did not seem related; that is, mastery motivation did not seem to encourage the use of particular study strategies.

Childhood Memories

Can you remember anything that happened to you before you were 3 years old? The chances are you can't. This inability to remember early events is called *infantile amnesia*. One explanation, held by Piaget (1969) and others, is that early events are not stored in memory at all. Freud believed that early memories are repressed because they are emotionally troubling. Some information-processing theorists suggested that early memories become inaccessible because they are not *encoded* (prepared for storage) as later memories are. None of these explanations is supported by recent research (K. Nelson, 1992, 1993). Very young children do seem to remember things that happened to them, much as adults do. Even children younger than 2 can talk about events that occurred a month before, and 4-year-olds remember trips they took at age 2 (K. Nelson, 1992). Why, then, don't these early memories last?

Explicit and Implicit Memory

A newer explanation arises from evidence that different *kinds* of memories are encoded in different ways. Memories that people know they have (such as knowledge of facts, names, and events) are encoded in a way that allows for intentional, or *explicit memory*. Other memories (for example, of how to throw a ball) seem to be encoded in a way that can produce behavioral change without intentional recall or even conscious awareness of the memory. This kind of memory is called *implicit memory* (Schacter, 1992), and it seems to exist before the brain structures necessary for explicit memory have formed (C. A. Nelson, 1995; Newcombe & Fox, 1994; see Chapter 6).

Memory in early childhood is rarely deliberate: young children simply remember events that made a strong impression, and most of these early conscious memories seem to be short-lived. However, implicit (unconscious) memories may persist much longer. In one study of implicit memory (Newcombe & Fox, 1994), 9- and 10-year-olds were shown photos of preschool classmates they had not seen for 5 years, along with photos of children they had never known. The children's *skin conductance* (movement of electrical impulses through the skin) was measured while they viewed the pictures. In a small but significant number of cases, positive responses appeared when the children saw pictures of their former classmates, even when they did not consciously recognize the faces. This finding suggests that people may retain memories from infancy or early childhood of which they are not aware, and that these submerged memories may affect behavior.

Generic, Episodic, and Autobiographical Memory

How, when, and why do children begin to form permanent conscious memories? To answer that question, let's look at three types of explicit childhood memory that serve different functions: *generic, episodic,* and *autobiographical* (K. Nelson, 1993).

Generic memory, which begins at about age 2, produces a **script**, or general outline of a familiar, repeated event without details of time or place. The script contains routines for situations that come up again and again; it helps a child know what to expect and how to act. For example, a child may have scripts for riding the bus to preschool or having lunch at Grandma's house.

Episodic memory refers to a particular incident that happened at a specific time and place. Young children remember more clearly events that are unique or new to them. Three-year-olds may recall details about a trip to the zoo for a year or longer (Fivush, Hudson, & Nelson, 1983), whereas generic memories of frequent events (such as going to the park) tend to blur together. However, given a young child's limited memory capacity, episodic memories are temporary. Unless they recur several times (in which case they are transferred to generic memory), they last for a few weeks or months and then fade. The reliability of children's episodic memory has become an important issue in lawsuits involving charges of child abuse (see Box 9-2).

generic memory Memory that produces a script of familiar routines to guide behavior.

script General remembered outline of a familiar, repeated event, used to guide behavior.

episodic memory Long-term memory of specific experiences or events, linked to time and place.

Box 9-2 How Reliable Is Young Children's Eyewitness Testimony?

Child abuse is a crime that often can be proved only by the testimony of preschool children (Doris, 1993). If a child's testimony is inaccurate, an innocent adult may be unfairly punished. The likelihood of tainted testimony may arise when, as often happens, a child is questioned again and again by multiple interviewers using a variety of methods and props (Steward & Steward, 1996).

Children responding to adults' suggestions have been known to "remember" events that never occurred. For 11 consecutive weeks, an interviewer told a 4-year-old, "You went to the hospital because your finger got caught in a mousetrap. Did this ever happen to you?" At first the boy said, "No, I've never been to the hospital." In the second interview he said, "Yes, I cried." By the eleventh interview, he gave a detailed recital of the event and the trip to the hospital, which he now said had happened the day before (Ceci, in Goleman, 1993).

According to some research, many children, given anatomically correct dolls, will insert fingers or sticks into a doll's vagina or anus, reporting that someone did that to them, even when it did not happen (S. J. Ceci & Bruck, 1993). In most other studies, however, use of dolls did *not* increase false reports but rather produced more complete reports. Young children may need such external cues as prods to memory (Steward & Steward, 1996).

Difficulty in *source monitoring* (identifying how memories originated) can be problematic if children do not know whether they "remember" something from experience or from imagining or being told or asked about it. Children as young as 3 can tell the difference between having seen, been told about, or imagined an object inside a box. This ability becomes significantly stronger by ages 4 and 5, depending on the source and the context (Woolley & Bruell, 1996).

Most research has found young preschoolers more suggestible than older children. This may be due to younger children's weaker episodic memory and also to their greater vulnerability to bribes, threats, or adult expectations. However, much of the older research was laboratory-based (S. J. Ceci & Bruck, 1993; Leichtman & Ceci, 1995).

To test young children's veracity in real-life circumstances, researchers had a man called "Sam Stone" visit a day-care center for a few minutes (Leichtman & Ceci, 1995). The visitor commented on a story that was being read, strolled around the room, and then waved goodbye and left. Each of the eight classes that witnessed the event was randomly assigned to one of four groups. All the children were interviewed once a week for 4 weeks. A *control* group were given no information about the visitor in advance and were questioned neutrally afterward. A *stereotype* group were repeatedly told stories about "Sam Stone" before his visit, depicting him as a well-meaning bumbler. A *suggestion* group, when questioned afterward, were given false suggestions that he had ripped a book and soiled a teddy bear. A *stereotype-plus-suggestion* group received both the stereotyped advance preparation and the misleading questioning.

In a fifth session with a new interviewer, nearly half of the 3- and 4-year-olds and 30 percent of 5- and 6-year-olds in the stereotype-plus-suggestion group spontaneously reported the book-ripping and teddy-bear-soiling; and when asked probing questions, nearly 3 out of 4 of the younger children claimed the visitor had done one or both. Lesser proportions of the groups that

(continued)

---

autobiographical memory
Memory of specific events in one's own life.

Autobiographical memory refers to memories that form a person's life history. These memories are specific and long-lasting. Although autobiographical memory is a type of episodic memory, not everything in episodic memory becomes part of it—only those memories that have a special, personal meaning. Autobiographical memory serves a social function, letting a person share something of the self with others.

Autobiographical memory begins for most people around age 4, and rarely before age 3. It increases slowly between ages 5 and 8; memories from then on may be recalled for 20, 40, or more years. Individuals differ in the onset of autobiographical memory; some people have vivid memories from the age of 3, while others do not remember much before age 8 (K. Nelson, 1992).

These findings suggest that autobiographical memory is linked with the development of language. Not until children can put memories into words can they hold them in their minds, reflect on them, and compare them with the memories of others. In line with Vygotsky's view of the importance of social interaction with adults, talking about shared events may help children learn how to formulate permanent memories to be called up when desired. As we have seen, this kind of talk may also help children learn to retell events, a skill related to the had received *only* stereotyped preparation or suggestive questioning gave false reports, generally in response to probing. Younger children were more suggestible than older ones.

By contrast, none of the children in the control group freely made false reports, and very few did so even when probed, showing that young children's testimony *can* be accurate when elicited neutrally. Reports may be more reliable if children are interviewed only once, soon after the event, by people who do not have an opinion about what took place, who do not ask leading questions, who ask open-ended rather than yes/no questions, who are patient and nonjudgmental, and who do not reward any responses (Leichtman & Ceci, 1995). Most 4- to 6-year-olds—4 out of 5 in one study—are unlikely to accept false suggestions concerning an event in which they were personally involved (being touched on the leg rather than the arm), but they still are more suggestible when asked leading questions. Suggestibility seems to diminish after age 4½ (Portwood & Repucci, 1996).

Young children are apt to err in recalling precise details of an event that varies with repetition, as is generally true of abuse. Researchers (Powell & Thomson, 1996) tested kindergartners and primary-grade students on recall of a staged sequence of activities, repeated six times with minor variations over a 3-week period. The activities included storytelling, puzzles, and a rest period, during which the teacher touched the children on either the arms or the legs. On the last occurrence, the children wore colorful badges, and this was the episode they were later questioned about.

The children who had repeatedly experienced the event recalled more general information than a control group who had experienced it only once, but their specific recollections were less accurate and consistent. When the control group did make errors, they reported things that had not been part of the event, whereas children with repeated exposure tended to confuse what had happened during the episode in question with what had happened during the other, similar episodes. This research supports the theory, discussed in this chapter, that several similar episodes blur together in young children's memory into a generic "script." Preschoolers may remember what happened to them, but not when and where. They may have trouble answering questions about a *specific instance* of abuse, even though they accurately remember a *pattern* of abuse.

Do children have difficulty remembering stressful events? Findings vary (Steward & Steward, 1996). Researchers interviewed 90 children, ages 2, 3, 4, 5, 9, and 13, who had been injured badly enough to go to a hospital emergency room. The stressfulness of the injury bore little relationship to the completeness and accuracy of their memory a few days or 6 months later. Both in free recall and in response to who, what, when, and where questions, children of all ages gave surprisingly good accounts; and the amount of detail increased with age. On the other hand, stressful hospital treatment did impair recall (C. Peterson & Bell, 1996).

Shame may inhibit some children from reporting sexual abuse. When questioned about doctors' examinations, 5- and 7-year-old girls, even when using dolls, gave almost no false reports of genital contact. They were far more likely to *fail* to report contact that *did* occur (Saywitz, Goodman, Nicholas, & Moan, 1991). The relative privacy and impersonality of a computer-assisted interview may encourage disclosure (Steward & Steward, 1996).

Issues concerning the reliability of young children's testimony are still being sorted out. Further research may discover more effective ways to expose adults who harm children while protecting those who may be falsely accused.

development of literacy (refer back to Box 9-1). Children of a higher social class, especially girls, who tend to show early language development, seem to develop autobiographical memory earlier than other children (K. Nelson, 1992, 1993). So do firstborns, who spend more time interacting with their parents than later-borns can (Mullen, 1994).

However, most research on memory has focused on middle-class American or western European children, most of whom have been talking since at least age 2. We know little about the relationship between memory and language among children who begin to speak later because of different social and cultural practices, or among deaf children of hearing parents who cannot as easily converse with them (K. Nelson, 1993).

Influences on Children's Memory

Why do some early episodic memories last longer than others? One factor, as we've seen, is the uniqueness of the event. Let's look at two other factors: children's active participation, either in the event itself or in its retelling or reenactment, and parents' way of talking with children about past events.

"Remember when we . . . ?" The development of language ability around age 4 helps young children remember past events. Children remember best an event that is unique or new; they may recall many details from a special trip or visit for a year or longer.

Active Participation

Preschoolers tend to remember things they did better than things they merely *saw* (D. C. Jones, Swift, & Johnson, 1988). In one study, sixty-five 3- and 4½-year-olds visited a replica of a turn-of-the-century farmhouse, where they did such things as pretend to sew a blanket on a treadle sewing machine and chop ice with a pick and hammer. When interviewed—either later the same day, 1 week later, or 8 weeks later—the children remembered best the objects they had used to do something, such as the sewing machine.

A study in New Zealand (Murachver, Pipe, Gordon, Owens, & Fivush, 1996) measured 5- and 6-year-olds' recall of a novel event (visiting a "pirate") that they either observed, were told a story about, or experienced directly. A few days later, the children recalled details (such as trying on pirate clothes, steering the ship, making a treasure map, and finding the treasure) more completely, more accurately, and in a more organized way when they themselves had participated, and they required less prompting or reminding. But while direct experience enhanced memory, this finding was qualified by other factors: how often the event was repeated and with what variations, how logically the event was structured, and whether the children were asked to reenact the event or just describe it (Murachver et al., 1996). These findings have practical implications when the accuracy of a child's report is in question, as in court testimony (refer back to Box 9-2).

Drawing, like reenactment, can help preschoolers remember. In one series of experiments, children who had visited a fire station where they had seen several unusual staged events were interviewed the next day or 1 month later. Half the children were asked to tell about what they had seen; the other half were asked to draw and describe it. Five- and 6-year-olds (but not 3- and 4-year-olds) who drew pictures reported more information verbally than those who did not draw (Butler, Gross, & Hayne, 1995).

Parental Styles of Discussing Events

The way adults talk with a child during a shared experience can influence how well the child will remember it. In one field experiment, ten 3-year-olds and their mothers visited a museum (Tessler, 1986, 1991). Half the mothers talked naturally with their children as they walked through the museum; the other half simply

This 4-year-old boy is more likely to remember the dolphins he saw at the aquarium if his mother talks naturally with him about this shared experience.

responded to the children's comments. A week later, the children recalled *only* those objects they had talked about with their mothers, and the children in the "natural conversation" group remembered them better.

Mothers' conversational styles also had an effect. Four mothers had a *narrative* style, reminiscing about shared experiences ("Remember when we went to New Jersey and saw Cousin Leroy?"). The other six mothers had a *pragmatic* style, using memory for practical purposes ("Where did you leave your mittens?"). When asked specific questions about the museum trip, children of "narrative" mothers recalled more than twice as many details as the "pragmatic" group.

Research on how adults talk with children about past events identified two styles among 24 white middle-class two-parent families (Haden & Fivush, 1996; E. Reese & Fivush, 1993). In a *repetitive* conversation, parents repeat either the general thrust or the exact content of their own previous statement or question. In an *elaborative* conversation, parents move on to a new aspect of the event or add more information. A repetitive-style parent might ask, "Do you remember how we traveled to Florida?" and then, receiving no answer, ask, "How did we get there? We went in the_____." An elaborative-style parent might instead follow up the first question by saying, "Did we go by car or by plane?" Elaborative parents seem more focused on having a mutually rewarding conversation and affirming the child's responses, whereas repetitive parents are more focused on checking the child's memory performance.

Adults' conversational styles may vary with the context. Mothers who talk either repetitively or elaboratively about past events do not necessarily use a similar style when playing with their children (Haden & Fivush, 1996). Whatever the case, adults' conversational styles are influential. Reminiscing and elaborating help children remember.

CHECKPOINT

Can you . . .

- Compare preschoolers' recognition and recall ability?

- Tell how the distinction between explicit and implicit memory, along with young children's limited language ability, helps to explain the impermanence of early memories?

- Identify factors that affect how well a child will remember an event?

Psychometric and Vygotskian Approaches: Development of Intelligence

One factor that may affect how early children develop both language and memory is intelligence. As children apply their intelligence to solving problems both at home and in preschool or kindergarten, individual differences become more apparent and more measurable. Let's look at two ways intelligence is measured—through traditional psychometric tests and through newer tests of cognitive potential—and at how parents influence children's performance.

Traditional Psychometric Measures

As we pointed out in Chapter 6, psychometric tests seek to measure quantitatively the factors that make up intelligence. The tests consist of questions or tasks, usually divided into verbal and performance categories, that indicate cognitive functioning.

Because children of 3, 4, and 5 are more proficient with language than younger children, intelligence tests can now include verbal items; and these tests produce more reliable results than the largely nonverbal tests used in infancy. As children approach age 5, there is a higher correlation between their scores on intelligence tests and the scores they will achieve later (M. H. Bornstein & Sigman, 1986). IQ tests given near the end of kindergarten are among the best predictors of future school success; other good predictors are linguistic ability, visual-motor and visual-perceptual performance, and attention span (Tramontana, Hooper, & Selzer, 1988).

Although preschool children are easier to test than infants and toddlers, they still need to be tested individually. The two most commonly used individual tests for preschoolers are the Stanford-Binet Intelligence Scale and the Wechsler Preschool and Primary Scale of Intelligence. The *Stanford-Binet Intelligence Scale,* the first individual childhood intelligence test to be developed, takes 30 to 40 minutes to complete. The child is asked to define words, string beads, build with blocks, identify the missing parts of a picture, trace mazes, and show an understanding of numbers. The child's score is supposed to measure memory, spatial orientation, and practical judgment in real-life situations.

The fourth edition of the Stanford-Binet, revised in 1985, includes an equal balance of verbal and nonverbal, quantitative, and memory items. Instead of providing the IQ as a single overall measure of intelligence, the revised version assesses patterns and levels of cognitive development. The updated standardization sample is well balanced geographically, ethnically, socioeconomically, and by gender, and it includes children with disabilities.

The *Wechsler Preschool and Primary Scale of Intelligence—Revised (WPPSI-R),* an hour-long individual test used with children ages 3 to 7, yields separate verbal and performance scores as well as a combined score. Its separate scales are similar to those in the Wechsler Intelligence Scale for Children (WISC-III), discussed in Chapter 12. The 1989 revision includes new subtests and new picture items. It too has been restandardized on a sample of children representing the population of preschool-age children in the United States. Because children of this age tire quickly and are easily distracted, the test may be given in two separate sessions.

Influences on Measured Intelligence

Many people believe that IQ scores represent a fixed quantity of intelligence a person is born with. This is not so: the score is simply a measure of how well a child can do certain tasks in comparison with others the same age. On the whole, test takers have done better in recent years, forcing test developers to

Stanford-Binet Intelligence Scale Individual intelligence test used with children to measure memory, spatial orientation, and practical judgment.

Wechsler Preschool and Primary Scale of Intelligence—Revised (WPPSI-R) Individual intelligence test for children ages 3 to 7, which yields verbal and performance scores as well as a combined score.

Parents of children with high IQs tend to be warm, loving, and sensitive and to encourage independence and creativity. Giving suggestions and strategies for solving a puzzle or problem—without showing strong approval or disapproval—can foster cognitive growth.

raise standardized norms (Anastasi, 1988). This improvement may reflect exposure to educational television, preschools, better-educated parents, and a wider variety of experiences, as well as changes in the tests themselves.

How well children do on intelligence tests is influenced by many factors. These include their temperament, the match between their cognitive style and the tasks they are asked to do, their social and emotional maturity, their ease in the testing situation, their preliteracy or literacy skills, and their socioeconomic status and ethnic background. (We will examine several of these factors in Chapter 12.) Specific kinds of training may also help (see Box 9-3).

Temperament and Parent-Child Interaction

Parents are a very important influence because they provide a child's earliest environment for learning. Parents of children with higher IQs tend to be warm, loving, and sensitive. They tend to use an *authoritative* style of child rearing (described in Chapter 10), which combines respect for the child with firm parental guidance.

Children's temperament—or at least the way parents perceive it—may contribute to the way parents treat them, and both of these factors may affect children's cognitive potential. In one longitudinal study (Fagot & Gauvain, 1997), researchers asked 93 mothers to rate their 18-month-olds' temperament. They also observed how mother and child interacted during play at home. A year later, at 2½, the children did two problem-solving tasks with their mothers in the laboratory. Finally, at age 5, the children did two independent laboratory problem-solving tasks and took an intelligence test (the WPSSI), and their kindergarten teachers were asked whether they had any learning problems.

Box 9-3 Can Musical Training Improve Spatial Reasoning?

Can musical training improve children's ability to learn such subjects as math and science, which involve reasoning about spatial relationships? One study suggests that the answer is yes.

One type of task on the revised Wechsler Preschool and Primary Scale of Intelligence (WPSSI-R) involves *spatial-temporal reasoning,* that is, the ability to manipulate and change patterns. For example, a child may be asked to arrange pieces of a puzzle to make a picture of an animal (see figure). To do this kind of task, a child must form a mental image of the whole animal, mentally reposition the pieces, and then arrange them to match the mental image. The order in which the pieces are put together makes a difference: starting with the head makes it easier to solve the puzzle, but putting the head and tail together first makes it harder.

This kind of reasoning, which involves changing a mental image in the absence of an actual model, is used at a more complex level in such fields as chess, mathematics, engineering, and music. Research with college students found that listening to classical music—specifically, a Mozart sonata—improved performance on spatial-temporal tasks. This suggests that experience with music can *prime,* or prepare, the parts of the brain that deal with spatial reasoning. However, the effect lasted only 10 minutes (Leng & Shaw, 1991).

Would giving preschool children music training have a more long-lasting effect? This hypothesis makes sense, since the neural connections in the cerebral cortex are still quite plastic (modifiable) at that age. Piano training was chosen to test the hypothesis because the keyboard provides a visual index of the intervals between higher and lower notes. Children are taught to associate the five fingers of each hand with specific numbered notes to be played by each finger; the numbers are shown in printed music and must be mentally applied to the piano keys.

In a pilot study in 1993, a group of 3-year-olds in a music school improved more on a spatial-temporal task after 9 months of individual piano lessons than the WPSSI-R norms would predict. So did a group of 3-year-olds from disadvantaged families who received 9 months of group singing lessons at a day-care center. However, neither group improved significantly on spatial *recognition* tasks, such as matching figures (refer to figure). To make sure that the musical training was the cause of the improvement in spatial reasoning, the researchers launched a controlled experiment with seventy-eight 3- and 4-year-olds of diverse ethnicity and normal intelligence (Rauscher et al., 1997).

The children, who attended three preschools, were divided into four groups. The experimental group received 6 to 8 months of private piano and group singing lessons. The other three groups received either singing lessons only, computer training in reading and number skills, or no special training. None of the children had had music or computer lessons before. Singing lessons were included in the treatment for the experimental group because the children normally had group singing activities at their preschools. By including a control group that had singing lessons alone, the researchers attempted to standardize the effects of group singing. They also wanted to find out whether singing instruction without piano instruction would have an effect, as it had in the pilot study.

All four groups were tested on spatial-temporal reasoning and spatial recognition tasks from the WPSSI-R, both before and after the training period. The results were striking (see graphs). The groups had shown no significant differences before the training. After the training, the experimental group improved dramatically on the spatial-temporal task; the other three groups did not. The improvement in the experimental group's performance was equivalent to a shift from the 50th percentile to the 85th percentile. None of the groups improved significantly on the spatial recognition tasks.

The computer-trained children's lack of improvement in spatial reasoning shows that such aspects of using a keyboard as attention, motivation, and motor-visual coordination do not affect that skill. The crucial factor seems to be experience in juggling the spatial relationships between musical notes, fingers, and piano keys. Furthermore, the effect of musical training, unlike the effect of just listening, seems to be more than immediate. Members of the experimental group who were tested a day or more after completing their musical training improved no less than those who were tested the same day the training ended. Further research is needed to determine how long this effect may last.

We cannot be sure whether singing lessons contributed to the success of the experimental group. Since the control group that had singing lessons alone did not improve significantly in spatial-temporal reasoning, it would seem that singing lessons are effective only when combined with keyboard training. Why, then, did the inner-city group in the pilot study improve after singing lessons alone? It may be that this improvement had to do with extra teacher attention or other aspects of this special experience for a disadvantaged group.

(continued)

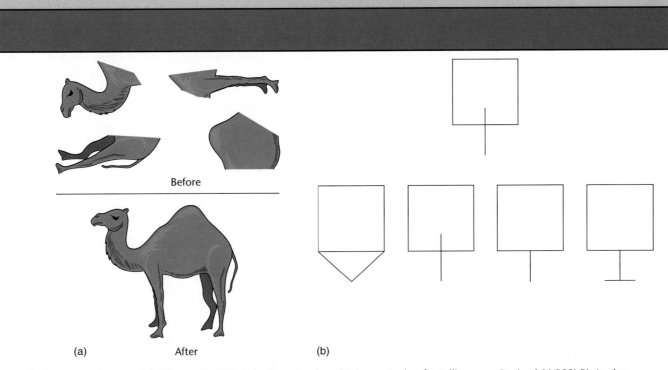

Tasks for measuring spatial skills on the Wechsler Preschool and Primary Scale of Intelligence—Revised (WPSSI-R). In the Object Assembly task (*a*), which tests spatial-temporal reasoning, the child arranges pieces of a puzzle to create a meaningful whole. On the Geometric Design task, which tests spatial recognition, the child points to the figure in the bottom row that matches the figure in the top row.

Source: Rauscher et al., 1997, Figure 3 A, p. 4.

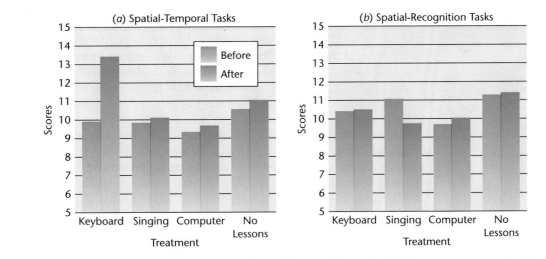

How four types of training affected spatial-temporal and spatial recognition skills. (*a*) The group that received keyboard training (along with group singing) improved significantly in the spatial-temporal task; the groups that received singing lessons only, computer training, or no lessons did not. (*b*) None of the groups improved significantly in spatial recognition.

Source: Adapted from Rauscher et al., 1997, Figure 4 A, p. 5.

The findings suggest that mothers who consider their children "difficult" tend to give them more assistance and instruction or to be more critical and coercive. Either way, such children may not develop independent problem-solving skills. They are likely to give up, make errors, and develop learning problems. Children whose mothers, when the children were 2½, gave them suggestions for solving problems or showed them effective strategies did better on the arithmetic and vocabulary subtests of the WPPSI at age 5, whereas children whose mothers had given *either* more approval *or* disapproval or had told them what to do did worse (Fagot & Gauvain, 1997).

Socioeconomic Factors

Family economic circumstances exert a powerful influence on measured intelligence. Poverty affects children not only through their parents' inability to provide educational resources but through the negative psychological effect poverty has on the parents. Poor children tend to have lower IQs at age 5 than more well-to-do children, especially if the family has been poor for a long time. This seems to be true regardless of related factors, such as family structure and the mother's educational level. These conclusions come from an analysis of a longitudinal survey of American households and a study of children originally identified as low birthweight (G. J. Duncan, Brooks-Gunn, & Klebanov, 1994). The average IQ of black children in the sample was about 18 points lower than that of white children; but adjustments for such factors as neighborhood economic conditions, family poverty, the mother's educational level, and the learning experiences provided in the home virtually eliminated this differential (Brooks-Gunn, Klebanov, & Duncan, 1996). This is important, because what looks like an ethnic or racial difference in intelligence may often turn out to reflect socioeconomic differences instead.

Socioeconomic status in itself is not a determining factor in intelligence scores, but only one of several social and family risk factors. Assessments of 152 children at ages 4 and 13 revealed no single pattern of risk. Instead, a child's IQ was related to *the total number* of such risk factors as the mother's behavior, mental health, anxiety level, education, and beliefs about children's development; family size and social support; stressful life events; parental occupations; and disadvantaged minority status. The more risk factors there were, the lower the child's IQ score (Sameroff, Seifer, Baldwin, & Baldwin, 1993).

An observational study (some of whose findings we reported in Chapter 6) shows how specific aspects of parenting in infancy and toddlerhood, often associated with socioeconomic status, can influence IQ. Once a month for more than 2 years, until the participating children turned 3, researchers visited the homes of 40 well-functioning families (B. Hart & Risley, 1992, 1996). In 32 of the families, both parents were present; 15 families were African American and 25 were white; 13 families were professional or white-collar, 23 were working-class, and 6 were on welfare.

The researchers noted how much attention parents gave a child, the nature of parent-child interactions, and what kinds of things parents said to children—prohibitions, questions, or repetitions and elaborations of the children's statements. There were considerable differences on some of these points, such as the number of words a parent addressed to a child in the course of an hour. Parents in higher-income families spent more time with their children, gave them more attention, talked more with them, and showed more interest in what they had to say; and children whose parents did these things tended to do well on IQ tests at age 3 and again at age 9. Much more of the talk of the lower-income parents included such words as "stop," "quit," and "don't"; and the children of parents who talked that way had lower IQs. This study pinpoints differences in parenting that may help account for typical differences in IQ and school performance of children from higher- and lower-income families and shows which specific parental practices can help children do better in school.

CHECKPOINT

Can you . . .

• Name and describe two commonly used individual intelligence tests for preschoolers?

• Discuss the influence of temperament, parent-child interaction, and socioeconomic factors on children's measured intelligence?

Testing and Teaching Based on Vygotsky's Theory

A form of testing developed in Russia and now becoming influential in the United States is based on Vygotsky's (1978) sociocultural theory of cognitive development. According to Vygotsky, children learn by internalizing the results of their interactions with adults. Adults direct children's learning most effectively in the *zone of proximal development (ZPD)*, that is, with regard to tasks children are almost ready to accomplish on their own (see Chapter 1).

Tests based on Vygotsky's approach emphasize potential rather than present achievement. These tests contain items up to 2 years above a child's current level of competence. The items a child can answer with help determine the ZPD, or potential level of development. Vygotsky (1956) gives an example of two children, each with a mental age of 7 years (based on ability to do various cognitive tasks). With the help of leading questions, examples, and demonstrations, Natasha can easily solve problems geared to a mental age of 9, two years beyond her mental age; but Ivan, with the same kind of help, can do tasks at only a 7½-year-old level. If we measure these children by what they can do on their own (as traditional IQ tests do), their intelligence seems about the same; but if we measure them by their immediate potential development (their ZPD), they are quite different.

The ZPD, in combination with the related concept of *scaffolding*, can help parents and teachers efficiently guide children's cognitive progress. Scaffolding (see Chapter 1) means that the less able a child is to do a task, the more direction an adult must give. As the child can do more and more, the adult helps less and less. When the child can do the job alone, the adult takes away the "scaffold" that is no longer needed.

In one study of scaffolding, parents worked with their 3-year-old children on three tasks: copying a model made of blocks; classifying by size, color, and shape; and having the children retell a story they had heard. As the experiment progressed, parents became more sensitive to how much support their children needed; the more finely tuned a parent's help became, the better the child did (Pratt, Kerig, Cowan, & Cowan, 1988). In another study, Mexican women were videotaped teaching young girls how to weave. When working with beginners, the teachers did not give spoken instruction. Instead, when the weaving became too difficult, the teachers simply took over, and the girls learned by watching. None of the 14 students experienced failure; the teachers intervened as soon as they saw the girls having the slightest problem (Greenfield, 1984).

In a more recent study, 3- and 4-year-olds were asked to give their parents directions for finding a hidden mouse in a dollhouse. The parents gave the children feedback when their directions needed clarifying. The parents proved to be highly sensitive to the children's scaffolding needs; they gave more directive prompts to 3-year-olds, whose directions tended to be less clear than those of 4-year-olds. The parents used fewer directive prompts as the children gained experience in giving clear directions (Plumert & Nichols-Whitehead, 1996).

Scaffolding seems to come naturally in so many situations that adults often do not recognize that they are using the method or even that they are teaching. One Mexican woman who was interviewed about how girls learn to weave said, "They learn by themselves." Similarly, many western parents, unaware of their role in teaching toddlers to talk, think that children learn how to talk by themselves rather than through interaction (N. Chomsky, 1965).

C H E C K P O I N T

Can you . . .

• Explain why an intelligence test score using the ZPD might be significantly different from a traditional psychometric test score?

• Give examples of how parents use scaffolding to help children learn?

Early Childhood Education

Today more young children than ever spend part of the day in preschool, day care, or kindergarten. Both preschools and day-care centers (discussed in Chapter 7) are *learning centers*—places where young children come together and learn—but preschools traditionally have a more developmental emphasis. Preschools have

Japanese preschools stress play. Academic competition will be intense once these children enter formal schooling.

flourished in the United States since 1919, when the first public nursery schools were established. Preschool enrollment has grown dramatically since 1970 despite a sharp decline in the birth rate. Many privately run preschools serve mainly well-educated, affluent families, but more and more public schools are moving into preschool education. The typical 5-year-old gets a preview of "real school" in kindergarten, the traditional introduction to formal schooling.

Goals of Preschool Education: A Cross-Cultural View

What makes a good preschool? The answer depends in part on the values of a culture and its goals for its children. In one study (Tobin, Wu, & Davidson, 1989), researchers videotaped preschool activities in Japan, China, and the United States, showed all three tapes to parents and educators in all three countries, and asked 750 teachers, administrators, parents, and child development specialists to fill out questionnaires. The classroom activities were consistent with the values expressed by people in each culture. Traditional Chinese preschools stressed academic instruction, Japanese preschools stressed play, and American preschools presented a more mixed picture.

More than half the Americans listed "to give children a good start academically" as one of the top three reasons for a society to have preschools. Only 2 percent of the Japanese gave this answer: they tended to see preschools as havens from the academic pressure and competition that children would face in the years to come. The Chinese emphasized academics even more than the Americans; 67 percent gave this answer. Their emphasis on early learning seemed to stem in part from the Confucian tradition of early, strenuous study; in part from the effects of the Cultural Revolution of the late 1960s and 1970s, with its discouragement of frivolity; and in part from the desire of parents to compensate for their own disrupted educations and their sense of responsiblity for their children's future academic success. This early stress on academics is controversial, however. A less academic preschool curriculum is becoming more popular in China, but schools taking that approach were not represented in this study.

In the United States, a good preschool is generally considered to be one that stimulates children's development in all domains—physical, social, emotional, and cognitive—through active interaction with teachers, other children, and carefully chosen materials. It offers an environment outside the home for children to

Compensatory preschool education, such as the Head Start program these children are enrolled in, often yields long-lasting gains. Some positive effects of Head Start have held up through high school.

explore, in which they can choose from activities tailored to their individual interests, abilities, and learning styles. Through these activities, children experience successes that build confidence and self-esteem.

A good preschool provides experiences that let children learn by doing. It stimulates their senses through art, music, and tactile materials—clay, water, and wood. It encourages children to observe, talk, create, and solve problems. Through storytelling, dramatic play, conversation, and written activities, it helps children develop preliteracy skills.

A good preschool helps children learn how to get along with others and to develop social and emotional skills, such as cooperation, negotiation, compromise, and self-control. Perhaps the preschool's most important contribution is to make children feel that school is fun, learning is satisfying, and they are competent.

Compensatory Preschool Programs

Children from deprived socioeconomic backgrounds often enter school at a considerable disadvantage. They may make as much progress as more advantaged classmates, but because they start out behind, they remain behind (Stipek & Ryan, 1997). Since the 1960s, large-scale programs have been developed to help such children compensate for what they have missed and to prepare them for school.

The best-known compensatory preschool program for children of low-income families in the United States is Project Head Start, launched in 1965. A committee of 14 experts in child development, health, and education formulated the initial plan. One of them, Urie Bronfenbrenner, was just beginning to work out his ecological approach to human development (see Chapter 1). He maintained that intervention must address the interrelationships among children, families, and communities (E. Zigler & Styfco, 1993).

Head Start's administrators adopted a "whole child" approach. Their goals were to improve physical health, enhance cognitive skills, and foster self-confidence, relationships with others, social responsibility, and a sense of dignity and self-worth for the child and the family. The program provides medical, dental, and mental health care; nutrition (at least one hot meal a day); cognitive enrichment; social services; and opportunity for parental involvement. Due to inadequate funding, Head Start serves only about one-third of eligible children: 798,513 in 1996 (Children's Defense Fund, 1997a). Recently, some communities have combined Head Start with all-day child care (Children's Defense Fund, 1996, 1997a).

Has Head Start lived up to its name? Because it is community-based and community-directed, the program varies around the country. With less funding in recent years, quality has been uneven, and evaluation has not kept current (E. Zigler & Styfco, 1993, 1994). Still, the program has had considerable success.

Head Start has probably had its strongest impact on physical health and well-being (E. Zigler & Styfco, 1994). Head Start children have also shown substantial cognitive and language gains, with the neediest children benefiting most. Being healthier, Head Start children are absent less. They do better on tests of motor control and physical development (R. C. Collins & Deloria, 1983). Head Start has had a positive impact on self-esteem, socialization, and social maturity (McKey et al., 1985). It has also had a favorable effect on families by offering parenting education, social support, and jobs and job training (E. Zigler & Styfco, 1993, 1994). The most successful Head Start programs have been those with the most parental participation, the best teachers, the smallest groups, and the most extensive services.

A major concern has been that gains in IQ do not last. Although Head Start children do better on intelligence tests than children from comparable backgrounds, this advantage disappears after the children start school. Nor have Head Start children equaled the average middle-class child in school achievement or on standardized tests (R. C. Collins & Deloria, 1983; E. Zigler & Styfco, 1993, 1994). These findings point to a need for earlier and longer-lasting intervention (E. Zigler & Styfco, 1993, 1994).

In another large-scale federally funded compensatory program, the Chicago Child Parent Centers, which extends from preschool through third grade, the added years of academic enrichment signicantly increased achievement (A. J. Reynolds, 1994). However, we must be wary of unrealistic expectations: "neither Head Start nor any preschool program can inoculate children against the ravages of poverty" (E. Zigler & Styfco, 1994, p. 129).

Some positive effects of Head Start and other compensatory preschool programs have persisted through elementary or high school or even beyond. A number of studies have found long-term benefits for children enrolled in high-quality compensatory preschool programs (Darlington, 1991; Haskins, 1989). A major benefit is a lesser likelihood of juvenile delinquency (see Chapter 16). Poor African American children who participated in the Perry Preschool Program of the High/Scope Educational Research Foundation (which predated Head Start) have been followed to age 27. They were much more likely than a comparison group who lacked preschool experience to finish high school, to enroll in college or vocational training, and to be employed. They also did better on tests of competence and were less likely to be on welfare or to have been arrested, and the women were less likely to have become pregnant in their teens (Berrueta-Clement, Schweinhart, Barnett, Epstein, & Weikart, 1985; Schweinhart, Barnes, & Weikart, 1993). It seems, then, that early childhood education can help compensate for deprivation and that well-planned programs produce long-term benefits that far exceed the original cost (Haskins, 1989; Schweinhart et al., 1993).

How Much Like "Real School" Should Preschool and Kindergarten Be?

As we have already mentioned, most preschools in the United States traditionally have followed a "child-centered" philosophy stressing social and emotional growth in line with young children's developmental needs. Some, such as those based on the theories of Piaget or the Italian educator Maria Montessori (see Chapter 1), have a strong cognitive emphasis. In some other countries, such as China, preschools are expected to provide academic preparation.

In recent years, as part of a debate over how to improve education in the United States, pressures have built to offer instruction in basic academic skills in U.S. preschools. Some of these pressures have filtered down from kindergarten.

Historically a year of transition between the relative freedom of home or preschool and the structure of the primary grades, kindergarten since the 1970s has become more like first grade. Children spend less time on freely chosen activities that stretch their muscles and imaginations and more time on worksheets and learning to read (Egertson, 1987).

Many educators and psychologists maintain that although children may learn more at first, too much teacher-directed instruction in early childhood may stifle their interest and interfere with self-directed learning. Furthermore, such instruction may neglect young children's needs for play, exploration, and freedom from undue demands (Elkind, 1986; E. F. Zigler, 1987).

One study compared 227 poor, minority, and middle-class 4- to 6-year-olds in highly academic and child-centered preschool and kindergarten classes. The children in the academic programs did better in recognizing letters and words, though not numbers. However, these children had lower motivation, a poorer opinion of their abilities, less pride in their accomplishments, and lower expectations for academic success. They were more dependent on adults for permission and approval and worried more about school. This was true of both disadvantaged and middle-class children and of both preschoolers and kindergartners (Stipek, Feiler, Daniels, & Milburn, 1995). In another study, children from both academic and child-centered preschools learned equally well in kindergarten, but the children from the academic preschools were more anxious about taking tests, less creative, and more negative about school (Hirsh-Pasek, 1991; Hirsh-Pasek, Hyson, & Rescorla, 1989).

What are the long-term effects of differing philosophies of early childhood education? One study (Schweinhart, Weikart, & Larner, 1986) compared what happened to low-income children in three high-quality preschool programs. The first was a traditional one that stressed child-initiated activities; the second was a highly structured, teacher-directed one that stressed academic preparation; and the third was the High/Scope program (mentioned in the previous section), which took a middle ground and emphasized joint planning by teachers and children. Children from all three programs did better in elementary school than children with no preschool experience, but the children from the academic program had more behavior problems. By 15 years of age, many of those children had lost interest in school and had become involved in vandalism or delinquency.

In part because of pressures for academic achievement and in part to meet the needs of working parents, many kindergartners now spend a full day in school rather than the traditional half day—with mixed results (Robertson, 1984; Rust, cited in Connecticut Early Childhood Education Council [CECEC], 1983). Longer blocks of time permit an unhurried atmosphere and more opportunities for pupil-teacher and parent-teacher contact; afternoon activities tend to be less structured, so as to match childrens' energy levels. However, opponents say some 5-year-olds cannot handle a 6-hour day and the long separation from parents. There is also a danger of overemphasizing academic skills and sedentary activities. One proposed solution is a half day of kindergarten followed by an optional half day of care by certified child caregivers for those who need it (E. F. Zigler, 1987).

Predicting School Success

Entrance into kindergarten is usually a major family transition. Some researchers therefore have explored a link between aspects of the parents' marriage and a child's adaptation to kindergarten. In a 6-year longitudinal study of 72 couples, beginning in late pregnancy, those who had had happy childhoods, were happily married in the child's early years, and had an authoritative parenting style (see Chapter 10) had children who did better in kindergarten, both socially and academically (P. A. Cowan, Cowan, Schulz, & Heming, 1994).

A number of measures, including psychometric tests, have been used to predict how well a young child will do in school later on. The best time for screening children with no known disability seems to be toward the end of the kindergarten year. Although no single measure or set of measures can accurately predict a child's academic future, it is often possible to identify children at either extreme of academic ability. IQ is among the best predictors of school achievement; children's ability to understand and to express themselves with language predicts reading competence; and visual-motor and visual-perceptual measures predict reading, math, and general achievement, at least through first grade. The most important behavioral measure is attentiveness (Tramontana, Hooper, & Selzer, 1988).

Many parents, concerned about the "speedup" in the curriculum, hold their children back from kindergarten for a year, especially if the child does not seem ready or has a fall birthday and would otherwise be one of the youngest in the class. About 12 percent of elementary and high school students enter school late and are nearly a year older, on average, than their classmates. Indeed, some experts advise delayed entrance, citing findings that the youngest children in a class tend to have less success than the oldest (Sweetland & DeSimone, 1987).

However, these studies generally have not considered such variables as IQ, day-care experience, and parents' education and occupations. Furthermore, the researchers typically compared year-end achievement of younger children with that of older ones, who tend to be more advanced to begin with, rather than looking at gains made during the year. More recent research in western Canada, which considered these factors, found that although younger first-graders did end the year with slightly lower achievement than older ones, they made just as much progress as their older classmates—and far more than older kindergartners whose birthdays missed the enrollment cutoff date and who were exposed to a less academically challenging curriculum. The study concluded that age of school entrance is not a good predictor of learning or of academic problems (F. J. Morrison, Griffith, & Alberts, 1997).

Furthermore, delayed school entrance can have negative behavioral effects which may not show up until adolescence, according to a large-scale U.S. study. In a nationally representative sample of 9,079 youngsters between the ages of 7 and 17 (Byrd, Weitzman, & Auinger, 1997), white adolescents who were older than their classmates—either because they had entered school late or had had to repeat a grade—were more likely to be seen by parents as having such behavioral problems as mood swings, anxiety or depression, bullying, cheating, lying, unpopularity, loss of temper, feelings of being unloved, and hanging around with peers who get in trouble. (No such effect emerged for black adolescents; it may be that for them, such factors as poverty and family structure are more closely associated with behavioral problems.)

Because this was cross-sectional research, we cannot be sure that late school entrance causes behavioral problems. However, it seems possible that earlier attainment of puberty may affect these young people's social relationships. Young people who are old for their grade also have been found to have higher rates of risky behaviors, such as drug use, sexual activity, and violence (Byrd, Weitzman, & Doniger, 1994, 1996). It seems wise for parents, pediatricians, and school counselors to consider this information in discussing a young child's readiness for kindergarten.

Going to preschool and kindergarten are important steps, widening a child's social environment. The growth of language and the other burgeoning physical and cognitive skills of these years have psychosocial implications as well, as we'll see in Chapter 10.

CHECKPOINT

Can you . . .

- Compare goals of preschool education in the United States, Japan, and China?

- Assess the long-term benefits of compensatory preschool education?

- Discuss the short-term and long-term effects of academic and child-centered preschool programs and of age of kindergarten entrance?

SUMMARY

Piagetian Approach: The Preoperational Child

- According to Piaget, a child is in the **preoperational stage** of cognitive development from approximately 2 years to 7 years of age.

- The **symbolic function**—as shown in deferred imitation, symbolic play, and language—enables children to mentally represent and reflect upon people, objects, and events. However, the child cannot yet think logically.

- Preoperational children can understand the concept of identity, are beginning to understand causal relationships, are becoming proficient at classification, and can understand principles of counting and quantity.

- Preoperational children do not understand principles of **conservation** because of **centration**, or inability to **decenter**. Their logic is also limited by **irreversibility, transduction**, and a focus on states rather than transformations.

- Research shows that in some ways, Piaget underestimated the abilities of the children he described as preoperational. Although preoperational children show **egocentrism**, they appear to be less egocentric than Piaget thought; for example, they do not generally exhibit **animism**, and they are capable of **empathy**.

- Children's **theory of mind**, which seems to develop markedly between the ages of 3 and 5, includes some awareness of their own thought processes, some ability to distinguish real and imagined events, understanding that people can hold false beliefs, and ability to distinguish appearance from reality.

Development of Language

- During early childhood, vocabulary increases greatly, apparently through **fast mapping**, and grammar and syntax become fairly sophisticated, although some immaturities remain.

- Piaget characterized much of early speech as egocentric, but recent research indicates that children learn **pragmatics** and engage in **social speech** earlier than he thought.

- **Private speech**—talking aloud to oneself—is normal and common; it usually disappears by age 9.

- Causes of delayed language development are unclear. If it is untreated, there may be serious cognitive, social, and emotional consequences.

- Conversations with adults, using relatively challenging vocabulary and subject matter, are important in preparing children for literacy, as is imaginative play. Educational television also can be helpful.

Information-Processing Approach: Development of Memory

- Studies of memory development indicate that **recognition** is better than **recall**, but both increase during early childhood.

- Inability to remember early childhood events at a later age may be due to the way young children encode memories; implicit memory precedes the development of explicit memory, and implicit (unconscious) memories persist longer.

- Early **episodic memory** is only temporary; it fades or is transferred to **generic memory,** which produces a **script** of familiar routines to guide behavior. **Autobiographical memory** begins at about age 4 and may be related to language development.

- Children are more likely to remember unusual activities that they actively participate in. The way adults talk with children about events influences memory formation.

Psychometric and Vygotskian Approaches: Development of Intelligence

- The two most commonly used psychometric intelligence tests for young children are the **Stanford-Binet Intelligence Scale** and the **Wechsler Preschool and Primary Scale of Intelligence—Revised (WPPSI-R).**

- Intelligence test scores are influenced by the child's temperament parent-child interaction, and socioeconomic factors.

- A newer form of intelligence testing is based on Vygotsky's concept of the zone of proximal development (ZPD). Tasks that children can perform with some adult help are an indication of current potential for achievement. Such tests, when combined with scaffolding (temporary support to do a task), can help parents and teachers guide children's progress.

Early Childhood Education

- Preschools and kindergartens prepare children for formal schooling. Goals of preschool education vary in different cultures. Since the 1970s, the academic content of early childhood education programs in the United States has increased, causing concern about the effects of academic pressure on young children.

- Compensatory preschool programs, such as Project Head Start, have had positive outcomes, but participants generally have not equaled the performance of middle-class children.

- IQ tests given near the end of kindergarten are good predictors of school achievement.

- Contrary to common belief, delayed school entrance may have negative cognitive and behavioral effects.

KEY TERMS

preoperational stage (312)	pragmatics (323)
symbolic function (313)	social speech (323)
centration (314)	private speech (324)
decenter (314)	recognition (328)
conservation (315)	recall (328)
irreversibility (315)	generic memory (329)
transduction (316)	script (329)
egocentrism (316)	episodic memory (329)
animism (317)	autobiographical memory (330)
empathy (317)	Stanford-Binet Intelligence Scale (334)
theory of mind (318)	Wechsler Preschool and Primary Scale of
fast mapping (322)	Intelligence—Revised (WPPSI-R) (334)

QUESTIONS FOR THOUGHT AND DISCUSSION

1. What do you see as the most important difference between the cognitive abilities of the sensorimotor period and of the preoperational period?

2. Is it better to let children develop such concepts as conservation naturally, or to teach them?

3. Suppose you wanted to set up a program to encourage literacy development in a group of children at high risk for literacy problems. What elements would you include in your program? How would you judge its success?

4. What information would you seek and what factors would you consider in deciding how much credence should be given to a preschooler's testimony in a child abuse case?

5. Since an elaborative conversational style seems most effective in jogging young children's memory, would you favor training mothers to use it? Why or why not? What difficulties or objections would you anticipate?

6. Given the importance of language to other aspects of cognitive development, do you think it is possible for a child who lacks language during the early years, such as the wild boy of Aveyron (see Chapter 1), to "catch up" cognitively with later language training?

7. How meaningful is intelligence testing of young children? If you were a preschool or kindergarten teacher, how helpful do you think it would be to know a child's IQ? The child's ZPD?

8. Can you think of an effective way in which you have used scaffolding, or seen it used?

9. Should the primary purpose of preschool and kindergarten be to provide a strong academic foundation for elementary school or to foster social and emotional development?

10. Is publicly funded compensatory education the best way to help poor children catch up?

Psychosocial Development in Early Childhood

"I love you,"
said a great mother.
"I love you for what you are
knowing so well what you are.
And I love you more yet, child,
deeper yet than ever, child,
for what you are going to be,
knowing so well you are going far,
knowing your great works are ahead,
ahead and beyond,
yonder and far over yet."

Carl Sandburg, *The People, Yes,* 1936

Focus

Eva Perón

E
va Perón was an enigma, a woman of myth and mystery who (as dramatized in Andrew Lloyd Webber's musical *Evita*) rose from tawdry origins to become first lady of Argentina, transforming herself from a bastard waif to one of the most powerful women of all time. Her followers depicted her as a selfless friend of downtrodden workers and a champion of women's rights. Her enemies denounced her as power-hungry, manipulative, and ruthless. Even the basic facts of her life are in question, for she destroyed records and intimidated interviewers, and her biographies are full of contradictions. One point, however, is clear: the origins of her resolute drive for advancement went back to early childhood.

Eva (affectionately known as Evita) began life on May 7, 1919, in the small, isolated, dusty village of Los Toldos, on the *pampas* (agricultural plains) about 200 miles west of Buenos Aires. She was the fifth and youngest illegitimate child of Juana Ibarguren, an uneducated peasant woman, and Juan Duarte, a small rancher and magistrate who had left a wife and three daughters in the nearby town of Chivilcoy. When Eva was nearly a year old, her father returned to his first family.

While Duarte was living with them, doña Juana and her children had enjoyed a comfortable lifestyle. Now they were reduced to poverty. They moved to a tiny house by the railroad tracks, and doña Juana took in sewing, often working into the night. She saw to it that her children were well-dressed and did not go hungry, but their few toys were damaged or secondhand.

The children were stung not only by abandonment and deprivation but by the stigma of illegitimacy and the whispers of villagers. Even after Duarte left, doña Juana was regarded as a kept woman. Although it was not unusual for an Argentinian man to have a mistress, Eva and her older brother and sisters were shunned by respectable people, and "nice" children were forbidden to play with them. These early years of poverty, shame, and insecurity awakened Eva's strong sense of injustice and led her to identify with the common people who accepted her and her family and to hate the "upstanding" people who would have nothing to do with them.

Eva was 6 years old when her father died. His funeral was a formative event, bringing home the humiliation of her dubious identity. There is disagreement as to whether her mother attempted to attend or only sent the children, and as to whether or not Duarte's wife had preceded him to the grave. Whatever the case, the dead man's legitimate daughters barred the interlopers' way. A violent argument erupted. According to one version of the story, Eva's godfather, a friend of her father's, got the children admitted to the wake and carried little Eva in on his arm, a perch from which she "stare[d] down at her half-sisters with . . . implacable animosity" (Flores, 1952, p. 18). In another version, it was the mayor of the town, the dead man's brother-in-law, who interceded and obtained permission for the outcasts to pay quick final respects and then trail behind the other mourners following the coffin to the cemetery. "Eva, the youngest, was last in line. . . . [She] swore to herself that, one day, she would be first" (Ortiz, 1996, p. 13).

An intense, frail girl given to tantrums and driven by dreams of glory, Eva at age 15 made her way to Buenos Aires and began her meteoric rise to become the consort and ultimately the wife of the military dictator Juan Perón. At the height of her power, Eva Perón, bedecked in diamonds, met the crowned heads of Europe, owned three newspapers, and established a multimillion-dollar foundation, which built hospitals, clinics, and schools with funds her opponents charged were extorted from workers. Still, she was beloved by the masses, and until the time of her death from cancer at age 33, she never forgot her humble origins. She knew from firsthand observation that hundreds of thousands of Argentine children lacked food, homes, education, and even basic hygiene. It was these early lessons that Eva had in mind when she called herself a "woman of the people."

*Sources of biographical information on Eva Perón are Barager (1968), J. Barnes (1978), Blanksten (1953), Flores (1952), N. Fraser & Navarro (1996), Guillermoprieto (1996), Ortiz (1996), Perón (1951), and J. M. Taylor (1979).

• • •

Eva Perón's experiences in early childhood fueled her hatred of the establishment, her will to power, and her hunger for love and esteem—themes that defined her personality. As a young child she learned what it meant in her society to be poor, illegitimate, and female. She saw that the path to security for a woman of her class was through a man—an insight she brilliantly turned to advantage.

The years from ages 3 to 6 are pivotal ones in children's psychosocial development, as they were for Eva Perón. As children's self-concept grows stronger, they learn what sex they are and begin to act accordingly. Their behavior also becomes more socially directed.

In this chapter we discuss preschool children's understanding of themselves and their feelings. We see how their identification of themselves as male or female arises and how it affects their behavior. We describe the activity on which children typically spend most of their time: play. We consider the influence, for good or ill, of what parents do. We then turn to specific developmental issues of this age group: why children help or hurt others and why they develop fears. Finally, we look at relationships with siblings and other children.

After reading this chapter, you should be able to answer and elaborate on such questions as these:

Preview Questions

- How does the self-concept develop during early childhood?

- How do young children advance in understanding their emotions?

- How do they develop initiative and self-esteem?

- How do boys and girls become aware of their gender, and what explains differences in behavior between the sexes?

- How do preschoolers play, and what does their play tell us about their social and cognitive development?

- How do parenting practices influence personality?

- How do young children get along with siblings and choose friends?

The Developing Self

"Who in the world am I? Ah, *that's* the great puzzle," said Alice in Wonderland, after her size had abruptly changed—again. Solving Alice's "puzzle" is a lifelong process of getting to know one's self.

The Self-Concept and Cognitive Development

self-concept Sense of self; descriptive and evaluative mental picture of one's abilities and traits.

The *self-concept* is our image of ourselves. It is what we believe about who we are—our total picture of our abilities and traits. It is a cognitive structure with emotional overtones and behavioral consequences, a "system of descriptive and evaluative representations about the self," which determines how we feel about ourselves and guides our actions (Harter, 1993, p. 1). The sense of self also has a social aspect: children incorporate into their self-image their growing understanding of how others see them.

The picture of the self comes into focus in toddlerhood and becomes clearer and more compelling as a person gains in cognitive abilities and deals with the developmental tasks of childhood, of adolescence, and then of adulthood. Let's look at the self-concept in early childhood.

Early Self-Concept Development: The Continuous Self

Infants gradually learn that they are separate from other people and things. At about 18 months, they may have their first moment of *self-recognition,* when they look in a mirror and realize that they are looking at themselves. During the next year they make attempts at *self-description* and *self-evaluation,* as their growing representational ability lets them reflect on themselves and their behavior (see Chapter 7).

A shift in self-awareness may occur near the age of 4, as autobiographical memory and a more sophisticated theory of mind develop (see Chapter 9). When 3½- and 4-year-olds were shown a videotape or photograph, taken a few minutes earlier, of a researcher unobtrusively placing a large sticker on their heads—an act of which they had been unaware—the children instantly reached up to feel and remove the sticker. Two-year-olds and younger 3-year-olds did not do that. Yet when shown the same thing happening in a mirror, the younger children did seem aware that a sticker was on their heads.

Does this mean that these children recognized themselves in a mirror but not in a photograph or videotape? That does not seem likely. Nor does it seem likely that they did not remember being photographed a few minutes earlier. A likelier explanation is that because younger children's memories are generic rather than autobiographical, they may not think of the events in the videotape or photograph as having happened to *them.* Also, until about 3½, children may not have a clear understanding of the self as being continuous in time. Perhaps, just as younger children have trouble accepting more than one representation of the same object as true, they do not identify the self-that-was with the self-that-is. Thus, they do not realize that the self who is now seeing the video or photograph is the same person as the self who was *in* it (Povinelli, Landau, & Perilloux, 1996).

Self-Definition: A Neo-Piagetian View

self-definition Cluster of characteristics used to describe oneself.

By age 4, Jason's attempts at *self-definition* are becoming more comprehensive as he begins to identify a cluster of characteristics to describe himself:

> My name is Jason and I live in an apartment with my mommy and daddy. I have a kitty and her name is Pumpkin. We have a television and I like to watch cartoons. I know all of my A-B-Cs. Listen: A-B-C-D-F-G-J-L-K-O-M-P-Q-X-Z. I can run faster

than anyone! I can climb to the top of the jungle gym, I'm not scared! Just happy. You can't be happy *and* scared, no way! I have black hair. I go to preschool. I'm really strong. I can lift this chair, watch me! (Adapted from Harter, 1993, p. 2)*

The way Jason describes himself is typical of children his age. He talks mostly about concrete, observable behaviors; external characteristics, such as physical features; preferences; possessions; and members of his household. He mentions particular skills (running and climbing) rather than general abilities (being athletic). His self-descriptions spill over into demonstrations; what he *thinks* about himself is almost inseparable from what he *does*. Not until middle childhood will he describe himself in generalized terms such as *popular, smart,* or *dumb*.

Neo-Piagetian thinkers describe this shift as occurring in three steps, which actually form a continuous progression (Fischer, 1980). At 4, Jason is at the first step: his statements about himself are **single representations,** isolated from one another. His thinking is still *transductive;* it jumps from particular to particular, without logical connections. At this stage he cannot imagine having two emotions at once ("You can't be happy and scared"). Because he cannot decenter, he cannot consider different aspects of himself at the same time. His thinking is all-or-nothing. He cannot acknowledge that his **real self,** the person he actually is, is not the same as his **ideal self,** the person he would like to be; so he describes himself as a paragon of virtue and ability.

At about ages 5 to 6, Jason moves up to the second step, as he begins to link one aspect of himself to another: "I can run fast, and I can climb high. I'm also strong. I can throw a ball real far, I'm going to be on a team some day!" (Harter, 1993, p. 9) However, these **representational mappings**—logical connections between parts of his image of himself—are still expressed in all-or-nothing terms. Since good and bad are opposites, he cannot see how he might be good at some things and not at others.

The third step, *representational systems,* takes place in middle childhood (see Chapter 13), when children begin to integrate specific features of the self into a general concept. As all-or-nothing thinking declines, Jason's self-descriptions will become more balanced ("I'm good at hockey but bad at arithmetic").

Understanding Emotions

"I hate you!" Maya, age 5, shouts to her mother. "You're a mean mommy!" Angry because her mother sent her to her room for pinching her baby brother, Maya cannot imagine ever loving her mother again. "Aren't you ashamed of yourself for making the baby cry?" her father asks Maya a little later. Maya nods, but only because she knows what response he wants. In truth, she feels a jumble of emotions—not the least of which is feeling sorry for herself.

Emotions Directed Toward the Self

Understanding one's own emotions is important to socialization. It helps children to control the way they show their feelings and to be sensitive to how others feel (P. W. Garner & Power, 1996). But Maya's confused emotional state is not unusual for her age. Shame—like its opposite, pride—is a complex emotion, which young children rarely understand.

Emotions directed toward the self, such as shame and pride, do not seem to develop until at least the second or third year, after children gain self-awareness (see Chapter 7). These emotions are "socially derived" (Harter, 1993, p. 20); they

single representations In neo-Piagetian terminology, first stage in development of self-definition, in which children describe themselves in terms of individual, unconnected characteristics and in all-or-nothing terms.

real self The self one actually is. Compare *ideal self.*

ideal self The self one would like to be. Compare *real self.*

representational mappings In neo-Piagetian terminology, the second stage in development of self-definition, in which a child makes logical connections between aspects of the self but still sees these characteristics in all-or-nothing terms.

---

*Much of this discussion of children's developing understanding of themselves from age 4 on, including their understanding of their emotions, is indebted to Susan Harter (1990, 1993).

The emotion of shame develops slowly. This 4-year-old boy may feel ashamed when his father scolds him, but it will be several years before he is ashamed of doing something unobserved.

depend on internalization of parental standards of behavior. Even children a few years older often lack the cognitive sophistication to recognize such emotions and what brings them on.

In one study (Harter, 1993), 4- to 8-year-olds were told two stories. In the first story, a child takes money after being told not to take it; in the second story, a child performs a difficult gymnastic feat. Each story was presented in two versions: one in which a parent sees the child doing the act, and one in which the child is not observed. The children were asked how they and their parents would feel in each circumstance.

The answers revealed a progression in understanding of feelings about the self. At ages 4 to 5, children did not say that either they or their parents would feel pride or shame. At 5 to 6, children said their parents would be ashamed or proud of them but did not mention feeling these emotions themselves. At 6 to 7, children said they would feel proud or ashamed, but only if they were observed. At 7 to 8, children acknowledged that even if no one saw them, they would feel ashamed or proud of themselves. By this age, the standards that produce pride and shame appear to be fully internalized. Until that happens, children need the prod of parental observation.

Simultaneous Emotions

Part of the confusion in young children's understanding of their feelings stems from the inability to recognize that they can experience different emotional reactions at the same time. The problem has two dimensions: the quality of the emotion (positive or negative) and the target toward which it is directed. One study found that children gradually acquire an understanding of simultaneous emotions as they move through five levels of development between ages 4 and 12 (Harter & Buddin, 1987):

- *Level 0:* At first children do not understand that *any* two feelings can coexist. At this stage, a child may say, "You can't have two feelings at the same time because you only have one mind!" The child cannot even acknowledge feeling two similar emotions at once (such as happy and glad).
- *Level 1:* Children can be aware of two emotions at the same time, but only if both are either positive or negative and are directed toward the same target ("If my brother hit me, I would be mad and sad"). A child at this level cannot understand the possibility of feeling simultaneous emotions toward two different people or feeling contradictory emotions toward the same person.
- *Level 2:* Children can recognize having two feelings of the same kind directed toward different targets ("I was excited about going to Mexico and glad to see my grandparents"). However, they cannot acknowledge holding contradictory feelings ("I couldn't feel happy and scared at the same time; I would have to be two people at once!").
- *Level 3:* Children can now understand having two opposing feelings at the same time, but only if they are directed toward two different targets. Maya can express a negative feeling toward her baby brother ("I was mad at Tony, so I pinched him") and a positive feeling toward her father ("I was happy my father didn't spank me"), but she cannot recognize that she has positive and negative feelings (anger and love) toward both.
- *Level 4:* Children can now describe opposite feelings toward the same target ("I'm excited about going to my new school, but I'm a little scared too").

In this study, not until children were 10 or 11 did they seem to understand conflicting emotions. However, in later research, children completing kindergarten, especially girls, showed such an understanding (J. R. Brown & Dunn, 1996). The difference may be one of methodology. In the earlier study, the children were asked to tell their own stories involving mixed feelings; thus narrative skills as well as understanding of emotions were involved. In the later study only 1 out of 4 kindergartners were able to recount such stories from their own experience. However, when *told* a story about, for example, a child receiving a present but not being allowed to open it, or riding a two-wheeled bicycle for the first time, 1 out of 3 could identify conflicting emotions, and most of the children were able to explain the emotions when told what they were.

Individual differences in emotional understanding seem to go back at least to age 3. Children who, at that age, could identify whether a face looked happy or sad and could tell how a puppet felt when enacting a situation involving happiness, sadness, anger, or fear were better able at the end of kindergarten to explain a story character's conflicting emotions. These children tended to come from families in which there was much discussion of why people behave as they do (J. R. Brown & Dunn, 1996).

Erikson: Initiative Versus Guilt

The need to deal with conflicting feelings about the self is at the heart of the third crisis of personality development identified by Erik Erikson (1950): *initiative versus guilt.* The conflict arises from the growing sense of purpose, which lets a child plan and carry out activities, and the growing pangs of conscience the child may have about such plans.

Preschool children can do—and want to do—more and more. At the same time, they are learning that some of the things they want to do (such as singing a cute song) meet social approval, while others (such as taking apart Mommy's clock) do not. How do they reconcile their desire to *do* with their desire for approval?

CHECKPOINT

Can you . . .

- Trace self-concept development between ages 3 and 6?
- Describe a typical progression in understanding of (1) emotions directed toward the self and (2) simultaneous emotions?

initiative versus guilt In Erikson's theory, the third crisis in psychosocial development, occurring between the ages of 3 and 6, in which children must balance the urge to pursue goals with the moral reservations that may prevent carrying them out.

A major source of young children's self-esteem is their parents' judgment of their competence. This mother's show of enthusiasm about her 3-year-old son's art work lets her child know that he matters. Feeling loved and respected, he is likely to feel good about himself.

This conflict marks a split between two parts of the personality: the part that remains a child, full of exuberance and a desire to try new things and test new powers, and the part that is becoming an adult, constantly examining the propriety of motives and actions. Children who learn how to regulate these opposing drives develop the "virtue" of *purpose*, the courage to envision and pursue goals without being unduly inhibited by guilt or fear of punishment (Erikson, 1982).

If this crisis is not resolved adequately, said Erikson, a child may turn into an adult who is constantly striving for success or showing off, or who is inhibited and unspontaneous or self-righteous and intolerant, or who suffers from impotence or psychosomatic illness. With ample opportunities to do things on their own—but under guidance and firm limits—children can attain a healthy balance between the tendency to overdo competition and achievement and the tendency to be repressed and guilt-ridden.

Self-Esteem

self-esteem The judgment a person makes about his or her self-worth.

Children cannot articulate a concept of self-worth until about age 8, but they show by their behavior that they have one (Harter, 1990, 1993). In young children, *self-esteem*—the judgment one makes about one's worth—is not based on a realistic appraisal of abilities or personality traits. In fact, children between 4 and 7 usually overrate their abilities. For one thing, they do not yet have the cognitive and social skills to compare themselves accurately with others. Also, although young children can make judgments about their competence at various activities, they are not yet able to rate them in importance; and they tend to accept the judgments of adults, who often give them positive, uncritical feedback (Harter, 1990).

In one study (Haltiwanger & Harter, 1988), preschool and kindergarten teachers were asked to describe behaviors of children with high or low self-esteem. Another group of teachers were asked to tell which of the 84 items cited by the first group were most typical of children at both extremes. The assessments of the two groups of teachers matched. Self-esteem was *not* related to actual competence, activity level, ability to pay attention, tendency to finish tasks, ability to make friends, or need for encouragement from teachers. Instead, differences in self-esteem seemed to be expressed chiefly in a child's confidence, curiosity, willingness to explore, and adaptability.

Self-esteem at this age tends to be global—"I am good" or "I am bad." This global view of the self may depend on adult approval (Burhans & Dweck, 1995). Parents' supportive behaviors—listening to a child, reading stories, making snacks, kissing away tears—are major contributors to self-esteem (Haltiwanger & Harter, 1988). Not until middle childhood do personal evaluations of competence and adequacy normally become critical in shaping and maintaining a sense of self-worth (Harter, 1990).

When self-esteem is high, a child is motivated to achieve (Harter, 1990). However, if self-esteem is *contingent* on success, children may view failure as an indictment of their worth and may feel helpless to do better. Between one-third and one-half of preschoolers show elements of this "helpless" pattern. Instead of trying a different way to complete a puzzle, as a child with unconditional self-esteem might do, "helpless" children feel ashamed and give up, or go back to an easier puzzle they have already done. They do not expect to succeed, and so they do not try. They interpet poor performance as a sign of being "bad" and believe that "badness" cannot be overcome. This sense of being a bad person may persist into adulthood. To avoid fostering the "helpless" pattern, parents and teachers can give children specific, focused feedback rather than criticizing the child as a person (Burhans & Dweck, 1995).

Gender

Being male or female affects how people look, how they move their bodies, and how they work, play, and dress. It influences what they think about themselves and what others think of them. All those characteristics—and more—are included in the word *gender:* what it means to be male or female.

Gender identity, the awareness of one's gender and all it implies, is an important aspect of the developing self-concept in early childhood. How different are young boys and girls, and how do they develop gender identity?

Gender Differences

Two 4-year-olds, Kendra and Michael, are neighbors. They were wheeled together in the park as babies. They learned to ride tricycles at about the same time and pedaled up and down the sidewalk, often colliding with each other. They go to preschool together. All in all, Kendra and Michael have followed very similar paths, but there are some definite differences between them. Besides having different sex organs, Kendra and Michael are different in size, strength, appearance, physical and cognitive abilities, and personality.

Which of their differences are due to the fact that Kendra is a girl and Michael is a boy, and which are simply differences between two individual human beings? In discussing this question, we need to distinguish between *sex differences,* the physical differences between males and females, and *gender differences,* the psychological or behavioral differences between the sexes.

Although some differences become more pronounced after age 3, boys and girls on average remain more alike than different. A landmark review of more than 2,000 studies found only a few significant gender differences. Three cognitive

CHECKPOINT

Can you . . .

- Explain the significance of Erikson's third crisis of personality development?
- Tell how young children's self-esteem differs from that of school-age children?

gender Significance of being male or female.

gender identity Awareness, developed in early childhood, that one is male or female.

sex differences Physical differences between males and females.

gender differences Psychological or behavioral differences between males and females.

differences—girls' superior verbal ability and boys' better mathematical and spatial abilities—did not appear until after age 10 or 11 (E. Maccoby & Jacklin, 1974). More recent analyses found gender differences in verbal abilities so small as to be almost meaningless (J. Hyde & Linn, 1988). Differences in mathematical and spatial abilities have decreased in recent years. In the general population, neither sex shows better understanding of mathematical concepts; girls excel in computation (adding, subtracting, and so on), and boys do not show superior problem-solving ability until high school (J. S. Hyde, Fennema, & Lamon, 1990). In a statistical analysis of 286 studies of spatial abilities, the male advantage increased with age and emerged at different ages for different abilities, with few significant differences appearing before adolescence (Voyer, Voyer, & Bryden, 1995).

Regarding personality, the clearest finding is that boys tend to be more aggressive than girls (P. J. Turner & Gervai, 1995). Some studies suggest that girls are more empathic, compliant, and cooperative with parents and seek adult approval more than boys do (N. Eisenberg, Fabes, Schaller, & Miller, 1989; M. L. Hoffman, 1977; E. Maccoby, 1980; P. J. Turner & Gervai, 1995). Also, as we'll discuss later in this chapter, boys and girls play differently. One of the earliest gender differences, appearing as early as age 2 and more consistently from age 3 on, is in the choice of toys and play activities and of playmates of the same sex (P. J. Turner & Gervai, 1995).

We need to remember, of course, that gender differences are valid for large groups of boys and girls but not necessarily for individuals (P. J. Turner & Gervai, 1995). By knowing a child's sex, we cannot predict whether that *particular* boy or girl will be faster, stronger, smarter, more obedient, or more assertive than another child.

Gender Development: Theoretical Explanations

Why do differences—especially cognitive and personality differences—between boys and girls increase with age? To answer that question, we need to consider two related aspects of gender identity: *gender roles* and *gender-typing*.

Gender roles are the behaviors, interests, attitudes, skills, and personality traits considered appropriate for males or females. All societies have gender roles. Historically, in most cultures, women have been expected to devote most of their time to caring for the household and children, while men were providers and protectors. Women were expected to be compliant and nurturant; men, to be active, aggressive, and competitive. Today, gender roles in western cultures have become more diverse and more flexible.

Gender-typing (see Chapter 7) is a child's learning of his or her gender role. Children learn these roles early through socialization. People vary in the degree to which they take on gender roles.

Gender stereotypes are exaggerated generalizations about male or female behavior ("All females are passive and dependent; all males are aggressive and independent"). Gender stereotypes pervade many cultures and are found in children as young as 3 (Haugh, Hoffman, & Cowan, 1980; J. E. Williams & Best, 1982). Gender stereotypes, if incorporated into gender roles, can restrict children's views of themselves and their future. Gender stereotypes can affect the simplest, most everyday tasks as well as far-reaching life decisions. Children who absorb these stereotypes may become men who are "all thumbs" when it comes to giving a baby a bottle or women who "can't" nail boards together (Bem, 1976).

How do children achieve gender identity and acquire gender roles? Let's look at four theoretical perspectives (summarized in Table 10-1). The *psychoanalytic* perspective emphasizes emotional ties to parents; the *social-learning* viewpoint stresses what and how children learn from models and from adult reinforcement; and the *cognitive* approach (represented by Kohlberg and Bem) notes children's own growing ability to take in and interpret information about the world and their place in it. Each theory contributes to our

gender roles Behaviors, interests, attitudes, skills, and traits that a culture considers appropriate for males or for females.

gender-typing Socialization process by which children, at an early age, learn behavior deemed by the culture appropriate for a boy or a girl.

gender stereotypes Exaggerated generalizations about male or female role behavior.

Table 10-1   Perspectives on Gender Identity

Theory	Major Theorist	Key Process	Basic Belief
Psychoanalytic	Sigmund Freud	Emotional	Gender identity occurs when child identifies with same-sex parent.
Social-learning	Albert Bandura	Learning	Gender identity is a result of observing and imitating models and being reinforced for gender-appropriate behavior.
Cognitive-developmental	Lawrence Kohlberg	Cognitive	Once child learns she is a girl or he is a boy, child actively sorts information by gender into what girls do and what boys do, and acts accordingly.
Gender-schema	Sandra Bem	Cognitive and learning	Child organizes information about what is considered appropriate for a boy or a girl on the basis of learning what a particular culture dictates, and behaves accordingly. Child sorts by gender because the culture dictates that gender is an important schema.

understanding, but none fully explains why boys and girls turn out differently in some respects and not in others.

Psychoanalytic Theory: Identification with a Parent

"Dad, where will you live when I grow up and marry Mommy?" asks Timmy, age 4. From the psychoanalytic perspective, Timmy's question is part of his acquisition of gender identity. That process, according to Freud, is one of *identification,* the adoption of characteristics, beliefs, attitudes, values, and behaviors of the parent of the same sex. Freud and other classical psychoanalytic theorists considered identification an important personality development of early childhood; some social-learning theorists also have used the term.

According to Freud, identification will occur for Timmy when he represses or gives up the wish to possess the parent of the other sex (his mother) and identifies with the parent of the same sex (his father). Although this explanation for gender identity has been influential, research has found that children's gender-typed behavior is often unlike that of their parents and that identification seems to be a result, not a cause, of gender-typing (E. E. Maccoby, 1992). Today, most psychologists favor explanations for gender identity advanced by social-learning or cognitive theorists.

identification In Freudian theory, the process by which a young child adopts characteristics, beliefs, attitudes, values, and behaviors of the parent of the same sex.

Social-Learning Theory: Observing and Imitating Models

Anna, at age 5, insisted on dressing in a new way. She wanted to wear leggings with a skirt over them, and boots—indoors and out. When Diane asked her why, Anna replied, "Because Katie dresses like this—and Katie's the king of the girls!"

In social-learning theory, children learn gender identity and gender roles in the same way as they learn other behavior: by observing and imitating models. Typically, one model is the parent of the same sex, but children also model themselves after other people.

Reinforcement strengthens the learning of gender roles. A boy sees that he is physically more like his father than his mother. He imitates his father and is rewarded for acting "like a boy." A comparable process takes place for a girl. By the end of early childhood, these lessons are internalized; a child no longer needs praise, punishment, or the model's presence to act in socially appropriate ways. However, since gender identity and gender roles are learned, they can later be modified through selection and imitation of new models or through reinforcement of different kinds of behavior.

Although social-learning theory seems to make sense, it has been hard to prove. Children do imitate adults, but not always those of the same sex. Children are no more like their parents in personality than like other parents chosen at random; and if they *are* like their own parents, they are no more like the same-sex parent than like the other parent (Hetherington, 1965; Mussen & Rutherford, 1963).

An analysis of a large number of studies suggests that parents, especially fathers, do encourage gender-typed activities in play and chores. However, it is not clear whether the behavior being reinforced arises from imitation, from the child's own preferences, or from some other cause (Lytton & Romney, 1991). Social learning may have something to do with children's acquisition of gender identity and gender roles, but simple imitation and reinforcement do not seem to fully explain how this occurs.

Cognitive-Developmental Theory: Mental Processes

Anna learns she is a girl because people call her a girl. She figures out what things girls are supposed to do and does them. She learns about gender the same way she learns everything else: by thinking about her experience. This is the heart of Lawrence Kohlberg's (1966) cognitive-developmental theory.

To learn their gender identity, Kohlberg says, children do not depend on adults as models or as dispensers of reinforcements and punishments. Instead, they classify themselves and others as male or female and then organize their behavior around that classification. They do this by adopting behaviors they perceive as consistent with their gender. From this perspective, the reason a girl may prefer dolls to trucks is not that she gets approval for playing with dolls (as in social-learning theory). Rather, the reason is her cognitive awareness that playing with dolls is consistent with her idea of herself as a girl. According to Kohlberg, gender identity typically arrives at about age 2; by 3, most children have a firm idea of which sex they belong to. A girl with a short haircut, for example, will indignantly correct people who mistake her for a boy.

gender constancy, or gender conservation Awareness that one will always be male or female.

Gender constancy, or *gender conservation*—a child's realization that his or her sex will always be the same—comes at age 4 or 5. At 3, Anna's friend David told his mother, "When I grow up, I want to be a mommy just like you so I can play tennis and drive a car." Anna, who was then 4, said she would always be a girl and David would always be a boy, even if he played with dolls. David had not achieved gender constancy; Anna had. According to Kohlberg, gender constancy precedes acquisition of gender roles. Once children realize they will always be male or female, they adopt what they see as gender-appropriate behaviors.

While research supports a connection between gender concepts and cognitive development, very little evidence directly links acquisition of gender constancy to gender-related behavior. One exception seems to be boys' television preferences. Five-year-old boys who have achieved gender constancy pay more attention to male characters on television and watch more sports and action programs than boys who have not yet achieved it (Luecke-Aleksa, Anderson, Collins, & Schmitt, 1995). Even before they attain gender constancy, however, children categorize activities and objects by gender, know a lot about what males and females do, and often acquire gender-appropriate behaviors (G. D. Levy & Carter, 1989; Luecke-Aleksa et al., 1995).

After achieving gender constancy, children at first have a rigid idea of gender categories; they seem to view gender differences as immutable and to believe that boys and girls are essentially different in nature, much as cats and dogs are. In one study, when asked how a baby boy raised on a desert island with only girls and women (or a girl raised with only boys and men) would turn out, 5- to 9-year-olds recognized *no* environmental influence on gender roles: they seemed to believe that a boy will develop stereotypically "male" characteristics (and a girl, "female" ones) regardless of upbringing. Ten-year-olds and college students, by contrast, distinguished between such characteristics as hair style, dress, play activities, and ambitions, which probably would be affected by the social environment, and biological characteristics, which would not (M. G. Taylor, 1996).

Apparently, then, development of gender constancy is not the whole story; as children gain more experience and information about what gender means, they develop more flexible ideas about what the categories of gender imply. It seems reasonable, then, to look for additional factors in gender-role development besides gender constancy.

Gender-Schema Theory: A Cognitive-Social Approach

Why—of all the differences among people—do children pay so much attention to sex in setting up the classifications by which they make sense of their world? To answer that question, Sandra Bem (1983, 1985) developed *gender-schema theory,* a cognitive-social approach that combines elements of cognitive-developmental theory and social-learning theory and emphasizes the role of culture. A *schema* (like the schemes in Piaget's theory) is a mentally organized pattern of behavior that helps a child sort information. A *gender schema* is a pattern of behavior organized around gender.

According to gender-schema theory, children socialize themselves in their gender roles by developing a concept of what it means to be male or female in their culture. They do this by organizing their observations around the schema of gender. They organize information on this basis because they see that their society classifies people that way: males and females wear different clothes, play with different toys, use separate bathrooms, and line up separately in school. Children then adapt their own attitudes and behavior to their culture's gender schema—what boys and girls are "supposed" to be and do. When they act gender-appropriately, their self-esteem rises; when they don't, they feel inadequate.

One variation on gender-schema theory, the *schema confirmation-deployment model* (Farrar & Goodman, 1990, 1992), sees the gender schema as a kind of script (see Chapter 9), which is based on experience and guides behavior. The script makes it easier to remember information consistent with it and harder to remember information that deviates from it. In this model, children go through three phases in assimilating and applying gender-related information: *information gathering,* in which they learn what kinds of information fit the script; *schema confirmation,* in which they notice and remember information compatible with their scripts; and *schema deployment,* in which they are now familiar enough with the script so that they can notice and remember information that contradicts it. Research suggests that 4-year-olds tend to fall in the information-gathering phase, 6-year-olds in the confirmation phase, and 8-year-olds in the deployment phase (Welch-Ross & Schmidt, 1996).

As in social-learning theory, since the gender schema is learned, it can be modified. Thus, Bem (1974, 1976) suggests, adults can teach children to substitute other schemas for a prevailing cultural schema that promotes gender-role stereotypes. Adults can do this by sharing household tasks, giving nonstereotyped gifts (dolls for boys and trucks for girls), exposing children to men and women in nontraditional occupations, and emphasizing anatomy and reproduction rather than clothing and behavior as the main distinctions between males and females. A child raised in this way may develop an *androgynous* personality, one that integrates positive characteristics normally thought of as masculine with those normally considered feminine. An androgynous person might be assertive, dominant, and self-reliant ("masculine" traits), as well as compassionate, sympathetic, and understanding ("feminine" traits). Androgynous men and women can do what seems best in a particular situation rather than confining themselves to what is considered "manly" or "womanly."

Anna's enjoyment of her truck shows that she is not restricted in her play by gender stereotypes. According to Bem's gender-schema theory, parents can help children avoid such stereotypes by encouraging them to pursue their own interests, even when these interests are unconventional for their sex.

gender-schema theory Theory, proposed by Bem, that children socialize themselves in their gender roles by developing a concept of what it means to be male or female in a particular culture.

gender schema In Bem's theory, a pattern of behavior organized around gender.

schema confirmation-deployment model Variation on gender-schema theory, in which a child builds a "script" based on gender-related information and then checks new information against the script.

androgynous Personality type integrating positive characteristics typically thought of as masculine and positive characteristics typically thought of as feminine.

CHECKPOINT

Can you . . .

• Compare how various theories explain the acquisition of gender identity and gender roles, and assess the research support for each theory?

Although ingrained cultural attitudes about gender can be highly resistant to change, in many places they *are* changing. In the United States and other industrialized countries, women have entered nontraditional occupations and are gaining power in business, government, and the family. Egalitarian attitudes and behavior have become more common, especially among younger, better-educated, and higher-income people. Men and women are exploring aspects of their personalities that were suppressed by the old gender stereotypes. If Bem is right, these cultural changes should be reflected in children's gender schemas, which in turn shape their attitudes and behavior.

Influences on Gender Development: Nature and Nurture

When Derek and his friend Shani play house in preschool, Shani, as the "mommy," is likely to "cook" and "take care of the baby" while Derek puts on a hat and "goes to work." When Derek "comes home," sits at the table, and says "I'm hungry," Shani drops what she is doing to wait on him. This scenario might seem perfectly normal, but for the fact that both children's mothers work outside the home and both fathers do a fair amount of housework. To what extent does the biological makeup of these children influence their behavior? Why do they seem to have absorbed the gender roles of their culture rather than those of their own households?

It seems clear that both nature and nurture play a part in what it means to be male or female. But do cultural influences *create* gender differences, or merely *accentuate* them? The existence of similar gender roles in many cultures suggests that some gender differences, at least, may be innate. On the other hand, psychological and behavioral differences among people of the same sex are larger than the average differences between the sexes, suggesting that the role of biology, if any, is limited. Research does not yield clear-cut answers to the nature-nurture question; as with other aspects of development, an interaction of factors may be at work.

Biological Influences

In animals, hormones circulating in the bloodstream before or about the time of birth seem to influence gender differences. The male hormone testosterone has been linked to aggressive behavior in mice, guinea pigs, rats, and primates, and the female hormone prolactin to motherly behavior in virgin or male animals (Bronson & Desjardins, 1969; D. M. Levy, 1966; R. M. Rose, Gordon, & Bernstein, 1972). Of course, human beings are influenced far more by learning than animals are, so conclusions drawn from animal studies may not apply.

However, a long-term follow-up of a classic case of sexual switching in infancy (Money & Ehrhardt, 1972), in which an 8-month-old boy whose penis had been accidentally destroyed during surgery was raised as a girl, points to the strength of basic biological makeup. Although initially described as developing into a normal female, the child was later found to have rejected female identity and, at puberty, to have successfully switched to living as a male. This case and several similar ones contradict the belief, prevalent among many physicians, that healthy psychosexual adjustment depends chiefly on the presence of appropriate sexual organs and on upbringing. Instead, it suggests that gender identity may be rooted in chromosomal structure or prenatal development and cannot easily be changed (Diamond & Sigmundson, 1997).

Parental Influences

Even in today's more "liberated" American society, parents treat sons and daughters differently, especially in toddlerhood (Fagot & Hagan, 1991; see Chapter 7). Parents accept aggression more in boys and show more warmth to girls.

According to some research, a father promotes gender-typing when he shows more affection and approval to a daughter than to a son.

An analysis of 172 studies that were done between 1952 and 1987 (Lytton & Romney, 1991) found that boys are gender-socialized more strongly than girls. Parents pressure boys more to act "like real boys" and avoid acting "like girls" than they pressure girls to avoid "boyish" behavior and to act in "feminine" ways. Parents are more likely to show discomfort if a boy plays with a doll than if a girl plays with a truck. Girls have much more freedom in the clothes they wear, the games they play, and the people they play with (Miedzian, 1991).

Some research has found that fathers, in particular, promote gender-typing (P. J. Turner & Gervai, 1995). For example, in one study, fathers were apt to be more social with, more approving of, and more affectionate toward their preschool daughters, but more controlling and directive toward their sons, and more concerned with their sons' cognitive achievements than with their daughters' (Bronstein, 1988). Still, according to an analysis of 67 studies of single-parent families, the father's absence seems to make little difference in a child's gender development. No differences appeared for girls, and those for boys were quite small (M. R. Stevenson & Black, 1988). Other research suggests that what fathers do has long-range implications: men and women who get along well at work and in relationships are most apt to have had warm ties to fathers who were competent, strong, secure in their own masculinity, and nurturant toward their children (Biller, 1981).

One reason for these mixed findings may be that researchers were studying different kinds of gender-related behavior and were using different measuring instruments. Gender-typing has many facets, and the particular combination of "masculine" and "feminine" traits and behaviors a child acquires is an individual matter. Jonathan may play mainly with boys, but not aggressively; Marguerite may insist on wearing dresses instead of jeans but may yell with all her lung-power when she doesn't get her way. Also, the child's age may make a difference (P. J. Turner & Gervai, 1995).

In one multidimensional study (P. J. Turner & Gervai, 1995), researchers talked with 4-year-old children in Cambridge, England, and Budapest, Hungary. The researchers showed the children pictures to determine their play prefer-ences, their knowledge of gender stereotypes, and which adult occupations ap-pealed to them. The children were observed at preschool to see how they played and with whom, and their parents were interviewed and filled out question-naires. One goal was to compare parents' and children's gender-typing; another was to find out whether parents' contribution to gender-typing differed for dif-ferent kinds of behavior.

The findings were complex. Highly gender-typed parents did tend to produce highly gender-typed children, but parents seemed to have more influence on chil-dren's *knowledge* of gender stereotypes than on their *behavior*. This was especially true of choice of playmates: children played with others of the same sex regard-less of what their parents thought. Indeed, same-sex peer groups may themselves be a major influence on gender-typing. Fathers were a more consistent influence than mothers. Surprisingly, though, they influenced both boys and girls in the same direction: daughters as well as sons of a highly "masculine" father tended to be more self-assertive and less expressive than sons and daughters of less "mascu-line" men. Not so surprisingly, children of fathers who did more housework and child care were less aware of gender stereotypes and engaged in less gender-typed play. More research on the multiple aspects of gender may help sort out the ways parents influence children's gender-related attitudes and behavior.

Cultural Influences

One important channel for the transmission of cultural attitudes about gender is television. The typical American high school graduate has watched 15,000 to 18,000 hours of television (Strasburger, 1992) and has absorbed highly gender-stereotyped attitudes from it. Although women seen on television are now more likely to be working outside the home and men are sometimes shown caring for children or doing the marketing, for the most part life as portrayed on television is more stereotyped than life in the real world.

Social-learning theory predicts that children who watch a lot of television will become more gender-typed by imitating the models they see on the screen. By the same token, young children who watched a series of nontraditional episodes, such as a father and son cooking together, had less stereotyped views than children who had not seen the series (J. Johnston & Ettema, 1982). Of course, children bring their own attitudes to the television set. Boys turn on more car-toons and action adventure programs than girls do, and both sexes remember television sequences that confirm the stereotypes they already hold better than they remember nonstereotypical sequences (Calvert & Huston, 1987).

Children's books are another source of gender stereotypes, as research in the 1970s pointed out. Today, friendship between boys and girls is portrayed more often, and girls are braver and more resourceful. Still, male characters predomi-nate, females are more likely to need help, and males are more likely to give it (Beal, 1994).

CHECKPOINT

Can you . . .

- Assess evidence for biological, parental, and cultural influences on gender development?

Play: The Business of Early Childhood

When Carmen, age 3, comes to breakfast, she pretends that the pieces of cereal floating in her bowl are "fishies" swimming in the milk, and she "fishes," spoonful by spoonful. After breakfast, she puts on her mother's old hat, picks up a discarded

Table 10-2	Types of Social and Nonsocial Play in Early Childhood

Category	Description
Unoccupied behavior	The child does not seem to be playing, but watches anything of momentary interest.
Onlooker behavior	The child spends most of the time watching other children play. The onlooker talks to them, asking questions or making suggestions, but does not enter into the play. The onlooker is definitely observing particular groups of children rather than anything that happens to be exciting.
Solitary independent play	The child plays alone with toys that are different from those used by nearby children and makes no effort to get close to them.
Parallel play	The child plays independently, but among the other children, playing with toys like those used by the other children, but not necessarily playing with them in the same way. Playing *beside* rather than *with* the others, the parallel player does not try to influence the other children's play.
Associative play	The child plays with other children. They talk about their play, borrow and lend toys, follow one another, and try to control who may play in the group. All the children play similarly if not identically; there is no division of labor and no organization around any goal. Each child acts as she or he wishes and is interested more in being with the other children than in the activity itself.
Cooperative or organized supplementary play	The child plays in a group organized for some goal—to make something, play a formal game, or dramatize a situation. One or two children control who belongs to the group and direct activities. By a division of labor, children take on different roles and supplement each other's efforts.

Source: Adapted from Parten, 1932, pp. 249–251.

briefcase, and is a "mommy" going to work. She runs outside to ride her tricycle through the puddles, comes in for an imaginary telephone conversation, then turns a wooden block into a truck and makes the appropriate sound effects. Carmen's day is one round of play after another.

An adult might be tempted to dismiss Carmen's activities as no more than "having fun." But that would be a mistake: play is the work of the young. Through play, children grow. They stimulate the senses, learn how to use their muscles, coordinate what they see with what they do, and gain mastery over their bodies. They find out about the world and themselves. They acquire new skills. They become more proficient with language, they try out different roles, and—by reenacting real-life situations—they cope with complex emotions.

Preschoolers engage in different types of play at different ages. Particular children have different styles of playing, and they play at different things. One kindergartner might put on dress-up clothes with a friend while another is absorbed in building a block tower. What can we learn about children by seeing how they play?

Types of Play

Researchers categorize children's play in both social and cognitive terms. *Social play* refers to the extent to which children interact with other children during play. *Cognitive play* reflects a child's level of mental development.

Social and Nonsocial Play

In the 1920s, Mildred B. Parten (1932) observed forty-two 2- to 5-year-olds during free-play periods at nursery school. She identified six types of play, ranging from the least to the most social (see Table 10-2). She found that as children get older,

social play Play in which children, to varying degrees, interact with other children.

cognitive play Forms of play that reveal children's mental development.

their play tends to become more social and more cooperative. At first they play alone, then alongside other children, and finally, together.

However, in a similar study done 40 years later, forty-four 3- and 4-year-olds played much less sociably than the children in Parten's group (K. E. Barnes, 1971). The difference may have reflected a changed environment. Because these children watched television, they may have become more passive; because they had more elaborate toys and fewer siblings, they may have played alone more.

We might expect children who have spent considerable time in group day care to play more sociably. That expectation has been borne out for children attending day-care centers that emphasize social skills, that have mixed age groups, and that have a high adult-child ratio. However, it does not seem applicable to children in small centers with same-age grouping and an emphasis on academic skills (Schindler, Moely, & Frank, 1987).

Is solitary play always less mature than social play? Parten thought so. She and some other observers suggest that young children who play alone may be at risk of developing social, psychological, and educational problems. Actually, though, much nonsocial play consists of activities that foster cognitive, physical, and social development. Among children in six kindergartens, about 33 percent of solitary play consisted of goal-directed activities such as block-building and art work; about 25 percent was large-muscle play; about 15 percent was educational; and only about 10 percent involved just looking (N. Moore, Evertson, & Brophy, 1974). In one study of 4-year-olds, some kinds of nonsocial play, such as *parallel constructive play* (for example, working on puzzles near another child) were most common among children who were good problem solvers, were popular with other children, and were seen by teachers as socially skilled (K. Rubin, 1982). Thus solitary play may reflect independence and maturity, not poor social adjustment.

Children need some time alone to concentrate on tasks and problems, and some simply enjoy nonsocial activities more than group activities. We need to look at what children *do* when they play, not just at whether they play alone or with someone else.

Cognitive Play

Carol, at 2½, "talked for" a doll, using a deeper voice than her own, as if the doll were a real person. Michael, at 3, wore a kitchen towel as a cape and "flew" around as Batman. Anna, at 3½, had several imaginary playmates (see Box 10-1). All these children were engaged in **pretend play** (also called *fantasy play, dramatic play, symbolic play,* or *imaginative play*), which involves make-believe people or situations.

Pretend play is one of the categories of play identified by Piaget and others as signs of cognitive development (Piaget, 1951; Smilansky, 1968). Young children progress from simple *repetitive play* involving muscular movements (such as rolling a ball) to three increasingly complex forms: *constructive play* (building a block tower), then *pretend play* (playing doctor), and then *formal games with rules* (hopscotch and marbles).

The ability to pretend rests on the ability to use and remember symbols (Piaget, 1962), which emerges near the end of the sensorimotor stage. Pretend play typically begins during the last part of the second year, increases during the next 3 to 4 years, and then declines as children become more interested in playing games with rules. About 10 to 17 percent of preschoolers' play is pretend play, and the proportion rises to about 33 percent among kindergartners (Bretherton, 1984; K. H. Rubin, Fein, & Vandenberg, 1983). The social dimension of imaginative play also changes during these years, from solitary pretending to sociodramatic play involving other children (D. G. Singer & Singer, 1990). Jessie, who at age 3 would climb inside a box by herself and pretend to be a train conductor, will by age 6 want to have passengers on her train.

pretend play Play involving imaginary people or situations; also called *fantasy play, dramatic play, symbolic play,* or *imaginative play.*

Box 10-1 Imaginary Playmates

At age 3½, Anna had 23 sisters with such names as Och, Elmo, Zeni, Aggie, and Ankie. She often talked to them on the telephone, since they lived about 100 miles away, in the town where her family used to live. During the next year, most of the sisters disappeared, but Och continued to visit, especially for birthday parties. Och had a cat and a dog (which Anna had begged for in vain), and whenever Anna was denied something she saw advertised on television, she announced that she already had one at her sister's house.

All 23 sisters—and some "boys" and "girls" who have followed them—lived only in Anna's imagination. Like about 15 to 30 percent of children between ages 3 and 10, she created imaginary companions, with whom she talked and played. This normal phenomenon of childhood is seen most often in bright, creative firstborn and only children (Manosevitz, Prentice, & Wilson, 1973). Girls are more likely than boys to have imaginary playmates (or at least to acknowledge them); girls' imaginary playmates are usually human, whereas boys' are more often animals (D. G. Singer & Singer, 1990).

Children who have imaginary companions can distinguish fantasy from reality, but in free-play sessions they are more likely to engage in pretend play than are children without imaginary companions (M. Taylor, Cartwright, & Carlson, 1993). They play more happily and more imaginatively than other children and are more cooperative with other children and adults (D. G. Singer & Singer, 1990; J. L. Singer & Singer, 1981). They are more fluent with language, watch less television, and show more curiosity, excitement, and persistence during play.

What role do imaginary companions play in a child's life? They are good company for an only child (like Anna). They provide wish-fulfillment mechanisms ("There was a monster in my room, but Elmo scared it off with magic dust"), scapegoats ("I didn't eat those cookies—Och must have done it!"), displacement agents for the child's own fears ("Aggie is afraid she's going to be washed down the drain"), and support in difficult situations. (One 6-year-old "took" her imaginary companion with her to see a scary movie.) In sum, children use imaginary companions to help them get along better in the real world.

Through pretending, children gain understanding of another person's viewpoint, develop skills in solving social problems, and express creativity. Children who often play imaginatively tend to cooperate more with other children and to be more popular and more joyful than those who don't (D. G. Singer & Singer, 1990).

Mothers and fathers of children who engage in frequent pretend play tend to get along well with each other, expose the children to interesting experiences, engage them in conversation, and do not spank (Fein, 1981). They provide a time and place to play, and such simple props as costumes, blocks, paints, and toy people (D. G. Singer & Singer, 1990). Children who watch a great deal of television tend to play less imaginatively, possibly because they get into the habit of passively absorbing images rather than generating their own. Children in high-quality day care play at more cognitively complex levels than children in barely adequate care (Howes & Matheson, 1992).

How Culture Influences Play

Both social and cognitive categories of play can be seen in many cultures. For example, categories similar to those described by Parten and by Smilansky showed up in the play of children in Taiwan (Pan, 1994). However, the frequency of specific forms of play differs across cultures and may be influenced by the environments adults set up for children, which in turn reflect cultural values.

One study compared 48 middle-class Korean American and 48 middle-class Anglo American children in separate full-day, year-round preschools (Farver, Kim, & Lee, 1995). The Anglo American preschools, in keeping with typical American values, encouraged independent thinking, problem solving, and active involvement in learning by letting children select from a wide range of activities. The Korean American preschool, in keeping with traditional Korean values, emphasized academic skills, perseverance in completing tasks, and passive learning. The Anglo American preschools encouraged social interchange among children

Preschools for Korean American children—in line with their culture's values—stress structure, passive learning, and perseverance in completing tasks. Korean American children tend to play more cooperatively but less imaginatively than Anglo American children.

and collaborative activities with teachers. In the Korean American preschool, with its structured schedule, children were allowed to talk and play only during outdoor recess.

Not surprisingly, the Anglo American children engaged in more social play, whereas the Korean Americans engaged in more unoccupied or parallel play. The Korean Americans showed less imaginative play—also not surprising, since their classroom offered few materials that would stimulate pretending, such as "dress-up" clothes or dolls. In addition, the greater amount of pretend play among the Anglo American children may have been influenced by the greater value American culture places on individuality and self-expression. Korean American children played more cooperatively, often offering toys to other children—very likely a reflection of their culture's emphasis on group harmony. Anglo American children were more aggressive and often responded negatively to other children's suggestions, reflecting the competitiveness of American culture.

Given the Korean American stress on "school-like" learning, it is again not surprising that these children scored higher on a picture vocabulary test, an indication of cognitive functioning.

Parenting Styles and Practices

As children gradually become their own persons, their upbringing can be a baffling, complex challenge. Parents must deal with small people who have minds and strong wills of their own, but who still have a lot to learn about what kinds of behavior work well in a civilized society. Parents struggle to make the right decisions in bringing up children. They want to raise human beings who enjoy life, think well of themselves, and fulfill their goals. They also want their children to learn to live harmoniously with other people and to form and maintain close, constructive relationships. To accomplish these ends, parents have to use discipline. How do parents discipline children and teach them self-discipline? Are some ways of parenting more effective than others?

Forms of Discipline

Discipline refers to methods of teaching children character, self-control, and acceptable behavior. It can be a powerful tool for socialization.

C**HECKPOINT**

Can you . . .

• Explain how social and cognitive development and cultural differences influence the types of play children engage in?

discipline Tool for socialization, which includes methods of molding children's character and of teaching them to exercise self-control and engage in acceptable behavior.

What forms of discipline work best? Social-learning research has compared reinforcement and punishment. Other researchers have looked at forms of discipline in terms of the quality of interaction between parent and child.

Reinforcement and Punishment

"What are we going to do with that child?" Noel's mother says. "The more we punish him, the more he misbehaves!"

Parents sometimes punish children to stop undesirable behavior, but research shows that children usually learn more from being reinforced for good behavior. *External* reinforcements may be tangible (candy, money, toys, or gold stars) or intangible (a smile, a word of praise, a hug, extra attention, or a special privilege). Whatever the reinforcement, the child must see it as rewarding and must receive it fairly consistently after showing the desired behavior. Eventually, the behavior should provide its own *internal* reward: a sense of pleasure or accomplishment. In Noel's case, his parents ignore him most of the time when he behaves well but scold or spank him when he acts up. In other words, they unwittingly reinforce his *mis*behavior by giving him attention when he does what they do *not* want him to do.

Unfortunately, spanking is very common. In the 1990 National Longitudinal Survey of Youth, more than 6 out of 10 mothers of 3- to 5-year-olds reported having spanked their children an average of three times during the previous week—a rate that works out to more than 150 spankings a year (Giles-Sims, Straus, & Sugarman, 1995).

Ironically, spanking often stimulates aggressive behavior. Aside from the risk of injury to the child, harsh physical or verbal punishment may encourage children to imitate the punisher and to consider violence an effective response to problems. Children who are punished harshly and frequently may have trouble interpreting other people's actions and words; they may attribute hostile intentions where none exist (B. Weiss, Dodge, Bates, & Pettit, 1992). On the other hand, such children may become passive because they feel helpless. Children may become frightened if parents lose control and yell, scream, chase, or hit the child. A child may eventually try to avoid a punitive parent, undermining the parent's ability to influence behavior (Grusec & Goodnow, 1994).

Despite the potentially negative effects of punishment, at times some kind of punishment does seem necessary. Children may have to be immediately and forcefully taught not to run out into traffic or bash one another over the head with heavy toys. When punishment must be used, the following factors influence its effectiveness (Parke, 1977):

1. *Timing:* The shorter the time between misbehavior and punishment, the more effective the punishment.
2. *Explanation:* Punishment is more effective when accompanied by a short, simple explanation.
3. *Consistency:* The more consistently a child is punished for the same misbehavior, the more effective the punishment will be.
4. *The person who punishes:* The better the relationship between the punishing adult and the child, the more effective the punishment.

Power Assertion, Induction, and Withdrawal of Love

From the point of view of a parent's interaction with a child, research has identified three types of discipline: *power assertion, induction,* and *temporary withdrawal of love.*

Power assertion includes demands, threats, withdrawal of privileges, spanking, and other physical punishment for undesirable behavior. *Inductive techniques* are used to induce desirable behavior; they include setting limits, demonstrating logical consequences of an action, explaining, reasoning, and getting ideas from the child. *Withdrawal of love* may take the form of ignoring, isolating, or showing dislike for a child.

Analysis of data from a number of studies suggests that induction is usually the most effective method, and power assertion the least effective, in getting children to accept parental standards (M. L. Hoffman, 1970a, 1970b). When the mothers of 54 poor, inner-city African American kindergartners were questioned about their disciplinary practices, children whose mothers used reasoning were more likely to see the moral wrongness of behavior that hurts others, as compared with behavior that merely violates rules. Children whose mothers took away privileges or ignored misbehavior did not show this moral understanding (Jagers, Bingham, & Hans, 1996).

Most parents call upon more than one of these strategies, depending on the situation. Parents tend to use reasoning in getting a child to show concern for others or in teaching table manners. They use power assertion to stop play that gets too rough, and they use both power assertion and reasoning to deal with lying and stealing. Sometimes parents use power assertion to get a child's attention (by raising their voices or picking up a child who will not move) and then use reasoning to make their position clear (Grusec & Goodnow, 1994).

The choice and effectiveness of a disciplinary strategy may depend in part on the personality of the parent, the personality and age of the child, and the quality of their relationship, as well as on culturally based customs and expectations (Grusec & Goodnow, 1994). A child interprets and responds to discipline in the context of ongoing interactions with a parent. Some researchers therefore have looked at overall styles, or patterns, of parenting.

Baumrind: Three Parenting Styles

Why does Stacy hit and bite the nearest person when she cannot finish a jigsaw puzzle? What makes David sit and sulk when he cannot finish the puzzle, even though his teacher offers to help him? Why does Consuelo work on the puzzle for 20 minutes and then shrug and try another? Why are children so different in their responses to the same situation? Temperament is a major factor, of course; but some research suggests that styles of parenting also may affect children's competence in dealing with their world.

In her pioneering research, Diana Baumrind (1971, 1996; Baumrind & Black, 1967) studied 103 preschool children from 95 families. Through interviews, testing, and home studies, she measured how children were functioning, identified three parenting styles, and described typical behavior patterns of children raised according to each.

Authoritarian parents value control and unquestioning obedience. They try to make children conform to a set standard of conduct and punish them arbitrarily and forcefully for violating it. They are more detached and less warm than other parents. Their children tend to be more discontented, withdrawn, and distrustful.

Permissive parents value self-expression and self-regulation. They consider themselves resources, not models. They make few demands and allow children to monitor their own activities as much as possible. When they do have to make rules, they explain the reasons for them. They consult with children about policy decisions and rarely punish. They are warm, noncontrolling, and undemanding. Their preschool children tend to be immature—-the least self-controlled and the least exploratory.

Authoritative parents respect a child's individuality but also stress social values. They have confidence in their ability to guide children, but they also respect children's independent decisions, interests, opinions, and personalities. They are loving, consistent, demanding, firm in maintaining standards, and willing to impose limited, judicious punishment—-even occasional, mild spanking—when necessary, within the context of a warm, supportive relationship. They explain the reasoning behind their stands and encourage verbal give-and-take.

CHECKPOINT

Can you . . .

• Compare various forms of discipline, and identify factors that influence their effectiveness?

authoritarian In Baumrind's terminology, parenting style emphasizing control and obedience. Compare *authoritative* and *permissive*.

permissive In Baumrind's terminology, parenting style emphasizing self-expression and self-regulation. Compare *authoritarian* and *authoritative*.

authoritative In Baumrind's terminology, parenting style blending respect for a child's individuality with an effort to instill social values. Compare *authoritarian* and *permissive*.

Their children apparently feel secure in knowing both that they are loved and what is expected of them. These preschoolers tend to be the most self-reliant, self-controlled, self-assertive, exploratory, and content.

Why does authoritative parenting seem to enhance children's competence? It may well be because authoritative parents set reasonable expectations and realistic standards. In authoritarian homes, children are so strictly controlled that often they cannot make independent choices about their own behavior. In permissive homes, children receive so little guidance that they may become uncertain and anxious about whether they are doing the right thing. In authoritative homes, children know when they are meeting expectations and can decide whether it is worth risking parental displeasure or other unpleasant consequences to pursue a goal. These children are expected to perform well, fulfill commitments, and participate actively in family duties as well as family fun. They know the satisfaction of meeting responsibilities and achieving success.

Baumrind's work has inspired much research, and the superiority of authoritative parenting has repeatedly been supported. However, because these findings seem to suggest that there is one "right" way to raise children well, they have caused some controversy. Sandra Scarr, for example, argues that heredity normally exerts a much greater influence than parenting practices (refer back to Box 2-3).

Since Baumrind's findings are correlational, they merely establish associations between each parenting style and a particular set of child behaviors; they do not show that different styles of child rearing *cause* children to be more or less competent. It is also impossible to know whether the children were, in fact, raised in a particular style. It may be that some of the better-adjusted children were raised inconsistently, but by the time of the study their parents had adopted the authoritative pattern. Furthermore, even if parents usually act toward their children in a certain way, they do not respond to all situations in that way.

In addition, Baumrind did not consider innate factors, such as temperament, that might have affected children's competence and exerted an influence on the parents. Parents of "easy" children may be more likely to respond to the child in a permissive or authoritative manner, while parents of "difficult" children may become more authoritarian.

Finally, Baumrind's categories reflect a child-centered, North American view of child development. These categories may be misleading when applied to some cultures or socioeconomic groups. For example, Asian American parenting, with its emphasis on respect for elders, is frequently described as authoritarian; but while authoritarian parenting typically leads to less competence, particularly in school achievement, Asian American children tend to do unusually well in school (see Box 12-2). Whereas an authoritarian style among European American parents is often associated with harshness and domination, among Asian Americans obedience and strictness have more to do with caring, concern, and involvement and with maintaining family harmony (R. K. Chao, 1994).

Specifically, Chinese culture emphasizes *chiao shun* ("training")—parents' (and teachers') responsibility to teach children socially proper behavior. This is done through *guan*—firm and just control and governance of the child. These concepts are derived from Confucian tradition, a system of hierarchical relationships intended to maintain the social order. Thus what looks like authoritarian parenting has different meaning in Chinese culture and may not capture what Chinese parenting is about. The warmth and supportiveness that characterize Chinese American family relationships more closely resemble Baumrind's authoritative parenting—but without the emphasis on the American values of individuality, choice, and freedom (R. K. Chao, 1994).

African American mothers, too, have been described as authoritarian, but a study of 42 low-income black mothers and grandmothers caring for 3- to 6-year-olds found a wide range of child-rearing attitudes and practices. Mothers who were more religious tended to be more sensitive to their children's

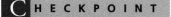

CHECKPOINT

Can you . . .

• Describe and evaluate Baumrind's model of parenting styles?

needs (in Baumrind's terminology, more "authoritative"), as did more mature, more educated, and married mothers. Younger, less educated single mothers, who were less religious, tended to emphasize obedience and respect for elders. Yet this latter approach may be adaptive for children in an inner-city community, in which respect for authority can lead to success in a highly structured school and work situation (Kelley, Power, & Wimbush, 1992). It may be misleading, then, to consider parenting styles without looking at the goals parents are trying to achieve and the constraints their life circumstances present.

Conflict, Autonomy, and Parenting Goals

A major difference among parenting styles, and a major source of conflict between parents and children in mainstream American culture, is the question of how much freedom children should be allowed. A child's area of autonomy typically enlarges in middle childhood (see Chapter 13), but even parents of preschoolers tend to believe that children are entitled to their own opinions and should have control over some aspects of their lives. This view is based on the belief that limited autonomy promotes important developmental goals—namely, competence and self-esteem (Nucci & Smetana, 1996).

What kinds of decisions do parents let children make for themselves? The precise boundaries are matters of negotiation and may vary among cultural and socioeconomic groups. In 40 white suburban middle-class families, 5-year-olds were more likely to be given choices about foods, whereas 7-year-olds were more likely to be allowed to choose their own activities. Even so, conflicts within a child's supposed area of autonomy tended to arise—with boys, over activities, and with girls over appearance (Nucci & Smetana, 1996).

With regard to conflicts within the larger domain over which parents seek to maintain control, an important goal of socialization is to help a child internalize parental teachings in the form of self-discipline. From an information-processing perspective, the effectiveness of parental discipline may hinge on how well the child understands and accepts the parent's message, both cognitively and emotionally (Grusec & Goodnow, 1994).

For children to perceive a message accurately, parents first need to get their children's attention. They need to get across the belief that the issue is important and that their intent is to help the child. They need to be clear and consistent about their expectations. For the child to accept the message, the child has to recognize it as appropriate; so parents need to be fair and truthful, and need to fit their actions to the misdeed and to the child's temperament and cognitive and emotional level. A child may be more motivated to accept the message as a guide to behavior if the parents are normally warm and responsive, making the child want to identify with or act like them; if they arouse the child's empathy (say, for another child who was the victim of the misdeed); and if they make the child feel less secure in their affections as a result of the misbehavior. It may help if parents deliver the message in humorous or indirect terms ("Who was your servant last year?" to a child who leaves things strewn around the house, or "What's the magic word?" to a child who doesn't say "Please") (Grusec & Goodnow, 1994).

Important as internalization is, it is not the only goal of parenting. In some situations, other goals—such as encouraging flexibility and initiative or preserving the child's self-esteem and a good parent-child relationship—may take precedence. When a child refuses to do as a parent says, the parent may take the opportunity to teach the child positive ways to communicate his or her own point of view and negotiate acceptable alternatives. ("If you don't want to throw away those smelly clam shells you found, where do you think we should keep them?") Internalization of this broader set of skills, not just of specific behavioral demands, may well be a key to the success of authoritative parenting

(Grusec & Goodnow, 1994). The outcome is not a child who acts just like the parent, but a unique individual who, while accepting a set of core values necessary for social functioning, is free to vary from those values or to apply them in her or his own way.

The processes by which parents and children resolve conflicts, then, may be more important than the specific outcomes. Through participation in family conflict, children learn about rules and standards of behavior and also learn what kinds of issues are worth arguing about and what strategies can be effective (A. R. Eisenberg, 1996).

Socioeconomic status seems to play a much greater role than culture in the way families deal with conflict. In one study of 80 Hispanic and Anglo American families with 4-year-old children in the San Antonio area, mother-child conflicts in working-class families, regardless of ethnicity, were longer, more intense, and less likely to be resolved than conflicts in middle-class families—perhaps because working-class mothers were less definite in saying no. Their children, especially girls, tended to pursue arguments in an attempt to justify their position. Also, working-class mother-child arguments were less likely to be over factual issues, such as the truth of a child's account, which tend to be more quickly resolved than other kinds of issues. Although clashes were no more frequent in working-class homes than in middle-class homes, there was less mother-child talk in working-class families, and so arguments made up a larger proportion of mother-child conversation (A. R. Eisenberg, 1996).

In the long run, specific parenting practices may be less important than how parents feel about their children, how they show their feelings, and whether they allow children to show theirs (see Box 10-2). That is the conclusion of a major study of young adults whose mothers had been interviewed about their child-rearing techniques 20 years earlier (McClelland, Constantian, Regalado, & Stone, 1978; Sears, Maccoby, & Levin, 1957). How these adults turned out bore little or no relation to specific parenting practices. The most important influence—dwarfing all others—was how much their parents had loved them, enjoyed them, and shown them affection.

The most beloved children grew up to be the most tolerant of other people, the most understanding, and the most likely to show active concern for others. The least mature adults had grown up in homes where they were considered a nuisance. Their parents had been intolerant of noise, mess, and roughhousing and had reacted unkindly to children's aggressiveness, to normal childhood sex play, and to expressions of dependency. The finding that children of easygoing, loving parents had been less well-behaved as they were growing up than children of stricter parents prompted the researchers to conclude that some childhood misbehavior may be necessary for the development of a person's own value system:

> Parents also need faith——faith that loving and believing in their children will promote maturity in the long run, even though some of their offsprings' behavior seems outrageous in the short run as they learn to make their own decisions. There are no shortcuts to perfection. Children have to explore some detours if they are to reach the heights. The best we parents can do to help is to love them, and not stand in the way of their groping attempts to grow up or force them at all times to conform to adult-centered codes of moral behavior. (McClelland et al., 1978, p. 114)

Dealing with Altruism, Aggression, and Fearfulness

Three specific issues of especial concern to parents, caregivers, and teachers of preschool children are how to promote altruism, curb aggression, and deal with fears that normally arise at this age.

C HECKPOINT

Can you . . .

- Discuss how parents' ways of resolving conflicts with young children over issues involving autonomy and control can contribute to internalization and other goals of child rearing?

Box 10-2 Can Parental Teaching "Poison" a Child for Life?

One of the most important aspects of parenting is the way parents teach a child to deal with feelings. According to Alice Miller, a Swiss psychotherapist, much pain in adult life stems from these early "lessons," which are passed on from generation to generation.

On the basis of her clinical experience and her study of central European child-rearing practices during the past two centuries, Miller (1984) identified a psychologically injurious cluster of child-rearing practices and attitudes called *poisonous pedagogy (PP)*. Through ridicule, criticism, teasing, scolding, impatience, and strict, authoritarian discipline, says Miller, parents break a child's will, undermine the child's self-confidence and curiosity, and force the child to suppress authentic feelings and impulses—whether sad, angry, or exuberant. PP undermines children's capacity to know, express, and act on their feelings. These suppressed emotions surface in adulthood in the form of rage and violence directed against the self and others. The end results can range from the stifling of empathy and creativity to drug addiction, mental illness, and suicide.

Why do parents do this to children? In Miller's view, they do it both consciously, in the belief that they are helping their children become more competent and self-sufficient, and unconsciously, in reaction to the emotional harm they themselves suffered as children. Only by breaking this generation-to-generation cycle of transmission, she says, can adults help children grow up to be psychologically healthy.

To test Miller's theory, David Harrington (1993) drew on data from a longitudinal study of 100 mostly middle-class families, begun in the late 1960s, when the children studied were 3 and 4 years old. About two-thirds were white, one-fourth were African American, and one-twelfth were Asian.

Near the outset of the study, the mothers and fathers had each completed a report of their parenting practices. Harrington asked a committee consisting of a psychologist, a graduate student, and four undergraduate psychology majors (who were also parents) to group the practices in the parents' reports according to their similarity to Miller's description of poisonous pedagogy (for example, "I do not allow my child to get angry with me"; "I believe too much affection and tenderness can harm or weaken a child"; I think children must learn early not to cry"; "I believe scolding and criticism make my child improve").

In addition, when the children were about 4½ years old, their mothers and fathers separately had taught them four thinking tasks while researchers observed and described the encounters. Again, Harrington asked his committee to examine these reports and sort the parents' behaviors into those most and least characteristic of PP. The most PP-like parents were critical and impatient, tended to control the task (and to overly control their own needs and impulses), and lacked pride in the child. They pressured the child to work at the tasks but rejected the child's ideas and suggestions. The least PP-like parents were warm and supportive, praised the child, encouraged the child to do the task independently, and valued the child's originality.

Finally, Harrington correlated the parents' self-reported and observed PP ratings with their children's scores on measures of psychological adjustment at ages 18 and 23. Strong correlations appeared between parents' early use of PP-like practices and their adult children's psychological ill health, as indicated by avoidance of close relationships, anxiety, self-pity, distrust, and other negative attributes (see Table 10-3). The correlations were stronger for observed practices than for self-reported ones. Young adults whose mothers had shown high levels of PP were deemed less comfortable with themselves and others and more vulnerable to

(continued)

Altruism, or Prosocial Behavior

altruism, or **prosocial behavior** Behavior intended to help others without external reward.

Anna, at 3½, responded to two fellow preschoolers' complaints that they did not have enough modeling clay, her favorite plaything, by giving them half of hers. Anna was showing *altruism, or prosocial behavior*—acting out of concern for another person with no expectation of reward. Prosocial acts like Anna's often entail cost, self-sacrifice, or risk.

Why do some children reach out to comfort a crying friend or stop to help someone who has fallen while crossing a street? What makes them empathic, generous, compassionate, and sensitive to other people's needs? Following Bronfenbrenner's ecological model, we can look at factors contributing to caring behavior within the child and influenced by the social context.

Prosocial behavior appears early. Even before the second birthday, children often help others, share belongings and food, and offer comfort. Such empathic behaviors emerge at a time when children are increasingly able to think representationally. The ability to imagine how another person might feel may enable children to develop a sense of responsibility for others (Zahn-Waxler, Radke-

| Table 10-3 | Personality Characteristics at Ages 18–23 Years Associated with Mothers' Poisonous Pedagogy (PP) in the Teaching Situation at 4.5 Years* |

Personality Characteristics of Adult Child of PP Mother	Characteristics of Adult Child of Non-PP Mother
Is disorganized and maladaptive when under stress	Is turned to for advice and reassurance
Is generally fearful	Appears straightforward, forthright, candid
Avoids close interpersonal relationships	Responds to humor
Gives up and withdraws in the face of frustration and adversity	Is personally charming
Is thin-skinned, sensitive to anything that can be construed as a criticism or slight	Has warmth; has the capacity for close relationships; is compassionate
Is concerned with own adequacy as a person	Has social poise and presence; appears socially at ease
Feels cheated and victimized by life; is self-pitying	Is socially perceptive of a wide range of interpersonal cues
Seeks reassurance from others	Tends to arouse liking and acceptance in people
Is anxious and tense; shows corresponding bodily symptoms	Is able to see to the heart of important problems
Feels a lack of personal meaning in life	Emphasizes being with others; is gregarious
Is basically distrustful of people in general	Is cheerful
Is subtly negativistic; tends to undermine and obstruct or sabotage	

*Listed characteristics yielded a significant correlation with mothers' observed PP.
Source: Adapted from Harrington, 1993, p. 306.

stress than young adults whose mothers had shown low levels of PP. A mother's use of PP seemed more influential than a father's, probably because the mothers spent more time with their young children than the fathers did.

Of course, as usual in correlational studies, we cannot be sure to what extent poisonous pedagogy itself caused psychological problems. Perhaps a bidirectional influence was at work, with child-raising practices being shaped at least in part by children's characteristics. Then too, aspects of the parents' personalities that led them to engage in PP could have independently contributed to the problems the children experienced as they grew up. We also don't know whether a more socioeconomically diverse sample might have yielded different results.

Still, the study seems to present striking support of one part of Miller's theory: the influence of poisonous pedagogy on adult personality. Within the next decade, as the young adults in this study become parents, it will be possible to test the other part of the theory: Miller's prediction of intergenerational transmission of PP.

Yarrow, Wagner, & Chapman, 1992). Altruistic children tend to be advanced in reasoning skills and able to take the role of others (Carlo, Knight, Eisenberg, & Rotenberg, 1991). They are also active and self-confident (C. H. Hart, DeWolf, Wozniak, & Burts, 1992). A tendency toward empathy may be genetic, according to a study of twins (Zahn-Waxler, Robinson, & Emde, 1992). Socioeconomic status is not a factor, and most studies show no differences between girls and boys.

The family, however, *is* important—as a model, as a source of explicit standards, and as a guide to adopting other models. Children who receive empathic, nurturant, responsive care as infants tend to develop those same qualities. Preschoolers who were securely attached as infants are more likely to respond to other children's distress. They have more friends, and their teachers consider them more socially competent (Kestenbaum, Farber, & Sroufe, 1989; Sroufe, 1983).

Parents of prosocial children typically are altruistic themselves. They point out models of prosocial behavior and steer children toward stories and television programs, such as *Mister Rogers' Neighborhood*, that depict cooperation, sharing, and empathy and encourage sympathy, generosity, and helpfulness (Mussen & Eisenberg-Berg, 1977; National Institute of Mental Health [NIMH], 1982; D. M. Zuckerman & Zuckerman, 1985).

Parents encourage prosocial behavior by using inductive disciplinary methods. When Sara took candy from a store, her father did not lecture her on honesty, spank her, or tell her what a bad girl she had been. Instead, he explained how the owner of the store would be harmed by her failure to pay for the candy, and he took her back to the store to return it. When such incidents occur, Sara's parents ask "How do you think Mr. Jones feels?" or "How would you feel if you were Mr. Jones?" In one study of 106 preschoolers, the most prosocial 3- to 6-year-olds were disciplined by such inductive techniques (C. H. Hart et al., 1992).

Teachers, like parents, can be models. Warm, empathic teachers foster helping and caring behavior (N. Eisenberg, 1992). In many countries, moral education is part of the curriculum. In China, teachers tell stories about prosocial heroes and encourage children to imitate them. In one program in a suburb of San Francisco, children hear about prosocial values and read books and see films depicting altruism. Children are encouraged to help other students and to perform community service, as well as classroom chores. After 5 years, children in the program were found to be more helpful, cooperative, and concerned about other people than a comparison group who were not in the program (Battistich, Watson, Solomon, Schaps, & Solomon, 1991).

Culture also plays a role. Why are children in some cultures more prosocial than in others? It may be because they experience more love and less rejection. Among the Papago Indians of Arizona, parents are warm, supportive, and nurturant; by contrast, Alorese parents in Java are hostile and neglectful. This, among other differences, may account for the cooperative, peaceful personality typical of Papago children, as compared with the hostile, distrustful, and aggressive behavior of Alorese children (N. Eisenberg, 1992).

Aggression

instrumental aggression Aggressive behavior used as a means of achieving a goal.

A young child who roughly snatches a toy away from another child is usually interested only in getting the toy, not in hurting or dominating the other child. This is *instrumental aggression,* or aggression used as an instrument to reach a goal—the most common type of aggression in early childhood. Between ages 2½ and 5, children commonly struggle over toys and the control of space. Aggression surfaces mostly during social play; the children who fight the most also tend to be the most sociable and competent. In fact, the ability to show some instrumental aggression may be a necessary step in social development.

As children become better able to express themselves verbally, they typically shift from showing aggression with blows to doing it with words (E. Maccoby, 1980). However, individual differences tend to be fairly stable, especially among boys; those who more frequently hit or grab toys from other children at age 2 are likely to remain more aggressive at age 5 (E. M. Cummings, Iannotti, & Zahn-Waxler, 1989). After age 6 or 7, most children become less aggressive as they become more cooperative, less egocentric, and more empathic. They can now put themselves into someone else's place, can understand why the other person may be acting in a certain way, and can develop more positive ways of dealing with that person. They also can communicate better.

hostile aggression Aggressive behavior intended to hurt another person.

Not all aggression is instrumental. *Hostile aggression*—action intended to hurt another person—normally increases during early childhood and then declines. However, some children do not learn to control hostile aggression; they become more and more destructive. Such aggression may be a reaction to major problems in a child's life. It may also *cause* major problems by making other children and adults dislike a child.

The male hormone testosterone may underlie aggressive behavior and may explain why males are more likely to be aggressive than females. (Gender differences in aggression are further discussed in Chapter 13.) Temperament may play a part: children who are intensely emotional and low in self-control tend to express anger through aggressive behavior rather than in more constructive ways (N. Eisenberg, Fabes, Nyman, Bernzweig, & Pinuelas, 1994). Social-learning research points to other contributing factors: imitation of models (real or televised) combined with reinforcement of aggressive behavior, often compounded by frustration.

Triggers of Aggression: Inadequate Parenting   Aggression may start with ineffective parenting (G. R. Patterson, DeBaryshe, & Ramsey, 1989). Parents of children who later become antisocial often fail to reinforce good behavior and are harsh or inconsistent, or both, in punishing misbehavior. Harsh punishment, especially spanking, may backfire, because children see aggressive behavior in an adult with whom they identify. As one classic study suggested, parents who spank provide a "living example of the use of aggression at the very moment they are trying to teach the child not to be aggressive" (Sears et al., 1957, p. 266).

The frustration, pain, and humiliation that result from physical punishment and insults can be added spurs to violence. A frustrated child is more apt to imitate aggressive models than a contented one. In one classic study, the social-learning theorist Albert Bandura and his colleagues (Bandura, Ross, & Ross, 1961) divided seventy-two 3- to 6-year-olds into two experimental groups and one control group. One by one, each child in the first experimental group went into a playroom. An adult model (male for half of the children, female for the other half) quietly played in a corner with toys. The model for the second experimental group began to assemble Tinker Toys, but then spent the rest of the 10-minute session punching, throwing, and kicking a life-size inflated doll. The children in the control group saw no model.

After the sessions, all the children were mildly frustrated by seeing toys they were not allowed to play with. They then went into another playroom. The children who had seen the aggressive model acted much more aggressively than those in the other groups, imitating many of the same things they had seen the model say and do. Both boys and girls were more strongly influenced by an aggressive male model than an aggressive female. The children who had been with the quiet model were less aggressive than those who had not seen any model, suggesting that a positive adult model can moderate the effects of frustration.

Effects of inadequate parenting extend beyond the home. Often parents of aggressive children are not positively involved in their children's lives. The children tend to do poorly in school, to be rejected by peers, and to have poor self-esteem. They may seek out and model themselves after other troubled children who engage in antisocial behavior (G. R. Patterson et al., 1989).

Influence of Real and Televised Violence
    . . . there was these guys in this car. . . . And they was drivin' around lookin' for the
    bad guys. But they couldn't tell who was the bad guys cause there was a big fire.
    Lotsa fire. So they took this gun and they shot the windows and all the doors and the
    tires on this car. And this guy comes and they kill all the people who was standin'
    there. And then somebody comes and punches this guy who was takin' stuff from
    this place. (Farver & Frosch, 1996, p. 28)

This story was told and enacted by a 4-year-old child who lived in a low-income, inner-city Los Angeles neighborhood during the riots of April 1992 that followed the acquittal of four white police officers on charges of beating a black motorist, Rodney King. Preschoolers directly exposed to the riots were much more likely than preschoolers in other communities to act out violent scenes similar to those they had seen or heard about (Farver & Frosch, 1996). This is but one of a number of studies which found that exposure to real-life violence and stressful events influences children's thoughts, feelings, and behavior.

Children often imitate what they see on television, including acts of violence. They may also absorb the value that aggression is appropriate behavior.

Children who do not see aggressive models in real life often see them on television. Indeed, research suggests that children are influenced more by filmed models of violence than by live ones (Bandura, Ross, & Ross, 1963). Preschool children watch an average of 3 hours of television each day (Farver & Frosch, 1996). A Canadian study found that 28 to 40 percent of children ages 3 to 10 watch violent television programs (Bernard-Bonnin, Gilbert, Rousseau, Masson, & Maheux, 1991).

Research since the 1950s shows that children who see televised violence behave more aggressively themselves (NIMH, 1982). This is true across geographic locations and socioeconomic levels, for both boys and girls, and for normal children as well as for those with emotional problems. These correlations do not, of course, prove that viewing televised violence *causes* aggression, though the findings strongly suggest it. It is possible that children already prone to aggression may watch more violent television and may become more aggressive after seeing violence on-screen. In fact, research suggests that aggressive children do watch more television than nonaggressive children, identify more strongly with aggressive characters, and are more likely to believe that aggression seen on television reflects real life (Eron, 1982). Then, too, some third factor may be involved: perhaps children who watch and react aggressively to televised violence are spanked more than other children.

Still, evidence from a wide range of research, including experimental and longitudinal studies, supports a causal relationship between watching televised violence and acting aggressively (Geen, 1994; Huston et al., 1992). Furthermore, the influence of televised violence may endure for years. Among 427 young adults whose viewing habits had been studied at age 8, the best predictor of aggressiveness in 19-year-old men and women was the degree of violence in the shows they had watched as children (Eron, 1980, 1982).

How might watching violence on television make children more aggressive? Two hypotheses involve mechanisms of cognitive processing. One mechanism is the *behavioral script,* which converts televised images into guides for behavior (Huesmann, 1986). The other mechanism is *cognitive priming* (L. Berkowitz, 1984). Seeing televised violence may stimulate associations with aggressive ideas and emotions. These associations are retrieved when a child is frustrated, attacked, in pain, or under stress, and they *prime,* or prepare, the child to respond aggressively.

Another explanation is that when children see televised violence, they absorb the values depicted and come to view aggression and lawbreaking as acceptable behavior (NIMH, 1982). Children who see both heroes and villains on television getting what they want through violence may become less sensitive to the pain that results from real-life aggression. They may, for instance, fail to protect the victim of a bully. They are also more likely to break rules and less likely to cooperate to resolve differences.

In 1993 the American Psychological Association called for a major effort to reduce violence on television, including limits on violence shown between 6 A.M. and 10 P.M. and warning labels on videotapes containing violent material. In 1996, Congress enacted a law requiring all new television sets to be equipped with an electronic blocking device that parents can use to screen out objectionable programs. The law also prods the networks to devise a violence rating system (Mifflin, 1996).

Influence of Culture How much influence does culture have on aggressive behavior? One research team asked closely matched samples of 30 Japanese and 30 U.S. middle- to upper-middle-class preschoolers to choose pictured solutions to hypothetical conflicts or stressful situations (such as having one's block tower knocked down, having to stop playing and go to bed, being hit, hearing parents argue, or fighting on a jungle gym). The children also were asked to act out and complete such situations using dolls and props. The U.S. children showed more anger, more aggressive behavior and language, and less control of emotions than the Japanese children. The Japanese children also were less able to acknowledge negative feelings (Zahn-Waxler, Friedman, Cole, Mizuta, & Hiruma, 1996).

These results are consistent with child-rearing values in the two cultures. In Japanese culture, anger and aggression are seen as clashing with the emphasis on harmonious relationships. Japanese mothers are more likely than U.S. mothers to discipline by reasoning and inducing guilt, pointing out how aggressive behavior hurts others. Japanese mothers also strongly show their disappointment when children do not meet their behavioral standards. However, the cross-cultural difference in children's anger and aggressiveness was significant even apart from mothers' encouragement or discouragement of emotional expression, suggesting that innate temperamental differences may also be at work (Zahn-Waxler et al., 1996).

Fearfulness

Passing fears are common in early childhood. Many 2- to 4-year-olds are afraid of animals, especially dogs. By 6 years, children are more likely to be afraid of the dark. Other common fears are of thunderstorms and doctors (DuPont, 1983). Most of these disappear as children grow older and lose their sense of powerlessness.

Young children's fears stem from their intense fantasy life and their tendency to confuse appearance with reality. Sometimes their imaginations get carried away, making them worry about being attacked by a lion or being abandoned. Young children are more likely to be frightened by something that looks scary, such as a cartoon monster, than by something capable of doing great harm, such as a nuclear explosion (Cantor, 1994). For the most part, older children's fears tend to be more realistic (see Table 10-4).

Experience may underlie some early fears. A preschooler whose mother is sick in bed may become upset by a story about a mother's death, even if it is an animal mother. Often fears come from appraisals of danger, such as the likelihood of being bitten by a dog, or are triggered by events, as when a child who was hit by a car becomes afraid to cross the street. Children who have lived through an earthquake, a kidnapping, or some other frightening event may fear that it will happen again (Kolbert, 1994).

Table 10-4	Childhood Fears

Age	Fears
0–6 months	Loss of support, loud noises
7–12 months	Strangers; heights, sudden, unexpected, and looming objects
1 year	Separation from parent, toilet, injury, strangers
2 years	A multitude of stimuli, including loud noises (vacuum cleaners, sirens and alarms, trucks, and thunder), animals, dark rooms, separation from parent, large objects or machines, changes in personal environment, unfamiliar peers
3 years	Masks, dark, animals, separation from parent
4 years	Separation from parent, animals, dark, noises (including noises at night)
5 years	Animals, "bad" people, dark, separation from parent, bodily harm
6 years	Supernatural beings (e.g., ghosts, witches), bodily injury, thunder and lightning, dark, sleeping or staying alone, separation from parent
7–8 years	Supernatural beings, dark, media events (e.g., news reports on the threat of nuclear war or child kidnapping), staying alone, bodily injury
9–12 years	Tests and examinations in school, school performances, bodily injury, physical appearance, thunder and lightning, death, dark

Source: Adapted from Morris & Kralochwill, 1983.

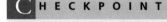

CHECKPOINT

Can you . . .

- Discuss how parental and other influences contribute to altruism, aggression, and fearfulness in young children?

Parents can help prevent children's fears by instilling a sense of trust and normal caution without being too protective and by overcoming their own unrealistic fears. They can help a child who is already fearful by reassurance and by encouraging open expression of feelings. Ridicule ("Don't be such a baby!"), coercion ("Pat the nice doggie—it won't hurt you"), and logical persuasion ("The closest bear is 20 miles away, locked in a zoo!") are not helpful. Not until elementary school can children tell themselves that what they fear is not real (Cantor, 1994).

Children can be helped to overcome fears by *systematic desensitization*, gradual exposure to a feared object or situation. In one study, first- through third-graders overcame their fear of snakes through increasingly close and frequent contact. After an average of two 15-minute sessions, 39 out of 45 children held snakes in their laps for 15 seconds, compared with only 5 of 22 children in a control group, who did not have the treatment (C. M. Murphy & Bootzin, 1973).

Relationships with Others

Although the most important people in young children's world are the adults who take care of them, relationships with siblings and playmates become more important in early childhood. Almost every characteristic activity and personality issue of this age, such as play, gender identity, and aggressive or prosocial behavior, involves other children.

Siblings—or Their Absence

Ties between brothers and sisters often set the stage for later relationships. Let's look at sibling relationships, and then at children who grow up with no siblings.

Brothers and Sisters

"It's mine!"

"No, it's mine!"

"Well, I was playing with it first!"

The earliest, most frequent, and most intense disputes among siblings are over property rights—who owns a toy or who is entitled to play with it—and some of these quarrels become so serious that parents or caregivers step in. Although exasperated adults may not always see it that way, sibling disputes and their settlement can be viewed as socialization opportunities, in which children learn to stand up for moral principles—even though those principles may not be precisely the same as the ones adults go by.

Among 40 pairs of 2- and 4-year-old siblings, property disputes arose, on average, about every 15 minutes during a 9-hour observation period. Even children as young as 2½ argued on the basis of clear principles: the owner's right to a toy should take precedence over who was currently using it, but when property was commonly owned (as was true in about half the disputes) the possessor should have exclusive rights. Parents, on the other hand, did not clearly favor claims based on either ownership or possession but were more inclined to stress sharing and avoidance of damage, or to suggest alternate playthings. Indeed, parents often seemed more interested in promoting a quick resolution than in defending children's rights (H. S. Ross, 1996). Fathers were more likely to emphasize justice and fairness, whereas mothers tended to stress care and concern for feelings and the need for siblings to get along (Lollis, Ross, & Leroux, 1996).

What happens when sibling disputes escalate into pushing, shoving, hitting, or other aggressive behavior? In judging the need for intervention and the appropriateness of a punishment, both parents and children (at least by age 4) pay attention to mitigating circumstances, such as intent ("I didn't mean to kick her"). Parents give more weight than children do to motivating factors, such as provocation ("He grabbed my doll!") and reciprocity ("She hit me first!"), while children are more likely to consider consent ("He told me to do it"), necessity ("If I hadn't pushed her out of the way, the blocks would have fallen on her"), and restitution ("I said I was sorry"). Thus experience with sibling conflict helps children recognize moral subtleties and think through their own beliefs about social and moral issues (J. L. Martin & Ross, 1996).

Despite the frequency of conflict, sibling rivalry is not the main pattern between brothers and sisters early in life. While some rivalry exists, so do affection, interest, companionship, and influence. Siblings (same-sex or mixed-sex) separated by as little as 1 year or as much as 4 years interact closely with each other in many ways. In observations spanning 3½ years, which began when younger siblings were about 1½ years old and the older ones ranged from 3 to 4½ (Abramovitch, Corter, & Lando, 1979; Abramovitch, Corter, Pepler, & Stanhope, 1986; Abramovitch, Pepler, & Corter, 1982), older siblings initiated more behavior, both friendly (sharing a toy, smiling, hugging, or starting a game) and unfriendly (hitting, fighting over a toy, teasing, or tattling). The younger children tended to imitate the older ones. As the younger children reached their fifth birthday, the siblings became less physical and more verbal, both in showing aggression (through commands, insults, threats, tattling, put-downs, bribes, and teasing) and in showing care and affection (by compliments and comforting rather than hugs and kisses).

The age difference between siblings had an effect: in closely spaced pairs, older siblings initiated more prosocial behavior. Same-sex siblings were a bit closer and played together more peaceably than boy-girl pairs. Siblings got along better when their mother was not with them. (Squabbling can be a bid for parental attention.) Overall, these researchers found prosocial and play-oriented behaviors to be more common than rivalry, hostility, and competition (Abramovitch et al., 1986).

The Only Child

People often think of only children as spoiled, selfish, lonely, or maladjusted, but research does not bear out this view. According to an analysis of 115 studies of children of various ages and backgrounds, "onlies" do comparatively well (Falbo & Polit, 1986; Polit & Falbo, 1987). In occupational and educational achievement

Box 10-3 A Nation of "Little Emperors"?

A group of Chinese kindergartners are learning how to fold paper to make toys. When the toys do not come out right, some of the children try again on their own or watch their classmates and copy what they do. Other children become bored and impatient and ask someone to do it for them, or else they give up, bursting into tears. In some research (Jiao, Ji, & Jing, 1986), the children in the second category tended to come from one-child families—a worrisome finding for the People's Republic of China, which in 1979 established an official policy of limiting families to one child each.

The Chinese government instituted this policy to control its exploding population. In addition to propaganda campaigns and incentives (housing, money, child care, health care, and preference in school placement) to induce voluntary compliance, there have been millions of involuntary abortions and sterilizations. People who have children without permission face fines and loss of their jobs. By 1985, at least 8 out of 10 young urban couples and half of those in rural areas had only one child (Yang, Ollendick, Dong, Xia, & Lin, 1995), and by 1997, the country's estimated population growth was holding steady at a little more than 1 percent—well within the planners' target. Today, the one-child policy is unevenly enforced; economic growth is exerting a natural check on family size and also making it easier for prosperous families who want a second child to pay the fine to local officials, who willingly bend the rules and pocket the money (Faison, 1997).

Still, in many Chinese cities, kindergartens and primary classrooms are almost completely filled with children who have no brothers or sisters. This situation marks a great change in Chinese society, in which newlyweds were traditionally congratulated with the wish, "May you have a hundred sons and a thousand grandsons." What kind of future population are the Chinese raising?

Some research has suggested that only children are more egocentric, less persistent, less cooperative, and less well liked than children with siblings. They were more likely to refuse to help another child or to help grudgingly, less likely to share their toys or to enjoy playing or working with other children, less modest, less helpful in group activities, and more irresponsible (Jiao et al., 1986).

However, later research contradicts previous findings that only children are spoiled, overindulged "little emperors." A sample of 4,000 third- and sixth-graders from urban and rural districts were assessed on academic achievement, physical growth, and personality. In academic achievement and physical growth, only children did about the same or better than those with siblings. They did especially well on verbal achievement; and in two of the four provinces studied, only children were taller or heavier than others. Personality differences, as rated by the children themselves and by parents, teachers, and peers, were few (Falbo & Poston, 1993).

Indeed, only children now seem to be at a distinct advantage in China. When questionnaires were administered to 731 urban children and adolescents, children with siblings reported higher levels of fear, anxiety, and depression than only children, regardless of sex or

Since 1979 the People's Republic of China has officially limited families to one child each. The implications of this policy for children growing up without siblings, cousins, or aunts and uncles are hotly debated by educators, researchers, and politicians.

age. Apparently children with siblings are less well adjusted in a society that favors and rewards the only child (Yang et al., 1995).

Only children seem to do better cognitively. A randomized study in Beijing schools (Jiao, Ji, & Jing, 1996) found that only children outperformed first-grade classmates with siblings in memory, language, and mathematics skills. This finding may reflect the greater attention, stimulation, hopes, and expectations that parents shower on a baby they know will be their first and last. Fifth grade only children, who were born before the one-child policy was strongly enforced—and whose parents may have originally planned on a larger family—did not show a pronounced cognitive edge.

(continued)

and intelligence, they surpass children with siblings, especially those with many siblings or older siblings. Only children also tend to be more mature and motivated to achieve and to have higher self-esteem. They do not differ, however, in overall adjustment or sociability. Perhaps these children do better because their parents spend more time and focus more attention on them, talk to them more, do more with them, and expect more of them. Research in China, which mandates one-child families, also produced encouraging findings about only children (see Box 10-3).

Playmates and Friends

Toddlers play alongside or near each other, but not until about age 3 do children begin to have friends—usually of the same sex. Yet, even in early childhood, the line between a playmate and a friend is not easy to draw. Let's look at how preschool boys and girls choose playmates and friends and at characteristics of popular children. We'll also look at benefits of friendship and at the bidirectional influences between family relationships and relationships with peers.

Sex Segregation in Play

By age 4, Anna much preferred to play with other girls than with boys. She constantly classified toys, games, and activities as "girls' " things or "boys' " things; when she was not sure how an item should be classified, she asked about it. Her friend Stephen also was more interested in playing with children of his own sex.

A tendency toward sex segregation in play seems to be universal across cultures. It is common among preschoolers as young as 3, who are more likely to welcome the overtures of playmates of the same sex. It becomes even more common in middle childhood, when boys often play in the streets and other public places, while girls meet in each other's homes or yards (E. E. Maccoby, 1988, 1990, 1994; Ramsey & Lasquade, 1996; J. Snyder, West, Stockemer, Gibbons, & Almquist-Parks, 1996).

Boys and girls typically play differently, and neither sex seems to like the other's style (Serbin, Moller, Gulko, Powlishta, & Colburne, 1994). Most boys like rough-and-tumble play (see Chapter 11) in fairly large groups, while girls are inclined to quieter play with one playmate (Benenson, 1993). The difference is not just based on liking different kinds of activities; even when boys and girls play with the same toys, they interact differently. At age 4, when playing in a large school-based group, boys pair off more frequently, but for a shorter time, than girls; and starting at age 6, boys engage in more coordinated group activity (Benenson, Apostoleris, & Parnass, 1997). Boys play more boisterously; girls tend to

CHECKPOINT

Can you . . .

- Explain how the resolution of sibling disputes contributes to socialization?

- Compare the cognitive and psychosocial development of only children with that of children with siblings?

set up rules, such as taking turns, to avoid clashes (E. Maccoby, 1980). It's not surprising, then, that preschool friends are usually of the same sex.

Choosing Playmates and Friends

Preschoolers are choosy about playmates. Not only do they usually like to play with children of their own sex, but they are quite selective about *which* children (of either sex) they play with. Given a choice of a number of playmates (for example, in a preschool classroom), they tend to spend most of their time with a few other children—usually those they have previously had positive experiences with. And children who have frequent positive experiences with each other are most likely to become friends (J. Snyder et al., 1996).

In one study, 4- to 7-year-olds rated the most important features of friendships as doing things together, liking and caring for each other, sharing and helping one another, and to a lesser degree, living nearby or going to the same school. Older children rated affection and support higher than did younger ones and rated physical traits, such as appearance and size, lower (Furman & Bierman, 1983). In another study, kindergartners liked having friends who played only with them. Friendships also were more satisfying—and more likely to last—when children saw them as relatively harmonious and as validating their self-worth. Being able to confide in friends and get help from them was less important at this age (Ladd, Kochenderfer, & Coleman, 1996).

The traits that make a child desirable or undesirable as a playmate are similar to the traits young children look for in friends. Children prefer prosocial preschoolers as playmates (C. H. Hart et al., 1992). They generally like to play with peers who smile and offer a greeting and a toy or a hand, and who fit in with what they are already doing or like to do. They tend to reject overtures from disruptive, demanding, intrusive, or aggressive children and ignore those who are shy, withdrawn, or tentative in their approach (Ramsey & Lasquade, 1996; J. Roopnarine & Honig, 1985).

Well-liked preschoolers and kindergartners, and those who are rated by parents and teachers as socially competent, generally cope well with anger. They respond in direct, active ways that minimize further conflict and keep relationships going. They avoid insults and threats. Unpopular children tend to hit back or tattle. Unpopular boys are more likely to express angry feelings or resist a child who provokes them, whereas girls are more apt to show disapproval of the other child (N. Eisenberg et al., 1994; Fabes & Eisenberg, 1992). Of course, children act differently with peers they like than with those they dislike. Although they get just as angry with someone they like—and, in the case of boys (who are more competitive than girls), do so more frequently—they are more likely to control their anger and express it constructively (Fabes, Eisenberg, Smith, & Murphy, 1996).

Not all children without playmates have poor social adjustment. In fact, among 567 kindergartners, almost 2 out of 3 socially withdrawn children were rated (through direct observation, teacher questionnaires, and interviews with classmates) as socially and cognitively competent; they simply preferred to play alone (Harrist, Zain, Bates, Dodge, & Pettit, 1997).

Benefits of Friendship

Through friendships, as well as interactions with more casual playmates, young children learn how to get along with others. They learn that being a friend is the way to have a friend. They learn how to solve problems in relationships, they learn how to put themselves in another person's place, and they see models of various kinds of behavior. They learn moral values and gender-role norms, and they practice adult roles. Children who have friends tend to talk more than other children and take turns directing and following (J. Roopnarine & Field, 1984). Of course, there are individual differences in interactions with friends, which may be affected

Young children learn the importance of being a friend in order to have a friend. Here, a sighted child helps a blind friend to enjoy the feel of the sand and the sound of the surf.

by cognitive development. Three-year-olds who can "read" how another person might feel about or interpret a situation are more likely to have back-and-forth conversations with friends and to coordinate their play (Slomkowski & Dunn, 1996).

Children with friends enjoy school more (Ladd & Hart, 1992). Among 125 kindergartners, those who had friends in their class when they entered in August liked school better two months later, and those who kept up these friendships continued to like school better the following May. Also, kindergartners who made new friends scored higher on achievement tests, whereas children rejected by classmates began to dislike school, were absent more, and did only half as well on academic tests (Ladd, 1990).

However, the quality of friendships makes a difference. Kindergartners whose friendships are conflict-filled, especially if they are boys, often have adjustment problems; they tend to be lonely and uninvolved and to dislike school. By contrast, children whose friendships are a source of self-validation and help are happier, have more positive attitudes toward school, and feel they can look to classmates for support. Children who are possessive about friendships tend to have academic difficulties; possibly they seek closer, more intense friendships to compensate for insecurity about schoolwork (Ladd et al., 1996).

CHECKPOINT

Can you . . .

• Explain how preschoolers choose playmates and friends, and how they benefit from friendships?

Family Relationships and Peer Relationships

Psychosocial development does not take place in compartments. Relationships at home have an impact on relationships outside the home, and the reverse may also be true.

Siblings and Friends

The quality of young children's relationships with their brothers and sisters often carries over to relationships with other children; a child who is aggressive with siblings is likely to be aggressive with friends as well. However, specific patterns established with siblings are not always repeated with friends. A child who is dominated by an older sibling can often step into a dominant role with a playmate. Usually children are more prosocial and playful with playmates than with siblings (Abramovitch et al., 1986).

Friendships can help prepare children for a younger sister or brother. In one longitudinal study of 30 firstborn 3- to 5-year-olds, which began during the last trimester of the mothers' second pregnancy, children who had a "best" friend, who played harmoniously with their friends, and who often participated in mutual pretend play had smoother relationships with the new baby 6 and 14 months after the birth. Learning to get along with a friend and manage conflicts may be a good "rehearsal" for getting along with a sibling, and intimate fantasy play lets children act out worries about the change in their lives. Of course, the same personality traits and social skills that make a child a good friend may also contribute to positive sibling relationships (Kramer & Gottman, 1992).

Parenting and Popularity

Parenting styles and practices influence peer relationships. Popular children generally have warm, positive relationships with both mother and father, who teach by reasoning more than by punishment (Isley, O'Neil, & Parke, 1996; Kochanska, 1992; J. Roopnarine & Honig, 1985). The parents are likely to be authoritative, and the children to be both assertive and cooperative. Parents of rejected or isolated children tend to have a different profile. The mothers do not have confidence in their parenting, rarely praise their children, and do not encourage independence. The fathers pay little attention to their children, dislike being disturbed by them, and consider child rearing women's work (Peery, Jensen, & Adams, 1984, in J. Roopnarine & Honig, 1985). Negative interaction between mother and daughter or father and son can be especially harmful, since they serve as models for interactions with peers (Isley et al., 1996).

Children whose parents rely on power-assertive discipline tend to use coercive tactics in peer relations, whereas children whose parents engage in give-and-take reasoning are more likely to resolve conflicts with peers that way (Crockenberg & Lourie, 1996). Children whose parents clearly communicate disapproval rather than anger, as well as strong positive feelings, are more prosocial, less aggressive, and better-liked (Boyum & Parke, 1995). Children who become involved in reciprocal exchanges of negative feelings (pouting, whining, anger, teasing, mocking, or boredom) during physical play with their fathers tend to share less than other children, to be more verbally and physically aggressive, and to avoid social contact (Carson & Parke, 1996).

The parents' own relationship may be a factor. Children whose parents do not get along sometimes respond to the resulting stress by trying to avoid conflict with other children. Consequently, they do not participate fully in play activities and do not learn how to get along with others (Gottman & Katz, 1989).

Helping Children with Peer Relations

Adults can help young children's relationships with peers by getting them together with other children, monitoring their play, and suggesting strategies to use in approaching other children.

Children whose parents arrange play dates for them have more playmates, see them more often, and initiate more get-togethers themselves (Ladd & Colter, 1988; Ladd & Hart, 1992). In arranging and supervising play dates, parents promote prosocial behavior as well as sociability by prompting children to think about the needs and wishes of their guests. Since children who behave prosocially tend to be more popular, such guidance can have long-lasting consequences (Ladd & Hart, 1992). Other helpful adult strategies include (1) making a special effort to find a play group for young children who do not often have the opportunity to be with other youngsters; (2) encouraging "loners" to play with another lone child or a small group of two or three children, or just to play side by side with other children at first; (3) praising signs of empathy and responsiveness; and (4) teaching friendship skills indirectly through puppetry, role-playing, and books about animals and children who learn to make friends (Ramsey & Lasquade, 1996; J. Roopnarine & Honig, 1985).

Parents who monitor preschoolers' play indirectly by staying nearby tend to have socially competent children. Children whose parents get right into the play activity are not so well adjusted in the classroom, but it is not clear which comes first. Parents' early monitoring styles may influence the way their children play with others; or parents of children who are aggressive or do not play well on their own may feel the need to maintain more of a presence (Ladd & Colter, 1988).

Coaching about how to handle problems with peers can be beneficial (Mize & Pettit, 1997). An Australian study found a close link between the social skills of kindergartners and of their mothers (Russell & Finnie, 1990). Mothers were asked to help their preschool children join the play of two other children whom the target child did not know. The mothers of popular children were most likely to offer effective, group-oriented suggestions that drew their own child's attention to what the other two were doing. They made positive comments about the playing children and gave ideas about joining the pair. The mothers of children who were either disliked or generally ignored by their classmates showed a lack of sensitivity toward the needs of the pair who were playing. They either disrupted the play by taking charge to make the other children let their own child play, or they gave little or no effective help to their child.

Since preschoolers respond to peers on the basis of past experience, it is important to help children learn effective strategies before they become tagged as outsiders (Ramsey & Lasquade, 1996). If that has already happened, a change in the child's behavior may not help unless something is done to change the other children's perceptions of that child—or to find a new group of children for the child to associate with (J. Snyder et al., 1996).

Children's play groups are powerful instruments of socialization, in which children learn social skills and approaches they will use throughout life. Changes in relationships with playmates and in kinds of play represent another advance in development as children enter middle childhood, the years we examine in Chapters 11, 12, and 13.

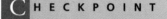

CHECKPOINT

Can you . . .

• Give examples of how parents influence relationships with peers?

SUMMARY

The Developing Self

- The **self-concept** is one's total picture of one's abilities and traits; it develops gradually throughout life.

- According to neo-Piagetians, **self-definition** in early childhood shifts from **single representations** to **representational mappings.** Young children cannot acknowledge the difference between the **real self** and the **ideal self.**

- Development of emotions directed toward the self depends upon socialization and cognitive development. Children gradually develop an understanding of simultaneous emotions. Individual differences in emotional understanding begin no later than age 3.

- According to Erikson, the chief developmental crisis of early childhood is **initiative versus guilt.** Successful resolution of this conflict results in the "virtue" of purpose.

- An important source of **self-esteem** in early childhood is social support from parents, teachers, and peers.

Gender

- **Gender identity,** the awareness of one's **gender** and its meaning, is an important aspect of the developing self-concept.

- **Sex differences** are physical differences between males and females; **gender differences** are psychological or behavioral differences. There are few gender differences in early childhood, and these differences are generally quite small.

- All societies hold beliefs about appropriate behaviors and attitudes for the two sexes. Children learn these **gender roles** at an early age through **gender-typing. Gender stereotypes** can restrict the development of both sexes.

- In Freudian theory, a child develops gender identity through **identification** with the same-sex parent after giving up the wish to possess the other parent.

- According to social-learning theory, gender identity develops through observing and imitating models and through reinforcement of gender-appropriate behavior.
- Cognitive-developmental theory maintains that gender identity develops from thinking about experience. According to Kohlberg, **gender constancy,** or **gender conservation,** precedes acquisition of gender roles.
- **Gender-schema theory** holds that children fit their self-concept to the **gender schema** for their culture, a socially organized pattern of behavior for males and females.
- According to the **schema confirmation-deployment model,** the gender schema serves as a script for assimilating and applying information about gender roles.
- A child raised with a nonstereotyped gender schema may develop an **androgynous** personality.
- Research suggests that both biological and environmental factors, such as the influence of parents and the media, affect gender-typing.

Play

- Changes in the type of play children engage in reflect social and cognitive development. **Social play** tends to increase during early childhood.
- Forms of **cognitive play** progress from simple repetitive play involving the muscles to constructive play, **pretend play,** and then formal games with rules.
- Pretend play becomes increasingly common during early childhood and helps children develop social and cognitive skills.
- Forms of play vary across cultures and are influenced by the environments adults create for children.

Parenting Styles and Practices

- **Discipline** is a powerful tool for socialization.
- Punishment is most effective when it is immediate, consistent, accompanied by an explanation, and carried out by someone who has a good relationship with the child. Harsh physical punishment can have damaging effects.
- Discipline based on induction is generally the most effective; temporary withdrawal of love is generally less effective, and power assertion the least effective, depending on the situation.
- Baumrind identified three child-rearing styles: **authoritarian, permissive,** and **authoritative.** According to much research, authoritative parents tend to raise more competent children. These categories and results may be misleading when applied to some cultures or socioeconomic groups.
- Internalization of parental teachings may depend on how accurately the child perceives the message and whether the child accepts it as appropriate.
- Parents' love may be the most important influence on the social maturity their children will exhibit as adults.
- Miller's theory of "poisonous pedagogy" suggests that certain parental behaviors can damage a child's future psychological health and may be transmitted to future generations.
- Whether children exhibit **altruism,** or **prosocial behavior,** is influenced by the child's own characteristics, as well as by the example of parents and teachers and by other cultural influences.
- **Instrumental aggression** is the most common type of aggression in early childhood and may be a necessary step in social development. Most children become less aggressive after age 6 or 7. **Hostile aggression,** too, generally declines, but some children do not learn to control it. Aggression may be triggered by inadequate parenting, media exposure, and cultural influences.
- Preschool children show many temporary fears of real and imaginary objects and events. Such fears can sometimes be overcome by systematic desensitization.

Relationships with Others

- Most sibling interactions are positive. Older siblings tend to initiate activities, and younger ones to imitate. Siblings tend to resolve disputes on the basis of moral principles, though not necessarily the same ones parents use.

- Only children seem to develop at least as well as children with siblings.
- Gender differences in play emerge early; children in all cultures increasingly segregate themselves by sex.
- Aggressive children tend to be less popular than prosocial children.
- The kind of relationship children have with siblings often carries over into other peer relationships, and vice versa.
- Parenting styles and direct parental coaching or monitoring of children's play can affect children's social competence with peers.

KEY TERMS

self-concept (352)
self-definition (352)
single representations (353)
real self (353)
ideal self (353)
representational mappings (353)
initiative versus guilt (355)
self-esteem (356)
gender (357)
gender identity (357)
sex differences (357)
gender differences (357)
gender roles (358)
gender-typing (358)
gender stereotypes (358)
identification (359)

gender constancy, or gender
  conservation (360)
gender-schema theory (361)
gender schema (361)
schema confirmation-deployment
  model (361)
androgynous (361)
social play (365)
cognitive play (365)
pretend play (366)
discipline (368)
authoritarian (370)
permissive (370)
authoritative (370)
altruism, or prosocial behavior (374)
instrumental aggression (376)
hostile aggression (376)

QUESTIONS FOR THOUGHT AND DISCUSSION

1. Looking back, can you think of ways in which your parents or other adults helped you develop self-esteem?

2. "Males are innately more aggressive, and females more nurturing. Although these traits can be altered to some degree, the basic tendencies will remain." Does research support these statements? Whether true or not, what implications do these widely held beliefs have for personality development?

3. Where would you place your own views on the continuum between the following extremes? Explain.
   - Family A thinks girls should wear only ruffly dresses and boys should never wash dishes or cry.
   - Family Z treats sons and daughters exactly alike, without making any references to the children's sex.

4. As a parent, what forms of discipline would you favor in what situations? Give specific examples, and tell why.

5. To what extent would you like your children to adopt your values and behavioral standards?

6. In a society in which "Good Samaritans" are sometimes reviled for "butting into other people's business" and sometimes attacked by the very persons they try to help, is it wise to encourage children to offer help to strangers?

7. Are there situations in which a child should be encouraged to be aggressive?

8. Since young children often find actual news broadcasts scarier than fictional shows, should parents try to prevent their viewing them? Or should parents try to reassure children that the frightening events depicted will not happen to them?

9. One way in which small children confront fears is to play at such potentially frightening activities as dressing up on Halloween, going on scary rides at amusement parks, and listening to ghost stories. Do you approve or disapprove of such play? Why?

Middle Childhood: *A Bird's-Eye View*

Chapter 11
Physical Development and Health in Middle Childhood

Growth slows.

Strength and athletic skills improve.

Respiratory illnesses are common, but health is generally better than at any other time in the life span.

Chapter 12
Cognitive Development in Middle Childhood

Egocentrism diminishes. Children begin to think logically but concretely.

Memory and language skills increase.

Cognitive gains permit children to benefit from formal schooling.

Some children show special educational needs and strengths.

Chapter 13
Psychosocial Development in Middle Childhood

Self-concept becomes more complex, affecting self-esteem.

Coregulation reflects gradual shift in control from parents to child.

Peers assume central importance.

Middle Childhood

The middle years of childhood, from about age 6 to about age 11, are often called the *school years* because school is the central experience during this time—a focal point for physical, cognitive, and psychosocial development. Children develop more competence in all realms. As we see in Chapter 11, they grow taller, heavier, and stronger and acquire the motor skills needed to participate in organized games and sports. Chapter 12 covers major advances in logical and creative thinking, moral judgments, memory, and literacy. Individual differences become more evident and special needs more important, as competencies affect success in school.

Competencies also affect self-esteem and popularity, as we see in Chapter 13. Although parents still have an important impact on personality, as well as on all other aspects of development, the peer group is more influential than before. Children develop physically, cognitively, and emotionally, as well as socially, through contacts with other youngsters.

Physical Development and Health in Middle Childhood

The healthy human child will keep
Away from home, except to sleep.
Were it not for the common cold,
Our young we never would behold.

Ogden Nash, *You Can't Get There from Here*

Focus

Theodore Roosevelt

Theodore Roosevelt, the twenty-sixth president of the United States, was a vigorous man who enjoyed the outdoor life. As a young boy, he showed an intense interest in nature and wanted to be a zoologist. He also loved adventure stories. As an adult, he had a number of adventures of his own. Before becoming president, he lived for two years on a ranch in North Dakota and organized and led a volunteer cavalry regiment, Roosevelt's Rough Riders. After leaving the White House, he conducted a big-game hunting expedition in East Africa, which captured 296 big-game animals, and an exploratory expedition to South America, which resulted in the discovery of a tributary of the Madeira River. He wrote several books on these experiences, one of which was called *The Strenuous Life* (1900).

Yet, as a child in Manhattan, "Teedie," as he was then called, was weak and sickly, subject to asthma. He and his two sisters and brother spent summers in the country, swimming, rowing, hiking, picking apples, hunting frogs, and riding a Shetland pony. Still, despite all this healthful exercise, he "continued to have his gasping nights, his days of exhausted reaction, his pipestem legs, his pale face, and his digestive upsets" (Putnam, 1958, p. 33). Too ill to go to school most of the time, he was tutored at home.

When Teedie was 10 or 11, his father—a big, powerful man, who came from sturdy Dutch stock—told him he must build up his physical condition. "You have the mind but not the body," the elder Roosevelt told him, "and without the help of the body the mind cannot go as far as it should" (Pringle, 1931, p. 17).

A large second-floor room in the family's brownstone house at 28 East Twentieth Street near Union Square was converted into a gymnasium. There the boy dutifully worked out with punching bag and dumbbells and on the horizontal bars. Later an asthma attack caused his family to send him to Moosehead Lake. On the way there, a couple of boys on the stagecoach teased him unmercifully, and he found himself too weak to fight them off. Humiliated, he resolved to improve his health and strength and immediately began boxing lessons. As he grew in stature and breadth of chest, he gained in self-confidence.

Focus—*Continued*

Asthma had not been his only problem. At 13, when he began learning to shoot, he discovered that he was nearsighted. At first he noticed his companions aiming at targets he could not see. One day they read aloud to him a distant billlboard advertisement. Although it was printed in huge letters, he could not make them out. Now he understood why, throughout his childhood, he had been at a disadvantage in studying nature: "the only things I could study were those I ran against or stumbled over" (Roosevelt, 1929, p. 17).

Putting on his first pair of glasses changed Roosevelt's outlook on life and "opened an entirely new world" to him. "I had been a clumsy and awkward little boy," he wrote in his autobiography, "and . . . a good deal of it was due to the fact that I could not see and yet was wholly ignorant that I was not seeing." The memory of his undiagnosed childhood handicap gave him "a keen sympathy" with efforts to "remove the physical causes of deficiency in children, who are often unjustly blamed for being obstinate or unambitious, or mentally stupid" (Roosevelt, 1929, p. 18).

Sources of biographical information about Theodore Roosevelt are Pringle (1931), Putnam (1958), and Roosevelt (1929).

•   •   •

As Theodore Roosevelt's father recognized, a sound body is a key to positive development. And, as Roosevelt himself discovered, physical competence has cognitive and psychosocial ramifications as well.

Although motor abilities improve less dramatically in middle childhood than before, these years are an important time for the development of the strength, stamina, endurance, and motor proficiency needed for active sports. Despite frequent colds and sore throats, this is a healthy time for most children; but many, like Theodore Roosevelt, are not as healthy or as physically fit as they should be, and some have eating problems, such as malnutrition and obesity. Debilitating diseases are rare, but among children living in poverty, without access to preventive and curative medical care, ill health is common.

In this chapter we look at these physical developments, beginning with normal growth, which depends on proper nutrition and good health. As we explore health concerns, we examine children's understanding of health and illness, which links physical, cognitive, and emotional issues. As children do more, their risk of accidents increases; we examine some ways to lower the risk.

After reading this chapter, you should be able to answer and elaborate on such questions as these:

Preview Questions

- What factors influence height and weight in middle childhood?
- What are the causes and implications of malnutrition, obesity, and dissatisfaction with body image?
- What gains in motor skills typically occur at this age?
- What kinds of play do school-age boys and girls engage in?
- What are the principal health and fitness problems and concerns in middle childhood?
- What can adults do to make the school years healthier and safer for children?

Table 11-1   Physical Growth, Age 6 to Age 11 (50th percentile)*

	Height, Inches				Weight, Pounds			
Age	White Males	Nonwhite Males	White Females	Nonwhite Females	White Males	Nonwhite Males	White Females	Nonwhite Females
6	46	47	46	47	48	49	47	46
7	49	49	49	49	53	55	52	51
8	51	52	50	51	61	61	57	58
9	53	53	53	53	66	66	63	65
10	55	55	57	57	73	72	70	78
11	57	58	58	59	81	80	87	90

*Fifty percent of children in each category are above this height or weight level, and 50 percent are below it.
Source: Adapted from Rauh, Schumsky, & Witt, 1967, pp. 515–530.

Growth

If we were to walk by a typical elementary school just after the three o'clock bell, we would see a virtual explosion of children of all shapes and sizes. Tall ones, short ones, husky ones, and skinny ones would be bursting out of the school doors into the open air. We would see that school-age children look very different from children a few years younger. They are taller, and most are fairly wiry; but more are likely to be overweight than in past decades, and some may be malnourished.

Height and Weight

Compared with its rapid pace in early childhood, growth in height and weight during middle childhood slows considerably. Still, although day-by-day changes may not be obvious, they add up to a startling difference between 6-year-olds, who are still small children, and 11-year-olds, many of whom are now beginning to resemble adults.

School-age children grow about 1 to 3 inches each year and gain about 5 to 8 pounds or more, doubling their average body weight (see Table 11-1). African American boys and girls tend to be a bit taller and heavier than white children of the same age and sex. Late in this stage, girls begin a growth spurt, gaining about 10 pounds a year. Suddenly they are taller and heavier than the boys in their class, and they remain so until about age 12 or 13, when the boys begin their spurt and overtake the girls (see Chapter 14). Girls retain somewhat more fatty tissue than boys, a characteristic that will persist through adulthood.

Variations in Growth

Of course, the figures given above are just averages. Individual children vary widely—so widely that "if a child who was of exactly average height at his seventh birthday grew not at all for two years, he would still be just within the normal limits of height attained at age nine" (Tanner, 1973, p. 35).

Children in different parts of the world grow at different rates. An international study of 8-year-old children (Meredith, 1969) yielded a range of about 9 inches between the average height of the shortest children (mostly from southeast Asia, Oceania, and South America) and the tallest ones (mostly from northern and central Europe, eastern Australia, and the United States). Although genetic differences account for some of this diversity, environmental influences such as nutrition and the prevalence of infectious disease are important too.

In the United States, as we have already seen, African American boys and girls tend to grow faster than white children. Furthermore, by about age 6,

African American girls have more muscle and bone mass than white or Hispanic girls, while Hispanic girls have a higher percentage of body fat than white girls the same size (K. J. Ellis, Abrams, & Wong, 1997).

Implicit in these variations in growth is a warning. When judging health or screening for abnormalities, observers often rely on measures of a child's physical growth and development. In the face of evidence that children from diverse ethnic groups develop differently, it would be useful to establish separate growth standards for different populations, as is already done for boys and girls.

Abnormal Growth

Of the many types of growth disorders, one arises from the body's failure to produce enough growth hormone. Human growth hormone is effective in improving short-term growth in height, and a synthetic form of this hormone is now available. Children whose own bodies fail to produce enough natural growth hormone may be given the synthetic hormone. In one study, after 4 years of treatment with synthetic growth hormone beginning at an average age of 6.3 years, such children showed increases in height with no side effects. However, how effective this therapy is in the long run will not be known until the children reach final adult height (Albanese & Stanhope, 1993).

This synthetic hormone is also being used for children who are much shorter than other children their age, but whose bodies *are* producing normal quantities of growth hormone. The synthetic hormone has risks. We have no clear idea what the long-term effects on health may be for a person whose height has been artificially "stretched" beyond what it otherwise would have been. Furthermore, the treatment is costly and lengthy, and there is as yet no evidence that the drug makes children who are normally short any taller as adults. It may also do psychological harm by creating unfulfilled expectations or by giving short children the feeling that something is wrong with them. Since many of the disadvantages associated with being short are due not to short stature itself but to feelings about it, genetically short people may gain more from counseling than from long-term hormone therapy. The American Academy of Pediatrics (AAP) Committee on Drugs and Committee on Bioethics (1997) therefore recommend caution in prescribing synthetic growth hormone.

Being short in itself does not necessarily lead to psychosocial problems. That conclusion emerged from a study of 180 boys and 78 girls, ages 4 to 18, who were referred for evaluation at a pediatric hospital because they were at or below the fifth percentile in height for their age and sex (Sandberg, Brook, & Campos, 1994). According to questionnaires completed by the children and their parents, the short girls were almost indistinguishable in social adjustment from a comparison group of normal height; and, while the boys were less well-adjusted than the normal sample, their problems did not reach clinical significance. However, some children, such as those with younger, taller siblings, seemed more likely to have social problems. Rather than across-the-board hormone therapy for short children, this study suggests the need for a closer look at such factors as the underlying medical condition and the family constellation, which may contribute to the way individuals deal with being unusually short.

Nutrition and Dentition

Parents of school-age children often have a hard time keeping the refrigerator stocked. Most 6- to 12-year-olds have good appetites and eat far more than younger children. They need the extra calories they are consuming: in these years, as we have seen, average body weight doubles, and physical play demands great expenditures of energy. Unfortunately, eating problems also become more prevalent during these years. And, with the arrival of the permanent teeth, proper dental care becomes more critical.

CHECKPOINT

Can you . . .

• Summarize typical growth patterns of boys and girls in middle childhood and give reasons for geographic or ethnic variations?

• Assess the advisability of administering synthetic growth hormone to unusually short children?

A good breakfast starts the day right. Children's play demands energy, and their body weight will double in these middle-childhood years. To support constant exertion and steady growth, children need high levels of complex carbohydrates, available in potatoes and grains, and a minimum of simple carbohydrates (sweets).

Nutritional Requirements

To support the steady growth and constant exertion of the middle years, children need, on average, 2,400 calories every day—more for older children and less for younger ones. Breakfast should supply about one-fourth of total calories; a healthy, balanced breakfast makes children more alert and productive in school. Daily food intake should include high levels of complex carbohydrates, found in such foods as potatoes, pasta, bread, and cereals. Simple carbohydrates, found in sweets, should be kept to a minimum. Although protein is necessary to build and repair muscles, most people in the United States eat more protein than they need. The government-recommended daily allowance (RDA) for 7- to 10-year-olds is 28 grams, but the average intake for both boys and girls is 71 grams (Bittman, 1993).

It used to be thought that sugar makes children hyperactive, interferes with learning, or has other negative effects on behavior or mood. However, although sweets are less desirable than nutritious foods in anyone's diet because they generally provide nonnutritive or "empty" calories, recent research suggests that neither sugar nor the artificial sweetener aspartame significantly affects most children's behavior, cognitive functioning, or mood (Kinsbourne, 1994; B. A. Shaywitz et al., 1994; Wolraich et al., 1994; Wolraich, Wilson, & White, 1995). Sugar's "bad press" may have resulted from its consumption in large amounts at such occasions as birthday parties, where disruptive behavior probably arises from the excitement of the situation, not the sweets.

Malnutrition

More than half of the young children in south Asia, 30 percent of those in sub-Saharan Africa, and 10 percent in the western hemisphere are believed to suffer from malnutrition. All told, an estimated 174 million children under 5 years old in developing countries are underweight due to malnourishment, and 230 million have stunted growth. Children who do not eat well have less resistance to illness; 54 percent of the 12.2 million deaths of children under 5 in developing countries each year are associated with malnutrition (World Health Organization [WHO], 1996).

Because undernourished children usually live in poverty and suffer other kinds of environmental deprivation, the specific effects of malnutrition may be hard to isolate. However, taken together, these deprivations may affect not only physical well-being but cognitive abilities and psychosocial development as well (Ricciuti, 1993; WHO, 1996).

African children in Kenya with mild-to-moderate undernutrition scored lower than well-nourished children on verbal abilities and on selecting a pattern to fit in with a set of other patterns (M. Sigman, Neumann, Jansen, & Bwibo, 1989). Another Kenyan study found better-nourished children happier, more active, and more likely to be leaders, while poorly nourished children were more anxious (Espinosa, Sigman, Neumann, Bwibo, & McDonald, 1992). When Kenya experienced a severe drought-induced famine, malnourished schoolchildren showed significant declines in rate of weight gain, activity on the playground, and attention in the classroom (M. A. McDonald, Sigman, Espinosa, & Neumann, 1994). In Massachusetts, when low-income third- to sixth-graders took part in a school breakfast program, their scores on achievement tests rose (A. F. Meyers, Sampson, Weitzman, Rogers, & Kayne, 1989).

Since malnutrition affects all aspects of development, its treatment may need to go beyond physical care. One longitudinal study (S. Grantham-McGregor, Powell, Walker, Chang, & Fletcher, 1994) followed two groups of Jamaican children with low developmental levels who were hospitalized for severe malnourishment in infancy or toddlerhood. The children came from extremely poor and often unstable homes. One group received only standard medical care, and their developmental levels remained low. Health care paraprofessionals played with a second, experimental group in the hospital and, after discharge, visited them at home every week for 3 years, showing the mothers how to use homemade toys and encouraging them to interact with their children.

Three years after the program stopped, the experimental group's IQs were well above those of the group who had not received the intervention (though not as high as those of a third, well-nourished group); and their IQs remained significantly higher 7, 8, 9, and 14 years after leaving the hospital. Apparently the continuity of the program was important; not only did it last 3 years, but the mothers in the experimental group enrolled their children in preschools at an earlier age than children in the malnourished group that did not receive the intervention. In other research on severely malnourished children (S. M. Grantham-McGregor, 1984), stimulation that stopped after the children went home from the hospital produced only passing improvement.

Formal schooling can make a difference. One longitudinal study followed approximately 1,400 Guatemalan children in impoverished rural villages, many of whom had stunted growth due to malnutrition and who lived in unsanitary, infection-causing conditions. Although schooling did not fully compensate for early biological and environmental risk factors, with regard to cognitive development it did seem to act as a partial buffer against their ill effects. Again, the length of schooling was significant: those who completed at least 4 years of school did better on tests of cognition during adolescence than those who dropped out earlier (Gorman & Pollitt, 1996).

Tooth Development and Dental Care

Most of the adult teeth arrive early in middle childhood. The primary teeth begin to fall out at about age 6 and are replaced by permanent teeth at a rate of about four teeth per year for the next 5 years. The first molars erupt at about age 6; the second molars at about age 13; and the third molars—the wisdom teeth—in the early twenties (Behrman, 1992).

Given the importance of sound teeth for nutrition, general health, and appearance, a major health concern in the United States until recently was the high rate of dental problems among children. Now, however, the picture is brighter, thanks to better nutrition, better dental care, and widespread use of fluoride in toothpaste, mouthwash, and water used for drinking and food preparation.

More than half (55 percent) of U.S. children ages 5 to 17 have cavity-free permanent teeth, compared with only about one-fourth (26 percent) of 6- to 17-year-olds in 1971–1974. Most of the decay in children's teeth is on the rough,

These girls proudly show off a childhood milestone—the normal loss of baby teeth, which will be replaced by permanent ones. American children today have fewer dental cavities than American children had in the early 1970s, probably owing to better nutrition, widespread use of fluoride, and better dental care.

CHECKPOINT

Can you . . .

- Summarize nutritional requirements of school-age children?

- Describe effects of malnutrition and identify factors that may influence the long-term outcome?

- Tell why dental care becomes more important in middle childhood and why dental health has improved in recent years?

chewing surfaces; much of this can be prevented with the use of adhesive sealants, plastic films that harden after being painted onto teeth. Much of the improvement in children's dental health is attributed to use of the sealants, which more than doubled between 1986–1987 and 1988–1991. Still, fewer than 1 in 5 school-age children have sealants on their permanent teeth (L. J. Brown, Kaste, Selwitz, & Furman, 1996).

Some children resist dental care because they are afraid of the dentist. Young children are usually cooperative at the dentist's office, especially after repeated visits, but in middle childhood some youngsters become more fearful. Perhaps modeling themselves after parents who are nervous about going to the dentist, children grow anxious themselves. Fears can be reduced if a child sees another person fearlessly doing something the child is afraid of and also if the child is repeatedly and gradually exposed to the fear-producing stimulus. If parents go to the dentist without showing anxiety, and if they take their children along on their own visits, the children will probably not become fearful (Winer, 1982).

Obesity and Other Eating Disorders

Obesity (extreme overweight) in children has become a major health issue in the United States. The proportion of U.S. children ages 6 to 17 who are obese more than doubled between 1981 and 1991—from 5 percent to nearly 11 percent (Centers for Disease Control and Prevention [CDC], 1994b). A child whose weight, in comparison with height, was in the 95th percentile (that is, higher than that of 95 percent of children of the same age and sex) was considered obese.

The problem seems to be escalating. In a series of cross-sectional studies of schoolchildren and young adults in Bogalusa, Louisiana, the prevalence of obesity, regardless of race or sex, approximately doubled between 1973 and 1994, and the increases were 50 percent greater from 1983 on than in the earlier part of the study. Furthermore, standards have become more lenient, obscuring the full extent of the problem. About one-third of 5- to 14-year-olds in 1992 to 1994 would have been considered obese by the standard used in 1973, which was based on the 85th percentile rather than the 95th (D. S. Freedman, Srinivasan, Valdez, Williamson, & Berenson, 1997).

Children, like adults, become overweight when they take in more calories than they expend, especially if they have an inherited tendency toward obesity. Physical activity, such as this tug-of-war, can help burn up calories.

What Causes Obesity?

What accounts for the increase in obesity? Research findings are most often correlational, and so we cannot draw conclusions about cause and effect. However, there is strong evidence that overweight often results from an inherited tendency, aggravated by too little exercise and too much food.

People become overweight when they consume more calories than they expend. But when two people eat the same amount of calories, why does only one get fat? What makes some people eat more than they need?

Several lines of research point to *genetic and hormonal factors.* As we reported in Chapter 2, twin and adoption studies show a strong genetic influence—as high as 80 percent (Leibel, 1997; A. Stunkard, Harris, Pedersen, & McClearn, 1990; A. J. Stunkard, Foch, & Hrubec, 1986), and researchers have now identified at least two genes that affect obesity (R. S. Jackson et al., 1997; Montague et al., 1997). One of these genes governs production of a protein called *leptin,* which seems to help regulate body fat. A defect in this gene, originally found in mice, can disrupt appetite control; giving obese mice large doses of leptin restores normal body size (Campfield, Smith, Guisez, Devos, & Burn, 1995; Halaas et al., 1995, Pelleymounter et al., 1995; Zhang et al., 1994). A mutation in the human gene for leptin was found in two young cousins whose leptin level was very low and who had been extremely obese from an early age. Other researchers have found a natural hormone that stimulates the production of fat cells (Forman et al., 1995; Kliewer et al., 1995). Such research may lead to identification and treatment of children predisposed to obesity.

Environment is also influential, since children tend to eat the same kinds of foods and develop the same kinds of habits as the people around them. Obesity is more common among lower socioeconomic groups, especially among women (Kolata, 1986). As we reported in Chapter 8, children of all ages eat too much fat and sugar and too few healthful foods, but diets of poor and minority children are especially unbalanced (Muñoz, Krebs-Smith, Ballard-Barbash, & Cleveland, 1997).

There is a negative correlation between *activity level* and weight. But are heavier children less active because they are fat, or do they become fat because they are less active? Professional opinion tends toward the second explanation. Since people claim to be eating no more than in the past, reduced activity may be a major factor in the sharp rise in obesity (D. S. Freedman et al., 1997).

Evidently, *television* is also a factor (Andersen, Crespo, Bartlett, Cheskin, & Pratt, 1998). Children who watch a lot of television tend to have lower metabolic rates than more active children, putting them at risk of obesity (Klesges, Shelton, & Klesges, 1993). Children who watch television a great deal also tend to eat more snacks (especially the high-calorie ones seen in commercials) and to be less active than other children. According to two major studies involving several thousand school-age children and adolescents, every hour per day spent watching television results in a 2 percent increase in the prevalence of obesity (Dietz & Gortmaker, 1985).

Treating Childhood Obesity

There are several compelling reasons for treating childhood obesity. First, obese children often suffer emotionally because of taunts from their peers. Indeed, they often compensate for their lack of popularity by indulging themselves with treats, making their physical and social problems even worse. An equally important reason for treating overweight children is that, without such treatment, they tend to become overweight adults. Both their self-esteem and their health are likely to suffer: they probably will be considered unattractive and will be at risk of high blood pressure, heart disease, orthopedic problems, and diabetes. Indeed, childhood overweight may be a better predictor of some diseases than adult overweight (Must, Jacques, Dallal, Bajema, & Dietz, 1992).

The basic treatment for obesity includes a restricted diet, more exercise, and behavior modification. "Lifestyle" exercise programs, which offer a wide choice of daily activities such as walking and bicycling that can be done from childhood into adulthood, seem to be more effective than aerobic programs based on a limited set of high-intensity, repetitive exercises. Behavioral therapies, which help children change their eating and exercise habits, have been somewhat effective (L. H. Epstein & Wing, 1987). Because these approaches focus on changing a child's daily routines, they are more productive when they involve parents. Parents can be taught not to use sweets as a reward for good behavior and to stop buying tempting high-calorie treats. Parents also can lose weight themselves, but whether they do or not does not seem to matter to children, as long as the adults support the children's efforts.

Health professionals warn against the indiscriminate use of diet pills for children. Some of these pills can raise blood pressure and cause dizziness, seizures, and strokes. Yet one study found that nearly 7 percent of U.S. eighth-grade and tenth-grade girls used diet pills or diet candies. Because of the dangers, especially to young people, doctors who specialize in treating obesity have called for making the most popular ingredient of such pills available only by prescription (Burros, 1990).

Body Image and Eating Disorders

body image Descriptive and evaluative beliefs about one's appearance.

Unfortunately, children who try to lose weight are not always the ones who need to do so. Concern with **body image**—how one believes one looks—begins to be important at this age, especially to girls, and may develop into eating disorders that become more common in adolescence (see Chapter 14). Children in the United States tend to develop a dislike of obesity between the ages of 6 and 9, largely, it seems, because the society equates thinness with beauty (W. Feldman, Feldman, & Goodman, 1988). As prepubertal girls begin to fill out and add body fat, some—influenced by the ultra-thin models in the media—see this normal development as undesirable.

According to one study, about 40 percent of 9- and 10-year-old girls work at trying to lose weight. White girls, although thinner than black girls, are more likely to be dissatisfied with their bodies and are more worried about overweight than African American girls, many of whom try to gain weight. Mothers exert a strong influence over their daughters' weight-control efforts. Girls whose

Table 11-2	Motor Development in Middle Childhood

Age	Selected Behaviors
6	Girls are superior in movement accuracy; boys are superior in forceful, less complex acts. Skipping is possible. Can throw with proper weight shift and step.
7	One-footed balancing without looking becomes possible. Can walk 2-inch-wide balance beams. Can hop and jump accurately into small squares. Can execute accurate jumping-jack exercise.
8	Have 12-pound pressure on grip strength. Number of games participated in by both sexes is greatest at this age. Can engage in alternate rhythmic hopping in a 2-2, 2-3, or 3-3 pattern. Girls can throw a small ball 40 feet.
9	Boys can run 16½ feet per second. Boys can throw a small ball 70 feet.
10	Can judge and intercept pathways of small balls thrown from a distance. Girls can run 17 feet per second.
11	Standing broad jump of 5 feet is possible for boys; 6 inches less for girls.

Source: Adapted from Cratty, 1986.

mothers have told them they are too fat or too thin are more likely to try to lose or gain weight (Schreiber et al., 1996).

Concern with body image may be related to the stirring of sexual attraction, which has been found to begin as early as age 9 or 10 (see Chapter 14).

Motor Development

If we were to follow a group of children on their way home from school, we would see some of them running or skipping and some leaping up onto narrow ledges and walking along, balancing till they jump off, trying to break distance records—but occasionally breaking a bone instead. Some of these youngsters will reach home (or a baby-sitter's apartment), get a snack, and dash outside again. There they will jump rope, play ball, skate, cycle, sled, throw snowballs, or splash in front of an open fire hydrant, depending on the season, the community, and the child. Others, especially those with working parents, may stay at school for organized after-school programs. Many children, however, go inside after school, not to emerge for the rest of the day. Instead of practicing new skills that stretch their bodies, they sit in front of the television set. When we talk about motor development in middle childhood, then, we need to look closely at individual children.

Motor Skills and Physical Play

During the middle years, children's motor abilities typically continue to improve (see Table 11-2). Children keep getting stronger, faster, and better coordinated—and they derive great pleasure from testing their bodies and learning new skills.

Rough-and-Tumble Play

Should you come across a couple of children tumbling over each other, you can often tell whether they are fighting or playing only by the expressions on their faces. About 10 percent of schoolchildren's free play on playgrounds consists of *rough-and-tumble play,* vigorous play that involves wrestling, hitting, and chasing, often accompanied by laughing and screaming.

> **C**HECKPOINT
>
> *Can you . . .*
>
> • Discuss the prevalence, possible causes, effects, and treatment of childhood obesity?

rough-and-tumble play
Vigorous play involving wrestling, hitting, and chasing, often accompanied by laughing and screaming.

This kind of play reminds us of our evolutionary heritage. Unlike symbolic play, which is distinctly human, rough-and-tumble play was first described in monkeys. It also seems to be universal, since it takes place from early childhood through adolescence in such diverse places as India, Mexico, Okinawa, the Kalahari in Africa, the Philippines, Great Britain, and the United States (Humphreys & Smith, 1984).

Anthropologists suggest that rough-and-tumble play evolved to provide practice in skills used in fighting and hunting (Symons, 1978). Today it serves other purposes, aside from physical exercise. There is a social function: children usually choose close friends to tussle with, possibly because they trust their friends not to become aggressive during play. Rough-and-tumble play also helps children assess their own strength as compared with that of other children.

In the United States, boys engage in rough-and-tumble play more than girls, a fact generally attributed to hormonal differences that are reinforced by societal attitudes (Humphreys & Smith, 1984); but in some societies this gender difference is slight or nonexistent (Blurton Jones & Konner, 1973). The amount of rough-and-tumble play typically diminishes between ages 7 and 11 (Humphreys & Smith, 1987) as children move into games with rules—such traditional games as hopscotch, leapfrog, hide-and-seek, and tag, which are played around the world (Opie & Opie, 1969).

Organized Sports

Many children, when they outgrow rough-and-tumble play and begin playing games with rules, concentrate on organized, adult-led sports. Nearly 20 million U.S. children under age 14 take part in team sports outside of school, but 3 out of 4 children who start to play a sport at age 6 or 7 quit by age 15 (Rubenstein, 1993). Too often, parents and coaches pressure children to practice long hours, focus on winning rather than playing the game, criticize children's skills, or offer bribes to make them do well (R. Wolff, 1993). All these tactics discourage rather than encourage participation. To help children improve their motor skills, organized athletic programs should offer the chance to try a variety of sports, should gear coaching to building skills rather than winning games, and should include as many youngsters as possible rather than concentrating on a few star athletes (AAP Committee on Sports Medicine and Committee on School Health, 1989).

Gender Differences in Motor Skills

Although there is little difference in the skills of young boys and girls, differences become greater as children approach puberty. Boys tend to run faster, jump higher, throw farther, and display more strength than girls (Cratty, 1986; refer back to Table 11-2). Part of this gender difference is due to boys' growing size and strength and girls' greater fleshiness, but much of it seems to be due to differing cultural expectations and experiences, differing levels of coaching, and differing rates of participation. Throwing, catching, and dribbling a ball are skills that have to be learned. Boys are routinely taught these skills, whereas girls generally are not. When prepubescent boys and girls take part in similar activities, their abilities are quite similar (E. G. Hall & Lee, 1984). Since girls' need for physical activity is getting more attention these days, the discrepancy between the sexes may narrow in the future.

To test the relationship between motor skills and body build, 2,142 students in grades 3, 7, and 11 did six motor tasks. The results were compared with their height, weight, and percentage of body fat. With age, boys showed progressively greater overall superiority. However, when it came to specific tasks, physical measurements—which may themselves be affected by the greater emphasis on physical activity for boys—played a declining role in that superiority. Thus, as children grow toward adolescence, environmental factors, such as encouragement

Playing little league baseball may be exciting, but nearly three out of four children who join such organized sports at age 6 or 7 drop out. Athletic programs that are widely inclusive and less competitive are more likely to contribute to lifetime fitness.

of boys' participation in sports, may play an increasing role in gender differences in motor skills (Smoll & Schutz, 1990).

The type of skill makes some difference. Among 2,309 five- to nine-year-olds, boys did better in the 50-meter dash, standing broad jump, 600-meter run, and shuttle run, and in strength of grip. Girls did better in the lateral jump, backward balancing, flexibility, and manual dexterity. Also, children from higher socioeconomic backgrounds and those who participated in sports outside of school had an advantage. However, the differences were not very great; no more than 10 percent of the variance in performance was attributable to gender or social class. Since physical differences between the sexes are fairly small before puberty, differences in skills may reflect the activities that boys and girls like or are encouraged to do (Krombholz, 1997). On the other hand, some tasks that require extensive movement or support of body weight, such as the standing long jump, are more affected by body fat and may be more subject to gender differences than tasks that require mainly eye-hand coordination, such as throwing a ball against a wall and catching it (Smoll & Schutz, 1990).

CHECKPOINT

Can you . . .

- Describe changes in the types of physical play children engage in as they grow older?
- Describe how gender differences in motor skills change with age, and compare the relative influences of physical and environmental factors?

Health, Fitness, and Safety

The development of vaccines for major childhood illnesses has made middle childhood a relatively safe time of life. Since immunizations are required for school admission, children this age are likely to be protected. The death rate in these years is the lowest in the life span. Still, many children get too little exercise to maintain physical fitness; some suffer from acute or chronic medical conditions; and some are injured in accidents. As children's experience with illness increases, so does their cognitive understanding of the causes of health and illness and of the steps people can take to promote their own health (see Box 11-1).

Maintaining Health and Fitness

Although the average U.S. schoolchild gets enough exercise to meet national goals, many children are not as active as they should be. By their own account, a multiethnic sample of 2,410 third-graders from 96 schools in 4 states averaged 125 minutes of moderate-to-vigorous or vigorous activity each day. However, more than 1 out of 3 youngsters (36.6 percent) spent less than 1 hour in moderate-to-vigorous exercise, and about 1 out of 8 (12.8 percent) spent less than half an hour. Boys were more active than girls, and white children were more active than black or Hispanic children. The most active children were those who were good at sports and were encouraged to participate (Simons-Morton et al., 1997).

Children who are not active enough tend to be those who are not fit. In the late 1980s, fewer than half of U.S. youth ages 6 to 17 could pass a full battery of fitness tests, including the mile run, flexed arm hang, sit and reach, and situps, though most children could pass some of the tests. About 20 to 30 percent failed to meet standards for cardiovascular fitness (Corbin & Pangrazi, 1992). While research does not show a decline in fitness, children do seem to be getting fatter, according to skinfold measurements and average weight (Kuntzleman & Reiff, 1992). This trend is ominous because overweight can increase the risk of heart disease in adulthood.

Why do some children get too little exercise? With cutbacks in funding, physical education classes may be offered less often. Outside of school, the most strenuous exercise some children engage in, particularly in cold weather, is switching television channels with a remote control. Furthermore, most physical activities, in and out of school, are team and competitive sports and games. These activities do not promote fitness, will usually be dropped after leaving school, and are typically aimed at the fittest and most athletic youngsters.

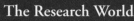
Box 11-1 Children's Understanding of Health and Illness

When Angela was sick, she overheard her doctor refer to *edema* (an accumulation of fluid, which causes swelling), and she thought her problem was "a demon." Being sick is frightening at any age. For young children, who do not understand what is happening, it can be especially distressing and confusing.

From a Piagetian perspective, children's understanding of health and illness is tied to cognitive development. As they mature, their explanations for disease change. Before middle childhood, children are egocentric; they tend to believe that illness is magically produced by human actions, often their own ("I was a bad boy, so now I feel bad"). Later they explain all diseases—only a little less magically—as being caused by all-powerful germs; the only "protection" is a variety of superstitious behaviors to ward them off. "Watch out for germs," a child may say. As children approach adolescence, they see that there can be multiple causes of disease, that contact with germs does not automatically lead to illness, and that people can do much to keep healthy.

As AIDS (acquired immune deficiency syndrome) has spread, attempts have been made to educate children about it. One study found that preschoolers knew practically nothing about AIDS. Third- and fifth-graders had a fair amount of accurate information about its causes, outcome, and prevention, but did hold mistaken beliefs—for example, that AIDS could be contracted from mosquito bites or that it could be prevented by good nutrition (Schvaneveldt, Lindauer, & Young, 1990).

Children's understanding of AIDS seems to follow the same developmental sequence as their understanding of colds and of cancer, but they understand the cause of colds earlier than they do the causes of the other two illnesses, probably because they are more familiar with colds. Interviews with 361 children in kindergarten through sixth grade (Schonfeld, Johnson, Perrin, O'Hare, & Cicchetti, 1993) found that children often give superficially correct explanations but lack real understanding of the processes involved. For example, although 96 children mentioned drug use as a cause of AIDS, most did not seem to realize that the disease is spread through blood adhering to a needle shared by drug users. One second-grader gave this version of how someone gets AIDS: "Well, by doing drugs and something like that . . . by going by a drug dealer who has AIDS. . . . Well, you go by a person who's a drug dealer and you might catch the AIDS from 'em by standing near 'em" (Schonfeld et al., 1993, p. 393).

From a young child's point of view, such a statement may be a logical extension of the belief that germs cause disease. The child may wrongly assume that AIDS can be caught, as colds are, from sharing cups and utensils, from being near someone who is coughing or sneezing, or from hugging and kissing. One AIDS education program (Sigelman et al., 1996) sought to replace such intuitive "theories" with scientifically grounded ones and to test Piaget's idea that if children have not mastered a concept, they are probably not yet ready to do so. The developers of the program hypothesized that what young children lack is knowledge about disease, not the ability to think about it.

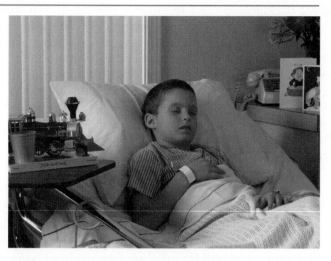

Being sick is less frightening when children understand what is happening and that they will recover soon. Children's understanding of causes of illness changes as they mature cognitively.

A carefully scripted program was tried on 306 third-, fifth-, and seventh-graders—mostly low-income Mexican Americans—in Catholic schools in Tucson. Trained health instructors conducted two 50-minute sessions consisting of lectures, video clips, drawings, and discussion, and using vocabulary appropriate for third-graders. Content included an introduction to contagious and noncontagious diseases; specific information about the AIDS virus; an overview of the immune system; the meaning of the letters in "AIDS"; differences between transmission of colds and of AIDS; misconceptions about how the AIDS virus is transmitted; risk factors for AIDS; how the disease develops; and how it can be prevented. The curriculum emphasized that there are only a few ways to get AIDS and that normal contact with people infected with the virus is not one of them. Flip charts summarized key points.

Experimental and control groups were tested before the program began and again about 2 weeks afterward. Students who had received instruction knew more about AIDS and its causes than those who had not, were no more (and no less) worried about it than before, and were more willing to be with people with AIDS. Another test almost a year later found that gains were generally retained. Third-graders gained about as much from the program as seventh-graders. It was somewhat less effective with fifth-graders, perhaps because children that age already know more about AIDS than younger children and find it less relevant to their own lives than older ones do. The success of this program shows that, contrary to Piaget, even relatively young children can grasp complex scientific concepts about disease if teaching is geared to their level of understanding.

The American Academy of Pediatrics Committee on Sports Medicine and Committee on School Health (1989) recommend that a sound physical education program include a variety of competitive and recreational sports for all children, emphasizing activities that can be part of a lifetime fitness regimen, such as tennis, bowling, running, swimming, golf, and skating. Although boxing was the sport Theodore Roosevelt turned to in his quest for physical fitness, today the American Academy of Pediatrics Committee on Sports Medicine and Fitness (1997) opposes boxing for children, adolescents, and young adults. Unlike other contact sports, such as football and ice hockey—some of which have a higher *overall* risk of injury—boxing is the only sport "where direct blows to the head are rewarded and the ultimate victory may be to render the opponent senseless" (p. 134).

Indoor play centers, where children run, climb, and crawl through colorful, complex structures, are becoming increasingly popular and may strengthen cardiovascular health. At one such center, 5- to 10-year-olds freely using the apparatus continuously for 20 minutes averaged 77 percent of their maximum heart rate—well above the 60 percent level required for improving circulatory and respiratory fitness (M. Whitehurst, Groo, & Brown, 1996; M. Whitehurst, Groo, Brown, & Findley, 1995).

Sometimes just changing everyday behavior brings about considerable improvement. Parents can make exercise a family activity, by regularly hiking or playing ball together, building strength on playground equipment, replacing driving with walking whenever possible, using stairs instead of elevators, and limiting television viewing.

Since adult hypertension has roots in childhood, blood pressure should be measured once a year from age 3 through adolescence. Treatment should be given if a child's blood pressure, after repeated measurements, is above the 95th percentile for age, sex, and size. (Blood pressure tables have now been adjusted for height because it is normal for tall children to have higher blood pressure than short children.) Taking off excess weight, moderately reducing salt intake, and increasing physical activity are usually beneficial; some children are also given drugs to avoid heart damage (AAP Task Force on Blood Pressure Control in Children, 1987; National High Blood Pressure Education Program Working Group, 1996).

Cholesterol is a waxy substance found in human and animal tissue. High levels of one type of cholesterol ("bad" cholesterol) can dangerously narrow blood vessels, leading to heart disease. This condition, called *atherosclerosis*, begins in childhood. In a randomized, controlled 3-year trial with 663 prepubertal boys and girls, a medically supervised low-fat, low-cholesterol diet brought modest improvement in cholesterol levels without endangering growth or nutrition (The Writing Group for the DISC Collaborative Research Group, 1995).

Programs of education and behavioral modification have had excellent results. In one randomized, controlled trial aimed at reducing cardiovascular risks—the largest and most rigorous such trial to date—5,106 third graders in ethnically diverse public schools in California, Louisiana, Minnesota, and Texas were given health education, along with heart-healthy school lunches and expanded physical education. After 2 years, no direct effects on blood pressure and cholesterol were observed, but—what may be more important in establishing lifetime health habits—the children in the program did report a significant reduction in fat intake (again, with no ill effects on growth and nutrition) and an increase in daily vigorous activity (Luepker et al., 1996).

More dramatic outcomes might have been achieved with more extensive family involvement. In a smaller, 3-month experiment with 342 four- to ten-year-olds, a home-based self-tutorial dietary education program proved effective in helping children with high cholesterol to learn about heart-healthy eating and reduce their fat consumption and cholesterol levels (B. M. Shannon et al., 1994). However, it may be that families who agree to have their children participate in such programs are more interested than the average family in improving health and more willing to make changes to achieve that goal.

cholesterol Waxy substance in human and animal tissue; excess deposits of one type can narrow blood vessels, leading to heart disease.

CHECKPOINT

Can you . . .

- Explain the importance of maintaining physical fitness, and give some recommendations for doing so?

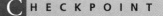

Richard, age 10, is home in bed with a cold. He sneezes, snoozes, watches television, and enjoys his break from the school routine. He is lucky. He has had no other illnesses this year, while some of his classmates have had six or seven bouts with colds, flu, or viruses. That number of respiratory infections is common during middle childhood, as germs pass freely among youngsters at school or at play (Behrman, 1992).

acute medical conditions
Illnesses that last a short time.

Illness in middle childhood tends to be brief and transient. A 6-year longitudinal study of mostly white, middle-class children in a health maintenance plan found that almost all the children had *acute medical conditions:* occasional, short-term conditions, such as upper-respiratory infections, viruses, allergies, or warts. Upper-respiratory illnesses, sore throats, strep throats, ear infections, and bed-wetting decreased with age; but acne, headaches, and transitory emotional disturbances increased as youngsters approached puberty (Starfield et al., 1984).

chronic medical conditions
Illnesses or impairments that persist for at least 3 months.

Most school-age children are free of *chronic medical conditions:* illnesses or impairments expected to last 3 months or longer, requiring special medical attention and care, lengthy hospitalization, or health services in the home (Starfield, 1991). In the 6-year study mentioned above, only 1 child in 9 had persistent conditions, such as migraine headaches or nearsightedness. However, the 1988 National Health Interview Survey (NHIS), which interviewed adults in households of 17,100 children under age 18, found, using a broad definition of chronic illness, that about 3 out of 10 children had chronic conditions (Newacheck, Stoddard, & McManus, 1993).

Socioeconomic status and ethnicity play an important part in children's health (see Chapter 8). Poor children (who are disproportionately minority children) and those living with a single parent or single adult are more likely than other children to be in fair or poor health, to have been hospitalized, and to have health-related limitations on activities. Also, children are more likely to have been hospitalized if the head of the household has less than a high school education. Why is this so? Parents with higher income and education tend to know more about good health habits and have better access to preventive health care; and two-parent families tend to have higher incomes and more wholesome diets than single-parent families (Collins & LeClere, 1997). Another factor in variations in health care is the difference in beliefs and attitudes about health and healing among cultural and ethnic groups (see Box 11-2).

Children with chronic conditions tend to be remarkably resilient. Most do not exhibit problems in mental health, behavior, or schooling; neither the severity nor the type of condition predicts who will have psychological difficulties and who will not. The young people who deal best with the stress of chronic illness seem to be those who have the inner resources of intelligence and adaptable temperament; whose parents have high self-esteem, good mental health, and positive beliefs about health care; and whose families are close, flexible, and communicative, and have strong social support networks (AAP Committee on Children with Disabilities and Committee on Psychosocial Aspects of Child and Family Health, 1993).

Still, certain conditions can greatly affect everyday living. An analysis of the 1988 NHIS data (Boyle, Decouflé, & Yeargin-Allsopp, 1994) revealed that 17 percent of the children were reported to have had one of six developmental disabilities: cerebral palsy, epilepsy or seizures, blindness, hearing impairment, stuttering, or other speech defects. Children with developmental disabilities suffer in educational functioning as well as in health. They miss more school, do worse when they are there, and are more likely to repeat a grade than children without these conditions. Of these six conditions, cerebral palsy and epilepsy have the greatest overall impact on a child's life.

Let's look at the impact of three other specific developmental conditions— stuttering and vision and hearing problems—and then at two chronic illnesses, asthma and AIDS.

Box 11-2   How Cultural Attitudes Affect Health Care

One morning Buddi Kumar Rai, a university-educated resident of Badel, a remote hill village in Nepal, carried his 2½-year-old daughter, Kusum, to the shaman, the local "medicine man." Kusum's little face was sober, her usually golden complexion pale, and her almond-shaped eyes droopy from the upper-respiratory infection she had been suffering the past week, complete with fever and a hacking cough.

Two days before, Kusum had been in her father's arms when he had slipped and fallen backwards off a veranda to the ground about 3 feet below, still tightly holding his little daughter. Neither was hurt, but little Kusum had screamed in fright.

Now the shaman told Buddi that Kusum's illness was due to that fright. He prescribed incantations and put a mark, a charcoal smudge the size of a silver dollar, on the child's forehead to drive away the evil spirit that had entered her body when she had her scare.

Two months before this incident, Buddi himself had gone to one of the ten shamans in Badel. "We have no doctors here, no medicine," he explains with a shrug. "One time I put on those stupid army boots my uncle gave me, and I walk with my wife to my father-in-law's house in Rakha, maybe two hours. And when I come home, my ankle hurt me so bad I can't walk on that foot. So I call the shaman, and he say my ankle hurts because I crossed the river without praying to the river god. So the shaman chanted over the ankle and told me to go back down to the river and pray, and after a couple of days my foot feels better."

Such adherence to ancient beliefs about illness is not unique to remote villages in the Himalayas. It is, in fact, common in many parts of the industrialized world, where many people cling to beliefs that are at odds with mainstream scientific and medical thinking. To provide better medical care to members of various ethnic minorities, policymakers need to understand the cultural beliefs and attitudes that influence what people do, what decisions they make, and how they interact with the broader society.

Many cultures see illness and disability as a form of punishment inflicted upon someone who either has transgressed (as did Buddi in failing to pray to the river god), has done something wrong in a previous life, or is paying for an ancestor's sin. People with such beliefs tend to distance themselves from, and often are unsympathetic to, the afflicted person. Another belief, common in Latin America and Southeast Asia, is that an imbalance of elements in the body causes illness and the patient has to reestablish his or her own equilibrium.

In many societies people believe that a severely disabled child will not survive. Since there is no hope, they do not expend time, effort, or money on the child—which often creates a self-fulfilling prophecy. Such a belief makes it nearly impossible for parents to plan realistically for the child's future. In some religious house-

This Peruvian healer treats a child by traditional methods, such as herbs and incantations. In many Latin American cultures, such practices are believed to cure illness by restoring the natural balance of elements in the body.

holds, parents hold out hope for a miracle and refuse surgery or other treatment.

Of course, standard medical practice in the United States is also governed by a cultural belief system. Here, parents are asked to make decisions about their child without consulting members of the extended family, as would be done in many nonwestern cultures. Independence and self-sufficiency are valued, and parents are discouraged from "babying" a disabled child. People from other cultures may not respond well to U.S. values: parents may feel a need to consult their own parents about medical decisions and may not consider it important, for example, for a disabled daughter to become self-supporting.

Professionals need to explain clearly, whenever possible in the language of the child's family, what course of treatment is being recommended, the reasoning behind it, and what can be expected to happen. Such concern can help prevent incidents like one in which an Asian mother became hysterical as an American nurse took the mother's baby to get a urine sample. The mother had had three children taken from her in Cambodia. None had returned.

Sources: Groce & Zola, 1993; Olds, in press.

Stuttering

Stuttering, involuntary, frequent repetition or prolongation of sounds or syllables, is a disorder that interferes with social functioning. As stutterers become frustrated and anxious about ordinary conversation, their self-esteem plummets.

What causes stuttering? Various theories point to faulty training in articulation and breathing; problems with brain functioning, including defective feedback about one's speech; parental pressures to speak properly; and deep-seated emotional conflicts. The condition runs in families, suggesting a genetic component, and is 3 times more common in boys than in girls. In 98 percent of cases, it begins before age 10; it is more prevalent among young children than older ones. Typically, stuttering starts gradually. About 10 percent of prepubertal children stutter; of these, 80 percent recover, typically before age 16. Sixty percent do so spontaneously, the other 20 percent in response to treatment (American Psychiatric Association [APA], 1994).

Treatments include psychotherapy and counseling, speech therapy, and drugs. The most effective training methods teach stutterers to unlearn their patterns of motor responses. With the aid of monitoring devices, such as videotape machines and computers, they learn to speak slowly and deliberately; to breathe slowly and deeply, using abdominal muscles rather than those of the upper chest; and to start up their voices gently, not in the abrupt and almost explosive way in which many stutterers begin to speak.

Vision and Hearing Problems

Most youngsters in middle childhood have keener vision than when they were younger because their visual apparatus is more developed. Children under 6 years old tend to be farsighted; their eyes have not matured and are shaped differently from those of adults. By age 6, vision is more acute; and because the two eyes are better-coordinated, they can focus better.

Still, some children have vision problems. Almost 13 percent of children under 18 are estimated to be blind or to have impaired vision (as Theodore Roosevelt did). Visual problems are reported more often for white and Latino children than for African Americans. Deafness and hearing loss affect an estimated 15.3 percent of those under 18, with 18 percent of white parents, 6 percent of black parents, and 15.2 percent of Latino parents reporting these problems in their children (Newacheck et al., 1993).

Asthma

Asthma, a chronic respiratory disease, which Roosevelt also suffered from, seems to have an allergic basis. It is characterized by sudden attacks of coughing, wheezing, and difficulty in breathing; and it can be fatal. Its prevalence increased by one-third between 1981 and 1988, and mortality rates are rising in the United States and several other countries. A reported 4.3 percent of U.S. children under 18 are asthmatic; poor, nonwhite, inner-city children are more likely to be severely affected (Halfon & Newacheck, 1993). Nearly 30 percent of children with asthma have limitations on daily activity (W. R. Taylor & Newacheck, 1992).

The disproportionate impact of asthma on poor and minority children seems to be related to access to health care. As we pointed out in Chapter 8, poor children are more likely to receive care in emergency rooms, hospital-based clinics, and neighborhood health centers than in doctors' offices. Poor children with asthma also miss more days of school, must limit their activities more, and spend more days in bed at home or in the hospital than do children from better-off families (Halfon & Newacheck, 1993). A study in Texas found that Puerto Rican children

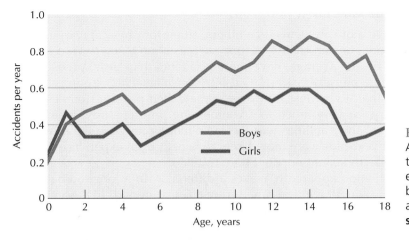

Figure 11-1

Average annual rates of injury by age and sex. Boys typically have a higher yearly accident rate than girls, except at age 1. Accident rates are especially high for both sexes in late middle childhood and early adolescence.

Source: Schor, 1987.

with asthma were likely to have more severe cases than children in other ethnic groups, probably because they tended to come from poor families that could not pay for medicine (P. R. Wood, Hidalgo, Prihoda, & Kromer, 1993).

HIV and AIDS

Children infected with the human immunodeficiency virus (HIV) are at a high risk to develop AIDS (acquired immune deficiency syndrome). As of the end of September 1996, 7,472 cases of AIDS in children less than 13 years old had been reported to the Centers for Disease Control and Prevention (1996a). Of these children, 58 percent were non-Hispanic blacks, 23 percent Hispanics, 18 percent non-Hispanic whites, and 1 percent from other racial or ethnic groups. Most of these children had acquired the AIDS virus from their mothers in the womb (see Chapter 3).

In addition to the devastating physical effects of this almost-always fatal disease, the child's entire family may be stigmatized, and the child may be shunned or kept out of school even though there is virtually no risk of infecting classmates. Infected people do not transmit HIV to others except through bodily fluids, even when they share toys, toothbrushes, eating utensils, toilets, or bathtubs (M. F. Rogers et al., 1990; refer back to Box 11-1). According to the American Academy of Pediatrics Task Force on Pediatric AIDS (1991), children who carry the HIV virus but do not show any disease symptoms should be treated like well children at home and in school. They do not need to be isolated, either for their own health or for that of other children. However, children who show symptoms of HIV infection need special care and special education.

Children with AIDS may develop central nervous system dysfunction that can interfere with their ability to learn and can also cause behavior problems (AAP Task Force on Pediatric AIDS, 1991). In one study at a developmental diagnostic and treatment center, most of the children in a sample of 5- to 14-year-olds who had been diagnosed with HIV infection had cognitive, linguistic, or emotional problems, although the children were living longer and doing better than predicted (Papola, Alvarez, & Cohen, 1994).

Accidental Injuries and Safety Concerns

Injuries increase between ages 5 and 14, as children become involved in more physical activities and are supervised less (see Figure 11-1). In the longitudinal study of children in a health maintenance plan, mentioned earlier, 80 percent of the children were treated for injuries during the 6 years of the study (Starfield et al., 1984). Accidental injuries continue to be the leading cause of death in middle childhood (U.S. Department of Health and Human Services [USDHHS], 1996a).

C HECKPOINT

Can you . . .

• Distinguish between acute and chronic medical conditions, and discuss how chronic conditions can affect everyday life?

Which Children Are Most Likely to Be Hurt?

Some children have more accidents than others, either for physical reasons, such as poor coordination, or personality factors, such as a tendency to take risks or daydream. Boys, on the average, have more accidents than girls, probably because they take more physical risks (H. Ginsburg & Miller, 1982). Young children may be subject to injuries because they overestimate their physical abilities, especially when they want very much to do something. In one study, 6-year-olds whose estimation of their abilities was the most inaccurate were the most accident prone. Eight-year-olds were more likely to benefit from experience in judging what they could and could not do (Plumert, 1995).

The family situation apparently makes a difference. In a longitudinal study of 693 families who sought medical care during a 6-year period, 10 percent of the families accounted for almost 25 percent of the injuries, after adjustment for family size (Schor, 1987). Families with high injury rates may be undergoing stress that interferes with the ability to make the home safe or watch over children. Children with siblings have more injuries than only children. Perhaps parents of more than one child are not as vigilant as parents of one child; or younger children may imitate their older siblings and take more risks; or children in larger families may be more active.

How Are Children Most Likely to Be Hurt?

Most childhood accidents occur in, or are inflicted by, automobiles or occur in the home; but between 10 and 20 percent take place in and around schools. Elementary school children are most likely to be injured from playground falls (Sheps & Evans, 1987).

Pedestrian deaths of children under 19 in the United States have decreased 48.8 percent since 1978, possibly because children today do less walking. Similar decreases have occurred in other countries. Still, pedestrian injuries accounted for 1,402 deaths of children in the United States in 1991 (Rivara & Grossman, 1996). Nonwhite children are 1½ times as likely as white children to die from such injuries (Agran, Winn, Anderson, Tran, & Del Valle, 1996).

Children are more likely to be hit by cars on the block in which they live if the street has a large number of apartment buildings and pedestrians and if more than half of the curb is occupied by parked vehicles, which can obscure a driver's view of a child darting out or a child's view of an oncoming car. Higher traffic speeds also increase the risk (Agran et al., 1996).

Parents tend to overestimate the safety skills of young children. Many kindergartners and first-graders walk alone to school, often crossing busy streets without traffic lights, although they do not have the skills to do this safely. Many such accidents could be prevented by making parents aware of their children's limitations as pedestrians and by providing school-operated transportation or more crossing guards (Dunne, Asher, & Rivara, 1992; Rivara, Bergman, & Drake, 1989).

Even on little-traveled streets close to home, young bicyclists are at risk and need to learn—and adhere to—the rules of the road. Each year about 140,000 head injuries and 400 deaths of children and adolescents, as well as about 450,000 visits to emergency rooms for treatment of nonfatal injuries, are attributed to bicycle accidents. Head injury is the leading cause of disability or death in these accidents and is most common among 5- to 9-year-olds (Sosin, Sacks, & Webb, 1996).

The dangers of riding a bicycle can be reduced dramatically by using safety-approved helmets (AAP Committee on Injury and Poison Prevention, 1995a; Sosin et al., 1996). In a study of bicycle accidents in Seattle, wearing a helmet reduced the risk of head injury by 85 percent and of brain injury by 88 percent (Thompson, Rivara, & Thompson, 1989). A later study of all bicyclists who were treated for head injuries in emergency rooms at seven Seattle hospitals, or who

Box 11-3 Keeping Children Safer

The following tips, based on research covered in this chapter, can help prevent accidental injuries to children:

- *In or near cars.* Children over age 5 should wear snug-fitting seat belts while riding in a car. Children should be taught to look both ways when crossing streets and to cross only at corners.
- *On the playground.* Children should play on soft surfaces such as sand, grass, or cedar chips. They should be taught to walk around swings and give them a wide berth; to slide down sliding boards feet first, sitting up—never head first; to use both hands on a jungle gym and never climb wet bars; and to sit facing one another on the seesaw, to grip it with both hands, never to stand on it, and never to jump off.

- *In other activities.* Children should wear approved headgear for cycling, football, roller blading, roller skating, skateboarding, horseback riding, hockey, speed sledding, skiing, snowboarding, and tobogganing. Cycling helmets should carry Snell or ANSI stickers, showing they have met standards for crash protection. Children should be taught how to fall properly; never to skate at night or wear skates on steps; to ride with the traffic; not to wear headphones, and not to carry anything in their arms while cycling; not to swing sticks, bats, or other sports equipment near other people; and to be sure all equipment is in good shape.

Many accidental injuries occur on school playgrounds. By wearing protective helmets when bicycling or roller skating, these children are dramatically reducing their risk of head injury.

died at the scene of an accident, confirmed the protective effect of helmets for all age groups. Helmets were as effective in car accidents as in other types of accidents (D. C. Thompson, Rivara, & Thompson, 1996). Protective headgear is also vital for football, roller skating, roller blading, skateboarding, horseback riding, hockey, speed sledding, skiing, and tobogganing. School programs to encourage helmet use can be effective (B. D. Weiss, 1992). (Box 11-3 summarizes tips for keeping children safer.)

One reason for some accidents is children's immaturity, both cognitive (preventing them from being aware of some dangers) and emotional (leading them to take dangerous risks). We discuss cognitive development in middle childhood in Chapter 12 and emotional and social development in Chapter 13.

CHECKPOINT

Can you . . .

- Identify factors that increase the risks of accidental injury?

SUMMARY

Growth

- Physical development is less rapid in middle childhood than in the earlier years. Boys are slightly larger than girls at the beginning of this period, but girls undergo the growth spurt of adolescence at an earlier age and thus tend to be larger than boys at the end of middle childhood.

- Wide differences in height and weight exist among individuals and groups.

- Proper nutrition is essential for normal growth and health. On average, children need 2,400 calories a day. Malnutrition can affect cognitive and psychosocial development.

- Because the permanent teeth arrive in middle childhood, dental care becomes important. Tooth decay rates have declined over the past few decades, mainly because of fluoride use and improved dental care.

- Obesity is increasingly common among U.S. children. It is influenced by genetic and environmental factors and can be treated. Concern with **body image,** especially among girls, may lead to eating disorders.

Motor Development

- Because of improved motor development, boys and girls in middle childhood can engage in a wider range of motor activities than preschoolers.

- About 10 percent of schoolchildren's play is **rough-and-tumble play,** which appears to be universal. From ages 7 to 11, rough-and-tumble play diminishes as children engage in games with rules.

- Differences in boys' and girls' motor abilities increase as puberty approaches, in part due to boys' greater strength and in part due to cultural expectations and experience.

Health, Fitness, and Safety

- Middle childhood is a relatively healthy period; most children are immunized against major illnesses, and the death rate is the lowest in the life span.

- Children today are less fit than in earlier years. Developing lifetime fitness habits and skills can reduce cardiovascular risks through control of blood pressure and **cholesterol.**

- Respiratory infections and other **acute medical conditions** are common, but most children this age are free of **chronic medical conditions,** though the prevalence of such maladies has increased.

- Children's understanding of health and illness is related to their cognitive level. Cultural beliefs affect expectations regarding health care.

- **Stuttering** is fairly common in middle childhood, especially among boys. Vision becomes keener; fewer than 16 percent of children have defective vision or hearing. **Asthma** has a disproportionate impact on poor and minority children, probably due to inadequate access to health care. Children who carry the HIV virus need not be isolated unless they show symptoms.

- Accidents are the leading cause of death in middle childhood. Most accidents occur in automobiles, at home, or in and around school.

KEY TERMS

body image (402)
rough-and-tumble play (403)
cholesterol (407)
acute medical conditions (408)

chronic medical conditions (408)
stuttering (410)
asthma (410)

QUESTIONS FOR THOUGHT AND DISCUSSION

1. Because height matters so much to so many people, should growth hormones be given to very short children who do not have a hormone deficiency?

2. In view of childhood malnutrition's long-term effects on physical, social, and cognitive development, what can and should various sectors of society—government agencies, community groups, and private organizations—do to combat it?

3. If obesity "runs in families," either because of heredity or lifestyle, or both, how can parents who have not been able to control their own weight help their children?

4. Some observers have suggested ways to help poor children with asthma. Which of the following possibilities do you think would be most helpful? How could these suggestions be implemented and how should they be funded? What other solutions might work?

   • Extended evening and weekend hours for community health centers

   • Education in detecting symptoms and avoiding triggers of attacks (such as cigarette smoking and allergy-causing substances in the home)

   • Classes in self-management of the disease

5. Medical evidence shows virtually no evidence that children with HIV infection who are symptom-free can transmit the virus to others except through bodily fluids. Yet many parents are afraid to have their children go to school with a child who is HIV-positive. Can you suggest ways to deal with this problem?

6. How would Piaget interpret the belief in some cultures that illness and disabilities are punishments for human actions? Does such a belief suggest that Piaget's theory is limited in its applicability to nonwestern cultures?

Cognitive Development in Middle Childhood

What we must remember above all in the education of our children is that their love of life should never weaken.

Natalia Ginzburg, *The Little Virtues*, 1985

Focus

Akira Kurosawa

The Japanese filmmaker Akira Kurosawa, who wrote and directed such classics as the Academy Award-winning *Rashomon* (1951) and *Seven Samurai* (1954), has been called a cinematographic genius. Kurosawa, who tried painting before going into filmmaking, uses the screen as if it were a canvas. Artistic intelligence—an unerring sense of composition, form, color, and texture—pervades his scenes.

Kurosawa's career began in his mid-twenties, when he won an apprenticeship to the great film director Kajiro Yamamoto. During the oral examination, he displayed unusual breadth and depth of knowledge and well-reasoned opinions. On the job, he was a quick study. Assigned to write scenarios, the talented novice polished off the first few and came up with idea after idea for more. He picked up editing with equal ease. A natural leader, he invariably brought Yamamoto and everyone else in the studio around to his way of thinking. "He is completely creative," Yamamoto said of him (Richie, 1984, p. 12).

Yet, as a child, during his first two years at a westernized school in Tokyo, Kurosawa remembers being a slow learner. Because he had trouble following the lessons, he just sat quietly, trying to amuse himself. Finally his teacher moved Akira's desk and chair away from the other students and frequently aroused snickers with such comments as "Akira probably won't understand this, but . . ." (Kurosawa, 1983, p. 8).

That initial school experience left an indelible mark on Kurosawa's psyche. He felt isolated and miserable. Then, toward the end of his second year of school, his family moved to another part of the city, and he was transferred to a traditional Japanese school. His new classmates, with their close-shaved heads, duck-cloth trousers, and wooden clogs, made fun of Akira's long hair and European-style clothing. The youngest of seven children, Akira had been a crybaby; now he became a laughingstock.

It was in third grade that he came out of his intellectual and emotional fog. The strongest catalyst for this change was his teacher, a man named Tachikawa, who later was forced to leave because of his progressive educational practices. In art class, instead of having all the students copy a picture and giving the top grade to the closest imitation, as was the custom, he let the youngsters draw whatever they liked. Akira became so carried away that he pressed on his colored pencils until they broke, and then he licked his fingertips and smeared the colors all over the paper. When Mr. Tachikawa held up Akira's drawing, the class laughed boisterously. But the teacher lavished it with praise and gave it the highest grade.

"From that time on," Kurosawa later wrote, ". . . I somehow found myself hurrying to school in anticipation on the days when we had art classes. . . . I became really good at drawing. At the same time my marks in other subjects suddenly began to improve. By the time Mr. Tachikawa left Kuroda, I was the president of my class, wearing a little gold badge with a purple ribbon on my chest" (1983, p. 13). Academically, his performance was uneven: the best in his class in the subjects he liked, he did barely passable work in science and math. Still, he graduated as valedictorian. According to his close friend and former classmate, Uekusa Keinosuke, who later became a scriptwriting colleague, "He certainly was not the little-genius type who merely gets good grades" but a "commanding" figure who became popular seemingly without effort (Richie, 1984, p. 10). (Uekusa, who had been a bigger crybaby than Akira, was also the beneficiary of Mr. Tachikawa's wise treatment; he blossomed after the teacher made him the class vice-president.)

It was Mr. Tachikawa who introduced Akira to the fine arts and to film. Akira's father—a descendant of the warrior class, the samurai—encouraged these interests, taking the whole family to foreign films and giving his son oil paints. So did Akira's brilliant older brother Heigo, who had once prodded him to give up his "sissy" ways but later discussed great literature with him and took him to Japanese vaudeville and western movies.

Even after Mr. Tachikawa left the school, Akira and his friend Uekusa would go to the teacher's home and sit around talking for hours: "We passed many a fulfilling day in the atmosphere of free education and respect for individuality he created" (Kurosawa, 1983, p. 21). So strong was Akira's spirit by this time that when Mr. Tachikawa's conservative successor lambasted one of his paintings, the boy simply made up his mind to "work so hard that this teacher would never be able to criticize me again" (Kurosawa, 1983, p. 25).

*Sources of biographical information about Akira Kurosawa are Goodwin, 1994, Kurosawa, 1983, and Richie, 1984.

• • •

W e can learn several lessons from Akira Kurosawa's school experience. First, children—even highly gifted ones—develop at different rates. A late bloomer should not be expected to progress as fast as a more precocious child. Second, Kurosawa's story illustrates the strong impact a teacher can have, for ill or for good, and how the influences of home and school interact. Finally, we see once again the tie-in between cognitive and psychosocial development. The flowering of Kurosawa's cognitive and social competence followed closely upon Mr. Tachikawa's effort to boost his self-esteem. As Kurosawa later wrote, "When someone is told over and over again that he's no good at something, he loses more and more confidence and eventually does become poor at it. Conversely, if he's told he's good at something, his confidence builds and he actually becomes better at it" (1983, p. 40).

School is a major formative experience in middle childhood, impinging on every aspect of development. Even today, when many children go to preschool and most go to kindergarten, the start of first grade is a milestone—a sign that a child has entered a new stage of development. During the next few years, children typically gain in self-confidence as they read, think, talk, play, and imagine in ways that were well beyond them only a few years before.

In this chapter we examine cognitive advances during the first 5 or 6 years of formal schooling, from about ages 6 to 11. Entry into Piaget's stage of concrete operations enables children to think logically and to make more mature moral judgments. As children improve in memory and problem solving, intelligence tests become more accurate in predicting school performance. The abilities to read and write open the door to a wider world. We describe all these changes, and we examine the controversies over IQ testing, bilingual education, and teaching of reading. Finally, we examine influences on school achievement and how schools try to meet special educational needs.

After reading this chapter, you should be able to answer and elaborate on such questions as these:

Preview Questions

- How is schoolchildren's thinking different from that of younger children?

- How is the development of moral reasoning related to cognitive development?

- What advances in memory, concepts, and language occur during middle childhood?

- How accurately can schoolchildren's intelligence be measured?

- What influences affect children's performance in school?

- How do schools meet the needs of children with disabilities?

- How can gifts, talents, and creativity be nurtured?

Table 12-1   Advances in Selected Cognitive Abilities During Middle Childhood

Ability	Example
Distinguishing between fantasy and reality	Miguel knows that what police officers do in real life is not as glamorous as what they do on television.
Classification	Elena can sort objects into categories, such as shape, color, or both. She knows that a subclass (roses) has fewer members than the class of which it is a part (flowers).
Inductive and deductive reasoning	Dara can solve both inductive and deductive problems and knows that inductive conclusions (based on particular premises) are less certain than deductive ones (based on general premises).
Cause and effect	Douglas knows which physical attributes of objects on each side of a balance scale will affect the result (i.e., number of objects matters but color does not). He does not yet know which spatial factors, such as position and placement of the objects, make a difference.
Seriation and transitive inference	Catherine can arrange a group of sticks in order, from the shortest to the longest, and can insert an intermediate-size stick into the proper place. She knows that if one stick is longer than a second stick, and the second stick is longer than a third, then the first stick is longer than the third.
Spatial thinking	Danielle can use a map or model to help her search for a hidden object and can give someone else directions for finding the object. She can find her way to and from school, can estimate distances, and can judge how long it will take her to go from one place to another.
Conservation	Stacy, at age 7, knows that if a clay ball is rolled into a sausage, it still contains the same amount of clay (conservation of substance). At age 9, she knows that the ball and the sausage weigh the same. Not until early adolescence will she understand that they displace the same amount of liquid if dropped in a glass of water.
Number and mathematics	Kevin can count in his head, can add by counting up from the smaller number, and can do simple story problems.

Piagetian Approach: The Concrete Operational Child

concrete operations Third stage of Piagetian cognitive development (approximately from ages 7 to 12), during which children develop logical but not abstract thinking.

At about age 7, according to Piaget, children enter the stage of **concrete operations.** They are less egocentric and can use mental operations to solve concrete (actual) problems. Children can now think logically because they can take multiple aspects of a situation into account rather than focus on only one aspect. Increased ability to understand other people's viewpoints helps them to communicate more effectively and to be more flexible in their moral judgments. However, children in this stage are still limited to thinking about real situations in the here and now. The ability to think abstractly does not develop until adolescence.

Advances in Cognitive Abilities

Children in the stage of concrete operations, roughly between ages 7 and 12, can perform many tasks at a much higher level than they could in the preoperational stage (see Table 12-1). They have a better understanding of the difference between fantasy and reality, of classification, of logical relationships, of cause and effect, of spatial concepts, and of conservation, and they are more proficient with numbers.

Distinguishing Between Fantasy and Reality

The ability to distinguish between what is real and what is imaginary becomes more sophisticated during the stage of concrete operations. When second- and fifth-graders were asked about what nurses and police officers do in real life and on television, the older children were more likely than the younger ones to recognize the television portrayals as unrealistic. Children who watched a lot of television were more likely to believe it was like real life and to want to be nurses and police officers like the ones on the screen (J. C. Wright et al., 1995).

Classification

One classification ability that develops in middle childhood is **class inclusion,** the ability to see the relationship between a whole and its parts. If preoperational children are shown a bunch of 10 flowers—7 roses and 3 carnations—and are asked whether there are more roses or more flowers, they are likely to say there are more roses, because they are comparing the roses with the carnations rather than with the whole bunch. Not until the stage of concrete operations do children come to realize that roses are a subclass of flowers and that, therefore, there cannot be more roses than flowers (Flavell, 1963).

class inclusion Understanding of the relationship between the whole and its parts.

Inductive and Deductive Reasoning

The ability to classify makes it possible for children to think logically. Both types of logical reasoning, *deduction* and *induction,* proceed from *premises* (statements that are known, believed, or assumed to be true) to *conclusions*. **Deduction** starts with a general statement (premise) about a class of people, animals, objects, or events and applies it to particular members of the class. If the premise is true of the whole class, and the reasoning is sound, then the conclusion must be true: "All dogs bark. Spot is a dog. Spot barks." *Induction* starts with particular observations and draws general conclusions: "My dog barks. So does Terry's dog and Melissa's dog. So it looks as if all dogs bark." Inductive conclusions are less certain than deductive ones because it is always possible to come across new information that does not support the conclusion.

Researchers gave 16 inductive and deductive problems to 16 kindergartners, 17 second graders, 16 fourth graders, and 17 sixth graders. The problems were designed so as not to call upon knowledge of the real world. For example, one deductive problem was: "All poggops wear blue boots. Tombor is a poggop. Does Tombor wear blue boots?" The corresponding inductive problem was: "Tombor is a poggop. Tombor wears blue boots. Do all poggops wear blue boots?" Second graders (but not kindergartners) were able not only to correctly answer both kinds of problems, but to see the difference between them and to explain their responses, and they (appropriately) expressed more confidence in their deductive answers than in their inductive ones. Sensitivity to the distinction between induction and deduction increased between second and sixth grade (Galotti, Komatsu, & Voelz, 1997).

deduction Type of logical reasoning that moves from a general premise about a class to a conclusion about a particular member or members of the class.

induction Type of logical reasoning that moves from particular observations to a general conclusion.

Cause and Effect

The ability to make judgments about cause and effect also increases during middle childhood. When 5- to 12-year-olds were asked to predict how levers and balance scales would perform under varying conditions, the older children gave more correct answers than the younger children. Children understood the influence of physical attributes (the number of objects on each side of a scale) earlier than they recognized the influence of spatial factors (the distance of objects from the center of the scale). Awareness of which variables have an effect does not seem to be related to awareness of which do not (for example, the color of the objects). Apparently, these two mental processes develop separately as experience

The ability to find a place on a map or globe is a sign of school-age children's progress in spatial thinking. Communication about spatial concepts also improves with age.

helps children revise their intuitive theories about how things work (Amsel, Goodman, Savoie, & Clark, 1996).

Seriation and Transitive Inference

seriation Ability to order items along a dimension.

Children show that they understand **seriation** when they can arrange objects in a series by placing them in order according to one or more dimensions, such as weight (lightest to heaviest) or color (lightest to darkest). Piaget (1952) tested this ability by asking children to put sticks in order from shortest to longest. By age 4 or 5, children can pick out the smallest and the largest sticks. By 5 or 6, they can arrange the rest of the sticks by trial and error. Finally, at 7 or 8, they can grasp the relationships among the sticks on sight, picking out the shortest, then the next shortest, and so on to the longest (see Figure 12-1).

transitive inference Understanding of the relationship between two objects by knowing the relationship of each to a third object.

Transitive inference, the ability to recognize a relationship between two objects by knowing the relationship between each of them and a third, also develops in middle childhood. Stacy is shown three sticks: a yellow one, a green one, and a blue one. She is shown that the yellow stick is longer than the green one, and the green one is longer than the blue. Without physically comparing the yellow and blue sticks, she can say that the yellow one is longer than the blue one. She bases her answer on her knowledge of how each of these sticks compares to the green stick (M. Chapman & Lindenberger, 1988; Piaget & Inhelder, 1967).

Spatial Thinking

Why can 6- or 7-year-olds be trusted to find their way to and from school, whereas most younger children cannot? One reason is that children in the stage

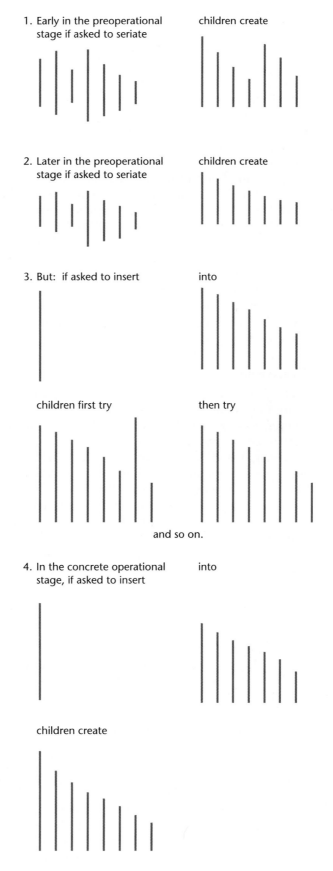

1. Early in the preoperational stage if asked to seriate

children create

2. Later in the preoperational stage if asked to seriate

children create

3. But: if asked to insert

into

children first try

then try

and so on.

4. In the concrete operational stage, if asked to insert

into

children create

Figure 12–1
Improvements in seriation between the preoperational and concrete operational stages.
Source: Adapted from Siegler, 1991, p. 43.

of concrete operations are better able to understand, visualize, and use spatial relationships. They have a better conception of how far it is from one place to another and how long it will take to get there, and they can better remember the route and the landmarks along the way. Experience plays a role in this development. Much as a baby who begins to crawl gains a better understanding of the immediate spatial environment by exploring it from a variety of positions and vantage points (refer back to Box 5-2), a child who goes to school becomes more familiar with the neighborhood outside the home.

Both the ability to use maps and models and the ability to communicate spatial information improve with age (Gauvain, 1993). Although 6-year-olds can search for and find hidden objects, they usually do not give well-organized directions for finding the same objects. In part, this may have to do with linguistic limitations or failure to recognize what information the listener needs (Plumert, Pick, Marks, Kintsch, & Wegesin, 1994). In one study (Gauvain & Rogoff, 1989), 9-year-olds were better able than 6-year-olds to give "mental tours" of a funhouse. The 9-year-olds were able to describe the layout, as well as the route through the funhouse; but the younger children, when asked to pay attention to the layout, merely listed places in no particular order. In another study (Waller & Harris, 1988), 8-year-olds gave route-like descriptions to younger children, but 5-year-olds did so only when told that this kind of description would make it easier for the younger child to understand.

Conservation

Piaget and other researchers have tested children's grasp of *conservation*, the ability to recognize that the amount of something remains the same even if the material is rearranged, as long as nothing is added or taken away (see Chapter 9). Tests of conservation deal with such attributes as number, substance, length, area, weight, and volume (refer back to Table 9-3). In solving conservation problems, concrete operational children can work out the answers in their heads; they do not have to measure or weigh the objects.

In a typical test of conservation of substance, an experimenter shows a child two identical clay balls. After the child acknowledges that the amount of clay in both balls is the same, the experimenter or the child rolls or kneads one of the balls into a different shape, say, a long, thin "sausage." The child is asked whether the two objects still contain the same amount of clay, and why. Felipe, who is still in the preoperational stage, is deceived by appearances. He says the long, thin roll contains more clay because it looks longer. Stacy, who has reached the stage of concrete operations, correctly answers that the ball and the "sausage" have the same amount of clay.

When asked about the reasoning behind her answer, Stacy shows that she understands the principle of *identity:* she knows the clay is still the same clay, even though it has a different shape. She also understands the principle of *reversibility:* she knows she can reverse the transformation and restore the original shape (change the sausage back into a ball). Felipe, the preoperational child, does not understand either of these principles. Stacy can also *decenter:* she can focus on more than one relevant dimension—in this case, on both length and width. She recognizes that although the ball is shorter than the "sausage," it is also thicker. Felipe centers on one dimension (length) while excluding the other (thickness).

Typically, children can solve problems involving conservation of substance (like the one just described) by about age 7 or 8. However, in tasks involving conservation of weight—in which they are asked, for example, whether the ball and the "sausage" weigh the same—children typically do not give correct answers until about age 9 or 10. In tasks involving conservation of volume—in which children must judge whether the "sausage" and the ball displace an equal amount of liquid when placed in a glass of water—correct answers are rare before age 12.

conservation In Piaget's terminology, awareness that two objects that are equal according to a certain measure (such as length, weight, or quantity) remain equal in the face of perceptual alteration (for example, a change in shape) so long as nothing has been added to or taken away from either object.

Children at first use objects to help them count. This girl is learning to *count on*—to count the red checkers and then continue with the black checkers to arrive at the total number of checkers.

Piaget's term for this inconsistency in the development of different types of conservation is *horizontal décalage.* Children's thinking at this stage is so concrete, so closely tied to a particular situation, that they cannot readily transfer what they have learned about one type of conservation to another type, even though the underlying principles are the same. Also, children who are just beginning to understand conservation may go through a transitional stage in which they do not always apply it. These children may answer correctly when they see a short "sausage" but fail to conserve if the "sausage" is very long and thin.

Horizontal décalage may apply to tasks other than conservation, as well; it suggests that higher levels of cognitive abilities do not emerge all at once, but gradually and continuously. As we will see, gradual gains in information processing ability may play a part in this improvement.

horizontal décalage In Piaget's terminology, a child's inability to transfer learning about one type of conservation to other types, hence, the child masters different types of conservation tasks at different ages.

Number and Mathematics

The cognitive advances described above help children tackle arithmetic. Their greater ability to manipulate symbols, understand class inclusion and seriation, and appreciate such concepts as reversibility make computation possible. Young children intuitively devise strategies for adding, by counting on their fingers or by using other objects. By age 6 or 7, they can count in their heads. They also learn to *count on:* to add 5 and 3, they start counting at 5 and then go on to 6, 7, and 8 to add the 3. They can reverse the numbers as well, starting with 3 and adding 5 to it. It may take 2 or 3 more years for them to perform a comparable operation for subtraction, but by age 9 most children can either count up from the smaller number or down from the larger number to get the answer (L. B. Resnick, 1989).

Children also become more adept at solving simple story problems, such as: "Pedro went to the store with $5 and spent $2 on candy. How much did he have left?" When the original amount is unknown ("Pedro went to the store, spent $2 and had $3 left. How much did he start out with?"), the problem is harder because the operation needed to solve it (addition) is not as clearly indicated. Few children can solve this kind of problem before age 8 or 9 (L. B. Resnick, 1989).

Influences of Culture and Schooling

According to Piaget, children's mastery of cognitive abilities depends on neurological maturation and on adaptation to the physical and social environment. Piaget believed that these processes are universal: that they are not tied to culture and are affected very little by schooling or training. What does other research say?

Does Culture Affect Cognitive Advances?

Some studies have found that children in nonwestern cultures achieve conservation and other Piagetian advances later than children in western cultures. Researchers have attributed these findings to differences in the importance various cultures attach to these abilities. However, most of the researchers conducting these studies have been European or American. Furthermore, they generally relied on standardized, highly structured interviews, rather than open-ended ones, which allow more insight into a child's thinking. It may well be, then, that the findings of cultural differences reflect the methods of the researchers rather than the abilities of the children.

A study of 48 Micmac Indian 10- and 11-year-olds on Cape Breton Island, Canada, supports this view. These children, who live on a government reservation, speak their native language at home but are taught in English at school. When tested in English by European examiners on conservation of substance, weight, and volume, the Indian children lagged behind a comparison group of white English-speaking Canadian children. They tended to give very short or incomplete explanations and were more frequently classified as "uncertain." However, when interviewed by examiners from their own culture, who spoke their native language, the Indian children did about as well as the comparison group (Nyiti, 1982).

Of course, cognitive abilities do not develop in a vacuum. Culture establishes the framework in which abilities are learned and used. For example, *activity theory*, which grows out of Vygotsky's sociocultural perspective, stresses the role of culturally organized spatial arrangements and tools, such as street layouts and maps, in helping children carry out such activities as searching and route-finding (Gauvain, 1993).

Does Schooling Affect Cognitive Advances?

Does schooling help children achieve conservation? Findings vary. Early research on African rural and urban children found that, by age 11 or 12, virtually all the children who had gone to school could conserve liquid quantity, compared with only half of the children who had not (Greenfield, 1966). However, a study of rural Guatemalan children suggests that the home environment may be the crucial factor. Before these children were 7 years old—old enough to go to school—those who came from more stimulating homes, and whose parents later enrolled them in school, conserved liquids better than those who came from less stimulating homes and did not later enter school (Irwin, Engle, Yarbrough, Klein, & Townsend, 1978). On the other hand, a study of nearly 1,100 Peruvian children ages 6 to 12 found effects of schooling which could not be explained by differences in home background (H. W. Stevenson, 1982).

Research with minimally schooled people in developing countries suggests that the ability to solve addition problems develops nearly universally and often intuitively, through concrete experience in a social and cultural context (Guberman, 1996; L. B. Resnick, 1989). For example, between ages 6 and 14, Brazilian children in shantytown communities who are sent to the store to buy bread or soda become increasingly proficient in making calculations involving money (Guberman, 1996). These intuitive procedures are different from the ones children are taught in school. In a study of Brazilian street vendors ages 9 to 15, a researcher acting as a customer gives a child a math problem. The "customer" says, "I'll take two coconuts." Each one costs 40 cruzeiros; she pays with a 500-cruzeiros bill and asks, "What do I get back?" The child counts up from 80: "Eighty, 90, 100, 420," to arrive at the correct answer, 420 cruzeiros. However,

This Malaysian newspaper boy must be able to add up a customer's bill and subtract to make change. Street vendors in developing countries, who often have little schooling, may develop intuitive ways to perform such computations.

when this same child is given a similar problem in the classroom ("What is 420 + 80?"), he arrives at the wrong answer by incorrectly using a series of steps he learned in school (Carraher, Schliemann, & Carraher, 1988).

Schooling—especially learning measurement skills—may contribute to the development of spatial thinking. Again, however, we can't be sure which comes first. Does schooling develop spatial awareness, or does the development of spatial awareness make children ready to learn about measurement in school? (Gauvain, 1993) It seems likely that both the activities that take place in school and those that arise within everyday cultural contexts influence cognitive abilities.

Moral Reasoning

According to Piaget, moral development is linked to cognitive growth. Piaget maintained that children make sounder moral judgments when they can look at things from more than one perspective. He proposed that moral reasoning develops in two stages (summarized in Table 12-2). Children may go through these stages at varying ages, but the sequence is the same.

In the first stage, *morality of constraint,* the young child thinks rigidly about moral concepts. In this stage children are quite egocentric; they cannot imagine more than one way of looking at a moral issue. They believe that rules cannot be changed, that behavior is right or wrong, and that any offense deserves punishment (unless they themselves are the offenders!).

The second stage, *morality of cooperation,* is characterized by flexibility. As children mature, they interact with more people and come into contact with an increasingly wide range of viewpoints. Some of these contradict what they have learned at home. They therefore discard the idea that there is a single, absolute standard of right and wrong, and they begin to formulate their own moral code. Because they can consider more than one aspect of a situation, they can make more subtle moral judgments. For example, they can consider the intent behind behavior.

CHECKPOINT

Can you . . .

- Identify cognitive abilities that emerge or strengthen during middle childhood?

- Name three principles that help school-aged children understand conservation, and explain why children master different kinds of conservation at different ages?

- Weigh the evidence for influences of schooling and culture on Piagetian tasks?

morality of constraint   First of Piaget's two stages of moral development, characterized by rigid, simplistic judgments.

morality of cooperation Second of Piaget's two stages of moral development, characterized by flexible, subtle judgments and formulation of one's own moral code.

Table 12-2 Piaget's Two Stages of Moral Development

	Stage I: Morality of Constraint	Stage II: Morality of Cooperation
Point of view	Child views an act as either totally right or totally wrong and thinks everyone sees it the same way. Children cannot put themselves in place of others.	Children put themselves in place of others. They are not absolutist in judgments but see that more than one point of view is possible.
Intention	Child judges acts in terms of actual physical consequences, not the motivation behind them.	Child judges acts by intentions, not consequences.
Rules	Child obeys rules because they are sacred and unalterable.	Child recognizes that rules are made by people and can be changed by people. Children consider themselves just as capable of changing rules as anyone else.
Respect for authority	Unilateral respect leads to feeling of obligation to conform to adult standards and obey adult rules.	Mutual respect for authority and peers allows children to value their own opinions and abilities and to judge other people realistically.
Punishment	Child favors severe punishment. Child feels that punishment itself defines the wrongness of an act; an act is bad if it will elicit punishment.	Child favors milder punishment that compensates the victim and helps the culprit recognize why an act is wrong, thus leading to reform.
Concept of justice	Child confuses moral law with physical law and believes that any physical accident or misfortune that occurs after a misdeed is a punishment willed by God or some other supernatural force.	Child does not confuse natural misfortune with punishment.

Source: Adapted partly from M. L. Hoffman, 1970b; Kohlberg, in M. L. Hoffman & Hoffman, 1964.

To draw out children's thinking on this point, Piaget (1932) would tell them a story about two little boys: "One day Augustus noticed that his father's inkpot was empty and decided to help his father by filling it. While he was opening the bottle, he spilled a lot of ink on the tablecloth. The other boy, Julian, played with his father's inkpot and spilled a little ink on the cloth." Then Piaget would ask, "Which boy was naughtier, and why?"

Children under about age 7, in the stage of constraint, usually consider Augustus naughtier, since he made the bigger stain. Older children, in the stage of cooperation, recognize that Augustus meant well and made the large stain by accident, whereas Julian made a small stain while doing something he should not have been doing. Immature moral judgments center only on the degree of offense; more mature judgments consider intent.

Lawrence Kohlberg's influential theory of moral development, which builds on Piaget's, is discussed in Chapter 15.

Information-Processing Approach: Memory and Other Processing Skills

Unlike Piaget, who described qualitative changes in the way children think, information-processing researchers focus on how children gain and deal with information. These researchers break down mental processes into separate components for study. They look at such questions as: How rapidly do children of different ages process information? How does memory work? What is involved in selective attention?

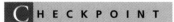

CHECKPOINT

Can you . . .

• Name and describe Piaget's two stages of moral development and explain how they are linked to cognitive maturation?

Improvements in Processing Speed and Memory Functioning

A big factor in schoolchildren's ability to acquire information is a steady improvement in the ability to process and retain it. Processing speed for such tasks as matching pictures, adding numbers in one's head, and recalling spatial information increases rapidly as unneeded synapses (neural connections in the brain) are pruned away (S. Hale, Bronik, & Fry, 1997; Kail, 1991, 1997; Kail & Park, 1994). Faster, more efficient processing increases the mind's capacity to hold and handle information. The amount of information a child can keep in mind increases, making possible better recall and more complex thinking (Flavell, Miller, & Miller, 1993).

Information-processing researchers think of memory as a filing system that has three steps: *encoding, storage,* and *retrieval.* In order to file something in memory, we first must decide which "folder" to put it in—for example, "people I know" or "places I've been." *Encoding* attaches a "code" or "label" to the information to prepare it for storage, so that it will be easier to find when needed. Next, we *store* the material (put the folder away in the filing cabinet). The last step is to *retrieve* the information when we need it (search for the file and take it out). Difficulties in any of these steps may cause memory problems.

Events are encoded along with information about the context in which they were encountered. As we reported in Chapter 6, infants can better recall the effect of kicking a mobile when placed in a setting that reminds them of their first exposure to this experience. Similarly, 7- to 11-year-olds who are asked to memorize three related words (say, "horse-pig-cow") can better retrieve the second and third words ("pig-cow") when cued with the first word ("horse") if they are given contextual information ("A boy named Barry saw these animals on a farm") both at the time they first see the words and when asked to recall them. With increasing age, children need less detailed reminders to reconstruct the original context (Ackerman, 1997).

Information that is being encoded or retrieved is kept in *working memory,* a short-term "storehouse" for information a person is actively working on, or trying to remember. The capacity of working memory increases rapidly in middle childhood. Researchers may assess working memory by asking children to recall a series of digits in reverse order (for example, "2-8-3-7-5-1" if they heard "1-5-7-3-8-2"). At ages 5 to 6, children usually remember only two digits; the typical adolescent remembers six.

According to a widely used model, an element of working memory called the *central executive* controls the processing of information (Baddeley, 1981, 1986). The central executive can temporarily expand the capacity of working memory by moving information into two separate subsidiary systems. One of these keeps verbal information, and the other, visual and spatial images, "on hold" while the central executive is occupied with other tasks. The central executive orders the encoding of information for transfer to *long-term memory,* a "storehouse" of virtually unlimited capacity that holds information for long periods of time. The central executive also retrieves information from long-term memory.

The central executive, which may be located in the brain's frontal lobes, seems to mature sometime between ages 8 and 10. We can infer this from the finding that 10-year-olds are less likely than younger children to become confused when given a visual task (identifying the color of each of a series of three numbers flashed on a computer screen) while trying to do a verbal task (committing the numbers to memory). This suggests that the visual and verbal components of working memory have become independent of each other by age 10 (S. Hale et al., 1997).

Metamemory: Understanding Memory

Even 3-year-olds know the difference between remembering and forgetting (O'Sullivan, Howe, & Marche, 1996). They are beginning to be aware of the

working memory Short-term storage of information being actively processed.

central executive In Baddeley's model, element of working memory that controls the processing of information.

long-term memory Storage of virtually unlimited capacity, which holds information for very long periods.

metamemory Understanding of processes of memory.

processes of memory. Knowledge about one's own memory is called *metamemory,* and it improves with age.

Four-year-olds understand that the passage of time affects memory. They know that if a doll saw two objects, the doll would be more likely to "remember" the one just seen than the one seen a long time before (Lyon & Flavell, 1993). From kindergarten through fifth grade, children advance steadily in understanding of memory (Kreutzer, Leonard, & Flavell, 1975). Kindergartners and first-graders know that people remember better if they study longer, that people forget things with time, and that relearning something is easier than learning it for the first time. By third grade, metamemory is fairly sophisticated; children typically know that some people remember better than others and that some things are easier to remember than others.

One pair of experiments looked at preschoolers', first-graders', and third-graders' beliefs about what influences remembering and forgetting. Most children in all three age groups believed that important events in a story about a birthday party were more likely to be retained than minor details. Most first- and third-graders, but not most preschoolers, believed that a later experience (playing with a friend who was not at the party) might color a child's recollection of who was at the party. But not until third grade did most children recognize that memory can be distorted by suggestions from others—say, a parent who suggests that the friend was at the party (O'Sullivan et al., 1996).

Mnemonics: Strategies for Remembering

mnemonic strategies Techniques to aid memory.

As children learn more about how memory works, they can take deliberate actions to help them remember. Devices to aid memory are called *mnemonic strategies.* Children may discover mnemonic techniques on their own, or they can be taught to use them. As children get older, they develop better strategies, use them more effectively, and tailor them to meet specific needs (Bjorklund, 1997). The most common mnemonic strategy among both children and adults is the use of *external memory aids.* Other common strategies include *rehearsal, organization,* and *elaboration.* (See Table 12-3.)

external memory aids Mnemonic strategies using something outside the person, such as a list.

Writing down a telephone number, making a list, setting a timer, and putting a library book by the front door are examples of *external memory aids:* prompting by something outside the person. Even kindergartners recognize the value of external aids, and as children mature, they use them more (Kreutzer et al., 1975). For example, third-graders are more likely than first-graders to think of putting their skates by their schoolbooks if they want to remember to take their skates to school the next day.

rehearsal Mnemonic strategy to keep an item in working memory through conscious repetition.

When Anna, at age 6, wanted to call her grandmother, she said the number out loud again and again as she went to the telephone. She was using *rehearsal,* or conscious repetition, a common mnemonic strategy to assist working memory. Some early research suggested that children do not usually use rehearsal spontaneously until after first grade. When an experimenter pointed to several pictures that children knew they would be asked to recall, first-graders typically sat, waited until they were asked for the information, and then tried to recall the pictures. Second- and fifth-graders moved their lips and muttered almost inaudibly between the time they saw the pictures and the time they were asked to recall them, and these children remembered the material better (Flavell, Beach, & Chinsky, 1966). When experimenters asked first-graders to name the pictures out loud when they first saw them (a form of rehearsal), the children recalled the order better. A later study showed that young children who were taught to rehearse applied the technique to the immediate situation but not spontaneously to new situations (Keeney, Canizzo, & Flavell, 1967).

organization Mnemonic strategy consisting of categorizing material to be remembered.

Another way to remember material is by mentally placing it into related groupings or categories, a mnemonic strategy known as *organization.* Adults tend to organize automatically. Children younger than 10 or 11 tend not to do

Table 12-3   Four Common Memory Strategies

Strategy	Definition	Development in Middle Childhood	Example
External memory aids	Prompting by something outside the person	5- and 6-year-olds can do this, but 8-year-olds are more likely to think of it.	Dana makes a list of the things she has to do today.
Rehearsal	Conscious repetition	6-year-olds can be taught to do this; 7-year-olds do it spontaneously.	Tim says the letters in his spelling words over and over until he knows them.
Organization	Grouping by categories	Most children do not do this until at least age 10, but younger children can be taught to do it.	Luis recalls the animals he saw in the zoo by thinking first of the mammals, then the reptiles, then the amphibians, then the fish, and then the birds.
Elaboration	Associating items to be remembered with something else, such as a phrase, scene or story	Older children are more likely to do this spontaneously and remember better if they make up their own elaboration; younger children remember better if someone else makes it up.	Yolanda remembers the lines of the musical staff (E, G, B, D, F) by associating them with the phrase "*Every good boy does fine.*"

this, but they can be taught to do it, or they may acquire the skill by imitation (Chance & Fischman, 1987). If they see randomly arranged pictures of, say, animals, furniture, vehicles, and clothing, they do not mentally sort the items into categories spontaneously; but if shown how to organize, they recall the pictures as well as older children. Again, however, the younger children do not generalize this learning to other situations.

In the mnemonic strategy called *elaboration,* children associate items with something else, such as an imagined scene or story. To remember to buy lemons, ketchup, and napkins, for example, a child might imagine a ketchup bottle balanced on a lemon, with a pile of napkins handy to wipe up spilled ketchup. Older children are more likely than younger ones to use elaboration spontaneously, and they remember better when they make up the elaborations themselves. Younger children remember better when a parent or someone else makes up the elaboration (Paris & Lindauer, 1976; H. W. Reese, 1977).

elaboration Mnemonic strategy of making mental associations involving items to be remembered, sometimes with an imagined scene or story.

Children often use more than one memory strategy for a task. They also may choose different strategies at different times. In one study aimed at gauging developmental changes in the effectiveness of multiple strategy use (Coyle & Bjorklund, 1997), second-, third-, and fourth-graders were given 2 minutes to study 18 words printed on separate index cards and then were asked to recall the words in any order. During the study period, the researchers noted the children's spontaneous use of four strategies: *rehearsal* (saying the words out loud or mouthing them), *examination* (visually scanning the cards), and two forms of *organization: sorting* (grouping the word cards by categories, such as fruits or tools), and *category naming* (saying the name of a category). The researchers also noted children's use of *clustering* during recall (naming the words in what appeared to be categorical groupings). The same procedure was repeated four more times with different sets of words.

Older children used more strategies than younger children, but even second-graders tended to use more than one strategy for each set of words; and children of all ages who used more strategies recalled more words. Many children, regardless of age, switched strategies or varied their combinations of strategies from one trial to another. However, children who stayed with the same combinations tended to have better recall, suggesting that they had hit on a method that worked for them. Fourth-graders seemed to use strategies more effectively from the start. There was a clear and consistent relationship between their use of multiple, varied strategies and their recall on all five trials, whereas second- and third-graders showed the benefits of multiple strategy use only after the initial trials.

Selective Attention

Most school-age youngsters can concentrate longer and can focus on the information they need and want while screening out irrelevant information. Children who cannot do this have problems in school, where attention and concentration are required.

School-age children learn to ignore outside distractions—and also those that come from their own memory. For example, as children grow older they are better able to summon up the appropriate meaning of a word in something they are reading and suppress other meanings that do not fit the context (G. B. Simpson & Foster, 1986; G. B. Simpson & Lorsbach, 1983). Fifth-graders are better able than first-graders to keep discarded information from reentering working memory and vying with other material for attention (Harnishfeger & Pope, 1996). This growing ability to control the intrusion of older thoughts and associations and redirect attention to current, relevant ones is believed to be due to neurological maturation. It is one of the reasons memory functioning improves during middle childhood (Bjorklund & Harnishfeger, 1990; Harnishfeger & Bjorklund, 1993).

The ability to consciously direct attention may help explain why older children make fewer mistakes in recall than younger ones. It may enable them to select what they want to remember and what they want to forget. In one study (Lorsbach & Reimer, 1997), second- and sixth-graders and college students were asked to guess the word that would complete each of a series of sentences (for example, "We made a sandwich with peanut butter and . . ."). Then the participants were told the correct ending and were asked to remember it. Some of the sentences had unexpected endings (for example, "We made a sandwich with peanut butter and *bananas.*").

Later the participants were asked to complete a new set of sentences with the first word that came to mind. Some of the expected words were ones that, in the previous exercise, had been called right ("The man peeled and ate two [*bananas*]") or wrong ("The fly landed on the jar of [*jelly*]"). Second-graders—but not sixth-graders or college students—tended to come up with words that had been called wrong, even though they had been asked to remember the "right" words.

Information Processing and Piagetian Tasks

Can advances in information processing help explain the advances Piaget described? Some researchers say yes.

The improvements in spatial thinking we described earlier, for example, are related to the underlying abilities to understand and use symbols, to coordinate perception and movement, and to remember spatial information. These abilities help children in everyday life. Why are 9-year-olds better than 5-year-olds at recognizing landmarks? It may be because they are better able to remember objects in context (say, a picture of a house in the woods). Similarly, 9-year-olds' greater ability to find their way to and from school seems related to their superior abilities to quickly scan a scene and take in its important features and to remember objects in the order in which they encountered them (G. L. Allen & Ondracek, 1995).

Improvements in memory also may contribute to the mastery of conservation tasks. Young children's working memory is so limited that, even if they are able to master the concept of conservation, they may not be able to remember all the relevant information (Siegler & Richards, 1982). They may forget that two differently shaped pieces of clay were originally identical. Gains in short-term memory may contribute to the ability to solve problems like this in middle childhood. Enhanced memory capacity also makes it easier to acquire and use knowledge; and children, like adults, can think more logically about things they know about (Flavell et al., 1993; refer back to Box 11-1).

Robbie Case is one of several neo-Piagetian psychologists who have tried to accommodate some aspects of Piaget's theory to the findings of information-processing research (see Chapter 1). Case (1985, 1992) suggests that as a child's understanding of a concept or scheme becomes more automatic, it frees space in working memory for dealing with new information. Practice in applying a scheme, together with the growing capacity of working memory, may help explain horizontal décalage: children may need to become comfortable enough with conservation of substance to use it without conscious thought before they can extend and adapt that scheme to other kinds of conservation. Recently Case has proposed a new model of cognitive development, based in part on information-processing research (see Box 12-1).

CHECKPOINT

Can you . . .

- Identify ways in which information processing improves during middle childhood?

- Describe the three steps in memory?

- Name four of the most common mnemonic aids and discuss developmental differences in their use?

- Give examples of how improved information processing may help explain cognitive advances Piaget described?

Psychometric Approach: Assessment of Intelligence

Intelligence tests (or IQ tests) are called *aptitude tests:* they claim to measure general intelligence, or the capacity to learn, as contrasted with *achievement tests,* which assess how much children have already learned in various subject areas. However, intelligence tests are validated against measures of achievement, such as school performance, and such measures are affected by factors beyond innate intelligence. For this and other reasons, there is strong disagreement over how accurately IQ tests assess differences among children.

aptitude tests Tests that measure children's general intelligence, or capacity to learn.

achievement tests Tests that assess how much children know in various subject areas.

Intelligence Tests and Their Critics

Most schools give group intelligence tests every few years, and scores are now more reliable than during the preschool period. In addition, children may be tested individually to help determine whether they might benefit from special treatment.

An individual intelligence test can help determine whether a child needs special help.

Box 12-1 Developing Concepts: A Neo-Piagetian Model

Does cognitive development take place in a universal series of stages leading to increasingly logical thought? Piaget thought so, and his view has been highly influential. However, beginning in the late 1960s, dissatisfaction with the idea of a single system of logical operations mounted. New research suggested that children's cognitive processes are more linked to content, context, and culture than Piaget imagined (Case & Okamoto, 1996; see Chapter 1).

Robbie Case (1985, 1992) and other neo-Piagetian psychologists have studied specific concepts, strategies, and skills, which develop within the constraints of the capacity of working memory. Now Case (Case & Okamoto, 1996) has proposed a new theory that blends elements of Piaget's work with insights from the neo-Piagetian position and other post-Piagetian branches of thought, which look at cognitive growth in specialized kinds of knowledge.

From Piaget, Case has taken the idea of centralized cognitive structures that develop in broad stages. However, the centralized structures Case describes are not, as in Piaget's theory, logical systems that can apply to any problem in any field. Instead, they are fundamental concepts central to particular *domains,* or fields of knowledge. Within each domain, children move through the same four levels of conceptual competency between ages 4 and 10: *predimensional, one-dimensional, two-dimensional,* and *multidimensional.* According to Case, progress through these stages comes from a combination of neurological maturation, social experience, and the natural desire for mastery.

In the domain of number, for example, 4-year-olds in the *predimensional stage* seem to have a schema for pointing-and-counting items one by one. They also have a schema for looking at, say, two groups of circles and estimating which group has more circles and which has fewer circles (see figure). These two schemas are separate; children this age cannot yet combine them to tell, for example, whether 4 is more or less than 5.

By about age 6, says Case, children have merged their schemas for counting and for knowing "more" and "less" into a central structure, the *mental number line,* which may stretch from 1 to 100 or more. In this *one-dimensional stage,* they can answer such questions as "What number comes after 7?" and "What number is the second one after 7?" They can count forward or backward and can tell whether numbers are bigger or smaller and which are closer to each other. This hypothetical number line "forms a sort of lens through which children view the world" (Case & Okamoto, 1996, p. 8). They use it to make sense of their culture's rules for measuring time and space and for regulating the buying and selling of goods.

However, this first mental number line is crude and incomplete. By age 8, children reach the *two-dimensional stage,* in which they can coordinate two number lines. They can understand the relationship between "ones" and "tens," and thus can do two-column arithmetic problems. Finally, by age 10, in the *multidimensional stage,* children advance to complex mastery of their culture's number system (in western cultures, the base-10 system). They can integrate multiple number lines (ones, tens, hundreds, thousands, and so forth) and can understand various mathematical operations, such as multiplication, division, and the use of fractions.

In a series of studies involving 6- to 10-year-olds in the United States, Canada, China, and Japan, Case and his colleagues (Case & Okamoto, 1996) found that children's numerical knowledge fell into stages like the ones described above. The studies also

---

Otis-Lennon School Ability Test Group intelligence test for kindergarten through twelfth grade.

Wechsler Intelligence Scale for Children (WISC-III) Individual intelligence test for schoolchildren, which yields verbal and performance scores as well as a combined score.

Kaufman Assessment Battery for Children (K-ABC) Nontraditional individual intelligence test for children ages 2½ to 12½, which seeks to provide fair assessments of minority children and children with disabilities.

One popular group test, the *Otis-Lennon School Ability Test,* has levels for kindergarten up to twelfth grade. Children are asked to classify items, to show an understanding of verbal and numerical concepts, to display general information, and to follow directions.

The most widely used individual test is the *Wechsler Intelligence Scale for Children (WISC-III).* This test measures verbal and performance abilities, yielding separate scores for each, as well as a total score. Separate subtest scores makes it easier to pinpoint a child's strengths and to diagnose specific problems. For example, if a child does well on verbal tests (such as understanding a written passage and knowing vocabulary words) but poorly on performance tests (such as figuring out mazes and copying a block design), the child may be slow in perceptual or motor development. A child who does well on performance tests but poorly on verbal tests may have a language problem. Another commonly used individual test is the Stanford-Binet Intelligence Scale (see Chapter 9).

A nontraditional individual test is the *Kaufman Assessment Battery for Children (K-ABC)* (A. S. Kaufman & Kaufman, 1983). This test for children 2½ to 12½ years old has separate scales for aptitude (mental processing abilities) and

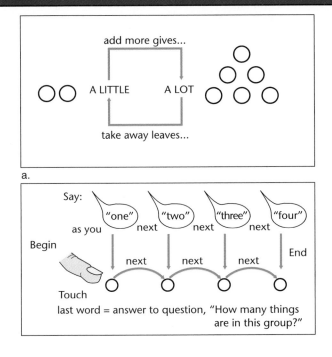

add more gives...

A LITTLE   A LOT

take away leaves...

a.

Say:
"one"   "two"   "three"   "four"

as you   next   next   next

Begin   End

next   next   next

Touch

last word = answer to question, "How many things are in this group?"

Central numerical structures at the predimensional stage (about age 4), according to Case's theory. (a) The *global quantity schema* lets children answer questions about "more" and "less." (b) The *counting schema* lets children tell how many objects are in a set or grouping.

Source: Case & Okamoto, 1996, p. 6.

suggested a parallel development in social and spatial skills, moving from one-dimensional to two-dimensional and finally multidimensional understanding. Six-year-olds who could integrate two schemas for number could also integrate two schemas for under-

standing human relationships: one for the sequence of events in a story and one for a character's feelings about the events. Next, at about 8, they could relate two story lines and the motivations of two characters. Finally, at about 10, they could integrate multiple story lines. They showed a similar age-related progression in spatial understanding, first putting together the ability to draw the shapes of objects with a sense of their relative size and location, and then moving to a partial and finally a complete understanding of perspective.

On tests of these three kinds of central conceptual structures—those for number, narrative, and spatial relations—children in all four cultures progressed through the same stages at the same rate. By contrast, on tests of more specific, culturally influenced knowledge, there were big differences. For example, in China, where much effort is devoted to teaching children how to draw, children's drawings were far more complex than in Canada, where there is relatively little stress on teaching drawing. Yet Chinese and Canadian children's drawings were similar in their representation of perspective, which is not emphasized in the Chinese training. The researchers concluded that if a culture values a particular task and devotes a great deal of effort to teaching it, children's performance will reflect that training. Still, even across cultures, widely varying experiences seem to lead to the same broad endpoints of development.

In line with Howard Gardner's theory of multiple intelligences (discussed in this chapter), Case and Okamoto (1996) speculate that there may be as many as eight central conceptual structures for eight separate domains. In addition to number, social relationships, and spatial relationships, these domains are language, logical analysis, motor ability, musical ability, and intrapersonal understanding (understanding of oneself). Further research is needed to support the theory and its application to various domains.

achievement. So as to fairly assess children from cultural minorities and children with disabilities, members of these groups were included in the standardization sample. There is also a nonverbal scale for children with hearing impairments or speech or language disorders and for those whose primary language is not English. The K-ABC incorporates Vygotsky's concept of scaffolding (see Chapters 1 and 9): if a child fails any of the first three items on a subtest, the examiner can clarify what kind of response is expected by using different words or gestures or a different language.

The use of psychometric intelligence tests is controversial. On the positive side, because IQ tests have been standardized, there is extensive information about their norms, validity, and reliability (see Chapter 6). IQ scores are good predictors of achievement in school, especially for highly verbal children, and they help identify youngsters who are either especially bright or in need of special help. On the other hand, there is serious concern that the tests may be unfair to many children. For one thing, they may underestimate the intelligence of children who, for one reason or another, do not do well on tests (Anastasi, 1988; S. J. Ceci, 1991). Also, because IQ tests are timed, they equate intelligence with speed. A child who works slowly and deliberately is penalized.

Table 12-4	Seven Intelligences, According to Gardner	

Intelligence	Definition	Fields or Occupations Where Used
Linguistic	Ability to use and understand words and nuances of meaning	Writing, editing, translating
Logical-mathematical	Ability to manipulate numbers and solve logical problems	Science, business, medicine
Musical	Ability to perceive and create patterns of pitch and rhythm	Musical composition, conducting
Spatial	Ability to find one's way around in an environment and judge relationships between objects in space	Architecture, carpentry, city planning
Bodily-kinesthetic	Ability to move with precision	Dancing, athletics, surgery
Interpersonal	Ability to understand and communicate with others	Teaching, acting, politics
Intrapersonal	Ability to understand the self	Counseling, psychiatry, spiritual leadership

A more fundamental criticism is that tests cannot assess aptitude directly; instead, they infer it from tasks that tap information and skills. Although some test makers have tried to separate what children have already learned (achievement) from their ability to acquire new knowledge (intelligence), critics maintain that it cannot be done. Experience, especially education, affects test results: scores, especially on verbal tasks, are more closely related to the amount of schooling a child has had than to the child's age (Cahan & Cohen, 1989).

The fact that IQs change is further evidence for the role of experience. According to Vygotsky, intelligence is not a fixed, inborn quantity; it results from the ongoing interaction between person and environment. Thus we should not be surprised if intelligence increases as children mature and grow more knowledgeable and more skillful in using their minds. Assessments should seek to capture this dynamic process. Tests based on Vygotsky's concept of the zone of proximal development (ZPD) offer an alternative to traditional IQ tests (see Chapter 9).

Finally, IQ tests do not cover important aspects of intelligent behavior, such as common sense, social skills, creative insight, and self-knowledge (H. Gardner, 1983; Sternberg, 1985a, 1987). Indeed, some followers of the psychometric approach maintain that intelligence is not a single ability, but several, and that conventional intelligence tests miss some of them. Two of the chief advocates of this position—and two of the most outspoken critics of IQ tests—are Howard Gardner and Robert Sternberg. Let's look at their theories of intelligence.

Gardner's Theory of Multiple Intelligences

Is a child who is good at analyzing paragraphs and making analogies more intelligent than someone who has perfect musical pitch, or someone who can organize a closet or design a group project, or someone who can pitch a curve ball at the right time? The answer is no, according to Howard Gardner's (1983) *theory of multiple intelligences.*

Gardner maintains that people have not just one but at least seven separate kinds of intelligence. IQ tests tap only three of these intelligences: *linguistic, logical-mathematical,* and, to some extent, *spatial.* The other four, which are not reflected in IQ scores, are *musical, bodily-kinesthetic, interpersonal,* and *intrapersonal.* (See Table 12-4 for definitions and examples of fields in which each "intelligence"

theory of multiple intelligences Gardner's theory that distinct, multiple forms of intelligence exist in each person.

is useful.) Gardner (in press) has recently proposed the possibility of three additional intelligences: *naturalist, spiritualist,* and *existential.*

High intelligence in one of these areas is not necessarily accompanied by high intelligence in any of the others. A person may be extremely gifted in art (a spatial ability), precision of movement (bodily-kinesthetic), social relations (interpersonal), or self-understanding (intrapersonal), but not have a high IQ. Thus the scientist Albert Einstein, the poet T. S. Eliot, and the cellist Pablo Casals may have been equally intelligent, each in a different area. The various intelligences also develop at different rates. For example, logical-mathematical ability tends to develop earlier and to decline more quickly in late life than interpersonal ability. However, these patterns vary from one person to another and may be modifiable.

Gardner sees intelligence as similar to talent; in fact, he uses the two words interchangeably. Talents, says Gardner, develop into "competencies" through training and practice, often revealing themselves in a "crystallizing moment" in which a person discovers an unsuspected ability. Children tend to develop competencies that their families and cultures value and encourage. A person who does not hear music, for example, is unlikely to develop competency in that field. Rather than try to measure inborn ability, as IQ tests attempt to do, Gardner would judge each intelligence by its products: how well a child can tell a story, remember a melody, or get around in an unfamiliar area. Assessments based on extended observation could be used to reveal strengths and weaknesses for purposes of guiding development, rather than to compare individuals (Scherer, 1985).

Gardner's theory has been particularly influential in the education of children with special gifts and talents (discussed later in this chapter). Brain research supports the existence of multiple intelligences, since different parts of the brain seem to process different kinds of information (R. J. Kirschenbaum, 1990). However, the theory needs more supporting research.

Sternberg's Triarchic Theory of Intelligence

Like Gardner, Robert Sternberg (1997) maintains that intelligence is most readily assessed by the behavior it produces. Sternberg defines *intelligence* as a group of mental abilities necessary for children or adults to adapt to any environmental context, and also to select and shape the contexts in which they live and act. Intelligent behavior may differ from one culture to another—in England it is intelligent to drive on the left side of the road, in the United States on the right—but the processes that produce such behavior are the same. These processes include recognizing and defining problems, designing strategies for solving them, obtaining and mentally representing information, allocating mental resources, and monitoring and evaluating the solution. By limiting his definition of intelligence to universally necessary mental abilities, Sternberg would exclude some of Gardner's "intelligences," such as musical and bodily-kinesthetic abilities.

Sternberg's (1985a) *triarchic theory of intelligence* embraces three elements, or aspects, of intelligence: *componential, experiential,* and *contextual.* According to Sternberg, everyone has these three kinds of abilities to a greater or lesser extent. As in Gardner's theory, a person may be strong in one, two, or all three.

- The *componential element* is the *analytic* aspect of intelligence; it determines how efficiently people process information. It tells people how to solve problems, how to monitor solutions, and how to evaluate the results.
- The *experiential element* is *insightful;* it determines how people approach novel or familiar tasks. It allows people to compare new information with what they already know and to come up with new ways of putting facts together—in other words, to think originally.
- The *contextual element* is *practical;* it determines how people deal with their environment. It is the ability to size up a situation and decide what to do: adapt to it, change it, or get out of it.

triarchic theory of intelligence Sternberg's theory describing three types of intelligence: componential (analytical ability), experiential (insight and originality), and contextual (practical thinking).

componential element In Sternberg's triarchic theory, term for the analytic aspect of intelligence, which determines how efficiently people process information and solve problems.

experiential element In Sternberg's triarchic theory, term for the insightful aspect of intelligence, which determines how effectively people approach both novel and familiar tasks.

contextual element In Sternberg's triarchic theory, term for the practical aspect of intelligence, which determines how effectively people deal with their environment.

Sternberg Triarchic Abilities
Test (STAT)   Test that seeks
to measure componential,
experiential, and contextual
intelligence in verbal,
quantitative, and figural (spatial)
domains.

Since componential ability is the kind most school tasks require, IQ tests that measure this kind of ability are fairly good predictors of school performance. However, because these tests do not focus on experiential (insightful) or contextual (practical) intelligence, says Sternberg, they may be less useful in predicting success in the outside world.

Like Gardner's theory, Sternberg's theory has helped to identify gifted students. The *Sternberg Triarchic Abilities Test (STAT)* (Sternberg, 1993) seeks to measure each of the three components of intelligence through multiple-choice and essay questions in three domains: verbal, quantitative, and figural (or spatial). For example, a test of practical-quantitative intelligence might be to solve an everyday math problem having to do with buying tickets to a ball game or following a recipe for making cookies. A creative-verbal item might ask children to solve deductive reasoning problems that start with factually false premises (such as, "Money falls off trees"). An analytical-figural item might ask children to identify the missing piece of a figure. The test has levels of increasing difficulty for elementary, high school, and college students. Preliminary validation has found correlations with several other tests of critical thinking, creativity, and practical problem solving. As predicted, the three kinds of abilities—componential, experiential, and contextual—are only weakly correlated with each other (Sternberg, 1997; Sternberg & Clinkenbeard, 1995).

Ethnic and Cultural Differences In IQ

Although there is considerable overlap in IQ among ethnic groups, with some African Americans scoring higher than most whites, on average African Americans score about 15 points lower than white Americans (N. Brody, 1985; Neisser et al., 1995; C. R. Reynolds, 1988). What accounts for this difference? Some writers have argued that part of the cause is genetic (Herrnstein & Murray, 1994; Jensen, 1969). However, while there is strong evidence of a genetic influence on differences in intelligence *within* a group (see Chapter 2), there is no direct evidence that differences *between* ethnic, cultural, or racial groups are hereditary (Neisser et al., 1995).

Most scholars attribute such differences to inequalities in environment—in income, nutrition, living conditions, intellectual stimulation, schooling, culture, or other circumstances that can affect self-esteem, motivation, and academic performance (Kamin, 1974, 1981; Kottak, 1994; Miller-Jones, 1989) and even the very structure of the brain (see Chapter 5). In one study of 5-year-olds who had been low-birthweight babies, when analysts adjusted for economic and social differences between black and white children (including differences in home environment), they virtually eliminated intergroup differences in IQ (Brooks-Gunn, Klebanov, & Duncan, 1996). The discrepancy in IQ between white and black Americans appears to be diminishing, perhaps as a result of efforts to improve the education and life circumstances of minority children (Neisser et al., 1995).

What about other ethnic groups? Asian Americans, whose scholastic achievements consistently outstrip those of other ethnic groups, do not seem to have a significant edge in IQ, despite earlier findings to the contrary (Neisser et al., 1995). Instead, Asian American children's strong scholastic achievement seems to be best explained by cultural factors (see Box 12-2). IQ scores do tend to predict the achievement of Hispanic children, as well as of African Americans. Average IQ scores of Hispanic children fall between those of black and white children, probably reflecting language difficulties; Latino children tend to do better on performance tasks than on verbal tasks (Neisser et al., 1995).

Language may play a part in the black-white differential as well. Differences between black and white children's test scores do not appear until about 2 or 3 years of age (Golden, Birns, & Bridger, 1973). In fact, some classic research suggests that African American babies are precocious on developmental tests (Bayley, 1965; Geber, 1962; Geber & Dean, 1957). The disadvantage that shows up later may reflect the switch from motor to verbal tasks, which may be confusing for children who hear black English rather than standard English around them.

Findings such as these lead some critics to attribute ethnic differences in IQ to the tests themselves. These critics claim that IQ tests are subject to *cultural bias:* a tendency to include questions that use language or call for information or skills more familiar or meaningful to some cultural groups than to others (Sternberg, 1985a, 1987). The contents of a test—the tasks it poses—tend to reflect the test-developers' values and experience. Critics argue that intelligence tests are built around the dominant thinking style and language of white people of European ancestry, putting minority children at a disadvantage. For example, most tests designate only one right answer to each question—the one that is considered appropriate according to standards of the dominant culture. But children socialized in a minority culture may see alternative answers, which are then marked wrong (Heath, 1989; Helms, 1992).

Since 1910, researchers have tried to design tests that can measure intelligence without introducing cultural bias, generally by posing tasks that do not require language. Testers use gestures, pantomime, and demonstrations for such tasks as tracing mazes, finding absurdities in pictures, putting the right shapes in the right holes, and completing pictures. However, test designers have not been able to eliminate all cultural influences. For example, when Lucas, an American child, was asked to identify the missing detail in a picture of a face with no mouth, he said, "the mouth." However, Ari, an Asian immigrant child in Israel, said the body was missing. Since the art he was familiar with would not present a head as a complete picture, he thought the absence of a body was more important than the omission of "a mere detail like the mouth" (Anastasi, 1988, p. 360).

It seems impossible to design a *culture-free* test, one with no culture-linked content. Instead, test developers have tried to produce *culture-fair* tests, dealing with experiences common to people in various cultures. However, it is almost impossible to screen for all culturally determined values and attitudes. On a simple sorting task, a child in a western culture will categorize things by what they *are* (say, putting *bird* and *fish* in the category *animal*). Kpelle tribespeople in Nigeria consider it more intelligent to sort things by what they *do* (grouping *fish* with *swim*, for example) (Sternberg, in Quinby, 1985; Sternberg, 1985a, 1986). In the United States, children in low-income homes, where tasks and roles are less clearly defined than in high-income households, tend to classify more like the Kpelle than like high-income Americans (Miller-Jones, 1989).

Cultural bias also can affect how well a child does in a particular testing situation. A child from a culture that stresses sociability and cooperation may be handicapped taking a test alone. A child from a nonindustrial culture that stresses slow, painstaking work may be handicapped in a timed test (Kottak, 1994). Rapport with the examiner and familiarity with the surroundings make a difference. African American and Latino children, disabled children, and children from low socioeconomic levels often achieve higher scores when tested in their own classrooms by their own teachers, rather than in unfamiliar rooms by examiners they do not know (D. Fuchs & Fuchs, 1986; L. S. Fuchs & Fuchs, 1986).

cultural bias   Tendency of intelligence tests to include items calling for knowledge or skills more familiar or meaningful to some cultural groups than to others, thus placing some test-takers at an advantage or disadvantage due to their cultural background.

culture-free   Describing an intelligence test that, if it were possible to design, would have no culturally linked content. Compare *culture-fair*.

culture-fair   Describing an intelligence test that deals with experiences common to various cultures, in an attempt to avoid cultural bias. Compare *culture-free*.

Development of Language

Language abilities continue to grow during middle childhood. Children are now better able to understand and interpret oral and written communication and to make themselves understood.

Vocabulary, Grammar, and Syntax

Six-year-olds use complex grammar and have a vocabulary of several thousand words, but they have yet to master many fine points of language. During the

Box 12-2   Why Are So Many Children of Asian Extraction High Achievers?

The striking academic success of many children of Asian origin, such as those from Chinese, Japanese, and Korean families—as well as the disproportionate success of adults from these ethnic groups in scientific and professional fields—has raised provocative questions. Why do so many students of East Asian extraction make such a strong showing? Is it because of superior innate ability, or other factors? To help answer these questions, some researchers have looked at differences in cognitive ability, educational practices, and family and cultural attitudes in these children's countries of origin, which may, at least initially, carry over to children of the immigrant generation.

Cognitive Ability

Chinese and Japanese students do not seem to start out with any overall cognitive superiority. In one cross-cultural study, U.S. first-graders did better on many tasks, possibly because they are more used to answering adults' questions, whereas Chinese children, for example, are expected to be "seen but not heard" (H. W. Stevenson et al., 1985). In another study, U.S. children did better at ages 4 to 6 in counting and in judging relative quantities, but by age 7 or 8, Korean children had surpassed them (Song & Ginsburg, 1987). U.S. students' mathematical skills decline from first to eleventh grade compared with the skills of Japanese and Chinese students, but their general information scores become increasingly similar (H. W. Stevenson, Chen, & Lee, 1993). Since children learn advanced math skills almost entirely in school, whereas general information can be learned outside of school, teaching seems to make the difference in math achievement.

Children of Asian extraction often do better in school than other U.S. youngsters. The reasons seem to be cultural, not genetic.

Educational Practices

Educational practices in such East Asian societies as Japan, Taiwan, and Korea differ markedly from those in the United States (Song & Ginsburg, 1987; H. W. Stevenson, 1995; Stigler, Lee, & Stevenson, 1987). Children spend more time in school each year and each day, and more time being taught mathematics, in part because the curriculum is set centrally. Classes are larger (about 40 to 50), and teachers spend more time teaching the whole class, whereas U.S. children spend more time working alone or in small

Continued

early school years, they rarely use the passive voice (as in "The sidewalk is being shoveled"), verb tenses that include the auxiliary *have* ("I have already shoveled the sidewalk"), and conditional sentences ("If Barbara were home, she would help shovel the sidewalk").

Up to and possibly after age 9, children develop an increasingly sophisticated understanding of *syntax*, how words are organized into phrases and sentences. Carol S. Chomsky (1969) found considerable variation in the ages at which children grasp certain syntactic structures (see Table 12-5). For example, most children under 5 or 6 years old think the sentences "John promised Bill to go shopping" and "John told Bill to go shopping" both mean that Bill is the one to go to the store. Their confusion is understandable, since almost all English verbs other than *promised* that might be used in such a sentence (such as *ordered*, *wanted*, and *expected*) would have that meaning. Many 6-year-olds have not yet learned how to deal with constructions such as the one in the first sentence, even though they know what a promise is and can use and understand the word correctly in other sentences. By age 8, most children can interpret the first sentence correctly.

groups. Although the approach in U.S. schools offers more individual attention, each child ends up with less total instruction. Still, East Asian teachers spend less of their total day in front of the class; about 40 percent of their time is allocated to preparing lessons, correcting papers, and working with individual students.

Family and Cultural Attitudes

In Japan, a child's entrance into school is a greater occasion for celebration than graduation from high school. First-graders receive such expensive gifts as desks, chairs, and leather backpacks. Japanese and Korean parents spend a great deal of time helping children with schoolwork. Japanese children who fall behind are tutored or go to *jukus,* private remedial and enrichment schools (McKinney, 1987; Song & Ginsburg, 1987).

Chinese and Japanese mothers view academic achievement as a child's most important pursuit and hold high standards for academic achievement (H. W. Stevenson, 1995; H. W. Stevenson et al., 1993; H. W. Stevenson, Lee, Chen, & Lummis, 1990; H. W. Stevenson, Lee, Chen, Stigler, et al., 1990). They are less satisfied than U.S. mothers with their children's school performance and their schools, and so are the children themselves (H. W. Stevenson, 1995; H. W. Stevenson et al., 1993). Chinese and Japanese children spend more time on homework, like it better, and get more help from parents than U.S. children (C. Chen & Stevenson, 1989). Whereas U.S. students socialize with friends after school and engage in sports and other activities, Asian students devote themselves almost entirely to study, alone or with friends (Fuligni & Stevenson, 1995; H. W. Stevenson, 1995; H. W. Stevenson et al., 1993). Most important, perhaps, Asian parents communicate an attitude that learning is valuable, mastery is satisfying, and effort is more important than ability. Perhaps that helps explain why Asian children are highly motivated to achieve (H. W. Stevenson, 1995).

A common belief is that high-achieving students in Japan and China suffer psychologically from pressure to achieve. Actually, lower-achieving U.S. students report more frequent feelings of stress, academic anxiety, and aggression; and school is their most commonly identified source of stress (H. W. Stevenson et al., 1993).

It is apparently culture, then, and not inborn cognitive superiority, that has helped East Asian students outperform U.S. students. Although Asian cultures vary greatly, East Asian cultures share certain values that foster educational success, such as obedience, responsibility, and respect for elders (R. K. Chao, 1994).

In addition to this cultural heritage, many Asian American families see education as the best route to upward mobility (R. Chao, 1996; Sue & Okazaki, 1990). The impact of immigrant Chinese Americans' parenting goals is already apparent when their children are preschool age. Along with Chinese American parents' emphasis on proper behavior (see Chapter 10) goes a strong motivation to see that their children succeed in school. This means training them early in the values of hard work and discipline, teaching them specific skills, and, if necessary, driving them to excel. The child's school success is seen as a central goal of parenting and a measure of its success; supervision of homework and teaching or tutoring are means to that end. Educated Chinese American mothers put more stress on academic achievement than their European American counterparts, who tend to see it as a by-product of building a child's self-confidence and self-esteem (R. Chao, 1996; R. K. Chao, 1994; Huntsinger & Jose, 1995).

Of course, as Asian American children grow up in U.S. culture and absorb its values, their attitudes toward learning may change, and their academic standing as well (C. Chen & Stevenson, 1995). The influence of the original Asian culture may well become weaker from one generation to the next. Research on second-, third-, and fourth-generation Asian Americans may help sort out the cultural influences on educational achievement.

Knowledge About Communication

Young children's misinterpretions of what others say often stem from difficulties in *metacommunication:* knowledge of how communication takes place. This knowledge increases during middle childhood.

metacommunication
Understanding of the processes involved in communication.

One aspect of metacommunication is awareness of the connection between instructions and results. In one experiment, kindergartners and second-graders were asked to construct block buildings exactly like those built by another child. They were to do this on the basis of the other child's audiotaped instructions without seeing the buildings themselves (Flavell, Speer, Green, & August, 1981). The instructions were often incomplete, ambiguous, or contradictory. The "builders" were then asked whether they thought their buildings looked like the ones the child on the tape had made and whether they thought the child's instructions were good or bad.

The second-graders were more likely than the younger children to notice when instructions were inadequate and to pause or look puzzled. They were much more likely to know when they did not understand something and to recognize that their buildings might not look exactly like those made by the child on

Table 12-5	Acquisition of Complex Syntactic Structures	
Structure	Difficult Concept	Age of Acquisition
John is easy to see.	Who is doing the seeing?	5.6 to 9 years*
John promised Bill to go.	Who is going?	5.6 to 9 years*
John asked Bill what to do.	Who is doing it?	Some 10-year-olds still have not learned this.
He knew that John was going to win the race.	Does the "he" refer to John?	5.6 years.

*All children 9 and over know this.
Source: C. S. Chomsky, 1969.

CHECKPOINT

Can you . . .

- Identify ways in which children's ability to communicate becomes more sophisticated between ages 6 and 9?

the tape because they had not received effective instructions. The kindergartners sometimes knew that the instructions were not clear, but they did not seem to realize that this would mean they might not be able to do the job well.

These findings have important implications. Young children often do not understand what they see, hear, or read, but they may not be aware that they do not understand. Adults need to realize that they cannot take children's understanding for granted and need to make sure that children know what the adults want them to know.

Literacy

School-age children use reading and writing for the same kinds of purposes adults do. They read for enjoyment, for learning facts and discovering ideas, and to stimulate their thinking. They write to express ideas, thoughts, and feelings.

Children's attitudes toward reading are influenced by ability, by experience, and by the social context (M. C. McKenna, 1994). While parents and teachers are important, peers exert a growing influence. According to a survey of 18,185 first-through sixth-graders across the United States (M. C. McKenna, Kear, & Ellsworth, 1995), attitudes toward reading—both recreational and academic—are most positive in first grade, and the trend is downward from then on (see Figure 12-2). Motivation for recreational reading declines fastest in the worst readers, and this trend grows stronger throughout elementary school. As a group, girls like reading better than boys do, perhaps because of social expectations or because boys may prefer sports and other activities. (Box 12-3 discusses approaches to teaching reading.)

As children become literate, they use storytelling to strengthen their participation in their culture and their social connections. An examination of journal entries and stories by 4- to 8-year-old African American children from working-class homes shows how peers' responses give social meaning to written communication (Dyson, 1993). The children initially "wrote" by talking and drawing. They expressed their thoughts and feelings to one another and talked about and acted out one another's stories. They put their friends into stories as characters and included words or actions designed to tease or amuse the other children. One third-grader wrote about rap stars on television.

Ironically, in the typical classroom children are discouraged from discussing their work with other children. This practice is based on the belief that children, especially friends, will distract one another, turn learning time into playtime, and prevent one another from doing their best work. Research based on Vygotsky's social interaction model suggests that this is not so.

One study of 60 fourth-graders found that children progress more when they write with other children, especially friends (Daiute, Hartup, Sholl, & Zajac,

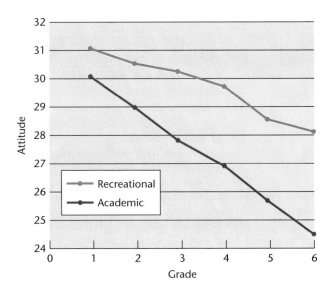

Figure 12–2
Changes in children's attitudes toward reading, grades 1–6.
Source: M. C. McKenna et al., 1995.

1993). The children were asked to write pieces for a class publication about the rain forest. Children working in pairs wrote stories with more solutions to problems, more explanations and goals, and fewer errors in syntax and word use than did children working alone. Children working with friends concentrated more intently than those paired with mere acquaintances. The acquaintances tended to stray from the task, joke around, and make less of a joint effort. The friends collaborated in complex ways, elaborating on each other's ideas, working as a team, and posing alternative ideas.

What makes collaboration between friends so fruitful? Since friends know one another well, they may better understand each other's needs, abilities, and likely behaviors. They can expect reciprocal commitment, and they are more comfortable and trusting; thus they may have more courage to take intellectual risks (Hartup, 1996a, 1996b).

Second-Language Education

More than 2.5 million school-age children in the United States come from non-English-speaking homes (Hakuta & Garcia, 1989). A goal of the federal Equal Education Opportunity Act of 1974 is for foreign-speaking students to learn English well enough to compete academically with native English-speakers. How can this best be done? That is a controversial issue with psychological and political ramifications. Identity is entwined with language and culture, and competence in school and in society affects self-esteem. In Canada, Canadian-born children are expected to learn both English and French, though some districts are populated more by one cultural group than the other. In the United States, the issue is how best to integrate newcomers.

Some schools use an *English-immersion* approach (sometimes called ESL, or English as a Second Language), in which minority children are immersed in English from the beginning, in special all-day or part-time classes. Other schools have adopted programs of *bilingual education,* in which children are taught in two languages, first learning academic subjects in their native language and then switching to English when they become more proficient in it. These programs can encourage children to become *bilingual* (fluent in two languages) and to feel pride in their cultural identity.

Advocates of early English-immersion claim that the sooner children are exposed to English and the more time they spend speaking it, the better they learn it (Rossel & Ross, 1986). Proponents of bilingual programs claim that children

CHECKPOINT

Can you . . .

- Summarize changes in children's attitudes toward reading during the elementary grades?

- Compare the whole-language and code-emphasis methods of teaching reading and present arguments for each?

- Explain why social interaction may improve children's writing?

English-immersion Approach to teaching English as a second language in which instruction is presented only in English from the outset of formal education.

bilingual education A system of teaching foreign-speaking children in two languages—their native language and English—and later switching to all-English instruction after the children develop enough fluency in English.

bilingual Fluent in two languages.

Box 12-3 Teaching Reading: Phonics Versus Whole-Language

Traditionally, most children learned to read by mastering a phonetic code that matches the printed alphabet to spoken sounds. A child who knows this code can "sound out," and thus "decode," unfamiliar words. Teaching methods that stress phonics take a *code emphasis* approach.

The *whole-language* approach (sometimes called *literature-based* or *process-oriented*), which is in widespread use today, is based on very different principles. Whole-language advocates believe that children can learn to read and write naturally, through discovery, much as they learn to understand and use speech. They claim that phonetic instruction hampers this natural process by obscuring the purpose of written language—to communicate meaning—and produces readers who can decode but cannot comprehend.

Proponents of whole-language instruction argue that children will learn to read and write better and with more enjoyment if they see written language as a way to gain information and express ideas and feelings, not as a system of isolated sounds and syllables that must be learned by memorization and drill. Whole-language programs encourage children to initiate and direct their own learning. They emphasize open-ended activities, in contrast with the more rigorous, teacher-directed tasks involved in phonics instruction. They use real literature in place of simplified "basal readers," which are said to be bland and boring.

Critics of the whole-language approach hold it largely responsible for the failure of an estimated 20 to 25 percent of schoolchildren to learn to read (Stedman & Kaestle, 1987). They claim that whole-language teaching encourages children to skim through a text, guessing at words and their meaning, and not to try to correct reading or spelling errors as long as the results "make sense." More fundamentally, these critics argue that reading is a skill which must almost always be taught. Children do not have an automatic biological mechanism for decoding the written word, as they seem to have for the spoken word. Therefore, "learning to read is . . . a cognitive . . . achievement in a way that learning to speak is not" (Liberman & Liberman, 1990, p. 52).

Despite the current popularity of the whole-language approach, reviews of the literature have found little support for its claims (Stahl, McKenna, & Pagnucco, 1994; Stahl & Miller, 1989). This may in part reflect the use of standardized achievement tests, which do not readily capture the kinds of skills taught in whole-language classes. Recently, there has been a shift away from measuring the method's effects on achievement and toward measuring its effects on attitudes toward reading (which also are not clear-cut).

Contrary to its stated aims, whole-language teaching seems to do better in developing word recognition than comprehension; however, traditional programs that stress decoding do an even better job of teaching that skill. Whole-language approaches seem to be more effective in kindergarten or first-grade reading readiness programs, which lay a conceptual foundation for reading and for the forms and functions of print, than in formal first-grade reading instruction.

A long line of research supports the view that phonological *awareness*—the knowledge that words are made up of separate sounds, or *phonemes*—and early phonics training are keys to reading proficiency (Hatcher, Hulme, & Ellis, 1994; Liberman & Liberman, 1990). One phonological ability that has been shown to predict later reading scores is recognition of words that have the same beginning sounds (alliteration) or ending sounds (rhyme).

In a well-known experiment in England (L. Bradley & Bryant, 1983, 1985), 4- and 5-year-olds who had tested poorly on alliteration and rhyme were trained not only in these skills but also in how letters "spell out" sounds. After 2 years of training, these children were 8 to 10 months ahead of a group that had been trained to categorize pictures and words by meaning, and they were also several months ahead of a third group trained only in alliteration and rhyme. A later longitudinal study of 7-year-olds who were having reading problems also concluded that phonological training is most effective when linked to reading and spelling skills (Hatcher et al., 1994).

The whole-language approach has made some important contributions to the teaching of reading. Open-ended, student-initiated activities seem to increase motivation, persistence, and willingness to risk being wrong. The use of high-quality literature in place of basal readers "continually remind[s] students of *why* they are learning to read" (Stahl et al., 1994, p. 182). But the whole-language philosophy should not be misinterpreted as giving children completely free rein. Challenge is fundamental to learning; indeed, the degree to which lessons challenge a child may be a better predictor of achievement than the teacher's philosophy of education (Stahl et al., 1994).

Some experts today seek to combine the best of both approaches by teaching children phonetic skills along with strategies to help them understand and interpret what they read. One example is Reading Recovery, a program for first-graders who are not making satisfactory progress. Like whole-language instruction, Reading Recovery uses only whole books, teaches skills and strategies through reading and writing rather than in isolation, and encourages children to develop a flexible repertoire of strategies rather than focus on only one (such as phonics). Unlike whole-language programs, the teacher, not the student, decides what books are to be read and what strategies need to be taught, and there is a stronger emphasis on mastery and achievement (Stahl et al., 1994). Especially when combined with phonetic instruction, Reading Recovery has enabled many at-risk students to catch up with their classmates (Pressley, 1994).

Other promising programs develop interpretive strategies in the context of group literary discussion. Teachers model effective strategies (such as making associations with prior knowledge, summarizing, visualizing relationships, and making predictions) and coach students on how to select and use them. After a year in one such program, low-achieving second-graders did significantly better on standardized measures of comprehension than a control group (R. Brown & Pressley, 1994; R. Brown, Pressley, Schuder, & Van Meter, 1994).

These Inupiat (Eskimo) children in Kotzebue, Alaska, are learning in their native language, Inupiaq, as well as in English, so as to preserve their cultural heritage. Although bilingual education is controversial, research suggests that knowing one language does not interfere with learning a second language, nor does learning a second language rob a child of fluency in the first. Bilingual children usually can switch readily from one language to the other.

progress faster academically in their native language and later make a smoother transition to all-English classrooms (Padilla et al., 1991). Some educators maintain that the English-only approach stunts children's cognitive growth; because foreign-speaking children can understand only simple English at first, the curriculum must be watered down, and children are less prepared to handle complex material later (Collier, 1995).

Findings on the relative success of these approaches have been mixed. Furthermore, most studies have focused only on how well children learn English, not on how well they do in school and society (Hakuta & Garcia, 1989). Now, large-scale research on the long-term academic achievement of children in high-quality bilingual and immersion programs offers strong support for a bilingual approach (Collier, 1995; W. P. Thomas & Collier, 1995).

Researchers examined the elementary and high school records of 42,000 foreign-speaking students in five districts across the United States and compared their standardized achievement test scores and grade-point averages with those of native English-speakers. In the primary grades, the type of language teaching made little difference; but from seventh grade on, differences were dramatic. Children who had remained in bilingual programs at least through sixth grade caught up with or even surpassed their native English-speaking peers, while the relative performance of those who had been in traditional immersion programs began to decline. By the end of high school, those in part-time ESL programs—the least successful type—scored lower than 80 percent of native English-speakers their age.

Most successful was the less common two-way, or dual-language, approach, in which English-speaking and foreign-speaking children learn together in their own and each other's languages. This approach avoids stigmatizing minority children by placement in segregated classes. Instead, by valuing both languages equally, it helps build self-esteem and thus improve school performance. An added advantage is that English-speakers learn a foreign language at an early age, when they can acquire it most easily (Collier, 1995; W. P. Thomas & Collier, 1995).

These findings echo earlier ones: the more bilingually proficient children are, the higher their cognitive achievement—as long as school personnel value bilingualism and the second language is added at no sacrifice to the first (Diaz, 1983;

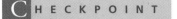

code switching Process of changing one's speech to match the situation, as with people who are bilingual.

CHECKPOINT

Can you . . .

- Describe and evaluate various types of second-language education?

- Assess the value of bilingualism?

Padilla et al., 1991). Knowing one language does not interfere with learning a second, and learning the second does not rob a child of fluency in the first (Hakuta, Ferdman, & Diaz, 1987; Hakuta & Garcia, 1989). Bilingual children usually switch easily from one language to the other (Zentella, 1981). *Code switching*—changing speech to match the situation—seems to come naturally to children; they learn very early, for example, to talk differently to parents than to friends. Also, bilingual children may learn to read earlier than children with only one language, because they better understand the symbolic nature of words (Bialystok, 1997). When bilingualism rises to the level of *biliteracy* (proficiency in reading and writing two languages), which makes possible full participation in both cultures, we see the most positive effects (Huang, 1995).

Influences on School Achievement

Children's school experience affects and is affected by every aspect of their development—cognitive, physical, emotional, and social. In addition to children's own characteristics, each level of the context of their lives, from the immediate family to what goes on in the classroom to the messages they receive from the larger culture (such as "It's not cool to be smart"), influences how well they do in school. Let's look at this "nest" of influences.

The Child

Most children, by the time they start school, have developed an impressive array of abilities that help them succeed. They can devise and use strategies to learn, remember, and solve problems. They can use language to show what they know, to ask and answer questions, to discuss ideas, and to seek help. They also become increasingly able to allocate time and take responsibility for doing assignments. Some children, of course, are better prepared for school than others. Differences in cognitive ability are important, but temperamental, attitudinal, and emotional factors also affect children's adjustment to school and their ability to apply themselves.

It isn't every day that a child gets a chance to see and touch a skull! Children who show curiosity, interest, attention, and active participation tend to do well in school.

Does a "teacher's pet" make better academic progress than a fidgety child who throws tantrums, cannot sit still, and has a short attention span? To find out, researchers followed 790 first-graders with a range of ethnic, racial, and economic backgrounds through fourth grade (K. L. Alexander, Entwisle, & Dauber, 1993). Children whose teachers rated them as cooperative and compliant were no more likely to get high scores on achievement tests or high marks in reading and math than children whose teachers rated them lower on those qualities. However, interest, attention, and active participation *were* associated with achievement test scores and, even more so, with teachers' marks. Furthermore, these influences carried over from first grade to later years.

Apparently, to make the most academic progress, a child need not be polite and helpful but does need to be involved in what is going on in class. A child who tries hard, pays attention, and participates eagerly tends to make a good impression on the teacher and is more likely to get high marks. A good report card, in turn, reinforces positive behavior and effort. Since patterns of classroom behavior seem to be set in first grade, this first year of formal schooling offers a "window of opportunity" for parents and teachers to help a child form good learning habits.

The Family

A small but growing number of parents—estimated at 500,000 to 1 million—school their children at home. These parents tend to be better educated than average and better off financially, and to have larger families; 3 out of 4 go to religious services every week, and 9 out of 10 are of white Anglo-Saxon extraction (Menendez, 1995).

Parents need not be their children's teachers in order to influence their education. Parents of achieving children provide a place to study and to keep books and supplies; they set and insist on times for meals, sleep, and homework; they monitor how much television their children watch and what their children do after school; and they show interest in their children's lives at school by talking about school events and about the children's problems and successes (U.S. Department of Education, 1986) and by being involved in school activities (D. L. Stevenson & Baker, 1987). Parents also influence achievement through the ways they motivate children and the attitudes they transmit, which may in turn be influenced by culture and socioeconomic status.

How do parents motivate children to do well? Some use *extrinsic* (external) means—giving children money or treats for good grades or punishing them for bad ones. Others encourage children to develop their own *intrinsic* (internal) motivation by praising them for ability and hard work. Intrinsic motivation seems more effective. In fact, some educators claim that even praise should be used cautiously, as it can shift the focus from the child's own motivation to the need to please others (Aldort, 1994). In a study of 77 third- and fourth-graders, those who were interested in the work itself did better in school than those who mainly sought grades or parents' approval (Miserandino, 1996).

Parenting styles may affect motivation. In one study, the highest achieving fifth-graders had *authoritative* parents (see Chapter 10). These children were curious and interested in learning; they liked challenging tasks and enjoyed solving problems by themselves. *Authoritarian* parents, who reminded children to do their homework, supervised closely, and relied on extrinsic motivation, tended to have lower-achieving children. Perhaps such external control undermines children's ability to trust their own judgment about what they need to do to achieve success. Children of *permissive* parents, who were uninvolved and did not seem to care how the children did in school, also tended to be low achievers (G. S. Ginsburg & Bronstein, 1993).

Since this was a correlational study, we cannot draw firm conclusions about the direction of causation. Parents of poor achievers may resort to bribes and threats and may feel obliged to make sure homework gets done, while parents of children who are motivated and successful may not feel the need to offer rewards or punishments or to take such an active supervisory role.

Parental Attitudes and Beliefs

Children are affected not only by what parents do but by what they think. In the study just described (G. S. Ginsburg & Bronstein, 1993), parents who assumed that outside forces were responsible for their fate—and who presumably communicated that belief to their children—had children who were less self-reliant, less self-motivated, less persistent, and less successful in their schoolwork.

Some beliefs come down via cultural routes. A California survey related parents' beliefs about child rearing, intelligence, and education to children's school performance (Okagaki & Sternberg, 1993). Of the 359 parents, some were immigrants from Mexico, Cambodia, Vietnam, and the Philippines; others were native-born Mexican Americans or Anglo Americans. Anglo American parents rated cognitive abilities (such as verbal ability, problem-solving skills, and creativity) as the most important factors in intelligence; the other groups held noncognitive elements to be equally or more important. Filipino and Vietnamese parents ranked motivation and hard work especially high; Latino parents emphasized social skills.

The one belief most clearly related to educational outcomes was approval of conformity to external standards. This value was rated low by U.S.-born parents (who tend to value autonomy and creativity) but high by immigrants (who may consider it important in adapting to a new culture). Children of parents who valued conformity did not do as well in U.S. schools as other children. Understanding the cultural sources of parents' beliefs may help teachers deal with students growing up in two different cultures at home and at school.

Socioeconomic Status

Socioeconomic status can have a major, lasting influence on school achievement. When 1,253 second- through fourth-graders were followed for 2 to 4 years, those from low-income families tended to have lower reading and math achievement test scores, and the income gap in math achievement widened as time went on. Regardless of income, African American children tended to do worse than white children. This finding may reflect the fact that their parents had lower-prestige occupations, and therefore lower socioeconomic status, than white parents with similar incomes. It may also reflect the stress of coping with racial prejudice (Pungello, Kupersmidt, Burchinal, & Patterson, 1996).

Apparently, socioeconomic status in itself does not determine school achievement; the difference comes from its effects on family life. In a study of 90 rural African American families with firstborn children ages 9 to 12, parents with more education were likely to have higher incomes and to be more involved in the child's schooling. Higher-income families also tended to be more supportive and harmonious. Children growing up in a positive family atmosphere, whose mothers were involved in their schooling, tended to develop better self-regulation and to do better in school (G. H. Brody, Stoneman, & Flor, 1995).

A longitudinal study of low-income African American children who had attended the Perry Preschool (discussed in Chapters 9 and 16) found that some did much better in school—and in adult life—than others. An important factor in the success of the higher-achieving children was the positive influence of parents who placed a high value on education and helped them overcome obstacles to obtaining it. Children who, in kindergarten, had higher IQs and whom teachers rated as more motivated to learn tended to have mothers who had completed more years of schooling and who were more cooperative with the teacher and more involved. These children did better on achievement tests in the first and eighth grades, spent more time on homework at age 15 than less successful students, and were more likely to finish high school. Parents' expectations for their children also seemed to play a role, though it is hard to know whether children did well because their parents expected them to achieve or whether parents expected more of children who showed the potential to succeed (Luster & McAdoo, 1996).

The Educational System

How can school best enhance children's development? Conflicting views, along with historical events, have brought great swings in educational theory and practice during the twentieth century. The traditional curriculum, centered on the "three R's" (reading, 'riting, and 'rithmetic), gave way first to "child-centered" methods that focused on children's interests and then, during the late 1950s, to an emphasis on science and mathematics to overcome the Soviet Union's lead in the space race. During the turbulent 1960s and early 1970s, rigorous studies were replaced by student-directed learning, electives, and "open classrooms," in which children chose their own activities and teachers served as "facilitators." Then, a decline in high school students' scores on the Scholastic Aptitude Test (SAT) in the mid-1970s sent schools back to the "basics" (Ravitch, 1983). In the 1980s, a series of governmental and educational commissions proposed plans for improvement, ranging from more homework to a longer school day and school year to a total reorganization of schools and curricula.

Today, educators who question the "back-to-basics" approach recommend teaching children in the primary grades in a way that integrates subject matter fields and builds on children's natural interests and talents: teaching reading and writing, for example, in the context of a social studies project or teaching math concepts through the study of music. They favor cooperative projects, hands-on experience, use of concrete materials to solve problems, and close parent-teacher cooperation (Rescorla, 1991).

Many contemporary educators emphasize a "fourth R": reasoning. Children who are taught thinking skills in the context of academic subject matter perform better on intelligence tests and in school (R. D. Feldman, 1986; Sternberg, 1984, 1985a, 1985b). Everyday activities also can be routes to enhancing thinking skills (see Table 12-6). Research on Sternberg's triarchic theory suggests that students learn better when taught in a variety of ways, emphasizing creative and practical skills as well as memorization and critical thinking (Sternberg, Torff, & Grigorenko, 1997, cited in Sternberg, 1997).

Computer literacy and the ability to navigate the World Wide Web are becoming classroom "musts," opening new possibilities for individualized instruction and early training in independent research skills. However, these new tools pose a danger of eclipsing the need for competency with the written word and of diverting financial resources from other areas of the curriculum. Nor does use of computers necessarily improve basic skills. In a major international math and science examination, fourth-graders from 7 other countries out of 26 significantly outperformed U.S. fourth-graders on the math section, and teachers in 5 of these countries reported that students never or almost never use computers in class (Mullis et al., 1997).

Some big-city school systems, such as New York's, Philadelphia's, and Chicago's, are experimenting with small elementary and high school programs, either freestanding or within larger school buildings—small enough for students,

Table 12-6	Everyday Ways to Enhance Children's Thinking Skills

- When reading to children, ask open-ended questions (beginning with what, why, and how).

- Help children find the most important points in what they read, see, or hear.

- Ask children to compare new information with what they already know. Identifying commonalities and differences can help children organize information, which helps them think as well as remember.

- Teach children not to accept a statement that contradicts common knowledge without reliable proof.

- Encourage children to write. Putting thoughts on paper forces them to organize their thoughts. Projects may include keeping a journal, writing a letter to a famous person, and presenting an argument to parents (say, for an increase in allowance or a special purchase or privilege).

- Encourage children to think imaginatively about what they have learned. ("How do you think the soldiers in the American Revolution felt at Valley Forge? What do you suppose they wore?")

- When writing a poem or drawing a picture, encourage children to produce a first version and then to polish or revise it.

- Show children how to approach a problem by identifying what they do and don't know about it, by designing a plan to solve it, by carrying out the plan, and then by deciding whether it has worked.

- Ask children to invent a new product, such as a gadget to ease a household chore.

- Teach children such skills as reading a map and using a microscope, and provide opportunities to practice them.

Sources: Marzano & Hutchins, 1987; Maxwell, 1987.

teachers, and parents to form a true learning community united by a common vision of good education. Teachers are usually handpicked and are given free rein to put their ideas into practice. The curriculum may have a special focus, such as ethnic studies. Teaching is flexible, innovative, and personalized; teachers work together more closely and get to know students better than in larger schools (Meier, 1995; R. Rossi, 1996). Results in some cases have been promising; in Central Park East, a complex of four small, ethnically diverse elementary and secondary schools in New York's East Harlem, 90 percent of the students finish high school and 9 out of 10 of those go on to college, as compared with an average citywide graduation rate of 50 percent (Meier, 1995).

The Culture

When a minority culture values behavioral styles different from those valued by the majority culture, minority children may be at a disadvantage in school. In the past, these children were considered to be suffering from a cultural *deficit*. Today many educators refer to cultural *difference*, with its own cognitive and behavioral strengths (Helms, 1992; Tharp, 1989).

The Kamehameha Early Education Program (KEEP) has produced dramatic improvements in primary-grade Hawaiian children's cognitive performance by designing educational programs to fit cultural patterns. Whereas children in non-KEEP classes score very low on standard achievement tests, children in KEEP classes approach national norms. To test KEEP's principles in a very different culture, a program was established on the Navajo reservation in northern Arizona. KEEP principles have also been applied to, or suggested for, other minorities.

To help teachers teach in a way that helps children learn, KEEP addresses the following issues:

- *Social organization of the classroom:* Since Hawaiian culture values collaboration, cooperation, and assisted performance, children are placed in small groups of four to five students, who continually teach and learn from one another. For Navajo children, who are trained in self-sufficiency and are separated by sex from about age 8, groupings are most effectively limited to two or three children of the same sex (Tharp, 1989).

- *Accommodation for language styles:* Hawaiians typically overlap one another's speech, a style of social involvement often interpreted by non-Hawaiian teachers as rude. By contrast, Navajos speak slowly, with frequent silent pauses. Non-Navajo teachers often interrupt, misinterpreting such pauses as signaling the end of a response. When teachers adjust their styles of speaking to their students', children participate more freely (Tharp, 1989).
- *Sensitivity to rhythms:* Both in speech and in movement, cultural groups maintain different tempos. When teachers adopt a rhythm children are familiar with, the children participate more in class and learn better. African American children and adults often interact in back-and-forth "challenge games" involving subtle nuances of meaning (J. Hale, 1982; Heath, 1989). Such patterns can be adapted to classroom teaching.
- *Adjustment for learning styles:* Most western teaching stresses verbal and analytic thought. This approach favors Japanese, Chinese, and white Americans, but not Native Americans, who tend to think in visual, holistic patterns and learn at home by imitation, with little verbal instruction. Contrary to typical American classroom practice, Native American parents expect children to listen to an entire story without interruption before discussing it. Teachers can help children by acknowledging culturally different learning styles and helping children adjust to an unfamiliar style (Tharp, 1989).

Educating for Special Needs and Strengths

Just as educators have become more sensitive to teaching children from varied cultural backgrounds, they have also sought to meet the needs of children with special abilities and disabilities.

Children with Learning Problems

Three of the most frequent sources of learning problems are mental retardation, attention deficit disorders, and learning disabilities.

Mental Retardation

Mental retardation is significantly subnormal intellectual functioning. It is indicated by an IQ of about 70 or less, coupled with a deficiency in age-appropriate adaptive behavior (such as communication, social skills, and self-care), appearing before age 18. About 1 percent of the population are mentally retarded; about 3 boys are affected for every 2 girls (American Psychiatric Association [APA], 1994).

In about 30 to 40 percent of cases, the cause of mental retardation is unknown. Known causes include problems in embryonic development, such as those caused by a mother's alcohol or drug use (30 percent); mental disorders, such as autism, and environmental influences, such as lack of nurturance (15 to 20 percent); problems in pregnancy and childbirth, such as fetal malnutrition or birth trauma (10 percent); hereditary conditions, such as Tay-Sachs disease (5 percent); and medical problems in childhood, such as trauma or lead poisoning (5 percent) (APA, 1994).

With a supportive and stimulating early environment and continued guidance and help, many mentally retarded children can expect a reasonably good outcome. Most mentally retarded children can benefit from schooling.

CHECKPOINT

Can you . . .

- Identify temperamental or attitudinal factors that contribute to school achievement?
- Identify parental beliefs and practices that influence school success?
- Discuss how socioeconomic status influences school achievement?
- Trace major changes in educational philosophy and practice during the twentieth century?
- Identify some ways of addressing cultural differences in the classroom?

mental retardation
Significantly subnormal cognitive functioning.

Hyperactivity and Attention Deficits

Attention-deficit/hyperactivity disorder (ADHD) is the psychiatric condition most commonly diagnosed in children ("Attention Deficit Disorder—Part II," 1995). It is marked by persistent inattention, impulsivity, low tolerance for frustration, distractibility, and a great deal of activity at the wrong time and the wrong place, such as the classroom. These characteristics appear to some degree in all children; but in about 3 to 5 percent of school-age children, they are so frequent and severe as to interfere with the child's functioning in school and in daily life (American Academy of Pediatrics [AAP] Committee on Children with Disabilities and Committee on Drugs, 1996; APA, 1994). Although some symptoms appear earlier, the disorder is often not recognized until the child starts school. However, a new test using computer measures of body movement and attention seems to be a reliable, objective indicator (Teicher, Ito, Glod, & Barber, 1996). Boys are 4 to 9 times as likely to be diagnosed as girls (APA, 1994), perhaps because girls' behavior may be less disruptive. More than 1 out of 4 learning-disabled children has ADHD (Roush, 1995; Zametkin, 1995).

ADHD seems to be at least partly inherited (APA, 1994; Zametkin, 1995). It is now believed to be caused by an irregularity in brain functioning in the region that inhibits impulses (Rosen, 1996). Family conflict may compound the problem ("Attention Deficit Disorder—Part II," 1995). Research has failed to substantiate any link between ADHD and food additives, such as artificial colorings and flavorings and the sugar substitute aspartame (B. A. Shaywitz et al., 1994; Zametkin, 1995).

If untreated, ADHD can lead to extreme frustration, alienation, failure in school, antisocial behavior, or substance abuse (Zametkin, 1995). By age 15 most hyperactive children continue to show poor cognitive skills and disruptive behavior (McGee, Partridge, Williams, & Silva, 1991). As adults, many have high rates of job changes, marital disruption, traffic accidents, and trouble with the law (Henker & Whalen, 1989).

ADHD is generally treated with drugs, combined with behavioral modification (see Chapter 1), counseling, and proper classroom placement. In about 70 to 80 percent of cases, stimulants such as Ritalin can help children concentrate and reduce antisocial behavior, but they do not seem to improve long-range academic achievement (AAP Committee on Children with Disabilities and Committee on Drugs, 1996; McDaniel, 1986; "Ritalin Improves Behavior," 1995; Zametkin, 1995).

Learning Disabilities

Nelson Rockefeller, former vice president of the United States, had so much trouble reading that he ad-libbed speeches instead of using a script. The inventor Thomas Edison never learned how to spell or write grammatically. General George Patton, a World War II hero, read poorly and got through West Point by memorizing entire lectures (Schulman, 1986). The actress Whoopi Goldberg had trouble learning to read. All these people apparently suffered from *dyslexia,* a developmental reading disorder in which reading achievement is at least 2 years below the level predicted by IQ.

Dyslexia is the most commonly diagnosed of a large number of *learning disabilities (LDs),* disorders that interfere with specific aspects of school achievement, resulting in performance substantially lower than would be expected given a child's age, intelligence, and amount of schooling (APA, 1994). A growing number of children are identified as learning-disabled—2.3 million in the 1992-1993 school year (Roush, 1995). Learning-disabled (LD) children often have near-average to higher-than-average intelligence and normal vision and hearing, but they seem to have trouble processing sensory information. They tend to be less

attention-deficit/hyperactivity disorder (ADHD) Syndrome characterized by persistent inattention, impulsivity, low tolerance for frustration, distractibility, and considerable activity at inappropriate times and places.

dyslexia Developmental disorder in learning to read.

learning disabilities (LDs) Disorders that interfere with specific aspects of learning and school achievement.

Children with dyslexia have trouble reading and writing, and often doing arithmetic, because they may confuse up and down and left and right. Dyslexia may be part of a more general language impairment.

task-oriented and more easily distracted than other children; they are less well-organized as learners and less likely to use memory strategies (Feagans, 1983). Because success in school is important for self-esteem, learning disabilities can have devastating effects on the psyche as well as on the report card.

Estimates of the prevalence of dyslexia range from 3 to 20 percent of the school population. There is disagreement about its definition and causes; some observers claim that what looks like dyslexia is often the result of poor teaching. Dyslexia is believed to affect boys and girls equally. It is more common in children from large families and in lower socioeconomic levels and may be at least partly genetic (Barinaga, 1996a; Council on Scientific Affairs of the American Medical Association, 1989; DeFries, Fulker, & LaBuda, 1987; M. D. Levine, 1987; Roush, 1995; S. E. Shaywitz, Shaywitz, Fletcher, & Escobar, 1990; Tallal et al., 1996; Tashman, 1995).

Dyslexia may be part of a generalized language impairment ("Dyslexia," 1989; Tallal et al., 1996). Language-impaired children are late in starting to talk, have trouble understanding what people say, speak and write unclearly, and have limited memory for verbal material. Some researchers have found subtle variations in brain structure and activity in language-impaired people, but it is not clear what role these differences may play or whether they are the causes or the effects of early learning problems (Hynd & Semrud-Clikeman, 1989; Merzenich et al., 1996; Roush, 1995). Some language-impaired children seem unable to hear subtle differences between sounds such as "da" and "ga" (Barinaga, 1996b; Kraus et al., 1996). A training technique in which short consonant sounds are stretched out and accentuated may help children who have trouble hearing brief consonant sounds, such as "ba" in "banana" (Merzenich et al., 1996; Tallal et al., 1996).

Mathematical disabilities may be even more common than reading disabilities, with which they are often associated. Math disabilities involve difficulty in counting, comparing numbers, calculating, and remembering basic arithmetic facts. One cause may be a neurological deficit, which may be partly inherited. Some children, however, have problems with arithmetic because they haven't learned it properly, because they are anxious or have trouble reading or hearing directions, or because of a developmental delay, which eventually disappears (Geary, 1993; Roush, 1995). Other learning disorders affect different aspects of

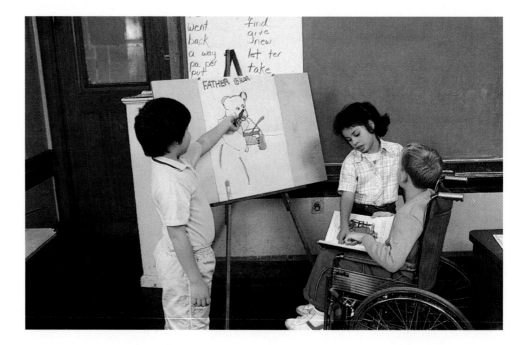

Under federal law, children with disabilities must be educated in the "least restrictive environment" that can meet their needs. This boy in a wheelchair may learn academic subjects in a regular classroom but may receive special physical training while his classmates go to gym.

learning. For example, poor coordination of fine motor movements can interfere with the ability to write.

Children generally do not outgrow learning disabilities but can learn to cope with them.

Educating Children with Disabilities

The Individuals with Disabilities Education Act (IDEA) assures a free, appropriate public education for all children with disabilities in the United States. More than half (51 percent) of covered children are learning-disabled, 22 percent are speech-impaired, 11 percent are mentally retarded, and 9 percent have serious emotional disturbances (D. L. Terman, Larner, Stevenson, & Behrman, 1996).

Under the law, an individualized program must be designed for each child, with parental involvement. Children must be educated in the "least restrictive environment" appropriate to their needs: that means, whenever possible, the regular classroom. Many of these students can be served by "inclusion" programs, in which they are integrated with nondisabled youngsters for all or part of the day. Inclusion can help children with disabilities learn to get along in society and can let nondisabled children know and understand people with disabilities.

Gifted, Creative, and Talented Children

Giftedness, like intelligence, is hard to define and measure. Educators disagree on who qualifies as gifted and on what basis, and what kinds of educational programs these children need. Another source of confusion is that creativity and artistic talent are sometimes viewed as aspects or types of giftedness and sometimes as independent of it (Hunsaker & Callahan, 1995).

Identifying Gifted Children

The way we define giftedness is important because it often determines who is identified for special treatment. The traditional criterion of giftedness is an IQ score of 130 or higher (Horowitz & O'Brien, 1986). This criterion tends to exclude

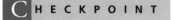

C HECKPOINT

Can you . . .

- Describe the causes and prognoses for three common conditions that interfere with learning?

- Summarize federal requirements for the education of children with disabilities?

Mahito Takahashi of New Jersey made a perfect score in a worldwide mathematics Olympiad and has won close to 200 other awards. A well-rounded youngster, he sings in a chamber choir and acted in a school production of Shakespeare's *Romeo and Juliet.* The key to helping such children achieve lies in recognizing and nurturing their natural gifts.

highly creative children (whose unusual answers often lower their test scores), children from minority groups (whose abilities may not be well developed, though the potential is there), and children with aptitudes in specific areas.

During the early 1970s a congressional commission proposed a broader criterion: "Gifted and talented children are those, identified by professionally qualified persons, who by virtue of outstanding abilities are capable of high performance" (Marland, 1972, p. 2). Most states and school districts have adopted this definition (Cassidy & Hossler, 1992). It includes children who have shown high *potential* or *achievement* in one or more of the following areas: general intellect, specific aptitude (such as in mathematics or science), creative or productive thinking, leadership, talent in the arts (such as painting, writing, or acting), and psychomotor ability.

Two ways of looking at giftedness stem from new theories of intelligence discussed earlier in this chapter. According to Howard Gardner's (1983) theory of multiple intelligences, a child may be gifted in one or more of at least seven separate "intelligences," each relatively independent of the others. (Akira Kurosawa's uneven school performance offers anecdotal evidence of this.) According to Robert Sternberg (1985a; J. E. Davidson & Sternberg, 1984), gifted children are distinguished by the ability to process information with unusual efficiency, especially on novel (creative) tasks requiring insight. In research using the Sternberg's Triarchic Abilities Test, students who tested high in creative or practical abilities were more ethnically and socioeconomically diverse than those who tested high in the analytical abilities measured by standard IQ tests, suggesting that IQ tests may fail to identify many promising minority students (Sternberg, 1997).

The Lives of Gifted Children

A classic longitudinal study of gifted children began in the 1920s, when Lewis Terman (who brought the Binet intelligence test to the United States) identified more than 1,500 California children with IQs of 135 or higher. The study demolished the widespread stereotype of the bright child as a puny, pasty-faced bookworm. These children were taller, healthier, better-coordinated, better-adjusted, and more popular than the average child (Wallach & Kogan, 1965), and their cognitive, scholastic, and vocational superiority has held up for more than 70 years. They were 10 times more likely than a comparison group to graduate from college and 3 times more likely to be elected to honorary societies such as Phi Beta Kappa. By midlife, they were highly represented in such listings as *Who's Who in America.* Almost 90 percent of the men were in the professions or in higher echelons of business, and the women also made a good showing at a time when there was far less emphasis on women's careers (L. M. Terman & Oden, 1959).

The lives of these people show that intelligence tests can spot children with promise and that cognitively gifted children tend to fulfill that promise. However, there were some methodological problems with Terman's study. For one, the sample was not representative of the United States population at large. All the participants were Californians, most came from relatively advantaged homes, Jewish children were overrepresented, and African American and Asian American children were underrepresented.

Later research found that cognitively gifted children tend to be relatively mature in social relationships and moral reasoning (though not always in behavior). On the whole, they show average or superior adjustment in their self-concept and in the way they handle their lives and get along with others. However, two groups of gifted children tend to have social and emotional problems: those with IQs over 180 and those with high IQs who do not do well in school. The problems of both groups seem to stem in part from unsatisfactory schooling: inflexibility, overemphasis on grades, lack of challenge, and unsupportive teachers (Janos & Robinson, 1985). Many bright children try to hide their intelligence to fit in with their classmates (R. D. Feldman, 1982).

Children identified as gifted tend to have well-educated, well-to-do, emotionally supportive, happily married parents who spend time with them, answer their questions, and encourage their curiosity. The homes of underachieving gifted children are often less harmonious (Janos & Robinson, 1985).

Defining, Measuring, and Fostering Creativity

The unusually bright people in the Terman study did not show signs of unusual creativity: the group did not produce a great musician, an exceptional painter, or a Nobel prize winner. Other classic research, too, found only modest correlations between creativity and IQ (Anastasi & Schaefer, 1971; Getzels, 1964, 1984; Getzels & Jackson, 1962, 1963), suggesting that creative thinking requires different abilities from those needed to do well in school (Renzulli & McGreevy, 1984).

creativity Ability to see things in a new light, resulting in a novel product, the identification of a previously unrecognized problem, or the formulation of new and unusual solutions.

convergent thinking Thinking aimed at finding the one "right" answer to a problem. Compare *divergent thinking.*

divergent thinking Thinking that produces a variety of fresh, diverse possibilities. Compare *convergent thinking.*

One definition of *creativity* is the ability to see things in a new light—to produce something never seen before or to discern problems others fail to recognize and find new and unusual solutions. IQ tests measure *convergent thinking,* the ability to give a single correct answer. Tests of creativity seek to measure *divergent thinking,* the ability to come up with a wide array of novel possibilities (Guilford, 1967).

The Torrance Tests of Creative Thinking (Torrance, 1966, 1974; Torrance & Ball, 1984), for example, include such tasks as listing unusual uses for a paper clip, thinking of ways to improve a toy, drawing a picture beginning with a few lines, and telling what such words as *crunch* and *pop* bring to mind. One problem with these tests is that the score depends partly on speed, which is not a hallmark of creativity. Moreover, although the tests are fairly *reliable* (they yield consistent results), there is little evidence that they are *valid*—that children who do well on them are creative in everyday life (Anastasi, 1988; Mansfield & Busse, 1981; Simonton, 1990). Divergent thinking may not be the only, or even the most important, factor in creativity. More research needs to be done to identify youngsters who will become creative adults.

Recognizing and Encouraging Talented Children

What do famous pianists, sculptors, athletes, mathematicians, and neurologists have in common? According to a Chicago study, success in all these fields depends on inborn talent, encouragement of that talent, and the drive to excel (Bloom, 1985).

First, talent has to be recognized. Most high achievers became intensely involved in their fields before age 10 to 12. Commonly, a parent or other relative talented in the same area recognized and encouraged the child's talent at an early age. Second, talent must be nurtured. Often the child's first teacher in the special field emphasized joy and playfulness. The child fell in love with the field and, even after discovering how demanding it was, wanted to master its discipline. Finally, the talented child must want to excel. The joys and rewards of the labor must seem full payment for its rigors.

The researchers recommended that teachers who give rigorous training take a "longitudinal" approach, getting to know children well, staying with them over several years, and emphasizing long-term goals and progress. Talented children also benefit from regular participation in public recitals or contests that provide short-term goals and benchmarks of progress. When children perform well, praise and rewards inspire them to persist in their efforts; when they do poorly, they may be spurred to try to do better the next time.

Educating Gifted, Creative, and Talented Children

How should gifted, creative, and talented children be educated? Do they need special programs? If so, what kinds, and how should participants be chosen?

In the United States, the achievement of the most promising students lags behind that in other technologically advanced countries (Feldhusen & Moon, 1992). Most states have officially recognized programs for the gifted and talented, but the economic recession of the early 1990s resulted in cutbacks in many communities (Purcell, 1995).

Programs for highly able learners take two main approaches: *enrichment* and *acceleration*. **Enrichment** broadens and deepens knowledge and skills through extra classroom activities, research projects, field trips, or coaching by mentors (experts in a child's field of talent or interest). **Acceleration,** often recommended for highly gifted children, speeds up their education, moving them through the curriculum quickly. This may be done by skipping grades, by placement in fast-paced classes or special schools, or by advanced classes in specific subjects, taken by correspondence or at a nearby high school, college, or university.

Many school districts use multiple criteria for admission to programs for the gifted, including achievement test scores, grades, classroom performance, creative production, parent and teacher nominations, and student interviews; but IQ remains an important, and sometimes the determining, factor (S. M. Reis, 1989). Some educators advocate moving away from an all-or-nothing definition of giftedness and including a wider range of students in flexible programs to develop a variety of academic and nonacademic talents (J. Cox, Daniel, & Boston, 1985; Feldhusen, 1992; R. D. Feldman, 1985).

African Americans are underrepresented in most programs for the gifted; about 1 out of 6 students in public schools, but only about 1 out of 12 participants in gifted programs, are black (U.S. Department of Education, 1993). One study in a mostly low-income all-black urban Ohio community (D. Y. Ford & Harris, 1996) explored how the perceptions and attitudes of fifth- and sixth-graders in a gifted program differed from the perceptions and attitudes of fifth- and sixth-grade schoolmates in regular classes and in an alternative program for the "potentially gifted." (Children identified as potentially gifted did better in school than on standardized tests. They were insightful, creative, and inquisitive and showed a need for more challenge than the regular curriculum provided.)

enrichment Approach to educating the gifted, which broadens and deepens knowledge and skills through extra activities, projects, field trips, or mentoring.

acceleration Approach to educating the gifted, which moves them through the entire curriculum, or part of it, at an unusually rapid pace.

CHECKPOINT

Can you . . .

- Explain why the definition of *giftedness* is important, and compare various definitions?

- State the relationship between IQ and creativity?

- Describe how creativity is measured, and evaluate the effectiveness of such instruments?

- Discuss issues concerning education of gifted, creative, and talented children?

When questioned, students identified as gifted appeared to be the most achievement-oriented and also saw their parents that way. There may well have been a bidirectional influence: children from achievement-oriented families may have had a better chance of qualifying for the gifted program, which then reinforced their efforts to achieve.

The greatest differences were between the students in regular classes and in the other two groups. Although nearly all the children acknowledged the importance of doing well in school, many "regular" students admitted not working up to capacity—in part, perhaps, because they found the curriculum uninteresting and claimed that their teachers (most of whom were white) did not understand them. "Regular" students also were more affected by negative peer pressure (such as calling gifted students "nerds" or saying they "acted white"). Gifted and potentially gifted students, because they were in full-time classes with others of like ability, were insulated from those pressures.

This study, though not representative of the national school population, exemplifies a fundamental educational dilemma. Children in gifted programs not only make academic gains but also tend to improve in self-concept and social adjustment (D. Y. Ford & Harris, 1996). For students left behind in regular classes, though, the lack of high-achieving classmates may reinforce a failure mentality. In the coming years, our nation will continue to grapple with how best to educate its most promising children while not shortchanging other children.

There is no firm dividing line between being gifted and not being gifted, creative and not creative, talented and not talented. All children benefit from being encouraged in their areas of interest and ability. What we learn about fostering intelligence, creativity, and talent in the most able youngsters may help all children make the most of their potential. The degree to which they do this will affect their self-concept and other aspects of personality, as we discuss in Chapter 13.

SUMMARY

Piagetian Approach: The Concrete Operational Child

- According to Piaget, a child from about age 7 to age 12 is in the stage of **concrete operations.** Children are less egocentric than before and are more proficient at tasks requiring logical reasoning, such as distinguishing fantasy from reality, classification (including **class inclusion**), **deduction** and **induction,** making judgments about cause and effect, **seriation, transitive inference,** spatial thinking, **conservation,** and working with numbers. However, their reasoning is largely limited to the here and now. The concreteness of their thinking results in **horizontal décalage,** uneven development of related skills.

- According to Piaget, moral development is linked with cognitive maturation and occurs in two stages. The first, **morality of constraint,** is characterized by rigidity. The second, **morality of cooperation,** is characterized by flexibility.

Information-Processing Approach: Development of Memory and Other Processing Skills

- Information-processing research suggests that the cognitive advances Piaget described result from gains in knowledge and in speed and efficiency of processing. Case's theory of central conceptual structures attempts to combine elements of Piagetian theory with findings of information-processing research.

- Memory improves greatly during middle childhood. Short-term memory capacity increases. The **central executive,** which controls the flow of information between **working memory** and **long-term memory,** seems to mature around age 9. **Metamemory** also improves, and children become more adept at using **mnemonic strategies,** such as **external memory aids, rehearsal, organization,** and **elaboration.** Selective attention and concentration increase.

Psychometric Approach: Assessment of Intelligence

- The intelligence of school-age children is assessed by group tests (such as the **Otis-Lennon School Ability Test**) and individual tests (such as the **Wechsler Intelligence Scale for Children (WISC-III)**, Stanford-Binet, and **Kaufman Assessment Battery for Children (K-ABC)**. Although these are intended as **aptitude tests,** not **achievement tests,** they are validated against measures of achievement.

- IQ tests are good predictors of school success but may miss important aspects of intelligent behavior. IQ tests tap only three of the "intelligences" in Howard Gardner's **theory of multiple intelligences.** According to Robert Sternberg's **triarchic theory of intelligence,** IQ tests measure mainly the **componential element** of intelligence, not the **experiential** and **contextual elements.** The **Sternberg Triarchic Abilities Test (STAT)** seeks to measure all three elements.

- Differences in IQ among ethnic groups appear to result primarily from environmental and cultural differences. Attempts to eliminate **cultural bias** by devising **culture-free** or **culture-fair** tests have not been successful.

Development of Language

- Children's understanding of increasingly complex syntax develops at least up to age 9, and **metacommunication** improves.

- Interaction with peers aids in the development of literacy.

- Many school districts have implemented programs of second-language education. Although some use an **English-immersion** approach, the most effective appear to be high-quality programs of **bilingual education. Code switching** enables **bilingual** children to use both languages in appropriate situations.

Influences on School Achievement

- Children's characteristics, such as temperament, attitudes, and emotional state, influence school performance.

- Parents influence children's learning by becoming involved in their schooling, motivating them to achieve, and transmitting beliefs about learning. The family's socioeconomic status and cultural background influence parental behavior and attitudes.

- The school system's educational philosophy affects learning. Minority children can benefit from educational programs adapted to their cultural styles.

Educating for Special Needs and Strengths

- Three frequent sources of learning problems are **mental retardation, attention-deficit/hyperactivity disorder (ADHD), and learning disabilities (LDs).**

- **Dyslexia** may be part of a general language impairment.

- In the United States, all children with disabilities are entitled to a free, appropriate education. Children must be educated in the least restrictive environment possible—which often means in the regular classroom.

- An IQ of 130 or higher is a common standard for identifying gifted children for special programs. Broader definitions of giftedness include **creativity,** artistic talent, and other attributes and rely on multiple criteria for identification. Tests of creativity attempt to measure **divergent thinking** rather than **convergent thinking.**

- Special educational programs for gifted, talented, and creative children stress **enrichment** or **acceleration.**

KEY TERMS

concrete operations (420)
class inclusion (421)
deduction (421)
induction (421)
seriation (422)
transitive inference (422)
conservation (424)
horizontal décalage (425)
morality of constraint (427)
morality of cooperation (427)
working memory (429)
central executive (429)
long-term memory (429)
metamemory (430)
mnemonic strategies (430)
external memory aids (430)
rehearsal (430)
organization (430)
elaboration (431)
aptitude tests (433)
achievement tests (433)
Otis-Lennon School Ability Test (434)
Wechsler Intelligence Scale for Children
   (WISC-III) (434)
Kaufman Assessment Battery for Children
   (K-ABC) (434)

theory of multiple intelligences (436)
triarchic theory of intelligence (437)
componential element (437)
experiential element (437)
contextual element (437)
Sternberg Triarchic Abilities Test
   (STAT) (438)
cultural bias (439)
culture-free (439)
culture-fair (439)
metacommunication (441)
English-immersion (443)
bilingual education (443)
bilingual (443)
code switching (446)
mental retardation (451)
attention-deficit/hyperactivity disorder
   (ADHD) (452)
dyslexia (452)
learning disabilities (LDs) (452)
creativity (456)
convergent thinking (456)
divergent thinking (456)
enrichment (457)
acceleration (457)

QUESTIONS FOR THOUGHT AND DISCUSSION

1. According to Piaget's theory of moral development, more mature moral judgments consider intent, not just the seriousness of the offense. Do you agree that intent is an important factor in morality? Should this hold true for adolescents and adults as well as for young children?

2. Select a mnemonic strategy and design a technique to train children how to use it. How would you assess the success of your teaching?

3. How would you define intelligence? How would you test your concept of intelligence? Would you use a traditional IQ test, a test such as the K-ABC, which incorporates scaffolding, or some other measure?

4. Which of Gardner's or Sternberg's types of intelligence are you strongest in? Did your education include a focus on any of these aspects? How might such teaching be integrated into a school curriculum?

5. Is intelligence related to how well a person adapts to the dominant culture, or should intelligence tests be designed to take a minority culture into account?

6. Which of the approaches to second-language education described in this chapter do you favor?

7. What do you consider the most important influence on school achievement?

8. Which approach to education do you favor for children in the primary grades: instruction in the "basics," or a more flexible, child-centered curriculum?

9. How would you define and assess giftedness? Creativity? Should schools actively seek out gifted, creative, and talented students and give them special learning opportunities? If so, what do you think would be the best approach for teaching them?

Psychosocial Development in Middle Childhood

Have you ever felt like nobody?
Just a tiny speck of air.
When everyone's around you,
And you are just not there.

Karen Crawford, age 9

Focus

Marian Anderson

The African American contralto Marian Anderson, had—in the words of the great Italian conductor Arturo Toscanini—a voice heard "once in a hundred years." She was also a pioneer in breaking racial barriers. Turned away by a music school in her hometown of Philadelphia, she studied voice privately and in 1925 won a national competition to sing with the New York Philharmonic. She performed in European capitals throughout the 1930s but was often forced to put up with second-class treatment at home. When she was refused the use of a concert hall in Washington, D.C., Eleanor Roosevelt—who was then First Lady—arranged for her to sing on the steps of the Lincoln Memorial. The unprecedented performance on Easter Sunday, 1939, drew 75,000 people and was broadcast to millions. Several weeks later, Marian Anderson was the first black singer to perform at the White House. But not until 1955, a year after the Supreme Court outlawed segregated public schools, did Anderson, at age 57, become the first person of her race to sing with New York's Metropolitan Opera.

A remarkable story lies behind this woman's "journey from a single rented room in South Philadelphia" (McKay, 1992, Preface, p. *xxx*). It is a story of nurturing family ties—bonds of mutual support, care, and concern that extended from generation to generation.

Marian Anderson was the eldest child of John and Annie Anderson. Two years after her birth, the family left their one-room apartment to move in with her father's parents and then, after two more baby girls came along, into a small rented house nearby. John Anderson supported his family by peddling coal and ice, among other jobs.

Marian's parents encouraged her love of singing. At the age of 6, she joined the junior choir at church. There she made a friend, Viola Johnson, who lived across the street from the Andersons. Within a year or two, they sang a duet together—Marian's first public performance. Two years later, Marian began singing with the senior choir, doing duets with her aunt, who also arranged for her to perform in a benefit concert.

At about this time, her father brought home a piano that had been sitting unused in his brother's house; she sat on his knee as she tried it out. When Marian decided she wanted a violin, she saved up the four-dollar price from money she earned running errands and scrubbing steps of neighbors' houses. Of course, there was no money for lessons.

When Marian was 10, her beloved father died, and the family again moved in with his parents, his sister, and her two daughters. Marian's grandfather had a steady job. Her grandmother took care of all the children, her aunt ran the house, and her mother contributed by cooking dinners, working as a cleaning woman, and taking in laundry, which Marian and her sister Alyce delivered.

Years later, the singer had vivid memories of her grandmother: "What she said was law. Everyone knew she was the boss, and if she wanted any of us at any time we came flying. . . . Grandmother loved children and always had scads of them living in her house. . . . [She] saw to it that we each had our little jobs to do. . . . [T]here may have been times when we were too much for Grandmother, but generally she knew how to keep us under control. And there were useful things for us to learn, . . . how to share a home with others, how to understand their ways and respect their rights and privileges" (Anderson, 1992, pp. 17-18).

But the most important influence in Marian Anderson's life was the counsel, example, and spiritual guidance of her hardworking, unfailingly supportive mother. Annie Anderson, who had been a teacher in her home state of Virginia, placed great importance on her children's schooling and saw to it that they didn't skimp on homework. Even when she was working full time, she cooked their dinner every night, and she taught Marian to sew her own clothes. "Not once can I recall. . . hearing Mother lift her voice to us in anger," Marian wrote. "When she corrected us she used a conversational tone. She could be firm, and we learned to respect her wishes" (Anderson, 1992, p. 92).

When Marian Anderson became a world-renowned concert artist, she often returned to her old neighborhood in Philadelphia. Her mother and sister Alyce shared a modest house, and the other sister, Ethel, lived next door with her son.

"It is the pleasantest thing in the world to go into that home and feel its happiness. . . ." the singer wrote. "They are all comfortable, and they cherish and protect one another. . . . I know that it warms [Mother] to have her grandson near her as he grows up, just as I think that when he gets to be a man, making his own life, he will have pleasant memories of his home and family" (1992, p. 93). In 1992, Marian Anderson—widowed, childless, and frail at age 95—went to live with that nephew, James DePriest, then music director of the Oregon Symphony. She died of a stroke at his home the following year.

The chief source of biographical material about Marian Anderson and her family is Anderson, 1992. Some details come from Heilbut, 1993; Kernan, 1993; "Marian Anderson, 1897–1993," 1993; "Marian Anderson Plans Move," 1992; "Song of Freedom," 1993; " 'Voice of Rights Struggle,' " 1993.

● ● ●

M arian Anderson "lived through momentous changes in America and the world" and in African American life (McKay, 1992, p. *xxiv*), but one thing that never changed was the strong, supportive network of relationships that sustained her and her family.

In less developed countries, children commonly grow up in multigenerational *extended-family households* (see Chapter 1), though that pattern is eroding due to modernization, industrialization, migration to urban centers, and the coming of western religions (N. M. Brown, 1990; M. Gorman, 1993). In the United States and other industrialized countries, the *nuclear family*—a two-generation family made up of parents and their growing children—is the usual household unit. But especially among minority families like Marian Anderson's, and especially in times of trouble, extended family members may live with each other. The kind of household a child lives in, and the web of relationships within that household, can have profound effects on psychosocial development in middle childhood, when children are developing a stronger sense of what it means to be responsible, contributing members, first of a family, and then of society.

In this chapter, we trace the rich and varied emotional and social lives of school-age children, and we look at personality changes that accompany physical and cognitive growth. We see how youngsters develop a more realistic concept of themselves and how they become more independent, self-reliant, and in control of their emotions. Through being with peers (like Marian Anderson's first friend, Viola Johnson) they make discoveries about their own attitudes, values, and skills. Still, as Marian Anderson's story shows, the family remains a vital influence. Children's lives are affected by parental employment, by the family's economic circumstances, and by its structure—whether it is a two-parent, single-parent, blended, or multigenerational family. Although most children are emotionally healthy, some suffer disorders; we look at several of these. We also describe resilient children, who emerge from the stresses of childhood healthier and stronger.

After reading this chapter, you should be able to answer and elaborate on such questions as these:

Preview Questions

- How do children develop a realistic self-concept?

- What are the sources of self-esteem?

- How do children grow in emotional control, social competence, and prosocial behavior?

- What is the impact on children of parents' work, divorce, and remarriage?

- How do siblings influence and get along with one another?

- What are the functions of the peer group?

- What influences popularity, and how do schoolchildren view friendship?

- What are some common childhood emotional disturbances, and how are they treated?

- What enables "resilient" children to withstand stress?

The Developing Self

The self-concept develops continuously from infancy on. The cognitive growth that takes place during middle childhood enables youngsters to develop more realistic and more complex concepts of themselves and of their self-worth. Children also grow in emotional understanding and control.

Representational Systems: A Neo-Piagetian View

"At school I'm feeling pretty smart in certain subjects, Language Arts and Social Studies," said 8-year-old Lisa. "I got A's in these subjects on my last report card and was really proud of myself. But I'm feeling really dumb in Arithmetic and Science, particularly when I see how well the other kids are doing. . . . I still like myself as a person, because Arithmetic and Science just aren't that important to me. How I look and how popular I am are more important" (Harter, 1993, p. 2).

Around age 7 or 8, children reach the third of the neo-Piagetian stages of self-concept development described in Chapter 10. Children now can form *representational systems:* broad, inclusive self-concepts that integrate different features of the self (Harter, 1993). Lisa no longer focuses on a single dimension of herself ("I am smart" or "I am popular" or "I am pretty") but on many. She has outgrown an all-or-nothing, black-or-white self-definition; she recognizes that she can be "smart" in certain subjects and "dumb" in others. Her self-descriptions are more balanced; she can verbalize her self-concept better, and she can weigh different aspects of it ("How I look and how popular I am are more important. . ."). She can compare her *real self* with her *ideal self* and can judge how well she measures up to social standards. All of these changes contribute to the development of self-esteem, her assessment of her personal worth ("I like myself as a person").

Self-Esteem

Children as young as 4 show that they possess a sense of self-worth, but judgments about the self become more realistic, more balanced, more comprehensive, and more clearly expressed in middle childhood. Self-esteem is an important component of the self-concept, linking cognitive, emotional, and social aspects of personality. Children with high self-esteem tend to be cheerful; those with low self-esteem tend to be depressed (Harter, 1990). A depressed mood can lower energy levels, which can affect how well a child does in school and elsewhere, leading to a downward spiral in self-esteem. Children with low self-esteem often retain a negative self-image long after childhood has been left behind.

Sources of Self-Esteem

Kendall has high self-esteem. He is confident, curious, and independent. He trusts his own ideas, approaches challenges and initiates new activities with confidence, describes himself positively, and takes pride in his work. He adjusts fairly easily to change, tolerates frustration, perseveres in pursuing a goal, and can handle criticism. Kerry, by contrast, has low self-esteem. He describes himself negatively, does not trust his own ideas, lacks confidence and pride in his work, sits apart from other children, and hangs back and watches instead of exploring on his own. He gives up easily when frustrated and reacts immaturely to stress.

What accounts for the striking difference between these two boys? Why does one have such positive feelings about himself, while the other has such negative ones?

According to Erikson (1982), a major determinant of self-esteem is children's view of their capacity for productive work; the issue to be resolved in the crisis of middle childhood is *industry versus inferiority.* The "virtue" that develops with successful resolution of this crisis is *competence,* a view of the self as able to master skills and complete tasks.

representational systems
In neo-Piagetian terminology, the third stage in development of self-definition, characterized by breadth, balance, and the integration and assessment of various aspects of the self.

Judgments about the self become clearer, more comprehensive, and more realistic during middle childhood. Anna is likely to feel good about herself if she considers herself attractive and competent, and if she feels that the important people in her life like and approve of her.

industry versus inferiority
In Erikson's theory, the fourth critical alternative of psychosocial development, occurring during middle childhood, in which children must learn the productive skills their culture requires or else face feelings of inferiority.

Middle childhood, according to Erikson, is a time for learning the skills one's culture considers important. In driving geese to market, this Vietnamese girl is developing a sense of competence and gaining self-esteem. In addition, by taking on responsibilities that match her growing cabilities, she learns about how her society works, her role in it, and what it means to do a job well.

Children have to learn skills valued in their society. Arapesh boys in New Guinea learn to make bows and arrows and to lay traps for rats; Arapesh girls learn to plant, weed, and harvest. Inuit children of Alaska learn to hunt and fish. Children in industrialized countries learn to read, write, count, and use computers. Like Marian Anderson, many children learn household skills and help out with odd jobs. Children compare their abilities with those of their peers; if they feel inadequate, they may retreat to the protective embrace of the family. If, on the other hand, they become too industrious, says Erikson, they may neglect social relationships and turn into "workaholics."

A more complex view of the sources of self-esteem, or *global self-worth,* comes from research by Susan Harter (1985, 1990, 1993). Harter (1985) asked 8- to 12-year-olds about their appearance, behavior, school performance, athletic ability, and acceptance by other children. The children rated themselves and assessed how much each of these five domains affected their opinion of themselves. They also answered questions about how much they liked themselves, how happy they were with the way they were, and how parents, teachers, classmates, and close friends treated them.

Among the five domains, the children rated physical appearance most important. Social acceptance came next. Less critical were schoolwork, conduct, and athletics. In contrast, then, to the high value Erikson placed on mastery of skills, Harter's research suggests that today's school-age children, at least in North America, judge themselves (as Lisa did) more by good looks and popularity.

The greatest contributor to self-esteem, though, seems to be how much social support a child feels—first, from parents and classmates, then from friends and teachers. Do these important people like and care about the child? Do they treat the child as a person who matters and has valuable things to say? Still, Harter and others have found, social support generally will not compensate for a poor self-evaluation. If Juanita thinks sports are important but feels she is not athletic, she will lose self-esteem no matter how much praise she gets from family and friends. On the other hand, even if Mike thinks it's important to be handsome and smart and considers himself both, his self-esteem will suffer if he does not feel valued by his family and other important people.

Parenting Style and Self-Esteem

Most parents of children with high self-esteem use what Diana Baumrind termed the *authoritative* parenting style (see Chapter 10). These parents combine love and acceptance of their children with strong demands for academic performance and good behavior (Coopersmith, 1967).

Parents who are both democratic and strict help a child's development in several ways. By setting clear, consistent rules, they let children know what behavior is expected of them. Knowing what to expect helps children gain internal control; as they function within rule systems, they learn to consider the demands of the outside world. Parents who make demands show that they believe their children can meet them—and that the parents care enough to insist that they do.

There is another way to look at the relationship between parenting and children's self-esteem. Children with high self-esteem may have characteristics that encourage their parents to be loving, firm, and democratic. Children who are self-confident, cooperative, and competent are easy to bring up. Once again we see the bidirectionality of influence between parents and children—how they continually affect each other.

Emotional Growth

Emotional life in middle childhood is quite complex. By age 7 or 8, children fully internalize shame and pride (see Chapter 10). These emotions, which depend on awareness of the implications of their actions and on what kind of socialization children have received, affect their opinion of themselves (Harter, 1993).

As children grow older, they can better understand and control negative emotions. They know what makes them angry, fearful, or sad and how other people are likely to react when they show these emotions, and they can control and adapt their behavior accordingly. They also understand the difference between having an emotion and expressing it. Kindergartners believe that a parent can make a child less sad by telling the child to stop crying, or can make a child less afraid of a dog by telling the child there is nothing to be afraid of, but sixth graders know that a suppressed emotion still exists (Rotenberg & Eisenberg, 1997).

When and why do children suppress emotion? The most common reason is self-protection—to avoid ridicule or rejection. Another reason is so as not to upset another person. Fifth graders are more aware of social "rules" about showing emotion than first graders and are less likely to show sadness or pain in front of their fathers than in front of their mothers. Girls are more willing than boys to reveal these feelings and are more likely to expect emotional support. Children are the most wary of showing their feelings to a friend. They feel freer to express pain than other emotions, since it can be considered beyond their control; but even so, they tend to believe peers will not be very accepting (Zeman & Garber, 1996).

Children whose mothers encourage them to express feelings constructively and help them focus on solving the root problem tend to cope more effectively and have better social skills—both in their own eyes and in the opinion of parents and teachers—than children whose mothers devalue their feelings by minimizing the seriousness of the situation. This pattern does not seem to apply to fathers, perhaps because mothers tend to discuss feelings with their children more than fathers do (N. Eisenberg, Fabes, & Murphy, 1996).

Even very young children show *empathy,* or understanding of what another person is feeling (see Chapter 10), but children become more empathic and more inclined to prosocial behavior with the cognitive growth of middle childhood. Prosocial behavior also has emotional roots; it is a sign of positive adjustment. Children whom peers consider prosocial tend to act appropriately in social situations, to be relatively free from negative emotion, and to cope with problems constructively (N. Eisenberg, Fabes, Karbon, et al., 1996). Acknowledging and accepting happiness, sadness, and fear, but keeping anger under control, seems to promote empathy and prosocial behavior (W. Roberts & Strayer, 1996).

CHECKPOINT

Can you . . .

- From a neo-Piagetian perspective, tell how the self-concept develops in middle childhood as compared with early childhood?

- Compare Erikson's and Harter's views about sources of self-esteem and explain its relationship to parenting style?

- Identify some aspects of emotional growth in middle childhood?

The Child in the Family

School-age children spend more time away from home than when they were younger, yet home and the people who live there remain the central part of their world. According to some research, parents in the United States spend only 30 minutes of the average workday interacting with their school-age children (Demo, 1992). Children spend much more time with their peers. Counting minutes and hours can be deceptive, however. Most parents continue to be highly supportive, loving, and involved with their children; and relationships with parents remain the most important ones in children's lives (Furman & Buhrmester, 1985).

The environment in a child's home has two major components. There is the *family structure:* whether there are two parents or one, or someone else raising the child. Then there is the economic, social, and psychological *family atmosphere.* Both factors have been affected by changes in family life.

As we will see, children generally perform better in school and have fewer emotional and behavior problems when they spend their childhood in an intact family with two parents who have a good relationship with each other. However, structure in itself is not the key; how parents get along and their ability to create a favorable atmosphere affect children's adjustment more than does marital status (Bray & Hetherington, 1993; Bronstein, Clauson, Stoll, & Abrams, 1993; D. A. Dawson, 1991; Emery, 1988; Hetherington, 1989).

To understand the child in the family, then, we need to look at the family environment—its atmosphere and structure; but these in turn are affected by what goes on beyond the walls of the home. As Bronfenbrenner points out (see Chapter 1), additional layers of influence—including parents' work and socioeconomic status and societal trends such as divorce and remarriage—help shape the family environment and, thus, children's development.

Beyond these influences are overarching cultural values that define rhythms of family life and roles of family members. Different ethnic groups have distinct adaptive strategies—cultural patterns that promote group survival and well-being and govern the socialization of children. African American, Native American, Asian-Pacific American, and Hispanic American families emphasize group values (such as loyalty) more than the individualistic ones (autonomy, competition, and self-reliance) stressed in western cultures. Children in these minority

One of the most important influences on a child's development is the atmosphere in the home. Loving, supportive parents who enjoy being with their children, like this mother, are likely to raise children who feel good about themselves—and about their parents.

families are encouraged to cooperate, share, and depend on each other. Social roles tend to be more flexible. Because of economic need, adults often share breadwinning, and children assume more responsibility for younger brothers and sisters. As Marian Anderson's family illustrates, the *extended family* provides close ties and strong support systems. These kinfolk are more likely than in white families to live in a child's household and interact daily with the child (Harrison, Wilson, Pine, Chan, & Buriel, 1990).

These cultural patterns affect social development. In a survey of 333 African American, Latino, and white schoolchildren ages 7 to 14, extended family members became increasingly important to older children as a bridge to the wider social world. African American and Latino children were more likely than white children to include extended family in their inner circle of support (Levitt, Guacci-Franco, & Levitt, 1993). As we look at the child in the family, then, we need to be aware of cultural differences.

Family Atmosphere

The most important influences of the family environment on children's development come from the atmosphere within the home: whether it is supportive and loving or conflict-ridden, and whether the family has enough money or not (Demo, 1991). Often these two facets of family atmosphere are interrelated.

Parenting Issues: Coregulation and Discipline

As children's lives change, so do the issues between them and their parents, and the ways in which issues are resolved. During the course of childhood, control of behavior gradually shifts from parents to child. A preschooler's acquisition of self-control and self-regulation reduces the need for constant supervision, but not until adolescence or even later are many young people permitted to decide how late to stay out and how to spend their money.

coregulation Transitional stage in the control of behavior in which parents exercise general supervision and children exercise moment-to-moment self-regulation.

Middle childhood is a transitional stage of *coregulation*, in which parent and child share power: parents oversee, but children make moment-by-moment decisions (E. E. Maccoby, 1984). Coregulation reflects social aspects of the child's developing self-concept. As children begin to coordinate what they want with what society demands, they can more readily anticipate how other people will react to what they do, or accept a reminder that others will think better of them if they behave differently. Children are more likely to follow their parents' wishes when they recognize that the parents are fair and have the family's well-being at heart and that they may "know better" because of experience. It also helps if parents try to defer to children's growing judgment and take strong stands only on important issues.

As children become preadolescents, and their striving for autonomy becomes more insistent, the quality of family problem solving and negotiation often deteriorates. In one study, 63 two-parent families with fourth-grade children videotaped home discussions of two problems that had come up within the past month—one topic of the child's choosing and one of the parents' choosing. The families repeated the procedure two years later. Between the ages of 9 and 11, the children's participation became more negative, especially when discussing topics the parents had chosen. It made no difference what the topic was; the basic issue, apparently, was "who is in charge" (Vuchinich, Angelelli, & Gatherum, 1996).

The shift to coregulation affects how parents handle *discipline:* the teaching of acceptable behavior. Most parents use somewhat different methods with older children than with younger ones (E. E. Maccoby, 1984; G. C. Roberts, Block, & Block, 1984). Parents of school-age children are more likely to use inductive techniques that include reasoning. For example, 8-year-old Jared's father points out how his actions affect others: "Hitting Jermaine hurts him and makes him feel bad." In other situations, Jared's parents may appeal to his self-esteem ("What happened to the helpful boy who was here yesterday?"), sense of humor ("If you go one more day without a bath, we'll know when you're coming without looking!"), moral values ("A big, strong boy like you shouldn't sit on the train and let an old person stand"), or appreciation ("Aren't you glad that your father cares enough to remind you to wear boots so that you won't catch a cold?"). Above all, Jared's parents let him know he must bear the consequences of his behavior ("No wonder you missed the school bus today—you stayed up too late last night! Now you'll have to walk to school").

Still, discipline remains fairly consistent throughout the child-raising years. In one study, parents filled out a questionnaire when their children were 3 years old and again when they were 12 (G. C. Roberts et al., 1984). The questions related to independence, control, handling aggression and sex, early training, emphasis on health and achievement, expression of feelings, protectiveness, supervision, and punishment. Over the 9-year period, the parents' basic approach to child rearing seemed to remain constant. Most of them, all along, emphasized rational guidance and praise while using specific techniques appropriate to a child's level of development.

Corporal (physical) punishment is common and widely accepted in the United States, and not only for preschoolers (see Chapter 10). Although corporal punishment is used less frequently as children get older, about half of early adolescents are still subjected to it (Straus, 1994; Straus & Donnelly, 1993). However, corporal punishment can be counterproductive. According to interviews with a national sample of mothers of 6- to 9-year-olds, it tends to increase rather than reduce antisocial behavior; the more frequent the spankings and the longer they continue, the greater the chance of problems (Straus, Sugarman, & Giles-Sims, 1997).

Furthermore, frequent corporal punishment can lead to distress or depression, and even a spanking or slapping once or twice a year can take a toll. According to a survey of a national random sample of 2,000 girls and boys ages 10 to 16, physical punishment was more stressful when it came from parents who were usually supportive. Perhaps this is because children then saw their parents as unpredictable or were less able to "write off" the parents' behavior as "mean" or "unfair" and were more likely to attribute the punishment to their own lack of worth (H. Turner & Finkelhor, 1996).

Parents' Work

A significant contributor to the atmosphere in the home is socioeconomic status, which largely reflects the work one or both parents do for pay. Parents' work has other, indirect effects on the family atmosphere and thus on children's development. Much of adults' time, effort, and emotional involvement go into their occupations. How do their jobs and their feelings about work affect children?

Today, about 3 out of 4 mothers of school-age children are in the work force (Children's Defense Fund, 1996). With more than half of all new mothers going to work soon after giving birth (Bachu, 1993), many children have never known a time when their mothers were not working for pay. The impact of a mother's work depends on many factors: the child's age, sex, temperament, and personality; whether the mother works full or part time, and for how many hours; how she feels about her work; whether she has a supportive or unsupportive mate, or none; the family's socioeconomic status; and the kind of care the child receives (see Box 13-1). When good child care is available and affordable, when men assume a large role in the home, and when employers support workers' family roles, children are more likely to do well.

The more satisfied a mother is with her employment status, the more effective she is as a parent (L. W. Hoffman, 1986, 1989). Despite the guilt some

The Everyday World

Box 13-1 After-School Care: What Kind Is Best?

When Kim, age 11, comes home from school, she unlocks the front door, throws down her books, and feeds her cat before sitting down for her own snack. Then she calls her mother to check in and to report whether she will be staying home, going outside to play, or visiting a friend's home.

Kim is among some 2 million *self-care children,* who regularly care for themselves at home without adult supervision because both parents or a single custodial parent works outside the home (C. Cole & Rodman, 1987). Although most self-care takes place after school, some children spend time alone in the morning or evening, too. However, most self-care children are alone for no more than 2 hours a day. Contrary to the stereotyped picture of the "latchkey child" as a lonely, neglected youngster from a poor, single-parent family in a high-risk inner-city setting, many self-care children are in well-educated, middle- to upper-class suburban or rural families (Cain & Hofferth, 1989).

Children who are not under self-care may be supervised after school by one or both parents or by baby-sitters or relatives. Some go to structured after-school programs, where they do their homework under adult supervision, take music or art lessons, or engage in other activities.

What difference does it make what kind of after-school care a child gets? As in many other aspects of development, there is no simple answer. Among 150 suburban middle-class children, mother-care and self-care children did about the same in classroom work, standardized tests, and parent and teacher ratings, and they were equally popular with other children. Children who went to after-school programs or stayed with baby-sitters tended to get lower school grades, to do worse on tests, and to be less popular. However, the type of care was not necessarily responsible for these children's poorer showing; it's possible that working parents who think their children are having problems may be more likely to see that they are supervised (Vandell & Corasaniti, 1988).

The picture seems to be different in low-income neighborhoods. There, both black and white third-graders from single-parent and two-parent families seem to thrive in formal after-school programs (Posner & Vandell, n.d.). These children get higher grades, have better work habits, and are better-adjusted than children who stay alone or are cared for by their mothers or baby-sitters. However, when family income and parental emotional support are controlled, the type of after-school care is less important than the quality of children's experiences with their families (Vandell & Ramanan, 1991).

This schoolboy letting himself into his home with his own key typifies some 2 million children of working parents who regularly care for themselves after school. Self-care children should have a regular time to check in with a parent by phone and need to know how to reach a responsible adult in an emergency.

How can parents tell whether a child is ready for self-care, and how can they make the situation as comfortable as possible (C. Cole & Rodman, 1987; S. W. Olds, 1989)? Before children take care of themselves, they should be able to control their bodies well enough to keep from injuring themselves; keep track of keys and handle doors well enough to avoid locking themselves in or out; safely operate necessary household equipment; stay alone without being afraid; be resourceful enough to handle the unexpected; be responsible enough to follow important rules; understand and remember spoken and written instructions; and read and write well enough to take telephone messages. They should know what to say and do about visitors and callers; for example, they should not tell strangers that they are alone, and they should not open the door to anyone but family and close friends. They should also know how to get help in an emergency: how to call police and firefighters, which friends and neighbors to call, and what other resources to call upon.

Parents and guardians should stay in touch by phone, preferably by setting up a regular time for check-in calls. They should establish safety procedures and tell children what to do and how to reach a responsible adult in an emergency. It is also advisable to set up a schedule to guide children during their self-care time.

employed mothers feel about being away from their children, many of these women feel more competent, more economically secure, and more in charge of their lives than mothers who do not work for pay. Their self-esteem, sense of personal effectiveness, and overall well-being tend to be higher than that of full-time homemakers, whose work is generally undervalued in American society (Demo, 1992).

The division of labor among dual-income couples tends to be different from that in one-paycheck families. Even though the mother typically does more housework and child care, the father is likely to do more of this work than the husband of a full-time homemaker (Almeida, Maggs, & Galambos, 1993; Demo, 1991). He can spend more time with his children, since he is less likely to have a second job. On weekends, both parents spend more time with their children than in families with at-home mothers (Demo, 1992). The father tends to be most involved when the mother works full time and earns close to what he does, when they have more than one child, and when the children are young (L. W. Hoffman, 1986).

School-age children of employed mothers tend to live in more structured homes than children of full-time homemakers, with clear-cut rules giving them more household responsibilities. They are also encouraged to be more independent (Bronfenbrenner & Crouter, 1982). Both boys and girls in low-income families seem to benefit academically from the more favorable environment a working mother's income can provide (Goldberg, Greenberger, & Nagel, 1996; Vandell & Ramanan, 1992). The pattern is more complex in middle-class families. Sons of middle-class working mothers tend to do less well in school than sons of homemakers, whereas a number of studies have found that girls do as well or better when mothers work (Goldberg et al., 1996; Heyns & Catsambis, 1986).

These gender differences in middle-class families may have to do with boys' greater need for supervision and guidance (Goldberg et al., 1996). Independence seems to help girls to become more competent, to achieve more in school, and to have higher self-esteem (Bronfenbrenner & Crouter, 1982). However, this is not necessarily true of the youngest school-age girls. One study looked at 100 mostly middle-class 5- to 7-year-olds, about three-fourths of whom had employed mothers. The findings suggest that if middle-class mothers do not work *at all*, young girls, as well as young boys, do better in school. But if we look only at families with *employed* mothers, an interesting switch emerges for girls: the more hours a mother works, the better her daughter does. Perhaps one explanation lies in a working mother's achievement motivation, which may transfer to her daughter: the more motivated an employed woman is to work, the more motivated her daughter is to achieve. Mothers who are highly motivated to work tend to be more supportive of their children's achievement and to give them better guidance in problem solving (Goldberg et al., 1996).

As boys approach adolescence, how well parents keep track of them may be more important than whether the mother works for pay. In one study, 9- to 12-year-old boys whose parents did not closely monitor their activities earned poorer grades than more closely monitored children (Crouter, MacDermid, McHale, & Perry-Jenkins, 1990). During school vacations, monitoring becomes harder. Fathers tend to do more monitoring in summer and to be more knowledgeable about children's activities. Mothers who do not work during the summer become more involved with their children then (Crouter & McHale, 1993).

Fathers' feelings about work, as well as mothers', can affect children. A New York Times-CBS poll in 1989 found that nearly as large a proportion of working men (72 percent) as of working women (83 percent) feel conflict between work and family responsibilities. Interviews with 300 husbands, ages 25 to 40, in two-earner couples, found that men's family roles were just as important to them as their work roles (Barnett, Marshall, & Pleck, 1992). Good relationships with wife and children often made up for a poor job experience; but when both job and family roles were unsatisfactory, men tended to feel distress.

Another study looked at 189 fathers of fourth- and fifth-graders in 10 Canadian elementary schools. These men held a variety of jobs, from unskilled to professional, and about two-thirds of the married men had working wives. Conflicts between work and family roles significantly affected men's job satisfaction, mood, and job-related tension; and men who were unhappier at work were more likely to punish or reject their children (W. Stewart & Barling, 1996).

Poverty and Parenting

What happens when parents cannot adequately support the family? Poverty can inspire people like Marian Anderson's mother to work hard and make a better life for their children—or it can crush their spirits. Vonnie McLoyd's (1990) ecological analysis of the pervasive effects of poverty traces a typical route that leads to adult psychological distress, to effects on child rearing, and finally to effects on children.

Parents who live in poor housing (or have none), who are worried about their next meal, and who feel a lack of control over their lives are likely to become anxious, depressed, and irritable. Their distress may lead them to be less affectionate with, and less supportive of, their children—in some cases, even abusive. They may discipline inconsistently and arbitrarily, with physical punishment and authoritarian commands. They may ignore good behavior and pay attention only to misbehavior. Their children may have social, emotional, and behavior problems. The children tend to become depressed themselves, to have trouble getting along with peers, to lack self-confidence, and to engage in antisocial acts. Marital conflict may make fathers, especially, more hostile and punitive, particularly toward unattractive or temperamentally "difficult" children.

This analysis may help explain why power-assertive discipline, including physical punishment, is more common among black families, who are more likely than white families to be poor. It may also help explain academic and behavioral problems. Families under economic stress are less likely to monitor their children's activities, and lack of monitoring is associated with poorer school performance and social adjustment (K. E. Bolger, Patterson, Thompson, & Kupersmidt, 1995).

Aggressive behavior tends to be bred from early childhood by a combination of a stressful and unstimulating home atmosphere; harsh discipline; lack of maternal warmth and social support; exposure to aggressive adults and neighborhood violence; and transient peer groups, which prevent stable friendships. Through such negative socializing experiences, children growing up in poor, high-risk surroundings may absorb antisocial attitudes despite their parents' best efforts (Dodge, Pettit, & Bates, 1994).

Lack of financial resources can make it harder for mothers and fathers to support each other in parenting. One study looked at African American 9- to 12-year-olds and their married parents in the rural south, with annual incomes ranging from $2,500 to $57,500. In many of the poor families, parents worked several fatiguing jobs, some of them at night, to make ends meet. These parents were less optimistic and more depressed than parents in better-off families; they found it harder to communicate and cooperate and often fought over child raising. Contradictory parental messages interfered with development of self-regulation and led to behavioral and scholastic problems (G. H. Brody et al., 1994).

Persistent poverty can be particularly damaging. Among 534 white and African American schoolchildren in Charlottesville, Virginia, those from persistently deprived families lagged in self-esteem, peer relations, and conduct from middle childhood into early adolescence in comparison with children whose families experienced intermittent hardship or none at all. Boys, especially, tended to show aggressive or antisocial behavior or to become anxious or shy (K. E. Bolger et al., 1995).

However, this bleak picture is not etched in stone. Parents who can turn to relatives (as Annie Anderson did) or to community representatives for emotional support, help with child care, and child-rearing information often can parent their children more effectively.

Family Structure

In the United States, most children under 18 live with two parents, though this proportion slipped from 85 percent in 1970 to 69 percent in 1995 (see Figure 13-1).

CHECKPOINT

Can you . . .

- Identify special characteristics of families in minority cultures?
- Describe how coregulation works and how discipline changes during middle childhood?
- Identify ways in which parents' work can indirectly affect children?
- Discuss effects of poverty on child raising?

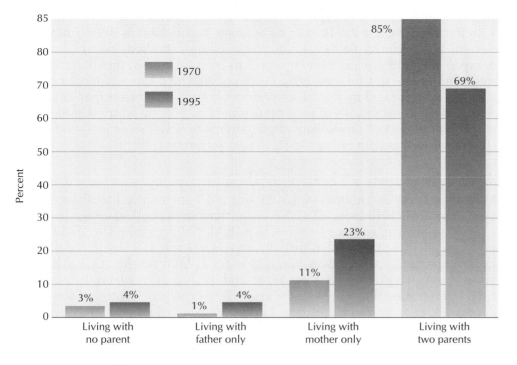

Figure 13-1
Living arrangements of children younger than 18, 1970–1995. Most children under 18 in the United States live with two parents, but this proportion dropped during the past quarter-century. Many of these two-parent families are stepfamilies.

Source: U.S. Department of Commerce, 1996.

A smaller proportion, but still more than 60 percent, live with both biological or adoptive parents (U.S. Department of Health and Human Services [USDHHS], 1996b). Many two-parent families are stepfamilies, resulting from divorce and re-marriage. There also are a growing number of other nontraditional families, including single-parent families and gay and lesbian families.

Intact Families

Much research has found that children tend to do better in traditional, or intact, families—those that include two biological parents or two parents who adopted the child in infancy (Bray & Hetherington, 1993; Bronstein et al., 1993; D. A. Dawson, 1991). In a nationwide study of 17,110 children under 18, those living with single or remarried mothers were more likely than those living with both biological parents to have repeated a grade of school, to have been expelled, to have health problems, or to have been treated for emotional or behavioral troubles in the previous year (D. A. Dawson, 1991).

Again, family atmosphere is an important factor. Traditional families do not have to deal with the stress and disruption experienced in families riven by divorce or the death of a parent; with the financial, psychological, and time pressures on single parents; or with the need to adjust to remarriage. Among 136 fifth-graders, those in traditional families were better-adjusted than children in nontraditional families. Traditional parents did more with their children, talked more with them, disciplined them more appropriately and consistently, and were likely to share parenting responsibilities more cooperatively than nontraditional parents. Deficiencies in family relationships in single-mother households were almost entirely linked to socioeconomic status (Bronstein et al., 1993).

In a traditional family, a father's involvement is usually deeper when there is at least one son. Fathers are more likely to play with, supervise, and discipline sons than daughters. A father's involvement with his children may be a gauge of whether the parents will stay together. When a father is heavily involved, the mother is likely to be more satisfied and to expect the marriage to last (Katzev, Warner, & Acock, 1994).

How couples deal with disagreements is another aspect of family atmosphere; and this, too, influences children's adjustment. In one study, 5-year-olds whose fathers expressed anger by withdrawing emotionally during conflicts with the mother tended to be seen by teachers 3 years later as self-blaming, distressed, and ashamed. Five-year-olds whose parents insulted, mocked, and disparaged each other were likely at age 8 to be disobedient, unwilling to obey rules, and unable to wait their turn. These patterns held true whether or not the parents had separated by then. The children's behavior problems may have been triggered by seeing models of poor conflict resolution or by worry that their parents might break up. Or perhaps these parents behaved negatively with their children as well as with each other (L. F. Katz & Gottman, 1993).

When Parents Divorce

More than 1 million children under the age of 18 are involved in divorces each year (Bray & Hetherington, 1993). No matter how unhappy a marriage has been, its breakup usually comes as a shock to a child. Children may feel afraid of the future, guilty about their own (usually imaginary) role in causing the divorce, hurt by the parent who moves out, and angry at both parents. Children of divorce tend to have more social, academic, and behavioral problems than children from intact homes; they may become aggressive, hostile, disruptive, disobedient, depressed, or withdrawn and may lose interest in schoolwork and social life (Amato & Keith, 1991a; Hetherington, Stanley-Hagan, & Anderson, 1989).

However, most children do gradually readjust (Masten, Best, & Garmezy, 1990). Although different children react differently, readjustment generally involves six "tasks" (Wallerstein, 1983; Wallerstein & Kelly, 1980), which are not necessarily completed in order: (1) acknowledging the reality of the marital rupture; (2) disengaging from parental conflict and distress and resuming customary pursuits; (3) resolving loss—of the parent they are not living with, of security in feeling loved and cared for by both parents, of familiar daily routines and family traditions; (4) resolving anger and self-blame; (5) accepting the permanence of the divorce; and (6) achieving realistic hope for their own intimate relationships.

What influences a child's adjustment to divorce? The child's own resilience is important, of course. Other important factors have to do with the way parents handle issues entailed in the separation and the challenge of raising children afterward—such factors as custody arrangements, finances, contact with the noncustodial parent, whether and when parents remarry, and the quality of the relationship with a stepparent. A child's age, gender, and temperament also make a difference. Younger children are more anxious at the time of a divorce and have less realistic perceptions of what caused it, but they may adapt more quickly than older children, who may feel more lasting effects. Boys find it especially hard to adjust (Hetherington et al., 1989; Masten et al., 1990).

Children's emotional or behavioral problems may stem from conflict between the parents, both before and after divorce, more than from the separation itself (Amato, Kurdek, Demo, & Allen, 1993). When parents argue frequently over child support and custody, their relationship with their children suffers (Donnelly & Finkelhor, 1992). Children whose parents can control their anger, cooperate in parenting, and avoid exposing the children to quarreling are less likely to have problems. Children of authoritative parents, especially boys, usually have fewer problems and do better in school than children of authoritarian or permissive parents (Bray & Hetherington, 1993; Guidubaldi & Perry, 1985; Hetherington, 1987).

In most divorce cases, the mother gets custody; in 1990, fathers received custody in about 17 percent of cases (S. C. Clark, 1995). Custodial fathers typically are older, make more money, and are better educated than custodial mothers (U.S. Bureau of the Census, 1993). Children do better when the custodial parent creates a stable, structured, and nurturing environment and does not expect the children to act more mature or take on more responsibility than they are ready for (Hetherington et al., 1989). Boys, especially, benefit from reliable, frequent

Children of divorce tend to be better adjusted if they have reliable, frequent contact with the noncustodial parent, usually the father.

contact with the noncustodial parent, typically the father (J. B. Kelly, 1987). The more recent the separation, the closer a divorced father lives to his children, and the higher his socioeconomic status, the more involved he is likely to be (Amato & Keith, 1991a). Fathers who see their children often, help to make child-rearing decisions, and feel that they have some control over their children's upbringing tend to make regular child support payments (Braver et al., 1993).

Some research suggests that *joint custody*—custody shared by both parents—does not improve a child's situation in an amicable divorce and may worsen it in a bitter one (M. Kline, Tschann, Johnston, & Wallerstein, 1988). Children in joint custody seem to have no better relationships with their parents than those in sole custody (Donnelly & Finkelhor, 1992).

Although most children of divorce adjust reasonably well, some remain troubled, and the effects can persist beyond childhood. An analysis of 37 studies involving more than 81,000 people found that adult children of divorced parents tend to be slightly more depressed, to have more marital problems, to be in poorer health, and to have lower socioeconomic status than adults who grew up in intact families (Amato & Keith, 1991b). These differences were smaller than in earlier studies (perhaps because divorce is more common than it used to be), weaker among African Americans (where one-parent families are more prevalent), and strongest among people who had sought counseling or therapy.

In a nationally representative British study based on data gathered on children from birth on, the vast majority of those whose parents divorced came through well. However, as a group, children of divorce were at greater risk than other children of having adjustment problems in their early twenties. The more recent the divorce, the greater the chance of problems carrying over to young adulthood. Divorce seemed to create greater difficulties at first for children whose previous lives had been relatively smooth, but these children eventually made a stronger recovery (Chase-Landale, Cherlin, & Kiernan, 1995).

Living in a One-Parent Family

In 1995, about 31 percent of U.S. families with children under 18—64 percent of African American families, 36 percent of Hispanic families, and 25 percent of white families—were single-parent families, as compared with only 13 percent in 1970 (Bryson, 1996). As of the mid-1980s, the United States had the

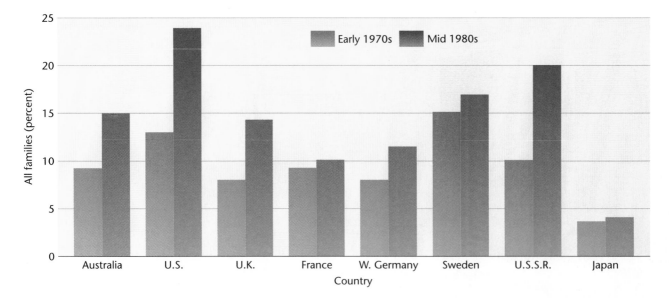

Figure 13-2
Single-parent families as a percentage of all families.
Source: A. Burns, 1992.

highest percentage of single-parent families (28.9 percent) among eight industrialized countries (Australia, United States, United Kingdom, France, West Germany, Sweden, U.S.S.R., and Japan). Japan had the lowest rate, 4.1 percent (A. Burns, 1992; see Figure 13-2). The increase in single-parent families in the United States slowed during the 1980s. Still, it is projected that 1 out of every 2 children born during that decade will spend time in a single-parent family (Bianchi, 1995).

Although most single-parent households are headed by women, the number of father-only families more than doubled between 1980 and 1992 (U.S. Bureau of the Census, 1993). By 1993, 15.5 percent of all single-parent families with children were headed by fathers (U.S. Bureau of the Census, 1995a). About one-third of single-father households also include the father's cohabiting partner (Eggebeen, Snyder, & Manning, 1996).

One-parent families result from divorce or separation, unwed parenthood, or death. Children in divorced families typically spend 5 years in a single-parent home, usually the mother's, before she remarries (Bray & Hetherington, 1993). However, the number of father-only families grew nearly 3 times as fast as the number of mother-only families during the 1980s (42 percent as compared with 15 percent), apparently due largely to an increase in the number of fathers having custody after divorce (Garasky & Meyer, 1996).

Since the 1970s, delayed marriage and unwed motherhood have created more single-mother families than has divorce (Bianchi, 1995). Between 1940 and 1990, births to unmarried mothers in the United States rose sevenfold—from fewer than 4 percent of all births to 28 percent; and 67 percent of all births to black mothers in 1990 were out of wedlock (National Center for Health Statistics [NCHS], 1993, 1994). By 1994 nearly 1 in 3 births was to an unwed mother (Rosenberg, Ventura, Maurer, Heuser, & Freedman, 1996). The trend has been especially marked among white and college-educated women but has also occurred among African American and Hispanic women (who still are far more likely to be unwed mothers) and among women of all educational levels (Bachu, 1993; U.S. Bureau of the Census, 1993). In 1995, the out-of-wedlock birthrate dropped 4 percent, for the first time in two decades, to about 45 births per 1,000 unmarried women ages 15 to 44 (Rosenberg et al., 1996). Out-of-wedlock births have increased dramatically in many other developed countries (Bruce, Lloyd, & Leonard, 1995; WuDunn, 1996).

Between 1960 and 1990, the proportion of U.S. children living in father-only households as a result of the mother's death declined fivefold, from 32 percent to less than 6 percent, as the proportion of never-married fathers jumped from 1.5 percent to 33.2 percent (Eggebeen et al., 1996). However, this picture may be changing as a result of the AIDS epidemic. Between 7,000 and 10,000 children in the United States lose their mothers to AIDS each year. Many of these families are poor, and the father is unemployed. Some of the children, whose fathers are not available or not fit to raise a child, must be placed in foster or adoptive homes (W. Gardner & Preator, 1996).

Compared with children in intact families, children in one-parent families are more on their own. They have more household responsibility, more conflict with siblings, less family cohesion, and less support, control, or discipline from fathers (Amato, 1987). They are also more likely to be poor, and financial hardship has negative effects on children's health, well-being, and school achievement. Mother-only families, in particular, often suffer from the mother's low earning capacity and the father's failure to pay child support (McLanahan & Booth, 1989). Nearly three times as many mother-only families as father-only families are poor—35 percent as compared with 13 percent (U.S. Bureau of the Census, 1996).

Students from one-parent homes tend to have more problems in school (D.A. Dawson, 1991), but what looks like a single-parent effect is often a low-income effect. A study of 18,000 students showed that low income affected school achievement more strongly than did the number of parents at home (Zakariya, 1982).

Some studies report that children with only one parent get into more trouble than those with two parents and that, as adults, they may be at greater risk of marital and parenting problems themselves (McLanahan & Booth, 1989; Rutter, 1979a). In general, though, children tend to be better-adjusted when they have had a good relationship with a single parent than when they have grown up in a two-parent home marked by discord and discontent (Bray & Hetherington, 1993; Hetherington et al., 1989; Rutter, 1983). An inaccessible, rejecting, or hostile parent can be more damaging than an absent one (Hetherington, 1980).

Living in a Stepfamily

Since about 75 percent of divorced mothers and 80 percent of divorced fathers remarry, families made up of "yours, mine, and ours" are common. Eighty-six percent of children in remarriages live with their biological mother and a stepfather (Bray & Hetherington, 1993).

The stepfamily—also called the *blended,* or *reconstituted,* family—is different from the "natural" family. It has a larger cast, which may include the relatives of up to four adults (the remarried pair, plus one or two former spouses); and it has many stressors. Because of losses from death or divorce, children and adults may be afraid to trust or to love. A child's loyalties to an absent or dead parent may interfere with forming ties to a stepparent. Past emotional and behavior problems often resurface. Adjustment is harder when there are many children, including those from both the man's and the woman's previous marriages, or when a new child is born (Hetherington et al., 1989).

Boys, who have more trouble than girls in adjusting to divorce and single-parent living, generally benefit from a stepfather. A girl, on the other hand, may find the new man in the house a threat to her independence and to her close relationship with her mother and is less likely to accept him (Bray & Hetherington, 1993; Hetherington, 1987; Hetherington et al., 1989; J. B. Kelly, 1987). Early adolescent boys and girls, perhaps because of their emerging concern with sexuality, have more trouble than younger children in adapting to remarriage and bonding with a stepparent (Hetherington et al., 1989).

Stepparents often take a "hands-off" attitude toward children of the custodial parent, though stepmothers may take a more active role than stepfathers

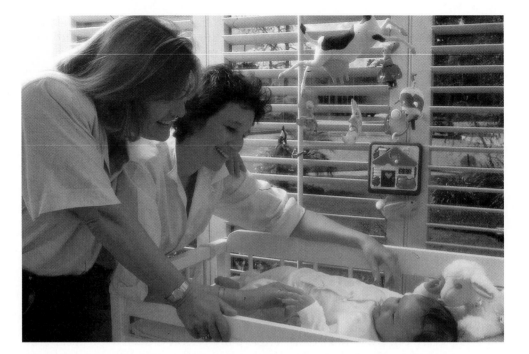

This baby has two mothers—and both obviously dote on the child. Contrary to popular stereotypes, children living with homosexual parents are no more likely than other children to have social or psychological problems or to turn out to be homosexual themselves.

CHECKPOINT

Can you . . .

- Differentiate between traditional (or intact) and nontraditional family structures?

- List the psychological "tasks" children face in adjusting to divorce, and identify factors which affect that adjustment?

- Assess the long-term effects of parental divorce?

- Tell three ways in which a one-parent family can be formed, and describe how it can affect children's well-being?

- Discuss how parents and stepparents handle the issues and challenges of a blended family?

- Identify three common, but false, beliefs about children raised by homosexual parents?

(Hetherington et al., 1989; Santrock, Sitterle, & Warshak, 1988). A stepchild's most enduring ties are with the custodial parent; and a positive relationship with that parent is "a key ingredient in helping the child . . . as the family [moves] from . . . intact to divorced to becoming a stepfamily" (Santrock et al., 1988, p. 161).

Children of Gay and Lesbian Parents

The number of children living with gay and lesbian parents is unknown; conservative estimates range from 6 to 14 million (C. J. Patterson, 1992). These numbers are probably low because many homosexual parents do not openly acknowledge their sexual orientation.

Several studies have focused on the sexual identity and gender-role behavior of children of homosexuals; on their personal development, including self-concept, moral judgment, and intelligence; and on their social relationships. Although research is still sparse and studies vary in methodology, none has indicated psychological risks (C. J. Patterson, 1992, 1995a, 1995b). Contrary to popular beliefs, openly homosexual parents usually have positive relationships with their children (P. H. Turner, Scadden, & Harris, 1990), and the children are no more likely than children raised by heterosexual parents to have social or psychological problems (C. J. Patterson, 1992, 1995a). Abuse by homosexual parents is rare (R. L. Barrett & Robinson, 1990; Cramer, 1986). Such findings can have social policy implications for legal decisions on custody and visitation disputes, foster care, and adoptions.

Children of homosexuals are no more likely to be homosexual themselves than are children of heterosexuals (B. M. King, 1996). In one study, the vast majority of adult sons of gay fathers were heterosexual (J. M. Bailey, Bobrow, Wolfe, & Mikach, 1995). Likewise, in a longitudinal study of adult children of lesbians, a large majority identified themselves as heterosexual (Golombok & Tasker, 1996).

Relationships with Grandparents

During the school years, children may spend less time with their grandparents, but these relationships remain important. The bond with grandparents is a special one, different from the relationship with parents. Grandparents' warmth, indulgence, and total, nondemanding acceptance can be a "release valve" from the pressure of parental expectations (Weissbourd, 1996). In one survey, 32 percent of grandparents had provided child care or supervision for at least one hour during the previous week, and 9 percent had done it for 20 or more hours (S. A. Bass & Caro, 1996). Some grandparents do even more, taking adult children and their children into their homes or, if need be, raising their grandchildren alone.

Grandparents Raising Grandchildren

An increasing number of grandparents and even great-grandparents are serving as "parents by default" for children whose parents are addicted to drugs or alcohol, divorced, dead, physically or mentally ill, unwed, underage, unemployed, abusive, neglectful, or in jail, or who have simply abandoned them (Chalfie, 1994; Minkler & Roe, 1996). More than 1 in 10 grandparents, a disproportionate number of whom are African American, low-income, or single women, have cared for a grandchild for at least 6 months, in most cases far longer (Fuller-Thomson, Minkler, & Driver, 1997). In 1991, nearly 1.1 million children under 18, including more than 5 percent of black children and about 1 percent of white and Hispanic children, lived with grandparents without a parent in the home (Furukawa, 1994). In some low-income urban areas, an estimated 30 to 50 percent of children are living in homes of grandparents or other relatives without their parents (Minkler & Roe, 1996).

Most grandparents who take on this responsibility do it because they love their grandchildren and do not want them placed in a stranger's foster home. However, the age difference can be a barrier, and both generations may feel cheated out of their traditional roles (Crowley, 1993; Larsen, 1990–1991). Also, there are many practical problems; for example, grandchildren are usually not covered under employer-provided health insurance even if the grandparent has custody (Chalfie, 1994; Simon-Rusinowitz, Krach, Marks, Piktialis, & Wilson, 1996). Like working parents, working grandparents need good, affordable child care and family-friendly workplace policies, such as time off to care for a sick child (Simon-Rusinowitz et al., 1996). The federal Family and Medical Leave Act of 1993 does cover grandparents who are raising grandchildren, but many do not realize it (H. Dabelko, personal communication, November 4, 1996).

Effects of Divorce

Unfortunately, one by-product of divorce and remarriage may be the weakening or even the severing of grandparent-grandchild relations. Because the mother usually has custody, her parents tend to have more contact and stronger relationships with their grandchildren (Cherlin & Furstenberg, 1986b; J. E. Myers & Perrin, 1993). The mother's remarriage increases the likelihood that the paternal grandparents will be displaced or that the family will move away, making contact more difficult (Cherlin & Furstenberg, 1986b). Since 1965 every state in the Union has given grandparents (and in some states, great-grandparents, siblings, and others) the right to visitation after a divorce or the death of a parent, if a judge finds it in the best interest of the child.

The remarriage of either parent often brings a new set of grandparents into the picture, and often stepgrandchildren as well. One-third of the grandparents in a national three-generational survey had at least one stepgrandchild (Cherlin & Furstenberg, 1986b). Stepgrandparents may find it hard to become close to their new stepgrandchildren, especially older children and those who do not live with the grandparent's adult child (Cherlin & Furstenberg, 1986b; Longino &

Although U.S. children do less active caretaking of younger siblings than do children in many other countries, scenes like this one are common. The special affection between this "big brother" and his baby sister is likely to last throughout their lives.

CHECKPOINT

Can you . . .

- Explain the increase in the number of grandparents raising grandchildren?
- Describe how divorce and a parent's remarriage affect children's relationships with the maternal and paternal grandparents?

Earle, 1996; J. E. Myers & Perrin, 1993). Such issues as birthday and Christmas presents for a "real" grandchild's half- or stepsiblings, or which grandparents are visited or included at holidays, can generate tension.

Still, a combined family can offer expanded opportunities for love and nurturing. Creating new family traditions; including *all* the grandchildren, step and otherwise, in trips, outings, and other activities; offering a safe haven for the children when they are unhappy or upset; and being understanding and supportive of all members of the new stepfamily are ways in which stepgrandparents can build bridges, not walls (T. S. Kaufman, 1993; Visher & Visher, 1991).

Sibling Relationships

"I fight more with my little brother than I do with my friends," reports Monique, age 10. "But when I fight with Billy, we always make up." The tie between Monique and Billy is deeper and more lasting than ordinary friendships, which may founder on a quarrel or just fade away. It is also ambivalent, marked by special affection as well as by intense competition and resentment.

How Siblings Affect Each Other's Development

Sibling relations are a laboratory for learning how to resolve conflicts. Siblings are impelled to make up after quarrels, since they know they will see each other every day. They learn that expressing anger does not end a relationship. Firstborns tend to be bossy and are more likely to attack, interfere with, ignore, or bribe their siblings. Younger siblings plead, reason, and cajole; they often become quite skillful at sensing other people's needs, negotiating, and compromising. Children are more apt to squabble with same-sex siblings; two brothers quarrel more than any other combination (Cicirelli, 1976a, 1995).

Siblings influence each other, not only *directly*, through their own interactions, but *indirectly* through their impact on each other's relationship with their parents. One direct influence is temperament: a "difficult" child is likely to have more trouble getting along with a sibling than an "easy" child. Because older children continue to take the lead in sibling relationships during middle childhood, their temperament has a stronger effect on the quality of those relationships than the temperament of younger brothers or sisters (G. H. Brody &

Stoneman, 1990, 1995; G. H. Brody, Stoneman, & Gauger, 1996; Stoneman & Brody, 1993).

Behavior patterns established with parents tend to "spill over" into behavior with siblings. An older child's positive relationship with the mother or father can mitigate the effects of that child's "difficult" temperament on sibling interactions. Also, a father's positive relationship with an "easy" younger sibling can bolster that child in dealing with a "difficult" older sibling (G. H. Brody, Stoneman, & Gauger, 1996).

Older children often mind younger ones and help them with homework. In one study, older siblings (who were in second or third grade) were better teachers of their younger siblings (in kindergarten or first grade) than were unrelated classmates of the older siblings. The older siblings were more likely to give spontaneous guidance, and the younger ones often prompted explanations and pressured their older siblings into giving them more control of the task (Azmitia & Hesser, 1993). Help is most likely to be effective (and accepted) when it comes from a sibling, especially a sister, who is at least 4 years older. Girls explain more to younger siblings than boys do, and when girls want younger siblings to do something, they are more apt to reason with them or to make them feel obligated. Older brothers tend to attack (Cicirelli, 1976a, 1976b, 1995).

Sibling Relationships in Cultural Context*

In nonindustrialized societies, such as those in remote rural areas or villages of Asia, Africa, Oceania, and Central and South America, it is common to see a 3-year-old rocking a baby. It is also common to see older girls stay home from school to care for three or four younger siblings: to feed, comfort, and toilet-train them; discipline them; assign chores; and generally keep an eye on them. By delegating these responsibilities to a daughter, the mother is free to work; the family's survival is at stake. Sometimes, even when the mother is present, girls or boys share in the care of younger children.

In a poor agricultural or pastoral community, group cooperation is essential to make the most of limited resources. Sibling care is continuous and obligatory; older children have an important, culturally defined role. Parents train children from an early age to teach their younger sisters and brothers skills such as gathering firewood, carrying water, tending animals, and growing food. At the same time, younger siblings absorb intangible values, such as respecting elders and placing the welfare of the group above that of the individual. Siblings may fight and compete, but they do so within the bounds of societally set rules and roles which carry over into adult life.

In industrialized societies, on the other hand, individual freedom and choice are important for advancement, and sibling ties in adulthood are voluntary. Parents generally try to treat children equally and not to "burden" older children with the care of younger ones (Weisner, 1993). Some caretaking does take place, but it is typically sporadic and mainly custodial: providing for basic needs, supervising, protecting, and sometimes entertaining younger children to keep them out of mischief when the parents are busy. Older siblings do teach younger ones, but this usually happens informally, by chance, and not as an established part of the social system. However, sibling relationships among some American working families and ethnic minority groups are closer to the pattern of nonindustrialized cultures than to that of the majority culture in the United States (C. L. Johnson, 1985).

The number of siblings in a family, as well as their spacing, birth order, and gender, determines roles and relationships more rigidly in nonindustrialized societies. The larger number of siblings in these societies helps the family carry on its work and provide for aging members. The definition of *siblings* may even

---

*Unless otherwise referenced, this discussion is based on Cicirelli (1994).

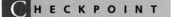

CHECKPOINT

Can you . . .

- Discuss how siblings affect each other's development during middle childhood?

- Compare the roles and responsibilities of siblings in industrialized and nonindustrialized countries?

include cousins, aunts, uncles, grandparents, or same-age peers, who are expected to fulfill the obligations of brothers and sisters. In industrialized societies, the number and spacing of siblings vary from family to family; siblings tend to be fewer and farther apart in age, making it easier for parents to pursue careers or other interests and to focus more resources and attention on each child.

The Child in the Peer Group

Babies are aware of one another, and preschoolers begin to make friends, but not until middle childhood does the peer group come into its own. Groups form naturally among children who live near one another or go to school together; thus peer groups often consist of children of the same racial or ethnic origin and similar socioeconomic status. Peers means "equals"; children who play together are usually close in age, though a neighborhood play group may include mixed ages. Too wide an age range brings differences, not only in size, but in interests and ability levels. Groups are usually all girls or all boys (Hartup, 1992). Children of the same sex have common interests; girls are generally more mature than boys, and (as we pointed out in Chapter 10) girls and boys play and talk to one another differently. Same-sex groups help children to learn gender-appropriate behaviors and to incorporate gender roles into their self-concept.

Today we are seeing new social patterns as technology changes the tools and habits of leisure. Television and videocassettes turn many children into "couch potatoes." Computer games demand few social skills. Children engage in more organized sports, which replace children's rules with adult rules and in which adult referees settle disputes so that children do not need to find ways to resolve matters among themselves. Still, children spend more time with others their own age than they did in early childhood.

How does the peer group influence children? What determines their acceptance by peers and their ability to make friends? Why do some children become bullies and others, victims?

Influence of the Peer Group

Children benefit in several ways from doing things with peers. They develop skills needed for sociability and intimacy, they enhance relationships, and they gain a sense of belonging. They are motivated to achieve, and they attain a sense of identity. They learn leadership, communication skills, cooperation, roles, and rules.

Such conclusions emerged from a study (Zarbatany, Hartmann, & Rankin, 1990) in which 91 Canadian fifth- and sixth-graders kept week-long diaries of what they did with other children and what they liked and disliked about their peers' behavior. Then another group of 81 children the same age rated the importance and prevalence of each activity and which behaviors they would most like or dislike in each (see Table 13-1). Noncompetitive activities (such as talking) offered opportunities for enhancing relationships: competitive ones (such as sports) helped children develop their self-concept.

As children begin to move away from parental influence, the peer group opens new perspectives and frees them to make independent judgments. Testing values they previously accepted unquestioningly against those of their peers helps them decide which to keep and which to discard. The peer group helps youngsters form opinions of themselves. In comparing themselves with others their age, children obtain a more realistic gauge of their abilities. The peer group helps children learn how to get along in society—how to adjust their needs and desires to those of others, when to yield, and when to stand firm. The peer group also offers emotional security. It is reassuring for children to find out that they are not alone in harboring thoughts that might offend an adult.

Table 13-1 Important and Prevalent Peer Activities as Rated by Fifth- and Sixth-Graders

Most Common Activities*		Most Important Activities*
Conversation		Noncontact sports
Hanging out		Watching TV or listening
Walking around at school		to records
Talking on the telephone		Conversation
Traveling to and from school		Talking on the telephone
Watching TV or listening		Physical games
to records		Going to parties
Physical games		Hanging out

Most Liked Behaviors

Invitations to participate	Sharing	Facilitating achievements
Performing admirably	Loyalty	Being nice or friendly
Physically helping	Humor	Absence of unpleasant
Complimenting or encouraging	Instructing	behavior
Giving permission	Helping	

Most Disliked Behaviors

Physical aggression	Teasing	Annoying or bothersome
Interfering with achievements	Ignoring	behavior
Verbal aggression	Violating rules	Expressing anger
Dishonesty	Criticizing	Unfaithfulness
		Greed or bossiness

*There were some gender differences. Boys liked sports more than girls did and spent more time in contact sports; girls spent more time shopping, talking on the telephone, and talking about hair styles and clothing than boys did.
Source: Zarbatany, Hartmann, & Rankin, 1990.

To be part of a peer group, a child must accept its values and behavioral norms; even though these may be undesirable, children may not have the strength to resist. It is usually in the company of peers that children shoplift, begin to use drugs, and act in other antisocial ways. Preadolescent children are especially susceptible to pressure to conform, and this pressure may change a troublesome child into a delinquent one. Children who already have antisocial leanings are the ones most likely to gravitate toward other antisocial youngsters and to be further influenced by them (Hartup, 1992). Peer group influence is especially strong when issues are unclear. Of course, some degree of conformity to group standards is healthy. It is unhealthy when it becomes destructive or prompts people to act against their own better judgment.

Another negative influence of the peer group may be a tendency to reinforce *prejudice:* unfavorable attitudes toward "outsiders," especially members of certain racial or ethnic groups. A study done in Montreal, Canada, where tensions exist between French-speaking and English-speaking citizens, found signs of prejudice in a sample of 254 English-speaking boys and girls in kindergarten through sixth grade (Powlishta, Serbin, Doyle, & White, 1994). The children were given brief descriptions of positive and negative traits (such as *helpful, smart, mean,* and *naughty*) and were asked whether one or both of two cartoon children—one English-speaking and the other French-speaking—would be likely to possess each trait. A similar procedure was followed with regard to male and

prejudice Unfavorable attitude toward members of certain groups outside one's own, especially racial or ethnic groups.

Among their peers, children get a sense of how smart, how athletic, and how likable they are. Both competition and shared confidences build the self-concept, helping children develop social skills and a sense of belonging. Peer groups tend to be of the same sex, enabling boys and girls to learn gender-appropriate behaviors.

CHECKPOINT

Can you . . .

- Tell some ways in which members of a peer group tend to be alike?
- Identify positive and negative effects of the peer group?

female figures (using gender stereotypes such as *ambitious* and *gentle*) and figures of overweight and normal-weight children. The researchers also asked the children which of two pictured children they would like to play with.

In general, children showed biases in favor of children like themselves, but these biases (except for a preference for children of the same sex) diminished with age and cognitive development. Girls were more biased with regard to gender, and boys with regard to ethnicity. However, individual differences were significant, and a child who was highly prejudiced in one respect was not necessarily prejudiced in another.

Prejudice may be lessened or eliminated by modifying children's experience. The most effective programs get children from different groups to work together toward a common goal, as on athletic teams (Gaertner, Mann, Murrell, & Dovidio, 1989).

Some unpopular children expect not to be liked, and so they do not try. Unpopular children often can gain acceptance from peers if they learn social skills.

Popularity

Popularity is not a frivolous issue. Unpopular children are deprived of a basic developmental experience—positive interaction with other youngsters—and may suffer sadness, a sense of rejection, and low self-esteem. Unpopularity during the preschool years is not necessarily cause for concern, but popularity gains importance in middle childhood, when youngsters spend more time with other children and their self-esteem is greatly affected by opinions of peers.

Peer relationships in middle childhood are strong predictors of later adjustment. Schoolchildren whose peers like them are likely to be well-adjusted as adolescents. Those who have trouble getting along with peers are more likely to develop psychological problems, drop out of school, or become delinquent (Hartup, 1992; Kupersmidt & Coie, 1990; P. Morison & Masten, 1991; Newcomb, Bukowski, & Pattee, 1993; Parker & Asher, 1987).

Popular and Unpopular Children

What are popular children like? Typically, they have good cognitive abilities, are good at solving social problems, are helpful to other children, and are assertive without being disruptive or aggressive. They are trustworthy, loyal, and self-disclosing enough to provide emotional support for other children. Their superior social skills make other people enjoy being with them (Newcomb et al., 1993).

Children can be unpopular for many reasons, some of which may not be fully within their control. Some unpopular youngsters are aggressive, some are hyperactive and inattentive, and some are withdrawn (Dodge, Coie, Pettit, & Price, 1990; Newcomb et al., 1993; A. W. Pope, Bierman, & Mumma, 1991). Others act silly and immature or anxious and uncertain. They are often insensitive to other children's feelings and cannot adapt to new situations (Bierman, Smoot, & Aumiller, 1993). Some show undue interest in being with groups of the other sex (Sroufe, Bennett, Englund, Urban, & Shulman, 1993). Some unpopular children expect not to be liked, and this becomes a self-fulfilling prophecy (Rabiner & Coie, 1989).

In one experiment, fifth- and sixth-graders were trained in social skills. They learned how to carry on a conversation: how to share information about themselves, how to show interest in others by asking questions, and how to give help, suggestions, invitations, and advice. When they had a chance to practice their new conversational skills in a group project with other children, they became better liked by the others and interacted more with them (Bierman & Furman, 1984). The experimental group who received the social skills training and took part in the group project showed more general and lasting improvement over a 6-week period (on measures of conversational skills, rates of interaction, peer acceptance, and self-perception) than did three other groups: a control group who received no training, an experimental group who received the training but did not participate in the group project, and another experimental group who took part in the group project but received no social skills teaching.

Family and Cultural Influences

It is often in the family that children acquire behaviors that affect popularity. Authoritative parenting tends to have better outcomes than authoritarian parenting (Dekovic & Janssens, 1992). Children of parents who punish and threaten are likely to threaten or act mean with other children; they are less popular than are children of parents who reason with them and try to help them understand how another person might feel (C. H. Hart, Ladd, & Burleson, 1990). Unpopular children report the least supportive relationships with their fathers (C. J. Patterson, Kupersmidt, & Griesler, 1990). Parents of aggressive children are likely to be either coercive or inept with them, and the children tend to be impulsive, mean, and disruptive (Hartup, 1989, 1992).

Culture helps determine what traits make children popular. In both Western and Chinese cultures, there is a bidirectional link between academic achievement and social competence. High achievers tend to be popular and socially skilled; and well-adjusted, well-liked children tend to do well in school (Chen, Rubin, & Li, 1997). One difference is that shyness and sensitivity are valued in China, but not in Western cultures. Thus children who show these traits are more likely to be popular in China—at least in middle childhood (see Box 13-2).

Friendship

Children may spend much of their free time in groups, but only as individuals do they form friendships. Popularity is the peer group's opinion of a child, but friendship is a two-way street. The strongest friendships involve equal commitment. They are not based on dominance or control, but on mutual give-and-take (T. P. George & Hartmann, 1996; Hartup, 1992; Newcomb & Bagwell, 1995).

Friendship begins with choice. A friend is someone a child feels affection for, is comfortable with, likes to do things with, and can share feelings and secrets with. Children look for friends who are like them: of the same age, sex, and ethnic group and with common interests (Hartup, 1992). Building on these commonalities, friendship becomes a complex pattern woven of the many positive experiences two children have with one another, which nourish and sustain their relationship (Newcomb & Bagwell, 1995).

School-age children typically have four or five friends with whom they spend most of their free time, but they usually play with only one or two at a time (Hartup, 1992). Girls care less about having many friends than about having a few close friends they can rely on; boys have more friendships, but they tend to

CHECKPOINT

Can you . . .

- Discuss the significance of unpopularity?
- Describe characteristics of popular and unpopular children?
- Identify family and cultural influences on popularity?

Box 13-2 Popularity: A Cross-Cultural View

How does culture affect popularity? Would a child who has what it takes to be popular in one culture be equally popular in another? Researchers compared 480 second- and fourth-graders in Shanghai, China, with 296 children the same ages in Ontario, Canada (X. Chen, Rubin, & Sun, 1992). Although the two samples were quite different—for example, none of the Canadian children came from peasant families, but many of the Chinese children did—both samples were representative of school-age children in the two countries.

The researchers assessed the children's popularity by means of two kinds of peer perceptions. First, each child was asked to name up to three classmates whose behavioral characteristics made them most suitable to take certain roles in a class play. Next, the children filled out a sociometric rating telling which three classmates they most and least liked to be with and which three classmates were their best friends.

The results showed that certain traits are valued similarly in both cultures. A sociable, cooperative child is likely to be popular in both China and Canada, and an aggressive child is likely to be rejected in both countries. However, one important difference emerged: shy, sensitive children are well-liked in China, but not in Canada. This is not surprising. Chinese children are encouraged to be cautious, to restrain themselves, and

to inhibit their urges; thus a quiet, shy youngster is considered well-behaved. In a western culture, by contrast, such a child is likely to be seen as socially immature, fearful, and lacking in self-confidence.

A follow-up study at ages 8 and 10 (X. Chen, Rubin, & Li, 1995) again found that shy, sensitive Chinese children were popular with peers. They were also rated by teachers as socially competent, as leaders, and as academic achievers. However, by age 12, an interesting twist had occurred: shy, sensitive Chinese children were no longer popular. In fact, they tended to be rejected by their peers, just as in western cultures.

It may be, then, that shyness and sensitivity take on different social meanings in China in the late part of middle childhood, as peer relationships become more important and adult approval becomes less so. As in the west, a shy preadolescent may lack the assertiveness and communication skills needed to establish and maintain strong peer relationships.

This research suggests that the influence of culture may interact with, and be tempered by, developmental processes that are more or less universal. Even in China, with its strong tradition of obedience to authority, the influence of adult social standards may wane as children's urges to make their own independent judgments of their peers assert themselves.

During middle childhood, shy, sensitive children are better liked in China than in western cultures, because they are considered well-behaved. Children this age tend to accept adult standards of behavior.

Table 13-2   Selman's Stages of Friendship

Stage	Description	Example
Stage 0: Momentary playmateship (ages 3 to 7)	On this *undifferentiated* level of friendship, children are egocentric and have trouble considering another person's point of view; they tend to think only about what they want from a relationship. Most very young children define their friends in terms of physical closeness and value them for material or physical attributes.	"She lives on my street" or "He has the Power Rangers."
Stage 1: One-way assistance (ages 4 to 9)	On this *unilateral* level, a "good friend" does what the child wants the friend to do.	"She's not my friend anymore, because she wouldn't go with me when I wanted her to" or "He's my friend because he always says yes when I want to borrow his eraser."
Stage 2: Two-way fair-weather cooperation (ages 6 to 12)	This *reciprocal* level overlaps stage 1. It involves give-and-take but still serves many separate self-interests, rather than the common interests of the two friends.	"We are friends; we do things for each other" or "A friend is someone who plays with you when you don't have anybody else to play with."
Stage 3: Intimate, mutually shared relationships (ages 9 to 15)	On this *mutual* level, children view a friendship as having a life of its own. It is an ongoing, systematic, committed relationship that incorporates more than doing things for each other. Friends become possessive and demand exclusivity.	"It takes a long time to make a close friend, so you really feel bad if you find out that your friend is trying to make other friends too."
Stage 4: Autonomous interdependence (beginning at age 12)	In this *interdependent* stage, children respect friends' needs for both dependency and autonomy.	"A good friendship is a real commitment, a risk you have to take; you have to support and trust and give, but you have to be able to let go too."

Source: Selman, 1980; Selman & Selman, 1979.

be less intimate and affectionate (Furman, 1982; Furman & Buhrmester, 1985). Boys tend to be more concerned about mastery and status in friendships, whereas girls are more concerned about having good relationships and enjoying them (Hartup, 1996b).

Even unpopular children can make and be friends. However, they have fewer friends than popular children and tend to find them among younger children, other unpopular children, or children in a different class or a different school (T. P. George & Hartmann, 1996).

Children's concepts of friendship, and the ways they act with their friends, change with age, reflecting cognitive and emotional growth (Hartup, 1992; Newcomb & Bagwell, 1995). Preschool friends play together, but friendship among school-age children is deeper and more stable (Hartup, 1992). Children cannot be or have true friends until they achieve the cognitive maturity to consider other people's views and needs as well as their own.

On the basis of interviews with more than 250 people between ages 3 and 45, Robert Selman (1980; Selman & Selman, 1979) traced changing conceptions of friendship through five overlapping stages (see Table 13-2). He found that most school-age children are in stage 2 (reciprocal friendship based on self-interest). Older children, from about age 9 up, may be in stage 3 (intimate, mutually shared relationships).

Friendship helps children to feel good about themselves; to become more sensitive and loving, more loyal and faithful, more able to give and receive respect. Friends know one another well, trust each other, feel a sense of commitment to each other, and treat each other as equals. They can help each other get

Friendship becomes deeper and more stable in middle childhood, reflecting cognitive and emotional growth. Although some boys develop just one or two close friendships, this is a more typical pattern among girls. Boys more commonly have a greater number of less intimate friends.

through stressful transitions, such as starting a new school or adjusting to parents' divorce. Of course, the bond needs to be sturdy enough to withstand the inevitable quarrels. Friends disagree more than children who are not friends; learning to resolve conflict is an important function of friendship (Furman, 1982; Hartup, 1992, 1996a, 1996b; Newcomb & Bagwell, 1995).

Friendship has cognitive benefits, too. As we reported in Chapter 12, friends who do written assignments together tend to produce more sophisticated writing. Friends also cooperate more effectively than mere acquaintances in creative exploration and in solving difficult or ambiguous problems (Hartup, 1996a, 1996b).

Friendship can have negative consequences, as well. Aggressive or antisocial children, who are generally disliked by other children, tend to seek out friends like themselves, and they egg each other on to antisocial acts (Hartup, 1989, 1992, 1996a). Let's look more closely at aggression in middle childhood.

Aggression and Bullying

Although aggression is common among preschoolers (see Chapter 10), by school age *overt* aggression (physical force and verbal threats) typically wanes, to give way to more subtle forms, such as teasing, manipulation, and bids for control (Crick, Bigbee, & Howes, 1996). As we have noted, highly aggressive children tend to be unpopular in middle childhood. If they are habitually aggressive and pick on weaker children, they are commonly called *bullies.*

Aggression and Social Information Processing

What makes children act aggressively? Part of the answer may lie in the way they process social information—what features of the social environment they pay attention to, and how they interpret what they perceive. When highly aggressive children become emotionally aroused, memories of past incidents may distort their current perceptions, so that they misinterpret others' intentions toward them. This faulty processing can lead to aggressive behavior (Crick & Dodge, 1994, 1996).

Children who engage in *hostile* (also called *reactive*) aggression tend to have a *hostile bias;* they frequently see other children as trying to hurt them, and they

CHECKPOINT

Can you . . .

- Distinguish between popularity and friendship?
- List characteristics children look for in friends?
- Compare boys' and girls' friendships?
- Summarize how friendships change with age?

strike out angrily either in retaliation or in self-defense (Crick & Dodge, 1996; Waldman, 1996). Since people often *do* become hostile toward someone who acts aggressively toward them, a hostile bias may become a self-fulfilling prophecy, setting in motion a cycle of aggression.

Children who engage in *instrumental* (or *proactive*) aggression see the world quite differently. They view force or coercion as effective ways to get what they want, and they act deliberately, not out of anger. In social learning terms, they are aggressive because they expect to be rewarded for it; and when they *are* rewarded, their belief in the effectiveness of aggression is reinforced (Crick & Dodge, 1996).

Adults can help children curb *hostile* aggression by teaching them how to recognize when they are getting angry and how to control their anger. *Instrumental* aggression tends to stop if it is not rewarded. Above all, aggressive children need help in altering the way they process social information, so that they do not interpret aggression as either justified or useful (Crick & Dodge, 1996).

Aggression and Gender

Are boys more aggressive than girls? Many people think so, but this may be because boys and girls show aggression in different ways.

Boys do show more overt aggression. Girls tend to engage in a more complex, subtle form—covert, or **relational aggression** (also called *indirect*, or *psychological aggression*). This kind of aggression consists of damaging or interfering with relationships, reputations, or psychological well-being. It may involve spreading rumors ("Did you hear that Christine stole a dollar out of my lunch money?"), name-calling, withholding friendship ("I won't be your friend if you play with Sally"), or excluding someone from a group ("You can't play with us"). Nine-year-olds recognize such behavior as aggressive; they realize that it stems from anger and is aimed at harming others (Crick, Bigbee, & Howes, 1996).

Aggressors of either kind tend to be unpopular and to have social and psychological problems, but it is not clear whether aggression causes these problems or is a reaction to them (Crick & Grotpeter, 1995). Overtly aggressive children tend to be impulsive and defiant and to blame others for their problems; relationally aggressive children show similar tendencies but also tend to be lonely and depressed. Overtly aggressive girls and relationally aggressive boys are more poorly adjusted than children who engage in the form of aggression more typical of their sex, perhaps because peers are less willing to tolerate such "offbeat" behavior (Crick, 1997).

Bullies and Victims

Aggression becomes **bullying** when it is deliberately, persistently directed against a particular target: a victim who is weak, vulnerable, and defenseless. Male bullies tend to use physical force (overt aggression) and to select either boys or girls as victims. Female bullies use verbal or psychological means (relational aggression) and are more likely to victimize other girls (M. J. Boulton, 1995).

Patterns of bullying and victimization may become established as early as kindergarten. As tentative peer groups form, aggression is directed at various targets. As the aggressors get to know which children make the easiest "marks," they begin to focus their aggression on them. Children who are victims of bullying tend to have trouble adjusting to school, though it is unclear whether victimization hampers their attention to schoolwork or whether children who are having school problems are more likely to be victimized (Kochenderfer & Ladd, 1996).

In one observational study, 186 six- and eight-year-old African American boys were assigned to play groups consisting of six boys who did not know each other. They were then observed during five daily 45-minute sessions. Thirteen boys became chronically victimized by the other children. These victims were

relational aggression
Aggression aimed at damaging or interfering with another person's relationships, reputation, or psychological well-being; also called *covert, indirect,* or *psychological aggression.*

bullying Aggression deliberately and persistently directed against a particular target, or victim, who is weak, vulnerable, and defenseless.

submissive, did not start conversations, did not try to persuade other children to do what they wanted, and played by themselves more than did the other boys. When other children teased or hit them, they showed pain, asked them to stop, gave up toys, or withdrew. The more they submitted, the more the other boys picked on them. Although the victims were not disliked at the beginning of the study, by the end they were not well liked (Schwartz, Dodge, & Coie, 1993).

Middle childhood is a prime time for bullying. The problem exists in many industrialized countries, and some, such as the United Kingdom, have undertaken extensive research and intervention efforts.

One British study suggests that bullying stems from the personalities of bully and victim, not the composition of the peer group. Among 158 eight- and nine-year-olds, about 1 out of 3 were identified by peers as bullies or victims, or both. All of the bullies were boys; victims were evenly divided between boys and girls. These identifications persisted throughout the school year and the beginning of the next, even when classes and classmates changed (M. J. Boulton & Smith, 1994).

Victims tend to have poor athletic skills and low self-esteem—though it is not clear whether low self-esteem leads to or follows from victimization. Although both bullies and victims are unpopular, bullies have more friends, who may egg them on (M. J. Boulton & Smith, 1994). In another British study, 8- to 10-year-old boys were observed on school playgrounds, the most frequent site of bullying. Bullies moved in large packs, though not necessarily with other bullies. Victims did not take part in organized games; they tended to spend time alone or to stand around talking with a few friends and thus stood out as potential targets (M. J. Boulton, 1995).

The likelihood of being bullied, but not of being a bully, seems to decrease steadily throughout middle childhood and adolescence. One reason may be that younger children are less able to defend themselves; however, since most bullying is done by and to agemates, this is probably not the primary factor. A more likely possibility arises from the fact that bullies are instrumental aggressors; their behavior tends to stop if it is not rewarded. As children get older, most of them may learn how to discourage bullying, leaving a smaller "pool" of available victims for bullies to pick on.

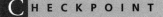

CHECKPOINT

Can you . . .

- Compare how social information processing contributes to hostile and instrumental aggression?

- Distinguish between overt and relational aggression and discuss gender differences in the incidence of each?

- Describe how patterns of bullying and victimization become established and change during middle childhood?

Mental Health

The mental health of American children seems to have worsened since the mid-1970s. When parent and teacher ratings of 2,466 children ages 7 to 16 who were not under psychological treatment in 1989 were compared with ratings of similar samples of children in 1976 and 1981, it appeared that emotional and behavioral problems had increased during those years (Achenbach & Howell, 1993). In 1976, only 10 percent of the children were judged to have problems that might need clinical treatment; in 1989, the comparable figure was more than 18 percent. Furthermore, nearly 3 times the proportion of children as in 1976 were excluded from the 1989 sample because they had required mental health services during the previous year.

Although poor children had more problems, the decline in mental health occurred across economic levels. When income was taken into account, black and white children were about equally affected. Conditions showing significant increases, according to parents and teachers, included *withdrawal or social problems* (wanting to be alone or to play with younger children or being secretive, sulky, overly dependent, or lethargic); *attention or thinking problems* (impulsiveness, hyperactivity, or difficulty in concentrating and doing schoolwork); *aggression or delinquency* (being mean, stubborn, hot-tempered, disobedient, destructive, or antisocial); and *anxiety or depression* (feeling sad, unloved, nervous, fearful, or lonely).

The growth in emotional disturbances may reflect the increasing stress of modern life. The trend is no better in several other countries, including France, Australia, Thailand, and Puerto Rico (Achenbach & Howell, 1993). However, different problems surface in different cultures. For example, Embu children of Kenya, whose parents emphasize obedience, tend to be troubled by fears, guilt, and bodily complaints without known medical causes. U.S. children, whose parents value independence, are more likely to argue excessively or to be cruel or disobedient (Weisz, Sigman, Weiss, & Mosk, 1993). Some problems seem to be associated with a particular phase of a child's life and will go away on their own, but others need to be treated to prevent future trouble.

Common Emotional Disturbances

Emotional disturbances can affect all aspects of development. According to one study of 776 children ages 9 to 18, girls who show anxiety disorders grow up to be, on average, one to two inches shorter than other women, apparently because such disorders affect the brain's release of growth hormones (Pine, Cohen, & Brook, 1996).

Let's look at one common type of anxiety disorder involving separation from parents. We'll also describe two other disorders often seen among U.S. schoolchildren: acting-out behavior and childhood depression.

Separation Anxiety Disorder and School Phobia

Nicole wakes up on a school morning complaining of nausea, stomachache, or headache. Soon after she receives permission to stay home, the symptom clears up. This goes on day after day, and the longer she is out of school, the harder it is to get her back.

school phobia Unrealistic fear of going to school; may be a form of separation anxiety disorder.

separation anxiety disorder Condition involving excessive, prolonged anxiety concerning separation from home or from people to whom a child is attached.

Nicole's behavior is typical of children with *school phobia,* an unrealistic fear of going to school. School phobia may be a type of *separation anxiety disorder,* a condition involving excessive anxiety for at least 4 weeks concerning separation from home or from people to whom the child is attached. Separation anxiety disorder affects some 4 percent of children and young adolescents and may persist through the college years. These children often come from close-knit, caring families. They may develop the disorder after the death of a pet, an illness, or a move to a new school (American Psychiatric Association [APA], 1994).

Some children have realistic reasons to avoid going to school: a sarcastic teacher, overly demanding work, or a bully in the schoolyard (Kochenderfer & Ladd, 1996). In such instances, the environment may need changing, not the child. True school phobia seems to have more to do with children's fear of leaving their mothers than with a fear of school. School-phobic children tend to be average or good students, ages 5 to 15, and are equally likely to be boys or girls. They tend to be timid and inhibited away from home, but willful, stubborn, and demanding with their parents. Their parents are more likely than other parents to be depressed, to suffer from anxiety disorders, and to report family dysfunction (G. A. Bernstein & Garfinkel, 1988). The most important element in treatment is an early, gradual return to school. Usually children go back without too much trouble once treatment is begun.

Acting-Out Behavior

acting-out behavior Misbehavior (such as lying or stealing) spurred by emotional difficulties.

When children continually fight, lie, steal, or destroy property, they may be showing *acting-out behavior,* misbehavior that is an outward expression of emotional turmoil. Almost all children lie occasionally, but when children past the age of 6 or 7 continue to tell tall tales, they are often signaling a sense of insecurity. They may be seeking attention and esteem or showing hostility toward their parents. Similarly, occasional minor stealing, while it needs to be dealt with, is not necessarily a sign of serious trouble; but children who steal repeatedly are often showing hostility. Sometimes the stolen items seem to symbolize the parents' love, power, or authority, of which the child feels deprived (A. H. Chapman, 1974).

Childhood Depression

"Nobody likes me" is a common complaint among school-age children, who tend to be popularity-conscious; but a prolonged sense of friendlessness may be one sign of *childhood depression*—an affective disorder, or disorder of mood, that goes beyond normal, temporary sadness. Other symptoms may include inability to have fun or concentrate, fatigue, extreme activity or apathy, crying, sleep problems, feelings of worthlessness, weight change, physical complaints, and frequent thoughts about death or suicide. Any five of these symptoms, lasting for at least 2 weeks, may point to depression (APA, 1994). If symptoms persist, the child should be given psychological help. Treatment is important, not only for immediate relief, but also because childhood depression may result in attempted suicide and often signals the beginning of a problem that may persist into adulthood.

Treatment Techniques

The choice of treatment depends on many factors: the nature of the problem, the child's personality, the family's willingness to participate and its finances, the facilities available in the community, and often, the orientation of the professional first consulted.

Psychological treatment can take several forms. In *individual psychotherapy*, a therapist sees a child one-on-one, to help the child gain insights into his or her personality and relationships and to interpret feelings and behavior. Such treatment may be helpful at a time of stress, such as the death of a parent, even when a child has not shown signs of disturbance. Child psychotherapy is usually more effective when combined with counseling for the parents.

In *family therapy*, the therapist sees the family together, observes how members interact, and points out both growth-producing and growth-inhibiting or destructive patterns of family functioning. Sometimes the child whose problem brings the family into therapy is, ironically, the healthiest member, responding openly to a troubled family situation. Therapy can help parents confront their own conflicts and begin to resolve them. This is often the first step toward resolving the child's problems as well.

Behavior therapy, or *behavioral modification,* is a form of psychotherapy that uses principles of learning theory (see Chapter 1) to eliminate undesirable behaviors (such as temper tantrums) or to develop desirable ones (such as putting away toys after play). In the latter example, every time the child puts toys away, she or he gets a reward, such as praise, a treat, or a token to be exchanged for a new toy.

A statistical analysis of many studies found that, in general, psychotherapy is effective with children and adolescents, especially with adolescent girls. Behavior therapy was more effective than nonbehavioral methods. Results were best when treatment was targeted to specific problems and desired outcomes (Weisz, Weiss, Han, Granger, & Morton, 1995).

During the 1980s, the use of *drug therapy* to treat childhood emotional disorders increased (Tuma, 1989). In Chapter 12, we mentioned the use of Ritalin to treat hyperactivity. Antidepressants are commonly prescribed for depression, and antipsychotics for severe psychological problems. Yet studies almost invariably find that antidepressants are no more effective than *placebos* (substances with no active ingredients) in treating depression in children and adolescents, and neither is fluoxetine (Prozac), another drug in wide use (R. L. Fisher &

childhood depression
Affective disorder characterized by such symptoms as a prolonged sense of friendlessness, inability to have fun or concentrate, fatigue, extreme activity or apathy, feelings of worthlessness, weight change, physical complaints, and thoughts of death or suicide.

Everyone feels "blue" at times, but a child's chronic depression can be a danger signal and should be taken seriously, especially when it represents a marked change from the child's usual behavior.

individual psychotherapy
Psychological treatment in which a therapist sees a troubled person one-on-one, to help the patient gain insight into his or her personality, relationships, feelings, and behavior.

family therapy Psychological treatment in which a therapist sees the whole family together to analyze patterns of family functioning.

behavior therapy Therapeutic approach using principles of learning theory to encourage desired behaviors or eliminate undesired ones; also called *behavioral modification.*

drug therapy Administration of drugs to treat emotional disorders.

Sometimes a child's difficulties bring the entire family into therapy. Family therapy can help all family members examine their interactions and resolve problems.

CHECKPOINT

Can you . . .

- Identify causes and symptoms of school phobia, acting-out behavior, and childhood depression?
- Describe and evaluate four common types of therapy for emotional disorders?

Fisher, 1996; Sommers-Flanagan & Sommers-Flanagan, 1996). Drugs may help some conditions, but they are usually most effective when combined with psychotherapy and should not be used in its place. Giving pills to change children's behavior is a radical step: many medicines have side effects. Furthermore, drugs may produce merely surface changes without getting at underlying causes. Many therapists therefore turn to drugs only as a last resort.

Stress and Resilience

Stressful events are part of childhood, and most children learn to cope. Stress that becomes overwhelming, however, can lead to psychological problems. Illness, the birth of a sibling, day-to-day frustration, and parents' temporary absence are common sources of stress for almost every child. Divorce or death of parents, hospitalization, and the day-in, day-out grind of poverty affect many children. Some children undergo the trauma of war, earthquakes, or kidnapping. Such severe stressors may have long-term effects on physical and psychological well-being (Garmezy, 1983; Pynoos et al., 1987). Yet some children show remarkable resilience in surviving such ordeals.

Stresses of Modern Life

The child psychologist David Elkind (1981, 1984, 1986) has called today's child the "hurried child." He warns that the pressures of modern life are forcing children to grow up too soon and are making their childhood too stressful. Today's children are expected to succeed in school, to compete in sports, and to meet parents' emotional needs. Children are exposed to many adult problems on television and in real life before they have mastered the problems of childhood. They know about sex and violence, and if they live in single-parent homes or dual-earner families, they often must shoulder adult responsibilities. Yet children are not small adults. They feel and think like children, and they need the years of childhood for healthy development.

One source of stress is the disruption that occurs when families move. Children in some countries, such as the United States, move much more often than in others (see Figure 13-3). Moving is hard on children. They feel the loss of friends, perhaps of extended family, and of control over their lives. They generally have to change schools and are less likely to know many adults well. Children who move three or more times have about twice the risk of emotional, behavior, health, or school problems as children who have never moved, even when

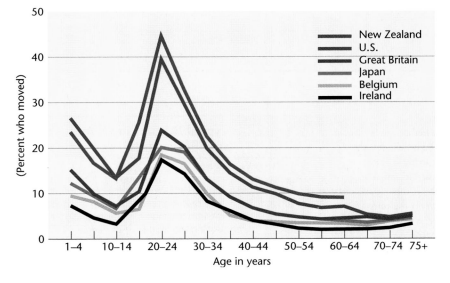

Figure 13-3

Percentage of population that changed usual residence in 1 year for six countries, by age, circa 1981. Children in some countries move much more often than those in others. In the United States such moves seem to be due largely to poverty and to parental separation.

Source: Long, 1992.

income and other social factors are taken into account (M. G. Fowler, Simpson, & Schoendorf, 1993; G. A. Simpson & Fowler, 1994).

Given how much stress children are exposed to, it should not be surprising that they worry a lot. What they worry about, however, may come as a surprise. We might expect that children would worry most about things that are part of their daily lives, such as how they are doing in school. Indeed, in a survey and interviews of 272 ethnically diverse second- through sixth-graders in a large metropolitan area (Silverman, La Greca, & Wasserstein, 1995), school did emerge as one of the children's chief concerns, as it has in previous studies. So did health—their own or someone else's. However, the worry reported by the largest number of children (56 percent of the sample) was personal harm from others: being robbed, stabbed, or shot.

These children were not in a high-crime area, nor had they personally experienced many attacks. Their intense anxiety about their safety seemed to reflect the high rates of crime and violence in the larger society. A steady diet of violence on television, in comic books and movies, and in the newspapers can make even relatively protected children feel that their world is not as safe as they had thought and that their parents cannot always guard them. How much more stressful life must be, then, for children who are in real, constant danger! (See Box 13-3.)

Among 918 children and adolescents ages 7 to 18 in Victoria, Australia, the 10 most common fears had to do with death and danger (for example, being threatened with a gun, being hit by a car or truck, nuclear war, and being kidnapped). However, most of these fears diminished during the three years of the study, while fears related to medical conditions and psychological stress (for example, having to speak in front of a class) increased. Apparently cognitive development leads children to focus on more realistic fears (Gullone & King, 1997).

Coping with Stress: The Resilient Child

Two children of the same age and sex are exposed to the same stressful experience; one crumbles while the other remains emotionally healthy. Why?

Resilient children are those who weather circumstances that would blight most others, who maintain their composure and competence under challenge or threat, or who bounce back from traumatic events. They are the children of the ghetto who distinguish themselves in the professions. They are the children of divorce who adjust and go on with their lives. They are the neglected or abused children who manage to form intimate relationships and be good parents. They

resilient children Children who weather adverse circumstances, function well despite challenges or threats, or bounce back from traumatic events that would have a highly negative impact on the emotional development of most children.

Box 13-3 Children Who Live in Chronic Danger

A 6-year-old in Washington, D.C., when asked whether she felt safe anywhere, said, "In my basement," because it had no windows where bullets could enter. A 10-year-old ran away in terror after seeing a man shot in the back on the street. A 6-year-old saw her mother punched in the face by a drug addict. These inner-city children are, unfortunately, typical of many who live in the midst of violence and, as a result, are fearful, anxious, distressed, and depressed (Garbarino, Dubrow, Kostelny, & Pardo, 1992).*

Possibly because the subject is so painful or because children may not report all that they see or experience, parents tend to underestimate the extent and effects of children's exposure to violence. Even if they are aware, some parents are powerless to shield their children from witnessing violence or becoming victims. Children may become desensitized to brutality; they may come to take it for granted and may not take necessary precautions to protect themselves.

Children who grow up surrounded by violence often have trouble concentrating and remembering because fears keep them from getting enough sleep. They may be afraid that their mothers will abandon them. Some become aggressive in order to hide their fear or protect themselves, or simply in imitation of what they have seen. Many do not allow themselves to become attached to other people, for fear of more hurt and loss. Children who first see or experience violence before age 11 are 3 times more likely to develop psychiatric symptoms than if first exposed to it as teenagers (J. Davidson & Smith, 1990). (Table 13-3 gives typical reactions to violence at different ages.) Children with multiple risks—those who live in violent communities, who are poor, and who receive inadequate parenting, education, and health care—are the most likely to suffer permanent developmental damage (Rutter, 1987).

These children need islands of safety in their lives. They need caring relationships with adults outside the family—teachers or community leaders—who can deal with their concerns in the day-to-day context of classroom or group meetings. Play and art activities can help a child express feelings about a traumatic event, restore a sense of inner control, build self-worth, and set the stage for dialogue with an adult whom the child can trust.

* Unless otherwise referenced, this discussion is based on Garbarino et al., 1992.

Table 13-3	Typical Reactions to Violence at Different Ages
Age	**Reaction**
Early childhood	Passive reactions and regression (such as bed-wetting, clinging, speaking less); fear of leaving the mother or of sleeping alone; aggressive play; sleep problems
School-age	Aggressiveness, inhibition, somatic complaints (headaches, stomachaches, etc.); learning difficulties (forgetfulness, trouble concentrating); psychological difficulties (anxiety, phobias, withdrawal, denial); grief and loss reactions (hopelessness, despair, depression, inability to play, suicidal thoughts, uncaring behavior, destructiveness); acting tough to hide fears; constricted activities
Adolescence	Some of the same reactions as school-age children, plus acting-out and self-destructive behavior (drug abuse, delinquency, promiscuity, life-threatening reenactments of the trauma); identification with the aggressor (becoming violent, joining a gang)

Source: Garbarino et al., 1992.

To reduce violence, the American Academy of Pediatrics (1992a) recommends regulating and restricting ownership of handguns and ammunition; stopping the romanticizing of gun use in television and movies; and targeting adolescents at high risk for becoming violent (chiefly teenage boys and drug and alcohol abusers) for community services. In addition, the American Psychological Association's Commission on Violence and Youth recommends community programs built around the interests and needs of youth, including health care, recreation, and vocational training (Youngstrom, 1992). Positive adult role models, peer-group discussions, and family intervention may help deter drug abuse and violence.

are the survivors of the Holocaust who went on to lead normal, successful adult lives. In spite of the bad cards they have been dealt, these children are winners.

Protective factors that seem to contribute to resilience (N. Eisenberg et al., 1997; Masten et al., 1990; E. E. Werner, 1993) include:

- *The child's personality:* Resilient children are adaptable. They are friendly, well liked, independent, and sensitive to others. They feel and are competent, have high self-esteem, and tend to be good students. They are creative, resourceful, independent, and pleasant to be with.

- *The family:* Resilient children are likely to have good relationships with one or two supportive parents. If not, an older child may be close to at least one other competent adult who is interested, caring, and trustworthy.
- *Learning experiences:* Resilient children are good learners and problem solvers. They have seen parents, older siblings, or others deal with frustration and make the best of a bad situation. They have faced challenges themselves, worked out solutions, and learned that they can exert some control over their lives.
- *Reduced risk:* Children who have been exposed to only one of a number of factors strongly related to psychiatric disorder (such as parental discord, low social status, a disturbed mother, a criminal father, and experience in foster care or an institution) are better able than children who have been exposed to more than one risk factor to overcome the stress.
- *Compensating experiences:* A supportive school environment or successful experiences in studies, in sports, in music, or with other children or interested adults can help make up for a destructive home life. In adulthood, a good marriage can compensate for poor relationships earlier in life.

All this does not mean that bad things which happen in a child's life do not matter. In general, children with unfavorable backgrounds have more problems in adjustment than children with more favorable backgrounds. What is heartening about these findings is that negative childhood experiences do not necessarily determine the outcome of a person's life and that many children have the strength to rise above the most difficult circumstances.

Adolescence, too, is a stressful, risk-filled time—more so than middle childhood. Yet most adolescents develop the skills and competence to deal with the challenges they face, as we'll see in Chapters 14, 15, and 16.

C HECK P O I N T

Can you. . .

- Explain Elkind's concept of the "hurried child"?
- Name the most common source of fear and anxiety in urban children and tell how fears change with age?
- Identify protective factors that contribute to resilience?

SUMMARY

The Developing Self

- The self-concept develops greatly during middle childhood. According to neo-Piagetian theory, cognitive development allows school-age children to form **representational systems** that are more balanced and realistic than before.
- Self-esteem links cognitive, emotional, and social aspects of personality. According to Erikson, the chief source of self-esteem is children's view of their own productive competence—the "virtue" that develops through resolution of the crisis of middle childhood, **industry versus inferiority.** According to Susan Harter's research, self-esteem, or global self-worth, arises primarily from social support as well as from a child's self-evaluation.
- Emotional development contributes to self-esteem. School-age children have internalized shame and pride and can better understand and control their emotions. Emotional expressiveness tends to be linked with empathy and prosocial behavior.

The Child in the Family

- Although school-age children spend less time with parents than with peers, relationships with parents continue to be the most important. Culture influences family relationships and roles, including the importance of extended family.
- Family structure and family atmosphere are two major components of the family environment. Family structure in itself is less influential than the atmosphere in the home, which includes emotional tone and economic well-being.
- **Coregulation** is an intermediate stage in the transfer of control from parent to child.
- The impact of mothers' working depends on such factors as the child's age, sex, temperament, and personality; whether the mother works full time or part time; how she feels about her work; whether she has a supportive mate; the family's socioeconomic status; and the kind of care the child receives. Fathers' family roles

seem to be as important to them as work roles; distress over work-family role conflicts can affect their children.

- Parents living in persistent poverty may be less able to offer children effective discipline and monitoring and emotional support.

- Many children in the United States today grow up in nontraditional family structures: one-parent families, stepfamilies, gay and lesbian families, and families headed by grandparents or other relatives.

- Children's reactions to divorce depend on a number of factors, including age, gender, and resilience; the way the parents handle the situation; the custody arrangement; financial circumstances; contact with the noncustodial parent; and circumstances surrounding a parent's remarriage. Some children show long-term negative effects of parental divorce.

- Children living with only one parent or in stepfamilies are at risk of lower achievement in school and other problems. In single-parent families, these effects seem to be largely related to low income.

- Despite public concern about children living with homosexual parents, studies have found no ill effects.

- Divorce can weaken ties between grandparents (usually the paternal grandparents) and grandchildren.

- Siblings exert a powerful influence on each other, either directly (through their interaction) or indirectly (through their impact on each other's relationship with parents).

- The roles and responsibilities of siblings in nonindustrialized societies are more significant and more structured throughout life than in industrialized societies.

The Child in the Peer Group

- Peer groups generally consist of children who are similar in age, sex, ethnicity, and socioeconomic status, and who live near one another.

- The peer group has several positive developmental functions: it helps children develop social skills, allows them to test and adopt values independent of parents, gives them a sense of belonging, and fosters the self-concept. One negative effect is encouragement of conformity; another is racial or ethnic segregation, which can reinforce **prejudice.**

- Popularity influences self-esteem. Behaviors that affect popularity may be derived from family relationships and may be culturally defined. Children rejected by peers are at risk of emotional and behavioral problems.

- Friendship involves mutual commitment and give-and-take. Friends typically are of the same age, sex, and ethnicity and have common interests. Intimacy and stability of relationships increases during middle childhood.

- Highly aggressive children tend to be disliked. Boys are more overtly aggressive, but girls are more likely to engage in **relational aggression.**

- Middle childhood is a prime time for **bullying.** Bullies generally are boys; victims may be boys or girls. Both bullies and victims are unpopular. Victims tend to have poor athletic skills and low self-esteem.

Mental Health

- Emotional and behavioral problems among school-age children have increased since the mid-1970s. Common disorders include **school phobia** (a form of **separation anxiety disorder**), **acting-out behavior,** and **childhood depression.**

- Treatment techniques include **individual psychotherapy, family therapy, behavior therapy,** and **drug therapy.**

- As a result of the pressures of modern life, many children are experiencing a shortened and stressful childhood. One source of stress is frequent mobility. Children tend to worry about their personal safety, about school, and about health.

- **Resilient children** are better able than others to withstand stress. Factors related to personality, family, experience, and degree of risk are associated with ability to bounce back from unfortunate circumstances.

KEY TERMS

representational systems (466)
industry versus inferiority (466)
coregulation (470)
prejudice (485)
relational aggression (492)
bullying (492)
school phobia (494)
separation anxiety disorder (494)

acting-out behavior (494)
childhood depression (495)
individual psychotherapy (495)
family therapy (495)
behavior therapy (495)
drug therapy (495)
resilient children (497)

QUESTIONS FOR THOUGHT AND DISCUSSION

1. Should schools give children "emotional education"?

2. If finances permit, should either the mother or the father stay home to take care of the children?

3. Would you advise parents who want a divorce to stay married until their children have grown up? Why or why not?

4. Should older siblings in industrialized societies have regular duties in taking care of younger ones, as is true in nonindustrialized societies?

5. How can or should society help grandparents who are raising grandchildren?

6. What can adults do to help unpopular children, bullies, and victims?

7. How can parents and schools reduce racial, religious, and ethnic prejudice?

8. How can adults contribute to children's resilience? Give examples.

Adolescence: *A Bird's-Eye View*

Adolescence

In adolescence, young people's appearance changes; as a result of the hormonal events of puberty, they take on the bodies of adults. Their thinking changes, too; they are better able to think abstractly and hypothetically. Their feelings change about almost everything. All areas of development converge as adolescents confront their major task: establishing an identity—including a sexual identity—that will carry over to adulthood.

In Chapters 14, 15, and 16, we see how adolescents incorporate their drastically changed appearances, their puzzling physical yearnings, and their new cognitive abilities into their sense of self. We see how the peer group serves as the testing ground for teenagers' ideas about life and about themselves. We look at risks and problems that arise during the teenage years, as well as at characteristic strengths of adolescents.

Physical Development and Health in Adolescence

What I like in my adolescents is that they have not yet hardened. We all confuse hardening and strength. Strength we must achieve, but not callousness.

Anaïs Nin, *The Diaries of Anaïs Nin*, Vol. IV

Focus

Anne Frank

F or her thirteenth birthday on June 12, 1942, Anne Frank's parents gave her a diary. This small, red-checkered cloth-covered volume was the first of three that Anne kept during the next two years. Little did she dream that her jottings would become one of the most famous, most poignant accounts of the experience of victims of the Holocaust during World War II, selling more than 13 million copies in 50 languages and being made into at least two plays and two motion pictures.

Anne Frank was born in Frankfurt, Germany, in 1929, into a well-to-do Jewish family. She, her parents, Otto and Edith Frank, and her older sister, Margot, fled to Amsterdam when Hitler came to power in 1933, only to see the Netherlands fall to Nazi conquest in May 1940. In her early diary entries, Anne—like a typical teenager—wrote about playing ping pong, about going to an ice cream store, about a math teacher who called her "the Incurable Chatterbox," and about her "strings of boyfriends." Only occasional references to the deteriorating situation of the Jews of Holland—to restrictions on what stores they could patronize or how late they could stay out at night—foreshadowed the ordeal that awaited Anne and her family.

In the summer of 1942, the Nazis began rounding up Jews for deportation to concentration camps. In July, when Margot received a call-up notice to report for work in the "East," the Frank family went into hiding. Taking only as much clothing as they could wear, they moved into a "Secret Annexe" behind the upper floors of the office and warehouse building occupied by Otto Frank's chemical and pharmaceutical firm. Behind a gray door concealed by a movable cupboard, a steep stairway led to the four rooms occupied by the Franks, another Jewish couple named Van Daan and their 15-year-old son, Peter, and a middle-aged dentist, Albert Dussel,* with whom Anne had to share a room. For two years, the eight of them stayed in those confined quarters, day and night, until German and Dutch security police, acting on a tip from an informant, discovered and raided the "Secret Annexe" and sent its occupants to concentration camps, where all but Anne's father died.

Anne's writings, found by friends of her family after the raid and later edited and published by her father in 1947, as *The Diary of a Young Girl,* recorded the life the fugitives led. During the day they had to be quiet so as not to alert people working in the offices below.

*The actual names of the other occupants of the "Annexe" were Hermann, Auguste, and Peter van Pels and Fritz Pfeffer. Anne invented the names used here, which appear in the originally published version of her diary.

F o c u s *—Continued*

They saw no one except a few trusted Christian friends who risked their lives to bring food, books, newspapers, and essential supplies. Anne, Margot, and Peter passed the time by carrying on their studies and playing Monopoly. From the attic window they witnessed brutal roundups of families like their own.

The *Diary* reveals the thoughts, feelings, daydreams, and mood swings of a high-spirited, introspective adolescent coming to maturity under traumatic conditions. Anne wrote of her concern about her appearance ("I asked Margot if she thought I was very ugly"), of her wish for "a real mother who understands me," and of her adoration for her father (Frank, 1958, pp. 36, 110). She expressed rage and despair at the adults' constant criticism of her failings and at her parents' apparent favoritism toward her sister. She wrote about her fears and frustrations, about her need for self-assertion and independence, about her hopes for a return to her old life, and about her aspirations for a future writing career.

Anne made rueful references to her physical growth—to shoes she could no longer get into and vests "so small that they don't even reach my tummy" (p. 71). Her worsening nearsightedness was a more serious problem, which could not be corrected without a dangerous venture outside the hideout.

As tensions rose among the closely closeted inhabitants of the "Secret Annexe" and the storm clouds of the outside world gathered around them, Anne lost her appetite and began taking antidepressant medication. But as time went on, she began to get along better with her mother and sister, to see her father's weaknesses, and to understand her own role in family conflicts. She became more self-critical, less self-pitying, and more serious-minded. When she thought back to her carefree existence before going into hiding, she felt like a different person from the Anne who had "grown wise within these walls" (p. 149).

An important factor in Anne's emotional growth was her awareness of the "wonders" happening inside her body: "I think what is happening to me is so wonderful, and not only what can be seen on my body, but all that is taking place inside. . . . Each time I have a period—and that has been only three times—I have the feeling that in spite of all the pain, unpleasantness, and nastiness, I have a sweet secret, and that is why, although it is nothing but a nuisance to me in a way, I always long for the time that I shall feel that secret within me again." She expressed fascination with the female form: "Sometimes, when I lie in bed at night, I have a terrible desire to feel my breasts and to listen to the quiet rhythmic beat of my heart" (pp. 115-116).

Anne had originally regarded Peter as shy and gawky—a not-very-promising companion; but her feelings gradually changed. She began visiting his attic room for long, intimate talks and finally, her first kiss. She struggled with her stirring sexual passion. "Peter has taken possession of me and turned me inside out. . . . I am afraid of myself, I am afraid that in my longing I am giving myself too quickly" (p. 194). Yet, a few days later, she wrote: "I am young and strong and living a great adventure. . . . Every day I feel that I am developing inwardly" (p. 198).

Anne wrote those words on May 2, 1944. She made her last diary entry on August 1, three days before the police raid and her arrest. About six months later, at the age of 15, Anne Frank died of typhus and starvation in the Nazi concentration camp at Bergen-Belsen, a few weeks before the camp was liberated by British soldiers.

Sources of biographical information about Anne Frank are Frank, 1958, 1995; Lindwer, 1991; and Netherlands State Institute for War Documentation, 1989. Page references are to the 1958 paperback version of Anne's diary.

• • •

The moving story of Anne Frank's tragically abbreviated adolescence points up the insistent role of biology and its interrelationships with inner and outer experience. Anne's "coming of age" occurred under highly stressful conditions—isolation from peers, lack of privacy, intense association with an adult "extended family," constant fear of discovery, and worry about the future. Yet her normal physical maturation went on, along with a host of cognitive and psychosocial changes.

In this chapter, we describe the physical transformations of adolescence and how they influence young people's feelings about themselves. We consider the impact of early and late maturation. We discuss health issues and risks associated with this time of life, and we examine two serious problems: maltreatment and teenage suicide.

After reading this chapter, you should be able to answer and elaborate on such questions as these:

Preview Questions

- What is adolescence, and when does it begin and end?
- What opportunities and risks does adolescence entail?
- What physical changes do adolescents experience, and how do these changes affect them psychologically?
- What are the most common health problems and risks of adolescence?

Adolescence: A Developmental Transition

Rituals to mark a child's "coming of age" are common in many societies. Rites of passage may include religious blessings, separation from the family, severe tests of strength and endurance, marking the body in some way (see Box 14-1), or acts of magic. The ritual may be held at a certain age, as are the bar mitzvah and bat mitzvah ceremonies that mark the assumption by 13-year-old Jewish boys and girls of responsibility for traditional religious observance; or it can be tied to a specific event, such as a girl's first menstruation, which Apache tribes celebrate with a four-day ritual of sunrise-to-sunset chanting.

In modern industrial societies, the passage to adulthood is generally less abrupt and less clearly marked. Instead, these societies recognize a long transitional period known as *adolescence,* a developmental transition between childhood and adulthood that entails major, interrelated physical, cognitive, and psychosocial changes.

Markers Of Adolescence

adolescence Developmental transition between childhood and adulthood entailing major physical, cognitive, and psychosocial changes.

puberty Process by which a person attains sexual maturity and the ability to reproduce.

Adolescence lasts about a decade, from about age 11 or 12 until the late teens or early twenties. Neither its beginning nor its end point is clearly marked. Adolescence is generally considered to begin with *puberty,* the process that leads to sexual maturity, or fertility—the ability to reproduce.* Before the twentieth century, children in western cultures entered the adult world when they matured physically or when they began a vocational apprenticeship. Today entry into adulthood takes longer and is less clear-cut. Puberty begins earlier than it used to, and entrance into a vocation tends to occur later, since complex societies require longer periods of education or vocational training before a young person can take on adult responsibilities.

Contemporary American society has a variety of markers of entrance into adulthood. There are *legal* definitions: at 17, young people may enlist in the armed forces; at age 18, in most states, they may marry without their parents' permission; at 18 to 21 (depending on the state), they may enter into binding contracts. Using *sociological* definitions, people may call themselves adults when they are self-supporting or have chosen a career, have married or formed a significant relationship, or have founded a family. There are also *psychological* definitions. Cognitive maturity is often considered to coincide with the capacity for abstract thought. Emotional maturity may depend on such achievements as discovering one's identity, becoming independent of parents, developing a system of values, and forming relationships. Some people never leave adolescence, no matter what their chronological age.

Opportunities and Risks of Adolescence

Early adolescence, the transition out of childhood, offers opportunities for growth—not only in physical dimensions, but also in cognitive and social competence, autonomy, self-esteem, and intimacy. It also carries great risks. Some young people have trouble handling so many changes at once and may need help in overcoming dangers along the way. Adolescence is a time of increasing divergence between the majority of young people, who are headed for a fulfilling and productive adulthood, and a sizable minority (about 1 out of 5) who will be dealing with major problems (Offer, 1987; Offer & Schonert-Reichl, 1992).

American adolescents today face greater hazards to their physical and mental well-being than did their counterparts in earlier years (Petersen, 1993; Takanishi, 1993). Among these hazards are early pregnancy and childbearing (see Chapter 16) and high death rates from accidents, homicide, and suicide (Centers

---

*Some people use the term *puberty* to mean the end point of sexual maturation and refer to the process as *pubescence,* but our usage conforms to that of most psychologists today.

Box 14-1 Female Genital Mutilation

Many traditional societies have coming-of-age rituals that signal membership in the adult community. These ceremonies often include putting an enduring mark on the body; for example, tattooing or scarring the face, removing the foreskin from the penis, or sharpening the teeth. One custom widely practiced in some parts of Africa, the Middle East, southeastern Asia, and Central and South America is surgery to alter the female genitals (Samad, 1996).

This 4,000-year-old practice, euphemistically called *female circumcision,* is termed *female genital mutilation (FGM)* by the World Health Organization. The operation—which is performed, usually without anesthesia, on girls of varying ages from infancy to puberty—entails clitoridectomy, the removal of part or all of the clitoris. Its most extreme form, infibulation, includes total clitoridectomy plus removal of parts of the labia (the lips of the vulva), the raw edges of which are then sewn together with catgut or held by thorns, leaving only a tiny opening for menstrual blood and urine. When a woman marries, the scar may be cut open and then enlarged for childbirth (Council on Scientific Affairs of the American Medical Association, 1995; Samad, 1996). About 80 to 100 million women worldwide have had such surgery, and 2 million girls undergo it each year (MacFarquhar, 1996; Samad, 1996).

The purposes of these procedures include preserving (and proving) virginity before marriage, reducing sexual appetite, maintaining cleanliness, increasing fertility, enhancing beauty, and affirming femininity through removal of the "malelike" clitoris. Some communities believe that the clitoris can poison men during intercourse and babies during childbirth, or that an unremoved clitoris will grow to the size of a penis. In such cultures, an uncircumcised girl may not be considered marriageable and may be ostracized. The operation also affirms the stability of established custom and reinforces respect for authority (Council on Scientific Affairs, 1995; Lightfoot-Klein, 1989; Samad, 1996).

Besides loss of sexual fulfillment, the consequences of FGM can include psychological dysfunction and various immediate or long-term medical problems, such as shock, infection, hemorrhaging, damage to the urethra or anus, tetanus, inability to urinate normally, painful intercourse, complications of childbirth, sterility, or even death (Council on Scientific Affairs, 1995; Lightfoot-Klein, 1989; Samad, 1996).

In more than 20 countries where these operations are practiced, government officials, physicians, and women's groups have tried to end them. Some western-educated African women have modified versions of the surgery done antiseptically, at home or in clinics, using anesthesia. Others have rejected it altogether (Samad, 1996). However, because many women believe in FGM and are often the ones who carry it out (or fear that their daughters will not be able to marry without it) and because it is sanctioned by some religious leaders, the practice continues (MacFarquhar, 1996; Samad, 1996). FGM has been practiced among African refugees in Europe and North America—an estimated 40,000 procedures each year in the United States alone (MacFarquhar, 1996). A number of countries, including Britain, France, Sweden, and Switzerland, have passed laws banning the practice; the United States Congress outlawed it in 1996. (Previously some states had made it a crime.) A ban by the Egyptian Health Ministry in 1996 met widespread local defiance but in late 1997 was upheld by the Supreme Administrative Court.

The World Health Organization, the World Medical Association, and the American Medical Association condemn FGM as medically unnecessary, harmful, and abusive. A British organization, the Foundation for Women's Health Research and Development (FORWARD), which was formed in 1981 to raise awareness of FGM, views it as a violation of human rights. Despite some resistance to interfering with a practice that reflects cultural beliefs (Samad, 1996), these organizations have urged physicians not to participate in such surgery and have supported efforts to abolish it. The AMA's Council on Scientific Affairs (1995) urges that doctors "provide culturally sensitive counseling" to awaken patients and their families to its dangers.

---

for Disease Control and Prevention [CDC], 1994b; Rivara & Grossman, 1996; U.S. Department of Health and Human Services [USDHHS], 1996a). These problems are not typical in other developed countries (Petersen, 1991). Behavior patterns that contribute to these risks, such as heavy drinking, drug abuse, sexual and gang activity, motorcycling without helmets, and use of firearms, are established early in adolescence (Petersen, 1993; Rivara & Grossman, 1996). Yet, despite the risks of this period, most young people come through the teenage years in good physical and mental health.

Puberty

The biological changes of puberty, which signal the end of childhood, result in rapid growth in height and weight (second only in pace to that in infancy), changes in body proportions and form, and attainment of sexual maturity. These

CHECKPOINT

Can you . . .

• Distinguish among three ways of defining entrance into adulthood?

• Identify some risky behavior patterns common during adolescence?

The Apache Indians of the southwestern United States celebrate a girl's entrance into puberty with a 4-day ritual that includes special clothing, a symbolic blanket, and singing from sunrise to sunset.

dramatic physical changes are part of a long, complex process of maturation that begins even before birth, and their psychological ramifications continue into adulthood.

How Puberty Begins

Puberty begins with a sharp increase in production of sex hormones. First, sometime between ages 5 and 9—well before any outward physical changes appear—the adrenal glands begin secreting larger amounts of androgens, which will play a part in the growth of pubic, axillary (armpit), and facial hair. A few years later, in girls, the ovaries step up their output of estrogen, which stimulates growth of female genitals and development of breasts. In boys, the testes increase the manufacture of androgens, particularly testosterone, which stimulate growth of male genitals, muscle mass, and body hair. Boys and girls have both types of hormones, but girls have higher levels of estrogen and boys have higher levels of androgens; in girls, testosterone influences growth of the clitoris, as well as of the bones and of pubic and axillary hair.

The precise time when this burst of hormonal activity begins may be related to reaching a critical weight level. Studies of mice suggest that leptin, a protein hormone secreted by fatty tissue and identified as having a possible role in obesity (see Chapter 11), may trigger the onset of puberty. When prepubertal female mice were injected with leptin, they showed earlier reproductive functioning than noninjected mice (Chehab, Mounzih, Lu, & Lim, 1997). An accumulation of leptin in the bloodstream may stimulate the hypothalamus, a structure at the base of the brain, to send pulsating signals to the nearby pituitary gland, which in turn may signal the sex glands to increase their secretion of hormones (see Figure 14-1). This may explain why overweight girls tend to enter puberty earlier than thin girls. Whether leptin or some other substance plays a similar role in males is yet to be determined.

Some research attributes the increased emotionality and moodiness of early adolescence to hormonal changes. For example, hormones are associated with

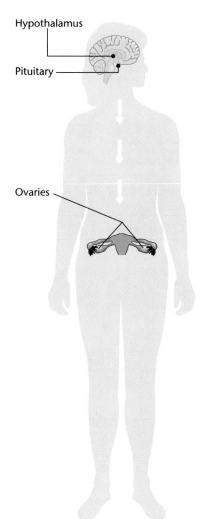

Hypothalamus

Pituitary

Ovaries

Figure 14-1

How puberty may begin. Research on female mice suggests the following scenario: At puberty, fat cells multiply and secrete a protein called *leptin,* which travels in the bloodstream to the brain. When the concentration of leptin is high enough, the hypothalamus sends out hormonal signals to the pituitary gland, telling it to release its own hormones, which then travel through the bloodstream to the ovaries. The ovaries then activate and release estrogen, the hormone that stimulates breast growth and other changes of puberty. Studies have not yet been done to determine whether a similar process may occur in males.

Source: Dr. Melvin M. Crumbach, 1997.

aggression in boys and with both aggression and depression in girls (Brooks-Gunn, 1988; Buchanan, Eccles, & Becker, 1992). However, other influences, such as sex, age, temperament, and the timing of puberty, may moderate or even override hormonal ones. Hormones seem more strongly related to moods in boys than in girls, and especially in early adolescents, who are still adjusting to pubertal changes.

Environmental factors also make a difference (Buchanan et al., 1992). Although there is a relationship between hormone production and sexuality, adolescents tend to begin sexual activity more in accord with what their friends do than with what their glands secrete (Brooks-Gunn & Reiter, 1990). A 12- to 16-year-old girl who has a father in the home or participates in sports may have less time and opportunity for sexual activity than some of her peers, despite the pressure of sex hormones (Uldry, 1988, cited in Buchanan et al., 1992). Further study is needed to sort out the effects of hormones from other influences.

Timing, Sequence, and Signs of Maturation

There is about a 7-year range for the onset of puberty in both boys and girls. The process typically takes about 4 years for both sexes and begins about 2 or 3 years earlier for girls than for boys. Some people move through puberty very quickly and others more slowly. Girls, on average, begin to show pubertal change at 8 to 10 years of age. However, it is normal for girls to show the first signs as early as

Table 14-1 Usual Sequence of Physiological Changes in Adolescence

Female Characteristics	Age of First Appearance
Growth of breasts	8–13
Growth of pubic hair	8–14
Body growth	9.5–14.5
Menarche	10–16.5
Underarm hair	About 2 years after appearance of pubic hair
Increased output of oil- and sweat-producing glands (which may lead to acne)	About the same time as appearance of underarm hair

Male Characteristics	Age of First Appearance
Growth of testes, scrotal sac	10–13.5
Growth of pubic hair	12–16
Body growth	10.5–16
Growth of penis, prostate gland, seminal vesicles	11–14.5
Change in voice	About the same time as growth of penis
First ejaculation of semen	About 1 year after beginning of growth of penis
Facial and underarm hair	About 2 years after appearance of pubic hair
Increased output of oil- and sweat-producing glands (which may lead to acne)	About the same time as appearance of underarm hair

age 7 or as late as 14. The average age for boys' entry into puberty is 12, but boys may begin to show changes any time between 9 and 16 (Chumlea, 1982; Herman-Giddens et al., 1997). African American girls, who tend to be heavier than white girls (K. J. Ellis, Abrams, & Wong, 1997), enter puberty about 1 to 1½ years earlier. At age 8, nearly half (48.3 percent) of black girls but only 14.7 percent of white girls have begun pubertal development (Herman-Giddens et al., 1997).

secular trend Trend that can be seen by observing several generations, such as the trend toward earlier attainment of adult height and sexual maturity, which began a century ago.

On the basis of historical sources, developmentalists have found a *secular trend* (a trend that spans several generations) in the onset of puberty: a lowering of the age when puberty begins and when young people reach adult height and sexual maturity. The trend, which also involves increases in adult height and weight, began about 100 years ago and has occurred in the United States, western Europe, and Japan (Chumlea, 1982). The most likely explanation seems to be a higher standard of living. Children who are healthier, better-nourished, and better cared for mature earlier and grow bigger. Thus, the age of sexual maturity is later in less developed countries than in more industrialized ones. For example, Bundi girls of New Guinea do not begin to menstruate until an average age of 18, about 5 years later than U. S. girls (Tanner, 1989). Although the secular trend is generally thought to have ended in the United States, recent data challenge this view. Girls typically appear to be maturing earlier than previous studies showed (Herman-Giddens et al., 1997).

Physical changes in both boys and girls during puberty include the adolescent growth spurt, the development of pubic hair, a deeper voice, and muscular growth, which peaks at age 12½ for girls and 14½ for boys. The maturation of reproductive organs brings the beginning of menstruation in girls and the production of sperm in boys. These changes unfold in a sequence that is much more consistent than their timing (see Table 14-1 and Figure 14–2), though it does vary somewhat. One girl, for example, may be developing breasts and body hair at about the same rate; in another, body hair may grow so fast that it shows an

During the years from ages 11 to 13, girls are, on the average, taller, heavier, and stronger than boys, who reach their adolescent growth spurt later than girls do.

adult pattern a year or so before her breasts develop. Similar variations occur among boys (Tobin-Richards, Boxer, McKavrell, & Petersen, 1984).

The Adolescent Growth Spurt

In Anne Frank's diary, she referred somewhat ruefully to her sudden growth. The *adolescent growth spurt* is a rapid increase in height and weight, which generally begins in girls between ages 9½ and 14½ (usually at about 10) and in boys, between 10½ and 16 (usually at 12 or 13). The growth spurt typically lasts about 2 years; soon after it ends, the young person reaches sexual maturity. Since girls' growth spurt usually occurs earlier than that of boys, girls between ages 11 and 13 are taller, heavier, and stronger than boys the same age. After their growth spurt, boys are again larger, as before. Both boys and girls reach virtually their full height by age 18 (Behrman, 1992).

Boys and girls grow differently, of course. A boy becomes larger overall: his shoulders wider, his legs longer relative to his trunk, and his forearms longer relative to his upper arms and his height. A girl's pelvis widens to make childbearing easier, and layers of fat are laid down just under the skin, giving her a more rounded appearance.

The adolescent growth spurt affects practically all skeletal and muscular dimensions. Even the eye grows faster, causing (as in Anne Frank's case) an increase in nearsightedness, a problem that affects about one-fourth of 12- to 17-year-olds (Gans, 1990). The lower jaw becomes longer and thicker, the jaw and nose project more, and the incisor teeth become more upright. Because each of these changes follows its own timetable, parts of the body may be out of proportion for a while. The result is the familiar teenage gawkiness Anne noticed in Peter Van Daan, which accompanies unbalanced, accelerated growth.

Primary and Secondary Sex Characteristics

The *primary sex characteristics* are the organs necessary for reproduction. In the female, the sex organs are the ovaries, uterus, and vagina; in the male, the testes, prostate gland, penis, and seminal vesicles (see Table 14-2). During puberty,

adolescent growth spurt
Sharp increase in height and weight that precedes sexual maturity.

primary sex characteristics
Organs directly related to reproduction, which enlarge and mature during adolescence. Compare *secondary sex characteristics*.

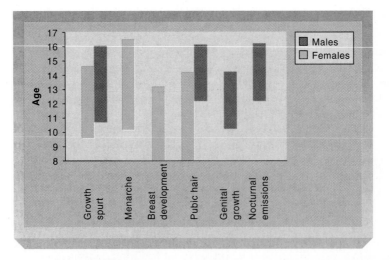

Figure 14-2
This graph shows typical age range of adolescent growth spurt as well as other milestones of adolescent development.

Table 14-2	Primary Sex Characteristics: Sex Organs

Female	Male
Ovaries	Testes
Fallopian tubes	Penis
Uterus	Scrotum
Vagina	Seminal vesicles
	Prostate gland

secondary sex characteristics
Physiological signs of sexual maturation (such as breast development and growth of body hair) that do not involve the sex organs. Compare *primary sex characteristics.*

these organs enlarge and mature. In boys, the first sign of puberty is the growth of the testes and scrotum.

The *secondary sex characteristics* are physiological signs of sexual maturation that do not directly involve the sex organs: for example, the breasts of females and the broad shoulders of males. Other secondary sex characteristics are changes in the voice and skin texture, muscular development, and the growth of pubic, facial, axillary, and body hair (see Table 14-3).

The first signs of puberty in girls are usually the budding of the breasts and the growth of pubic hair. The nipples enlarge and protrude, the *areolae* (the pigmented areas surrounding the nipples) enlarge, and the breasts assume first a conical and then a rounded shape. Some adolescent boys, much to their distress, experience temporary breast enlargement; this is normal and may last up to 18 months.

The voice deepens, partly in response to the growth of the larynx and partly, especially in boys, in response to the production of male hormones. The skin becomes coarser and oilier. Increased activity of the sebaceous glands (which secrete a fatty substance) may give rise to pimples and blackheads. Acne is more common in boys and seems related to increased amounts of testosterone.

Pubic hair, which at first is straight and silky and eventually becomes coarse, dark, and curly, appears in different patterns in males and females. Adolescent boys are usually happy to see hair on the face and chest; but girls are usually dismayed at the appearance of even a slight amount of hair on the face or around the nipples, though this is normal.

Signs of Sexual Maturity: Sperm Production and Menstruation

In males, the principal sign of sexual maturity is the production of sperm. Its timing is highly variable, but nearly one-fourth of 15-year-old boys have sperm in

Table 14-3	Secondary Sex Characteristics	
Girls	**Boys**
Breasts	Pubic hair
Pubic hair	Axillary (underarm) hair
Axillary (underarm) hair	Muscular development
Changes in voice	Facial hair
Changes in skin	Changes in voice
Increased width and depth of pelvis	Changes in skin
Muscular development	Broadening of shoulders

the urine (D. W. Richardson & Short, 1978). A boy may wake up to find a wet spot or a hardened, dried spot on the sheets—the result of a *nocturnal emission,* an involuntary ejaculation of semen (commonly referred to as a *wet dream).* Most adolescent boys have these emissions, sometimes in connection with an erotic dream. There is little research on boys' feelings about the first ejaculation *(spermarche),* which occurs at an average age of 13; most boys in one study reported positive reactions, though about two-thirds were somewhat frightened (Gaddis & Brooks-Gunn, 1985).

spermarche Boy's first ejaculation.

The principal sign of sexual maturity in girls is *menstruation,* a monthly shedding of tissue from the lining of the womb. The first menstruation, called *menarche,* occurs fairly late in the sequence of female development (refer back to Table 14-1). On average, a girl in the United States first menstruates before her thirteenth birthday—about 2 years after her breasts have begun to develop and her uterus has begun to grow, and shortly after her growth spurt has slowed down. However, the normal timing of menarche can vary from ages 10 to 16½.

menarche Girl's first menstruation.

Strenuous exercise, as in competitive athletics, can delay menarche (Graber, Brooks-Gunn, & Warren, 1995), and nutrition is a factor. One study suggests a combination of genetic, physical, emotional, and environmental influences on its timing (Graber et al., 1995). Seventy-five girls were examined at ages 10 to 14, before starting to menstruate, and again after menarche. Their age of first menstruation turned out to be similar to that of their mothers. Bigger girls and those whose breasts were more developed tended to menstruate earlier. Even when these factors were controlled, girls with early menarche tended to show aggression or depression or reported poor family relationships (conflict with parents, lack of parental approval and warmth, or negative feelings about the home environment). This last finding supports previous suggestions of a link between family conflict and early menarche (Moffitt, Caspi, Belsky, & Silva, 1992; Steinberg, 1988). The mechanism by which family problems may affect menarche is not clear, though it may be related to hormonal activity.

Menarche is more than a physical event; it is "a concrete symbol of a shift from girl to woman" (Ruble & Brooks-Gunn, 1982, p. 1557)—what Anne Frank described as her "sweet secret." Although in many cultures menarche is taken as the sign that a girl has become a woman, early menstrual periods usually do not include ovulation, and many girls are unable to conceive for 12 to 18 months. However, since ovulation and conception do sometimes occur in these early months, girls who have begun to menstruate should assume that they can become pregnant.

In her diary, Anne Frank expressed the ambivalence about menstruation felt by many young girls, describing it as a nuisance but also as a "sweet secret."

Although many girls have mixed feelings about starting to menstruate, most take it in stride. The better-prepared a girl is for menarche, the more positive her feelings and the less her distress (Koff, Rierdan, & Sheingold, 1982; Rierdan, Koff, & Flaherty, 1986; Ruble & Brooks-Gunn, 1982; Stubbs, Rierdan, & Koff, 1989). Young girls need information from parents, teachers, or health professionals that addresses both the affirmative and negative aspects of menstruation—information geared to their biological, cognitive, and social readiness (Stubbs et al., 1989). They need to understand that menstruation is a normal, universal female experience, different from injury or disease.

Psychological Issues Related to Physical Changes

It is not surprising that the dramatic physical changes of adolescence have psychological ramifications. In addition to feelings about wet dreams or the onset of menstruation, many young people have strong reactions to changes in physical appearance and to early or late maturation.

Feelings About Physical Appearance

Most young teenagers are more concerned about their looks than about any other aspect of themselves, and many do not like what they see in the mirror (Siegel, 1982). Boys want to be tall, broad-shouldered, and athletic; girls want to be pretty, slim but shapely, with nice hair and skin (Tobin-Richards et al., 1984). Anything that makes boys think that they look feminine or girls think that they look masculine makes them miserable. Teenagers of both sexes worry about their weight, their complexion, and their facial features.

Girls tend to be unhappier about their looks than boys of the same age, reflecting the greater cultural emphasis on women's physical attributes. Girls, especially those who are advanced in pubertal development, tend to think they are too fat even when they are not, and this negative body image can lead to eating problems (Richards, Boxer, Petersen, & Albrecht, 1990).

Psychological Effects of Early and Late Maturation

One of the great paradoxes of adolescence is the conflict between a young person's yearning to assert a unique self and an overwhelming desire to be exactly like his or her friends. Anything that sets an adolescent apart from the crowd can be unsettling, and youngsters may be disturbed if they mature sexually either much earlier or much later than usual. However, the effects of early and late maturing are not clear-cut and differ in boys and girls.

Some research has found early-maturing boys to be more poised, relaxed, good-natured, popular with peers, likely to be leaders, and less impulsive than late maturers. Other studies have found them to be more worried about being liked, more cautious, and more bound by rules and routines. Some studies suggest that early maturers retain a head start in cognitive performance into late adolescence and adulthood (R. T. Gross & Duke, 1980; M. C. Jones, 1957; Tanner, 1978). Late maturers have been found to feel more inadequate, rejected, and dominated; to be more dependent, aggressive, and insecure; to rebel more against their parents; and to think less of themselves (Mussen & Jones, 1957; Peskin, 1967, 1973; Siegel, 1982).

Apparently there are pluses and minuses in both situations. Boys like to mature early, and those who do so seem to gain in self-esteem (Alsaker, 1992; Clausen, 1975). Being more muscular than late maturers, they are stronger and better in sports and have a more favorable body image. They also have an edge in dating (Blyth et al., 1981). However, an early maturer sometimes has trouble living up to expectations that he should act as mature as he looks.

Unlike most boys, girls tend not to like maturing early; they are generally happier if their timing is about the same as that of their peers. Early-maturing girls tend to be less sociable, less expressive, and less poised; more introverted and shy; and more negative about menarche (M. C. Jones, 1958; Livson & Peskin, 1980; Ruble & Brooks-Gunn, 1982; Stubbs et al., 1989). Perhaps because they feel rushed into confronting the pressures of adolescence before they are ready, they are more vulnerable to psychological distress and remain so at least through the mid-teens. They are more likely to associate with antisocial peers and to be especially sensitive to an irritable or hostile father (Ge, Conger, & Elder, 1996). Some research suggests that they are apt to have a poor body image and lower self-esteem than later-maturing girls (Alsaker, 1992; Simmons, Blyth, Van Cleave, & Bush, 1979). However, other research has found that maturational status in itself does not affect self-esteem, which depends more on the overall context of the girl's social surroundings (Brooks-Gunn, 1988).

An early-maturing girl may feel less attractive if her new curviness clashes with cultural standards equating beauty with thinness (Crockett & Petersen, 1987). She may feel dismayed if she sees herself as changing for the worse, not for the better (Simmons, Blyth, & McKinney, 1983).

Early-maturing girls may also react to other people's concerns about their sexuality. Parents and teachers sometimes assume that girls who look mature are sexually active and may treat an early-maturing girl more strictly or disapprovingly. Other adolescents may put pressures on her that she is ill-equipped to handle. She may "hang out" with older boys and young men and may be faced with sexual demands appropriate to her appearance but not to her age (Petersen, 1993).

It is hard to generalize about the psychological effects of timing of puberty, because they depend so much on how the adolescent and other people in his or her world interpret the accompanying changes. Effects of early or late maturation are most likely to be negative when adolescents are much more or less developed than their peers; when they do not see the changes as advantageous; and when several stressful events occur at about the same time (Petersen, 1993; Simmons et al., 1983). As we'll see later in this chapter, early maturation is associated with a tendency toward risky behavior (D. P. Orr & Ingersoll, 1995). Adults need to be sensitive to the potential impact of pubertal changes so as to help young people experience these changes as positively as possible.

CHECKPOINT

Can you . . .

- Tell how puberty begins and how its timing and length vary?
- Describe typical pubertal changes in boys and girls, and identify factors that affect psychological reactions to these changes?

Sexuality

Although present in younger children, it is in adolescence that a person's *sexual orientation* generally becomes a pressing issue: whether that person will consistently be sexually, romantically, and affectionately attracted to persons of the other sex (*heterosexual*), the same sex (*homosexual*), or both sexes (*bisexual*).

Origins of Sexual Orientation

The incidence of sexual orientation is hard to pinpoint. In one study of 38,000 American students in grades 7 through 12, about 88 percent described themselves as predominantly heterosexual and only 1 percent as predominantly homosexual or bisexual. About 11 percent, mostly younger students, were unsure of their sexual orientation. Those who were unsure were more likely to report homosexual fantasies and attractions and were less likely to have had heterosexual experiences (Remafedi, Resnick, Blum, & Harris, 1992).

Much research on sexual orientation has been spurred by efforts to explain homosexuality. Although it was once considered a mental illness, several decades of research have found no association between homosexuality and emotional or social problems (American Psychological Association, n.d.; C. J. Patterson, 1992, 1995a, 1995b). These findings (along with political lobbying and changes in public attitudes) eventually led the psychiatric profession to stop classifying homosexuality as a mental disorder. The 1994 edition of the American Psychiatric Association's *Diagnostic and Statistical Manual of Mental Disorders* contains no references to it at all.

sexual orientation Focus of consistent sexual, romantic, and affectionate interest, either heterosexual, homosexual, or bisexual.

heterosexual Describing a person whose sexual orientation is toward the other sex.

homosexual Describing a person whose sexual orientation is toward the same sex.

bisexual Describing a person whose sexual orientation is toward both sexes.

Although sexual orientation may well be shaped before birth or very early in life, it is in adolescence that it becomes a pressing issue. Here, a Massachusetts high school girl who "came out" as a lesbian sits in front of a banner for a student support group.

Other theories of the sources of homosexuality—all of which lack convincing scientific support—point to disturbed relationships with parents; parental encouragement of unconventional, cross-gender behavior; imitation of homosexual parents; or chance learning through seduction by a homosexual. Many young people have one or more homosexual experiences as they are growing up, usually before age 15. However, isolated experiences, or even homosexual attractions or fantasies, do not determine sexual orientation.

According to one theory, sexual orientation may be influenced by a complex prenatal process involving both hormonal and neurological factors (L. Ellis & Ames, 1987). If the levels of sex hormones in a fetus of either sex are in the typical female range between the second and fifth months of gestation, the person is likely to be attracted to males after puberty. If the hormone levels are in the male range, the person is likely to be attracted to females. Whether and how hormonal activity may affect brain development, and whether and how differences in brain structure may affect sexual orientation have not been established (Golombok & Tasker, 1996), but an anatomical difference between homosexual and heterosexual men in an area of the brain that governs sexual behavior has been reported (LeVay, 1991).

There also is growing evidence that sexual orientation may be at least partly genetic. One series of studies links male homosexuality to a small region of the X chromosome inherited from the mother; no such effect was found for women (Hamer, Hu, Magnuson, Hu, & Pattatucci, 1993; Hu et al., 1995). An identical twin of a homosexual has about a 50 percent probability of being homosexual himself or herself, while a fraternal twin has only about a 20 percent likelihood and an adopted sibling 10 percent or less (Gladue, 1994).

Controversy remains as to whether or not sexual orientation is decisively shaped either before birth or at an early age. There is also dispute as to the relative contributions of biological, psychological, and social influences (Baumrind, 1995; C. J. Patterson, 1995b). These influences may well be "impossible to untangle," and their relative strength may differ among individuals (Baumrind, 1995, p. 132).

Some people have sought treatment to change their sexual orientation, but there is no good evidence that such therapy works. Furthermore, many mental health providers question the ethics of trying to alter a trait that is not a disorder and that is important to a person's identity (American Psychological Association, n.d.).

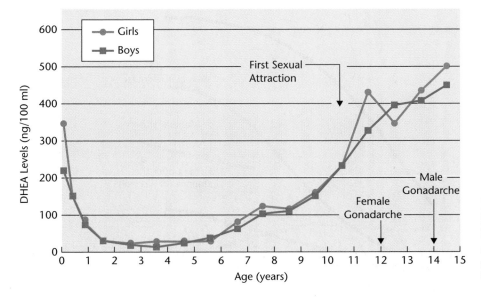

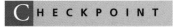

Figure 14-3
Levels of the hormone DHEA secreted by the adrenal glands, birth through age 15.

Source: McClintock & Herdt, 1996, Fig. 2, p. 181. Data redrawn from De Peretti & Forest, 1976.

Sexual Attraction*

Do you remember the first time you were sexually attracted to someone? If so, how old were you?

It is commonly believed that the first stirrings of sexual attraction follow *go-nadarche*, maturation of the testes and ovaries. Yet in three recent studies, adolescent boys and girls—whether homosexual or heterosexual—recalled their earliest sexual attraction as having taken place at about age 10, about 2 to 4 years before sexual maturation.

What could prompt this earliest sexual attraction, well before gonadarche, when the sex organs step up hormone production? It does not seem likely that children are merely picking up cultural signals or mimicking the adults they see around them. Given the strong taboo on homosexual behavior, we would then be hard put to explain why some 10-year-olds are attracted to the same sex.

The answer may lie in the maturation of the adrenal glands (*adrenarche*), which occurs several years before gonadarche. Between ages 6 and 11, these glands, located above the kidneys, secrete gradually increasing levels of androgens, principally *dehydroepiandrosterone* (DHEA). DHEA is present in high levels at birth and then declines sharply, only to rise again when the adrenal glands mature. By age 10, levels of DHEA are 10 times what they were between ages 1 and 4. The maturing of the sex organs triggers a second burst of DHEA production, which then rises to adult levels (see Figure 14-3). DHEA is responsible for the initial sprouting of pubic hair and also for faster growth, oilier skin, and the development of body odor.

These findings suggest that the transition to puberty may begin earlier and may be more gradual than is generally recognized. Puberty may consist of two stages: the maturing of the adrenal glands, which may bring on the earliest sexual attraction, followed a few years later by the maturing of the sex organs and the more obvious pubertal changes.

Health

These years are generally healthy ones. Most adolescents have low rates of disability and chronic disease, and dental health has improved among both children and adolescents (see Chapter 11). Still, a report to the U.S. Congress suggests that about one-fifth of the nation's 10- to 18-year-olds have at least one serious health problem, often related to mental health, and that many more young people need counseling or other health services (D. M. Dougherty, 1993).

*The discussion in this section is based on McClintock and Herdt, 1996.

gonadarche   Maturation of testes or ovaries.

adrenarche   Maturation of adrenal glands.

C HECKPOINT

Can you . . .

- Compare the estimated incidence of homosexuality and heterosexuality in American adolescents?

- Discuss theories and research regarding origins of sexual orientation?

- Identify the age of first sexual attraction and discuss its implications for the timing of puberty?

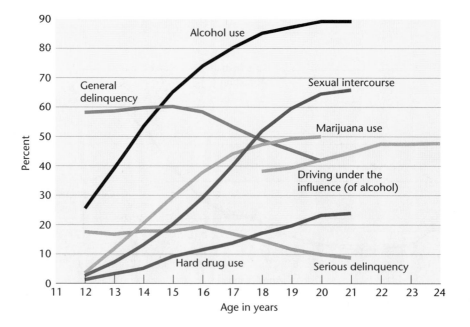

Figure 14-4
Age-specific rates for prevalence of some high-risk behaviors, averaged out over 3 years.
Source: Adapted from Elliott, 1993.

Health problems frequently stem from lifestyle or poverty. Across ethnic and social-class lines, many young adolescents (ages 12 to 14) use drugs, drive while intoxicated, and become sexually active, and these behaviors increase throughout the teenage years (see Figure 14-4). Adolescents whose families have been disrupted by parental separation or death are more likely to start these activities early and to engage in them more frequently over the next few years (Millstein et al., 1992). Boys and girls who enter puberty early or whose cognitive maturation is delayed are especially prone to risky behavior (D. P. Orr & Ingersoll, 1995).

The health status of adolescents is expected to worsen during the next few decades, largely because more young people will be poor. Adolescents from poor families are 3 times as likely to be in fair or poor health and 1½ times as likely to have disabling chronic illnesses as adolescents from families above the poverty line (Newacheck, 1989).

Adolescents are less likely than younger children to see a physician regularly. An estimated 14 percent of young people under age 18 do not receive the medical care they need. Reasons include lack of money or insurance coverage, medical office hours that conflict with school hours, requirements for parental consent, and a lack of assurance of confidentiality on the part of the health care provider. Adolescents consult physicians most often for skin and cosmetic problems, coughs and sore throats, and (for girls) prenatal care (Gans, 1990). Adolescents with mental health problems are more likely to turn to family or friends (if anyone) than to professionals (Offer & Schonert-Reichl, 1992). Black and Hispanic adolescents have greater health needs but less access to medical care than white adolescents, and they visit doctors less often (Lieu, Newacheck & McManus, 1993).

Adolescents are more likely to go to school-based health centers than to other sources of care. Among 3,818 students who used such health facilities at three Denver high schools during a four-year period (see Table 14-4), 29 percent had emotional problems. Other major reasons for seeking care were for health supervision (13 percent), respiratory problems (11 percent), reproductive health problems (11 percent), and substance abuse problems (8 percent) (Anglin, Naylor, & Kaplan, 1996).

Let's look at several specific health concerns of adolescence: physical fitness, depression, nutrition and eating disorders, use and abuse of drugs, sexually transmitted diseases, abuse and neglect, and causes of death in adolescence, including suicide. We'll also look at factors that seem to protect some adolescents from health risks.

Table 14-4	Diagnoses of Denver High School Students Visiting Three School-Based Health Centers, April 1988 Through 1992 School Year	
Diagnostic Category*	**Number of Diagnoses**	**Percent**
Emotional problem	11,780	29%
Health supervision	5,285	13%
Respiratory problem	4,251	11%
Drug/alcohol problem	3,264	8%
Skin problem	2,674	7%
Injury/poisoning	1,937	5%
Gynecologic problem	1,850	5%
Symptoms without diagnosis	1,698	4%
Pregnancy/contraception	1,669	4%
Eye problem	935	2%
Ear problem	904	2%
Sexually transmitted disease	754	2%
Musculoskeletal problem	740	2%
Urinary problem	669	2%
Infection (nonrespiratory, non-sexually transmitted disease	432	1%
Metabolic problem	380	1%
Dental problem	205	0.5%
Cardiovascular problem	198	0.5%
Gastrointestinal problem	198	0.5%
Neurologic problem	147	0.4%
Hematologic problem	118	0.3%
Endocrine problem	88	0.2%
Total	40,176	100%†

*There are two remaining diagnostic categories: congenital anomaly (five visits) and neoplasm (four visits).

†There are 560 missing values, representing missing diagnostic codes for 1.3% of visits.

Note: A maximum of three diagnoses could be made per visit.

Source: Adapted from Anglin et al., 1996, Table 5, p. 321.

Physical Fitness

Most American high school students do not engage in regular vigorous physical activity. As girls grow older, they become less active than boys, and both sexes become less active during the course of adolescence (NIH Consensus Development Panel on Physical Activity and Cardiovascular Health, 1996). Only 35 percent of ninth grade girls and 53 percent of ninth grade boys participate in 20 minutes of vigorous activity 3 times a week, and participation rates drop to only 25 to 50 percent, respectively, for high school seniors (CDC, 1994a). What does that mean for young people's health, now and in the future?

Exercise—or lack of it—affects both mental and physical health. Even moderate physical activity, such as brisk walking, bicycling, swimming, or yard work, has health benefits if done regularly for at least 30 minutes on most, or preferably all, days of the week. A sedentary lifestyle that carries over into adulthood may result in increased risk of obesity, diabetes, heart disease, and cancer (NIH Consensus Development Panel, 1996).

In a British study, 16-year-olds who participated in team or individual sports had fewer physical or emotional problems and felt better about themselves than less active classmates (Steptoe & Butler, 1996). On the other hand, injuries to high

Participation in team sports has benefits for physical and emotional health, but also is a frequent source of injuries.

school students most often result from sports; some of these injuries could be avoided by grouping players by size, skill, and maturational level instead of by age (American Academy of Pediatrics [AAP] Committee on Sports Medicine and Committee on School Health, 1989).

In one study, the highest injury rate for either sex was for girls who go out for cross-country running. The next most dangerous sports were, in order, football, wrestling, girls' soccer, and boys' cross-country (about two-thirds the girls' rate) (S. G. Rice, 1993). The high rate of girls' injuries seems to stem partly from biological factors. Prepubescent girls suffer many stress fractures, in part because with their low estrogen levels they have not yet developed maximum bone density. In addition, heavy training often inhibits menstruation, keeping estrogen levels low. Girls' body build may contribute to injuries: they have wider hips than boys, sharper angles to the thigh bones, and weaker muscles on the inside of the knee.

After puberty, girls should not be playing heavy-collision sports with boys because their lighter, smaller frames make them too subject to injury (AAP Committee on Pediatric Aspects of Physical Fitness, Recreation, and Sports, 1981). Postpubertal girls still need to be physically active, however, for general fitness and for the benefit that weight-bearing exercise offers in the prevention of *osteoporosis,* a thinning of the bones that occurs mostly among middle-aged and older women. Engaging in athletics or other exercise, besides being emotionally satisfying in itself, also helps slim and trim the figure, reduces stress, gives girls a sense of mastery and competence, and makes them feel better about their appearance (Richards et al., 1990).

Depression

Most young people negotiate adolescence without major emotional problems, but some undergo mild to severe bouts of depression, which may lead to thoughts of, or attempts at, suicide (discussed later in this chapter). Research among adolescents who have not sought psychotherapy suggests that somewhere between 10 and 35 percent of boys and 15 to 40 percent of girls experience depressed moods (Petersen et al., 1993). Before puberty, rates for depression are the same in boys and girls; but after age 15, females are about twice as likely to be depressed as males. Possibly girls have less assertive ways of coping with challenge and change, and this, coupled with the greater challenges and changes girls face during early adolescence, puts them at more risk (Nolen-Hoeksema & Girgus, 1994).

Girls are more likely than boys to experience several stressful life changes at about the same time. One such change is the move from elementary to secondary school. A young person who makes this move either at or just after puberty runs a higher risk of depression, and since girls enter puberty earlier, they are more likely than boys to experience these two events simultaneously (Petersen, Sarigiani, & Kennedy, 1991). Then, because parents of daughters have a higher divorce rate than parents of sons, adolescent girls are more likely to experience their parents' divorce (Petersen et al., 1993). Still another factor is worry about appearance. Adolescent girls tend to be unhappier about their looks than adolescent boys, perhaps because of a greater cultural emphasis on women's physical attributes (Tobin-Richards, Boxer, & Petersen, 1983). In addition, males may have more effective ways of coping with a depressed mood: they typically distract themselves until the mood lifts, whereas females tend to look for reasons for their depression. These patterns may begin in adolescence (Petersen, Kennedy, & Sullivan, 1991).

Drug treatment, which often works well with depressed adults, has not proved effective for adolescent depression, for reasons that are not clear. However, psychotherapy has achieved improvement (Petersen et al., 1993).

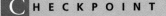

CHECKPOINT

Can you . . .

- Summarize the status of adolescents' health and health care?
- Explain why physical activity is important in adolescence?
- Assess risks and benefits of athletic activity for adolescent girls?
- Explain why adolescent girls are more likely to be depressed than adolescent boys?

Nutrition and Eating Disorders

The average teenage girl needs about 2,200 calories per day; the average teenage boy needs about 2,800. Teenagers (like everyone else) should avoid "junk foods" such as french fries, soft drinks, ice cream, and snack chips and dips, which are high in cholesterol, fat, and calories, and low in nutrients.

Adolescents' most common mineral deficiencies are of calcium, zinc, and iron. The need for calcium, which supports bone growth, is best met by drinking enough milk; young people who suffer from lactose intolerance (the inability to digest milk) may obtain calcium from other foods. Girls who avoid milk for fear of gaining weight should try skim milk, which actually has a higher calcium content than whole milk. Calcium supplements can increase bone density and may protect against osteoporosis (Lloyd et al., 1993). Regular weight-bearing exercise, such as walking or running, also protects against osteoporosis.

Iron-deficiency anemia is common among American adolescents because their diet tends to be iron-poor. Teenagers need a steady source of iron-fortified breads, dried fruits, and green leafy vegetables (E. R. Williams & Caliendo, 1984). Iron has important cognitive benefits; giving iron supplements to adolescent girls who were not anemic but did have iron deficiency improved their verbal learning and memory (A. B. Bruner, Joffe, Duggan, Casella, & Brandt, 1996). Foods containing zinc—meats, eggs, seafood, and whole-grain cereal products—belong in the diet; even a mild zinc deficiency can delay sexual maturity (E. R. Williams & Caliendo, 1984).

Obesity

Many adolescents eat more calories than they expend and thus accumulate excess body fat. Obesity is the most common eating disorder in the United States; 11.5 percent of 12- to 17-year-olds are in the 95th percentile of body mass (weight for height) for their age and sex (National Center for Health Statistics [NCHS], 1997).

Some causes of obesity—too little physical activity and poor eating habits—are within a person's control, and weight-loss programs using behavioral modification to help adolescents make changes in diet and exercise have had some success. However, genetic and other factors having nothing to do with willpower or lifestyle choices seem to make some people susceptible to obesity (see Chapter 11). Among these factors are faulty regulation of metabolism, inability to recognize body cues about hunger and satiation, and development of an abnormally large number of fat cells.

Obese teenagers tend to become obese adults, subject to physical, social, and possibly psychological risks. According to a 60-year longitudinal study, overweight in adolescence can lead to life-threatening chronic conditions in adulthood, even if the excess weight is lost. The effects are particularly strong for heavy boys, who as adults have death rates nearly double those of men who were more slender as teenagers (Must, Jacques, Dallal, Bajema, & Dietz, 1992).

In another longitudinal study, 370 people, ages 16 to 24, who were above the 95th percentile of weight for their age and sex, were compared with normal-weight people, some of whom had chronic health conditions. After 7 years, the women in the overweight group had completed fewer years of school and were more likely to be poor, and both the overweight women and the overweight men were less likely to be married. These differences held even when original socio-economic circumstances were taken into account (Gortmaker, Must, Perrin, Sobol, & Dietz, 1993). These social and economic consequences may in part be attributable to discrimination against, or social disapproval of, heavy people. Although this study found no effect of overweight on self-esteem or psychological disturbance, other research did find an association between overweight and poor psychological adjustment (Alsaker, 1992).

Anorexia Nervosa and Bulimia Nervosa

Sometimes a determination not to become obese can result in even graver problems than obesity itself. For the sake of health and beauty, some adolescents—especially girls—embark on a lifelong struggle to reduce, which in some cases becomes pathological.

With puberty, girls show a normal increase in body fat, and this may lead to an excessive concern with body image and weight control (Swarr & Richards, 1996). In one survey of fifth- through eighth-grade girls, 31 percent said they were dieting, 9 percent sometimes fasted, and 5 percent had induced vomiting ("Eating Disorders—Part II," 1997). Among 497 urban and suburban high school seniors, about 66 percent of the girls were preoccupied with weight and dieting, compared with only 15 percent of the boys (R. C. Casper & Offer, 1990). Although in the past white girls were found to be more weight- and diet-conscious than black girls, recent surveys suggest that eating disorders are equally common in both races and in all social classes ("Eating Disorders—Part II," 1997). They are especially common among girls driven to excel in ballet, competitive swimming, figure skating, and gymnastics ("Eating Disorders—Part II," 1997; Skolnick, 1993).

Relationships with parents and peers may be a factor in the development of eating disorders. In one study, 240 suburban white girls in grades 5 through 9 were asked how strongly they agreed or disagreed with such statements as "I am terrified about being overweight," "I like my stomach to be empty," and "Eating too much makes me feel gross and ugly." The girls also filled out questionnaires about how much time they spent with each parent and how close and friendly their relationship was. Girls who had positive relationships with their parents had fewer weight and eating concerns, both at the time of the original testing and two years later (Swarr & Richards, 1996). However, it is not clear that negative relationships with parents cause eating disorders; it is possible that the strain of dealing with an eating disorder may undermine parent-child relationships ("Eating Disorders—Part I," 1997).

Girls who have begun dating, particularly if they are physically intimate with a boyfriend or if they have recently begun menstruating, tend to be more concerned with dieting and are more susceptible to eating disorders. Relationships with boys put girls under pressure to be "sexy"; this pressure may be greater on girls who have recently begun sexual activity or have gained weight due to the changes of puberty (Cauffman & Steinberg, 1996).

Let's look more closely at two eating disorders—*anorexia nervosa* and *bulimia nervosa*—which are being diagnosed with increasing frequency. Both are complex, often chronic, illnesses with physical and psychological ramifications, and both tend to run in families, suggesting a possible genetic basis ("Eating Disorders—Part I," 1997; Kendler et al., 1991).

Anorexia Someone suggests to Susanna, 14, that she would perform better in gymnastics if she lost a few pounds. She loses them—and then continues to diet obsessively. She is preoccupied with food—cooking it, talking about it, and urging others to eat—but she eats very little herself. Yet she has a distorted body image: she thinks she is too fat. Her body weight becomes less than 85 percent of what is considered normal for her height and age (APA, 1994). Meanwhile, she stops menstruating, and thick soft hair spreads over her body. Her skin becomes dry, her nails brittle, and her joints swollen. She may become anemic, constipated, and lethargic. To hide what she is doing to herself, she may wear baggy clothes or quietly pocket food and later throw it away; yet she denies that her behavior is abnormal or dangerous. She is a good student, described by her parents as a "model" child, and is compulsive about exercising. She is also withdrawn and depressed and engages in repetitive, perfectionist behavior ("Eating Disorders—Part I," 1997; D. M. Garner, 1993).

This is a typical scenario for **anorexia nervosa,** or self-starvation, a potentially life-threatening eating disorder seen mostly in young white women. Anorexia occurs across socioeconomic levels, typically beginning during adolescence. Ninety percent of people with anorexia are females; an estimated 0.5 to 1 percent of late adolescent girls and an unknown, but growing, percentage of boys are affected (APA, 1994; "Eating Disorders—Part I," 1997; D. M. Garner, 1993).

The cause of anorexia is unknown; it may be due to a combination of genetic and environmental factors. Some authorities point to a deficiency of a crucial chemical in the brain, a disturbance of the hypothalamus, or high levels of opiate-like substances in the spinal fluid ("Eating Disorders—Part I," 1997). Researchers in London, Sweden, and Germany have found reduced blood flow to certain parts of the brain, including an area thought to control visual self-perception and appetite (Gordon, Lask, Bryantwaugh, Christie, & Timini, 1997). Others see anorexia as a psychological disturbance related to fear of growing up or fear of sexuality or to a malfunctioning family that seems harmonious while members are actually overdependent, overly involved in each other's lives, and unable to deal with conflict. People with anorexia may feel that controlling their weight is the only way to control any part of their lives (Dove, n.d.; "Eating Disorders—Part I," 1997; D. M. Garner, 1993).

Anorexia may in part be a reaction to extreme societal pressure to be slender. The disorder is most prevalent in industrialized societies, such as the United States, Canada, Europe, Australia, Japan, New Zealand, and South Africa, where food is abundant and attractiveness is equated with thinness (APA, 1994).

Gymnast Christy Henrich died of multiple organ failure at age 22, after having suffered from anorexia and bulimia as a teenager. These eating disorders are especially common among female gymnasts, figure skaters, ballet dancers, and competitive swimmers.

anorexia nervosa Eating disorder characterized by self-starvation.

Early warning signs include determined, secret dieting; dissatisfaction after losing weight; setting new, lower weight goals after reaching an initial desired weight; excessive exercising; and interruption of regular menstruation. Diagnosis and treatment (discussed below) should occur as soon as such symptoms appear.

bulimia nervosa Eating disorder in which a person regularly eats huge quantities of food and then purges the body by laxatives, induced vomiting, fasting, or excessive exercise.

Bulimia In *bulimia nervosa,* a person—usually an adolescent girl or a young woman—regularly goes on huge eating binges within a short time, usually 2 hours or less, and then tries to undo the high caloric intake by self-induced vomiting, strict dieting or fasting, engaging in excessively vigorous exercise, or taking laxatives, enemas, or diuretics to purge the body. These episodes occur at least twice a week for at least 3 months (APA, 1994). (Binge eating without purging is a separate disorder associated with obesity.)

Bulimia is at least 2 or 3 times as common as anorexia, and, as with anorexia, most sufferers are females. An estimated 1 to 3 percent of adolescent girls and young women have the disorder, about 10 times the number of males. Estimates are that between 4 and 10 percent of women may become bulimic at some time in their lives, and larger numbers show bulimia-like behavior (APA, 1994; "Eating Disorders—Part I," 1997; Kendler et al., 1991).

People with bulimia are obsessed with their weight and shape. They do not become abnormally thin, but they become overwhelmed with shame, self-contempt, and depression over their abnormal eating habits. They also suffer extensive tooth decay (caused by repeated vomiting of stomach acid), gastric irritation, skin lesions, and loss of hair. There is some overlap between anorexia and bulimia; some victims of anorexia have bulimic episodes, and some people with bulimia lose weight ("Eating Disorders—Part I," 1997; K. I. Edwards, 1993; Kendler et al., 1991). However, the two are separate disorders.

Bulimia is about equally common in each of the industrialized countries with high rates of anorexia, noted above (APA, 1994). One theory attributes the prevalence of bulimia in these countries to the same pressures that create a social climate for anorexia. However, bulimia may have a biological basis; it seems to be related to low levels of the brain chemical serotonin. There is also a psychoanalytic explanation: people with bulimia use food to satisfy their hunger for love and attention. This interpretation rests on reports by some bulimic patients that they felt abused, neglected, and deprived of parental nurturing ("Eating Disorders—Part I," 1997; Humphrey, 1986). Women likely to become bulimic are age 30 or under. They have low self-esteem, a slim ideal body image, and a history of wide weight fluctuation, dieting, or frequent exercise (Kendler et al., 1991). Many bulimics are also alcoholics or substance abusers or have other mental health problems, which may arise from the physical effects of the disorder ("Eating Disorders—Part I," 1997; K. I. Edwards, 1993; Kendler et al., 1991). Although childhood sexual abuse has been suggested as a risk factor for both bulimia and anorexia, there is no evidence that women with these disorders are more likely to have been abused than women in the general population or anxious and depressed women in general ("Eating Disorders—Part I," 1997; H. G. Pope & Hudson, 1992).

Treatment and Outcomes for Anorexia and Bulimia Anorexia and bulimia can be treated, but the relapse rate is very high. Treatment for bulimia tends to be more successful, because bulimia patients generally want treatment. Treatment may speed recovery at first but does not seem to affect the long-term outcome; symptoms often disappear by the age of 40, even without treatment. About 50 percent of women diagnosed as bulimic have fully recovered 5 to 10 years later, but 20 percent still exhibit the disorder, and 30 percent show some symptoms. Nearly one-third of patients who initially recover relapse during the first 4 years, but a second recovery is common. Certain personality traits, such as impulsiveness, may increase the likelihood of relapse ("Eating Disorders—Part II," 1997; Keel &

Mitchell, 1997). The prognosis is worse for anorexia. Up to 25 percent of anorexic patients progress to chronic invalidism, and between 2 and 10 percent die prematurely (APA, 1994; Beumont, Russell, & Touyz, 1993; "Eating Disorders—Part I," 1997; Herzog, Keller, & Lavori, 1988).

The immediate goal of treatment for anorexia is to get patients to eat and gain weight. They are likely to be admitted to a hospital, where they may be given 24-hour nursing, drugs to encourage eating and inhibit vomiting, and behavior therapy, which rewards eating with such privileges as being allowed to get out of bed and leave the room (Beumont et al., 1993). Bulimia also may be treated with behavior therapy, either group or individual. Patients keep daily diaries of their eating patterns and are taught ways to avoid the temptation to binge. Both anorexia and bulimia are also treated by psychotherapy. Since these patients are at risk for depression and suicide, antidepressant drugs can be helpful (K. I. Edwards, 1993; Fluoxetine-Bulimia Collaborative Study Group, 1992; Hudson & Pope, 1990; Kaye, Weltzin, Hsu, & Bulik, 1991).

People with anorexia seem to need long-term support even after they have stopped starving themselves. Some 27 months after completion of treatment, most of the 63 females in one study were gaining weight, had resumed menstruating, and were functioning in school or at work. Still, they continued to have problems with body image. Even though they averaged 8 percent below ideal weight, most thought of themselves as being overweight and as having excessive appetites, and many felt depressed and lonely (Nussbaum, Shenker, Baird, & Saravay, 1985). Similarly, a Canadian study that followed anorexic patients for 9 years, starting 5 years after treatment, found a tendency toward depression or anxiety disorders (Toner, Garfinkel, & Garner, 1986).

Use and Abuse of Drugs

Although the great majority of adolescents do not abuse drugs, a significant minority do. They turn to drugs out of curiosity or a desire for sensation, because of peer pressure, or as an escape from overwhelming problems, and thereby endanger their present and future physical and psychological health.

Substance abuse means harmful use of alcohol or other drugs. It is a poorly adaptive behavior pattern, lasting more than 1 month, in which a person continues to use a substance after knowingly being harmed by it or uses it repeatedly in a hazardous situation, such as driving while intoxicated (APA, 1994). Abuse can lead to *substance dependence* (addiction), which may be physiological or psychological, or both, and is likely to continue into adulthood (Kandel, Davies, Karus, & Yamaguchi, 1986).

Drug use among American adolescents has been on the upswing during the 1990s (see Table 14-5), though it is not as prevalent as during the late 1970s and early 1980s and considerably less so than at its peak in the 1960s. Marijuana has shown the sharpest increase; eighth and tenth graders are becoming less likely to regard marijuana as risky, while the perceived risk of most other drugs has increased or stayed the same. However, marijuana use often leads to use of other illicit drugs.

These findings come from a series of annual surveys of a nationally representative sample of approximately 49,000 eighth-, tenth-, and twelfth-graders in 435 public and private schools across the United States (National Institute on Drug Abuse [NIDA], 1996). The proportion of eighth-graders who admit to having taken illicit drugs during the previous year has more than doubled since 1991, from 11 to 24 percent. Since 1992, illicit drug use among tenth-graders has almost doubled, from 20 to 38 percent, and among twelfth-graders, has risen from 27 to 40 percent. These surveys probably underestimate adolescent drug use since they do not reach high school dropouts, who are likely to have higher rates.

CHECKPOINT

Can you . . .

- Summarize the normal nutritional needs of adolescent boys and girls?
- Discuss risk factors, effects, treatment, and prognosis for obesity, anorexia nervosa, and bulimia nervosa?

substance abuse Repeated, harmful use of a substance, usually alcohol or another drug.

substance dependence Addiction (physical or psychological, or both) to a harmful substance.

Drug	Eighth-Graders, %	Tenth-Graders, %	Twelfth-Graders, %
Table 14-5 Percentage of Students Who Have Ever Used Drugs, 1992–1996			
Marijuana	1992: 11.2	1992: 21.4	1992: 32.6
	1994: 16.7	1994: 30.4	1994: 38.2
	1996: 23.1	1996: 39.8	1996: 44.9
Cocaine	1992: 2.9	1992: 3.3	1992: 6.1
	1994: 3.6	1994: 4.3	1994: 5.9
	1996: 4.5	1996: 6.5	1996: 7.1
Crack cocaine	1992: 1.6	1992: 1.5	1992: 2.6
	1994: 2.4	1994: 2.1	1994: 3.0
	1996: 2.9	1996: 3.3	1996: 3.3
Inhalants	1992: 17.4	1992: 16.6	1992: 16.6
	1994: 19.9	1994: 18.0	1994: 17.7
	1996: 21.2	1996: 19.3	1996: 16.6
LSD	1992: 3.2	1992: 5.8	1992: 8.6
	1994: 3.7	1994: 7.2	1994: 10.5
	1996: 5.1	1996: 9.4	1996: 12.6
Alcohol*	1992: 69.3	1992: 82.3	1992: 87.5
	1994: 55.8	1994: 71.7	1994: 80.4
	1996: 55.3	1996: 71.8	1996: 79.2
Cigarettes	1992: 45.2	1992: 53.5	1992: 61.8
	1994: 46.1	1994: 56.9	1994: 62.0
	1996: 49.2	1996: 61.2	1996: 63.5
All illicit drugs	1992: 20.6	1992: 29.8	1992: 40.7
	1994: 25.7	1994: 37.4	1994: 45.6
	1996: 31.2	1996: 45.4	1996: 50.8

*Note: After 1993, the question was reworded to indicate that a "drink" meant "more than a few sips."
Source: Adapted from NIDA, 1996.

The rise in drug use has accompanied a decline in perception of its dangers and a softening of peer disapproval. Still, the great majority of young people disapprove of trying illicit drugs other than marijuana; and even for marijuana, disapproval rates range from 67.5 percent of eighth-graders to 52.5 percent of twelfth-graders, with much larger proportions disapproving of regular use (NIDA, 1996).*

Legal restrictions, social norms, and economic factors such as price and taxation affect the availability and desirability of drugs and thus the extent of their use; but what makes it likely that a particular young person will abuse drugs? Research has pinpointed a number of characteristics of the individual and the environment: (1) poor impulse control and a tendency to seek out sensation rather than avoid harm (which may have a biochemical basis and may show up as early as kindergarten), (2) family influences (such as a genetic predisposition to alcoholism, parental use or acceptance of drugs, poor or inconsistent parenting practices, family conflict, troubled or distant family relationships, and not living with

*The 1997 NIDA survey, published as we went to press, shows a small decline in eighth-graders' use of illicit drugs, especially marijuana, and a slight rise in disapproval and perception of risk.

Heavy alcohol use is widespread among high school students. The combination of drinking and driving can be lethal.

two biological or adoptive parents), (3) "difficult" temperament, (4) early and persistent behavior problems, particularly aggression, (5) academic failure and lack of commitment to education, (6) peer rejection, (7) associating with drug users, (8) alienation and rebelliousness, (9) favorable attitudes toward drug use, and (10) early initiation into drug use. The earlier young people start using a drug, the more frequently they are likely to use it and the greater the tendency to abuse it. Contrary to popular belief, poverty is not linked with drug abuse unless deprivation is extreme (Hawkins, Catalano, & Miller, 1992; R. A. Johnson, Hoffmann, & Gerstein, 1996; Masse & Tremblay, 1997; USDHHS, 1996b).

Of course, these characteristics do not necessarily cause drug abuse, but they are fairly reliable predictors of it. The more risk factors that are present, the greater the chance that an adolescent or young adult will abuse drugs.

Alcohol, marijuana, and tobacco, the three drugs most popular with adolescents, are sometimes called *gateway drugs,* because their use often leads to use of more addictive substances, such as cocaine and heroin.

gateway drugs Drugs such as alcohol, tobacco, and marijuana, the use of which tends to lead to use of more addictive drugs.

Alcohol

Many of the same people who worry about the illegal use of marijuana forget that alcohol too is a potent, mind-altering drug, that in most states it is illegal for adolescents to consume and that it is a much more serious problem nationwide. Alcohol use among high school students has remained fairly stable in recent years, but at high levels, and alcohol use by eighth-graders has increased. About 30 percent of twelfth-graders, 25 percent of tenth-graders, and 16 percent of eighth-graders report having had five or more drinks in a row during the previous 2 weeks. Thirty-one percent of seniors, 21 percent of tenth-graders, and 10 percent of eighth-graders admit to having been drunk during the past month (NIDA, 1996).

Marijuana

Marijuana has been used all over the world for centuries, but only since the 1960s has it become popular among the American middle class. Despite a decline in use since 1979 (when more than 50 percent of high school seniors had smoked marijuana during the previous year), it is still by far the most widely used illicit drug in the United States; and usage has increased dramatically since the low

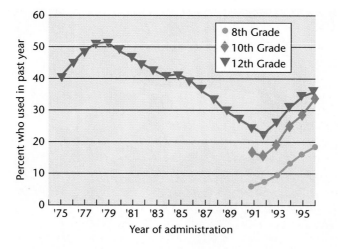

point in the early 1990s (see Figure 14-5). In 1996, 36 percent of twelfth-graders had smoked marijuana during the previous year—an increase of more than half from the 22 percent who reported using it in 1992. Increases for younger students were even greater: usage among tenth-graders more than doubled, from 15 percent to 34 percent; and among eighth-graders, it rose to 18 percent, 2½ times as high as in 1991 (NIDA, 1996).

Heavy use of marijuana can damage the brain, heart, lungs, and immune system; its smoke typically contains more than 400 carcinogens. Using marijuana can impede memory, learning, perception, judgment, and the motor skills needed to drive a vehicle. It can contribute to traffic accidents, nutritional deficiencies, respiratory infections, and other physical problems. It may also lessen motivation, interfere with schoolwork and other activities, cut down on alertness and attention span, and cause family problems (AAP Committee on Drugs, 1980; Farrow, Rees, & Worthington-Roberts, 1987; NIDA, 1996).

Contrary to many young people's belief, marijuana may be addictive. Injecting rats with marijuana initially produces a "high" by increasing levels of a brain chemical called *dopamine.* But, as with heroin, cocaine, and other addictive drugs, the brain's ability to produce dopamine gradually diminishes, creating a greater craving for the drug. Marijuana's addictive nature tends to be masked in most users; they normally do not experience sudden withdrawal symptoms, because the drug's active ingredient stays in the bloodstream for a long time. However, when rats were injected with marijuana and then with a counteractive drug, they went into withdrawal, suggesting that the underlying changes in brain chemistry are the same as for other addictive drugs (Tanda, Pontieri, & DiChiara, 1997).

Tobacco

A U.S. Surgeon General's report in 1964 linked smoking to lung cancer, heart disease, emphysema, and several other illnesses. Many adolescents eventually got the message, and the percentage of high school seniors who were daily smokers dropped by 34 percent between 1976 and 1993. Most of that drop reflected a nearly 84 percent decline among black teenagers (McIntosh, 1995). Smoking, both frequent and occasional, is far less prevalent among black teenagers, especially girls, than among white and Hispanic youth. Only about 12 percent of black girls smoke at all, and only about 1 percent smoke heavily (CDC, 1996c). This may in part be because black girls are less concerned about weight control than white girls, who often use smoking as a way to keep from overeating (Center on Addiction and Substance Abuse at Columbia University [CASA], 1996).

Smoking among adolescents has taken a recent upturn; by 1996, about one-third (34 percent) of high school seniors, 30 percent of tenth-graders, and

21 percent of eighth-graders were smoking regularly, up from 28 percent and 14 percent, respectively, in 1991 (NIDA, 1996). The average age of starting a smoking habit has dropped to 14½; about 9 out of 10 smokers begin before age 18 (Bartecchi, MacKenzie, & Schrier, 1995; CDC, 1996c).

Apparent peer influence on smoking has been documented extensively (CASA, 1996). However, many studies have failed to distinguish between influence and similarity of behavior. Adolescents who smoke may choose friends who smoke. Or they and their friends may both be subject to the same outside influences. In a study of sixth-, eighth-, and tenth-graders, which attempted to control for these factors and also for gender, grade level, and ethnicity, the influence of close friends or friendship groups on both cigarette and alcohol use over the course of a school year was only modest. This finding suggests that interventions focused on teaching young people to resist peer influence are likely to be largely ineffective. Instead, programs might be targeted to those adolescents who select substance users as friends, or to those who can be identified as most susceptible to peer influence (Urberg, Degirmencioglu, & Pilgrim, 1997).

Other research points to the influence of family factors. One 6-year longitudinal study followed 312 adolescents—most of them from white, college-educated, two-parent families—who were not smoking at ages 11 and 13. Those whose families were not close and whose parents smoked were more than twice as likely as others in the sample to smoke by ages 17 to 19 (Doherty & Allen, 1994). Tobacco advertising may be an even stronger factor (N. Evans, Farkas, Gilpin, Berry, & Pierce, 1995). National Health Interview Surveys found a sudden, marked increase in cigarette smoking by girls under 18 after the launching in 1967 of advertising campaigns specifically targeted to women (Pierce, Lee, & Gilpin, 1994).

All states and the District of Columbia have laws forbidding the sale of tobacco to minors, but these laws are poorly enforced. Now a number of states and cities are enacting stiffer penalties, including imprisonment, for minors who buy or possess cigarettes or chewing tobacco. Proposed federal legislation contains measures designed to reduce teenage smoking: restrictions on tobacco advertising, removal of cigarette vending machines, and a ban on tobacco companies' sponsorship of rock concerts and sporting events. Prices of cigarette would rise (making them less affordable to young people), and tobacco companies would face large fines unless youth smoking declined.

CHECKPOINT

Can you . . .

- Summarize trends in drug use among adolescents?

Sexually Transmitted Diseases (STDs)

Sexually transmitted diseases (STDs), also called *venereal diseases,* are diseases spread by sexual contact. The prevalence of STDs has soared since the 1960s. Rates in the United States are among the highest in the industrialized world; 1 out of 4 Americans is likely to contract an STD (Alan Guttmacher Institute, 1994).

The most prevalent STD, according to some estimates, is human papilloma virus (HPV), which sometimes produces warts on the genitals (AAP Committee on Adolescence, 1994). Next is genital herpes simplex, a chronic, recurring, often painful, and highly contagious disease caused by a virus (Alan Guttmacher Institute, 1994). The condition can be fatal to a person with a deficiency of the immune system or to the newborn infant of a mother who has an outbreak at the time of delivery. There is no cure, but the antiviral drug acyclovir can prevent active outbreaks. Both diseases have been associated, in women, with increased incidence of cervical cancer.

The most common *curable* STD is chlamydia, which causes infections of the urinary tract, rectum, and cervix and can lead, in women, to pelvic inflammatory disease (PID), a serious abdominal infection. In 1995, chlamydia was the infectious disease most frequently reported to the Centers for Disease Control and

sexually transmitted diseases (STDs) Diseases spread by sexual contact; also called *venereal diseases.*

Prevention (1996b), followed by gonorrhea and AIDS (acquired immune deficiency syndrome). AIDS was 4 times as common among men as among women. Also among the 10 most commonly reported diseases were hepatitis A, syphilis, and hepatitis B. (Not all diseases are reported, and reports are believed to vastly underestimate true incidence.) Gonorrhea was the infectious disease most commonly reported among 15- to 24-year-olds. Table 14-6 summarizes some common STDs: their causes, most frequent symptoms, treatment, and consequences.

One out of three cases of STDs occurs among adolescents; the younger the teenager, the greater the chance of infection. The chief reasons for the spread of STDs among adolescents are early sexual activity, which increases the likelihood of having multiple high-risk partners, and failure to use condoms or to use them regularly and correctly. Half of all young people are sexually active by age 17, and an estimated 25 percent may develop an STD before high school graduation (AAP Committee on Adolescence, 1994).

Adolescents at high risk for contracting STDs—besides those who engage in unprotected sex—are those who experiment with alcohol and drugs, which can impair judgment; homosexual males; young people who "hang out" on the streets, are in jail, or engage in prostitution; and pregnant girls (AAP Committee on Adolescence, 1994).

STDs are more likely to develop undetected in women than in men, and in adolescents as compared with adults. Symptoms may not show up until the disease has progressed to the point of causing serious long-term complications. Programs that promote abstaining from or postponing sexual activity, responsible decision making, and ready availability of condoms for those who are sexually active may have some effect in controlling the spread of STDs. It is important to target programs to women and teenagers, since they are disproportionately affected by many STDs (AAP Committee on Adolescence, 1994; Alan Guttmacher Institute, 1994).

Although AIDS is not as prevalent as some other STDs, it has reached epidemic proportions since 1980. AIDS results from the human immunodeficiency virus (HIV), which attacks the body's immune system, leaving affected persons vulnerable to a variety of fatal diseases. HIV is transmitted through bodily fluids (mainly blood and semen) and is believed to stay in the body for life, even though the person carrying it may show no signs of illness. Symptoms of AIDS—which include extreme fatigue, fever, swollen lymph nodes, weight loss, diarrhea, and night sweats—may not appear until 6 months to 10 or more years after initial infection. As of now, AIDS is incurable, but in many cases the related infections that kill people can be stopped with antibiotics. Many HIV-infected people lead active lives for years.

Worldwide, most HIV-infected adults are heterosexual. In the United States, HIV is most prevalent among drug abusers who share contaminated hypodermic needles, homosexual and bisexual men, people who have received transfusions of infected blood or blood products, people who have had sexual contact with someone in one of these high-risk groups, and infants who have been infected in the womb or during birth. Unprotected heterosexual activity with multiple partners (for example, among users of crack cocaine selling sex to support their drug habit) is an increasingly high-risk factor for contracting HIV (Edlin et al., 1994).

AIDS can be avoided by changes in behavior. Prevention efforts focus on education about safer sex practices (such as using condoms, which offer some protection, and avoiding promiscuity) and screening of blood used in transfusions. Among 15- to 19-year-old boys, those who receive AIDS education and sex education have fewer sex partners and less frequent intercourse and use condoms more consistently (Ku, Sonenstein, & Pleck, 1992). More controversial are proposals to reduce sharing of hypodermic needles by distributing clean ones to drug users. Box 14-2 lists steps that people can take to protect themselves from AIDS and other STDs.

CHECKPOINT

Can you . . .

- Summarize the prevalence, causes, symptoms, treatment, and consequences of the most common sexually transmitted diseases?

- Identify risk factors for developing an STD and ways of protecting against STDs?

Table 14-6   Common Sexually Transmitted Diseases

Disease	Cause	Symptoms: Male	Symptoms: Female	Treatment	Consequences if Untreated
Chlamydia	Bacterial infection	Pain during urination, discharge from penis	Vaginal discharge, abdominal discomfort†	Tetracycline or erythromycin	Can cause pelvic inflammatory disease or eventual sterility
Trichomoniasis	Parasitic infection, sometimes passed on in moist objects such as towels and bathing suits	Often absent	May be absent, or may include vaginal discharge, discomfort during intercourse, odor, painful urination	Oral antibiotic	May lead to abnormal growth of cervical cells
Gonorrhea	Bacterial Infection	Discharge from penis, pain during urination*	Discomfort when urinating, vaginal discharge, abnormal menses†	Penicillin or other antibiotics	Can cause pelvic inflammatory disease or eventual sterility; can also cause arthritis, dermatitis, and meningitis
HPV (genital warts)	Human papiloma virus	Painless growths that usually appear on penis, but may also appear on urethra or in rectal area*	Small, painless growths on genitals and anus; may also occur inside the vagina without external symptoms*	Removal of warts; but infection often reappears	May be associated with cervical cancer. In pregnancy, warts enlarge and may obstruct birth canal.
Herpes	Herpes simplex virus	Painful blisters anywhere on the genitalia, usually on the penis*	Painful blisters on the genitalia, sometimes with fever and aching muscles; women with sores on cervix may be unaware of outbreaks*	No known cure, but controlled with antiviral drug acyclovir	Possible increased risk of cervical cancer
Hepatitis B	Hepatitis B virus	Skin and eyes become yellow	Skin and eyes become yellow	No specific treatment; no alcohol	Can cause liver damage, chronic hepatitis
Syphillis	Bacterial infection	In first stage, reddish-brown sores on the mouth or genitalia, or both which may disappear, though the bacteria remain; in the second more infectious stage, a widespread skin rash*	Same as in men	Penicillin or other antibiotics	Paralysis, convulsions, brain damage, and sometimes death
AIDS (acquired immune deficiency syndrome)	Human immunodeficiency virus (HIV)	Extreme fatigue, fever, swollen lymph nodes, weight loss, diarrhea, night sweats, susceptibility to other diseases*	Same as in men	No known cure; protease inhibitors and other drugs appear to extend life	Death, usually due to other diseases, such as cancer

*May be asymptomatic.
†Often asymptomatic.

Box 14-2 Protecting Against Sexually Transmitted Diseases

How can people protect themselves against sexually transmitted diseases (STDs)? Abstinence is safest, of course. For those who are sexually active, the following guidelines minimize the possibility of acquiring an STD and maximize the chances of getting good treatment if one is acquired.

- Have regular medical checkups. All sexually active persons should request tests specifically aimed at diagnosing STDs.
- Know your partner. The more discriminating you are, the less likely you are to be exposed to STDs. Partners with whom you develop a relationship are more likely than partners you do not know well to inform you of any medical problems they have.
- Avoid having sexual intercourse with many partners, promiscuous persons, and drug abusers.
- Practice "safer sex": avoid sexual activity involving exchange of bodily fluids. Use a latex condom during intercourse and oral sex. Avoid anal intercourse.
- Use a contraceptive foam, cream, or jelly during vaginal intercourse; it will kill many germs and help to prevent certain STDs.
- Learn the symptoms of STDs: vaginal or penile discharge; inflammation, itching, or pain in the genital or anal area; burning during urination; pain during intercourse; genital,

body, or mouth sores, blisters, bumps, or rashes; pain in the lower abdomen or in the testicles; discharge from or itching of eyes; and fever or swollen glands.

- Inspect your partner for any visible symptoms.
- If you develop any symptoms yourself, get immediate medical attention.
- Just before and just after sexual contact, wash genitals and rectal area with soap and water; males should urinate after washing.
- Do not have any sexual contact if you suspect that you or your partner may be infected. Abstinence is the most reliable preventive measure.
- Avoid exposing any cut or break in the skin to anyone else's blood (including menstrual blood), body fluids, or secretions.
- Make sure needles used for ear piercing, tattooing, acupuncture, or any kind of injection are either sterile or disposable. Never share a needle.
- If you contract any STD, notify all recent sexual partners immediately so that they can obtain treatment and avoid passing the infection back to you or on to someone else. If you have HIV or hepatitis B infection, inform your doctor or dentist of your condition so that precautions can be taken to prevent transmission. Do not donate blood, plasma, sperm, body organs, or other body tissue.

Source: Adapted from American Foundation for the Prevention of Venereal Disease [AFPVD], 1988; Upjohn Company, 1984.

Abuse and Neglect

Of the 1 million children found by state agencies to be victims of substantiated or indicated abuse or neglect in 1995, 26 percent were 8 to 12 years old, and 21 percent were ages 13 to 18 (National Clearinghouse on Child Abuse and Neglect Information, 1997). Maltreatment of adolescents is believed to be less prevalent than in younger age groups, but only because of disproportionate increases in maltreatment among younger children (Sedlak & Broadhurst, 1996).

One difficulty in assessing the extent of the problem among older children is that teenagers are more likely to fight back or run away (Sedlak & Broadhurst, 1996). Also, adolescents are often perceived as bearing at least part of the blame for provoking parents; physically abused teenagers are more likely than other adolescents to use violence against parents and siblings. Parents who maltreat adolescents tend to have higher socioeconomic and educational levels than parents who abuse younger children, and they are less likely to have been abused themselves. They tend to be either authoritarian or overindulgent and to use excessive force as a means of discipline (Council on Scientific Affairs, 1993).

Although abuse of teenagers is less likely to result in death or severe injury than abuse of younger children, it can have serious long-term results. Sexually abused teenagers are more likely than their peers to engage in early or heavy sexual activity; to become pregnant or delinquent; to abuse alcohol or other drugs; to be confused about their sexual identity; to be depressed or anxious; and to attempt suicide. Physically abused teenagers also tend to be anxious and depressed. They may show severe behavioral, academic, or sleeping problems; self-destructive or reckless actions; heavy drug use; or suicidal tendencies (Council on Scientific Affairs, 1993).

Death in Adolescence

When adolescents die, it is usually from violence. The leading causes of death among 15- to 24-year-olds in the United States—accidents, homicide, and suicide (Anderson, Kochanek, & Murphy, 1997)—reflect cultural pressures and adolescents' inexperience and immaturity, which often lead to risk taking and carelessness. The death rate is about 3 times as high for 15- to 24-year-old males as for females; boys and young men are about 6 times more likely to die of homicide or suicide than girls and young women (Anderson et al., 1997).

Death rates among 15- to 24-year-olds are almost twice as high for black as for white youths (159.8 versus 84.3 deaths per 100,000). Automobile accidents are the leading cause for young whites. For African Americans, homicide is the number one killer—among black males, at a rate about 8 times greater than among white males (Anderson et al., 1997).

Suicide is now the second leading cause of death for 15- to 24-year-old white males and the third leading cause for this age group generally. Furthermore, the leading cause is accidents, some of which may actually be suicides (Anderson et al., 1997). In a 1990 Gallup poll, more than 60 percent of teenagers said they knew someone who had attempted suicide, and 6 percent said they had attempted to kill themselves (G. L. Ackerman, 1993). Far fewer completed suicides are reported—13.3 per 100,000 15- to 24-year-olds in 1995—but that rate has tripled since 1950. The suicide rate for 15- to 24-year-old males in 1995—22.5 per 100,000—was almost twice the rate for the population as a whole and more than three times the rate for young males in the 1950s. The rate for females the same age was only 3.7 per 100,000 (NCHS, 1997).

Whether by homicide or suicide, firearms are the leading cause of death among both African American and white adolescent boys (M.I. Singer, Anglin, Song, & Lunghofer, 1995). Between 1985 and 1991, killings of 15- to 19-year-old boys—nearly 9 out of 10 firearm-related—increased 154 percent (CDC, 1994b). Many teenagers grow up with handgun violence as a fact of daily life (M. I. Singer et al., 1995). The American Academy of Pediatrics and the Center for the Prevention of Handgun Violence have developed a program to help doctors educate parents about the dangers of guns in the home, which increase the risk of teenage homicide more than threefold and of suicide more than tenfold and have been a major factor in the rise in teenage suicide (Rivara & Grossman, 1996).

Teenagers who attempt suicide tend to have histories of emotional illness—commonly depression, substance abuse, antisocial or aggressive behavior, or unstable personality. They also tend to have attempted suicide before, or to have friends or family members who did (A. F. Garland & Zigler, 1993; Meehan, 1990; Slap, Vorters, Chaudhuri, & Centor, 1989; "Suicide—Part I," 1996). Drugs and alcohol play a part in one-third or more of teenage suicides and probably account for much of the rise in incidence (A. F. Garland & Zigler, 1993). Although school problems—academic or behavioral—are common among would-be suicides, they are not universal (National Committee for Citizens in Education [NCCE], 1986).

Suicidal teenagers tend to think poorly of themselves, to feel hopeless, and to have poor impulse control and low tolerance for frustration and stress. Their feelings of depression may be masked as boredom, apathy, hyperactivity, or physical problems. Some of these young people are alienated from their parents and have no one outside the family to turn to. Many come from troubled families—often with a history of divorce, unemployment, imprisonment, or suicidal behavior—and a high proportion have been abused or neglected (Deykin, Alpert, & McNamara, 1985; A. F. Garland & Zigler, 1993; Slap et al., 1989; "Suicide—Part I," 1996; Swedo et al., 1991).

Box 14-3 Preventing Suicide

What can be done to stem the alarming rise in suicide among young people? Many people intent on killing themselves keep their plans secret, but others send out signals well in advance. An attempt at suicide is sometimes a call for help, and some people die because they are more successful than they intended to be.

Warning signs include withdrawal from relationships; talking about death, the hereafter, or suicide; giving away prized possessions; drug or alcohol abuse; personality changes, such as a rise in anger, boredom, or apathy; unusual neglect of appearance; difficulty concentrating at work or in school; staying away from work, school, or other usual activities; complaints of physical problems when nothing is organically wrong; and eating or sleeping much more or much less than usual. Friends or family may be able to help by talking to a young person about his or her suicidal thoughts to bring them out in the open; telling others who are in a position to do something—the person's parents or spouse, other family members, a close friend, a therapist, or a counselor; and showing the person that she or he has other options besides death, even though none of them may be ideal.

Telephone hotlines are the most prevalent type of suicide intervention for adolescents, but their effectiveness appears to be minimal. The few studies that have been done of school suicide prevention programs found them of limited value. In fact, some of these programs may do harm by exaggerating the extent of teenage suicide and painting it as a reaction to normal stresses of adolescence rather than a pathological act. A review of the research on adolescent suicide suggests that programs should instead seek to identify and treat young people at particular risk of suicide, including those who have already attempted it. Equally important is to attack the risk factors—for example, through programs to reduce substance abuse and strengthen families (A. F. Garland & Zigler, 1993). Programs to enhance self-esteem and build problem solving and coping abilities can be directed toward young children and continued throughout the school years (Meehan, 1990).

Steps can also be taken to reduce access to common methods of suicide. Many suicides are impulsive; if a convenient means is not at hand, a depressed person may not go any further or may at least defer action long enough to get help. Furthermore, a person who leans toward one method may be reluctant to use another (L. Eisenberg, 1980). In England and Wales between 1960 and

Access to guns is a major factor in the rise in teenage suicide.

1975, suicide rates declined, apparently as a result of the elimination of coal gas containing carbon monoxide, the inhalation of which had been a popular method of suicide (J. H. Brown, 1979). In the United States and in Australia, the number of suicides from barbiturates dropped in proportion to the number of prescriptions written. The number of suicides involving guns has risen in recent years; the ready availability of firearms in the home is associated with a higher risk of suicide (Kellermann et al., 1992). Although most young people who *attempt* suicide do it by taking pills or ingesting other substances, those who succeed are most likely to use firearms (A. F. Garland & Zigler, 1993). Thus limiting access to firearms might well reduce the suicide rate.

However, we need to be cautious in assessing claims that family problems put young people at risk of suicide. Many studies have not considered whether these problems preceded or followed a suicide attempt. A review of the literature did find consistent evidence that a history of physical or sexual abuse is a risk factor for suicide. Evidence is less strong that poor family communication, loss of a parent through separation or death, or a family history of personality disorders is likely to lead to suicide (B. M. Wagner, 1997). (Box 14-3 discusses suicide prevention.)

Protective Factors: Health in Context

Adolescents' physical development, like that of younger children, does not occur in a vacuum. Young people live and grow in a social world. As we have pointed out throughout this book, the influences of the family and school environments, particularly, play an important part in physical and mental health.

A study of 12,118 seventh- through twelfth-graders in a random sample of 134 schools across the country (M. D. Resnick et al., 1997) took a broad overview of risk factors and protective factors affecting four major aspects of adolescent health and well-being: emotional distress and suicidal behavior; involvement in violence (fighting or threats or use of weapons); use of cigarettes, alcohol, and marijuana; and sexuality (including age of sexual initiation and any history of pregnancy). The students completed questionnaires and had 90-minute home interviews; during the sensitive portions of the interview, the young people listened to the questions through earphones and entered their answers on laptop computers. The youngsters' school administrators also filled out questionnaires.

The findings emphasize the interconnectedness of physical, cognitive, emotional, and social development. Perceptions of connectedness to others, both at home and at school, consistently affect young people's health and well-being in all domains. The findings underline the importance of parents' spending time with, and being available to, their children. Even more important, however, is an adolescent's sense that parents and teachers are warm and caring and that they have high expectations for the youngster's achievement. The data also support the advisability of restrictions on adolescents' access to tobacco, alcohol, and guns.

Does an after-school job help or harm adolescents' development? This question is a complex one, which we address more fully in Chapter 15. According to this study, teenagers who work 20 or more hours a week are more likely to suffer emotional stress; to smoke, drink, or use marijuana; and to begin sexual activity at an early age. Young people with low grade point averages, those who are held back in school, and those who look older than their peers face similar risks and also are more likely than other teenagers to be involved in violence.

This study is continuing; future analyses will incorporate longitudinal data and parent interviews. However, the main thrust of the findings is clear and consistent with other research: youngsters who are getting emotional support at home and are doing well in school have the best chance of avoiding the health hazards of adolescence.

Despite the perils of adolescence, most young people emerge from these years with a mature, healthy body and a zest for life. While their bodies have been developing, their intellect has continued to develop too, as we will see in Chapter 15.

SUMMARY

Adolescence: A Developmental Transition

- Neither the beginning nor the end of **adolescence** is clearly marked in western societies. In some nonwestern cultures, attainment of adulthood is signified by special rites.
- Adolescence is fraught with risks to healthy development, as well as with opportunities for physical, cognitive, and psychosocial growth.

Puberty

- **Puberty** has a wide age range. It is triggered by hormonal changes, which may affect moods and behavior. Puberty takes about 4 years, typically begins earlier in girls than in boys, and ends when a person can reproduce.

CHECKPOINT

Can you . . .

- Tell how maltreatment of adolescents differs from maltreatment of younger children?
- Name the three leading causes of death among adolescents?
- Assess risk factors and prevention programs for teenage suicide?
- Identify factors that tend to protect adolescents from health risks?

- During puberty, both boys and girls undergo an **adolescent growth spurt.** A **secular trend** toward earlier attainment of adult height and sexual maturity began about 100 years ago, probably because of improvements in living standards.
- **Primary sex characteristics** (the reproductive organs) enlarge and mature during puberty. **Secondary sex characteristics** also appear.
- The principal signs of sexual maturity are production of sperm (for males) and menstruation (for females). **Spermarche,** a boy's first ejaculation, typically occurs at age 13. **Menarche,** the first menstruation, occurs, on average, between the ages of 12 and 13 in the United States.
- Teenagers, especially girls, tend to be sensitive about their physical appearance. Girls who mature early tend to adjust less easily than early-maturing boys.

Sexuality

- **Sexual orientation—heterosexual, homosexual,** or **bisexual**—appears to be influenced by an interaction of biological and environmental factors.
- Sexual attraction seems to begin at **adrenarche** (about age 10), when the adrenal glands increase their hormonal output, and well before **gonadarche.**

Health

- For the most part, the adolescent years are relatively healthy. Health problems often result from poverty, a risk-taking lifestyle, or a sedentary one. Adolescents are less likely than younger children to get regular medical care.
- Between 10 and 40 percent of adolescents experience depressed moods. Depression is often associated with concern about appearance.
- Three common eating disorders in adolescence are obesity, **anorexia nervosa,** and **bulimia nervosa.** Anorexia and bulimia affect mostly girls.
- In general, **substance abuse,** which can lead to **substance dependence,** is less common among adolescents today than during recent decades, but use of marijuana has increased. Marijuana, alcohol, and tobacco are called **gateway drugs** because their use often leads to use of more addictive drugs.
- **Sexually transmitted diseases (STDs)** have become far more prevalent since the 1960s; rates in the United States are among the highest in the industrialized world. One out of three cases occurs among adolescents.
- Maltreatment of adolescents can lead to serious behavior problems.
- The three leading causes of death among adolescents are accidents, homicide, and suicide. Access to firearms is a major factor in increases in homicide and suicide.
- Protective factors against physical and mental health risks include close, caring relationships with parents and teachers and high expectations for achievement.

KEY TERMS

adolescence (508)
puberty (508)
secular trend (512)
adolescent growth spurt (513)
primary sex characteristics (513)
secondary sex characteristics (514)
spermarche (515)
menarche (515)
sexual orientation (517)
heterosexual (517)

homosexual (517)
bisexual (517)
gonadarche (519)
adrenarche (519)
anorexia nervosa (525)
bulimia nervosa (526)
substance abuse (527)
substance dependence (527)
gateway drugs (529)
sexually transmitted diseases (STDs) (531)

QUESTIONS FOR THOUGHT AND DISCUSSION

1. Do western adolescents miss something by not having a specific rite of passage from childhood? If so, what kind of observance would be appropriate?

2. How would you define the end of adolescence and entry into adulthood?

3. What are some implications of attaining sexual maturity years before the customary age of marriage and attaining physical maturity years before attaining independence from parents?

4. Did you mature early, late, or "on time"? How did the timing of your maturation affect you psychologically?

5. Can you suggest ways to reduce the prevalence of eating disorders?

6. How can adolescents be helped to avoid or change risky behaviors, such as the use of drugs and firearms and unsafe sexual activity?

7. Should marijuana be legal, like alcohol? Why or why not?

8. Should there be tighter restrictions on cigarette advertising? If so, what kinds of restrictions would you favor?

9. Some people argue that banning female genital mutilation is imposing western cultural values on nonwestern cultures. How would you respond?

Cognitive Development in Adolescence

I should place [the prime of a man's life] at between fifteen and sixteen. It is then, it always seems to me, that his vitality is at its highest; he has greatest sense of the ludicrous and least sense of dignity. After that time, decay begins to set in.

Evelyn Waugh, aged 16, in a school debate, 1920

Focus

Nelson Mandela

The name Nelson Mandela's father gave him at birth, Rolihlahla, means "stirring up trouble"—something he did throughout his long and finally successful struggle to topple apartheid, South Africa's rigid system of racial separation and subjugation. Mandela's election as his country's first black president in April, 1994—only 4 years after his emergence from 28 years behind bars for conspiring to overthrow the white-dominated government—was the realization of a dream formed in his youth. It was a dream kindled as Mandela sat quietly listening to his tribal elders reminisce about a bygone era of self-government more than a century earlier, before the coming of white people—an era of peace, freedom, and equality.

"The land . . . belonged to the whole tribe and there was no individual ownership whatsoever," Mandela told the court that sentenced him to prison in 1962. "There were no classes, no rich or poor and no exploitation of man by man. . . . The council was so completely democratic that all members of the tribe could participate in its deliberations. Chief and subject, warrior and medicine man, all took part" (Meer, 1988, p. 12). Mandela recognized that his forebears' primitive way of life would not be viable in the modern world. But the vision of a society "in which none will be held in slavery or servitude, and in which poverty, want and insecurity shall be no more" served as a lifelong inspiration.

Mandela was born July 18, 1918, at Mvezo, a small, isolated village in a native reserve, or homeland, called the Transkei. He had royal blood: one of his ancestors had ruled his Thembu tribe. He seems to have inherited his "proud rebelliousness" and "stubborn sense of fairness" (Mandela, 1994, p. 6): not long after his birth, his father, the chief of Mvezo and a counselor to tribal kings, was deposed for refusing to honor a summons to appear before the local British magistrate. For standing on his traditional prerogatives and defying the magistrate's authority, Mandela's father paid with his lands and fortune.

Mandela's mother, the third of his father's four wives, moved to the nearby village of Qunu. There Mandela and his three sisters grew up in a compound of mud huts. The family raised all their own food—cows and goats for milk, and mealies (a form of corn), which his mother ground between two stones to make bread or boiled over an open fire. At 5, Mandela became a herd boy, driving sheep and cattle through the fertile grasslands. His was a simple life, governed for the most part by the time-honored rules of his tribe. But his mother, who had become a Christian, had him baptized in the Methodist church; and at 7, he became the first member of his family to go to school. It was his first teacher who gave him his English name, Nelson.

When Mandela was 9, his father died, and his life changed completely. His mother sent him to live at the tribal headquarters at Mqhekezweni. The acting regent, who owed his position to Mandela's father, had offered to become his guardian and raise him as his own son.

As Mandela grew into adolescence, he observed tribal meetings, where any member could speak and the regent listened quietly before summing up the consensus. This style of leadership deeply impressed Mandela and influenced his own demeanor as a leader in later years. He also watched his guardian preside over council meetings to which minor chiefs brought disputes to be tried. His fascination with the presentation of cases and the cross-examination of witnesses planted the seeds of an ambition to be a lawyer—an ambition he eventually fulfilled. From the visiting chiefs and headmen, he heard tales about early African warriors who had fought against Western domination. These stories stirred his interest in his people's history and laid the groundwork for his political activism.

At the age of 16, Mandela underwent circumcision, the traditional ritual by which a boy becomes recognized as a man and a participant in tribal councils. At the concluding ceremony, the main speaker, Chief Meligqili, struck a discordant note. The promise of manhood, he said, was an empty one in a land where Africans were a conquered people. "Among these young men," he said, "are chiefs who will never rule because we have no power to govern ourselves; soldiers who will never fight for we have no weapons to fight with; scholars who will never teach because we have no place for them to study. The abilities, the intelligence, the promise of these young men will be squandered in their attempt to eke out a living doing the simplest, most mindless chores for the white man. These gifts [we give them] today are naught, for we cannot give them the greatest gift of all, which is freedom and independence." Although Mandela did not appreciate it at the time, that speech began his political awakening.

The main sources of biographical information about Nelson Mandela's youth are M. Benson, 1986, Hargrove, 1989, Harwood, 1987, Mandela, 1994, and Meer, 1988.

• • •

The formative influences of Mandela's adolescent years helped shape his moral and political thinking and his life's work. The lessons he had learned about leadership and about his people's past glory stood him in good stead as he directed the resistance to an increasingly repressive regime, first in the streets and then from his island prison. Those lessons remained with him as he eventually managed to negotiate a new nonracial constitution and free elections—accomplishments for which he received the Nobel Peace Prize in 1993.

In this chapter, we first examine the Piagetian stage of formal operations, which makes it possible for a young person like Nelson Mandela to visualize an ideal world. We also look at what David Elkind has identified as some immature aspects of adolescents' thought and at their moral development. Finally, we explore practical aspects of cognitive growth—issues of school and vocational choice.

After reading this chapter, you should be able to answer and elaborate on such questions as these:

Preview Questions:

- How does adolescent thinking differ from that of younger children?
- How do adolescents make moral judgments and life decisions?
- How does the transition to secondary school affect adolescents' development?
- What factors affect success in school?
- What factors influence high school students' educational and vocational planning?

What determines how fast the pendulum swings: the length of the string? the weight of the object suspended from it? the height from which the object is released? the amount of force used to push the object? According to Piaget, an adolescent who has achieved the stage of formal operations can form a hypothesis and figure out a logical way to test it. However, many people never figure out how to solve this problem.

Aspects of Cognitive Maturation

Adolescents not only look different from younger children; they also think differently. Their speed of information processing continues to increase, though not as dramatically as in middle childhood (Kail, 1991, 1997). For the first time, they are capable of abstract reasoning and idealistic thinking.

Piaget's Stage of Formal Operations

What distinguishes adolescent thinking is awareness of the concept "What if . . . ?" Much of childhood appears to be a struggle to come to grips with the world as it is. Adolescents become aware of the world as it could be.

According to Piaget, adolescents enter the highest level of cognitive development—*formal operations*—when they develop the capacity for abstract thought. This development, which usually occurs around age 12, gives them a new way to manipulate (or operate on) information. No longer limited to thinking about the here and now, they can think in terms of what might be true, not just in terms of what is true. They can imagine possibilities, test hypotheses, and form theories.

formal operations In Piaget's theory, the final stage of cognitive development, characterized by the ability to think abstractly.

Evidence of Cognitive Maturity

To appreciate the advancement in thinking that the stage of formal operations brings, let's follow the progress of a typical child in dealing with a classic Piagetian problem, the pendulum problem.* The child, Adam, is shown the pendulum—an object hanging from a string. He is then shown how he can change any of four factors: the length of the string, the weight of the object, the height from which the object is released, and the amount of force he may use to

*This description of age-related differences in the approach to the pendulum problem is adapted from H. Ginsburg & Opper, 1979.

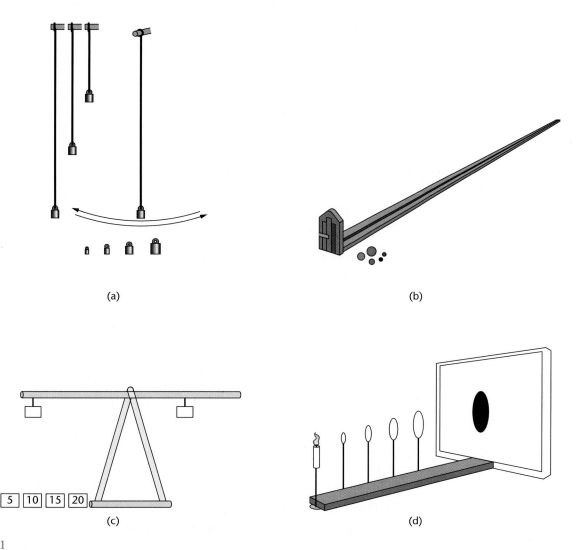

Figure 15-1

Piagetian tasks for measuring attainment of formal operations. (*a*) Pendulum. The pendulum's string can be shortened or lengthened, and weights of varying sizes can be attached to it. The student must determine what variables affect the speed of the pendulum's swing. (*b*) Motion in a horizontal plane. A spring device launches balls of varying sizes, which roll in a horizontal plane. The student must predict their stopping points. (*c*) Balance beam. A balance scale comes with weights of varying sizes, which can be hung at different points along the crossbar. The student must determine what factors affect whether or not the scale will balance. (*d*) Shadows. A baseboard containing a row of peg holes is attached to a screen. A light source and rings of varying diameters can be placed in the holes, at varying distances from the screen. The student must produce two shadows of the same size, using different-sized rings.

Source: Adapted from Small, 1990, Fig. 8-12.

push the object. He is asked to figure out which factor or combination of factors determines how fast the pendulum swings. (This and other Piagetian tasks for assessing the achievement of formal operations are shown in Figure 15-1.)

When Adam first sees the pendulum, he is not yet 7 years old and is in the preoperational stage. Unable to formulate a plan for attacking the problem, he tries one thing after another in a hit-or-miss manner. First he puts a light weight on a long string and pushes it; then he tries swinging a heavy weight on a short string; then he removes the weight entirely. Not only is his method random; he also cannot understand or report what has happened.

Adam next encounters the pendulum at age 11, when he is in the stage of concrete operations. This time, he discovers that varying the length of the string and the weight of the object affect the speed of the swing. However, because he varies both factors at the same time, he cannot tell which is critical or whether both are.

Adam is confronted with the pendulum for a third time at age 15, and this time he goes at the problem systematically. He designs an experiment to test all the possible hypotheses, varying one factor at a time—first, the length of the string; next, the weight of the object; then the height from which it is released; and finally, the amount of force used—each time holding the other three factors constant. In this way, he is able to determine that only one factor—the length of the string—determines how fast the pendulum swings.

Adam's solution of the pendulum problem shows that he has arrived at the stage of formal operations. Since he can imagine a variety of possibilities, he is now capable of *hypothetical-deductive reasoning.* He can develop a hypothesis and can design an experiment to test it. He considers all the relationships he can imagine and goes through them one by one, to eliminate the false and arrive at the true.

hypothetical-deductive reasoning Ability, believed by Piaget to accompany the stage of formal operations, to develop, consider, and test hypotheses.

What Brings About Cognitive Maturity?

According to Piaget, neurological and environmental influences combine to bring about cognitive maturity. The adolescent's brain has matured, and the wider social environment offers more opportunities for experimentation and cognitive growth. Interaction between the two kinds of change is essential: even if young people's neurological development has advanced enough to allow them to reach the stage of formal reasoning, they may never attain it without environmental stimulation. One way this happens is through peer interaction.

In one study, researchers gave college students (average age, 18½ years) a chemistry problem, asked them questions about it, and told them to set up their own experiments (Dimant & Bearison, 1991). Students were randomly assigned to work alone or with a partner. Those working in twosomes were told to discuss their answers with each other. Their videotaped statements were categorized as (1) disagreement, (2) explanation, (3) question, (4) agreement, or (5) extraneous. The researchers coded one dialogue as follows (Dimant & Bearison, 1991, p. 280):

Student A: "What you said can't be. It's no sense." *(disagreement)*

Student B: "I'm right. I know it." *(disagreement)*

Student A: "Look here, see B [a container in the experiment] didn't work with D and E, so it can't be B." *(explanation)*

Student B: "Oh, you're right." *(agreement)*

Students who worked in pairs solved more problems than those who worked alone. Quality as well as frequency of feedback was important. The more disagreeing, explaining, and questioning a student received—that is, the more a partner challenged his or her reasoning—the greater were the advances in thinking.

Of course, formal reasoning does not develop overnight. One study compared the theories and reasoning strategies used by preadolescents (fifth- and sixth-graders) with those used by noncollege-educated adults in designing a series of experiments to understand two physical science phenomena (Schauble, 1996). One, the *canal task,* involved varying the depth of water in a model canal and the size, shape, and weight of boats traveling in it, so as to maximize their speed. The second task, the *spring task,* involved lowering an object suspended from a spring into a container of water and discovering what variables would affect the extent to which the spring contracted due to the buoyancy of the object. Although most of the preadolescents were less systematic than most of the adults in exploring these problems—typically varying more than one factor at the same time, as Adam did with the pendulum at that age—they did show progress as they went along.

This study underlines the bidirectional influence between reasoning and conceptual understanding. As we discussed in Chapter 1, theories and experimental methods are intimately related, and this is true not only for scientists but for

According to Piaget, adolescents who have attained the ability to think hypothetically can imagine and make commitments to an ideal world—as in this demonstration for racial unity.

ordinary people thinking about everyday problems. Beliefs about the factors involved in, say, the speed of a boat in the water, affect the development of strategies for testing those beliefs. Conversely, errors in reasoning about the results of an experiment can lead to false beliefs. An expanding knowledge of the world goes hand in hand with cognitive maturation in giving adolescents better tools to think and solve problems.

Applying Formal Reasoning

The ability to systematically consider and test possibilities applies to all sorts of problems, from fixing the family car to constructing political and philosophical theories. As Nelson Mandela did during his adolescence, people in the stage of formal operations can integrate what they have learned in the past with the challenges of the present and make plans for the future. Thought at this stage has a flexibility not possible in the stage of concrete operations. The ability to think abstractly has emotional implications too. Earlier, a child could love a parent or hate a classmate. Now "the adolescent can love freedom or hate exploitation. . . . The possible and the ideal captivate both mind and feeling" (H. Ginsburg & Opper, 1979, p. 201).

Of course, people who are capable of formal thought do not always use it. For example, the object of the familiar game Twenty Questions is to ask as few yes-or-no questions as necessary to determine the identity of an unknown person, place, or thing. The efficiency with which young people can do this, by systematically narrowing down the categories within which the answer might fall, generally improves between middle childhood and late adolescence. However, in one study (Drumm & Jackson, 1996), high school students (average age, 16.8 years), especially boys, showed a greater tendency than either early adolescents (average age, 13.5 years) or college students to jump to guessing the answer. This pattern may reflect a penchant for impulsive, risky behavior—whether it be in driving, drug use, or sexual activity—in middle adolescence, a time when young people have more autonomy than before and more choices to make.

Limitations of Piaget's Theory

Does Piaget's stage of formal operations represent the highest reaches of cognitive development? Some critics say no.

The telephone is often a battleground for parents and teenagers. According to the psychologist David Elkind, argumentativeness is one of several immature aspects of adolescent thought.

Perhaps one-third to one-half of American adults never attain the stage of formal operations as measured by the pendulum problem and conservation of volume (Kohlberg & Gilligan, 1971; Papalia, 1972). Even by late adolescence or adulthood not everyone seems to be capable of abstract thought as Piaget defined it, and those who are capable do not always use it. Are these people cognitively immature? Or are there other aspects of mature thought not captured by Piaget's theory?

According to Piaget's critics, formal reasoning is not the only, and perhaps not even the most important, aspect of mature thinking. Such Piagetian measures as the pendulum problem and conservation of volume seem to imply that cognition is bounded by mathematical and scientific thinking—a narrow view of a person as "living in a timeless world of abstract rules" (Gilligan, 1987a, p. 67). Formal logic may be less important in such nonscientific fields as history, languages, writing, and the arts. And Piaget's theory may not give enough weight to such aspects of mature intelligence as the role of experience and intuition in practical problem solving and the wisdom that helps people cope with an often chaotic world.

Elkind: Immature Aspects Of Adolescent Thought

Adolescents can solve complex problems and envision ideal societies. Yet sometimes, as any parent of a teenager will attest, adolescent thought seems immature. On the basis of clinical work with adolescents, the psychologist David Elkind (1984) described typical behaviors and attitudes that may stem from young people's inexperienced ventures into abstract thought:

- *Finding fault with authority figures:* Adolescents now realize that the adults they once worshipped fall far short of their ideals, and they feel compelled to say so—loudly and often.
- *Argumentativeness:* Adolescents often become argumentative as they practice their new abilities to explore the nuances of a problem and to build a case for their viewpoint.
- *Indecisiveness:* Because they are now more aware of how many choices life offers, many teenagers have trouble making up their minds even about such simple things as whether to go to the mall with a friend or to the library to work on a school assignment.

- *Apparent hypocrisy:* Young adolescents often do not recognize the difference between expressing an ideal and living up to it. Matthew marches against pollution while littering along the way, and Beth aggressively protests for peace.
- *Self-consciousness:* Adolescents often assume that everyone else is thinking about the same thing they are thinking about: themselves. The extreme self-consciousness of young adolescents has a great deal to do with the *imaginary audience,* a conceptualized "observer" who is as concerned with their thoughts and behavior as they are.
- *Assumption of invulnerability:* Elkind uses the term *personal fable* to denote a belief by adolescents that they are special, that their experience is unique, and that they are not subject to the rules that govern the rest of the world ("Other people get hooked from taking drugs, not me"). According to Elkind, this special form of egocentrism underlies much risky, self-destructive behavior in early adolescence.

imaginary audience
In Elkind's terminology, an observer who exists only in an adolescent's mind and is as concerned with the adolescent's thoughts and actions as the adolescent is.

personal fable   In Elkind's terminology, conviction that one is special, unique, and not subject to the rules that govern the rest of the world.

Although the concepts of the imaginary audience and the personal fable have been widely accepted, their validity as cognitive earmarks of adolescence has little support. One study testing the personal fable compared three groups: 86 mostly white, middle-class teenagers; their parents; and 95 mostly male, nonwhite teenagers in homes for adolescents with legal and substance abuse problems. Participants were asked to estimate their risk, compared with other people they knew, of being in a car accident, having an unwanted pregnancy, becoming alcoholic, being mugged, or becoming sick from air pollution. All three groups saw themselves as facing less risk than others; this attitude was no more pronounced in teenagers than in adults. In fact, contrary to what Elkind's model would predict, for some risks adolescents considered themselves *more* vulnerable than their parents considered themselves (Quadrel, Fischoff, & Davis, 1993). Similarly, in another study, adolescents were more likely than college students or adults to see themselves as vulnerable to alcohol and other drug problems (Millstein, in press).

It has been proposed that the imaginary audience and the personal fable are linked with emergence of the cognitive ability to take an outsider's perspective. However, a longitudinal study of 96 sixth- to eighth-graders found no such link for the imaginary audience, and only a *temporary* link for the personal fable, in sixth grade only. The researchers suggested that an upsurge in belief in the personal fable at that time may be connected with the transition to middle school, which may disrupt social relationships and increase the sense of isolation and uniqueness (Vartanian & Powlishta, 1996).

All in all, the imaginary audience and personal fable do *not* seem to be universal features of cognitive development in adolescence; instead, they may be related to specific social experiences. Since these concepts grew out of Elkind's clinical observations, they may be more characteristic of youngsters who are experiencing difficulties in adjustment (Vartanian & Powlishta, 1996). Furthermore, if these frequently cited concepts are invalid, perhaps other beliefs about "immature" adolescent thinking patterns are equally so.

CHECKPOINT

Can you . . .

- Explain the difference between formal operational and concrete operational thinking, as exemplified by the pendulum problem?
- Discuss factors influencing adolescents' use of formal operational thinking?
- List Elkind's six proposed immature aspects of adolescent thought, and evaluate their validity?

Moral Reasoning

A woman is near death from cancer. A druggist has discovered a drug that doctors believe might save her. The druggist is charging $2,000 for a small dose—10 times what the drug costs him to make. The sick woman's husband, Heinz, borrows from everyone he knows but can scrape together only $1,000. He begs the druggist to sell him the drug for $1,000 or let him pay the rest later. The druggist refuses, saying "I discovered the drug and I'm going to make money from it." Heinz, desperate, breaks into the man's store and steals the drug. Should Heinz have done that? Why or why not? (Kohlberg, 1969).

Table 15-1   Kohlberg's Six Stages of Moral Reasoning

Levels	Stages of Reasoning	Typical Answers to Heinz's Dilemma
Level 1: Preconventional morality (ages 4 to 10) Emphasis in this level is on external control. The standards are those of others, and they are observed either to avoid punishment or to reap rewards.	*Stage 1: Orientation toward punishment and obedience.* "What will happen to me?" Children obey the rules of others to avoid punishment. They ignore the motives of an act and focus on its physical form (such as the size of a lie) or its consequences (for example, the amount of physical damage).	*Pro:* "He should steal the drug. It isn't really bad to take it. It isn't as if he hadn't asked to pay for it first. The drug he'd take is worth only $200; he's not really taking a $2,000 drug." *Con:* "He shouldn't steal the drug. It's a big crime. He didn't get permission; he used force and broke and entered. He did a lot of damage, stealing a very expensive drug and breaking up the store, too."
	Stage 2: Instrumental purpose and exchange. "You scratch my back, I'll scratch yours." Children conform to rules out of self-interest and consideration for what others can do for them in return. They look at an act in terms of the human needs it meets and differentiate this value from the act's physical form and consequences.	*Pro:* "It's all right to steal the drug, because his wife needs it and he wants her to live. It isn't that he wants to steal, but that's what he has to do to get the drug to save her." *Con:* "He shouldn't steal it. The druggist isn't wrong or bad; he just wants to make a profit. That's what you're in business for—to make money."
Level II: Conventional morality (ages 10 to 13 or beyond) Children now want to please other people. They still observe the standards of others, but they have internalized these standards to some extent. Now they want to be considered "good" by those persons whose opinions are important to them. They are now able to take the roles of authority figures well enough to decide whether an action is good by their standards.	*Stage 3: Maintaining mutual relations, approval of others, the golden rule.* "Am I a good boy or girl?" Children want to please and help others, can judge the intentions of others, and develop their own ideas of what a good person is. They evaluate an act according to the motive behind it or the person performing it, and they take circumstances into account.	*Pro:* "He should steal the drug. He is only doing something that is natural for a good husband to do. You can't blame him for doing something out of love for his wife. You'd blame him if he didn't love his wife enough to save her." *Con:* "He shouldn't steal. If his wife dies, he can't be blamed. It isn't because he's heartless or that he doesn't love her enough to do everything that he legally can. The druggist is the selfish or heartless one."
	Stage 4: Social concern and conscience. "What if everybody did it?" People are concerned with doing their duty, showing respect for higher authority, and maintaining the social order. They consider an act always wrong, regardless of motive or circumstances, if it violates a rule and harms others.	*Pro:* "You should steal it. If you did nothing, you'd be letting your wife die. It's your responsibility if she dies. You have to take it with the idea of paying the druggist." *Con:* "It is a natural thing for Heinz to want to save his wife, but it's still always wrong to steal. He still knows that he's stealing and taking a valuable drug from the man who made it."

Heinz's problem is the most famous example of Lawrence Kohlberg's approach to studying moral development. Starting in the 1950s, Kohlberg and his colleagues posed hypothetical dilemmas like this one to 75 boys ages 10, 13, and 16, and continued to question them periodically for more than 30 years. At the heart of each dilemma was the concept of justice. By asking respondents how they arrived at their answers, Kohlberg concluded that how people think about moral issues reflects cognitive development and that people arrive at moral judgments on their own, rather than merely internalizing standards of parents, teachers, or peers.

Table 15-1 *(continued)*

Levels	Stages of Reasoning	Typical Answers to Heinz's Dilemma
Level III: Postconventional morality (early adolescence, or not until young adulthood, or never) This level marks the attainment of true morality. For the first time, the person acknowledges the possibility of conflict between two socially accepted standards and tries to decide between them. The control of conduct is now internal, both in the standards observed and in the reasoning about right and wrong. Stages 5 and 6 may be alternative expressions of the highest level of moral reasoning.	*Stage 5: Morality of contract, of individual rights, and of democratically accepted law.* People think in rational terms, valuing the will of the majority and the welfare of society. They generally see these values as best supported by adherence to the law. While they recognize that there are times when human need and the law conflict, they believe that it is better for society in the long run if they obey the law.	*Pro:* "The law wasn't set up for these circumstances. Taking the drug in this situation isn't really right, but it's justified." *Con:* "You can't completely blame someone for stealing, but extreme circumstances don't really justify taking the law into your own hands. You can't have people stealing whenever they are desperate. The end may be good, but the ends don't justify the means."
	Stage 6: Morality of universal ethical principles. People do what they as individuals think is right, regardless of legal restrictions or the opinions of others. They act in accordance with internalized standards, knowing that they would condemn themselves if they did not.	*Pro:* "This is a situation that forces him to choose between stealing and letting his wife die. In a situation where the choice must be made, it is morally right to steal. He has to act in terms of the principle of preserving and respecting life." *Con:* "Heinz is faced with the decision of whether to consider the other people who need the drug just as badly as his wife. Heinz ought to act not according to his particular feelings toward his wife, but considering the value of all the lives involved."

Source: Adapted from Kohlberg, 1969; Lickona, 1976.

Kohlberg's Levels and Stages

Moral development in Kohlberg's theory bears some similarity to Piaget's (see Chapter 12), but his model is more complex. On the basis of thought processes shown by responses to his dilemmas, Kohlberg (1969) described three levels of moral reasoning, each divided into two stages (see Table 15-1):

- *Level I: Preconventional morality.* People, under external controls, obey rules to avoid punishment or reap rewards, or act out of self-interest. This level is typical of children ages 4 to 10.
- *Level II: Conventional morality (or morality of conventional role conformity).* People have internalized the standards of authority figures. They are concerned about being "good," pleasing others, and maintaining the social order. This level is typically reached after age 10; many people never move beyond it, even in adulthood.
- *Level III: Postconventional morality (or morality of autonomous moral principles).* People now recognize conflicts between moral standards and make their own judgments on the basis of principles of right and wrong, fairness, and justice. People generally do not reach this level of moral reasoning until at least early adolescence, or more commonly in young adulthood, if ever.

preconventional morality
First level of Kohlberg's theory of moral reasoning, in which control is external and rules are obeyed in order to gain rewards or avoid punishment.

conventional morality (or morality of conventional role conformity) Second level in Kohlberg's theory of moral reasoning, in which the standards of authority figures are internalized.

postconventional morality (or morality of autonomous moral principles) Third level in Kohlberg's theory of moral reasoning, in which people follow internally held moral principles of right and wrong, fairness, and justice, and can decide among conflicting moral standards.

Box 15-1   Cross-Cultural Perspectives on Care of the Environment

In Kohlberg's proposed seventh stage of moral development, people reflect on their connection to the universe and recognize the connectedness of all existence. They see moral issues "from the standpoint of the universe as a whole" (Kohlberg & Ryncarz, 1990, p. 207. They understand that the consequences of one person's actions affect and are affected by everything and everyone else.

Concern for the environment would seem to be a logical manifestation of this highest stage of moral development, which, according to Kohlberg, is rarely attained even by adults. Yet, in cross-cultural research, adolescents in urban and rural parts of the Brazilian Amazon and black inner-city children in Houston, Texas, whose environment is far from a pristine natural one, showed sensitivity to nature and awareness of the moral dimensions of environmental problems.

In the Brazilian study (Howe, Kahn, & Friedman, 1996), researchers interviewed 30 boys and girls from Manaus, a city of nearly 1 million people, and 14 youngsters from Novo Ayrao, a small, remote village. Both Manaus and Novo Ayrao border the Rio Negro, a river that runs through the Amazon rainforest. The average age of the children was a little more than 13½.

After probing the youngsters' attitudes toward plants and animals and their awareness of environmental issues, the interviewers asked whether or not it was all right to throw garbage in the local river and whether it would make a difference in the rightness or wrongness of the act if everyone in the neighborhood did it, or if the river was in a faraway place. The researchers also asked whether throwing garbage in the river would harm birds, insects, people, and other specific aspects of the environment. Finally, they asked a series of questions designed to determine how much the young people knew about the rainforest and how they felt about its value. The researchers then compared the results with the findings of a study of 24 African American 11-year-olds in the Houston area, who had been asked about throwing garbage in a bayou half a mile from their school (Kahn & Friedman, 1995).

As Table 15-2 shows, the overwhelming majority of preadolescents and early adolescents in both Brazilian communities and in Houston were aware of environmental problems, discussed them with their families, and cared about harm to the environment. For example, the Brazilian youngsters talked about large-scale burning of the Amazon jungle. Children in both Brazil and Houston brought up air pollution, harm to animals, and garbage or litter. Many said they did things to help the environment: the Brazilian children mentioned planting trees and caring for animals, while the Houston children mentioned recycling bottles and

newspapers. The Brazilian children also showed understanding of the importance of the rainforest, and virtually all could name at least one thing the forest provided, such as food, clean air, and lumber. Most believed that cutting down the rainforest was wrong and should be stopped.

Practically all the children in all three communities thought it would be wrong to pollute a waterway, even if local customs permitted it and even if the waterway were far from their homes. Their reasons fell into two main categories: *homocentric* and *biocentric*. *Homocentric* reasons were based on human welfare (polluting water could make people sick), aesthetics (people enjoy the beauty of nature), or personal interests (it's fun to play with animals, and they could be harmed by drinking polluted water). *Biocentric* reasons focused on the value of nature itself, apart from how it serves human needs, or on the idea that plants and animals have rights that deserve respect.

In both Brazil and Houston, the reasons youngsters gave for moral judgments about nature were largely homocentric, though some biocentric thinking did appear. It is possible that studies with older adolescents would find a developmental increase in biocentric reasoning.

Many of the responses across cultures were strikingly similar (Howe, et al., 1996, p. 985). For example:

Brazilian child (homocentric): [It is not all right to throw garbage in the river] because it causes pollution and that is dangerous for us. Because now we have cholera, a very dangerous disease and there are others attacking us like the malaria.

Houston child (homocentric): Because some people that don't have homes, they go and drink out of the rivers and stuff and they could die because they get all of that dirt and stuff inside of their bodies.

Brazilian child (biocentric): Because the river was not made to have trash thrown in it, because the river belongs to nature.

Houston child (biocentric): Because water is what nature made. . . . When you're dealing with what nature made, you need not destroy it.

Such responses suggest that, among both urban and rural children in diverse cultures, affinity with nature may form a universal basis of moral thinking about the nonhuman world.

Continued

Kohlberg later added a transitional level between levels II and III, when people no longer feel bound by society's moral standards but have not yet developed rationally derived principles of justice. Instead, they base their moral decisions on personal feelings.

In Kohlberg's theory, it is the reasoning underlying a person's response to a moral dilemma, not the answer itself, which indicates the stage of moral

Table 15-2

Brazilian and African American Children's Environmental Values, Knowledge, and Practices

Environmental Criterion	Percent Responding Postivitely		
	Manaus (*n* = 30)	Novo Ayrao (*n* = 14)	Houston (*n* = 24)
Animals an important part of your life.	100	100	91
Plants an important part of your life.	97	100	79
Aware of environmental problems in general.	69	57	—
Aware of environmental problems affecting self and community.	81	86	80
Discuss environmental issues with family.	62	64	71
Initiate discussions on environmental issues.	31	43	—
Act to help solve environmental problems.	41	79	—
Thinks that throwing garbage in a river harms birds.	97	86	96
Cares that birds would be harmed.	96	100	95
Thinks that throwing garbage in a river harms insects.	57	64	68
Cares that insects would be harmed.	61	58	89
Thinks that throwing garbage in a river harms the view.	97	100	91
Cares that the view would be harmed.	93	92	95
Thinks that throwing garbage in a river harms people along the river.	93	100	95
Cares that people would be harmed.	89	85	81

Note: Children were first asked if they thought harm occurred (to birds, insects, the view, or people). Only those children who thought harm did occur were then asked if they cared about the harm. The dash indicates that a comparable question was not asked of the Houston children.

Source: Adapted from Howe et al., 1996, Table 2, p. 983.

development. As illustrated in Table 15-1, two people who give opposite answers may be at the same stage if their reasoning is based on similar factors.

Kohlberg's early stages correspond roughly to Piaget's stages of moral development in childhood (see Chapter 12), but his advanced stages go into adulthood. Some adolescents, and even some adults, remain at Kohlberg's level I. Like young children, they seek to avoid punishment or satisfy their own needs. Most adolescents, and most adults, seem to be at level II. They conform to social conventions, support the status quo, and do the "right" thing to please others or to obey the law. Very few people reach level III, when they can choose between two socially accepted standards. In fact, at one point Kohlberg questioned the validity of stage 6, since so few people seem to attain it. Later, however, he proposed a seventh, "cosmic" stage, in which people consider the effect of their actions not only on other people but on the universe as a whole (Kohlberg, 1981; Kohlberg & Ryncarz, 1990; see Box 15-1).

One reason the ages attached to Kohlberg's levels are so variable is that factors besides cognition, such as emotional development and life experience, affect moral judgments. People who have achieved a high level of cognitive development do not always reach a comparably high level of moral development. Thus a certain level of cognitive development is *necessary* but not *sufficient* for a comparable level of moral development.

Evaluating Kohlberg's Theory

Kohlberg's work and that of his colleagues and followers has had a major impact. His theory has enriched our thinking about how morality develops, has supported an association between cognitive maturation and moral maturation, and has stimulated much research and other theories of moral development.

Research has supported some aspects of Kohlberg's theory but has left others in question. The American boys that Kohlberg and his colleagues followed through adulthood progressed through Kohlberg's stages in sequence, and none skipped a stage. Their moral judgments correlated positively with age, education, IQ, and socioeconomic status (Colby, Kohlberg, Gibbs, & Lieberman, 1983). However, as we'll see, Kohlberg's stages may be limited in their applicability to women and girls and to people in nonwestern cultures. Also, his theory pays little attention to environmental influences, such as the family.

Another serious criticism is the lack of a clear relationship between moral reasoning and behavior. Studies suggest that people at postconventional levels of reasoning do not necessarily act more morally than those at lower levels (Colby & Damon, 1992; Kupfersmid & Wonderly, 1980). Perhaps one problem is the remoteness from young people's experience of such dilemmas as the "Heinz" situation (see Box 16-3 in Chapter 16).

One practical problem in evaluating Kohlberg's system is its time-consuming testing procedures. The standard dilemmas need to be presented to each person individually and then scored by trained judges. One alternative is the Defining Issues Test (DIT), which can be given quickly to a group and scored objectively (Rest, 1975). The DIT has 12 questions about each of 6 moral dilemmas; its results correlate moderately well with scores on Kohlberg's traditional tasks.

Family Influences

Neither Piaget nor Kohlberg considered parents important to children's moral development. More recent research, however, emphasizes parents' contribution in both the cognitive and the emotional realms.

In one study, parents of 63 students in grades 1, 4, 7, and 10 were asked to talk with their children about two dilemmas: a hypothetical one and an actual one that the child described (L. J. Walker & Taylor, 1991). The children and adolescents who, during the next 2 years, showed the greatest progress through Kohlberg's stages were those whose parents had used humor and praise, listened to them, and asked their opinions. These parents had asked clarifying questions, reworded answers, and checked to be sure the children understood the issues. They reasoned with their children at a slightly higher level than the children were currently at, much as in Vygotsky's method of scaffolding. The children who advanced the least were those whose parents had lectured them or challenged or contradicted their opinions.

Validity for Women and Girls

Carol Gilligan (1982), on the basis of research on women, argued that Kohlberg's theory is oriented toward values more important to men than to women. According to Gilligan, women see morality not so much in terms of justice and fairness, but rather in terms of responsibility to show care and avoid harm.

Some studies based on Kohlberg's dilemmas have shown differences in the levels achieved by men and women—differences that consistently favored men. However, a large-scale analysis comparing results from many studies found no

The psychologist Carol Gilligan studied moral development in women and concluded that they are more concerned about responsibility to others than about abstract justice. However, most research does not support a gender difference in moral judgments. Gilligan's own later research suggests that for *both* women and men, concern for others is at the highest level of moral thought.

significant differences in men's and women's responses to Kohlberg's dilemmas across the lifespan (L. J. Walker, 1984). In the few studies in which men scored slightly higher, the findings were not clearly gender-related, since the men generally were better educated and had better jobs than the women. A more recent study of male and female college and university students found no evidence that men's thinking is more principled and women's more relationship-oriented (Orr & Luszcz, 1994). Thus the weight of evidence does not appear to back up either of Gilligan's original contentions: a male bias in Kohlberg's theory or a distinctly female perspective on morality. Gilligan has since modified her position on gender differences in moral judgments, suggesting that moral development in *both* sexes involves an evolution from abstract principles to compassion and care and the ability to see gray areas (Gilligan, Murphy, & Tappan, 1990).

Cross-Cultural Validity

Cross-cultural studies support Kohlberg's sequence of stages—up to a point. Older people from countries other than the United States do tend to score at higher stages than younger people. However, people in nonwestern cultures rarely score above stage 4 (C. P. Edwards, 1981; Nisan & Kohlberg, 1982; Snarey, 1985). It is possible that these cultures do not foster higher moral development, but it seems more likely that some aspects of Kohlberg's definition of morality may not fit the cultural values of some societies.

For example, people born and raised on a kibbutz (collective farming or industrial settlement) in Israel are imbued with a socialist perspective. How do such people score on a problem such as Heinz's dilemma, which weighs the value of human life against a druggist's right to charge what the market will bear?

Interviewers using Kohlberg's standardized scoring manual ran into trouble in trying to classify responses like the following:

> The medicine should be made available to all in need; the druggist should not have the right to decide on his own. . . . The whole community or society should have control of the drug.

Responses such as this one were coupled with statements about the importance of obeying the law and thus were confusing to the interviewers, who estimated them as fitting in with conventional stage 4 reasoning or as being in transition between stages 4 and 5. However, from the perspective of an Israeli kibbutz dweller, such a response may represent a postconventional moral principle missing from Kohlberg's description of stage 5. If membership in a kibbutz is viewed as a commitment to certain social values, including cooperation and equality for all, then concern about upholding the system may be not merely for its own sake, but aimed at protecting those principles (Snarey, 1985).

When Kohlberg's dilemmas were tested in India, Buddhist monks from Ladakh, a Tibetan enclave, scored lower than laypeople. Apparently Kohlberg's model, while capturing the preconventional and conventional elements of Buddhist thinking, was inadequate for understanding postconventional Buddhist principles of cooperation and nonviolence (Gielen & Kelly, 1983).

Heinz's dilemma was revised for use in Taiwan. In the revision, a shopkeeper will not give a man *food* for his sick wife. This version would seem unbelievable to Chinese villagers, who are more accustomed to hearing a shopkeeper in such a situation say, "You have to let people have things whether they have money or not" (Wolf, 1968, p. 21).

Whereas Kohlberg's system is based on justice, the Chinese ethos leans toward conciliation and harmony. In Kohlberg's format, respondents make an either-or decision based on their own value systems. In Chinese society, people faced with such a dilemma discuss it openly, are guided by community standards, and try to find a way of resolving the problem to please as many parties as possible. In the west, even good people may be harshly punished if, under the force of circumstances, they break a law. The Chinese are unaccustomed to universally applied laws; they prefer to abide by the decisions of a wise judge (Dien, 1982).

Kohlberg himself observed that people, before they can develop a fully principled morality, must recognize the relativity of moral standards. Adolescents begin to understand that every society evolves its own definitions of right and wrong; in some cases, the values of one culture may even seem shocking to members of another (see Box 3-3 and Box 14-1). Many young people question their earlier views about morality when they enter high school or college and encounter people whose values, culture, and ethnic background are different from their own.

CHECKPOINT

Can you . . .

• List Kohlberg's levels and stages, and discuss factors that influence how rapidly children and adolescents progress through them?

• Evaluate Kohlberg's theory, especially with regard to family influences, gender, and cultural validity?

Educational and Vocational Issues

School is a central organizing experience in most adolescents' lives. It offers opportunities to learn information, master new skills, and sharpen old ones; to participate in sports, the arts, and other activities; to explore vocational choices; and to be with friends. It widens intellectual and social horizons. Some adolescents, however, experience school not as an opportunity but as one more hindrance on the road to adulthood.

The move from elementary school to secondary school sets the stage for the high school experience, and the way that transition takes place can have a profound effect on psychological adjustment, as well as on educational attainment. Let's look first at that transition. Then we'll examine contextual influences on school achievement: the school, the neighborhood, the family, and the peer group. Finally, we'll consider planning for college and careers.

Leaving Elementary School

At the end of sixth grade, most American children leave the familiar surroundings of elementary school to enter a junior high school or middle school with many more students and a more impersonal setting in which teachers, classrooms, and classmates change constantly throughout the day. In 3 more years they move again, to an even larger high school. This typical sequence is known as the *6-3-3 pattern*. A minority of children follow the *8-4 pattern*, staying in elementary school through eighth grade and then going directly to high school.

Research has found a number of stresses associated with the typical sequence. Typically, junior high school students have fewer opportunities to make decisions than elementary school students; they have less personal, less positive relationships with their teachers; and they are more likely to be grouped by ability, a practice that increases competitiveness and concerns about evaluation. Furthermore, teachers tend to judge them by higher standards than elementary school teachers do, often resulting in lowered grades and a drop in self-esteem (Eccles et al., 1993).

One 5-year study followed 594 white students in the Milwaukee public schools from sixth through tenth grade, comparing students in the 6-3-3 pattern with those in the 8-4 pattern (Blyth, Simmons, & Carlton-Ford, 1983). Students in the 6-3-3 group had more problems than those in the 8-4 group. Both boys and girls in the 6-3-3 pattern had a decrease in grade-point averages, participated less in extracurricular activities, and saw their schools as more anonymous. Girls were especially vulnerable; their self-esteem dropped, an effect that persisted into tenth grade (Blyth et al., 1983).

Why did the girls have more problems? As we mentioned in Chapter 14, girls who enter puberty at the same time they change schools are likely candidates for depression (Petersen, Sarigiani, & Kennedy, 1991). The more major changes that take place at once, the greater the likelihood that grade-point averages, extracurricular participation, and self-esteem will decline (Simmons, Burgeson, Carlton-Ford, & Blyth, 1987). Since girls usually enter puberty sooner than boys and begin to date earlier, they are more likely to experience "life-change overload" (Petersen, 1993). Also, there is more emphasis on girls' looks and popularity at this age, and they may miss the security of being with old friends.

As Bronfenbrenner's model suggests, a change in parents' work status can affect a child's adjustment to a new school. A 2-year study found that when parents had been demoted or laid off at about the same time their children were moving into junior high school, the youngsters had a hard time adjusting. They had more trouble getting along with other students and were more disruptive than children of parents with stable employment or those whose parents had just been rehired or promoted (Flanagan & Eccles, 1993).

Moving to a more "grown-up" school is a challenge that offers opportunities for social and emotional, as well as cognitive, growth. The research suggests that young adolescents may cope better with this challenge if they can deal with one change at a time. Although this is not always possible, educators and families can help by designing environments that involve opportunities for decision making, participation in rule making, continued close relationships with adults both within and outside the family, and a level of independence appropriate for youngsters' age and level of development.

School Achievement: Contextual Influences

Today, nearly 82 percent of Americans age 25 or older—more than ever before—have graduated from high school or the equivalent. Furthermore, the proportion is growing. Among 25- to 29-year-olds, it is approximately 86 percent, including—again for the first time—statistically equal percentages of blacks and whites (J. Day & Curry, 1996). The 1980s and 1990s have seen a greater emphasis on academics, though English skills have scarcely improved. College entrance test scores have risen somewhat, especially for minorities; but for most minorities, an achievement gap remains (American College Testing Program, 1995; National Center for Education Statistics [NCES], 1995).

Quality of Schooling

An important factor in students' achievement is the quality of the schools they attend. A good high school has an orderly, unoppressive atmosphere, an active,

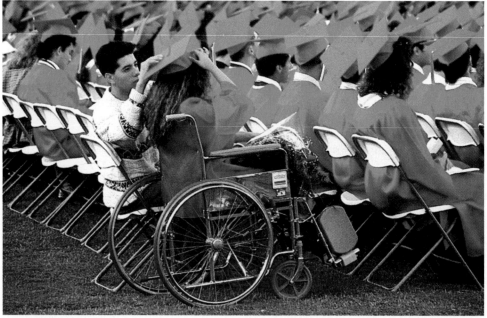

These high school graduates are taking an important step toward their future careers. Today, more young people in the United States than ever before graduate from high school.

energetic principal, and teachers who take part in making decisions. Principal and teachers should have high expectations for students, place greater emphasis on academics than on extracurricular activities, and closely monitor student performance (Linney & Seidman, 1989). Schools largely populated by students from low-income families often fall far short of these conditions and generally have the fewest material resources. Despite the efforts of some dedicated educators and parents, such schools often fail to help students build the skills they need for successful adult lives (National Research Council [NRC], 1993a).

The educational practice known as *tracking,* or grouping students by abilities, may contribute to failure. Students placed in low-track classes lack the stimulation of higher-ability peers and often get poorer teaching. They rarely move up to higher tracks, and many lose interest in trying to do better (NRC, 1993a). Furthermore, since school failure and contact with antisocial peers are often related to antisocial behavior, grouping poor achievers together may solidify problem behaviors (Dishion, Patterson, Stoolmiller, & Skinner, 1991). Some research suggests that mixed-ability classes have cognitive, social, and psychological benefits for these young people while not holding back more competent students (Oakes, Gamoran, & Page, 1992; Rutter, 1983). However, other research has found that gifted students achieve better and are more motivated when grouped with their intellectual peers (Feldhusen & Moon, 1992).

Schools that tailor teaching to students' abilities get better results than schools that try to teach all students in the same way. Research on Sternberg's triarchic theory of intelligence (see Chapter 12) has found that students high in practical or creative intelligence do better when taught in a way that allows them to capitalize on those strengths and compensate for their weaknesses.

In one study, 199 high school students, selected on the basis of scores on the Sternberg Triarchic Abilities Test (STAT), were randomly assigned to afternoon sections of an introductory college-level psychology course. Each section primarily emphasized either memorization, analysis, creative thinking, or practical thinking. All students heard the same lectures in the morning. Students in the memory-based sections were tested on the main points of theories; those in the analytical sections compared theories; those in the creatively oriented sections came up with their own theories; and those in the practically oriented sections applied theories. All the students were then evaluated on all four kinds of

Table 15-3   Parents' Involvement and High School Students' Grades

| | Self-Reported Grades | | | |
Survey Item	Mostly A's	Mostly B's	Mostly C's	Mostly D's
Mother keeps close track of how well child does in school.	92%	89%	84%	80%
Father keeps close track of how well child does in school.	85%	79%	69%	64%
Parents almost always know child's whereabouts.	88%	81%	72%	61%
Child talks with mother and father almost every day.	75%	67%	59%	45%
Parents attend PTA meetings at least once in a while.	25%	22%	20%	15%
Child lives in household with both parents.	80%	71%	64%	60%

Note: This table, based on a survey of more than 30,000 high school seniors, shows the percentage of students with various grade averages who gave positive answers to each survey item. In each instance, the higher the grades were, the more likely the parents were to be involved with the child.
Source: NCES, 1985.

achievement. Students whose abilities were well-matched to the instructional emphasis of their assigned sections did substantially better on homework, examinations, and independent projects than those who were poorly matched (Sternberg, 1997).

Parenting

Even though adolescents are more independent than elementary school children, the atmosphere in the home influences how well they do in school. Students whose parents are closely involved in their lives and monitor their progress fare best, according to a survey of more than 30,000 high school seniors in more than 1,000 schools (NCES, 1985; see Table 15-3). Parents of high-achieving adolescents make time to talk to them and know what is going on in their lives. They go to PTA meetings. They take the children seriously, and the children reward that interest. This is particularly true of fathers, whose involvement varies more than that of mothers. In this survey, 85 percent of the A students but only 64 percent of the D students had fathers who kept close track of how they were doing. The father's importance is also evident from the fact that students who live with both parents earn better grades.

Parents' involvement may be related to their style of child rearing (see Chapter 10). *Authoritative parents* urge adolescents to look at both sides of issues, admit that children sometimes know more than parents, and welcome their participation in family decisions. These parents strike a balance between making demands and being responsive. Their children receive praise and privileges for good grades; poor grades bring encouragement to try harder and offers of help. *Authoritarian parents* tell adolescents not to argue with or question adults and tell them they will "know better when they are grown up." Good grades bring admonitions to do even better; poor grades upset the parents, who may punish by reducing allowances or "grounding." *Permissive parents* seem not to care about grades, make no rules about watching television, do not attend school functions, and neither help with nor check their children's homework. These parents may not be neglectful or uncaring, but simply convinced that teenagers should be responsible for their own lives.

Research has consistently found that the positive effects of authoritative parenting continue during adolescence. Among about 6,400 California high school students, children of authoritative parents tended to do better in school than children of authoritarian and permissive parents (Dornbusch, Ritter, Leiderman, Roberts, & Fraleigh, 1987; Steinberg & Darling, 1994; Steinberg, Lamborn, Dornbusch, & Darling, 1992). Adolescents raised authoritatively not only achieve

Even though adolescents are more independent than younger children, the home atmosphere continues to influence school achievement. Parents help not only by monitoring homework but by taking an active interest in other aspects of teenagers' lives. Children of authoritative parents who discuss issues openly and offer praise and encouragement tend to do best in school.

better academically but are more socially competent, are more emotionally healthy, and show fewer behavior problems than children raised in an authoritarian or permissive manner. This is true regardless of gender, family structure, age, and social class (Glasgow, Dornbusch, Troyer, Steinberg, & Ritter, 1997)— but not, as we'll see, regardless of ethnicity.

What accounts for the academic success of authoritatively raised adolescents? Several factors may be important, including authoritative parents' greater involvement in schooling and their encouragement of positive attitudes toward work. A more subtle mechanism may be parents' influence on how children explain success or failure. In a study of 2,353 students at 6 high schools in California and 3 high schools in Wisconsin, youngsters who saw their parents as nonauthoritative were more likely than their peers to attribute poor grades to external causes or to low ability—forces beyond their control—rather than to their own efforts. A year later, such students tended to pay less attention in class and to spend less time on homework (Glasgow et al., 1997). Thus a sense of helplessness associated with nonauthoritative parenting may become a self-fulfilling prophecy, discouraging students from even trying to succeed. Conversely, among 279 eleven- to fourteen-year-olds in a socioeconomically mixed community outside Rome, Italy, academic achievement was linked to belief in the ability to control their own learning (Bandura, Barbaranelli, Caprara, & Pastorelli, 1996).

Ethnicity

The findings about the value of authoritative parenting do not seem to hold true among some minority groups in the United States. In one study, Latino and African American students—even those with authoritative parents—did not do as well as white students, apparently because of lack of peer support for academic achievement (Steinberg, Dornbusch, & Brown, 1992). On the other hand, Asian American students, whose parents tend to be authoritarian, get high grades and score higher than white students on math achievement tests, apparently because both parents and peers prize achievement (C. Chen & Stevenson, 1995). In addition to having parents and peers with high academic standards, who value hard work, Asian American students tend to go to good schools, to take challenging courses, and to like math. They also spend more time studying than white students and less time socializing with friends, and they are less likely to hold outside jobs (see Box 15-2).

Box 15-2 Should Teenagers Hold Part-Time Jobs?

Many teenage students today hold part-time jobs. This trend fits in with a longstanding American belief in the moral benefits of work. However, some research challenges the value of part-time employment for high school students who do not have to work to help support their families. Let's look at both sides of the issue.

On the positive side, paid work is generally believed to teach young people to handle money and to help them develop good habits, such as promptness, reliability, and efficient management of time. A good part-time job requires a teenager to assume responsibility and to get along with people of different ages and backgrounds. It enables an adolescent to learn workplace skills, such as how to find a job and how to get along with employers, coworkers, and sometimes the public. It may improve the self-concept by giving young people a greater sense of competence, independence from parents, and status with peers. By helping them learn more about particular fields of work, it may guide them in choosing careers and may lead to higher attainment in those fields (Elder & Caspi, 1990; Mortimer & Shanahan, 1991; National Commission on Youth, 1980; S. Phillips & Sandstrom, 1990; Steel, 1991). Also, by showing adolescents how demanding and difficult the world of work is and how unprepared they are for it, part-time jobs, especially menial ones, sometimes motivate young people to continue their education.

On the negative side, studies have questioned the benefits of part-time work and have pointed to serious drawbacks. Most high school students who work part time have low-level, repetitive jobs in which they do not learn useful skills for later in life (Hamilton & Crouter, 1980). According to some research, teenagers who work are no more independent in making financial decisions and are unlikely to earn any more money as adults than those who do not hold jobs during high school. By assuming adult burdens they are not yet ready to deal with, young people may miss out on the opportunity to explore their identity and develop close relationships. Outside work may require a stressful juggling of other commitments and cut down on active involvement in school (Greenberger & Steinberg, 1986). There is some evidence that long hours of work may undermine school performance and increase the likelihood of dropping out, especially when teenagers work more than 15 to 20 hours per week (NCES, 1987). However, findings about the influence of employment on grades are mixed (Mortimer, Finch, Ryu, Shanahan, & Call, 1996).

Paid work can have other hidden costs. Young people who work long hours are less likely to eat breakfast, exercise, get enough sleep, or have enough leisure time (Bachman & Schulenberg, 1993). They spend less time with their families and may feel less close to them. They have little contact with adults on the job, and their jobs usually reinforce gender stereotypes. Some teenagers spend their earnings on alcohol or drugs, develop cynical attitudes toward work, and cheat or steal from their employers (Green-

berger & Steinberg, 1986; Steinberg, Fegley, & Dornbusch, 1993). Such conduct may be tied in with a premature assumption of adult roles—an effort to grow up too soon (Bachman & Schulenberg, 1993). Some of the undesirable effects that have been attributed to part-time work may result, not from working itself, but from the factors that motivate some teenagers to take jobs. Some may want to work because they are already uninterested in school or feel alienated from their families or because they want money to buy drugs or liquor.

However, a longitudinal study that followed 1,000 randomly selected ninth graders in St. Paul, Minnesota, through 4 years of high school suggests that some of the harmful effects of work may have been overstated (Mortimer et al., 1996). Each year, the students filled out questionnaires designed to measure their mental health and behavioral adjustment. They were asked about their grade point average, how much time they spent doing homework, and how much they drank and smoked. They also reported on whether they worked for pay and, if so, for how many hours a week.

The number of hours an adolescent worked did not seem to reduce self-esteem or mastery motivation. Nor were employed students unusually likely to be depressed. During the first 3 years, working had no effect on homework time or grades. Only during senior year did students who worked more than 20 hours a week tend to do less homework than other students, and even so, their grades and motivation to do well in school did not suffer in comparison with nonworking peers. Furthermore, students who worked 20 or fewer hours during their senior year had *higher* grades than either those who worked longer hours or those who did not work at all. Working was not related to smoking or behavioral problems at school. However, working more than 20 hours a week was associated with increased alcohol use.

This research does not give a definitive answer to the question of whether outside work is good or bad for adolescents. For one thing, the data come entirely from self-reports. Furthermore, they do not deal with the influence of working on illegal drug use, cheating in school, delinquency, sexual behavior, or a number of other possible concerns. Finally, the study addressed only how *much* young people work, and not the quality of their work experience. Another study discussed in Chapter 14 (also based largely on self-reports) found that teenagers who work 20 or more hours a week are more likely to feel stress, to smoke, drink, or use marijuana, and to begin sexual activity early (M. D. Resnick et al., 1997). Still other studies suggest that such factors as advancement opportunity, the chance to learn useful skills, and the kinds of responsibilities adolescents have at work may determine whether the experience is a positive or negative one (Call, Mortimer, & Shanahan, 1995; Finch, Shanahan, Mortimer, & Ryu, 1991; Shanahan, Finch, Mortimer, & Ryu, 1991).

Among some ethnic groups, then, parenting styles may be less important than other factors that affect motivation. Young people who are interested in what they are learning and whose parents and peers esteem education are more motivated to succeed. The strong school achievement of many first- and second-generation youngsters from immigrant backgrounds—not only East Asian, but also Filipino, Mexican, and European—reflects their families' and friends' strong emphasis on and support of educational success. Of course, students who have not yet surmounted the language barrier have a harder time in school (Fuligni, 1997).

Socioeconomic Status and the Family Environment

Socioeconomic status can be a powerful factor in educational achievement through its influence on family atmosphere, on choice of neighborhood, and on parents' way of rearing children (NRC, 1993a). Is the family stable and harmonious, or conflict-ridden? Do the parents talk to their children? What goals do they have for their children, and how do they help them reach those goals? Do parents show interest in schoolwork and expect children to go to college? Whether a family is rich or poor, the answers to questions like these are important, but the answers are more likely to be positive in a higher-income, better-educated family.

It is not parents' occupation, income, or education that makes the difference, but the indirect effect that socioeconomic status tends to have on parenting (K. R. White, 1982). Children of poor, uneducated parents are more likely to experience negative family and school atmospheres and more stressful events (Felner et al., 1995). The neighborhood a family can afford generally determines the quality of schooling available, as well as opportunities for higher education; and the availability of such opportunities, together with attitudes in the neighborhood peer group, affect motivation.

When a school has a predominance of low-income children, negative effects of low socioeconomic status spread through the school population as a whole. This may help explain why schools in which a majority of students come from single-parent homes tend to have lower eighth-grade math and reading achievement scores (Pong, 1997).

Still, some young people from nontraditional families and from disadvantaged neighborhoods do well in school and improve their condition in life. What may make the difference is *social capital:* the family and community resources children can draw upon. Parents who invest time and effort in their children and who have a strong network of community support build the family's social capital (Coleman, 1988). For example, single parents and stepparents who establish relationships with other parents may become better aware of school programs and operations and thus foster their children's achievement (Pong, 1997). African American adolescents whose parents get social support from relatives are more likely to see their homes as well-organized; and the better organized the youngsters perceive their home environment to be, the more self-reliant they are and the better they do in school (R. D. Taylor, 1996).

In a 20-year study of 252 children born to mostly poor and African American teenage mothers in Baltimore, those who—regardless of parents' income, education, and employment—had more social capital (according to such measures as those listed in Table 15-4) were more likely by the end of adolescence to have completed high school and in some cases to have gone to college or to have entered the labor force and to be enjoying stable incomes (Furstenberg & Hughes, 1995). (Box 15-3 discusses other factors that affect the likelihood of finishing school.)

College and Career Planning

How do young people develop career goals? How do they decide whether or not to go to college and, if not, how to enter the world of work? Many factors enter

social capital Family and community resources upon which a person can draw.

Table 15-4	Factors Contributing to Social Capital

Within Family

Family cohesion

Mother's support to and from own mother

Parents see siblings or grandparents weekly?

Father in home:

   Biological father or long-term stepfather?

Parents' help with homework

Child's activities with parents

Parents' expectations for school performance

Parents' educational aspirations for child

Mother's encouragement of child

Mother's attendance at school meetings

Number of child's friends mother knows

Family Links to Community

Religious involvement

Strong help network

Mother sees close friend weekly?

Child ever changed schools due to move?

Child's friends' educational expectations

School quality

Neighborhood as a place to grow up

Source: Adapted from Furstenberg & Hughes, 1995.

in, including individual ability and personality, education, socioeconomic and ethnic background, the advice of school counselors, life experiences, and societal values. Let's look at a classic model of stages in vocational planning during childhood and adolescence and then at influences on vocational aspirations. Then we'll examine what happens to young people who do not go to college.

Stages in Vocational Planning

At the age of 6, Julie wanted to be an astronaut. By the time she was 12, she realized that mathematics and science were not her best subjects and she would never make it into the space program. At 15, after doing some volunteer work at a hospital, she decided that she would like to go into one of the helping professions, possibly psychiatry. But by her senior year in high school she had given up the idea of medical school (again, her weakness in math and science would have hurt her chances) and instead was applying to colleges that offered 5-year programs leading to a master's degree in social work.

Julie's development followed three classic stages in career planning: the *fantasy period,* the *tentative period,* and the *realistic period* (Ginzberg et al., 1951).* During the *fantasy period* in elementary school, Julie's ambitions were active and exciting, and her decisions were based on emotions rather than on practical considerations. In the *tentative period,* at about puberty, she began to try to more accurately match her interests with her abilities and values. By the end of high

fantasy period In Ginzberg's theory of career planning, period during elementary school years when occupational ambitions are based on emotion and excitement, not on practical considerations.

tentative period In Ginzberg's theory of career planning, period around puberty when young people begin to try to match their interests with their abilities and values.

*Ginzberg (1972, 1984) has reformulated aspects of his theory that apply to adulthood, particularly women's career development.

Box 15-3 Dropping Out of High School

Students who leave school before receiving a diploma reduce their opportunities. Many employers require a high school diploma, and many jobs require skills based on a solid education. Dropouts have trouble getting and keeping jobs, and the jobs they do get tend to be low-level and poorly paying.

Society suffers when young people do not finish school. Dropouts are more likely to end up on welfare, to be unemployed, and to become involved with drugs, crime, and delinquency. In addition, the loss of taxable income burdens the public treasury (NCES, 1987).

Fewer students are dropping out these days, and some eventually go back to school to earn a high school equivalency certificate. The dropout rate declined from 13.9 percent in 1982 to 11 percent in 1993. Latino students are about twice as likely to drop out as African Americans (27.5 percent as compared with 13.6 percent), and African Americans are nearly twice as likely to drop out as non-Latino whites (7.9 percent). However, rates for all three groups have improved (NCES, 1995). In all three groups, low-income students are more likely to drop out than middle- or high-income students (Children's Defense Fund, 1995; see figure). The higher dropout rates among minority groups living in poverty may stem in part from the poor quality of their schools as compared with those attended by more advantaged children. Among other possible reasons for the high Latino dropout rates are language difficulties, financial pressures, and a culture that puts family first, since these students often leave school to help support their families (U.S. Department of Education, 1992).

Students in single-parent and remarried households—even relatively affluent ones—are more likely to drop out than students living with both parents (Finn & Rock, 1997; Zimiles & Lee,

1991). Frequent moves may contribute to the effects of family instability. Changing schools may reduce a family's *social capital* (resources for enhancing children's development). Families that move a lot generally have weaker social connections, know less about the children's school, and are less able to make wise decisions about schooling (Teachman, Paasch, & Carver, 1996).

Other factors associated with dropping out include having repeated a grade in elementary school, working more than 15 hours a week while in high school, being married, having a child, being alienated from family and community, and displaying such signs of antisocial behavior as suspension, probation, or trouble with the law (NCES, 1987; S. B. Williams, 1987). Dropouts tend to be risk takers; they are less likely to use safety belts in a car and more likely to ride with a drinking driver, carry a weapon, use drugs, or have sexual intercourse than youngsters who stay in school (Centers for Disease Control and Prevention [CDC], 1994a). Dropping out may be related to lack of motivation and self-esteem, lack of parental encouragement, low expectations by teachers, inappropriate skill training for noncollege-bound youth, and disciplinary problems (Hamilton, 1990; Rule, 1981).

Perhaps the most important factor in whether or not a student will finish school is *active engagement:* the extent to which the student is actively involved in schooling. On the most basic level, active engagement means coming to class on time, being prepared, listening and responding to the teacher, and obeying school rules. A second level of engagement consists of getting involved with the coursework—asking questions, taking the initiative to seek help when needed, or doing extra projects. Both levels of active

Continued

---

realistic period In Ginzberg's theory of career planning, period toward the end of the high school years when adolescents select future occupations on the basis of an accurate match between interests, abilities, and values and plan for appropriate preparation for those occupations.

school, she was in the *realistic period.* She was attempting to objectively size up what she wanted to, and would be able to, achieve and was planning for the right education to meet her career goals.

Marco's aspirations are less sharply focused. At 6 he wanted to be a baseball player. At 12 baseball still sounded good, but so did becoming a dancer. As the time to apply to college draws closer, he bounces from one interest to another—baseball, choreography, law, geology, and psychology—and hates to have to drop any of them.

Marco has not yet reached the realistic period. He is not alone. In one study, more than 6,000 high school seniors in Texas were asked to name their top three career choices and to report on their educational plans. At a time in their lives when they had to make crucial choices about education and work, these students knew little about occupations. Of those who felt that they had a good understanding of their first career choice, only about half planned to get the appropriate amount of education; some thought they needed much more education for their chosen careers than they actually did, and others were not planning on getting enough training. Furthermore, most students did not seem to be making

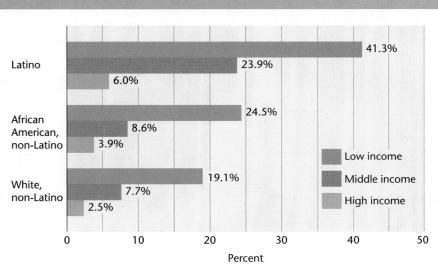

School dropout rates among youths ages 16 to 24, by income and ethnicity, 1993. Both family income and minority status greatly affect the likelihood of dropping out.

Source: Children's Defense Fund, 1995, p. 94; attributed to U.S. Department of Education, National Center for Education Statistics.
Note: The National Education Goals Panel (1997) reports no change in high school completion rates during the 1990s.

engagement tend to pay off in positive school performance by at-risk students. In a nationwide sample of 1,803 low-income African American and Hispanic students, active engagement was the chief distinction between those who graduated from high school on time, got reasonably good grades, and did fairly well on achievement tests and those who did not (Finn & Rock, 1997).

What factors promote active engagement? Family encouragement is undoubtedly one. Others may be small class size and a warm, supportive school environment. Since engaged or alienated behavior patterns tend to be set early in a child's school career, dropout prevention should start early too (Finn & Rock, 1997). Indeed, dropping out of high school can sometimes be predicted as early as the seventh grade. In a longitudinal study of 475 seventh-graders who were followed for 5 years,

dropout rates were higher for students who, when first seen, showed aggressive behavior *and* did poorly in school (Cairns, Cairns, & Neckerman, 1989).

Public and private organizations have developed a variety of programs aimed at keeping young people from low-income families in school. One federally funded program, Upward Bound, established in 1964, stresses high expectations, has a rigorous curriculum, and offers tutoring and peer counseling. It also offers counseling on drug abuse, self-esteem, study skills, preparing for the Scholastic Aptitude Test (SAT), applying to college, and career planning (A. S. Wells, 1988). The success of such programs as Upward Bound—by 1988, 80 percent of its graduates had gone on to 4-year colleges—shows that it is possible to help prevent able, engaged students from dropping out.

good matches between their career choices and their interests (Grotevant & Durrett, 1980). It may be that many young people do not think seriously about career choices until college.

Influences on Vocational Aspirations

How do black inner-city boys, who tend to face a life of limited opportunity, evaluate their vocational prospects? One study (T. D. Cook et al., 1996) compared the occupational ambitions and expectations of second-, fourth-, sixth-, and eighth-grade boys in three low-income, virtually all-African American schools and three middle-income, predominantly white schools in Memphis, Tennessee. Researchers asked the children what jobs they would like to have and thought they probably would have when they grew up. Then they repeated the questions, this time giving the children a choice among nine occupations of varying prestige: physician, reporter, teacher, insurance agent, mail carrier, policeman, plumber, auto mechanic, and taxi driver.

In line with Ginzberg's model, both groups of boys became more realistic about their occupational aspirations and expectations as they grew older, outgrowing

Is this career counselor influenced by the student's sex in advising him about possible career choices? Even though there is little or no difference between boys and girls in mathematical or verbal ability, many school counselors still steer young people into gender-typed careers.

their fascination with such exciting, high-profile jobs as policeman and fireman. However, the African American eighth-graders were more likely to continue to aspire to these occupations, which presumably seemed more desirable and more attainable to them than some of the other choices. More than one-fourth (27 percent) of the white eighth-graders, but only 4 percent of the African American eighth-graders, wanted to be doctors or lawyers. As compared with their white counterparts, African American boys, from second grade on, showed a larger and widening gap between aspirations and expectations. For them, the reality that they were unlikely to get their dream jobs hit home at an early age.

Parents' encouragement and financial support influence aspiration and achievement; in fact, parental encouragement predicts high ambition better than social class does. When 2,622 sixth-, eighth-, tenth-, and twelfth-grade students, black and white and from all social strata, were asked to describe their own expectations for their education and their fathers' and mothers' expectations for them, more than half the students agreed with the perceived goals of each parent (T. E. Smith, 1981).

Despite the greater flexibility in career goals today, gender—and gender-stereotyping—often influence vocational choice. Although there is little or no difference between boys and girls in mathematical or verbal ability and although girls' grades are on average better than boys', many girls are not encouraged to continue in gifted programs, to take advanced science and math courses, or to pursue demanding careers. Many parents, teachers, and counselors still steer young people into gender-typed occupations, even though there is no real basis for doing so (J. E. Hyde & Linn, 1988; Maccoby & Jacklin, 1974; McCormick & Wolf, 1993; Read, 1991; S. M. Reis, 1991).

The educational system itself may act as a subtle influence on vocational aspirations. The relatively narrow range of abilities valued and cultivated in many schools gives certain students the inside track. Students who can memorize and analyze tend to do well on intelligence tests that hinge on those abilities and in classrooms where teaching is geared to those abilities; thus, as predicted by the tests, these students are achievers in a system that stresses the abilities in which they happen to excel. Meanwhile, students whose strength happens to be in creative or practical thinking—areas critical to success in certain fields—never get a chance to show what they can do. Thus the young people with the greatest actual potential may be frozen out of career paths or forced into less challenging and rewarding ones because of test scores and grades too low to put them on the fast track—"or perhaps any track"—to success (Sternberg, 1997, p. 1036). Recognition of a broader range of "intelligences" (see Chapter 12), combined with more flexible teaching and career counseling at all levels, could allow more students to get the education and enter the occupations they truly desire and to make the contributions of which they are capable.

Guiding Students Not Bound for College

About half the high school graduates in the United States do not go on to college; of those who do, fewer than half earn 4-year degrees. Still, although some 75 percent of high school students will not finish college, most vocational counseling in high schools is oriented toward college-bound youth (NRC, 1993a).

Most other industrialized countries offer some kind of structured guidance to noncollege-bound students. Germany, for example, has an apprenticeship system, in which high school students go to school part time and spend the rest of the week in paid on-the-job training supervised by an employer-mentor. About 60 percent of German high school students take advantage of this program each year, and 85 percent of those who complete it find jobs (Hopfensperger, 1996).

The United States, by contrast, has relied almost entirely on market forces to help noncollege-bound youths find work. Whatever vocational training programs do exist are less closely tied in with the needs of businesses and industries than the German apprenticeship program. Most young people get their training on the job or in community college courses. Many, ignorant about the job market, do not obtain the skills they need. Others take jobs beneath their abilities. Some do not find work at all. For people under age 20, being raised in a low-income family is the strongest predictor of joblessness (NRC, 1993a).

In some communities, demonstration programs help in the school-to-work transition. The most successful ones offer instruction in basic skills, counseling, peer support, mentoring, apprenticeship, and job placement (NRC, 1993a). In 1994, the U.S. Department of Labor and U.S. Department of Education created a School to Work Opportunities office, which has awarded more than $100 million in grants to state and local governments to develop vocational training programs (Hopfensperger, 1996).

Vocational planning is closely tied to an adolescent's search for identity. The question "What shall I do?" is very close to "Who shall I be?" People who feel they are doing something worthwhile, and doing it well, feel good about themselves. Those who feel that their work does not matter—or that they are not good at it—may wonder about the meaning of their lives. A prime personality issue in adolescence, which we discuss in Chapter 16, is the effort to define the self.

SUMMARY

Aspects of Cognitive Maturation

- People in Piaget's stage of **formal operations** can engage in **hypothetical-deductive reasoning.** They can think in terms of possibilities, deal flexibly with problems, and test hypotheses. Since experience plays an important part in attaining this stage, not all people become capable of formal operations.

- According to Elkind, immature thought patterns characteristic of adolescence include finding fault with authority figures, argumentativeness, indecisiveness, apparent hypocrisy, self-consciousness (which he calls the **imaginary audience**), and an assumption of uniqueness and invulnerability (which he calls the **personal fable**). However, research has cast doubt on the prevalence of the latter two patterns.

C H E C K P O I N T

Can you . . .

- Compare the psychological effects of the transition from elementary school in the 6-3-3 pattern and the 8-4 pattern of school organization?

- Assess factors in adolescents' academic achievement?

- Discuss influences on college and vocational planning?

Moral Reasoning

- According to Kohlberg, moral reasoning is rooted in the development of a sense of justice and occurs on three main levels: **preconventional morality, conventional morality** (or **morality of conventional role conformity**), and **postconventional morality** (or **morality of autonomous moral principles**).

- Family influences play a part in the attainment of the more advanced levels of moral judgment.

- The applicability of Kohlberg's system to women and girls and to people in nonwestern cultures has been questioned.

Educational and Vocational Issues

- Stress is associated with the transition to secondary school, especially in the 6-3-3 pattern and especially for girls.

- Quality of schooling, parenting styles, ethnicity, and socioeconomic status influence educational achievement—the latter, through its effects on home atmosphere, choice of neighborhood, and peer attitudes, which influence motivation to achieve. Poor families whose children do well in school tend to have more **social capital.**

- Although most Americans graduate from high school, the dropout rate is particularly high among poor Latino and African American students and among those not living with both parents. Active engagement in studies is an important factor in keeping adolescents in school.

- According to Ginzberg's model, young people go through three stages in career planning: the **fantasy period,** the **tentative period,** and the **realistic period.** However, many high school students are not realistic in their career aspirations.

- Vocational choice is influenced by several factors, including ethnicity, parental encouragement, gender, and parental support. About half of American high school graduates do not go to college.

- Outside work seems to have both positive and negative effects on educational, social, and occupational development.

KEY TERMS

formal operations (544)
hypothetical-deductive reasoning (546)
imaginary audience (549)
personal fable (549)
preconventional morality (551)
conventional morality (or morality of conventional role conformity) (551)

postconventional morality (or morality of autonomous moral principles) (551)
social capital (562)
fantasy period (563)
tentative period (563)
realistic period (564)

QUESTIONS FOR THOUGHT AND DISCUSSION

1. How can parents and teachers help adolescents improve their reasoning ability?

2. In your experience, are the attitudes Elkind called the *imaginary audience* and *personal fable* characteristic of most adolescents?

3. Kohlberg's method of assessing moral development by evaluating participants' reactions to moral dilemmas is widely used. Does this seem like the most appropriate method? Why or why not? Can you suggest an alternative measure?

4. In what ways can parents and teachers help students with the transitions to junior high, middle school, and high school?

5. How can parents, educators, and other societal institutions encourage young people to finish high school?

6. Imagine you are a high school counselor. What kind of program would you put in place to help students make career plans?

7. Would you favor an apprenticeship program like Germany's in the United States? How successful do you think it would be in helping young people make realistic career plans? What negative effects, if any, might it have?

8. Compare the factors influencing girls' occupational aspirations and those of African American boys. What, if anything, might Ginzberg's theory have to say about these issues? What interventions might help narrow the gap between African American boys' occupational aspirations and expectations?

Psychosocial Development in Adolescence

This face in the mirror
stares at me
demanding Who are you? What will you become?
And taunting, You don't even know.
Chastened, I cringe and agree
and then
because I'm still young,
I stick out my tongue.

Eve Merriam, "Conversation with Myself," 1964

Focus

Jackie Robinson

On April 15, 1947, when 28-year-old Jack Roosevelt ("Jackie") Robinson put on a Brooklyn Dodgers uniform and strode onto Ebbets Field, he became the first African American in the twentieth century to play major league baseball. By the end of a spectacular first season in which he was named Rookie of the Year, Robinson had become a household word, the symbol of a revolution against institutionalized prejudice and discrimination. Two years later, he was voted baseball's Most Valuable Player. During his 10 years with the Dodgers, the team won six pennants, and Robinson played in six consecutive All-Star games. After his retirement, he won first-ballot election to the Hall of Fame.

As Robinson made plain in the title of his autobiography, *I Never Had It Made* (1995), his triumph did not come easily. When the Dodgers' manager, Branch Rickey, decided to break the color bar that had been in effect since the 1890s by bringing Robinson up from the Negro Leagues, several players petitioned to keep him off the team. To avoid racial confrontations that might have sabotaged the "noble experiment," Robinson promised Rickey to hold his hot temper no matter what the provocation—a promise he kept during his first three seasons with the Dodgers (until Rickey released him from it) in the face of racist taunts and jibes, threats, hate mail, and attempts at bodily harm. Once, after he safely slid into second base, the opposing baseman smacked him hard on the cheek with a gratuitous late tag. Robinson simply stood up, brushed himself off, and stole third base.

Robinson's athletic prowess and dignified demeanor won the respect of the baseball world. Within the next decade, most major league teams signed African American players. Baseball had become "one of the first institutions in modern society to accept blacks on a relatively equal basis" (Tygiel, 1983).

Behind the Jackie Robinson legend is the story of a prodigiously talented boy growing up in a nation in which opportunities for black youth were extremely limited. The grandson of a slave and the son of a Georgia sharecropper, he seemed to have at least two strikes against him. He was poor and fatherless; when Jackie was 6 months old, his father had left his mother, Mallie Robinson, and she was forced to support her five children alone. This determined, deeply religious woman imbued her children with moral strength and pride. Intent on providing them with a good education, she moved her family to Pasadena, California, where her brother lived, and got a job doing domestic work.

Pasadena turned out to be almost as rigidly segregated as the Deep South. Movie theaters had separate sections for blacks, and they could swim at the public pool only one day a week, when the water was changed. Nevertheless, Mallie Robinson eventually managed to buy a house in an all-white neighborhood, and the family stayed put despite neighbors' initial attempts to force them out.

Jackie Robinson wasn't much of a student; he lived for sports and excelled in every game he tried. Intensely competitive, he was also a good team player. At first he tagged along with his older brothers in sandlot games. He idolized his brother Mack, a gifted athlete who later won a silver medal in the 1936 Olympics. Another brother, Frank, was Jackie's "greatest fan" (J. Robinson, 1995, p. 9). By the time Jackie Robinson was in junior high school, he was a star in his own right, with a growing reputation. He also worked after school, delivering newspapers, cutting grass, and running errands.

Still, he had time on his hands. The neighborhood was now more diverse, and he became a member of a street gang of poor black, Mexican, and Japanese boys who seethed with "a growing resentment at being deprived of some of the advantages the white kids had" (J. Robinson, 1995, p. 6). Robinson was frequently brought into the police station for questioning; once he and his friends were taken to jail at gunpoint for swimming in the reservoir. The gang's activities were not much more than youthful high-jinks, but serious enough to get them in trouble: throwing rocks at cars and street lamps, smashing windows, swiping apples from fruitstands and food from local stores, and stealing stray golf balls to resell to their owners. Once, while at Pasadena Junior College, where he broke his brother Mack's national broad-jump record, Robinson—never one to shrink from a fight—landed in jail after a racial altercation with a white motorist.

Robinson later reflected that he "might have become a full-fledged juvenile delinquent" had it not been for the influence of two men. One was an auto mechanic named Carl Anderson, who pointed out that "it didn't take guts to follow the crowd, that courage and intelligence lay in being willing to be different" (J. Robinson, 1995, pp. 6–7). The other was a young African American minister named Karl Downs, who lured Robinson and his friends into church-sponsored sports, listened to their worries, helped them find jobs, and got them to help build a youth center—"an alternative to hanging out on street corners" (J. Robinson, 1995, p. 8). Later, while at UCLA, where Robinson earned an unprecedented four letters in football, basketball, baseball, and track and met his future wife, he served as a volunteer Sunday school teacher at the church.

Sources of biographical information about Jackie Robinson are Falkner, 1995, Rampersad, 1997, J. Robinson, 1995, S. Robinson, 1996, and Tygiel, 1983, 1997.

• • •

Adolescence is a time of opportunities and risks. Teenagers are on the threshold of love, of life's work, and of participation in adult society. Yet adolescence is also a time when some young people engage in behavior that closes off their options and limits their possibilities. Today, research is increasingly focusing on how to help adolescents whose environments are not optimal to avoid hazards that can keep them from fulfilling their potential. What saved Jackie Robinson—in addition to the influence of his indomitable, hardworking mother, his brothers, and his adult mentors—were his talent and passion for athletics, which ultimately enabled him to channel his drive, energy, audacity, and rebellion against racism in a positive direction.

Adolescents need to embrace values and make commitments. Whatever their abilities, they need to discover what they can do and take pride in their accomplishments. They need to form close ties with people their own age and to be liked and loved and respected for who they are and what they stand for. This means they have to find out what they stand for. These tasks are not easy. While teenagers look to peers as comrades in the struggle for independence, they still turn to parents and other adults for guidance and support.

In Chapters 14 and 15 we looked at some important factors that contribute to an adolescent's sense of self: appearance and other physical attributes, cognitive abilities, moral reasoning, school achievement, and preparation for the world of work. In this chapter, we turn to psychosocial aspects of the quest for identity. We discuss how adolescents come to terms with their sexuality and what factors increase the risks of early sexual activity and teenage pregnancy. We consider how teenagers' burgeoning individuality expresses itself in relationships with parents, siblings, and peers. We examine sources of antisocial behavior and ways of reducing the risks of adolescence so as to make it a time of positive growth and expanding possibilities. Finally, we compare adolescents' views of themselves and their lives in countries around the world.

After reading this chapter, you should be able to answer and elaborate on such questions as these:

Preview Questions

- How do adolescents form an identity?

- What influences sexual orientation?

- What are the prevailing sexual practices and attitudes among adolescents, and what leads some to engage in high-risk sexual behavior?

- How typical is "adolescent rebellion"?

- How are adolescents' attitudes and behavior influenced by parents, siblings, and peers?

- What are the causes and consequences of teenage pregnancy and juvenile delinquency, and what can be done to reduce these and other risks of adolescence?

The Search for Identity

The search for identity comes into focus during the teenage years. As Erikson (1950) emphasized, the teenager's effort to make sense of the self is not "a kind of maturational malaise." It is part of a healthy, vital process that builds on the achievements of earlier stages—on trust, autonomy, initiative, and industry—and lays the groundwork for coping with the crises of adult life. Let's look at Erikson's view of identity formation and at research that has tested and extended it.

Identity Versus Identity Confusion

identity versus identity confusion In Erikson's theory, the fifth crisis of psychosocial development, in which an adolescent seeks to develop a coherent sense of self, including the role she or he is to play in society. Also called *identity versus role confusion*.

Erikson's concept of the identity crisis was based on his own life and his research on adolescents in various societies (see Chapter 1). The chief task of adolescence, said Erikson (1968), is to confront the crisis of *identity versus identity confusion* (or *role confusion*), so as to become a unique adult with a coherent sense of self and a valued role in society. The identity crisis is seldom fully resolved in adolescence; issues concerning identity may crop up again and again throughout adult life.

According to Erikson, adolescents form their identity not by modeling themselves after other people, as younger children do, but by modifying and synthesizing earlier identifications into "a new psychological structure, greater than the sum of its parts" (Kroger, 1993, p. 3). To form an identity, adolescents must ascertain and organize their abilities, needs, interests, and desires so they can be expressed in a social context.

Erikson saw the prime danger of this stage as identity (or role) confusion, which can greatly delay reaching psychological adulthood—even until after age 30. (He himself did not resolve his own identity crisis until his mid-twenties.) Some degree of identity confusion is normal. It accounts for both the seemingly chaotic nature of much adolescent behavior and teenagers' painful self-consciousness. Cliquishness and intolerance of differences—both hallmarks of the adolescent social scene—are defenses against identity confusion. Adolescents may also show confusion by regressing into childishness to avoid resolving conflicts or by committing themselves impulsively to poorly thought-out courses of action.

This flutist's musical talent and interest can, according to Erikson, help her resolve the adolescent conflict of *identity versus identity confusion*. Assessing her abilities, interests, and desires may help her decide whether to pursue a career in music or in some other field, thus fulfilling a major task in the search for identity.

Identity forms as young people resolve three major issues: the choice of an occupation, the adoption of values to believe in and live by, and the development of a satisfying sexual identity. During the crisis of middle childhood, that of *industry versus inferiority,* children acquire skills needed for success in their culture. Now, as adolescents, they need to find ways of using these skills. When young people have trouble settling on an occupational identity—or when their opportunities are artificially limited, as may be true for racial minorities—they are at risk of behavior with serious negative consequences, such as criminal activity or early pregnancy.

During the *psychosocial moratorium*—the "time out" period that adolescence provides—many young people search for commitments to which they can be faithful. These youthful commitments, both ideological and personal, may shape a person's life for years to come. Jackie Robinson's commitments, which remained lifelong goals, were to develop his athletic potential and to help improve the position of African Americans in society. The extent to which young people remain faithful to commitments influences their ability to resolve the identity crisis. Adolescents who satisfactorily resolve that crisis develop the "virtue" of *fidelity:* sustained loyalty, faith, or a sense of belonging to a loved one or to friends and companions. Fidelity can also mean identification with a set of values, an ideology, a religion, a political movement, a creative pursuit, or an ethnic group (Erikson, 1982). Self-identification emerges when young people choose values and people to be loyal to, rather than simply accepting their parents' choices.

Fidelity is an extension of trust. In infancy, it is important to trust others, especially parents; in adolescence, it becomes important to be trustworthy oneself. In addition, adolescents now extend their trust from parents to mentors or loved ones. In sharing thoughts and feelings, an adolescent clarifies a tentative identity by seeing it reflected in the eyes of the beloved. However, these adolescent "intimacies" differ from mature intimacy, which involves greater commitment, sacrifice, and compromise.

Erikson's theory, which was based largely on interviews with men, describes male development as the norm. According to Erikson, a man is not capable of real intimacy until after he has achieved a stable identity, whereas women define themselves through marriage and motherhood (something that may have been truer when Erikson developed his theory than it is today). Thus, said Erikson, women (unlike men) develop identity through intimacy, not before it. As we'll see, the male orientation of Erikson's theory has prompted criticism. Still, Erikson's concept of the identity crisis has inspired much valuable research.

Identity Status: Crisis and Commitment

Kate, Andrea, Nick, and Mark are all about to graduate from high school. Kate has considered her interests and her talents and plans to become a social worker. She has narrowed her college choices to three schools that offer good programs in this field. She knows that college will either confirm her interest in social work or lead her in another direction. She is open to both possibilities.

Andrea knows exactly what she is going to do with her life. Her mother, a union leader at a plastics factory, has arranged for Andrea to enter an apprenticeship program there. Andrea has never considered doing anything else.

Nick, on the other hand, is agonizing over his future. Should he attend a community college or join the army? He cannot decide what to do now or what he wants to do eventually.

Mark still has no idea of what he wants to do, but he is not worried. He figures he can get some sort of a job—maybe at a supermarket or fast-food restaurant—and make up his mind about the future when he is ready.

These four young people are involved in identity formation. What accounts for the differences in the way they go about it, and how will these differences affect the outcome? According to research by the psychologist James E. Marcia,

Table 16-1 — Identity-Status Interview

Sample Questions	Typical Answers for the Four Statuses
About occupational commitment "How willing do you think you'd be to give up going into _____ if something better came along?"	*Identity achievement.* "Well, I might, but I doubt it. I can't see what 'something better' would be for me." *Foreclosure.* "Not very willing. It's what I've always wanted to do. The folks are happy with it and so am I." *Moratorium.* "I guess that if I knew for sure, I could answer that better. It would have to be something in the general area—something related . . ." *Identity diffusion.* "Oh, sure. If something better came along, I'd change just like that."
About ideological commitment: "Have you ever had any doubts about your religious beliefs?"	*Identity achievement.* "Yes, I even started wondering whether there is a God. I've pretty much resolved that now, though. The way it seems to me is . . ." *Foreclosure.* "No, not really; our family is pretty much in agreement on these things." *Moratorium.* "Yes, I guess I'm going through that now. I just don't see how there can be a God and still so much evil in the world . . ." *Identity diffusion.* "Oh, I don't know. I guess so. Everyone goes through some sort of stage like that. But it really doesn't bother me much. I figure that one religion is about as good as another!"

Source: Adapted from Marcia, 1966.

Table 16-2 — Criteria for Identity Statuses

Identity Status	Crisis (Period of Considering Alternatives)	Commitment (Adherence to a Path of Action)
Identity achievement	Resolved	Present
Foreclosure	Absent	Present
Moratorium	In crisis	Absent
Identity diffusion	Absent	Absent

Source: Adapted from Marcia, 1980.

identity statuses   In Marcia's terminology, states of ego development which depend on the presence or absence of crisis and commitment.

crisis   In Marcia's terminology, period of conscious decision making related to identity formation.

commitment   In Marcia's terminology, personal investment in an occupation or system of beliefs.

these students are in four different states of ego (self) development, or *identity statuses,* which seem to be related to certain aspects of personality.

Marcia's definition of *identity* is similar to Erikson's: "an internal, self-constructed, dynamic organization of drives, abilities, beliefs, and individual history" (Marcia, 1980, p. 159). Through 30-minute, semistructured *identity-status interviews* (see Table 16-1), Marcia found four types of identity status: *identity achievement, foreclosure, moratorium, and identity diffusion.* The four categories differ according to the presence or absence of **crisis** and **commitment,** the two elements Erikson saw as crucial to forming identity (see Table 16-2). Marcia defines *crisis* as a period of conscious decision making, and *commitment* as a personal investment in an occupation or system of beliefs (ideology). He found relationships between identity status and such characteristics as anxiety, self-esteem, moral reasoning, and patterns of behavior. Building on Marcia's theory, other researchers have identified other personality and family variables related to

Table 16-3   Family and Personality Factors Associated with Adolescents in Four Identity Statuses*

Factor	Identity Achievement	Foreclosure	Moratorium	Identity Diffusion
Family	Parents encourage autonomy and connection with teachers; differences are explored within a context of mutuality.	Parents are overly involved with their children; families avoid expressing differences; parents use denial and repression to avoid dealing with unwelcome thoughts and events.	Adolescents are often involved in an ambivalent struggle with parental authority.	Parents are laissez-faire in child-rearing attitudes; are rejecting or not available to children.
Personality	High levels of ego development, moral reasoning, internal locus of control, self-certainty, self-esteem, performance under stress, and intimacy.	Highest levels of authoritarianism and stereotypical thinking, obedience to authority, external locus of control, dependent relationships, low levels of anxiety.	Most anxious and fearful of success; high levels of ego development, moral reasoning, and self-esteem.	Mixed results, with low levels of ego development, moral reasoning, cognitive complexity, and self-certainty; poor cooperative abilities.

*These associations have emerged from a number of separate studies. Since the studies have all been correlational, rather than longitudinal, it is impossible to say that any factor caused placement in any identity status.
Source: Kroger, 1993.

identity status (see Table 16-3.) Marcia and other researchers have also studied differences in identity formation between males and females and among ethnic groups. Here is a thumbnail sketch of people in each of the four identity statuses:

- *Identity achievement* (*crisis leading to commitment*). Kate has resolved her identity crisis. During the crisis period, she devoted much thought and some emotional struggle to major issues in her life; she has made choices and expresses strong commitment to them. Her parents have encouraged her to make her own decisions; they have listened to her ideas and given their opinions without pressuring her to adopt them. Kate has *flexible strength:* she is thoughtful but not so introspective as to be unable to act. She has a sense of humor, functions well under stress, is capable of intimate relationships, and holds to her standards while being open to new ideas. Research in a number of cultures has found people in this category to be more mature and more competent in relationships than people in the other three (Marcia, 1993).

- *Foreclosure* (*commitment without crisis*). Andrea has made commitments, not as a result of a crisis, which would involve questioning and exploring possible choices, but by accepting someone else's plans for her life. She has rigid strength: she is happy and self-assured, perhaps even smug and self-satisfied, and she becomes dogmatic when her opinions are questioned. She has close family ties, is obedient, and tends to follow a powerful leader (like her mother), who accepts no disagreement.

- *Moratorium* (*crisis with no commitment yet*). Nick is in crisis, struggling with decisions. He is lively, talkative, self-confident, and scrupulous, but also anxious and fearful. He is close to his mother but also resists her authority. He wants to have a girlfriend but has not yet developed a close relationship. He will probably come out of his crisis eventually with the ability to make commitments and achieve identity.

- *Identity diffusion* (*no commitment, no crisis*). Mark has not seriously considered options and has avoided commitments. He is unsure of himself and tends to be uncooperative. His parents do not discuss his future with him; they say it's up to him. Some people in this category become aimless drifters without goals. They tend to be unhappy, and they are often lonely because they have only superficial relationships.

identity achievement   Identity status, described by Marcia, which is characterized by commitment to choices made following a crisis, a period spent in exploring alternatives.

foreclosure   Identity status, described by Marcia, in which a person who has not spent time considering alternatives (that is, has not been in crisis) is committed to other people's plans for his or her life.

moratorium   Identity status, described by Marcia, in which a person is currently considering alternatives (in crisis) and seems headed for commitment.

identity diffusion   Identity status, described by Marcia, which is characterized by absence of commitment and lack of serious consideration of alternatives.

These categories are not permanent, of course; they may change as people continue to develop (Marcia, 1979). From late adolescence on, more and more people are in moratorium or achievement: seeking or finding their own identity. Still, many people, even as young adults, remain in foreclosure or diffusion (Kroger, 1993). Although people in foreclosure seem to have made final decisions, that is often not so; when adults in midlife look back on their lives, they most commonly trace a path from foreclosure to moratorium to achievement (Kroger & Haslett, 1991).

Gender Differences in Identity Formation

Freud's statement "Biology is destiny" suggests that the differing patterns of male and female development in almost all cultures are an inevitable result of anatomical differences. Today, many people believe that most gender differences arise from societal attitudes and practices (see Chapter 10). Whatever the reasons, the sexes (at least in the United States) seem to differ somewhat in rates of emotional and social maturation and perhaps also in routes to identity.

To explore female identity, Marcia (1979) asked questions about attitudes toward premarital intercourse, views on women's roles, and concerns related to lifestyle. His findings were surprising. In their answers to his questions, men in moratorium (in crisis) most closely resembled men who had achieved identity. But the women whose answers most closely resembled those of male identity achievers were in foreclosure: they had made commitments without undergoing a crisis. Marcia's explanation was that society expects women to carry on social values from one generation to the next, and therefore stability of identity is extremely important for them. He suggested that, for women, early foreclosure of identity may be just as adaptive as a struggle to achieve identity. (This may no longer be true in light of the changes in women's roles that have taken place since the 1970s.)

Much research supports Erikson's view that, for women, identity and intimacy develop together. Indeed, intimacy matters more to girls than to boys even in grade school friendships (Blyth & Foster-Clark, 1987). Rather than view this pattern as a departure from a male norm, however, some researchers who have studied girls and women see it as pointing to a weakness in Erikson's theory, which, they claim, is based on male-centered western concepts of individuality, autonomy, and competitiveness. According to Carol Gilligan (1982, 1987a, 1987b; L. M. Brown & Gilligan, 1990), the female sense of self develops not so much through achieving a separate identity as through establishing relationships. Girls and women, says Gilligan, judge themselves on their handling of their responsibilities and on their ability to care for others as well as for themselves. Even high-achieving women attain identity more through cooperation than through competition.

Some developmentalists, however, have begun to question how different the male and female paths to identity really are—especially today—and whether individual differences may be more important than gender differences (Archer, 1993; Marcia, 1993). Indeed, Marcia (1993) argues that relationships and an ongoing tension between independence and connectedness are at the heart of all of Erikson's psychosocial stages for both men and women.

Self-esteem, during adolescence, develops largely in the context of relationships with peers, particularly those of the same sex. In line with Gilligan's view, male self-esteem seems to be linked with striving for individual achievement, whereas female self-esteem depends more on connections with others. In one longitudinal study, 84 mostly white, socioeconomically diverse young adults, whose self-esteem had been measured at ages 14 and 18, described memories about important experiences with others. Men who had had high self-esteem during adolescence tended to recall wanting to assert themselves with male friends, whereas women who had had high self-esteem recalled efforts to help female friends—efforts that involved asserting themselves in a collaborative rather than a competitive way (Thorne & Michaelieu, 1996).

Interviews with 99 girls from kindergarten through twelfth grade suggest that girls' self-confidence and self-esteem stay fairly high until age 11 or 12 and then tend to falter (L. M. Brown & Gilligan, 1990). Among 174 girls and boys who filled out questionnaires during each of their high school years, ninth-grade boys tended to have higher self-esteem than girls their age, and the picture changed little during the next 4 years (Chubb, Fertman, & Ross, 1997).

Preadolescent girls, according to Gilligan, tend to be perceptive about relationships and assertive about expressing feelings. As adolescents, however, they often accept stereotyped notions of the way they should act and repress their true feelings for the sake of being "nice". Only those who continue to acknowledge their true feelings and express them appropriately stay in healthy relationship with themselves, with others, and with society and retain high self-esteem. They see themselves as competent and are more apt than other girls to choose nontraditional careers (L. M. Brown & Gilligan, 1990).

Ethnic Factors in Identity Formation

What happens to young people's identity when the values of their own ethnic community conflict with those of the larger society—for example, when Native Americans are expected to participate in a tribal ceremony on a day when they are also supposed to be in school? Or when young people face and perhaps internalize (take into their own value system) prejudice against their group? Or when discrimination limits their occupational choice, as it did for Jackie Robinson's brother Mack, who, after his Olympic glory, came home to a succession of menial jobs? All these situations can lead to identity confusion.

Identity formation is especially complicated for young people in minority groups, who need to integrate multiple identities. In fact, for some adolescents ethnicity may be central to identity formation (Phinney, 1993). Skin color and other physical features, language differences, and stereotyped social standing are extremely influential in molding minority adolescents' self-concept (Spencer & Markstrom-Adams, 1990).

Some research using Marcia's (1966) identity-status measures has shown a disproportionately large number of minority teenagers in foreclosure (Spencer & Markstrom-Adams, 1990). However, for them, this status may be adaptive. For example, Latino adolescents living in predominantly Latino communities may find social recognition, strength, and a robust sense of identity through following the customs and values of their culture. In a survey sponsored by the American Association of University Women, many more black girls than white and Hispanic girls remained self-confident in high school; white girls lost their self-assurance the earliest. African American girls may feel more self-confident because they often see strong women around them. They seem less dependent on school achievement for their self-esteem, drawing their sense of themselves more from family and community (Daley, 1991).

Sexuality

Seeing oneself as a sexual being, recognizing one's sexual orientation (see Chapter 14), coming to terms with sexual stirrings, and forming romantic or sexual attachments are all parts of achieving sexual identity. This urgent awareness of sexuality is an important aspect of identity formation, profoundly affecting self-image and relationships. This process is biologically driven, but its expression is in part culturally defined.

Identity development can be especially complicated for young people from minority groups. Ethnicity—and the conflicts with the dominant culture it entails—may play a central part in their self-concept.

CHECKPOINT

Can you . . .

List the three major issues involved in identity formation, according to Erikson?

• Describe four types of identity status found by Marcia?

• Discuss how gender and ethnicity can affect identity formation?

Attitudes toward sexuality have liberalized during the past fifty years. This "sexual evolution" includes more open acceptance of sexual activity and a decline in the double standard by which males are freer sexually than females.

How have sexual attitudes and behavior changed in recent decades? What factors affect the likelihood, risks, and consequences of sexual activity during the teenage years?

Sexual Attitudes and Behavior

It is difficult to do research on sexual expression. People willing to answer questions about sex tend to be sexually active and liberal in their attitudes toward sex and thus are not representative of the population. Also, there is often a discrepancy between what people say about sex and what they do, and there is no way to corroborate what people say. Some may conceal sexual activity; others may exaggerate. Problems multiply in surveying young people. For one thing, parental consent is often required, and parents who grant permission may not be typical. Still, even if we cannot generalize findings to the population as a whole, within the groups that take part in surveys we can see trends that reveal changes in sexual mores.

The early 1920s through the late 1970s witnessed an evolution in sexual attitudes and behavior. This "sexual evolution" has brought greater acceptance of and indulgence in premarital sex, especially in a committed relationship, together with a decline in the *double standard:* the code that gives males more sexual freedom than females. One reason for this change is a gradual decline in the age at which young people reach sexual maturity (see Chapter 14), coupled with a trend toward later marriage. The average age at marriage today is 24, about 3 or 4 years later than during the 1950s and about 12 years after sexual maturation (Children's Defense Fund, 1997a).

In 1965, at a large southern university, 33 percent of male students and 70 percent of female students called premarital sexual intercourse immoral. By 1985, only about 16 percent of the men and 17 percent of the women thought so (I. Robinson, Ziss, Ganza, Katz, & Robinson, 1991). Rates of premarital sexual activity have risen accordingly, especially among girls. In the mid-1950s, 1 out of 4 girls had sexual experience by age 18. Today, more than half of adolescent boys *and* girls have had intercourse by that age, and 4 out of 5 by age 20 (Abma, Chandra, Mosher, Peterson, & Piccinino, 1997a; Alan Guttmacher Institute [AGI], 1994;

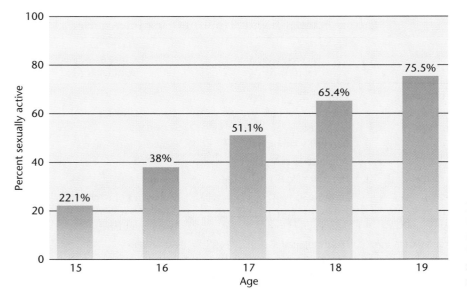

Figure 16-1

Percentage of teenage girls who have had intercourse after menarche, by age, 1995. More than half of teenage girls become sexually active by age 17.

Source: Based on data from Abma et al., 1997.

Children's Defense Fund, 1997a; see Figure 16-1). The average girl has her sexual initiation at 17, only one year later than the average boy (Children's Defense Fund, 1997a).

The double standard is not dead, however. In a telephone survey of 500 high school students, more boys said that sex was pleasurable and that they felt good about their sexual experiences, whereas more girls said that they were in love with their last sexual partner and that they should have waited until they were older before having sex (G. Lewin, 1994). A girl is likely to experience her first sexual relations with a steady boyfriend; a boy is likely to have his with someone he knows casually (Dreyer, 1982; Zelnik, Kantner, & Ford, 1981; Zelnik & Shah, 1983). In a study of 1,880 fifteen- to nineteen-year-old males, the average sexually active boy had had sexual relationships with two girls at different times during the previous year, each one lasting a few months (Sonenstein, Pleck, & Ku, 1991).

A national longitudinal survey of 11,725 white, African American, and Hispanic adolescents showed more ethnic variation in average age of first intercourse among boys than among girls (R. D. Day, 1992). Girls in all ethnic groups typically had their sexual initiation around age 17. African American boys became sexually active the earliest—at about 14. White, Mexican, and Mexican American boys began having intercourse at 16, but Cuban and Puerto Rican boys started at 15. Still, differences in sexual activity based on gender, race, religion, and socioeconomic status have narrowed considerably (AGI, 1994).

The wave of sexual liberation may be ebbing. After a steady rise since the 1970s, two government surveys found a decline between 1990 and 1995 in the proportion of 15- to 19-year-olds who report being sexually active. Among girls, the percentage who have had intercourse dropped from 55 to 50 percent (Abma et al., 1997), and among never-married boys, from 60 to 55 percent ("Teen Sex Down," 1997).

The sexual evolution has brought more acceptance of homosexuality. In 1995, 31 percent of 240,082 college freshmen in a major survey said homosexual relations should be prohibited, down from 53 percent in 1987 (Sax, Astin, Korn, & Mahoney, 1996). Still, teenagers who openly identify themselves as gay or lesbian often feel isolated in a hostile environment and may be subject to prejudice and even violence. In high school they generally keep their sexual activity private, do not discuss their sexuality, and may become depressed or suicidal (C. J. Patterson, 1995b).

CHECKPOINT

Can you . . .

- Describe trends in sexual attitudes and activity among teenage boys and girls?

Table 16-4	Factors Associated with Timing of First Intercourse	
	Factors Associated with Early Age	**Factors Associated with Later Age**
Timing of puberty	Early	Late
Personality style and behavior	Risk taking, impulsive	Traditional values, religious orientation
	Depressive symptoms	Prosocial or conventional behavior
	Antisocial or delinquent	
Substance use	Use of drugs, alcohol, tobacco	Nonuse
Education	Fewer years of schooling	More years of schooling; valuing academic achievement
Family structure	Single-parent family	Two-parent family
Socioeconomic status	Disadvantaged	Advantaged
Race	African American	White, Latino

Source: B. C. Miller & Moore, 1990; Sonenstein et al., 1991.

Sexual Risk Taking

Some patterns of sexual behavior are especially risky. Most in danger are young people who start sexual activity early, who have multiple partners, and who do not use contraceptives, or use them improperly.

Two major concerns about early sexual activity are the risks of sexually transmitted disease (see Chapter 14) and of pregnancy. Delinquency may also be a danger. In a survey of 1,167 mostly white, Catholic, middle-class, suburban high school sophomores and juniors, those who began sexual activity earliest, and engaged in it frequently, were more likely to show antisocial behavior than those who abstained. The sexually active group may have been less mature than those who waited to engage in sex, or they may have been steered toward both sexual activity and delinquency by rebellion against authority and by the influence of antisocial peers. They were also more likely to be depressed, to have alcohol problems, and to have low grades (Tubman, Windle, & Windle, 1996).

Let's look at some factors in sexual risk taking. In the next section and in Box 16-1, we focus on the problem of teenage pregnancy.

Early Sexual Activity

Teenage girls (and, to a lesser extent, boys) often feel under pressure to engage in activities they do not feel ready for. Social pressure was the chief reason given by 73 percent of the girls and 50 percent of the boys in a Harris poll when asked why many teenagers do not wait to engage in sex until they are older. Both boys and girls also mentioned curiosity as a reason for early sexual intimacy. More boys than girls cited sexual feelings and desires. Only 6 percent of the boys and 11 percent of the girls gave love as a reason (Louis Harris & Associates, 1986). Often, girls who begin having sexual relations early are coerced into it by an older man (AGI, 1994; Children's Defense Fund, 1997a); 16 percent of women ages 15 to 44 whose first intercourse took place before age 16, and 22 percent of those whose first experience was before age 15, report that it was not voluntary (Abma et al., 1997).

Various factors—including timing of puberty, personality style, drug use, education, family structure, socioeconomic status, age, ethnicity, and gender—influence the likelihood of early sexual activity (see Table 16-4). In general, girls are more influenced by such psychological factors as self-esteem, religiosity, desire for a career, and perceived control of their lives, whereas boys are more affected by factors having to do with family and community, such as the presence of a father in the home, the father's educational level, and living in a rural or urban setting. Rural teens are more likely to have intercourse, and among younger (but not older) adolescents, those with lower self-esteem and less autonomy are more likely to do so (R. D. Day, 1992).

Girls who move frequently are more likely to engage in premarital sex (Stack, 1994). These girls may use sexuality to overcome loneliness. Their bonds with family and community may be weakened: they may be less closely supervised by parents, they may be removed from extended family, and they may have come to regard relationships as casual and temporary.

Use of Contraceptives

The best safeguard for sexually active teens is regular use of condoms, which gives some protection against sexually transmitted disease as well as against pregnancy. Most sexually active adolescents do take precautions. About two-thirds use some kind of protection, usually a condom, the first time they engage in sex, and between 72 percent and 84 percent of teenage girls use contraceptives regularly (AGI, 1994). Condom use has increased dramatically in recent years, probably due to educational campaigns aimed at preventing AIDS. More than half (54 percent) of girls and women who first had intercourse between 1990 and 1995 report that their partners used condoms, as compared with only 18 percent of those whose first sexual experience was before 1980 (Abma et al., 1997).

Adolescents who do not use contraceptives, or who use them irregularly or ineffectively, tend to be in their early teens. They tend to have low educational and career aspirations, to be uninvolved in sports or other activities, and to use alcohol or drugs. They are relatively inexperienced with sex, ignorant about it, and ashamed of engaging in it, and typically they are not in committed relationships. African American and Latina girls, girls who live with a single parent, girls from impoverished families, and girls whose parents are relatively uneducated tend to use no birth control or to use less effective methods (AGI, 1994; Louis Harris & Associates, 1986; Luster & Small, 1994; B. C. Miller & Moore, 1990).

Many teenagers with multiple sex partners do not use reliable protection (Luster & Small, 1994). Nationally, among high school seniors, 38.5 percent of all boys and 17 percent of girls have had four or more sex partners. Teenagers in this high-risk group tend to have low grades, to be frequent drinkers, and to have little parental supervision or support; they are more likely to have been abused by parents than teenagers who abstain from sex or use contraceptives responsibly (Luster & Small, 1994).

Where Do Teenagers Get Information About Sex?

Recent declines in sexual activity and in the teenage pregnancy and birth rates (discussed in the next section) have gone hand in hand with an increase in adolescents' knowledge about sexual matters. About 96 percent of 18- to 19-year-olds (as compared with only 80 percent of 25- to 29-year-olds and 65 percent of 35- to 39-year-olds) report having had formal sex instruction, usually covering birth control methods, sexually transmitted diseases, safe sex to prevent HIV infection, and how to say no to sex (Abma et al., 1997). This is important because teenagers, especially girls, who are knowledgeable about sex are more likely to use contraceptives and to use them consistently (Louis Harris & Associates, 1986; Luster & Small, 1994). They are also more likely to postpone sexual intimacy—the most effective means of birth control (Conger, 1988; Jaslow, 1982). Teenagers who can go to their parents or other adults with questions about sex and those who get sex education from school or community programs have a better chance of avoiding pregnancy and other risks connected with sexual activity (see Box 16-1).

Box 16-1   Preventing Teenage Pregnancy

Teenage pregnancy rates in the United States are many times higher than in most Western European industrialized countries where adolescents begin sexual activity just as early or earlier (Children's Defense Fund, 1997a; E. F. Jones et al., 1985). Although many people believe that welfare programs encourage pregnancy, industrial countries that have been more generous than the United States in their support of poor mothers have much lower teenage pregnancy rates.

In 1996, the White House announced a National Campaign to Prevent Teen Pregnancy, with a stated goal of cutting the teenage pregnancy rate by one-third by 2005. The campaign will study a wide range of possible causes of teenage pregnancy and will evaluate several types of prevention programs.

Experts disagree about the causes of teenage pregnancy. Some observers point to such factors as the reduced stigma on unwed motherhood, media glorification of sex, the lack of a clear message that sex and parenthood are for adults, the influence of childhood sexual abuse, and failure of parents to communicate with children. However, the European experience suggests the importance of two other factors: inadequate sex education and lack of accessible family planning services.

Europe's industrialized countries have long provided comprehensive sex education—a more recent development in the United States. Realistic programs to prevent early pregnancy encourage young teenagers to delay intercourse but also aim to improve contraceptive use among adolescents who are sexually active. Such programs include education about sexuality and acquisition of skills for responsible sexual decision making and communication with partners. They provide information about risks and consequences of teenage pregnancy, about birth control methods, and about where to get medical and contraceptive help (AGI, 1994; I. C. Stewart, 1994).

Contrary to some critics, community- and school-based sex education does not lead to more sexual activity (Eisen & Zellman,

1987). The content of sex education programs has become a political issue. The 1996 federal welfare reform law funded a massive, state-administered sex education program, to begin in 1998. The program is to stress abstinence only, with no authorization for teaching about contraception. Some experts fear that this program may actually increase teenage pregnancy by failing to teach sexually active young people how to prevent it (Children's Defense Fund, 1997a).

Of course, parents are young people's first and often best teachers. Teenagers whose parents have talked with them about sex from an early age, have communicated healthy attitudes, and have been available to answer questions tend to wait longer for sexual activity (J. J. Conger, 1988; Jaslow, 1982). However, many adolescents are uncomfortable talking about sex with parents. Programs that include peer counseling can be effective; teenagers often heed peers when they might not pay attention to the same advice from an older person (Jay, DuRant, Shoffitt, Linder, & Litt, 1984).

Community programs can help young people stand up against peer pressure to be more sexually active than they want to be and can teach them how to say no gracefully (Howard, 1983). The two arguments for delaying sex that teenagers find most convincing are the risk of STDs and the danger that pregnancy will ruin their lives (Louis Harris & Associates, 1986). The media should present sexual situations responsibly and should permit advertising of contraceptives (AAP Committee on Communications, 1995).

Another important factor in preventing pregnancy is access to reproductive services. Contraceptives are provided free to adolescents in Britain, France, Sweden, and, in many cases, the Netherlands. In Sweden, parents cannot be told that their children have sought contraceptives if the teenagers request privacy. When similar programs are proposed in the United States, they generally

(continued)

The media also exert a powerful influence on adolescents' sexual attitudes and behavior. Unfortunately, that influence is negative. The media present a distorted view of sexual activity. It is often associated with fun, excitement, danger, or violence, but the risks of unprotected sexual relations are seldom shown (American Academy of Pediatrics [AAP] Committee on Communications, 1995).

Not surprisingly, then, adolescents who get their information about sex from television and who lack well-formed value systems, critical viewing skills, and strong family influence may accept the idea of premarital and extramarital intercourse with multiple partners and without protection against pregnancy and disease. Furthermore, television tends to reinforce a stereotypical double standard, in which women, but not men, consider marriage important. Movies and rock music lyrics have become more and more sexually explicit; music videos are full of sexual images and violence against women (AAP Committee on Communications, 1995).

In ironic contrast to the blatantly irresponsible portrayals of sexuality in television programming, network executives have almost universally refused to show contraceptive advertisements, claiming that they would be controversial and offensive and might encourage sexual activity. However, there is no are not adopted for fear that they might seem to endorse sexual activity among teenagers. U.S. teenagers say that making birth control services free, readily accessible (close to schools), and confidential are the three most effective ways to encourage contraception (Louis Harris & Associates, 1986; Zabin & Clark, 1983). Many say they would not go to a clinic that insisted on notifying their parents or obtaining parental consent (Jaslow, 1982).

In the long run, preventing teenage pregnancy requires attention to underlying factors that put teenagers and families at risk: reducing poverty, school failure, and family problems, and expanding employment and social and recreational opportunities (AGI, 1994; Children's Defense Fund, 1995, 1996, 1997a, 1997b). The Perry Preschool Project (discussed in this chapter) has shown how a comprehensive, long-term approach could reduce pregnancy rates among its former participants (Schweinhart, Barnes, & Weikart, 1993).

Adolescents who have high aspirations for the future are less likely to become pregnant. Programs that focus on motivating young people to achieve and raising their self-esteem, rather than merely on the mechanics of contraception, have achieved some success (Carrera, 1986).

One promising program, Teen Outreach, has grown dramatically within the past decade; by the 1994–1995 school year, it was offered in 45 schools in 13 states. At 25 randomly assigned sites where the program was given between 1991 and 1995, rates of teenage pregnancy, school failure, and suspension were less than half the rates in a control group (J. P. Allen, Philliber, Herrling, & Kuperminc, 1997). Teen Outreach does not explicitly focus on these problem behaviors; instead, it seeks to help teenagers make decisions, handle emotions, and deal with peers and adults. The program includes volunteer community service linked to classroom discussions of future life decisions. By allowing students to select their volunteer activity, the program helps them see themselves as autonomous and competent. This is further evidence that teenage pregnancy and school failure are not isolated problems but are part of a larger developmental picture.

IT'S LIKE BEING GROUNDED FOR EIGHTEEN YEARS.

Having a baby when you're a teenager can do more than just take away your freedom, it can take away your dreams.

THE CHILDREN'S DEFENSE FUND

To teenagers, one of the most persuasive arguments against sexual risk-taking is the danger that pregnancy will ruin their lives. Teenage girls respond better when the advice comes from other girls close to their own age.

evidence for the latter claim, and trial advertisements in limited markets have brought mostly commendations instead of complaints (AAP Committee on Communications, 1995).

Teenage Pregnancy and Childbearing

In the United States, about 1 in 10 girls age 15 to 19—about 1 million girls—become pregnant each year, and 4 out of 5 of these pregnancies are unplanned (Children's Defense Fund, 1996, 1997a; Ventura, Taffel, Mosher, Wilson, & Henshaw, 1995). The younger a girl is when becoming sexually active, the less likely she is to use contraception at first intercourse (Abma et al., 1997), the longer she is likely to wait before seeking help with contraception, and the more likely she is to become pregnant (Tanfer & Horn, 1985). Low-income girls and those who do not do well in school are more likely to become pregnant than those who are more affluent or are academic achievers (Children's Defense Fund, 1997a). Most fathers of babies born to teenage mothers are no longer teenagers themselves, and the younger the girl, the greater the age difference tends to be. Nearly one-third of the fathers of babies born to 15-year-old girls are 21 or older (AGI, 1994).

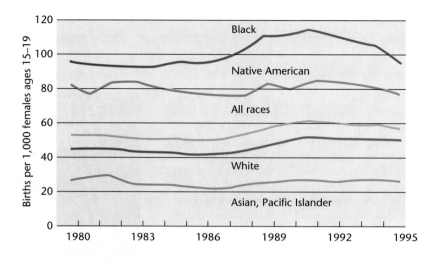

Figure 16-2
Trends in teenage birth rates by race of mother, 1980–1995. The birth rate among black teenagers has fallen much farther than teenage birth rates for other ethnic groups, but still remains much higher.

Source: Children's Defense Fund, 1997b; data from National Center for Health Statistics.

About half of pregnant teenagers have their babies and plan to raise them themselves; very few place their children for adoption. About one-third have abortions, and one-seventh miscarry (AGI, 1994; Children's Defense Fund, 1997a).

Teenage pregnancy and birth rates have declined during the 1990s, probably reflecting the decline in sexual activity and the increase in use of contraceptives due in part to fear of AIDS (Children's Defense Fund, 1995, 1996, 1997a, 1997b; "Preventing Teenage Pregnancy," 1996; "Teen Sex Down," 1997). The teenage birth rate has dropped steadily since its high point in 1991, from about 62 births per 1,000 to fewer than 57 in 1995, a modest reversal of the sharp increase of 5 percent or more each year during the late 1980s (Children's Defense Fund, 1997a, 1997b; National Center for Health Statistics [NCHS], 1995; Rosenberg, Ventura, Maurer, Heuser, & Freedman, 1996).

However, a greater proportion of these births than in the past—about 3 out of 4—are to unmarried mothers. As the overall teenage birth rate has fallen, the birth rate for unwed teens has risen. In 1995, the birth rate for unmarried teens was 3 times as high as in 1960—when girls tended to marry younger—though the overall teenage birth rate was one-third lower. Still, the 1995 rate—44.4 births per 1,000 unmarried teenagers—did represent a 4 percent drop from 1994 (Children's Defense Fund, 1997a, 1997b).

The decline in the birth rate during the early 1990s was almost entirely among black teenagers, but black girls—who are more likely to be poor and to do poorly in school—are still twice as likely to have babies as white girls (Children's Defense Fund, 1997a, 1997b; see Figure 16-2). More than 8 out of 10 adolescent mothers are from low-income families (AGI, 1994); pregnant girls from advantaged families are more likely to have abortions.

Helping Pregnant Teenagers Adjust to Parenthood

An unmarried pregnant teenager is especially vulnerable to emotional upheaval. However she handles her pregnancy, she is likely to have conflicting feelings. Just when she needs the most emotional support, she may get the least: her boyfriend may be frightened by the responsibility and turn away, her family may be angry, and she may be isolated from her school friends. If a young mother and her baby need additional support, an interested, sympathetic, and knowledgeable counselor may be of great help.

Expectant and new mothers need to learn parenting skills. In one program, 80 low-income teenage mothers learned such skills either from biweekly home visits by a graduate student and a teenage aide or through paid training as teachers' aides in the nursery of a medical school. The infants of trained mothers

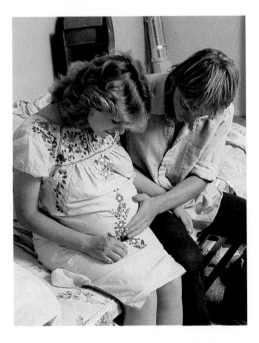

Among the frequent consequences of teenage parenthood are medical complications for mother and baby and social problems for adolescents who must assume the responsibilities of parenthood before they are mature enough to handle them. Expectant teenage parents, like this 14-year-old prospective mother and her 18-year-old husband, have many difficult issues to deal with, not the least of which is the emotional unheaval caused by this momentous—and usually unplanned—change in their lives.

developed better than babies of untrained mothers. They weighed more, displayed more advanced motor skills, and interacted better with their mothers. The mothers who worked as teachers' aides and their children showed the most gains: more mothers returned to work or school, fewer became pregnant again, and their babies made the most progress (T. M. Field, Widmayer, Greenberg, & Stoller, 1982).

The mother usually bears the major impact of teenage parenthood, but a young father's life is often affected as well. A boy who feels committed to the girl he has impregnated has decisions to make. At a time when his financial resources may be meager and his prospects uncertain, he may pay for an abortion or become obligated to continuing child support; or he may marry the girl, a move that may drastically affect his educational and career plans. The father, too, needs someone to talk to, to help him sort out his own feelings so that he and the mother can make the best decisions for themselves and their child.

Teenage Parenthood: Problems and Outcomes

Teenage pregnancies often have poor outcomes. Many of the mothers are impoverished and poorly educated, do not eat properly, and get inadequate prenatal care or none at all; and their babies are likely to be dangerously small. Nearly 1 out of 10 babies born to 15- to 19-year-olds, and more than 1 out of 8 born to black mothers in that age group, have low birthweight (S. S. Brown, 1985; Children's Defense Fund, 1995, 1997a). Babies of more affluent teenage mothers are also at risk. Among more than 134,000 white, largely middle-class girls and women in Utah who had their first babies between 1970 and 1990, 13- to 19-year-olds were more likely than 20- to 24-year-olds to have low-birthweight babies, even when the mothers were married and well-educated and had adequate prenatal care. Thirteen- to 17-year-old girls were nearly twice as likely to have premature deliveries as older teenage mothers. Although prenatal care is a factor in prematurity, good prenatal care apparently cannot overcome the biological disadvantage inherent in being born to a still-growing girl whose own body may be competing with the developing fetus for vital nutrients (A. M. Fraser, Brockert, & Ward, 1995).

Birth complications are just the beginning of the problems likely to beset a teenage mother and her child. Adolescent mothers are 3 times as likely to drop out of high school as agemates who do not have babies until their twenties (Children's Defense Fund, 1995). However, many do finish later on. In one large study, 5 years after giving birth, only half of urban black adolescent mothers had graduated from high school; but 10 years later, two-thirds had graduated (Furstenberg, Brooks-Gunn, & Morgan, 1987).

Teenage mothers and their families are likely to suffer financial hardship. About one-fourth of women in their twenties and thirties who became mothers in adolescence are poor. Most of them were poor before becoming mothers and probably would have remained poor even without having had a baby. Still, early childbearing does restrict opportunity (AGI, 1994). Also, teenage mothers are at high risk of repeat pregnancies; the risk is greatest for those who drop out of school and do not use reliable birth control (McAnarney & Hendee, 1989).

Many states require fathers to pay child support at least for the first 18 years of a child's life, sometimes through payroll deductions. However, these laws are spottily enforced, and court-ordered payments are often inadequate. Even though paternity can be clearly established through biological testing, many men assume little or no responsibility for their children. In the past, many teenage mothers went on public assistance, but under the 1996 federal welfare reform law such assistance is severely limited. Unmarried parents under age 18 are now eligible only if they live with their parents and go to school.

The children of teenage mothers are more likely than children born to older mothers to be sickly, to grow up fatherless, to be abused and neglected, to spend time in foster care, to run away from home, to have academic problems, to be unproductive workers, to go to prison, and to become teenage parents themselves (Children's Defense Fund, 1997a). However, these outcomes are far from universal. A 20-year study of more than 400 teenage mothers in Baltimore found that two-thirds of their daughters did not become teenage mothers themselves, and most graduated from high school (Furstenberg, Levine, & Brooks-Gunn, 1990).

What factors affect the way children of teenage mothers develop? In one follow-up study of disadvantaged teenage mothers enrolled at an adolescent health center in New York City, 13 percent of the children at 28 to 36 months of age had behavior problems severe enough to need clinical treatment, according to a checklist filled out by the mothers. These were most likely to be African American boys whose mothers had shown symptoms of depression or had experienced stressful events during the first year after giving birth. Problems were less likely if the mothers received emotional support from friends or family, and particularly if they were living with their grandmothers, who may have been more supportive than their own mothers (Leadbeater & Bishop, 1994).

Living with Grandma: Pros and Cons

For practical reasons, many teenage mothers—particularly poor, single African American girls—live with their mothers. This living arrangement can have both benefits and drawbacks. On the positive side, the young mothers are more likely to stay in school (Chase-Lansdale, Brooks-Gunn, & Zamsky, 1994; Unger & Cooley, 1992). Low-birthweight infants tend to do better when mother and baby live with the infant's grandmother, who can help with caregiving (S. K. Pope et al., 1993). Early studies found beneficial effects on children's social and emotional health when they lived with both mother and grandmother. But a later study found that infants are most likely to form secure attachments when the mother lives with a partner while the grandmother plays a more traditional, supportive role (Spieker & Bensley, 1994).

Positive effects of living with a grandmother lessen, and may even be reversed, when the arrangement continues for a long time. For example, babies living in three-generation households had more favorable home environments, as measured by the HOME scale (see Chapter 6), than babies living only with a single mother, though no more so than babies whose mothers lived with a partner

(Spieker & Bensley, 1994). Yet, in a longitudinal study of 338 teenage mothers, those who still lived with their own mothers several years after giving birth tended to provide a *lower* quality home environment than mothers who were on their own or lived with a husband or partner. In white families, especially, the children tended to have behavior problems and to perform poorly on cognitive tests (Unger & Cooley, 1992).

Teenage mothers living with their own mothers may maintain their adolescent roles and may not develop parenting skills, or may resent their mothers' interference. Conversely, the grandmothers, unless their daughters are in their *early* teens, may resent the daughters' lack of independence. Many of these grandmothers were teenage mothers themselves. Now they must balance midlife work and parenting responsibilities with the need to help raise grandchildren. Economic hardship may increase strain and provoke conflict (Chase-Lansdale et al., 1994; Spieker & Bensley, 1994; Wakschlag, Chase-Lansdale, & Brooks-Gunn, 1996).

Relationships with Family, Peers, and Adult Society

The teenage years have been called a time of *adolescent rebellion,* involving emotional turmoil, conflict within the family, alienation from adult society, and hostility toward adults' values. Yet research on adolescents in the United States and other countries the world over suggests that fewer than 1 out of 5 teenagers—at least among those who remain in school—fit this pattern of tumult, alienation, and disturbance (Brooks-Gunn, 1988; Offer, 1987; Offer, Ostrov, & Howard, 1989; Offer, Ostrov, Howard, & Atkinson, 1988; Offer & Schonert-Riechl, 1992).

Adolescence does not typically bring wide emotional swings, though negative moods do increase as boys and girls move through these years (R. Larson & Lampman-Petraitis, 1989). Cross-cultural research suggests that adolescents do not show major personality shifts—they remain pretty much the people they have always been (see Box 16-2). Furthermore, although adolescents defy parental authority with some regularity, the emotions attending this transition do not normally lead to family conflict of major proportions or to a "generation gap"—a sharp break with parental or societal standards (Offer & Church, 1991; Offer et al., 1989). Even as adolescents turn to peers for companionship and intimacy, they look to parents to provide a "secure base" from which they can try their wings (Laursen, 1996).

Age does become a powerful bonding agent in adolescence—more powerful than race, religion, community, or gender. Adolescents sometimes seem to believe that most other adolescents share their values and that most older people do not. Actually, though, most teenagers' fundamental values remain closer to their parents' values than is generally realized (Offer & Church, 1991). "Adolescent rebellion" frequently amounts to little more than a series of minor skirmishes.

One reason teenagers get into trouble is their lack of skills or knowledge; they may not know how to use a condom, when to stop drinking, or when a friend is leading them into dangerous activities. They also face more new, nonroutine situations than adults generally do. Then too, their missteps may be more noticeable; they are often committed in the presence of other people and are often dealt with by parents and teachers (Quadrel, Fischoff, & Davis, 1993).

The biggest danger in assuming that adolescent turmoil is normal and necessary is that parents, teachers, community leaders, and makers of social policy may erroneously assume that teenagers will "outgrow" problems and may fail to recognize when a young person needs help. In addition to spotting individual characteristics of troubled adolescents, we need to pay attention to the influence of the environment—the family, the peer group, and the community—to find ways of reducing young people's exposure to high-risk settings (National Research Council [NRC], 1993a).

CHECKPOINT

Can you . . .

- Identify and discuss factors that increase the risks of sexual activity?
- Summarize recent trends in teenage pregnancy and birth rates?
- Discuss problems and outcomes of teenage pregnancy?
- Identify ways to prevent teenage pregnancy and to help teenage parents?

adolescent rebellion Pattern of emotional turmoil, characteristic of a minority of adolescents, which may involve conflict with family, alienation from adult society, and hostility toward adults' values.

Box 16-2 Continuity of Personality from Childhood to Adolescence

"I hardly recognize Sean any more—he's like a different person," says the mother of a teenage boy. Yet, in important ways, personality changes very little from childhood through adolescence, according to cross-cultural research.

Studies of children in New Zealand (Caspi & Silva, 1995), the Netherlands (van Lieshout, Haselager, Riksen-Walraven, & van Aken, 1995), and Iceland (D. Hart, Hofmann, Edelstein, & Keller, 1997), as well as of inner-city African American and white children in the United States (Robins, John, Caspi, Moffitt, & Stouthamer-Loeber, 1996), have identified three basic personality types: *resilient, overcontrolled,* and *undercontrolled.* Children of these three types differ in *ego-resiliency,* or adaptability, and *ego-control,* or self-control.

Resilient (well-adjusted) children are self-confident, independent, articulate, attentive, helpful, cooperative, and task-focused; they tend to do better in school than the other two groups. *Overcontrolled* (inhibited) children are shy, quiet, anxious, and dependable; they tend to keep their thoughts to themselves and to withdraw from conflict, and they are the most subject to depression. *Undercontrolled* children are active, energetic, impulsive, stubborn, and easily distracted; they are the most likely to have behavior problems in school and to become delinquent.

In the New Zealand study, personality types at age 3, as rated by observers, showed predictable relationships to self-reported personality characteristics at age 19 (Caspi & Silva, 1995). For example, adolescents who had been identified as inhibited preschoolers reported a tendency to avoid risk, whereas those who had been identified as undercontrolled were most likely to describe themselves as aggressive, alienated, and unhappy.

In a longitudinal study of a socioeconomically diverse group of 168 seven-year-olds in urban and rural Iceland (D. Hart et al.,

1997), intensive interviews were used to determine personality type through a Q-sort technique (see Chapter 7). Children identified as resilient tended to have higher IQs than the other two groups and were more likely to have been rated by teachers as "very well-developed" at school entry.

From childhood through age 15, the resilient children had much higher school grades than the other two groups, and teachers consistently rated them as having fewer concentration problems. In terms of social cognition (understanding of social relationships and situations), their development was more rapid and more advanced. Apparently because of their ability to adapt and succeed, they were more likely to see themselves, rather than external forces, as controlling their lives. And, perhaps because they were better able to enter into and learn from positive peer relationships, they had a more sophisticated understanding of friendship, according to Selman's (1980) model (see Chapter 13).

By contrast, overcontrolled children were more withdrawn and had lower self-esteem than the other two groups. Undercontrolled children were more aggressive—increasingly so during late childhood and adolescence. Yet their self-esteem was higher than that of the resilient children, suggesting that they did not see themselves as others saw them.

Of course, this finding of a tendency toward continuity of attitudes and behavior does not mean that personalities never change, or that certain children are condemned to a life of maladjustment. Undercontrolled children may get along better in late adolescence and early adulthood if they find niches in which their energy and spontaneity are considered a plus rather than a minus. Overcontrolled children may "come out of their shell" somewhat if they find that their quiet dependability is valued.

How Adolescents Spend Their Time—and with Whom

What do teenagers do on a typical day? With whom do they do it, and how do they feel about what they are doing? To answer these questions, 75 high school students in a suburb of Chicago carried beepers that rang at random once in every 2 waking hours for 1 week. Each student was asked to report what she or he was doing when the beeper sounded, and where and with whom. From the 4,489 self-reports, the researchers put together a picture of the everyday life of a teenager (Csikszentmihalyi & Larson, 1984).

These adolescents spent more than half their waking hours with peers: 29 percent with friends and 23 percent with classmates. They spent only 5 percent of their time alone with one or both parents and 8 percent with parents and siblings together. They felt happiest when with friends—free, open, involved, excited, and motivated. They had more fun with friends—joking, gossiping, and fooling around—than at home, where the atmosphere tended to be more serious and humdrum. Friends were the people they most wanted to be with. Being with the family ranked second; next came being alone; and last, being with classmates.

Age is a powerful bond for adolescents—more so than race, religion, community, or gender. But while adolescents look to peers for companionship and intimacy, their fundamental values seldom depart much from those they were raised with.

According to sequential research with 220 white middle- and working-class suburban youngsters, using this "beeper" method, the amount of time young people spend with their families declines dramatically between ages 10 and 18, from 35 percent to 14 percent of waking hours (R. W. Larson, Richards, Moneta, Holmbeck, & Duckett, 1996). This disengagement from family life is not a rejection of the family, but a response to the "pull" of developmental needs. Early adolescents often retreat to their rooms; they seem to need time alone to step back from the demands of social relationships, regain emotional stability, and reflect on identity issues (R. W. Larson, 1997). High schoolers spend more of their free time with peers, with whom they identify and feel comfortable (R. Larson & Richards, 1991).

The character of family interactions changes during these years. The time adolescents do spend with their families tends to be "quality time": they may spend less time than before watching television together, but just as much—and among girls, more—in one-to-one conversations with parents. As adolescents grow older, they increasingly see themselves as taking the lead in these discussions, and their feelings about contact with parents become more positive (R. W. Larson et al., 1996).

Another study of 121 rural New England high school students (average age, 17) considered not only how much time teenagers spent with the important people in their lives, but the kinds of things they did together and how much influence these people had. By these three criteria, the students were closest to romantic partners, followed by friends and mothers, then by fathers, and finally by siblings. Parents' influence remained high even as contact dropped (Laursen, 1996).

African American teenagers maintain more intimate family relationships and less intense peer relations than white teenagers, according to interviews with a representative cross section of 942 adolescents in Toledo, Ohio. Black teenagers also tend to be more flexible in their choice of friends and less dependent on peer approval. Black adolescents may look upon their families as havens in a hostile world and thus may be less likely to distance themselves from parents (Giordano, Cernkovich, & DeMaris, 1993).

In a cross-cultural study, researchers asked a representative sample of eleventh-graders in Minneapolis how they spent their time at and after school. The investigators then compared the results with similar interviews of teenagers in Taiwanese and Japanese cities (Fuligni & Stevenson, 1995). The American students spent much more time socializing with friends, whereas the Chinese and Japanese students spent more time in school, in studying, and in reading for pleasure. Not surprisingly, the Asian teens were better academic performers than the Americans, as measured by math achievement tests. Also, young people in the three cultures did different kinds of things with friends. American students were more likely to go to parties, dances, movies, concerts, or sporting events or to engage in athletics or watch television together; Chinese and Japanese students spent more time studying with friends or just "hanging out."

Keeping such cultural differences in mind, let's look more closely at relationships with parents, siblings, and peers.

The Adolescent in the Family

The idea that parents and teenagers do not get along may have been born in the first formal theory of adolescence, that of the psychologist G. Stanley Hall. Hall (1904/1916) believed that young people's efforts to adjust to their changing bodies and to the imminent demands of adulthood usher in a period of "storm and stress," which inevitably leads to conflict between the generations. Sigmund Freud (1935/1953) and his daughter, Anna Freud (1946), also described parent-child friction as inevitable, growing out of adolescents' need to free themselves from dependency on their parents. However, the anthropologist Margaret Mead (1928, 1935), who studied adolescence in nonwestern cultures, concluded that when a culture provides a gradual, serene transition from childhood to adulthood, adolescent rebellion is not typical.

It now appears that full-fledged rebellion is uncommon even in western societies, at least among middle-class youngsters who are in school, and that teenagers who are very rebellious may well need special help. In his classic studies of midwestern American boys, Daniel Offer (1969) found a high level of bickering over unimportant issues between 12- and 14-year-olds and their parents, but little turmoil. A follow-up study (Offer & Offer, 1974) found that most of the participants—now out of their teens—were happy, had a realistic self-image, and were reasonably well-adjusted. Less than one-fifth had experienced a tumultuous adolescence. More recent research has found that most young people feel close to and positive about their parents, share similar opinions on major issues, and value their parents' approval (J. P. Hill, 1987; Offer et al., 1988; Offer et al., 1989). Only 15 to 25 percent of families report significant conflict, and these families often had problems before the children approached adolescence (W. A. Collins, 1990; J. P. Hill, 1987; Offer et al., 1989).

Some conflict between teenagers and parents is normal, of course. Let's look at its levels and sources, what forms it takes, and what kind of parenting is most effective. We'll also look at the impact of mothers' employment, divorce and single parenting, and economic stress. Then we'll consider adolescents' relationships with siblings.

Patterns of Family Conflict: Influences of Age and Ethnicity

Just as adolescents feel tension between dependency on their parents and the need to break away, parents often have mixed feelings too. They want their children to be independent, yet they find it hard to let go. Parents have to walk a fine line between giving adolescents enough independence and protecting them from immature lapses in judgment.

Many arguments between teenagers and their parents focus on "how much" or "how soon": how much freedom teenagers should have to plan their own activities or how soon they can take the family car. Parents and teenagers rarely clash over economic, religious, social, or political values or even about sexual activity and drug use. Most arguments concern day-to-day matters: chores, family relations, schoolwork, dress, money, curfews, and friends (B. K. Barber, 1994).

Subjects of conflict are similar in married and divorced families (Smetana, Yau, Restrepo, & Braeges, 1991) and across ethnic lines. However, white parents report more frequent clashes with teenagers than black or Hispanic parents, who tend to enforce higher behavioral expectations as a means of survival in the majority culture (B. K. Barber, 1994). Working-class Chinese adolescents in Hong Kong, whose culture stresses family obligations and harmony, report fewer conflicts with parents than European American adolescents (Yau & Smetana, 1996).

Family conflict generally rises during early adolescence, stabilizes in middle adolescence, and then decreases in late adolescence. The increased strife in early adolescence may be related to the strains of puberty and the need to assert autonomy. The calmer climate in late adolescence may signify adjustment to the momentous changes of the teenage years and a renegotiation of the balance of power between parent and child (Fuligni & Eccles, 1993; Molina & Chassin, 1996; Steinberg, 1988).

This pattern, too, has ethnic variations. Mexican-American boys, unlike non-Hispanic white boys, tend to become closer to their parents during puberty. This may reflect the unusually close-knit nature of Mexican-American families and their greater adaptability to change. Or—since this ethnic difference does not exist among girls—it may reflect the importance Hispanic families place on the traditional male role (Molina & Chassin, 1996).

In African American families in the rural South, religiosity influences the levels of family cohesion and conflict during preadolescence and early adolescence. Highly religious parents tend to get along better with each other and with their children, and the children are less likely to become either overly aggressive or depressed (G. H. Brody, Stoneman, & Flor, 1996).

Asian American youngsters experience more family conflict during late adolescence than during early adolescence, and their perceptions of their parents' warmth and understanding do not seem to improve as much as in European American families. This may be because Asian cultures stress control of emotions and expectations for respect and obedience. By college age, when many European American young people have already renegotiated their relationships with parents, Asian American parents and adolescents are struggling over control of the young person's friends, activities, and private life (Greenberger & Chen, 1996). Conflict in both cultures is more likely with mothers than with fathers (Greenberger & Chen, 1996; Steinberg, 1981, 1987), perhaps because most mothers have been more closely involved with their children and may be more ambivalent about giving up that involvement.

Family Conflict, Family Atmosphere, and Parenting Styles

Regardless of ethnicity, the level of family discord seems to hinge primarily on teenagers' personalities and on their parents' treatment of them. These factors may explain why disagreements in some families tend to blow over, whereas in other families they escalate into major confrontations. Dissension is most likely when parents see a teenager as having negative personality characteristics (such as a hot temper, meanness, or anxiety) and a history of problem behavior, and when parents use coercive discipline (B. K. Barber, 1994). Among 335 two-parent rural midwestern families with teenagers, conflict declined in warm, supportive families during early to middle adolescence but worsened in a hostile, coercive, or critical family atmosphere (Rueter & Conger, 1995). Parents who are not getting along with each other tend to be more hostile toward an adolescent child, and their children tend to become more hostile, anxious, or depressed (Harold & Conger, 1997).

In looking at teenagers' adjustment, then, we need to consider the emotional "fit" between the adolescent and the family. Young people may react to a negative family atmosphere by distancing themselves emotionally from the parents; and this can be an effective adaptive strategy, according to a study of 96 white

The warmth and acceptance this mother shows to her son are characteristic of an authoritative parenting style. Authoritative parents set reasonable rules about, for example, what time a child must come home, but are willing to listen to and respect the child's point of view. Authoritative parenting may be especially effective as children enter adolescence and want to be treated more like adults.

and African American 10- to 18-year-olds from two-parent, single-parent, and stepfamilies. When the family atmosphere was stressful and conflict-ridden, youngsters who were emotionally independent of their parents tended to be relatively well-adjusted. However, emotional distance did not indicate good adjustment when mothers were warm and supportive and when conflict levels were low (Fuhrman & Holmbeck, 1995).

Warmth and acceptance are characteristic of an authoritative parenting style. Although adolescents need to be treated differently from younger children, authoritative parenting still works best. Authoritative parents insist on important rules, norms, and values, but are willing to listen, explain, and negotiate. They encourage teenagers to form their own opinions (Lamborn, Mounts, Steinberg, & Dornbusch, 1991). They exercise appropriate control over the child's conduct but not over the child's sense of self (Steinberg & Darling, 1994).

Overly strict, authoritarian parenting may be counterproductive, especially as children enter adolescence and feel a need to be treated more as adults. When parents do not adjust to this need, their children may reject parental influence and seek peer support and approval at all costs. Among 1,771 predominantly white, middle-class sixth- and seventh-graders, those who saw their parents as giving them little opportunity to be involved in decisions affecting them were apt to do virtually anything to gain popularity with peers, even if it meant breaking family rules and neglecting schoolwork and their own talents. This was not true of students whose parents simply monitored their activities. Apparently it is power assertion, not appropriate supervision, that evokes negative reactions (Fuligni & Eccles, 1993).

As we discussed in Chapter 10, inductive discipline, which encourages young children to think about the effect of their actions on others, promotes prosocial behavior. This is true of 12-year-olds as well. Apparently, inductive techniques foster the development of empathy, whereas power assertion tends to focus young people's concern on themselves and leads to less prosocial behavior. Parents who express disappointment are more effective in motivating young people to behave more responsibly than parents who punish them harshly (Krevans & Gibbs, 1996).

Effects of Parents' Life Situation

Many adolescents today live in families that are very different from families of a few decades ago. Most mothers, like Jackie Robinson's, work outside the home, and teenagers often care for themselves after school. Many youngsters, like Robinson, live with single parents or stepparents. Many families, like Robinson's, must cope with severe economic stress.

How do these family situations affect adolescents? A combination of factors may be involved. The impact of a mother's employment, for example, may depend upon whether there are two parents or only one in the home. Often a single mother must work to stave off economic disaster; how her working affects her teenage children may hinge on how much time and energy she has left over to spend with them and what sort of role model she provides. These factors, in turn, may be influenced by others: what kind of work she does, how many hours she works, how much she earns, and how much she likes her work (B. L. Barber & Eccles, 1992).

Parents' Employment Most research about how parents' work affects adolescents deals with mothers' employment. Some research has found that adolescent children of working mothers tend to be better-adjusted socially than other teenagers; they feel better about themselves, have more of a sense of belonging, and get along better with families and friends. On the negative side, they tend to spend less time on homework and leisure reading and more time watching television (Gold & Andres, 1978; Milne, Myers, Rosenthal, & Ginsburg, 1986).

Teenagers may like being freer to direct their own activities when their mothers are out of the house. However, with less supervision adolescents are more susceptible to peer pressure. A survey of 3,993 ninth-graders in six school districts in southern California, who came from a wide range of ethnic and socioeconomic backgrounds, found that students who are unsupervised after school tend to smoke, drink, use marijuana, or engage in other risky behavior; to be depressed; and to have low grades. Being unsupervised does not in itself significantly increase the risk of problems as long as parents know where their son or daughter is; the less consistently parents monitor their child's activities and the more hours the young person is unsupervised, the greater the risk. Lack of supervision seems to have the most detrimental effect on girls, who otherwise are less prone to problems than boys (J. L. Richardson, Radziszewska, Dent, & Flay, 1993).

Parents' work stress seems to affect early adolescents differently, depending on which parent is under stress. Mothers who feel overloaded with work tend to become less caring and accepting, and their children often show behavior problems. When fathers are overloaded—and especially when both parents are overworked—parent-child conflict tends to rise (Galambos, Sears, Almeida, & Kolaric, 1995).

In the 1950s, 1960s, and 1970s, when most mothers who could afford to stay home did so, adolescent sons of working women held less stereotyped attitudes about female roles than did sons of at-home mothers. Also, daughters of employed women had higher and less gender-stereotyped career aspirations, were more outgoing, scored higher on several academic measures, and seemed better-adjusted on social and personality measures (L. W. Hoffman, 1979). Today, however, a mother's work status seems to be just one of many factors that shape attitudes toward women's roles (Galambos, Petersen, & Lenerz, 1988). In fact, maternal employment in itself does not seem to affect teenagers much; whatever effect it has is filtered through other factors, such as the warmth in a relationship (Galambos et al., 1995) or a woman's satisfaction with her dual roles as mother and worker. Teenage sons of working mothers tend to have more flexible attitudes toward gender roles when they have warm relationships with their mothers, and teenage daughters show unstereotyped attitudes when their mothers are happy with their roles (Galambos et al., 1988).

Family Structure Growing up in a household with two parents is an advantage during childhood (see Chapter 13), and it continues to be an advantage during adolescence, at least in terms of avoidance of risky behaviors. An analysis of data on approximately 22,000 young people ages 12 to 17 from the 1991, 1992, and 1993 National Household Survey of Drug Abuse found that adolescents living with two biological or adoptive parents are less likely than adolescents living in other family structures to use alcohol, cigarettes, or illegal drugs, or to report problems associated with their use. This finding holds true when effects of gender, age, family income, and race or ethnicity are controlled. Living with a single father or a father and stepmother is riskier than living with a single mother or a mother and stepfather. However, the risks of living with a single mother are greater for girls than for boys. Teenagers who are married and live with a spouse, as well as those who live with a mother and a nonrelative (presumably, the mother's boyfriend) are also at high risk (R. A. Johnson, Hoffmann, & Gerstein, 1996).

Still, divorce and single parenting do not necessarily produce problem adolescents. Indeed, a review of the literature suggests that some of the detrimental effects of living in a "broken home" may have been overgeneralized (B. L. Barber & Eccles, 1992). For example, a number of studies suggest that children of divorce do worse in school than those in two-parent families. However, in younger children, the differences depend on such factors as age, gender, the type of skill tested, and the length of time since the marriage ended. In adolescents, the differences are usually minor and may be nonexistent when other factors, such as socioeconomic status and parental conflict, are held constant. Similarly, findings of lower self-esteem and differences in attitudes toward gender roles are small, inconsistent, or inconclusive. Furthermore, most of these studies are cross-sectional and thus do not show changes in the same young person before and after a divorce.

In evaluating the effects of divorce and single parenting, then, we need to look at particular circumstances. Divorce affects different children differently. Sometimes divorce can improve the situation by reducing the amount of conflict within the home. And, while the immediate effects of a marital breakup may be traumatic, in the long run some adolescents may benefit from having learned new coping skills that make them more competent and independent (B. L. Barber & Eccles, 1992).

Parental support may be more important than family structure, especially in some minority cultures. In one study of 254 urban African American adolescent boys, those living with a single mother were no more likely than those in two-parent, stepparent, or extended family households to use alcohol or drugs, to become delinquent, to drop out of school, or to have psychological problems. The only difference was a positive one: sons in single-mother households experienced more parental support than other youths. It may be that the mothers provided extra support to compensate for the fathers' absence. However, many fathers also continued to be involved in their sons' lives, and this involvement was related to positive outcomes. Almost 2 out of 3 boys not living with their fathers considered them role models. In addition, African American parents and children may be more able than white families to draw on support from extended family (M. A. Zimmerman, Salem, & Maton, 1995).

Economic Stress The major problem in many single-parent families is economic stress. Poverty can complicate family relationships and harm children's development through its impact on parents' emotional state (see Chapter 13). Such indirect effects of economic hardship may be felt by adolescents too. On the other hand, many adolescents, like Jackie Robinson, benefit from the social capital they and their families have accumulated—the support of kin and community (see Chapter 15).

One study looked at single African American mothers of seventh- and eighth-graders in a midwestern city that was experiencing widespread manufacturing layoffs. Unemployed mothers, especially those without outside help and support, tended to become depressed; and depressed mothers tended to be negative in their perception of their maternal role and punitive with their children. Young people who saw their relationships with their mothers deteriorate tended to be depressed themselves and to have trouble in school (McLoyd, Jayaratne, Ceballo, & Borquez, 1994).

Another study looked at 51 poor, urban African American families, in which teenagers were living with their mothers, grandmothers, or aunts. The women who had strong kinship networks to rely on tended to be psychologically healthy, and so were their youngsters. The more social support the women received, the greater their self-esteem and acceptance of their children. The women with stronger support exercised firmer control and closer monitoring while granting appropriate autonomy, and their teenage children were more self-reliant and had fewer behavior problems (R. D. Taylor & Roberts, 1995).

Of course, economic distress can strike two-parent families as well. Among 378 intact white families in an economically declining area of rural Iowa, financial conflicts between parents and adolescents were worsened by parental depression and marital conflict. Parents who fought with each other and with their children over money tended to be hostile and coercive, increasing the risk of teenage behavior problems (R. C. Conger, Ge, Elder, Lorenz, & Simons, 1994).

Sibling Relationships

As teenagers begin to separate from their families and spend more time with peers, they have less time and less need for the emotional gratification they used to get from the sibling bond. The decline in time spent with siblings is greater than the decline in time spent with parents (R. W. Larson et al., 1996). Adolescents are less close to siblings than to either parents or friends, are less influenced by them, and become even more distant as they move through adolescence (Laursen, 1996).

Changes in sibling relationships may well precede similar changes in the relationship between adolescents and parents: more independence on the part of the younger person and less authority exerted by the older person. As children reach high school, their relationships with their siblings become progressively more equal and more distant (Buhrmester & Furman, 1990).* Adolescents still show intimacy, affection, and admiration for their brothers and sisters, but they spend less time with them (Raffaelli & Larson, 1987), and their relationships are less intense. Older siblings exercise less power over younger ones, fight with them less, are not as close to them, and are less likely to look to them for companionship.

These changes seem to be fairly complete by the time the younger sibling is about 12 years old. By this time, the younger child no longer needs as much supervision, and differences in competence and independence between older and

---

* Unless otherwise noted, this discussion is indebted to Buhrmester and Furman, 1990.

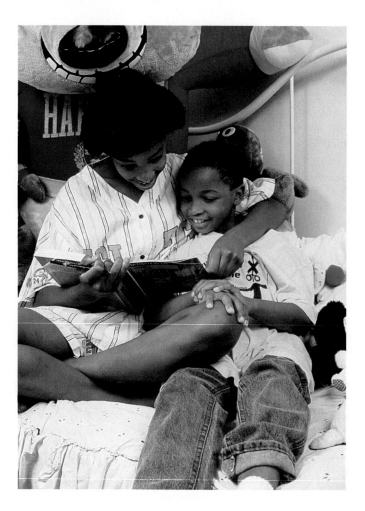

Adolescents show intimacy and affection for younger siblings, even though they spend less time together than before. Although differences in power and status lessen, younger siblings still look up to older ones.

younger siblings are shrinking. (A 6-year-old is vastly more competent than a 3-year-old, but a 15-year-old and a 12-year-old are more nearly equal.)

Older and younger siblings tend to have different feelings about their changing relationship. As the younger sibling grows up, the older one has to give up some of his or her accustomed power and status and may look on a newly assertive younger brother or sister as a pesky annoyance. On the other hand, younger siblings still tend to look up to older ones—as Jackie Robinson did to his brother Mack—and try to feel more "grown up" by identifying with and emulating them (Buhrmester & Furman, 1990). Even by age 17, younger siblings are more likely to get advice about plans and problems from older siblings, to be influenced by them, and to be satisfied with the support they receive from them. There is more advice-giving between sisters than between brothers or between a brother and sister (Tucker, Barber, & Eccles, 1997).

Siblings born farther apart tend to be more affectionate toward each other and to get along better than those who are closer in age. The quarreling and antagonism between closely spaced brothers and sisters may reflect more intense rivalry, since their capabilities are similar enough to be frequently compared—by themselves and others. Same-sex siblings are usually closer than a brother and sister.

These effects of birth order, spacing, and gender have held up across several studies. Still, these factors are less important in the quality of sibling relationships than the youngsters' ages and temperaments and how their parents treat them (Stocker, Dunn, & Plomin, 1989).

Young people are sensitive to parental favoritism. If siblings believe that parents treat them differently, their own relationship may suffer. However, this may not be true if children can see a justification for a parent's behavior. In interviews with 61 early adolescents, ages 11 to 13, and their siblings, 3 out of 4 children who recognized the existence of differential treatment did *not* find this treatment unfair. Youngsters most frequently gave five types of reasons for such treatment: (1) *disparity in age* ("My sister is older and so she gets punished more than me because my parents think she ought to know better"); (2) *personal attributes* ("My mom listens to my sister more because my sister is a very talkative person"); (3) *family alliances* ("My mom and I just get along better, so we do more things together"); (4) *individual needs* ("My brother has really low self-esteem. My parents praise him more because he needs it to feel better about himself"); and (5) *sibling-driven behaviors* ("My brother gets punished more because he asks for it. He knows he shouldn't kick the ball in the house"). Children who explained their parents' behavior in terms of individual needs were most likely to maintain close, warm, harmonious sibling relationships. Older siblings were more aware of differential treatment than younger ones (Kowal & Kramer, 1997).

The Adolescent in the Peer Group

As Jackie Robinson found, an important source of emotional support during the complex transition of adolescence, as well as a source of pressure for behavior that parents may deplore, is young people's growing involvement with their peers.

Adolescents going through rapid physical changes take comfort from being with others going through like changes. Young people challenging adult standards and parental authority find it reassuring to turn for advice to friends who are in the same position themselves. Adolescents questioning their parents' adequacy as models of behavior, but not yet sure enough of themselves to stand alone, look to peers to show them what's "in" and what's "out." The peer group is a source of affection, sympathy, understanding, and moral guidance (see Box 16-3); a place for experimentation; and a setting for achieving autonomy and independence of parents. It is a place to form intimate relationships that serve as "rehearsals" for adult intimacy in romantic relationships (Buhrmester, 1996; Coleman, 1980; Gecas & Seff, 1990; Laursen, 1996; P. R. Newman, 1982).

Peer Group Status

In sociometric studies, children are generally asked to name the classmates they like most and those they like least. Such studies have identified five *peer status groups: popular* (youngsters who receive many positive nominations), *rejected* (those who receive many negative nominations), *neglected* (those who receive few nominations of either kind), *controversial* (those who receive many positive and many negative nominations), and *average* (those who do not receive an unusual number of nominations of either kind).

A study of 1,041 preteens (ages 10 to 12) and 862 teenagers (ages 13 to 16) in northern Greece (Hatzichristou & Hopf, 1996) used this technique but added teacher ratings and self-ratings. The young people also were asked to name two classmates who best fit certain behavioral descriptions (for example, "quarrels often with other students," "liked by everybody and helps everybody," or "gets into trouble with the teacher"). By combining and comparing the various evaluations, the researchers were able to fill out a portrait of rejected, neglected, and controversial adolescents. The findings generally agree with and extend those of studies done in other countries; however, owing to the strong emphasis on school achievement in Greece, academic prowess may have more strongly influenced peer evaluations there than in some other societies.

As in U.S. studies, *rejected* youngsters had the greatest adjustment problems. They also had academic difficulties and low achievement test scores. Rejected boys, particularly younger ones, tended to be aggressive and antisocial; rejected girls were more likely to be shy, isolated, and unhappy, and to have a negative self-image. The latter characteristics also were typical of rejected boys in junior

Can you . . .

- Identify age and cultural differences in how young people spend their time?
- Identify factors that affect conflict with parents?
- Discuss the impact on adolescents of parents' employment, marital status, and socioeconomic status?
- Describe typical changes in sibling relationships during adolescence?

Box 16-3   How Do Psychosocial Issues Affect Adolescents' Moral Judgments?

How many adolescents face the problem of having to get a rare and expensive medicine for a mortally ill spouse? Not many do. And yet, Kohlberg's theory of moral development (see Chapter 15) is based on responses to dilemmas like this one. Today, researchers, often using methods based on Kohlberg's, are interviewing adolescents to find out what principles lie behind their thinking on moral issues they are more likely to confront in everyday life—such issues as whether and how a bystander should respond to aggression, under what circumstances it might be all right to break a school rule, and whether to admit someone from a minority group to an exclusive club. The findings suggest that psychosocial issues, such as the needs for peer acceptance and personal autonomy, may be important factors in adolescents' moral choices.

In one study, interviewers told stories about aggressive behavior to 111 working-class and middle-class preadolescents and early adolescents (ages 10, 12, and 14) in rural Ohio (Tisak & Tisak, 1996). The youngsters were asked what a person their age *would* do and *should* do, and why, when witnessing a good friend or a younger sibling hit or push someone, tear a book, or break a game. Their justifications fell into five main categories: looking out for others' welfare ("He [the victim] will get hurt if he doesn't do something to stop it"), helping the aggressor avoid punishment ("She will get in trouble if she continues to hit"), family responsibility ("He is supposed to make sure his brother doesn't do that"), maintaining solidarity with friends ("She will lose her as a friend [if she intervenes]"), and importance of the consequences ("Why should she do anything, it's not important").

Older participants were more likely than younger ones to weigh several of these factors. They were less likely to consider the welfare of the victim and more likely to be concerned about maintaining solidarity with the aggressor or helping him or her avoid punishment, perhaps reflecting adolescents' growing need for peer acceptance. Respondents of all ages thought a bystander would be more likely to stop a sibling's aggression than a friend's and had a greater obligation to do so. However, the older children were less inclined to expect or favor either kind of intervention, perhaps because they felt that the aggressor and the victim should be able to resolve the dispute themselves. Girls were more apt to expect a bystander to intervene, though boys were just as likely to think it would be wrong not to. This finding may reflect girls' greater confidence in their ability to influence a peer's behavior.

In another study, 120 fifth-, seventh-, ninth-, and eleventh-graders were asked about the legitimacy of school rules (Smetana & Bitz, 1996). Preadolescents and adolescents of all ages agreed that three kinds of conduct should be regulated in school: *immoral* behavior violating the rights and welfare of others, such as stealing, fighting, or failing to return textbooks; *unconventional* behavior violating customary standards, such as acting up in class, swearing, coming late, or talking back to the teacher; and *imprudent* behavior, such as smoking, drinking, taking drugs, and eating junk food for lunch. On the other hand, the young people viewed *personal* behavior, such as whom to sit next to and talk to, choice of clothing or hairstyle, and eating or reading comics in class, as matters to decide for themselves.

The respondents were almost evenly split in their judgments about behavior that is customarily regulated in school but not in other contexts, such as kissing a boyfriend or girlfriend in the hall, leaving class without permission, keeping forbidden items in a school locker, or passing notes to friends in class. As compared with fifth-graders, older youngsters were more likely to view this kind of behavior as a matter of personal discretion rather than a proper subject for regulation. Adolescents' views about the legitimacy of rules were important predictors of how often they broke the rules, according to their own and teachers' reports.

In a third study (Phinney & Cobb, 1996), 120 European American (Anglo) and Hispanic American fifth-, eighth-, and eleventh-graders were asked how they would respond to a Hispanic or Anglo student's request to join an exclusive school club in which all the members were of the other ethnic group. In half of the cases, the hypothetical applicant was of the same ethnic group as the respondent; in the other half, of the other ethnic group.

About three-fourths of the students favored accepting the applicant. The main reason given was fairness ("Everybody should be treated the same"). Next came a concern with individual welfare ("So they won't hurt her feelings"). Other reasons involved upholding social principles ("If they choose their own people, then they're never going to get along with each other") and the benefits of cultural diversity ("They can get to meet new people . . . learn about different cultures").

A small minority, less than 10 percent, favored excluding the outsider, citing the right of club members to select their associates ("They're the ones who started this club and . . . they should have the right . . . to choose who they want"). Many of these students also mentioned cultural barriers ("If they start speaking Spanish, she's going to feel left out").

In contrast to these two groups, who strongly held to their views even when challenged, about 12 percent of the respondents (mostly fifth- and eighth-graders) originally favored admission but switched when the interviewer suggested that "some people" would consider exclusion appropriate. The original reasons given by those who switched were largely pragmatic rather than principled ("Let him in, otherwise it'll cause a lot of tension").

Ethnicity did not affect which way participants decided, but did seem to influence the reasons. Anglo students—in line with dominant values in western cultures—tended to appeal to rights of free choice and rules ("The school says they could choose their own members") as reasons for exclusion, Hispanics to cultural barriers. Girls also tended to refer to rules. In line with Kohlberg's theory, older adolescents who favored inclusion were more likely than younger ones to show awareness of the impact on the social order ("If you start getting your own little groups . . . that hurts the country").

Friendships are closer and more intense in adolescence than at any other time in the life span. As young people separate from parents, they look to friends for intimacy. This is especially true of girls, who confide more in their friends and count more on their emotional support than boys do.

high or high school, apparently because shyness and sensitivity become more of a social liability as young people move into their teens (refer back to Box 13-2).

The *neglected* group—which, by high school age, included more boys than girls—were not much different from the average, except that they were less prosocial and had some learning difficulties, which contributed to a poor self-image. The transitions from elementary to junior high school and from junior high to high school seem to be particularly hard for rejected and neglected youngsters.

Controversial youngsters often were viewed differently by teachers and peers. Since the controversial group tended to do well in school, teachers did not see them as having behavioral problems. Peers, particularly in elementary school, often rated the girls in this category as well-behaved but snobbish and arrogant—perhaps reflecting girls' tendency to form cliques at this age. The boys were seen as aggressive and antisocial—but also as leaders, perhaps because peers expect and accept aggressiveness in young boys. By high school, the girls in the controversial category were better liked and were also seen as leaders.

Friendships

Friendships are fundamentally different from family relationships. They are more egalitarian than relationships with parents, who hold greater power, or with siblings, who are usually older or younger. Friendships are based on choice and commitment. By the same token, they are more unstable than family relationships. Awareness of the distinct character of friendships, and of what it takes to maintain them, emerges in adolescence. Adolescents quarrel less angrily and resolve conflicts more equitably with friends than with family members, perhaps because they realize that too much conflict could cost them a friendship (Laursen, 1996).

Adolescents tend to choose friends who are like them, and friends influence each other to become even more alike (Berndt, 1982; Berndt & Perry, 1990). Friends usually are of the same race (Giordano et al., 1993) and have similar status within the peer group (Berndt & Perry, 1990). Friendships become more reciprocal in adolescence: there is a greater likelihood that both friends will perceive their relationship in the same way (Buhrmester, 1990).

The intensity and importance of friendships is probably greater in adolescence than at any other time in the life span. Early adolescents begin to rely more on friends than on parents for intimacy and support. Friends now regard loyalty as more critical, and they share more than younger friends. Intimacy, loyalty, and sharing are features of adult friendship; their appearance in adolescence marks a transition to adultlike relationships (Berndt & Perry, 1990; Buhrmester, 1996; Laursen, 1996). Intimacy with same-sex friends increases during early to mid-adolescence, after which it declines as intimacy with the other sex generally increases (Laursen, 1996).

The increased intimacy of adolescent friendship reflects cognitive development. Adolescents are now better able to express their private thoughts and feelings. They can also more readily consider another person's point of view, and so it is easier for them to understand a friend's thoughts and feelings.

Increased intimacy also reflects early adolescents' concern with getting to know themselves. Confiding in a friend helps young people explore their own feelings, define their identity, and validate their self-worth. Friendship provides a safe place to venture opinions, admit weaknesses, and get help in coping with problems (Buhrmester, 1996). The way young people respond when a friend is upset changes during adolescence (Denton & Zarbatany, 1996). Distraction—trying to take the friend's mind off the problem—remains the most common response, as during preadolescence, but it offers less relief and becomes less common by the end of adolescence. Instead, adolescents try to bolster a friend's self-image by making excuses ("The accident wasn't your fault—that intersection is really dangerous").

The capacity for intimacy is related to psychological adjustment and social competence. Adolescents who have close friends generally have a high opinion of themselves, do well in school, and are unlikely to be hostile, anxious, or depressed (Berndt & Perry, 1990; Buhrmester, 1990). A bidirectional process seems to be at work: intimate friendships foster adjustment, which in turn fosters intimate friendships.

Friendship in adolescence requires more advanced social skills than friendship in early or middle childhood. Because friendships become more talk-oriented, teenagers need to be able to start and sustain conversations. They need to know how to seek out friends, call them up, and make plans. They need to know how to handle conflicts and disagreements. They need to know how and when to share confidences and how and when to offer emotional support. Friendships help adolescents develop these skills by offering opportunities to use them and feedback on their effectiveness (Buhrmester, 1996).

Sharing of confidences and emotional support are more vital to female friendships than to male friendships during adolescence and throughout life. Boys and men typically have more friends than girls and women, but their friendships focus less on conversation than on shared activity, usually sports and competitive games (Blyth & Foster-Clark, 1987; Buhrmester, 1996; Bukowski & Kramer, 1986). Girls feel better after telling a friend about an upsetting experience than boys do; boys may express support by just spending time doing things together (Denton & Zarbatany, 1996). As we have seen, boys tend to gain self-esteem from competition with friends, girls from helping them.

Adolescents in Trouble: Antisocial Behavior and Juvenile Delinquency

What influences young people to engage in—or refrain from—antisocial acts? What determines whether or not a juvenile delinquent will grow up to be a hardened criminal?

How Parental and Peer Influences Interact

Delinquency is often attributed to the influence of the peer group; parents worry about a child's "falling in with the wrong crowd" and feel powerless against peer influence. Young people who take drugs, drop out of school, and commit delinquent acts usually do all these in the company of friends. However, children do not usually "fall in" with a group; as we have seen, they tend to seek out friends like themselves. The more we look at factors that contribute to delinquency, the less satisfactory such a simplistic answer as "peer influence" becomes.

Peer influence may be strongest in borderline cases: a young person with moderately deviant tendencies can be pushed in one direction or the other by peers. In one study of 868 early adolescent low-income boys in French-speaking schools in Montreal, those who had been identified by teachers at ages 11 and 12 as moderately disruptive in class were more delinquent at age 13 if they had friends who were rated by peers as highly aggressive and disturbing. Boys who were either highly disruptive or very conforming to teachers' expectations were not affected by friends' aggressiveness; the highly disruptive boys tended to become delinquent with or without friends' influence, while the highly conforming ones did not (Vitaro, Tremblay, Kerr, Pagani, & Bukowski, 1997).

Although this research found little or no connection between parenting practices and delinquency, it does not tell us what earlier factors contributed to antisocial tendencies. Here parents' influence may play a vital role.

As we examine the roots of delinquency, we need to keep in mind an important distinction. Some adolescents occasionally commit an antisocial act. A smaller group of chronic (repeat) offenders *habitually* commit a *variety* of antisocial acts, such as stealing, setting fires, breaking into houses or cars, destroying property, physical cruelty, frequent fighting, and rape. Chronic offenders are responsible for most juvenile crime and are most likely to continue their criminal activity in adulthood (Yoshikawa, 1994). Adolescents who were aggressive or got in trouble when they were younger—lying, being truant, stealing, or doing poorly in school—are more likely than other youngsters to become chronic delinquents (Loeber & Dishion, 1983; Yoshikawa, 1994).

How do "problem behaviors" escalate into chronic delinquency? Some research points to early patterns of parent-child interaction that may lead to negative peer influence.

As we have seen, parenting practices help shape prosocial or antisocial behavior (Krevans & Gibbs, 1996). Parents of chronic delinquents often failed to reinforce good behavior in early childhood and were harsh or inconsistent, or both, in punishing misbehavior. Through the years these parents have not been closely and positively involved in their children's lives (G. R. Patterson, DeBaryshe, & Ramsey, 1989). The children may get payoffs for antisocial behavior: when they act up, they may gain attention or get their own way. Antisocial behavior interferes with schoolwork and with the ability to get along with well-behaved classmates. Unpopular and low-achieving children tend to gravitate toward each other and influence one another toward further misconduct (G. R. Patterson, Reid, & Dishion, 1992). Grouping children with similar academic skills in the same classroom may make the problem worse by keeping low-achieving, anti-social children together (Dishion, Patterson, Stoolmiller, & Skinner, 1991).

Ineffective parenting tends to continue in adolescence. Antisocial behavior at this age is closely related to parents' tendency to use lenient discipline and inability to keep track of their children's activities (G. R. Patterson & Stouthamer-Loeber, 1984). A longitudinal study of 132 white families found that the way mothers communicate with early adolescent children about such issues as the young person's keeping his or her room clean can predict whether the adolescent will engage in severely delinquent behavior at age 19. The highest rates of criminal arrests and convictions occurred in families in which poor maternal communication and problem-solving skills were combined with parental conflict, divorce, or a mother's depression (Klein, Forehand, Armistead, & Long, 1997).

Parents also have considerable indirect influence on their children's choice of friends. In a study of 3,781 high school students (B. B. Brown, Mounts, Lamborn,

& Steinberg, 1993), the extent to which parents monitored adolescents' behavior and schoolwork, encouraged achievement, and allowed joint decision making were related to academic achievement, drug use, and self-reliance. These behaviors, in turn, were linked with membership in such peer groups as "populars, jocks, brains, normals, druggies, and outcasts" (p. 471).

Authoritative parenting can help young people internalize standards that insulate them against negative peer influences and open them to positive ones. In a study of 500 ninth- through eleventh-graders, students whose close friends were drug users tended to increase their own self-reported drug use, but that was less true of those who saw their parents as highly authoritative. Adolescents whose close friends were academic achievers tended to improve their grades, but that was less true of students whose parents were not authoritative (Mounts & Steinberg, 1995).

Teenagers' behavior also can be indirectly influenced by the way their friends are brought up. Among 4,431 high school students of varied ethnic backgrounds, those whose friends described their parents as authoritative were more likely to do well in school and less likely to use drugs or get in trouble with the law; this was true over and above the effect of a youngster's own parenting. Boys whose friends had authoritative parents were less likely to misbehave in school and were less susceptible to antisocial peer pressure; girls were more self-reliant and work-oriented, had higher self-esteem, and were less likely to be anxious or depressed (Fletcher, Darling, Steinberg, & Dornbusch, 1995). Apparently, authoritative parents tend to raise well-adjusted teenagers, who seek out other well-adjusted teenagers as friends. Thus the peer group reinforces and enhances the beneficial effects of effective parenting.

Long-Term Prospects

Most delinquents do not grow up to become criminals; many who are not hard-core offenders simply outgrow their "wild oats" (L. W. Shannon, 1982). Delinquency peaks at about age 15 and then declines, unlike alcohol use and sexual activity, which become more prevalent with age (refer back to Figure 14-4). Since alcohol and sexual activity are accepted parts of adult life, it is not surprising that as teenagers grow older they increasingly want to engage in them (Petersen, 1993). Antisocial behavior that is not accepted in adulthood may diminish as most adolescents and their families come to terms with young people's need to assert independence.

Most teenagers who experiment with delinquent behavior, such as minor shoplifting, grow up to be law-abiding citizens. Those who become chronic offenders tend to be products of a combination of risk factors going back to early childhood, including poverty and ineffective parenting.

Middle- and high-income adolescents may experiment with problem behaviors and then drop them, but low-income teenagers who do not see positive alternatives are more likely to adopt a permanently antisocial lifestyle (Elliott, 1993). Both delinquency and crime tend to be concentrated in poor, overcrowded urban neighborhoods with dilapidated housing, high unemployment rates, and predominantly minority populations (NRC, 1993a; Yoshikawa, 1994). A youth who sees that the only rich people in the neighborhood are drug dealers may be seduced into a life of crime.

Predicting and Preventing Delinquency

Can we predict who will become a juvenile delinquent? Some studies suggest a genetic influence, but this is relatively small in comparison with such factors as parenting style, family atmosphere, and socioeconomic status. However, the risk is far greater when influences combine.

Chronic delinquency may be predictable from a complex network of interacting early risk factors (Yoshikawa, 1994). Children at genetic risk—whose biological parents are antisocial or alcoholic, or both—are more likely to become chronic delinquents if exposed to family conflict at an early age. Those who had complications at birth, such as prematurity, low birthweight, anoxia, or other trauma, are at greater risk if they grow up in poor, unstable families. Infants who are insecurely attached or whose parents are constantly arguing and fighting are more at risk if the parents are hostile, rejecting, insensitive, or neglectful. Young people in impoverished circumstances are more at risk if they come from large, quarrelsome families, if they had birth complications, or if their parents are poorly educated or mentally ill. On the other hand, low-income youngsters are at less risk if they have been raised with a mixture of discipline and affection and if their verbal ability is normal for their age (Yoshikawa, 1994).

Since juvenile delinquency apparently has roots early in childhood, so must preventive efforts. Young people who suffer from poor parenting are at less risk if their parents get effective community support. Effective programs attack the multiple risk factors that can lead to delinquency (Yoshikawa, 1994; E. Zigler, Taussig, & Black, 1992).

Researchers analyzing the long-term effects of some early childhood intervention programs have found that adolescents who had taken part in these programs as children were less likely to get in trouble with the law (Yoshikawa, 1994; E. Zigler et al., 1992). For example, the Perry Preschool Project (see Chapters 9 and 12), which focused on preparing children for school, had a "snowball effect." The children's teachers had a more positive attitude toward better-prepared kindergartners, the children liked school better, and they achieved more in later grades. The children developed higher self-esteem and aspirations for the future, both of which tend to deter antisocial behavior (Berrueta-Clement, Schweinhart, Barnett, & Weikart, 1987). Even though the early benefits to school performance did not always hold up, Perry "graduates" showed less antisocial behavior than equally disadvantaged peers. Other programs that have achieved impressive long-term results in preventing antisocial behavior and delinquency include the Syracuse Family Development Research Project, the Yale Child Welfare Project, and the Houston Parent Child Development Center.

Although each of these programs had a different character and focus, all targeted high-risk urban children and lasted for at least 2 years during the child's first 5 years of life. All influenced children directly, through high-quality day care or education, and at the same time indirectly, by offering families assistance and support geared to their needs (Yoshikawa, 1994; E. Zigler et al., 1992). Some programs have taught parents how to discipline and motivate their children and to build relationships with the children's teachers, all of which may help school performance (Seitz, 1990).

In terms of Bronfenbrenner's ecological model (see Chapter 1), these programs operated on the mesosystem by affecting interactions between two or more settings (the home and the educational or child-care center) of which a child was a part. The programs also went one step further to the exosystem, by creating supportive parent networks and linking parents with community providers of prenatal and postnatal health care, educational and vocational counseling, and other services (Yoshikawa, 1994; E. Zigler et al., 1992). Through their multipronged approach, these programs have made an impact on several early risk factors for delinquency.

Still, effective as such early preventive efforts may be, they cannot buffer a child against years of negative influences during middle childhood and adolescence. Programs need to be designed for older at-risk youngsters as well. Parent training may help, especially in families undergoing parental conflict, divorce, or depression (Klein et al., 1997). Interventions also need to focus on such factors as peer rejection, chronic poverty, media influences, and availability of drugs and guns. Some programs have helped delinquents by teaching them social and vocational skills (NRC, 1993a).

Fortunately, the great majority of adolescents do not get into serious trouble. Those who do show disturbed behavior can—and should—be helped. With love, guidance, and support, adolescents can avoid risks, build on their strengths, and explore their possibilities as they approach adult life.

CHECKPOINT

Can you . . .

• Explain how parental and peer influences promote or prevent antisocial behavior and juvenile delinquency?

• Give examples of programs that have been successful in preventing juvenile delinquency?

Is There a "Universal Adolescent"?

Do teenagers growing up in Hungary go through more or fewer "growing pains" than adolescents in the United States? Do adolescents in Taiwan and Japan, whose cultures traditionally show great respect to parents, have any special advantages or difficulties in navigating the transition to adulthood? How much does the psychological world of adolescence vary in cultures as diverse as those of Australia and Bangladesh? Is the communication revolution making the world a "global village" and breaking down cultural differences among the young people who inhabit it?

To answer questions like these, Daniel Offer and his colleagues (Offer et al., 1988) administered the Offer Self-Image Questionnaire to 5,938 adolescents in 10 countries: Australia, Bangladesh, Hungary, Israel, Italy, Japan, Taiwan, Turkey, the United States, and West Germany. The young people answered questions about five aspects of themselves: (1) the *psychological self:* impulse control, fluctuations in mood and emotions, and feelings about their bodies, (2) the *social self:* peer relations, moral attitudes, and educational and vocational goals, (3) the *sexual self:* attitudes toward sexuality and sexual behavior, (4) the *familial self:* feelings about parents and the atmosphere in the home, and (5) the *coping self:* ability to deal with the world.

The researchers found cross-cultural commonalities in each of the five "selves," particularly familial, social, and coping. For example, about 9 out of 10 adolescents in each country had positive feelings toward their parents, valued work and friendship, and tried to learn from failure. There was less consistency in the psychological and sexual areas; here socioeconomic circumstances and local customs were more crucial. In general, however, these "universal adolescents" described themselves as happy; felt able to cope with life, make decisions, and use self-control; cared about others and liked being with and learning from them; enjoyed a job well done; were confident about their sexuality; did not harbor grudges against their parents; saw their mothers and fathers as getting along well most of the time; and expected to be able to take responsibility for themselves as they grew older. All in all, the researchers judged at least 73 percent of the total sample as having "a healthy adolescent self-image" (p. 124).

These Israeli adolescents, growing up in a small nation wracked by internal tensions and surrounded by hostile neighbors, have had very different experiences from those of teenagers in the United States. Yet Daniel Offer and his colleagues found underlying similarities in self-image between adolescents in these and other countries the world over.

Teenagers in each country showed strengths and weaknesses; in no country were adolescents better- or worse-adjusted in all respects. In Bangladesh, the third poorest country in the world, even middle-class teenagers were low in impulse control; felt lonely, sad, and vulnerable; and had a poor body image. They also reported the most problems with peers and the highest rate of depression (48 percent). In Taiwan, where traditional sexual taboos still operate, large numbers of young people seemed to be afraid of sex or inhibited about it. On the other hand, Bengali and Taiwanese youths seemed superior in their enjoyment of solving difficult problems and in their willingness to find out how to deal with new situations.

The lower a country's economic output and the higher the proportion of adolescents who must compete for places in school and for jobs, the less positive were the teenagers' emotional tone and peer relationships: "very positive peer relationships seem to be a luxury of relatively well-advantaged adolescents" (p. 105). This finding echoes surveys of U. S. adolescents in the 1960s, 1970s, and 1980s. Although most young people in all three cohorts had no major problems, teenagers in the 1960s seemed to be the best-adjusted and those in the 1970s the worst (Offer et al., 1989). Adolescents in the 1960s were at the end of a "baby bust" generation; those in the 1970s were in the middle of a "baby boom," which ran its course by the 1980s. In "boom" periods, competition for jobs and college admission is keener, and this pressure may help explain the greater unease of teenagers in the 1970s, as well as in less-developed countries today.

Some consistent age and gender differences emerged in the cross-cultural study (Offer et al., 1988). Older adolescents were less self-conscious than younger ones, more willing to learn from others, and better able to take criticism without resentment. These findings point to normal developmental growth in self-confidence and self-esteem and a smooth transition toward adulthood. Older adolescents were also more comfortable with their sexuality and more realistic in their view of family relationships.

Boys felt surer of themselves than girls, less afraid of competition, more in control of their emotions, and more interested in sex. Boys were also prouder of their bodies; girls in both early and late adolescence were more likely to feel unattractive. Girls were more empathic, caring, and socially responsible—more likely to help a friend and to refrain from actions that harm others. Girls were also more committed to work and study.

Another study of adolescents' identity in Turkey, where women have lower social standing than men and girls are subject to stricter social control, found similar gender differences. In questionnaires completed by 154 urban and rural high school boys and 119 girls, the boys tended to evaluate themselves in terms of physical attributes and cognitive abilities, whereas girls stressed altruism and social and communication skills (Yildirim, 1997).

Offer and his colleagues attributed the "surprising unity of adolescent experience" across cultures largely to the media, which give young people a "collective consciousness" of what is going on in one another's lives all over the world (Offer et al., 1988, p. 114). Through the eye of television, adolescents see themselves as part of a world culture.

We do need to be careful about drawing overly broad generalizations from these findings. The samples included only young people in school, mostly urban or suburban and middle-class. Also, some of the questionnaire items may have taken on different meanings in translation. Nevertheless, this research draws a fascinating picture of the universal and not-so-universal aspects of adolescence and raises many questions for future research.

The normal developmental changes in the early years of life are obvious and dramatic signs of growth. The infant lying in the crib becomes an active, exploring toddler. The young child enters and embraces the worlds of school and society. The adolescent, with a new body and new awareness, prepares to step into adulthood. But growth and development do not screech to a stop with adolescence. People change in many ways throughout early, middle, and late adulthood. Some capacities emerge relatively late in life, and human beings continue to shape their own development, as they have been doing since birth. What occurs in a child's world is significant, but it is not the whole story. We each continue to write our own story of human development for as long as we live.

SUMMARY

The Search for Identity

- A central concern during adolescence is the search for identity, which has occupational, sexual, and values components. Erik Erikson described the psychosocial crisis of adolescence as the conflict of **identity versus identity confusion.** The "virtue" that should arise from this crisis is *fidelity.*

- James Marcia, in research based on Erikson's theory, described four **identity statuses** with differing combinations of **crisis** and **commitment: identity achievement** (crisis leading to commitment), **foreclosure** (commitment without crisis), **moratorium** (crisis with no commitment yet), and **identity diffusion** (no commitment, no crisis).

- Marcia, Carol Gilligan, and other researchers have found differences in the ways males and females define themselves. Ethnic differences also seem to exist.

Sexuality

- Sexual attitudes and behaviors are more liberal than in the past. There is more acceptance of premarital sexual activity, and there has been a decline in the double standard.

CHECKPOINT

Can you . . .

- Identify cross-cultural commonalities and differences in adolescents' self-image, attitudes, and personalities?

- This more liberal sexual climate involves increased risks. Teenagers at greatest risk are those who begin sexual activity early, have multiple partners, and do not use contraceptives.
- Although teenage pregnancy and birth rates in the United States have declined, more of those births are to unmarried mothers. Teenage pregnancy often has negative consequences for mother, father, child, and society. Adolescents who are knowledgeable about sex and contraception are less likely to become pregnant.

Relationships with Family, Peers, and Adult Society

- Although relationships between adolescents and their parents are not always smooth, full-scale **adolescent rebellion** does not seem usual, and parents and their teenage children often hold similar values.
- Adolescents spend most of their time with their peers, but relationships with parents continue to play an important role in their development.
- While there are ethnic variations, conflict with parents tends to rise during early adolescence, stabilize during middle adolescence, and decrease during late adolescence. Authoritative parenting appears to be associated with the most positive outcomes.
- The effect of maternal employment on adolescents' development is filtered through other factors, such as mothers' warmth and role satisfaction. Although adolescents not living with biological fathers are at greater risk of trouble, the effects of divorce and single parenting may be less severe than has been believed and may depend on individual circumstances. Economic stress affects relationships in both single-parent and two-parent families.
- Relationships with siblings tend to become more equal and more distant during adolescence.
- The peer group can have both positive and negative influences. Youngsters who are rejected by peers tend to have the greatest adjustment problems.
- Friendships become more intimate and supportive in adolescence, especially among girls.
- Most juvenile delinquents grow up to be law-abiding citizens. Chronic delinquency is associated with multiple interacting risk factors, including ineffective parenting, school failure, peer influence, and low socioeconomic status. Programs that attack such risk factors at an early age have had success.

Is There a "Universal Adolescent"?

- Cross-cultural research has found striking commonalities in adolescents' self-image, attitudes, and coping ability.

KEY TERMS

identity versus identity confusion (574)
identity statuses (576)
crisis (576)
commitment (576)

identity achievement (577)
foreclosure (577)
moratorium (577)
identity diffusion (577)
adolescent rebellion (589)

QUESTIONS FOR THOUGHT AND DISCUSSION

1. Can you think of values you hold that are different from those of your parents? How did you come to develop these values?

2. Which of Marcia's identity statuses do you think you fit into? Has your identity status changed since adolescence?

3. How can adults help raise teenage girls' self-esteem?

4. Since girls generally bear the burdens of adolescent pregnancy, should teenage girls be urged to follow a stricter standard of sexual behavior than teenage boys? Should more emphasis be placed on encouraging teenage boys to be more responsible sexually? Or both?

5. Under what circumstances do you think each of the following choices might be best for a teenage girl who discovers that she is pregnant: marry the father and raise the child, stay single and raise the child, give the baby to adoptive parents, or have an abortion?

6. When teenagers complain that their parents "don't understand" them, what do you think they mean?

Glossary

A

acceleration Approach to educating the gifted, which moves them through the entire curriculum, or part of it, at an unusually rapid pace.

accommodation In Piaget's terminology, changes in an existing cognitive structure to include new information.

achievement tests Tests that assess how much children know in various subject areas.

acquired immune deficiency syndrome (AIDS) Viral disease that undermines effective functioning of the immune system.

acting-out behavior Misbehavior (such as lying or stealing) spurred by emotional difficulties.

acute medical conditions Illnesses that last a short time.

adaptation In Piaget's terminology, adjustment to new information about the environment through the complementary processes of assimilation and accommodation.

adolescence Developmental transition between childhood and adulthood entailing major physical, cognitive, and psychosocial changes.

adolescent growth spurt Sharp increase in height and weight that precedes sexual maturity.

adolescent rebellion Pattern of emotional turmoil, characteristic of a minority of adolescents, which may involve conflict with family, alienation from adult society, and hostility toward adults' values.

adrenarche Maturation of adrenal glands.

Adult Attachment Interview (AAI) Instrument for measuring the clarity, coherence, and consistency of an adult's memories of attachment to her or his parents.

alleles Paired genes (alike or different) that affect a particular trait.

altruism, or prosocial behavior Behavior intended to help others without external reward.

ambivalent (resistant) attachment Attachment pattern in which an infant becomes anxious before the primary caregiver leaves, is extremely upset during his or her absence, and both seeks and resists contact on his or her return.

amniocentesis Prenatal diagnostic procedure in which a sample of amniotic fluid is withdrawn and analyzed to determine whether any of certain genetic defects are present.

androgynous Personality type integrating positive characteristics typically thought of as masculine and positive characteristics typically thought of as feminine.

animism Tendency to attribute life to objects that are not alive.

anorexia nervosa Eating disorder characterized by self-starvation.

anoxia Lack of oxygen, which may cause brain damage.

Apgar scale Standard measurement of a newborn's condition; it assesses appearance, pulse, grimace, activity, and respiration.

aptitude tests Tests that measure children's general intelligence, or capacity to learn.

artificial insemination Injection of sperm into a woman's cervix in order to enable her to conceive.

assimilation In Piaget's terminology, incorporation of new information into an existing cognitive structure.

asthma A chronic respiratory disease characterized by sudden attacks of coughing, wheezing, and difficulty in breathing.

attachment Reciprocal, enduring relationship between infant and caregiver, each of whom contributes to the quality of the relationship.

Attachment Q-Set (AQS) Instrument for measuring attachment, developed by Waters and Deane, in which observer sorts descriptive words and phrases into those most and least characteristic of a child and compares these descriptors with descriptions of the "hypothetical most secure child."

attention-deficit/hyperactivity disorder (ADHD) Syndrome characterized by persistent inattention, impulsivity, low tolerance for frustration, distractibility, and considerable activity at inappropriate times and places.

authoritarian In Baumrind's terminology, parenting style emphasizing control and obedience. Compare *authoritative* and *permissive*.

authoritative In Baumrind's terminology, parenting style blending respect for a child's individuality with an effort to instill social values. Compare *authoritarian* and *permissive*.

autism One of a group of *pervasive developmental disorders (PDD)* of the brain that develops within the first 2½ years and is characterized by lack of sociability, impaired communication, and a narrow range of repetitive, often obsessive behaviors.

autobiographical memory Memory of specific events in one's own life.

autonomy versus shame and doubt In Erikson's theory, the second crisis in psychosocial development, occurring between about 18 months and 3 years, in which children achieve a balance between self-determination and control by others.

autosomes The 22 pairs of chromosomes not related to sexual expression.

avoidant attachment Attachment pattern in which an infant rarely cries when separated from the primary caregiver and avoids contact upon his or her return.

B

basic trust versus basic mistrust In Erikson's theory, the first crisis in psychosocial development, occurring between birth and about 18 months, in which infants develop a sense of the reliability of people and objects in their world.

battered child syndrome Condition showing symptoms of physical abuse of a child.

Bayley Scales of Infant Development Standardized test of infants' mental and motor development.

behavior therapy Therapeutic approach using principles of learning theory to encourage desired behaviors or eliminate undesired ones; also called *behavioral modification.*

behavioral genetics Quantitative study of relative genetic and environmental influences on behavioral and psychological traits.

behaviorism Learning theory that emphasizes the study of observable behaviors and events and the predictable role of environment in causing behavior.

behaviorist approach Approach to the study of cognitive development based on learning theory, which is concerned with the basic mechanics of learning.

bilingual Fluent in two languages.

bilingual education A system of teaching foreign-speaking children in two languages—their native language and English—and later switching to all-English instruction after the children develop enough fluency in English.

birth trauma Injury sustained at the time of birth due to oxygen deprivation, mechanical injury, infection, or disease.

bisexual Describing a person whose sexual orientation is toward both sexes.

body image Descriptive and evaluative beliefs about one's appearance.

Brazelton Neonatal Behavioral Assessment Scale Neurological and behavioral test to measure neonate's response to the environment; it assesses interactive behaviors, motor behaviors, physiological control, and response to stress.

bulimia nervosa Eating disorder in which a person regularly eats huge quantities of food and then purges the body by laxatives, induced vomiting, fasting, or excessive exercise.

bullying Aggression deliberately and persistently directed against a particular target, or victim, who is weak, vulnerable, and defenseless.

C

canalization Limitation on variance of expression of certain inherited characteristics.

case study Scientific study covering a single case or life, based on notes taken by observers or on published biographical materials.

causality Awareness that one event causes another.

central executive In Baddeley's model, element of working memory that controls the processing of information.

central nervous system Brain and spinal cord.

centration In Piaget's theory, a limitation of preoperational thought that leads the child to focus on one aspect of a situation and neglect others, often leading to illogical conclusions.

cephalocaudal principle Principle that development proceeds in a head-to-toe direction (i.e., that upper parts of the body develop before lower parts).

cesarean delivery Delivery of a baby by surgical removal from the uterus.

child development Scientific study of change and continuity throughout childhood.

child-directed speech (CDS) Form of speech often used in talking to babies or toddlers; includes slow, simplified speech, a high-pitched tone, exaggerated vowel sounds, short words and sentences, and much repetition. Also called *parentese.*

childhood depression Affective disorder characterized by such symptoms as a prolonged sense of friendlessness, inability to have fun or concentrate, fatigue, extreme activity or apathy, feelings of worthlessness, weight change, physical complaints, and thoughts of death or suicide.

cholesterol Waxy substance in human and animal tissue; excess deposits of one type can narrow blood vessels, leading to heart disease.

chorionic villus sampling (CVS) Prenatal diagnostic procedure in which tissue from villi (hairlike projections

of the membrane surrounding the fetus) is analyzed for birth defects.

chromosome One of 46 rod-shaped structures that carry the genes.

chronic medical conditions Illnesses or impairments that persist for at least 3 months.

circular reactions In Piaget's terminology, processes by which an infant learns to reproduce desired occurrences originally discovered by chance.

class inclusion Understanding of the relationship between the whole and its parts.

classical conditioning Kind of learning in which a previously neutral stimulus (one that does not originally elicit a particular response) acquires the power to elicit the response after the stimulus is repeatedly associated with another stimulus that ordinarily does elicit the response.

code switching Process of changing one's speech to match the situation, as with people who are bilingual.

code-mixing Use of elements of two languages, sometimes in the same utterance, by young children in households where both languages are spoken.

cognitive neuroscience approach Approach to the study of cognitive development by examining brain structures and measuring neurological activity.

cognitive perspective View of development concerned with thought processes and the behavior that reflects those processes.

cognitive play Forms of play that reveal children's mental development.

cohort Group of people who share a similar experience, such as growing up at the same time and in the same place.

commitment In Marcia's terminology, personal investment in an occupation or system of beliefs.

committed compliance In Kochanska's terminology, a toddler's wholehearted obedience of a parent's orders without reminders or lapses.

componential element In Sternberg's triarchic theory, term for the analytic aspect of intelligence, which determines how efficiently people process information and solve problems.

concordant Term describing twins who share the same trait or disorder.

concrete operations Third stage of Piagetian cognitive development (approximately from ages 7 to 12), during which children develop logical but not abstract thinking.

conscience Internal standards of behavior, which usually control one's conduct and produce emotional discomfort when violated.

conservation In Piaget's terminology, awareness that two objects that are equal according to a certain measure (such as length, weight, or quantity) remain equal in the face of perceptual alteration (for example, a change in shape) so long as nothing has been added to or taken away from either object.

contextual element In Sternberg's triarchic theory, term for the practical aspect of intelligence, which determines how effectively people deal with their environment.

contextual perspective View of development that sees the individual as inseparable from the social context.

control group In an experiment, a group of people who are similar to the people in the experimental group but who do not receive the treatment whose effects are to be measured; the results obtained with this group are compared with the results obtained with the experimental group.

conventional morality (or morality of conventional role conformity) Second level in Kohlberg's theory of moral reasoning, in which the standards of authority figures are internalized.

convergent thinking Thinking aimed at finding the one "right" answer to a problem. Compare *divergent thinking*.

coregulation Transitional stage in the control of behavior in which parents exercise general supervision and children exercise moment-to-moment self-regulation.

correlational study Research design intended to discover whether a statistical relationship between variables exists, either in direction or in magnitude.

creativity Ability to see things in a new light, resulting in a novel product, the identification of a previously unrecognized problem, or the formulation of new and unusual solutions.

crisis In Marcia's terminology, period of conscious decision making related to identity formation.

critical period Specific time during development when a given event will have the greatest impact.

cross-modal transfer Ability to identify by sight an item earlier felt but not seen.

cross-sectional study Study design in which people of different ages are assessed on one occasion, providing comparative information about different age cohorts.

cross-sequential study Study design that combines cross-sectional and longitudinal techniques by assessing people in a cross-sectional sample more than once.

cultural bias Tendency of intelligence tests to include items calling for knowledge or skills more familiar or meaningful to some cultural groups than to others, thus placing some test-takers at an advantage or disadvantage due to their cultural background.

culture A society's or group's total way of life, including customs, traditions, beliefs, values, language, and physical products—all learned behavior passed on from adults to children.

culture-fair Describing an intelligence test that deals with experiences common to various cultures, in an attempt to avoid cultural bias. Compare *culture-free*.

culture-free Describing an intelligence test that, if it were possible to design, would have no culturally linked content. Compare *culture-fair*.

D

data Information obtained through research.

decenter In Piaget's terminology, to think simultaneously about several aspects of a situation; characteristic of operational thought.

deduction Type of logical reasoning that moves from a general premise about a class to a conclusion about a particular member or members of the class.

deferred imitation In Piaget's terminology, reproduction of an observed behavior after the passage of time by calling up a stored symbol of it.

Denver Developmental Screening Test Screening test given to children 1 month to 6 years old to determine whether they are developing normally; it assesses gross motor skills, fine motor skills, language development, and personality and social development.

deoxyribonucleic acid (DNA) Chemical of which genes are composed that controls the functions of body cells.

dependent variable In an experiment, the condition that may or may not change as a result of changes in the independent variable.

depression Affective disorder in which a person feels unhappy and often has trouble eating, sleeping, and concentrating.

depth perception Ability to perceive objects and surfaces three-dimensionally.

developmental priming mechanisms Preparatory aspects of the home environment that seem to be necessary for normal cognitive and psychosocial development to occur.

difficult children Children with irritable temperament, irregular biological rhythms, and intense emotional responses.

discipline Tool for socialization, which includes methods of molding children's character and of teaching them to exercise self-control and engage in acceptable behavior.

dishabituation Increase in responsiveness after presentation of a new stimulus. Compare *habituation*.

disorganized-disoriented attachment Attachment pattern in which an infant, after being separated from the primary caregiver, shows contradictory behaviors upon his or her return.

divergent thinking Thinking that produces a variety of fresh, diverse possibilities. Compare *convergent thinking*.

dizygotic (two-egg) twins Twins conceived by the union of two different ova (or a single ovum that has split) with two different sperm cells within a brief period of time; also called *fraternal twins*.

dominant inheritance Pattern of inheritance in which, when an individual receives contradictory alleles for a trait, only the dominant one is expressed.

Down syndrome Chromosomal disorder characterized by moderate-to-severe mental retardation and by such physical signs as a downward-sloping skin fold at the inner corners of the eyes.

drug therapy Administration of drugs to treat emotional disorders.

dyslexia Developmental disorder in learning to read.

E

early intervention Systematic process of planning and providing therapeutic and educational services to families that need help in meeting infants', toddlers', or preschool children's developmental needs.

easy children Children with a generally happy temperament, regular biological rhythms, and a readiness to accept new experiences.

ecological approach Bronfenbrenner's system of understanding development, which identifies five interlocking levels of environmental influence: the microsystem, mesosystem, exosystem, macrosystem, and chronosystem.

ego In Freudian theory, an aspect of personality that develops during infancy and operates on the reality principle, seeking acceptable means of gratification in dealing with the real world.

egocentrism In Piaget's terminology, inability to consider another person's point of view; a characteristic of preoperational thought.

elaboration Mnemonic strategy of making mental associations involving items to be remembered, sometimes with an imagined scene or story.

electronic fetal monitoring Mechanical monitoring of fetal heartbeat during labor and delivery.

elicited imitation Research method in which a child copies a researcher's use of specific objects and later remembers how to repeat the procedure without further instruction.

embryonic stage Second stage of gestation (2 to 8 weeks), characterized by rapid growth and development of major body systems and organs.

embryoscopy Prenatal medical procedure in which a scope is inserted in the abdomen of a pregnant woman to permit viewing of the embryo for diagnosis and treatment of abnormalities.

emotional (psychological) abuse Nonphysical action that may damage children's behavioral, cognitive, emotional, or physical functioning.

emotional (psychological) neglect Failure to give a child emotional support, love, and affection.

emotions Subjective feelings, such as sadness, joy, and fear, which arise in response to situations and experiences and are expressed through altered behavior.

empathy Ability to put oneself in another person's place and feel what that person feels.

English-immersion Approach to teaching English as a second language in which instruction is presented only in English from the outset of formal education.

enrichment Approach to educating the gifted, which broadens and deepens knowledge and skills through extra activities, projects, field trips, or mentoring.

enuresis Repeated urination in clothing or in bed.

environment Totality of nongenetic influences on development, external to the self.

episodic memory Long-term memory of specific experiences or events, linked to time and place.

equilibration In Piaget's terminology, the tendency to strive for equilibrium (balance) among cognitive elements within the organism and between it and the outside world.

ethnic group Group united by ancestry, race, religion, language, and/or national origins, which contribute to a sense of shared identity.

ethological perspective View of development that focuses on the biological and evolutionary bases of behavior.

experiential element In Sternberg's triarchic theory, term for the insightful aspect of intelligence, which determines how effectively people approach both novel and familiar tasks.

experiment Rigorously controlled, replicable (repeatable) procedure in which the researcher manipulates variables to assess the effect of one on the other.

experimental group In an experiment, the group receiving the treatment under study; any changes in these people are compared with changes in the control group.

explicit memory Memory, generally of facts, names, and events, which is intentional and conscious. Compare *implicit memory.*

exploratory competence Cognitive capacity underlying the variance in toddlers' ability to sustain attention and engage in sophisticated symbolic play.

extended family Multigenerational kinship network of parents, children, and more distant relatives, sometimes living together in an *extended-family household.*

external memory aids Mnemonic strategies using something outside the person, such as a list.

F

family therapy Psychological treatment in which a therapist sees the whole family together to analyze patterns of family functioning.

fantasy period In Ginzberg's theory of career planning, period during elementary school years when occupational ambitions are based on emotion and excitement, not on practical considerations.

fast mapping Process by which a child absorbs the meaning of a new word after hearing it only once or twice in conversation.

fertilization Union of sperm and ovum to produce a zygote; also called *conception.*

fetal alcohol syndrome (FAS) Combination of mental, motor, and developmental abnormalities affecting the offspring of some women who drink heavily during pregnancy.

fetal stage Final stage of gestation (from 8 weeks to birth), characterized by increased detail of body parts and greatly enlarged body size.

fine motor skills Physical skills that involve the small muscles and eye-hand coordination.

fontanels Soft spots on head of young infant.

foreclosure Identity status, described by Marcia, in which a person who has not spent time considering alternatives (that is, has not been in crisis) is committed to other people's plans for his or her life.

formal operations In Piaget's theory, the final stage of cognitive development, characterized by the ability to think abstractly.

G

gateway drugs Drugs such as alcohol, tobacco, and marijuana, the use of which tends to lead to use of more addictive drugs.

gender Significance of being male or female.

gender constancy, or **gender conservation** Awareness that one will always be male or female.

gender differences Psychological or behavioral differences between males and females.

gender identity Awareness, developed in early childhood, that one is male or female.

gender roles Behaviors, interests, attitudes, skills, and traits that a culture considers appropriate for males or for females.

gender schema In Bem's theory, a pattern of behavior organized around gender.

gender stereotypes Exaggerated generalizations about male or female role behavior.

gender-schema theory Theory, proposed by Bem, that children socialize themselves in their gender roles by developing a concept of what it means to be male or female in a particular culture.

gender-typing Socialization process by which children, at an early age, learn behavior deemed appropriate by the culture for a boy or a girl.

gene Basic functional unit of heredity that contains all inherited material passed from biological parents to children.

generic memory Memory that produces a script of familiar routines to guide behavior.

genetic counseling Clinical service that advises couples of their probable risk of having children with particular hereditary defects.

genetic testing Procedure for ascertaining a person's genetic makeup for purposes of identifying predispositions to specific hereditary diseases or disorders.

genome imprinting Process by which genes that have been temporarily chemically altered in the mother or father have differing effects when transmitted to offspring.

genotype Genetic makeup of a person, containing both expressed and unexpressed characteristics.

genotype-environment correlation Tendency of certain genetic and environmental influences to occur together; may be passive, reactive (evocative), or active. Also called *genotype-environment covariance.*

genotype-environment interaction The portion of phenotypic variation that results from the reactions of genetically different individuals to similar environmental conditions.

germinal stage First 2 weeks of prenatal development, characterized by rapid cell division, increasing complexity and differentiation, and implantation in the wall of the uterus.

gestation The approximately 266-day period of development between fertilization and birth.

gonadarche Maturation of testes or ovaries.

goodness of fit Appropriateness of environmental demands and constraints to a child's temperament.

gross motor skills Physical skills that involve the large muscles.

guided participation In Vygotsky's terminology, participation of an adult in a child's activity in a manner that helps to structure the activity and to bring the child's understanding of it closer to the understanding of the adult.

H

habituation Simple type of learning in which familiarity with a stimulus reduces, slows, or stops a response. Compare *dishabituation.*

handedness Preference for using a particular hand.

haptic perception Ability to acquire information about properties of objects, such as size, weight, and texture, by handling them.

heredity Inborn influences on development, carried on the genes inherited from the parents.

heritability Statistical estimate of contribution of heredity to individual differences in a specific trait within a given population.

heterosexual Describing a person whose sexual orientation is toward the other sex.

heterozygous Possessing differing alleles for a trait.

holophrase Single word that conveys a complete thought.

Home Observation for Measurement of the Environment (HOME) Instrument to measure the influence of the home environment on children's cognitive growth.

homosexual Describing a person whose sexual orientation is toward the same sex.

homozygous Possessing two identical alleles for a trait.

horizontal décalage In Piaget's terminology, a child's inability to transfer learning about one type of conservation to other types, hence, the child masters different types of conservation tasks at different ages.

hostile aggression Aggressive behavior intended to hurt another person.

hypotheses Possible explanations for phenomena, used to predict the outcome of research.

hypothetical-deductive reasoning Ability, believed by Piaget to accompany the stage of formal operations, to develop, consider, and test hypotheses.

I

id In Freudian theory, the instinctual aspect of personality (present at birth) that operates on the pleasure principle, seeking immediate gratification.

ideal self The self one would like to be. Compare *real self.*

identification In Freudian theory, the process by which a young child adopts characteristics, beliefs, attitudes, values, and behaviors of the parent of the same sex.

identity achievement Identity status, described by Marcia, which is characterized by commitment to choices made following a crisis, a period spent in exploring alternatives.

identity diffusion Identity status, described by Marcia, which is characterized by absence of commitment and lack of serious consideration of alternatives.

identity statuses In Marcia's terminology, states of ego development which depend on the presence or absence of crisis and commitment.

identity versus identity confusion In Erikson's theory, the fifth crisis of psychosocial development, in which an adolescent seeks to develop a coherent sense of self, including the role she or he is to play in society. Also called *identity versus role confusion.*

imaginary audience In Elkind's terminology, an observer who exists only in an adolescent's mind and is as concerned with the adolescent's thoughts and actions as the adolescent is.

implicit memory Memory, generally of habits and skills, which does not require conscious recall; sometimes called *procedural memory.* Compare *explicit memory.*

imprinting Instinctive form of learning in which, during a critical period in early development, a young animal forms an attachment to the first moving object it sees, usually the mother.

in vitro fertilization (IVF) Fertilization of an ovum outside the mother's body.

independent variable In an experiment, the condition over which the experimenter has direct control.

individual psychotherapy Psychological treatment in which a therapist sees a troubled person one-on-one, to help the patient gain insight into his or her personality, relationships, feelings, and behavior.

induction Type of logical reasoning that moves from particular observations to a general conclusion.

industry versus inferiority In Erikson's theory, the fourth critical alternative of psychosocial development, occurring during middle childhood, in which children must learn the productive skills their culture requires or else face feelings of inferiority.

infant mortality rate Proportion of babies born alive who die within the first year.

infertility Inability to conceive after 12 to 18 months of trying.

information-processing approach Approach to the study of cognitive development by observing and analyzing the mental processes involved in perceiving and handling information.

initiative versus guilt In Erikson's theory, the third crisis in psychosocial development, occurring between the ages of 3 and 6, in which children must balance the urge to pursue goals with the moral reservations that may prevent carrying them out.

instrumental aggression Aggressive behavior used as a means of achieving a goal.

intelligent behavior Behavior that is goal-oriented (conscious and deliberate) and adaptive to circumstances and conditions of life.

internalization Process by which children accept societal standards of conduct as their own; fundamental to socialization.

invisible imitation Imitation with parts of one's body that one cannot see (e.g., the mouth).

IQ (intelligence quotient) tests Psychometric tests that seek to measure how much intelligence a person has by comparing her or his performance with standardized norms.

irreversibility In Piaget's terminology, a limitation on preoperational thinking consisting of failure to understand that an operation can go in two or more directions.

K

Kaufman Assessment Battery for Children (K-ABC) Nontraditional individual intelligence test for children ages 2½ to 12½, which seeks to provide fair assessments of minority children and children with disabilities.

L

laboratory observation Research method in which the behavior of all participants is noted and recorded in the same situation, under controlled conditions.

language Communication system based on words and grammar.

language acquisition device (LAD) In Chomsky's terminology, an inborn mechanism that enables children to infer linguistic rules from the language they hear.

lanugo Fuzzy prenatal body hair, which drops off within a few days after birth.

learning Long-lasting change in behavior that occurs as a result of experience.

learning disabilities (LDs) Disorders that interfere with specific aspects of learning and school achievement.

learning perspective View of development concerned with changes in behavior that result from experience, or adaptation to the environment; the two major branches are behaviorism and social-learning theory.

linguistic speech Verbal expression designed to convey meaning.

literacy Ability to read and write.

long-term memory Storage of virtually unlimited capacity, which holds information for very long periods.

longitudinal study Study design in which data are collected about the same people over a period of time, to assess developmental changes that occur with age.

low birthweight Weight of less than 5½ pounds at birth because of prematurity or being small for date.

M

maternal blood test Prenatal diagnostic procedure to detect the presence of fetal abnormalities, used particularly when the fetus is at risk of defects in the central nervous system.

maturation Unfolding of a genetically influenced, often age-related, sequence of physical changes and behavior patterns, including the readiness to master new abilities.

mechanistic model Model, based on the machine as a metaphor, that views development as a passive, predictable response to internal and external stimuli, focuses on quantitative development, and studies phenomena by analyzing the operation of their component parts.

meconium Fetal waste matter, excreted during the first few days after birth.

menarche Girl's first menstruation.

mental retardation Significantly subnormal cognitive functioning.

metacommunication Understanding of the processes involved in communication.

metamemory Understanding of processes of memory.

mnemonic strategies Techniques to aid memory.

monozygotic (one-egg) twins Twins resulting from the division of a single zygote after fertilization; also called *identical twins*.

morality of constraint First of Piaget's two stages of moral development, characterized by rigid, simplistic judgments.

morality of cooperation Second of Piaget's two stages of moral development, characterized by flexible, subtle judgments and formulation of one's own moral code.

moratorium Identity status, described by Marcia, in which a person is currently considering alternatives (in crisis) and seems headed for commitment.

mother-infant bond Mother's feeling of close, caring connection with her newborn.

multifactorial transmission Combination of genetic and environmental factors to produce certain complex traits.

mutual regulation Process by which infant and caregiver communicate emotional states to each other and respond appropriately.

N

nativism Theory that human beings have an inborn capacity for language acquisition.

natural childbirth Method of childbirth, developed by Dr. Grantly Dick-Read, that seeks to prevent pain by eliminating the mother's fear of childbirth through education about the physiology of reproduction and training in methods of breathing and relaxation during delivery.

naturalistic observation Research method in which behavior is studied in natural settings without the observer's intervention or manipulation.

negativism Behavior characteristic of toddlers, in which they express their desire for independence by resisting authority.

neonatal jaundice Condition, in many newborn babies, caused by immaturity of liver and evidenced by yellowish appearance; can cause brain damage if not treated promptly.

neonatal period First 4 weeks of life, a time of transition from intrauterine dependency to independent existence.

neonate Newborn baby, up to 4 weeks old.

neurons Nerve cells.

niche-picking Tendency of a person, especially after early childhood, to seek out environments compatible with his or her genotype.

nonshared environmental effects The unique environment in which each child grows up, consisting of dissimilar influences or influences that affect each child differently.

nuclear family Two-generational economic, kinship, and living unit made up of parents and their biological or adopted children.

O

obesity Extreme overweight in relation to age, sex, height, and body type; sometimes defined as having a body mass index (weight-for-height) at or above the 85th percentile of growth curves for children of the same age and sex.

object permanence In Piaget's terminology, the understanding that a person or object still exists when out of sight.

observational learning In social-learning theory, learning that occurs through watching the behavior of others.

observer bias Tendency of an observer to misinterpret or distort data to fit his or her expectations.

operant conditioning Kind of learning in which a person tends to repeat a behavior that has been reinforced or to cease a behavior that has been punished.

organismic model Model that views development as internally initiated by an active person, or organism, and as occurring in a universal sequence of qualitatively different stages of maturation.

organization (1) In Piaget's terminology, integration of knowledge into a system to make sense of the environment. (2) Mnemonic strategy consisting of categorizing material to be remembered.

Otis-Lennon School Ability Test Group intelligence test for kindergarten through twelfth grade.

ovum transfer Method of fertilization in which a woman who cannot produce normal ova receives an ovum donated by a fertile woman.

P

permissive In Baumrind's terminology, parenting style emphasizing self-expression and self-regulation. Compare *authoritarian* and *authoritative*.

personal fable In Elkind's terminology, conviction that one is special, unique, and not subject to the rules that govern the rest of the world.

personality Person's unique and relatively consistent way of feeling, reacting, and behaving.

phenotype Observable characteristics of a person.

physical abuse Action taken to endanger a child involving potential injury to the body.

physical neglect Failure to meet a child's basic bodily needs, such as food, clothing, medical care, protection, and supervision.

Piagetian approach Approach to the study of cognitive development based on Piaget's theory, which describes qualitative stages, or typical changes, in children's and adolescents' cognitive functioning.

plasticity (1) Modifiability of performance. (2) Modifiability, or "molding," of the brain through early experience.

polygenic inheritance Interaction of several sets of genes to produce a complex trait.

postconventional morality (or morality of autonomous moral principles) Third level in Kohlberg's theory of moral reasoning, in which people follow internally held moral principles of right and wrong, fairness, and justice, and can decide among conflicting moral standards.

postmature Referring to a fetus not yet born as of 2 weeks after the due date or 42 weeks after the mother's last menstrual period.

pragmatics The practical knowledge needed to use language for communicative purposes.

preconventional morality First level of Kohlberg's theory of moral reasoning, in which control is external and rules are obeyed in order to gain rewards or avoid punishment.

preimplantation genetic diagnosis Medical procedure in which cells from an embryo conceived by in vitro fertilization are analyzed for genetic defects prior to implantation of the embryo in the mother's uterus.

prejudice Unfavorable attitude toward members of certain groups outside one's own, especially racial or ethnic groups.

prelinguistic speech Forerunner of linguistic speech; utterance of sounds that are not words. Includes crying, cooing, babbling, and accidental and deliberate imitation of sounds without understanding their meaning.

preoperational stage In Piaget's theory, the second major stage of cognitive development (approximately from age 2 to age 7), in which children become more sophisticated in their use of symbolic thought but are not yet able to use logic.

prepared childbirth Method of childbirth, developed by Dr. Ferdinand Lamaze, that uses instruction, breathing exercises, and social support to induce controlled physical responses to uterine contractions and reduce fear and pain.

Preschool Assessment of Attachment (PAA) Instrument for measuring attachment after 20 months of age, which takes into account the complexity of preschoolers' relationships and linguistic abilities.

pretend play Play involving imaginary people or situations; also called *fantasy play, dramatic play, symbolic play,* or *imaginative play.*

preterm (premature) infants Infants born before completing the thirty-seventh week of gestation.

primary sex characteristics Organs directly related to reproduction, which enlarge and mature during adolescence. Compare *secondary sex characteristics.*

private speech Talking aloud to oneself with no intent to communicate.

proximodistal principle Principle that development proceeds from within to without (i.e., that parts of the body near the center develop before the extremities).

psychoanalytic perspective View of development concerned with unconscious forces motivating behavior.

psychometric approach Approach to the study of cognitive development that seeks to measure the quantity of intelligence a person possesses.

psychosexual development In Freudian theory, an unvarying sequence of stages of personality development during infancy, childhood, and adolescence, in which gratification shifts from the mouth to the anus and then to the genitals.

psychosocial development In Erikson's theory, the socially and culturally influenced process of development of the ego, or self; it consists of eight maturationally determined stages throughout the life span, each revolving around a particular crisis or turning point in which the person is faced with achieving a healthy balance between alternative positive and negative traits.

puberty Process by which a person attains sexual maturity and the ability to reproduce.

punishment In operant conditioning, a stimulus experienced following a behavior, which decreases the probability that the behavior will be repeated.

Q

qualitative change   Change in kind, structure, or organization, such as the change from nonverbal to verbal communication.

quantitative change   Change in number or amount, such as in height, weight, or size of vocabulary.

R

random assignment   Technique used in assigning members of a study sample to experimental and control groups, in which each member of the sample has an equal chance to be assigned to each group and to receive or not receive the treatment.

random selection   Sampling method that ensures representativeness because each member of the population has an equal and independent chance to be selected.

reaction range   Potential variability, depending on environmental conditions, in the expression of a hereditary trait.

real self   The self one actually is. Compare *ideal self.*

realistic period   In Ginzberg's theory of career planning, period toward the end of the high school years when adolescents select future occupations on the basis of an accurate match between interests, abilities, and values and plan for appropriate preparation for those occupations.

recall   Ability to reproduce material from memory. Compare *recognition.*

recessive inheritance   Pattern of inheritance in which an individual receives identical recessive alleles from both parents, resulting in expression of a recessive (nondominant) trait.

reciprocity   In Maccoby's terminology, system of mutually binding, mutually responsive relationships into which a child is socialized.

recognition   Ability to identify a previously encountered stimulus. Compare *recall.*

reflex behaviors   Automatic, involuntary, innate responses to stimulation.

rehearsal   Mnemonic strategy to keep an item in working memory through conscious repetition.

reinforcement   In operant conditioning, a stimulus experienced following a behavior, which increases the probability that the behavior will be repeated.

relational aggression   Aggression aimed at damaging or interfering with

another person's relationships, reputation, or psychological well-being; also called *covert, indirect,* or *psychological aggression.*

relational theory   Theory, proposed by Miller, that all personality growth occurs within emotional connections, not separate from them.

reliability   Consistency of a test in measuring performance.

representational ability   In Piaget's terminology, capacity to mentally represent objects and experiences, largely through the use of symbols.

representational mappings   In neo-Piagetian terminology, the second stage in development of self-definition, in which a child makes logical connections between aspects of the self but still sees these characteristics in all-or-nothing terms.

representational systems   In neo-Piagetian terminology, the third stage in development of self-definition, characterized by breadth, balance, and the integration and assessment of various aspects of the self.

resilient children   Children who weather adverse circumstances, function well despite challenges or threats, or bounce back from traumatic events that would have a highly negative impact on the emotional development of most children.

rough-and-tumble play   Vigorous play involving wrestling, hitting, and chasing, often accompanied by laughing and screaming.

S

sample   Group of participants chosen to represent the entire population under study.

scaffolding   Temporary support given to a child who is mastering a task.

schema confirmation-deployment model   Variation on gender-schema theory, in which a child builds a "script" based on gender-related information and then checks new information against the script.

schemes   In Piaget's terminology, basic cognitive structures consisting of organized patterns of behavior used in different kinds of situations.

school phobia   Unrealistic fear of going to school; may be a form of separation anxiety disorder.

scientific method   System of established principles and processes of scientific inquiry, including identification of a problem to be studied, formulation and testing of alternative hypotheses,

collection and analysis of data, and public dissemination of findings so that other scientists can check, learn from, analyze, repeat, and build on the results.

script   General remembered outline of a familiar, repeated event, used to guide behavior.

secondary sex characteristics   Physiological signs of sexual maturation (such as breast development and growth of body hair) that do not involve the sex organs. Compare *primary sex characteristics.*

secular trend   Trend that can be seen by observing several generations, such as the trend toward earlier attainment of adult height and sexual maturity, which began a century ago.

secure attachment   Attachment pattern in which an infant separates readily from the primary caregiver and actively seeks out the caregiver upon the caregiver's return.

self-awareness   Realization that one's existence is separate from other people and things.

self-concept   Sense of self; descriptive and evaluative mental picture of one's abilities and traits.

self-definition   Cluster of characteristics used to describe oneself.

self-esteem   The judgment a person makes about his or her self-worth.

self-regulation   Child's independent control of behavior to conform to understood social expectations.

sensorimotor stage   In Piaget's theory, the first stage in cognitive development, during which infants (from birth to approximately 2 years) learn through their developing senses and motor activity.

separation anxiety   Distress shown by an infant when a familiar caregiver leaves.

separation anxiety disorder   Condition involving excessive, prolonged anxiety concerning separation from home or from people to whom a child is attached.

seriation   Ability to order items along a dimension.

sex chromosomes   Pair of chromosomes that determines sex: XX in the normal female, XY in the normal male.

sex differences   Physical differences between males and females.

sex-linked inheritance   Pattern of inheritance in which certain characteristics carried on the X chromosome inherited from the mother are transmitted differently to her male and female offspring.

sexual abuse Sexual activity involving a child and an older person.

sexual orientation Focus of consistent sexual, romantic, and affectionate interest, either heterosexual, homosexual, or bisexual.

sexually transmitted diseases (STDs) Diseases spread by sexual contact; also called *venereal diseases.*

single representations In neo-Piagetian terminology, first stage in development of self-definition, in which children describe themselves in terms of individual, unconnected characteristics and in all-or-nothing terms.

situational compliance In Kochanska's terminology, a toddler's obedience of a parent's orders only in the presence of prompting or other signs of ongoing parental control.

slow-to-warm-up children Children whose temperament is generally mild but who are hesitant about accepting new experiences.

small-for-date (small-for-gestational age) infants Infants whose birthweight is less than that of 90 percent of babies of the same gestational age, as a result of slow fetal growth.

social capital Family and community resources upon which a person can draw.

social play Play in which children, to varying degrees, interact with other children.

social referencing Understanding an ambiguous situation by seeking out another person's perception of it.

social speech Speech intended to be understood by a listener.

social-contextual approach Approach to the study of cognitive development by focusing on the influence of environmental aspects of the learning process, particularly parents and other caregivers.

social-learning theory Theory, proposed by Bandura, that behaviors are learned by observing and imitating models. Also called *social-cognitive theory.*

socialization Process of developing the habits, skills, values, and motives shared by responsible, productive members of a particular society.

sociocultural theory Vygotsky's theory that analyzes how specific cultural practices, particularly social interaction with adults, affect children's development.

socioeconomic status (SES) Combination of economic and social factors, including income, education, and occupation.

spermarche Boy's first ejaculation.

spontaneous abortion Natural expulsion from the uterus of an embryo or fetus that cannot survive outside the womb; also called *miscarriage.*

standardized norms Standards for evaluating performance of persons who take an intelligence test, obtained from scores of a large, representative sample who took the test while it was in preparation.

Stanford-Binet Intelligence Scale Individual intelligence test used with children to measure memory, spatial orientation, and practical judgment.

state of arousal An infant's degree of alertness; his or her condition, at a given moment, in the periodic daily cycle of wakefulness, sleep, and activity.

Sternberg Triarchic Abilities Test (STAT) Test that seeks to measure componential, experiential, and contextual intelligence in verbal, quantitative, and figural (spatial) domains.

Strange Situation Laboratory technique used to study attachment.

stranger anxiety Wariness of strange people and places, shown by some infants during the second half of the first year.

stuttering Involuntary, frequent repetition or prolongation of sounds or syllables.

substance abuse Repeated, harmful use of a substance, usually alcohol or another drug.

substance dependence Addiction (physical or psychological, or both) to a harmful substance.

sudden infant death syndrome (SIDS) Sudden and unexpected death of an apparently healthy infant.

superego In Freudian theory, the aspect of personality that represents socially-approved values; it develops around the age of 5 or 6 as a result of identification with the parent of the same sex.

surrogate motherhood Method of conception in which a woman who is not married to a man agrees to bear his baby and then give the child to the father and his mate.

symbolic function In Piaget's terminology, ability to use mental representations (words, numbers, or images) to which a child has attached meaning.

syntax Rules for forming sentences in a particular language.

systems of action (1) Combinations of motor skills that permit increasingly complex activities. (2) Increasingly complex combinations of simpler, previously acquired skills, which permit a wider or more precise range of movement and more control of the environment.

T

telegraphic speech Early form of sentence consisting of only a few essential words.

temperament Person's characteristic disposition, or style of approaching and reacting to people and situations.

tentative period In Ginzberg's theory of career planning, period around puberty when young people begin to try to match their interests with their abilities and values.

teratogenic Capable of causing birth defects.

theory Coherent set of related concepts that seeks to organize and explain data.

theory of mind Awareness and understanding of mental processes.

theory of multiple intelligences Gardner's theory that distinct, multiple forms of intelligence exist in each person.

transduction In Piaget's terminology, a preoperational child's tendency to mentally link particular experiences, whether or not there is logically a causal relationship.

transitional objects Objects used repeatedly by a child as bedtime companions.

transitive inference Understanding of the relationship between two objects by knowing the relationship of each to a third object.

triarchic theory of intelligence Sternberg's theory describing three types of intelligence: componential (analytical ability), experiential (insight and originality), and contextual (practical thinking).

U

ultrasound Prenatal medical procedure using high-frequency sound waves to detect the outline of a fetus and its movements, so as to determine whether a pregnancy is progressing normally.

umbilical cord sampling Prenatal medical procedure in which samples of a fetus's blood are taken from the umbilical cord to assess body functioning; also called *fetal blood sampling.*

V

validity Capacity of a test to measure what it is intended to measure.

vernix caseosa Oily substance on a neonate's skin that protects against infection.

violation-of-expectations Research method in which an infant's tendency to dishabituate to a stimulus that conflicts with previous experience is taken as evidence that the infant recognizes the new stimulus as surprising.

visible imitation Imitation with parts of one's body that one can see (e.g., the hands and the feet).

visual cliff Apparatus designed to give an illusion of depth and used to assess depth perception in infants.

visual novelty preference Infant's preference for new rather than familiar sights.

visual preference An infant's tendency to look longer at certain stimuli than at others, which depends on the ability to make visual distinctions.

visual-recognition memory Ability to distinguish a familiar visual stimulus from an unfamiliar one.

W

Wechsler Intelligence Scale for Children (WISC-III) Individual intelligence test for schoolchildren, which yields verbal and performance scores as well as a combined score.

Wechsler Preschool and Primary Scale of Intelligence—Revised (WPPSI-R) Individual intelligence test for children ages 3 to 7, which yields verbal and performance scores as well as a combined score.

working memory Short-term storage of information being actively processed.

Z

zone of proximal development (ZPD) Vygotsky's term for the level at which children can *almost* perform a task on their own and, with appropriate teaching, *can* perform it.

zygote One-celled organism resulting from fertilization.

Bibliography

Abbey, A., Andrews, F. M., & Halman, J. (1992). Infertility and subjective well being: The mediating roles of self-esteem, internal control, and interpersonal conflict. *Journal of Marriage and the Family, 54,* 408–417.

Abma, J. C., Chandra, A., Mosher, W. D., Peterson, L., & Piccinino, L. (1997). Fertility, family planning, and women's health: New data from the 1995 National Survey of Family Growth. *Vital Health Statistics, 23* (19). Washington, DC: National Center for Health Statistics.

Abramovitch, R., Corter, C., & Lando, B. (1979). Sibling interaction in the home. *Child Development, 50,* 997–1003.

Abramovitch, R., Corter, C., Pepler, D., & Stanhope, L. (1986). Sibling and peer interactions: A final follow-up and comparison. *Child Development, 57,* 217–229.

Abramovitch, R., Pepler, D., & Corter, C. (1982). Patterns of sibling interaction among preschool-age children. In M. E. Lamb (Ed.), *Sibling relationships: Their nature and significance across the lifespan.* Hillsdale, NJ: Erlbaum.

Abrams, B., & Parker, J. D. (1990). Maternal weight gain in women with good pregnancy outcome. *Obstetrics and Gynecology, 76* (1), 1–7.

Abravanel, E., & Sigafoos, A. D. (1984). Exploring the presence of imitation during early infancy. *Child Development, 55,* 381–392.

Abroms, K., & Bennett, J. (1981). Changing etiological perspectives in Down's syndrome: Implications for early intervention. *Journal of the Division for Early Childhood, 2,* 109–112.

Achenbach, T. M., & Howell, C. T. (1993). Are American children's problems getting worse? A 13-year comparison. *Journal of the American Academy of Child and Adolescent Psychiatry, 32,* 1145–1154.

Achievers after the age of 90. (1993, September 26). *Parade,* p. 17.

Ackerman, B. P. (1997). The role of setting information in children's memory retrieval. *Journal of Experimental Child Psychology, 65,* 238–260.

Ackerman, G. L. (1993). A Congressional view of youth suicide. *American Psychologist, 48(2),* 183–184.

Acredolo, L., & Goodwyn, S. (1988). Symbolic gesturing in normal infants. *Child Development, 59,* 450–466.

Adams, L. A., & Rickert, V. I. (1989). Reducing bedtime tantrums: Comparison between positive routines and graduated extinction. *Pediatrics, 84,* 756–761.

Agran, P. F., Winn, D. G., Anderson, C. L., Tran, C., & Del Valle, C. P. (1996). The role of the physical and traffic environment in child pedestrian injuries. *Pediatrics, 98,* 1096–1103.

Ainsworth, M. D. (1964). Patterns of attachment behavior shown by the infant in interaction with his mother. *Merrill-Palmer Quarterly, 10,* 51–58.

Ainsworth, M. D. S. (1967). *Infancy in Uganda: Infant care and the growth of love.* Baltimore: Johns Hopkins University Press.

Ainsworth, M. D. S. (1969). Object relations, dependency, and attachment: A theoretical review of the infant-mother relationship. *Child Development, 40,* 969–1025.

Ainsworth, M. D. S. (1979). Infant-mother attachment. *American Psychologist, 34* (10), 932–937.

Ainsworth, M. D. S., & Bell, S. (1977). Infant crying and maternal responsiveness: A rejoinder to Gerwitz and Boyd. *Child Development, 48,* 1208–1216.

Ainsworth, M. D. S., Blehar, M. C., Waters, E., & Wall, S. (1978). *Patterns of attachment: A psychological study of the strange situation.* Hillsdale, NJ: Erlbaum.

Alan Guttmacher Institute (AGI). (1994). *Sex & America's teenagers.* New York: Author.

Albanese, A., & Stanhope, R. (1993). Growth and metabolic data following growth hormone treatment of children with intrauterine growth retardation. *Hormone Research, 39,* 8–12.

Aldort, N. (1994, Summer). Getting out of the way. *Mothering,* pp. 38–43.

Alessandri, S. M., Sullivan, M. W., Imaizumi, S., & Lewis, M. (1993). Learning and emotional responsivity in cocaine-exposed infants. *Developmental Psychology, 29,* 989–997.

Alexander, K. L., Entwisle, D. R., & Dauber, S. L. (1993). First-grade classroom behavior: Its short- and long-term consequences for school performance. *Child Development, 64,* 801–814.

Aligne, C. A., & Stoddard, J. J. (1997). Tobacco and children: An economic evaluation of the medical effects of parental smoking. *Archives of Pediatric and Adolescent Medicine, 151,* 648–653.

Allen, G. L., & Ondracek, P. J. (1995). Age-sensitive cognitive abilities related to children's acquisition of spatial knowledge. *Developmental Psychology, 31,* 934–945.

Allen, J. P., Philliber, S., Herrling, S., & Kuperminc, G. P. (1997). Preventing teen pregnancy and academic failure: Experimental evaluation of a developmentally based approach. *Child Development, 64,* 729–742.

Allore, R., O'Hanlon, D., Price, R., Neilson, K., Willard, H. F., Cox, D. R., Marks, A., & Dun, R. J. (1988). Gene encoding the B subunit of S100 protein is on chromosome 21: Implications for Down syndrome. *Science, 239,* 1311–1313.

Almeida, D. M., Maggs, J. L., & Galambos, N. L. (1993). Wives' employment hours and spousal participation in family work. *Journal of Family Psychology, 7,* 233–244.

Alsaker, F. D. (1992). Pubertal timing, overweight, and psychological adjustment. *Journal of Early Adolescence, 12(4),* 396–419.

Amabile, T. A., & Rovee-Collier, C. (1991). Contextual variation and memory retrieval at six months. *Child Development, 62,* 1155–1166.

Amato, P. R. (1987). Family processes in one-parent, stepparent, and intact families: The child's point of view. *Journal of Marriage and the Family, 49,* 327–337.

Amato, P. R., & Keith, B. (1991a). Parental divorce and adult well-being: A meta-analysis. *Journal of Marriage and the Family, 53,* 43–58.

Amato, P. R., & Keith, B. (1991b). Parental divorce and the well-being of children: A meta-analysis. *Psychological Bulletin, 110,* 26–46.

Amato, P. R., Kurdek, L. A., Demo, D. H., & Allen, K. R. (1993). Children's adjustment to divorce: Theories, hypotheses, and empirical support. *Journal of Marriage and the Family, 55,* 23–54.

American Academy of Pediatrics (AAP). (1986). *Positive approaches to day care dilemmas: How to make it work.* Elk Grove Village, IL: Author.

American Academy of Pediatrics (AAP). (1989a, November). *The facts on breast feeding* [Fact sheet]. Elk Grove, IL: Author.

American Academy of Pediatrics (AAP). (1989b). Follow-up on weaning formulas. *Pediatrics, 83,* 1067.

American Academy of Pediatrics (AAP). (1992a, January 15). *AAP proposes handgun ban, other measures to curb firearm deaths, injuries* [News release]. Elk Grove Village, IL: Author.

American Academy of Pediatrics (AAP). (1992b, Spring). Bedtime doesn't have to be a struggle. *Healthy Kids,* pp. 4–10.

American Academy of Pediatrics (AAP). (1996, October). *Where we stand.* Available: http://www.aap.org/advocacy/wwestand.htm[1997, May 24]

American Academy of Pediatrics (AAP) and Center to Prevent Handgun Violence. (1994). *Keep your family safe from firearm injury.* Washington, DC: Center to Prevent Handgun Violence.

American Academy of Pediatrics (AAP) Committee on Accident and Poison Prevention. (1990). Bicycle helmets. *Pediatrics, 85,* 229–230.

American Academy of Pediatrics (AAP) Committee on Adolescence. (1994). Sexually transmitted diseases. *Pediatrics, 94,* 568–572.

American Academy of Pediatrics (AAP) Committee on Bioethics. (1992). Infants with anencephaly as organ sources: Ethical considerations. *Pediatrics, 89,* 1116–1119.

American Academy of Pediatrics (AAP) Committee on Children with Disabilities and Committee on Drugs. (1996). Medication for children with attentional disorders. *Pediatrics, 98,* 301–304.

American Academy of Pediatrics (AAP) Committee on Children with Disabilities and Committee on Psychosocial Aspects of Child and Family Health. (1993). Psychosocial risks of chronic health conditions in childhood and adolescence. *Pediatrics, 92,* 876–877.

American Academy of Pediatrics (AAP) Committee on Communications. (1995). Sexuality, contraception, and the media. *Pediatrics, 95,* 298–300.

American Academy of Pediatrics (AAP) Committee on Community Health Services. (1996). Health needs of homeless children and families. *Pediatrics, 88,* 789–791.

American Academy of Pediatrics (AAP) Committee on Drugs. (1980). Marijuana. *Pediatrics, 65,* 652–656.

American Academy of Pediatrics (AAP) Committee on Drugs. (1994). The transfer of drugs and other chemicals into human milk. *Pediatrics, 93,* 137–150.

American Academy of Pediatrics (AAP) Committee on Drugs and Committee on Bioethics. (1997). Considerations related to the use of recombinant human growth hormone in children. *Pediatrics, 99,* 122–128.

American Academy of Pediatrics (AAP) Committee on Environmental Health. (1993). Lead poisoning: From screening to primary prevention. *Pediatrics, 92,* 176–183.

American Academy of Pediatrics (AAP) Committee on Environmental Health. (1997). Environmental tobacco smoke: A hazard to children. *Pediatrics, 99,* 639–642.

American Academy of Pediatrics (AAP) Committee on Fetus and Newborn. (1986). Use and abuse of the Apgar scale. *Pediatrics, 78,* 1148–1149.

American Academy of Pediatrics (AAP) Committee on Fetus and Newborn and American College of Obstetricians and Gynecologists Committee on Obstetric Practice. (1996). Use and abuse of the Apgar score. *Pediatrics, 98,* 141–142.

American Academy of Pediatrics (AAP) Committee on Genetics. (1993). Folic acid for the prevention of neural tube defects. *Pediatrics, 92,* 493–494.

American Academy of Pediatrics (AAP) Committee on Genetics. (1996). Newborn screening fact sheet. *Pediatrics, 98,* 1–29.

American Academy of Pediatrics (AAP) Committee on Infectious Diseases. (1994). *Red book* (23rd ed.). Elk Grove Village, IL: Author.

American Academy of Pediatrics (AAP) Committee on Infectious Diseases. (1998). 1998 recommended childhood immunization schedule. *Pediatrics, 101,* 154–157.

American Academy of Pediatrics (AAP) Committee on Injury and Poison Prevention. (1995a). Bicycle helmets. *Pediatrics, 95,* 609–610.

American Academy of Pediatrics (AAP) Committee on Injury and Poison Prevention. (1995b). Injuries associated with infant walkers. *Pediatrics, 95,* 778–780.

American Academy of Pediatrics (AAP) Committee on Nutrition. (1986). Prudent life-style for children: Dietary fat and cholesterol. *Pediatrics, 78,* 521–525.

American Academy of Pediatrics (AAP) Committee on Nutrition. (1992a). Statement on cholesterol. *Pediatrics, 90,* 469–473.

American Academy of Pediatrics (AAP) Committee on Nutrition. (1992b). The use of whole cow's milk in infancy. *Pediatrics, 89,* 1105–1109.

American Academy of Pediatrics (AAP) Committee on Nutrition. (1993). *Pediatric nutrition handbook.* Elk Grove Village, IL: Author.

American Academy of Pediatrics (AAP) Committee on Pediatric Aspects of Physical Fitness, Recreation, and Sports. (1981). Competitive athletics for children of elementary school age. *Pediatrics, 67,* 927–928.

American Academy of Pediatrics (AAP) Committee on Sports Medicine and Committee on School Health. (1989). Organized athletics for preadolescent children. *Pediatrics, 84,* 583–584.

American Academy of Pediatrics (AAP) Committee on Sports Medicine and Fitness. (1992). Fitness, activity, and sports participation in the preschool child. *Pediatrics, 90,* 1002–1004.

American Academy of Pediatrics (AAP) Committee on Sports Medicine and Fitness. (1997). Participation in boxing by children, adolescents, and young adults. *Pediatrics, 99,* 134–135.

American Academy of Pediatrics (AAP) Committee on Substance Abuse and Committee on Children with Disabilities. (1993). Fetal alcohol syndrome and fetal alcohol effects. *Pediatrics, 91,* 1004–1006.

American Academy of Pediatrics (AAP) Provisional Committee on Pediatric AIDS. (1995). Perinatal human immunodeficiency virus testing. *Pediatrics, 95,* 303–307.

American Academy of Pediatrics (AAP) Task Force on Blood Pressure Control in Children. (1987). Report of the second Task Force on Blood Pressure Control in Children. *Pediatrics, 79,* 1–25.

American Academy of Pediatrics (AAP) Task Force on Infant Positioning and SIDS. (1992). Positioning and SIDS. *Pediatrics, 89,* 1120–1126.

American Academy of Pediatrics (AAP) Task Force on Infant Positioning and SIDS. (1996). Positioning and sudden infant death syndrome (SIDS): Update. *Pediatrics, 98,* 1216–1218.

American Academy of Pediatrics (AAP) Task Force on Infant Positioning and SIDS. (1997). Does bed sharing affect the risk of SIDS? *Pediatrics, 100,* 272.

American Academy of Pediatrics (AAP) Task Force on Pediatric AIDS. (1991). Education of children with human immunodeficiency virus infection. *Pediatrics, 88,* 645–648.

American Academy of Pediatrics (AAP) Work Group on Breastfeeding. (1997). Breastfeeding and the use of human milk. *Pediatrics, 100,* 1035–1039.

American Cancer Society. (1997). *Cancer facts and figures—1997.* Atlanta, GA: Author.

American College of Obstetrics and Gynecology. (1994). *Exercise during pregnancy and the postpartum pregnancy* (Technical Bulletin No. 189). Washington, DC: Author.

American College Testing Program. (1995). *ACT high school profile report, 1995.* Iowa City: Author.

American Foundation for the Prevention of Venereal Disease (AFPVD). (1988). *Sexually transmitted disease [venereal disease]: Prevention for everyone* (16th rev. ed.). New York: Author.

American Heart Association (AHA). (1994). *Fact sheet: Risk factors—cigarette/tobacco smoke.* Dallas, TX: Author.

American Psychiatric Association (APA). (1994). *Diagnostic and statistical manual of mental disorders* (4th ed.). Washington, DC: Author.

American Psychological Association. (n.d.). *Answers to your questions about sexual orientation and homosexuality* [Brochure]. Washington, DC: Author.

American Psychological Association. (1992). Ethical principles of psychologists and code of conduct. *American Psychologist, 47,* 1597–1611.

American Psychological Association. (1997, June 4). Mirror images: Depressed mothers, depressed newborns [News release]. *APA Experts.* Washington, DC: Author.

Ames, E. W. (1997). *The development of Romanian orphanage children adopted to Canada: Final report* (National Welfare Grants Program, Human Resources Development, Canada). Burnaby, BC, Canada: Simon Fraser University, Psychology Dept.

Amsel, E., Goodman, G., Savoie, D., & Clark, M. (1996). The development of reasoning about causal and noncausal influences on levers. *Child Development, 67,* 1624–1646.

Anastasi, A. (1988). *Psychological testing* (6th ed.). New York: Macmillan.

Anastasi, A., & Schaefer, C. E. (1971). Note on concepts of creativity and intelligence. *Journal of Creative Behavior, 3,* 113–116.

Andersen, R. E., Crespo, C. J., Bartlett, S. J., Cheskin, L. J., & Pratt, M. (1998). Relationship of physical activity and television watching with body weight and level of fatness among children: Results from the Third National Health and Nutrition Examination Survey. *Journal of the American Medical Association, 279,* 938–942.

Anderson, M. (1992). *My Lord, what a morning.* Madison: University of Wisconsin Press.

Anderson, R. N., Kochanek, K. D., & Murphy, S. L. (1997). *Report of final mortality statistics, 1995* (Monthly Vital Statistics Report, 45[11, Suppl. 2]). Washington, DC: U.S. Department of Health and Human Services.

Andersson, B. E. (1992). Effects of daycare on cognitive and socioemotional competence of thirteen-year-old Swedish children. *Child Development, 63,* 20–36.

Angell, M. (1990). New ways to get pregnant. *New England Journal of Medicine, 323,* 1200–1202.

Angier, N. (1997, January 7). Chemical tied to fat control could help trigger puberty. *The New York Times,* pp. C1, C3.

Anglin, T. M., Naylor, K. E., & Kaplan, D. W. (1996). Comprehensive school-based health care: High school students' use of medical, mental health, and substance abuse services. *Pediatrics, 97,* 318–330.

Anisfeld, M. (1996). Only tongue protrusion modeling is matched by neonates. *Developmental Review, 16,* 149–161.

Antonarakis, S. E., & Down Syndrome Collaborative Group. (1991). Parental origin of the extra chromosome in trisomy 21 as indicated by analysis of DNA polymorphisms. *New England Journal of Medicine, 324,* 872–876.

Apgar, B. S., & Churgay, C. A. (1993). Spontaneous abortion. *Primary Care, 20,* 621–627.

Apgar, V. (1953). A proposal for a new method of evaluation of the newborn infant. *Current Research in Anesthesia and Analgesia, 32,* 260–267.

Apostal, R. A., & Helland, C. (1993). Commitment to and role changes in dual career families. *Journal of Career Development, 20*(2), 121–129.

Archer, S. L. (1993). Identity in relational contexts: A methodological proposal. In J. Kroger (Ed.), *Discussions on ego identity* (pp. 75–99). Hillsdale, NJ: Erlbaum.

Arcus, D., & Kagan, J. (1995). Temperament and craniofacial variation in the first two years. *Child Development, 66,* 1529–1540.

Arend, R., Gove, F., & Sroufe, L. A. (1979). Continuity of individual adaptation from infancy to kindergarten: A predictive study of ego-resiliency and curiosity in preschoolers. *Child Development, 50,* 950–959.

Ariès, P. (1962). *Centuries of childhood.* New York: Vintage.

Armstrong, B. G., McDonald, A. D., & Sloan, M. (1992). Cigarette, alcohol, and coffee consumption and spontaneous abortion. *American Journal of Public Health, 81,* 85.

Arnold, D. S., & Whitehurst, G. J. (1994). Accelerating language development through picture book reading: A summary of dialogic reading and its effects. In D. K. Dickinson (Ed.), *Bridges to literacy: Children, families, and schools* (pp. 103–128). Oxford: Blackwell.

Aslin, R. N. (1987). Visual and auditory development in infancy. In J. D. Osofsky (Ed.), *Handbook of infant development* (2nd ed.). New York: Wiley.

Astington, J. W. (1993). *The child's discovery of the mind.* Cambridge, MA: Harvard University Press.

Attention deficit disorder—Part II. (1995, May). *The Harvard Mental Health Letter,* pp. 1–3.

Aureli, T., & Colecchia, N. (1996). Day care experience and free play behavior in preschool children. *Journal of Applied Developmental Psychology, 17,* 1–17.

Autism—Part II. (1997, April). *The Harvard Mental Health Letter,* pp. 1–4.

Aylward, G. P., Pfeiffer, S. I., Wright, A., & Verhulst, S. J. (1989). Outcome studies of low birth weight infants published in the last decade: A meta-analysis. *Journal of Pediatrics, 115,* 515–520.

Azmitia, M., & Hesser, J. (1993). Why siblings are important agents of cognitive development: A comparison of siblings and peers. *Child Development, 64,* 430–444.

Azuma, S. D., & Chasnoff, I. J. (1993). Outcome of children prenatally exposed to cocaine and other drugs: A path analysis of three-year data. *Pediatrics, 92,* 396–402.

Babson, S. G., & Clarke, N. G. (1983). Relationship between infant death and maternal age. *Journal of Pediatrics, 103,* 391–393.

Babu, A., & Hirschhorn, K. (1992). *A guide to human chromosome defects* (Birth Defects: Original Article Series, 28[2]). White Plains, NY: March of Dimes Birth Defects Foundation.

Bachman, J. G., & Schulenberg, J. (1993). How part-time work intensity relates to drug use, problem behavior, time use, and satisfaction among high school seniors: Are these consequences or merely correlates? *Developmental Psychology, 29,* 220–235.

Bachrach, C. A., London, K. A., & Maza, P. L. (1991). On the path to adoption: Adoption seeking in the United States, 1988. *Journal of Marriage and the Family, 53,* 705–718.

Bachu, A. (1993). *Fertility of American women: June 1992* (Current Population Report No. P24-470). Washington, DC: U.S. Government Printing Office.

Backett, K. (1987). The negotiation of fatherhood. In C. Lewis & M. O'Brien (Eds.), *Reassessing fatherhood: New observations on fathers and the modern family.* London: Sage.

Baddeley, A. D. (1981). The concept of working memory: A view of its current state and probable future development. *Cognition, 10,* 17–23.

Baddeley, A. D. (1986). *Working memory.* London: Oxford University Press.

Baghurst, P. A., McMichael, A. J., Wigg, N. R., Vimpani, G. V., Robertson, E. F., Roberts, R. J., & Tong, S. L. (1992). Environmental exposure to lead and children's intelligence at the age of seven years. *New England Journal of Medicine, 327,* 1279–1284.

Bailey, A., Le Couteur, A., Gottesman, I., & Bolton, P. (1995). Autism as a strongly genetic disorder: Evidence from a British twin study. *Psychological Medicine, 25,* 63–77.

Bailey, J. M., Bobrow, D., Wolfe, M., & Mikach, S. (1995). Sexual orientation of adult sons of gay fathers. *Developmental Psychology, 31,* 124–129.

Bailey, W. T. (1994). A longitudinal study of fathers' involvement with young children: Infancy to age 5 years. *Journal of Genetic Psychology, 155,* 331–339.

Baillargeon, R. (1994). How do infants learn about the physical world? *Current Directions in Psychological Science, 3,* 133–140.

Baillargeon, R., & DeVos, J. (1991). Object permanence in young infants: Further evidence. *Child Development, 62,* 1227–1246.

Baldwin, D. A., & Moses, L. J. (1996). The ontogeny of social information gathering. *Child Development, 67,* 1915–1939.

Baldwin, J. (1972). *No name in the street*. New York: Dial.

Baltes, P. B., Reese, H. W., & Lipsitt, L. (1980). Life-span developmental psychology. *Annual Review of Psychology, 31,* 65–110.

Bandura, A. (1977). *Social learning theory*. Englewood Cliffs, NJ: Prentice-Hall.

Bandura, A. (1989). Social cognitive theory. In R. Vasta (Ed.), *Annals of child development*. Greenwich, CT: JAI.

Bandura, A., Barbaranelli, C., Caprara, G. V., & Pastorelli, C. (1996). Multifaceted impact of self-efficacy beliefs on academic functioning. *Child Development, 67,* 1206–1222.

Bandura, A., Ross, D., & Ross, S. A. (1961). Transmission of aggression through imitation of aggressive models. *Journal of Abnormal and Social Psychology, 63,* 575–582.

Bandura, A., Ross, D., & Ross, S. A. (1963). Imitation of film-mediated aggressive models. *Journal of Abnormal and Social Psychology, 66,* 3–11.

Barager, J. R. (Ed.). (1968). *Why Perón came to power: The background to Peronism in Argentina*. New York: Knopf.

Barber, B. K. (1994). Cultural, family, and personal contexts of parent-adolescent conflict. *Journal of Marriage and the Family, 56,* 375–386.

Barber, B. L., & Eccles, J. S. (1992). Long-term influence of divorce and single parenting on adolescent family- and work-related values, behaviors, and aspirations. *Psychological Bulletin, 111* (1), 108–126.

Barinaga, M. (1996a). Giving language skills a boost. *Science, 271,* 27–28.

Barinaga, M. (1996b). Learning defect identified in brain. *Science, 273,* 867–868.

Barnes, A., Colton, T., Gunderson, J., Noller, K., Tilley, B., Strama, T., Townsend, D., Hatab, P., & O'Brien, P. (1980). Fertility and outcome of pregnancy in women exposed in utero to diethylstilbestrol. *New England Journal of Medicine, 302* (11), 609–613.

Barnes, J. (1978). *Evita, first lady: A biography of Eva Perón*. New York: Grove.

Barnes, K. E. (1971). Preschool play norms: A replication. *Developmental Psychology, 5,* 99–103.

Barnett, R. C., Brennan, R., Raudenbush, S. W., & Marshall, N. L. (1994). Gender and the relationship between marital-role quality and psychological distress. *Psychology of Women Quarterly, 18*(1), 105–127.

Barnett, R. C., Marshall, N. L., & Pleck, J. H. (1992). Men's multiple roles and their relationship to men's psychological distress. *Journal of Marriage and the Family, 54,* 358–367.

Barrett, R. L., & Robinson, B. E. (1990). *Gay fathers*. Lexington, MA: Lexington.

Bartecchi, C. E., MacKenzie, T. D., & Schrier, R. W. (1995, May). The global tobacco epidemic. *Scientific American,* pp. 44–51.

Barthel, J. (1982, May). Just a normal, naughty three-year-old. *McCall's,* pp. 78, 136–144.

Bartoshuk, L. M., & Beauchamp, G. K. (1994). Chemical senses. *Annual Review of Psychology, 45,* 419–449.

Bass, J. L., Brennan, P., Mehta, K. A., & Kodzis, S. (1990). Pediatric problems in a suburban shelter for homeless families. *Pediatrics, 85,* 33–38.

Bass, M., Kravath, R. E., & Glass, L. (1986). Death-scene investigation in sudden infant death. *New England Journal of Medicine, 315,* 100–105.

Bass, S. A., & Caro, F. G. (1996). The economic value of grandparent assistance. *Generations, 20*(1), 29–33.

Bassuk, E. L. (1991). Homeless families. *Scientific American, 265*(6), 66–74.

Bassuk, E. L., & Rosenberg, L. (1990). Psychosocial characteristics of homeless children and children with homes. *Pediatrics, 85,* 257–261.

Bassuk, E. L., Weinreb, L. F., Dawson, R., Perloff, J. N., & Buckner, J. C. (1997). Determinants of behavior in homeless and low-income housed preschooler children. *Pediatrics, 100,* 92–100.

Bates, E., Bretherton, I., & Snyder, L. (1988). *From first words to grammar: Individual differences and dissociable mechanisms*. New York: Cambridge University Press.

Bates, E., O'Connell, B., & Shore, C. (1987). Language and communication in infancy. In J. D. Osofsky (Ed.), *Handbook of infant development* (2nd ed.). New York: Wiley.

Bateson, M. C. (1984). *With a daughter's eye: A memoir of Margaret Mead and Gregory Bateson*. New York: William Morrow & Co.

Battistich, V., Watson, M., Solomon, D., Schaps, E., & Solomon, J. (1991). The Child Development Project: A comprehensive program for the development of prosocial character. In W. M. Kurtines & J. L. Gewirtz (Eds.), *Handbook of moral behavior and development: Vol. 3. Application* (pp. 1–34). Hillsdale, NJ: Erlbaum.

Bauer, P. J. (1996). What do infants recall of their lives? Memory for specific events by one- to two-year-olds. *American Psychologist, 51,* 29–41.

Baumrind, D. (1971). Harmonious parents and their preschool children. *Developmental Psychology, 41,* 92–102.

Baumrind, D. (1993). The average expectable environment is not good enough: A response to Scarr. *Child Development, 38,* 1299–1317.

Baumrind, D. (1995). Commentary on sexual orientation: Research and social policy implications. *Developmental Psychology, 31,* 130–136.

Baumrind, D. (1996). The discipline controversy revisited. *Family Relations, 45,* 405–414.

Baumrind, D., & Black, A. E. (1967). Socialization practices associated with dimensions of competence in preschool boys and girls. *Child Development, 38,* 291–327.

Baumwell, L., Tamis-Lemonda, C. S., & Bornstein, M. H. (1997). Maternal verbal sensitivity and child language comprehension. *Infant Behavior and Development, 20,* 247–258.

Bayley, N. (1965). Comparisons of mental and motor test scores for age 1–15 months by sex, birth order, race, geographic location, and education of parents. *Child Development, 36,* 379–411.

Bayley, N. (1969). *Bayley Scales of Infant Development*. New York: Psychological Corporation.

Bayley, N. (1993). *Bayley Scales of Infant Development: II*. New York: Psychological Corporation.

Beal, C. R. (1994). *Boys and girls: The development of gender roles*. New York: McGraw-Hill.

Beautrais, A. L., Fergusson, D. M., & Shannon, F. T. (1982). Life events and childhood morbidity: A prospective study. *Pediatrics, 70,* 935–940.

Begley, S. (1997, September 22). The nursery's littlest victims: Hundreds of cases of "crib death," or SIDS, may in fact be infanticide. *Newsweek,* pp. 72–73.

Behrman, R. E. (1992). *Nelson textbook of pediatrics* (13th ed.). Philadelphia: Saunders.

Behrman, R. E., & Vaughan, V. C. (Eds.). (1983). *Nelson textbook of pediatrics*. Philadelphia: Saunders.

Bell, S., & Ainsworth, M. D. S. (1972). Infant crying and maternal responsiveness. *Child Development, 43,* 1171–1190.

Bellinger, D., Leviton, A., Watermaux, C., Needleman, H., & Rabinowitz, M. (1987). Longitudinal analyses of prenatal and postnatal lead exposure and early cognitive development. *New England Journal of Medicine, 316* (17), 1037–1043.

Bellinger, D. C., Stiles, K. M., & Needleman, H. L. (1992). Low-level lead exposure, intelligence, and academic achievement: A long-term follow-up study. *Pediatrics, 90,* 855–861.

Belsky, J. (1984). Two waves of day care research: Developmental effects and conditions of quality. In R. Ainslie (Ed.), *The child and the day care setting*. New York: Praeger.

Belsky, J. (1993). Etiology of child maltreatment: A developmental-ecological analysis. *Psychological Bulletin, 114,* 413–434.

Belsky, J. (1996). Parent, infant, and social-contextual antecedents of father-son attachment security. *Developmental Psychology, 32,* 905–913.

Belsky, J., Fish, M., & Isabella, R. (1991). Continuity and discontinuity in infant negative and positive emotionality: Family antecedents and attachment consequences. *Developmental Psychology, 27,* 421–431.

Belsky, J., Lang, M., & Huston, T. L. (1986). Sex typing and division of labor as determinants of marital change across the transition to parenthood. *Journal of Personality and Social Psychology, 50,* 517–522.

Belsky, J., & Rovine, M. (1990). Patterns of marital change across the transition to parenthood: Pregnancy to three years postpartum. *Journal of Marriage and the Family, 52,* 5–19.

Belsky, J., & Rovine, M. J. (1988). Non-maternal care in the first year of life and the security of infant-parent attachment. *Child Development, 59,* 157–167.

Beltramini, A. U., & Hertzig, M. E. (1983). Sleep and bedtime behavior in preschool-aged children. *Pediatrics, 71,* 153–158.

Bem, S. L. (1974). The measurement of psychological androgyny. *Journal of Consulting and Clinical Psychology, 42,* 155–162.

Bem, S. L. (1976). Probing the promise of androgyny. In A. G. Kaplan & J. P. Bean (Eds.), *Beyond sex-role stereotypes: Readings toward a psychology of androgyny.* Boston: Little, Brown.

Bem, S. L. (1983). Gender schema theory and its implications for child development: Raising gender-aschematic children in a gender-schematic society. *Signs, 8,* 598–616.

Bem, S. L. (1985). Androgyny and gender schema theory: A conceptual and empirical integration. In T. B. Sondregger (Ed.), *Nebraska Symposium on Motivation, 1984: Psychology and gender.* Lincoln: University of Nebraska Press.

Benenson, J. F. (1993). Greater preference among females than males for dyadic interaction in early childhood. *Child Development, 64,* 544–555.

Benenson, J. F., Apostoleris, N. H., & Parnass, J. (1997). Age and sex differences in dyadic and group interaction. *Developmental Psychology, 33,* 538–543.

Benson, J. B. (1993). Season of birth and onset of locomotion: Theoretical and methodological implications. *Infant Behavior and Development, 16,* 69–81.

Benson, J. B., & Uzgiris, I. C. (1985). Effect of self-inflicted locomotion on infant search activity. *Developmental Psychology, 21,* 923–931.

Benson, M. (1986). *Nelson Mandela: The man and the movement.* New York: Norton.

Benson, P. L., Sharma, A. R., & Roehlkepartain, E. C. (1994). *Growing up adopted: A portrait of adolescents and their families.* Minneapolis: Search Institute.

Bergeman, C. S., & Plomin, R. (1989). Genotype-environment interaction. In M. Bornstein & J. Bruner (Eds.), *Interaction in human development* (pp. 157–171). Hillsdale, NJ: Erlbaum.

Berk, L. E. (1986). Private speech: Learning out loud. *Psychology Today, 20*(5), 34–42.

Berk, L. E., & Garvin, R. A. (1984). Development of private speech among low-income Appalachian children. *Developmental Psychology, 20,* 271–286.

Berkowitz, G. S., Skovron, M. L., Lapinski, R. H., & Berkowitz, R. L. (1990). Delayed childbearing and the outcome of pregnancy. *New England Journal of Medicine, 322,* 659–664.

Berkowitz, L. (1984). Some effects of thoughts on anti- and prosocial influences of media events: A cognitive-neoassociation analysis. *Psychological Bulletin, 95,* 410–427.

Berman, S. M., MacKay, H. T., Grimes, D. A., & Binkin, N. J. (1985). Deaths from spontaneous abortion in the United States. *Journal of the American Medical Association, 253,* 3119–3123.

Bernard, J., & Sontag, L. W. (1947). Fetal reactivity to sound. *Journal of Genetic Psychology, 70,* 205–210.

Bernard-Bonnin, A. C., Gilbert, S., Rousseau, E., Masson, P., & Maheux, B. (1991). Television and the 3- to 10-year-old child. *Pediatrics, 88,* 48–54.

Berndt, T. J. (1982). The features and effects of friendship in early adolescence. *Child Development, 53,* 1447–1460.

Berndt, T. J., & Perry, T. B. (1990). Distinctive features and effects of early adolescent friendships. In R. Montemayor, G. R. Adams, & T. P. Gullotta (Eds.), *From childhood to adolescence: A transitional period?* Newbury Park, CA: Sage.

Bernstein, G. A., & Garfinkel, B. D. (1988). Pedigrees, functioning, and psychopathology in families of school phobic children. *American Journal of Psychiatry, 145,* 70–74.

Bernstein, J. (1973). *Einstein.* New York: Viking.

Berrueta-Clement, J. R., Schweinhart, L. J., Barnett, W. S., Epstein, A. S., & Weikart, D. P. (1985). *Changed lives: The effects of the Perry Preschool Program on youths through age 19.* Ypsilanti, MI: High/Scope.

Berrueta-Clement, J. R., Schweinhart, L. J., Barnett, W. S., & Weikart, D. P. (1987). The effects of early educational intervention on crime and delinquency in adolescence and early adulthood. In J. D. Burchard & S. N. Burchard (Eds.), *Primary prevention of psychopathology: Vol. 10. Prevention of delinquent behavior* (pp. 220–240). Newbury Park, CA: Sage.

Bertenthal, B. I., & Campos, J. J. (1987). New directions in the study of early experience. *Child Development, 58,* 560–567.

Bertenthal, B. I., Campos, J. J., & Barrett, K. C. (1984). Self-produced locomotion: An organizer of emotional, cognitive, and social development in infancy. In R. N. Emde & R. J. Harmon (Eds.), *Continuities and discontinuities in development.* New York: Plenum.

Bertenthal, B. I., Campos, J. J., & Kermoian, R. (1994). An epigenetic perspective on the development of self-produced locomotion and its consequences. *Current Directions in Psychological Science, 3*(5), 140–145.

Beumont, P. J. V., Russell, J. D., & Touyz, S. W. (1993). Treatment of anorexia nervosa. *The Lancet, 341,* 1635–1640.

Bialystok, E. (1997). Effects of bilingualism and biliteracy on children's emerging concepts of print. *Developmental Psychology, 33,* 429–440.

Bianchi, S. M. (1995). The changing demographic and socioeconomic characteristics of single parent families. *Marriage and Family Review, 20*(1–2), 71–97.

Bierman, K. L., & Furman, W. (1984). The effects of social skills training and peer involvement on the social adjustment of preadolescents. *Child Development, 55,* 151–162.

Bierman, K. L., Smoot, D. L., & Aumiller, K. (1993). Characteristics of aggressive-rejected, aggressive (non-rejected), and rejected (non-aggressive) boys. *Child Development, 64,* 139–151.

Biller, H. B. (1981). The father and sex role development. In M. E. Lamb (Ed.), *The role of the father in child development.* New York: Wiley.

Birch, L. L., Johnson, S. L., Andersen, G., Peters, J. C., & Schulte, M. C. (1991). The variability of young children's energy intake. *New England Journal of Medicine, 324,* 232–235.

Birns, B. (1976). The emergence and socialization of sex differences in the earliest years. *Merrill-Palmer Quarterly, 22,* 229–254.

Bithoney, W. G., Vandeven, A. M., & Ryan, A. (1993). Elevated lead levels in reportedly abused children. *Journal of Pediatrics, 122,* 719–720.

Bittman, M. (1993, October 27). Eating well: Need more protein? Probably not. *The New York Times,* p. C11.

Bjorklund, D. F. (1997). The role of immaturity in human development. *Psychological Bulletin, 122,* 153–169.

Bjorklund, D. F., & Harnishfeger, K. K. (1990). The resources construct in cognitive development: Diverse sources of evidence and a theory of inefficient inhibition. *Developmental Review, 10,* 48–71.

Blakeslee, S. (1997, April 17). Studies show talking with infants shapes basis of ability to think. *The New York Times,* p. D21.

Blanksten, G. I. (1953). *Perón's Argentina.* Chicago: University of Chicago Press.

Blass, E. M., Ganchrow, J. R., & Steiner, J. E. (1984). Classical conditioning in newborn humans 2–24 hours of age. *Infant Behavior and Development, 7,* 223–235.

Bloom, B. S. (1985). *Developing talent in young people.* New York: Ballantine.

Bloom, L. (1993). *The transition from infancy to language: Acquiring the power of expression.* Cambridge, England: Cambridge University Press.

Bloom, L., Margulis, C., Tinker, E., & Fujita, N. (1996). Early conversations and word learning: Contributions from child and adult. *Child Development, 67,* 3154–3175.

Blurton Jones, N. G., & Konner, M. J. (1973). Sex differences in behavior of London and Bushman children. In R. P. Michael & J. H. Crook (Eds.), *Comparative ecology and behavior of primates.* London: Academic Press.

Blyth, D. A., & Foster-Clark, F. S. (1987). Gender differences in perceived intimacy with different members of adolescents' social networks. *Sex Roles, 17,* 689–718.

Blyth, D. A., Simmons, R. G., Bulcroft, R., Felt, D., Van Cleave, E. F., & Bush, D. M. (1981). The effects of physical development on self-image and satisfaction with body-image for early adolescent males. In R. G. Simmons (Ed.), *Research on community and mental health* (Vol. 2, pp. 43–73). Greenwich, CT: JAI.

Blyth, D. A., Simmons, R. G., & Carlton-Ford, S. (1983). The adjustment of early adolescents to school transitions. *Journal of Early Adolescence*, 3(1–2), 105–120.

Bolger, K. E., Patterson, C. J., Thompson, W. W., & Kupersmidt, J. B. (1995). Psychosocial adjustment among children experiencing persistent and intermittent family economic hardship. *Child Development*, 66, 1107–1129.

Bond, C. A. (1989, September). A child prodigy from China wields a magical brush. *Smithsonian*, pp. 70–79.

Bone marrow transplant in fetus staves off immune disease. (1996, December 12). *The New York Times*, p. A27.

Bornstein, M., Kessen, W., & Weiskopf, S. (1976). The categories of hue in infancy. *Science*, 191, 201–202.

Bornstein, M. H. (1985a). Habituation of attention as a measure of visual information processing in human infants. In G. Gottlieb & N. A. Krasnegor (Eds.), *Development of audition and vision in the first year of post-natal life: A methodological overview*. Norwood, NJ: Ablex.

Bornstein, M. H. (1985b). How infant and mother jointly contribute to developing cognitive competence in the child. *Proceedings of the National Academy of Science*, 82, 7470–7473.

Bornstein, M. H., & Lamb, M. E. (1992). *Development in infancy: An introduction*. New York: McGraw-Hill.

Bornstein, M. H., & Sigman, M. D. (1986). Continuity in mental development from infancy. *Child Development*, 57, 251–274.

Bornstein, M. H., & Tamis-LeMonda, C. S. (1989). Maternal responsiveness and cognitive development in children. In M. H. Bornstein (Ed.), *Maternal responsiveness: Characteristics and consequences* (New Directions for Child Development No. 43). San Francisco: Jossey-Bass.

Bornstein, M. H., & Tamis-LeMonda, C. S. (1994). Antecedents of information processing skills in infants: Habituation, novelty responsiveness, and cross-modal transfer. *Infant Behavior and Development*, 17, 371–380.

Bouchard, T. J. (1994). Genes, environment, and personality. *Science*, 264, 1700–1701.

Boulton, M. G. (1983). *On being a mother: A study of women with pre-school children*. London: Tavistock.

Boulton, M. J. (1995). Playground behaviour and peer interaction patterns of primary school boys classified as bullies, victims and not involved. *British Journal of Educational Psychology*, 65, 165–177.

Boulton, M. J., & Smith, P. K. (1994). Bully/victim problems in middle-school children: Stability, self-perceived competence, peer perception, and peer acceptance. *British Journal of Developmental Psychology*, 12, 315–329.

Bouza, A. V. (1990). *The police mystique: An insider's look at cops, crime, and the criminal justice system*. New York: Plenum.

Bower, B. (1985). The left hand of math and verbal talent. *Science News*, 127, 263.

Bower, B. (1993). A child's theory of mind. *Science News*, 144, 40–42.

Bowlby, J. (1951). Maternal care and mental health. *Bulletin of the World Health Organization*, 3, 355–534.

Bowman, J. A., Sanson-Fisher, R. W., & Webb, G. R. (1987). Interventions in preschools to increase the use of safety restraints by preschool children. *Pediatrics*, 79, 103–109.

Boyle, C. A., Decouflé, P., & Yeargin-Allsopp, M. (1994). Prevalence and health impact of developmental disabilities in U.S. children. *Pediatrics*, 93, 399–403.

Boyum, L. A., & Parke, R. D. (1995). The role of family emotional expressiveness in the development of children's social competence. *Journal of Marriage and the Family*, 57, 593–608.

Brackbill, Y., & Broman, S. H. (1979). *Obstetrical medication and development in the first year of life*. Unpublished manuscript.

Bradley, L., & Bryant, P. E. (1983). Categorizing sounds and learning to read—A causal connection. *Nature*, 30, 419–421.

Bradley, L., & Bryant, P. E. (1985). Rhyme and reason in reading and spelling. *International Academy for Research in Learning Disabilities Monograph Series*, 1 .

Bradley, R., & Caldwell, B. (1982). The consistency of the home environment and its relation to child development. *International Journal of Behavioral Development*, 5, 445–465.

Bradley, R., Caldwell, B., & Rock, S. (1988). Home environment and school performance: A ten-year follow-up and examination of three models of environmental action. *Child Development*, 59, 852–867.

Bradley, R. H. (1989). Home measurement of maternal responsiveness. In M. H. Bornstein (Ed.), *Maternal responsiveness: Characteristics and consequences* (New Directions for Child Development No. 43). San Francisco: Jossey-Bass.

Bradley, R. H., Caldwell, B. M., Rock, S. L., Ramey, C. T., Barnard, K. E., Gray, C., Hammond, M. A., Mitchell, S., Gottfried, A. W., Siegel, L., & Johnson, D. L. (1989). Home environment and cognitive development in the first 3 years of life: A collaborative study involving six sites and three ethnic groups in North America. *Developmental Psychology*, 25, 217–235.

Braine, M. (1976). Children's first word combinations. *Monographs of the Society for Research in Child Development*, 41 (1, Serial No. 164).

Brandes, J. M., Scher, A., Itzkovits, J., Thaler, I., Sarid, M., & Gershoni-Baruch, R. (1992). Growth and development of children conceived by in vitro fertilization. *Pediatrics*, 90, 424–429.

Brass, L. M., Isaacsohn, J. L., Merikangas, K. R., & Robinette, C. D. (1992). A study of twins and stroke. *Stroke*, 23(2), 221–223.

Braungart, J. M., Plomin, R., DeFries, J. C., & Fulker, D. W. (1992). Genetic influence on tester-rated infant temperament as assessed by Bayley's Infant Behavior Record: Nonadoptive and adoptive siblings and twins. *Developmental Psychology*, 28, 40–47.

Braver, S. L., Wolchik, S. A., Sandler, I. N., Sheets, V. L., Fogas, B., & Bay, R. C. (1993). A longitudinal study of noncustodial parents: Parents without children. *Journal of Family Psychology*, 7, 9–23.

Bray, J. H., & Hetherington, E. M. (1993). Families in transition: Introduction and overview. *Journal of Family Psychology*, 7, 3–8.

Brazelton, T. B. (1973). *Neonatal behavioral assessment scale*. Philadelphia: Lippincott.

Bretherton, I. (1990). Communication patterns, internal working models, and the intergenerational transmission of attachment relationships. *Infant Mental Health Journal*, 11(3), 237–252.

Bretherton, I. (Ed.). (1984). *Symbolic play: The development of social understanding*. Orlando, FL: Academic.

Brian, D. (1996). *Einstein: A life*. New York: Wiley.

Briss, P. A., Sacks, J. J., Addiss, D. G., Kresnow, M., & O'Neil, J. (1994). A nationwide study of the risk of injury associated with day care center attendance. *Pediatrics*, 93, 364–368.

Broberg, A. G., Wessels, H., Lamb, M. E., & Hwang, C. P. (1997). Effects of day care on the development of cognitive abilities in 8-year-olds: A longitudinal study. *Developmental Psychology*, 33, 62–69.

Brody, G. H., & Stoneman, Z. (1990). Sibling relationships. In I. E. Sigel & G. H. Brody (Eds.), *Methods of family research: Biographies of research projects: Vol. 1. Normal families* (pp. 182–212). Hillsdale, NJ: Erlbaum.

Brody, G. H., & Stoneman, Z. (1995). Sibling relationships in middle childhood. In R. Vata (Ed.), *Annals of child development* (Vol. 11, pp. 73–93). London: Kingsley.

Brody, G. H., Stoneman, Z., & Flor, D. (1995). Linking family processes and academic competence among rural African American youths. *Journal of Marriage and the Family*, 57, 567–579.

Brody, G. H., Stoneman, Z., & Flor, D. (1996). Parental religiosity, family processes, and youth competence in rural, two-parent African American families. *Developmental Psychology*, 32, 696–706.

Brody, G. H., Stoneman, Z., Flor, D., McCrary, C., Hastings, L., & Conyers, O. (1994). Financial resources, parent psychological functioning, parent co-caregiving, and early adolescent competence in rural two-parent African-American families. *Child Development*, 65, 590–605.

Brody, G. H., Stoneman, Z., & Gauger, K. (1996). Parent-child relationships, family problem-solving behavior, and sibling relationship quality: The moderating role of sibling temperaments. *Child Development, 67,* 1289–1300.

Brody, J. E. (1995, June 28). Preventing birth defects even before pregnancy. *The New York Times,* p. C10.

Brody, L. R., Zelazo, P. R., & Chaika, H. (1984). Habituation-dishabituation to speech in the neonate. *Developmental Psychology, 20,* 114–119.

Brody, N. (1985). The validity of tests of intelligence. In B. B. Wolman (Ed.), *Handbook of intelligence* (pp. 353–389). New York: Wiley.

Bronfenbrenner, U. (1979). *The ecology of human development.* Cambridge, MA: Harvard University Press.

Bronfenbrenner, U. (1986). Ecology of the family as a context for human development: Research perspectives. *Developmental Psychology, 22,* 723–742.

Bronfenbrenner, U. (1994). Ecological models of human development. In T. Husen & T. N. Postlethwaite (Eds.), *International encyclopedia of education* (2nd ed., Vol. 3). Oxford: Pergamon Press/Elsevier Science.

Bronfenbrenner, U., Belsky, J., & Steinberg, L. (1977). *Daycare in context: An ecological perspective on research and public policy.* Review prepared for Office of the Assistant Secretary for Planning and Evaluation, U.S. Department of Health, Education, and Welfare.

Bronfenbrenner, U., & Crouter, A. (1982). Work and family through time and space. In S. B. Kamerman & C. D. Hayes (Eds.), *Families that work: Children in a changing world.* Washington, DC: National Academy of Science.

Bronson, F. H., & Desjardins, C. (1969). Aggressive behavior and seminal vesicle function in mice: Differential sensitivity to androgen given neonatally. *Endocrinology, 85,* 871–975.

Bronstein, P. (1988). Father-child interaction: Implications for gender role socialization. In P. Bronstein & C. P. Cowan (Eds.), *Fatherhood today: Men's changing role in the family.* New York: Wiley.

Bronstein, P., Clauson, J., Stoll, M. F., & Abrams, C. L. (1993). Parenting behavior and children's social, psychological, and academic adjustment in diverse family structures. *Family Relations, 42,* 268–276.

Brooks-Gunn, J. (1988). Pubertal processes and the early adolescent transition. In W. Damon (Ed.), *Child development today and tomorrow.* San Francisco: Jossey-Bass.

Brooks-Gunn, J., Klebanov, P. K., & Duncan, G. J. (1996). Ethnic differences in children's intelligence test scores: Role of economic deprivation, home environment, and maternal characteristics. *Child Development, 67,* 396–408.

Brooks-Gunn, J., Klebanov, P. K., Liaw, F., & Spiker, D. (1993). Enhancing the development of low-birthweight, premature infants: Changes in cognition and behavior over the first three years. *Child Development, 64,* 736–753.

Brooks-Gunn, J., McCarton, C. M., Casey, P. H., et al. (1994). Early intervention in low-birthweight premature infants: Results through age 5 years from the Infant Health Development Program. *Journal of the American Medical Association, 272,* 1257–1262.

Brooks-Gunn, J., & Reiter, E. O. (1990). The role of pubertal processes. In S. S. Feldman & G. R. Elliott (Eds.), *At the threshold: The developing adolescent.* Cambridge, MA: Harvard University Press.

Brown, B. B., Mounts, N., Lamborn, S. D., & Steinberg, L. (1993). Parenting practices and peer group affiliation in adolescence. *Child Development, 64,* 467–482.

Brown, J. H. (1979). Suicide in Britain: More attempts, fewer deaths, lessons for public policy. *Archives of General Psychiatry, 36,* 1119–1124.

Brown, J. L. (1987). Hunger in the U.S. *Scientific American, 256*(2), 37–41.

Brown, J. R., & Dunn, J. (1996). Continuities in emotion understanding from three to six years. *Child Development, 67,* 789–802.

Brown, L. J., Kaste, L. M., Selwitz, R. H., & Furman, L. J. (1996). Dental caries and sealant usage in U.S. children, 1988–1991. *Journal of the American Dental Association, 127,* 335–343.

Brown, L. M., & Gilligan, C. (1990, April). *The psychology of women and the development of girls.* Paper presented at the Laurel-Harvard Conference on the Psychology of Women and the Education of Girls, Cleveland, OH.

Brown, N. M. (1990). Age and children in the Kalahari. *Health and Human Development Research, 1,* 26–30.

Brown, P. (1993, April 17). Motherhood past midnight. *New Scientist,* pp. 4–8.

Brown, R. (1973a). Development of the first language in the human species. *American Psychologist, 28*(2), 97–106.

Brown, R. (1973b). *A first language: The early stage.* Cambridge, MA: Harvard University Press.

Brown, R., & Pressley, M. (1994). Self-regulated reading and getting meaning from text: The transactional strategies instruction model and its ongoing validation. In D. Schunk & B. Zimmerman (Eds.), *Self-regulation of learning and performance: Issues and educational applications* (pp. 155–179). Hillsdale, NJ: Erlbaum.

Brown, R., Pressley, M., Schuder, T., & Van Meter, P. (1994) *A quasi-experimental validation of transactional strategies instruction with previously low-achieving grade-2 readers.* Buffalo and Albany: State University of New York.

Brown, S. S. (1985). Can low birth weight be prevented? *Family Planning Perspectives, 17*(3), 112–118.

Browne, A., & Finkelhor, D. (1986). Impact of child sexual abuse: A review of research. *Psychological Bulletin, 99*(1), 66–77.

Bruce, J., Lloyd, C. B., & Leonard, A. (1995). *Families in focus: New perspectives on mothers, fathers, and children.* New York: Population Council.

Brumfield, C. G., Lin, S., Conner, W., Cosper, P., Davis, R. O., & Owen, J. (1996). Pregnancy outcome following genetic amniocentesis at 11–14 versus 16–19 weeks' gestation. *Obstetrics and Gynecology, 88,* 114–118.

Bruner, A. B., Joffe, A., Duggan, A. K., Casella, J. F., & Brandt, J. (1996). Randomised study of cognitive effects of iron supplementation in non-anaemic iron-deficient adolescent girls. *Lancet, 348,* 992–996.

Bruner, J. (1983). The acquisition of pragmatic commitments. In R. Golinkoff (Ed.), *The transition from prelinguistic to linguistic communication* (pp. 27–42). Hillsdale, NJ: Erlbaum.

Bryer, J. B., Nelson, B. A., Miller, J. J., & Krol, P. A. (1987). Childhood sexual and physical abuse as factors in adult psychiatric illness. *American Journal of Psychiatry, 144*(11), 1426–1430.

Bryson, K. (1996, October). *Household and family characteristics: March 1995* (Current Population Report No. P20-488; PPL-46). Washington, DC: U.S. Bureau of the Census.

Buchanan, C. M., Eccles, J. S., & Becker, J. B. (1992). Are adolescents the victims of raging hormones: Evidence for activational effects of hormones on moods and behavior at adolescence. *Psychological Bulletin, 111,* 62–107.

Buhrmester, D. (1990). Intimacy of friendship, interpersonal competence, and adjustment during preadolescence and adolescence. *Child Development, 61,* 1101–1111.

Buhrmester, D. (1996). Need fulfillment, interpersonal competence, and the developmental contexts of early adolescent friendship. In W. M. Bukowski, A. F. Newcomb, & W. W. Hartup (Eds.), *The company they keep: Friendship in childhood and adolescence* (pp. 158–185). New York: Cambridge University Press.

Buhrmester, D., & Furman, W. (1990). Perceptions of sibling relationships during middle childhood and adolescence. *Child Development, 61,* 138–139.

Bukowski, W. M., & Kramer, T. L. (1986). Judgments of the features of friendship among early adolescent boys and girls. *Journal of Early Adolescence, 6,* 331–338.

Burchinal, M. R., Campbell, F. A., Bryant, D. M., Wasik, B. H., & Ramey, C. T. (1997). Early intervention and mediating processes in cognitive performance of children of low-income African American families. *Child Development, 68,* 935–954.

Burchinal, M. R., Roberts, J. E., Nabors, L. A., & Bryant, D. M. (1996). Quality of center child care and infant cognitive and language development. *Child Development, 67,* 606–620.

Burgess, A. W., Hartman, C. R., & McCormack, A. (1987). Abused to abuser: Antecedents of socially deviant behaviors. *American Journal of Psychiatry, 144*(11), 1431–1436.

Burhans, K. K., & Dweck, C. S. (1995). Helplessness in early childhood: The role of contingent worth. *Child Development, 66*, 1719–1738.

Burns, A. (1992). Mother-headed families: An international perspective and the case of Australia. *Social Policy Report of the Society for Research in Child Development, 6*(1).

Burns, J. F. (1994, August 27). India fights abortion of female fetuses. *The New York Times*, p. A5.

Burros, M. (1990, October 3). Children are focus of diet-pill issue. *The New York Times*, pp. C1, C4.

Bushnell, E. W., & Boudreau, J. P. (1993). Motor development and the mind: The potential role of motor abilities as a determinant of aspects of perceptual development. *Child Development, 64*, 1005–1021.

Butler, S., Gross, J., & Hayne, H. (1995). The effect of drawing on memory performance in young children. *Developmental Psychology, 31*, 597–608.

Butterfield, E., & Siperstein, G. (1972). Influence of contingent auditory stimulation upon nonnutritional suckle. In J. Bosma (Ed.), *Oral sensation and perception: The mouth of the infant*. Springfield, IL: Thomas.

Byrd, R. S., Weitzman, M., & Auinger, P. (1997). Increased behavior problems associated with delayed school entry and delayed school progress. *Pediatrics, 100*, 654–661.

Byrd, R. S., Weitzman, M., & Doniger, A. S. (1994). Increase in risk taking behaviors among old-for-grade adolescents [Abstract]. *Archives of Pediatric and Adolescent Medicine, 148*, P78.

Byrd, R. S., Weitzman, M., & Doniger, A. S. (1996). Increased drug use among old-for-grade adolescents. *Archives of Pediatric and Adolescent Medicine, 150*, 470–476.

Cahan, S., & Cohen, M. (1989). Age versus schooling effects on intelligence development. *Child Development, 60*, 1239–1249.

Cain, V. S., & Hofferth, S. L. (1989). Parental choice of self-care for school-age children. *Journal of Marriage and the Family, 51*, 65–77.

Cairns, R. B., Cairns, B. D., & Neckerman, H. J. (1989). Early school dropout: Configurations and determinants. *Child Development, 60*, 1437–1452.

Calkins, S. D., & Fox, N. A. (1992). The relations among infant temperament, security of attachment, and behavioral inhibition at twenty-four months. *Child Development, 63*, 1456–1472.

Call, K. T., Mortimer, J. T., & Shanahan, M. (1995). Helpfulness and the development of competence in adolescence. *Child Development, 66*, 129–138.

Calvert, S. L., & Huston, A. C. (1987). Television and children's gender schemata. In L. S. Liben & M. S. Signorella (Eds.), *Children's gender schemata*. San Francisco: Jossey-Bass.

Calvo, E. B., Galindo, A. C., & Aspres, N. B. (1992). Iron status in exclusively breast-fed infants. *Pediatrics, 90*, 375–379.

Campbell, F. A., & Ramey, C. T. (1994). Effects of early intervention on intellectual and academic achievement: A follow-up study of children from low-income families. *Child Development, 65*, 684–698.

Campbell, S. B., Cohn, J. F., & Meyers, T. (1995). Depression in first-time mothers: Mother-infant interaction and depression chronicity. *Developmental Psychology, 31*, 349–357.

Campfield, L. A., Smith, F. J., Guisez, Y., Devos, R., & Burn, P. (1995). Recombinant mouse OB protein: Evidence for a peripheral signal linking adiposity and central neural networks. *Science, 269*, 546–549.

Campos, J., Bertenthal, B., & Benson, N. (1980, April). *Self-produced locomotion and the extraction of form invariance*. Paper presented at the meeting of the International Conference on Infant Studies, New Haven, CT.

Campos, J. J., Langer, A., & Krowitz, A. (1970). Cardiac responses on the visual cliff in prelocomotor human infants. *Science, 170*, 196–197.

Camras, L. A., Oster, H., Campos, J. J., Miyake, K., & Bradshaw, D. (1992). Japanese and American infants' responses to arm restraint. *Developmental Psychology, 28*, 578–583.

The Canadian Early and Mid-Trimester Amniocentesis Trial (CEMAT) Group. (1998). Randomized trial to assess safety and fetal outcome of early and midtrimester amniocentesis. *Lancet, 351*, 242–247.

Cantor, J. (1994). Confronting children's fright responses to mass media. In D. Zillman, J. Bryant, & A. C. Huston (Eds.), *Media, children, and the family: Social scientific, psychoanalytic, and clinical perspectives*. Hillsdale, NJ: Erlbaum.

Caplan, M., Vespo, J., Pedersen, J., & Hay, D. F. (1991). Conflict and its resolution in small groups of one- and two-year olds. *Child Development, 62*, 1513–1524.

Capute, A. J., Shapiro, B. K., & Palmer, F. B. (1987). Marking the milestones of language development. *Contemporary Pediatrics, 4*(4), 24.

Carlo, G., Knight, G. P., Eisenberg, N., & Rotenberg, K. J. (1991). Cognitive processes and prosocial behaviors among children: The role of affective attributions and reconciliations. *Developmental Psychology, 27*, 456–461.

Carpenter, M. W., Sady, S. P., Hoegsberg, B., Sady, M. A., Haydon, B., Cullinane, E. M., Coustan, D. R., & Thompson, P. D. (1988). Fetal heart rate response to maternal exertion. *Journal of the American Medical Association, 259*(20), 3006–3009.

Carraher, T. N., Schliemann, A. D., & Carraher, D. W. (1988). Mathematical concepts in everyday life. In G. B. Saxe & M. Gearhart (Eds.), Children's mathematics. *New Directions in Child Development, 41*, 71–87.

Carrera, M. A. (1986, April). *Future directions in teen pregnancy prevention*. Paper presented at the annual meeting of the Society for the Scientific Study of Sex, Eastern Region.

Carson, J. L., & Parke, R. D. (1996). Reciprocal negative affect in parent-child interactions and children's peer competency. *Child Development, 67*, 2217–2226.

Caruso, D. (1993). Dimensions of quality in infants' exploratory competence at one year. *Infant Behavior and Development, 16*(4), 441–454.

Casaer, P. (1993). Old and new facts about perinatal brain development. *Journal of Child Psychology and Psychiatry, 34*(1), 101–109.

Case, R. (1985). *Intellectual development: Birth to adulthood*. Orlando, FL: Academic Press.

Case, R. (1992). Neo-Piagetian theories of child development. In R. Sternberg & C. Berg (Eds.), *Intellectual development*. New York: Cambridge University Press.

Case, R., & Okamoto, Y. (1996). The role of central conceptual structures in the development of children's thought. *Monographs of the Society for Research in Child Development, 61*(1–2, Serial No. 246).

Casper, L. M. (1996). *Who's minding our preschoolers?* (Current Population Reports No. P-70-53). Washington, DC: U.S. Bureau of the Census.

Casper, R. C., & Offer, D. (1990). Weight and dieting concerns in adolescents, fashion or symptom? *Pediatrics, 86*, 384–390.

Caspi, A., & Silva, P. (1995). Temperamental qualities at age 3 predict personality traits in young adulthood: Longitudinal evidence from a birth cohort. *Child Development, 66*, 486–498.

Cassidy, J., & Hossler, A. (1992). State and federal definitions of the gifted: An update. *Gifted Child Quarterly, 15*, 46–53.

Cauffman, E., & Steinberg, L. (1996). Interactive effects of menarcheal status and dating on dieting and disordered eating among adolescent girls. *Developmental Psychology, 32*, 631–635.

Ceci, S. J. (1991). How much does schooling influence general intelligence and its cognitive components? A reassessment of the evidence. *Developmental Psychology, 27*, 703–722.

Ceci, S. J., & Bruck, M. (1993). Child witnesses: Translating research into policy. *Social Policy Report of the Society for Research in Child Development, 7*(3).

Celis, W. (1990). More states are laying school paddle to rest. *The New York Times*, pp. A1, B12.

Center on Addiction and Substance Abuse at Columbia University (CASA). (1996, June). *Substance abuse and the American woman*. New York: Author.

Centers for Disease Control and Prevention (CDC). (1991). *Preventing lead poisoning in young children: A statement by the Centers for Disease Control*. Atlanta, GA: U.S. Department of Health and Human Services.

Centers for Disease Control and Prevention (CDC). (1993). Rates of cesarean delivery—United States, 1991. *Morbidity and Mortality Weekly Report, 42,* 285–289.

Centers for Disease Control and Prevention (CDC). (1994a). Health risk behaviors among adolescents who do and do not attend school—United States, 1992. *Journal of the American Medical Association, 271,* 1068–1070.

Centers for Disease Control and Prevention (CDC). (1994b). Homicides among 15- to 19-year-old males—United States, 1963–1991. *Morbidity and Mortality Weekly Report, 43,* 725–727.

Centers for Disease Control and Prevention (CDC). (1995). Update: Trends in fetal alcohol syndrome—United States, 1979–1993. *Morbidity and Mortality Weekly Report, 44,* 249–251.

Centers for Disease Control and Prevention (CDC). (1996a). AIDS among children—United States, 1996. *Morbidity and Mortality Weekly Report, 45,* 1005–1010.

Centers for Disease Control and Prevention (CDC). (1996b). Summary of notifiable diseases, United States, 1995. *Morbidity and Mortality Weekly Report, 44*(53), 1–13.

Centers for Disease Control and Prevention (CDC). (1996c, May 24). Tobacco use and usual source of cigarettes among high school students—United States, 1995. *Morbidity and Mortality Weekly Report, 45*(20), 413–418.

Centers for Disease Control and Prevention (CDC). (1997, April 25). Alcohol consumption among pregnant and childbearing-aged women—United States, 1991 and 1995. *Morbidity and Mortality Weekly Report, 46*(16), 346–350.

Cernoch, J. M., & Porter, R. H. (1985). Recognition of maternal axillary odors by infants. *Child Development, 56,* 1593–1598.

Chalfie, D. (1994). *Going it alone: A closer look at grandparents parenting grandchildren.* Washington, DC: AARP Women's Initiative.

Chance, P., & Fischman, J. (1987). The magic of childhood. *Psychology Today, 21*(5), 48–58.

Chao, R. (1996). Chinese and European American mothers' beliefs about the role of parenting in children's school success. *Journal of Cross-Cultural Psychology, 27,* 403–423.

Chao, R. K. (1994). Beyond parental control and authoritarian parenting style: Understanding Chinese parenting through the cultural notion of training. *Child Development, 65,* 1111–1119.

Chapman, A. H. (1974). *Management of emotional problems of children and adolescents* (2nd ed). Philadelphia: Lippincott.

Chapman, M., & Lindenberger, U. (1988). Functions, operations, and décalage in the development of transitivity. *Developmental Psychology, 24,* 542–551.

Chase-Lansdale, P. L., Brooks-Gunn, J., & Zamsky, E. S. (1994). Young African-American multigenerational families in poverty: Quality of mothering and grandmothering. *Child Development, 65,* 373–393.

Chase-Lansdale, P. L., Cherlin, A. J., & Kiernan, K. E. (1995). The long-term effects of parental divorce on the mental health of young adults: A developmental perspective. *Child Development, 66,* 1614–1634.

Chavkin, W., & Kandall, S. R. (1990). Between a "rock" and a hard place: Perinatal drug abuse. *Pediatrics, 85,* 223–225.

Chehab, F. F., Mounzih, K., Lu, R., & Lim, M. E. (1997, January 3). Early onset of reproductive function in normal female mice treated with leptin. *Science, 275,* 88–90.

Chen, C., & Stevenson, H. W. (1989). Homework: A cross-cultural examination. *Child Development, 60,* 551–561.

Chen, C., & Stevenson, H. W. (1995). Motivation and mathematics achievement: A comparative study of Asian-American, Caucasian-American, and East Asian high school students. *Child Development, 66,* 1215–1234.

Chen, X., Rubin, K. H., & Li, D. (1997). Relation between academic achievement and social adjustment: Evidence from Chinese children. *Developmental Psychology, 33,* 518–525.

Chen, X., Rubin, K. H., & Li, Z. (1995). Social functioning and adjustment in Chinese children: A longitudinal study. *Developmental Psychology, 31,* 531–539.

Chen, X., Rubin, K. H., & Sun, Y. (1992). Social reputation and peer relationships in Chinese and Canadian children: A cross-cultural study. *Child Development, 63,* 1336–1343.

Cherlin, A., & Furstenberg, F. F. (1986a). Grandparents and family crisis. *Generations, 10*(4), 26–28.

Cherlin, A., & Furstenberg, F. F. (1986b). *The new American grandparent.* New York: Basic Books.

Chervenak, F. A., Isaacson, G., & Mahoney, M. J. (1986). Advances in the diagnosis of fetal defects. *New England Journal of Medicine, 315*(5), 305–307.

Chess, S. (1997, November). Temperament: Theory and clinical practice. *The Harvard Mental Health Letter,* pp. 5–7.

Chess, S., & Thomas, A. (1982). Infant bonding: Mystique and reality. *American Journal of Orthopsychiatry, 52*(2), 213–222.

Cheung, M. C., Goldberg, J. D., & Kan, Y. W. (1996). Prenatal diagnosis of sickle cell anaemia and thalassaemia by analysis of fetal cells in maternal blood. *Nature Genetics, 14,* 264–268.

Children's Defense Fund. (1995). *The state of America's children: Yearbook 1995.* Washington, DC: Author.

Children's Defense Fund. (1996). *The state of America's children: Yearbook 1996.* Washington, DC: Author.

Children's Defense Fund. (1997a). *The state of America's children: Yearbook 1997.* Washington, DC: Author.

Children's Defense Fund. (1997b, October). U.S. teen birth rate drops for fourth year in a row. *CDF Reports, 18*(11), 1–2.

Chisholm, J. S. (1983). *Navajo infancy: An ethological study of child development.* New York: Aldine.

Chomitz, V. R., Cheung, L. W. Y., & Lieberman, E. (1995). The role of lifestyle in preventing low birth weight. *The Future of Children, 5*(1), 121–138.

Chomsky, C. S. (1969). *The acquisition of syntax in children from five to ten.* Cambridge, MA: MIT Press.

Chomsky, N. (1957). *Syntactic structures.* The Hague: Mouton.

Chomsky, N. (1965). *Aspects of a theory of syntax.* Cambridge, MA: MIT Press.

Chomsky, N. (1972). *Language and mind* (2nd ed.). New York: Harcourt Brace Jovanovich.

Christie, J. F. (1991). *Psychological research on play: Connections with early literacy development.* Albany: State University of New York Press.

Chubb, N. H., Fertman, C. I., & Ross, J. L. (1997). Adolescent self-esteem and locus of control: A longitudinal study of gender and age differences. *Adolescence, 32,* 113–129.

Chumlea, W. C. (1982). Physical growth in adolescence. In B. B. Wolman (Ed.), *Handbook of developmental psychology.* Englewood Cliffs, NJ: Prentice-Hall.

Cicirelli, V. G. (1976a). Family structure and interaction: Sibling effects on socialization. In M. F. McMillan & S. Henao (Eds.), *Child psychiatry: Treatment and research.* New York: Brunner/Mazel.

Cicirelli, V. G. (1976b). Siblings teaching siblings. In V. L. Allen (Ed.), *Children as teachers: Theory and research on tutoring.* New York: Academic Press.

Cicirelli, V. G. (1994). Sibling relationships in cross-cultural perspective. *Journal of Marriage and the Family, 56,* 7–20.

Cicirelli, V. G. (1995). *Sibling relationships across the life span.* New York: Plenum.

Cigales, M., Field, T., Lundy, B., Cuandra, A., & Hart, S. (1997). Massage enhances recovery from habituation in normal infants. *Infant Behavior and Development, 20*(1), 29–34.

Clark, E. V. (1983). Meanings and concepts. In P. H. Mussen (Ed.), *Handbook of child psychology.* New York: Wiley.

Clark, S. C. (1995). Advance report of final divorce statistics, 1989, 1990. *Monthly Vital Statistics Report, 43*(8, Suppl.), 27.

Clarke-Stewart, K. A. (1987). Predicting child development from day care forms and features: The Chicago study. In D. A. Phillips (Ed.), *Quality in child care: What does the research tell us?* (Research Monographs of the National Association for the Education of Young Children). Washington, DC: National Association for the Education of Young Children.

Clarke-Stewart, K. A. (1989). Infant day care: Maligned or malignant. *American Psychologist, 44*(2), 266–273.

Clarke-Stewart, K. A. (1992). Consequences of child care for children's development. In A. Booth (Ed.), *Child care in the 1990s: Trends and consequences.* Hillsdale, NJ: Erlbaum.

Clausen, J. A. (1975). The social meaning of differential physical and sexual maturation. In S. E. Dragastin & G. H. Elder, Jr. (Eds.), *Adolescence in the life cycle.* New York: Halsted.

Clausen, J. A. (1993). *American lives.* New York: Free Press.

Clay, R. A. (1995, November). Working mothers: Happy or haggard? *APA Monitor*, pp. 1, 37.

Clayton, R., & Heard, D. (Eds.). (1994). *Elvis up close: In the words of those who knew him best.* Atlanta, GA: Turner.

Cobrinick, P., Hood, R., & Chused, E. (1959). Effects of maternal narcotic addiction on the newborn infant. *Pediatrics, 24,* 288–290.

Cohn, J. F., & Tronick, E. Z. (1983). Three-month-old infants' reaction to simulated maternal depression. *Child Development, 54,* 185–193.

Colby, A., & Damon, W. (1992). *Some do care: Contemporary lives of moral commitment.* New York: Free Press.

Colby, A., Kohlberg, L., Gibbs, J., & Lieberman, M. (1983). A longitudinal study of moral development. *Monographs of the Society for Research in Child Development, 48*(1–2, Serial No. 200).

Cole, C., & Rodman, H. (1987). When school-age children care for themselves: Issues for family life educators and parents. *Family Relations, 36,* 92–96.

Cole, M., & Cole, S. R. (1989). *The development of children.* New York: Freeman.

Cole, P. M., Barrett, K. C., & Zahn-Waxler, C. (1992). Emotion displays in two-year-olds during mishaps. *Child Development, 63,* 314–324.

Coleman, J. (1980). Friendship and the peer group in adolescence. In J. Adelson (Ed.), *Handbook of adolescent development.* New York: Wiley.

Coleman, J. S. (1988). Social capital in the creation of human capital. *American Journal of Sociology, 94*(Suppl. 95), S95–S120.

Collier, V. P. (1995). Acquiring a second language for school. *Directions in Language and Education, 1*(4), 1–11.

Collins, C. (1994, November 10). Baby walkers: The question of safety. *The New York Times*, p. C2.

Collins, J. G., & LeClere, F. B. (1997). *Health and selected socioeconomic characteristics of the family: United States, 1988–90* (DHHS No. PHS 97-1523). Washington, DC: U.S. Government Printing Office.

Collins, R. C., & Deloria, D. (1983). Head Start research: A new chapter. *Children Today, 12*(4), 15–19.

Collins, W. A. (1990). Parent-child relationships in transition to adolescence: Continuity and change in interaction, affect, and cognition. In R. Montemayor, G. R. Adams, & T. P. Gullotta (Eds.), *From childhood to adolescence: A transitional period?* Newbury Park, CA: Sage.

Colombo, J. (1993). *Infant cognition: Predicting later intellectual functioning.* Thousand Oaks, CA: Sage.

Conel, J. L. (1959). *The postnatal development of the human cerebral cortex.* Cambridge, MA: Harvard University Press.

Conger, J. J. (1988). Hostages to fortune: Youth, values, and the public interest. *American Psychologist, 43*(4), 291–300.

Conger, R. C., Ge, X., Elder, G. H., Lorenz, F. O., & Simons, R. L. (1994). Economic stress, coercive family processes, and developmental problems of adolescents. *Child Development, 65,* 541–561.

Connecticut Early Childhood Education Council (CECEC). (1983). *Report on full-day kindergarten.* Author.

Cook, E. H., Courchesne, R., Lord, C., Cox, N. J., Yan, S., Lincoln, A., Haas, R., Courchesne, E., & Leventhal, B. L. (1997). Evidence of linkage between the serotonin transporter and autistic disorder. *Molecular Psychiatry, 2,* 247–250.

Cook, T. D., Church, M. B., Ajanaku, S., Shadish, W. R., Jr., Kim, J., & Cohen, R. (1996). The development of occupational aspirations and expectations among inner-city boys. *Child Development, 67,* 3368–3385.

Coons, S., & Guilleminault, C. (1982). Development of sleep-wake patterns and non–rapid eye movement sleep stages during the first six months of life in normal infants. *Pediatrics, 69,* 793–798.

Cooper, R. P., & Aslin, R. N. (1990). Preference for infant-directed speech in the first month after birth. *Child Development, 61,* 1584–1595.

Coopersmith, S. (1967). *The antecedents of self-esteem.* San Francisco: Freeman.

Corbet, A., Long, W., Schumacher, R., Gerdes, J., Cotton, R., & the American Exosurf Neonatal Study Group 1. (1995). Double-blind developmental evaluation at 1-year corrected age of 597 premature infants with birth weights from 500 to 1350 grams enrolled in three placebo-controlled trials of prophylactic synthetic surfactant. *Journal of Pediatrics, 126,* S5–S12.

Corbin, C. (1973). *A textbook of motor development.* Dubuque, IA: Brown.

Corbin, C. B., & Pangrazi, R. P. (1992). Are American children and youth fit? *Research Quarterly for Exercise and Sport, 63*(2), 96–106.

Coren, S. (1992). *The left-hander syndrome: The causes and consequences of left-handedness.* New York: Free Press.

Coren, S., & Halpern, D. F. (1991). Lefthandedness: A marker for decreased survival fitness. *Psychological Bulletin, 109*(1), 90–106.

Costello, S. (1990, December). Yani's monkeys: Lessons in form and freedom. *School Arts*, pp. 10–11.

Coster, W. J., Gersten, M. S., Beeghly, M., & Cicchetti, D. (1989). Communicative functioning in maltreated toddlers. *Developmental Psychology, 25,* 1020–1029.

Council on Scientific Affairs of the American Medical Association. (1989). Dyslexia. *Journal of the American Medical Association, 261,* 2236–2239.

Council on Scientific Affairs of the American Medical Association. (1993). Adolescents as victims of family violence. *Journal of the American Medical Association, 276,* 1850–1856.

Council on Scientific Affairs of the American Medical Association. (1995). Female genital mutilation. *Journal of the American Medical Association, 274,* 1714–1716.

Cowan, M. W. (1979). The development of the brain. *Scientific American, 241,* 112–133.

Cowan, P. A., Cowan, C. P., Schulz, M. S., & Heming, G. (1994). Prebirth to preschool family factors in children's adaptation to kindergarten. In R. D. Parke & S. G. Kellam (Eds.), *Exploring family relationships with other social contexts. Family research consortium: Advances in family research* (pp. 75–114). Hillsdale, NJ: Erlbaum.

Cox, J., Daniel, N., & Boston, B. O. (1985). *Educating able learners: Programs and promising practices.* Austin: University of Texas Press.

Cox, M. J., Owen, M. T., Henderson, V. K., & Margand, N. A. (1992). Prediction of infant-father and infant-mother attachment. *Developmental Psychology, 28,* 474–483.

Coyle, T. R., & Bjorklund, D. F. (1997). Age differences in, and consequences of, multiple- and variable-strategy use on a multitrial sort-recall task. *Developmental Psychology, 33,* 372–380.

Craft, M. J., Montgomery, L. A., & Peters, J. (1992, October). *Comparative study of responses in preschool children to the birth of an ill sibling.* Nursing seminar series presentation, University of Iowa College of Nursing, Iowa City, IA.

Crain-Thoreson, C., & Dale, P. S. (1992). Do early talkers become early readers? Linguistic precocity, preschool language, and emergent literacy. *Developmental Psychology, 28,* 421–429.

Cramer, D. (1986). Gay parents and their children: A review of research and practical implications. *Journal of Counseling and Development, 64,* 504–507.

Cratty, B. (1979). *Perceptual and motor development in infants and children* (2nd ed.). Englewood Cliffs, NJ: Prentice-Hall.

Cratty, B. J. (1986). *Perceptual and motor development in infants and children* (3rd ed.). Englewood Cliffs, NJ: Prentice-Hall.

Crick, N. R. (1997). Engagement in gender normative versus nonnormative forms of aggression: Links to social-psychological adjustment. *Developmental Psychology, 33,* 610–617.

Crick, N. R., Bigbee, M. A., & Howes, C. (1996). Gender differences in children's normative beliefs about aggression: How do I hurt thee? Let me count the ways. *Child Development, 67,* 1003–1014.

Crick, N. R., & Dodge, K. A. (1994). A review and reformulation of social information-processing mechanisms in children's social adjustment. *Psychological Bulletin, 115,* 74–101.

Crick, N. R., & Dodge, K. A. (1996). Social information-processing mechanisms in reactive and proactive aggression. *Child Development, 67,* 993–1002.

Crick, N. R., & Grotpeter, J. K. (1995). Relational aggression, gender, and social-psychological adjustment. *Child Development, 66,* 710–722.

Crittenden, P. M. (1993). Comparison of two systems for assessing quality of attachment in the preschool years. In P. M. Crittenden (Chair), *Quality of attachment in the preschool years.* Symposium conducted at the Ninth Biennial Meeting of the International Conference on Infant Studies, Paris.

Crockenberg, S., & Lourie, A. (1996). Parents' conflict strategies with children and children's conflict strategies with peers. *Merrill-Palmer Quarterly, 42,* 495–518.

Crockett, L. J., & Petersen, A. C. (1987). Pubertal status and psychosocial development: Findings from the Early Adolescent Study. In R. M. Lerner & T. T. Foch (Eds.), *Biological-psychosocial interactions in early adolescence: A life-span perspective.* Hillsdale, NJ: Erlbaum.

Crouter, A. C., MacDermid, S. M., McHale, S. M., & Perry-Jenkins, M. (1990). Parental monitoring and perception of children's school performance and conduct in dual- and single-earner families. *Developmental Psychology, 26,* 649–657.

Crouter, A. C., & McHale, S. M. (1993). Temporal rhythms in family life: Seasonal variation and the relation between parental work and family processes. *Developmental Psychology, 29,* 198–205.

Crow, J. F. (1993). How much do we know about spontaneous human mutation rates? *Environmental and Molecular Mutagenesis, 21,* 122–129.

Crow, J. F. (1995). Spontaneous mutation as a risk factor. *Experimental and Clinical Immunogenetics, 12*(3), 121–128.

Crowley, S. L. (1993, October). Grandparents to the rescue. *AARP Bulletin,* pp. 1, 16–17.

Csikszentmihalyi, M., & Larson, R. (1984). *Being adolescent: Conflict and growth in the teenage years.* New York: Basic Books.

Culp, A. M., Osofsky, J. D., & O'Brien, M. (1996). Language patterns of adolescent and older mothers and their one-year-old children: A comparison study. *First Language, 16,* 61–75.

Cummings, E. M., Iannotti, R. J., & Zahn-Waxler, C. (1989). Aggression between peers in early childhood: Individual continuity and developmental change. *Child Development, 60,* 887–895.

Cummings, P., Grossman, D. C., Rivara, F. P., & Koepsell, T. D. (1997). State gun safe storage laws and child mortality due to firearms. *Journal of the American Medical Association, 278,* 1084–1086.

Cunningham, A. S., Jelliffe, D. B., & Jelliffe, E. F. P. (1991). Breastfeeding and health in the 1980s: A global epidemiological review. *Journal of Pediatrics, 118,* 659–666.

Cunningham, F. G., & Leveno, K. J. (1995). Childbearing among older women—The message is cautiously optimistic. *New England Journal of Medicine, 333,* 1002–1004.

Curtin, S. C. (1997, July 16). *Rates of cesarean birth and vaginal birth after previous cesarean, 1991–95* (Monthly Vital Statistics Report, 45[11, Suppl. 3], DHHS Publication No. PHS 97-1120). Washington, DC: National Center for Health Statistics.

Cutz, E., Perrin, D. G., Hackman, R., & Czegledy-Nagy, E. N. (1996). Maternal smoking and pulmonary neuroendocrine cells in sudden infant death syndrome. *Pediatrics, 88,* 668–672.

Daiute, C., Hartup, W. W., Sholl, W., & Zajac, R. (1993, March). *Peer collaboration and written language development: A study of friends and acquaintances.* Paper presented at the meeting of the Society for Research in Child Development, New Orleans, LA.

Dale, P. S., Crain-Thoreson, C., Notari-Syverson, A., & Cole, J. (1996). Parent-child book reading as an intervention technique for young children with language delays. *Topics in Early Childhood Special Education, 16,* 213–235.

Daley, S. (1991, January 9). Little girls lose their self-esteem on the way to adolescence, study finds. *The New York Times,* p. B6.

D'Alton, M. E., & DeCherney, A. H. (1993). Prenatal diagnosis. *New England Journal of Medicine, 32*(2), 114–120.

Daly, L. E., Kirke, P. N., Molloy, A., Weir, D. G., & Scott, J. M. (1995). Folate levels and neural tube defects: Implications for prevention. *Journal of the American Medical Association, 274,* 1698–1702.

Daniels, D., & Plomin, R. (1985). Origins of individual differences in infant shyness. *Developmental Psychology, 21,* 118–121.

Darlington, R. B. (1991). The long-term effects of model preschool programs. In L. Okagaki & R. J. Sternberg (Eds.), *Directors of development: Influences on the development of children's thinking.* Hillsdale, NJ: Erlbaum.

Darwin, C. (1877). A biographical sketch of an infant. *Mind, 2,* 285–294.

David, R. J., & Collins, J. W., Jr. (1997). Differing birth weight among infants of U.S.-born blacks, African-born blacks, and U.S.-born whites. *New England Journal of Medicine, 337,* 1209–1214.

Davidson, J., & Smith, R. (1990). Traumatic experiences in psychiatric outpatients. *Journal of Traumatic Stress, 3,* 459–475.

Davidson, J. E., & Sternberg, R. J. (1984). The role of insight in intellectual giftedness. *Gifted Child Quarterly, 28(2),* 58–64.

Davidson, R. J., & Fox, N. A. (1989). Frontal brain asymmetry predicts infants' response to maternal separation. *Journal of Abnormal Psychology, 948*(2), 58–64.

Davis, M., & Emory, E. (1995). Sex differences in neonatal stress reactivity. *Child Development, 66,* 14–27.

Dawson, D. A. (1991). Family structure and children's health and well-being: Data from the 1988 National Health Interview Survey on child health. *Journal of Marriage and the Family, 53,* 573–584.

Dawson, G., Frey, K., Panagiotides, H., Osterling, J., & Hessl, D. (1997). Infants of depressed mothers exhibit atypical frontal brain activity: A replication and extension of previous findings. *Journal of Child Psychology & Allied Disciplines, 38,* 179–186.

Dawson, G., Klinger, L. G., Panagiotides, H., Hill, D., & Spieker, S. (1992). Frontal lobe activity and affective behavior of infants of mothers with depressive symptoms. *Child Development, 63,* 725–737.

Dawson, J. M., & Langan, P. A. (1994, July). *Murder in families* (Bureau of Justice Statistics Special Report). Washington, DC: U.S. Government Printing Office.

Day, J., & Curry, A. (1996, August). *Educational attainment in the United States: March 1995* (Current Population Reports Publication No. P20-489). Washington, DC: U.S. Government Printing Office.

Day, R. D. (1992). The transition to first intercourse among racially and culturally diverse youth. *Journal of Marriage and the Family, 54,* 749–762.

DeCasper, A. J., & Fifer, W. P. (1980). Of human bonding: Newborns prefer their mothers' voices. *Science, 208,* 1174–1176.

DeCasper, A. J., Lecanuet, J. P., Busnel, M. C., Granier-Deferre, C., & Maugeais, R. (1994) Fetal reactions to recurrent maternal speech. *Infant Behavior and Development, 17,* 159–164.

DeCasper, A. J., & Spence, M. J. (1986). Prenatal maternal speech influences newborns' perceptions of speech sounds. *Infant Behavior and Development, 9,* 133–150.

DeFries, J. C., Fulker, D. W., & LaBuda, M. C. (1987). Evidence for a genetic etiology in reading disability of twins. *Nature, 329,* 537–539.

DeFries, P. J., Plomin, R., & Fulker, D. W. (1994). *Nature and nurture during middle childhood.* Cambridge, England: Blackwell.

Dekovic, M., & Janssens, J. M. A. M. (1992). Parents' child-rearing style and child's sociometric status. *Developmental Psychology, 28,* 925–932.

de Lafuente, D. (1994, September 11). Fertility clinics: Trying to cut the cost of high-tech baby making. *Chicago Sun-Times,* p. C4.

Del Carmen, R. D., Pedersen, F. A., Huffman, L. C., & Bryan, Y. E. (1993). Dyadic distress management predicts subsequent security of attachment. *Infant Behavior and Development, 16,* 131–147.

Demo, D. H. (1991). A sociological perspective on parent-adolescent disagreements. In R. L. Paikoff (Ed.), *Shared views in the family during adolescence* (New Directions for Child Development No. 51, pp. 111–118). San Francisco: Jossey-Bass.

Demo, D. H. (1992). Parent-child relations: Assessing recent changes. *Journal of Marriage and the Family, 54,* 104–117.

Denney, N. W. (1972). Free classification in preschool children. *Child Development, 43,* 1161–1170.

Dennis, W. (1936). A bibliography of baby biographies. *Child Development, 7,* 71–73.

Dennison, B. A., Rockwell, H. L., & Baker, S. L. (1997). Excess fruit juice consumption by preschool-aged children is associated with short stature and obesity. *Pediatrics, 99,* 15–22.

Denny, F. W., & Clyde, W. A. (1983). Acute respiratory tract infections: An overview [Monograph]. *Pediatric Research, 17,* 1026–1029.

Denton, K., & Zarbatany, L. (1996). Age differences in support in conversations between friends. *Child Development, 67,* 1360–1373.

De Peretti, E., & Forest, M. G. (1976). Unconjugated dehydroepiandrosterone plasma levels in normal subjects from birth to adolescence in humans: The use of a sensitive radioimmunoassay. *Journal of Clinical Endocrinology and Metabolism, 43,* 982–991.

Devlin, B., Daniels, M., & Roeder, K. (1997). The heritability of IQ. *Nature, 388,* 468–471.

Dewey, K. G., Heinig, M. J., & Nommsen-Rivers, L. A. (1995). Differences in morbidity between breast-fed and formula-fed infants. *Journal of Pediatrics, 126,* 696–702.

De Wolff, M. S., & van IJzendoorn, M. H. (1997). Sensitivity and attachment: A meta-analysis on parental antecedents of infant attachment. *Child Development, 68,* 571–591.

Deykin, E. Y., Alpert, J. J., & McNamara, J. J. (1985). A pilot study of the effect of exposure to child abuse or neglect on adolescent suicidal behavior. *American Journal of Psychiatry, 142*(11), 1299–1303.

Diamond, M., & Sigmundson, H. K. (1997). Sex reassignment at birth: Long-term review and clinical implications. *Archives of Pediatric and Adolescent Medicine, 151,* 298–304.

Diamond, M. C. (1988). *Enriching heredity.* New York: Free Press.

Diaz, R. M. (1983). Thought and two languages: The impact of bilingualism on cognitive development. *Review of Research in Education, 10,* 23–54.

Dickinson, D. K., Cote, L., & Smith, M. W. (1993). Learning vocabulary in preschool: Social and discourse contexts affecting vocabulary growth. In C. Daiute (Ed.), *The development of literacy through social interaction* (New Directions for Child Development No. 61, pp. 67–78). San Francisco: Jossey-Bass.

Dien, D. S. F. (1982). A Chinese perspective on Kohlberg's theory of moral development. *Developmental Review, 2,* 331–341.

Dietrich, K. N., Berger, O. G., & Succop, P. A. (1993). Lead exposure and the motor developmental status of urban six-year-old children in the Cincinnati Prospective Study. *Pediatrics, 91,* 301–307.

Dietz, W. H., & Gortmaker, S. L. (1985). Do we fatten our children at the television set? Obesity and television viewing in children and adolescents. *Pediatrics, 75,* 807–812.

DiFranza, J. R., & Lew, R. A. (1995, April). Effect of maternal cigarette smoking on pregnancy complications and sudden infant death syndrome. *Journal of Family Practice, 40,* 385–394.

DiLalla, L. F., Kagan, J., & Reznick, J. S. (1994). Genetic etiology of behavioral inhibition among 2-year-old children. *Infant Behavior and Development, 17,* 405–412.

Dimant, R. J., & Bearison, D. J. (1991). Development of formal reasoning during successive peer interactions. *Developmental Psychology, 27,* 277–284.

DiPietro, J. A., Hodgson, D. M., Costigan, K. A., Hilton, S. C., & Johnson, T. R. B. (1996). Fetal neurobehavioral development. *Child Development, 67,* 2553–2567.

DiPietro, J. A., Hodgson, D. M., Costigan, K. A., & Johnson, T. R. B. (1996). Fetal antecedents of infant temperament. *Child Development, 67,* 2568–2583.

Dishion, T. J., Patterson, G. R., Stoolmiller, M., & Skinner, M. L. (1991). Family, school, and behavioral antecedents to early adolescent involvement with antisocial peers. *Developmental Psychology, 27,* 172–180.

Dodge, K. A., Bates, J. E., & Pettit, G. S. (1990). Mechanisms in the cycle of violence. *Science, 250,* 1678–1683.

Dodge, K. A., Coie, J. D., Pettit, G. S., & Price, J. M. (1990). Peer status and aggression in boys' groups: Developmental and contextual analysis. *Child Development, 61,* 1289–1309.

Dodge, K. A., Pettit, G. S., & Bates, J. E. (1994). Socialization mediators of the relation between socioeconomic status and child conduct problems. *Child Development, 65,* 649–665.

Doherty, W. J., & Allen, W. (1994). Family functioning and parental smoking as predictors of adolescent cigarette use: A six-year prospective study. *Journal of Family Psychology, 8*(3), 347–353.

Donnelly, D., & Finkelhor, D. (1992). Does equality in custody arrangement improve the parent-child relationship? *Journal of Marriage and the Family, 54,* 837–845.

Doris, J. (1993). Paper presented at the Child Witness Conference, Family Life Development Center, Cornell University, Ithaca, NY.

Dornbusch, S. M., Ritter, P. L., Leiderman, P. H., Roberts, D. F., & Fraleigh, M. J. (1987). The relation of parenting style to adolescent school performance. *Child Development, 58,* 1244–1257.

Dorris, M. (1989). *The broken cord.* New York: Harper & Row.

Dougherty, D. M. (1993). Adolescent health. *American Psychologist, 48*(2), 193–201.

Dougherty, T. M., & Haith, M. M. (1997). Infant expectations and reaction time as predictors of childhood speed of processing and IQ. *Developmental Psychology, 33,* 146–155.

Dove, J. (n.d.). *Facts about anorexia nervosa.* Bethesda, MD: National Institutes of Health, Office of Research Reporting, National Institute of Child Health and Human Development.

Dreher, M. C., Nugent, K., & Hudgins, R. (1994). Prenatal marijuana exposure and neonatal outcomes in Jamaica: An ethnographic study. *Pediatrics, 93,* 254–260.

Dreyer, P. H. (1982). Sexuality during adolescence. In B. B. Wolman (Ed.), *Handbook of developmental psychology.* Englewood Cliffs, NJ: Prentice-Hall.

Drumm, P., & Jackson, D. W. (1996). Developmental changes in questioning strategies during adolescence. *Journal of Adolescent Research, 11,* 285–305.

Duncan, G. J., Brooks-Gunn, J., & Klebanov, P. K. (1994). Economic deprivation and early childhood development. *Child Development, 65,* 296–318.

Dundy, E. (1985). *Elvis and Gladys.* New York: Dell.

Dunham, P. J., Dunham, F., & Curwin, A. (1993). Joint-attentional states and lexical acquisition at 18 months. *Developmental Psychology, 29,* 827–831.

Dunn, J. (1983). Sibling relationships in early childhood. *Child Development, 54,* 787–811.

Dunn, J. (1985). *Sisters and brothers.* Cambridge, MA: Harvard University Press.

Dunn, J. (1991). Young children's understanding of other people: Evidence from observations within the family. In D. Frye & C. Moore (Eds.), *Children's theories of mind: Mental states and social understanding.* Hillsdale, NJ: Erlbaum.

Dunn, J., Brown, J., Slomkowski, C., Tesla, C., & Youngblade, L. (1991). Young children's understanding of other people's feelings and beliefs: Individual differences and antecedents. *Child Development, 62,* 1352–1366.

Dunn, J., & Kendrick, C. (1982). *Siblings: Love, envy and understanding.* Cambridge, MA: Harvard University Press.

Dunn, J., & Munn, P. (1985). Becoming a family member: Family conflict and the development of social understanding in the second year. *Child Development, 56,* 480–492.

Dunn, J., & Shatz, M. (1989). Becoming a conversationalist despite (or because of) having an older sibling. *Child Development, 60,* 399–410.

Dunne, R. G., Asher, K. N., & Rivara, F. P. (1992). Behavior and parental expectations of child pedestrians. *Pediatrics, 89,* 486–490.

DuPont, R. L. (1983). Phobias in children. *Journal of Pediatrics, 102,* 999–1002.

Durand, A. M. (1992). The safety of home birth: The Farm study. *American Journal of Public Health, 82,* 450–452.

Durkin, D. (1966). *Children who read early.* New York: Teacher's College Press.

Dwyer, T., Ponsonby, A. B., Newman, N. M., & Gibbons, L. E. (1991). Prospective cohort study of prone sleeping position and sudden infant death syndrome. *The Lancet, 337,* 1244–1247.

Dwyer, T., Ponsonby, A. L., Blizzard, L., Newman, N. M., & Cochrane, J. A. (1995). The contribution of changes in the prevalence of prone sleeping position to the decline in sudden infant death syndrome in Tasmania. *Journal of the American Medical Association, 273,* 783–789.

Dyslexia. (1989, September 23). *The Lancet,* pp. 719–720.

Dyson, A. H. (1993). A sociocultural perspective on symbolic development in primary grade classrooms. In C. Daiute (Ed.), *The development of literacy through social interaction* (New Directions for Child Development No. 61, pp. 25–39). San Francisco: Jossey-Bass.

Easterbrooks, M. A., & Goldberg, W. A. (1984). Toddler development in the family: Impact of father involvement and parenting characteristics. *Child Development, 55,* 740–752.

Eating disorders—Part I. (1997, October). *The Harvard Mental Health Letter,* pp. 1–5.

Eating disorders—Part II. (1997, November). *The Harvard Mental Health Letter,* pp. 1–5.

Eaton, W. O., & Enns, L. R. (1986). Sex differences in human motor activity level. *Psychological Bulletin, 100,* 19–28.

Eccles, J. S., Midgley, C., Wigfield, A., Buchanan, C. M., Reuman, D., Flanagan, C., & MacIver, D. (1993). Development during adolescence: The impact of stage-environment on young adolescents' experiences in schools and in families. *American Psychologist, 48*(2), 90–101.

Echeland, Y., Epstein, D. J., St-Jacques, B., Shen, L., Mohler, J., McMahon, J. A., & McMahon, A. P. (1993). Sonic hedgehog, a member of a family of putative signality molecules, is implicated in the regulation of CNS polarity. *Cell, 75,* 1417–1430.

Eckenrode, J., Laird, M., & Doris, J. (1993). School performance and disciplinary problems among abused and neglected children. *Developmental Psychology, 29,* 53–62.

Eckerman, C. O., Davis, C. C., & Didow, S. M. (1989). Toddlers' emerging ways of achieving social coordination with a peer. *Child Development, 60,* 440–453.

Eckerman, C. O., & Stein, M. R. (1982). The toddler's emerging interactive skills. In K. H. Rubin & H. S. Ross (Eds.), *Peer relationships and social skills in childhood.* New York: Springer-Verlag.

Edlin, B. R., Irwin, K. L., Farugue, S., McCoy, C. B., Word, C., Serrano, Y., Inciardi, J. A., Bowser, B. P., Schilling, R. F., Holmberg, S. D., & Multicenter Crack Cocaine and HIV Infection Study Team. (1994, November 24). Intersecting epidemics—Crack cocaine use and HIV infection among inner-city young adults. *New England Journal of Medicine, 331,* 1422–1427.

Edwards, C. P. (1981). The comparative study of the development of moral judgment and reasoning. In R. Monroe, R. Monroe, & B. B. Whiting (Eds.), *Handbook of cross-cultural human development.* New York: Garland.

Edwards, K. I. (1993). Obesity, anorexia, and bulimia. *Clinical Nutrition, 77,* 899–909.

Effects of open adoption vary. (1995, May). *The Menninger Letter,* p. 3.

Egbuono, L., & Starfield, B. (1982). Child health and social status. *Pediatrics, 69,* 550–557.

Egeland, B., Jacobvitz, D., & Sroufe, L. A. (1988). Breaking the cycle of abuse. *Child Development, 59,* 1080–1088.

Egeland, B., & Sroufe, L. A. (1981). Attachment and early maltreatment. *Child Development, 52,* 44–52.

Egertson, H. A. (1987, May 20). Recapturing kindergarten for 5-year-olds. *Education Week,* pp. 28, 19.

Eggebeen, D. J., Snyder, A. R., & Manning, W. D. (1996). Children in single-father families in demographic perspective. *Journal of Family Issues, 17,* 441–465.

Eiberg, H., Berendt, I., & Mohr, J. (1995). Assignment of dominant inherited nocturnal enuresis (ENUR1) to chromosome 13q. *Nature Genetics, 10,* 354–356.

Eiden, R. D., Teti, D. M., & Corns, K. M. (1995). Maternal working models of attachment, marital adjustment, and the parent-child relationship. *Child Development, 66,* 1504–1518.

Eiger, M. S., & Olds, S. W. (in press). *The complete book of breastfeeding* (3rd ed.). New York: Workman.

Eimas, P. (1985). The perception of speech in early infancy. *Scientific American, 252*(1), 46–52.

Eimas, P., Siqueland, E., Jusczyk, P., & Vigorito, J. (1971). Speech perception in infants. *Science, 171,* 303–306.

Einbender, A. J., & Friedrich, W. N. (1989). Psychological functioning and behavior of sexually abused girls. *Journal of Consulting and Clinical Psychology, 57*(1), 155–157.

Eisen, M., & Zellman, G. L. (1987). Changes in incidence of sexual intercourse of unmarried teenagers following a community-based sex education program. *Journal of Sex Research, 23*(4), 527–544.

Eisenberg, A. R. (1996). The conflict talk of mothers and children: Patterns related to culture, SES, and gender of child. *Merrill-Palmer Quarterly, 42,* 438–452.

Eisenberg, L. (1980). Adolescent suicide: On taking arms against a sea of troubles. *Pediatrics, 66,* 315–320.

Eisenberg, N. (1992). *The caring child.* Cambridge, MA: Harvard University Press.

Eisenberg, N., Fabes, R. A., Karbon, M., Murphy, B. C., Wosinski, M., Polazzi, L., Carlo, G., & Juhnke, C. (1996). The relations of children's dispositional prosocial behavior to emotionality, regulation, and social functioning. *Child Development, 67,* 974–992.

Eisenberg, N., Fabes, R. A., & Murphy, B. C. (1996). Parents' reactions to children's negative emotions: Relations to children's social competence and comforting behavior. *Child Development, 67,* 2227–2247.

Eisenberg, N., Fabes, R. A., Nyman, M., Bernzweig, J., & Pinuelas, A. (1994). The relations of emotionality and regulation to children's anger-related reactions. *Child Development, 65,* 109–128.

Eisenberg, N., Fabes, R. A., Schaller, M., & Miller, P. A. (1989). Sympathy and personal distress: Development, gender differences, and interrelations of indexes. In N. Eisenberg (Ed.), *Empathy and related emotional responses* (New Directions for Child Development No. 44). San Francisco: Jossey-Bass.

Eisenberg, N., Guthrie, I. K., Fabes, R. A., Reiser, M., Murphy, B. C., Holgren, R., Maszk, P., & Losoya, S. (1997). The relations of regulation and emotionality to resiliency and competent social functioning in elementary school children. *Child Development, 68 ,* 295–311.

Eisenson, J., Auer, J. J., & Irwin, J. V. (1963). *The psychology of communication.* New York: Appleton-Century-Crofts.

Elder, G. H., Jr., & Caspi, A. (1990). Studying lives in a changing society: Sociological and personological explorations. In A. I. Rabin, R. A. Zucker, R. Emmons, & S. Franks (Eds.), *Studying persons and lives.* New York: Springer.

Elicker, J., Englund, M., & Sroufe, L. A. (1992). Predicting peer competence and peer relationships in childhood from early parent-child relationships. In R. Parke & G. Ladd (Eds.), *Family-peer relationships: Modes of linkage* (pp. 77–106). Hillsdale, NJ: Erlbaum.

Elkind, D. (1981). *The hurried child.* Reading, MA: Addison-Wesley.

Elkind, D. (1984). *All grown up and no place to go.* Reading, MA: Addison-Wesley.

Elkind, D. (1986). *The miseducation of children: Superkids at risk.* New York: Knopf.

Elliott, D. S. (1993). Health enhancing and health compromising lifestyles. In S. G. Millstein, A. C. Petersen, & E. O. Nightingale (Eds.), *Promoting the health of adolescents: New directions for the twenty-first century.* New York: Oxford University Press.

Ellis, K. J., Abrams, S. A., & Wong, W. W. (1997). Body composition of a young, multiethnic female population. *American Journal of Clinical Nutrition, 65,* 724–731.

Ellis, L., & Ames, M. A. (1987). Neuro-hormonal functioning and sexual orientation: A theory of homosexuality-heterosexuality. *Psychological Bulletin, 101*(2), 233–258.

Emde, R. N. (1992). Individual meaning and increasing complexity: Contributions of Sigmund Freud and René Spitz to developmental psychology. *Developmental Psychology, 28,* 347–359.

Emde, R. N., Plomin, R., Robinson, J., Corley, R., DeFries, J., Fulker, D. W., Reznick, J. S., Campos, J., Kagan, J., & Zahn-Waxler, C. (1992). Temperament, emotion, and cognition at 14 months: The MacArthur longitudinal twin study. *Child Development, 63,* 1437–1455.

Emery, R. E. (1988). *Marriage, divorce, and children's adjustment.* Newbury Park, CA: Sage.

Enloe, C. F. (1980). How alcohol affects the developing fetus. *Nutrition Today, 15*(5), 12–15.

Epstein, L. H., & Wing, R. R. (1987). Behavioral treatment of childhood obesity. *Psychological Bulletin, 101*(3), 331–342.

Erikson, E. H. (1950). *Childhood and society.* New York: Norton.

Erikson, E. H. (1968). *Identity: Youth and crisis.* New York: Norton.

Erikson, E. H. (1973). The wider identity. In K. Erikson (Ed.), *In search of common ground: Conversations with Erik H. Erikson and Huey P. Newton.* New York: Norton.

Erikson, E. H. (1982). *The life cycle completed.* New York: Norton.

Erikson, E. H., Erikson, J. M., & Kivnick, H. Q. (1986). *Vital involvement in old age: The experience of old age in our time.* New York: Norton.

Eron, L. D. (1980). Prescription for reduction of aggression. *American Psychologist, 35,* 244–252.

Eron, L. D. (1982). Parent-child interaction, television violence, and aggression in children. *American Psychologist, 37,* 197–211.

Escarce, M. E. W. (1989). A cross-cultural study of Nepalese neonatal behavior. In J. K. Nugent, B. M. Lester, & T. B. Brazelton (Eds.), *The cultural context of infancy: Vol. 1. Biology, culture, and infant development* (pp. 65–86). Norwood, NJ: Ablex.

Espinosa, M. P., Sigman, M. D., Neumann, C. G., Bwibo, N. O., & McDonald, M. A. (1992). Playground behavior of school-age children in relation to nutrition, schooling, and family characteristics. *Developmental Psychology, 28,* 1188–1195.

European Collaborative Study. (1994). Natural history of vertically acquired human immunodeficiency virus-1 infection. *Pediatrics, 94,* 815–819.

Evans, G. (1976). The older the sperm . . . *Ms., 4*(7), 48–49.

Evans, N., Farkas, A., Gilpin, E., Berry, C., & Pierce, J. P. (1995). Influence of tobacco marketing and exposure to smoking on adolescent susceptibility to smoking. *Journal of the National Cancer Institute, 87,* 1538–1545.

Evans, R. I. (1967). *Dialogue with Erik Erikson.* New York: Harper & Row.

Ewigman, B. G., Crane, J. P., Frigoletto, F. D., LeFevre, M. L., Bain, R. P., McNellis, D., & the RADIUS Study Group. (1993). Effect of prenatal ultrasound screening on perinatal

outcome. *New England Journal of Medicine, 329,* 821–827.

Fabes, R. A., & Eisenberg, N. (1992). Young children's coping with interpersonal anger. *Child Development, 63,* 116–128.

Fabes, R. A., Eisenberg, N., Smith, M. C., & Murphy, B. C. (1996). Getting angry at peers: Associations with liking of the provocateur. *Child Development, 67,* 942–956.

Fagen, J. W., Morrongiello, B. A., Rovee-Collier, C., & Gekoski, M. J. (1984). Expectancies and memory retrieval in three-month-old infants. *Child Development, 55,* 936–943.

Fagot, B. I. (1997). Attachment, parenting, and peer interactions of toddler children. *Developmental Psychology, 33,* 489–499.

Fagot, B. I., & Gauvain, M. (1997). Mother-child problem solving: Continuity through the early childhood years. *Developmental Psychology, 33,* 480–488.

Fagot, B. I., & Hagan, R. (1991). Observations of parent reaction to sex-stereotyped behaviors: Age and sex effects. *Child Development, 62,* 617–628.

Faison, S. (1997, August 17). Chinese happily break the "one child" rule. *The New York Times,* pp. 1, 10.

Falbo, T., & Polit, D. F. (1986). Quantitative review of the only child literature: Research evidence and theory development. *Psychological Bulletin, 100*(2), 176–189.

Falbo, T., & Poston, D. L. (1993). The academic, personality, and physical outcomes of only children in China. *Child Development, 64,* 18–35.

Falkner, D. (1995). *Great time coming: The life of Jackie Robinson, from baseball to Birmingham.* New York: Simon & Schuster.

Faltermayer, C., Horowitz, J. M., Jackson, D., Lofaro, L., Maroney, T., Morse, J., Ramirez, A., & Rubin, J. C. (1996, August 5). Where are they now? *Time,* p. 18.

Fantuzzo, J. W., Jurecic, L., Stoval, A., Hightower, A. D., Goiins, C., & Schachtel, D. (1988). Effects of adult and peer social initiations on the social behavior of withdrawn, maltreated preschool children. *Journal of Consulting and Clinical Psychology, 56,* 34–39.

Fantz, R. L. (1963). Pattern vision in newborn infants. *Science, 140,* 296–297.

Fantz, R. L. (1964). Visual experience in infants: Decreased attention to familiar patterns relative to novel ones. *Science, 146,* 668–670.

Fantz, R. L. (1965). Visual perception from birth as shown by pattern selectivity. In H. E. Whipple (Ed.), New issues in infant development. *Annals of the New York Academy of Science, 118,* 793–814.

Fantz, R. L., Fagen, J., & Miranda, S. B. (1975). Early visual selectivity. In L. Cohen & P. Salapatek (Eds.), *Infant perception: From sensation to cognition: Vol. 1. Basic visual processes* (pp. 249–341). New York: Academic Press.

Fantz, R. L., & Nevis, S. (1967). Pattern preferences and perceptual-cognitive development in early infancy. *Merrill-Palmer Quarterly, 13,* 77–108.

Farrar, M. J., & Goodman, G. S. (1990). Developmental differences in the relation between scripts and episodic memory: Do they exist? In R. Fivush & J. Hudson (Eds.), *Knowing and remembering in young children* (pp. 30–64). Cambridge, England: Cambridge University Press.

Farrar, M. J., & Goodman, G. S. (1992). Developmental changes in event memory. *Child Development, 66,* 173–187.

Farrow, J. A., Rees, J. M., & Worthington-Roberts, B. S. (1987). Health, developmental, and nutritional status of adolescent alcohol and marijuana abusers. *Pediatrics, 79,* 218–223.

Farver, J. A. M., & Frosch, D. L. (1996). L.A. stories: Aggression in preschoolers' spontaneous narratives after the riots of 1992. *Child Development, 67,* 19–32.

Farver, J. A. M., Kim, Y. K., & Lee, Y. (1995). Cultural differences in Korean- and Anglo-American preschoolers' social interaction and play behavior. *Child Development, 66,* 1088–1099.

Feagans, L. (1983). A current view of learning disabilities. *Journal of Pediatrics, 102*(4), 487–493.

Fein, G. (1981). Pretend play in childhood: An integrative review. *Child Development, 52,* 1095–1118.

Feinman, S., & Lewis, M. (1983). Social referencing at ten months: A second-order effect on infants' responses. *Child Development, 54,* 878–887.

Feldhusen, J. F. (1992). *Talent identification and development in education (TIDE).* Sarasota, FL: Center for Creative Learning.

Feldhusen, J. F., & Moon, S. M. (1992). Grouping gifted students: Issues and concerns. *Gifted Child Quarterly, 36*(2), 63–67.

Feldman, H., Goldin-Meadow, S., & Gleitman, L. (1979). Beyond Herodotus: The creation of language by linguistically deprived deaf children. In A. Lock (Ed.), *Action, gesture and symbol: The emergence of language.* New York: Academic Press.

Feldman, R. D. (1982). *Whatever happened to the Quiz Kids: Perils and profits of growing up gifted.* Chicago: Chicago Review Press.

Feldman, R. D. (1985, August 6). Libraries open the books on local adult illiteracy. *Chicago Sun-Times School Guide,* pp. 10–11.

Feldman, R. D. (1986, April). What are thinking skills? *Instructor,* pp. 62–71.

Feldman, W., Feldman, E., & Goodman, J. T. (1988). Culture versus biology: Children's attitudes toward thinness and fatness. *Pediatrics, 81,* 190–194.

Felner, R. D., Brand, S., DuBois, D. L., Adan, A. M., Mulhall, P. F., & Evans, E. G. (1995). Socioeconomic disadvantage, proximal environmental experiences, and socioemotional and academic adjustment in early adolescence: Investigation of a mediated effect. *Child Development, 66,* 774–792.

Ferber, R. (1985). *Solve your child's sleep problems.* New York: Simon & Schuster.

Fergusson, D. M., Horwood, L. J., & Shannon, F. T. (1986). Factors related to the age of attainment of nocturnal bladder control: An 8-year longitudinal study. *Pediatrics, 78,* 884–890.

Fernald, A. (1984). The perceptual and affective salience of mothers' speech to infants. In L. Feagans, C. Garvey, & R. Golinkoff (Eds.), *The origins and growth of communication* (pp. 5–29). Norwood, NJ: Ablex.

Fernald, A., & Morikawa, H. (1993). Common themes and cultural variations in Japanese and American mothers' speech to infants. *Child Development, 64,* 637–656.

Fernald, A., & O'Neill, D. K. (1993). Peekaboo across cultures: How mothers and infants play with voices, faces, and expectations. In K. MacDonald (Ed.), *Parent-child play* (pp. 259–285). Albany: State University of New York Press.

Fernald, A., & Simon, T. (1984). Expanded intonation contours in mothers' speech to newborns. *Developmental Psychology, 20,* 104–113.

Fetters, L., & Tronick, E. Z. (1996). Neuromotor development of cocaine-exposed and control infants from birth through 15 months: Poor and poorer performance. *Pediatrics, 98,* 1–6.

Field, D. (1981). Can preschool children really learn to conserve? *Child Development, 52,* 326–334.

Field, T. (1991). Quality infant day-care and grade school behavior and performance. *Child Development, 62,* 863–870.

Field, T. (1995). Infants of depressed mothers. *Infant Behavior and Development, 18,* 1–13.

Field, T., Fox, N. A., Pickens, J., Nawrocki, T., & Soutollo, D. (1995). Right frontal EEG activation in 3- to 6-month-old infants of depressed mothers. *Developmental Psychology, 31,* 358–363.

Field, T., Grizzle, N., Scafidi, F., Abrams, S., Richardson, S., Kuhn, C., & Schanberg, S. (1996). Massage therapy for infants of depressed mothers. *Infant Behavior and Development, 19,* 107–112.

Field, T., Morrow, C., & Adelstein, D. (1993). Depressed mothers' perceptions of infant behavior. *Infant Behavior and Development, 16,* 99–108.

Field, T. M. (1978). Interaction behaviors of primary versus secondary caretaker fathers. *Developmental Psychology, 14,* 183–184.

Field, T. M. (1986). Interventions for premature infants. *Journal of Pediatrics, 109*(1), 183–190.

Field, T. M. (1987). Interaction and attachment in normal and atypical infants. *Journal of Consulting and Clinical Psychology, 55*(6), 853–859.

Field, T. M., & Roopnarine, J. L. (1982). Infant-peer interaction. In T. M. Field, A. Huston, H. C. Quay, L. Troll, & G. Finley (Eds.), *Review of human development.* New York: Wiley.

Field, T. M., Sandberg, D., Garcia, R., Vega-Lahr, N., Goldstein, S., & Guy, L. (1985). Pregnancy problems, postpartum depression, and early infant-mother interactions. *Developmental Psychology, 21,* 1152–1156.

Field, T. M., Widmayer, S., Greenberg, R., & Stoller, S. (1982). Effects of parent training on teenage mothers and their infants. *Pediatrics, 69,* 703–707.

Fifer, W. P., & Moon, C. M. (1995). The effects of fetal experience with sound. In J. P. Lecanuet, W. P. Fifer, N. A. Krasnegor, & W. P. Smotherman (Eds.), *Fetal development: A psychobiological perspective* (pp. 351–366). Hillsdale, NJ: Erlbaum.

Finch, M. D., Shanahan, M. J., Mortimer, J. T., & Ryu, S. (1991). Work experience and control orientation in adolescence. *American Sociological Review, 56,* 597–611.

Finegan, J. A. K., Quarrington, B. J., Hughes, H. E., Mervyn, J. M., Hood, J. E., Zacher, J. E., & Boyden, M. (1990). Child outcome following mid-trimester amniocentesis: Development, behaviour, and physical status at age 4 years. *British Journal of Obstetrics and Gynaecology, 97,* 32.

Finn, J. D., & Rock, D. A. (1997). Academic success among students at risk for dropout. *Journal of Applied Psychology, 82,* 221–234.

The first test-tube baby. (1978, July 31). *Time,* pp. 58–70.

Fischer, K. (1980). A theory of cognitive development: The control and construction of hierarchies of skills. *Psychological Review, 87,* 477–531.

Fiscus, S. A., Adimora, A. A., Schoenbach, V. J., Lim, W., McKinney, R., Rupar, D., Kenny, J., Woods, C., & Wilfert, C. (1996). Perinatal HIV infection and the effect of zidovudine therapy on transmission in rural and urban counties. *Journal of the American Medical Association, 275,* 1483–1488.

Fisher, C. B. (1993). Integrating science and ethics in research with high-risk children and youth. *Social Policy Report of the Society for Research in Child Development, 7*(Whole No. 4).

Fisher, M. (1992, November 30). Dead mother, living fetus: Rights prevail, but whose? *International Herald Tribune,* p. 2.

Fisher, R. L., & Fisher, S. (1996). Antidepressants for children: Is scientific support necessary? *Journal of Nervous Mental Disorders (United States), 184,* 99–102.

Fivush, R., Hudson, J., & Nelson, K. (1983). Children's long-term memory for a novel event: An exploratory study. *Merrill-Palmer Quarterly, 30,* 303–316.

Flake, A. W., Roncarolo, M. G., Puck, J. M., Almeida-Porada, G., Evans, M. I., Johnson, M. P., Abella, E. M., Harrison, D. D., & Zanjani, E. D. (1996). Treatment of X-linked severe combined immunodeficiency by in utero transplantation of paternal bone marrow. *New England Journal of Medicine, 335,* 1806–1810.

Flanagan, C. A., & Eccles, J. S. (1993). Changes in parents' work status and adolescents' adjustment at school. *Child Development, 64,* 246–257.

Flavell, J. (1963). *The developmental psychology of Jean Piaget.* New York: Van Nostrand.

Flavell, J. H. (1992). Cognitive development: Past, present, and future. *Developmental Psychology, 28,* 998–1005.

Flavell, J. H. (1993). Young children's understanding of thinking and consciousness. *Current Directions in Psychological Science, 2,* 40–43.

Flavell, J. H., Beach, D., & Chinsky, J. (1966). Spontaneous verbal rehearsal in a memory task as a function of age. *Child Development, 37,* 283–299.

Flavell, J. H., Green, F. L., & Flavell, E. R. (1986). Development of knowledge about the appearance-reality distinction. *Monographs of the Society for Reseach in Child Development, 51*(1, Serial No. 212).

Flavell, J. H., Green, F. L., & Flavell, E. R. (1995). Young children's knowledge about thinking. *Monographs of the Society for Research in Child Development, 60*(1, Serial No. 243).

Flavell, J. H., Green, F. L., Flavell, E. R., & Grossman, J. B. (1997). The development of children's knowledge about inner speech. *Child Development, 68,* 39–47.

Flavell, J. H., Miller, P. H., & Miller, S. A. (1993). *Cognitive development.* Englewood Cliffs, NJ: Prentice-Hall.

Flavell, J. H., Speer, J. R., Green, F. L., & August, D. L. (1981). The development of comprehension monitoring and knowledge about communication. *Monographs of the Society for Research in Child Development, 46*(5, Serial No. 192).

Flavell, J. H., Zhang, X. D., Zou, H., Dong, Q., & Qi, S. (1983). A comparison between development of the appearance-reality distinction in the People's Republic of China and the United States. *Cognitive Development, 15,* 459–466.

Fletcher, A. C., Darling, N. E., Steinberg, L., & Dornbusch, S. M. (1995). The company they keep: Relation of adolescents' adjustment and behavior to their friends' perceptions of authoritative parenting in the social network. *Developmental Psychology, 31,* 300–310.

Flores, J. (1952). *The woman with the whip: Eva Perón.* Garden City, NY: Doubleday.

Fluoxetine-Bulimia Collaborative Study Group. (1992). Fluoxetine in the treatment of bulimia nervosa: A multicenter placebo-controlled, double-blind trial. *Archives of General Psychiatry, 49,* 139–147.

Ford, D. Y., & Harris, J. J., III. (1996). Perceptions and attitudes of black students toward school, achievement, and other educational variables. *Child Development, 67,* 1141–1152.

Forman, B. M., Thotonoz, P., Chen, J., Brun, R. P., Spiegelman, B. M., & Evans, R. M. (1995). 15-deoxy-delta 12,

14-prostaglandin J2 is a ligand for the adopocyte determination factor PPAR gamma. *Cell, 83,* 803–812.

Fowler, M. G., Simpson, G. A., & Schoendorf, K. C. (1993). Families on the move and children's health care. *Pediatrics, 91,* 934–940.

Fox, N. A., Kimmerly, N. L., & Schafer, W. D. (1991). Attachment to mother/attachment to father: A meta-analysis. *Child Development, 62,* 210–225.

Fraga, C. G., Motchnik, P. A., Shigenaga, M. K., Helbock, H. J., Jacob, R. A., & Ames, B. N. (1991). Ascorbic acid protects against endogenous oxidative DNA damage in human sperm. *Proceedings of the National Academy of Sciences of the United States, 88,* 11003–11006.

Frank, A. (1958). *The diary of a young girl* (B. M. Mooyaart-Doubleday, Trans.). New York: Pocket.

Frank, A. (1995). *The diary of a young girl: The definitive edition* (O. H. Frank & M. Pressler, Eds.; S. Massotty, Trans.). New York: Doubleday.

Frankenburg, W. K., Dodds, J., Archer, P., Bresnick, B., Maschka, P., Edelman, N., & Shapiro, H. (1992). *Denver II training manual.* Denver: Denver Developmental Materials.

Frankenburg, W. K., Dodds, J. B., Fandal, A. W., Kazuk, E., & Cohrs, M. (1975). *The Denver Developmental Screening Test: Reference manual.* Denver: University of Colorado Medical Center.

Fraser, A. M., Brockert, J. F., & Ward, R. H. (1995). Association of young maternal age with adverse reproductive outcomes. *New England Journal of Medicine, 332*(17), 1113–1117.

Fraser, N., & Navarro, M. (1996). *Evita: The real life of Eva Perón.* New York: Norton.

Freedman, D. G. (1979, January). Ethnic differences in babies. *Human Nature,* pp. 15–20.

Freedman, D. G., & Freedman, M. (1969). Behavioral differences between Chinese-American and American newborns. *Nature, 224,* 1227.

Freedman, D. S., Srinivasan, S. R., Valdez, R. A., Williamson, D. F., & Berenson, G. S. (1997). Secular increases in relative weight and adiposity among children over two decades: The Bogalusa Heart Study. *Pediatrics, 88,* 420–426.

French, A. P. (Ed.). (1979). *Einstein: A centenary volume.* Cambridge, MA: Harvard University Press.

Fretts, R. C., Schmittdiel, J., McLean, F. H., Usher, R. H., & Goldman, M. B. (1995). Increased maternal age and the risk of fetal death. *New England Journal of Medicine, 333,* 953–957.

Freud, A. (1946). *The ego and the mechanisms of defense.* New York: International Universities Press.

Freud, S. (1953). *A general introduction to psychoanalysis* (J. Riviere, Trans.). New York: Perma-books. (Original work published 1935)

Freud, S. (1964a). New introductory lectures on psycho-analysis. In J. Strachey (Ed. & Trans.), *The standard edition of the complete psychological works of Sigmund Freud*

(Vol. 22). London: Hogarth. (Original work published 1933)

Freud, S. (1964b). An outline of psycho-analysis. In J. Strachey (Ed. & Trans.), *The standard edition of the complete psychological works of Sigmund Freud* (Vol. 23). London: Hogarth. (Original work published 1940)

Fried, P. A., Watkinson, B., & Willan, A. (1984). Marijuana use during pregnancy and decreased length of gestation. *American Journal of Obstetrics and Gynecology, 150,* 23–27.

Friend, M., & Davis, T. L. (1993). Appearance-reality distinction: Children's understanding of the physical and affective domains. *Developmental Psychology, 29,* 907–914.

Frith, U. (1989). *Autism: Explaining the enigma.* Oxford: Basil Blackwell.

Fuchs, D., & Fuchs, L. S. (1986). Test procedure bias: A meta-analysis of examiner familiarity effects. *Review of Educational Research, 56,* 243–262.

Fuchs, F. (1980). Genetic amniocentesis. *Scientific American, 242*(6), 47–53.

Fuchs, L. S., & Fuchs, D. (1986). Effects of systematic formative evaluation of student achievement: A metaanalysis. *Exceptional Children, 53,* 199–205.

Fuhrman, T., & Holmbeck, G. N. (1995). A contextual-moderator analysis of emotional autonomy and adjustment in adolescence. *Child Development, 66,* 793–811.

Fuligni, A. J. (1997). The academic achievement of adolescents from immigrant families: The roles of family background, attitudes, and behavior. *Child Development, 68,* 351–363.

Fuligni, A. J., & Eccles, J. S. (1993). Perceived parent-child relationships and early adolescents' orientation toward peers. *Developmental Psychology, 29,* 622–632.

Fuligni, A. J., & Stevenson, H. W. (1995). Time use and mathematics achievement among American, Chinese, and Japanese high school students. *Child Development, 66,* 830–842.

Fuller-Thomson, E., Minkler, M., & Driver, D. (1997). A profile of grandparents raising grandchildren in the United States. *The Gerontologist, 37.* 406–411.

Furman, W. (1982). Children's friendships. In T. M. Field, A. Huston, H. C. Quay, L. Troll, & G. E. Finley (Eds.), *Review of human development.* New York: Wiley.

Furman, W., & Bierman, K. L. (1983). Developmental changes in young children's conception of friendship. *Child Development, 54,* 549–556.

Furman, W., & Buhrmester, D. (1985). Children's perceptions of the personal relationships in their social networks. *Developmental Psychology, 21,* 1016–1024.

Furstenberg, F. F., Brooks-Gunn, J ., & Morgan, S. P. (1987). Adolescent mothers and their children in later life. *Family Planning Perspectives, 19,* 142–152.

Furstenberg, F. F., & Hughes, M. E. (1995). Social capital in successful development. *Journal of Marriage and the Family, 57,* 580–592.

Furstenberg, F. F., Levine, J. A., & Brooks-Gunn, J. (1990). The children of teenage mothers: Patterns of early child bearing in two generations. *Family Planning Perspectives, 22*(2), 54–61.

Furukawa, S. (1994). *The diverse living arrangements of children: Summer 1991* (U.S. Bureau of the Census, Current Population Reports, Series P70, No. 38). Washington, DC: U.S. Government Printing Office.

Gabriel, T. (1996, January 7). High-tech pregnancies test hope's limit. *The New York Times,* pp. 1, 18–19.

Gaddis, A., & Brooks-Gunn, J. (1985). The male experience of pubertal change. *Journal of Youth and Adolescence, 14,* 61–69.

Gaensbauer, T., & Hiatt, S. (1984). *The psychobiology of affective development.* Hillsdale, NJ: Erlbaum.

Gaertner, S. L., Mann, J., Murrell, A., & Dovidio, J. F. (1989). Reducing inter-group bias: The benefits of recategorization. *Journal of Personality and Social Psychology, 57,* 239–249.

Galambos, N. L., Petersen, A. C., & Lenerz, K. (1988). Maternal employment and sex typing in early adolescence: Contemporaneous and longitudinal relations. In A. D. Gottfried & A. W. Gottfried (Eds.), *Maternal employment and children's development: Longitudinal research.* New York: Plenum.

Galambos, N. L., Sears, H. A., Almeida, D. M., & Kolaric, G. C. (1995). Parents' work overload and problem behavior in young adolescents. *Journal of Research on Adolescence, 5*(2), 201–223.

Gale, J. L., Thapa, P. B., Wassilak, S. G., Bobo, J. K., Mendelman, P. M., & Foy, H. M. (1994). Risk of serious acute neurological illness after immunization with diptheria-tetanus-pertussis vaccine: A population-based case-control study. *Journal of the American Medical Association, 271,* 37–41.

Galotti, K. M., Komatsu, L. K., & Voelz, S. (1997). Children's differential performance on deductive and inductive syllogisms. *Developmental Psychology, 33,* 70–78.

Gans, J. E. (1990). *America's adolescents: How healthy are they?* Chicago: American Medical Association.

Garai, J. E., & Scheinfeld, A. (1968). Sex differences in mental and behavioral traits. *Genetic Psychology Monographs, 77,* 169–299.

Garasky, S., & Meyer, D. R. (1996). Reconsidering the increase in father-only families. *Demography, 33,* 385–393.

Garbarino, J., Dubrow, N., Kostelny, K., & Pardo, C. (1992). *Children in danger: Coping with the consequences of community violence.* San Francisco: Jossey-Bass.

Garbarino, J., & Kostelny, K. (1993). Neighborhood and community influences on parenting. In T. Luster & L. Okagaki (Eds.), *Parenting: An ecological perspective* (pp. 203–226). Hillsdale, NJ: Erlbaum.

Garcia-Coll, C., Kagan, J., & Reznick, J. S. (1984). Behavioral inhibition in young children. *Child Development, 55,* 1005–1019.

Gardner, H. (1983). *Frames of mind: The theory of multiple intelligences.* New York: Basic Books.

Gardner, H. (in press). Are there additional intelligences? In J. Kane (Ed.), *Education, information, and transformation.* Englewood Cliffs, NJ: Prentice-Hall.

Gardner, W., & Preator, K. (1996). Children of seropositive mothers in the U.S. AIDS epidemic. *Journal of Social Issues, 52*(3), 177–195.

Garland, A. F., & Zigler, E. (1993). Adolescent suicide prevention: Current research and social policy implications. *American Psychologist, 48*(2), 169–182.

Garland, J. B. (1982, March). *Social referencing and self-produced locomotion.* Paper presented at the meeting of the International Conference on International Studies, Austin, TX.

Garmezy, N. (1983). Stressors of childhood. In N. Garmezy & M. Rutter (Eds.), *Stress, coping and development in children.* New York: McGraw-Hill.

Garmezy, N., Masten, A., & Tellegen, A. (1984). The study of stress and competence in children. A building block for developmental psychopathology. *Child Development, 55,* 97–111.

Garner, D. M. (1993). Pathogenesis of anorexia nervosa. *The Lancet, 341,* 1631–1635.

Garner, P. W., & Power, T. G. (1996). Preschoolers' emotional control in the disappointment paradigm and its relation to temperament, emotional knowledge, and family expressiveness. *Child Development, 67,* 1406–1419.

Gauvain, M. (1993). The development of spatial thinking in everyday activity. *Developmental Review, 13,* 92–121.

Gauvain, M., & Rogoff, B. (1989). Ways of speaking about space: The development of children's skill at communicating spatial knowledge. *Cognitive Development, 4,* 295–307.

Geary, D. C. (1993). Mathematical disabilities: Cognitive, neuropsychological, and genetic components. *Psychological Bulletin, 114,* 345–362.

Geber, M. (1962). Longitudinal study and psychomotor development among Baganda children. *Proceedings of the Fourteenth International Congress of Applied Psychology, 3,* 50–60.

Geber, M., & Dean, R. F. A. (1957, June 16). The state of development of newborn African children. *The Lancet,* pp. 1216–1219.

Gecas, V., & Seff, M. A. (1990). Families and adolescents: A review of the 1980s. *Journal of Marriage and the Family, 52,* 941–958.

Geen, R. G. (1994). Television and aggression: Recent developments in research and theory. In D. Zillman, J. Bryant, & A. C. Huston (Eds.), *Media, children, and the family: Social scientific, psychoanalytic, and clinical perspectives.* Hillsdale, NJ: Erlbaum.

Gelfand, D. M., & Teti, D. M. (1995, November). How does maternal depression affect children? *The Harvard Mental Health Letter,* p. 8.

Gelman, R., Bullock, M., & Meck, E. (1980). Preschoolers' understanding of simple object transformations. *Child Development, 51,* 691–699.

Gelman, R., & Gallistel, C. R. (1978). *The child's understanding of number.* Cambridge, MA: Harvard University Press.

Gelman, R., Spelke, E. S., & Meck, E. (1983). What preschoolers know about animate and inanimate objects. In D. R. Rogers & J. S. Sloboda (Eds.), *The acquisition of symbolic skills* (pp. 297–326). New York: Plenum.

Genesee, F., Nicoladis, E., & Paradis, J. (1995). Language differentiation in early bilingual development. *Journal of Child Language, 22,* 611–631.

Gentner, D. (1982). Why nouns are learned before verbs: Linguistic relativity versus natural partitioning. In S. A. Kuczaj (Ed.), *Language development: Vol. 2. Language, thought and culture* (pp. 301–334). Hillsdale, NJ: Erlbaum.

George, C., Kaplan, N., & Main, M. (1985). *The Berkeley Adult Attachment Interview.* Unpublished protocol, Department of Psychology, University of California, Berkeley, CA.

George, T. P., & Hartmann, D. P. (1996). Friendship networks of unpopular, average, and popular children. *Child Development, 67,* 2301–2316.

Gertner, B. L., Rice, M. L., & Hadley, P. A. (1994). Influence of communicative competence on peer preferences in a preschool classroom. *Journal of Speech and Hearing Research, 37,* 913–923.

Geschwind, N., & Galaburda, A. M. (1985). Cerebral lateralization. Biological mechanisms, associations and pathology: I. A hypothesis and a program for research. *Archives of Neurology, 42,* 428–459.

Gesell, A. (1929). Maturation and infant behavior patterns. *Psychological Review, 36,* 307–319.

Getzels, J. W. (1964). Creative thinking, problem-solving, and instruction. In *Yearbook of the National Society for the Study of Education* (Pt. 1, pp. 240–267). Chicago: University of Chicago Press.

Getzels, J. W. (1984, March). *Problem-finding in creativity in higher education* [The Fifth Rev. Charles F. Donovan, S.J., Lecture]. Boston College, School of Education, Boston, MA.

Getzels, J. W., & Jackson, P. W. (1962). *Creativity and intelligence: Explorations with gifted students.* New York: Wiley.

Getzels, J. W., & Jackson, P. W. (1963). The highly intelligent and the highly creative adolescent: A summary of some research findings. In C. W. Taylor & F. Baron (Eds.), *Scientific creativity: Its recognition and development* (pp. 161–172). New York: Wiley.

Gielen, U., & Kelly, D. (1983, February). *Buddhist Ladakh: Psychological portrait of a nonviolent culture.* Paper presented at the Annual Meeting of the Society for Cross-Cultural Research, Washington, DC.

Giles-Sims, J., Straus, M., & Sugarman, D. B. (1995). Child, maternal, and family characteristics associated with spanking. *Family Relations, 44,* 170–176.

Gilligan, C. (1982). *In a different voice: Psychological theory and women's development.* Cambridge, MA: Harvard University Press.

Gilligan, C. (1987a). Adolescent development reconsidered. In E. E. Irwin (Ed.), *Adolescent social behavior and health.* San Francisco: Jossey-Bass.

Gilligan, C. (1987b). Moral orientation and moral development. In E. F. Kittay & D. T. Meyers (Eds.), *Women and moral theory* (pp. 19–33). Totowa, NJ: Rowman & Littlefield.

Gilligan, C., Murphy, J. M., & Tappan, M. B. (1990). Moral development beyond adolescence. In C. N. Alexander & E. J. Langer (Eds.), *Higher stages of human development* (pp. 208–228). New York: Oxford University Press.

Ginsburg, G. S., & Bronstein, P. (1993). Family factors related to children's intrinsic/extrinsic motivational orientation and academic performance. *Child Development, 64,* 1461–1474.

Ginsburg, H., & Miller, S. M. (1982). Sex differences in children's risk-taking behavior. *Child Development, 53,* 426–428.

Ginsburg, H., & Opper, S. (1979). *Piaget's theory of intellectual development* (2nd ed.). Englewood Cliffs, NJ: Prentice-Hall.

Ginzberg, E. (1972). Toward a theory of occupational choice: A restatement. *Vocational Guidance Quarterly, 20,* 169–176.

Ginzberg, E. (1984). Career development. In D. Brown & L. Brooks (Eds.), *Career choice and development: Applying contemporary theories to practice* (pp. 169–191). San Francisco: Jossey-Bass.

Ginzberg, E., Ginsberg, S. W., Axelrad, S., & Herma, J. (1951). *Occupational choice: An approach to a general theory.* New York: Columbia University Press.

Giordano, P. C., Cernkovich, S. A., & DeMaris, A. (1993). The family and peer relations of black adolescents. *Journal of Marriage and the Family, 55,* 277–287.

Gladue, B. A. (1994). The biopsychology of sexual orientation. *Current Directions in Psychological Science, 3,* 150–154.

Glasgow, K. L., Dornbusch, S. M., Troyer, L., Steinberg, L., & Ritter, P. L. (1997). Parenting styles, adolescents' attributions, and educational outcomes in nine heterogeneous high schools. *Child Development, 68,* 507–529.

Glass, R. B. (1986). Infertility. In S. S. C. Yen & R. B. Jaffe (Eds.), *Reproductive endocrinology: Physiology, pathophysiology, and clinical management* (pp. 571–613). Philadelphia: Saunders.

Gleitman, L. R., Newport, E. L., & Gleitman, H. (1984). The current status of the motherese hypothesis. *Journal of Child Language, 11,* 43–79.

Glick, P. C., & Lin, S. L. (1986). Recent changes in divorce and remarriage. *Journal of Marriage and the Family, 48,* 737–747.

Gold, D., & Andres, D. (1978). Developmental comparison between adolescent children with employed and nonemployed mothers. *Merrill-Palmer Quarterly, 24,* 243–254.

Goldberg, W. A., Greenberger, E., & Nagel, S. K. (1996). Employment and achievement: Mothers' work involvement in relation to children's achievement behaviors and mothers' parenting behaviors. *Child Development, 67*, 1512–1527.

Golden, M., Birns, B., & Bridger, W. (1973). *Review and overview: Social class and cognitive development.* Paper presented at the meeting of the Society for Research in Child Development, Philadelphia, PA.

Goldenberg, R. L., & Tamura, T. (1996). Prepregnancy weight and pregnancy outcome. *Journal of the American Medical Association, 275*, 1127–1128.

Goldenberg, R. L., Tamura, T., Neggers, Y., Copper, R. L., Johnston, K. E., DuBard, M. B., & Hauth, J. C. (1995). The effect of zinc supplementation on pregnancy outcome. *Journal of the American Medical Association, 274*, 463–468.

Goldin-Meadow, S., & Mylander, C. (1998). Spontaneous sign systems created by deaf children in two cultures. *Nature, 391*, 279–281.

Goldman, A. (1981). *Elvis.* New York: McGraw-Hill.

Goldsmith, M., Mackay, A., & Woudhuysen, J. S. (Eds.). (1980). *Einstein: The first hundred years.* Oxford: Pergamon.

Goleman, D. (1993, June 11). Studies reveal suggestibility of very young as witnesses. *The New York Times,* pp. A1, A23.

Goleman, D. (1995, July 1). A genetic clue to bed-wetting is located: Researchers say discovery shows the problem is not emotional. *The New York Times,* p. 8.

Golinkoff, R. M., Jacquet, R. C., Hirsh-Pasek, K., & Nandakumar, R. (1996). Lexical principles may underlie the learning of verbs. *Child Development, 67*, 3101–3119.

Golomb, C., & Galasso, L. (1995). Make believe and reality: Explorations of the imaginary realm. *Developmental Psychology, 31*, 800–810.

Golombok, S., Cook, R., Bish, A., & Murray, C. (1995). Families created by the new reproductive technologies: Quality of parenting and social and emotional development of the children. *Child Development, 66*, 285–298.

Golombok, S., & Tasker, F. (1996). Do parents influence the sexual orientation of their children? Findings from a longitudinal study of lesbian families. *Developmental Psychology, 32*, 3–11.

Goodwin, J. (1994). *Akira Kurosawa and intertextual cinema.* Baltimore: Johns Hopkins University Press.

Gopnik, A., & Meltzoff, A. N. (1994). Minds, bodies, and persons: Young children's understanding of the self and others as reflected in imitation and "theory of mind" research. In S. Parker & R. Mitchell (Eds.), *Self-awareness in animals and humans* (pp. 166–186). New York: Cambridge University Press.

Gopnik, A., & Meltzoff, A. N. (in press). *Words, thoughts and theories.* Cambridge, MA: MIT Press.

Gordon, I., Lask, B., Bryantwaugh, R., Christie, D., & Timini, S. (1997). Childhood onset anorexia nervosa: Towards identifying a biological substrate. *International Journal of Eating Disorders, 22*(2), 159–165.

Gorman, K. S., & Pollitt, E. (1996). Does schooling buffer the effects of early risk? *Child Development, 67*, 314–326.

Gorman, M. (1993). Help and self-help for older adults in developing countries. *Generations, 17*(4), 73–76.

Gortmaker, S. L., Must, A., Perrin, J. M., Sobol, A. M., & Dietz, W. H. (1993). Social and economic consequences of overweight in adolescence and young adulthood. *New England Journal of Medicine, 329*, 1008–1012.

Gottesman, I. I. (1993). Origins of schizophrenia: Past and prologue. In R. P. Plomin & G. E. McClearn (Eds.), *Nature, nurture, and psychology.* Washington, DC: American Psychological Association.

Gottman, J. M., & Katz, L. F. (1989). Effects of marital discord on young children's peer interaction and health. *Developmental Psychology, 25*, 373–381.

Graber, J. A., Brooks-Gunn, J., & Warren, M. P. (1995). The antecedents of menarcheal age: Heredity, family environment, and stressful life events. *Child Development, 66*, 346–359.

Graham, C. J., Dick, R., Rickert, V. I., & Glenn, R. (1993). Left-handedness as a risk factor for unintentional injury in children. *Pediatrics, 92*, 823–826.

Gralinski, J. H., & Kopp, C. B. (1993). Everyday rules for behavior: Mothers' requests to young children. *Developmental Psychology, 29*, 573–584.

Grantham-McGregor, S., Powell, C., Walker, S., Chang, S., & Fletcher, P. (1994). The long-term follow-up of severely malnourished children who participated in an intervention program. *Child Development, 65*, 428–439.

Grantham-McGregor, S. M. (1984). Rehabilitation following clinical malnutrition. In J. Brozek & B. Schurch (Eds.), *Malnutrition and behavior: Critical assessment of key issues* (pp. 531–554). Lausanne, Switzerland: Nestle Foundation.

Graziano, A. M., & Mooney, K. C. (1982). Behavioral treatment of "nightfears" in children: Maintenance and improvement at 2½ to 3-year follow-up. *Journal of Counseling and Clinical Psychology, 50*, 598–599.

Greenberger, E., & Chen, C. (1996). Perceived family relationships and depressed mood in early and late adolescence: A comparison of European and Asian Americans. *Developmental Psychology, 32*, 707–716.

Greenberger, E., & Steinberg, L. (1986). *When teenagers work.* New York: Basic Books.

Greenfield, P. (1966). On culture and conservation. In J. S. Bruner, R. R. Olver, & P. Greenfield (Eds.), *Studies in cognitive growth* (pp. 225–256). New York: Wiley.

Greenfield, P. M. (1984). A theory of the teacher in the learning activities of everyday life. In B. Rogoff & J. Lave (Eds.), *Everyday cognition: Its development in social context.* Cambridge, MA: Harvard University Press.

Greenough, W. T., Black, J. E., & Wallace, C. S. (1987). Experience and brain development. *Child Development, 58*, 539–559.

Greenstein, T. N. (1995). Gender ideology, marital disruption, and the employment of married women. *Journal of Marriage and the Family, 57*, 31–42.

Groce, N. E., & Zola, I. K. (1993). Multiculturalism, chronic illness, and disability. *Pediatrics, 91*, 1048–1055.

Gross, R. T., & Duke, P. (1980). The effect of early versus late physical maturation on adolescent behavior. [Special issue: I. Litt (Ed.), Symposium on adolescent medicine.] *Pediatric Clinics of North America, 27*, 71–78.

Grotevant, H., & Durrett, M. (1980) Occupational knowledge and career development in adolescence. *Journal of Vocational Behavior, 17*, 171–182.

Groth-Marnat, G. (1984). *Handbook of psychological assessment.* New York: Van Nostrand Reinhold.

Grubman, S., Gross, E., Lerner-Weiss, N., Hernandez, M., McSherry, G. D., Hoyt, L. G., Boland, M., & Oleske, J. M. (1995). Older children and adolescents living with perinatally acquired human immunodeficiency virus. *Pediatrics, 95*, 657–663.

Grusec, J. E., & Goodnow, J. J. (1994). Impact of parental discipline methods on the child's internalization of values: A reconceptualization of current points of view. *Developmental Psychology, 30*, 4–19.

Gruson, L. (1992, April 22). Gains in deciphering genes set off effort to guard data against abuses. *The New York Times,* p. C12.

Guberman, S. R. (1996). The development of everyday mathematics in Brazilian children with limited formal education. *Child Development, 67*, 1609–1623.

Guerin, D. W., & Gottfried, A. W. (1994). Temperamental consequences of infant difficultness. *Infant Behavior and Development, 17*, 413–421.

Guidubaldi, J., & Perry, J. D. (1985). Divorce and mental health sequelae for children: A two year follow-up of a nationwide sample. *Journal of the American Academy of Child Psychiatry, 24*, 531–537.

Guilford, J. P. (1967). *The nature of human intelligence.* New York: McGraw-Hill.

Guillermoprieto, A. (1996, December 2). Little Eva. *The New Yorker,* pp. 98–106.

Guisinger, S., & Blatt, S. J. (1994). Individuality and relatedness: Evolution of a fundamental dialectic. *American Psychologist, 49*, 104–111.

Gullone, E., & King, N. J. (1997). Three-year-old follow-up of normal fear in children and adolescents aged 7 to 18 years. *British Journal of Developmental Psychology, 15*, 97–111.

Gunnar, M. R., Larson, M. C., Hertsgaard, L., Harris, M. L., & Brodersen, L. (1992). The stressfulness of separation among nine-month-old infants: Effects of social context variables and infant temperament. *Child Development, 63*, 290–303.

Guralnick, P. (1994). *Last train to Memphis: The rise of Elvis Presley*. Boston: Little, Brown.

Guyer, B., Strobino, D. M., Ventura, S. J., MacDorman, M., & Martin, J. A. (1996). Annual summary of vital statistics—1995. *Pediatrics, 98*, 1007–1019.

Hack, M., Friedman, H., & Fanaroff, A. A. (1996). Outcomes of extremely low birth weight infants. *Pediatrics, 98*, 931–937.

Haddow, J. E., Palomaki, G. E., Knight, G. J., Williams, J., Polkkiner, A., Canick, J. A., Saller, D. N., & Bowers, G. B. (1992). Prenatal screening for Down's syndrome with use of maternal serum markers. *New England Journal of Medicine, 327*, 588–593.

Haden, C. A., & Fivush, F. (1996). Contextual variation in maternal conversational styles. *Merrill-Palmer Quarterly, 42*, 200–227.

Haden, C. A., Haine, R. A., & Fivush, R. (1997). Developing narrative structure in parent-child reminiscing across the preschool years. *Developmental Psychology, 33*, 295–307.

Haglund, B. (1993). Cigarette smoking and sudden infant death syndrome: Some salient points in the debate. *Acta Paediatrica, 389*(Suppl.), 37–39.

Haith, M. M. (1986). Sensory and perceptual processes in early infancy. *Journal of Pediatrics, 109*(1), 158–171.

Hakuta, K., Ferdman, B. M., & Diaz, R. M. (1987). Bilingualism and cognitive development: Three perspectives. In S. Rosenberg (Ed.), *Advances in applied psycholinguistics: Vol. 2. Reading, writing, and language learning* (pp. 284–319). New York: Cambridge University Press.

Hakuta, K., & Garcia, E. E. (1989). Bilingualism in education. *American Psychologist, 44*(2), 374–379.

Hala, S., & Chandler, M. (1996). The role of strategic planning in accessing false-belief understanding. *Child Development, 67*, 2948–2966.

Halaas, J. L., Gajiwala, K. S., Maffei, M., Cohen, S. L., Chait, B. T., Rabinowitz, D., Lallone, R. L., Burley, S. K., & Friedman, J. M. (1995). Weight reducing effects of the plasma protein encoded by the obese gene. *Science, 269*, 543–546.

Hale, J. (1982). *Black children: Their roots, culture, and learning styles*. Provo, UT: Brigham Young University Press.

Hale, S., Bronik, M. D., & Fry, A. F. (1997). Verbal and spatial working memory in school-age children: Developmental differences in susceptibility to interference. *Developmental Psychology, 33*, 364–371.

Halfon, N., & Newacheck, P. W. (1993). Childhood asthma and poverty: Differential impacts and utilization of health services. *Pediatrics, 91*, 56–61.

Hall, E. G., & Lee, A. M. (1984). Sex differences in motor performance of young children: Fact or fiction? *Sex Roles, 10*, 217–230.

Hall, G. S. (1916). *Adolescence*. New York: Appleton. (Original work published 1904)

Hallé, P. A., & de Boysson-Bardies, B. (1994). Emergence of an early receptive lexicon: Infants' recognition of words. *Infant Behavior and Development, 17*, 119–129.

Halpern, D. F., & Coren, S. (1993). Left-handedness and life span: A reply to Harris. *Psychological Bulletin, 114*(2), 235–241.

Haltiwanger, J., & Harter, S. (1988). *A behavioral measure of young children's presented self-esteem*. Unpublished manuscript, University of Denver, Denver, CO.

Hamer, D. H., Hu, S., Magnuson, V. L., Hu, N., & Pattatucci, A. M. L. (1993). A linkage between DNA markers on the X chromosome and male sexual orientation. *Science, 261*, 321–327.

Hamilton, S. (1990). *Apprenticeship for adulthood*. New York: Free Press.

Hamilton, S., & Crouter, A. (1980). Work and growth: A review of research on the impact of work experience on adolescent development. *Journal of Youth and Adolescence, 9*, 323–338.

Handyside, A. H., Lesko, J. G., Tarin, J. J., Winston, R. M. L., & Hughes, M. R. (1992). Birth of a normal girl after in vitro fertilization and preimplantation diagnostic testing for cystic fibrosis. *New England Journal of Medicine, 327*(13), 905–909.

Hanna, E., & Meltzoff, A. N. (1993). Peer imitation by toddlers in laboratory, home, and day care contexts: Implications for social learning and memory. *Developmental Psychology, 29*, 701–710.

Hardy-Brown, K., & Plomin, R. (1985). Infant communicative development: Evidence from adoptive and biological families for genetic and environmental influences on rate differences. *Developmental Psychology, 21*, 378–385.

Hardy-Brown, K., Plomin, R., & DeFries, J. C. (1981). Genetic and environmental influences on rate of communicative development in the first year of life. *Developmental Psychology, 17*, 704–717.

Hardyck, C., & Petrinovich, L. F. (1977). Left-handedness. *Psychological Bulletin, 84*, 385–404.

Hargrove, J. (1989). *Nelson Mandela: South Africa's silent voice of protest*. Chicago: Children's Press.

Harlow, H. F., & Harlow, M. K. (1962). The effect of rearing conditions on behavior. *Bulletin of the Menninger Clinic, 26*, 213–224.

Harlow, H. F., & Zimmerman, R. R. (1959). Affectional responses in the infant monkey. *Science, 130*, 421–432.

Harnishfeger, K. K., & Bjorklund, D. F. (1993). The ontogeny of inhibition mechanisms: A renewed approach to cognitive development. In M. L. Howe & R. P. Pasnak (Eds.), *Emerging themes in cognitive development* (Vol. 1, pp. 28–49). New York: Springer-Verlag.

Harnishfeger, K. K., & Pope, R. S. (1996). Intending to forget: The development of cognitive inhibition in directed forgetting. *Journal of Experimental Psychology, 62*, 292–315.

Harold, & Conger, R. (1997). Marital conflict and adolescent distress. *Child Development, 68*, 333–350.

Harrington, D. M. (1993). Child-rearing antecedents of suboptimal personality development: Exploring aspects of Alice Miller's concept of the poisonous pedagogy. In D. C. Funder, R. D. Parke, C. Tomlinson-Keasey, & K. Widamen (Eds.), *Studying lives through time: Personality and development* (pp. 289–313). Washington, DC: American Psychological Association.

Harris, L. J. (1993a). Do left-handers die sooner than right-handers? Commentary on Coren and Halpern's (1991) "Left-handedness: A marker for decreased survival fitness." *Psychological Bulletin, 114*(2), 203–234.

Harris, L. J. (1993b). Reply to Halpern and Coren. *Psychological Bulletin, 114*(2), 242–247.

Harris, P. L., Brown, E., Marriott, C., Whittall, S., & Harmer, S. (1991). Monsters, ghosts, and witches: Testing the limits of the fantasy-reality distinction in young children. In G. E. Butterworth, P. L. Harris, A. M. Leslie, & H. M. Wellman (Eds.), *Perspective on the child's theory of mind*. Oxford: Oxford University Press.

Harrison, A. O., Wilson, M. N., Pine, C. J., Chan, S. Q., & Buriel, R. (1990). Family ecologies of ethnic minority children. *Child Development, 61*, 347–362.

Harrist, A. W., Zain, A. F., Bates, J. E., Dodge, K. A., & Pettit, G. S. (1997). Subtypes of social withdrawal in early childhood: Sociometric status and social-cognitive differences across four years. *Child Development, 68*, 278–294.

Hart, B., & Risley, T. (1996, August). *Individual differences in early intellectual experience of typical American children: Beyond SES, race, and IQ*. Address at the annual convention of the American Psychological Association, Toronto, Canada.

Hart, B., & Risley, T. R. (1989). The longitudinal study of interactive systems. *Education and Treatment of Children, 12*, 347–358.

Hart, B., & Risley, T. R. (1992). American parenting of language-learning children: Persisting differences in family-child interactions observed in natural home environments. *Developmental Psychology, 28*, 1096–1105.

Hart, C. H., DeWolf, M., Wozniak, P., & Burts, D. C. (1992). Maternal and paternal disciplinary styles: Relations with preschoolers' playground behavioral orientation and peer status. *Child Development, 63*, 879–892.

Hart, C. H., Ladd, G. W., & Burleson, B. R. (1990). Children's expectations of the outcome of social strategies: Relations with sociometric status and maternal disciplinary style. *Child Development, 61*, 127–137.

Hart, D., Hofmann, V., Edelstein, W., & Keller, M. (1997). The relation of childhood personality types to adolescent behavior and development: A longitudinal study of Icelandic children. *Developmental Psychology, 33,* 195–205.

Hart, S. N., & Brassard, M. R. (1987). A major threat to children's mental health: Psychological maltreatment. *American Psychologist, 42*(2), 160–165.

Harter, S. (1985). Competence as a dimension of self-worth. In R. Leahy (Ed.), *The development of the self.* New York: Academic Press.

Harter, S. (1990). Causes, correlates, and the functional role of global self-worth: A life-span perspective. In J. Kolligan & R. Sternberg (Eds.), *Competence considered: Perceptions of competence and incompetence across the life-span* (pp. 67–97). New Haven: Yale University Press.

Harter, S. (1993). Developmental changes in self-understanding across the 5 to 7 shift. In A. Sameroff & M. Haith (Eds.), *Reason and responsibility: The passage through childhood.* Chicago: University of Chicago Press.

Harter, S., & Buddin, B. J. (1987). Children's understanding of the simultaneity of two emotions: A five-stage developmental acquisition sequence. *Developmental Psychology, 23,* 388–389.

Hartmann, E. (1981). The strangest sleep disorder. *Psychology Today, 15*(4), 14–18.

Hartup, W. W. (1989). Social relationships and their developmental significance. *American Psychologist, 44,* 120–126.

Hartup, W. W. (1992). Peer relations in early and middle childhood. In V. B. Van Hasselt & M. Hersen (Eds.), *Handbook of social development: A lifespan perspective* (pp. 257–281). New York: Plenum.

Hartup, W. W. (1996a). The company they keep: Friendships and their developmental significance. *Child Development, 67,* 1–13.

Hartup, W. W. (1996b). Cooperation, close relationships, and cognitive development. In W. M. Bukowski, A. F. Newcomb, & W. W. Hartup (Eds.), *The company they keep: Friendship in childhood and adolescence* (pp. 213–237). New York: Cambridge University Press.

Harvey, B. (1990). Toward a national child health policy. *Journal of the American Medical Association, 264,* 252–253.

Harwood, R. (1987). *Mandela.* New York: New American Library.

Harwood, R. L., Schoelmerich, A., Ventura-Cook, E., Schulze, P. A., & Wilson, S. P. (1996). Culture and class influences on Anglo and Puerto Rican mothers' beliefs regarding long-term socialization goals and child behavior. *Child Development, 67,* 2446–2461.

Haskett, M. E., & Kistner, J. A. (1991). Social interaction and peer perceptions of young physically abused children. *Child Development, 62,* 979–990.

Haskins, R. (1989). Beyond metaphor: The efficacy of early childhood education. *American Psychologist, 44*(2), 274–282.

Haswell, K., Hock, E., & Wenar, C. (1981). Oppositional behavior of preschool children: Theory and prevention. *Family Relations, 30,* 440–446.

Hatcher, P. J., Hulme, C., & Ellis, A. W. (1994). Ameliorating early reading failure by integrating the teaching of reading and phonological skills: The phonological linkage hypothesis. *Child Development, 65,* 41–57.

Hatzichristou, C., & Hopf, D. (1996). A multiperspective comparison of peer sociometric status groups in childhood and adolescence. *Child Development, 67,* 1085–1102.

Haugh, S., Hoffman, C., & Cowan, G. (1980). The eye of the very young beholder: Sex typing of infants by young children. *Child Development, 51,* 598–600.

Hawkins, J. D., Catalano, R. F., & Miller, J. Y. (1992). Risk and protective factors for alcohol and other drug problems in adolescence and early adulthood: Implications for substance abuse programs. *Psychological Bulletin, 112*(1), 64–105.

Hawley, T. L., & Disney, E. R. (1992). Crack's children: The consequences of maternal cocaine abuse. *Social Policy Report of the Society for Research in Child Development, 6*(4), 1–23.

Hay, D. F., Pedersen, J., & Nash, A. (1982). Dyadic interaction in the first year of life. In K. H. Rubin & H. S. Ross (Eds.), *Peer relationships and social skills in children.* New York: Springer.

Hayes, A., & Batshaw, M. L. (1993). Down syndrome. *Pediatric Clinics of North America, 40,* 523–535.

Hayne, H., & Campbell, B. A. (1997, October). *Declarative memory during the first year of life.* Paper presented at the meeting of the Society for Neuroscience, New Orleans, LA.

Hayne, H., & Rovee-Collier, C. (1995). The organization of reactivated memory in infancy. *Child Development, 66,* 893–906.

Health Care Financing Administration. (1997, September 10). *HCFA announces state allotments for children's health insurance program* [Press release]. Washington, DC: Author.

Heath, S. B. (1989). Oral and literate tradition among black Americans living in poverty. *American Psychologist, 44,* 367–373.

Heilbut, A. (1993, April 26). Postscript: Marian Anderson. *New Yorker,* pp. 82–83.

Helms, J. E. (1992). Why is there no study of cultural equivalence in standardized cognitive ability testing? *American Psychologist, 47,* 1083–1101.

Henker, B., & Whalen, C. K. (1989). Hyperactivity and attention deficits. *American Psychologist, 44,* 216–223.

Henly, W. L., & Fitch, B. R. (1966). Newborn narcotic withdrawal associated with regional enteritis in pregnancy. *New York Journal of Medicine, 66,* 2565–2567.

Herman-Giddens, M. E., Slora, E. J., Wasserman, R. C., Bourdony, C. J., Bhapkar, M. V., Koch, G. G., & Hasemeier, C. M. (1997). Secondary sexual characteristics and menses in young girls seen in office practice: A study from the Pediatric Research in Office Settings network. *Pediatrics, 99,* 505–512.

Herrmann, H. J., & Roberts, M. W. (1987). Preventive dental care: The role of the pediatrician. *Pediatrics, 80,* 107–110.

Herrnstein, R. J., & Murray, C. (1994). *The bell curve: Intelligence and class structure in American life.* New York: Free Press.

Herzog, D. B., Keller, M. B., & Lavori, P. W. (1988). Outcome in anorexia nervosa and bulimia. *Journal of Nervous and Mental Disease, 176,* 131–143.

Hetherington, E. M. (1965). A developmental study of the effects of sex of the dominant parent on sex role preference, identification, and imitation in children. *Journal of Personality and Social Psychology, 2,* 188–194.

Hetherington, E. M. (1980). Children and divorce. In R. Henderson (Ed.), *Parent-child interaction: Theory, research and prospects.* New York: Academic Press.

Hetherington, E. M. (1987). Family relations six years after divorce. In K. Pasley & M. Ihinger-Tallman (Eds.), *Remarriage and parenting today: Research and theory.* New York: Guilford.

Hetherington, E. M. (1989). Coping with family transitions: Winners, losers, and survivors. *Child Development, 60,* 1–14.

Hetherington, E. M., Stanley-Hagan, M., & Anderson, E. (1989). Marital transitions: A child's perspective. *American Psychologist, 44,* 303–312.

Hewlett, B. S. (1987). Intimate fathers: Patterns of paternal holding among Aka pygmies. In M. E. Lamb (Ed.), *The father's role: Cross-cultural perspectives.* Hillsdale, NJ: Erlbaum.

Heyns, B., & Catsambis, S. (1986). Mother's employment and children's achievement: A critique. *Sociology of Education, 59,* 140–151.

Hill, J. P. (1987). Research on adolescents and their families: Past and prospect. In E. E. Irwin (Ed.), *Adolescent social behavior and health.* San Francisco: Jossey-Bass.

Hirsch, H. V., & Spinelli, D. N. (1970). Visual experience modifies distribution of horizontally and vertically oriented receptive fields in cats. *Science, 168,* 869–871.

Hirsch, J. (1972). Can we modify the number of adipose cells? *Postgraduate Medicine, 51*(5), 83–86.

Hirsh-Pasek, K. (1991). Pressure or challenge in preschool? How academic environments affect children. In L. Rescorla, M. C. Hyston, & K. Hirsh-Pasek (Eds.), *Academic instruction in early childhood: Challenge or pressure?* San Francisco: Jossey-Bass.

Hirsh-Pasek, K., Hyson, M. C., & Rescorla, L. (1989, August). *Academic environments in early childhood: Challenge and pressure.* Paper presented at the annual meeting of the American Psychological Association, New Orleans, LA.

Ho, W. C. (1989). *Yani: The brush of innocence.* New York: Hudson Hills.

Hoff-Ginsberg, E. (1991). Mother-child conversation in different social classes and communicative settings. *Child Development, 62,* 782–796.

Hoff-Ginsberg, E., & Shatz, M. (1982). Linguistic input and the child's acquisition of language. *Psychological Bulletin, 92*(1), 3–26.

Hoffman, L. W. (1979). Maternal employment. *American Psychologist, 34*(10), 859–865.

Hoffman, L. W. (1986). Work, family, and the child. In M. S. Pallak & R. O. Perloff (Eds.), *Psychology and work: Productivity, change, and employment.* Washington, DC: American Psychological Association.

Hoffman, L. W. (1989). Effects of maternal employment in the two-parent family: A review of recent research. *American Psychologist, 44*(2), 283–292.

Hoffman, M. L. (1970a). Conscience, personality, and socialization techniques. *Human Development, 13,* 90–126.

Hoffman, M. L. (1970b). Moral development. In P. H. Mussen (Ed.), *Carmichael's manual of child psychology* (Vol. 2, 3rd ed., pp. 261–360). New York: Wiley.

Hoffman, M. L. (1977). Sex differences in empathy and related behaviors. *Psychological Bulletin, 84,* 712–722.

Hoffman, M. L., & Hoffman, L. W. (Eds.). (1964). *Review of child development research.* New York: Russell Sage Foundation.

Holden, C. (1994). A cautionary genetic tale: The sobering story of D2. *Science, 264,* 1696–1697.

Hook, B., Kiwi, R., Amini, S. B., Fanaroff, A., & Hack, M. (1997). Neonatal morbidity after elective repeat cesarean section and trial of labor. *Pediatrics, 100,* 348–353.

Hopfensperger, J. (1996, April 15). Germany's fast track to a career. *Minneapolis Star-Tribune,* pp. A1, A6.

Horbar, J. D., Wright, E. C., Onstad, L., & the Members of the National Institute of Child Health and Human Development Neonatal Research Network. (1993). Decreasing mortality associated with the introduction of surfactant therapy: An observational study of neonates weighing 601 to 1300 grams at birth. *Pediatrics, 92,* 191–196.

Horn, J. (1983). The Texas Adoption Project: Adopted children and their intellectual resemblance to biological and adoptive parents. *Child Development, 54,* 268–275.

Horowitz, F. D., & O'Brien, M. (1986). Gifted and talented children: State of knowledge and directions for research. *American Psychologist, 41*(10), 1147–1152.

Horwood, L. J., & Fergusson, D. M. (1998). Breastfeeding and child achievement. *Pediatrics* [On-line], *101*(1). Available: http://www.pediatrics.org/cgi/content/full/101/1/e9[1998, January 5]

Hossain, Z., & Roopnarine, J. L. (1994). African-American fathers' involvement with infants: Relationship to their functioning style, support, education, and income. *Infant Behavior and Development, 17*(2), 175–184.

Householder, J., Hatcher, R., Burns, W., & Chasnoff, I. (1982). Infants born to narcotics-addicted mothers. *Psychological Bulletin, 92,* 453–468.

Howard, M. (1983). Postponing sexual involvement: A new approach. *SIECUS Report, 11*(4), 5–6, 8.

Howe, D. C., Kahn, P. H., Jr., & Friedman, B. (1996). Along the Rio Negro: Brazilian children's environmental views and values. *Developmental Psychology, 32,* 979–987.

Howes, C., Hamilton, C. E., & Matheson, C. C. (1994). Children's relationships with peers: Differential associations with aspects of the teacher-child relationship. *Child Development, 65,* 253–263.

Howes, C., & Matheson, C. C. (1992). Sequences in the development of competent play with peers: Social and social pretend play. *Developmental Psychology, 28,* 961–974.

Howes, C., Matheson, C. C., & Hamilton, C. E. (1994). Maternal, teacher, and child care history correlates of children's relationships with peers. *Child Development, 65,* 264–273.

Hu, S., Pattatucci, A. M. L., Patterson, C., Li, L., Fulker, D. W., Cherny, S. S., Kruglyak, L., & Hamer, D. H. (1995). Linkage between sexual orientation and chromosome Xq28 in males but not in females. *Nature Genetics, 11,* 248–256.

Huang, G. G. (1995). Self-reported biliteracy and self-esteem: A study of Mexican American 8th graders. *Applied Psycholinguistics, 16,* 271–291.

Hudson, J. I., & Pope, H. G. (1990). Affective spectrum disorder: Does antidepressant response identify a family of disorders with a common pathophysiology? *American Journal of Psychiatry, 147*(5), 552–564.

Huesmann, L. R. (1986). Psychological processes promoting the relation between exposure to media violence and aggressive behavior by the viewer. *Journal of Social Issues, 42,* 125–139.

Hughes, M. (1975). *Egocentrism in preschool children.* Unpublished doctoral dissertation, Edinburgh University, Edinburgh, Scotland.

Humphrey, L. L. (1986). Structural analysis of parent-child relationships in eating disorders. *Journal of Abnormal Psychology, 95*(4), 395–402.

Humphreys, A. P., & Smith, P. K. (1984). Rough-and-tumble in preschool and playground. In P. K. Smith (Ed.), *Play in animals and humans.* Oxford: Blackwell.

Humphreys, A. P., & Smith, P. K. (1987). Rough and tumble, friendship, and dominance in schoolchildren: Evidence for continuity and change with age. *Child Development, 58,* 201–212.

Hunsaker, S. L., & Callahan, C. M. (1995). Creativity and giftedness: Published instrument uses and abuses. *Gifted Child Quarterly, 39*(2), 110–114.

Hunt, C. E. (1996). Prone sleeping in healthy infants and victims of sudden infant death syndrome. *Journal of Pediatrics, 128,* 594–596.

Hunt, C. E., & Brouillette, R. T. (1987). Sudden infant death syndrome: 1987 perspective. *Journal of Pediatrics, 110*(5), 669–678.

Huntsinger, C. S., & Jose, P. E. (1995). Chinese American and Caucasian American family interaction patterns in spatial rotation puzzle solutions. *Merrill-Palmer Quarterly, 41,* 471–496.

Huston, A., Donnerstein, E., Fairchild, H., Feshbach, N. D., Katz, P. A., Murray, J. P., Rubenstein, E. A., Wilcox, B. L., & Zuckerman, D. (1992). *Big world, small screen: The role of television in American society.* Lincoln: University of Nebraska Press.

Hutchings, G. (1997, April 11). Female infanticide "will lead to army of bachelors." *International News* [On-line], *686.* Available: http://www.telegraph.co.uk:80/et?ac=000289500536618&rtmo=336916d2&atmo=336916d2&pg=/et/97/4/11/wchi11.html

Huttenlocher, J., Haight, W., Bryk, A., Seltzer, M., & Lyons, T. (1991). Early vocabulary growth: Relation to language input and gender. *Developmental Psychology, 27,* 236–248.

Huxley, A. (1932). *Brave new world.* New York: Harper & Bros.

Hwang, C. P., & Broberg, A. G. (1992). The historical and social context of child care in Sweden. In M. E. Lamb, K. J. Sternberg, C. P. Hwang, & A. G. Broberg (Eds.), *Child care in context.* Hillsdale, NJ: Erlbaum.

Hwang, S. J., Beaty, T. H., Panny, S. R., Street, N. A., Joseph, J. M., Gordon, S., McIntosh, I., & Francomano, C. A. (1995). Association study of transforming growth factor alpha (TGFa) TaqI polymorphism and oral clefts: Indication of gene-environment interaction in a population-based sample of infants with birth defects. *American Journal of Epidemiology, 141,* 629–636.

Hyde, J., & Linn, M. C. (1988). Gender differences in verbal abilities: A meta-analysis. *Psychological Bulletin, 104*(1), 53–69.

Hyde, J. S., Fennema, E., & Lamon, S. J. (1990). Gender differences in mathematics performance: A meta-analysis. *Psychological Bulletin, 107*(2), 139–155.

Hynd, G. W., & Semrud-Clikeman, M. (1989). Dyslexia and brain morphology. *Psychological Bulletin, 106*(3), 447–482.

Infant Health and Development Program (IHDP). (1990). Enhancing the outcomes of low-birth-weight, premature infants. *Journal of the American Medical Association, 263*(22), 3035–3042.

Infante-Rivard, C., Fernández, A., Gauthier, R., David, M., & Rivard, G. E. (1993). Fetal loss associated with caffeine intake before and during pregnancy. *Journal of the American Medical Association, 270,* 2940–2943.

Ingram, D. D., Makuc, D., & Kleinman, J. C. (1986). National and state trends in use of prenatal care, 1970–1983. *American Journal of Public Health, 76*(4), 415–423.

Institute of Medicine (IOM) National Academy of Sciences. (1993, November). *Assessing genetic risks: Implications for health and social policy.* Washington, DC: National Academy of Sciences.

Institute of Medicine (IOM) National Academy of Sciences. (1994). *Overcoming barriers to immunization: A workshop summary.* Washington, DC: National Academy Press.

Irwin, M., Engle, P. L., Yarbrough, C., Klein, R. E., & Townsend, J. W. (1978). The relationship of prior ability and family characteristics to school attendance and school achievement in rural Guatemala. *Child Development, 49,* 415–427.

Isabella, R. A. (1993). Origins of attachment: Maternal interactive behavior across the first year. *Child Development, 64,* 605–621.

Isley, S., O'Neil, R., & Parke, R. (1996). The relation of parental affect and control behaviors to children's classroom acceptance: A concurrent and predictive analysis. *Early Education and Development, 7,* 7–23.

Izard, C. E., Haynes, O. M., Chisholm, G., & Baak, K. (1991). Emotional determinants of infant-mother attachment. *Child Development, 62,* 906–917.

Izard, C. E., Huebner, R. R., Resser, D., McGinness, G. C., & Dougherty, L. M. (1980). The young infant's ability to produce discrete emotional expressions. *Developmental Psychology, 16,* 132–140.

Izard, C. E., & Malatesta, C. Z. (1987). Perspectives on emotional development I: Differential emotions theory of early emotional development. In J. D. Osofsky (Ed.), *Handbook of infant development* (2nd ed.). New York: Wiley.

Izard, C. E., Porges, S. W., Simons, R. F., Haynes, O. M., & Cohen, B. (1991). Infant cardiac activity: Developmental changes and relations with attachment. *Developmental Psychology, 27,* 432–439.

Jackson, J. F. (1993). Human behavioral genetics, Scarr's theory, and her views on interventions: A critical review and commentary on their implications for African American children. *Child Development, 64,* 1318–1332.

Jackson, R. S., Creemers, J. W. M., Ohagi, S., Raffin-Sanson, M. L., Sanders, L., Montague, C. T., Hutton, J. C., & O'Rahilly, S. (1997). Obesity and impaired prohormone processing associated with mutations in the human prohormone convertase 1 gene. *Nature Genetics, 16,* 303–306.

Jacobsen, T., & Hofmann, V. (1997). Children's attachment representations: Longitudinal relations to school behavior and academic competency in middle childhood and adolescence. *Developmental Psychology, 33,* 703–710.

Jacobson, J. L., & Jacobson, S. W. (1996). Intellectual impairment in children exposed to polychlorinated biphenyls in utero. *New England Journal of Medicine, 335,* 783–789.

Jacobson, J. L., & Wille, D. E. (1986). The influence of attachment pattern on developmental changes in peer interaction from the toddler to the preschool period. *Child Development, 57,* 338–347.

Jacobson, S. W., Jacobson, J. L., Sokol, R. J., Martier, S. S., & Ager, J. W. (1993). Prenatal alcohol exposure and infant information processing ability. *Child Development, 64,* 1706–1721.

Jagers, R. J., Bingham, K., & Hans, S. L. (1996). Socialization and social judgments among inner-city African-American kindergartners. *Child Development, 67,* 140–150.

Janos, P. M., & Robinson, N. M. (1985). Psychosocial development in intellectually gifted children. In F. D. Horowitz & M. O'Brien (Eds.), *The gifted and talented: Developmental perspectives* (pp. 251–295). Washington, DC: American Psychological Association.

Jaslow, C. K. (1982). *Teenage pregnancy (ERIC/CAPS Fact Sheet).* Ann Arbor, MI: Counseling and Personnel Services Clearing House.

Jay, M. S., DuRant, R. H., Shoffitt, T., Linder, C. W., & Litt, I. F. (1984). Effect of peer counselors on adolescent compliance in use of oral contraceptives. *Pediatrics, 73,* 126–131.

Jensen, A. R. (1969). How much can we boost IQ and scholastic achievement? *Harvard Educational Review, 39,* 1–123.

Ji, B. T., Shu, X. O., Linet, M. S., Zheng, W., Wacholder, S., Gao, Y. T., Ying, D. M., & Jin, F. (1997). Paternal cigarette smoking and the risk of childhood cancer among offspring of nonsmoking mothers. *Journal of the National Cancer Institute, 89,* 238–244.

Jiao, S., Ji, G., & Jing, Q. (1986). Comparative study of behavioral qualities of only children and sibling children. *Child Development, 57,* 357–361.

Jiao, S., Ji, G., & Jing, Q. (1996). Cognitive development of Chinese urban only children and children with siblings. *Child Development, 67,* 387–395.

Johnson, C. L. (1985). *Growing up and growing old in Italian-American families.* New Brunswick, NJ: Rutgers University Press.

Johnson, R. A., Hoffmann, J. P., & Gerstein, D. R. (1996). *The relationship between family structure and adolescent substance use* (DHHS Publication No. SMA 96-3086). Washington, DC: U.S. Department of Health and Human Services.

Johnson, S. L., & Birch, L. L. (1994). Parents' and children's adiposity and eating styles. *Pediatrics, 94,* 653–661.

Johnston, J., & Ettema, J. S. (1982). *Positive images: Breaking stereotypes with children's television.* Newbury Park, CA: Sage.

Jones, D. C., Swift, D. J., & Johnson, M. A. (1988). Nondeliberate memory for a novel event among preschoolers. *Developmental Psychology, 24,* 641–645.

Jones, E. F., Forrest, J. D., Goldman, N., Henshaw, S. K., Lincoln, R., Rosoff, J. I., Westoff, C. F., Wulf, W., & Wulf, D. (1985). Teenage pregnancy in developed countries: Determinants and policy implications. *Family Planning Perspectives, 17,* 53–63.

Jones, H. W., & Toner, J. P. (1993). The infertile couple. *New England Journal of Medicine, 329,* 1710–1715.

Jones, M. C. (1957). The late careers of boys who were early- or late-maturing. *Child Development, 28,* 115–128.

Jones, M. C. (1958). The study of socialization patterns at the high school level. *Journal of Genetic Psychology, 93,* 87–111.

Jones, N. A., Field, T., Fox, N. A., Davalos, M., Malphurs, J., Carraway, K., Schanberg, S., & Kuhn, C. (1997). Infants of intrusive and withdrawn mothers. *Infant Behavior and Development, 20,* 175–186.

Jones, N. A., Field, T., Fox, N. A., Lundy, B., & Davalos, M. (in press). *EEG activation in one-month-old infants of depressed mothers.* Unpublished manuscript, Touch Research Institute, University of Miami School of Medicine.

Jones, S. S. (1996). Imitation or exploration? Young infants' matching of adults' oral gestures. *Child Development, 67,* 1952–1969.

Jusczyk, P. W., Cutler, A., & Redanz, N. J. (1993). Infants' preference for the predominant stress patterns of English words. *Child Development, 64,* 675–687.

Jusczyk, P. W., & Hohne, E. A. (1997). Infants' memory for spoken words. *Science, 277,* 1984–1986.

Kaback, M., Lim-Steele, J., Dabholkar, D., Brown, D., Levy, N., & Zeiger, K., for the International TSD Data Collection Network. (1993). Tay-Sachs disease—Carrier screening, prenatal diagnosis, and the molecular era. *Journal of the American Medical Association, 270,* 2307–2315.

Kagan, J. (1984). *The nature of the child.* New York: Basic Books.

Kagan, J. (1989). *Unstable ideas: Temperament, cognition, and self.* Cambridge, MA: Harvard University Press.

Kagan, J. (1997). Temperament and the reactions to unfamiliarity. *Child Development, 68,* 139–143.

Kagan, J., Arcus, D., Snidman, N., Wang, Y. F., Hendler, J., & Greene, S. (1994). Reactivity in infants: A cross-national comparison. *Developmental Psychology, 30,* 342–345.

Kagan, J., Reznick, J. S., Clarke, C., Snidman, N., & Garcia-Coll, C. (1984). Behavioral inhibition to the unfamiliar. *Child Development, 55,* 2212–2225.

Kagan, J., Reznick, J. S., & Gibbons, J. (1989). Inhibited and uninhibited types of children. *Child Development, 60,* 838–845.

Kagan, J., & Snidman, N. (1991a). Infant predictors of inhibited and uninhibited behavioral profiles. *Psychological Science, 2,* 40–44.

Kagan, J., & Snidman, N. (1991b). Temperamental factors in human development. *American Psychologist, 46,* 856–862.

Kahn, P. H., Jr., & Friedman, B. (1995). Environmental views and values of children in an inner-city Black community. *Child Development, 66,* 1403–1417.

Kail, R. (1991). Processing time declines exponentially during childhood and adolescence. *Developmental Psychology, 27,* 259–266.

Kail, R. (1997). Processing time, imagery, and spatial memory. *Journal of Experimental Child Psychology, 64,* 67–78.

Kail, R., & Park, Y. (1994). Processing time, articulation time, and memory span. *Journal of Experimental Child Psychology, 57,* 281–291.

Kaitz, M., Meschulach-Sarfaty, O., Auerbach, J., & Eidelman, A. (1988). A reexamination of newborns' ability to imitate facial expressions. *Developmental Psychology, 24,* 3–7.

Kamin, L. J. (1974). *The science and politics of IQ.* Potomac, MD: Erlbaum.

Kamin, L. J. (1981). Commentary. In S. Scarr (Ed.), *Race, social class, and individual differences in I.Q.* Hillsdale, NJ: Erlbaum.

Kandel, D. B., Davies, M., Karus, D., & Yamaguchi, K. (1986). The consequences in young adulthood of adolescent drug involvement. *Archives of General Psychiatry, 43,* 746–754.

Kaplan, H., & Dove, H. (1987). Infant development among the Ache of East Paraguay. *Developmental Psychology, 23,* 190–198.

Katz, L. F., & Gottman, J. M. (1993). Patterns of marital conflict predict children's internalizing and externalizing behaviors. *Developmental Psychology, 29,* 940–950.

Katzev, A. R., Warner, R. L., & Acock, A. C. (1994). Girl or boy? Relationship of child gender to marital instability. *Journal of Marriage and the Family, 56,* 89–100.

Katzman, R. (1993). Education and prevalence of Alzheimer's disease. *Neurology, 43,* 13–20.

Kaufman, A. S., & Kaufman, N. L. (1983). *Kaufman assessment battery for children: Administration and scoring manual.* Circle Pines, MN: American Guidance Service.

Kaufman, J., & Zigler, E. (1987). Do abused children become abusive parents? *American Journal of Orthopsychiatry, 57*(2), 186–192.

Kaufman, T. S. (1993). *The combined family: A guide to creating successful step-relationships.* New York: Plenum.

Kaye, W. H., Weltzin, T. E., Hsu, L. K. G., & Bulik, C. M. (1991). An open trial of fluoxetine in patients with anorexia nervosa. *Journal of Clinical Psychiatry, 52,* 464–471.

Keegan, R. T., & Gruber, H. E. (1985). Charles Darwin's unpublished "Diary of an Infant": An early phase in his psychological work. In G. Eckardt, W. G. Bringmann, & L. Sprung (Eds.), *Contributions to a history of developmental psychology: International William T. Preyer Symposium* (pp. 127–145). Berlin, Germany: Walter de Gruyter.

Keel, P. K., & Mitchell, J. E. (1997). Outcome in bulimia nervosa. *American Journal of Psychiatry, 154,* 313–321.

Keeney, T. J., Canizzo, S. R., & Flavell, J. H. (1967). Spontaneous and induced verbal rehearsal in a recall task. *Child Development, 38,* 953–966.

Kelleher, K. J., Casey, P. H., Bradley, R. H., Pope, S. K., Whiteside, L., Barrett, K. W., Swanson, M. E., & Kirby, R. S. (1993). Risk factors and outcomes for failure to thrive in low birth weight preterm infants. *Pediatrics, 91,* 941–948.

Keller, H. (1905). *The story of my life.* New York: Grosset & Dunlap.

Keller, H. (1920). *The world I live in.* New York: Century. (Original work published 1908)

Keller, H. (1929). *The bereaved.* New York: Leslie Fulenwider, Inc.

Kellermann, A. L., Rivara, F. P., Somes, G., Reay, D. T., Francisco, J., Banton, J. G., Prodzinski, J., Flinger, C., & Hackman, B. B. (1992). Suicide in the home in relation to gun ownership. *New England Journal of Medicine, 327,* 467–472.

Kelley, J. L., Power, T. G., & Wimbush, D. D. (1992). Determinants of disciplinary practices in low-income black mothers. *Child Development, 63,* 573–582.

Kellogg, R. (1970). Understanding children's art. In P. Cramer (Ed.), *Readings in developmental psychology today.* Delmar, CA: CRM.

Kelly, J. B. (1987, August). *Longer-term adjustment in children of divorce: Converging findings and implications for practice.* Paper presented at the annual meeting of the American Psychological Association, New York, NY.

Kemp, J. S., Livne, M., White, D. K., & Arfken, C. L. (1998). Softness and potential to cause rebreathing: Differences in bedding used by infants at high and low risk for sudden infant death syndrome. *Journal of Pediatrics, 132,* 234–239.

Kempe, C. H., Silverman, F. N., Steele, B. N., Droegemueller, W., & Silver, H. K. (1962). The battered child syndrome. *Journal of the American Medical Association, 181,* 17–24.

Kendall-Tackett, K. A., Williams, L. M., & Finkelhor, D. (1993). Impact of sexual abuse on children: A review and synthesis of recent empirical studies. *Psychological Bulletin, 113*(1), 164–180.

Kendler, K. S., MacLean, C., Neale, M., Kessler, R., Heath, A., & Eaves, L. (1991). The genetic epidemiology of bulimia nervosa. *American Journal of Psychiatry, 148,* 1627–1637.

Kennell, J., Klaus, M., McGrath, S., Robertson, S., & Hinckley, C. (1991). Continuous emotional support during labor in a US hospital. *Journal of the American Medical Association, 265,* 2197–2201.

Kenny, P., & Turkewitz, G. (1986). Effects of unusually early visual stimulation on the development of homing behavior in the rat pup. *Developmental Psychobiology, 19,* 57–66.

Kernan, M. (1993, June). The object at hand. *Smithsonian,* pp. 14–16.

Kestenbaum, R., Farber, E. A., & Sroufe, L. A. (1989). Individual differences in empathy among preschoolers: Relation to attachment history. In N. Eisenberg (Ed.), *Empathy and related emotional responses* (New Directions for Child Development No. 44). San Francisco: Jossey-Bass.

Kimbrough, R. D., LeVois, M., & Webb, D. R. (1994). Management of children with slightly elevated blood lead levels. *Pediatrics, 93,* 188–191.

King, B. M. (1996). *Human sexuality today.* Englewood Cliffs, NJ: Prentice-Hall.

Kinney, H. C., Filiano, J. J., Sleeper, L. A., Mandell, F., Valdes-Dapena, M., & White, W. F. (1995). Decreased muscarinic receptor binding in the arcuate nucleus in Sudden Infant Death Syndrome. *Science, 269,* 1446–1450.

Kinsbourne, M. (1994). Sugar and the hyperactive child. *New England Journal of Medicine, 330,* 355–356.

Kirkley-Best, E., & Kellner, K. R. (1982). The forgotten grief: A review of the psychology of stillbirth. *American Journal of Orthopsychiatry, 52,* 420–429.

Kirschenbaum, R. J. (1990, November–December). An interview with Howard Gardner. *The Gifted Child Today,* pp. 26–32.

Kisilevsky, B. S., Muir, D. W., & Low, J. A. (1992). Maturation of human fetal responses to vibroacoustic stimulation. *Child Development, 63,* 1497–1508.

Kistin, N., Benton, D., Rao, S., & Sullivan, M. (1990). Breast-feeding rates among black urban low-income women: Effects of prenatal education. *Pediatrics, 86,* 741–746.

Klar, A. J. S. (1996). A single locus, RGHT, specifies preference for hand utilization in humans. In *Cold Spring Harbor Symposia on Quantitative Biology* (Vol. 61, pp. 59–65). Cold Spring Harbor, NY: Cold Spring Harbor Laboratory Press.

Klaus, M. H., & Kennell, J. H. (1976). *Maternal-infant bonding.* St. Louis, MO: Mosby.

Klaus, M. H., & Kennell, J. H. (1982). *Parent-infant bonding* (2nd ed.). St. Louis, MO: Mosby.

Klebanov, P. K., Brooks-Gunn, J., & McCormick, M. C. (1994). Classroom behavior of very low birth weight elementary school children. *Pediatrics, 94,* 700–708.

Klein, K., Forehand, R., Armistead, L., & Long, P. (1997). Delinquency during the transition to early adulthood: Family and parenting predictors from early adolescence. *Adolescence, 32,* 61–80.

Kleinberg, F. (1984). Sudden infant death syndrome. *Mayo Clinic Proceedings, 59,* 352–357.

Kleinman, J. C., Cooke, M., Machlin, S., & Kessel, S. S. (1983). *Variations in use of obstetric technology* (DHHS Publication No. PHS 84-1232). Washington, DC: U.S. Government Printing Office.

Klesges, R. C., Klesges, L. M., Eck, L. H., & Shelton, M. L. (1995). A longitudinal analysis of accelerated weight gain in preschool children. *Pediatrics, 95,* 126–130.

Klesges, R. C., Shelton, M. L., & Klesges, L. M. (1993). Effects of television on metabolic rate: Potential implications for childhood obesity. *Pediatrics, 91,* 281–295.

Kliegman, R., Madura, D., Kiwi, R., Eisenberg, I., & Yamashita, T. (1994). Relation of maternal cocaine use to the risk of prematurity and low birth weight. *Journal of Pediatrics, 124,* 751–756.

Kliewer, S. A., Lenhard, J. M., Willson, T. M., Patel, I., Morris, D. C., & Lehmann, J. M. (1995). A prostaglandin JZ metabolite binds peroxisome proliferator-activated receptor gamma and promotes adipocyte differentiation. *Cell, 83,* 813–819.

Kline, M., Tschann, J. M., Johnston, J., & Wallerstein, J. (1988, March). *Child outcome in joint and sole custody families.* Paper presented at the annual meeting of the American Orthopsychiatry Association, San Francisco, CA.

Klonoff-Cohen, H. S., Edelstein, S. L., Lefkowitz, E. S., Srinivasan, I. P., Kaegi, D., Chang, J. C., & Wiley, K. J. (1995). The effects of passive smoking and tobacco exposure through breast milk on sudden infant death syndrome. *Journal of the American Medical Association, 273,* 795–798.

Kochanska, G. (1992). Children's interpersonal influence with mothers and peers. *Developmental Psychology, 28,* 491–499.

Kochanska, G. (1993). Toward a synthesis of parental socialization and child temperament in early development of conscience. *Child Development, 64,* 325–437.

Kochanska, G. (1995). Children's temperament, mothers' discipline, and security of attachment: Multiple pathways to emerging internalization. *Child Development, 66,* 597–615.

Kochanska, G. (1997a). Multiple pathways to conscience for children with different temperaments: From toddlerhood to age 5. *Developmental Psychology, 33,* 228–240.

Kochanska, G. (1997b). Mutually responsive orientation between mothers and their young children: Implications for early socialization. *Child Development, 68,* 94–112.

Kochanska, G., & Aksan, N. (1995). Mother-child positive affect, the quality of child compliance to requests and prohibitions, and maternal control as correlates of early internalization. *Child Development, 66,* 236–254.

Kochanska, G., Aksan, N., & Koenig, A. L. (1995). A longitudinal study of the roots of preschoolers' conscience: Committed compliance and emerging internalization. *Child Development, 66,* 1752–1769.

Kochanska, G., Casey, R. J., & Fukumoto, A. (1995). Toddlers' sensitivity to standard violations. *Child Development, 66,* 643–656.

Kochanska, G., Murray, K., & Coy, K. C. (1997). Inhibitory control as a contributor to conscience in childhood: From toddler to early school age. *Child Development, 68,* 263–277.

Kochenderfer, B. H., & Ladd, G. W. (1996). Peer victimization: Cause or consequence of school maladjustment? *Child Development, 67,* 1305–1317.

Koff, E., Rierdan, J., & Sheingold, K. (1982). Memories of menarche: Age, preparation, and prior knowledge as determinants of initial menstrual experience. *Journal of Youth and Adolescence, 11,* 1–9.

Kohlberg, L. (1966). A cognitive-developmental analysis of children's sex-role concepts and attitudes. In E. E. Maccoby (Ed.), *The development of sex differences.* Stanford, CA: Stanford University Press.

Kohlberg, L. (1969). Stage and sequence: The cognitive-developmental approach to socialization. In D. A. Goslin (Ed.), *Handbook of socialization theory and research.* Chicago: Rand McNally.

Kohlberg, L. (1981). *Essays on moral development.* San Francisco: Harper & Row.

Kohlberg, L., & Gilligan, C. (1971, Fall). The adolescent as a philosopher: The discovery of the self in a postconventional world. *Daedalus,* pp. 1051–1086.

Kohlberg, L., & Ryncarz, R. A. (1990). Beyond justice reasoning: Moral development and consideration of a seventh stage. In C. N. Alexander & E. J. Langer (Eds.), *Higher stages of human development* (pp. 191–207). New York: Oxford University Press.

Kohlberg, L., Yaeger, J., & Hjertholm, E. (1968). Private speech: Four studies and a review of theories. *Child Development, 39,* 691–736.

Köhler, L., & Markestad, T. (1993). Consensus statement on prevention programs for SIDS. *Acta Paediatrica, 38* (Suppl.), 126–127.

Kolata, G. (1986). Obese children: A growing problem. *Science, 232,* 20–21.

Kolata, G. (1988, March 29). Fetuses treated through umbilical cords. *The New York Times,* p. C3.

Kolb, B. (1989). Brain development, plasticity, and behavior. *American Psychologist, 44*(9), 1203–1212.

Kolbert, E. (1994, January 11). Canadians curbing TV violence. *The New York Times,* pp. C15, C19.

Kolder, V. E., Gallagher, J., & Parsons, M. T. (1987). Court-ordered obstetrical interventions. *New England Journal of Medicine, 316,* 1192–1196.

Kopp, C. B. (1982). Antecedents of self-regulation. *Developmental Psychology, 18,* 199–214.

Kopp, C. B., & Kaler, S. R. (1989). Risk in infancy: Origins and implications. *American Psychologist, 44*(2), 224–230.

Kopp, C. B., & McCall, R. B. (1982). Predicting later mental performance for normal, at-risk, and handicapped infants. In P. B. Baltes & O. G. Brim (Eds.), *Life-span development and behavior* (Vol. 4). New York: Academic Press.

Korner, A. (1996). Reliable individual differences in preterm infants' excitation management. *Child Development, 67,* 1793–1805.

Korner, A. F., Zeanah, C. H., Linden, J., Berkowitz, R. I., Kraemer, H. C., & Agras, W. S. (1985). The relationship between neonatal and later activity and temperament. *Child Development, 56,* 38–42.

Korte, D., & Scaer, R. (1984). *A good birth, a safe birth.* New York: Bantam.

Kottak, C. P. (1994). *Cultural anthropology.* New York: McGraw-Hill.

Kowal, A., & Kramer, L. (1997). Children's understanding of parental differential treatment. *Child Development, 68,* 113–126.

Kraemer, H. C., Korner, A., Anders, T., Jacklin, C. N., & Dimiceli, S. (1985). Obstetric drugs and infant behavior: A reevaluation. *Journal of Pediatric Psychology, 10,* 345–353.

Kramer, L., & Gottman, J. (1992). Becoming a sibling: "With a little help from my friends." *Developmental Psychology, 28,* 685–699.

Kraus, N., McGee, T. J., Carrell, T. D., Zecker, S. G., Nicol, T. G., & Koch, D. B. (1996). Auditory neurophysiologic responses and discrimination deficits in children with learning problems. *Science, 273,* 971–973.

Krauss, S., Concordet, J. P., & Ingham, P. W. (1993). A functionally conserved homolog of the Drosophila segment polarity gene hh is expressed in tissues with polarizing activity in zebrafish embryos. *Cell, 75,* 1431–1444.

Kreutzer, M., & Charlesworth, W. R. (1973). *Infant recognition of emotions.* Paper presented at the meeting of the Society for Research in Child Development, Philadelphia, PA.

Kreutzer, M., Leonard, C., & Flavell, J. (1975). An interview study of children's knowledge about memory. *Monographs of the Society for Research in Child Development, 40*(1, Serial No. 159).

Krevans, J., & Gibbs, J. C. (1996). Parents' use of inductive discipline: Relations to children's empathy and prosocial behavior. *Child Development, 67,* 3263–3277.

Kristof, N. D. (1991, June 17). A mystery from China's census: Where have young girls gone? *The New York Times,* pp. A1, A8.

Kristof, N. D. (1993, July 21). Peasants of China discover new way to weed out girls. *The New York Times,* pp. A1, A6.

Kroger, J. (1993). Ego identity: An overview. In J. Kroger (Ed.), *Discussions on ego identity.* Hillsdale, NJ: Erlbaum.

Kroger, J., & Haslett, S. J. (1991). A comparison of ego identity status transition pathways and change rates across five identity domains. *International Journal of Aging and Human Development, 32,* 303–330.

Krombholz, H. (1997). Physical performance in relation to age, sex, social class and sports activities in kindergarten and elementary school. *Perceptual and Motor Skills, 84,* 1168–1170.

Kropp, J. P., & Haynes, O. M. (1987). Abusive and nonabusive mothers' ability to identify general and specific emotion signals of infants. *Child Development, 58,* 187–190.

Ku, L. C., Sonenstein, F. L., & Pleck, J. H. (1992). The association of AIDS education and sex education with sexual behavior and condom use among teenage men. *Family Planning Perspectives, 24,* 100–106.

Kuczynski, L., & Kochanska, G. (1995). Function and content of maternal demands: Developmental significance of early demands for competent action. *Child Development, 66,* 616–628.

Kuhl, P. K., Andruski, J. E., Chistovich, I. A., Chistovich, L. A., Kozhevnikova, E. V., Ryskina, V. L., Stolyarova, E. I., Sundberg, U., & Lacerda, F. (1997). Cross-language analysis of phonetic units in language addressed to infants. *Science, 277,* 684–686.

Kuhl, P. K., Williams, K. A., Lacerda, F., Stevens, K. N., & Lindblom, B. (1992). Linguistic experience alters phonetic perception in infants by 6 months of age. *Science, 255,* 606–608.

Kuntzleman, C. T., & Reiff, G. G. (1992). The decline in American children's fitness levels. *Research Quarterly for Exercise and Sport, 63*(2), 107–111.

Kupersmidt, J. B., & Coie, J. D. (1990). Preadolescent peer status, aggression, and school adjustment as predictors of externalizing problems in adolescence. *Child Development, 61,* 1350–1362.

Kupfersmid, J., & Wonderly, D. (1980). Moral maturity and behavior: Failure to find a link. *Journal of Youth and Adolescence, 9*(3), 249–261.

Kurosawa, A. (1983). *Something like an autobiography* (A. E. Bock, Trans.). New York: Vintage.

Lach, J. (1997, Spring–Summer). Cultivating the mind. *Newsweek,* pp. 38–39.

Ladd, G. W. (1990). Having friends, keeping friends, making friends, and being liked by peers in the classroom: Predictors of children's early school adjustment. *Child Development, 61,* 1081–1100.

Ladd, G. W., & Colter, B. S. (1988). Parents' management of preschoolers' peer relations: Is it related to children's social competence? *Developmental Psychology, 24,* 109–117.

Ladd, G. W., & Hart, C. H. (1992). Creating informal play opportunities: Are parents' and preschoolers' initiations related to children's competence with peers? *Developmental Psychology, 28,* 1179–1187.

Ladd, G. W., Kochenderfer, B. J., & Coleman, C. C. (1996) Friendship quality as a predictor of young children's early school adjustment. *Child Development, 67,* 1103–1118.

Lagercrantz, H., & Slotkin, T. A. (1986). The "stress" of being born. *Scientific American, 254*(4), 100–107.

Lalonde, C. E., & Werker, J. F. (1995). Cognitive influences on cross-language speech perception in infancy. *Infant Behavior and Development, 18,* 459–475.

Lamb, M. E. (1977). Father-infant and mother-infant interaction in the first year of life. *Child Development, 48,* 167–181.

Lamb, M. E. (1978). Influence of the child on marital quality and family interaction during the prenatal, perinatal, and infancy periods. In R. Lerner & G. Spanier (Eds.), *Child influences on marital and family interaction: A life-span perspective.* New York: Academic Press.

Lamb, M. E. (1981). The development of father-infant relationships. In M. E. Lamb (Ed.), *The role of the father in child development* (2nd ed.). New York: Wiley.

Lamb, M. E. (1982a). The bonding phenomenon: Misinterpretations and their implications. *Journal of Pediatrics, 101* (4), 555–557.

Lamb, M. E. (1982b). Early contact and maternal-infant bonding: One decade later. *Pediatrics, 70,* 763–768.

Lamb, M. E. (1987a). Predictive implications of individual differences in attachment. *Journal of Consulting and Clinical Psychology, 55*(6), 817–824.

Lamb, M. E. (1987b). *The father's role: Cross-cultural perspectives.* Hillsdale, NJ: Erlbaum.

Lamb, M. E., Frodi, A. M., Frodi, M., & Hwang, C. P. (1982). Characteristics of maternal and paternal behavior in traditional and non-traditional Swedish families. *International Journal of Behavior Development, 5,* 131–151.

Lamb, M. E., & Sternberg, K. J. (1992). Sociocultural perspectives on non-parental childcare. In M. E. Lamb, K. J. Sternberg, C. P. Hwang, & A. G. Broberg (Eds.), *Child care in context.* Hillsdale, NJ: Erlbaum.

Lamborn, S. D., Mounts, N. S., Steinberg, L., & Dornbusch, S. M. (1991). Patterns of competence and adjustment among adolescents from authoritative, authoritarian, indulgent, and neglectful families. *Child Development, 62,* 1049–1065.

Landesman-Dwyer, S., & Emanuel, I. (1979). Smoking during pregnancy. *Teratology, 19,* 119–126.

Lane, H. (1976). *The wild boy of Aveyron.* Cambridge, MA: Harvard University Press.

Lange, G., MacKinnon, C. E., & Nida, R. E. (1989). Knowledge, strategy, and motivational contributions to preschool children's object recall. *Developmental Psychology, 25,* 772–779.

Lanphear, B. P., Weitzman, M., & Eberly, S. (1996). Racial differences in urban child environmental exposures to lead. *American Journal of Public Health, 86,* 1460–1463.

Lanting, C. I., Fidler, V., Huisman, M., Touwen, B. C. L., & Boersma, E. R. (1994). Neurological differences between 9-year-old children fed breast-milk or formula-milk as babies. *The Lancet, 334,* 1319–1322.

LaRossa, R. (1988). Fatherhood and social change *Family Relations, 34,* 451–457.

LaRossa, R., & LaRossa, M. M. (1981). *Transition to parenthood: How infants change families.* Beverly Hills, CA: Sage.

Larsen D. (1990, December–1991, January). Unplanned parenthood. *Modern Maturity,* pp. 32–36.

Larson, R., & Lampman-Petraitis, C. (1989). Daily emotional states as reported by children and adolescents. *Child Development, 60,* 1250–1260.

Larson, R., & Richards, M. H. (1991). Daily companionship in late childhood and early adolescence: Changing developmental contexts. *Child Development, 62,* 284–300.

Larson, R. W. (1997). The emergence of solitude as a constructive domain of experience in early adolescence. *Child Development, 68,* 80–93.

Larson, R. W., Richards, M. H., Moneta, G., Holmbeck, G., & Duckett, E. (1996). Changes in adolescents' daily interactions with their families from ages 10 to 18: Disengagement and transformation. *Developmental Psychology, 32,* 744–754.

Lash, J. P. (1980). *Helen and teacher: The story of Helen Keller and Anne Sullivan Macy.* New York: Delacorte.

Laucht, M., Esser, G., & Schmidt, M. H. (1994). Contrasting infant predictors of later cognitive functioning. *Journal of Child Psychology and Psychiatry, 35,* 649–652.

Laursen, B. (1996). Closeness and conflict in adolescent peer relationships: Interdependence with friends and romantic partners. In W. M. Bukowski, A. F. Newcomb, & W. W. Hartup (Eds.), *The company they keep: Friendship in childhood and adolescence* (pp. 186–210). New York: Cambridge University Press.

Lawson, C. (1993, October 4). Celebrated birth aside, teen-ager is typical now. *The New York Times,* p. A18.

Leadbeater, B. J., & Bishop, S. J. (1994). Predictors of behavior problems in preschool children of inner-city Afro-American and Puerto Rican adolescent mothers. *Child Development, 65,* 638–648.

Leary, W. E. (1994, April 24). Barriers to immunization peril children, expert says. *The New York Times,* p. A26.

Lecanuet, J. P., Granier-Deferre, C., & Busnel, M.-C. (1995). Human fetal auditory perception. In J. P. Lecanuet, W. P. Fifer, N. A. Krasnegor, & W. P. Smotherman (Eds.), *Fetal development: A psychobiological perspective* (pp. 239–262). Hillsdale, NJ: Erlbaum.

Leibel, R. L. (1997). And finally, genes for human obesity. *Nature Genetics, 16,* 218–220.

Leichtman, M. D., & Ceci, S. J. (1995). The effects of stereotypes and suggestions on preschoolers' reports. *Developmental Psychology, 31,* 568–578.

Lelwica, M., & Haviland, J. (1983). *Ten-week-old infants' reactions to mothers' emotional expressions.* Paper presented at the biennial meeting of the Society for Research in Child Development, Detroit, MI.

Lemish, D., & Rice, M. L. (1986). Television as a talking picture book: A prop for language acquisition. *Journal of Child Language, 13,* 251–274.

Leng, X., & Shaw, G. L. (1991). Toward a neural theory of higher brain function using music as a window. *Concepts in Neuroscience, 2,* 229–258.

Lenneberg, E. H. (1967). *Biological functions of language.* New York: Wiley.

Lenneberg, E. H. (1969). On explaining language. *Science, 164* (3880), 635–643.

Lerner, J. V., & Galambos, N. L. (1985). Maternal role satisfaction, mother-child interaction, and child temperament: A process model. *Child Development, 21,* 1157–1164.

Lesch, K. P., Bengel, D., Heils, A., Sabol, S. Z., Greenberg, B. D., Petri, S., Benjamin, J., Müller, C. R., Hamer, D. H., & Murphy, D. L. (1996). Association of anxiety-related traits with a polymorphism in the serotonin transporter gene regulatory region. *Science, 274,* 1527–1531.

Leslie, A. M. (1982). The perception of causality in infants. *Perception, 11,* 173–186.

Lester, B. M. (1987). Developmental outcome prediction from acoustic cry analysis in term and preterm infants. *Pediatrics, 80,* 529–534.

Lester, B. M., Anderson, L. T., Boukydis, C. F. Z., Garcia-Coll, C. T., Vohr, B., & Peucker, M. (1989). Early detection of infants at risk for late handicap through acoustic cry analysis. *Research in Infancy, 25*(6), 99–118.

Lester, B. M., Corwin, M. J., Sepkoski, C., Seifer, R., Peuker, M., McLaughlin, S., & Golub, H. L. (1991). Neurobehavioral syndromes in cocaine exposed newborn infants. *Child Development, 62,* 694–705.

Lester, B. M., & Dreher, M. (1989). Effects of marijuana use during pregnancy on newborn cry. *Child Development, 60,* 765–771.

Lester, R., & Van Theil, D. H. (1977). Gonadal function in chronic alcoholic men. *Advances in Experimental Medicine and Biology, 85A,* 339–414.

LeVay, S. (1991). A difference in hypothalamic structure between heterosexual and homosexual men. *Science, 253,* 1034–1037.

Levine, M. D. (1987). *Developmental variation and learning disorders.* Cambridge, MA: Educators Publishing.

Levitt, M. J., Guacci-Franco, N., & Levitt, J. L. (1993). Convoys of social support in childhood and early adolescence: Structure and function. *Developmental Psychology, 29,* 811–818.

Levy, D. M. (1966). *Maternal overprotection.* New York: Norton.

Levy, G. D., & Carter, D. B. (1989). Gender schema, gender constancy, and gender-role knowledge: The roles of cognitive factors in preschoolers' gender-role stereotype attributions. *Developmental Psychology, 25,* 444–449.

Levy-Shiff, R. (1994). Individual and contextual correlates of marital change across the transition to parenthood. *Developmental Psychology, 30,* 591–601.

Levy-Shiff, R., Goldschmidt, I., & Har-Even, D. (1991). Transition to parenthood in adoptive families. *Developmental Psychology, 27,* 131–140.

Levy-Shiff, R., Hoffman, M. A., Mogilner, S., Levinger, S., & Mogilner, M. B. (1990). Fathers' hospital visits to their preterm infants as a predictor of father-infant relationship and infant development. *Pediatrics, 86,* 289–293.

Lewin, G. (1994, May 18). Boys are more comfortable with sex than girls are, survey finds. *The New York Times,* p. A20.

Lewis, M. (1987). Social development in infancy and early childhood. In J. D. Osofsky (Ed.), *Handbook of infant development* (2nd ed.). New York: Wiley.

Lewis, M. (1992). Shame, the exposed self. *Zero to Three, 12*(4), 6–10.

Lewis, M., & Brooks, J. (1974). Self, other, and fear: Infants' reaction to people. In H. Lewis & L. Rosenblum (Eds.), *The origins of fear: The origins of behavior* (Vol. 2). New York: Wiley.

Lewis, M., Worobey, J., Ramsay, D. S., & McCormack, M. K. (1992). Prenatal exposure to heavy metals: Effect on childhood cognitive skills and health status. *Pediatrics, 89,* 1010–1015.

Lewit, E. M., Baker, L. S., Corman, H., & Shiono, P. H. (1995). The direct cost of low birth weight. *The Future of Children, 5*(1), 35–56.

Li, C. Q., Windsor, R. A., Perkins, L., Goldenberg, R. L., & Lowe, J. B. (1993). The impact on infant birth weight and gestational age of cotinine-validated smoking reduction during pregnancy. *Journal of the American Medical Association, 269,* 1519–1524.

Liaw, F., & Brooks-Gunn, J. (1993). Patterns of low-birth-weight children's cognitive development. *Developmental Psychology, 29,* 1024–1035.

Liberman, I. Y., & Liberman, A. M. (1990). Whole language vs. code emphasis: Underlying assumptions and their implications for reading instruction. *Annals of Dyslexia, 40,* 51–76.

Lickliter, R., & Hellewell, T. B. (1992). Contextual determinants of auditory learning in bobwhite quail embryos and hatchlings. *Developmental Psychobiology, 25,* 17–24.

Lickona, T. (Ed.). (1976). *Moral development and behavior.* New York: Holt.

Lieberman, E., Lang, J. M., Frigoletto, F., Jr., Richardson, D. K., Ringer, S. A., & Cohen, A. (1997). Epidural analgesia, intrapartum fever, and neonatal sepsis evaluation. *Pediatrics, 99,* 415–419.

Lieu, T. A., Newacheck, P. W., & McManus, M. A. (1993). Race, ethnicity, and access to ambulatory care among U.S. adolescents. *American Journal of Public Health, 83,* 960–965.

Lieven, E. M. (1978). Conversations between mothers and young children. In N. Waterson & E. Snow (Eds.), *The development of communication: Social and pragmatic factors in language acquisition.* New York: Wiley.

Lightfoot-Klein, H. (1989). *Prisoners of ritual.* Binghamton, NY: Haworth.

Lindberg, L. D. (1996). Women's decisions about breast feeding and maternal employment. *Journal of Marriage and the Family, 58,* 239–251.

Lindwer, W. (1991). *The last seven months of Anne Frank* (A. Meersschaert, Trans.). New York: Pantheon.

Linney, J. A., & Seidman, E. (1989). The future of schooling. *American Psychologist, 44*(2), 336–340.

Livson, N., & Peskin, H. (1980). Perspectives on adolescence from longitudinal research. In J. Adelson (Ed.), *Handbook of adolescent psychology.* New York: Wiley.

Lloyd, T., Andon, M. B., Rollings, N., Martel, J. K., Landis, J. R., Demers, L. M., Eggli, D. F., Kieselhorst, K., & Kulin, H. E. (1993). Calcium supplementation and bone mineral density in adolescent girls. *Journal of the American Medical Association, 270,* 841–844.

Lo, Y. M. D., Patel, P., Wainscoat, J. S., Sampietro, M., Gillmer, M. D. G., & Fleming, K. A. (1989, December 9). Prenatal sex determination by DNA amplification from maternal peripheral blood. *The Lancet,* pp. 1363–1365.

Lock, A., Young, A., Service, V., & Chandler, P. (1990). Some observations on the origin of the pointing gesture. In V. Volterra & C. J. Erting (Eds.), *From gesture to language in hearing and deaf children.* New York: Springer.

Loda, F. A. (1980). Day care. *Pediatrics in Review, 1*(9), 277–281.

Loeber, R., & Dishion, T. (1983). Early predictors of male delinquency: A review. *Psychological Bulletin, 94,* 68–99.

Lollis, S. Ross, H., & Leroux, L. (1996). An observational study of parents' socialization of moral orientation during sibling conflicts. *Merrill-Palmer Quarterly, 42,* 475–494.

Long, L. (1992). International perspectives on the residential mobility of America's children. *Journal of Marriage and the Family, 54,* 861–869.

Longino, C. F., & Earle, J. R. (1996). Who are the grandparents at century's end? *Generations, 20*(1), 13–16.

Lonigan, C. J., Fischel, J. E., Whitehurst, G. J., Arnold, D. S., & Valdez-Menchaca, M. C. (1992). The role of otitis media in the development of expressive language disorder. *Developmental Psychology, 28,* 430–440.

Lorenz, K. (1957). Comparative study of behavior. In C. H. Schiller (Ed.), *Instinctive behavior.* New York: International Universities Press.

Lorsbach, T. C., & Reimer, J. F. (1997). Developmental changes in the inhibition of previously relevant information. *Journal of Experimental Child Psychology, 64*, 317–342.

Louis Harris & Associates. (1986). *American teens speak: Sex, myths, TV and birth control: The Planned Parenthood poll.* New York: Planned Parenthood Federation of America.

Louise Brown: From miracle baby to regular teen. (1994, February 7). *People Weekly*, p. 12.

Louise Brown: The world's first "test-tube baby" ushered in a revolution in fertility. (1984, March). *People Weekly*, p. 82.

Lowrey, G. H. (1978). *Growth and development of children* (7th ed.). Chicago: Year Book Medical.

Lozoff, B., Wolf, A., & Davis, N. S. (1985). Sleep problems seen in pediatric practice. *Pediatrics, 75*, 477–483.

Luecke-Aleksa, D., Anderson, D. R., Collins, P. A., & Schmitt, K. L. (1995). Gender constancy and television viewing. *Developmental Psychology, 31*, 773–780.

Luepker, R. V., Perry, C. L., McKinlay, S. M., Nader, P. R., Parcel, G. S., Stone, E. J., Webber, L. S., Elder, J. P., Feldman, H. A., Johnson, C. C., Kelder, S. H., & Wu, M., for the CATCH Collaborative Group. (1996). Outcomes of a field trial to improve children's dietary patterns and physical activity. *Journal of the American Medical Association, 275*, 768–776.

Luke, B., Mamelle, N., Keith, L., Munoz, F., Minogue, J., Papiernik, E., Johnson, T. R., & Timothy, R. B. (1995). The association between occupational factors and preterm birth: A United States nurses' study. *American Journal of Obstetrics and Gynecology, 173*, 849–862.

Lundy, B., Field, T., & Pickens, J. (1996). Newborns of mothers with depressive symptoms are less expressive. *Infant Behavior and Development, 19*, 419–424.

Luster, T., & McAdoo, H. (1996). Family and child influences on educational attainment: A secondary analysis of the High/Scope Perry Preschool data. *Developmental Psychology, 32*, 26–39.

Luster, T., & Small, S. A. (1994). Factors associated with sexual risk-taking among adolescents. *Journal of Marriage and the Family, 56*, 622–632.

Lutjen, P., Trounson, A., Leeton, J., Findlay, J., Wood, C., & Renou, P. (1984). The establishment and maintenance of pregnancy using in vitro fertilization and embryo donation in a patient with primary ovarian failure. *Nature, 307*, 174–175.

Lyman, R. (1997, April 15). Michael Dorris dies at 52: Wrote of his son's suffering. *The New York Times*, p. C24.

Lyon, T. D., & Flavell, J. H. (1993). Young children's understanding of forgetting over time. *Child Development, 64*, 789–800.

Lyons-Ruth, K., Alpern, L., & Repacholi, B. (1993). Disorganized infant attachment classification and maternal psychosocial problems as predictors of hostile-aggressive behavior in the preschool classroom. *Child Development, 64*, 572–585.

Lytton, H., & Romney, D. M. (1991). Parents' differential socialization of boys and girls: A meta-analysis. *Psychological Bulletin, 109*(2), 267–296.

Maccoby, E. (1980). *Social development.* New York: Harcourt Brace Jovanovich.

Maccoby, E., & Jacklin, C. (1974). *The psychology of sex differences.* Stanford, CA: Stanford University Press.

Maccoby, E. E. (1984). Middle childhood in the context of the family. In W. A. Collins (Ed.), *Development during middle childhood.* Washington, DC: National Academy.

Maccoby, E. E. (1988). Gender as a social category. *Developmental Psychology, 24*, 755–765.

Maccoby, E. E. (1990). Gender and relationships: A developmental account. *American Psychologist, 45*(11), 513–520.

Maccoby, E. E. (1992). The role of parents in the socialization of children: An historical overview. *Developmental Psychology, 28*, 1006–1017.

Maccoby, E. E. (1994). Commentary: Gender segregation in childhood. In C. Leaper (Ed.), *Childhood gender segregation: Causes and consequences* (New Directions for Child Development No. 65, pp. 87–97). San Francisco: Jossey-Bass.

Maccoby, E. E., & Martin, J. A. (1983). Socialization in the context of the family: Parent-child interaction. In P. H. Mussen (Series Ed.) & E. M. Hetherington (Vol. Ed.), *Handbook of child psychology: Vol. 4. Socialization, personality, and social development* (pp. 1–101). New York: Wiley.

Macfarlane, A. (1975). Olfaction in the development of social preferences in the human neonate. In *Parent-infant interaction* (CIBA Foundation Symposium No. 33). Amsterdam: Elsevier.

MacFarquhar, N. (1996, August 8). Mutilation of Egyptian girls: Despite ban, it goes on. *The New York Times*, p. A3.

MacGowan, R. J., MacGowan, C. A., Serdula, M. K., Lane, J. M., Joesoef, R. M., & Cook, F. H. (1991). Breast-feeding among women attending women, infants, and children clinics in Georgia, 1987. *Pediatrics, 87*, 361–366.

Main, M. (1983). Exploration, play, and cognitive functioning related to infant-mother attachment. *Infant Behavior and Development, 6*, 167–174.

Main, M. (1995). Recent studies in attachment: Overview, with selected implications for clinical work. In S. Goldberg, R. Muir, & J. Kerr (Eds.), *Attachment theory: Social, developmental, and clinical perspectives* (pp. 407–470). Hillsdale, NJ: Analytic Press.

Main, M., & Hesse, E. (1990). Parents' unresolved traumatic experiences are related to infant disorganized attachment status: Is frightened and/or frightening parental behavior the linking mechanism? In M. T. Greenberg, D. Cicchetti, & E. M. Cummings (Eds.), *Attachment in preschool years: Theory, research, and intervention* (pp. 161–184). Chicago: University of Chicago Press.

Main, M., Kaplan, N., & Cassidy, J. (1985). Security in infancy, childhood and adulthood: A move to the level of representation. In I. Bretherton & E. Waters (Eds.), Growing points in attachment. *Monographs of the Society for Research in Child Development, 50*(1–20), 66–104.

Main, M., & Solomon, J. (1986). Discovery of an insecure, disorganized/disoriented attachment pattern: Procedures, findings, and implications for the classification of behavior. In M. Yogman & T. B. Brazelton (Eds.), *Affective development in infancy.* Norwood, NJ: Ablex.

Makrides, M., Neumann, M., Simmer, K., Pater, J., & Gibson, R. (1995). Are long-chain polyunsaturated fatty acids essential nutrients in infancy? *The Lancet, 345*, 1463–1468.

Mandela, N. (1994). *Long walk to freedom: The autobiography of Nelson Mandela.* Boston: Little, Brown.

Mandler, J. M. (1990). A new perspective on cognitive development in infancy. *American Scientist, 78*, 236–243.

Mangelsdorf, S. C., Shapiro, J. R., & Marzolf, D. (1995). Developmental and temperamental differences in emotion regulation in infancy. *Child Development, 66*, 1817–1828.

Manosevitz, M., Prentice, N. M., & Wilson, F. (1973). Individual and family correlates of imaginary companions in preschool children. *Developmental Psychology, 8*, 72–79.

Mansfield, R. S., & Busse, T. V. (1981). *The psychology of creativity and discovery: Scientists and their work.* Chicago: Nelson-Hall.

Maratsos, M. (1973). Nonegocentric communication abilities in preschool children. *Child Development, 44*, 697–700.

March of Dimes Birth Defects Foundation. (1987). *Genetic counseling: A public health information booklet* (Rev. ed.). White Plains, NY: Author.

Marcia, J. E. (1966). Development and validation of ego identity status. *Journal of Personality and Social Psychology, 3*(5), 551–558.

Marcia, J. E. (1979, June). *Identity status in late adolescence: Description and some clinical implications.* Address given at symposium on identity development, Rijksuniversitat Groningen, Netherlands.

Marcia, J. E. (1980). Identity in adolescence. In J. Adelson (Ed.), *Handbook of adolescent psychology.* New York: Wiley.

Marcia, J. E. (1993). The relational roots of identity. In J. Kroger (Ed.), *Discussions on ego identity* (pp. 101–120). Hillsdale, NJ: Erlbaum.

Marian Anderson, 1897–1993. (1993, April 19). *Time*, p. 24.

Marian Anderson plans move to Portland, Oregon with her nephew, James DePriest. (1992, July 13). *Jet*, p. 33.

Markoff, J. (1992, October 12). Miscarriages tied to chip factories. *The New York Times*, pp. A1, D2.

Marland, S. P., Jr. (1972). *Education of the gifted and talented: Vol. 1. Report to the Congress of the United States by the U.S. Commissioner of Education.* Washington, DC: U.S. Government Printing Office.

Marling, K. A. (1996). *Graceland: Going home with Elvis.* Cambridge, MA: Harvard University Press.

Martin, G. B., & Clark, R. D. (1982). Distress crying in neonates: Species and peer specificity. *Developmental Psychology, 18,* 3–9.

Martin, J. L., & Ross, H. S. (1996). Do mitigating circumstances influence family reaction to physical aggression? *Child Development, 67,* 1455–1466.

Marzano, R. J., & Hutchins, C. L. (1987). *Thinking skills: A conceptual framework* (ERIC Document Reproduction Service No. ED 266436).

Masataka, N. (1996). Perception of motherese in a signed language by 6-month-old deaf infants. *Developmental Psychology, 32,* 874–879.

Masse, L. C., & Tremblay, R. E. (1997). Behavior of boys in kindergarten and the onset of substance use during adolescence. *Archives of General Psychiatry, 54,* 62–68.

Masten, A., Best, K., & Garmezy, N. (1990). Resilience and development: Contributions from the study of children who overcome adversity. *Development and Psychopathology, 2,* 425–444.

Mathews, T. J., & Ventura, S. J. (1997). *Birth and fertility rates by educational attainment: United States, 1994* (Monthly Vital Statistics Report, 45[10, Suppl.], DHHS Publication No. PHS 97-1120). Hyattsville, MD: National Center for Health Statistics.

Maxwell, L. (1987, January). *Eight pointers on teaching children to think* (Research in Brief No. IS 87-104 RIB). Washington, DC: U.S. Department of Education, Office of Educational Research and Improvement.

May, K. A., & Perrin, S. P. (1985). Prelude: Pregnancy and birth. In S. M. H. Hanson & F. W. Bozett (Eds.), *Dimensions of fatherhood.* Beverly Hills, CA: Sage.

Mayaux, M. J., Teglas, J. P., Mandelbrot, L., Berrebi, A., Gallais, H., Matheron, S., Ciraru-Vigneron, N., Parnet-Mathieu, F., Bongain, A., Rouzioux, C., Delfraissy, J. F., & Blanchu, S. (1997). Acceptability and impact of zidovudine for prevention of mother-to-child human immunodeficiency virus-1 transmission in France. *Journal of Pediatrics, 131,* 857–62.

Mayes, L. C., Granger, R. H., Frank, M. A., Schottenfeld, R., & Bornstein, M. H. (1993). Neurobehavioral profiles of neonates exposed to cocaine prenatally. *Pediatrics, 91,* 778–783.

McAnarney, E. R., & Hendee, W. R. (1989). Adolescent pregnancy and its consequences. *Journal of the American Medical Association, 262,* 74–77.

McCall, R. B., & Carriger, M. S. (1993). A meta-analysis of infant habituation and recognition memory performance as predictors of later IQ. *Child Development, 64,* 57–79.

McCartney, K. (1984). Effect of quality of daycare environment on children's language development. *Developmental Psychology, 20,* 244–260.

McCarton, C. M., Brooks-Gunn, J., Wallace, I. F., Bauer, C. R., Bennett, F. C., Bernbaum, J. C., Broyles, S., Casey, P. H., McCormick, M. C., Scott, D. T., Tyson, J., Tonascia, J., & Meinert, C. L., for the Infant Health and Development Program Research Group. (1997). Results at age 8 years of early intervention for low-birth-weight premature infants. *Journal of the American Medical Association, 277,* 126–132.

McCarton, C. M., Wallace, I. F., Divon, M., & Vaughan, H. G. (1996). Cognitive and neurologic development of the preterm, small for gestational age infant through age 6: Comparison by birth weight and gestational age. *Pediatrics, 98,* 1167–1178.

McClearn, G. E., Johansson, B., Berg, S., Pedersen, N. L., Ahern, F., Petrill, S. A., & Plomin, R. (1997). Substantial genetic influence on cognitive abilities in twins 80 or more years old. *Science, 276,* 1560–1563.

McClelland, D., Constantian C., Regalado, D., & Stone, C. (1978, January). Making it to maturity. *Psychology Today 12*(1), pp. 42–53, 114.

McClintock, M. K., & Herdt, G. (1996). Rethinking puberty: The development of sexual attraction. *Current Directions in Psychological Science, 5*(6), 178–183.

McCormick, M. E., & Wolf, J. S. (1993). Intervention programs for gifted girls. *Roeper Review, 16*(2), 85–88.

McCurdy, K., & Daro, D. (1993, April). *Current trends in child abuse reporting and fatalities: The results of the 1992 annual fifty state survey* (Working Paper No. 808). Chicago: National Committee for the Prevention of Child Abuse.

McDaniel, K. D. (1986). Pharmacological treatment of psychiatric and neuro-developmental disorders in children and adolescents (Part 1, Part 2, Part 3). *Clinical Pediatrics, 25*(2, 3, 4), 65–71, 198–224.

McDonald, A. D., Armstrong, B. G., & Sloan, M. (1992). Cigarette, alcohol, and coffee consumption and prematurity. *American Journal of Public Health, 82,* 87.

McDonald, M. A., Sigman, M., Espinosa, M. P., & Neumann, C. G. (1994). Impact of a temporary food shortage on children and their mothers. *Child Development, 65,* 404–415.

McGauhey, P. J., Starfield, B., Alexander, C., & Ensminget, M. E. (1991). Social environment and vulnerability of low birth weight children: A social-epidemiological perspective. *Pediatrics, 88,* 943–953.

McGee, R., Partridge, F., Williams, S., & Silva, P. A. (1991). A twelve-year follow-up of preschool hyperactive children. *Journal of the American Academy of Child and Adolescent Psychiatry, 30,* 224–232.

McGue, M. (1997). The democracy of the genes. *Nature, 388,* 417–418.

McGue, M., Bouchard, T. J., Jr., Iacono, W. G., & Lykken, D. T. (1993). Behavioral genetics of cognitive ability: A life-span perspective. In R. Plomin & G. E. McClearn (Eds.), *Nature, nurture and psychology* (pp. 59–76). Washington, DC: American Psychological Association.

McGuffin, P., Owen, M. J., & Farmer, A. E. (1995). Genetic basis of schizophrenia. *The Lancet, 346,* 678–682.

McIntosh, H. (1995). Black teens not smoking in great numbers. *Journal of National Cancer Institute, 87,* 564.

McKay, N. Y. (1992). Introduction. In M. Anderson, *My Lord, what a morning* (pp. ix–xxxiii). Madison: University of Wisconsin Press.

McKenna, J. J., & Mosko, S. (1993). Evolution and infant sleep: An experimental study of infant-parent co-sleeping and its implications for SIDS. *Acta Paediatrica, 389* (Suppl.), 31–36.

McKenna, J. J., Mosko, S. S., & Richard, C. A. (1997). Bedsharing promotes breastfeeding. *Pediatrics, 100,* 214–219.

McKenna, M. C. (1994). Toward a model of reading attitude acquisition. In E. H. Cramer & M. Castle (Eds.), *Fostering the life-long love of reading: The affective domain in reading education* (pp. 18–40). Newark, DE: International Reading Association.

McKenna, M. C., Kear, D. J., & Ellsworth, R. A. (1995). Children's attitudes toward reading: A national survey. *Reading Research Quarterly, 30,* 934–956.

McKey, R. H., Condelli, L., Ganson, H., Barrett, B. J., McConkey, C., & Plantz, M. C. (1985). *The impact of Head Start on children, families, and communities.* Washington, DC: CSR, Inc.

McKinney, K. (1987, March). *A look at Japanese education today* (Research in Brief No. IS 87-107 RIB). Washington, DC: U.S. Department of Education, Office of Educational Research and Improvement.

McLanahan, S., & Booth, K. (1989). Mother-only families: Problems, prospects, and politics. *Journal of Marriage and the Family, 51,* 557–580.

McLoyd, V. C. (1990). The impact of economic hardship on black families and children: Psychological distress, parenting, and socioemotional development. *Child Development, 61,* 311–346.

McLoyd, V. C., Jayaratne, T. E., Ceballo, R., & Borquez, J. (1994). Unemployment and work interruption among African American single mothers: Effects on parenting and adolescent socioemotional functioning. *Child Development, 65,* 562–589.

McMahon, M. J., Luther, E. R., Bowes, W. A., & Olshan, A. F. (1996). Comparison of a trial of labor with an elective second cesarean section. *New England Journal of Medicine, 335,* 689–695.

McManus, M. A., & Newacheck, P. (1993). Health insurance differentials among minority children with chronic conditions and the role of federal agencies and private foundations in improving financial access. *Pediatrics, 91*, 1040–1047.

Mead, M. (1928). *Coming of age in Samoa.* New York: Morrow.

Mead, M. (1935). *Sex and temperament in three primitive societies.* New York: Morrow.

Mead, M. (1972). *Blackberry winter: My earlier years.* New York: Morrow.

Meehan, P. J. (1990). Prevention: The endpoint of suicidology. *Mayo Clinic Proceedings, 65*, 115–118.

Meer, F. (1988). *Higher than hope: The authorized biography of Nelson Mandela.* New York: Harper & Row.

Meier, D. (1995). *The power of their ideas.* Boston: Beacon.

Melnick, S., Cole, P., Anderson, B. A., & Herbst, A. (1987). Rates and risks of diethylstilbestrol-related clear-cell adenocarcinoma of the vagina and cervix. *New England Journal of Medicine, 316*, 514–516.

Meltzoff, A. N. (1988). Infant imitation after a one-week delay: Long-term memory for novel acts and multiple stimuli. *Developmental Psychology, 24*, 470–476.

Meltzoff, A. N., & Borton, R. W. (1979). Intermodal matching by human neonates. *Nature, 282*, 403–404.

Meltzoff, A. N., & Moore, M. K. (1983). Newborn infants imitate adult facial gestures. *Child Development, 54*, 702–709.

Meltzoff, A. N., & Moore, M. K. (1989). Imitation in newborn infants: Exploring the range of gestures imitated and the underlying mechanisms. *Developmental Psychology, 25*, 954–962.

Meltzoff, A. N., & Moore, M. K. (1994). Imitation, memory, and the representation of persons. *Infant Behavior and Development, 17*, 83–99.

Menendez, A. (1995, Fall). Home schooling: The facts. *Voice of Reason* (Newsletter of Americans for Religious Liberty), pp. 6–8.

Mennella, J. A., & Beauchamp, G. K. (1996a). The early development of human flavor preferences. In E. D. Capaldi (Ed.), *Why we eat what we eat: The psychology of eating* (pp. 83–112). Washington, DC: American Psychological Association.

Mennella, J. A., & Beauchamp, G. K. (1996b). The human infants' response to vanilla flavors in mother's milk and formula. *Infant Behavior and Development, 19*, 13–19.

Meredith, N. V. (1969). Body size of contemporary groups of eight-year-old children studied in different parts of the world. *Monographs of the Society for Research in Child Development, 34*(1).

Merzenich, M. M., Jenkins, W. M., Johnston, P., Schreiner, C., Miller, S. L., & Tallal, P. (1996). Temporal processing deficits of language-learning impaired children ameliorated by training. *Science, 271*, 77–81.

Meyers, A. F., Sampson, A. E., Weitzman, M., Rogers, B. L., & Kayne, H. (1989). School breakfast program and school performance. *American Journal of Diseases of Children, 143*, 1234–1239.

Meyers, B. J., Jarvis, P. A., & Creasey, G. L. (1987). Infants' behavior with their mothers and grandmothers. *Infant Behavior and Development, 10*, 245–259.

Michelmore, P. (1962). *Einstein: Profile of the man.* London: Frederick Muller, Ltd.

Miedzian, M. (1991). *Boys will be boys: Breaking the link between masculinity and violence.* New York: Doubleday.

Mifflin, L. (1996, February 15). 4 networks plan a ratings system for their shows. *The New York Times,* pp. A1, C24.

Milberger, S., Biederman, J., Faraone, S. V., Chen, L., & Jones, J. (1996). Is maternal smoking during pregnancy a risk factor for attention hyperactivity disorder in children? *American Journal of Psychiatry, 153*, 1138–1142.

Milerad, J., & Sundell, H. (1993). Nicotine exposure and the risk of SIDS. *Acta Paediatrica, 389* (Suppl.), 70–72.

Miller, A. (1984). *For your own good: Hidden cruelty in child-rearing and the roots of violence* (2nd ed.). New York: Farrar, Straus, & Giroux.

Miller, B. C., & Moore, K. A. (1990). Adolescent sexual behavior, pregnancy, and parenting: Research through the 1980s. *Journal of Marriage and the Family, 52*, 1025–1044.

Miller, E., Cradock-Watson, J. E., & Pollock, T. M. (1982, October 9). Consequences of confirmed maternal rubella at successive stages of pregnancy. *The Lancet,* pp. 781–784.

Miller, J. B. (1991). The development of women's sense of self. In J. V. Jordan, A. G. Kaplan, J. B. Miller, I. P. Stiver, & J. L. Surrey (Eds.), *Women's growth in connection: Writings from the Stone Center.* New York: Guilford.

Miller, P. H. (1993). *Theories of personality development* (3rd ed.). New York: Freeman.

Miller, V., Onotera, R. T., & Deinard, A. S. (1984). Denver Developmental Screening Test: Cultural variations in Southeast Asian children. *Journal of Pediatrics, 104*(3), 481–482.

Miller-Jones, D. (1989). Culture and testing. *American Psychologist, 44*(2), 360–366.

Mills, J. L., Graubard, B. I., Harley, E. E., Rhoads, G. G., & Berendes, H. W. (1984). Maternal alcohol consumption and birth weight: How much drinking is safe during pregnancy? *Journal of the American Medical Association, 252*, 1875–1879.

Mills, J. L., Holmes, L. B., Aarons, J. H., Simpson, J. L., Brown, Z. A., Jovanovic-Peterson, L. G., Conley, M. R., Graubard, B. I., Knopp, R. H., & Metzger, B. E. (1993). Moderate caffeine use and the risk of spontaneous abortion and intrauterine growth retardation. *Journal of the American Medical Association, 269*, 593–597.

Mills, J. L., McPartlin, J. N., Kirke, P. N., Lee, Y. J., & Conley, M. R. (1995). Homocysteine metabolism in pregnancies complicated by neural tube defects. *The Lancet, 345*, 149–151.

Millstein, S. (in press). Perceptual, attributional, and affective processes in perceptions of vulnerability through the life span. In N. J. Bell & R. W. Bell (Eds.), *Perspectives on adolescent risk taking.* Newbury Park, CA: Sage.

Millstein, S. G., Irwin, C. E., Adler, N. E., Cohn, L. D., Kegeles, S. M., & Dolcini, M. M. (1992). Health-risk behaviors and health concerns among young adolescents. *Pediatrics, 89*, 422–428.

Milne, A. M., Myers, D. E., Rosenthal, A. S., & Ginsburg, A. (1986). Single parents, working mothers, and the educational achievement of school children. *Sociology of Education, 59*, 125–139.

Milunsky, A. (1992). *Heredity and your family's health.* Baltimore: Johns Hopkins University Press.

Minami, M., & McCabe, A. (1995). Rice balls and bear hunts: Japanese and North American family narrative patterns. *Journal of Child Language, 22*, 423–445.

Minkler, M., & Roe, K. M. (1996). Grandparents as surrogate parents. *Generations, 20*(1), 34–38.

Miranda, S., Hack, M., Fantz, R., Fanaroff, A., & Klaus, M. (1977). Neonatal pattern vision: Predictor of future mental performance? *Journal of Pediatrics, 91*(4), 642–647.

Miserandino, M. (1996). Children who do well in school: Individual differences in perceived competence and autonomy in above-average children. *Journal of Educational Psychology, 88*(2), 203–214.

Mishell, D. R. (1993). Recurrent abortion. *Journal of Reproductive Medicine, 38*, 250–259.

Misrahi, M., Teglas, J. P., N'Go, N., Burgard, M., Mayaux, M. J., Rouzioux, C., Delfraissy, J. F., Blanche, S., for the French Pediatric HIV Infection Study Group. (1998). CCR5 chemokine receptor variant in HIV-1 mother-to-child transmission and disease progression in children. *Journal of the American Medical Association, 279*, 277–80.

Mitchell, E. A., Ford, R. P. K., Stewart, A. W., Taylor, B. J., Bescroft, D. M. O., Thompson, J. M. P., Scragg, R., Hassall, I. B., Barry, D. M. J., Allen, E. M., & Roberts, A. P. (1993). Smoking and the sudden infant death syndrome. *Pediatrics, 91*, 893–896.

Miyake, K., Chen, S., & Campos, J. (1985). Infants' temperament, mothers' mode of interaction and attachment in Japan: An interim report. In I. Bretherton & E. Waters (Eds.), Growing points of attachment theory and research. *Monographs of the Society for Research in Child Development, 50*(1–2, Serial No. 109), 276–297.

Mize, J., & Pettit, G. S. (1997). Mothers' social coaching, mother-child relationship style, and children's peer competence: Is the medium the message? *Child Development, 68*, 312–332.

Moffitt, T. E., Caspi, A., Belsky, J., & Silva, P. A. (1992). Childhood experience and the onset of menarche: A test of a sociobiological model. *Child Development, 63*, 47–58.

Molina, B. S. G., & Chassin, L. (1996). The parent-adolescent relationship at puberty: Hispanic ethnicity and parent alcoholism as moderators. *Developmental Psychology, 32,* 675–686.

Money, J., & Ehrhardt, A. A. (1972). *Man and woman/Boy and girl.* Baltimore: Johns Hopkins University Press.

Montague, C. T., Farooqi, I. S., Whitehead, J. P., Soos, M. A., Rau, H., Wareham, N. J., Sewter, C. P., Digby, J. E., Mohammed, S. N., Hurst, J. A., Cheetham, C. H., Earley, A. R., Barnett, A. H., Prins, J. B., & Orahilly, S. (1997). Congenital leptin deficiency is associated with severe early onset obesity in humans. *Nature, 387,* 903–908.

Montgomery, L. E., Kiely, J. L., & Pappas, G. (1996). The effects of poverty, race, and family structure on U.S. children's health: Data from the NHIS, 1978 through 1980 and 1989 through 1991. *American Journal of Public Health, 86,* 1401–1405.

Moon, C., Cooper, R. P., & Fifer, W. P. (1993). Two-day-olds prefer their native language. *Infant Behavior and Development, 16,* 495–500.

Moon, C., & Fifer, W. P. (1990, April). *Newborns prefer a prenatal version of mother's voice.* Paper presented at the biannual meeting of the International Society of Infant Studies, Montreal, Canada.

Moore, C., Jarrold, C., Russell, J., Lumb, A., Sapp, F., & MacCallum, F. (1995). Conflicting desire and the child's theory of mind. *Cognitive Development, 10,* 467–482.

Moore, C. A., Khoury, M. J., & Liu, Y. (1997). Does light-to-moderate alcohol consumption during pregnancy increase the risk for renal anomalies among offspring? *Pediatrics* [On-line], *99.* Available: http://www.pediatrics.org/cgi/content/full/99/4/e11

Moore, N., Evertson, C., & Brophy, J. (1974). Solitary play: Some functional reconsiderations. *Developmental Psychology, 10,* 830–834.

Moore, S. E., Cole, T. J., Poskitt, E. M. E., Sonko, B. J., Whitehead, R. G., McGregor, I. A., & Prentice, A. M. (1997). Season of birth predicts mortality in rural Gambia. *Nature, 388,* 434.

Morelli, G. A., Rogoff, B., Oppenheim, D., & Goldsmith, D. (1992). Cultural variation in infants' sleeping arrangements: Questions of independence. *Developmental Psychology, 28,* 604–613.

Morison, P., & Masten, A. S. (1991). Peer reputation in middle childhood as a predictor of adaptation in adolescence: A seven-year follow-up. *Child Development, 62,* 991–1007.

Morison, S. J., Ames, E. W., & Chisholm, K. (1995). The development of children adopted from Romanian orphanages. *Merrill-Palmer Quarterly Journal of Developmental Psychology, 41,* 411–430.

Morris, R., & Kralochwill, T. (1983). *Treating children's fears and phobias: A behavioral approach.* Elmsford, NY: Pergamon.

Morrison, F. J., Griffith, E. M., & Alberts, D. M. (1997). Nature-nurture in the classroom: Entrance age, school readiness, and learning in children. *Developmental Psychology, 33,* 254–262.

Mortimer, J. T., Finch, M. D., Ryu, S., Shanahan, M. J., & Call, K. T. (1996). The effects of work intensity on adolescent mental health, achievement, and behavioral adjustment: New evidence from a prospective study. *Child Development, 67,* 1243–1261.

Mortimer, J. T., & Shanahan, M. J. (1991). *Adolescent work experience and relations with peers.* Paper presented at the American Sociological Association Annual Meeting, Cincinnati, OH.

Moses, L. J., & Flavell, J. H. (1990). Inferring false belief from actions and reactions. *Child Development, 61,* 929–945.

Mosher, W. D., & Pratt, W. F. (1991). Fecundity and infertility in the United States: Incidence and trends. *Fertility and Sterility, 56,* 192–193.

Mossberg, H. O. (1989, August 26). 40-year follow-up of overweight children. *The Lancet,* pp. 491–493.

Mounts, N. S., & Steinberg, L. (1995). An ecological analysis of peer influence on adolescent grade point average and drug use. *Developmental Psychology, 31,* 915–922.

Mullen, M. K. (1994). Earliest recollections of childhood: A demographic analysis. *Cognition, 52,* 55–79.

Mullis, I. V. S., Martin, M. O., Beaton, A. E., Gonzalez, E. J., Kelly, D. L., & Smith, T. A. (1997). *Mathematics achievement in the primary school years: IEA's Third International Mathematics and Science Study (TIMSS).* Chestnut Hill, MA: TIMSS International Study Center, Boston College.

Muñoz, K. A., Krebs-Smith, S. M., Ballard-Barbash, R., & Cleveland, L. E. (1997). Food intakes of U.S. children and adolescents compared with recommendations. *Pediatrics, 100,* 323–329.

Murachver, T., Pipe, M., Gordon, R., Owens, J. L., & Fivush, R. (1996). Do, show, and tell: Children's event memories acquired through direct experience, observation, and stories. *Child Development, 67,* 3029–3044.

Murchison, C., & Langer, S. (1927). Tiedemann's observations on the development of the mental facilities of children. *Journal of Genetic Psychology, 34,* 205–230.

Murphy, C. M., & Bootzin, R. R. (1973). Active and passive participation in the contact desensitization of snake fear in children. *Behavior Therapy, 4,* 203–211.

Murray, A. D., Dolby, R. M., Nation, R. L., & Thomas, D. B. (1981). Effects of epidural anesthesia on newborns and their mothers. *Child Development, 52,* 71–82.

Murray, L., Fiori-Cowley, A., Hooper, R., & Cooper, P. (1996). The impact of postnatal depression and associated adversity on early mother-infant interactions and later infant outcome. *Child Development, 67,* 2512–2526.

Mussen, P. H., & Eisenberg-Berg, N. (1977). *Roots of caring, sharing, and helping: The development of prosocial behavior in children.* San Francisco: Freeman.

Mussen, P. H., & Jones, M. C. (1957). Self-conceptions, motivations, and interpersonal attitudes of late- and early-maturing boys. *Child Development, 28,* 243–256.

Mussen, P. H., & Rutherford, E. (1963). Parent-child relations and parental personality in relation to young children's sex role preferences. *Child Development, 34,* 589–607.

Must, A., Jacques, P. F., Dallal, G. E., Bajerna, C. J., & Dietz, W. H. (1992). Long-term morbidity and mortality of overweight adolescents: A follow-up of the Harvard Growth Study of 1922 to 1935. *New England Journal of Medicine, 327*(19), 1350–1355.

Myers, J. E., & Perrin, N. (1993). Grandparents affected by parental divorce: A population at risk? *Journal of Counseling and Development, 72,* 62–66.

Myers, N., & Perlmutter, M. (1978). Memory in the years from 2 to 5. In P. Ornstein (Ed.), *Memory development in children.* Hillsdale, NJ: Erlbaum.

Naeye, R. L., & Peters, E. C. (1984). Mental development of children whose mothers smoked during pregnancy. *Obstetrics and Gynecology, 64,* 601.

Napiorkowski, B., Lester, B. M., Freier, C., Brunner, S., Dietz, L., Nadra, A., & Oh, W. (1996). Effects of in utero substance exposure on infant neurobehavior. *Pediatrics, 98,* 71–75.

Nash, J. M. (1997, February 3). Fertile minds. *Time,* pp. 49–56.

Nathanielsz, P. W. (1995). The role of basic science in preventing low birth weight. *The Future of Our Children, 5*(1), 57–70.

National Center for Education Statistics (NCES). (1985). *The relationship of parental involvement to high school grades* (Publication No. NCES-85-205b). Washington, DC: U.S. Government Printing Office.

National Center for Education Statistics (NCES). (1987). *Who drops out of high school? From high school and beyond.* Washington, DC: U.S. Department of Education, Office of Educational Research and Improvement.

National Center for Education Statistics (NCES). (1995). *Condition of education, 1995.* Washington, DC: U.S. Department of Education.

National Center for Health Statistics (NCHS). (1990). *Health, United States, 1989 and prevention profile* (DHHS Publication No. 90-1232). Washington, DC: U.S. Public Health Service.

National Center for Health Statistics (NCHS). (1993). *Health, United States, 1992 and prevention profile.* Washington, DC: U.S. Public Health Service.

National Center for Health Statistics (NCHS). (1994). *Health, United States, 1993.* Hyattsville, MD: U.S. Public Health Service.

National Center for Health Statistics (NCHS). (1995). *Statistics.* Washington, DC: Author.

National Center for Health Statistics (NCHS). (1996). *Vital statistics of the United States, 1992: Volume I—Natality.* Hyattsville, MD: U.S. Public Health Service.

National Center for Health Statistics (NCHS). (1997). *Health United States, 1996–97 and injury chartbook* (DHHS Publication No., PHS 97-1232). Hyattsville, MD: U.S. Department of Health and Human Services.

National Clearinghouse on Child Abuse and Neglect Information. (1997, May 16). *National child abuse and neglect statistical fact sheet.* Washington, DC: U.S. Department of Health and Human Services. (Available: http://www.calib.com/nccanch/pubs/stats.htm)

National Commission for the Protection of Human Subjects of Biomedical and Behavioral Research. (1978). *Report.* Washington, DC: Author.

National Commission on Youth. (1980). *The transition to adulthood: A bridge too long.* New York: Westview.

National Committee for Citizens in Education (NCCE). (1986, Winter Holiday). Don't be afraid to start a suicide prevention program in your school. *Network for Public Schools,* pp. 1, 4.

National Education Goals Panel. (1997). *The national education goals report summary 1997: Mathematics and science achievement for the 21st century.* Washington, DC: Author.

National High Blood Pressure Education Program Working Group on Hypertension Control in Children and Adolescents. (1996). Update on the 1987 task force report on high blood pressure in children and adolescents: A working group report from the National High Blood Pressure Education Program. *Pediatrics, 98,* 649–658.

National Institute of Mental Health (NIMH). (1982). *Television and behavior: Ten years of scientific progress and implications for the eighties: Vol. 1. Summary report* (DHHS Publication No. ADM 82-1195). Washington, DC: U.S. Government Printing Office.

National Institute on Drug Abuse (NIDA). (1996). *Monitoring the future.* Washington, DC: National Institutes of Health.

National Institute on Drug Abuse (NIDA). (1997). *Monitoring the future.* Washington, DC: National Institutes of Health.

National Research Council (NRC). (1993a). *Losing generations: Adolescents in high-risk settings.* Washington, DC: National Academy Press.

National Research Council (NRC). (1993b). *Understanding child abuse and neglect.* Washington, DC: National Academy Press.

Neal, A. G., Grout, H. T., & Wicks, J. W. (1989). Attitudes about having children: A study of 600 couples in the early years of marriage. *Journal of Marriage and the Family, 51,* 313–328.

Needleman, H. L., & Gatsonis, C. A. (1990). Low-level lead exposure and the IQ of children: A meta-analysis of modern studies. *Journal of the American Medical Association, 263,* 673–678.

Needleman, H. L., Riess, J. A., Tobin, M. J., Biesecker, G. E., & Greenhouse, J. B. (1996). Bone lead levels and delinquent behavior. *Journal of the American Medical Association, 275,* 363–369.

Neisser, U., Boodoo, G., Bouchard, T. J., Jr., Boykin, A. W., Brody, N., Ceci, S. J., Halpern, D. F., Loehlin, J. C., Perloff, R., Sternberg, R. J., & Urbina, S. (1995). *Intelligence: Knowns and unknowns.* Washington, DC: American Psychological Association.

Nelson, C. A. (1995). The ontogeny of human memory: A cognitive neuroscience perspective. *Developmental Psychology, 31,* 723–738.

Nelson, C. A., & Collins, P. F. (1991). Event-related potential and looking-time analysis of infants' responses to familiar and novel events: Implications for visual recognition memory. *Developmental Psychology, 27,* 50–58.

Nelson, C. A., & Collins, P. F. (1992). Neural and behavioral correlates of recognition memory in 4- and 8-month-old infants. *Brain and Cognition, 19,* 105–121.

Nelson, C. A., Henschel, M., & Collins, P. F. (1993). Neural correlates of cross-modal recognition memory in 8-month-old infants. *Developmental Psychology, 29,* 411–420.

Nelson, K. (1973). Structure and strategy in learning to talk. *Monographs of the Society for Research in Child Development, 38* (1–2).

Nelson, K. (1974). Concept, word and sentence: Interrelations in development. *Psychological Review, 81,* 267–285.

Nelson, K. (1981). Individual differences in language development: Implications for development and language. *Developmental Psychology, 17,* 170–187.

Nelson, K. (1992). Emergence of autobiographical memory at age 4. *Human Development, 35,* 172–177.

Nelson, K. (1993). The psychological and social origins of autobiographical memory. *Psychological Science, 47,* 7–14.

Nelson, K. B., Dambrosia, J. M., Ting, T. Y., & Grether, J. K. (1996). Uncertain value of electronic fetal monitoring in predicting cerebral palsy. *New England Journal of Medicine, 334,* 613–618.

Netherlands State Institute for War Documentation. (1989). *The diary of Anne Frank: The critical edition* (D. Barnouw & G. van der Stroom, Eds.; A. J. Pomerans & B. M. Mooyaart-Doubleday, Trans.). New York: Doubleday.

Newacheck, P. W. (1989). Improving access to health services for adolescents from economically disadvantaged families. *Pediatrics, 84,* 1056–1063.

Newacheck, P. W., Stoddard, J. J., Hughes, D. C., & Pearl, M. (1988). Health insurance and access to primary care for children. *New England Journal of Medicine, 338,* 513–519.

Newacheck, P. W., Stoddard, J. J., & McManus, M. (1993). Ethnocultural variations in the prevalence and impact of childhood chronic conditions. *Pediatrics, 91,* 1031–1047.

Newcomb, A. F., & Bagwell, C. L. (1995). Children's friendship relations: A meta-analytic review. *Psychological Bulletin, 117*(2), 306–347.

Newcomb, A. F., Bukowski, W. M., & Pattee, L. (1993). Children's peer relations: A meta-analytic review of popular, rejected, neglected, controversial, and average sociometric status. *Psychological Bulletin, 113,* 99–128.

Newcombe, N., & Fox, N. A. (1994). Infantile amnesia: Through a glass darkly. *Child Development, 65,* 31–40.

Newman, D. L., Caspi, A., Moffitt, T. E., & Silva, P. A. (1997). Antecedents of adult interpersonal functioning: Effects of individual differences in age 3 temperament. *Developmental Psychology, 33,* 206–217.

Newman, J. (1995). How breast milk protects newborns. *Scientific American, 273,* 76–79.

Newman, P. R. (1982). The peer group. In B. Wolman (Ed.), *Handbook of developmental psychology.* Englewood Cliffs, NJ: Prentice-Hall.

Newnham, J. P., Evans, S. F., Michael, C. A., Stanley, F. J., & Landau, L. I. (1993). Effects of frequent ultrasound during pregnancy: A randomised controlled trial. *The Lancet, 342,* 887–891.

Newson, J., Newson, E., & Mahalski, P. A. (1982). Persistent infant comfort habits and their sequelae at 11 and 16 years. *Journal of Child Psychology and Psychiatry, 23,* 421–436.

NICHD Early Child Care Research Network. (1997a). The effects of infant child care on infant-mother attachment security: Results of the NICHD study of early child care. *Child Development, 68,* 860–879.

NICHD Early Child Care Research Network. (1997b). Familial factors associated with the characteristics of nonmaternal care for infants. *Journal of Marriage and the Family, 59,* 389–408.

Nielsen, K., McSherry, G., Petru, A., Frederick, T., Wara, D., Bryson, Y., Martin, N., Hutto, C., Ammann, A. J., Grubman, S., Oleske, J., & Scott, G. B. (1997). A descriptive survey of pediatric human immunodeficiency virus-infected long-term survivors. *Pediatrics* [On-line], *99.* Available: http://www.pediatrics.org/cgi/content/full/99/4/e4

NIH Consensus Development Panel on Physical Activity and Cardiovascular Health. (1996). Physical activity and cardiovascular health. *Journal of the American Medical Association, 276,* 241–246.

Nisan, M., & Kohlberg, L. (1982). Universality and variation in moral judgment: A longitudinal and cross-sectional study in Turkey. *Child Development, 53,* 865–876.

Noirot, E., & Algeria, J. (1983). Neonate orientation towards human voice differs with type of feeding. *Behavioral Processes, 8,* 65–71.

Nolen-Hoeksema, S., & Girgus, J. S. (1994). The emergence of gender differences in depression during adolescence. *Psychological Bulletin, 115* (3), 424–443.

Notzon, F. C. (1990). International differences in the use of obstetric interventions. *Journal of the American Medical Association, 263*(24), 3286–3291.

Nozyce, M., Hittelman, J., Muenz, L., Durako, S. J., Fischer, M. L., & Willoughby, A. (1994). Effect of perinatally acquired human immunodeficiency virus infection on neurodevelopment in children during the first two years of life. *Pediatrics, 94,* 883–891.

Nucci, L., & Smetana, J. G. (1996). Mothers' concepts of young children's areas of personal freedom. *Child Development, 67,* 1870–1886.

Nugent, J. K. (1991). Cultural and psychological influences on the father's role in infant development. *Journal of Marriage and the Family, 53,* 475–485.

Nugent, J. K., Lester, B. M., Greene, S. M., Wieczorek-Deering, D., & O'Mahony, P. (1996). The effects of maternal alcohol consumption and cigarette smoking during pregnancy on acoustic cry analysis. *Child Development, 67,* 1806–1815.

Nussbaum, M., Shenker, I. R., Baird, D., & Saravay, S. (1985). Follow-up investigation in patients with anorexia nervosa. *Journal of Pediatrics, 106,* 835–840.

Nyiti, R. M. (1982). The validity of "cultural differences explanations" for cross-cultural variation in the rate of Piagetian cognitive development. In H. W. Stevenson & D. A. Wagner (Eds.), *Cultural perspectives on child development* (pp. 146–166). San Francisco: W. H. Freeman.

Oakes, J., Gamoran, A., & Page, R. N. (1992). Curriculum differentiation: Opportunities, outcomes, and meanings. In P. W. Jackson (Ed.), *Handbook of research on curriculum* (pp. 570–608). New York: Macmillan.

Oates, R. K., Peacock, A., & Forrest, D. (1985). Long-term effects of nonorganic failure to thrive. *Pediatrics, 75,* 36–40.

O'Connell, M. (1991). *Late expectations: Childbearing patterns of American women for the 1990s* (Current Population Reports, Series P23-176). Washington, DC: U.S. Government Printing Office.

O'Connor, M. J., Cohen, S., & Parmelee, A. H. (1984). Infant auditory discrimination in preterm and full-term infants as a predictor of 5-year intelligence. *Developmental Psychology, 20,* 159–165.

O'Connor, M. J., Sigman, M., & Kasari, C. (1993). Interactional model for the association among maternal alcohol use, mother-infant interaction, and infant cognitive development. *Infant Behavior and Development, 16,* 177–192.

Offer, D. (1969). *The psychological world of the teenager: A study of normal adolescent boys.* New York: Basic Books.

Offer, D. (1987). In defense of adolescents. *Journal of the American Medical Association, 257,* 3407–3408.

Offer, D., & Church, R. B. (1991). Generation gap. In R. M. Lerner, A. C. Petersen, & J. Brooks-Gunn (Eds.), *Encyclopedia of adolescence* (pp. 397–399). New York: Garland.

Offer, D., & Offer, J. B. (1974). Normal adolescent males: The high school and college years. *Journal of the American College Health Association, 22,* 209–215.

Offer, D., Ostrov, E., & Howard, K. I. (1989). Adolescence: What is normal? *American Journal of Diseases of Children, 143,* 731–736.

Offer, D., Ostrov, E., Howard, K. I., & Atkinson, R. (1988). *The teenage world: Adolescents' self-image in ten countries.* New York: Plenum.

Offer, D., & Schonert-Reichl, K. A. (1992). Debunking the myths of adolescence: Findings from recent research. *Journal of the American Academy of Child and Adolescent Psychiatry, 31,* 1003–1014.

Ogden, C. L., Troiano, R. P., Briefel, R. R., Kuczmarski, R. J., Flegal, K. M., & Johnson, C. L. (1997). Prevalence of overweight among preschool children in the United States, 1971 through 1994. *Pediatrics* [On-line], *99.* Available: http://www.pediatrics.org/cgi/content/full/99/4/e1

Okagaki, L., & Sternberg, R. J. (1993). Parental beliefs and children's school performance. *Child Development, 64,* 36–56.

Olds, D. L., Eckenrode, J., Henderson, C. R., Jr., Kitzman, H., Powers, J., Cole, R., Sidora, K., Morris, P., Pettitt, L. M., & Luckey, D. (1997). Long-term effects of home visitation on maternal life course and child abuse and neglect: Fifteen-year follow-up of a randomized trial. *Journal of the American Medical Association, 278,* 637–643.

Olds, D. L., Henderson, C. R., & Tatelbaum, R. (1994a). Intellectual impairment in children of women who smoke cigarettes during pregnancy. *Pediatrics, 93,* 221–227.

Olds, D. L., Henderson, C. R., & Tatelbaum, R. (1994b). Prevention of intellectual impairment in children of women who smoke cigarettes during pregnancy. *Pediatrics, 93,* 228–233.

Olds, S. (in press). *That is our way.* Kathmandu, Nepal: Mandala Book Point.

Olds, S. W. (1989). *The working parents' survival guide.* Rocklin, CA: Prima.

Olmsted, P. P., & Weikart, D. P. (Eds.). (1994). *Family speak: Early childhood care and education in eleven countries.* Ypsilanti, MI: High/Scope.

Olsen-Fulero, L. (1982). Style and stability in mother conversational behavior: A study of individual differences. *Journal of Child Language, 9,* 543–564.

Opie, I., & Opie, P. (1969). *Children's games in street and playground.* London: Oxford University Press.

Orr, D. P., & Ingersoll, G. M. (1995). The contribution of level of cognitive complexity and pubertal timing to behavioral risk in young adolescents. *Pediatrics, 95,* 528–533.

Orr, R., & Luszcz, M. (1994). Rethinking women's ways: Gender commonalities and intersections with postformal thought. *Journal of Adult Development, 1,* 225–234.

Ortiz, A. D. (1996). *Eva Perón* (S. Fields, Trans.). New York: St. Martin's.

Oshima-Takane, Y., Goodz, E., & Derevensky, J. L. (1996). Birth order effects on early language development: Do secondborn children learn from overheard speech? *Child Development, 67,* 621–634.

Ostrea, E. M., & Chavez, C. J. (1979). Perinatal problems (excluding neonatal withdrawal) in maternal drug addiction: A study of 830 cases. *Journal of Pediatrics, 94*(2), 292–295.

O'Sullivan, J. T., Howe, M. L., & Marche, T. A. (1996). Children's beliefs about long-term retention. *Child Development, 67,* 2989–3009.

Oswald, P. F., & Peltzman, P. (1974). The cry of the human infant. *Scientific American, 230*(3), 84–90.

Padilla, A. M., Lindholm, K. J., Chen, A., Durán, R., Hakuta, K., Lambert, W., & Tucker, G. R. (1991). The English-only movement: Myths, reality, and implications for psychology. *American Psychologist, 46*(2), 120–130.

Palkovitz, R. (1985). Fathers' birth attendance, early contact, and extended contact with their newborns: A critical review. *Child Development, 56,* 392–406.

Pally, R. (1997). How brain development is shaped by genetic and environmental factors. *International Journal of Psycho-Analysis, 78,* 587–593.

Pan, W. H. L. (1994). Children's play in Taiwan. In J. L. Roopnarine, J. E. Johnson, & F. H. Hooper (Eds.), *Children's play in diverse cultures.* Albany: State University of New York Press.

Papalia, D. (1972). The status of several conservation abilities across the life-span. *Human Development, 15,* 229–243.

Papola, P., Alvarez, M., & Cohen, H. J. (1994). Developmental and service needs of school-age children with human immunodeficiency virus infection: A descriptive study. *Pediatrics, 94,* 914–918.

Papousek, H. (1959). A method of studying conditioned food reflexes in young children up to age six months. *Pavlovian Journal of Higher Nervous Activity, 9,* 136–140.

Papousek, H. (1960a). Conditioned motor alimentary reflexes in infants: 1. Experimental conditioned sucking reflex. *Ceskoslovenska Pediatrie, 15,* 861–872.

Papousek, H. (1960b). Conditioned motor alimentary reflexes in infants: 2. A new experimental method of investigation. *Ceskoslovenska Pediatrie, 15,* 981–988.

Papousek, H. (1961). Conditioned head rotation reflexes in infants in the first months of life. *Acta Paediatrica, 50,* 565–576.

Paris, S. G., & Lindauer, B. K. (1976). The role of inference in children's comprehension and memory for sentences. *Cognitive Psychology, 8,* 217–227.

Park, S., Belsky, J., Putnam, S., & Crnic, K. (1997). Infant emotionality, parenting, and 3-year inhibition: Exploring stability and lawful discontinuity in a male sample. *Developmental Psychology, 33,* 218–227.

Parke, R. (1977). Some effects of punishment on children's behavior—Revisited. In P. Cantor (Ed.), *Understanding a child's world.* New York: McGraw-Hill.

Parke, R. D., Grossman, K., & Tinsley, R. (1981). Father-mother-infant interaction in the newborn period: A German-American comparison. In T. M. Field, A. M. Sostek, P. Viete, & P. H. Leideman (Eds.), *Culture and early interaction.* Hillsdale, NJ: Erlbaum.

Parke, R. D., Ornstein, P. A., Rieser, J. J., & Zahn-Waxler, C. (1994). The past as prologue: An overview of a century of developmental psychology. In R. D. Parke, P. A. Ornstein, J. J. Rieser, & C. Zahn-Waxler (Eds.), *A century of developmental psychology* (pp. 1–70). Washington, DC: American Psychological Association.

Parke, R. D., & Tinsley, B. R. (1981). The father's role in infancy: Determinants of involvement in caregiving and play. In M. E. Lamb (Ed.), *The role of the father in child development* (2nd ed.). New York: Wiley.

Parker, J. G., & Asher, S. R. (1987). Peer relations and later personal adjustment: Are low-accepted children at risk? *Psychological Bulletin, 102,* 357–389.

Parker, J. G., & Herrera, C. (1996). Interpersonal processes in friendship: A comparison of abused and nonabused children's experiences. *Developmental Psychology, 32,* 1025–1038.

Parmelee, A. H. (1986). Children's illnesses: Their beneficial effects on behavioral development. *Child Development, 57,* 1–10.

Parmelee, A. H., Wenner, W. H., & Schulz, H. R. (1964). Infant sleep patterns: From birth to 16 weeks of age. *Journal of Pediatrics, 65,* 576.

Parmentier, M., Libert, F., Schurmans, S., Schiffmann, S., Lefort, A., Eggerickx, D., Mollereau, C., Gerard, C., Perret, J., et al. (1992). Expression of members of the putative olfactory receptor gene family in mammalian germ cells. *Nature, 355* (6359), 243–269.

Parrish, K. M., Holt, V. L., Easterling, T. R., Connell, F. A., & LeGerfo, J. P. (1994). Effect of changes in maternal age, parity, and birth weight distribution on primary cesarean delivery rates. *Journal of the American Medical Association, 271,* 443–447.

Parten, M. B. (1932). Social play among preschool children. *Journal of Abnormal and Social Psychology, 27,* 243–269.

Pasnak, R., Hansbarger, A., Dodson, S. L., Hart, J. B., & Blaha, J. (1996). Differential results of instruction at the preoperational/concrete operational transition. *Psychology in the Schools, 33,* 70–83.

Patterson, C. J. (1992). Children of lesbian and gay parents. *Child Development, 63,* 1025–1042.

Patterson, C. J. (1995a). Lesbian mothers, gay fathers, and their children. In A. R. D'Augelli & C. J. Patterson (Eds.), *Lesbian, gay, and bisexual identities over the lifespan: Psychological perspectives* (pp. 293–320). New York: Oxford University Press.

Patterson, C. J. (1995b). Sexual orientation and human development: An overview. *Developmental Psychology, 31,* 3–11.

Patterson, C. J., Kupersmidt, J. B., & Griesler, P. C. (1990). Children's perceptions of self and of relationships with others as a function of socioeconomic status. *Child Development, 61,* 1335–1349.

Patterson, G. R., DeBaryshe, B. D., & Ramsey, E. (1989). A developmental perspective on antisocial behavior. *American Psychologist, 44*(2), 329–335.

Patterson, G. R., Reid, J. B., & Dishion, T. J. (1992). *Antisocial boys.* Eugene, OR: Castalia.

Patterson, G. R., & Stouthamer-Loeber, M. (1984). The correlation of family management practices and delinquency. *Child Development, 55,* 1299–1307.

Pease, D., & Gleason, J. B. (1985). Gaining meaning: Semantic development. In J. B. Gleason (Ed.), *The development of language.* Columbus, OH: Merrill.

Pedersen, F. A., Cain, R., & Zaslow, M. (1982). Variation in infant experience associated with alternative family roles. In L. Laosa & I. Sigel (Eds.), *The family as a learning environment.* New York: Plenum.

Pedersen, F. A., Huffman, L. C., del Carmen, R., & Bryan, Y. E. (1996). Prenatal maternal reactivity to infant cries predicts postnatal perceptions of infant temperament and marriage appraisal. *Child Development, 67,* 2541–2552.

Pelleymounter, N. A., Cullen, M. J., Baker, M. B., Hecht, R., Winters, D., Boone, T., & Collins, F. (1995). Effects of the obese gene product on body regulation in ob/ob mice. *Science, 269,* 540–543.

Pepper, S. C. (1942). *World hypotheses.* Berkeley: University of California Press.

Perón, E. (1951). *La razón de mi vida.* Buenos Aires: Ediciones Peuser.

Peskin, H. (1967). Pubertal onset and ego functioning. *Journal of Abnormal Psychology, 72,* 1–15.

Peskin, H. (1973). Influence of the developmental schedule of puberty on learning and ego functioning. *Journal of Youth and Adolescence, 2,* 273–290.

Petersen, A. C. (1991, April). *American adolescence: How it affects girls.* Paper presented at the Gisela Konopka Lecture, University of Minnesota, Minneapolis.

Petersen, A. C. (1993). Presidential address: Creating adolescents: The role of context and process in developmental transitions. *Journal of Research on Adolescents, 3*(1), 1–18.

Petersen, A. C., Compas, B. E., Brooks-Gunn, J., Stemmler, M., Ey, S., & Grant, K. E. (1993). Depression in adolescence. *American Psychologist, 48* (2), 155–168.

Petersen, A. C., Kennedy, R. E., & Sullivan, P. (1991). Coping with adolescence. In M. E. Colten & S. Gore (Eds.), *Adolescent stress: Causes and consequences* (pp. 93–110). New York: Aldine de Gruyter.

Petersen, A. C., Sarigiani, P. A., & Kennedy, R. E. (1991). Adolescent depression: Why more girls? *Journal of Youth and Adolescence, 20,* 247–271.

Peterson, C., & Bell, M. (1996). Children's memory for traumatic injury. *Child Development, 67,* 3045–3070.

Peterson, C., & McCabe, A. (1994). A social interactionist account of developing decontextualized narrative skill. *Developmental Psychology, 30,* 937–948.

Petitto, L. A., & Marentette, P. F. (1991). Babbling in the manual mode: Evidence for the ontogeny of language. *Science, 251,* 1493–1495.

Phillips, D., McCartney, K., & Scarr, S. (1987). Child-care quality and children's social development. *Developmental Psychology, 23,* 537–543.

Phillips, R. B., Sharma, R., Premachandra, B. R., Vaughn, A. I., & Reyes-Lee, M. (1996). Intrauterine exposure to cocaine: Effect on neurobehavior of neonates. *Infant Behavior and Development, 19,* 71–81.

Phillips, S., & Sandstrom, K. L. (1990). Parental attitudes towards youth work. *Youth and Society, 22,* 160–183.

Phinney, J. S. (1993). Multiple group identities: Differentiation, conflict, and integration. In J. Kroger (Ed.), *Discussions on ego identity* (pp. 47–73). Hillsdale, NJ: Erlbaum.

Phinney, J. S., & Cobb, N. J. (1996). Reasoning about intergroup relations among Hispanic and Euro-American adolescents. *Journal of Adolescent Research, 11,* 306–324.

Piaget, J. (1929). *The child's conception of the world.* New York: Harcourt Brace.

Piaget, J. (1932). *The moral judgment of the child.* New York: Harcourt Brace.

Piaget, J. (1951). *Play, dreams, and imitation* (C. Gattegno & F. M. Hodgson, Trans.). New York: Norton.

Piaget, J. (1952). *The origins of intelligence in children.* New York: International Universities Press. (Original work published 1936)

Piaget, J. (1962). Comments on Vygotsky's critical remarks concerning *The Language and Thought of the Child* and *Judgment and Reasoning in the Child.* In L. S. Vygotsky (Ed.), *Thought and language.* Cambridge, MA: MIT Press.

Piaget, J. (1969). *The child's conception of time* (A. J. Pomerans, Trans.). London: Routledge & Kegan Paul.

Piaget, J., & Inhelder, B. (1967). *The child's conception of space.* New York: Norton.

Pickens, J., & Field, T. (1993). Facial expressivity in infants of depressed mothers. *Developmental Psychology, 29,* 986–988.

Pierce, J. P., Lee, L., & Gilpin, E. A. (1994). Smoking initiation by adolescent girls, 1944 through 1988: An association with targeted advertising. *Journal of the American Medical Association, 271,* 608–611.

Pillow, B. H., & Henrichon, A. J. (1996). There's more to the picture than meets the eye: Young children's difficulty understanding biased interpretation. *Child Development, 67,* 803–819.

Pine, D. S., Cohen, P., & Brook, J. (1996). Emotional problems during youth as predictors of stature during early adulthood: Results from a prospective epidemiologic study. *Pediatrics, 97,* 856–863.

Pirkle, J. L., Brody, D. J., Gunter, E. W., Kramer, R. A., Raschal, D. C., Flegal, K. M., & Matte, T. D. (1994). The decline in blood lead levels in the United States. *Journal of the American Medical Association, 272,* 284–291.

Pirkle, J. L., Flegal, K. M., Bernert, J. T., Brody, D. J., Etzel, R. A., & Maurer, K. R. (1996). Exposure of the U.S. population to environmental tobacco smoke: The Third National Health and Nutrition Examination Survey, 1988–1991. *Journal of the American Medical Association, 275,* 1233–1240.

Plomin, R. (1989). Environment and genes: Determinants of behavior. *American Psychologist, 44*(2), 105–111.

Plomin, R. (1990). The role of inheritance in behavior. *Science, 248,* 183–188.

Plomin, R. (1996). Nature and nurture. In M. R. Merrens & G. G. Brannigan (Eds.), *The developmental psychologist: Research adventures across the life span* (pp. 3–19). New York: McGraw-Hill.

Plomin, R., & Daniels, D. (1987). Why are children in the same family so different from one another? *Behavioral and Brain Sciences, 10,* 1–16.

Plomin, R., Owen, M. J., & McGuffin, P. (1994). The genetic bases of behavior. *Science, 264,* 1733–1739.

Plomin, R., & Rende, R. (1991). Human behavioral genetics. In M. R. Rosenzweig & L. W. Porter (Eds.), *Annual review of psychology* (Vol. 42). Palo Alto, CA: Annual Reviews, Inc.

Plumert, J., & Nichols-Whitehead, P. (1996). Parental scaffolding of young children's spatial communication. *Developmental Psychology, 32,* 523–532.

Plumert, J. M. (1995). Relations between children's overestimation of their physical abilities and accident proneness. *Developmental Psychology, 31,* 866–876.

Plumert, J. M., Pick, H. L., Jr., Marks, R. A., Kintsch, A. S., & Wegesin, D. (1994). Locating objects and communicating about locations: Organizational differences in children's searching and direction-giving. *Developmental Psychology, 30,* 443–453.

Polit, D. F., & Falbo, T. (1987). Only children and personality development: A quantitative review. *Journal of Marriage and the Family, 49,* 309–325.

Pollock, L. A. (1983). *Forgotten children.* Cambridge, England: Cambridge University Press.

Pong, S. L. (1997). Family structure, school context, and eighth-grade math and reading achievement. *Journal of Marriage and the Family, 59,* 734–746.

Pope, A. W., Bierman, K. L., & Mumma, G. H. (1991). Aggression, hyperactivity, and inattention-immaturity: Behavior dimensions associated with peer rejection in elementary school boys. *Developmental Psychology, 27,* 663–671.

Pope, H. G., Jr., & Hudson, J. I. (1992). Is childhood sexual abuse a risk factor for bulimia nervosa? (Review). *American Journal of Psychiatry, 149,* 455–463.

Pope, S. K., Whiteside, L., Brooks-Gunn, J., Kelleher, K. J., Rickert, V. I., Bradley, R. H., & Casey, P. H. (1993). Low-birth-weight infants born to adolescent mothers: Effects of coresidency with grandmother on child development. *Journal of the American Medical Association, 269,* 1396–1400.

Porac, C., & Coren, S. (1981). *Lateral preferences and human behavior.* New York: Springer-Verlag.

Portwood, S. G., & Repucci, N. D. (1996). Adults' impact on the suggestibility of preschoolers' recollections. *Journal of Applied Developmental Psychology, 17,* 175–198.

Posada, G., Gao, Y., Wu, F., Posada, R., Tascon, M., Schoelmerich, A., Sagi, A., Kondo-Ikemura, K., Haaland, W., & Synnevaag, B. (1995). The secure-base phenomenon across cultures: Children's behavior, mothers' preferences, and experts' concepts. In E. Waters, B. E. Vaughn, G. Posada, & K. Kondo-Ikemura (Eds.), Caregiving, cultural, and cognitive perspectives on secure-base behavior and working models: New growing points of attachment theory and research (pp. 27–48). *Monographs of the Society for Research in Child Development, 60*(2–3, Serial No. 244).

Posner, J. K., & Vandell, D. L. (n.d.). *Low-income children's afterschool care: Are there beneficial effects of afterschool programs?* Unpublished manuscript, University of Wisconsin—Madison.

Post, S. G. (1994). Ethical commentary: Genetic testing for Alzheimer's disease. *Alzheimer Disease and Associated Disorders, 8,* 66–67.

Povinelli, D. J., Landau, K. R., & Perilloux, H. K. (1996). Self-recognition in young children using delayed versus live feedback: Evidence of a developmental asynchrony. *Child Development, 67,* 1540–1554.

Powell, M. B., & Thomson, D. M. (1996). Children's memory of an occurrence of a repeated event: Effects of age, repetition, and retention interval across three question types. *Child Development, 67,* 1988–2004.

Power, T. G., & Chapieski, M. L. (1986). Childrearing and impulse control in toddlers: A naturalistic investigation. *Developmental Psychology, 22,* 271–275.

Powlishta, K. K., Serbin, L. A., Doyle, A. B., & White, D. R. (1994). Gender, ethnic, and body type biases: The generality of prejudice in childhood. *Developmental Psychology, 30,* 526–536.

Pratt, M. W., Kerig, P., Cowan, P. A., & Cowan, C. P. (1988). Mothers and fathers teaching 3-year-olds: Authoritative parenting and adult scaffolding of young children's learning. *Developmental Psychology, 24,* 832–839.

Prechtl, H. F. R., & Beintema, D. J. (1964). The neurological examination of the full-term newborn infant. *Clinics in Developmental Medicine* (No. 12). London: Heinemann.

Pressley, M. (1994). State-of-the-science primary-grades reading instruction or whole language? *Educational Psychologist, 29,* 211–215.

Preventing teenage pregnancy. (1996, October 4). *HHS fact sheet.* Washington, DC: U.S. Department of Health and Human Services.

Price, J. M. (1996). Friendships of maltreated children and adolescents: Contexts for expressing and modifying relationship history. In W. M. Bukowski, A. F. Newcomb, & W. W. Hartup (Eds.), *The company they keep: Friendship in childhood and adolescence* (pp. 262–285). New York: Cambridge University Press.

Pringle, H. F. (1931). *Theodore Roosevelt, a biography.* New York: Harcourt, Brace.

Pruett, K. D. (1987). *The nurturing father.* New York: Warner.

Pugliese, M. T., Weyman-Daum, M., Moses, N., & Lifschitz, F. (1987). Parental health beliefs as a cause of nonorganic failure to thrive. *Pediatrics, 80,* 175–182.

Pungello, E. P., Kupersmidt, J. B., Burchinal, M. R., & Patterson, C. J. (1996). Environmental risk factors and children's achievement from middle childhood to early adolescence. *Developmental Psychology, 32,* 755–767.

Purcell, J. H. (1995). Gifted education at a crossroads: The program status study. *Gifted Child Quarterly, 39*(2), 57–65.

Putnam, C. (1958). *Theodore Roosevelt: Vol. 1. The formative years.* New York: Scribner's.

Pynoos, R. S., Frederick, C., Nader, K., Arroyo, W., Steinberg, A., Eth, S., Nunez, F., & Fairbanks, L. (1987). Life threat and post-traumatic stress in school-age children. *Archives of General Psychiatry, 44,* 1057–1063.

Quadrel, M. J., Fischoff, B., & Davis, W. (1993). Adolescent (in)vulnerability. *American Psychologist, 48,* 102–116.

Quasha, S. (1980). *Albert Einstein: An intimate portrait.* Larchmont, NY: Forest.

Quinby, N. (1985, October). On testing and teaching intelligence: A conversation with Robert Sternberg. *Educational Leadership,* pp. 50–53.

Quintero, R. A., Abuhamad, A., Hobbins, J. C., & Mahoney, M. J. (1993). Transabdominal thin-gauge embryofetoscopy: A technique for early prenatal diagnosis and its use in the diagnosis of a case of Meckel-Gruber syndrome. *American Journal of Obstetrics and Gynecology, 168,* 1552–1557.

Rabiner, D., & Coie, J. (1989). Effect of expectancy induction on rejected peers' acceptance by unfamiliar peers. *Developmental Psychology, 25,* 450–457.

Racine, A., Joyce, T., & Anderson, R. (1993). The association between prenatal care and birth weight among women exposed to cocaine in New York City. *Journal of the American Medical Association, 270,* 1581–1586.

Raffaelli, M., & Larson, R. W. (1987). *Sibling interactions in late childhood and early adolescence.* Paper presented at the biennial meeting of the Society for Research in Child Development, Baltimore, MD.

Rafferty, Y., & Shinn, M. (1991). Impact of homelessness on children. *American Psychologist, 46*(11), 1170–1179.

Ragozin, A. S., Basham, R. B., Crnic, K. A., Greenberg, M. T., & Robinson, N. M. (1982). Effects of maternal age on parenting role. *Developmental Psychology, 18,* 627–634.

Ramey, C. T., & Campbell, F. A. (1991). Poverty, early childhood education, and academic competence. In A. Huston (Ed.), *Children reared in poverty* (pp. 190–221). Cambridge, England: Cambridge University Press.

Ramey, C. T., & Ramey, S. L. (1996). Early intervention: Optimizing development for children with disabilities and risk conditions. In M. Wolraich (Ed.), *Disorders of development and learning: A practical guide to assessment and management* (2nd ed., pp. 141–158). Philadelphia: Mosby.

Ramey, C. T., & Ramey, S. L. (1998). Early intervention and early experience. *American Psychologist, 53,* 109–120.

Ramey, C. T., & Ramey, S. L. (in press). Prevention of intellectual disabilities: Early interventions to improve cognitive development. *Preventive Medicine.*

Ramey, S. L., & Ramey, C. T. (1992). Early educational intervention with disadvantaged children—To what effect? *Applied and Preventive Psychology, 1,* 131–140.

Rampersad, A. (1997). *Jackie Robinson: A biography.* New York: Knopf.

Ramsey, P. G., & Lasquade, C. (1996). Preschool children's entry attempts. *Journal of Applied Developmental Psychology, 17,* 135–150.

Rapin, I. (1997). Autism. *New England Journal of Medicine, 337,* 97–104.

Rappaport, L. (1993). The treatment of nocturnal enuresis—Where are we now? *Pediatrics, 92,* 465–466.

Rates of homicide, suicide, and firearm-related death among children—26 industrialized countries. (1997, February 7). *Morbidity and Mortality Weekly Report, 46*(5), 101–105.

Ratner, H. H., & Foley, M. A. (1997, April). *Children's collaborative learning: Reconstructions of the other in the self.* Paper presented at the meeting of the Society for Research in Child Development, Washington, DC.

Rauh, J. L., Schumsky, D. A., & Witt, M. T. (1967). Heights, weights, and obesity in urban school children. *Child Development, 38,* 515–530.

Rauscher, F. H., Shaw, G. L., Levine, L. J., Wright, E. L., Dennis, W. R., & Newcomb, R. L. (1997). Music training causes long-term enhancement of preschool children's spatial-temporal reasoning. *Neurological Research, 19,* 2–8.

Ravitch, D. (1983). The education pendulum. *Psychology Today, 17*(10), 62–71.

Read, C. R. (1991). Gender distribution in programs for the gifted. *Roeper Review, 13,* 188–193.

Redding, R. E., Harmon, R. J., & Morgan, G. A. (1990). Maternal depression and infants' mastery behaviors. *Infant Behavior and Development, 113,* 391–396.

Rees, J. M., Lederman, S. A., & Kiely, J. L. (1996). Birth weight associated with lowest neonatal mortality: Infants of adolescent and adult mothers. *Pediatrics, 98,* 1161–1166.

Reese, E. (1995). Predicting children's literacy from mother-child conversations. *Cognitive Development, 10,* 381–405.

Reese, E., & Fivush, R. (1993). Parental styles of talking about the past. *Developmental Psychology, 29,* 596–606.

Reese, H. W. (1977). Imagery and associative memory. In R. V. Kali & J. W. Hagen (Eds.), *Perspectives on the development of memory and cognition.* Hillsdale, NJ: Erlbaum.

Reid, J. D. (1995). Development in late life: Older lesbian and gay life. In A. R. D'Augelli & C. J. Patterson (Eds.), *Lesbian, gay, and bisexual identities over the lifespan: Psychological perspectives* (pp. 215–240). New York: Oxford University Press.

Reid, J. R., Patterson, G. R., & Loeber, R. (1982). The abused child: Victim, instigator, or innocent bystander? In D. J. Berstein (Ed.), *Response structure and organization.* Lincoln: University of Nebraska Press.

Reijo, R., Alagappan, R. K., Patrizio, P., & Page, D. C. (1996). Severe oligozoospermia resulting from deletions of azoospermia factor gene on Y chromosome. *The Lancet, 347,* 1290–1293.

Reinisch, J. M., Sanders, S. A., Mortensen, E. L., Psych, C., & Rubin, D. B. (1995). In utero exposure to phenobarbital and intelligence deficits in adult men. *Journal of the American Medical Association, 274,* 1518–1525.

Reis, S. M. (1989). Reflections on policy affecting the education of gifted and talented students: Past and future perspectives. *American Psychologist, 44,* 399–408.

Reis, S. M. (1991). The need for clarification in research designed to examine gender differences in achievement and accomplishment. *Roeper Review, 13,* 193–198.

Remafedi, G., Resnick, M., Blum, R., & Harris, L. (1992). Demography of sexual orientation in adolescents. *Pediatrics, 89,* 714–721.

Renzulli, J. S., & McGreevy, A. M. (1984). *A study of twins included and not included in gifted programs.* Storrs: University of Connecticut, School of Education.

Repacholi, B. M., & Gopnik, A. (1997). Early reasoning about desires: Evidence from 14- and 18-month-olds. *Developmental Psychology, 33,* 12–21.

Rescorla, L. (1991). Early academics: Introduction to the debate. In L. Rescorla, M. C. Hyson, & K. Hirsh-Pasek (Eds.), *Academic instruction in early childhood: Challenge or pressure?* (New Directions for Child Development No. 53, pp. 5–11). San Francisco: Jossey-Bass.

Resnick, L. B. (1989). Developing mathematical knowledge. *American Psychologist, 44,* 162–169.

Resnick, M. D., Bearman, P. S., Blum, R. W., Bauman, K. E., Harris, K. M., Jones, J., Tabor, J., Beuhring, T., Sieving, R. E., Shew, M., Ireland, M., Bearinger, L. H., & Udry, J. R. (1997). Protecting adolescents from harm: Findings from the National Longitudinal Study on Adolescent Health. *Journal of the American Medical Association, 278,* 823–832.

Rest, J. R. (1975). Longitudinal study of the Defining Issues Test of moral judgment: A strategy for analyzing developmental change. *Developmental Psychology, 11,* 738–748.

Restak, R. (1984). *The brain.* New York: Bantam.

Reynolds, A. J. (1994). Effects of a preschool plus follow-on intervention for children at risk. *Developmental Psychology, 30,* 787–804.

Reynolds, C. R. (1988, Winter). Race differences in intelligence: Why the controversy. *MENSA Research Journal,* pp. 4–7.

Reznick, J. S., Kagan, J., Snidman, N., Gersten, M., Baak, K., & Rosenberg, A. (1986). Inhibited and uninhibited children: A follow-up study. *Child Development, 57,* 660–680.

Rheingold, H. L. (1985). Development as the acquisition of familiarity. *Annual Review of Psychology, 36,* 1–17.

Ricciuti, H. M. (1993). Nutrition and mental development. *Current Directions in Psychological Science, 2*(2), 43–46.

Rice, C., Koinis, D., Sullivan, K., Tager-Flusberg, H., & Winner, E. (1997). When 3-year-olds pass the appearance-reality test. *Developmental Psychology, 33,* 54–61.

Rice, M., Oetting, J. B., Marquis, J., Bode, J., & Pae, S. (1994). Frequency of input effects on SLI children's word comprehension. *Journal of Speech and Hearing Research, 37,* 106–122.

Rice, M. L. (1982). Child language: What children know and how. In T. M. Field, A. Huston, H. C. Quay, L. Troll, & G. E. Finley (Eds.), *Review of human development research.* New York: Wiley.

Rice, M. L. (1989). Children's language acquisition. *American Psychologist, 44*(2), 149–156.

Rice, M. L., Hadley, P. A., & Alexander, A. L. (1993). Social biases toward children with speech and language impairments: A correlative causal model of language limitations. *Applied Psycholinguistics, 14,* 445–471.

Rice, M. L., Huston, A. C., Truglio, R., & Wright, J. (1990). Words from "Sesame Street": Learning vocabulary while viewing. *Developmental Psychology, 26,* 421–428.

Rice, S. G. (1993). [Injury rates among high school athletes, 1979–1992]. Unpublished raw data.

Richards, M. H., Boxer, A. M., Petersen, A. C., & Albrecht, R. (1990). Relation of weight to body image in pubertal girls and boys from two communities. *Developmental Psychology, 26,* 313–321.

Richardson, D. W., & Short, R. V. (1978). Time of onset of sperm production in boys. *Journal of Biosocial Science, 5,* 15–25.

Richardson, J. L., Radziszewska, B., Dent, C. W., & Flay, B. R. (1993). Relationship between after-school care of adolescents and substance use, risk-taking, depressed mood, and academic achievement. *Pediatrics, 92,* 32–38.

Richardson, L. (1993, November 25). Adoptions that lack papers, not purpose. *The New York Times,* pp. C1, C6.

Richie, D. (1984). *The films of Akira Kurosawa.* Berkeley: University of California Press.

Riddle, R. D., Johnson, R. L., Laufer, E., & Tabin, C. (1993). Sonic hedgehog mediates the polarizing activity of the ZPA. *Cell, 75,* 1401–1416.

Rierdan, J., Koff, E., & Flaherty, J. (1986). Conceptions and misconceptions of menstruation. *Women and Health, 10*(4), 33–45.

Rieser, J., Yonas, A., & Wilkner, K. (1976). Radial localization of odors by human newborns. *Child Development, 47,* 856–859.

Ritalin improves behavior of ADHD children. (1995, October). *The Menninger Letter,* p. 3.

Rivara, F. P., Bergman, A. B., & Drake, C. (1989). Parental attitudes and practices toward children as pedestrians. *Pediatrics, 84,* 1017–1021.

Rivara, F. P., & Grossman, D. C. (1996). Prevention of traumatic deaths to children in the United States: How far have we come and where do we need to go? *Pediatrics, 97,* 791–798.

Roberts, G. C., Block, J. H., & Block, J. (1984). Continuity and change in parents' child-rearing practices. *Child Development, 55,* 586–597.

Roberts, I., Kramer, M., & Suissa, S. (1996). Does home visiting prevent childhood injury? A systematic review of randomized controlled trials. *British Medical Journal, 312,* 29–33.

Roberts, W., & Strayer, J. (1996). Empathy, emotional expressiveness, and prosocial behavior. *Child Development, 67,* 449–470.

Robertson, L. F. (1984, November). Why we went back to half-days. *Principal,* pp. 22–24.

Robins, R. W., John, O. P., Caspi, A., Moffitt, T. E., & Stouthamer-Loeber, M. (1996). Resilient, overcontrolled, and undercontrolled boys: Three replicable personality types. *Journal of Personality and Social Psychology, 70,* 157–171.

Robinson, I., Ziss, K., Ganza, B., Katz, S., & Robinson, E. (1991). Twenty years of the sexual revolution, 1965–1985: An update. *Journal of Marriage and the Family, 53,* 216–220.

Robinson, J. (as told to A. Duckett). (1995). *I never had it made.* Hopewell, NJ: Ecco.

Robinson, J. L., Kagan, J., Reznick, J. S., & Corley, R. (1992). The heritability of inhibited and uninhibited behavior: A twin study. *Developmental Psychology, 28,* 1030–1037.

Robinson, S. (1996). *Stealing home.* New York: HarperCollins.

Robison, L. L., Buckley, J. D., Daigle, A. E., Wells, R., Benjamin, D., Arthur, D. C., & Hammond, G. D. (1989). Maternal drug use and risk of childhood nonlymphoblastic leukemia among offspring. *Cancer, 63,* 1904–1911.

Roche, A. F. (1981). The adipocyte-number hypothesis. *Child Development, 52,* 31–43.

Rogers, M. F., White, C. R., Sanders, R., Schable, C., Ksell, T. E., Wasserman, R. L., Ballanti, J. A., Peters, S. M., & Wray, B. B. (1990). Lack of transmission of human immunodeficiency virus from infected children to their household contacts. *Pediatrics, 85,* 210–214.

Rogoff, B., Mistry, J., Göncü, A., & Mosier, C. (1993). Guided participation in cultural activity by toddlers and caregivers. *Monographs of the Society for Research in Child Development, 58* (8, Serial No. 236).

Rogoff, B., & Morelli, G. (1989). Perspectives on children's development from cultural psychology. *American Psychologist, 44,* 343–348.

Rome-Flanders, T., Cronk, C., & Gourde, C. (1995). Maternal scaffolding in mother-infant games and its relationship to language development: A longitudinal study. *First Language, 15,* 339–355.

Ronca, A. E., & Alberts, J. R. (1995). Maternal contributions to fetal experience and the transition from prenatal to postnatal life. In J. P. Lecanuet, W. P. Fifer, N. A. Krasnegor, & W. P. Smotherman (Eds.), *Fetal development: A psychobiological perspective* (pp. 331-350). Hillsdale, NJ: Erlbaum.

Roopnarine, J., & Field, T. (1984). Play interaction of friends and acquaintances in nursery school. In T. Field, J. Roopnarine, & M. Segal (Eds.), *Friendships in normal and handicapped children.* Norwood, NJ: Ablex.

Roopnarine, J., & Honig, A. S. (1985, September). The unpopular child. *Young Children,* pp. 59–64.

Roopnarine, J. L., Brown, J., Snell-White, P., & Riegraft, N. B. (1995). Father involvement in children and household work in common-law dual-earner and single-earner Jamaican families. *Journal of Applied Developmental Psychology 16* (1), 35–52.

Roopnarine, J. L., Hooper, F. H., Ahmeduzzaman, M., & Pollack, B. (1993). Gentle play partners: Mother-child and father-child play in New Delhi, India. In K. MacDonald (Ed.), *Parent-child play* (pp. 287–304). Albany: State University of New York Press.

Roopnarine, J. L., Talokder, E., Jain, D., Josh, P., & Srivastav, P. (1992). Personal well-being, kinship ties, and mother-infant and father-infant interactions in single-wage and dual-wage families in New Delhi, India. *Journal of Marriage and the Family, 54,* 293–301.

Roosevelt, T. (1900). *The strenuous life.* New York: Century.

Roosevelt, T. (1929). *Theodore Roosevelt: An autobiography.* New York: Scribner's.

Rose, R. M., Gordon, T. P., & Bernstein, I. S. (1972). Plasma testosterone levels in the male rhesus: Influences of sexual and social stimuli. *Science, 178*(4061), 643–645.

Rose, S. A. (1994). Relation between physical growth and information processing in infants born in India. *Child Development, 65,* 889–902.

Rose, S. A., & Feldman, J. F. (1995). Prediction of IQ and specific cognitive abilities at 11 years from infancy measures. *Developmental Psychology, 31,* 685–696.

Rose, S. A., & Feldman, J. F. (1997). Memory and speed: Their role in the relation of infant information processing to later IQ. *Child Development, 68,* 630–641.

Rosen, D. (1996, September 17). Attention deficit disorder. *HealthNews,* p. 4.

Rosenberg, H. M., Ventura, S. J., Maurer, J. D., Heuser, R. L., & Freedman, M. A. (1996). *Births and deaths: United States, 1995* (Monthly Vital Statistics Report, 45[3, Suppl. 2], DHHS Publication No. 96-1120). Hyattsville, MD: National Center for Health Statistics.

Rosenblatt, R. A., Dobie, S. A., Hart, L. G., Schneeweiss, R., Gould, D., Raine, T. R., Benedetti, T. J., Pirani, M. J., & Perrin, E. B. (1997). Interspeciality differences in the obstetric care of low risk women. *American Journal of Public Health, 87,* 344–351.

Rosenzweig, M. R. (1984). Experience, memory, and the brain. *American Psychologist, 39,* 365–376.

Rosenzweig, M. R., & Bennett, E. L. (Eds.). (1976). *Neural mechanisms of learning and memory.* Cambridge, MA: MIT Press.

Ross, G., Lipper, E. G., & Auld, P. A. M. (1991). Educational status and school-related abilities of very low birth weight premature children. *Pediatrics, 8,* 1125–1134.

Ross, H. S. (1996). Negotiating principles of entitlement in sibling property disputes. *Developmental Psychology, 32,* 90–101.

Rossel, C., & Ross, J. M. (1986). *The social science evidence on bilingual education.* Boston: Boston University Press.

Rossi, R. (1996, August 30). Small schools under microscope. *Chicago Sun-Times,* p. 24.

Rotenberg, K. J., & Eisenberg, N. (1997). Developmental differences in the understanding of and reaction to others' inhibition of emotional expression. *Developmental Psychology, 33,* 526–537.

Rothenberg, K., Fuller, B., Rothstein, M., Duster, T., Kahn, M. J. E., Cunningham, R., Fine, B., Hudson, K., King, M. C., Murphy, P., Swergold, G., & Collins, F. (1997). Genetic information and the workplace: Legislative approaches and policy challenges. *Science, 275,* 1755–1757.

Rothman, K. J., Moore, L. L., Singer, M. R., Nguyen, U. S., Mannino, S., & Milunsky, A. (1995). Teratogenicity of high vitamin A intake. *New England Journal of Medicine, 333,* 1369–1373.

Roush, W. (1995). Arguing over why Johnny can't read. *Science, 267,* 1896–1898.

Rovee-Collier, C. (1987). Learning and memory in infancy. In J. D. Osofsky (Ed.), *Handbook of infant development* (2nd ed.). New York: Wiley.

Rovee-Collier, C. (1996). Shifting the focus from what to why. *Infant Behavior and Development, 19,* 385–400.

Rovee-Collier, C., & Lipsitt, L. (1982). Learning, adaptation, and memory in the newborn. In P. Stratton (Ed.), *Psychobiology of the human newborn.* New York: Wiley.

Rovee-Collier, C., Schechter, A., Shyi, G., & Shields, P. (1992). Perceptual identification of contextual attributes and infant memory retrieval. *Developmental Psychology, 28,* 307–318.

Rubenstein, C. (1993, November 18). Child's play, or nightmare on the field? *The New York Times,* pp. C1, C10.

Rubin, D. H., Erickson, C. J., San Agustin, M., Cleary, S. D., Allen, J. K., & Cohen, P. (1996). Cognitive and academic functioning of homeless children compared with housed children. *Pediatrics, 97,* 289–294.

Rubin, D. H., Krasilnikoff, P. A., Leventhal, J. M., Weile, B., & Berget, A. (1986, August 23). Effect of passive smoking on birth-weight. *The Lancet,* pp. 415–417.

Rubin, K. (1982). Nonsocial play in preschoolers: Necessary evil? *Child Development, 53,* 651–657.

Rubin, K. H., Fein, G. G., & Vandenberg, B. (1983). Play. In P. H. Mussen (Series Ed.) & E. M. Hetherington (Vol. Ed.), *Handbook of child psychology: Vol. 4. Socialization, personality, and social development* (pp. 694–774). New York: Wiley.

Ruble, D. M., & Brooks-Gunn, J. (1982). The experience of menarche. *Child Development, 53,* 1557–1566.

Rueter, M. A., & Conger, R. D. (1995). Antecedents of parent-adolescent disagreements. *Journal of Marriage and the Family, 57,* 435–448.

Ruff, H. A., Bijur, P. E., Markowitz, M., Ma, Y. C., & Rosen, J. F. (1993). Declining blood lead levels and cognitive changes in moderately lead-poisoned children. *Journal of the American Medical Association, 269,* 1641–1646.

Rule, S. (1981, June 11). The battle to stem school dropouts. *The New York Times,* pp. A1, B10.

Russell, A., & Finnie, V. (1990). Preschool children's social status and maternal instructions to assist group entry. *Developmental Psychology, 26,* 603–611.

Rutter, M. (1979a). Maternal deprivation, 1972–1978: New findings, new concepts, new approaches. *Child Development, 50,* 283–305.

Rutter, M. (1979b). Separation experiences: A new look at an old topic. *Pediatrics, 95,* 147–154.

Rutter, M. (1983). Stress, coping, and development: Some issues and some questions. In N. Garmezy & M. Rutter (Eds.), *Stress, coping, and development in children.* New York: McGraw-Hill.

Rutter, M. (1987). Continuities and discontinuities from infancy. In J. Osofsky (Ed.), *Handbook of infant development.* New York: Wiley.

Ryan, A. S. (1997). The resurgence of breastfeeding in the United States. *Pediatrics* [On-line], *99.* Available: http://www.pediatrics.org/cgi/content/full/99/4/e12

Sabatelli, R. M., Meth, R. L., & Gavazzi, S. M. (1988). Factors mediating the adjustment to involuntary childlessness. *Family Relations, 37,* 338–343.

Sachs, B. P., McCarthy, B. J., Rubin, G., Burton, A., Terry, J., & Tyler, C. W. (1983). Cesarean section. *Journal of the American Medical Association, 250*(16), 2157–2159.

Sadowitz, P. D., & Oski, F. A. (1983). Iron status and infant feeding practices in an urban ambulatory center. *Pediatrics, 72,* 33–36.

Sagan, C. (1977). The dragons of Eden: Speculations on the evolution of human intelligence. New York: Random House.

Sagi, A., & Hoffman, M. (1976). Empathic distress in newborns. *Developmental Psychology, 12,* 175–176.

Saigal, S., Feeny, D., Rosenbaum, P., Furlong, W., Burrows, E., & Stoskopf, B. (1996). Self-perceived health status and health-related quality of life of extremely low-birth-weight infants at adolescence. *Journal of the American Medical Association, 276,* 453–459.

Salzinger, S., Feldman, R. S., Hammer, M., & Rosario, M. (1993). Effects of physical abuse on children's social relations. *Child Development, 64,* 169–187.

Sameroff, A. J., Seifer, R., Baldwin, A., & Baldwin, C. (1993). Stability of intelligence from preschool to adolescence: The influence of social and family risk factors. *Child Development, 64,* 80–97.

Sandberg, D. E., Brook, A. E., & Campos, S. P. (1994). Short stature: A psychosocial burden requiring growth hormone therapy? *Pediatrics, 94,* 832–840.

Sandler, D. P., Everson, R. B., Wilcox, A. J., & Browder, J. P. (1985). Cancer risk in adulthood from early life exposure to parents' smoking. *American Journal of Public Health, 75,* 487–492.

Santer, L. J., & Stocking, C. B. (1991). Safety practices and living conditions of low-income urban families. *Pediatrics, 88,* 111–118.

Santrock, J. W., Sitterle, K. A., & Warshak, R. A. (1988). Parent-child relationships in stepfather families. In P. Bronstein & C. P. Cowan (Eds.), *Fatherhood today: Men's changing role in the family.* New York: Wiley.

Sapienza, C. (1990, October). Parental imprinting of genes. *Scientific American,* pp. 52–60.

Sauer, M. V., Paulson, R. J., & Lobo, R. A. (1990). A preliminary report on oocyte donation extending the reproductive potential to women over forty. *New England Journal of Medicine, 323,* 1157–1160.

Sauer, M. V., Paulson, R. J., & Lobo, R. A. (1993). Pregnancy after age 50: Application of oocyte donation to women after natural menopause. *The Lancet, 341,* 321–323.

Saunders, N. (1997, March). Pregnancy in the 21st century: Back to nature with a little assistance. *The Lancet, 349,* s17–s19.

Savage, S. L., & Au, T. K. (1996). What word learners do when input contradicts the mutual exclusivity assumption. *Child Development, 67,* 3120–3134.

Sax, L. J., Astin, L. W., Korn, W. F., & Mahoney, K. M. (1996). *The American freshman: Norms for fall, 1995.* Los Angeles: UCLA Higher Education Institute.

Saxe, G. B., Guberman, S. R., & Gearhart, M. (1987). Social processes in early number development. *Monographs of the Society for Research in Child Development, 52*(216).

Saywitz, K. J., Goodman, G. S., Nicholas, E., & Moan, S. F. (1991). Children's memories of a physical examination involving genital touch: Implications for reports of child sexual abuse. *Journal of Consulting and Clinical Psychology, 59,* 682–691.

Scarborough, H. S. (1990). Very early language deficits in dyslexic children. *Child Development, 61,* 1728–1743.

Scariati, P. D., Grummer-Strawn, L. M., & Fein, S. B. (1997a). A longitudinal analysis of infant morbidity and the extent of breastfeeding in the United States. *Pediatrics, 99,* e5.

Scariati, P. D., Grummer-Strawn, L. M., & Fein, S. B. (1997b). Water supplementation of infants in the first month of life. *Archives of Pediatric and Adolescent Medicine, 151,* 830–832.

Scarr, S. (1992). Developmental theories for the 1990s: Development and individual differences. *Child Development, 63,* 1–19.

Scarr, S. (1993). Biological and cultural diversity: The legacy of Darwin for development. *Child Development, 64,* 1333–1353.

Scarr, S. (1997). Behavior-genetics and socialization theories of intelligence: Truce and reconciliation. In R. J. Sternberg & E. Grigorenko (Eds.), *Intelligence, heredity, and environment* (pp. 3–41). Cambridge, England: Cambridge University Press.

Scarr, S., & McCartney, K. (1983). How people make their own environments: A theory of genotype→environment effects. *Child Development, 54,* 424–435.

Scarr, S., & Weinberg, R. (1983). The Minnesota Adoption Study: Genetic differences and malleability. *Child Development, 54,* 260–264.

Schacter, D. L. (1992). Understanding implicit memory: A cognitive neuroscience approach. *American Psychologist, 47,* 559–569.

Schanberg, S. M., & Field, T. M. (1987). Sensory deprivation illness and supplemental stimulation in the rat pup and preterm human neonate. *Child Development, 58,* 1431–1447.

Schauble, L. (1996). The development of scientific reasoning in knowledge-rich contexts. *Developmental Psychology, 32,* 102–119.

Schechtman, V. L., Harper, R. M., Wilson, A. J., & Southall, D. P. (1992). Sleep state organization in normal infants and victims of the sudden infant death syndrome. *Pediatrics, 89,* 865–870.

Schendel, D. E., Berg, C. J., Yeargin-Allsopp, M., Boyle, C. A., & Decoufle, P. (1996). Prenatal magnesium sulfate exposure and the risk for cerebral palsy or mental retardation among very low-birthweight children aged 3 to 5 years. *Journal of the American Medical Association, 276,* 1805–1810.

Scherer, M. (1985, January). How many ways is a child intelligent? *Instructor,* pp. 32–35.

Schilpp, P. A. (1970). *Albert Einstein: Philosopher-scientist* (3rd ed.). La Salle, IL: Open Court. (Original work published 1949)

Schindler, P. J., Moely, B. E., & Frank, A. L. (1987). Time in day care and social participation in young children. *Developmental Psychology, 23,* 255–261.

Schizophrenia update—Part I. (1995, June). *The Harvard Mental Health Letter,* pp. 1–4.

Schmitt, B. D., & Kempe, C. H. (1983). Abused and neglected children. In R. E. Behrman & V. C. Vaughn (Eds.), *Nelson textbook of pediatrics* (12th ed.). Philadelphia: Saunders.

Schmitz, S., Saudino, K. J., Plomin, R., Fulker, D. W., & DeFries, J. C. (1996). Genetic and environmental influences on temperament in middle childhood: Analyses of teacher and tester ratings. *Child Development, 67,* 409–422.

Schoendorf, K. C., Hogue, C. J. R., Kleinman, J. C., & Rowley, D. (1992). Mortality among infants of black as compared with white college-educated parents. *New England Journal of Medicine, 326,* 1522–1526.

Schoendorf, K. C., & Kiely, J. L. (1992). Relationship of sudden infant death syndrome to maternal smoking. *Pediatrics, 90,* 905–908.

Scholer, S. J., Mitchel, E. F., & Ray, W. A. (1997). Predictors of injury mortality in early childhood. *Pediatrics, 100,* 342–347.

Schonfeld, D. J., Johnson, S. R., Perrin, E. C., O'Hare, L. L., & Cicchetti, D. V. (1993). Understanding of acquired immunodeficiency syndrome by elementary school children—A developmental survey. *Pediatrics, 92,* 389–395.

Schor, E. L. (1987). Unintentional injuries: Patterns within families. *American Journal of the Diseases of Children, 141,* 1280.

Schreiber, J. B., Robins, M., Striegel-Moore, R., Obarzanek, E., Morrison, J. A., & Wright, D. J. (1996). Weight modification efforts reported by preadolescent girls. *Pediatrics, 96,* 63–70.

Schulman, S. (1986). Facing the invisible handicap. *Psychology Today, 20*(2), 58–64.

Schvaneveldt, J. D., Lindauer, S. L. K., & Young, M. H. (1990). Children's understanding of AIDS: A developmental viewpoint. *Family Relations, 39,* 330–335.

Schwartz, D., Dodge, K. A., & Coie, J. D. (1993). The emergence of chronic peer victimization in boys' play groups. *Child Development, 64,* 1755–1772.

Schweinhart, L. J., Barnes, H. V., & Weikart, D. P. (1993). *Significant benefits: The High/Scope Perry Preschool Study through age 27* (Monographs of the High/Scope Educational Research Foundation No. 10). Ypsilanti, MI: High/Scope.

Schweinhart, L. J., Weikart, D. P., & Larner, M. B. (1986). A report on the High/Scope preschool curriculum comparison study. *Early Childhood Research Quarterly, 1,* 15–45.

Sears, R. R., Maccoby, E. E., & Levin, H. (1957). *Patterns of child rearing.* New York: Harper & Row.

Sedlak, A. J., & Broadhurst, D. D. (1996). *Executive summary of the third national incidence study of child abuse and neglect* (NIS-3). Washington, DC: U.S. Department of Health and Human Services.

Seifer, R., Schiller, M., Sameroff, A. J., Resnick, S., & Riordan, K. (1996). Attachment, maternal sensitivity, and infant temperament during the first year of life. *Developmental Psychology, 32,* 12–25.

Seiner, S. H., & Gelfand, D. M. (1995). Effects of mother's simulated withdrawal and depressed affect on mother-toddler interactions. *Child Development, 60,* 1519–1528.

Seitz, V. (1990). Intervention programs for impoverished children: A comparison of educational and family support models. *Annals of Child Development, 7,* 73–103.

Selman, R. L. (1980). *The growth of interpersonal understanding: Developmental and clinical analyses.* New York: Academic.

Selman, R. L., & Selman, A. P. (1979, April). Children's ideas about friendship: A new theory. *Psychology Today,* pp. 71–80.

Serbin, L. A., Moller, L. C., Gulko, J., Powlishta, K. K., & Colburne, K. A. (1994). The emergence of gender segregation in toddler playgroups. In C. Leaper (Ed.), *Childhood gender segregation: Causes and consequences* (New Directions for Child Development No. 65, pp. 7–17). San Francisco: Jossey-Bass.

Sexton, M., & Hebel, R. (1984). A clinical trial of change in maternal smoking and its effect on birth weight. *Journal of the American Medical Association, 251*(7), 911–915.

Shafer, M. B., & Moscicki, A. (1991). Sexually transmitted disease. In W. R. Hendee (Ed.), *Health of adolescents: Understanding and facilitating biological behavior and social development* (pp. 211–249). San Francisco: Jossey-Bass.

Shanahan, M. J., Finch, M. D., Mortimer, J. T., & Ryu, S. (1991). Adolescent work experience and depressive affect. *Social Psychology Quarterly, 54,* 299–317.

Shannon, B. M., Tershakovec, A. M., Martel, J. K., Achterberg, C. L., Cortner, J. A., Smiciklas-Wright, H. S., Stallings, V. A., & Stolley, P. D. (1994). Reduction of elevated LDL-cholesterol levels of 4- to 10-year-old children through home-based dietary education. *Pediatrics, 94,* 923–927.

Shannon, D. C., & Kelly, D. H. (1982a). SIDS and near-SIDS (Part 1). *New England Journal of Medicine, 306*(16), 959–965.

Shannon, D. C., & Kelly, D. H. (1982b). SIDS and near-SIDS (Part 2). *New England Journal of Medicine, 306*(17), 1022–1028.

Shannon, L. W. (1982). *Assessing the relationship of adult criminal careers to juvenile careers.* Iowa City: University of Iowa, Iowa Urban Community Research Center.

Shatz, M., & Gelman, R. (1973). The development of communication skills: Modifications in the speech of young children as a function of listener. *Monographs of the Society for Research in Child Development, 38*(5, Serial No. 152).

Shaw, G. M., Velie, E. M., & Schaffer, D. (1996). Risk of neural tube defect-affected pregnancies among obese women. *Journal of the American Medical Association, 275,* 1093–1096.

Shaw, G. M., Wasserman, C. R., Lammer, E. J., O'Malley, C. D., Murray, J. C., Basart, A. M., & Tolarova, M. M. (1996). Orofacial clefts, parental cigarette smoking, and transforming growth factor-alpha gene variants. *American Journal of Human Genetics, 58,* 551–561.

Shaywitz, B. A., Sullivan, C. M., Anderson, G. M., Gillespie, S. M., Sullivan, B., & Shaywitz, S. E. (1994). Aspartame, behavior, and cognitive function in children with attention deficit disorder. *Pediatrics, 93,* 70–75.

Shaywitz, S. E., Shaywitz, B. A., Fletcher, J. M., & Escobar, M. D. (1990). Prevalence of reading disability in boys and girls. *Journal of the American Medical Association, 246*(8), 998–1002.

Shea, S., Basch, C. E., Stein, A. D., Contento, I. R., Irigoyen, M., & Zybert, P. (1993). Is there a relationship between dietary fat and stature or growth in children three to five years of age? *Pediatrics, 92,* 579–586.

Sheps, S., & Evans, G. D. (1987). Epidemiology of school injuries: A 2-year experience in a municipal health department. *Pediatrics, 79,* 69–75.

Shields, P. J., & Rovee-Collier, C. (1992). Long-term memory for context-specific category information at six months. *Child Development, 63,* 245–259.

Shiono, P. H., & Behrman, R. E. (1995). Low birth weight: Analysis and recommendations. *The Future of Children, 5*(1), 4–18.

Shu, X.-O., Ross, J. A., Pendergrass, T. W., Reaman, G. H., Lampkin, B., & Robison, L. L. (1996). Prenatal alcohol consumption, cigarette smoking, and risk of infant leukemia: A Children's Cancer Group Study. *Journal of the National Cancer Institute, 88,* 24–31.

Siegel, O. (1982). Personality development in adolescence. In B. B. Wolman (Ed.), *Handbook of developmental psychology.* Englewood Cliffs, NJ: Prentice-Hall.

Siegler, R. S. (1991). *Children's thinking* (2nd ed.). Englewood Cliffs, NJ: Prentice-Hall.

Siegler, R. S., & Richards, D. (1982). The development of intelligence. In R. Sternberg (Ed.), *Handbook of human intelligence.* London: Cambridge University Press.

Sigelman, C., Alfeld-Liro, C., Derenowski, E., Durazo, O., Woods, T., Maddock, A., & Mukai, T. (1996). Mexican-American and Anglo-American children's responsiveness to a theory-centered AIDS education program. *Child Development, 67,* 253–266.

Sigman, M., Cohen, S. E., & Beckwith, L. (1997). Why does infant attention predict adolescent intelligence? *Infant Behavior and Development, 20,* 133–140.

Sigman, M., Neumann, C., Jansen, A. A. J., & Bwibo, N. (1989). Cognitive abilities of Kenyan children in relation to nutrition, family characteristics, and education. *Child Development, 60,* 1463–1474.

Sigman, M. D., Kasari, C., Kwon, J. H., & Yirmiya, N. (1992). Responses to the negative emotions of others by autistic, mentally retarded, and normal children. *Child Development, 63,* 796–807.

Silverman, W. K., La Greca, A. M., & Wasserstein, S. (1995). What do children worry about? Worries and their relation to anxiety. *Child Development, 66,* 671–686.

Simmons, R. G., Blyth, D. A., & McKinney, K. L. (1983). The social and psychological effect of puberty on white females. In J. Brooks-Gunn & A. C. Petersen (Eds.), *Girls at puberty: Biological and psychological perspectives.* New York: Plenum.

Simmons, R. G., Blyth, D. A., Van Cleave, E. F., & Bush, D. M. (1979). Entry into early adolescence: The impact of school structure, puberty, and early dating on self-esteem. *American Sociological Review, 44*(6), 948–967.

Simmons, R. G., Burgeson, R., Carlton-Ford, S., & Blyth, D. A. (1987). The impact of cumulative change in early adolescence. *Child Development, 58,* 1220–1234.

Simner, M. L. (1971). Newborn's response to the cry of another infant. *Developmental Psychology, 5,* 135–150.

Simon, T. J., Hespos, S. J., & Rochat, P. (1995). Do infants understand simple arithmetic: A replication of Wynn (1992). *Cognitive Development, 10,* 253–269.

Simon-Rusinowitz, L., Krach, C. A., Marks, L. N., Piktialis, D., & Wilson, L. B. (1996). Grandparents in the workplace: The effects of economic and labor trends. *Generations, 20*(1), 41–44.

Simons-Morton, B. G., McKenzie, T. J., Stone, E., Mitchell, P., Osganian, V., Strikmiller, P. K., Ehlinger, S., Cribb, P., & Nader, P. R. (1997). Physical activity in a multiethnic population of third graders in four states. *American Journal of Public Health, 87,* 45–50.

Simonton, D. K. (1990). Creativity and wisdom in aging. In J. E. Birren & K. W. Schaie (Eds.), *Handbook of the psychology of aging* (pp. 320–329). New York: Academic Press.

Simpson, G., Bloom, B., Cohen, R. A., & Parsons, E. (1997). Access to health care: Part 1. Children. *Vital and Health Statistics* (Series 10; data from National Health Survey No. 196, DHHS Publication No. PHS 97-1524). Hyattsville, MD: U.S. Department of Health and Human Services.

Simpson, G. A., & Fowler, M. G. (1994). Geographic mobility and children's emotional/behavioral adjustment and school functioning. *Pediatrics, 93,* 303–309.

Simpson, G. B., & Foster, M. R. (1986). Lexical ambiguity and children's word recognition. *Developmental Psychology, 22,* 147–154.

Simpson, G. B., & Lorsbach, T. C. (1983). The development of automatic and conscious components of contextual facilitation. *Child Development, 54,* 760–772.

Simpson, J. L., & Elias, S. (1993). Isolating fetal cells from maternal blood: Advances in prenatal diagnosis through molecular technology. *Journal of the American Medical Association, 270,* 2357–2361.

Singer, D. G., & Singer, J. L. (1990). *The house of make-believe: Play and the developing imagination.* Cambridge, MA: Harvard University Press.

Singer, J. L., & Singer, D. G. (1981). *Television, imagination, and aggression: A study of preschoolers.* Hillsdale, NJ: Erlbaum.

Singer, L. T., Yamashita, T. S., Hawkins, S., Cairns, D., Baley, J., & Kliegman, R. (1994). Increased incidence of intraventricular hemorrhage and developmental delay in cocaine-exposed, very low birth weight infants. *Journal of Pediatrics, 124,* 765–771.

Singer, M. I., Anglin, T. M., Song, L. Y., & Lunghofer, L. (1995). Adolescents' exposure to violence and associated symptoms of psychological trauma. *Journal of the American Medical Association, 273,* 477–482.

Singh, S., Forrest, J. D., & Torres, A. (1989). *Prenatal care in the United States: A state and country inventory.* New York: Alan Guttmacher Institute.

Skadberg, B. T., Morild, I., & Markestad, T. (1998). Abandoning prone sleeping: Effect on the risk of sudden infant death syndrome. *Journal of Pediatrics, 132,* 340–343.

Skinner, B. F. (1938). *The behavior of organisms: An experimental approach.* New York: Appleton-Century.

Skinner, B. F. (1957). *Verbal behavior.* New York: Appleton-Century-Crofts.

Skinner, D. (1989). The socialization of gender identity: Observations from Nepal. In J. Valsiner (Ed.), *Child development in cultural context* (pp. 181–192). Toronto: Hogrefe & Huber.

Skolnick, A. A. (1993). 'Female athlete triad' risk for women. *Journal of the American Medical Association, 270,* 921–923.

Skuse, D. H., James, R. S., Bishop, D. V. M., Coppin, B., Dalton, P., Aamodt-Leeper, G., Bacarese-Hamilton, M., Creswell, C., McGurk, R., & Jacobs, P. A. (1997). Evidence from Turner's syndrome of an imprinted X-linked locus affecting cognitive function. *Nature, 387,* 705–708.

Slap, G. B., Vorters, D. F., Chaudhuri, S., & Centor, R. M. (1989). Risk factors for attempted suicide during adolescence. *Pediatrics, 84,* 762–772.

Slobin, D. (1971). Universals of grammatical development in children. In W. Levett & G. B. Flores d'Arcais (Eds.), *Advances in psycholinguistic research.* Amsterdam: New Holland.

Slobin, D. (1973). Cognitive prerequisites for the acquisition of language. In C. Ferguson & D. Slobin (Eds.), *Studies of child language development.* New York: Holt, Rinehart, & Winston.

Slobin, D. (1983). Universal and particular in the acquisition of grammar. In E. Wanner & L. Gleitman (Eds.), *Language acquisition: The state of the art.* Cambridge, England: Cambridge University Press.

Slomkowski, C., & Dunn, J. (1996). Young children's understanding of other people's beliefs and feelings and their connected communication with friends. *Developmental Psychology, 32,* 442–447.

Slomkowski, C. L., Nelson, K., Dunn, J., & Plomin, R. (1992). Temperament and language: Relations from toddlerhood to middle childhood. *Developmental Psychology, 28,* 1090–1095.

Small, M. Y. (1990). *Cognitive development.* New York: Harcourt Brace.

Smetana, J. G., & Bitz, B. (1996). Adolescents' conceptions of teachers' authority and their relations to rule violations in school. *Child Development, 67,* 1153–1172.

Smetana, J. G., Yau, J., Restrepo, A., & Braeges, J. L. (1991). Adolescent-parent conflict in married and divorced families. *Developmental Psychology, 27,* 1000–1010.

Smilansky, S. (1968). *The effects of sociodramatic play on disadvantaged preschool children.* New York: Wiley.

Smith, B. A., & Blass, E. M. (1996). Taste-mediated calming in premature, preterm, and full-term human infants. *Developmental Psychology, 32,* 1084–1089.

Smith, D. W., & Brodzinsky, D. M. (1994). Stress and coping in adopted children: A developmental study. *Journal of Clinical Child Psychology, 23*(1), 91–99.

Smith, M. M., & Lifshitz, F. (1994). Excess fruit juice consumption as a contributing factor in nonorganic failure to thrive. *Pediatrics, 93,* 438–443.

Smith, T. E. (1981). Adolescent agreement with perceived maternal and paternal educational goals. *Journal of Marriage and the Family, 43,* 85–93.

Smoll, F. L., & Schutz, R. W. (1990). Quantifying gender differences in physical performance: A developmental perspective. *Developmental Psychology, 26,* 360–369.

Smotherman, W. P., & Robinson, S. R. (1995). Tracing developmental trajectories into the prenatal period. In J. P. Lecanuet, W. P. Fifer, N. A. Krasnegor, & W. P. Smotherman (Eds.), *Fetal development: A psychobiological perspective* (pp. 15–32). Hillsdale, NJ: Erlbaum.

Smotherman, W. P., & Robinson, S. R. (1996). The development of behavior before birth. *Developmental Psychology, 32,* 425–434.

Snarey, J. R. (1985). Cross-cultural universality of social-moral development: A critical review of Kohlbergian research. *Psychological Bulletin, 97,* 202–232.

Snow, C. E. (1972). Mother's speech to children learning language. *Child Development, 43,* 549–565.

Snow, C. E. (1977). Mother's speech research: From input to interaction. In C. E. Snow & C. A. Ferguson (Eds.), *Talking to children: Language input and acquisition.* London: Cambridge University Press.

Snow, C. E. (1990). The development of definitional skill. *Journal of Child Language, 17,* 697–710.

Snow, C. E. (1993). Families as social contexts for literacy development. In C. Daiute (Ed.), *The development of literacy through social interaction* (New Directions for Child Development No. 61, pp. 11–24). San Francisco: Jossey-Bass.

Snow, C. E., Arlman-Rupp, A., Hassing, Y., Jobse, J., Jootsen, J., & Verster, J. (1976). Mother's speech in three social classes. *Journal of Psycholinguistic Research, 5,* 1–20.

Snow, M. E., Jacklin, C. N., & Maccoby, E. E. (1983). Sex-of-child differences in father-child interaction at one year of age. *Child Development, 54,* 227–232.

Snyder, J., West, L., Stockemer, V., Gibbons, S., & Almquist-Parks, L. (1996). A social learning model of peer choice in the natural environment.

Journal of Applied Developmental Psychology, 17, 215–237.

Society for Assisted Reproductive Technology, The American Fertility Society. (1993). Assisted reproductive technology in the United States and Canada: 1991 results from the Society for Assisted Reproductive Technology generated from The American Fertility Society Registry. *Fertility and Sterility, 59,* 956–962.

Society for Research in Child Development. (1993). Ethical standards for research with children. In *Directory of members* (pp. 337–339). Ann Arbor, MI: Author.

Solomons, H. (1978). The malleability of infant motor development. *Clinical Pediatrics, 17*(11), 836–839.

Sommers-Flanagan, J., & Sommers-Flanagan, R. (1996). Efficacy of antidepressant medication with depressed youth: What psychologists should know. *Professional Psychology: Research & Practice, 27,* 145–153.

Sonenstein, F. L., Pleck, J. H., & Ku, L. C. (1991). Levels of sexual activity among adolescent males in the United States. *Family Planning Perspectives, 23*(4), 162–167.

Song, M., & Ginsburg, H. P. (1987). The development of informal and formal mathematical thinking in Korean and U.S. children. *Child Development, 58,* 1286–1296.

Song of freedom: Marian Anderson broke barriers by touching hearts. (1993, April 26). *People Weekly,* p. 126.

Sontag, L. W. (1966). Implications of fetal behavior and environment for adult personality. *Annals of the New York Academy of Science, 134,* 782–786.

Sontag, L. W., & Richards, T. W. (1938). Studies in fetal behavior: Fetal heart rate as a behavioral indicator. *Child Development Monographs, 3* (Whole No. 4).

Sontag, L. W., & Wallace, R. I. (1934). Preliminary report on the Fels fund: A study of fetal activity. *American Journal of Diseases of Children, 48,* 1050–1057.

Sontag, L. W., & Wallace, R. I. (1936). Changes in the heart rate of the human fetal heart in response to vibratory stimuli. *American Journal of Diseases of Children, 51,* 583–589.

Sophian, C. (1988). Early developments in children's understanding of number: Inferences about numerosity and one-to-one correspondence. *Child Development, 59,* 1397–1414.

Sorce, J. F., Emde, R. N., Campos, J., & Klinnert, M. D. (1985). Maternal emotional signalling: Its effect on the visual cliff behavior of 1-year-olds. *Developmental Psychology, 21,* 195–200.

Sorensen, T., Nielsen, G., Andersen, P., & Teasdale, T. (1988). Genetic and environmental influence of premature death in adult adoptees. *New England Journal of Medicine, 318,* 727–732.

Sosin, D. M., Sacks, J. J., & Webb, K. W. (1996). Pediatric head injuries and death from bicycling, United States. *Pediatrics, 98,* 868–870.

Southall, D. P., Plunkett, M. C. B., Banks, M. W., Falkov, A. F., & Samuels, M. P. (1997). Covert video recordings of life-threatening child abuse: Lessons for child protection. *Pediatrics, 100,* 735–760.

Spelke, E. (1994). Initial knowledge: Six suggestions. *Cognition, 50,* 431–445.

Spencer, M. B., & Markstrom-Adams, C. (1990). Identity processes among racial and ethnic minority children. *Child Development, 61,* 290–310.

Sperling, R. S., Shapiro, D. E., Coombs, R. W., Todd, J. A., Herman, S. A., McSherry, G. D., O'Sullivan, M. J., Van Dyke, R. B., Jimenez, E., Rouzioux, C., Flynn, P. M., & Sullivan, J. L. (1996). Maternal viral load, zidovudine treatment, and the risk of transmission of human immunodeficiency virus type 1 from mother to infant. *New England Journal of Medicine, 335,* 1621–1629.

Spieker, S., & Bensley, L. (1994). Roles of living arrangements and grandmother social support in adolescent mothering and infant attachment. *Developmental Psychology, 30,* 102–111.

Spiker, D., Ferguson, J., & Brooks-Gunn, J. (1993). Enhancing the maternal interactive behavior and child social competence in low birth weight, premature infants. *Child Development, 64,* 754–768.

Spitz, M. R., & Johnson, C. C. (1985). Neuroblastoma and paternal occupation: A case-control analysis. *American Journal of Epidemiology, 121*(6), 924–929.

Spitz, R. A. (1945). Hospitalism: An inquiry into the genesis of psychiatric conditioning in early childhood. In D. Fenschel et al. (Eds.), *Psychoanalytic studies of the child* (Vol. 1, pp. 53–74). New York: International Universities Press.

Spitz, R. A. (1946). Hospitalism: A follow-up report. In D. Fenschel et al. (Eds.), *Psychoanalytic studies of the child* (Vol. 1, pp. 113–117). New York: International Universities Press.

Spock, B., & Rothenberg, M. B. (1992). *Baby and child care* (6th ed.). New York: Dutton.

Spohr, H. L., Willms, J., & Steinhausen, H.-C. (1993). Prenatal alcohol exposure and long-term developmental consequences. *The Lancet, 341,* 907–910.

Squire, L. R. (1992). Memory and the hippocampus: A synthesis of findings with rats, monkeys, and humans. *Psychological Review, 99,* 195–231.

Sroufe, L. A. (1977). Wariness of strangers and the study of infant development. *Child Development, 48,* 731–746.

Sroufe, L. A. (1979). Socioemotional development. In J. Osofsky (Ed.), *Handbook of infant development.* New York: Wiley.

Sroufe, L. A. (1983). Individual patterns of adaptation from infancy to preschool. In M. Perlmutter (Ed.), *Proceedings of the Minnesota Symposium on Child Psychology.* Hillsdale, NJ: Erlbaum.

Sroufe, L. A., Bennett, C., Englund, M., Urban, J., & Shulman, S. (1993). The significance of gender boundaries in preadolescence: Contemporary correlates and antecedents of boundary violation and maintenance. *Child Development, 64,* 455–466.

Sroufe, L. A., Carlson, E., & Shulman, S. (1993). Individuals in relationships: Development from infancy through adolescence. In D. C. Funder, R. D. Parke, C. Tomlinson-Keasey, & K. Widaman (Eds.), *Studying lives through time: Personality and development* (pp. 315–342). Washington, DC: American Psychological Association.

Sroufe, L. A., Fox, N. E., & Pancake, V. R. (1983). Attachment and dependency in a developmental perspective. *Child Development, 54,* 1615–1627.

Sroufe, L. A., & Waters, E. (1976). The ontogenesis of smiling and laughter: A perspective on the organization of development in infancy. *Psychological Review, 83,* 173–189.

Sroufe, L. A., & Wunsch, J. (1972). The development of laughter in the first year of life. *Child Development, 43,* 1326–1344.

St. James-Roberts, I., & Plewis, I. (1996). Individual differences, daily fluctuations, and developmental changes in amounts of infant waking, fussing, crying, feeding, and sleeping. *Child Development, 67,* 2527–2540.

Stack, S. (1994). The effect of geographic mobility on premarital sex. *Journal of Marriage and the Family, 56,* 204–208.

Stager, C. L., & Werker, J. F. (1997). Infants listen for more phonetic detail in speech perception than in word-learning tasks. *Nature, 388,* 381–382.

Stahl, S. A., McKenna, M. C., & Pagnucco, J. R. (1994). The effects of whole-language instruction: An update and a reappraisal. *Educational Psychologist, 29,* 175–185.

Stahl, S. A., & Miller, P. D. (1989). Whole language and language experience approaches for beginning reading: A quantitative research synthesis. *Review of Educational Research, 59,* 87–116.

Stainton, M. C. (1985). The fetus: A growing member of the family. *Family Relations, 34,* 321–326.

Starfield, B. (1991). Childhood morbidity: Comparisons, clusters, and trends. *Pediatrics, 88,* 519–526.

Starfield, B., Katz, H., Gabriel, A., Livingston, G., Benson, P., Hankin, J., Horn, S., & Steinwachs, D. (1984). Morbidity in childhood—a longitudinal view. *New England Journal of Medicine, 310,* 824–829.

Staub, S. (1973). *The effect of three types of relationships on young children's memory for pictorial stimulus pairs.* Unpublished doctoral dissertation, Harvard University Graduate School of Education, Cambridge, MA.

Stedman, L. C., & Kaestle, C. E. (1987). Literacy and reading performance in the United States from 1880 to the present. *Reading Research Quarterly, 22,* 8–46.

Steel, L. (1991). Early work experience among white and non-white youths: Implications for subsequent enrollment and employment. *Youth and Society, 22,* 419–447.

Steinberg, L. (1981). Transformations in family relations at puberty. *Developmental Psychology, 17,* 833–840.

Steinberg, L. (1987). Impact of puberty on family relations: Effect of pubertal status and pubertal timing. *Developmental Psychology, 23,* 451–460.

Steinberg, L. (1988). Reciprocal relation between parent-child distance and pubertal maturation. *Developmental Psychology, 24,* 122–128.

Steinberg, L., & Darling, N. (1994). The broader context of social influence in adolescence. In R. Silberstein & E. Todt (Eds.), *Adolescence in context.* New York: Springer.

Steinberg, L., Dornbusch, S. M., & Brown, B. B. (1992). Ethnic differences in adolescent achievement: An ecological perspective. *American Psychologist, 47,* 723–729.

Steinberg, L., Fegley, S., & Dornbusch, S. M. (1993). Negative impact of part-time work on adolescent adjustment: Evidence from a longitudinal study. *Developmental Psychology, 29,* 171–180.

Steinberg, L., Lamborn, S. D., Dornbusch, S. M., & Darling, N. (1992). Impact of parenting practices on adolescent achievement: Parenting, school involvement, and encouragement to succeed. *Child Development, 47,* 723–729.

Steiner, J. E. (1979). Human facial expressions in response to taste and smell stimulation. *Advances in Child Development and Behavior, 13,* 257.

Steptoe, A., & Butler, N. (1996). Sports participation and emotional wellbeing in adolescents. *The Lancet, 347,* 1789–1792.

Stern, M., & Hildebrandt, K. A. (1986). Prematurity stereotyping: Effects on mother-infant interaction. *Child Development, 57,* 308–315.

Sternberg, R. J. (1984, September). How can we teach intelligence? *Educational Leadership,* pp. 38–50.

Sternberg, R. J. (1985a). *Beyond IQ: A triarchic theory of human intelligence.* New York: Cambridge University Press.

Sternberg, R. J. (1985b, November). Teaching critical thinking, Part I: Are we making critical mistakes? *Phi Delta Kappan,* pp. 194–198.

Sternberg, R. J. (1986). *Intelligence applied: Understanding and increasing your intellectual skills.* San Diego: Harcourt Brace.

Sternberg, R. J. (1987, September 23). The use and misuse of intelligence testing: Misunderstanding meaning, users over-rely on scores. *Education Week,* pp. 22, 28.

Sternberg, R. J. (1993). *Sternberg Triarchic Abilities Test.* Unpublished manuscript.

Sternberg, R. J. (1997). The concept of intelligence and its role in lifelong learning and success. *American Psychologist, 52,* 1030–1037.

Sternberg, R. J., & Clinkenbeard, P. (1995). A triarchic view of identifying, teaching, and assessing gifted children. *Roeper Review, 17,* 255–260.

Sternberg, R. J., Torff, B., & Grigorenko, E. L. (1997). *Teaching triarchically improves school achievement.* Manuscript submitted for publication.

Stevens, J. H., & Bakeman, R. (1985). A factor analytic study of the HOME scale for infants. *Developmental Psychology, 21,* 1106–1203.

Stevenson, D. L., & Baker, D. P. (1987). The family-school relation and the child's school performance. *Child Development, 58,* 1348–1357.

Stevenson, H. W. (1982). Influences of schooling on cognitive development. In H. W. Stevenson & D. A. Wagner (Eds.), *Cultural perspectives on child development* (pp. 208–224). San Francisco: W. H. Freeman.

Stevenson, H. W. (1995). Mathematics achievement of American students: First in the world by the year 2000? In C. A. Nelson (Ed.), *The Minnesota Symposia on Child Psychology: Vol. 28. Basic and applied perspectives on learning, cognition, and development* (pp. 131–149). Mahwah, NJ: Erlbaum.

Stevenson, H. W., Chen, C., & Lee, S. Y. (1993). Mathematics achievement of Chinese, Japanese, and American children: Ten years later. *Science, 258* (5081), 53–58.

Stevenson, H. W., Lee, S., Chen, C., & Lummis, M. (1990). Mathematics achievement of children in China and the United States. *Child Development, 61,* 1053–1066.

Stevenson, H. W., Lee, S. Y., Chen, C., Stigler, J. W., Hsu, C. C., & Kitamura, S. (1990). Contexts of achievement: A study of American, Chinese, and Japanese children. *Monographs of the Society for Research in Child Development, 55*(1–2, Serial No. 221).

Stevenson, H. W., Stigler, J. W., Lee, S., Lucker, G. W., Kitamura, S., & Hsu, C. (1985). Cognitive performance and academic achievement of Japanese, Chinese, and American children. *Child Development, 56,* 718–734.

Stevenson, M. R., & Black, K. N. (1988). Paternal absence and sex-role development: A meta-analysis. *Child Development, 59,* 793–814.

Steward, M. S., & Steward, D. S. (1996). Interviewing young children about body touch and handling. *Monographs of the Society for Research in Child Development, 61*(4–5, Serial No. 248).

Stewart, I. C. (1994, January 29). Two-part message [Letter to the editor]. *The New York Times,* p. A18.

Stewart, R. B. (1983). Sibling attachment relationships: Child-infant interactions in the strange situation. *Developmental Psychology, 19,* 192–199.

Stewart, W., & Barling, J. (1996). Fathers' work experiences effect children's behaviors via job-related affect and parenting behaviors. *Journal of Organizational Behavior, 17,* 221–232.

Stick, S. M., Burton, P. R., Gurrin, L., Sly, P. D., & LeSouëf, P. N. (1996). Effects of maternal smoking during pregnancy and a family history of asthma on respiratory function in newborn infants. *The Lancet, 348,* 1060–1064.

Stifter, C. A., Coulehan, C. M., & Fish, M. (1993). Linking employment to attachment: The mediating effects of maternal separation anxiety and interactive behavior. *Child Development, 64,* 1451–1460.

Stigler, J. W., Lee, S., & Stevenson, H. W. (1987). Mathematics classrooms in Japan, Taiwan, and the United States. *Child Development, 58,* 1272–1285.

Stipek, D., Feiler, R., Daniels, D., & Milburn, S. (1995). Effect of different instructional approaches on young children's achievement and motivation. *Child Development, 66,* 209–233.

Stipek, D. J., Gralinski, H., & Kopp, C. B. (1990). Self-concept development in the toddler years. *Developmental Psychology, 26,* 972–977.

Stipek, D. J., & Ryan, R. H. (1997). Economically disadvantaged preschoolers: Ready to learn but further to go. *Developmental Psychology, 33,* 711–723.

Stocker, C., Dunn, J., & Plomin, R. (1989). Sibling relationships: Links with child temperament, maternal behavior, and family structure. *Child Development, 60,* 715–727.

Stolberg, S. G. (1997, May 16). Senate tries to define fetal viability: Murky concepts still clouding the debate over abortion laws. *The New York Times,* p. A18.

Stoneman, Z., & Brody, G. H. (1993). Sibling temperaments, conflict, warmth, and role asymmetry. *Child Development, 64,* 1786–1800.

Strasburger, V. C. (1992). Children, adolescents, and television. *Pediatrics Review, 13,* 144–151.

Straus, M. A. (1994). *Beating the devil out of them: Corporal punishment in American families.* San Francisco: Jossey-Bass/Lexington.

Straus, M. A., & Donnelly, D. A. (1993). Corporal punishment of adolescents by American parents. *Youth and Society, 24,* 419–442.

Straus, M. A., Sugarman, D. B., & Giles-Sims, J. (1997). Spanking by parents and subsequent antisocial behavior of children. *Archives of Pediatric and Adolescent Medicine, 151,* 761–767.

Strauss, M., Lessen-Firestone, J., Starr, R., & Ostrea, E. (1975). Behavior of narcotics-addicted newborns. *Child Development, 46,* 887–893.

Strawn, J. (1992). The states and the poor: Child poverty rises as the safety net shrinks. *Social Policy Report of the Society for Research in Child Development, 6*(3).

Streissguth, A. P., Aase, J. M., Clarren, S. K., Randels, S. P., LaDue, R. A., & Smith, D. F. (1991). Fetal alcohol syndrome in adolescents and adults. *Journal of the American Medical Association, 265,* 1961–1967.

Streissguth, A. P., Martin, D. C., Barr, H. M., Sandman, B. M., Kirchner, G. L.,

& Darby, B. L. (1984). Intrauterine alcohol and nicotine exposure: Attention and reaction time in 4-year-old children. *Developmental Psychology, 20,* 533–541.

Streitfeld, D. (1997, July 13). Sad story. *Washington Post,* p. F1.

Strom, R., Collinsworth, P., Strom, S., & Griswold, D. (1992–1993). Strengths and needs of black grandparents. *International Journal of Aging and Human Development, 36,* 255–268.

Strömland, K., & Hellström, A. (1996). Fetal alcohol syndrome—An ophthalmological and socioeducational prospective study. *Pediatrics, 97,* 845–850.

Stubbs, M. L., Rierdan, J., & Koff, E. (1989). Developmental differences in menstrual attitudes. *Journal of Early Adolescence , 9*(4), 480–498.

Stunkard, A., Harris, J. R., Pedersen, N. L., & McClearn, G. E. (1990). The body-mass index of twins who have been reared apart. *New England Journal of Medicine, 322*(21), 1483–1487.

Stunkard, A. J., Foch, T. T., & Hrubec, Z. (1986). A twin study of human obesity. *Journal of the American Medical Association, 256*(1), 51–54.

Sue, S., & Okazaki, S. (1990). Asian-American educational achievements: A phenomenon in search of an explanation. *American Psychologist, 45* (8), 913–920.

Suicide—Part I. (1996, November). *The Harvard Mental Health Letter,* pp. 1–5.

Sullivan-Bolyai, J., Hull, H. F., Wilson, C., & Corey, L. (1983). Neonatal herpes simplex virus infection in King County, Washington. *Journal of the American Medical Association, 250,* 3059–3062.

Suomi, S., & Harlow, H. (1972). Social rehabilitation of isolate-reared monkeys. *Developmental Psychology, 6,* 487–496.

Susman-Stillman, A., Kalkoske, M., Egeland, B., & Waldman, I. (1996). Infant temperament and maternal sensitivity as predictors of attachment security. *Infant Behavior and Development, 19,* 33–47.

Swain, I. U., Zelazo, P. R., & Clifton, R. K. (1993). Newborn infants' memory for speech sounds retained over 24 hours. *Developmental Psychology, 29,* 312–323.

Swanston, H. Y., Tebbutt, J. S., O'Toole, B. I., & Oates, R. K. (1997). Sexually abused children 5 years after presentation: A case-control study. *Pediatrics, 100,* 600–608.

Swarr, A. E., & Richards, M. H. (1996). Longitudinal effects of adolescent girls' pubertal development, perceptions of pubertal timing, and parental relations on eating problems. *Developmental Psychology, 32,* 636–646.

Swedo, S., Rettew, D. C., Kuppenheimer, M., Lum, D., Dolan, S., & Goldberger, E. (1991). Can adolescent suicide attemptors be distinguished from at-risk adolescents? *Pediatrics, 88,* 620–629.

Sweetland, J. D., & DeSimone, P. A. (1987). Age of entry, sex, and academic achievement in elementary school children. *Psychology in the Schools, 24,* 406–412.

Symons, D. (1978). *Play and aggression: A study of rhesus monkeys.* New York: Columbia University Press.

Tabor, A., Philip, J., Masden, M., Bang, J., Obel, E. B., & Norgaard-Pedersen, B. (1986, June 7). Randomized controlled trial of genetic amniocentesis in 4606 low-risk women. *The Lancet,* pp. 1287–1293.

Taddio, A., Katz, J., Ilersich, A. L., & Koren, G. (1997). Effect of neonatal circumcision on pain response during subsequent routine vaccination. *The Lancet, 349,* 599–603.

Takanishi, R. (1993). The opportunities of adolescence—Research, interventions, and policy. *American Psychologist, 48,* 85–87.

Tallal, P., Miller, S. L., Bedi, G., Byma, G., Wang, X., Nagarajan, S. S., Schreiner, C., Jenkins, W. M., & Merzenich, M. M. (1996). Language comprehension in language-learning impaired children improved with acoustically modified speech. *Science, 271,* 81–84.

Tamis-LeMonda, C. S., & Bornstein, M. H. (1993). Antecedents of exploratory competence at one year. *Infant Behavior and Development, 16*(4), 423–440.

Tanda, G., Pontieri, F. E., & DiChiara, G. (1997). Cannabinoid and heroin activation of mesolimbic dopamine transmission by a common N_1 opiod receptor mechanism. *Science, 276,* 2048–2050.

Tanfer, K., & Horn, M. C. (1985). Contraceptive use, pregnancy and fertility patterns among single American women in their 20's. *Family Planning Perspectives, 17*(1), 10–19.

Tanner, J. M. (1973). Growing up. *Scientific American, 229*(3), 35–43.

Tanner, J. M. (1978). *Fetus into man: Physical growth from conception to maturity.* Cambridge, MA: Harvard University Press.

Tanner, J. M. (1989). *Fetus into man: Physical growth from conception to maturity* (2nd ed.). Cambridge, MA: Harvard University Press.

Tardif, T. (1996). Nouns are not always learned before verbs: Evidence from Mandarin speakers' early vocabularies. *Developmental Psychology, 32,* 492–504.

Tashman, B. (1995, August). Misreading dyslexia: Researchers debate the causes and prevalence of the disorder. *Scientific American,* pp. 14, 16.

Taylor, J. A., Krieger, J. W., Reay, D. T., Davis, R. L., Harruff, R., & Cheney, L. K. (1996). Prone sleep position and the sudden infant death syndrome in King's County, Washington: A case-control study. *Journal of Pediatrics, 128,* 626–630.

Taylor, J. A., & Sanderson, M. (1995). A reexamination of the risk factors for sudden infant death syndrome. *Journal of Pediatrics, 126,* 887–891.

Taylor, J. M. (1979). *Eva Perón: The myths of a woman.* Chicago: University of Chicago Press.

Taylor, M., Cartwright, B. S., & Carlson, S. M. (1993). A developmental investigation of children's imaginary companions. *Developmental Psychology, 28*, 276–285.

Taylor, M. G. (1996). The development of children's beliefs about social and biological aspects of gender differences. *Child Development, 67*, 1555–1571.

Taylor, R. D. (1996). Adolescents' perceptions of kinship support and family management practices: Association with adolescent adjustment in African American families. *Developmental Psychology, 32*, 687–695.

Taylor, R. D., & Roberts, D. (1995). Kinship support in maternal and adolescent well-being in economically disadvantaged African-American families. *Child Development, 66*, 1585–1597.

Taylor, W. R., & Newacheck, P. W. (1992). Impact of childhood asthma on health. *Pediatrics, 90*, 657–662.

Teachman, J. D., Paasch, K., & Carver, K. (1996). Social capital and dropping out of school early. *Journal of Marriage and the Family, 58*, 773–783.

Teen sex down, new study shows: Secretary Shalala announces new teen pregnancy prevention grant programs [Press release]. (1997, May 1). Washington, DC: National Center for Health Statistics.

Teicher, M. H., Ito, Y., Glod, C. A., & Barber, N. I. (1996). Objective measurements of hyperactivity and attention problems in ADHD. *Journal of the American Academy of Child and Adolescent Psychiatry, 35*(3), 334–342.

Teller, D. Y., & Bornstein, M. H. (1987). Infant color vision and color perception. In P. Salapatek & L. B. Cohen (Eds.), *Handbook of infant perception: Vol. 1. From sensation to perception* (pp. 185–236). Orlando, FL: Academic Press.

Terman, D. L., Larner, M. B., Stevenson, C. S., & Behrman, R. E. (1996). Special education for students with disabilities. *The Future of Children, 6*(1), 4–24.

Terman, L. M., & Oden, M. H. (1959). *Genetic studies of genius: Vol. 5. The gifted group at mid-life.* Stanford, CA: Stanford University Press.

Termine, N. T., & Izard, C. E. (1988). Infants' responses to their mothers' expressions of joy and sadness. *Developmental Psychology, 24*, 223–229.

Terry, D. (1996, August 17). In Wisconsin, a rarity of a fetal-harm case: Attempted-murder charges for alcoholic. *The New York Times*, p. 6.

Tesman, J. R., & Hills, A. (1994). Developmental effects of lead exposure in children. *Social Policy Report* (Society for Research in Child Development), *8*(3), 1–16.

Tessler, M. (1986). *Mother-child talk in a museum: The socialization of a memory.* Unpublished manuscript, City University of New York, Graduate Center.

Tessler, M. (1991). *Making memories together: The influence of mother-child joint encoding on the development of autobiographical memory style.* Unpublished doctoral dissertation, City University of New York, Graduate Center.

Test-tube baby: It's a girl. (1978, August 7). *Time*, p. 68.

Teti, D. M., & Ablard, K. E. (1989). Security of attachment and infant-sibling relationships: A laboratory study. *Child Development, 60*, 1519–1528.

Teti, D. M., Gelfand, D. M., Messinger, D. S., & Isabella, R. (1995). Maternal depression and the quality of early attachment: An examination of infants, preschoolers, and their mothers. *Developmental Psychology, 31*, 364–376.

Teti, D. M., Sakin, J. W., Kucera, E., Corns, K. M., & Eiden, R. D. (1996). And baby makes four: Predictors of attachment security among preschool-age firstborns during the transition to siblinghood. *Child Development, 67*, 579–596.

Thacker, S. B., Addiss, D. G., Goodman, R. A., Holloway, B. R., & Spencer, H. C. (1992). Infectious diseases and injuries in child day care: Opportunities for healthier children. *Journal of the American Medical Association, 268*, 1720–1726.

Tharp, R. G. (1989). Psychocultural variables and constants: Effects on teaching and learning in schools. *American Psychologist, 44*, 349–359.

Thelen, E. (1995). Motor development: A new synthesis. *American Psychologist, 50* (2), 79–95.

Thelen, E., & Fisher, D. M. (1982). Newborn stepping: An explanation for a "disappearing" reflex. *Developmental Psychology, 18*, 760–775.

Thelen E., & Fisher, D. M. (1983). The organization of spontaneous leg movements in newborn infants. *Journal of Motor Behavior, 15*, 353–377.

Thomas, A., & Chess, S. (1977). *Temperament and development.* New York: Brunner/Mazel.

Thomas, A., & Chess, S. (1984). Genesis and evolution of behavioral disorders: From infancy to early adult life. *American Journal of Orthopsychiatry, 141* (1), 1–9.

Thomas, A., Chess, S., & Birch, H. G. (1968). *Temperament and behavior disorders in children.* New York: New York University Press.

Thomas, D. G., & Lykins, M. S. (1995). Event-related potential measures of 24-hour retention in 5-month-old infants. *Developmental Psychology, 31*, 946–957.

Thomas, R. M. (1996). *Comparing theories of child development* (4th ed.). Pacific Grove, CA: Brooks-Cole.

Thomas, W. P., & Collier, V. P. (1995). *Language minority student achievement and program effectiveness.* Manuscript in preparation.

Thompson, B., Wasserman, J. D., Gyurke, J. S., Matula, K., Mitchell, J. H., & Carr, B. (1994, January). *The validity of mental and motor scores from the new Bayley Scales of Infant Development—II: A second-order factor analysis.* Paper presented at the annual meeting of the Southwest Educational Research Association, San Antonio, TX.

Thompson, D. C., Rivara, F. P., & Thompson, R. S. (1996). Effectiveness of bicycle safety helmets in preventing head injuries: A case-control study. *Journal of the American Medical Association, 276*, 1968–1973.

Thompson, L. A., Fagan, J. F., & Fulker, D. W. (1991). Longitudinal prediction of specific cognitive abilities from infant novelty preference. *Child Development, 62*, 530–538.

Thompson, R. S., Rivara, F. P., & Thompson, D. C. (1989). A case-control study of the effectiveness of bicycle safety helmets. *New England Journal of Medicine, 320*, 1361–1367.

Thorne, A., & Michaelieu, Q. (1996). Situating adolescent gender and self-esteem with personal memories. *Child Development, 67*, 1374–1390.

Tiedemann, D. (1897). *Beobachtungen über die entwickelung der seelenfähigkeiten bei kindern* [Record of an infant's life]. Altenburg, Germany: Oscar Bonde. (Original work published 1787)

Timiras, P. S. (1972). *Developmental psychology and aging.* New York: Macmillan.

Tinsley, B. J., & Parke, R. D. (1987). Grandparents as interactive and social support agents for families with young children. *International Journal of Aging and Human Development, 25*(4), 259–277.

Tisak, M. S., & Tisak, J. (1996). My sibling's but not my friend's keeper: Reasoning about responses to aggressive acts. *Journal of Early Adolescence, 16*, 324–339.

Tisdale, S. (1988). The mother. *Hippocrates, 2*(3), 64–72.

Tobin, J. J., Wu, D. Y. H., & Davidson, D. H. (1989). *Preschools in three cultures: Japan, China, and the United States.* New Haven: Yale University Press.

Tobin-Richards, M. H., Boxer, A. M., McKavrell, S. A., & Petersen, A. C. (1984). Puberty and its psychological and social significance. In R. M. Lerner & N. L. Galambos (Eds.), *Experiencing adolescence: A sourcebook for parents, teachers, and teens.* New York: Garland.

Tobin-Richards, M. H., Boxer, A. M., & Petersen, A. C. (1983). The psychological significance of pubertal change: Sex differences in perceptions of self during early adolescence. In J. Brooks-Gunn & A. C. Petersen (Eds.), *Girls at puberty: Biological, social, and psychological perspectives.* New York: Plenum.

Tomasello, M., Mannle, S., & Kruger, A. C. (1986). Linguistic environment of 1- and 2-year-old twins. *Developmental Psychology, 22*, 169–176.

Toner, B. B., Garfinkel, P. E., & Garner, D. M. (1986). Long-term follow-up of anorexia nervosa. *Psychosomatic Medicine, 48*(7), 520–529.

Torrance, E. P. (1966). *The Torrance Tests of Creative Thinking: Technical-norms manual* (Research ed.). Princeton, NJ: Personnel Press.

Torrance, E. P. (1974). *The Torrance Tests of Creative Thinking: Technical-norms manual*. Bensonville, IL: Scholastic Testing Service.

Torrance, E. P., & Ball, O. E. (1984). *Torrance Tests of Creative Thinking: Streamlined (revised) manual, Figural A and B*. Bensonville, IL: Scholastic Testing Service.

Tramontana, M. G., Hooper, S. R., & Selzer, S. C. (1988). Research on the preschool prediction of later academic achievement: A review. *Developmental Review, 8*, 89–146.

Treffers, P. E., Eskes, M., Kleiverda, G., & van Alten, D. (1990). Home births and minimal medical interventions. *Journal of the American Medical Association, 246*(17), 2203, 2207–2208.

Trehub, S. E., Unyk, A. M., Kamanetsky, S. B., Hill, D. S., Trainor, L. J., Henderson, J. L., & Saraza, M. (1997). Mothers' and fathers' singing to infants. *Developmental Psychology, 33*, 500–507.

Tronick, E. (1972). Stimulus control and the growth of the infant's visual field. *Perception and Psychophysics, 11*, 373–375.

Tronick, E. Z. (1980). On the primacy of social skills. In D. B. Sawin, L. O. Walker, & J. H. Penticuff (Eds.), *The exceptional infant: Psychosocial risk in infant environment transactions*. New York: Brunner/Mazel.

Tronick, E. Z. (1989). Emotions and emotional communication in infants. *American Psychologist, 44*(2), 112–119.

Tronick, E. Z., Frank, D. A., Cabral, H., Mirochnick, M., & Zuckerman, B. (1996). Late dose-response effects of prenatal cocaine exposure on newborn neurobehavioral performance. *Pediatrics, 98*, 76–83.

Tronick, E. Z., & Gianino, A. F. (1986). The transmission of maternal depression to the infant. In E. Z. Tronick & T. Field (Eds.), *Maternal depression and infancy disturbance*. San Francisco: Jossey-Bass.

Tronick, E. Z., Morelli, G. A., & Ivey, P. (1992). The Efe forager infant and toddler's pattern of social relationships: Multiple and simultaneous. *Developmental Psychology, 28*, 568–577.

Trotter, R. J. (1983). Baby face. *Psychology Today, 17*(8), 14–20.

Tubman, J. G., Windle, M., & Windle, R. C. (1996). The onset and cross-temporal patterning of sexual intercourse in middle adolescence: Prospective relations with behavior and emotional problems. *Child Development, 67*, 327–343.

Tucker, C. J., Barber, B. L., & Eccles, J. S. (1997). Advice about life plans and personal problems in late adolescent sibling relationships. *Journal of Youth and Adolescence, 26*, 63–76.

Tuma, J. M. (1989). Mental health services for children: The state of the art. *American Psychologist, 44*, 188–199.

Turner, H., & Finkelhor, D. (1996). Corporal punishment as a stressor among youth. *Journal of Marriage and the Family, 58*, 155–156.

Turner, P. H., Scadden, L., & Harris, M. B. (1990). Parenting in gay and lesbian families. *Journal of Gay and Lesbian Psychotherapy, 1*, 55–66.

Turner, P. J., & Gervai, J. (1995). A multidimensional study of gender typing in preschool children and their parents: Personality, attitudes, preferences, behavior, and cultural differences. *Developmental Psychology, 31*, 759–772.

Tygiel, J. (1983). *Baseball's great experiment: Jackie Robinson and his legacy*. New York: Oxford University Press.

Tygiel, J. (Ed.). (1997). *The Jackie Robinson reader*. New York: Dutton.

Tyler, P. E. (1994, January 11). Chinese start a vitamin program to eliminate a birth defect. *The New York Times*, p. C3.

Uldry, J. R. (1988). Biological predispositions and social control in adolescent sexual behavior. *American Sociological Review, 53*, 709–722.

Umberger, F. G., & Van Reenen, J. S. (1995). Thumb sucking management: A review. *International Journal of Orofacial Myology, 21*, 41–47.

Unger, D., & Cooley, M. (1992). Partner and grandmother contact in black and white teen parent families. *Journal of Adolescent Health Care, 13*, 546–552.

UNICEF. (1992). *State of the world's children*. New York: Oxford University Press.

UNICEF. (1996). *State of the world's children*. New York: Oxford University Press.

Upjohn Company. (1984). *Writer's guide to sex and health*. Kalamazoo, MI: Author.

Urberg, K. A., Degirmencioglu, S. M., & Pilgrim, C. (1997). Close friend and group influence on adolescent cigarette smoking and alcohol use. *Developmental Psychology, 33*, 834–844.

U.S. Advisory Board on Child Abuse and Neglect. (1995, October). *A nation's shame: Fatal child abuse and neglect in the United States*. Washington, DC: U.S. Government Printing Office.

U.S. Bureau of the Census. (1993). *Statistics on characteristics of single-parent households*. Washington, DC: Author.

U.S. Bureau of the Census. (1995a). *Household and family characteristics: March 1994* (Current Population Reports, Series P20-483). Washington, DC: U.S. Government Printing Office.

U.S. Bureau of the Census. (1995b). *Statistical abstract of the United States, 1995*. Washington, DC: U.S. Government Printing Office.

U.S. Bureau of the Census. (1996, February). *How we're changing: Demographic state of the nation: 1996* (Current Population Reports, Special Studies, Series P-23-191). Washington, DC: U.S. Government Printing Office.

U.S. Consumer Product Safety Commission. (1991). *Statistics on shopping cart safety*. Washington, DC: Author.

U.S. Department of Commerce. (1996). *Statistical abstract of the United States, 1996*. Washington, DC: U.S. Government Printing Office.

U.S. Department of Education. (1986). *What works: Research about reading and learning*. Washington, DC: Office of Educational Research and Improvement. (Available from What Works, Pueblo, CO 81009)

U.S. Department of Education. (1992). *Dropout rates in the U.S., 1991* (Publication No. NCES 92–129). Washington, DC: U.S. Government Printing Office.

U.S. Department of Education. (1993). *National excellence: A case for developing America's talent*. Washington, DC: Author.

U.S. Department of Education. (1997). *The national education goals report summary 1997: Mathematics and science achievement for the 21st century*. Washington, DC: Author.

U.S. Department of Health and Human Services (USDHHS). (1982). *Prevention 82* (DHHS Publication No. PHS 82-50157). Washington, DC: U.S. Government Printing Office.

U.S. Department of Health and Human Services (USDHHS). (1984). *Child abuse prevention: Tips to parents*. Washington, DC: Office of Human Development Services, Administration for Children, Youth, and Families, National Center on Child Abuse and Neglect.

U.S. Department of Health and Human Services (USDHHS). (1990). *Health, United States, 1989* (DHHS Publication No. PHS 90-1232). Washington, DC: U.S. Government Printing Office.

U.S. Department of Health and Human Services (USDHHS). (1996a). *Health, United States, 1995* (DHHS Publication No. PHS 96-1232). Washington, DC: U.S. Government Printing Office.

U.S. Department of Health and Human Services (USDHHS). (1996b). *HHS releases study of relationship between family structure and adolescent substance abuse* [Press release, on-line]. Available: http://www.hhs.gov.[1996, September 6]

U.S. Environmental Protection Agency. (1994). *Setting the record straight: Secondhand smoke is a preventable health risk* (EPA Publication No. 402-F-94-005). Washington, DC: U.S. Government Printing Office.

Valdez-Menchaca, M. C., & Whitehurst, G. J. (1992). Accelerating language development through picture book reading: A systematic extension to Mexican daycare. *Developmental Psychology, 28*, 1106–1114.

Valentine, D. P. (1982). The experience of pregnancy: A developmental process. *Family Relations, 31*, 243–248.

Vandell, D. L., & Bailey, M. D. (1992). Conflicts between siblings. In C. U. Shantz & W. W. Hartup (Eds.), *Confict in child and adolescent development* (pp. 242–269). New York: Cambridge University Press.

Vandell, D. L., & Corasaniti, M. A. (1988). The relation between third graders' after-school care and social, academic, and emotional functioning. *Child Development, 59*, 868–875.

Vandell, D. L., & Ramanan, J. (1991). Children of the National Longitudinal Survey of Youth: Choices in after-school care and child development. *Developmental Psychology, 27*, 637–643.

Vandell, D. L., & Ramanan, J. (1992). Effects of early and recent maternal employment on children from low-income families. *Child Development, 63,* 938–949.

Van Dyck, J. (1995). *Manufacturing babies and public consent: Debating the new reproductive technologies.* New York: New York University Press.

van IJzendoorn, M. H. (1995). Adult attachment representations, parental responsiveness, and infant attachment: A meta-analysis on the predictive validity of the Adult Attachment Interview. *Psychological Bulletin, 117*(3), 387–403.

van Lieshout, C. F. M., Haselager, G. J. T., Riksen-Walraven, J. M., & van Aken, M. A. G. (1995, April). Personality development in middle childhood. In D. Hart (Chair), *The contribution of childhood personality to adolescent competence: Insights from longitudinal studies from three societies.* Symposium conducted at the Biennial Meeting of the Society for Research in Child Development, Indianapolis, IN.

van Noord-Zaadstra, B., Looman, C. W., Alsbach, H., Habbema, J. D., teVelde, E. R., & Karbaat, J. (1991). Delayed childbearing: Effect of age on fecundity and outcome of pregnancy. *British Medical Journal, 302,* 1361–1365.

Vargha-Khadem, F., Gadian, D. G., Watkins, K. E., Connelly, A., Van Paesschen, W., & Mishkin, M. (1997). Differential effects of early hippocampal pathology on episodic and semantic memory. *Science, 277,* 376–380.

Vartanian, L. R., & Powlishta, K. K. (1996). A longitudinal examination of the social-cognitive foundations of adolescent egocentrism. *Journal of Early Adolescence, 16,* 157–178.

Vaughn, B. E., Goldberg, S., Atkinson, L., Marcovitch, S., MacGregor, D., & Seifer, R. (1994). Quality of toddler-mother attachment in children with Down syndrome: Limits to interpretation of Strange Situation behavior. *Child Development, 65,* 95–108.

Vaughn, B. E., Stevenson-Hinde, J., Waters, E., Kotsaftis, A., Lefever, G. B., Shouldice, A., Trudel, M., & Belsky, J. (1992). Attachment security and temperament in infancy and early childhood: Some conceptual clarifications. *Developmental Psychology, 28,* 463–473.

Ventura, S. J., Martin, J. A., Curtin, S. C., & Mathews, T. J. (1997, June 10). *Report of final natality statistics, 1995* (Monthly Vital Statistics Report, 45[11, Suppl. 2], DHHS Publication No. PHS 97-1120). Washington, DC: National Center for Health Statistics.

Ventura, S. J., Taffel, S. M., Mosher, W. D., Wilson, J. B., & Henshaw, S. (1995, May 25). *Trends in pregnancies and pregnancy rates: Estimates for the United States, 1980–92* (Monthly Vital Statistics Report, 43[11, Suppl.]). Washington, DC: Centers for Disease Control and Prevention/National Center for Health Statistics.

Verloove-Vanhorick, S. P., Veen, S., Ens-Dokkum, M. H., Schreuder, A. M., Brand, R., & Ruys, R. H. (1994). Sex differences in disability and handicap at five years of age in children born at very short gestation. *Pediatrics, 93,* 576–579.

Verschueren, K., Marcoen, A., & Schoefs, V. (1996). The internal working model of the self, attachment, and competence in five-year-olds. *Child Development, 67,* 2493–2511.

Visher, E. B., & Visher, J. S. (1991). *How to win as a step-family* (2nd ed.). New York: Brunner/Mazel.

Vitaro, F., Tremblay, R. E., Kerr, M., Pagani, L., & Bukowski, W. M. (1997). Disruptiveness, friends' characteristics, and delinquency in early adolescence: A test of two competing models of development. *Child Development, 68,* 676–689.

'Voice of rights struggle' Marian Anderson, 96, opera pioneer succumbs. (1993, April 26). *Jet,* pp. 14–16, 18, 54.

Volling, B. L., & Feagans, L. V. (1995). Infant day care and children's social competence. *Infant Behavior and Development, 18,* 177–188.

Vosniadou, S. (1987). Children and metaphors. *Child Development, 58,* 870–885.

Voyer, D., Voyer, S., & Bryden, M. P. (1995). Magnitude of sex differences in spatial abilities: A meta-analysis and consideration of critical variables. *Psychological Bulletin, 117*(2), 250–270.

Vuchinich, S., Angelelli, J., & Gatherum, A. (1996). Context and development in family problem solving with preadolescent children. *Child Development, 67,* 1276–1288.

Vuori, L., Christiansen, N., Clement, J., Mora, J., Wagner, M., & Herrera, M. (1979). Nutritional supplementation and the outcome of pregnancy: 2. Visual habituation at 15 days. *Journal of Clinical Nutrition, 32,* 463–469.

Vygotsky, L. S. (1956). *Selected psychological investigations.* Moscow: Izdstel'sto Akademii Pedagogicheskikh Nauk USSR.

Vygotsky, L. S. (1962). *Thought and language.* Cambridge, MA: MIT Press.

Vygotsky, L. S. (1978). *Mind in society: The development of higher psychological processes.* Cambridge, MA: Harvard University Press.

Wagner, B. M. (1997). Family risk factors for child and adolescent suicidal behavior. *Psychological Bulletin, 121,* 246–298.

Wakschlag, L. S., Chase-Lansdale, P. L., & Brooks-Gunn, J. (1996). Not just "Ghosts in the Nursery": Contemporaneous intergenerational relationships and parenting in young African-American families. *Child Development, 67,* 2131–2147.

Wakschlag, L. S., Lahey, B. B., Loeber, R., Green, S. M., Gordon, R. A., & Leventhal, B. L. (1997). Maternal smoking during pregnancy and the risk of conduct disorder in boys. *Archives of General Psychiatry, 54,* 670–676.

Waldman, I. D. (1996). Aggressive boys' hostile perceptual and response biases: The role of attention and impulsivity. *Child Development, 67,* 1015–1033.

Walk, R. D., & Gibson, E. J. (1961). A comparative and analytical study of visual depth perception. *Psychology Monographs, 75*(15).

Walker, D., Greenwood, C., Hart, B., & Carta, J. (1994). Prediction of school outcomes based on early language production and socioeconomic factors. *Child Development, 65,* 606–621.

Walker, L. J. (1984). Sex differences in the development of moral reasoning: A critical review. *Child Development, 55,* 677–691.

Walker, L. J., & Taylor, J. H. (1991). Family interactions and the development of moral reasoning. *Child Development, 62,* 264–283.

Wallach, M. A., & Kogan, M. (1965). *Modes of thinking in young children: A study of the creativity-intelligence distinction.* New York: Holt.

Waller, G., & Harris, P. L. (1988). Who's going where? Children's route descriptions for peers and younger children. *British Journal of Developmental Psychology, 6,* 137–143.

Wallerstein, J. S. (1983). Children of divorce: The psychological tasks of the child. *American Journal of Orthopsychiatry, 53,* 230–243.

Wallerstein, J. S., & Kelly, J. B. (1980). *Surviving the break-up: How children actually cope with divorce.* New York: Basic Books.

Wasik, B. H., Ramey, C. T., Bryant, D. M., & Sparling, J. J. (1990). A longitudinal study of two early intervention strategies: Project CARE. *Child Development, 61,* 1682–1696.

Waters, E., & Deane, K. E. (1985). Defining and assessing individual differences in attachment relationships: Q-methodology and the organization of behavior in infancy and early childhood. *Monographs of the Society for Research in Child Development, 50,* 41–65.

Waters, E., Wippman, J., & Sroufe, L. A. (1979). Attachment, positive affect, and competence in the peer group: Two studies in construct validation. *Child Development, 50,* 821–829.

Waters, K. A., Gonzalez, A., Jean, C., Morielli, A., & Brouillette, R. T. (1996). Face-straight-down and face-near-straight-down positions in healthy prone-sleeping infants. *Journal of Pediatrics, 128,* 616–625.

Watson, J. B., & Rayner, R. (1920). Conditioned emotional reactions. *Journal of Experimental Psychology, 3,* 1–14.

Weathers, W. T., Crane, M. M., Sauvain, K. J., & Blackhurst, D. W. (1993). Cocaine use in women from defined populations: Prevalence at delivery and effects on growth in infants. *Pediatrics, 91,* 350–354.

Wegman, M. E. (1992). Annual summary of vital statistics—1991. *Pediatrics, 90,* 835–845.

Wegman, M. E. (1993). Annual summary of vital statistics—1992. *Pediatrics, 92,* 743–754.

Wegman, M. E. (1994). Annual summary of vital statistics—1993. *Pediatrics, 94,* 792–803.

Wegman, M. E. (1996). Infant mortality: Some international comparisons. *Pediatrics, 98,* 1020–1027.

Weinberg, M. K., & Tronick, E. Z. (1996). Infant affective reactions to the resumption of maternal interaction after still face. *Child Development, 67,* 905–914.

Weinberg, R. A. (1989). Intelligence and IQ: Landmark issues and great debates. *American Psychologist, 44*(2), 98–104.

Weisman, S. R. (1988, July 20). No more guarantees of a son's birth. *The New York Times,* pp. A1, A9.

Weisner, T. S. (1993). Ethnographic and ecocultural perspectives on sibling relationships. In Z. Stoneman & P. W. Berman (Eds.), *The effects of mental retardation, visibility, and illness on sibling relationships* (pp. 51–83). Baltimore: Brooks.

Weiss, B., Dodge, K. A., Bates, J. E., & Pettit, G. S. (1992). Some consequences of early harsh discipline: Child aggression and a maladaptive social information processing style. *Child Development, 63,* 1321–1335.

Weiss, B. D. (1992). Trends in bicycle helmet use by children: 1985 to 1990. *Pediatrics, 89,* 78–80.

Weissbourd, B. (1996, February–March). There will always be lullabies: Enduring connections between grandparents and young children. In *Zero to Three, 16* (4, pp. 1, 3–8). Washington, DC: National Center for Infants, Toddlers and Families.

Weisz, J. R., Sigman, M., Weiss, B., & Mosk, J. (1993). Parent reports of behavioral and emotional problems among children in Kenya, Thailand, and the United States. *Child Development, 64,* 98–109.

Weisz, J. R., Weiss, B., Han, S. S., Granger, D. A., & Morton, T. (1995). Effects of psychotherapy with children and adolescents revisited: A meta-analysis of treatment outcome studies. *Psychological Bulletin, 117*(3), 450–468.

Weitzman, M., Gortmaker, S., & Sobol, A. (1992). Maternal smoking and behavior problems of children. *Pediatrics, 90,* 342–349.

Welch-Ross, M. K., & Schmidt, C. R. (1996). Gender-schema development and children's story memory: Evidence for a developmental model. *Child Development, 67,* 820–835.

Wellman, H., & Lempers, J. (1977). The naturalistic communicative abilities of two-year-olds. *Child Development, 48,* 1052–1057.

Wellman, H. M., & Banerjee, M. (1991). Mind and emotion: Children's understanding of the emotional consequences of beliefs and desires. *British Journal of Developmental Psychology, 9,* 191–214.

Wells, A. S. (1988, September 7). For those at risk of dropping out, an enduring program that works. *The New York Times,* p. B9.

Wells, G. (1985). Preschool literacy-related activities and success in school. In D. R. Olson, N. Torrence, & A. Hilyard (Eds.), *Literacy, language, and learning* (pp. 229–255). New York: Cambridge University Press.

Werker, J. F. (1989). Becoming a native listener. *American Scientist, 77,* 54–59.

Werker, J. F., Pegg, J. E., & McLeod, P. J. (1994). A cross-language investigation of infant preference for infant-directed communication. *Infant Behavior and Development, 17,* 323–333.

Werler, M. M., Louik, C., Shapiro, S., & Mitchell, A. A. (1996). Prepregnant weight in relation to risk of neural tube defects. *Journal of the American Medical Association, 275,* 1089–1092.

Werner, E., Bierman, L, French, F. E., Simonian, K., Conner, A., Smith, R., & Campbell, M. (1968). Reproductive and environmental casualties: A report on the 10-year follow-up of the children of the Kauai pregnancy study. *Pediatrics, 42,* 112–127.

Werner, E. E. (1985). Stress and protective factors in children's lives. In A. R. Nichol (Ed.), *Longitudinal studies in child psychology and psychiatry.* New York: Wiley.

Werner, E. E. (1987, July 15). *Vulnerability and resiliency: A longitudinal study of Asian Americans from birth to age 30.* Invited address at the Ninth Biennial Meeting of the International Society for the Study of Behavioral Development, Tokyo, Japan.

Werner, E. E. (1989). Children of the garden island. *Scientific American, 260*(4), 106–111.

Werner, E. E. (1993). Risk and resilience in individuals with learning disabilities: Lessons learned from the Kauai longitudinal study. *Learning Disabilities Research and Practice, 8,* 28–34.

Werner, E. E. (1995). Resilience in development. *Current Directions in Psychological Science, 4*(3), 81–85.

West Berlin Human Genetics Institute. (1987). *Study on effects of nuclear radiation at Chernobyl on fetal development.* Berlin: Author.

Whiffen, V. E., & Gotlib, I. H. (1989). Infants of postpartum depressed mothers: Temperament and cognitive status. *Journal of Abnormal Psychology, 98* (3), 274–279.

Whitaker, R. C., Wright, J. A., Pepe, M. S., Seidel, K. D., & Dietz, W. H. (1997). Predicting obesity in young adulthood from childhood and parental obesity. *New England Journal of Medicine, 337,* 869–873.

White, B. L. (1971, October). *Fundamental early environmental influences on the development of competence.* Paper presented at the Third Western Symposium on Learning: Cognitive Learning, Western Washington State College, Bellingham, WA.

White, B. L., Kaban, B., & Attanucci, J. (1979). *The origins of human competence.* Lexington, MA: Heath.

White, K. R. (1982). The relation between socioeconomic status and academic achievement. *Psychological Bulletin, 91* (3), 461–481.

Whitehurst, G. I., Fischel, J. E., Caulfield, M., DeBaryshe, B. D., & Valdez-Menchaca, M. C. (1989). Assessment and treatment of early expressive language delay. In P. R. Zelazo & R. G. Barr (Eds.), *Challenges to developmental paradigms: Implications for theory, assessment and treatment.* Hillsdale, NJ: Erlbaum.

Whitehurst, G. J., Falco, F. L., Lonigan, C. J., Fischel, J. E., DeBaryshe, B. D., Valdez-Menchaca, M. D., & Caufield, M. (1988). Accelerating language development through picture book reading. *Developmental Psychology, 24,* 552–559.

Whitehurst, M., Groo, D., & Brown, L. E. (1996). Prepubescent heart response to indoor play. *Pediatric Exercise Science, 8* (3), 245–250.

Whitehurst, M., Groo, D., Brown, L. E., & Findley, B. W. (1995). Prepubescent heart rate response to indoor play. *Medicine and Science in Sport and Exercise, 27*(5), S115.

Whitrow, G. J. (1967). *Einstein: The man and his achievement.* New York: Dover.

WHO/UNICEF Constitution on HIV Transmission and Breastfeeding. (1992). Consensus statement from the WHO/UNICEF Constitution on HIV Transmission and Breastfeeding, Geneva. *Weekly Epidemiological Record, 67,* 177–184.

Wideman, M. V., & Singer, J. F. (1984). The role of psychological mechanisms in preparation for childbirth. *American Psychologist, 34,* 1357–1371.

Widom, C. S. (1989). The cycle of violence. *Science, 244,* 160–166.

Wilcox, A. J., Weinberg, C. R., & Baird, D. D. (1995). Timing of sexual intercourse in relation to ovulation: Effects on the probability of conception, survival of the pregnancy, and sex of the baby. *New England Journal of Medicine, 333,* 1563–1565.

Williams, B. C., & Miller, C. A. (1991). *Preventive health care for young children: Findings from a 10-country study and directions for United States policy.* Arlington, VA: National Center for Clinical Infant Programs.

Williams, B. C., & Miller, C. A. (1992). Preventive health care for young children: Findings from a 10-country study and directions for the United States policy. *Pediatrics, 89* (Suppl.).

Williams, E. R., & Caliendo, M. A. (1984). *Nutrition: Principles, issues, and applications.* New York: McGraw-Hill.

Williams, J. E., & Best, D. L. (1982). *Measuring sex stereotypes: A thirty-nation study.* Beverly Hills, CA: Sage.

Williams, S. B. (1987). A comparative study of black dropouts and black high school graduates in an urban public school system. *Education and Urban Society, 19,* 311–319.

Willinger, M. (1995). Sleep position and sudden infant death. *Journal of the*

American Medical Association, 273(10), 818–819.

Willinger, M., Hoffman, H. T., & Hartford, R. B. (1994). Infant sleep position and risk for sudden infant death syndrome: Report of meeting held January 13 and 14, 1994. *Pediatrics, 93,* 814–819.

Wilson, G., McCreary, R., Kean, J., & Baxter, J. (1979). The development of preschool children of heroin-addicted mothers: A controlled study. *Pediatrics, 63,* 135–141.

Winer, G. A. (1982). A review and analysis of children's fearful behavior in dental settings. *Child Development, 53,* 1111–1133.

Winick, M. (1981, January). Food and the fetus. *Natural History,* pp. 16–81.

Wittrock, M. C. (1980). Learning and the brain. In M. C. Wittrock (Ed.), *The brain and psychology.* New York: Academic Press.

Wolf, M. (1968). *The house of Lim.* Englewood Cliffs, NJ: Prentice-Hall.

Wolfe, D. A. (1985). Child-abusive parents: An empirical review and analysis. *Psychological Bulletin, 97*(3), 462–482.

Wolfe, D. A., Edwards, B., Manion, I., & Koverola, C. (1988). Early intervention for parents at risk of child abuse and neglect: A preliminary investigation. *Journal of Consulting and Clinical Psychology, 56,* 40–47.

Wolff, P. H. (1963). Observations on the early development of smiling. In B. M. Foss (Ed.), *Determinants of infant behavior* (Vol. 2). London: Methuen.

Wolff, P. H. (1966). The causes, controls, and organizations of behavior in the newborn. *Psychological Issues, 5* (1, Whole No. 17), 1–105.

Wolff, P. H. (1969). The natural history of crying and other vocalizations in early infancy. In B. M. Foss (Ed.), *Determinants of infant behavior* (Vol. 4). London: Methuen.

Wolff, R. (1993). *Good sports: The concerned parent's guide to Little League and other competitive youth sports.* New York: Dell.

Wolraich, M. L., Lindgren, S. D., Stumbo, P. J., Stegink, L. D., Appelbaum, M. I., & Kiritsky, M. C. (1994). Effects of diets high in sucrose or aspartame on the behavior and cognitive performance of children. *New England Journal of Medicine, 330,* 301–307.

Wolraich, M. L., Wilson, D. B., & White, J. W. (1995). The effect of sugar on behavior or cognition in children: A meta-analysis. *Journal of the American Medical Association, 274*(20), 1617–1621.

Woman delivers a baby boy after refusing a caesarean. (1993, December 30). *The New York Times,* p. A12.

Wood, D. L., Hayward, R. A., Corey, C. R., Freeman, H. E., & Shapiro, M. F. (1990). Access to medical care for children and adolescents in the United States. *Pediatrics, 86,* 666–673.

Wood, P. R., Hidalgo, H. R., Prihoda, T. J., & Kromer, M. E. (1993). Hispanic children with asthma. *Pediatrics, 91,* 62–69.

Woodward, A. L., Markman, E. M., & Fitzsimmons, C. M. (1994). Rapid word learning in 13- and 18-month olds. *Developmental Psychology, 30,* 553–566.

Woolley, J. D., & Bruell, M. J. (1996). Young children's awareness of the origins of their mental representations. *Developmental Psychology, 32,* 335–346.

World Health Organization (WHO). (1996, May). *WHO Fact Sheet, 119,* pp. 1–3.

Wright, A. L., Holberg, C. J., Taussig, L. M., & Martinez, F. D. (1995). Relationship of infant feeding to recurrent wheezing at age 6 years. *Archives of Pediatric Adolescent Medicine, 149,* 758–763.

Wright, J. C., Huston, A. C., Truglio, R., Fitch, M., Smith, E., & Piemyat, S. (1995). Occupational portrayals on television: Children's role schemata, career aspirations, and perceptions of reality. *Child Development, 66,* 1706–1718.

Wright, J. T., Waterson, E. J., Barrison, I. G., Toplis, P. J., Lewis, I. G., Gordon, M. G., MacRae, K. D., Morris, N. F., & Murray Lyon, I. M. (1983, March 26). Alcohol consumption, pregnancy, and low birth weight. *The Lancet,* pp. 663–665.

Wright, L. (1996, January 15). Silent sperm. *The New Yorker,* pp. 42–55.

The Writing Group for the DISC Collaborative Research Group. (1995). Efficacy and safety of lowering dietary intake of fat and cholesterol in children with elevated low-density lipoprotein cholesterol. *Journal of the American Medical Association, 273,* 1429–1435.

WuDunn, S. (1996, March 23). Japan's single mothers face discrimination. *Cleveland Plain Dealer,* p. 5E.

WuDunn, S. (1997, January 14). Korean women still feel demands to bear a son. *The New York Times* (International Ed.), p. A3.

Wynn, K. (1992). Evidence against empiricist accounts of the origins of numerical knowledge. *Mind and Language, 7,* 315–332.

Wynn, K. (1996). Infants' individuation and enumeration of actions. *Psychological Science, 7,* 164–169.

Yamazaki, J. N., & Schull, W. J. (1990). Perinatal loss and neurological abnormalities among children of the atomic bomb. *Journal of the American Medical Association, 264,* 605–609.

Yang, B., Ollendick, T. H., Dong, Q., Xia, Y., & Lin, L. (1995). Only children and children with siblings in the People's Republic of China: Levels of fear, anxiety, and depression. *Child Development, 66,* 1301–1311.

Yarrow, M. R. (1978, October). *Altruism in children.* Paper presented at program, Advances in Child Development Research, New York Academy of Sciences, New York, NY.

Yau, J., & Smetana, J. G. (1996). Adolescent-parent conflict among Chinese adolescents in Hong Kong. *Child Development, 67,* 1262–1275.

Yazigi, R. A., Odem, R. R., & Polakoski, K. L. (1991). Demonstration of specific binding of cocaine to human spermatozoa. *Journal of the American Medical Association, 266,* 1956–1959.

Yildirim, A. (1997). Gender role influences on Turkish adolescents' self-identity. *Adolescence, 32,* 217–231.

Yogman, M. J. (1984). Competence and performance of fathers and infants. In A. MacFarlane (Ed.), *Progress in child health.* London: Churchill Livingston.

Yogman, M. J., Dixon, S., Tronick, E., Als, H., & Brazelton, T. B. (1977, March). *The goals and structure of face-to-face interaction between infants and their fathers.* Paper presented at the meeting of the Society for Research in Child Development, New Orleans, LA.

Yoshikawa, H. (1994). Prevention as cumulative protection: Effects of early family support and education on chronic delinquency and its risks. *Psychological Bulletin, 115*(1), 28–54.

Youngblade, L. M., & Belsky, J. (1992). Parent-child antecedents of 5-year-olds' close friendships: A longitudinal analysis. *Developmental Psychology, 28,* 700–713.

Youngstrom, N. (1992, January). Inner-city youth tell of life in "a war zone." *APA Monitor,* pp. 36–37.

Zabin, L. S., & Clark, S. D. (1983). Institutional factors affecting teenagers' choice and reasons for delay in attending a family planning clinic. *Family Planning Perspectives, 15,* 25–29.

Zahn-Waxler, C., Friedman, R. J., Cole, P. M., Mizuta, I., & Hiruma, N. (1996). Japanese and U.S. preschool children's responses to conflict and distress. *Child Development, 67,* 2462–2477.

Zahn-Waxler, C., & Kochanska, G. (1990). The origins of guilt. In R. Thompson (Ed.), *The 36th National Symposium on Motivation: Socioemotional development* (pp. 183–258). Lincoln: University of Nebraska Press.

Zahn-Waxler, C., Radke-Yarrow, M., Wagner, E., & Chapman, M. (1992). Development of concern for others. *Developmental Psychology, 28,* 126–136.

Zahn-Waxler, C., Robinson, J. L., & Emde, R. N. (1992). The development of empathy in twins. *Developmental Psychology, 28,* 1038–1047.

Zakariya, S. B. (1982, September). Another look at the children of divorce: Summary report of the study of school needs of one-parent children. *Principal,* pp. 34–37.

Zametkin, A. J. (1995). Attention-deficit disorder: Born to be hyperactive. *Journal of the American Medical Association, 273*(23), 1871–1874.

Zarbatany, L., Hartmann, D. P., & Rankin, D. B. (1990). The psychological functions of preadolescent peer activities. *Child Development, 61,* 1067–1080.

Zeifman, D., Delaney, S., & Blass, E. M. (1996). Sweet taste, looking, and calm in 2- and 4-week-old infants: The eyes have it. *Developmental Psychology, 32,* 1090–1099.

Zelazo, N. A., Zelazo, P. R., Cohen, K. M., & Zelazo, P. D. (1993). Specificity of practice effects on elementary neuromotor patterns. *Developmental Psychology, 29,* 686–691.

Zelazo, P. R., Zelazo, N. A., & Kolb, S. (1972). "Walking" in the newborn. *Science, 176,* 314–315.

Zell, E. R., Dietz, V., Stevenson, J., Cochi, S., & Bruce, R. H. (1994). Low vaccination levels of U.S. preschool and school-age children. *Journal of the American Medical Association, 271,* 833–839.

Zelnik, M., Kantner, J. F., & Ford, K. (1981). *Sex and pregnancy in adolescence.* Beverly Hills, CA: Sage.

Zelnik, M., & Shah, F. K. (1983). First intercourse among young Americans. *Family Planning Perspectives, 15,* 64–72.

Zeman, J., & Garber, J. (1996). Display rules for anger, sadness, and pain: It depends on who is watching. *Child Development, 67,* 957–973.

Zentella, A. C. (1981). Language variety among Puerto Ricans. In C. A. Ferguson & S. B. Heath (Eds.), *Language in the USA* (pp. 218–238). New York: Cambridge University Press.

Zeskind, P. S., & Iacino, R. (1984). Effects of maternal visitation to preterm infants in the neonatal intensive care unit. *Child Development, 55,* 1887–1893.

Zeskind, P. S., & Marshall, T. R. (1988). The relation between variations in pitch and maternal perceptions of infant crying. *Child Development, 59,* 193–196.

Zhang, Y., Proenca, R., Maffei, M., Barone, M., Leopold, L., & Friedman, J. M., (1994). Positional cloning of the mouse obese gene in its human homologue. *Nature, 372,* 425–431.

Zhensun, Z., & Low, A. (1991). *A young painter: The life and paintings of Wang Yani—China's extraordinary young artist.* New York: Scholastic.

Zigler, E., & Styfco, S. J. (1993). Using research and theory to justify and inform Head Start expansion. *Social Policy Report of the Society for Research in Child Development, 7*(2).

Zigler, E., & Styfco, S. J. (1994). Head Start: Criticisms in a constructive context. *American Psychologist, 49*(2), 127–132.

Zigler, E., Taussig, C., & Black, K. (1992). Early childhood intervention: A promising preventative for juvenile delinquency. *American Psychologist, 47,* 997–1006.

Zigler, E. F. (1987). Formal schooling for four-year-olds? *North American Psychologist, 42*(3), 254–260.

Zimiles, H., & Lee, V. E. (1991). Adolescent family structure and educational progress. *Developmental Psychology, 27,* 314–320.

Zimmerman, M. A., Salem, D. A., & Maton, K. I. (1995). Family structure and psychosocial correlates among urban African-American adolescent males. *Child Development, 66,* 1598–1613.

Zimrin, H. (1986). A profile of survival. *Child Abuse and Neglect, 10,* 339–349.

Zuckerman, B., Frank, D., Hingson, R., Amaro, H., Levenson, S. M., Kayne, H., Parker, S., Vinci, R., Aboagye, K., Fried, L., Cabral, H., Timperi, R., & Bauchner, H. (1989). Effects of maternal marijuana and cocaine use on fetal growth. *New England Journal of Medicine, 320*(12), 762–768.

Zuckerman, B. S., & Beardslee, W. R. (1987). Maternal depression: A concern for pediatricians. *Pediatrics, 79,* 110–117.

Zuckerman, D. M., & Zuckerman, B. S. (1985). Television's impact on children. *Pediatrics, 75,* 233–24.

Acknowledgments

The authors wish to thank the copyright owners for permission to reprint the following copyrighted material.

Chapter 1

Figure 1-1: Cole, M., and S. R. Cole. (1989) From *The Development of children* by Cole and Cole. Copyright © 1989 by Michael Cole, Sheila R. Cole, and Judith Boies. Used with permission of W. H. Freeman and Company.

Table 1-4, Table 1-5, Figure 1-6, & Figure 1-7: Papalia, D., and S. W. Olds. (1997) From *Human Development*, Seventh Edition, by Diane Papalia and Sally Wendkos Olds. Copyright © 1997. Reproduced with permission of The McGraw-Hill Companies.

Box 1-2: Bjorklund, D. F. (1997) From "The role of immaturity in human development," *Psychological Bulletin, 122,* 1997, pp. 153–169. Copyright © 1997 by the American Psychological Association. Reprinted with permission.

Chapter 2

Opener: Leonard, W. E. (1923) From *Two Lives* by William Ellery Leonard. Copyright 1923 by B. W. Huebsch. Copyright renewed © 1951 by Charlotte Charlton Leonard. Used by permission of Viking-Penguin, a division of Penguin Putnam, Inc.

Figure 2-2, Figure 2-4, & Box 2-1: Papalia, D., and S. W. Olds. (1997) From *Human Development*, Seventh Edition, by Diane Papalia and Sally Wendkos Olds. Copyright © 1997. Reproduced with permission of The McGraw-Hill Companies.

Table 2-1: AAP Committee on Genetics. (1996) Adapted from American Academy of Pediatrics Committee on Genetics 1996. Copyright American Academy of Pediatrics. Used with permission. Fahey, V. (1988) Adapted from "The Gene Screen: Looking in on baby," (in Tisdale, "The Mother"), *Hippocrates*, Vol. 2, No. 3,

1988, pp. 68–69. Reprinted by permission of Time Inc., Health.

Table 2-2: Milunsky, A. (1992) Adapted from *Heredity and Your Family's Health* by A. Milunsky, p. 122. © 1992. The Johns Hopkins University Press.

Box 2-1 (fig.): Babu, A., and K. Hirschhorn. (1992) From *A Guide to Human Chromosome Defects,* Third Edition. Birth Defects: Original Article Series 28(2), 1987. White Plains, NY: March of Dimes Birth Defects Foundation.

Chapter 3

Opener: Sexton, A. (1966). Excerpt from "Little Girl, My String Bean, My Lovely Woman," *Live or Die* by Anne Sexton. Copyright © 1966 by Anne Sexton. Reprinted by permission of Houghton Mifflin Company and Sterling Lord Literistic, Inc. All rights reserved.

Figure 3-2: Brody, J. E. (1995) From "Preventing birth defects even before pregnancy," *The New York Times*, June 28, 1995, p. C10. Copyright © 1995 by The New York Times Co. Reprinted by permission.

Figure 3-4: Fuchs, F. (1980) From "Genetic Amniocentesis." *Scientific American,* 242(6), 1980, 47–53. © Carol Donner. Reprinted by permission.

Chapter 4

Figure 4-1: Lagercrantz, H., and T. A. Slotkin. (1986) From "The 'stress' of being born," *Scientific American, 254*(4), 1986, pp. 100–107. Reprinted by permission of Patricia J. Wynne.

Figure 4-2: Casaer, P. (1993) From "Old and New Facts about Perinatal Brain Development," *Journal of Child Psychology & Psychiatry*, Vol. 34, 1993. Reprinted by permission of Cambridge University Press.

Restak, R. (1984) From "Illustration," from *The Brain* by Richard Restak, M.D. Copyright © 1984 by Educational Broadcasting Corporation and Richard M.

Restak, M.D. Used by permission of Bantam Books, a division of Bantam Doubleday Dell Publishing Group, Inc. and Sterling Lord Literistic.

Figure 4-3: Nash, J. M. (1997) From "Fertile Lands," *Time*, February 3, 1997, pp. 49–56. © 1997 Time Inc. Reprinted by permission.

Table 4-1: Timiras, P. S. (1972) From *Developmental Physiology and Aging* by P. S. Timiras, Macmillan Publishing Co. Reprinted by permission of the author.

Table 4-4: Apgar, V. (1953) Adapted from "A proposal for a new method of evaluation of the newborn infant," *Current Research in Anesthesia & Analgesia, 32,* 1953, pp. 260–267. Reprinted by permission of Williams & Williams.

Box 4-1: Olds, S. W. (1995) From *Having a baby in the Himalayas.* Copyright 1995 by Sally Wendkos Olds. Reprinted by permission.

Box 4-3: Eiger, M. S., and S. W. Olds. (1987) Excerpted from *The Complete Book of Breastfeeding*, pp. 152–153. Copyright © 1987 by Marvin S. Eiger, M.D. and Sally Wendkos Olds. Used by permission of Workman Publishing Co., Inc., New York. All Rights Reserved.

Chapter 5

Figure 5-3: Lach, J. (1997) From "Cultivating the mind," from *Newsweek*, Special Issue, Spring/Summer, 1997, pp. 38–39. © 1997, Newsweek, Inc. All rights reserved. Reprinted by permission.

Figure 5-4: Conel, J. L. (1939–1967) Reprinted by permission of the publisher from *The Postnatal Development of the Cerebral Cortex* by J. L. Conel, Cambridge, Mass.: Harvard University Press, Copyright © 1939–1967 by the President and Fellows of Harvard College.

Figure 5-5: Zelazo, N. A., P. R. Zelazo, K. M. Cohen, and P. D. Zelazo. (1993) From "Specificity of practice effects on elementary neuromotor patterns." *Developmental Psychology, 29,* pp. 686–691.

Chapter 6

Chapter 7

Chapter 8

Chapter 9

Chapter 10

Chapter 11

Frances Nash, Isabel Nash Eberstat, and Linnel Nash Smith. By permission of Little, Brown and Company, and Curtis Brown Ltd.

Figure 11-1: Schor, E. L. (1987) From "Unintentional injuries: Patterns within families." *American Journal of the Diseases of Children, 141,* 1987, 1280. Copyright 1987, American Medical Association. Reprinted by permission.

Table 11-1: Rauh, J. L., D. A. Schumsky, and M. T. Witt (1967) Adapted from "Heights, weights and obesity in urban school children." *Child Development, 38,* 1967, 515–530. © 1967 by The Society for Research in Child Development, Inc. Adapted by permission.

Table 11-2: Cratty, B. J. (1986) Adapted from Bryant J. Cratty, *Perceptual and Motor Development in Infants and Children,* Third Edition. Copyright © 1986 by Allyn & Bacon. Adapted by permission.

Box 11-2: Groce, N. E., and I. K. Zola. (1993) From "Multiculturalism, chronic illness, and disability." Reproduced by permission of *Pediatrics,* Vol. 91, pages 1048–55, 1993.

Chapter 12

Figure 12-1: Siegler, R. S. (1998) Adapted from *Children's Thinking,* Third Edition, by Siegler, p. 48. © 1998. Reprinted by permission of Prentice-Hall, Inc., Upper Saddle River, NJ.

Figure 12-2: McKenna, M. C., D. J. Kear, and R. A. Ellsworth. (1995) From "Children's attitudes toward reading: A national survey," *Reading Research Quarterly, 30*(4), 1995, pp. 934–956. Reprinted with permission of Michael C. McKenna and the International Reading Association. All rights reserved.

Table 12-2: Hoffman, M. L. (1970) From "Moral development," in *Carmichael's Manual of Child Psychology, Vol. 2,* edited by P. H. Mussen, pp. 261–360. Copyright © 1970. Reprinted by permission of John Wiley & Sons, Inc.

Kohlberg, L. (1964) From "The development of moral character and moral ideology," in *Review of Child Development Research,* M. Hoffman and L. Hoffman, editors. © 1964 Russell Sage Foundation 1964.

Table 12-5: Chomsky, C. S. (1969) From *The Acquisition of Syntax in Children from Five to Ten* by C. S. Chomsky. Copyright © 1969. Reprinted by permission of MIT Press.

Table 12-7: Amabile, Theresa M. (1983) From *The Social Psychology of Creativity,* Springer-Verlag, 1983. Reprinted by permission.

Miller, B., and D. Gerard. (1979) From "Family influences on the development of creativity in children: An integrative review," *Family Coordinator, 28,* 1979, pp. 295–312. Copyrighted 1979 by the National Council on Family Relations, 3989 Central Ave. NE, Suite 550,

Minneapolis, MN 55421. Reprinted by permission.

Box 12-1 (fig.): Case, R., and Y. Okamoto. (1996) From "The role of central conceptual structures in the development of children's thought," *Monographs of the Society for Research in Child Development, 61*(1-2, Serial No. 246), 1996, p. 6. © Society for Research in Child Development, Inc.

Chapter 13

Figure 13-2: Burns, A. (1992) From "Mother-headed families: An international perspective and the case of Australia," *Social Policy Report of the Society for Research in Child Development, VI*(1), Spring, 1992. Reprinted by permission of the Society for Research in Child Development, Inc.

Figure 13-3: Long, L. (1992) From "International perspectives on the residential mobility of America's children," *Journal of Marriage and the Family, 54,* 1992, pp. 861–869. Copyrighted 1992 by the National Council on Family Relations, 3989 Central Ave. NE, Suite 550, Minneapolis, MN 55421. Reprinted by permission.

Table 13-1: Zarbatany, L., D. P. Hartmann, and D. B. Rankin. (1990) From "The psychological functions of preadolescent peer activities," *Child Development, 61,* 1990, pp. 1067–1080. © The Society for Research in Child Development, Inc.

Table 13-2: Selman, R. L. (1980) From *The Growth of Interpersonal Understanding: Developmental and Clinical Analyses* by R. L. Selman, 1980. Reprinted by permission of Academic Press, Inc.

Selman, R. L., and A. P. Selman. (1979) From "Children's ideas about friendship: A new theory," *Psychology Today,* April 1979, pp. 71–80. Reprinted with permission from *Psychology Today* Magazine, Copyright © 1979 (Sussex Publishers, Inc.).

Table 13-3: Garbarino, J., N. Dobrow, K. Kostelny, and C. Pardo. (1992) Adapted from *Children in Danger: Coping with the Consequences of Community Violence* by J. N. Garbarino et al., pp. 51–52. Copyright 1992 Jossey-Bass Inc., Publishers.

Chapter 14

Figure 14-1: Crumbach, M. (1997) From *The New York Times,* January 7, 1997, p. C3. Copyright © 1997 by The New York Times Company. Reprinted by permission.

Figure 14-2: Bornstein, M. H., and M. E. Lamb. (1992) From *Development in Infancy: An Introduction,* Third Edition, p. 111, Figure 14-2. Copyright © 1992. Reproduced with permission of The McGraw-Hill Companies.

Dacey, J. S., and M. E. Kenny. (1997) From *Adolescent Development,* 2nd ed., by John S. Dacey and Maureen E. Kenny.

Reproduced with permission of the McGraw-Hill Companies.

Tanner, J. M. (1978) Adapted from *Foetus into Man: Physical Growth from Conception to Maturity* by J. M. Tanner, Open Books Publishing, Ltd., 1978.

Figure 14-3: McClintock, M. K., and G. Herdt. (1996) From "Rethinking puberty: The development of sexual attraction," *Current Directions in Psychological Science, 5*(6), 1996, pp. 178–183. Reprinted with the permission of Cambridge University Press.

De Peretti, E., and M. G. Forest. (1976) Figure redrawn from data in "Unconjugated dehydroepiandrosterone plasma levels in normal subjects from birth to adolescence in humans: The use of sensitive radioimmunoassay," *Journal of Clinical Endocrinology and Metabolism, 43,* 1976, pp. 982–991. © The Endocrine Society.

Figure 14-4: Elliott, D. S., and B. J. Morse. (1989) Adapted from "Delinquency and drug use as risk factors in teenage sexual activity," *Youth and Society, 21,* 1989, pp. 21–60. Reprinted by permission of Sage Publications, Inc.

Table 14-4: Anglin, T. M., K. E. Naylor, and D. W. Kaplan. (1996) Adapted from "Comprehensive school-based health care: High school students' use of medical, mental health, and substance abuse services." Reproduced by permission of *Pediatrics,* Vol. 97, Table 5, pp. 328–330, 1996.

Box 14-2: American Foundation for the Prevention of Venereal Disease, Inc. (1988) From *Sexually Transmitted Disease [Venereal Disease]: Prevention for Everyone,* 16th Edition, 1988. Reprinted by permission.

Upjohn. (1988) Adapted from American Foundation for the Prevention of Venereal Disease (AFPVD), 1988; The Upjohn Co.

Chapter 15

Figure 15-1: Small, M. Y., and J. Kagan. (1990) Figure adapted from *Cognitive Development* by Melinda Y. Small and Jerome Kagan, copyright © 1990 by Harcourt Brace & Company, reproduced by permission of the publisher.

Figure 15-2: Children's Defense Fund. (1995) From *The State of America's Children Yearbook 1995,* p. 94. © Children's Defense Fund. All rights reserved.

Table 15-1: Kohlberg, L. (1969) Adapted from "Stage and sequence: The cognitive-developmental approach to socialization," in *Handbook of Socialization Theory and Research,* by David A. Goslin, Rand McNally, 1969. Reprinted by permission of David A. Goslin.

Lickona, T. E. (1976) From *Moral Development and Behavior* by Thomas E. Lickona, Holt, Rinehart and Winston, 1976. Reprinted by permission Thomas E. Lickona.

Table 15-2: Howe, D. C., P. H. Kahn, Jr., and B. Friedman. (1996) Adapted from "Along the Rio Negro: Brazilian children's environmental views and values," *Developmental Psychology, 32,* 1996, p. 983. Copyright © 1996 by the American Psychological Association. Reprinted with permission.

Table 15-4: Furstenberg, F. F., and M. E. Hughes. (1995) Adapted from "Social capital in successful development," *Journal of Marriage and the Family, 57,* 1995, pp. 580–592. Copyrighted 1995 by the National Council on Family Relations, 3989 Central Ave. NE, Suite 550, Minneapolis, MN 55421. Reprinted by permission.

Box 15-1 (list): Howe, D. C., P. H. Kahn, Jr., and B. Friedman. (1996) From "Along the Rio Negro: Brazilian children's environmental views and values," *Developmental Psychology, 32,* 1996, p. 985. Copyright © 1996 by the American Psychological Association. Reprinted with permission.

Chapter 16

Opener: Merriam, E. (1964) From *A Sky full of Poems* by Eve Merriam. Copyright © 1964, © 1970, 1973, 1986 by Eve Merriam. © renewed Eve Merriam. Reprinted by permission of Marian Reiner.

Figure 16-2: Children's Defense Fund. (1997) From "Trends in teen birth rates, by race of mother, 1980–1995," *CDF Reports,* Vol. 18, No. 11, October 1997, p. 2. © Children's Defense Fund. All rights reserved.

Table 16-1: Marcia, J. E. (1966) Adapted from "Development and validation of ego identity status," *Journal of Personality and Social Psychology, 3*(5), 1966, pp. 551–558. Copyright 1966 by the American Psychological Association. Adapted by permission.

Table 16-2: Marcia, J. E. (1980) From "Identity in adolescence," in *Handbook of Adolescent Psychology,* edited by J. Adelson. Copyright © 1980 by John Wiley & Sons, Inc. Reprinted by permission of John Wiley & Sons, Inc.

Table 16.3: Kroger, J. (1993) From "Ego identity: An overview," in *Discussions of Ego Identity,* edited by J. Kroger, Lawrence Erlbaum Associates, Inc., 1993. Reprinted by permission.

Table 16.4: Miller, B. C., and K. A. Moore. (1990) From "Adolescent sexual behavior, pregnancy, and parenting: Research through the 1980s," *Journal of Marriage and the Family, 52,* 1990, pp. 1025–1044. Copyrighted 1990 by the National Council on Family Relations, 3989 Central Ave. NE, Suite 550, Minneapolis, MN 55421. Reprinted by permission.

Sonnenstein, F. L., J. H. Pleck, and L. C. Ku. (1991) From "Levels of sexual activity among adolescent males in the United States," *Family Planning Perspectives, 23*(4), July/August 1991, pp. 162–167.

Photo Credits

Photo Research by Inge King

Chapter 1

Chapter 1 opening photo © Jon Feingersh/The Stock Market; **p. 11** © Robert Fried/Stock, Boston; **p. 17** (Locke) Library of Congress; **p. 17** (Rousseau) Corbis-Bettmann; **p. 17** (Darwin and Hall) Corbis; **p. 17** (Binet) National Library of Medicine; **p. 17** (Dewey) Corbis; **p. 17** (Baldwin) The Ferdinand Hamburger, Jr., Archives of the Johns Hopkins University; **p. 17** (Montessori) American Montessori Society; **p. 17** (Watson) Archives of the History of Psychology, University of Akron, Akron, OH; **p. 17** (Gesell) UPI/Corbis-Bettmann; **p.23** Mary Evans/Sigmund Freud Copyrights; **p. 25** UPI/Corbis-Bettmann; **p. 26** C. Fatta Studio, Boston/Courtesy of the Wellesley College News Office; **p. 28** Joe McNally; **p. 31** © Yves De Braine/Black Star; **p. 35** © Richard Hutchings/Photo Researchers; **p. 41** © James Wilson/Woodfin Camp & Assoc.

Chapter 2

Chapter 2 opening photo PhotoDisc, Volume 2, People & Lifestyles; **p. 56** Margaret Roche; **p. 59** © John Coletti/The Picture Cube; **p. 61** © CC Studio/Science Photo Library/Photo Researchers; **p. 63** © Myrleen Ferguson/PhotcEdit; **p. 80** © Jalandoni/Monkmeyer; **p. 82** Rhoda Baer; **p. 83** (both) Jane Scherr; **p. 84** © Barbara Campbell/Liaison International.

Chapter 3

Chapter 3 opening photo © Pollak/Monkmeyer; **p. 96** (1 month) © Petit Format/Nestle/Science Source/Photo Researchers; **p. 96** (7 wks) © Petit Format/Nestle/Science Source/Photo Researchers; **p. 96** (3 months) © Lennart Nilsson, A CHILD IS BORN. English translation © 1966, 1977 by Dell Publishing Co. Inc. **p. 96** (4 months) © J. S. Allen/Daily Telegraph/International Stock; **p. 97** (5 months) © James Stevenson/Photo Researchers; **p. 97** (6 months) © Lennart Nilsson, BEING BORN. **p. 97** (7 months) © Petit Format/Nestle/Science Source/Photo Researchers; **p. 97** (8 months) © Petit Format/Nestle/Science Source/Photo Researchers; **p. 97** (9 months) © Ronn Maratea/International Stock Photo; **p. 102** © David Schaefer/Monkmeyer; **p. 105** © L. Rorke/The Image Works; **p. 108** © Mugshots/The Stock Market; **p. 110** Fred R. Conrad/NYT Pictures; **p. 118** © Mark M. Walker/The Picture Cube.

Chapter 4

Chapter 4 opening photo © Kindra Clineff/The Picture Cube; **p. 128** © Lawrence Migdale/Photo Researchers; **p. 131** J.T. Miller; **p. 137** (top left) © Mimi Forsyth/Monkmeyer; **p. 137** (top middle) © Lew Merrim/Monkmeyer; **p. 137** (top right) © Laura Dwight/Black Star; **p. 137** (bottom left) © Mimi Forsyth/Monkmeyer; **p. 137** (bottom middle) Elizabeth Crews; **p. 137** (bottom right) Elizabeth Crews; **p. 141** © Hank Morgan/Science Source/Photo Researchers; **p. 146** Thomas McAvoy/Life Magazine © Time Inc. **p. 149** © Bob Daemmrich/Stock, Boston.

Chapter 5

Chapter 5 opening photo PhotoDisc/Volume 2, People and Lifestyles; **p. 162** © Laima Druskis/Stock, Boston; **p. 163** © Myrleen Ferguson Cate/PhotoEdit; **p. 165** © Camille Tokerud/Photo Researchers; **p. 167** (both) Courtesy of Children's Hospital of Michigan; **p. 170** (both) © J. Guichard/Sygma; **p. 175** Elizabeth Crews; **p. 176** Innervisions; **p. 177** © Margaret Miller/Photo Researchers.

Chapter 6

Chapter 6 opening photo © Laura Dwight/PhotoEdit; **p. 191** Mary Ellen Mark; **p. 192** Courtesy of Carolyn Rovee-Collier; **p. 196** Nancy Olds; **p. 201** (top) © Joel Gordon; **p. 201** (bottom) © Doug Goodman/Monkmeyer; **p. 206** James Kilkelly **p. 217** Shirley Zeiberg; **p. 220** © Jose Pelaez/The Stock Market; **p. 225** © Tony Freeman/PhotoEdit; **p. 227** © Anthony Wood/Stock, Boston.

Chapter 7

Chapter 7 opening photo © Jim Erickson/The Stock Market; **p. 235** PhotoDisc, Volume 2, People and Lifestyles; **p. 236** Digital Stock, Babies and Children; **p. 241** Harry Harlow Primate Laboratory/University of Wisconsin; **p. 242** © Joel Gordon; **p. 245** Jonathan Finlay; **p. 249** © David Young-Wolff/PhotoEdit; **p. 251** © Carl Purcell/Photo Researchers; **p. 255** © Kathy McLoughlin/The Image Works; **p. 258** © George Goodwin/Monkmeyer; **p. 265** © Eastcott/The Image Works; **p. 270** © Joseph Schuyler/Stock, Boston.

Chapter 8

Chapter 8 opening photo © Bob Daemmrich/Stock, Boston; **p. 284** © George Zimbel/Monkmeyer; **p. 288** © Laura Dwight; **p. 293** © Bob Daemmrich/Stock, Boston; **p. 299** © Sybil Shackman/Monkmeyer; **p. 305** Janet Fries.

Chapter 9

Chapter 9 opening photo © Jeff Isaac Greenberg/Photo Researchers; **p. 315** © Erika Stone; **p. 318** © Brady/Monkmeyer; **p. 323** © Erika Stone; **p. 332** © Sybil Shackman/Monkmeyer; **p. 333** © K. Preuss/The Image Works; **p. 335** © Erika Stone/Photo Researchers; **p. 340** © Collins/The Image Works; **p. 341** © Laura Dwight/Peter Arnold, Inc.

Chapter 10

Chapter 10 opening photo © Joan Teasdale/The Stock Market; **p. 354 & 356** © Nancy Richmond/The Image Works; **p. 361** © Erika Stone/Photo Researchers; **p. 363** © Tom McCarthy/PhotoEdit; **p. 368** © Michael Newman/PhotoEdit; **p. 378** © Bob Daemmrich/Stock, Boston; **p. 382** © Owen Franken/Stock, Boston; **p. 385** Nita Winter.

Chapter 11

Chapter 11 opening photo © Robert Finken/The Picture Cube; **p. 398** © Lawrence Migdale/Photo Researchers; **p. 400** © Mary Kate Denny/PhotoEdit; **p. 401** © Bob Daemmrich/Stock, Boston; **p. 404** © Miro Vintoniv/Stock, Boston; **p. 406** PhotoDisc/Volume 18, Health and Medicine; **p. 409** © Martin Rogers/Stock, Boston; **p. 413** © Lawrence Migdale/Stock, Boston.

Chapter 12

Chapter 12 opening photo © Erika Stone; **p. 422** PhotoDisc, Volume 2, People and Lifestyles; **p. 425** © Laura Dwight; **p. 427** © David R. Frazier/Photo Researchers; **p. 433** © Laura Dwight/ PhotoEdit; **p. 440** © Peter Dublin/ Stock, Boston; **p. 445** © Lawrence Migdale/Stock, Boston; **p. 446** © Tony Freeman/PhotoEdit; **p. 453** Richard S. Orton; **p. 454** © Andrew Brilliant/The Picture Cube; **p. 455** © Ken Kerbs/Monkmeyer.

Chapter 13

Chapter 13 opening photo © Tom McCarthy/The Stock Market; **p. 466** © Erika Stone; **p. 467** © M. Justice/The Image Works; **p. 469** © Bernager/Explorer/Photo Researchers; **p. 472** © Jeff Dunn/Stock, Boston; **p. 477** © Erika Stone; **p. 480** © Deborah Davis/PhotoEdit; **p. 482** © Brady/Monkmeyer; **p. 486** (top) © Tony Freeman/PhotoEdit; **p. 486** (bottom)

© Mindy E. Klarman/Photo Researchers; **p. 487** © Myrleen Ferguson Cate/PhotoEdit; **p. 489** © Dallas & John Heaton/Stock, Boston; **p. 491** © Ken Lax/Photo Researchers; **p. 495** © Gabe Palmer Mugshots/The Stock Market; **p. 496** © David Young-Wolff/PhotoEdit.

Chapter 14

Chapter 14 opening photo © Eric Draper/AP/Wide World Photos; **p. 510** © Bill Gillette/Stock, Boston; **p. 513** © Laima Druskis/Photo Researchers; **p. 515** Culver Pictures; **p. 518** © Paula Lerner/The Picture Cube; **p. 522** © Kathy McLaughlin/The Image Works; **p. 525** Kelley Chin-The Kansas City Star/AP/Wide World Photo; **p. 529** © Louis Fernandez/Black Star; **p. 536** © Roy Morsch/The Stock Market.

Chapter 15

Chapter 15 opening photo © Charles Gupton/The Stock Market; **p. 544** © Mimi Forsyth/Monkmeyer; **p. 547** © David Young-Wolff/PhotoEdit; **p. 548** © Jeffry W. Myers/Stock, Boston; **p. 555** Richard E. Schultz; **p. 558** © Spencer Grant/Photo Researchers; **p. 560** © Erika Stone; **p. 566** © Richard Pasley/Stock, Boston.

Chapter 16

Chapter 16 opening photo © Paula Lerner/The Picture Cube; **p. 574** © Erika Stone; **p. 579** © Bob Daemmrich/The Image Works; **p. 580** © Ellen Skye/Monkmeyer; **p. 584** The Children's Defense Fund; **p. 587** © Bob Daemmrich/Stock, Boston; **p. 591** © Myrleen Ferguson/PhotoEdit; **p. 594** © David Young-Wolff/PhotoEdit; **p. 598** © Steve Skjold/PhotoEdit; **p. 601** © Nancy Sheehan/The Picture Cube; **p. 604** © Mike Kagan/Monkmeyer; **p. 607** © A. Ramey/Stock, Boston.

Index

Burhans, K. K., 357
Buriel, R., 470
Burleson, B. R., 488
Burn, P., 401
Burns, A., 478
Burns, J. F., 116
Burns, W., 109
Burros, M., 402
Burton, P. R., 107
Burts, D. C., 375
Bush, D. M., 517
Bushnell, E. W., 169, 174, 176
Busnel, M. C., 216
Busse, T. V., 456
Butler, N., 521
Butler, S., 332
Butterfield, E., 191
Bwibo, N. O., 399
Byrd, R. S., 344

Cahan, S., 436
Cain, R., 242
Cain, V. S., 472
Cairns, B. D., 565
Cairns, R. B., 565
Caldwell, B., 195
Caliendo, M. A., 283, 284, 523
Calkins, S. D., 249, 252
Call, K. T., 561
Callahan, C. M., 454
Calvert, S. L., 364
Campbell, B. A., 205
Campbell, F. A., 195, 196
Campbell, S. B., 253
Campfield, L. A., 401
Campos, J., 175, 248, 256
Campos, J. J., 174, 175, 235
Campos, S. P., 397
Camras, L. A., 235
Canadian Early and Mid-Trimester
        Amniocentesis Trial (CEMAT)
        Group, 115
Canizzo, S. R., 430
Cantor, J., 379, 380
Caplan, M., 267
Caprara, G. V., 560
Carlo, G., 375
Carlson, S. M., 367
Carlton-Ford, S., 557
Caro, F. G., 481
Carpenter, M. W., 105
Carraher, D. W., 427
Carraher, T. N., 427
Carrera, M. A., 585
Carriger, M. S., 194, 206, 207, 208
Carson, J. L., 386
Carta, J., 224
Carter, D. B., 360
Cartwright, B. S., 367
Caruso, D., 208
Carver, K., 564
Casaer, P., 134
Case, R., 32, 33, 433, 434, 435
Casella, J. F., 523
Casey, R. J., 261
Casper, L. M., 244, 267
Casper, R. C., 524
Caspi, A., 239, 515, 561, 590
Cassidy, J., 250, 455
Catalano, R. F., 529
Catsambis, S., 473
Cauffman, E., 525
Caulfield, M., 325
Ceballo, R., 597

Ceci, S. J., 330, 331, 435
Celis, W., 302
Center on Addiction and Substance Abuse
        at Columbia University (CASA),
        530, 531
Centers for Disease Control and Prevention
        (CDC), 106, 128, 183, 299, 411,
        508–509, 521, 530, 531–532, 535, 564
Centor, R. M., 535
Cernkovich, S. A., 591
Cernoch, J. M., 169
Chaika, H., 170
Chalfie, D., 481
Chan, S. Q., 470
Chance, P., 431
Chandler, M., 320
Chandler, P., 217
Chandra, A., 580
Chang, S., 399
Chao, R. K., 371, 441
Chapieski, M. L., 259
Chapman, A. H., 495
Chapman, M., 374–375, 422
Charlesworth, W. R., 236
Chase-Lansdale, P. L., 477, 588, 589
Chasnoff, I. J., 109, 110
Chassin, L., 593
Chaudhuri, S., 535
Chavez, C. J., 109
Chavkin, W., 103
Chehab, F. F., 510
Chen, C., 440, 441, 560, 593
Chen, L., 107
Chen, S., 248
Chen, X., 488, 489
Cherlin, A. J., 244, 477, 481
Chervenak, F. A., 117
Chess, S., 84, 147, 237, 238, 239
Cheung, L. W. Y., 107, 139
Cheung, M. C., 117
Children's Defense Fund, 183, 295, 296–297,
        298, 341, 471, 564, 580, 581, 582, 585,
        586, 587, 588
Chinsky, J., 430
Chisholm, J. S., 178, 256
Chisholm, K., 168
Chomitz, V. R., 107, 139, 140
Chomsky, C. S., 322, 440
Chomsky, N., 221, 339
Christie, D., 525
Christie, J. F., 328
Chubb, N. H., 579
Chumlea, W. C., 512
Church, R. B., 589
Churgay, C. A., 99
Chused, E., 109
Cicchetti, D., 302–303
Cicirelli, V. G., 482, 483
Cigales, M., 168
Clark, E. V., 224
Clark, M., 422
Clark, R. D., 266
Clark, S. C., 476
Clark, S. D., 585
Clarke, N. G., 181
Clarke-Stewart, K. A., 247, 269, 271, 272
Clausen, J. A., 44, 516
Clauson, J., 469
Clay, R. A., 150
Clayton, R., 123, 124
Cleveland, L. E., 284, 401
Clifton, R. K., 207
Clinkenbeard, P., 438
Clyde, W. A., 291

Cobb, N. J., 600
Cobrinick, P., 109
Cochi, S., 182–183
Cochrane, J. A., 182
Cohen, B., 250
Cohen, H. J., 411
Cohen, K. M., 178
Cohen, M., 436
Cohen, P., 494
Cohen, R. A., 296
Cohen, S. E., 171, 207, 212
Cohn, J. F., 253
Cohrs, M., 172
Coie, J. D., 487, 488, 493
Colburne, K. A., 383
Colby, A., 554
Cole, C., 472
Cole, K., 326
Cole, P. M., 106, 254
Colecchia, N., 269
Coleman, C. C., 384
Coleman, J. S., 562, 599
Collier, V. P., 445
Collins, C., 179
Collins, J. G., 408
Collins, J. W., Jr., 140
Collins, P. F., 212
Collins, R. C., 342
Collins, W. A., 592
Collinsworth, P., 244
Colombo, J., 194, 206, 207
Colter, B. S., 386, 387
Concordet, J. P., 94
Conger, J. J., 583, 585
Conger, R. C., 593, 597
Conger, R. D., 593
Conley, M. R., 105
Connecticut Early Childhood Education
        Council (CECEC), 343
Connell, F. A., 129
Cook, E. H., 86
Cook, R., 62
Cook, T. D., 565
Cooke, M., 112
Cooley, M., 588, 589
Coons, S., 147
Cooper, P., 254
Cooper, R. P., 102, 171, 216, 226
Coopersmith, S., 468
Corasaniti, M. A., 472
Corbet, A., 140
Corbin, C., 287, 288
Corbin, C. B., 405
Coren, S., 288, 289
Corey, C. R., 297
Corey, L., 111
Corley, R., 85
Corman, H., 140
Corns, K. M., 251, 264
Corter, C., 381
Coster, W. J., 302–303
Costigan, K. A., 99, 100, 239
Cote, L., 326
Coulehan, C. M., 249
Council on Scientific Affairs of the American
        Medical Association, 453, 509,
        534, 535
Cowan, C. P., 339, 343
Cowan, G., 358
Cowan, M. W., 134
Cowan, P. A., 339, 343
Cox, J., 457
Cox, M. J., 249
Coy, K. C., 260

Coyle, T. R., 431
Cradock-Watson, J. E., 111
Craft, M. J., 295
Crain-Thoreson, C., 226, 326
Cramer, D., 480
Crane, M. M., 110
Cratty, B., 288
Cratty, B. J., 404
Creasey, G. L., 244
Crick, N. R., 491, 492
Crittenden, P. M., 248
Crnic, K., 240
Crnic, K. A., 58
Crockenberg, S., 386
Crockett, L. J., 517
Cronk, C., 202
Crouter, A. C., 473, 561
Crowley, S. L., 481
Crown, J. F., 113
Csikszentmihalyi, M., 590
Cuandra, A., 168
Culp, A. M., 224
Cummings, E. M., 376
Cummings, P., 292
Cunningham, A. S., 162
Cunningham, F. G., 112
Curry, A., 557
Curtin, S. C., 57, 115, 128, 129
Curwin, A., 223
Cutler, A., 216
Cutz, E., 181, 182
Czegledy-Nagy, E. N., 181

Daiute, C., 442–443
Dale, P. S., 226, 326
Daley, S., 589
Dallal, G. E., 402, 524
D'Alton, M. E., 117
Daly, L. E., 104
Dambrosia, J. M., 129
Damon, W., 554
Daniel, N., 457
Daniels, D., 77, 78, 81, 85
Daniels, M., 84
Darling, N. E., 559, 594, 604
Darlington, R. B., 342
Daro, D., 305
Dauber, S. L., 447
Davalos, M., 254
David, M., 108
David, R. J., 140
Davidson, D. H., 340
Davidson, J., 498
Davidson, J. E., 455
Davidson, R. J., 255
Davies, M., 527
Davis, C. C., 266
Davis, M., 243
Davis, N. S., 286
Davis, T. L., 320
Dawson, D. A., 469, 475, 479
Dawson, G., 165, 254
Dawson, J. M., 300
Dawson, R., 298
Day, J., 557
Day, R. D., 581, 583
Dean, R. F. A., 438
Deane, K. E., 248
DeBaryshe, B. D., 325, 603
de Boysson-Bardies, B., 218
DeCasper, A. J., 101, 102, 171, 216
DeCherney, A. H., 116, 117
Decouflé, P., 140, 195, 408
DeFries, J. C., 85, 222, 239, 453

DeFries, P. J., 77
Degirmencioglu, S. M., 531
Deinard, A. S., 172
Dekovic, M., 488
de Lafuente, D., 61
Delaney, S., 170
Del Carmen, R. D., 238, 248
Deloria, D., 342
DeMaris, A., 591
Demo, D. H., 469, 470, 472, 473, 476
Denney, N. W., 313
Dennis, W., 16
Dennison, B. A., 164
Denny, F. W., 291
Dent, C. W., 595
Denton, K., 602
Derevensky, J. L., 225
DeSimone, P. A., 344
Desjardins, C., 362
Devlin, B., 84
DeVos, J., 209
Devos, R., 401
Dewey, K. G., 162
DeWolf, M., 375
De Wolff, M. S., 248
Deykin, E. Y., 535
Diamond, M., 362
Diamond, M. C., 164, 167
Diaz, R. M., 445, 446
DiChiara, G., 530
Dick, R., 289
Dickinson, D. K., 326
Didow, S. M., 266
Dien, D. S. F., 556
Dietrich, K. N., 299
Dietz, V., 182–183
Dietz, W. H., 402, 524
DiFranza, J. R., 107
DiLalla, L. F., 85
Dimant, R. J., 546
Dimiceli, S., 127
DiPietro, J. A., 94, 99, 100, 239
Dishion, T. J., 558, 603
Disney, E. R., 110
Divon, M., 140
Dixon, S., 243
Dodds, J. B., 172
Dodge, K. A., 303, 369, 384, 474, 487, 491,
        492, 493
Dodson, S. L., 321
Doherty, W. J., 531
Dong, Q., 321
Doniger, A. S., 344
Donnelly, D. A., 471, 476, 477
Doris, J., 303, 330
Dornbusch, S. M., 559, 560, 561, 594, 604
Dorris, M., 91, 92
Dougherty, D. M., 519
Dougherty, L. M., 234
Dougherty, T. M., 206, 207
Dove, H., 177, 178
Dove, J., 525
Dovidio, J. F., 486
Down Snydrome Collaborative Group, 74, 113
Doyle, A. B., 485
Drake, C., 412
Dreher, M. C., 108
Driver, D., 481
Droegemueller, W., 300
Drumm, P., 547
Dryer, P. H., 581
Dubrow, N., 291, 498
Duckett, E., 591
Duggan, A. K., 523

Duke, P., 516
Duncan, G. J., 338, 438
Dunham, F., 223
Dunham, P. J., 223
Dunn, J., 222, 226, 264, 265, 318, 355, 385, 598
Dunne, R. G., 412
DuPont, R. L., 379
Durand, A. M., 131
DuRant, R. H., 585
Durkin, D., 226
Durrett, M., 565
Dweck, C. S., 357
Dwyer, T., 182
Dyson, A. H., 442

Earle, J. R., 481–482
Easterbrooks, M. A., 242, 243
Easterling, T. R., 129
Eaton, W. O., 243
Eberly, S., 299
Eccles, J. S., 511, 557, 593, 594, 595, 596, 598
Echeland, Y., 94
Eck, L. H., 284
Eckenrode, J., 303
Eckerman, C. O., 266
Edelstein, W., 590
Edlin, B. R., 532
Edwards, B., 304
Edwards, C. P., 555
Edwards, K. I., 526, 527
Egbuono, L., 296
Egeland, B., 249, 304
Egertson, H. A., 343
Eggebeen, D. J., 240, 478, 479
Ehrhardt, A. A., 362
Eiberg, H., 286
Eidelman, A., 203
Eiden, R. D., 251, 264
Eiger, M. S., 149, 163
Eimas, P., 170, 216, 221
Einbender, A. J., 304
Eisen, M., 585
Eisenberg, A. R., 373
Eisenberg, I., 109
Eisenberg, L., 536
Eisenberg, N., 358, 375, 376, 377, 384, 468, 498
Eisenberg-Berg, N., 376
Eisenson, J., 216
Elder, G. H., Jr., 561, 597
Elias, S., 117
Elicker, J., 251, 252
Elkind, D., 15, 343, 496, 548
Elliott, D. S., 605
Ellis, A. W., 444
Ellis, K. J., 397, 512
Ellis, L., 518
Ellsworth, R. A., 442
Emanuel, I., 107
Emde, R. N., 25, 239, 256, 375
Emery, R. E., 469
Emory, E., 243
Engle, P. L., 426
Englund, M., 488
Enloe, C. F., 92
Enns, L. R., 243
Ensminget, M. E., 142
Entwisle, D. R., 447
Epstein, A. S., 342
Epstein, L. H., 402
Erikson, E. H., 25, 245, 258, 355, 356, 466,
        574, 575
Erikson, J. M., 25
Eron, L. D., 378
Escarce, M. E. W., 94

Escobar, M. D., 453
Eskes, M., 129
Espinosa, M. P., 399
Esser, G., 208
Ettema, J. S., 364
European Collaborative Study, 110
Evans, G. D., 113, 412
Evans, N., 531
Evans, R. I., 25
Evans, S. F., 115
Everson, R. B., 113
Evertson, C., 366
Ewigman, B. G., 115

Fabes, R. A., 358, 377, 384, 468
Fagan, J. F., 206
Fagen, J., 169
Fagen, J. W., 192
Fagot, B. I., 243, 251, 335, 338, 362
Faison, S., 382
Falbo, T., 381, 382, 383
Faltermayer, C., 54
Fanaroff, A. A., 140, 169
Fantuzzo, J. W., 306
Fantz, F. L., 169
Fantz, R., 169
Faraone, S. V., 107
Farber, E., 375
Farkas, A., 531
Farrar, M. J., 361
Farrow, J. A., 530
Farver, J. A. M., 367, 377, 378
Feagans, L. V., 272, 453
Fegley, S., 561
Feiler, R., 343
Fein, G. G., 366, 367
Fein, S. B., 162
Feinman, S., 256
Feldhusen, J. F., 457, 558
Feldman, E., 402
Feldman, J. F., 208
Feldman, R. D., 449, 456, 457
Feldman, R. S., 303
Feldman, W., 402
Felner, R. D., 562
Fennema, E., 358
Ferdman, B. M., 446
Ferguson, J., 142
Fergusson, D. M., 162, 286, 295
Fernald, A., 202, 224, 225
Fernández, A., 108
Fertman, C. I., 579
Fetters, L., 109
Fidler, V., 162
Field, D., 321
Field, T., 168, 254, 255, 270, 272, 384
Field, T. M., 141, 168, 247, 254, 266, 587
Fifer, W. P., 102, 171, 216
Finch, M. D., 561
Findley, B. W., 407
Finegan, J. A. K., 115
Finkelhor, D., 303, 304, 471, 476, 477
Finn, J. D., 564, 565
Finnie, V., 387
Fiori-Cowley, A., 254
Fischel, J. E., 325
Fischer, K., 353
Fischman, J., 431
Fish, M., 240, 249
Fisher, C. B., 45
Fisher, D. M., 172
Fisher, M., 103
Fisher, R. L., 495–496
Fisher, S., 495–496

Fitch, B. R., 109
Fitzsimmons, C. M., 218
Fivush, F., 333
Fivush, R., 327, 329, 333
Flaherty, J., 515
Flake, A. W., 118
Flanagan, C. A., 557
Flavell, E. R., 44, 318, 319
Flavell, J., 421, 430
Flavell, J. H., 32, 44, 221, 318, 319, 320, 321, 429, 430, 433, 441
Flay, B. R., 595
Fletcher, A. C., 604
Fletcher, J. M., 453
Fletcher, P., 399
Flor, D., 448, 593
Flores, J., 350
Fluoxetine-Bulimia Collaborative Study Group, 527
Foch, T. T., 161, 401
Foley, M. A., 34
Ford, D. Y., 457, 458
Ford, K., 581
Forehand, R., 603
Forman, B. M., 401
Forrest, D., 303
Forrest, J. D., 119
Foster, M. R., 432
Foster-Clark, F. S., 578, 602
Fowler, M. G., 497
Fox, N. A., 249, 252, 254, 255, 329
Fox, N. E., 251–252
Fraga, C. G., 113
Fraleigh, M. J., 559
Frank, A. L., 366, 506
Frank, M. A., 109
Frankenburg, W. K., 172
Fraser, A. M., 587
Freedman, D. G., 85, 136
Freedman, D. S., 400, 401
Freedman, M., 85
Freedman, M. A., 478, 586
Freeman, H. E., 297
Freets, R. C., 112
Freud, A., 592
Freud, S., 22, 592
Frey, K., 165
Fried, P. A., 108
Friedman, B., 552
Friedman, H., 140
Friedrich, W. N., 304
Friend, M., 320
Frodi, A. M., 243
Frosch, D. L., 377, 378
Fry, A. F., 429
Fuchs, D., 439
Fuchs, L. S., 439
Fuhrman, T., 594
Fujita, N., 223
Fukumoto, A., 261
Fuligni, A. J., 441, 562, 591, 593, 594
Fulker, D. W., 77, 85, 206, 239, 453
Fuller-Thomson, E., 481
Furman, L. J., 400
Furman, W., 384, 469, 488, 490, 491, 597, 598
Furstenberg, F. F., 244, 481, 562, 588
Furukawa, S., 240, 481

Gabarino, J., 291, 302, 498
Gabriel, T., 61, 62
Gaddis, A., 515
Gaensbauer, T., 235
Gaertner, S. L., 486
Galaburda, A. M., 289

Galambos, N. L., 240, 473, 595, 596
Galasso, L., 319
Gale, J. L., 183
Gallagher, J., 103
Gallistel, C. R., 314
Galotti, K. M., 421
Gamoran, A., 558
Gans, J. E., 513, 520
Ganza, B., 580
Garai, J. E., 288
Garasky, S., 478
Garber, J., 468
Garcia, E. E., 443, 445, 446
Gardner, H., 436, 437, 455
Gardner, W., 479
Garfinkel, B. D., 494
Garfinkel, P. E., 527
Garland, A. F., 535, 536
Garland, J. B., 175
Garmezy, N., 304, 476, 496
Garner, D. M., 525, 527
Garner, P. W., 353
Gatherum, A., 470
Gatsonis, C. A., 112
Gauger, K., 483
Gauthier, R., 108
Gauvain, M., 335, 338, 424, 426, 427
Gavazzi, S. M., 60
Ge, X., 597
Gearhart, M., 314
Geary, D. C., 453
Gecas, V., 599
Geen, R. G., 378
Gekoski, M. J., 192
Gelfand, D. M., 248, 253, 254
Gelman, R., 313, 314, 317, 323
Genesee, F., 219
Gentner, D., 218
George, C., 250
George, T. P., 488, 490
Gerber, M., 438
Gerstein, D. R., 529, 596
Gersten, M. S., 302–303
Gertner, B. L., 325
Gervai, J., 358, 363, 364
Geschwind, N., 289
Gesell, A., 178
Getzels, J. W., 456
Gianino, A. F., 252
Gibbons, J., 85
Gibbons, L. E., 182
Gibbons, S., 383
Gibbs, J. C., 554, 595, 603
Gibson, E. J., 174
Gibson, R., 162
Gielen, U., 556
Gilbert, S., 378
Giles-Sims, J., 369, 471
Gilgan, C., 548, 554, 555, 578, 579
Gilpin, E. A., 531
Ginsberg, S. W., 563
Ginsburg, A., 595
Ginsburg, G. S., 447, 448
Ginsburg, H. P., 412, 440, 441, 547
Ginzberg, E., 563
Giordano, P. C., 591, 601
Girgus, J. S., 523
Gladue, B. A., 518
Glasgow, K. L., 560
Glass, L., 181
Glass, R. B., 60
Gleason, J. B., 322
Gleitman, H., 225
Gleitman, L. R., 225

Glenn, R., 289
Glick, P. C., 240
Glod, C. A., 452
Gold, D., 595
Goldberg, J. D., 117
Goldberg, W. A., 242, 243, 473
Golden, M., 438
Goldenberg, R. L., 104, 105, 107
Goldin-Meadow, S., 221
Goldman, A., 123
Goldman, M. B., 112
Goldschmidt, I., 150
Goldsmith, M., 309
Goleman, D., 286, 330
Golinkoff, R. M., 322
Golomb, C., 319
Golombok, S., 62, 63, 480, 518
Göncü, A., 214
Gonzalez, A., 181
Goodman, G. S., 331, 361, 422
Goodman, J. T., 402
Goodman, R. A., 293
Goodnow, J. J., 259, 369, 370, 372, 373
Goodwyn, S., 217
Goodz, E., 225
Gopnik, A., 203, 204
Gordon, I., 525
Gordon, T. P., 362
Gorman, K. S., 399
Gorman, M., 465
Gortmaker, S. L., 107, 402, 524
Gotlib, I. H., 254
Gottesman, I. I., 86
Gottfried, A. W., 239
Gottman, J. M., 386, 476
Gourde, C., 202
Gove, F., 251
Graber, J. A., 515
Graham, C. J., 289
Gralinski, H., 235
Gralinski, J. H., 261
Granger, D. A., 495
Granger, R. H., 109
Granier-Deferre, C., 216
Grantham-McGregor, S., 399
Graubard, B. I., 106
Graziano, A. M., 283
Green, F. L., 44, 318, 319, 441
Greenberg, M. T., 58
Greenberg, R., 587
Greenberger, E., 473, 561, 593
Greene, S. M., 85, 107
Greenfield, P., 426
Greenfield, P. M., 339
Greenhouse, J. B., 299
Greenough, W. T., 167
Greenstein, T. N., 150
Greenwood, C., 224
Grether, J. K., 129
Griesler, P. C., 488
Griffith, E. M., 344
Grigorenko, E. L., 449
Grimes, D. A., 99
Griswold, D., 244
Groo, D., 407
Gross, J., 332
Gross, R. T., 516
Grossman, D. C., 292, 412, 509, 535
Grossman, J. B., 319
Grossman, K., 243
Grotevant, H., 565
Groth-Marnat, G., 291
Grotpeter, J. K., 492
Grout, H. T., 56

Gruber, H. E., 187, 188
Grubman, S., 111
Grummer-Strawn, L. M., 162
Grusec, J. E., 259, 369, 370, 372, 373
Gruson, L., 76
Guacci-Franco, N., 470
Guberman, S. R., 314, 426
Guerin, D. W., 239
Guidubaldi, J., 476
Guilford, J. P., 456
Guilleminault, C., 147
Guisez, Y., 401
Guisinger, S., 26
Gulko, J., 383
Gullone, E., 497
Gunnar, M. R., 256
Guralnick, P., 124
Gurrin, L., 107
Guyer, B., 60, 68, 181

Hack, M., 140, 169
Hackman, R., 181
Haddow, J. E., 117
Haden, C. A., 327, 333
Hadley, P. A., 325
Hagan, R., 243, 362
Haglund, B., 181
Haight, W., 222–223
Haine, R. A., 327
Haith, M. M., 168, 169, 170, 206, 207
Hakuta, K., 443, 445, 446
Hala, S., 320
Halaas, J. L., 401
Hale, J., 451
Hale, S., 429
Halfon, N., 410
Hall, E. G., 404
Hall, G. S., 16, 592
Hallé, P. A., 218
Halman, J., 60
Halpern, D. F., 289
Haltiwanger, J., 357
Hamer, D. H., 518
Hamilton, C. E., 272
Hamilton, S., 561, 564
Hammer, M., 303
Han, S. S., 495
Handyside, A., 117
Hanna, E., 205, 266
Hans, S. L., 370
Hansbarger, A., 321
Hardy-Brown, K., 222
Hardyck, C., 289
Har-Even, D., 150
Harley, E. E., 106
Harlow, H. F., 242
Harlow, M. K., 242
Harmer, S., 319
Harmon, R. J., 254
Harnishfeger, K. K., 432
Harold, R., 593
Harper, R. M., 181
Harrington, D. M., 374
Harris, J. J., III, 457, 458
Harris, J. R., 81, 161, 401
Harris, L. J., 289, 517
Harris, M. B., 480
Harris, M. L., 256
Harris, P. L., 319, 424
Harrison, A. O., 470
Harrist, A. W., 384
Hart, B., 224, 338
Hart, C. H., 375, 376, 384, 385, 386, 388
Hart, D., 590

Hart, J. B., 321
Hart, S. N., 168, 304
Harter, S., 352, 353, 354, 355, 356, 357, 466, 467, 468
Hartford, R. B., 182
Hartman, C. R., 303
Hartmann, D. P., 484, 488, 490
Hartmann, E., 286
Hartup, W. W., 442–443, 484, 485, 487, 488, 490, 491
Harvey, B., 183
Harwood, R. L., 262, 263
Haselager, G. J. T., 590
Haskett, M. E., 303
Haskins, R., 342
Haslett, S. J., 578
Haswell, K., 259
Hatcher, P. J., 444
Hatcher, R., 109
Hatzichristou, C., 599
Haugh, S., 358
Haviland, J., 253
Hawkins, J. D., 529
Hawley, T. L., 110
Hay, D. F., 266, 267
Hayes, A., 73, 74
Hayne, H., 192, 205, 332
Haynes, O. M., 249, 250, 301
Hayward, R. A., 297
Health Care Financing Administration, 296, 297
Heard, D., 123, 124
Heath, S. B., 58, 439, 451
Hebel, R., 107
Heinig, M. J., 162
Helland, C., 150
Hellewell, T. B., 34
Hellström, A., 106
Helms, J. E., 439, 450
Heming, G., 343
Hendee, W. R., 588
Henderson, C. R., 107
Henderson, V. K., 249
Hendler, J., 85
Henker, B., 452
Henly, W. L., 109
Henrichon, A. J., 320
Henschel, M., 212
Henshaw, S., 585
Herbst, A., 106
Herma, J., 563
Herman-Giddens, M. E., 512
Herrera, C., 303
Herrling, S., 585
Herrmann, H. J., 282
Herrnstein, R. J., 438
Hertsgaard, L., 256
Hertzig, M. E., 285
Herzog, D. B., 527
Hespos, S. J., 209
Hesse, E., 247
Hesser, J., 483
Hessl, D., 165
Hetherington, E. M., 360, 469, 475, 476, 478, 479, 480
Heuser, R. L., 478, 586
Hewlett, B. S., 243
Heyns, B., 473
Hiatt, S., 235
Hidalgo, H. R., 411
Hildebrandt, K. A., 141
Hill, J. P., 592
Hills, A., 297, 299
Hinckley, C., 131
Hirsch, H. V., 165
Hirsch, J., 165

Solomons, H., 177
Sommers-Flanagan, J., 496
Sommers-Flanagan, R., 496
Sonenstein, F. L., 532, 581
Song, L. Y., 535
Song, M., 440, 441
Sontag, L. W., 100, 101
Sophian, C., 314
Sorce, J. F., 256
Sorensen, T., 82
Sosin, D. M., 412
Southall, D. P., 181
Soutollo, D., 254
Sparling, J. J., 195
Speer, J. R., 441
Spelke, E. S., 189, 317
Spence, M. J., 101, 102, 171
Spencer, H. C., 293
Spencer, M. B., 579
Spieker, S., 588, 589
Spiker, D., 142
Spinelli, D. N., 165
Spitz, M. R., 113
Spitz, R. A., 256
Spock, B., 264
Spohr, H. L., 106
Squire, L. R., 212
Srinivasan, S. R., 400
Srivastav, P., 243
Sroufe, L. A., 236, 237, 251–252, 256, 304,
   375, 488
Stack, S., 583
Stager, C. L., 218
Stahl, S. A., 444
Stainton, M. C., 94
Stanhope, R., 397
Stanley, F. J., 115
Stanley-Hagan, M., 476
Starfield, B., 142, 296, 408, 411
Starr, R., 109
Staub, S., 328
Stedman, L. C., 444
Steel, L., 561
Steele, B. N., 300
Stein, M. R., 266
Steinberg, L., 270, 515, 525, 559, 560, 561, 593,
   594, 603–604
Steiner, J. E., 169
Steinhausen, H. C., 106
Steptoe, A., 521
Stern, M., 141
Sternberg, K. J., 268
Sternberg, R. J., 436, 437, 438, 439, 448, 449, 455,
   559, 567
Stevens, J. H., 195
Stevens, K. N., 216
Stevenson, C. S., 454
Stevenson, D. L., 447
Stevenson, H. W., 426, 440, 441, 560, 591
Stevenson, J., 182–183
Stevenson, M. R., 363
Steward, D. S., 330, 331
Steward, M. S., 330, 331
Stewart, I. C., 584
Stewart, R. B., 264, 266
Stewart, W., 473
Stick, S. M., 107
Stifter, C. A., 249
Stigler, J. W., 440
Stiles, K. M., 299
Stipek, D., 343
Stipek, D. J., 235, 257, 258, 261, 341
Stockemer, V., 383
Stocker, C., 598

Stocking, C. B., 296
Stoddard, J. J., 181, 294, 297, 408
Stoll, M. F., 469
Stoller, S., 587
Stoneman, Z., 448, 482–483, 593
Stoolmiller, M., 558, 603
Stouthamer-Loeber, M., 590, 603
Straus, M. A., 369, 471
Strauss, M., 109
Strawn, J., 295
Strayer, J., 468
Streissguth, A. P., 106, 107
Streitfeld, D., 92
Strobino, D. M., 60, 181
Strom, R., 244
Strom, S., 244
Strömland, K., 106
Stubbs, M. L., 515, 516
Stunkard, A., 81, 161, 165, 401
Stunkard, A. J., 161, 165, 401
Styfco, S. J., 341, 342
Succop, P. A., 299
Sue, S., 441
Sugarman, D. B., 369, 471
Suissa, S., 293
Sullivan, K., 321
Sullivan, M. W., 109, 163
Sullivan, P., 523
Sullivan-Bolyai, J., 111
Sun, Y., 489
Sundell, H., 182
Suomi, S., 242
Susman-Stillman, A., 249, 250
Swain, I. U., 207
Swanston, H. Y., 304
Swarr, A. E., 524, 525
Swedo, S., 535
Sweetland, J. D., 344
Swift, D. J., 332
Symons, D., 404

Tabin, C., 95
Tabor, A., 115
Taddio, A., 168
Taffel, S. M., 585
Tager-Flusberg, H., 321
Takanishi, R., 508
Tallal, P., 453
Talokder, E., 243
Tamis-LeMonda, C. S., 208, 212, 223
Tamura, T., 105
Tanda, G., 530
Tanfer, K., 585
Tanner, J. M., 396, 512, 516
Tappan, M. B., 555
Tardif, T., 218
Tarin, J. J., 117
Tashman, B., 453
Tasker, F., 480, 518
Tatelbaum, R., 107
Taussig, C., 605
Taussig, L. M., 162
Taylor, J. A., 182
Taylor, J. H., 554
Taylor, M., 367
Taylor, M. G., 361
Taylor, R. D., 562, 597
Taylor, W. R., 410
Teachman, J. D., 564
Teasdale, T., 82
Tebbutt, J. S., 304
Teicher, M., 452
Tellegen, A., 304
Teller, D. Y., 169

Terman, D. L., 454
Terman, L. M., 456
Termine, N. T., 253
Terry, D., 103
Tesla, C., 318
Tesman, J. R., 297, 299
Tesslre, M., 332
Teti, D. M., 248, 251, 253, 254, 264
Thacker, S. B., 293, 295
Tharp, R. G., 450, 451
Thelen, E., 171, 172
Thomas, A., 84, 147, 237, 238, 239
Thomas, D. G., 212
Thomas, R. M., 33
Thomas, W. P., 445
Thompson, B., 194
Thompson, D. C., 412, 413
Thompson, L. A., 206, 207
Thompson, R. S., 412, 413
Thompson, W. W., 474
Thomson, D. M., 331
Thorne, A., 579
Tiedemann, D., 15–16
Timini, S., 525
Ting, T. Y., 129
Tinker, E., 223
Tinsley, B. J., 244
Tinsley, B. R., 243
Tisak, J., 600
Tisak, M. S., 600
Tobin, J. J., 340
Tobin, M. J., 299
Tobin-Richards, M. H., 513, 516, 523
Tomasello, M., 223
Toner, B. B., 527
Toner, J. P., 60
Torff, B., 449
Torrance, E. P., 456
Torres, A., 119
Touwen, B. C. L., 162
Touyz, S. W., 527
Townsend, J. W., 426
Tramontana, M. G., 334, 344
Treffers, P. E., 129
Trehub, S. E., 224
Tremblay, R. E., 529, 603
Tronick, E., 169, 243
Tronick, E. Z., 109, 241, 252, 253
Trotter, R. J., 235, 243
Troyer, L., 560
Truglio, R., 326
Tschann, J. M., 477
Tubman, J. G., 582
Tucker, C. J., 598
Turkewitz, G., 34
Turner, H., 471
Turner, P. H., 480
Turner, P. J., 358, 363, 364
Tygiel, J., 571
Tyler, P. E., 104

Umberger, F. G., 282
Unger, D., 588, 589
UNICEF, 139
U. S. Advisory Board on Child Abuse and
   Neglect, 300
U. S. Bureau of the Census, 57, 476, 478, 479
U. S. Consumer Product Safety
   Commission, 293
U. S. Department of Education, 447, 457, 564
U. S. Department of Health and Human
   Services (USDHHS), 99, 114, 119,
   181, 292, 305, 411, 475, 509, 529
U. S. Environmental Protection Agency, 294

Subject Index

Aptitude tests, **433**
Arapesh people, self-esteem among, 467
Areolae, 514
Arithmetic, understanding of
during early childhood, 314
during infancy and toddlerhood, 209
during middle childhood, 425
Armenians, genetic defect risks of, 72
Artificial insemination by a donor (AID), **61**, 61
Artistic development, during early childhood, 290–291
Art therapy, 291
Asian(s)
genetic defect risks of, 72
motor development in, 172–173
Asian Americans
adolescent/family conflict and, 593
intelligence of, 438–442
play among, 367–368
school achievement of, during adolescence, 560
temperament of, 85
Aspirations, vocational, influences on, 565–567
Assimilation, **31**
Assisted reproductive technology, 53–54, 61–62
Asthma, **410**
during middle childhood, 410–411
Atherosclerosis, 407
Athletics
accidental injuries due to, during adolescence, 522
during middle childhood, 404
Attachment, **245**, 245–252
establishment of, 248–249
long-term effects of, 251–252
patterns of, 246–248
intergenerational transmission of, 250–251
temperament and, 249–250
Attachment Q-set (AQS), **248**
Attention, selective, 432
Attention-deficit/hyperactivity disorder (ADHD), **452**
Attitudes
parental, school achievement during middle childhood and, 448
sexual, 580–581
Authoritarian parenting, 370
adolescent/family conflict and, 594
school achievement and
during adolescence, 559
during middle childhood, 447
socialization success and, 262
Authoritative parenting, 370–371
adolescent/family conflict and, 594
intelligence and, 335, 338
school achievement and
during adolescence, 559
during middle childhood, 447
self-esteem and, 467–468
socialization success and, 262–263
Autism, **86**
heredity and environment and, 86
Autobiographical memory, **330**, 330–331
Automobile accidents
during adolescence, 535
during middle childhood, 412, 413
Autonomy, development of, 258–259
parenting styles and, 372
Autonomy versus shame and doubt, **258**, 258–259
Autosomes, **65**
Avoidant attachment, **246**
Axons, 134, 164

Babbling, 216
Babinski reflex, 137
Baby biographies, 15–16
Baldwin, James Mark, 17, 21
Bandura, Albert, 29
Basal ganglia, 166
Basic trust versus basic mistrust, **245**
Bateson, Gregory, 231, 232
Bateson, Mary Catherine, 231–233
Battered child syndrome, **300**. *See also* Maltreatment
Baumrind, Diana, 82–83
Bayley Scales of Infant Development, **194**
Bedtime. *See* Sleep
Bed wetting, 286
Behavioral genetics, **74**. *See also* Nature-nurture debate
Behavioral measures, 38
Behavioral modification, 29, 495
Behavioral scripts, aggression and, 378
Behaviorism, **27**, 27–29
classical conditioning and, 27–28
operant conditioning and, 28–29
Behaviorist approach, **190**
classical conditioning and, 190–192
operant conditioning and, 190–193
memory and, 192–193
Behavior therapy, **495**
for obesity during middle childhood, 402
Beliefs
false, knowledge about, during early childhood, 320
parental, school achievement during middle childhood and, 448
Berkeley Growth and Guidance Studies, 16
Beta thalassemia, 68
Bias
cultural, 439
observer, 39
Bicycle accidents, during middle childhood, 412–413
Bilingual children, **443**
Bilingual education, **443**, 445
Bilingual households, language development and, 219
Binet
Albert, 193
Alfred, 17, 21
Binocular cues, 176
Binocular vision, 169
Birth. *See* Childbirth
Birth defects, 68–74
genome imprinting and, 74
prediction from maternal blood tests, 117
transmitted by dominant inheritance, 70
transmitted by recessive inheritance, 70–71
transmitted by sex-linked inheritance, 71–73
Birth rate, decline in, 57
Birth trauma, **138**
Birthweight, low. *See* Low birthweight
Bisexuality, **516**
Blastocyst, 95
Blended families, during middle childhood, 479–480
Blood type, prenatal development and, 112
Body image, **402**
Body proportions, change with age, 160, 161
Bonding. *See also* Attachment
childbirth and, 146–147
Bone marrow transplantation, fetal, 117–118
Bowlby, John, 33

Brain
development during infancy and toddlerhood, 164–168
memory structures of, 212–213
neonatal, 134–136
plasticity of, 164
Brain stem, 166, 213
neonatal, 134
Brazelton Neonatal Behavioral Assessment Scale, **145**
Brazil, care about environment in, 552
Breast development, 514
Breastfeeding, 161–163
smell sense and, 169
taste sense and, 170
Bronfenbrenner, Urie, 341
Brown, Louise, 53–55
Bulimia nervosa, **526**
treatment for, 526–527
Bullying, 491–493, **492**
Bundi people, age of menarche in, 512

Caffeine, maternal use of, prenatal development and, 107–108
Canalization, **78**, 78–79
Cardinality principle, 314
Caregivers
cognitive development and, 212
emotional communication with, 252–255
maternal depression and, 253–255
mutual regulation and, 252–255
language development and, 222–223
learning from interactions with, 213–214
Carriers, for genetic defects, 70–71
Casals, Pablo, 437
Case, Robbie, 33, 433
Case studies, **39**, 39–40
Causality, **209**
understanding of, during infancy and toddlerhood, 209
Cause and effect
during middle childhood, 421–422
symbolic function and, 313
Central executive, **429**
Central nervous system, **134**
neonatal, 134–136
Centration, **314**, 314–315
Cephalocaudal principle, **95**, 160
Cerebellum, 166, 213
neonatal, 134
Cerebral cortex
development during infancy and toddlerhood, 164
neonatal, 134
Cerebrum, 166
neonatal, 134
Cesarean delivery, **128**, 128–129
Chemical exposures, prenatal development and, 112
Chicago Child Parent Centers, 342
Child abuse, 300. *See also* Maltreatment
Childbirth, 126–132
adolescent (*see* Teen pregnancy)
bonding and, 146–147
Cesarean delivery and, 128–129
medicated, 127
natural and prepared, 128
settings and attendants for, 129–132
stages of, 126–127
Child development, **8**. *See also specific periods and types of development*
active versus passive nature of, 20–21
aspects and periods of, 8–9
contexts of, 14–15
evolution of study of, 15–18

heredity versus environment and, 20
influences on, 9, 11–15
perspectives on (see specific perspectives)
science and goals of study of, 16–18
stages versus continuous development
and, 21–22
Child-directed speech (CDS), **224,** 224–225
Childhood depression, **495**
Child-rearing practices. See also Fathers;
Mother(s); Parent(s); Parenting;
Parenting styles
psychosocial development and, 240–244
father's role and, 242–243
grandparent's role and, 244
mother's role and, 241–242
shaping of gender differences and, 243
China
moral reasoning in, 556
neural-tube defects in, 104–105
only children in, 382–383
parenting styles in, 371
preference for male babies in, 116
word choice in, 218
Chinese Americans. See Asian Americans
Chlamydia, 531–533
Cholesterol, **407**
Chomsky, Noam, 221
Chorionic villus sampling (CVS), **115,** 115–116
Chromosomal abnormalities. See Birth defects;
specific birth defects
Chromosomes, **64**
sex (see Sex chromosomes)
Chronic medical conditions, **408**
Chronosystem, 15
Cigarette smoking. See Nicotine use
Cilia, 58
Cingulate cortex, 166
Circular reactions, **198,** 198–200
Circulatory system, neonatal, 133
Circumcision, pain with, 168
Classical conditioning, **27,** 27–28, **190,** 190–192
Classification
during middle childhood, 421
symbolic function and, 313–314
Class inclusion, **421**
Clinical method, of Piaget, 30
Clitoridectomy, 509
Cocaine use
maternal, prenatal development and, 109–110
paternal, prenatal development and, 113
Code-mixing, **219**
Code-switching, 219, **446**
Cognitive development, 8. See also Gifted
children; Intelligence; *specific age
periods*
Cognitive-developmental theory of gender
development, 360–361
Cognitive maps, 193
Cognitive neuroscience approach, **205**
during infancy and toddlerhood, 212–213
Cognitive perspective, 18, 19, **30,** 30–33
information-processing approach and,
32–33
non-Piagetian theories and, 33
of Piaget (see Piaget, Jean)
Cognitive play, **365,** 366–367
Cognitive priming, aggression and, 378
Cognitive theory, of gender development,
359–360
Cohorts, 13
College, 562–563
Colorado Adoption Project, 85
Comforting crying infants, 149
Commitment, **576**
Committed compliance, **261**

Companionate pattern of grandparent-child
relationships, 244
Compensatory preschool programs, 341–342
Competence
exploratory, 208
fostering, 196
planful, 43–44
Compliance, committed and situational, 261
Componential element, **437,** 438
Computer literacy, teaching of, 449
Conception, difficulty with. See Infertility
Concordance, **78**
Concrete operations, **420,** 420–428
advances in cognitive abilities and, 420–425
cultural and schooling effects and, 425–427
influences of culture and schooling and,
425–427
moral reasoning and, 427–428
Conditioning
classical, 27–28, 190–192
operant, 28–29, 190–193
memory and, 192–193
Confidentiality, right to, research and, 46
Conflict
between adolescents and their families,
592–595
family atmosphere and parenting styles
and, 593–595
patterns of, 592–593
parenting styles and, 372
among siblings
during early childhood, 380–381
during toddlerhood, 265–266
Conscience, **260**
development of, 260–262
Consent, informed, right to, research and, 45
Conservation, **315,** 316, **424**
during middle childhood, 424–425
Constraint, morality of, 427, 428
Constructive play, 366
Contextual cues, infant memory and, 192–193
Contextual element, **437,** 438
Contextual perspective, 18, 19, **36**
Contraceptives, adolescent use of, 583, 585
Control, inhibitory, 260
Control group, **41**
Controversial adolescents, 601
Conventional morality, **551**
Conventional social gestures, during infancy
and toddlerhood, 217
Convergent thinking, **456**
Conversation, parental style of, memory and,
332–333
Cooing, 216
Cooley's anemia, 68
Cooperation, morality of, 427, 428
Coregulation, **470**
during middle childhood, 470–471
Corporal punishment, during middle
childhood, 471
Correlational studies, 39, **40**
Counting, during infancy and toddlerhood, 209
Cow's milk, infants feed on, 164
Crawling, 175
Creative children. See Gifted children
Creativity, **456**
Crisis, **576**
Critical periods, **13**
Cross-cultural research, purposes of, 12
Cross-modal transfer, **207,** 207–208
Cross-sectional studies, **44**
Cross-sequential studies, **44**
Crying, 216
comforting crying infants and, 149
types of cries and, 235

Cultural bias, **439**
Culture, **11,** 11–12. See also Ethnic groups;
specific groups
aggression and, 379
attachment patterns and, 247–248
care about environment and, 552
child-directed speech and, 226
cognitive development and
in Asian countries, 441–442
intelligence and, 438–441
during middle childhood, 425–426
cross-cultural commonalities among
adolescents and, 606–608
emotional development and, 234
environmental influences on motor
development during infancy and
toddlerhood and, 177–178
family atmosphere and, 470
gender development and, 364
handedness and, 289
home environment's impact on intelligence
and, 195
interactions with caregivers and, 214
maltreatment and, 302
moral reasoning and, 555–556
parenting styles and, 371–372
play and, 367–368
popularity during middle childhood and, 488
preschool education and, 340–341
school achievement during middle
childhood and, 450–451
sibling relationships and, during middle
childhood, 483–484
sleep and, during infancy and
toddlerhood, 183
socialization and, 263
stranger anxiety and, 256
Culture-fair tests, **439**
Culture-free tests, **439**
Custody, following divorce, during middle
childhood, 477
Cystic fibrosis, 68

Darwin, Charles, 16, 17
Darwin, William Erasmus, 187–189
Darwinian reflex, 137
Data, **18**
collection of, 37–39
behavioral methods for, 38
observation for, 38–39
self-reports for, 37–38
Day care, 267–272
cognitive development and, 269–271
emotional development and, 271
good, qualities of, 269
social development and, 271–272
in Sweden, 268
Death
during adolescence, 535–536
suicide and, 535–536
violent, 535
during early childhood, maltreatment as
cause of, 300
fetal, 98–99, 105
during infancy, 179–183
neonatal, 99, 105, 143–144
sudden infant death syndrome and,
107, 179–183
trends in, 179–181
Decentering, **314**
during middle childhood, 424
Deception, knowledge about, during early
childhood, 320
Deduction, **421**
during middle childhood, 421

Deferred imitation, **201,** 203–205, 313
Defining Issues Test (DIT), 554
Dehydroepiandrosterone (DHEA), 519
Delinquency, 602–606
    interaction of parental and peer influences
        and, 602–604
    long-term prospects for, 604–605
    predicting and preventing, 605–606
Delivery. *See* Childbirth
Dendrites, 134, 164
Denver Developmental Screening Test, **172**
Deoxyribonucleic acid (DNA), **64**
Dependent variables, **41,** 41–42
Depression
    during adolescence, 523
    childhood, 495
    maternal, mutual regulation and,
        253–255
Depth perception, **174,** 176
Description, as goal of study of child
    development, 16–17
Developmental priming mechanisms, **195**
Developmental quotients, 194
Dewey, John, 17
Diaries, 37, 38
Dick-Read, Grantly, 128
Diethylstilbestrol (DES), maternal use of,
    prenatal development, 106
Diet pills, during middle childhood, 402
Difficult children, **238**
Discipline, **368,** 368–370
    during middle childhood, 470–471
    power assertion, induction, and
        withdrawal of love and, 369–370
    reinforcement and punishment
        and, 369
Diseases. *See* Illness
Dishabituation, **207**
Disorganized-disoriented attachment, **246,**
    246–247
Divergent thinking, **456**
Divorce
    during adolescence, 596
    during middle childhood, 476–477,
        481–482
Dizygotic twins, **59,** 60
Dominant inheritance, **66**
    defects transmitted by, 70
Donor eggs, 61–62
Dopamine, marijuana use and, 530
Dorris, Abel, 91–93
Dorris, Michael, 91–92
Double standard, sexual, 580–581
Doulas, 131
Down syndrome, 68, 73–74
    prenatal prediction of, 117
Dramatic play, 366
Drawing, 290–291
Dropping out, of high school, 564–565
Drug therapy, **495**
    for childbirth, 127
    maternal use of, prenatal development
        and, 106
    for mental disorders, 495–496
Drug use and abuse
    during adolescence, 527–531
        alcohol and, 529
        marijuana and, 529–530
        tobacco and, 530–531
    maternal, prenatal development and,
        105–110
    paternal, prenatal development
        and, 113
Duchenne's muscular dystrophy, 68
Dyslexia, **452,** 453

Early childhood, 10
    artistic development during, 290–291
    cognitive development during, 309–346
        animism and, 317
        cognitive advances and, 312–314
        early childhood education and, 339–344
        egocentrism and, 317
        empathy and, 317–318
        gender differences in, 357–358
        information-processing approach to,
            328–333
        limitations of preoperational thought
            and, 314–316
        psychometric measures and, 334–338
        testing and teaching based on zone of
            proximal development and, 339
        theories of mind and, 318–320
        training and, 320–321
    health and safety during, 291–299
        accidental injuries and, 291–294
        environmental influences on health
            and, 294–299
        minor illnesses and, 291
    language development during, 321–328
        communicative and noncommunicative
            speech and, 323–325
        delayed, 325–326
        grammar and syntax and, 322–323
        social interaction and, 326–328
        vocabulary and, 322
    maltreatment during, 300–306
        ecological view of, 301–302
        helping families in trouble or at risk
            for, 304–306
        long-term effects of, 302–304
    memory development during, 328–333
        autobiographical memory and, 330–331
        childhood memories and, 328–331
        episodic memory and, 329
        explicit and implicit memory and, 329
        generic memory and, 329
        influences on, 331–333
        recognition and recall and, 328
    motor development during, 286–291
        artistic development and, 290–291
        handedness and, 288–290
        motor skills and, 287–288
    physical development during, 282–286
        diet and, 283–284
        sleep and, 284–286
    psychosocial development during, 349–389
        altruism, aggression, and fearfulness
            and, 373–380
        conflict, autonomy, and parenting
            goals and, 372–375
        discipline and, 368–370
        emotions and, 353–355
        family and peer relationships and,
            385–387
        gender development and, 358–364
        gender differences in, 357–358
        initiative versus guilt stage and,
            355–356
        parenting styles and, 370–372
        play and, 364–368
        playmates and friends and, 383–385
        self-concept and, 352–353
        self-esteem and, 356–357
        sibling relationships and, 380–383
Early intervention, **195,** 197–198
Easy children, **238**
Eating disorders. *See also* Obesity
    during adolescence, 524–527
    during middle childhood, 402–403
Ecological approach, **14,** 14–15

Ectoderm, 95, 98
Edison, Thomas, 452
Education. *See also* Preschool
    in Asian societies, 440–441
    bilingual, 443, 445
    for children with learning problems, 451–454
        attention-deficit/hyperactivity disorder,
            452
        learning disabilities, 452–454
        mental retardation, 451
    cognitive development during middle
        childhood and, 426–427
    during early childhood
        based on zone of proximal development,
            339
        instruction in, 342–343
        predicting success in, 343–344
    for gifted children, 454–458
        defining, measuring, and fostering
            creativity and, 456
        identifying gifted children and, 454–455
    leaving elementary school and, 556–557
    during middle childhood
        school achievement and, 449–450
        second-language, 443, 445–446
    nutrition and, 399
    preschool, 339–344
        compensatory programs, 341–342
        goals of, 340–341
        instruction in, 342–343
    quality of, achievement and, 557–559
Edwards, Robert, 53
Efe people, child-rearing practices of, 241
Effacement, 126
Ego, **23**
Egocentricity, of young children, 34
Egocentrism, **316**
    challenges to Piaget's conclusions about, 317
Einstein, Albert, 309–311, 325, 437
Elaboration, **431**
Elaborative conversation, memory and, 333
Electronic fetal monitoring, **144**
Elementary school, leaving, 556–557
Elicited imitation, **205**
Eliot, T. S., 437
Embryonic disk, 95
Embryonic stage, **98,** 98–99
Embryoscopy, **116,** 116–117
Emotion(s), **234,** 234–237
    during early childhood, 353–355
        directed toward self, 353–354
        simultaneous, 354–355
    during infancy and toddlerhood
        day care and, 271
        expression by infants, 235–237
        timing of development of emotions
            and, 234–235
    mutual regulation of, 252–255
        maternal depression and, 253–255
Emotional abuse, **300.** *See also* Maltreatment
Emotional neglect, **300.** *See also* Maltreatment
Empathy, **317**
    challenges to Piaget's conclusions about,
        317–318
    development of, 204
    self-esteem and, 468
Employment
    during adolescence, 561
    influences on vocational aspirations and,
        565–567
    maternal
        adolescents and, 595–596
        psychosocial development during
            middle childhood and, 471–473
    stages in vocational planning and, 563–565

Gender roles, **358**
Gender schemas, **361**
Gender-schema theory, **361,** 361–362
Gender stereotypes, **358**
Gender-typing, **243, 358**
Gene(s), **64,** 64–65
Generalization, of research results, 37, 42–43
Generic memory, **329**
Gene therapy, 76
Genetic abnormalities. *See* Birth defects; *specific birth defects*
Genetic counseling, **74,** 75
Genetic determinism, 76
Genetics. *See also* Heredity; Nature-nurture debate
  behavioral, 74
Genetic testing, **74,** 76
Genital herpes simplex virus (HSV), 533
  maternal, prenatal development and, 111
Genital mutilation, of females, 509
Genital stage, 23, 24
Genital warts, 533
Genome imprinting, 74
Genotype, **67,** 67–68
Genotype-environment correlation (covariance), **79,** 79–80
Genotype-environment interaction, **79**
German measles, maternal, prenatal development and, 111
Germinal stage, **95,** 98
Gesell, Arnold, 17, 21
Gestation, **94.** *See also* Fetal stage; Pregnancy; Prenatal development; Prenatal environmental hazards
Gestational age, 94
  infants small for, 138
Gestures, during infancy and toddlerhood, 217
Gifted children, 454–458
  defining, measuring, and fostering creativity and, 456
  educating, 457–458
  identifying gifted, 454–455
  lives of, 455–456
Glaucoma, 69
Glial cells, 164
  neonatal, 134
Goldberg, Whoopi, 452
Gonadarche, **519**
Gonorrhea, 533
Goodness-of-fit, **238,** 238–239
Grammar, 219
  during early childhood, 322
  during middle childhood, 439–440
Grandparents
  living with, teen pregnancy and, 588–589
  psychosocial development and, 244
  relationships with, during middle childhood, 480–482
Grasping reflex, 137, 173
Greek Americans, genetic defect risks of, 72
Gross motor skills, **287**
  during early childhood, 286, 287
Growth. *See specific age periods*
Growth hormone, 397
Guatemala, interactions with caregivers in, 214
Guided participation, **213,** 213–214
Guns, during adolescence, 535

Habituation, **206,** 206–207
Halford, Graeme, 33
Hall, G. Stanley, 17, 21
Hand-babbling, 221
Hand control, during infancy, 173
Handedness, **288**
  during early childhood, 288–290

Handgun violence, during adolescence, 535
Haptic perception, **176**
Harlow, Harry, 241–242
Hawaii, school achievement during middle childhood in, 450–451
Head
  development of control of, 173
  proportion relative to body, 160, 161
Head Start program, 341–342
Health. *See specific age periods*
Health care
  cultural attitudes and, 409
  lack of, poverty and, 296–297
  for victims of maltreatment, 305
Hearing
  impairment of, during middle childhood, 410
  during infancy and toddlerhood, 170–171, 207
Height, during middle childhood, 396–397
Hemophilia, 68
Henrich, Christy, 525
Hepatitis B, 533
Heredity, **9,** 64–74. *See also* Nature-nurture debate
  dominant and recessive inheritance and, 66–67
  environment versus, 20
  genes and chromosomes and, 64–65
  genetic and chromosomal abnormalities and, 68–74
  genotypes and phenotypes and, 67–68
  language development and, 222
  obesity and, during middle childhood, 401
  patterns of genetic transmission and, 66
  sex determination and, 65–66
Heritability, **77**
Herpes simplex virus (HSV), genital, 533
  maternal, prenatal development and, 111
Heterosexuality, **516**
Heterozygous inheritance, **66**
Hippocampus, 166, 213
Hispanic Americans
  adolescent/family conflict and, 593
  adolescent moral reasoning among, 600
  AIDS among, 411
  asthma among, 410–411
  growth rate of, 397
  intelligence of, 438
  low birthweight among, 139
  poverty among, health during early childhood and, 295
  school achievement of, during adolescence, 560
  sexual behavior of, 581
  single-parent families among, 477
HIV. *See* Acquired immunodeficiency syndrome (AIDS); Human immunodeficiency virus (HIV) infection
Holophrases, **218**
Home birth, 129, 130–131
Home environment, intelligence and, 195, 196
Homelessness, 298
Home Observation for Measurement of the Environment (HOME), **195**
Homosexuality, **516,** 516–517
  gay and lesbian parents during middle childhood and, 480
Homozygous inheritance, **66**
Hope, in psychosocial theory, 25
Horizontal décalage, **425**
Hormones
  aggressive behavior and, 376–377
  gender development and, 362
  growth and, 397
  obesity and, during middle childhood, 401

Hostile aggression, **376**
  during middle childhood, 491–492
Human development, 16
Human Genome Project, 76
Human immunodeficiency virus (HIV) infection. *See also* Acquired immunodeficiency syndrome (AIDS)
  maternal, prenatal development and, 110–111
  during middle childhood, 411
Human milk, 161–163
Human papillomavirus (HPV), 533
Hunger cry, 235
Huntington's disease, 69, 70, 74
Huxley, Aldous, 53
Hyaline membrane disease, 140
Hyperactivity, 452
Hypotheses, **18**
Hypothetical-deductive reasoning, **546**

Id, **23**
Ideal self, **353**
Identical twins, 59–60
Identification, **359**
  with parents, gender development and, 359
Identities
  during middle childhood, 424
  symbolic function and, 313
Identity
  adolescent search for, 574–579
    gender differences in identity formation and, 578–579
    identity status and, 575–578
    identity versus identity confusion and, 574–575
  in psychosocial theory, 25
Identity achievement, **577**
Identity diffusion, **577**
Identity statuses, 575–578, **576**
Identity versus identity confusion, **574**
Illness
  children's understanding of, 406
  during early childhood, 291
  exposure to, during early childhood, 295
  maternal, prenatal development and, 110–111
  during middle childhood, 408–411
  in neonates, screening for, 145
Imaginary audience, **549**
Imaginary playmates, 367
Imaginative play, 366
  preparation for literacy and, 326, 328
Imitation
  deferred, 201, 203–205
  elicited, 205
  invisible, 203–205
  of language sounds, 216
  visible, 203–205
Immaturity, adaptive value of, 34–35
Immunization, during infancy and toddlerhood, 182–184
Implicit memory, **212,** 212–213, 329
Imprinting, **146**
Independent variables, **41,** 41–42
India
  interactions with caregivers in, 214
  moral reasoning in, 556
  preference for male babies in, 116
Indirect aggression, 492
Individual psychotherapy, **495**
Individuals with Disabilities Education Act (IDEA), 454
Individuation, 26
Induction, **421**
  as discipline, 370
  during middle childhood, 421

Industry versus inferiority, **466,** 575
Infancy, 10. *See also* Infancy and toddlerhood;
    Neonates
   cocaine addiction during, 109
   comforting crying infants and, 149
   cultural preference for males and, 116
   emotional expression during, 235–237
   parent-child relationship and, 145–150
   psychosocial development during, 244–257
     attachments and, 245–252
     emotional communication with
      caregivers and, 252–255
     social referencing and, 256–257
     stranger anxiety and separation anxiety
      and, 255–256
     trust and, 244–245
Infancy and toddlerhood. *See also* Infancy;
    Neonates; Toddlerhood
   body growth during, 160–164
     nutrition and, 161–164
     obesity and, 165
   brain development during, 164–168
   cognitive development during, 187–229
     behaviorist approach to study of,
      190–193
     cognitive neuroscience approach to,
      212–213
     day care and, 269–271
     information-processing approach to,
      205–212
     psychometric approach to (*see*
      Psychometric approach)
     social-contextual approach to, 213–214
   fostering competence during, 196
   health during, 179–184
     breastfeeding and, 162
     immunization and, 182–184
     infant mortality and, 179–183
   language development during, 214–227
     child-directed speech and, 224–226
     early, sequence of, 215–219
     early speech characteristics and, 219–220
     family characteristics and, 223–224
     genetic influences on, 222
     nature-nurture debate and, 220–222
     reading aloud and, 226–227
     social interaction and, 222–223
     temperament and, 222
   motor development during, 171–179
     environmental influences on, 176–179
     milestones of, 172–174
     perception and, 174, 176
   psychosocial development during, 231–273
     day care and, 267–272, 271–272
     emotions and, 234–237
     family and, 240–244
     siblings and, 263–266
     sociability with nonsiblings and, 266–267
     temperament and, 237–240
   sensory development during, 168–171,
     207–208
     hearing and, 170–171
     smell and taste senses and, 169–170
     touch and pain senses and, 168
     vision and, 169
Infantile amnesia, 329
Infant mortality, 179–183
   sudden infant death syndrome and, 179–183
   trends in, 179–181
Infant mortality rate, **179**
Inference, transitive, 422
Infertility, **60,** 60–64
   adoption and, 63–64
   assisted reproductive technology and,
     53–54, 61–62

Infibulation, 509
Information processing, of social information,
    aggression during middle
    childhood and, 491–492
Information-processing approach, **32,** 32–33, **205**
   during early childhood, 328–333
     childhood memories and, 328–331
     influences on memory and, 331–333
     recognition and recall and, 328
   during infancy and toddlerhood, 205–212
     caregivers' influence and, 212
     exploratory competence and, 208
     predicting intelligence and, 206–208
     violation of expectations and
      development of thought and,
      208–211
   during middle childhood, 428–433
     Piagetian tasks and, 432–435
     processing speed and memory function
      and, 429–434
     selective attention and, 432
Informed consent, right to, research and, 45
Inheritance. *See* Heredity; Nature-nurture
    debate
Inhibition to the unfamiliar, 239
Inhibitory control, 260
Initiative versus guilt, **355,** 355–356
Injuries. *See* Accidental injuries
Innate learning mechanisms, 211
Instrumental aggression, **376**
   during middle childhood, 492
Intelligence. *See also* Cognitive development;
    Gifted children
   development during early childhood,
     334–339
     measured, influences on, 334–338
     psychometric measures of, 334
     testing and teaching based on zone of
      proximal development and, 339
   heredity and environment and, 82–84
   infants' information processing as
     predictor of, 206–208
   low birthweight and, 140
   in mental retardation, 451
   theory of multiple intelligences and,
     436–437
   triarchic theory of, 437–438
Intelligence quotient (IQ) tests, **193.** *See also*
    Psychometric approach
   during infancy and toddlerhood, 193–194
Intelligence tests. *See* Psychometric approach
Intelligent behavior, **190**
Intentionality model, language development
    and, 223
Internalization, **259.** *See also* Socialization
   parenting styles and, 372
Internal rewards, discipline and, 369
Interviews, for research, 37–38
Invisible imitation, **203,** 203–205
In vitro fertilization (IVF), 53–54, **61**
IQ (intelligence quotient) tests, **193.** *See also*
    Psychometric approach
   during infancy and toddlerhood, 193–194
Iron-deficiency anemia, during adolescence, 523
Irreversibility, **315**
Isolettes, 141
Italian Americans, genetic defect risks of, 72
Itard, Jean-Marc-Gaspard, 5–7

Jackson, Jacquelyn Faye, 82, 83
Jamaica, marijuana use in, 108–109
James, William, 168–171
Japan
   adolescent activities in, 591–592
   aggression in, 379

attachment patterns in, 247–248
child-directed speech in, 225, 226
emotional development in, 234
Japanese Americans. *See* Asian Americans
Jaundice, neonatal, 133
Jews, genetic defect risks of, 72
Joint custody, 477
Juvenile delinquency, 602–606
   interaction of parental and peer influences
     and, 602–604
   long-term prospects for, 604–605
   predicting and preventing, 605–606

Kamehameha Early Education Program
    (KEEP), 450–451
Karyotype, 75
Kaufman Assessment Battery for Children
    (K-ABC), **434,** 434–435
Keller, Helen, 157–159
Kenya, malnutrition in, 399
Kidney disease, polycystic, 69
Kindergarten
   holding children back from, 344
   instruction in, 342–343
   predicting success in, 343–344
Kinetic cues, 176
Kleinfelter syndrome, 73
Kohlberg, Lawrence, moral reasoning stages
    of, 550–556
Korea, preference for male babies in, 116
Korean Americans. *See* Asian Americans
Kurosawa, Akira, 417–418

Labor, 126
Laboratory experiments, 42–43
Laboratory observation, **38,** 38–39
Lamaze, Fernand, 128
Language, **215**
   ethnic differences in intelligence and,
     438–439
   symbolic function and, 313
Language acquisition devices (LADs), **221**
Language development. *See specific age periods*
Lanugo, **132**
Latency stage, 23
Latinos. *See* Hispanic Americans
Laughing, during infancy, 236–237
Lead exposure, 297, 299
Learning, **26**
   behaviorist approach and (*see* Behaviorist
     approach)
   fetal, 101–102
   innate mechanisms of, 211
   observational, 29–30
Learning disabilities (LDs), **452,** 452–454
Learning perspective, 18, 19, **26,** 26–30
   behaviorism and, 27–29
   social-learning (cognitive) theory and,
     29–30
Lesbians, 516–517
   as parents, during middle childhood, 480
Life events, normative, 13
Linguistic speech, **218**
Literacy, **215.** *See also* Reading
   during middle childhood, 442–444
   reading aloud and, 226–227
   social interaction and, 326–328
Literature-based approach, phonics versus, 444
"Little Albert," 191
Locke, John, 17, 20
Locomotion, during infancy and toddlerhood,
    173–175
Logs, 37, 38
Longitudinal studies, **43,** 43–44
Long-term memory, **429**

language development and, 220–222
nonshared environment of siblings and, 80–83
personality and, 84–86
physical and physiological traits and, 81–82
reaction range and canalization and, 78–79
studying heredity and environment and, 77–78
Navajo Indians
newborn reflexes in, 138
stranger anxiety among, 256
Negative reinforcement, 28–29
Negativism, **259**
Neglect, 300. *See also* Maltreatment
Neglected adolescents, 601
Neighborhood, maltreatment and, 302
Neonatal jaundice, **133**
Neonatal mortality, 179
Neonatal period, **132**
Neonates, **132,** 132–150
body systems of, 132–133
central nervous system development in, 134–136
classical conditioning of, 190–191
death of, maternal obesity and, 105
low birthweight, 138–142
medical and behavioral screening of, 144–145
pain experience in, 168
parent-child relationship and, 145–150
postmature, 142–143
reflexes of, 135–138
grasping reflex, 173
size and appearance of, 132
stillborn, 99, 105, 143–144
Nepal, childbirth in, 130
Netherlands, childbirth settings in, 129
Neural-tube defects, 69
folic acid and, 104–105
Neurologic assessment, of neonates, 145
Neurons, **134**
Neuroticism, 85
Neurotransmitters, 134
Newborn reflexes, 135–136
Newborns. *See* Neonates
New York Longitudinal Study (NYLS), 84–85, 237–240
New Zealand, deferred imitation in, 205
Niche-picking, **80**
Nicotine use
during adolescence, 530–531
maternal
low birthweight and, 138–139
prenatal development and, 107
by parents, health effects of, 294
paternal, prenatal development and, 113
sudden infant death syndrome and, 181–182
Nightmares, 286
Night terrors, 286
Nocturnal emissions, 515
Nonshared environmental effects, 80–83, **81**
Norm(s), standardized, 193
Normative age-graded influences, 12
Normative history-graded influences, 13
Normative life events, 13
Nuclear families, **9,** 244, 465
Number concepts, understanding of
during early childhood, 314
during infancy and toddlerhood, 209
during middle childhood, 425
Nursing, of infants, 161–163

Nutrition
during adolescence, 523
during early childhood, 283–284
during infancy and toddlerhood, 161–168
body growth and, 161–164
brain development and, 164–165
maternal, prenatal development and, 104–105
during middle childhood, 397–399
malnutrition and, 398–399
requirements for, 398

Oakland (Adolescent) Growth Study, 16, 43–44
Obesity, **81**
during adolescence, 524
during early childhood, 284
heredity and environment and, 81–82
during infancy, 165
maternal, prenatal development and, 105
during middle childhood, 400–402
causes of, 401–402
treatment of, 402
Object permanence, **201,** 201–202
Observation, 38–39
Observational learning, **29,** 29–30
Observer bias, **39**
Obstetrics. *See* Childbirth
One-egg twins, **59,** 59–60
1-to-1 principle, 314
Only children, 381–383
Operant conditioning, **28,** 28–29, 190–193, **191**
memory and, 192–193
Opiates, maternal use of, prenatal development and, 109
Oral stage, 22, 24
Order-irrelevance principle, 314
Organismic model, **21**
Organization, **31, 430,** 430–431
Organized sports, during middle childhood, 404
Osteoporosis, 522
Otis-Lennon School Ability Test, **434**
Ova, 58
donor, 61–62
Overcontrolled children, 590
Overgeneralization (overextending), 219–220
Overregularization of rules, 220
Ovulation, 58
Ovum transfer, **61,** 61–62

Pain cry, 235
Pain sense, during infancy and toddlerhood, 168
Papalia, Diane E., 63
Paraguay, environmental influences on motor development in, 178
Parallel constructive play, 366
Parent(s). *See also* Fathers; Mother(s)
adolescent (*see* Teen pregnancy)
attitudes and beliefs of, school achievement during middle childhood and, 448
discussion with children, memory and, 332–333
divorce of
during adolescence, 596
during middle childhood, 476–477, 481–482
effects of parenthood on marriage of, 150
gay and lesbian, during middle childhood, 480
gender development and, 362–364
identification with, gender development and, 359
interaction of parental and peer influences during adolescence, antisocial behavior and, 602–604

language development and, 222–223
maltreatment by, 301–302, 304
reasons for having children and, 56
self-reports of, 37, 38
sensitivity to differences in babies' cries, 235
shaping of gender differences by, 243
single
during adolescence, 596
during middle childhood, 477–479
smoking by (*see* Nicotine use)
stepparents, during middle childhood, 479–480
timing of having children and, 57–58
Parent-child relationship, during infancy, 145–150
Parenting
coregulation and, 470–471
"good enough," 82–83
inadequate, aggression and, 377
popularity and, during early childhood, 386
poverty and, 474
Parenting styles
during adolescence
adolescent/family conflict and, 593–595
school achievement and, 559–560
during early childhood, 368–380
altruism, aggression, and fearfulness and, 373–380
conflict, autonomy, and parenting goals and, 372–375
discipline and, 368–370
intelligence and, 335, 338
poisonous pedagogy, 374–375
school achievement during middle childhood and, 447–448
self-esteem during middle childhood and, 467–468
socialization success and, 262–263
Parietal lobe, 166
Pascual-Leone, Juan, 33
Passive vocabulary, 218
Pattern vision, 169
Patton, George, 452
Pavlov, Ivan, 28
Pedestrian injuries, during middle childhood, 412
Peekaboo, 202
Peer relationships
during adolescence, 599–602
friendships and, 601–602
interaction with parental influence, antisocial behavior and, 602–604
peer group status and, 599, 601
during early childhood, 383–385
benefits of friendship and, 384–385
choosing playmates and friends and, 384
helping children with, 386–387
parenting and popularity and, 386
sex segregation in play and, 383–384
siblings and, 385–386
during middle childhood, 484–493
aggression and bullying and, 491–493
friendship and, 488, 490–491
influence of peer group and, 484–486
popularity and, 487–489
during toddlerhood, 266–267
Penis envy, 23
Perception
of depth, 174, 176
haptic, 176
motor development and, 174, 176
Permissive parenting, 370
school achievement and, during adolescence, 559

Perón, Eva, 349–350
Perry Preschool Program, 342, 585
Personal fables, **549**
Personality, **8,** 8–9
    androgynous, 361
    continuity from childhood to adolescence, 590
    gender differences in, during early childhood, 358
    heredity and environment and, 84–85
Personality disorders, heredity and environment and, 86
Pervasive developmental disorders, 86
Phallic stage, 22–24
Phenotype, **67**
Phenylketonuria (PKU), 69, 79
    in neonates, screening for, 145
Phobia, school, 494
Phonics, whole-language approach versus, 444
Physical abuse, **300.** *See also* Maltreatment
Physical activity
    during adolescence, 521–522
    maternal, prenatal development and, 105
    obesity and, during middle childhood, 401, 402
Physical development, 8. *See also specific age periods*
Physical neglect, **300.** *See also* Maltreatment
Physical punishment, during middle childhood, 471
Piaget, Jean, 21
    cognitive stage theory of, 24, 30–32, 198–205
        elicited interaction and, 205
        invisible and deferred imitation and, 203–205
    concrete operations of, 420–428
        advances in cognitive abilities and, 420–425
        influences of culture and schooling and, 425–427
        moral reasoning and, 427–428
    formal operations stage of, 544–548
        evidence of cognitive maturity and, 544–546
        factors bringing about cognitive maturity and, 546–547
        limitations of Piaget's theory and, 547–548
    on moral reasoning, 427–428
    preoperational stage of, 312–321
    sensorimotor stage of, 198–202
Piagetian approach, **190**
Picasso, Pablo, 289
Placenta, 98
Placing reflex, 137
Planful competence, 43–44
Plasticity, **13,** 34, **164**
Play
    during early childhood, 364–368
        cultural influences on, 367–368
        sex segregation in, 383–384
        types of, 365–367
    during middle childhood, 403–404
        organized sports, 404
        rough-and-tumble, 403–404
    peekaboo, 202
    preparation for literacy and, 326, 328
    pretend, 201
    symbolic function and, 313
Playmates. *See also* Peer relationships
    imaginary, 367
Pleasure principle, 23
Poisonous pedagogy (PP), 374–375
Polychlorinated biphenyls (PCBs), prenatal development and, 112

Polycystic kidney disease, 69
Polygenic inheritance, **66,** 66–67
Polymorphic genes, 64–65
Popularity
    during adolescence, 599, 601
    during early childhood, parenting and, 386
    during middle childhood, 487–489
Population, sampling and, 37
Positive reinforcement, 28
Positron-emission tomography (PET), 135
Postconventional morality, **551**
Postmaturity, **142,** 142–143
Postneonatal mortality, 179
Poverty
    during adolescence, 597
    during early childhood, 295–298
    parenting and, 474
Power assertion, as discipline, 369–370
Pragmatics, **323**
    during middle childhood, 441–442
Preconventional morality, **551**
Prediction, as goal of study of child development, 17
Preferences, for visual novelty, 207
Prefrontal cortex, 213
Pregnancy, 94. *See also* Prenatal development; Fetal stage; Prenatal environmental hazards
    among adolescents (*see* Teen pregnancy)
    future of, 114
    loss of, 98–99
        maternal obesity and, 105
    multiple births and, 59–60
    risks of, 114
Preimplantation genetic diagnosis, **117**
Prejudice, **485**
    peer relationships during middle childhood and, 485–486
Prelinguistic speech, **215,** 215–217
Preliteracy skills, 226
    social interaction and, 326–328
Prenatal care, 118–120
Prenatal development, 10, 94–120
    assessment techniques for, 113–117
    embryonic stage of, 98–99
    environmental hazards during (*see* Prenatal environmental hazards)
    fetal stage of (*see* Fetal stage)
    germinal stage of, 95, 98
    prenatal care during, 118–120
Prenatal environmental hazards, 102–113
    age of father and, 113
    age of mother and, 111–112
    blood type incompatibility, 112
    chemical exposures, 112
    drug intake of mother and, 105–110
    drug use by father and, 113
    illnesses of mother and, 110–111
    nutrition of mother and, 104–105
    physical activity of mother and, 105
    radiation exposure, 112
Preoperational stage, **312,** 312–321
    challenges to Piaget's conclusions about, 316–320
        egocentrism, animism, and empathy and, 317–318
        theories of mind and, 318–320
        training and, 320–321
    cognitive advances during, 312–314
    limitations of preoperational thought and, 314–316
Prepared childbirth, **128**

Preschool, 339–344
    compensatory programs, 341–342
    goals of, 340–341
    instruction in, 342–343
Preschool Assessment of Attachment (PAA), **248**
Preschool children. *See* Early childhood
Prescription drugs
    for childbirth, 127
    maternal use of, prenatal development, 106
    for mental disorders, 495–496
Presley, Elvis, 123–125
Pretend play, **201,** 366, **366**
Preterm (premature) infants, **138**
Primary sex characteristics, **513,** 513–514
Priming, cognitive, aggression and, 378
Priming mechanisms, developmental, 195
Primitive reflexes, 135–136
Privacy, right to, research and, 46
Private speech, **324,** 324–325
Proactive aggression, during middle childhood, 492
Process-oriented approach, phonics versus, 444
Project Head Start, 341–342
Prosocial behavior
    during early childhood, 374–376
    self-esteem and, 468
Proximodistal principle, **95,** 160
Psychoanalysis, 22
Psychoanalytic perspective, 18, 19, **22,** 22–26
    on gender development, 359
    psychosexual, 22–25 (*see also* Freud, Sigmund)
    psychosocial, 35 (*see also* Erikson, Erik H., psychosocial theory of)
    relational, 26
Psychological abuse, **300.** *See also* Maltreatment
Psychological aggression, 492
Psychological neglect, **300.** *See also* Maltreatment
Psychometric approach, **190**
    during early childhood, 334–338
        influences on measured intelligence and, 334–338
        traditional measures and, 334
    during infancy and toddlerhood, 193–205
        assessment home environment's impact and, 195, 196
        cognitive stages and, 198–205
        early intervention and, 195, 197–198
        testing and, 193–194
    during middle childhood, 433–439
        ethnic and cultural differences in IQ and, 438–441
        intelligence tests and, 433–438
Psychosexual development, **22,** 22–25
Psychosocial development, 8–9, 24, **25.** *See also specific age periods*
Psychosocial moratorium, 575
Psychotherapy, individual, 495
Puberty, **508,** 509–517
    onset of, 510–511
    timing, sequence, and signs of maturation and, 511–516
        psychological issues related to physical changes of, 516–517
Pubic hair, 514
Puerto Ricans
    asthma among, 410–411
    low birthweight among, 139
Punishment, **28**
    corporal, during middle childhood, 471
    discipline and, 369

Social-contextual approach, **205**
  during infancy and toddlerhood, 213–214
Social development, 8. *See also* Psychosocial
    development; *specific age periods*
Social gestures, conventional, during infancy
    and toddlerhood, 217
Social interaction
  language development and, 222–223
  preparation for literacy and, 326–328
Socialization, **259,** 259–263
  conscience and, 260–262
  factors influencing success of, 262–263
  self-regulation and, 260
Social-learning theory, **29,** 29–30
  of gender development, 359–360
Social play, **365,** 365–366
Social referencing, 175, **256,** 256–257
Social speech, **323**
Social support, maltreatment and, 302
Sociocultural theory, **36**
Socioeconomic status, **11.** *See also* Poverty
  breastfeeding and, 162–163
  development and, 11.
  intelligence and, 347
  school achievement and, during
      adolescence, 562–565
  school achievement during middle
      childhood and, 448–449
  socialization and, 263
Solid foods, introduction of, 164
Sonograms, prenatal, 99–100, 114–115, 116
South Korea, preference for male babies in, 116
Spatial reasoning
  during middle childhood, 422, 424
  training in music and, 336–337
Speech. *See also specific age periods*
  early, characteristics of, 219–220
  linguistic, 218
  prelinguistic, 215–217
  private, 324–325
  social, 323
  telegraphic, 219
Sperm, 58–69
Spermarche, **515**
Spina bifida, 69
Spontaneous abortion, **98,** 98–99
  maternal obesity and, 105
Sports
  accidental injuries due to, during
      adolescence, 522
  organized, during middle childhood, 404
Squabbling, among siblings
  during early childhood, 380–381
  during toddlerhood, 265–266
Stable-order principle, 314
Standardized norms, **193**
Stanford-Binet Intelligence Scale, 193, **334**
Stanford Studies of Gifted Children, 16
"Startle" reflex, 135–138
State of arousal, **147**
  of neonates, parent-infant relationship
      and, 147–148
Stepfamilies, during middle childhood, 479–480
Steptoe, Patrick, 53
Sternberg Triarchic Abilities Test (STAT), **438**
Stillbirths, 99, 143–144
  maternal obesity and, 105
Storage, 429
Stranger anxiety, **255,** 255–256
Strange Situation, 34, **246**
Stress
  during early childhood, 295
  during middle childhood, 496–501
    coping with, 497–499
    sources of, 496–498

Striatum, 213
Structured interviews, 38
Stuttering, **410**
Substance abuse, **527.** *See also* Drug use
    and abuse
Substance dependence, **527**
Sudden infant death syndrome (SIDS), 107,
    179–183, **181**
Suicide
  during adolescence, 535–536
  warning signs of, 536
Sullivan, Annie, 158
Superego, **23**
Supportive environment, for infants with birth
    complications, 143
Surfactant, for preterm infants, 140
Surrogate motherhood, **62**
Sweden
  day care in, 268
  family policy in, 268
Swimming reflex, 137
Symbolic function, **313**
Symbolic gestures, during infancy and
    toddlerhood, 217
Symbolic play, 313, 366
Synapses, 134
  development during infancy and
      toddlerhood, 164
Syntax, **219**
  during early childhood, 322–323
  during middle childhood, 440
Syphilis, 533
Systematic desensitization, for fears, 380
Systems of action, **171, 288**

Tabula rasa, 20
Taiwan
  adolescent activities in, 591–592
  moral reasoning in, 556
Takahashi, Mahito, 455
Talented children. *See* Gifted children
Taste sense, during infancy and
    toddlerhood, 170
Tay-Sachs disease, 69
Teen Outreach, 585
Teen pregnancy, 583–589
  adjustment to parenthood and, 586–587
  living arrangements and, 588–589
  low birthweight and, 138–139
  preventing, 583–585
  problems and outcomes of teenage
      parenthood and, 587–588
Teething, 160
Telegraphic speech, **219**
Television
  obesity and, during middle childhood, 402
  violence on, aggression and, 377–379
Temperament, 59, 237–240
  attachment and, 249–250
  components and patterns of, 237–238
  during infancy, stability of, 239–240
  intelligence and, 335, 338
  language development and, 222
Temperature regulation, neonatal, 133
Temporal lobe, medial, 213
Tentative period, **563**
Teratogenic factors, **103,** 103–104
"Terrible twos," 259
Testing, psychometric. *See* Psychometric
    approach
Testosterone
  aggressive behavior and, 376–377
  gender development and, 362
Thalamus, 166
Thalassemia, 68

Theories, **18.** *See also specific theories*
Theory of mind, 204, 257, **318**
  challenges to Piaget's conclusions about,
      318–322
Theory of multiple intelligences, **436,** 436–437
Thinking/thought. *See also* Reasoning
  adolescent, immature aspects of, 548–549
  development of, violation of expectations
      and, 208–211
  knowledge about, during early
      childhood, 319
  spatial, during middle childhood, 422, 424
Thumb-sucking, 282
Tinbergen, Niko, 33
Tobacco. *See* Nicotine use
Toddlerhood, 10. *See also* Infancy and
    toddlerhood
  psychosocial development during, 257–263
    autonomy and, 258–259
    day care and, 271–272
    internalization and, 259–263
    self-concept and, 257–258
Tonic neck reflex, 137
Torrance Tests of Creative Thinking, 456
Touch sense, during infancy and
    toddlerhood, 168
Toxoplasmosis, maternal, prenatal
    development and, 111
Tracking, school achievement and, during
    adolescence, 558
Training
  cognitive development and, 320–321
  in music, spatial reasoning and, 336–337
Transduction, **316**
Transforming growth factor alpha, 104
Transitional objects, **285**
Transitive inference, **422**
Triarchic theory of intelligence, **437,**
    437–438
Trichomoniasis, 533
Trimesters, 98
Triple X syndrome, 73
Trisomy-21, 68, 73–74
Trophoblast, 98
Trust, development of, 244–245
Trust versus mistrust, 25
Turkey, interactions with caregivers in, 214
Turner syndrome, 73
Twins, 59–60
Twin studies, 77–78
Two-egg twins, **59,** 60

Ultrasound, **99**
  prenatal, 99–100, 114–115, 116
Umbilical cord, 98
Umbilical cord sampling, **117**
Undercontrolled children, 590
Underextension, 219
Unstructured interviews, 38

Vaccinations, during infancy and toddlerhood,
    182–184
Validity, **193**
Variables, independent and dependent, 41–42
Venereal diseases, during adolescence,
    531–534
Vernix caseosa, **132**
Victor, the Wild Boy of Aveyron, 5–7
Vinci, Leonardo da, 289
Violation of expectations method, 203, **208**
  development of thought and, 208–211
Violence. *See also* Aggression
  during adolescence, 535
  fear of, during middle childhood, 497, 498
Visible imitation, **203,** 203–205